MANAGEMENT

605

MANAGEMENT

RICHARD L. DAFT, MARTYN KENDRICK, NATALIA VERSHININA

SOUTH-WESTERN
CENGAGE Learning™

Australia • Brazil • Japan • Korea • Mexico • Singapore • Spain • United Kingdom • United States

Management: International Edition
Richard Daft, Martyn Kendrick,
Natalia Vershinina

Publishing Director: Linden Harris

Publisher: Thomas Rennie

Development Editor: Jennifer Seth

Content Project Editor: Lucy Arthy

Senior Production Controller: Paul Herbert

Marketing Manager: Amanda Cheung

Typesetter: KnowledgeWorks Global, India

Cover design: Adam Renvoize

Text design: Design Deluxe

For product information and technology assistance,
contact **emea.info@cengage.com**.

For permission to use material from this text or product,
and for permission queries,
email **clsuk.permissions@cengage.com**.

Adapted from *Management*, 8th Edition by Richard L. Daft,
published by South-Western Higher Education, a division of
Cengage Learning, Inc. © 2008.

British Library Cataloguing-in-Publication Data
A catalogue record for this book is available from the British
Library.

ISBN: 978-1-84480-882-3

Cengage Learning EMEA
Cheriton House, North Way, Andover, Hampshire. SP10 5BE.
United Kingdom

Cengage Learning products are represented in Canada by Nelson
Education Ltd.

For your lifelong learning solutions, visit
www.cengage.co.uk

Purchase your next print book, e-book or e-chapter at
www.CengageBrain.com

Printed by Seng Lee Press, Singapore
1 2 3 4 5 6 7 8 9 10 – 12 11 10

BRIEF CONTENTS

CONTENTS

PART 2 THE ENVIRONMENT AND CORPORATE CULTURE OF MANAGEMENT 79

PART 4 ORGANIZING 345

LIST OF CASES

PREFACE

Managing for Innovation in a Changing World

In recent years, organizations have been buffeted by massive and far-reaching social, technological, and economic changes. The recent world financial crisis has put a lot of pressure on businesses from all sectors and of all sizes. Any manager who still believed in the myth of stability was rocked out of complacency when, one after another, large financial institutions all over the world began to fail. Business schools, as well as managers and businesses, were scrambling to keep up with the fast-changing story and evaluate its impact. This adaptation of *Management*, prepared for students in Europe, the Middle East and Africa (EMEA), addresses themes and issues that are directly relevant to the current, fast-shifting business environment. We revised *Management* with a goal of helping current and future managers find innovative solutions to the problems that plague today's organizations—whether they are everyday challenges or once-in-a-lifetime crises. The world in which most students will work as managers is undergoing a tremendous upheaval. Ethical turmoil, the need for crisis management skills, e-business, diversity, rapidly changing technologies, globalization, outsourcing, global virtual teams, knowledge management, global supply chains, and other changes place demands on managers that go beyond the techniques and ideas traditionally taught in management courses. Managing today requires the full breadth of management skills and capabilities. This text provides comprehensive coverage of both traditional management skills and the new competencies needed in a turbulent environment characterized by economic turmoil, political confusion, and general uncertainty.

In the traditional world of work, management was to control and limit people, enforce rules and regulations, seek stability and efficiency, design a top-down hierarchy, and achieve bottom-line results. To spur innovation and achieve high performance, however, managers need different skills to engage workers' hearts and minds as well as take advantage of their physical labour. The new workplace asks that managers focus on leading change, harnessing people's creativity and enthusiasm, finding shared visions and values, and sharing information and power. Teamwork, collaboration, participation, and learning are guiding principles that help managers and employees manoeuvre the difficult terrain of today's turbulent business environment. Managers focus on developing, not controlling, people to adapt to new technologies and extraordinary environmental shifts, and thus achieve high performance and total corporate effectiveness.

Our vision for this adaptation of *Management* is to present the newest management ideas for turbulent times in a way that is interesting and valuable to students while retaining the best of traditional management thinking. To achieve this vision, we have included the most recent management concepts and research and have shown the contemporary application of management ideas in organizations. We have added a questionnaire at the beginning of each chapter that draws students personally into the topic and gives them some insight into their own management skills.

Chapter 9 gives an overview of managerial decision making with an expanded discussion of how conflicting interests among managers can create uncertainty regarding decisions. A new section on why managers often make bad decisions looks at the biases that can cloud judgment. The chapter also includes a new section on innovative group decision making and the dangers of groupthink.

Chapter 10 discusses basic principles of organizing and describes both traditional and contemporary organizational structures in detail. The chapter includes a discussion of organic versus mechanistic structures and when each is more effective. Chapter 10 also provides a description of the virtual network organization form.

Chapter 11 includes a more focused discussion of the critical role of managing change and innovation today. The chapter includes a new discussion of the ambidextrous approach for both creating and using innovations and has expanded material on exploration and creativity, the importance of internal and external cooperation, and the growing trend toward open innovation.

Chapter 12 includes an expanded discussion of the strategic role of HRM in building human capital. The chapter has new sections on coaching and mentoring and the trend toward part-time and contingent employment. New ways of doing background checks on applicants, such as checking their pages on social networks, are discussed, and the chapter also looks at the changing social contract between employers and employees.

Chapter 13 has been revised and updated to reflect the most recent thinking on organizational diversity issues. The chapter looks at how diversity is changing the domestic and global workforce and includes a new section on the traditional versus inclusive models for managing diversity. This chapter also contains new coverage of the dividends of diversity; an expanded discussion of prejudice, discrimination, and stereotypes; and a new look at the difference between stereotyping and valuing cultural differences. The chapter includes a new five-step process for achieving cultural competence.

Chapter 14 continues its solid coverage of the basics of organizational behaviour, including personality, values and attitudes, perception, emotional intelligence, learning and problem-solving styles, and stress management. Many exercises and questionnaires throughout this chapter enhance students' understanding of organizational behaviour topics and their own personalities and attitudes.

Chapter 15 has been enriched with a discussion of followership. The chapter emphasizes that good leaders and good followers share common characteristics. Good leadership can make a difference, often through subtle, everyday actions. The discussion of power and influence has been expanded to include the sources of power that are available to followers as well as leaders. The discussions of charismatic, transformational, and interactive leadership have all been revised and refocused.

Chapter 16 covers the foundations of motivation and also incorporates recent thinking about motivational tools for today, including an expanded treatment of employee engagement. The chapter looks at new motivational ideas such as the importance of helping employees achieve work-life balance, incorporating fun and learning into the workplace, giving people a chance to fully participate, and helping people fi nd meaning in their work.

Chapter 17 begins with a discussion of how managers facilitate strategic conversations by using communication to direct everyone's attention to the vision, values, and goals of the organization. The chapter explores the foundations of good communication and includes a new section on gender differences in communication, an enriched discussion of dialogue, and a refocused look at the importance of effective written communication in today's technologically connected workplace, including the use of new forms of manager communication such as blogs.

Chapter 18 includes a new section on the dilemma of teams, acknowledging that teams are sometimes ineffective and looking at the reasons for this, including such problems as free riders, lack of trust among team members, and so forth. The chapter then looks at how to make teams effective, including a signifi cantly revised discussion of what makes an effective team leader. The chapter covers the types of teams and includes a new look at effectively using technology in virtual teams. The chapter also includes a section on managing conflict, including the use of negotiation.

Chapter 19 provides an overview of financial and quality control, including Six Sigma, ISO certification, and a new application of the balanced scorecard, which views employee learning and growth as the foundation of high performance. The discussion of hierarchical versus decentralized control has been updated and expanded. The chapter also addresses current concerns about corporate governance and finding a proper balance of control and autonomy for employees.

Chapter 20 has been thoroughly revised to discuss recent trends in information technology, and e-business. The discussion of information technology has been updated to include the trend toward user-generated content through wikis, blogs, and social networking. The chapter explores how these new technologies are being applied within organizations along with traditional information systems. The chapter also discusses e-commerce strategies, the use of business intelligence software, and knowledge management.

Chapter 21 has been updated to discuss recent trends in operations management, and begins by looking at the organization as a value chain and includes an expanded discussion of supply chain management and new technologies such a radio frequency identification (RFID). The chapter discusses major techniques for the management of materials and inventory, and explains why and how managers seek to improve productivity.

Organization

The chapter sequence in *Management* is organized around the management functions of planning, organizing, leading, and controlling and in presenting these the book has been colour-coordinated. These four functions effectively encompass both management research and characteristics of the manager's job.

Part One introduces the world of management, including the nature of management, issues related to today's chaotic environment, the learning organization, historical perspectives on management, and the technology-driven workplace.

Part Two examines the environments of management and organizations. This section includes material on the business environment and corporate culture, the global environment, ethics and social responsibility, and the natural environment.

Part Three presents four chapters on planning, including entrepreneurial start-ups, organizational goal setting and planning, strategy formulation and implementation, and the decision-making process.

Part Four focuses on organizing processes. These chapters describe dimensions of structural design, the design alternatives managers can use to achieve strategic objectives, structural designs for promoting innovation and change, the design and use of the human resource function, and the ways managing diverse employees are significant to the organizing function.

Part Five is devoted to leadership. The section begins with a chapter on organizational behaviour, providing grounding in understanding people in organizations. This foundation paves the way for subsequent discussion of leadership, motivation of employees, communication, and team management.

Part Six describes the controlling function of management, including basic principles of total quality management, the design of control systems, information technology, emerging e-business models, and techniques for control of operations management.

Innovative Features

A major goal of this book is to offer better ways of using the textbook medium to convey management knowledge to the reader. To this end, the book includes several innovative features that draw students in and help them contemplate, absorb, and comprehend management concepts. Cengage Learning has brought together a team of experts to create and coordinate colour photographs, beautiful artwork, and supplemental materials for the best management textbook and package on the market.

Chapter Outline and Objectives. Each chapter begins with a clear statement of its learning objectives and an outline of its contents. These devices provide an overview of what is to come and can also be used by students to guide their study and test their understanding and retention of important points.

Opening Questionnaire. The text grabs student attention immediately by giving the student a chance to participate in the chapter content actively by completing a short questionnaire related to the topic.

Take a Moment. At strategic places through the chapter, students are invited to Take a Moment to apply a particular concept or think about how they would apply it as a practicing manager. This call to action further engages students in the chapter content. Some of the Take a Moment features also refer students to the associated New Manager Self-Test, or direct students from the chapter content to relevant end-of chapter materials, such as an experiential exercise or an ethical dilemma.

New Manager Self-Test. A New Manager Self-Test in each chapter of the text provides opportunities for self-assessment as a way for students to experience management issues in a personal way. The change from individual performer to new manager is dramatic, and these self-tests provide insight into what to expect and how students might perform in the world of the new manager.

Concept Connection Photo Essays. A key feature of the book is the use of photographs accompanied by detailed photo essay captions that enhance learning. Each caption highlights and illustrates one or more specific concepts from the text to reinforce student understanding of the concepts. Although the photos are beautiful to look at, they also convey the vividness, immediacy, and concreteness of management events in today's business world.

Innovative Way. Every chapter of the text contains several written examples of management incidents. They are placed at strategic points in the chapter and are designed to illustrate the application of concepts to specific companies. These in-text examples—indicated by an icon in the margin—include well-known international companies such as Toyota, Facebook, UPS, LG Electronics, Google, Unilever, Siemens, Monsanto, and Caterpillar, as well as less-well-known companies and not-for-profit organizations such as Imagination Ltd, SOL Cleaning, Tom's of Maine, Aldi, Shewee, and Interface. These examples put students in touch with the real world of organizations so that they can appreciate the value of management concepts.

Manager's Shoptalk Boxes. A Manager's Shoptalk box in each chapter addresses a specific topic straight from the field of management that is of special interest to students. These boxes may describe a contemporary topic or problem that is relevant to chapter content, or they may contain a diagnostic questionnaire or a special example of how managers handle a problem. The boxes heighten student interest in the subject matter and provide an auxiliary view of management issues not typically available in textbooks.

Exhibits. Several exhibits have been added or revised in this edition to enhance student understanding. Many aspects of management are research based, and some concepts tend to be abstract and theoretical. The many exhibits throughout this book enhance students' awareness and understanding of these concepts. These exhibits consolidate key points, indicate relationships among concepts, and visually illustrate concepts. They also make effective use of colour to enhance their imagery and appeal.

Glossaries. Learning the management vocabulary is essential to understanding contemporary management. This process is facilitated in three ways. First, key concepts are boldfaced and completely defined where they first appear in the text. Second, brief definitions are set out in the margin for easy review and follow-up. Third, a glossary summarizing all key terms and definitions appears at the end of the book for handy reference.

A Manager's Essentials and Discussion Questions. Each chapter closes with a summary of the essential points that students should retain. The discussion questions are a complementary learning tool that will enable students to check their understanding of key issues, to think beyond basic concepts, and to determine areas that require further study. The summary and discussion questions help students discriminate between main and supporting points and provide mechanisms for self-teaching.

Management in Practice Exercises. End-of-chapter exercises called "Management in Practice: Experiential Exercise" and "Management in Practice: Ethical Dilemma" provide a self-test for students and an opportunity to experience management issues in a personal way. These exercises take the form of questionnaires, scenarios, and activities, and many also provide an opportunity for students to work in teams. The exercises are tied into the chapter through the Take a Moment feature that refers students to the end-of-chapter exercises at the appropriate point in the chapter content.

Case for Critical Analysis. Also appearing at the end of each chapter is a brief but substantive case that provides an opportunity for student analysis and class discussion. Some of these cases are about companies whose names students will recognize; others are based on real management events but the identities of companies and managers have been disguised. These cases allow students to sharpen their diagnostic skills for management problem solving.

Continuing Case. Located at the end of each part, the Continuing Case is a running discussion of management topics appropriate to that part as experienced by IKEA. Focusing on one company allows students to follow the managers' and the organization's long-term problems and solutions in a sustained manner.

ACKNOWLEDGEMENTS

Acknowledgements for the first EMEA edition
Martyn Kendrick and Natalia Vershinina

It has been an amazing experience working on this book together, and making this book more international in context and rewriting and introducing case study examples from Europe, Middle East and Africa. Although this has taken a long time, this book now reflects better the diversity of issues modern organisations outside of the U.S. are facing and have to deal with. The major backdrop which was taken into account was the current world financial crisis.

This contribution would not have taken place without the reviewers who kindly helped develop the book. We would like to thank the following people from Cengage Learning, who have been most supportive of this adaptation:

Tom Rennie – Publisher
Jennifer Seth – Development Editor
Linda Dhondy – Development Editor
Charlotte Green – Editorial Assistant
Lucy Arthy – Content Production Editor

The Publisher would like to thank the following academics who supplied feedback on the original proposal and during the writing process:

Zella King, Reading University
Jennifer Hennessey, Waterford Institute of Technology
Jo Cullinane, University of Greenwich
Sandra Penger, University of Ljubljana
Roger Brown, Coventry Business School
Sharon Clarke, Manchester Business School
Graham Leask, Aston Business School
Gideon Nieman, University of Pretoria
Robert Mackie, University of the West of Scotland

The Publisher would also like to thank Alan Hogarth, Glasgow Caledonian University, for supplying the extended case study based on the Swedish firm IKEA and for the Chapter 1 Case for Critical Analysis. The Publisher also thanks various copyright holders for granting permission to reproduce material throughout the text. Every effort has been made to trace all copyright holders, but if anything has been inadvertently overlooked the Publisher will be pleased to make the necessary arrangements at the first opportunity (please contact the Publisher directly).

ABOUT THE AUTHORS

RICHARD L. DAFT is the Brownlee O. Currey, Jr., Professor of Management in the Owen Graduate School of Management at Vanderbilt University. Professor Daft has served on the editorial boards of *Academy of Management Journal, Administrative Science Quarterly*, and *Journal of Management Education*. He was the Associate Editor-in-Chief of *Organization Science* and served for three years as associate editor of *Administrative Science Quarterly*.

Professor Daft has authored or co-authored 12 books, including *The Leadership Experience* (Thomson Learning/South-Western, 2005), and *What to Study: Generating and Developing Research Questions* (Sage, 1982). He recently published *Fusion Leadership: Unlocking the Subtle Forces That Change People and Organizations* (Berrett-Koehler, 2000, with Robert Lengel).

Professor Daft has been involved in management development and consulting for many companies and government organizations, including the American Banking Association, Bell Canada, National Transportation Research Board, NL Baroid, Nortel, TVA, Pratt & Whitney, State Farm Insurance, Tenneco, the United States Air Force, the United States Army, J. C. Bradford & Co., Central Parking System, Entergy Sales and Service, Bristol-Myers Squibb, First American National Bank, and the Vanderbilt University Medical Center.

MARTYN KENDRICK is Deputy Head, Department of Strategy and Management and Principal Lecturer in International Management and Strategy, at the Leicester Business School, De Montfort University, England.

Martyn lectures and researches in the areas of international business and emerging markets, business ethics, corporate social responsibility, leadership, strategic management and reputation and relationship management. Martyn is also the Faculty International Academic Director, chairing the Faculty International Committee responsible for developing international collaborative and commercial activities, and facilitating overseas student recruitment to UK.

Martyn is particularly interested in emerging markets, such as BRIC, and in 2010/11 will be delivering guest lectures at universities in China, Hong Kong, India, Brazil and Russia. Martyn has previously acted as a consultant to the Government of Cuba, as a member of the Cuban Financial Reform group, and made significant contributions to the university's international programmes in China, Hong Kong, India, Malaysia, Singapore and Southern Africa. He has also recently helped to establish the Anglo-China Open Research Network (ACORN).

Martyn has extensive business and consultancy experience, and has worked with a broad spectrum of clients, including: Alliance and Leicester plc, Britannia Building Society, British Telecom plc, Charnwood Borough Council, East Midlands Development Agency (emda), General Motors, GMAC RFC, Nottingham City Council, Norfolk and Suffolk Constabularies, Office Depot, RWE npower plc, and Severn Trent plc. Martyn has also acted as lead academic for three DTI-sponsored Knowledge

Transfer Partnerships (KTP) schemes, working closely with local SMEs to help them further develop their strategic capabilities.

Prior to embarking on an academic career Martyn worked in the insurance and financial services industry, and ran his own consultancy company. He is a Chartered Insurance Practitioner, and a member of the Chartered Insurance Institute's Society of Fellows, as well as a Fellow of the Higher Education Academy.

NATALIA VERSHININA is a Principal Lecturer in the Department of Strategy and Management specialising in small business, enterprise, creative management and innovation at undergraduate and post graduate levels. She is currently Programme Director for MSc International Business and Entrepreneurship, and Module Leader for Entrepreneurial Organisations and Dissertation at Post Graduate level.

Born in Russia, Natalia graduated from St. Petersburg State University of Technology and Design with a degree in foreign economic relations major with distinction. Natalia worked for a large wool processing firm in St. Petersburg called "Nevskaya Manufactura", where she was responsible for all foreign contacts of the firm, sales negotiations within international activity of the company, and managed creative Design Studio where the new fabrics were tested through garments.

After completion of her MBA with distinction at Leicester Business School, Natalia went on to continue her further education through research route, thus working towards her PhD in the area of business relationships with a closer investigation of mergers and acquisitions. Her study looked at MNCs within industrial textiles sector and explored their growth patterns through relationship building.

She is now a part of the research group within the Centre for Research in Ethnic Minority Entrepreneurship at Leicester Business School and her recent research was focused on the role of forms of capital in developing entrepreneurial activity amongst new migrants to UK. Her main publications are based on Polish and Russian nationals. She is currently supervising three PhD students at De Montfort University working in the area of ethnic minority entrepreneurship, family firms and female entrepreneurship.

Natalia is a Fellow of Higher Education Academy (UK) and is passionate about teaching on a variety of courses in Leicester, as well as in other locations including India and China. She has also been involved with in-company training programmes on management and leadership, including the Office Depot, nPower as part of RWE, Police, General Motors, St. Petersburg Academy of Economics and Management and Nottingham City Council.

WALK-THROUGH TOUR

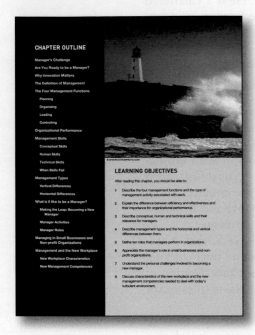

Learning Objectives each chapter starts with a list of objectives to help you monitor your understanding and progress through the chapter

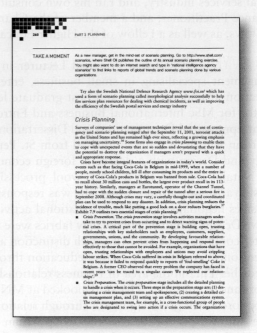

Take a Moment tasks appear regularly throughout each chapter to stimulate critical thinking and highlight key questions for discussion

Concept Connection photos accompany detailed captions discussing and illustrating specific concepts

Innovative Way mini case study examples demonstrate how management concepts are applied to real-world companies

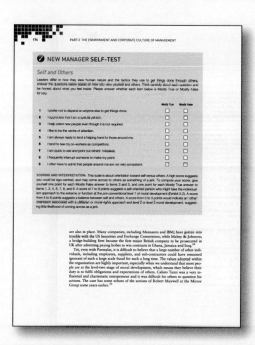

New Manager Self-Test provide opportunities for self assessment as a way for students to experience management issues in a personal way

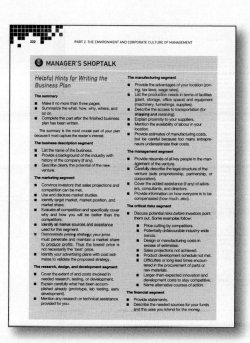

Manager's Shoptalk addresses a specific topic or problem straight from the field of management that is of particular interest to students

A Manager's Essentials: What Have We Learned? a summary of the essential points covered in each chapter, to track learning and promote thinking beyond basic concepts

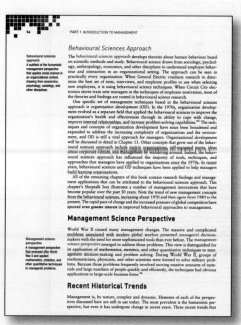

Marginal Glossary Terms key terms are highlighted throughout the text and explained in full in the margins as well as in a full glossary at the end of the book

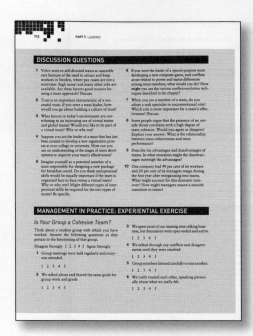

Discussion Questions are provided at the end of each chapter to help reinforce and test your knowledge and understanding, and provide a basis for group discussions and activities

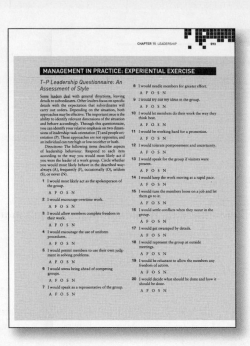

Management in Practice exercises at the end of each chapter provide a self-test for student and stimulate group discussion

Case for Critical Analysis provides an opportunity for student analysis and class discussion, and allowing students to sharpen their diagnostic skills for management problem solving

Continuing Case an extended case study focusing on one company providing a running discussion of management topics appears at the end of each part section

ABOUT THE WEBSITE

Discover a rich array of online teaching and learning resources on the *Management* companion website at www.cengage.co.uk/dkv:

For Lecturers:
- "Sustainable Management" Module Booster Notes
- "Enterprising Management" Module Booster Notes
- Instructor's Manual
- Test Bank
- PowerPoint Slides

For Students:
- Revision Quizzes
- Flashcards
- Crossword Puzzles

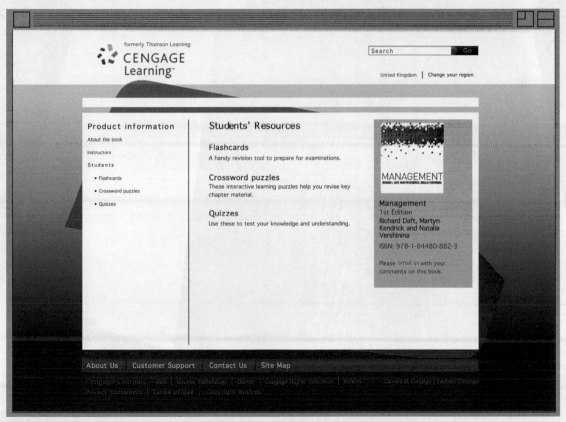

CengageNOW™

Designed by lecturers for lecturers, CengageNOW™ for Daft, Kendrick & Vershinina's *Management* mirrors the natural teaching workflow with an easy-to-use online suite of services and resources, all in one programme. With this system, lecturers can easily plan their courses, manage student assignments, automatically grade, teach with dynamic technology, and assess student progress. CengageNOW™ operates seamlessly with Blackboard/WebCT, Moodle and other virtual learning environments. Ask your Cengage Learning sales representative for a demonstration of what CengageNOW™ for Daft, Kendrick and Vershinina's *Management* can bring to your courses (http://edu.cengage.co.uk/contact_us.aspx).

PART 1

INTRODUCTION TO MANAGEMENT

Innovation can be used to drive changes, such as new materials, ideas, or fashions, to shifting needs and to bring those components into harmony. Of the countless changes that came from the Industrial Revolution, cast iron emerged as a new alternative to wood or stone, which made it possible to build tall structures with thin walls. This, in turn, led Sir Joseph Paxton to design the Crystal Palace, a building with a frame of cast iron and walls of glass to house the Great Exhibition of 1851. The first of its kind, the Crystal Palace was considered by many to be a symbol of modernity and civilization.

Architecture is a blend of art and science, and since the time of Caesar Augustus it has been held that a structure must have "firmness, commodity, and delight," also commonly known as fit, function, and form. Firmness is typically understood to mean a structure's stability; commodity or value pertains to how well a structure performs its function. Delight is commonly understood as the structure's aesthetics: It must be pleasing to the eye, as well as the other senses, in the context of its use.

Management can be judged by much the same standards. Whether small, medium or large, a whole company or simply one department, good professional management will result in a business that is structurally fit, functions as intended, and is innovative and creative as well as being a desirable place to work or conduct business.

However, in today's dynamic global economy, managers face having to also manage a complex series of external relationships with customers, suppliers including outsourcing partners, competitors, financial institutions, and government, as well as deal with the opportunities and challenges presented by external environmental factors such as rapid technological change, fluctuating economic conditions, and the debate over climate change and the natural environment.

CHAPTER OUTLINE

© SHAUN/ISTOCKPHOTO.COM

LEARNING OBJECTIVES

After reading this chapter, you should be able to:

1   Describe the four management functions and the type of
    management activity associated with each.

2   Explain the difference between efficiency and effectiveness and
    their importance for organizational performance.

3   Describe conceptual, human and technical skills and their
    relevance for managers.

4   Describe management types and the horizontal and vertical
    differences between them.

5   Define ten roles that managers perform in organizations.

6   Appreciate the manager's role in small businesses and non-
    profit organizations.

7   Understand the personal challenges involved in becoming a
    new manager.

8   Discuss characteristics of the new workplace and the new
    management competencies needed to deal with today's
    turbulent environment.

CHAPTER 1

INNOVATIVE MANAGEMENT FOR TURBULENT TIMES

Manager's Challenge

The nature of management is to motivate and coordinate others to cope with diverse and far-reaching challenges. For example, imagine that you are the busy CEO of a railway company and enjoying a well-earned family holiday in the Swiss Alps. One day you're enjoying a relaxing day on the ski slopes. That evening you are told that there has just been a serious accident involving the derailment of one of your company's trains that has resulted in a number of serious, possibly life-threatening injuries to passengers. What do you do? Do you abandon you holiday and fly home to take charge of the situation? Or do you continue the holiday, but ask to be kept informed of developments, reasoning that you have employed some experienced mid-level managers to handle such a situation, and that they can contact you if they need any help and advice?

Well this was the situation facing Sir Richard Branson, the founder of Virgin Trains, in February 2007. Sir Richard didn't hesitate but got on a plane as fast as he could, and got out to the crash scene in Cumbria early the next morning to view the wreckage, having to walk on foot, as he was not allowed to drive beyond a police cordon. Later, speaking to the press, Sir Richard said, 'It is a very sad day because of the loss of one life and the injuries caused to other people'. He said the actions of the emergency services, the RAF and the police in dealing with the crash had been 'wonderful'. He also praised the bravery of the train driver, who could 'have run from his seat and dashed to the next carriage, where he might have been safe, but instead tried to steer the train to safety, and he's ended up quite badly injured. I am honestly not worried at this moment who is to blame'. Sir Richard also praised the strength of type of train used by Virgin, saying 'the (Pendolino) train was magnificent – it's built like a tank. I think if it had been any of the old trains the injuries and the mortalities would have been horrendous'.

Are you ready to be a manager?[1]

Welcome to the world of management. Are you ready for it? This questionnaire will help you see whether your priorities align with the demands placed on today's managers. Rate each of the following items based on what you think is the appropriate emphasis for that task to your success as a new manager of a department. Your task is to rate the top four priority items as 'High Priority' and the other four as 'Low Priority'. You will have four of the items rated high and four rated low.

		High Priority	Low Priority
1	Spend 50 per cent or more of your time in the care and development of people.	☐	☐
2	Make sure people understand that you are in control of the department.	☐	☐
3	Use lunches to meet and network with peers in other departments.	☐	☐
4	Implement the changes you believe will improve department performance.	☐	☐
5	Spend as much time as possible talking with and listening to subordinates.	☐	☐
6	Make sure jobs get out on time.	☐	☐
7	Meet regularly with your boss to discuss her expectations for you and your department.	☐	☐
8	Make sure you set clear expectations and policies for your department.	☐	☐

SCORING & INTERPRETATION All eight items in the list may be important, but the odd-numbered items are considered more important than the even-numbered items for long-term success as a manager. If you ticked three or four of the odd-numbered items, consider yourself ready for a management position. A successful new manager discovers that a lot of time has to be spent in the care and feeding of people, including direct reports and colleagues. People who fail in new management jobs often do so because they have poor working relationships or they misjudge management philosophy or cultural values. Developing good relationships in all directions is typically more important than holding on to old work skills or emphasizing control and task outcomes. Successful outcomes typically will occur when relationships are solid. After a year or so in a managerial role, successful people learn that more than half their time is spent networking and building relationships.

Many new managers expect to have power, to be in control, and to be personally responsible for departmental outcomes. A big surprise for many people when they first step into a management role is that they are much less in control of things than they expected. Managers are dependent on subordinates more than vice-versa because they are evaluated on the work of other people rather than on their own work. In a world of rapid change, unexpected events and uncertainty, organizations need managers who can build networks and pull people together toward common goals.

In the past, many managers did exercise tight control over employees. But the field of management is undergoing a revolution that asks managers to do more with less, to engage whole employees, to see change rather than stability as natural, and to inspire vision and cultural values that allow people to create a truly collaborative and productive workplace. In today's work environment, managers rely less on command and control and more on coordination and communication. This approach differs significantly from a traditional mind-set that emphasizes tight top-down control, employee separation and specialization, and management by impersonal measurement and analysis.

This textbook introduces and explains the process of management and the changing ways of thinking about the world that are critical for managers. By reviewing the actions of some successful and not-so-successful managers, you will learn the fundamentals of management. By the end of this chapter, you will already recognize some of the skills managers use to keep organizations on track, and you will begin to understand how managers can achieve astonishing results through people. By the end of this book, you will understand fundamental management skills for planning, organizing, leading and controlling a department or entire organization.

Sue Crawford, news editor of the local News and Star newspaper in Carlisle said later that Virgin managed to emerge from the crisis with its reputation unscathed, and that Sir Richard Branson's presence at the site on Saturday morning was very important: 'Because of their reaction, Branson coming, and because the train itself was intact, people have a lot of confidence in the company.'

Think about the situation Richard Branson and other managers at Virgin Trains were in and try to imagine what you would do. What management style and systems do you think would enable the kind of rapid, flexible response needed to accomplish seemingly impossible goals amid chaos and confusion? Jot down two or three elements that you think might play a role in this success story.

TAKE A MOMENT

Why Innovation Matters

The theme of this text is innovation. To gain or keep a competitive edge, managers have renewed their emphasis on innovation, shifting away from a relentless focus on controlling costs toward investing in the future. In a survey of nearly 1000 executives in North America, Europe, South America, and Asia, 86 per cent agreed that 'innovation is more important than cost reduction for long-term success'.[2]

Why does innovation matter? Innovations in products, services, management systems, production processes, corporate values and other aspects of the organization are what keep companies growing, changing and thriving. Without innovation, no company can survive over the long run. The growing clout and expertise of companies in developing countries, particularly China and India, have many Western managers worried. In a hyper-competitive global environment, companies must innovate more – and more quickly – than ever. Throughout this text, we will spotlight various companies that reflect this new innovation imperative. In addition, Chapter 10 discusses innovation and change in detail. First, let's begin our adventure into the world of management by learning some basics about what it means to be a manager.

The Definition of Management

Every day, managers solve difficult problems, turn organizations around, and achieve astonishing performances. To be successful, every organization needs good managers.

What characteristic do all good managers have in common? They get things done through their organizations. Managers are the *executive function* of the organization, responsible for building and coordinating an entire system rather than performing specific tasks. That is, rather than doing all the work themselves, good managers create the systems and conditions that enable others to perform those tasks. As a boy, Wal-Mart founder Sam Walton made $4000 a year at his paper route. How? Walton had a natural talent for management, and he created a system whereby he hired and coordinated others to help deliver papers rather than simply delivering what he could on his own.[3]

By creating the right systems and environment, managers ensure that the department or organization will survive and thrive beyond the tenure of any specific supervisor or manager. Consider that Jack Welch was CEO of General Electric through 20 amazingly successful years, but the leadership transition to Jeff Immelt in 2001 was as smooth as silk, and GE has stayed at or near the top of lists such as *Fortune* magazine's 'Most Admired Companies', and the *Financial Times*' 'most respected' survey. In 2009, Forbes ranked GE as the world's largest company. With products and services ranging from aircraft engines, power generation, water processing and security technology to medical imaging, business and consumer financing, media content and industrial products, GE has sales in over 100 countries and employs more than 320 000 people worldwide. People who have studied GE are not surprised. The company has thrived for more than a century because managers created the right environment and systems. In the late 1800s, CEO Charles Coffin emphasized that GE's most important product was not light bulbs or transformers, but managerial talent. Managers at GE spend a huge amount of time on human resources issues – recruiting, training, appraising, mentoring and developing leadership talent for the future.[4]

It takes good management to keep people motivated, focused and productive. Customers are not very forgiving of a negligent brand. It is normally better at times of crisis to be open and honest, and by being proactive prevent the company being put in a weakened defensive situation. However, note it was not just the way that Virgin Trains handled the crisis in the aftermath of the train crash discussed earlier. The design of the Pendolino train helped to keep fatalities and serious injuries low, and this was down to Virgin's foresight and commitment to new rolling stock designed with public safety in mind.

Recognizing the role and importance of other people is a key aspect of good management. Early twentieth-century management scholar Mary Parker Follett defined management as 'the art of getting things done through people'.[5] More recently, noted management theorist Peter Drucker stated that the job of managers is to give direction to their organizations, provide leadership, and decide how to use organizational resources to accomplish goals.[6] Getting things done through people and other resources and providing leadership and direction are what managers do. These activities apply not only to top executives such as Eric Schmidt of Google, Richard Branson of Virgin Group, or Indra Nooyi of PepsiCo, but also to the manager of a restaurant in your home town, the leader of an airport security team, a supervisor of an accounting department, or a director of sales and marketing. Thus, our definition of management is as follows:

© CHRIS WILKINS/GETTY IMAGES

CONCEPT CONNECTION   One of the world's worst environmental accidents in history, the Exxon Valdez oil spillage, is widely regarded as one of the clearest examples of mismanagement in history because of the lack of coordination between management, communications and operations. It took the Exxon CEO, Lawrence Rawl, two weeks to visit the scene and make any kind of substantive comment about what had happened.

Management is the attainment of organizational goals in an effective and efficient manner through planning, organizing, leading and controlling organizational resources.

This definition holds two important ideas:

1 the four functions of planning, organizing, leading and controlling; and

2 the attainment of organizational goals in an effective and efficient manner.

Let's first take a look at the four primary management functions. Later in the chapter, we'll discuss organizational effectiveness and efficiency, as well as the multitude of skills managers use to perform their jobs successfully.

> **Management**
> The attainment of organizational goals in an effective and efficient manner through planning, organizing, leading and controlling organizational resources.

As a new manager, remember that management means getting things done through other people. You can't do it all yourself. As a manager, your job is to create the environment and conditions that engage other people in goal accomplishment.

TAKE A MOMENT

The Four Management Functions

Exhibit 1.1 illustrates the process of how managers use resources to attain organizational goals through the functions of planning, organizing, leading and controlling. Although some management theorists identify additional management functions, such as staffing, communicating or decision making, those additional functions will be discussed as subsets of the four primary functions in Exhibit 1.1. Chapters of this book are devoted to the multiple activities and skills associated with each function, as well as to the environment, global competitiveness and ethics, which influence how managers perform these functions.

Planning

Planning means identifying goals for future organizational performance and deciding on the tasks and use of resources needed to attain them. In other words, managerial

> **Planning**
> The management function concerned with defining goals for future organizsational performance and deciding on the tasks and resources needed to attain them.

Exhibit 1.1 The Process of Management

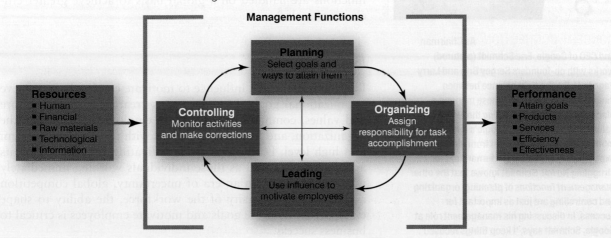

Organizing
The management function concerned with assigning tasks, grouping tasks into departments, and allocating resources to departments.

Leading
The management function that involves the use of influence to motivate employees to achieve the organization's goals.

planning defines where the organization wants to be in the future and how to get there. An example of good planning comes from Time Warner, Inc., where the marketing chiefs of the various divisions – HBO, Time Inc., Turner Broadcasting, Warner Bros., AOL, New Line Cinema, and Time Warner Cable – get together every three weeks to talk about future projects and how the divisions can work together to make them more successful. Thanks to careful planning, for example, almost every division is involved in promoting major films such as *The Golden Compass*, *Hairspray* and *The Lord of the Rings* trilogy.[7]

A lack of planning – or poor planning – alternatively will damage an organization's performance. Marks & Spencer, the UK retailer suffered a surprise slump in the early 1990s partly caused by its then refusal to accept any credit cards other than its own store card. This lack of planning was compounded by its failure to follow the example of rival retailers to shift clothes production to cheaper suppliers overseas, and when it did belatedly make this move, it then suffered negative publicity for the way it terminated long-standing relationships with its UK suppliers. Top managers' lack of vision in perceiving market direction and weak planning efforts regarding overseas outsourcing and supplier relationships seriously damaged the company for some time.

Organizing

Organizing typically follows planning and reflects how the organization tries to accomplish the plan. **Organizing** involves assigning tasks, grouping tasks into departments, delegating authority, and allocating resources across the organization. In recent years, companies as diverse as IBM, Ericsson, Barclays Bank and the UK National Health Service (NHS) have undergone structural reorganizations to accommodate their changing plans. For instance, Ericsson Microwave Systems created and implemented a 'competence shift process', which reduced the total headcount of the division by almost 25 per cent, at a cost approximately 20 per cent less than a traditional restructuring, without any reduction in turnover. Similarly, at Avon Products, where sales have stalled and overhead costs were escalating, CEO Andrea Jung recently trimmed seven layers of management and reorganized the company into a structure where more decisions and functions are handled on a global basis to achieve greater efficiency of scale.[8]

Leading

Leading is the use of influence to motivate employees to achieve organizational goals. Leading means creating a shared culture and values, communicating goals to employees throughout the organization, and infusing employees with the desire to perform at a high level. Leading involves motivating entire departments and divisions as well as those individuals working immediately with the manager. In an era of uncertainty, global competition and a growing diversity of the workforce, the ability to shape culture, communicate goals and motivate employees is critical to business success.

© TORSTEN BLACKWOOD/GETTY IMAGES

CONCEPT CONNECTION As Chairman and CEO of Google, Eric Schmidt (pictured) works with co-founders Sergey Brin and Larry Page to strike the right balance between innovation and discipline. These managers place a high priority on *leading* through shared values and goals to keep Google's employees motivated and energized. Yet from his experience of engineering a turnaround at struggling Novell, Schmidt knows that the other *management functions* of planning, organizing and controlling are just as important for success. In discussing his management role at Google, Schmidt says, 'I keep things focused'.

One does not have to be a well-known top manager to be an exceptional leader. Many managers working quietly in both large and small organizations around the world also provide strong leadership within departments, teams, non-profit organizations and small businesses. For instance, Greg Mortenson runs the Central Asia Institute, a non-profit organization he founded to promote secular education for girls in northern Pakistan and neighbouring Afghanistan. Mortensen's vision, determination, courage and enthusiasm encouraged others to join him in this innovative long-term approach to fighting terrorism.[9]

Controlling

Controlling is the fourth function in the management process. Controlling means monitoring employees' activities, determining whether the organization is on target toward its goals, and making corrections as necessary. Managers must ensure that the organization is moving toward its goals. Trends toward empowerment and trust of employees have led many companies to place less emphasis on top-down control and more emphasis on training employees to monitor and correct themselves.

Information technology is helping managers provide needed organizational control without strict top-down constraints. Companies such as Cisco Systems, Amazon and Oracle use the internet and other information technology to coordinate and monitor virtually every aspect of operations, which enables managers to keep tabs on performance without maintaining daily authoritarian control over employees.[10]

Controlling
The management function concerned with monitoring employees' activities, keeping the organization on track toward its goals, and making corrections as needed.

Organizational Performance

The other part of our definition of management is the attainment of organizational goals in an efficient and effective manner. Management is so important because organizations are so important. In an industrialized society where complex technologies dominate, organizations bring together knowledge, people and raw materials to perform tasks no individual could do alone. Without organizations, how could technology be provided that enables us to share information around the world in an instant; electricity be produced from huge dams and nuclear power plants; and thousands of videogames, compact discs and DVDs be made available for our entertainment? Organizations pervade our society and managers are responsible for seeing that resources are used wisely to attain organizational goals.

Our formal definition of an **organization** is a social entity that is goal directed and deliberately structured. *Social entity* means being made up of two or more people. *Goal directed* means designed to achieve some outcome, such as make a profit (Wal-Mart, Royal-Dutch Shell, Toyota, Starbucks), win pay increases for members (Trade Unions), meet spiritual needs (United Methodist Church), or provide social satisfaction (amateur sports team). *Deliberately structured* means that tasks are divided and responsibility for their performance is assigned to organization members. This definition applies to all organizations, including both profit and not-for-profit. Small, off-beat, niche and non-profit organizations are more numerous than large, visible corporations – and just as important to society.

Based on our definition of management, the manager's responsibility is to coordinate resources in an effective and efficient manner to accomplish the organization's goals. Organizational **effectiveness** is the degree to which the organization achieves a *stated goal*, or succeeds in accomplishing what it tries to do. Organizational effectiveness means providing a product or service that customers value. Organizational **efficiency** refers to the amount of resources used to achieve an organizational goal. It is based on how much raw materials, money and people are necessary for producing

Organization
A social entity that is goal directed and deliberately structured.

Effectiveness
The degree to which the organization achieves a stated goal.

Efficiency
The use of minimal resources – raw materials, money and people – to produce a desired volume of output.

Technical Skills

Technical skill
The understanding of and proficiency in the performance of specific tasks.

Technical skill is the understanding of and proficiency in the performance of specific tasks. Technical skill includes mastery of the methods, techniques and equipment involved in specific functions such as engineering, manufacturing or finance. Technical skill also includes specialized knowledge, analytical ability and the competent use of tools and techniques to solve problems in that specific discipline. Technical skills are particularly important at lower organizational levels. Many managers get promoted to their first management jobs by having excellent technical skills. However, technical skills become less important than human and conceptual skills as managers move up the hierarchy. For example, in his seven years as a manufacturing engineer at Boeing, Bruce Moravec developed superb technical skills in his area of operation. But when he was asked to lead the team designing a new fuselage for the Boeing 757, Moravec found that he needed to rely heavily on human skills in order to gain the respect and confidence of people who worked in areas he knew little about.[18]

TAKE A MOMENT   Complete the Experiential Exercise on page 29 that pertains to management skills. Reflect on the strength of your preferences among the three skills and the implications for you as a manager.

When Skills Fail

Everyone has flaws and weaknesses, and these shortcomings become most apparent under conditions of rapid change and uncertainty.[19] Therefore, during turbulent times, managers really have to stay on their toes and apply all their skills and competencies in a way that benefits the organization and its stakeholders – employees, customers, investors, the community, and so forth. In recent years, numerous highly publicized examples showed us what happens when managers fail to effectively and ethically apply their skills to meet the demands of an uncertain, rapidly changing world. Companies such as Enron, Parmalat and WorldCom were flying high in the 1990s but came crashing down under the weight of financial scandals. Others, such as Woolworths, Northern Rock, General Motors and Chrysler have failed or are struggling partly because of management failures over a long period of time.

Although corporate greed and deceit grab the headlines, many more companies falter or fail less spectacularly. Managers fail to listen to customers, misinterpret signals from the marketplace, or can't build a cohesive team and execute a strategic plan. Over the past years, many CEOs, including Carly Fiorina at Hewlett-Packard, and Michael Eisner at Disney have been ousted due to their failure to implement their strategic plans or keep stakeholders happy.

Recent examinations of struggling organizations and executives offer a glimpse into the mistakes managers often make in a turbulent environment.[20] One of the biggest blunders is managers' failure to comprehend and adapt to the rapid pace of change in the world around them. A related problem is top managers who create a climate of fear in the organization so that people are afraid to tell the truth and strive primarily to avoid the boss's wrath. Thus, bad news gets hidden and important signals from the marketplace are missed. People stop thinking creatively, avoid responsibility, and may even slide into unethical behaviour if it keeps them on the boss's good side.[21]

Other critical management missteps include poor communication skills and failure to listen; poor interpersonal skills; treating employees as instruments to be used; a failure to clarify direction and performance expectations; suppressing dissenting viewpoints; and the inability to build a management team characterized by mutual trust and respect.[22] Bob Nardelli was forced out at Home Depot, the largest home-improvement retailer in the United States, largely because he was unable to build trust and cohesiveness among his board and management team, and his brusque and unfeeling style alienated executives and rank and file workers alike. Using expletives for emphasis at one meeting soon after his arrival as CEO, Nardelli reportedly said, 'You guys don't know how to run a business'. At the annual meeting where shareholder advocates were protesting Nardelli's extravagant pay package, the CEO limited shareholder questions to one minute, sealing his image as a callous executive unwilling to listen and compromise. He tried to redeem himself by going on a 'listening tour', but the damage had been done.[23] Although primarily a US based company, Home Depot does have plans for expansion overseas and, in December 2006, the company announced its acquisition of the Chinese home improvement retailer, The Home Way. Home Depot is a relatively latecomer to China, where competitors such as Sweden's IKEA, Britain's B&Q and Chinese retailers are already established in its sector. As we will discuss in a later chapter an appropriate management style can also be heavily influenced by the organizational, market and national context in which it has to operate, and it is likely that Home Depot will face very different management and cultural challenges in China than it does in the United States.

Contrast Nardelli's approach with that of Jim McNerney, who spent his first six months as CEO of Boeing, the world's leading aerospace company, talking with employees around the company to understand Boeing's strengths and challenges and emphasizing the need for cooperation and teamwork. Unlike Home Depot, Boeing has customers in more than 90 countries around the world and is one of the largest US exporters in terms of sales.[24]

Management Types

Managers use conceptual, human and technical skills to perform the four management functions of planning, organizing, leading and controlling in all organizations – large and small, manufacturing and service, profit and non-profit, traditional and internet-based. But not all managers' jobs are the same. Managers are responsible for different departments, work at different levels in the hierarchy, and meet different requirements for achieving high performance. Twenty-five-year-old Daniel Wheeler is a first-line supervisor in his first management job at Del Monte Foods, where he is directly involved in promoting products, approving packaging sleeves and organizing people to host sampling events.[25] Alan Forrest is a middle manager for B&Q, where he works as warehouse manager for Scotland and is responsible for expansion and development of new stores,[26] and James Mwangi is CEO of Equity Bank, a Kenyan based Bank that has a 50 per cent share of the Kenyan market and is opening 4000 new accounts a day by focusing on the millions of low wage earners who had previously been excluded from the banking system.[27] All three are managers and must contribute to planning, organizing, leading and controlling their organizations – but in different amounts and ways.

Vertical Differences

An important determinant of the manager's job is hierarchical level. Exhibit 1.3 illustrates the three levels in the hierarchy. A recent study of more than 1400 managers examined how the manager's job differs across these three hierarchical levels and found that the primary focus changes at different levels.[28] For first-level managers, the main concern is facilitating individual employee performance. Middle managers,

Exhibit 1.3 Management Levels in the Organizational Hierarchy

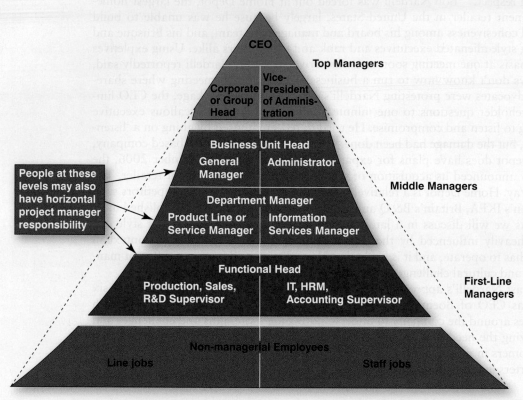

SOURCE: Adapted from Thomas V. Bonoma and Joseph C. Lawler, 'Chutes and Ladders: Growing the General Manager', *Sloan Management Review* (Spring 1989), 27–37.

though, are concerned less with individual performance and more with linking groups of people, such as allocating resources, coordinating teams or putting top management plans into action across the organization. For top-level managers, the primary focus is monitoring the external environment and determining the best strategy to be competitive.

Top manager
A manager who is at the top of the organizational hierarchy and is responsible for the entire organization.

Let's look in more detail at differences across hierarchical levels. **Top managers** are at the top of the hierarchy and are responsible for the entire organization. They have such titles as president, chairperson, executive director, chief executive officer (CEO) and managing director. Top managers are responsible for setting organizational goals, defining strategies for achieving them, monitoring and interpreting the external environment, and making decisions that affect the entire organization. They look to the long-term future and concern themselves with general environmental trends and the organization's overall success. Top managers are also responsible for communicating a shared vision for the organization, shaping corporate culture, and nurturing an entrepreneurial spirit that can help the company innovate and keep pace with rapid change.[29]

Middle manager
A manager who works at the middle levels of the organization and is responsible for business units and major departments.

Middle managers work at middle levels of the organization and are responsible for business units and major departments. Examples of middle managers are department head, division head, manager of quality control, and director of the research lab. Middle managers typically have two or more management levels beneath them. They are responsible for implementing the overall strategies and policies defined by top managers. Middle managers generally are concerned with the near future rather than with long-range planning.

The middle manager's job has changed dramatically over the past two decades. Many organizations improved efficiency by laying off middle managers and slashing middle management levels. Traditional pyramidal organization charts were flattened to allow information to flow quickly from top to bottom and decisions to be made with greater speed. Exhibit 1.3 illustrates the shrinking middle management.

Yet even as middle management levels have been reduced, the middle manager's job has taken on a new vitality. Rather than managing the flow of information up and down the hierarchy, middle managers create horizontal networks that can help the organization act quickly. Research shows that middle managers play a crucial role in driving innovation and enabling organizations to respond to rapid shifts in the environment.[30] 'Leaders can design wonderful strategies, but the success of the organization resides in the execution of those strategies. The people in the middle are the ones who make it work.'[31]

Middle managers' status has also escalated because of the growing use of teams and projects. Strong project managers are in hot demand. A project manager is responsible for a temporary work project that involves the participation of people from various functions and levels of the organization, and perhaps from outside the company as well. Many of today's middle managers work with a variety of projects and teams at the same time, some of which cross geographical and cultural as well as functional boundaries.

First-line managers are directly responsible for the production of goods and services. They are the first or second level of management and have such titles as supervisor, line manager, section chief, and office manager. They are responsible for groups of non-management employees. Their primary concern is the application of rules and procedures to achieve efficient production, provide technical assistance, and motivate subordinates. The time horizon at this level is short, with the emphasis on accomplishing day-to-day goals. For example, Alistair Boot manages the menswear department for a John Lewis department store in Cheadle, England.[32] Boot's duties include monitoring and supervising shop floor employees to make sure sales procedures, safety rules and customer service policies are followed. This type of managerial job might also involve motivating and guiding young, often inexperienced workers, providing assistance as needed, and ensuring adherence to company policies.

Horizontal Differences

The other major difference in management jobs occurs horizontally across the organization. **Functional managers** are responsible for departments that perform a single functional task and have employees with similar training and skills. Functional departments include advertising, sales, finance, human resources, manufacturing, and accounting. *Line managers* are responsible for the manufacturing and marketing departments that make or sell the product or service. *Staff managers* are in charge of departments such as finance and human resources that support line departments.

General managers are responsible for several departments that perform different functions. A general manager is responsible for a self-contained division, such as a Sainsbury's store or a Hyundai Motors assembly plant, and for all the functional

CONCEPT CONNECTION Afghan radio personalities Jamila Restin (L) and Farida Helleh (R) read the news on the "Good Morning Afghanistan" program in Kabul, February 25, 2002. The hour-long radio show, a mixture of news, interviews and feature packages, differs from traditional programs which focus on government propaganda and Islamic teachings.

Project manager
A manager responsible for a temporary work project that involves the participation of other people from various functions and levels of the organization.

First-line manager
A manager who is at the first or second management level and is directly responsible for the production of goods and services.

Functional manager
A manager who is responsible for a department that performs a single functional task and has employees with similar training and skills.

General manager
A manager who is responsible for several departments that perform different functions.

departments within it. Project managers also have general management responsibility because they coordinate people across several departments to accomplish a specific project.

What is it Like to be a Manager?

Unless someone has actually performed managerial work, it is hard to understand exactly what managers do on an hour-by-hour, day-to-day basis. The manager's job is so diverse that a number of studies have been undertaken in an attempt to describe exactly what happens. The question of what managers actually do to plan, organize, lead and control was answered by Henry Mintzberg, who followed managers around and recorded all their activities.[33] He developed a description of managerial work that included three general characteristics and ten roles. These characteristics and roles, discussed in the following sections, have been supported in subsequent research.[34]

More recent research has looked at what managers *like* to do. The research found that both male and female managers across five different countries reported that they most enjoy activities such as leading others, networking and leading innovation. Activities managers like least include controlling subordinates, handling paperwork and managing time pressures.[35] Many new managers in particular find the intense time pressures of management, the load of administrative paperwork, and the challenge of directing others to be quite stressful as they adjust to their new roles and responsibilities. Indeed, the initial leap into management can be one of the scariest moments in a person's career.

TAKE A MOMENT   How will you make the transition to a new manager's position? Complete the New Manager Self-Test on page 17 to see how prepared you are to step into a management role.

Making the Leap: Becoming a New Manager

Many people who are promoted into a management position have little idea what the job actually entails and receive little training about how to handle their new role. It's no wonder that, among managers, first-line supervisors tend to experience the most job burnout and attrition.[36]

Organizations often promote the star performers – those who demonstrate individual expertise in their area of responsibility and have an ability to work well with others – both to reward the individual and to build new talent into the managerial ranks. But making the shift from individual contributor to manager is often tricky.[37] Harvard professor Linda Hill followed a group of 19 managers over the first year of their managerial careers and found that one key to success is to recognize that becoming a manager involves more than learning a new set of skills. Rather, becoming a manager means a profound transformation in the way people think of themselves, called *personal identity*, that includes letting go of deeply held attitudes and habits and learning new ways of thinking.[38] Exhibit 1.4 outlines the transformation from individual performer to manager.

Recall our earlier discussion of the role of the manager as the executive function of the organization, the person who builds systems rather than doing specific tasks. The individual performer is a specialist and a 'doer'. His or her mind is conditioned to think in terms of performing specific tasks and activities as expertly as possible.

Exhibit 1.4 Making the Leap from Individual Performer to Manager

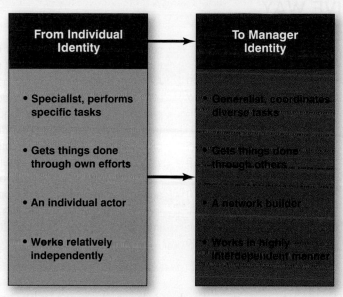

From Individual Identity

- **Specialist, performs specific tasks**
- **Gets things done through own efforts**
- **An individual actor**
- **Works relatively independently**

To Manager Identity

- **Generalist, coordinates diverse tasks**
- **Gets things done through others**
- **A network builder**
- **Works in highly interdependent manner**

SOURCE: Based on Exhibit 1.1, 'Transformation of Identity', in Linda A. Hill, *Becoming a Manager: Mastery of a New Identity,* 2nd ed. (Boston, MA: Harvard Business School Press, 2003): 6.

✔ NEW MANAGER SELF-TEST

Manager Achievement

Rate each item below based on your orientation toward personal achievement. Read each item and tick either Mostly True or Mostly False as you feel right now.

		Mostly True	Mostly False
1	I enjoy the feeling I get from mastering a new skill.	☐	☐
2	Working alone is typically better than working in a group.	☐	☐
3	I like the feeling I get from winning.	☐	☐
4	I like to develop my skills to a high level.	☐	☐
5	I rarely depend on anyone else to get things done.	☐	☐
6	I am frequently the most valuable contributor to a team.	☐	☐
7	I like competitive situations.	☐	☐
8	To get ahead, it is important to be viewed as a winner.	☐	☐

SCORING AND INTERPRETATION Give yourself one point for each Mostly True answer. In this case, a *low score* is better. A high score means a focus on personal achievement separate from others, which is ideal for a specialist or individual contributor. However, a manager is a generalist who gets things done through others. A desire to be a winner may put you in competition with your people rather than a focus on developing their skills. As a manager, you will not succeed as a lone achiever who does not facilitate and coordinate others. If you ticked three or fewer as Mostly True, your basic orientation is good. If you scored six or higher, your focus is on being an individual winner. You will want to shift your perspective to become an excellent manager.

INNOVATIVE WAY

Lisa Drakeman, Genmab AS

Lisa Drakeman was teaching religion at Princeton when her husband asked her to help out at Medarex, a new biotechnology company he founded to develop antibody-based medicines for cancer, inflammation and infectious disease. Drakeman began performing various tasks part-time, but soon found herself heading up a spin-off company, Genmab AS of Denmark.

One of the toughest things Drakeman had to learn was to stop doing everything herself. In the beginning, she attended every meeting, interviewed every job candidate, and read every draft of clinical trial designs. She soon realized that she couldn't master every detail and that trying to do so would stall the company's growth. Although it was hard to step back, Drakeman eventually made the transition from doing individual tasks to performing the executive function. She established clear procedures and began delegating the details of products and clinical trials to others. Rather than interviewing job candidates herself, she set up human resources systems to enable others to interview, hire and train employees. By developing from individual performer to manager, Drakeman helped Genmab grow from 25 employees to around 200 within a few years.[39]

The manager, on the other hand, has to be a generalist and learn to coordinate a broad range of activities. Whereas the individual performer strongly identifies with his or her specific tasks, the manager has to identify with the broader organization and industry.

In addition, the individual performer gets things done mostly through his or her own efforts, and develops the habit of relying on self rather than others. The manager, though, gets things done through other people. Indeed, one of the most common mistakes new managers make is wanting to do all the work themselves rather than delegating to others and developing others' abilities.[40] Lisa Drakeman made this mistake when she moved from teaching religion to being CEO of a biotechnology start-up.

Another problem for many new managers is that they expect to have greater freedom to do what they think is best for the organization. In reality, though, managers find themselves hemmed in by interdependencies. Being a successful manager means thinking in terms of building teams and networks, becoming a motivator and organizer within a highly interdependent system of people and work. Although the distinctions may sound simple in the abstract, they are anything but. In essence, becoming a manager means becoming a new person and viewing oneself in a completely new way.

TAKE A MOMENT   Can you make a personal transformation from individual performer to manager, accomplishing work by engaging and coordinating other people? Look back at your results on the questionnaire at the beginning of this chapter to see how your priorities align with the demands placed on a manager.

Many new managers have to make the transformation in a 'trial by fire', learning on the job as they go, but organizations are beginning to be more responsive to the need for new manager training. The cost to organizations of losing good employees who can't make the transition is greater than the cost of providing training to help new managers cope, learn and grow. In addition, some of today's organizations are using great care in selecting people for managerial positions, including ensuring that

MANAGER'S SHOPTALK

Do You Really Want to be a Manager?

Is management for you? Becoming a manager is considered by most people to be a positive, forward-looking career move and, indeed, life as a manager offers appealing aspects. However, it also holds many challenges, and not every person will be happy and fulfilled in a management position. Here are some of the issues would-be managers should consider before deciding they want to pursue a management career:

1 **The increased workload.** It isn't unusual for managers to work 70 to 80 hours per week, and some work even longer. A manager's job always starts before a shift and ends hours after the shift is over. When Ray Sarnacki was promoted to manager at an aerospace company, he found himself frustrated by the incessant travel, endless paperwork and crowded meeting schedule. He eventually left the job and found happiness in a position earning about one-fifth of his peak managerial salary.

2 **The challenge of supervising former peers.** This issue can be one of the toughest for new managers. They frequently struggle to find the right approach, with some trying too hard to remain 'one of the gang', and others asserting their authority too harshly. In almost all cases, the transition from a peer-to-peer relationship to a manager-to-subordinate one is challenging and stressful.

3 **The headache of responsibility for other people.** A lot of people get into management because they like the idea of having power, but the reality is that many managers feel overwhelmed by the responsibility of hiring, supervising and disciplining others. New managers are often astonished at the amount of time it takes to handle 'people problems'. Kelly Cannell, who quit her job as a manager, puts it this way: 'What's the big deal [about managing people]? The big deal is that people are human . . . To be a good manager, you have to mentor them, listen to their problems, counsel them, and at the end of the day you still have your own work on your plate . . . Don't take the responsibility lightly, because no matter what you think, managing people is not easy.'

4 **Being caught in the middle.** Except for those in the top echelons, managers find themselves acting as a backstop, caught between upper management and the workforce. Even when managers disagree with the decisions of top executives, they are responsible for implementing them.

For some people, the frustrations of management aren't worth it. For others, management is a fulfilling and satisfying career choice and the emotional rewards can be great. One key to being happy as a manager may be carefully evaluating whether you can answer yes to the question, 'Do I really want to be a manager?'

SOURCES Erin White, 'Learning to Be the Boss', *The Wall Street Journal*, November 21, 2005; Jared Sandberg, 'Down Over Moving Up: Some New Bosses Find They Hate Their Jobs', *The Wall Street Journal*, July 27, 2005; Heath Row, 'Is Management for Me? That Is the Question', *Fast Company* (February–March 1998): 50–52; Timothy D. Schellhardt, 'Want to Be a Manager? Many People Say No, Calling Job Miserable', *The Wall Street Journal*, April 4, 1997; and Matt Murray, 'Managing Your Career – The Midcareer Crisis: Am I in This Business to Become a Manager?', *The Wall Street Journal*, July 25, 2000.

each candidate understands what management involves and really wants to be a manager. A career as a manager can be highly rewarding, but it can also be stressful and frustrating. The Manager's Shoptalk further examines some of the challenges new managers face. After reading the Shoptalk, can you answer 'Yes' to the question 'Do I really want to be a manager?'

Manager Activities

Most new managers are unprepared for the variety of activities managers routinely perform. One of the most interesting findings about managerial activities is how busy managers are and how hectic the average workday can be.

Adventures in Multitasking

Managerial activity is characterized by variety, fragmentation and brevity.[41] The widespread and voluminous nature of a manager's involvements leaves little time for quiet reflection. The average time spent on any one activity is less than nine minutes. Managers shift gears quickly. Significant crises are interspersed with trivial events in no predictable sequence. One example of just two typical hours for a fictional manager Julia Jones follows. Note the frequent interruptions and the brevity and variety of tasks.

7:30A.M.	Julia arrives at work and begins to plan her day.
7:37A.M.	Andy Smith, calls into Julia's office to discuss a meeting with a client and to review the cost-benefit analysis for a proposed customer relationship management planning system.
7:45A.M.	Julia's administrative assistant, Pat, motions for her to pick up the telephone. 'Julia, they have had serious water damage at the warehouse last night. A water pipe burst, causing over £50 000 of damage. It will take around a week to get everything back to normal. Thought you should know.'
8:00A.M.	Pat brings in the mail. She also asks instructions for formatting a report Julia gave her yesterday.
8:14A.M.	Julia gets a phone call from the accounting manager, who is returning a call from the day before. They talk about an accounting problem.
8:25A.M.	A Mr Newton is ushered in. Mr Newton is here to complain that a sales manager has been rude to his employees and insists something must be done. Julia rearranges her schedule to investigate this claim.
9:00A.M.	Julia returns to the mail. One letter is from an irate customer. Janet types out a helpful, restrained reply. Pat brings in phone messages.
9:15A.M.	Janet receives an urgent phone call from Mike Baldwin. They discuss a lost contract, problems with unhappy subordinates, and a potential promotion.[42]

Life on Speed Dial

The manager performs a great deal of work at an unrelenting pace.[43] Managers' work is fast paced and requires great energy. The managers observed by Mintzberg processed 36 pieces of mail each day, attended eight meetings and took a tour through the building or plant. As soon as a manager's daily calendar is set, unexpected disturbances erupt. New meetings are required. During time away from the office, executives catch up on work-related reading, paperwork, phone calls and email. Technology, such as email, instant messaging, mobile phones and laptops, intensifies the pace.[44]

Heather Coin, a restaurant manager, says. 'I really try to keep the plates spinning', and compares her management job to a circus act. 'If I see a plate slowing down, I go and give it a spin and move on.' She arrives at work about 9:30a.m. and checks the financials for how the restaurant performed the day before. Next comes a staff meeting and various personnel duties. Before and after the lunch shift, she's pitching in with whatever needs to be done – making salads in the kitchen, expediting the food, serving tables or talking with guests. After lunch, from 3:00p.m. to 4:30p.m., Heather takes care of administrative duties, paperwork or meetings with upper management, media or community organizations. At 4:30p.m., she holds a shift-change meeting to ensure a smooth transition from the day crew to the night crew. Throughout the day, Heather also mentors staff members, which she considers the most rewarding part of her job. After the evening rush, she usually heads for home about 10p.m., the end of another 12.5-hour day.[45]

Manager Roles

Mintzberg's observations and subsequent research indicate that diverse manager activities can be organized into ten roles.[46] A role is a set of expectations for a manager's behaviour. Exhibit 1.5 provides examples of each of the roles. These roles are divided into three conceptual categories: informational (managing by information); interpersonal (managing through people); and decisional (managing through action). Each role represents activities that managers undertake to ultimately accomplish the functions of

Role
A set of expectations for one's behaviour.

Exhibit 1.5 Ten Manager Roles

Category	Role	Activity
Informational	Monitor	Seek and receive information, scan periodicals and reports, maintain personal contacts.
	Disseminator	Forward information to other organization members; send memos and reports, make phone calls.
	Spokesperson	Transmit information to outsiders through speeches, reports, memos.
Interpersonal	Figurehead	Perform ceremonial and symbolic duties such as greeting visitors, signing legal documents.
	Leader	Direct and motivate subordinates; train, counsel, and communicate with subordinates.
	Liaison	Maintain information links both inside and outside the organization; use email, phone calls, meetings.
Decisional	Entrepreneur	Initiate improvement projects; identify new ideas, delegate idea responsibility to others.
	Disturbance handler	Take corrective action during disputes or crises; resolve conflicts among subordinates; adapt to environmental crises.
	Resource allocator	Decide who gets resources; schedule, budget, set priorities.
	Negotiator	Represent department during negotiation of union contracts, sales, purchases, budgets; represent departmental interests.

SOURCE: Adapted from Henry Mintzberg, *The Nature of Managerial Work* (New York: Harper & Row, 1973), pp. 92–93; and Henry Mintzberg, 'Managerial Work: Analysis from Observation', *Management Science* 18 (1971): B97–B110.

needs of the organization. Managers stay alert to needs both within and outside the organization to determine what roles are most critical at various times.

Managing in Small Businesses and Non-profit Organizations

Small businesses are growing in importance. Hundreds of small businesses are opened every month, but the environment for small business today is highly complicated. Small companies sometimes have difficulty developing the managerial dexterity needed to survive in a turbulent environment. One survey on trends and future developments in small business found that nearly half of respondents saw inadequate management skills as a threat to their companies, as compared to less than 25 per cent of larger organizations.[52]

One interesting finding is that managers in small businesses tend to emphasize roles different from those of managers in large corporations. Managers in small companies often see their most important role as that of spokesperson because they must promote the small, growing company to the outside world. The entrepreneur role is also critical in small businesses because managers have to be innovative and help their organizations develop new ideas to remain competitive. Small-business managers tend to rate lower on the leader role and on information-processing roles, compared with their counterparts in large corporations.

Non-profit organizations also represent a major application of management talent. Organizations such as the Salvation Army, RSPCA, Amnesty International, and the Red Cross all require excellent management. The functions of planning, organizing, leading and controlling apply to non-profits just as they do to business organizations, and managers in non-profit organizations use similar skills and perform similar activities. The primary difference is that managers in businesses direct their activities toward earning money for the company, whereas managers in non-profits direct their efforts toward generating some kind of social impact. The unique characteristics and needs of non-profit organizations created by this distinction present unique challenges for managers.[53]

Financial resources for non-profit organizations typically come from government appropriations, grants and donations rather than from the sale of products or services to customers. In businesses, managers focus on improving the organization's products and services to increase sales revenues. In non-profits, however, services are typically provided to non-paying clients, and a major problem for many organizations is securing a steady stream of funds to continue operating. Non-profit managers, committed to serving clients with limited resources, must focus on keeping organizational costs as low as possible.[54] Donors generally want their money to go directly to helping clients rather than for overhead costs. If non-profit managers can't demonstrate a highly efficient use of resources, they might have a hard time securing additional donations or government appropriations. In the US, the Sarbanes–Oxley Act (the 2002 corporate governance reform law) doesn't apply to non-profits, for example, but many are adopting its guidelines, striving for greater transparency and accountability to boost credibility with constituents and be more competitive when seeking funding.[55]

In addition, because non-profit organizations do not have a conventional *bottom line*, managers often struggle with the question of what constitutes results and effectiveness. It is easy to measure dollars and cents, but the metrics of success in non-profits are much more ambiguous. Managers have to measure intangibles such as 'improve public health', 'make a difference in the lives of the disenfranchised' or 'increase appreciation for the arts'. This intangible nature also makes it more difficult to gauge the performance of employees and managers. An added complication is that managers often depend on volunteers and donors who cannot be supervised and controlled in the same way a business manager deals with employees.

The roles defined by Mintzberg also apply to non-profit managers, but these may differ somewhat. We might expect managers in non-profit organizations to place more emphasis on the roles of spokesperson (to 'sell' the organization to donors and the public), leader (to build a mission-driven community of employees and volunteers), and resource allocator (to distribute government resources or grant funds that are often assigned top-down).

Managers in all organizations – large corporations, small businesses and non-profit organizations – carefully integrate and adjust the management functions and roles to meet challenges within their own circumstances and keep their organizations healthy.

Management and the New Workplace

Rapid environmental shifts, such as changes in technology, globalization and shifting social values, are causing fundamental transformations that have a dramatic impact on the manager's job. These transformations are reflected in the transition to a new workplace, as illustrated in Exhibit 1.7.

New Workplace Characteristics

The primary characteristic of the new workplace is the *digitization* of business, which has radically altered the nature of work, employees and the workplace itself.[56] The *old workplace* is characterized by routine, specialized tasks and standardized control procedures. Employees typically perform their jobs in one specific company facility, such as a car factory located in Sunderland or Milan, or an insurance company located in Sydney or Norwich. Individuals concentrate on doing their own specific tasks, and managers are cautious about sharing knowledge and information across boundaries. The organization is coordinated and controlled through the vertical hierarchy, with decision-making authority residing with upper-level managers.

In the *new workplace*, by contrast, work is free-flowing and *flexible*. Structures are flatter, and lower-level employees make decisions based on widespread

Exhibit 1.7 The Transition to a New Workplace

	The New Workplace	The Old Workplace
Characteristics		
Technology	Digital	Mechanical
Work	Flexible, virtual	Structured, localized
Workforce	Empowered; diverse	Loyal employees; homogeneous
Management Competencies		
Leadership	Empowering	Autocratic
Doing Work	By teams	By individuals
Relationships	Collaboration	Conflict, competition

© DIBYANGSHU SARKAR/GETTY IMAGES

CONCEPT CONNECTION The internet and other new technologies are also tied closely though *globalization* to the development of the *new workplace*. Global interconnections bring many opportunities, but they also bring new threats, raise new risks, and accelerate complexity and competitiveness. Think about the trend towards outsourcing to low-cost providers overseas. European and US companies have been sending manufacturing work to other countries for many years to cut costs. Now, high-level knowledge work is also being outsourced to countries such as India, Malaysia and South Africa. For example, India's Wipro Ltd. writes software, performs consulting work, integrates back-office solutions, performs systems integration and handles technical support for some of the biggest corporations in the world – and they do it for 40 per cent less than comparable domestic companies can do the work.[60]

Interim manager
A manager who is not affiliated with a specific organization but works on a project-by-project basis or provides expertise to organizations in a specific area.

information and guided by the organization's mission and values.[57] *Empowered employees* are expected to seize opportunities and solve problems as they emerge. Knowledge is widely shared, and people throughout the company keep in touch with a broad range of colleagues via advanced technology. The valued worker is one who learns quickly, shares knowledge, and is comfortable with risk, change and ambiguity. People expect to work on a variety of projects and jobs throughout their careers rather than staying in one field or with one company.

The new workplace is organized around *networks* rather than rigid hierarchies, and work is often *virtual*, with managers having to supervise and coordinate people who never actually 'come to work' in the traditional sense.[58] Flexible hours, telecommuting and virtual teams are increasingly popular ways of working that require new skills from managers. Using virtual teams allows organizations to tap the best people for a particular job, no matter where they are located. Teams may include outside contractors, suppliers, customers, competitors and interim managers. **Interim managers** are managers who are not affiliated with a specific organization but work on a project-by- project basis or provide expertise to organizations in a specific area.[59] This approach enables a company to benefit from specialist skills without making a long-term commitment, and it provides flexibility for managers who like the challenge, variety and learning that comes from working in a wide range of organizations.

Diversity of the population and the workforce is another fact of life for organizations in many countries. For example, the general population of the UK and France, and thus of their workforce, is growing more ethnically and racially diverse. In addition, generational and gender diversity is a powerful force in today's workplace, with male and female employees of all ages working together on teams and projects in a way rarely seen in the past.

New Management Competencies

In the face of these transitions, managers must rethink their approach to organizing, directing and motivating employees. Today's best managers give up their command-and-control mind-set to focus on coaching and providing guidance, creating organizations that are fast, flexible, innovative and relationship-oriented.

Instead of 'management-by-keeping-tabs', managers employ an *empowering leadership* style.[61] When people are working at scattered locations, managers can't

Read the Ethical Dilemma on page 30 that pertains to managing in the new workplace. Think about what you would do and why to begin to understand how you will solve thorny management problems.

TAKE A MOMENT

continually monitor behaviour. In addition, they are sometimes coordinating the work of people who aren't under their direct control, such as those in partner organizations. They have to set clear expectations, guide people toward goal accomplishment through vision, values and regular communication, and develop a level of trust in employees' commitment to getting the job done.

Success in the new workplace depends on the strength and quality of *collaborative relationships*. New ways of working emphasize collaboration across functions and hierarchical levels as well as with other companies. *Team-building skills* are crucial. Instead of managing a department of employees, many managers act as team leaders of ever-shifting, temporary projects. When a manager at IBM needs to staff a project, he or she gives a list of skills needed to the human resources department, which provides a pool of people who are qualified. The manager then puts together the best combination of people for the project, which often means pulling people from many different locations. IBM estimates that about 40 per cent of its employees participate in virtual teams.[62]

The shift to a new way of managing isn't easy for traditional managers who are accustomed to being 'in charge', making all the decisions, and knowing where their subordinates are and what they're doing at every moment. Many new managers have a hard time with today's flexible work environment, which in theory allows employees to work anywhere, anytime as long as they complete assignments and meet goals, and for example, find it difficult to keep themselves from checking to see who's logged onto the company network.[63]

Even more changes and challenges are on the horizon for organizations and managers. It's an exciting time to be entering the field of management. Throughout this book, you will learn much more about the new workplace, about the new and dynamic roles managers are playing in the twenty-first century, and about how you can be an effective manager in a complex, ever-changing world.

An important management challenge in the new workplace is to build a *learning organization* by creating an organizational climate that values experimentation and risk taking, applies current technology, tolerates mistakes and failure, and rewards non-traditional thinking and the sharing of knowledge. Everyone in the organization participates in identifying and solving problems, enabling the organization to continuously experiment, improve and increase its capability. The role of managers is not to make decisions, but to create learning capability, where everyone is free to experiment and learn what works best.

© MIKE HEWITT/GETTY IMAGES

CONCEPT CONNECTION Manchester United manager Sir Alex Ferguson knows how to use new management competencies to build high performance teams capable of winning English Premiership and European Cup titles. His management style is a paradox. Born in Glasgow to a Protestant, working class family, his leadership skills first came to the fore as a shop steward in the Clyde shipyards, when Ferguson led an unofficial walk-out over a pay dispute. His management style has been thoroughly analysed by lovers of the sport. They have attributed his success to factors as diverse as a 'working class ability' to assess the qualities of men around him, and 'tunnel vision'. However, he is also fiercely loyal to his players in public, although never shy to give them a blast of his temper in private. Ferguson claims his success is down to inspiring discipline and confidence, and trust in the relationships developed within the team.

A MANAGER'S ESSENTIALS: WHAT HAVE WE LEARNED?

■ This chapter introduced the topic of management and defined the types of roles and activities managers perform. Managers are responsible for attaining organizational goals in an efficient and effective manner through the four management functions of planning, organizing, leading, and controlling. Managers are the executive function of the organization. Rather than performing specific tasks, they are responsible for creating systems and conditions that enable others to achieve high performance.

■ To perform the four functions, managers need three types of skills – conceptual, human and technical. Conceptual skills are more important at top levels of the organization; human skills are important at all levels; and technical skills are most important for first-line managers.

■ A manager's job varies depending on whether one is a top manager, middle manager or first-line manager. A manager's job may also differ across the organization, to include project managers and interim managers as well as functional managers (including line managers and staff managers) and general managers.

■ Becoming a manager requires a shift in thinking. New managers often struggle with the challenges of coordinating a broad range of people and activities, delegating to and developing others, and relating to former peers in a new way.

■ Managers' activities are associated with ten roles: the informational roles of monitor, disseminator and spokesperson; the interpersonal roles of figurehead, leader and liaison; and the decisional roles of entrepreneur, disturbance handler, resource allocator and negotiator.

■ Rapid and dramatic change in recent years has caused significant shifts in the workplace and the manager's job. Rather than managing by command and control, managers of today and tomorrow use an empowering leadership style that focuses on vision, values and communication. Team-building skills are crucial. Instead of just directing tasks, managers focus on building relationships, which may include customers, partners and suppliers.

DISCUSSION QUESTIONS

1 How do you feel about having a manager's responsibility in today's world characterized by uncertainty, ambiguity and sudden changes or threats from the environment? Identify and discuss some skills and qualities that are important to managers under these conditions.

2 Assume you are a project manager at a biotechnology company, working with managers from research, production and marketing on a major product modification. You notice that every email and memo you receive from the marketing manager has been copied to senior management. At every company function, she spends time talking to the CEO and other members of the Board. You are also aware that sometimes when you and the other project members are slaving away over the project, she is playing golf with senior managers. What is your

evaluation of her behaviour? As project manager, what do you do?

3 Jeff Immelt of GE said that the most valuable thing he learned in business school was that 'there are 24 hours in a day, and you can use all of them'. Do you agree or disagree? What are some of the advantages to this approach to being a manager? What are some of the drawbacks?

4 Why do some organizations seem to have a new CEO every year or two, whereas others have top leaders who stay with the company for many years (e.g. Jack Welch's 20 years as CEO at General Electric)? What factors about the manager or about the company do you believe might account for this difference?

5 Is efficiency or effectiveness more important to organizational performance? Can managers

improve both simultaneously? Explain the difference between effectiveness and efficiency.

6 You are a bright, hard-working entry-level manager who fully intends to rise up through the ranks. Your performance evaluation gives you high marks for your technical skills but low marks when it comes to people skills. Do you think people skills can be learned, or do you need to rethink your career path? If people skills can be learned, how would you go about it?

7 If managerial work is characterized by variety, fragmentation and brevity, how do managers perform basic management functions such as planning, which would seem to require reflection and analysis?

8 A professor once told her students, 'The purpose of a management course is to teach students about management, not to teach them to

be managers'. Do you agree or disagree with this statement? Discuss.

9 Discuss some of the ways organizations and jobs have changed over the past ten years. What changes do you anticipate over the next ten years? How might these changes affect the manager's job and the skills a manager needs to be successful?

10 How might the teaching of a management course be designed to help people make the transition from individual performer to manager in order to prepare them for the challenges they will face as new managers?

11 Is Management more of an art, science or practice? Explain your view.

12 What problems and opportunities do you think globalization, climate change and workplace diversity present for managers?

MANAGEMENT IN PRACTICE: EXPERIENTIAL EXERCISE

Management Aptitude Questionnaire

Rate each of the following questions according to the following scale:

1   I am never like this.

2   I am rarely like this.

3   I am sometimes like this.

4   I am often like this.

5   I am always like this.

1 When I have a number of tasks or homework to do, I set priorities and organize the work around deadlines.

   1   2   3   4   5

2 Most people would describe me as a good listener.

   1   2   3   4   5

3 When I am deciding on a particular course of action for myself (such as hobbies to pursue,

languages to study, which job to take, special projects to be involved in), I typically consider the long-term (three years or more) implications of what I would choose to do.

   1   2   3   4   5

4 I prefer technical or quantitative courses rather than those involving literature, psychology or sociology.

   1   2   3   4   5

5 When I have a serious disagreement with someone, I stick with it and talk it out until it is completely resolved.

   1   2   3   4   5

6 When I have a project or assignment, I really get into the details rather than the 'big picture' issues.

   1   2   3   4   5

7 I would rather sit in front of my computer than spend a lot of time with people.

   1   2   3   4   5

8 I try to include others in activities or discussions.

1　2　3　4　5

9 When I take a course, I relate what I am learning to other courses I took or concepts I learned elsewhere.

1　2　3　4　5

10 When somebody makes a mistake, I want to correct the person and let her or him know the proper answer or approach.

1　2　3　4　5

11 I think it is better to be efficient with my time when talking with someone, rather than worry about the other person's needs, so that I can get on with my real work.

1　2　3　4　5

12 I know my long-term vision of career, family, and other activities and have thought it over carefully.

1　2　3　4　5

13 When solving problems, I would much rather analyse some data or statistics than meet with a group of people.

1　2　3　4　5

14 When I am working on a group project and someone doesn't pull a fair share of the load, I am more likely to complain to my friends rather than confront the slacker.

1　2　3　4　5

15 Talking about ideas or concepts can get me really enthused or excited.

1　2　3　4　5

16 The type of management course for which this questionnaire is used is really a waste of time.

1　2　3　4　5

17 I think it is better to be polite and not to hurt people's feelings.

1　2　3　4　5

18 Data or things interest me more than people.

1　2　3　4　5

Scoring and Interpretation

Subtract your scores for questions 6, 10, 14, and 17 from the number 6, and then add the total points for the following sections:

1, 3, 6, 9, 12, 15 Conceptual skills total score _____

2, 5, 8, 10, 14, 17 Human skills total score _____

4, 7, 11, 13, 16, 18 Technical skills total score _____

These skills are three abilities needed to be a good manager. Ideally, a manager should be strong (though not necessarily equal) in all three. Anyone noticeably weaker in any of the skills should take courses and read to build up that skill. For further background on the three skills, please refer to the explanation on pages 8–9.

This exercise was contributed by Dorothy Marcic.

MANAGEMENT IN PRACTICE: ETHICAL DILEMMA

Can Management Afford to Look the Other Way?

Harry Rull had been with Shellington Pharmaceuticals for 30 years. After a tour of duty in the various plants and seven years overseas, Harry was back at headquarters, looking forward to his new role as vice president of global marketing.

Two weeks into his new job, Harry received some unsettling news about one of the managers under his supervision. Over casual lunch conversation, the Director of Human Resources mentioned that Harry should expect a phone call about Roger Jacobs, manager of new product development. Jacobs had a history of being 'pretty horrible' to his subordinates, she said, and one disgruntled employee asked to speak to someone in senior management. After lunch, Harry did some follow-up work. Jacobs' performance reviews had been stellar, but his personnel file also contained a large number of notes documenting charges of Jacobs' mistreatment of subordinates. The complaints ranged from 'inappropriate and derogatory remarks' to subsequently dropped charges of sexual harassment. What was more disturbing was that the amount as well as the severity of complaints had increased with each of Jacobs' ten years with Shellington.

When Harry questioned the company CEO about the issue, he was told, 'Yeah, he's had some problems, but you can't just replace someone with an eye for new products. You're a bottom-line guy; you understand why we let these things slide'. Not sure how to handle the situation, Harry met briefly with Jacobs and reminded him to 'keep the team's morale up'. Just after the meeting, Sally Barton from HR called to let him know that the problem she'd mentioned over lunch had been worked out. However, she warned, another employee had now come forward demanding that her complaints be addressed by senior management.

What Would You Do?

1 Ignore the problem. Jacobs' contributions to new product development are too valuable to risk

losing him, and the problems over the past ten years have always worked themselves out anyway. No sense starting something that could make you look bad.

2 Launch a full-scale investigation of employee complaints about Jacobs, and make Jacobs aware that the documented history over the past ten years has put him on thin ice.

3 Meet with Jacobs and the employee to try to resolve the current issue, then start working with Sally Barton and other senior managers to develop stronger policies regarding sexual harassment and treatment of employees, including clear-cut procedures for handling complaints.

SOURCE Based on Doug Wallace, 'A Talent for Mismanagement: What Would You Do?', *Business Ethics* 2 (November–December 1992): 3–4.

CASE FOR CRITICAL ANALYSIS 1.1

Down but Not Out: Managing Organizations in Turbulent Times
By Alan Hogarth

Given the effect of the 'credit crunch' of 2007/2008 on the global economic landscape governments and organizations are attempting to stimulate their economies by encouraging financial institutions to keep on lending, in the hope of recovery. But there is a great deal of uncertainty. In times such as this, leadership is vital. Employees working for organizations who are vulnerable are justifiably worried. Furthermore, they are bombarded constantly with stories in the media of companies losing massive amounts of capital, and they more than likely know friends or family members who have recently lost their jobs. As such it is up to leaders to reassure them that while the rest of the economy may be in trouble, their organization has the strength to weather the financial storm.

With the benefit of hindsight there may have been some indication of the signs of the economic meltdown but few people saw it coming, and even fewer prepared for it.

Leaders, who expect to be able to shape the world to their purpose, can become paralysed when suddenly dealing with a big unpredicted event. However there are steps leaders can take to reduce their vulnerability to unexpected events and to increase their ability to respond when they happen. As FPM Managing Partner, Feargal McCormack states, 'The quality of leadership more than any other single factor determines the success or failure of an organization and would be key in assisting businesses navigate through the current credit crunch. Leadership should not be about position or hierarchy, but is about attitude, definite characteristics and behaviours such as vision, passion, culture, people, team building and inspiring others. During this age of credit crunch it is time for real leaders to stand-up and deliver'.

However, with UK liquidations reaching highs of 3689 during the second quarter of 2008 some accounting experts working in the field of working capital consultancy are dealing with an increased demand for professional advice from large companies with a need for company information to improve their cash flow. As such leaders of these companies have taken a strategic decision that could have a knock-on effect on smaller companies who are financially tied to them. As Martin Williams, Managing Director, Graydon UK says: 'Companies can vastly improve their cash flow situation by negotiating or in some cases imposing extended payment terms on their suppliers while at the same time honing their skills at collecting money at the other end from their customers. As a result, their financial position strengthens at the expense of those smaller companies around them.' John Wright, Federation of Small Businesses National Chairman agrees when he says that, 'Big companies appear to be aware that small businesses are afraid of taking them on over payment terms and are abusing their power as a result. Making small businesses wait 105 days for payment and charging them for the privilege of doing so is nothing short of outrageous.' This cash flow situation for SMEs in the current economic climate has also been recognized by the UK Government. The Prime Minister alerted the House of Commons in October 2008 to the growing cash flow problems that have become a particular problem for small to medium companies at this critical time for the economy. Late payment problems have intensified, with all firms lengthening the time they take to pay their suppliers. Gordon Brown says, 'The government can ease the situation, and we can help cash flow through prompt payment. The government has already agreed to move its procurement rules from payments within 30 days to a commitment to pay as soon as possible. In the current climate, we need to go further with harder targets. We will therefore aim to make SME payments within ten days. The government will pick up the cost of that, but it is a small price to pay for greatly increasing cash flow associated with £8bn of contracts with SMEs.'

Unfortunately situations such as the aforementioned problems are having a knock-on effect with regard to employee morale. For example, pay deals are proving difficult and budgets for staffing have been cut dramatically. Furthermore, figures released by the Office for National Statistics (UK) in July 2008 indicate that this is the toughest economic climate in recent memory. A global example of the effect that the economic downturn is having on employment and staff morale is in China where, as a survey suggests, nearly 70 per cent of multinational companies plan to cut recruitment this year, and more than a quarter have laid off staff already. Of the more than 350 companies questioned in different sectors across the country, finance, communications and IT firms were the hardest hit. White collar jobs in multinational companies are much sought after in China. The pay is often higher than you might get as a public servant or the employee of a state-owned enterprise. However, since the financial crisis, jobs are less secure in multinational firms whose parent companies have run into trouble overseas like CitiGroup, General Motors or Motorola.

As a result of tighter budgets and the freeze on recruitment John Sylvester, executive director of motivation and benefits specialist P&MM says, 'Many companies are now seeking to develop non-financial rewards that can alleviate the financial pressure employees find themselves under.' One way of doing this is to offer staff access to retail discount schemes. At Cambridgeshire County Council, all employees receive a 'CamCard' on joining, which gives them discounts in local book stores, restaurants and shops. The council also offers reduced BUPA membership for staff, preferential rates at gyms and subsidized public transport schemes. Another option organizations are considering is salary sacrifice schemes. A salary sacrifice happens when an employee gives up the right to receive part of the cash pay due under his or her contract of employment. Usually the sacrifice is made in return for the employer's agreement to provide the employee with some form of non-cash benefit. Sylvia Doyle, director of Reward First People Consulting says, 'The most cost-effective plan from a monetary point of view is salary sacrifice. Childcare vouchers can be a huge saving, particularly when you've got a couple with children and they both get the benefit.' Also Nottingham City Council, for example, offers a tax-free annual bus pass, a plan through which employees can purchase tax-free bicycles and another initiative that allows staff to hire bicycles worth up to £1000 from local retailers. Eunice Campbell, HR customer services and consultation, estimates that, '25 per cent of the organization's employees already participate in the scheme, run by

P&MM. Siemens Enterprise Communications have developed the Applause programme, through Capital Incentives, which allows managers to directly reward staff who have excelled in any of five key business drivers, with a budget of £40 per employee'. Staff receives points in Capital's online banking system, which can then be redeemed against purchases or experiences from a reward catalogue. Some HR departments, however, are concentrating on 'working smarter' in making cost savings and focusing on their return on investment (ROI). For example, companies are looking at their recruitment processes and mobility costs, and looking to see what changes they can implement internally to reduce cost and maximize performance.

Due to the credit crunch HR departments have recognized that there are some good opportunities for reducing overall costs around the hiring process, including: using IT to reduce the time HR staff and managers spend on activities such as requisition management, sourcing, screening and assessment; consistent objective pre-screening methods to reduce the administrative burden of narrowing down a candidate shortlist; strong business intelligence to enable strategic management of any metrics which an organization needs to measure; promoting the use of technology to drive internal mobility in organizations, which reduces costs, increases staff satisfaction and improves retention rates. By automating and streamlining these processes, HR managers are cutting time and costs and increasing their own efficiency. Claire Grove, marketing manager, Taleo UK states that, 'One of our customers spent heavily on advertising positions on a well-know job board. Once they started reporting and analysing their methods in more detail, they found that although they attracted the largest number of applicants through this source, they subsequently hired very few people this way. Most effective for them was their employee referral scheme, where they had a tiny proportion of applicants in comparison but the hire rate was much more effective and cost of hire was in fact very low'.

In the above HR scenario Information Technology (IT) has been shown to be beneficial, however the global growth in IT spending is slowing for the fourth year in a row as the credit crunch adds to the problems that the IT industry is facing. Many companies, just over 60 per cent, will cut their IT budgets, according to market analyst Datamonitor. The stagnant market has been exacerbated by a sharp fall in businesses planning to significantly increase their IT budget, down from 21 per cent in 2006 to 9 per cent in 2009. Daniel Okubo, a technology analyst with Datamonitor, says, 'For the past couple of years enterprises have been cutting back IT budget increases as they adopt a more cautious viewpoint of the global economy. More recently, the financial services market, as seen by the recent collapse of Lehman Brothers, is suffering from a crisis in confidence, caused by a spate of write-downs and concerns over liquidity.' However, despite this, the European IT market is flouting the credit crunch and is predicted to grow to €315bn next year. Strong sales in IT services will fuel 2 per cent growth in the IT market in Western Europe, according to forecasts by the European Information Technology Observatory (EITO). It is predicted that the 15 core countries in Western Europe are more likely to survive the economic downturn than the US, where IT turnover is forecast to grow by only 0.8 per cent to €347bn. EITO chairman Bruno Lamborghini says, 'IT will be of strategic importance to companies during the downturn by helping them to save cash and boost efficiency'.

Taking a similar stance, Kishore Swaminathan, chief scientist at Accenture agrees that business must continue to invest in strategic research and development during the recession when he says that, 'This is the time to invent new products. The recession will change the business landscape. This is the time for R&D to ignore the current economic conditions in order to sow the seeds for when the economy improves.' Swaminathan believes four key technological advancements will make an impact on business when the recovery comes. These include cloud and internet computing, mobility, collaboration and business intelligence technologies.

With the credit crunch causing plant closings, rising unemployment and shifting demand on supply chains because of the global recession, now may seem a hard time to focus on the recovery. Therefore, 2009 will be anything but business as usual, with this recession predicted to go longer and be more profound than any other in most of our lifetimes. What should companies do in response? Lora Cecere of AMR Research, suggests that, 'The answer is simple: improve capabilities to better sense demand. Companies need to reduce demand latency to see the upturn quicker. If not, decisions will be made two weeks too late.' She suggests seven ways to sense demand and predict the upturn:

- *Make better use of downstream data from retailers.* Point-of-sale (POS) and inventory movement data can be used to reduce channel latency and shorten the time for replenishment and sensing true shopper demand, e.g. Del Monte and Wal-Mart.
- *Implement vendor-managed inventory (VMI) with customers.* The use of RFID in this process triggers a demand signal two weeks earlier than the receipt of a new order, e.g. Dow Chemical.
- *Use downstream data from distributors.* Companies are using the recession as an opportunity to redefine distributor relationships in multi-tier distribution channels to encourage data sharing on inventory movement, e.g. Anheuser-Busch, McDonalds.
- *Move from passive to active forecasting.* The use of this technique improved Procter & Gamble's distribution-level demand signal by 33 per cent.
- *Tap into sales contract information.* Sales contract information is critical for planning processes for make-to-order and configure-to-order supply chains.
- *Use market data actively.* Now is the perfect time to use channel data and third-party data to sense market trends.
- *Sense service requirements.* For products with long lifecycles, service data is a way to improve demand sensing, e.g. Caterpillar.

Questions

1 Discuss the importance of a strong organizational leadership ethos in a turbulent economic environment. How might this type of leadership manifest itself?

2 What can small- to medium-enterprises (SMEs) do to cope with the supply chain issues caused by larger organizations imposing extended payment terms upon them?

3 How can human resource departments adapt to changing personnel and recruitment issues during times of economic downturn?

4 Why do you think the European Information Technology (IT) market is flouting the 'credit crunch' as opposed to the US where IT growth has stagnated?

SOURCE Grove, C. (2008), HR works smarter to beat the credit crunch, *Taleo UK*, online at: http://www.changeboard.com/hrcir cles/blogs/human_resources/archive/2008/09/18/hr-works-smarter-to-beat-the-credit-crunch.aspx; Martindale, N. (2008), Rewarding staff during the credit crunch. *Personneltoday.com*, online at: http://www.personneltoday.com/articles/2008/08/14/47104/reward ing-staff-during-the-credit-crunch.html; Saran, C. (2009), Four technologies to boost business in the recovery. *Computer weekly*, online at: http://www.computerweekly.com/Articles/2009/03/25/ 235394/four-technologies-to-boost-business-in-the-recovery.htm; Credit Crunch Ushers in Corporate 'Law of the Jungle', *Response Source* (2008), online at: http://www.responsesource.com/releas es/rel_display.php?relid=41354&chilite=; Leadership Key in Navigating Through Credit Crunch, *FPM Chartered Accountants*, Quarterly News Letter (2009), online at: http://www.fpm ca.com/docs/CM21_web.pdf; *No gov't funding for faster SME payments*, IT Management News (2008), online at: http://news. zdnet.co.uk/itmanagement/0,1000000308,39517298,00.htm; British workers 'fear job losses', *BBC News* (2008), online at: http://news.bbc.co.uk/1/hi/uk/7585129.stm; Effective Leadership and the Credit Crunch, *Leadership Expert* (2008), online at http://www.leadershipexpert.co.uk/effective-leadership-credit-crunch. html.

CASE FOR CRITICAL ANALYSIS 1.2

Elektra Products, Inc.

Barbara Russell, a manufacturing vice president, walked into the monthly companywide meeting with a light step and a hopefulness she hadn't felt in a long time. The company's new, dynamic CEO was going to announce a new era of employee involvement and empowerment at Elektra Products, an 80-year-old, publicly held company that had once been a leading manufacturer and retailer of electrical products and supplies. In recent years, the company experienced a host of problems: market share was declining in the face of increased foreign and domestic competition; new product ideas were few and far between; departments such as manufacturing and sales barely spoke to one another; morale was at an all-time low, and many employees were actively seeking other jobs. Everyone needed a dose of hope.

Martin Griffin, who had been hired to revive the failing company, briskly opened the meeting with a challenge: 'As we face increasing competition, we need new ideas, new energy, new spirit to make this company great. And the source for this change is you – each one of you.' He then went on to explain that under the new empowerment campaign, employees would be getting more information about how the company was run and would be able to work with their fellow employees in new and creative ways. Martin proclaimed a new era of trust and cooperation at Elektra Products. Barbara felt the excitement stirring within her; but as she looked around the room, she saw many of the other employees, including her friend Simon, rolling their eyes. 'Just another pile of corporate crap', Simon said later. 'One minute they try downsizing, the next re-engineering. Then they dabble in restructuring. Now Martin wants to push empowerment. Garbage like empowerment isn't a substitute for hard work and a little faith in the people who have been with this company for years. We made it great once, and we can do it again. Just get out of our way.' Simon had been a manufacturing engineer with Elektra Products for more than 20 years. Barbara knew he was extremely loyal to the company, but he – and a lot of others like him – were going to be an obstacle to the empowerment efforts.

Top management assigned selected managers to several problem-solving teams to come up with ideas for implementing the empowerment campaign. Barbara loved her assignment as team leader of the manufacturing team, working on ideas to improve how retail stores got the merchandize they needed when they needed it. The team thrived, and trust blossomed among the members. They even spent nights and weekends working to complete their report. They were proud of their ideas, which they believed were innovative but easily achievable: permit a manager to follow a product from design through sales to customers; allow salespeople to refund up to $500 worth of merchandise on the spot; make information available to salespeople about future products; and swap sales and manufacturing personnel for short periods to let them get to know one another's jobs.

When the team presented its report to department heads, Martin Griffin was enthusiastic. But shortly into the meeting he had to excuse himself because of a late-breaking deal with a major hardware store chain. With Martin absent, the department heads rapidly formed a wall of resistance. The director of human resources complained that the ideas for personnel changes would destroy the carefully crafted job categories that had just been completed. The finance department argued that allowing salespeople to make $500 refunds would create a gold mine for unethical customers and salespeople. The legal department warned that providing information to salespeople about future products would invite industrial spying.

The team members were stunned. As Barbara mulled over the latest turn of events, she considered her options: keep her mouth shut; take a chance and confront Martin about her sincerity in making empowerment work; push slowly for reform and work for gradual support from the other teams; or look for another job and leave a company she really cares about. Barbara realized she was looking at no easy choices and no easy answers.

Questions

1 How might top management have done a better job changing Elektra Products into a new kind of organization? What might they do now to get the empowerment process back on track?

2 Can you think of ways Barbara could have avoided the problems her team faced in the meeting with department heads?

3 If you were Barbara Russell, what would you do now? Why?

SOURCE Based on Lawrence R. Rothstein, 'The Empowerment Effort That Came Undone', *Harvard Business Review* (January–February 1995): 20–31.

ENDNOTES

1. This questionnaire is adapted from research findings reported in Linda A. Hill, *Becoming a Manager: How New Managers Master the Challenges of Leadership*, 2nd ed. (Harvard Business School Press, Boston, MA: 2003); and John J. Gabarro, *The Dynamics of Taking Charge* (Boston, MA: Harvard Business School Press, 1987).

2. Darrell Rigby and Barbara Bilodeau, 'The Bain 2005 Management Tool Survey', *Strategy & Leadership* 33, no. 4 (2005): 4–12.

3. Todd G. Buchholz, 'The Right Stuff to be CEO', *The Conference Review Board* (November–December 2007): 13.

4. Geoffrey Colvin, 'What Makes GE Great?', *Fortune* (March 6, 2006): 90–96; and Betsy Morris, 'The GE Mystique', *Fortune* (March 6, 2006): 98–104.

5. James A. F. Stoner and R. Edward Freeman, *Management*, 4th ed. (Englewood Cliffs, NJ: Prentice Hall, 1989).

6. Peter F. Drucker, *Management Tasks, Responsibilities, Practices* (New York: Harper & Row, 1974).

7. George Anders, 'AOL's True Believers', *Fast Company* (July 2002): 96–104.

8. Nanette Byrnes, 'Avon: More Than Cosmetic Changes', *BusinessWeek* (March 12, 2007): 62–63.

9. Kevin Fedarko, 'He Fights Terror with Books', *Parade* (April 6, 2003): 4–6; and David Oliver Relin, 'With Your Help, He's Fighting On', *Parade* (February 29, 2004): 12–14.

10. Eryn Brown, 'Nine Ways to Win on the Web', *Fortune* (May 24, 1999): 112–125.

11. Jennifer Reingold, 'Target's Inner Circle', *Fortune* (March 31, 2008): 74–86.

12. Robert L. Katz, 'Skills of an Effective Administrator', *Harvard Business Review* 52 (September–October 1974): 90–102.

13. Troy V. Mumford, Michael A. Campion and Frederick P. Morgeson, 'The Leadership Skills Strataplex: Leadership Skills Requirements Across Organizational Levels', *The Leadership Quarterly* 18 (2007): 154–166.

14. Geoffrey Colvin, 'The Bionic Manager', *Fortune* (September 19, 2005): 88–100.

15. Kate Bonamici, 'The Shoe-In', *Fortune* (January 23, 2006): 116.

16. Sue Shellenbarger, 'From Our Readers: The Bosses That Drove Me to Quit My Job', *The Wall Street Journal* (February 7, 2000): B1.

17. Quoted in Linda Tischler, 'The CEO's New Clothes', *Fast Company* (September 2005): 27–28.

18. Eric Matson, 'Congratulations, You're Promoted. (Now What?)', *Fast Company* (June–July 1997): 116–130.

19. Clinton O. Longenecker, Mitchell J. Neubert and Laurence S. Fink, 'Causes and Consequences of Managerial Failure in Rapidly Changing Organizations', *Business Horizons* 50 (2007): 145–155.

20. Based on Sydney Finkelstein, '7 Habits of Spectacularly Unsuccessful Executives', *Fast Company* (July 2003): 84–89; Sydney Finkelstein, *Why Smart Executives Fail* (New York: Portfolio, 2003); Ram Charan and Jerry Useem, 'Why Companies Fail'; and John W. Slocum Jr., Cass Ragan, and Albert Casey, 'On Death and Dying: The Corporate Leadership Capacity of CEOs', *Organizational Dynamics* 30, no. 3 (Spring 2002): 269–281.

21. Patricia Wallington, 'Toxic!' *CIO* (April 15, 2006): 34–36.

22. Based on Longenecker, *et al.*, *Causes and Consequences of Managerial Failure in Rapidly Changing Organizations*; Sydney Finkelstein, '7 Habits of Spectacularly Unsuccessful Executives'; Ram Charan and Jerry Useem, 'Why Companies Fail'; and Slocum *et al.*, 'On Death and Dying'.

23. Alan Murray, 'Behind Nardelli's Abrupt Exit; Executive's Fatal Flaw: Failing to Understand New Demands on CEOs', *The Wall Street Journal*, January 4, 2007; Brian Grow, 'Out at Home Depot', *Business-Week* (January 15, 2007): 56–62.

24. Diane Brady, 'Being Mean is So Last Millennium', *Business-Week* (January 15, 2007), sidebar in Murray, 'Behind Nardelli's Abrupt Exit'.

25. Eileen Sheridan, 'Rise: Best Day, Worst Day', *The Guardian* (September 14, 2002): 3.

26. BBC available at http://news.bbc.co.uk/1/hi/scotland/1470902.stm.

27. *The Guardian*, 'Three million customers and still counting: the bank getting rich by helping the poor', (January 2, 2009): 22.

28. A. I. Kraut, P. R. Pedigo, D. D. McKenna, and M. D. Dunnette, 'The Role of the Manager: What's Really Important in Different Management Jobs', *Academy of Management Executive* 19, no. 4 (2005): 122–129.

29. Christopher A. Bartlett and Sumantra Ghoshal, 'Changing the Role of Top Management: Beyond Systems to People', *Harvard Business Review* (May–June 1995): 132–142; and Sumantra Ghoshal and Christopher A. Bartlett, 'Changing the Role of Top Management: Beyond Structure to Processes', *Harvard Business Review* (January–February 1995): 86–96.

30. Quy Nguyen Huy, 'In Praise of Middle Managers', *Harvard Business Review* (September 2003): 72–79; Rosabeth Moss Kanter, *On the Frontiers of Management* (Boston: Harvard-Business School Press, 2003).

31. Lisa Haneberg, 'Reinventing Middle Management', *Leader to Leader* (Fall 2005): 13–18.

32. Miles Brignall, 'Rise; Launch Pad: The Retailer; Alistair Boot, An Assistant Manager at the John Lewis Store in Cheadle, Talks to Miles Brignall', *The Guardian* (October 4, 2003): 3.

33. Henry Mintzberg, *The Nature of Managerial Work* (New York: Harper & Row, 1973); and Henry Mintzberg, 'Rounding Out the Manager's Job', *Sloan Management Review* (Fall 1994): 11–26.

34. Robert E. Kaplan, 'Trade Routes: The Manager's Network of Relationships', *Organizational Dynamics* (Spring 1984): 37–52; Rosemary Stewart, 'The Nature of Management: A Problem for Management Education', *Journal of Management Studies* 21 (1984): 323–330; John P. Kotter, 'What Effective General Managers Really Do', *Harvard Business Review* (November–December 1982): 156–167; and Morgan W. McCall, Jr., Ann M. Morrison and Robert L. Hannan, 'Studies of Managerial Work: Results and Methods', Technical Report No. 9, Center for Creative Leadership, Greensboro, NC, 1978.

35. Alison M. Konrad, Roger Kashlak, Izumi Yoshioka, Robert Waryszak and Nina Toren, 'What Do Managers *Like* to Do? A Five-Country Study', *Group and Organizational Management* 26, no. 4 (December 2001): 401–433.

36. For a review of the problems faced by first-time managers, see Linda A. Hill, 'Becoming the Boss', *Harvard Business Review* (January 2007): 49–56; Loren B. Belker and Gary S. Topchik, *The First-Time Manager: A Practical Guide to the Management of People*, 5th ed. (New York: AMACOM, 2005); J. W. Lorsch and P. F. Mathias, 'When Professionals Have to Manage', *Harvard Business Review* (July–August 1987): 78–83; R. A. Webber, *Becoming a Courageous Manager: Overcoming Career Problems of New Managers* (Englewood Cliffs, NJ: Prentice Hall, 1991); D. E. Dougherty, *From Technical Professional to Corporate Manager: A Guide to Career Transition* (New York: John Wiley and Sons Inc., 1984); J. Falvey, 'The Making of a Manager',

Sales and Marketing Management (March 1989): 42–83; M. K. Badawy, *Developing Managerial Skills in Engineers and Scientists: Succeeding as a Technical Manager* (Van Nostrand Reinhold, New York: 1982); and M. London, *Developing Managers: A Guide to Motivating and Preparing People for Successful Managerial Careers* (San Francisco: Jossey-Bass, 1985).

37. Erin White, 'Learning to Be the Boss; Trial and Error Is the Norm as New Managers Figure Out How to Relate to Former Peers,' *The Wall Street Journal*, November 21, 2005.

38. This discussion is based on Linda A. Hill, *Becoming a Manager: How New Managers Master the Challenges of Leadership*, 2nd ed. (Boston, MA: Harvard Business School Press, 2003), pp. 6–8; and Linda A. Hill, 'Becoming the Boss', *Harvard Business Review* (January 2007): 49–56.

39. Jeanne Whalen, 'Chance Turns a Teacher into a CEO; Religion Lecturer Leaves Academic Path and Learns to Run a Biotech Start-Up', Theory & Practice column, *The Wall Street Journal*, October 17, 2005.

40. See also 'Boss's First Steps', sidebar in White, 'Learning to Be the Boss'; and Loren Belker and Gary Topchik, *The First-Time Manager*.

41. Henry Mintzberg, 'Managerial Work: Analysis from Observation', *Management Science* 18 (1971): B97–B110.

42. Based on Carol Saunders and Jack William Jones, 'Temporal Sequences in Information Acquisition for Decision Making: A Focus on Source and Medium', *Academy of Management Review* 15 (1990): 29–46.

43. Mintzberg, 'Managerial Work'.

44. Matthew Boyle and Jia Lynn Yang, "All in a Day's Work," *Fortune* (March 20, 2006): 97–104.

45. Susan Spielberg, 'The Cheesecake Factory'.

46. Lance B. Kurke and Howard E. Aldrich, 'Mintzberg Was Right!: A Replication and Extension of *The Nature of Managerial Work*', *Management Science* 29 (1983): 975–984; Cynthia M. Pavett and Alan W. Lau, 'Managerial Work: The Influence of Hierarchical Level and Functional Specialty', *Academy of Management Journal* 26 (1983): 170–177; and Colin P. Hales, 'What Do Managers Do? A Critical Review of the Evidence', *Journal of Management Studies* 23 (1986): 88–115.

47. Mintzberg, 'Rounding out the Manager's Job'.

48. Andy Serwer, 'Inside the Rolling Stones Inc.', *Fortune* (September 30, 2002): 58–72.

49. Valerie Darroch, 'High Flyer with Feet on Home Ground; Gorbals-Born Stephen Baxter Combines His Role as Glasgow Airport Boss with Heading the City's Chamber of Commerce', *Sunday Herald*, February 6, 2005.

50. Harry S. Jonas III, Ronald E. Fry, and Suresh Srivastva, 'The Office of the CEO: Understanding the Executive Experience', *Academy of Management Executive* 4 (August 1990): 36–48.

51. Carol Hymowitz, 'Smart Executives Shed Some Traditional Tasks to Focus on Key Areas', *The Wall Street Journal*, (June 19, 2006).

52. Edward O. Welles, 'There Are No Simple Businesses Anymore', *The State of Small Business* (1995): 66–79.

53. This section is based on Peter F. Drucker, *Managing the Non-Profit Organization: Principles and Practices* (New York: Harper Business, 1992); and Thomas Wolf, *Managing a Non-profit Organization* (New York: Fireside/Simon & Schuster, 1990).

54. Christine W. Letts, William P. Ryan and Allen Grossman, *High Performance Non-profit Organizations* (New York: Wiley & Sons, 1999), pp. 30–35.

55. Carol Hymowitz, 'In Sarbanes—Oxley Era, Running a Non-profit Is Only Getting Harder', *The Wall Street Journal* (June 21, 2005); and Bill Birchard, 'Non-profits by the Numbers' *CFO* (June 2005): 50–55.

56. This section is based on 'The New Organization: A Survey of the Company', *The Economist* (January 21, 2006); Harry G. Barkema, Joel A. C. Baum and Elizabeth A. Mannix, 'Management Challenges in a New Time', *Academy of Management Journal* 45, no. 5 (2002): 916–930; Michael Harvey and M. Ronald Buckley, 'Assessing the 'Conventional Wisdoms' of Management for the 21st Century Organization', *Organizational Dynamics* 30, no. 4 (2002): 368–378; and Toby J. Tetenbaum, 'Shifting Paradigms: From Newton to Chaos', *Organizational Dynamics* (Spring 1998): 21–32.

57. Caroline Ellis, 'The Flattening Corporation', *MIT Sloan Management Review* (Summer 2003): 5.

58. Christopher Rhoads and Sara Silver, 'Working at Home Gets Easier', *The Wall Street Journal* (December 29, 2005); Cliff Edwards, 'Wherever You Go, You're on the Job'; and Kelley Holland, 'When Work Time Isn't Face Time', *The New York Times* (December 3, 2006).

59. Kerr Inkson, Angela Heising and Denise M. Rousseau, 'The Interim Manager: Prototype of the 21st Century Worker', *Human Relations* 54, no. 3 (2001): 259–284.

60. Keith H. Hammonds, 'Smart, Determined, Ambitious, Cheap: The New Face of Global Competition', *Fast Company* (February 2003): 91–97.

61. Keeley Holland, 'When Work Time Isn't Face Time'.

62. Carla Johnson, 'Managing Virtual Teams', *HR Magazine* (June 2002): 69–73; 'The New Organization', *The Economist* (January 21, 2006).

63. Keeley Holland, 'When Work Time Isn't Face Time'.

CHAPTER OUTLINE

© SEAN NEL/SHUTTERSTOCK

LEARNING OBJECTIVES

After reading this chapter, you should be able to:

1   Understand how historical forces influence the practice of management.

2   Identify and explain major developments in the history of management thought.

3   Describe the major components of the classical and humanistic management perspectives.

4   Discuss the management science perspective and its current use in organizations.

5   Explain the major concepts of systems theory, the contingency view and total quality management.

6   Describe the learning organization and the changes in structure, empowerment and information sharing that managers make to support it.

7   Discuss the technology-driven workplace and the role of outsourcing, supply chain management, enterprise resource planning, knowledge management systems and customer relationship management.

CHAPTER 2

THE EVOLUTION OF MANAGEMENT THINKING

Manager's Challenge

Cementos Mexicanos (Cemex), based in Monterrey, Mexico, and with cement plants throughout Europe, has been making and delivering concrete for nearly a century. The company specializes in delivering concrete in developing areas of the world, places where anything can, and usually does, go wrong. Even in Monterrey, for example, Cemex copes with unpredictable weather and traffic conditions, spontaneous labour disruptions, building permit problems, and arbitrary government inspections of construction sites. In addition, more than half of all orders are changed or cancelled by customers, usually at the last minute. Considering that a load of concrete is never more than 90 minutes from spoiling, these chaotic conditions mean high costs, complex scheduling and frustration for employees, managers and customers. As competition in the industry increased, Cemex managers began looking for ways to stand out from the crowd. One idea was a guaranteed delivery time, but despite the efforts of employees, the best Cemex could do was promise delivery within a three-hour window. To make matters worse, the construction business itself was becoming increasingly complex and competitive, leading to even more disruptions and cancellations. Builders were sometimes lucky to get their orders delivered on the right day, let alone at the right hour. Cemex managers began to consider that the company needed a whole new approach to doing business – one that accepted rather than resisted the natural chaos of the marketplace. It would mean massive changes in operations, as well as finding ways to get dispatchers and drivers to think like entrepreneurs.[1]

If you were a manager at Cemex, what changes would you implement to help the organization thrive in the face of constant chaos? What advice would you give managers concerning their management approach and the kind of company they might create?

TAKE A MOMENT

Are You a New-Style or an Old-Style Manager?[2]

The following are various behaviours that a manager may engage in when relating to subordinates. Read each statement carefully and rate each one Mostly True or Mostly False to reflect the extent to which you would use that behaviour.

	Mostly True	Mostly False
1 Closely supervise my subordinates in order to get better work from them.	☐	☐
2 Set the goals and objectives for my subordinates and sell them on the merits of my plans.	☐	☐
3 Set up controls to ensure that my subordinates are getting the job done.	☐	☐
4 Make sure that my subordinates' work is planned out for them.	☐	☐
5 Check with my subordinates daily to see if they need any help.	☐	☐
6 Step in as soon as reports indicate that the job is slipping.	☐	☐
7 Push my people to meet schedules if necessary.	☐	☐
8 Have frequent meetings to learn from others what is going on.	☐	☐

SCORING AND INTERPRETATION Add the total number of Mostly True answers and mark your score on the scale below. Theory X tends to be 'old-style' management and Theory Y 'new-style', because the styles are based on different assumptions about people. To learn more about these assumptions, you can refer to Exhibit 2.4 (later) and review the assumptions related to Theory X and Theory Y. Strong Theory X assumptions are typically considered inappropriate for today's workplace. Where do you fit on the X–Y scale? Does your score reflect your perception of yourself as a current or future manager?

X–Y Scale

Theory X	10	5	0	Theory Y

Cemex is faced with a situation similar to many companies. The methods and patterns that kept the organization successful in the past no longer seem enough to keep it thriving in today's turbulent environment. Unexpected market forces or other changes in the environment can devastate a company. Retail chains in the US such as Kmart and Sears are fighting to stay alive in the face of Wal-Mart's growing dominance; in the UK Tesco's dominance is worrying many. Major airlines in the US are being hammered by new low-cost carriers such as JetBlue; while in Europe easyJet and Ryanair to name a couple have caused major airlines to launch their own low-cost options. And widespread financial and ethical scandals in the early 2000s affected companies in all industries. Lutheran Health Network, which runs six hospitals in and around Fort Wayne, Indiana, now spends about $250 000 more per year to make sure the organization has documentation to show they are complying with health care regulators and other oversight boards.[3] Confronted by ever-shifting conditions, managers have to make continual changes in their organizations, and sometimes create a new kind of company, as at Cemex, one with which they have little experience or skill.

As discussed in Chapter 1, we are currently shifting to a new kind of workplace and a new approach to management. Managers today face the ultimate paradox: (1) keep everything running efficiently and profitably, while, at the same time, (2) change everything.[4] It is no longer enough just to learn how to measure and control things. Success accrues to those who learn how to be leaders, to initiate change, and to create organizations with fewer managers and less hierarchy that can shift gears quickly.

Management philosophies and organizational forms change over time to meet new needs. The workplace of today is different from what it was 50 years ago – indeed, from what it was even ten years ago. Yet some ideas and practices from the past are still highly relevant and applicable to management today. Many students wonder why history matters to managers. A historical perspective provides a broader way of thinking, a way of searching for patterns and determining whether they recur across time periods. For example, certain management techniques that seem modern, such as share ownership programmes, have repeatedly gained and lost popularity since the early twentieth century because of historical forces.[5] William Cooper Procter, grandson of the cofounder of Procter & Gamble, introduced a profit-sharing plan in 1887, and expanded it by tying it to stock ownership a few years later. Sam Walton opened Wal-Mart's financial records, including salaries, to all employees in the 1960s, long before business magazines were touting the value of *open-book management.*[6] Currently across the UK there are approximately 3.5 million employees participating in 5000 company schemes: 83 per cent of the FTSE 100 currently offer an All Employee Share Plan; 77 per cent offer a Save as You Earn Plan; and 46 per cent offer a Share Incentive Plan.[7] SAYE (also know as Sharesave, introduced in 1980) and SIP (introduced in 2000) form the foundation of employee share ownership in the UK.

Research has shown that the benefits of employee share schemes include higher productivity and financial performance, greater innovation and lower staff turnover. A study of the past contributes to understanding both the present and the future. It is a way of learning from others' mistakes so as not to repeat them; learning from others' successes so as to repeat them in the appropriate situation; and most of all, learning to understand why things happen to improve our organizations in the future. This chapter provides an overview of the ideas, theories and management philosophies that have contributed to making the workplace what it is today. We examine several management approaches that have been popular and successful throughout the twentieth century. The final section of the chapter looks at recent trends and current approaches that build on this foundation of management understanding. This foundation illustrates that the value of studying management lies not in learning current facts and research but in developing a perspective that will facilitate the broad, long-term view needed for management success.

Management and Organization

A historical perspective on management provides a context or environment in which to interpret current opportunities and problems. However, studying history doesn't mean merely arranging events in chronological order; it means developing an understanding of the impact of societal forces on organizations. Studying history is a way to achieve strategic thinking, see the big picture and improve conceptual skills. Let's start by examining how social, political and economic forces have influenced organizations and the practice of management.[8]

Social forces
The aspects of a culture that guide and influence relationships among people – their values, needs, and standards of behaviour.

Social forces refer to those aspects of a culture that guide and influence relationships among people. What do people value? What do people need? What are the standards of behaviour among people? These forces shape what is known as the *social contract*, which refers to the unwritten, common rules and perceptions about relationships among people and between employees and management.

A significant social force today is the changing attitudes, ideas, and values of Generation X and Generation Y employees.[9] Generation X employees, those now in their thirties and forties, have had a profound impact on the workplace, and Generation Y workers (sometimes called Nexters) may have an even greater one. These young workers, the most educated generation so far, grew up technologically adept and globally conscious. Unlike many workers of the past, they aren't hesitant to question their superiors and challenge the status quo. They want a work environment that is challenging and supportive, with access to cutting-edge technology, opportunities to learn and further their careers and personal goals, and the power to make substantive decisions and changes in the workplace. In addition, Gen X and Gen Y workers have prompted a growing focus on work/life balance, reflected in trends such as telecommuting, flexitime, shared jobs and organization-sponsored sabbaticals.

Political forces
The influence of political and legal institutions on people and organizations.

Political forces refer to the influence of political and legal institutions on people and organizations. Political forces include basic assumptions underlying the political system, such as the desirability of self-government, property rights, contract rights, the definition of justice, and the determination of innocence or guilt of a crime. The spread of capitalism throughout the world has dramatically altered the business landscape. The dominance of the free-market system and growing interdependencies among the world's countries require organizations to operate differently and managers to think in new ways.

Economic forces
Forces that affect the availability, production, and distribution of a society's resources among competing users.

Economic forces pertain to the availability, production and distribution of resources in a society. Governments, military agencies, churches, schools and business organizations in every society require resources to achieve their goals, and economic forces influence the allocation of scarce resources. Less-developed countries such as China and India are growing in economic power, and the economy of the US, Great Britain and Japan, and other developed countries, is shifting dramatically, with the sources of wealth, the fundamentals of distribution and the nature of economic decision-making undergoing significant changes.[10]

Today's economy is based as much on ideas, information and knowledge as it is on material resources. Supply chains and distribution of resources have been revolutionized by digital technology. Surplus inventories, which once could trigger recessions, are declining or completely disappearing. Another economic trend is the booming importance of small- and medium-sized businesses, including start-ups, which early in the twenty-first century grew at three times the rate of the national economy. 'I call it "the invisible economy", yet it is *the* economy', says David Birch of Cognetics Inc., a Cambridge, Massachusetts firm that tracks business formation.[11]

A massive shift in the economy is not without its upheavals, of course. In the early 2000s, years of seemingly endless growth ground to a halt as stock prices fell, particularly for dot-com and technology companies. Numerous internet-based companies went out of business, and organizations throughout the United States and Europe and Asia began laying off hundreds of thousands of workers. However, this economic downturn may also be a stimulus for even greater technological innovation and small business vitality.

TAKE A MOMENT

As a new manager do you appreciate a historical perspective to help you interpret current opportunities and problems? Social, economic and political forces often repeat themselves, so your understanding will facilitate a broader view of how organizations adapt and succeed in today's environment.

Management practices and perspectives vary in response to these social, political and economic forces in the larger society. During difficult times, managers look for ideas to help them cope with environmental turbulence and keep their organizations vital. A management tools survey conducted by Bain & Company, for example, reveals a dramatic increase over the past dozen or so years in the variety of management ideas and techniques used by managers. Challenges such as a tough economy and rocky stock market, environmental and organizational crises, lingering anxieties over war and terrorism, and the public suspicion and scepticism resulting from corporate scandals, leave executives searching for any management tool – new or old – that can help them get the most out of limited resources.[12] This search for guidance is also reflected in a proliferation of books, scholarly articles, and conferences dedicated to examining management fashions and trends.[13] Exhibit 2.1 illustrates the evolution of significant management perspectives over time, each of which will be examined in the remainder of this chapter. The timeline reflects the dominant timeperiod for each approach, but elements of each are still used in today's organizations.

Classical Perspective

The practice of management can be traced to 3000 BC to the first government organizations developed by the Sumerians and Egyptians, but the formal study of management is relatively recent.[14] The early study of management as we know it today began with what is now called the **classical perspective**.

The classical perspective on management emerged during the nineteenth and early twentieth centuries. The factory system that began to appear in the 1800s posed challenges that earlier organizations had not encountered. Problems arose in tooling the plants, organizing managerial structure, training employees (many of them non-English-speaking immigrants), scheduling complex manufacturing operations, and dealing with increased labour dissatisfaction and resulting strikes.

Classical perspective
A management perspective that emerged during the nineteenth and early twentieth centuries that emphasized a rational, scientific approach to the study of management and sought to make organizations efficient operating machines.

Exhibit 2.1 Management Perspectives over Time

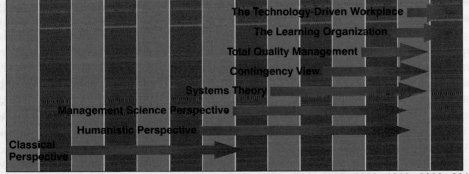

The Technology-Driven Workplace	
The Learning Organization	
Total Quality Management	
Contingency View	
Systems Theory	
Management Science Perspective	
Humanistic Perspective	
Classical Perspective	

1870 1880 1890 1900 1910 1920 1930 1940 1950 1960 1970 1980 1990 2000 2010

© THE GRANGER COLLECTION, NEW YORK.

CONCEPT CONNECTION
Frederick Winslow Taylor (1856–1915). Taylor's theory that labour productivity could be improved by scientifically determined management practices earned him the status of 'father of scientific management'.

Scientific management
A subfield of the classical management perspective that emphasized scientifically determined changes in management practices as the solution to improving labour productivity.

These myriad new problems and the development of large, complex organizations demanded a new approach to coordination and control, and a 'new sub-species of economic man – the salaried manager'[15] – was born. Between 1880 and 1920, the number of professional managers in the US grew from 161 000 to more than 1 million.[16] This trend was reflected in other countries such as Germany and France. These professional managers began developing and testing solutions to the mounting challenges of organizing, coordinating and controlling large numbers of people and increasing worker productivity. Thus began the evolution of modern management with the classical perspective.

This perspective contains three subfields, each with a slightly different emphasis: scientific management, bureaucratic organizations and administrative principles.[17]

Scientific Management

Organizations' somewhat limited success in achieving improvements in labour productivity led a young engineer to suggest that the problem lay more in poor management practices than in labour. Frederick Winslow Taylor (1856–1915) insisted that management itself would have to change and, further, that the manner of change could be determined only by scientific study; hence, the label *scientific management* emerged. Taylor suggested that decisions based on rules of thumb and tradition be replaced with precise procedures developed after careful study of individual situations.[18]

Taylor's philosophy is encapsulated in his statement, 'In the past the man has been first. In the future, the system must be first'.[19] The **scientific management** approach is illustrated by the unloading of iron from rail cars and reloading finished steel for the Bethlehem Steel plant in 1898. Taylor calculated that with correct movements, tools, and sequencing, each man was capable of loading 47.5 tons per day instead of the typical 12.5 tons. He also worked out an incentive system that paid each man $1.85 a day for meeting the new standard, an increase from the previous rate of $1.15. Productivity at Bethlehem Steel shot up overnight.

Although known as the *father of scientific management*, Taylor was not alone in this area. Henry Gantt, an associate of Taylor's, developed the *Gantt chart* – a bar graph that measures planned and completed work along each stage of production by time elapsed. Two other important pioneers in this area were the husband-and-wife team of Frank B. and Lillian M. Gilbreth. Frank B. Gilbreth (1868–1924) pioneered *time and motion study* and arrived at many of his management techniques independently of Taylor. He stressed efficiency and was known for his quest for the one best way to do work. Although Gilbreth is known for his early work with bricklayers, his work had great impact on medical surgery by drastically reducing the time patients spent on the operating table. Surgeons were able to save countless lives through the application of time and motion study. Lillian M. Gilbreth (1878–1972) was more interested in the human aspect of work. When her husband died at the age of 56, she had 12 children ages two to 19. The undaunted 'first lady of management' went right on with her work. She presented a paper in place of her late husband, continued their seminars and consulting, lectured, and eventually became a professor at Purdue University.[20] She pioneered in the field of industrial psychology and made substantial contributions to human resource management.

The basic ideas of scientific management are shown in Exhibit 2.2. To use this approach, managers should develop standard methods for doing each job, select workers with the appropriate abilities, train workers in the standard methods, support workers and eliminate interruptions, and provide wage incentives.

The ideas of scientific management that began with Taylor dramatically increased productivity across all industries, and they are still important today. Indeed, the concept of arranging work based on careful analysis of tasks for maximum productivity is deeply embedded in our organizations.[21] However, because scientific management ignored the social context and workers' needs, it led to increased conflict and sometimes violent clashes between managers and employees. Under this system, workers often felt exploited – a sharp contrast from the harmony and cooperation that Taylor and his followers had envisioned.

Chinese industrialists, officials and academics embraced Frederick W. Taylor's ideas of scientific management during 1920s and 1930s. Scientific management was introduced a wider scale than is commonly realized. It influenced the redesign of personnel systems and work organization, and promoted employee welfare and production efficiency outcomes.[22]

Frederick Taylor's *scientific management* techniques were also expanded by car maker Henry Ford, who replaced workers with machines for heavy lifting and moving. One of the first applications of the moving assembly line was the Magneto assembly operation at Ford's Highland Park plant in 1913. Magnetos moved from one worker to the next, reducing production time by one half. The same principle was applied to total-car assembly, improving efficiency and reducing worker-hours required to produce a Model-T Ford to less than two. Under this system, a Ford rolled off the assembly line every ten seconds.

CONCEPT CONNECTION Lillian M. Gilbreth (1878–1972), Frank B. Gilbreth (1868–1924). This husband-and-wife team contributed greatly to the principles of scientific management. His development of time and motion studies and her work in industrial psychology pioneered many of today's management and human resource techniques.

Bureaucratic Organizations

A systematic approach developed in Europe that looked at the organization as a whole is the **bureaucratic organizations** approach, a subfield within the classical perspective. Max Weber (1864–1920), a German theorist, introduced most of the concepts on bureaucratic organizations.[23]

During the late 1800s, many European organizations were managed on a personal, family-like basis. Employees were loyal to a single individual rather than to the organization or its mission. The dysfunctional consequence of this management practice was that resources were used to realize individual desires rather than organizational goals. Employees in effect owned the organization and used resources for their own gain rather than to serve customers. Weber envisioned organizations that would be managed on an impersonal, rational basis. This form of organization was called a *bureaucracy*. Exhibit 2.3 summarizes the six characteristics of bureaucracy as specified by Weber.

Weber believed that an organization based on rational authority would be more efficient and adaptable to change because continuity is related to formal structure and positions rather than to a particular person, who may leave or die. To Weber, rationality in organizations meant employee selection and advancement based not on who you know, but rather on competence and technical qualifications, which are assessed by examination or according to training and experience. The organization relies on rules and written records for continuity. In addition, rules and procedures are impersonal and applied uniformly to all employees. A clear division of labour arises from distinct definitions of authority and responsibility, legitimized as official duties. Positions are organized in a hierarchy, with each position under the authority of a higher one. The manager depends not on his or her personality for successfully giving orders but on the legal power invested in the managerial position.

Bureaucratic organizations
A subfield of the classical management perspective that emphasized management on an impersonal, rational basis through such elements as clearly defined authority and responsibility, formal record-keeping, and separation of management and ownership.

Bureaucratic Rationality vs. Emotions[25]

Since Max Weber wrote about the ideal bureaucracy, a good deal of work, for example by Merton, Gouldner and Selznick, has focused on the dysfunctions of the bureaucratic form – the menace of bureaucracy. These writers, as well as questioning the perfection of the 'ideal type' discussed whether the opposition between organizational efficiency and the freedom of the individual was possible.

The routine and oppressive aspects of bureaucracy were highlighted to show it as a 'vicious circle' that develops from the resistance of the human factor to the mechanistic rationalist theory of behaviour which is being imposed on it. The very resistance tends to reinforce the use of the bureaucracy. For example in Gouldner's view, impersonal bureaucratic rules evolve because they alleviate the tensions created by subordination and control, but at the same time they enable the very tensions that bring them into being. They particularly reinforce the low motivation of the workforce that makes close supervision necessary.

As we have seen the ideal type of bureaucracy is governed by a formal set of rules and procedures which ensures that operations and activities are carried out in a predictable, uniform, and impersonal manner. Personal relationships are excluded from organizational life. Zygmunt Bauman shows the importance of bureaucratic organization to the death camps in Nazi Germany. Can bureaucracy be devoid of emotion? We think of bureaucracy, organizational order, and efficiency as matters of rational, non-emotional activity. Cool clear strategic thinking should not be sullied by messy feelings. Fineman wrote that good organizations are places where feelings are managed, designed out or tamed. It is thought that emotions interfere with rationality. But can organizations, and in particular bureaucracy, be free of emotion?

Administrative Principles

Another major subfield within the classical perspective is known as the administrative principles approach. Whereas scientific management focused on the productivity of the individual worker, the **administrative principles** approach focused on the total organization. The contributors to this approach included Henri Fayol, Mary Parker Follett and Chester I. Barnard.

Administrative principles
A subfield of the classical management perspective that focuses on the total organization rather than the individual worker, delineating the management functions of planning, organizing, commanding, coordinating and controlling.

Henri Fayol (1841–1925) was a French mining engineer who worked his way up to become head of a major mining group known as Comambault. Comambault survives today as part of Le Creusot-Loire, the largest mining and metallurgical group in central France. In his later years, Fayol wrote down his concepts on administration, based largely on his own management experiences.[26]

In his most significant work, *General and Industrial Management*, Fayol discussed 14 general principles of management, several of which are part of management philosophy today. For example:

- *Unity of command.* Each subordinate receives orders from one – and only one – superior.
- *Division of work.* Managerial and technical work are amenable to specialization to produce more and better work with the same amount of effort.
- *Unity of direction.* Similar activities in an organization should be grouped together under one manager.
- *Scalar chain.* A chain of authority extends from the top to the bottom of the organization and should include every employee.

Fayol felt that these principles could be applied in any organizational setting. He also identified five basic functions or elements of management: *planning*, *organizing*, *commanding*, *coordinating* and *controlling*. These functions underlie much of the general approach to today's management theory.

Mary Parker Follett (1868–1933) was trained in philosophy and political science at what today is Radcliffe College. She applied herself in many fields, including social psychology and management. She wrote of the importance of common superordinate goals for reducing conflict in organizations.[27] Her work was popular with business people of her day but was often overlooked by management scholars.[28] Follett's ideas served as a contrast to scientific management and are re-emerging as applicable for modern managers dealing with rapid changes in today's global environment. Her approach to leadership stressed the importance of people rather than engineering techniques. She offered the pithy admonition, 'Don't hug your blueprints', and analyzed the dynamics of management-organization interactions. Follett addressed issues that are timely today, such as ethics, power and how to lead in a way that encourages employees to give their best. The concepts of *empowerment*, facilitating rather than controlling employees, and allowing employees to act depending on the authority of the situation opened new areas for theoretical study by Chester I. Barnard and others.[29]

Chester I. Barnard (1886–1961) studied economics at Harvard but failed to receive a degree because he lacked a course in laboratory science. He went to work in the statistical department of AT&T and in 1927 became president of New Jersey Bell. One of Barnard's significant contributions was the concept of the informal organization. The *informal organization* occurs in all formal organizations and includes cliques and naturally occurring social groupings. Barnard argued that organizations are not machines and informal relationships are powerful forces that can help the organization if properly managed. Another significant contribution was the *acceptance theory of authority*, which states that people have free will and can choose whether to follow management orders. People typically follow orders because they perceive positive benefit to themselves, but they do have a choice. Managers should treat employees properly because their acceptance of authority may be critical to organization success in important situations.[30]

The overall classical perspective as an approach to management was very powerful and gave companies fundamental new skills for establishing high productivity and effective treatment of employees. Indeed, the US surged ahead of the world in management techniques, and other countries, especially Japan, borrowed heavily from American ideas.

COURTESY OF MARY PARKER FOLLETT FOUNDATION AND READING UNIVERSITY, UK

CONCEPT CONNECTION
Mary Parker Follett (1868–1933). Follett was a major contributor to the administrative principles approach to management. Her emphasis on worker participation and shared goals among managers was embraced by many business-people of the day and has been recently 'rediscovered' by corporate America.

Humanistic Perspective

Mary Parker Follett and Chester Barnard were early advocates of a more **humanistic perspective** on management that emphasized the importance of understanding human behaviours, needs, and attitudes in the workplace as well as social interactions and group processes.[31] We will discuss three subfields based on the humanistic perspective: the human relations movement, the human resources perspective and the behavioural sciences approach.

Humanistic perspective
A management perspective that emerged near the late nineteenth century and emphasized understanding human behaviour, needs, and attitudes in the workplace.

Human Relations Movement

The US always espoused the spirit of human equality. However, this spirit did not always translate into practice when it came to power sharing between managers and workers. The human relations school of thought considers that truly effective control comes from within the individual worker rather than from strict, authoritarian

Behavioural Sciences Approach

Behavioural sciences approach
A subfield of the humanistic management perspective that applies social science in an organizational context, drawing from economics, psychology, sociology and other disciplines.

The **behavioural sciences approach** develops theories about human behaviour based on scientific methods and study. Behavioural science draws from sociology, psychology, anthropology, economics and other disciplines to understand employee behaviour and interaction in an organizational setting. The approach can be seen in practically every organization. When General Electric conducts research to determine the best set of tests, interviews and employee profiles to use when selecting new employees, it is using behavioural science techniques. When Circuit City electronics stores train new managers in the techniques of employee motivation, most of the theories and findings are rooted in behavioural science research.

One specific set of management techniques based in the behavioural sciences approach is *organization development* (OD). In the 1970s, organization development evolved as a separate field that applied the behavioural sciences to improve the organization's health and effectiveness through its ability to cope with change, improve internal relationships and increase problem-solving capabilities.[45] The techniques and concepts of organization development have since been broadened and expanded to address the increasing complexity of organizations and the environment, and OD is still a vital approach for managers. Organizational development will be discussed in detail in Chapter 11. Other concepts that grew out of the behavioural sciences approach include matrix organizations, self-managed teams, ideas about corporate culture and management by wandering around. Indeed, the behavioural sciences approach has influenced the majority of tools, techniques and approaches that managers have applied to organizations since the 1970s. In recent years, behavioural sciences and OD techniques have been applied to help managers build learning organizations.

All of the remaining chapters of this book contain research findings and management applications that can be attributed to the behavioural sciences approach. This chapter's Shoptalk box illustrates a number of management innovations that have become popular over the past 50 years. Note the trend of new management concepts from the behavioural sciences, increasing about 1970 and then again from 1980 to the present. The rapid pace of change and the increased pressure of global competition have spurred even greater interest in improved behavioural approaches to management.

Management Science Perspective

Management science perspective
A management perspective that emerged after World War II and applied mathematics, statistics and other quantitative techniques to managerial problems.

World War II caused many management changes. The massive and complicated problems associated with modern global warfare presented managerial decision-makers with the need for more sophisticated tools than ever before. The **management science perspective** emerged to address those problems. This view is distinguished for its application of mathematics, statistics, and other quantitative techniques to management decision-making and problem solving. During World War II, groups of mathematicians, physicists, and other scientists were formed to solve military problems. Because those problems frequently involved moving massive amounts of materials and large numbers of people quickly and efficiently, the techniques had obvious applications to large-scale business firms.[46]

Recent Historical Trends

Management is, by nature, complex and dynamic. Elements of each of the perspectives discussed here are still in use today. The most prevalent is the humanistic perspective, but even it has undergone change in recent years. Three recent trends that

MANAGER'S SHOPTALK

Operations research grew directly out of the World War II groups (called *operational research teams* in Great Britain and *operations research teams* in the US).[47] It consists of mathematical model building and other applications of quantitative techniques to managerial problems.

Operations management refers to the field of management that specializes in the physical production of goods or services. Operations management specialists use quantitative techniques to solve manufacturing problems. Some commonly used methods are forecasting, inventory modelling, linear and non-linear programming, queuing theory, scheduling, simulation, and break-even analysis.[48]

Information technology (IT) is the most recent subfield of the management science perspective, which is often reflected in management information systems.

These systems are designed to provide relevant information to managers in a timely and cost-efficient manner. More recently, information technology within organizations evolved to include intranets and extranets, as well as various software programs that help managers estimate costs, plan and track production, manage projects, allocate resources or schedule employees. When in the US Weyerhaeuser Company's door factory implemented an intranet combined with software to track inventory, calculate estimates, schedule production and automate order taking, it applied management science to cut both manufacturing costs and production time.[49] Most of today's organizations have departments of information technology specialists who use management science techniques to solve complex organizational problems.

---

grew out of the humanistic perspective are systems theory, the contingency view and total quality management.

Systems Theory

A **system** is a set of interrelated parts that function as a whole to achieve a common purpose.[50] A system functions by acquiring inputs from the external environment, transforming them in some way, and discharging outputs back to the environment. Exhibit 2.6 shows the basic **systems theory** of organizations. It consists of five components: inputs, a transformation process, outputs, feedback and the environment. *Inputs* are the material, human, financial, or information resources used to produce goods and services. The *transformation process* is management's use of production technology to change the inputs into outputs. *Outputs* include the organization's products and services. *Feedback* is knowledge of the results that influence the selection of inputs during the next cycle of the process. The *environment* surrounding the organization includes the social, political, and economic forces noted earlier in this chapter.

Some ideas in systems theory significantly affected management thinking. They include open and closed systems, entropy, synergy and subsystem interdependencies.[51]

Open systems must interact with the environment to survive; **closed systems** need not. In the classical and management science perspectives, organizations were frequently thought of as closed systems. In the management science perspective, closed system assumptions – the absence of external disturbances – are sometimes used to simplify problems for quantitative analysis. In reality, however, all organizations are open systems, and the cost of ignoring the environment may be failure.

Entropy is a universal property of systems and refers to their tendency to run down and die. If a system does not receive fresh inputs and energy from its environment, it will eventually cease to exist. Organizations must monitor their environments, adjust to changes, and continuously bring in new inputs in order to survive

System
A set of interrelated parts that function as a whole to achieve a common purpose.

Systems theory
An extension of the humanistic perspective that describes organizations as open systems characterized by entropy, synergy and subsystem interdependence.

Open system
A system that interacts with the external environment.

Closed system
A system that does not interact with the external environment.

Entropy
The tendency for a system to run down and die.

Exhibit 2.5 Ebbs and Flows of Management Innovations, 1950–2000

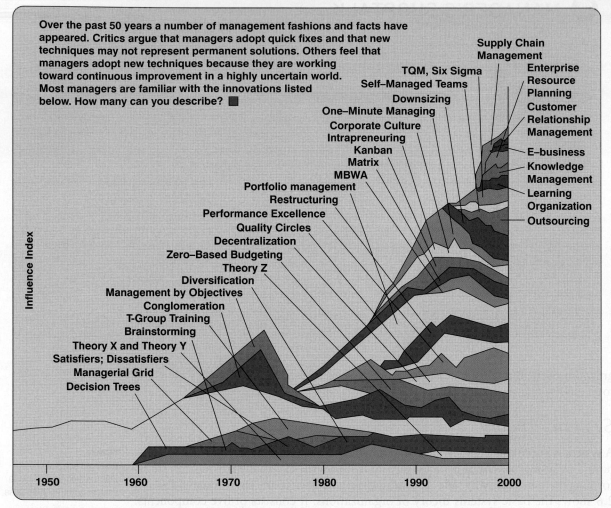

Over the past 50 years a number of management fashions and facts have appeared. Critics argue that managers adopt quick fixes and that new techniques may not represent permanent solutions. Others feel that managers adopt new techniques because they are working toward continuous improvement in a highly uncertain world. Most managers are familiar with the innovations listed below. How many can you describe? ■

Influence Index

Supply Chain Management
TQM, Six Sigma
Self–Managed Teams
Downsizing
One–Minute Managing
Corporate Culture
Intrapreneuring
Kanban
Matrix
MBWA
Portfolio management
Restructuring
Performance Excellence
Quality Circles
Decentralization
Zero–Based Budgeting
Theory Z
Diversification
Management by Objectives
Conglomeration
T-Group Training
Brainstorming
Theory X and Theory Y
Satisfiers; Dissatisfiers
Managerial Grid
Decision Trees

Enterprise Resource Planning
Customer Relationship Management
E–business
Knowledge Management
Learning Organization
Outsourcing

1950   1960   1970   1980   1990   2000

SOURCE: Adapted from Fig 1.3, Richard Tanner Pascale, *Managing on the Edge* (New York: Touchstone/Simon & Schuster, 1990), 20. Copyright © 1990 by Richard Pascale.

Synergy
The concept that the whole is greater than the sum of its parts.

Subsystems
Parts of a system that depend on one another for their functioning.

and prosper. Managers try to design the organization/environment interface to reduce entropy.

Synergy means that the whole is greater than the sum of its parts. When an organization is formed, something new comes into the world. Management, coordination and production that did not exist before are now present. Organizational units working together can accomplish more than those same units working alone. The sales department depends on production, and vice versa.

Subsystems depend on one another as parts of a system. Changes in one part of the organization affect other parts. The organization must be managed as a coordinated whole. Managers who understand subsystem interdependence are reluctant to make changes that do not recognize subsystem impact on the organization as a whole. Consider Toyota's highly successful application of the 'just-in-time' inventory control system, which aims to keep inventory at its lowest. Managers knew that the best way to make the system work was to let employees on the factory floor control the flow of materials. Thus the change in production required that the company also make changes in culture and structure. Toyota decentralized decision-making so that employees doing the work were empowered to make choices about how to

Exhibit 2.6 The Systems View of Organizations

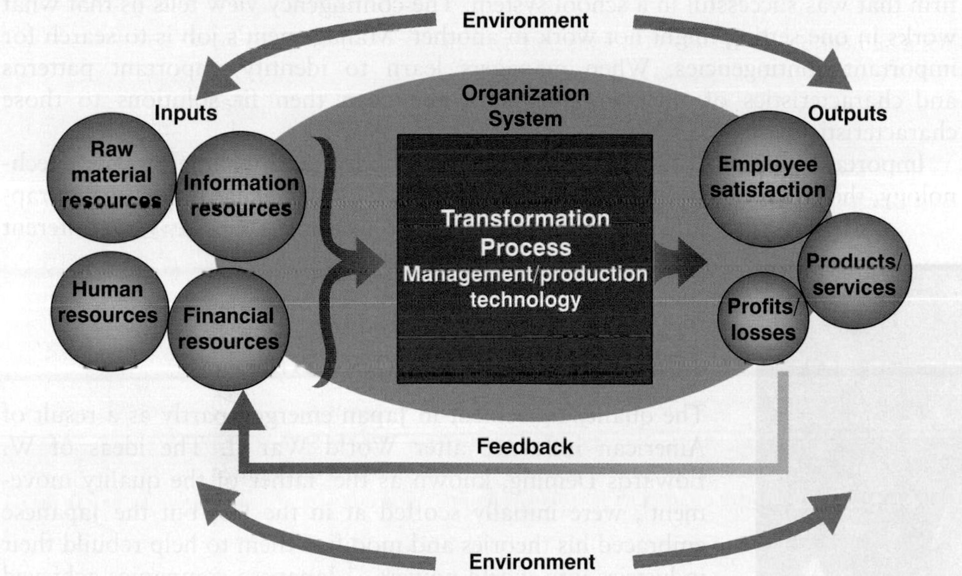

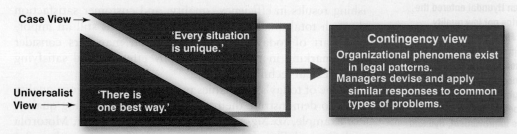

accomplish it. Cultural values were shifted to encourage every employee to think creatively about improving his or her particular piece of the organization and to see problems as opportunities for learning and improving.[52] Major changes in an organization often take quite some time because of the interconnection of the organization's subsystems.

Contingency View

A second contemporary extension to management thinking is the **contingency view**. The classical perspective assumed a *universalist* view. Management concepts were thought to be universal; that is, whatever worked – leader style, bureaucratic structure – in one organization would work in another. In business education, however, an alternative view exists. In this *case* view, each situation is believed to be unique. Principles are not universal, and one learns about management by experiencing a large number of case problem situations. Managers face the task of determining what methods will work in every new situation.

To Integrate these views the contingency view emerged, as illustrated in Exhibit 2.7.[53] Here neither of the other views is seen as entirely correct. Instead, certain contingencies, or variables, exist for helping management identify and understand situations. The contingency view means that a manager's response depends on identifying key contingencies in an organizational situation. For example, a consultant might mistakenly

Contingency view
An extension of the humanistic perspective in which the successful resolution of organizational problems is thought to depend on managers' identification of key variations in the situation at hand.

Exhibit 2.7 Contingency View of Management

Case View → 'Every situation is unique.'

Universalist View → 'There is one best way.'

Contingency view
Organizational phenomena exist in legal patterns.
Managers devise and apply similar responses to common types of problems.

Total Quality Management (TQM)
A concept that focuses on managing the total organization to deliver quality to customers. Four significant elements of TQM are employee involvement, focus on the customer, benchmarking and continuous improvement.

recommend the same *management by objectives* (MBO) system for a manufacturing firm that was successful in a school system. The contingency view tells us that what works in one setting might not work in another. Management's job is to search for important contingencies. When managers learn to identify important patterns and characteristics of their organizations, they can then fit solutions to those characteristics.

Important contingencies that managers must understand include industry, technology, the environment and international cultures. Management practices in a rapidly changing industry, for example, will be very different from those in a stable one.

Total Quality Management

The quality movement in Japan emerged partly as a result of American influence after World War II. The ideas of W. Edwards Deming, known as the 'father of the quality movement', were initially scoffed at in the US, but the Japanese embraced his theories and modified them to help rebuild their industries into world powers.[54] Japanese companies achieved a significant departure from the American model by gradually shifting from an inspection-oriented approach to quality control towards an approach emphasizing employee involvement in the prevention of quality problems.[55]

During the 1980s and into the 1990s, **total quality management (TQM)**, which focuses on managing the total organization to deliver quality to customers, was at the forefront in helping managers deal with global competition. The approach infuses quality values throughout every activity within a company, with front-line workers intimately involved in the process. Four significant elements of quality management are employee involvement, focus on the customer, benchmarking and continuous improvement.

Employee involvement means that TQM requires companywide participation in quality control. All employees are *focused on the customer;* TQM companies find out what customers want and try to meet their needs and expectations. *Benchmarking* refers to a process whereby companies find out how others do something better than they do and then try to imitate or improve on it. *Continuous improvement* is the implementation of small, incremental improvements in all areas of the organization on an ongoing basis. TQM is not a quick fix, but companies such as General Electric, Texas Instruments, Procter & Gamble and DuPont achieved astonishing results in efficiency, quality, and customer satisfaction through total quality management.[56] TQM is still an important part of today's organizations, and managers consider benchmarking in particular a highly effective and satisfying management technique.[57]

Some of today's companies pursue highly ambitious quality goals to demonstrate their commitment to improving quality. For example, *Six Sigma*, popularized by Caterpillar, Motorola and General Electric, specifies a goal of no more than 3.4 defects per million parts. However, the term also refers to a

COURTESY OF HYUNDAI

CONCEPT CONNECTION The inclusion of Hyundai Motor Company's Elantra SE and Santa Fe in the 2008 top ten autos by *Consumer Reports* shows how commitment to total quality management can improve a company's products and market position. When Hyundai entered the US market in 1999, its autos got low quality ratings from consumers. First, managers increased the quality team from 100 to 865 people and held quality seminars to train employees. They also benchmarked products, using vehicle lifts and high-intensity spotlights to compare against competing brands. Committing to continuous improvement, Hyundai delayed several new models to resolve problems. Within five years Hyundai earned quality ratings comparable to Honda and just behind Toyota.

broad quality control approach that emphasizes a disciplined and relentless pursuit of higher quality and lower costs. TQM will be discussed in detail in Chapter 19.

Innovative Management Thinking for Turbulent Times

All of the ideas and approaches discussed so far in this chapter go into the mix that makes up modern management. A recent book on management thinking indicates dozens of ideas and techniques in current use that can trace their roots to these historical perspectives.[58] In addition, innovative concepts continue to emerge to address management challenges in today's turbulent world. Organizations experiment with new ways of managing that more adequately respond to the demands of today's environment and customers. Two current innovations in management thinking are the shift to a learning organization and managing the technology-driven workplace.

The Learning Organization

One of the toughest challenges for managers today is to get people focused on adaptive change to meet the demands of a turbulent and rapidly changing environment. Few problems come with ready-made solutions, and they require that people throughout the company think in new ways and learn new values and attitudes.[59] These needs demand a new approach to management and a new kind of organization. Managers began thinking about the concept of the learning organization after the publication of Peter Senge's book, *The Fifth Discipline: The Art and Practice of Learning Organizations*.[60] Senge described the kind of changes managers needed to undergo to help their organizations adapt to an increasingly chaotic world. These ideas gradually evolved to describe characteristics of the organization itself. No single view describes what the learning organization looks like. The learning organization is an attitude or philosophy about what an organization can become.

The learning organization can be defined as one in which everyone is engaged in identifying and solving problems, enabling the organization to continuously experiment, change and improve, thus increasing its capacity to grow, learn and achieve its purpose. The essential idea is problem solving, in contrast to the traditional organization designed for efficiency. In the learning organization all employees look for problems, such as understanding special customer needs. Employees also solve problems, which means putting things together in unique ways to meet a customer's needs. Many of today's managers are quite aware that sustained competitive advantage can come only by developing the learning capacity of everyone in the organization. This awareness is reflected in a survey conducted by *Strategy Business* in the US. The magazine asked its online subscribers, along with a group of thinkers, educators, interview subjects and scholars, to vote for the ideas discussed in *Strategy Business* over the past ten years that they consider most likely to remain relevant for at least the next decade. The concept of the learning organization ranked second on the list of top ten ideas.[61]

To develop a learning organization, managers make changes in all the subsystems of the organization. Three important adjustments to promote continuous learning are shifting to a team-based structure, empowering employees and sharing information. These three characteristics are illustrated in Exhibit 2.8 and each is described here.

Learning organization
An organization in which everyone is engaged in identifying and solving problems, enabling the organization to continuously experiment, improve and increase its capability.

Exhibit 2.8 Elements of a Learning Organization

Team–Based
Structure

Learning
Organization

Empowered
Employees

Open
Information

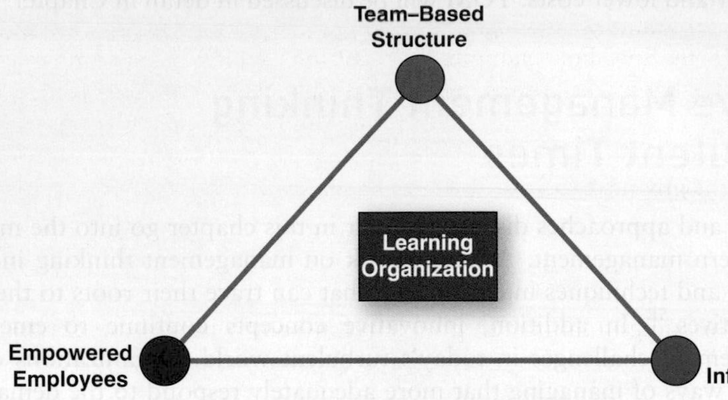

Team-Based Structure

An important value in a learning organization is collaboration and communication across departmental and hierarchical boundaries. Self-directed teams are the basic building block of the structure. These teams are made up of employees with different skills who share or rotate jobs to produce an entire product or service. Traditional management tasks are pushed down to lower levels of the organization, with teams often taking responsibility for training, safety, scheduling, and decisions about work methods, pay and reward systems, and coordination with other teams. Although team leadership is critical, in learning organizations the traditional boss is practically eliminated. People on the team are given the skills, information, tools, motivation and authority to make decisions central to the team's performance and to respond creatively and flexibly to new challenges or opportunities that arise.

Employee Empowerment

Empowerment means unleashing the power and creativity of employees by giving them the freedom, resources, information, and skills to make decisions and perform effectively. Traditional management tries to limit employees, while empowerment expands their behaviour. Empowerment may be reflected in self-directed work teams, quality circles, job enrichment and employee participation groups as well as through decision-making authority, training and information so that people can perform jobs without close supervision.

In learning organizations, people are a manager's primary source of strength, not a cost to be minimized. Companies that adopt this perspective believe in treating employees well by providing competitive wages and good working conditions, as well as by investing time and money in training programmes and opportunities for personal and professional development. In addition, they often provide a sense of employee ownership by sharing gains in productivity and profits.[62]

Open Information

A learning organization is flooded with information. To identify needs and solve problems, people have to be aware of what's going on. They must understand the whole organization as well as their part in it. Formal data about budgets, profits, and departmental expenses are available to everyone. 'If you really want to respect individuals', says Solectron Corporation's Winston Chen, 'you've got to let them know how they're doing – and let them know soon enough so they can do something about it'.[63] Managers know that providing too much information is better than providing too little. In addition, managers encourage people throughout the organization to share information. For example, at Viant Inc., which helps companies build and maintain web-based businesses, people are rewarded for their willingness to absorb and share knowledge. Rather than encouraging consultants to hoard specialized knowledge, CEO Bob Gett says, 'We value you more for how much information you've given to the guy next to you.'[64]

Managing the Technology-Driven Workplace

The shift to the learning organization goes hand-in-hand with the current transition to a technology-driven workplace. The physical world that Frederick Taylor and other proponents of scientific management measured determines less and less of what is valued in organizations and society. Our lives and organizations have been engulfed by information technology. Ideas, information, and relationships are becoming more important than production machinery, physical products and structured jobs.[65] Many employees perform much of their work on computers and may work in virtual teams, connected electronically to colleagues around the world. Even in factories that produce physical goods, machines have taken over much of the routine and uniform work, freeing workers to use more of their minds and abilities. Managers and employees in today's companies focus on opportunities rather than efficiencies, which requires that they be flexible, creative and unconstrained by rigid rules and structured tasks.

The Shifting World of e-Business

Today, much business takes place by digital processes over a computer network rather than in physical space. **E-business** refers to the work an organization does by using electronic linkages (including the internet) with customers, partners, suppliers, employees, or other key constituents. For example, organizations that use the internet or other electronic linkages to communicate with employees or customers are engaged in e-business.

E-commerce is a narrower term referring specifically to business exchanges or transactions that occur electronically. E-commerce replaces or enhances the exchange of money and products with the exchange of data and information from one computer to another. Three types of e-commerce – *business-to-consumer*, *business-to-business* and *consumer-to-consumer* – are illustrated in Exhibit 2.9. Companies such as Amazon.com, 800-Flowers, Expedia.com and Progressive are engaged in what is referred to as *business-to-consumer (B2C) e-commerce*, because they sell products and services to consumers over the internet. Although this type of exchange is probably the most visible expression of e-commerce to the public, the fastest growing area of e-commerce is *business-to-business (B2B) e-commerce*, which refers to electronic transactions between organizations. Today, much B2B e-commerce takes place over the internet.[66] Large organizations such as Tesco, Wal-Mart, Marks & Spencer, Carrefour, General Motors and Ford Motor Company buy and sell billions of dollars worth of goods and services a year via either public or private internet linkages.[67] For example, General Motors sells about 300 000 previously owned vehicles a year online through SmartAuction. Ford purchases a large portion of the steel it uses to build cars through e-Steel.[68]

Some companies take e-commerce to high levels to achieve amazing performance through supply chain management. **Supply chain management** refers to managing

E-business
Work an organization does by using electronic linkages.

E-commerce
Business exchanges or transactions that occur electronically.

Supply chain management
Managing the sequence of suppliers and purchasers, covering all stages of processing from obtaining raw materials to distributing finished goods to final customers.

Exhibit 2.9 Three Types of e-Commerce

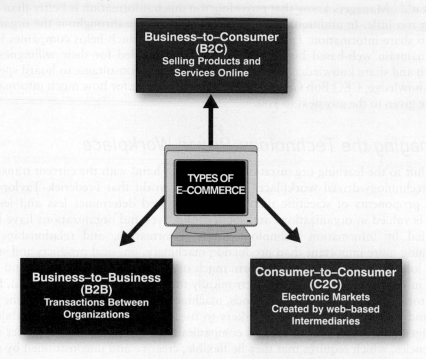

the sequence of suppliers and purchasers, covering all stages of processing from obtaining raw materials to distributing finished goods to consumers.[69] Dell Computer was a pioneer in the use of end-to-end digital supply-chain networks to keep in touch with customers, take orders, buy components from suppliers, coordinate with manufacturing partners and ship customized products directly to consumers. This trend is affecting every industry, prompting a group of consultants at a Harvard University conference to conclude that businesses today must either 'Dell or be Delled'.[70]

The third area of e-commerce, *consumer-to-consumer* (C2C), is made possible when an internet-based business acts as an intermediary between and among consumers. One of the best-known examples of C2C e-commerce is Web-based auctions such as those made possible by eBay. Internet auctions create a large electronic marketplace where consumers can buy and sell directly with one another, usually handling practically the entire transaction via the Web. To the end of 2006, eBay has nearly 222 million eBay users, 133 million PayPal accounts and 171 million Skype users. Members of eBay in the US alone sold approximately $10.6 billion in merchandize during the first six months of 2005. Merchandize sales worldwide in the previous year were approximately $36 billion.[71] Another growing area of C2C commerce is peer-to-peer (P2P) file-sharing networks. Companies such as iTunes, Kazaa and Grokster provide the technology for swapping music, movies, software and other files. Online music sharing, in particular, has zoomed in popularity, and although music companies and record retailers are currently engaged in a heated battle with file-sharing services, these companies are likely here to stay.[72]

Innovative Technology in the Workplace

New electronic technologies also shape the organization and how it is managed. A century ago, Frederick Taylor described the kind of worker needed in the iron industry: 'Now one of the first requirements for a man who is fit to handle pig iron as a regular occupation is that he shall be so stupid and so phlegmatic that he more nearly resembles in his mental makeup the ox than any other type'.[73] The philosophy of scientific management was that managers structured and controlled jobs so carefully that thinking on the part of employees wasn't required – indeed, it was usually discouraged. How different things are today! Many organizations depend on employees' minds more than their physical bodies. In companies where the power of an idea determines success, managers' primary goal is to tap into the creativity and knowledge of every employee.

TAKE A MOMENT

As a new manager in today's workplace, how would you develop your employees' abilities to think independently, build relationships and share knowledge? Be prepared to learn to use technology as a tool to tap into the insight and creativity of each person in the organization.

Technology provides the architecture that supports and reinforces this new workplace. One approach to information management is **enterprise resource planning (ERP)** systems, which weave together all of a company's major business functions, such as order processing, product design, purchasing, inventory, manufacturing, distribution, human resources, receipt of payments and forecasting of future demand.[74] ERP supports a companywide management system in which everyone, from the CEO down to a machine operator on the factory floor, has instant access to critical information. People can see the big picture and act quickly, based on up-to-the-minute information. Thus, ERP also supports management attempts to harness and leverage organizational *knowledge*.

Peter Drucker coined the term *knowledge work* more than 40 years ago,[75] but only in recent years did managers begin to genuinely recognize knowledge as an important organizational resource that should be managed just as they manage cash flow or raw materials. **Knowledge management** refers to the efforts to systematically find, organize, and make available a company's intellectual capital and to foster a culture of continuous learning and knowledge sharing so that a company's activities build on what is already known.[76] One growing segment of knowledge management is the use of sophisticated **customer relationship management (CRM)** systems, which collect and manage large amounts of data about customers and make them available to employees, enabling better decision-making and superior customer service. The use of CRM has virtually exploded over the past several years. In Bain and Company's 2005 management tool survey, for example, three out of four companies reported using CRM, up from only 35 per cent of companies in 2000, one of the largest and fastest usage increases ever revealed by the survey.[77]

Information technology also contributes to the rapid growth of **outsourcing**, which means contracting out selected functions or activities to other organizations that can do the work more cost-efficiently. Today's companies are outsourcing like crazy to free up cash for investment in long-term research and innovation. Outsourcing – along with other trends such as supply chain management, customer relationship management, telecommuting and virtual teamwork – requires that managers not only be technologically savvy, but that they also learn to manage a complex web of relationships. These relationships might reach far beyond the boundaries of the physical organization; they are often built through flexible e-links between a company and its employees, suppliers, partners and customers.[78]

Enterprise resource planning (ERP)
Systems that unite a company's major business functions – order processing, product design, purchasing, inventory and so on.

Knowledge management
The efforts to systematically find, organize and make available a company's intellectual capital and to foster a culture of continuous learning and knowledge sharing.

Customer relationship management (CRM)
Systems that help companies track customers' interaction with the firm and allow employees to call up information on past transactions.

Outsourcing
Contracting out selected functions or activities of an organization to other organizations that can do the work more cost-efficiently.

CONCEPT CONNECTION The BMW subsidiary MINI offers customers a voice in everything from personalizing their credit cards to designing their cars. BMW Financial Services' MINI Platinum Visa cardholders can customize the MINI image that graces their card by accessing the web page, shown here. There they can choose from four body styles, 36 different wheels, 21 body colours and 24 roof options. Similar software allows individuals to customize their actual MINI vehicles. 'No two MINIs are exactly alike', the MINI website proclaims. This type of collaborative customer experience is the next step in customer relationship management (CRM), as companies court internet-savvy Gen X and Gen Y consumers.

Non-Linear Development[79]

This chapter leads you to understand that there has been a linear development of management thinking from early theorists like Taylor and Webber to the present day. An alternative view is presented by Tsoukas and Cummings. They argue that we should abandon the idea that there is a development of thinking about organization and management that is underpinned by progression, that we are part of a continuous progress. Rather than seeing the history of management as a 'stairway to heaven' upwards and onwards, it should be viewed as a kaleidoscope, containing a number of discrete fragments, revealing a pattern, as Foucault did. The sequence of patterns from the kaleidoscope obeys no inner logic and conforms to no universal norm of reason. Fragments from the past will reappear now and again.

1 What support do you find for this thought?

2 Would you agree with Tsoukas and Cummings?

3 What would be the rationale for presenting a non-linear view of management thinking?

A MANAGER'S ESSENTIALS: WHAT HAVE WE LEARNED?

■ An understanding of the evolution of management helps current and future managers appreciate where we are now and continue to progress toward better management. Elements of various historical approaches go into the mix that makes up modern management.

■ Three major perspectives on management evolved since the late 1800s: the classical perspective, the humanistic perspective and the management science perspective. Each perspective encompasses several specialized subfields that provided important ideas still relevant in organizations today.

■ Recent extensions of those perspectives include systems theory, the contingency view and total quality management. Systemic thinking, which means looking not just at discrete parts of a situation but also at the continually changing interactions among the parts, is a powerful tool for managing in a complex environment.

■ The most recent thinking about organizations was brought about by today's turbulent times and the shift to a new workplace described in Chapter 1. Many managers are redesigning their companies toward the learning organization, which fully engages all employees in identifying and solving problems.

■ The shift to a learning organization goes hand-in-hand with the transition to a technology-driven workplace. Important new management approaches include supply chain management, customer relationship management, and outsourcing. These approaches require managers to think in new ways about the role of employees, customers and partners. Today's best managers value employees for their ability to think, build relationships and share knowledge, which is quite different from the scientific management perspective of a century ago.

One century-old company that is thriving as a technology-driven learning organization is Cementos Mexicanos (Cemex), described at the beginning of the chapter. To help the organization compete in a turbulent environment, managers looked for both technological and management innovations. A core element of the new approach is the company's complex information technology infrastructure, which includes a global positioning satellite system and on-board computers in all delivery trucks that are continuously fed with streams of day-to-day data on customer orders, production schedules, traffic problems, weather conditions, and so forth. Even more important are changes in how managers and employees think about and do their work. All drivers and dispatchers attended weekly secondary education classes for two years.

Regular training in quality, customer service, and computer skills continues, with Cemex devoting at least 8 per cent of total work time to employee training and development. The company abolished strict and demanding work rules so that workers have more discretion and responsibility for identifying and solving problems.

As a result, Cemex trucks now operate as self-organizing business units, run by well-trained employees who think like business people. The three-hour delivery window has been reduced to 20 minutes, and managers believe a goal of 10 minutes is within reach. According to Francisco Perez, operations manager at Cemex in Guadalajara, 'They used to think of themselves as drivers. But anyone can deliver concrete. Now our people know that they're delivering a service that the competition cannot deliver.' Cemex transformed the industry by combining extensive networking technology with a new management approach that taps into the mind power of everyone in the company. People at Cemex learn constantly – on the job, in training classes, and through visits to other organizations. As a result, the company achieves a startling capacity to anticipate customer needs, solve problems and innovate quickly.[80]

DISCUSSION QUESTIONS

1 Why is it important to understand the different perspectives and approaches to management theory that have evolved throughout the history of organizations?

2 How do societal forces influence the practice and theory of management? Do you think new management techniques are a response to these forces? What are the differences in societal forces in Europe, the US, Asia and the Middle East, and how does the application of management theory differ in across those regions?

3 Based on your experience at work or school, describe some ways in which the principles of scientific management and bureaucracy are still used in organizations. Do you believe these characteristics will ever cease to be a part of organizational life? Discuss.

4 A management professor once said that for successful management, studying the present was most important, studying the past was next, and studying the future was least important. Do you agree? Why?

5 Which of the three characteristics of learning organizations do you find most appealing? As a manager, which would be hardest for you to adopt? Why?

6 As organizations become more technology-driven, which do you think will become more important – the management of the human element of the organization or the management of technology? Discuss.

7 Why do you think Mary Parker Follet's ideas tended to be popular with business people of her day, but were ignored by management

scholars? Why are her ideas appreciated more today?

8 Explain the basic idea underlying the contingency view. How would you go about identifying the key contingencies facing an organization?

9 Why can an event such as the Hawthorne studies be a major turning point in the history of management even if the idea is later shown to be in error? Discuss.

10 Identify the major components of systems theory. Is this perspective primarily internal or external to the organization? Explain.

11 Do you think management theory will ever be as precise as theories in the fields of finance,

accounting or experimental psychology? Why or why not?

12 To what degree do you think that effective control comes from within the individual worker, or do workers need rules, rewards and punishments to perform effectively? Explain your reasoning.

13 In the Bain survey of management tools, corporate blogs were used in 30 per cent of companies and also have the highest projected growth rates among managers. What might explain this? Do you think corporate blogs will ever become as popular as customer relationship management systems?

MANAGEMENT IN PRACTICE: EXPERIENTIAL EXERCISE

Theory X and Theory Y Scale

The following are various types of behaviour that a manager may engage in when relating to subordinates. Read each statement carefully and rate each one in terms of the extent to which you would use that behaviour, according to the following scale.

1 Make a great effort to do this

2 Tend to do this

3 Tend to avoid doing this

4 Make a great effort to avoid this

1 Closely supervize my subordinates in order to get better work from them.

    1   2   3   4

2 Set the goals and objectives for my subordinates and sell them on the merits of my plans.

    1   2   3   4

3 Set up controls to assure that my subordinates are getting the job done.

    1   2   3   4

4 Encourage my subordinates to set their own goals and objectives.

    1   2   3   4

5 Make sure that my subordinates' work is planned out for them.

    1   2   3   4

6 Check with my subordinates daily to see if they need any help.

    1   2   3   4

7 Step in as soon as reports indicate that the job is slipping.

    1   2   3   4

8 Push my people to meet schedules if necessary.

    1   2   3   4

9 Have frequent meetings to keep in touch with what is going on.

    1   2   3   4

10 Allow subordinates to make important decisions.

    1   2   3   4

Scoring and Interpretation

Subtract each of your scores for Questions 4 and 10 from the number 5. Then, add the total points and mark your score on the scale below. Refer back to

Exhibit 2.4 and review the assumptions related to Theory X and Theory Y. A person who fully subscribes to the assumptions of Theory X would have a score of 10, whereas a person who fully subscribes to the assumptions of Theory Y would have a score of 40. Strong Theory X assumptions are typically considered inappropriate for today's workplace. Where do you fit on the X–Y scale? Does your score reflect your perception of yourself as a current or future manager?

Theory X	10	20	30	40	Theory Y

SOURCE J. William Pfeiffer and John E. Jones, eds, 'Supervisory Attitudes: The X–Y Scale,' *The 1972 Annual Handbook for Group Facilitators* (New York: John Wiley & Sons Inc., 1972): 65–68. This material is used by permission of John Wiley & Sons, Inc. The X–Y scale was adapted from an instrument developed by Robert N. Ford of AT&T for in-house manager training.

MANAGEMENT IN PRACTICE: ETHICAL DILEMMA

The Supervisor

Karen Moore, manager of Health and Social Care Services a social service agency in Cork, South of Ireland, loved to see her employees learn and grow to their full potential. When a rare opening for a supervising clerk occurred, Karen quickly decided to give Charlotte Mullins a shot at the job. Charlotte had been with the agency for ten years and had shown herself to be a true leader. Charlotte worked hard at being a good supervisor, just as she had always worked hard at being a first-class clerk. She paid attention to the human aspects of employee problems and introduced modern management techniques that strengthened the entire organization.

However, the Health and Social Care Services Board decided that a promotional exam should be given to find a permanent placement for the supervising clerk position. For the sake of fairness, the exam was an open competition – anyone, even a new employee, could sign up and take it. The board wanted the candidate with the highest score to get the job but allowed Karen, as manager of the agency, to have the final say-so.

Since she had accepted the provisional opening and proven herself on the job, Charlotte was upset that the entire clerical force was deemed qualified to take the test. When the results came back, she was

devastated. Charlotte placed twelfth in the field of candidates, while one of her newly hired clerks placed first. The Health and Social Care Services Board, impressed by the new clerk's high score, is urging Karen to give her the permanent supervisory job. Karen wonders whether it's fair to base her decision solely on the test results.

What Would You Do?

1 Ignore the test. Charlotte has proven herself and deserves the job.

2 Give the job to the candidate with the highest score. You don't need to make enemies on the Health and Social Care Services Board and, after all, it is an objective way to select a permanent placement.

3 Devise a more comprehensive set of selection criteria – including test results as well as supervisory experience, ability to motivate employees, and knowledge of agency procedures – that can be explained and justified to the board and to employees.

SOURCE Based on Betty Harrigan, 'Career Advice', *Working Woman* (July 1986): 22–24.

CASE FOR CRITICAL ANALYSIS 2.1

Ivanovskaya Manufactura

In the early years of the new century, it wasn't hard to see that Ivanovskaya Manufactura, the Russian wool

processing plant, with over 3300 employees couldn't keep doing business the old-fashioned twentieth century way. The newly appointed Vice Director for foreign relations Maria Ivanova, having completed her

MBA in the UK and now back in Russia to support her family business, fully realized that she had to rise to this challenge to justify her new position in the recently formed foreign relations department.

Headquartered in Moscow, Ivanovskaya Manufactura was the only wool processing company in central Russia, offering a wide range of wool fabrics, and woollen blankets for the army and civilians, as well as producing screens and felts for paper machines to commercial customers of all sizes throughout the country. Over the years it had diversified into various types of activities by dividing the company into smaller business units until it consisted of more than 30 separate such units. 'Like mother, like son' each had its own hierarchy, characterized by strong top-down administration and the well-defined rules and procedures typical of the textile industry; virtually every employee possessed specialized knowledge about a narrowly defined market niche.

After Maria's presentation on the development of trends in management science and how the company should adapt its business practices, the upper-level management gave the matter considerable attention and concluded that Ivanovskaya Manufactura's refined division of labour into technical specialisms needed to give way to a collaborative learning organization, one where employee empowerment and open information made it possible for anyone, from workers at the shop floor to the management in each business unit to be knowledgeable about a variety of products the other units were producing, and as a result to join forces on the R&D front.

Since it was Maria's idea, she was given responsibility to start implementing the learning organization environment. She wanted to introduce newsletters as vehicles of information sharing – an idea she had seen working well abroad. However, she was stuck, as she was obstructed at every step and could not print the necessary information as a newsletter, could not summarize the information on the website and if newsletters were sent via email then only the top management would have access to these and then only during working hours. It appeared that there was always a reason why things were not possible.

Alexey Ivanov, the president of the company, clued her in. After weathering a turbulent period, one that had seen plenty of layoffs in the textile industry, many employees viewed the restructuring and new information-sharing methods as the first step in a process that would lead to redundancy letters landing on their desks. Some employees, in fact, saw their own highly specialized knowledge as a kind of job insurance policy. 'They know that if they don't share their specialist information now, they become a lot more important to the company.' However, Maria thought that it was not the workers that were not ready to share their expertise and experience, it was also management that did not want any ideas to be shared. She thought, 'They simply do not want to devolve the power to lower levels!'

Questions

1 What are some of the social, political and economic forces that are influencing Ivanovskaya Manufactura's decision to move with the time and become a learning organization?

2 If you were a specialist at Ivanovskaya Manufactura, how and why would you respond to the proposed changes? What steps would you suggest Maria take to increase employee utilization of the knowledge-sharing system in particular? How can she encourage management and employees to share information?

3 What general obstacles would you foresee in a company such as Ivanovskaya Manufactura trying to make the transition from a hierarchical, or bureaucratic, to a learning organization? What are some general measures managers can take to smooth the way?

ENDNOTES

1. Thomas Petzinger, Jr., *The New Pioneers: The Men and Women Who Are Transforming the Workplace and Marketplace* (New York: Simon & Schuster, 1999): 91–93: 'In Search of the New World of Work', *Fast Company* (April 1999): 214–220+; and Peter Katel, 'Bordering on Chaos', *Wired* (July 1997): 98–107.

2. This questionnaire is from William Pfeiffer and John E. Jones, eds. 'Supervisory Attitudes: The X–Y Scale', *The 1972 Annual Handbook for Group Facilitators* (New York: John Wiley and Sons Inc., 1972), pp. 65–68. This material is used by permission of John Wiley and Sons, Inc. The X–Y scale was adapted from an instrument developed

by Robert N. Ford of AT&T for in-house manager training.

3. Jeffrey Zaslow, 'Feeling the Shivers of Faraway Scandals in Fort Wayne, Ind.', *The Wall Street Journal* (February 6, 2004): A1, A10.

4. John Huey, 'Managing in the Midst of Chaos', *Fortune* (April 5, 1993): 38–48; and Toby J. Tetenbaum, 'Shifting Paradigms: From Newton to Chaos', *Organizational Dynamics* (Spring 1998): 21–32.

5. Eric Abrahamson, 'Management Fashion', *Academy of Management Review* 21, no. 1 (January 1996): 254–285. Also see '75 Years of Management Ideas and Practice', a supplement to the *Harvard Business Review* (September–October 1997), for a broad overview of historical trends in management thinking.

6. 'Of Water Coolers and Coffee Breaks', timeline in Matthew Boyle, 'How the Workplace Was Won', *Fortune* (January 22, 2001): 139+.

7. HMRC Share Scheme Statistics, June 2006.

8. Daniel A. Wren, *The Evolution of Management Thought*, 2d ed. (New York: Wiley, 1979): 6–8. Much of the discussion of these forces comes from Arthur M. Schlesinger, *Political and Social History of the United States, 1829–1925* (New York: Macmillan, 1925); and Homer C. Hockett, *Political and Social History of the United States, 1492–1828* (New York: Macmillan, 1925).

9. Based on Stephanie Armour, 'Generation Y: They've Arrived at Work with a New Attitude', *USA Today* (November 6, 2005): www.usatoday.com/money/workplace/2005-11-06-gen-y_x.htm; and Marnie E. Green, 'Beware and Prepare: The Government Workforce of the Future', *Public Personnel Management* (Winter 2000): 435+.

10. This section is based heavily on Thomas Petzinger, Jr., 'So Long Supply and Demand,' *The Wall Street Journal* (January 1, 2000): R31.

11. Petzinger, 'So Long Supply and Demand'.

12. Darrell Rigby and Barbara Bilodeau, 'The Bain 2005 Management Tool Survey', *Strategy & Leadership* 33, no. 4 (2005): 4–12; and Darrell Rigby, 'Management Tools Survey 2003: Usage Up as Companies Strive to Make Headway in Tough Times', *Strategy & Leadership* 31, no. 5 (2003): 4–11.

13. See Daniel James Rowley, 'Resource Reviews', *Academy of Management Learning and Education* 2, no. 3 (2003): 313–321; Jane Whitney Gibson, Dana V. Tesone and Charles W. Blackwell, 'Management Fads: Here Yesterday, Gone Today?', *SAM Advanced Management Journal* (Autumn 2003): 12–17; David Collins, *Management Fads and Buzzwords: Critical-Practices Perspective*, (London, UK: Routledge, 2000); Timothy Clark, 'Management Research on Fashion: A Review and Evaluation', *Human Relations* 54, no. 12 (2001): 1650–1661; Brad Jackson, *Management Gurus and Management Fashions* (London: Routledge, 2001); Patrick Thomas, *Fashions in Management Research: An Empirical Analysis* (Aldershot, UK: Ashgate, 1999).

14. Daniel A. Wren, 'Management History: Issues and Ideas for Teaching and Research', *Journal of Management* 13 (1987): 339–350.

15. Business historian Alfred D. Chandler, Jr., quoted in Jerry Useem, 'Entrepreneur of the Century', *Inc.* (20th Anniversary Issue, 1999): 159–174.

16. Useem, 'Entrepreneur of the Century'.

17. The following is based on Wren, *Evolution of Management Thought*, Chapters 4, 5; and Claude S. George, Jr., *The History of Management Thought* (Englewood Cliffs, N.J.: Prentice Hall, 1968): Chapter 4.

18. Alan Farnham, 'The Man Who Changed Work Forever', *Fortune* (July 21, 1997): 114; Charles D. Wrege and Ann Marie Stoka, 'Cooke Creates a Classic: The Story Behind F. W. Taylor's Principles of Scientific Management', *Academy of Management Review* (October 1978): 736–749; Robert Kanigel, *The One Best Way: Frederick Winslow Taylor and the Enigma of Efficiency* (New York: Viking, 1997); and 'The X and Y Factors: What Goes Around Comes Around', in 'The New Organisation: A Survey of the Company', *The Economist* (January 21–27, 2006): special section pp. 17–18.

19. Quoted in Ann Harrington, 'The Big Ideas', *Fortune* (November 22, 1999): 152–154.

20. Wren, *Evolution of Management Thought*, 171; and George, *History of Management Thought*, 103–104.

21. Geoffrey Colvin, 'Managing in the Info Era', *Fortune* (March 6, 2000): F-5–F-9.

22. Stephen L. Morgan, 'Scientific Management in China, 1910–1930s'. Working Paper 2003/10012, Department of Management, University of Melbourne.

23. Max Weber, *General Economic History*, trans. Frank H. Knight (London: Allen & Unwin, 1927); Max Weber, *The Protestant Ethic and the Spirit of Capitalism*, trans. Talcott Parsons (New York: Scribner, 1930); and Max Weber, *The Theory of Social and Economic Organizations*, ed. and trans. A. M. Henderson and Talcott Parsons (New York: Free Press, 1947).

24. Kelly Barron, 'Logistics in Brown', *Forbes* (January 10, 2000): 78–83; Scott Kirsner, 'Venture Vérité: United Parcel Service', *Wired* (September 1999): 83–96; 'UPS', *The Atlanta Journal and Constitution* (April 26, 1992): H1; and Kathy Goode, Betty Hahn, and Cindy Seibert, 'United Parcel Service: The Brown Giant' (unpublished manuscript, Texas A&M University, 1981).

25. Fiona Wilson (1999) 'Rationalization and Rationality 2: Weber, McDonald's, and Bureaucracy', *Organizational Behaviour* (1999): 35–49; Z. Bauman, *Modernity and the Holocaust*. (Cambridge: Polity, 1959); Fineman, S. (1996) 'Emotion and Organizing', in S. R. Clegg, C. Hardy, and W. R. Nord (eds), (London: Sage), *Handbook of Organization Studies*: ch. 3.3; Gouldner, A. *Patterns of Industrial Bureaucracy* (Glencoe, Ill.: The Free Press, 1954); Merton, R. K. 'The Unanticipated Consequences of Purposive Social Action', *American Sociological Review*, 1(1936):894–904; P. Selznick, *TVA and the Grass Roots* (Berkeley, Calif.: University of California Press, 1949).

26. Henri Fayol, *Industrial and General Administration*, trans. J. A. Coubrough (Geneva: International Management Institute, 1930); Henri Fayol, *General and Industrial Management*, trans. Constance Storrs (London: Pitman and Sons, 1949); and W. J. Arnold *et al.*, *Business Week, Milestones in Management* (New York: McGraw-Hill, vol. I, 1965; vol. II, 1966).

27. Mary Parker Follett, *The New State: Group Organization: The Solution of Popular Government* (London: Longmans, Green, 1918); and Mary Parker Follett, *Creative Experience* (London: Longmans, Green, 1924).

28. Henry C. Metcalf and Lyndall Urwick, eds. *Dynamic Administration: The Collected Papers of Mary Parker Follett* (New York: Harper & Row, 1940); Arnold, *Milestones in Management*.

29. Follett, *The New State*; Metcalf and Urwick, *Dynamic Administration* (London: Sir Isaac Pitman, 1941).

30. William B. Wolf, *How to Understand Management: An Introduction to Chester I. Barnard* (Los Angeles: Lucas-Brothers, 1968); and David D. Van Fleet, 'The Need-Hierarchy and Theories of Authority', *Human Relations* 9 (Spring 1982): 111–118.

31. Gregory M. Bounds, Gregory H. Dobbins, and Oscar S. Fowler, *Management: A Total Quality Perspective* (Cincinnati, OH: South-Western Publishing, 1995): 52–53.

32. Curt Tausky, *Work Organizations: Major Theoretical Perspectives* (Itasca, IL: F. E. Peacock, 1978): 42.

33. Charles D. Wrege, 'Solving Mayo's Mystery: The First Complete Account of the Origin of the Hawthorne Studies – The Forgotten Contributions of Charles E. Snow and Homer Hibarger' (paper presented to the Management History Division of the Academy of Management, August 1976).

34. Ronald G. Greenwood, Alfred A. Bolton, and Regina A. Greenwood, 'Hawthorne a Half Century Later: Relay Assembly Participants Remember', *Journal of Management* 9 (Fall/Winter 1983): 217–231.

35. F. J. Roethlisberger, W. J. Dickson, and H. A. Wright, *Management and the Worker* (Cambridge, MA: Harvard University Press, 1939).

36. H. M. Parson, 'What Happened at Hawthorne?', *Science* 183 (1974): 922–932; John G. Adair, 'The Hawthorne Effect: A Reconsideration of the Methodological Artifact', *Journal of Applied Psychology* 69, no. 2 (1984): 334–345; and Gordon Diaper, 'The Hawthorne Effect: A Fresh Examination', *Educational Studies* 16, no. 3 (1990): 261–268.

37. R. G. Greenwood, A. A. Bolton, and R. A. Greenwood, 'Hawthorne a Half Century Later', 219–221.

38. F. J. Roethlisberger and W. J. Dickson, *Management and the Worker*.

39. Ramon J. Aldag and Timothy M. Stearns, *Management*, 2d ed. (Cincinnati, OH: South-Western Publishing, 1991): 47–48.

40. Elton Mayo. (1945) *The Social Problems of an Industrial Civilization.* New Hampshire: Ayer

41. Tausky, *Work Organizations: Major Theoretical Perspectives*, 55.

42. Douglas McGregor, *The Human Side of Enterprise* (New York: McGraw-Hill, 1960): 16–18.

43. Based on SOL online available from http://www.sonera.fi/english/reachingout/jan97/sol/page1.html; R.D. Becker and F. Steele, 'Chapter 8: Making Effective Use of Nonterritorial Offices, Workplace by Design', (San Francisco: Jossey-Bass Inc., 1995): 116–135; Gina Imperato, 'Dirty Business, Bright Ideas', Fast Company (February–March 1997), 89–93; Superbrands online available from http://www.superbrands.fi/pages/SOLPalvelut.pdf

44. Jack Ewing, 'No-Cubicle Culture', *BusinessWeek* (August 20 and 27, 2006): 60

45. Julie Gehrke, 'Power to the Painters', *Painting and Wallcovering Contractor* (September–October 2003): 84.

46. Wendell L. French and Cecil H. Bell Jr., 'A History of Organizational Development', in Wendell L. French, Cecil H. Bell Jr., and Robert A. Zawacki, *Organization Development and Transformation: Managing Effective Change* (Burr Ridge, IL: Irwin McGraw-Hill, 2000): 20–42

47. Mansel G. Blackford and K. Austin Kerr, *Business Enterprise in American History* (Boston: Houghton Mifflin, 1986): Chapters 10, 11; and Alex Groner et al. of *American Heritage and BusinessWeek, The American Heritage History of American Business and Industry* (New York: American Heritage Publishing, 1972): Chapter 9.

48. Larry M. Austin and James R. Burns, *Management Science* (New York: Macmillan, 1985).

49. Marcia Stepanek, 'How an Intranet Opened Up the Door to Profits', *BusinessWeek E.Biz* (July 26, 1999): EB32–EB38.

50. Ludwig von Bertalanffy, Carl G. Hempel, Robert E. Bass, and Hans Jonas, 'General Systems Theory: A New Approach to Unity of Science', *Human Biology* 23 (December 1951): 302–361; and Kenneth E. Boulding, 'General Systems Theory – The Skeleton of Science', *Management Science* 2 (April 1956): 197–208.

51. Fremont E. Kast and James E. Rosenzweig, 'General Systems Theory: Applications for Organization and Management', *Academy of Management Journal* (December 1972): 447–465.

52. 'Teaming with Bright Ideas', in 'The New Organisation: A Survey of the Company', *The Economist* (January 21–27, 2006): special section pp. 4–16.

53. Fred Luthans, 'The Contingency Theory of Management: A Path Out of the Jungle', *Business Horizons* 16 (June 1973): 62–72; and Fremont E. Kast and James E. Rosenzweig, *Contingency Views of Organization and Management* (Chicago: Science Research Associates, 1973).

54. Samuel Greengard, '25 Visionaries Who Shaped Today's Workplace', *Workforce* (January 1997): 50–59; and Harrington, 'The Big Ideas'.

55. Mauro F. Guillen, 'The Age of Eclecticism: Current Organizational Trends and the Evolution of Managerial Models', *Sloan Management Review* (Fall 1994): 75–86.

56. Jeremy Main, 'How to Steal the Best Ideas Around', *Fortune* (October 19, 1992): 102–106.

57. Rigby and Bilodeau, 'The Bain 2005 Management Tool Survey'.

58. Thomas H. Davenport and Laurence Prusak, with Jim Wilson, *What's the Big Idea? Creating and Capitalizing on the Best Management Thinking* (Boston, MA: Harvard Business School Press, 2003). Also see Theodore Kinni, 'Have We Run Out of Big Ideas?', *Across the Board* (March–April 2003): 16–21

59. Ronald A. Heifetz and Donald L. Laurie, 'The Leader as Teacher: Creating the Learning Organization', *Ivey Business Journal* (January–February 2003): 1–9.

60. Peter Senge, *The Fifth Discipline: The Art and Practice of Learning Organizations* (New York: Doubleday/Currency, 1990).

61. Art Kleiner, 'Our 10 Most Enduring Ideas', *Strategy + Business*, no. 41 (December 12, 2005): 36–41.

62. Khoo Hsien Hui and Tan Kay Chuan, 'Nine Approaches to Organizational Excellence', *Journal of Organizational Excellence* (Winter 2002): 53–65; Leon Martel, 'The Principles of High Performance – And How to Apply Them', *Journal of Organizational Excellence* (Autumn 2002): 49–59; and Jeffrey Pfeffer, 'Producing Sustainable Competitive

Advantage through the Effective Management of People', *Academy of Management Executive* 9, no. 1 (1995): 55–69.

63. Alex Markels, 'The Wisdom of Chairman Ko', *Fast Company* (November 1999): 258–276.

64. Edward O. Welles, 'Mind Gains', *Inc.* (December 1999): 112–124.

65. Kevin Kelly, *New Rules for the New Economy: 10 Radical Strategies for a Connected World* (New York: Viking Penguin, 1998).

66. Nick Wingfield, 'In the Beginning . . .', *The Wall Street Journal* (May 21, 2001): R18.

67. Andy Reinhardt, 'From Gearhead to Grand High PoohBah', *BusinessWeek* (August 28, 2000): 129–130.

68. Julia Angwin, 'Used Car Auctioneers, Dealers Meet Online', *The Wall Street Journal* (November 20, 2003): B1, B13; William J. Holstein and Edward Robinson, 'The ReEducation of Jacques Nasser', *Business2.Com* (May 29, 2001): 60–73.

69. Definition based on Steven A. Melnyk and David R. Denzler, *Operations Management: A Value Driven Approach* (IL: Burr Ridge, Richard D. Irwin, 1996): 613.

70. Bernard Wysocki, Jr., 'Corporate Caveat: Dell or Be Delled', *The Wall Street Journal* (May 10, 1999): A1.

71. Michelle Singletary, 'Beating a Path to the Power Sellers', *Washington Post* (August 7, 2005): F1; and Patricia Sellers, 'EBay's Secret', *Fortune* (October 18, 2004): 160–178.

72. Amber Chung, 'Music Retailers Face Tough Times as File-Sharing Grows', *Taipei Times* (February 10, 2004): 11; www.taipeitimes.com (accessed on February 10, 2004).

73. Quoted in Colvin, 'Managing in the Info Era'.

74. Jeffrey Zygmont, 'The Ties That Bind', *Inc. Tech* no. 3, (1998): 70–84; and Nancy Ferris, 'ERP: Sizzling or Stumbling?', *Government Executive* (July 1999): 99–102.

75. Harrington, 'The Big Ideas'. Also see Peter Drucker, *Post-Capitalist Society*, (Oxford: Butterworth Heinemann, 1993): 5.

76. Based on Andrew Mayo, 'Memory Bankers', *People Management* (January 22, 1998): 34–38; William Miller, 'Building the Ultimate Resource', *Management Review* (January 1999): 42–45; and Todd Datz, 'How to Speak Geek', *CIO Enterprise*, Section 2 (April 15, 1999): 46–52.

77. Rigby and Bilodeau, 'The Bain 2005 Management Tool Survey', and Edward Prewitt, 'CRM Gains Ground as Management Tool', *CIO* (September 1, 2005): 28.

78. Reinhardt, 'From Gearhead to Grand High Pooh-Bah'.

79. Fiona Wilson 'Rationalization and Rationality 2: Weber, McDonald's, and Bureaucracy', *Organizational Behaviour* (1999): pp. 35–49; Michael Foucault, *The Order of Things: An Archaeology of the Humanities*. (London: Tavistock and Routledge 1966); H. Tsoukas and S. Cummings 'Marginalization and Recovery: The Emergence of Aristotelian Themes in Organization Studies', *Organization Studies*, 18/4: (1997) 655–83.

80. Petzinger, *The New Pioneers: The Men and Women Who Are Transforming the Workplace and Marketplace*; 'In Search of the New World of Work'; Katel, 'Bordering on Chaos'; and Oren Harari, 'The Concrete Intangibles', *Management Reviews*, (May 1999): 30–33.

CONTINUING CASE
BY ALAN HOGARTH

IKEA
PART ONE: ASSEMBLING THE COMPANY

IKEA was founded in 1943 in Sweden by Ingvar Kamprad. In 1947, IKEA issued its first primitive mail-order catalogue. Then in 1950, Kamprad set the foundation for the future direction of IKEA by introducing furniture and home furnishings to the mail-order line. In 1952, the stability of home furnishings in the IKEA product line was solidified when customers were impressed by the high-quality, low-priced furniture items in his line. IKEA items had been typically obtained from other sources and sold by Kamprad, making his enterprise solely a retail operation. However in 1953 Kamprad bought a small furniture factory and opened a small furniture and home-furnishing showroom in Älmhult. Then, IKEA began designing its own furniture items in 1955. The first IKEA store opened outside Sweden, near Oslo in Norway, in 1963.

IKEA's home base is in Denmark and it is now one of the world's top retailers of furniture, home furnishings and house wares. The company designs its own items, and sells them in the more than 140 IKEA stores that are spread throughout approximately 30 different countries worldwide. IKEA is characterized by its efforts to offer high-quality items at low prices. A critical point in IKEA's history was when Kamprad opened a store just outside Stockholm. This new IKEA revolutionized furniture manufacturing and selling. To make this possible, the furniture was specially designed by IKEA staff. Almost all of the components of each piece of furniture could be put together by the customers themselves, but in some cases IKEA staff could help the customer assemble the furniture at home. Another innovative marketing tool employed was a self-service method of selling, which was largely unknown in the furniture and home furnishing retail trades

at the time. The IKEA concept was an immediate success, particularly for kitchenware and children's furniture. Additional stores were opened in Sweden in 1966 and 1967, and in 1969 a store was opened in Denmark. Soon the first stores outside the Scandinavian territory – in Switzerland in 1973, and in Germany in 1974 – were opened. The stores employed a total of 1500 people, and sales in 1974 were SKr 616 million. However, Sweden remained the company's main market, with 75 per cent of total sales.

Next came expansion into new markets worldwide. After the first major expansion in Germany, ten more were opened by 1980, more than were in operation in Sweden, and by 1990 there were 17 stores in Western Germany. Elsewhere in Europe, stores were opened in Austria in 1977 and in the Netherlands in 1979. The company was expanding outside of Europe, as well. In 1975 the first IKEA in Australia was opened; in 1976 a store opened in Canada; and in 1978 a store was placed in Singapore followed by more stores in the Far East and the Middle East.

To counter any problematic situations arising from the fact that IKEA's operations were situated all around the world, management organized the company as a whole into four different main areas with interlocking functions. The first area – *Product Range and Development* – was primarily carried out by IKEA of Sweden. Thus, product development tasks were completed in a more centralized fashion, and then filtered down to all other areas of IKEA's operations. Second, *Purchasing* of materials for production and other small retail items was conducted by agents responsible for placing orders to the specifications laid down by IKEA of Sweden and the product development teams. Third, the *Distribution Service* undertook the transport and distribution of the finished products to 12 regional distribution centres and stores throughout the world. Finally, *Retailing* functions were carried out by those operating under the same retail concept, ensuring that selling methods and customer service were of the same standards in all IKEA stores.

In addition to its strong corporate organization of operations, another factor in IKEA's success was its effective sales promotion campaigns around the world. Targeted customers were mainly 20–35 year-olds, and the high quality of modern Swedish design was emphasized. IKEA continued to open stores in new locations throughout the world and by 1998 IKEA had also opened a store in mainland China. In 1997, IKEA in keeping with times joined thousands of other companies online when it introduced its site on the World Wide Web, aptly named the 'World Wide Living Room Web Site'.

On how IKEA functions Kerry Capell, of *Business Week*, says, 'To understand what makes the IKEA Group tick, you need to understand the values and vision of its 79-year-old founder, Ingvar Kamprad. IKEA's complicated corporate structure allows Kamprad to maintain tight control over the operations of Ingka Holding, and thus the operation of most IKEA stores.' She further acknowledges that, 'The Ingka Foundation's five-person executive committee is chaired by Kamprad. It appoints the board of Ingka Holding, approves any changes to Ingka Holding's bylaws, and has the right to pre-empt new share issues. If a member of the executive committee quits or dies, the other four members appoint his or her replacement.'

'Kamprad has long been a cultural icon and the chief spreader of the IKEA gospel, and he believes it's best spread from mouth to ear', says Harvard Business School professor Christopher Bartlett. 'When he speaks, whether it's to customers or employees, people are electrified.' Kamprad had once written in a manifesto that 'the true IKEA spirit is still founded on our enthusiasm, on our constant will to renew, on our cost consciousness, on our willingness to assume responsibility and to help, on our humbleness before the task and on the simplicity in our behaviour. We must take care of each other, inspire each other.' Although Kamprad gave up day-to-day management of the company in 1986, he remains involved, appearing at store openings to greet customers or showing up unannounced at sales-training meetings, shaking hands, and making small talk with staff. 'He's an entrepreneur, and he will never fully let go of the business before he dies', says IKEA CEO Anders Dahlvig. 'IKEA is his life.'

Operationally IKEA's organizational 'function' is a specific department that the business must perform in as efficiently as it can to enable the business to make money. Catherine O'Mahoney, of the *Sunday Business Post*, states that: 'There's a kind of Superquinn-ish vibe to IKEA, certainly when it comes to the staff. Everyone is decked out in yellow and blue, and the frequent tannoy announcements refer to employees as "co-workers". For example there are 550 "co-workers" at IKEA in Glasgow, where the policy is to take on staff from a wide age range and give them little family-friendly perks, like a day off when their child has its first day at school.'

In all its branches the world over, IKEA has a flat management structure. Senior staff don't generally wear suits, and managers are expected to stock shelves like everyone else. There are several different sections to these fundamental functions: production, marketing, sales, accounting and finance, and few others. The managing directors of IKEA have a specific job; controlling how to perform these functions. It is vital that these separate functions of IKEA all perform well to enable the business to succeed. Each function of the business interlinks with the mission statement and the businesses objectives. Depending on the business structure you can follow the path of the different functions. Each function has its own co-workers that report back to the managing director of that function. IKEA must find the optimum balance of between production, marketing, sales, human resources, administration, research and development and finance to maintain its accomplishment. IKEA have several smaller internal functions that also are carried out through the whole of IKEA worldwide. These interior functions consist of: Bathrooms, Beds, Checkouts, Children, Cooking, Eating, Kitchen, Lighting, Living Rooms,

Showrooms and Wall Units (shelving). IKEA insist on sticking to this easily followed structure.

Essentially, IKEA's success can be put down to a high level of fundamental control. Preservation worldwide, stability of the IKEA brand name and its image is all-important if it wants to continue its market domination. IKEA has currently performed remarkably well, it has set the standards for its competitors to meet and there are very few that can offer the same quality and assurance. It would take major changes in the business environment to remove IKEA from the top spot.

Questions

1 Discuss the *'vertical differences'* and *'horizontal differences'* of the organizational hierarchy in relation to IKEA's management structure.

2 Evaluate the social and economic forces that may have led to IKEA's organizational culture?

3 In turbulent times how well placed is IKEA to become a Learning Organization? Explain.

SOURCES 'Sweden's Answer to Sam Walton', Kerry Capell, November 14, 2005, online at: http://www.businessweek.com/magazine/content/05_46/b3959011.htm; Funding Universe (2008): http://www.fundinguniverse.com/company-histories/IKEA-International-AS-Company-History.html; 'The IKEA Experience', Catherine O'Mahoney (2005), *Sunday Business Post*, online at: http://archives.tcm.ie/businesspost/2005/01/23/story1663.asp 'Ikea's Innovative Human Resource Management Practices and Work Culture', (2008), online at: http://www.icmrindia.org/casestudies/catalogue/Human%20Resource%20and%20Organization%20Behavior/HROB066.htm

PART 2

THE ENVIRONMENT AND CORPORATE CULTURE OF MANAGEMENT

The cultural environment into which a structure is constructed has enormous impact on the final design. Both in terms of the surrounding public culture, as well as any private culture, religious structures reveal the importance of this invisible environment in different physical forms.

The Parthenon in Athens was the ancient temple of Athena. Although only some of the sculptures survived, it is believed the Parthenon was full of images related to Greek ideas, mythology, and gods. Churches and mosques likewise exhibit fundamental elements of theology. Notre Dame Cathedral in Paris, France, uses images of the Virgin Mary and Christian symbols and saints, and the nave is shaped like a cross. The Koutoubia mosque in Marrakech, Morocco, although built at roughly the same time as Notre Dame, features an open courtyard for prayer, a repeating pattern to symbolize the infinity of God, and no human images.

Overall environmental factors are considered when creating and operating a business. Managers must consider both internal and external environments, which are often intertwined. These elements dictate how the manager will bring firmness, commodity, and delight into harmony. The creative environment is tied to the creative culture. A creative company, Pixar values imagination and expression. As such, paper airplane contests and toy collecting at work are not only acceptable but encouraged because they reinforce the company's culture. A company's culture dictates what is acceptable and what is not acceptable, as different theologies dictate the shape, images, and space in any house of worship.

CHAPTER OUTLINE

© BUZ BUZZER/ISTOCK

LEARNING OBJECTIVES

After reading this chapter, you should be able to:

1   Describe the general and task environments and the
dimensions of each.

2   Explain the strategies managers use to help organizations
adapt to an uncertain or turbulent environment.

3   Define corporate culture and give organizational examples.

4   Explain organizational symbols, stories, heroes, slogans and
ceremonies, and their relationship to corporate culture.

5   Describe how corporate culture relates to the environment.

6   Define a cultural leader and explain the tools a cultural leader
uses to create a high-performance culture.

CHAPTER 3

THE ENVIRONMENT AND CORPORATE CULTURE

Manager's Challenge

Many people think of Microsoft and software as being almost synonymous, the same way folks once thought of Xerox and photocopying. But Xerox learned the hard way that a dominant position is not guaranteed. To avoid the same fate at Microsoft, managers recently warned founder and chairman Bill Gates that his company's PC software business is in danger of becoming 'increasingly defunct'. It could be a warning that came too late. For years, Microsoft exerted significant control over what appears on the PC desktop and what software programs the majority of customers use, but that control is about to change. Most people, especially home users, set up a new PC by clicking through a series of introductory screens and selecting the software and services they want. Microsoft historically controlled this 'first-boot' sequence and the software that comes preinstalled on the computer. Now, though, PC makers are taking back control, selling desktop space to competing software and service providers and giving end users broader choices of software during setup. Google, for example, was negotiating in early 2006 to have its software preinstalled on millions of Dell PCs. Hewlett-Packard is already giving users the option to sign up for a variety of programs and services from companies other than Microsoft, for instance since April 2009 HP brought to the market first-ever standard business laptop with Linux software pre-installed on it. Because Microsoft has long garnered its largest source of revenue and profit from PC software, it's a shift that could spell big trouble.[1]

If you were a manager at Microsoft, how might you have been more prepared for this shift in the way PC makers do business with software companies? What steps would you take to help Microsoft maintain its status in the software industry as it faces new threats from competitors in the environment?

TAKE A MOMENT

Are You Fit for Managerial Uncertainty?²

Do you approach uncertainty with an open mind? Think back to how you thought or behaved during a time of uncertainty when you were in a formal or informal leadership position. Answer whether each of the following items was Mostly True or Mostly False in that circumstance.

		Mostly True	Mostly False
1	Enjoyed hearing about new ideas even when working toward a deadline.	☐	☐
2	Welcomed unusual viewpoints of others even if we were working under pressure.	☐	☐
3	Made it a point to attend industry trade shows and company events.	☐	☐
4	Specifically encouraged others to express opposing ideas and arguments.	☐	☐
5	Asked 'dumb' questions.	☐	☐
6	Always offered comments on the meaning of data or issues.	☐	☐
7	Expressed a controversial opinion to bosses and peers.	☐	☐
8	Suggested ways of improving my and others' ways of doing things.	☐	☐

SCORING AND INTERPRETATION Give yourself one point for each item you marked as Mostly True. If you scored less than 5 you might want to start your career as a manager in a stable rather than unstable environment. A score of 5 or above suggests a higher level of mindfulness and a better fit for a new manager in an organization with an uncertain environment.

In an organization in a highly uncertain environment everything seems to be changing. In that case, an important quality for a new manager is 'mindfulness', which includes the qualities of being open-minded and an independent thinker. In a stable environment, a manager with a closed mind may perform okay because much work can be done in the same old way. In an uncertain environment, even a new manager needs to facilitate new thinking, new ideas and new ways of working. A high score on the preceding items suggests higher mindfulness and a better fit with an uncertain environment.

In high-tech industries, environmental conditions are volatile. Microsoft is currently in a situation similar to the one Xerox faced in the early 1990s. Xerox was dominant in its industry for many years, but managers missed cues from the environment and got blindsided by rivals Canon and Ricoh when they began selling comparable copy machines at lower prices. Moreover, Xerox failed to keep pace with changing methods of document management, failed to satisfy customer requirements and had no new products to fill the gaps in the declining copy business. Consequently, the company struggled for more than decade to find its footing in a vastly changed world. Current CEO Anne Mulcahy has used her management skills to mastermind a hot turnaround at Xerox and get the company moving forward again.³ Similar to Xerox, Microsoft has held a dominant position for nearly 30 years, but the environment is shifting dramatically and Microsoft will have to change significantly to remain competitive.

Another example from the UK is Marks & Spencer, which started out more than 100 years ago. With its products designed to appeal to the broad mass of the population, it became Britain's largest and most popular clothing chain. But in the late 1990s, its phenomenal growth came to a halt and profits slumped. Every year, it began new initiatives aimed at different segments of the market that failed to catch on. This was not just a failure of design or pricing. Rather, Britain's ever-increasing demographic changes and social polarization had a logic of its own, and people' shopping habits reflected this with the ever-greater market segmentation. It was no longer so easy to cater to all social layers.

In the toy industry, Mattel was shaken when it learned that a Chinese subcontractor used lead paint while manufacturing its toys. Because of the potential health hazard, Mattel recalled nearly 850 000 of its most popular toys – months before its holiday selling season. Not only did the recall frighten consumers, but it sparked a global debate about the safety of Chinese-made products. Mattel managers moved swiftly to reassure nervous parents of its high safety standards in its Chinese factories. In addition, CEO Robert Eckert explained the recall to consumers on the company's website and announced steps Mattel was taking to prevent further recalls.[4]

Mattel's prompt response, teamed with its long-standing history of successful manufacturing in China, led many independent analysts and watchdog groups to say that it may be the best role model for how to operate prudently in China. 'Mattel realized very early that they were always going to be in the crosshairs of sensitivities about child labour and product safety, and they knew they had to play it straight. Mattel was in China before China was cool, and they learned to do business there in a good way', says M. Eric Johnson, a Dartmouth management professor.[5]

Environmental surprises, like the one Mattel faced in China, leave some managers unable to adapt their companies to new competition, shifting consumer interests or new technologies. The study of management traditionally focused on factors within the organization – a closed-systems view – such as leading, motivating and controlling employees. The classical, behavioural and management science schools described in Chapter 2 looked at internal aspects of organizations over which managers have direct control. These views are accurate but incomplete. To be effective, managers must monitor and respond to the environment – an open-systems view. The events that have the greatest impact on an organization typically originate in the external environment. In addition, globalization and worldwide societal turbulence affect companies in new ways, making the international environment of growing concern to managers everywhere.

The environment surprises many managers and leaves them unable to adapt their companies to new competition, shifting consumer interests or new technologies. The study of management traditionally focused on factors within the organization – a closed systems view – such as leading, motivating and controlling employees. The classical, behavioural and management science schools described in Chapter 2 looked at internal aspects of organizations over which managers have direct control. These views are accurate but incomplete. To be effective, managers must monitor and respond to the environment – an open systems view. The events that have the greatest impact on an organization typically originate in the external environment. In addition, globalization and worldwide societal turbulence affect companies in new ways, making the international environment of growing concern to managers everywhere.

This chapter explores in detail components of the external environment and how they affect the organization. We also examine a major part of the organization's internal environment – corporate culture. Corporate culture is shaped by the external environment and is an important part of the context within which managers do their jobs.

The External Environment

Organizational environment
All elements existing outside the organization's boundaries that have the potential to affect the organization.

General environment
The layer of the external environment that affects the organization indirectly.

Task environment
The layer of the external environment that directly influences the organization's operations and performance.

Internal environment
The environment that includes the elements within the organization's boundaries.

The tremendous and far-reaching changes occurring in today's world can be understood by defining and examining components of the external environment. The external organizational environment includes all elements existing outside the boundary of the organization that have the potential to affect the organization.[6] The environment includes competitors, resources, technology and economic conditions that influence the organization. It does not include those events so far removed from the organization that their impact is not perceived.

The organization's external environment can be further conceptualized as having two layers: general and task environments, as illustrated in Exhibit 3.1.[7] The general environment is the outer layer that is widely dispersed and affects organizations indirectly. It includes social, demographic and economic factors that influence all organizations about equally. Increases in the inflation rate or the percentage of dual-career couples in the workforce are part of the organization's general environment. These events do not directly change day-to-day operations, but they do affect all organizations eventually. The task environment is closer to the organization and includes the sectors that conduct day-to-day transactions with the organization and directly influence its basic operations and performance. It is generally considered to include competitors, suppliers and customers.

The organization also has an internal environment, which includes the elements within the organization's boundaries. The internal environment is composed of current employees, management, and especially corporate culture, which defines employee

Exhibit 3.1 Location of the Organization's General, Task and Internal Environments

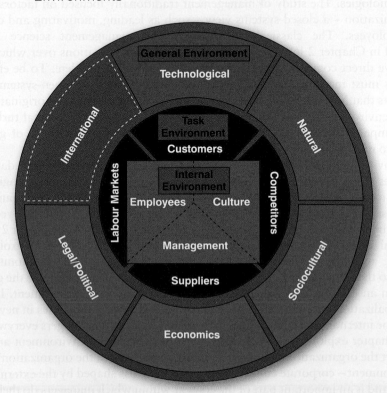

behaviour in the internal environment and how well the organization will adapt to the external environment.

Exhibit 3.1 illustrates the relationship among the general, task, and internal environments. As an open system, the organization draws resources from the external environment and releases goods and services back to it. We will now discuss the two layers of the external environment in more detail. Then we will discuss corporate culture, the key element in the internal environment. Other aspects of the internal environment, such as structure and technology, will be covered in Parts 4 and 5 of this book.

General Environment

The general environment represents the outer layer of the environment. These dimensions influence the organization over time but often are not involved in day-to-day transactions with it. The dimensions of the general environment include international, technological, sociocultural, economic, legal-political and natural.

International

The **international dimension** of the external environment represents events originating in foreign countries as well as opportunities for companies in other countries. Note in Exhibit 3.1 that the international dimension represents a context that influences all other aspects of the external environment. The international environment provides new competitors, customers and suppliers, and shapes social, technological and economic trends, as well.

International dimension
Portion of the external environment that represents events originating in foreign countries as well as opportunities for US companies in other countries.

Today, every company has to compete on a global basis. High-quality, low-priced automobiles from India and Korea have permanently changed the world automobile industry. For instance, the launch of Tata Nano – the 'people's car' – at a price of 100 000 rupees (£1300) is the cheapest in the world and comparable with the price of the DVD player in a Lexus. In mobile phones and PDAs, companies face stiff competition from Korea's Samsung, Finland's Nokia and Taiwan's High Tech Computer Corporation (HTC). For many companies originating in the US, such as Starbucks and Wal-Mart, domestic markets have become saturated and the only potential for growth lies overseas. E-commerce organizations, too, are making international expansion a priority. The US share of worldwide e-commerce is falling as foreign companies set up their own e-commerce ventures.

The most dramatic change in the international environment in recent years is the shift of economic power to China and India. Together, these countries have the population, brainpower and dynamism to transform the twenty-first century global economy. If things continue on the current track, analysts predict that India will overtake Germany as the world's third-largest economy within three decades, and that China will overtake the US as number one by mid-century. In China, per capita income has tripled in a generation, and leaders are building the infrastructure for decades of expansion, as reflected in the country's hunger for raw materials. In 2005, China represented roughly 47 per cent of the global cement consumption, 30 per cent of coal and 26 per cent of crude steel, and hence China is playing a critical role in consumption trends. It was recorded that in 2007 about 20 per cent of cement consumption growth occurred outside of China and the industrialized world, mostly in other Asian nations, the Middle East, Eastern Europe and South America. 'While the major developed economies like the US and Western Europe have generally performed well', PCA Chief Economist Ed Sullivan said, 'world economic growth has been characterized by buoyant growth outside these industrial countries'. No one can predict the future, but it is clear that however things in India and China shake out, European, American and other firms have no choice but to pay attention.

Cloning technology and stem cell research are raising both scientific and ethical concerns. Nanotechnology, which refers to manipulating matter at its tiniest scale, is moving from the research lab to the marketplace. Although only a few products incorporated nanoparticles in 2005, within a few years, nanotechnology could affect every industry. General Electric is researching how nanoceramics can make turbines more efficient. Medical researchers are looking at the potential for portable labs that offer instant analysis for everything from diabetes to HIV. Nanoparticles could someday give us golf balls designed to fly straight, army fatigues that resist chemical weapons, dent-free automobiles and super-charged fuel cells that could replace fossil-fuel engines. Some 1200 nanotechnology start-ups have emerged around the world, and smart managers at established organizations such as 3M, Dow Chemical, Samsung, NASA, Intel, Johnson & Johnson and IBM are investing research dollars in this technological breakthrough.[12]

Sociocultural

Sociocultural dimension
The dimension of the general environment representing the demographic characteristics, norms, customs, and values of the population within which the organization operates.

The **sociocultural dimension** of the general environment represents the demographic characteristics as well as the norms, customs and values of the general population. Important sociocultural characteristics are geographical distribution and population density, age and education levels. Today's demographic profiles are the foundation of tomorrow's workforce and consumers. Forecasters see increased globalization of both consumer markets and the labour supply, with increasing diversity both within organizations and consumer markets.[13] Consider the following key demographic trends in different countries:

1 The US is experiencing the largest influx of immigrants in more than a century. By 2050, non-Hispanic whites will make up only about half of the population, down from 74 per cent in 1995 and 69 per cent in 2004. Hispanics are expected to make up about a quarter of the US population.[14]

2 People are staying in the workforce longer, and many members of the huge post-World War II baby-boom generation are choosing to work well past traditional retirement age. At the same time, the 76 million or so members of Generation Y, which rivals the baby boom in size, are beginning to flood the job market. For the first time, a significant number of organizations are dealing with four generations working side-by-side.[15]

3 The fastest-growing type of living arrangement is single-father households, which rose 62 per cent in ten years, even though two-parent and single-mother households are still much more numerous.[16]

4 In an unprecedented demographic shift, married couple households have slipped from 80 per cent in the 1950s to just over 50 per cent in 2003. Couples with children total just 25 per cent, with the number projected to drop to 20 per cent by 2010. By that year, it is expected that 30 per cent of homes will be inhabited by someone who lives alone.[17]

Demographic trends affect organizations in other countries just as powerfully. Japan, Italy, and Germany are all faced with an ageing workforce and customer base due to years of declining birth rates. In both Italy and Japan, the proportion of people over the age of 65 reached 20 per cent in 2006.[18] The first effects of an ageing population in Europe are already being felt in the field of social protection, particularly on retirement pensions but also on health. This will place great strain on the future funding of social protection which is largely dependent upon the contributions of the working population. The regions which will still have a relatively younger population will be more limited in number and include Southern Spain and Northern Portugal, Ireland and northern France.

The companies utilize advances in the *technological dimension* of their environment to understand the complexities of today's ever-changing energy market.

'The highly fluctuating power input is expected to increase in the future, if only because of the planned massive expansion of wind energy. Therefore it is important to address this challenge and develop concepts for efficient storage in due time', explains Dr Johannes Lambertz, CEO of RWE Power AG, Fossil-Fired Power Plants portfolio.

'We believe that thanks to GE's vast experience in compressor technology, we have the capability to study and propose unique solutions as an alternative to the current state of art', said Claudi Santiago, president and CEO of GE's Oil & Gas, which will study the compressor technology required.

> **Economic dimension**
> The dimension of the general environment representing the overall economic health of the country or region in which the organization operates.

Economic

The **economic dimension** represents the general economic health of the country or region in which the organization operates. Consumer purchasing power, the unemployment rate and interest rates are part of an organization's economic environment. Because organizations today are operating in a global environment, the economic dimension has become exceedingly complex and creates enormous uncertainty for managers. The economies of countries are more closely tied together now. For example, the early 2000s economic recession and the decline of consumer confidence in the US affected economies and organizations around the world. Similarly, economic problems in Asia and Europe had a tremendous impact on companies and the stock market in the US.

One significant recent trend in the economic environment is the frequency of mergers and acquisitions. Citibank and Travelers merged to form Citigroup, IBM purchased Pricewaterhouse Coopers Consulting, and Cingular acquired AT&T Wireless. Similarly Arcelor (France) and Mittal Steel (India) merged to become the biggest producer and distributor of steel products in the world. Wal-Mart's acquisition of Asda supermarket chain gave the company access to the UK market. In the toy industry, the three largest toy makers – Hasbro, Mattel and Tyco – gobbled up at least a dozen smaller competitors within a few years. At the same time, however, a tremendous vitality is evident in the small business sector of the economy. Entrepreneurial start-ups are a significant aspect of today's world economy and will be discussed in Chapter 6.

Legal–Political

The **legal-political dimension** includes government regulations at the local, regional, and national levels, as well as political activities designed to influence company behaviour. The Anglo-American political system encourages capitalism, and the government tries not to overregulate business. However, government laws do specify rules of the game. The government

© PETER DENCH/ALAMY

CONCEPT CONNECTION The sociocultural dimension also includes societal norms and values. The low-carb craze replaced the low-fat craze, spurring restaurants to alter their menus and supermarkets to revise their product mix.[19] Use of celebrity chefs like Jamie Oliver advertising Sainsburys through 'Jamie's School Dinners' series tackled the shameful state of school dinners. Children were eating piles of processed junk and recoiled at the sight of fresh vegetables. And the terrible diet was leading to a health time-bomb, with soaring rates of obesity and hugely increased risks of heart disease and other life-threatening conditions for Britain's children. And after a huge campaign, newspaper headlines and a 300 000-signature petition, Tony Blair agreed to set new standards for school meals, and committed £280 million for proper ingredients, equipment and training. With the healthy eating culture emerging in the UK, even the fast food chains like McDonald's and KFC through their 'Eat Smart' campaigns are offering healthier salads and sandwich options for the new and young generation of health cautious customers.

Customers today have greater power because of the internet, which presents threats as well as opportunities for managers. Today's customers can directly affect the organization's reputation and sales, for example, through gripe sites such as *walmartsucks.com*, where customers and sales associates cyber-vent about the worlds largest retailer, and *untied.com*, where United Airlines employees and disgruntled fliers grumble against the air carrier. 'In this new information environment', says Kyle Shannon, CEO of e-commerce consultancy Agency.com, 'you've got to assume everyone knows everything'.[29]

Competitors

Competitors
Other organizations in the same industry or type of business that provide goods or services to the same set of customers.

Other organizations in the same industry or type of business that provide goods or services to the same set of customers are referred to as **competitors**. Each industry is characterized by specific competitive issues. The recording industry differs from the steel industry and the pharmaceutical industry.

Competitive wars are being waged worldwide in all industries. Coke and Pepsi continue to battle it out for the soft-drink market. UPS and FedEx fight the overnight delivery wars. Homebase and B&Q brawl in the UK retail home improvement market, trying to out-do one another in terms of price, service and selection.[30] In the travel and tourism industry, internet companies such as Lastminute.com, Expedia. com and Hotels.com have hurt the big hotel chains. These chains are fighting back by undercutting the brokers' prices on the hotels' own websites.

Suppliers

Suppliers
People and organizations who provide the raw materials the organization uses to produce its output.

The raw materials the organization uses to produce its output are provided by **suppliers**. A steel mill requires iron ore, machines and financial resources. A small, private university may utilize hundreds of suppliers for paper, pencils, cafeteria food, computers, trucks, fuel, electricity and textbooks. Companies from toolmakers to construction firms and auto manufacturers were hurt recently by an unanticipated jump in the price of steel from suppliers. Just as they were starting to see an upturn in their business, the cost of raw materials jumped 30 per cent in a two-month period.[31] Consider also that China now produces more than 85 per cent of the Vitamin C used by companies in the US. An agreement among China's four largest producers led to an increase in the price of vitamin C from $3 a kilogram to as high as $9 a kilogram.[32]

Many companies are using fewer suppliers and trying to build good relationships with them so that they will receive high-quality parts and materials at lower prices. The relationship between manufacturers and suppliers has traditionally been an adversarial one, but managers are finding that cooperation is the key to saving money, maintaining quality and speeding products to market.

TAKE A MOMENT   As a new manager, you can get ahead by paying attention to the external environment and international events. Stay in tune with what's going on in the general environment, including social, economic, technological and political trends. Pay particular attention to the task environment, including your customers, competitors and suppliers. Be sure to connect the dots among the things you see.

Labour Market

The **labour market** represents people in the environment who can be hired to work for the organization. Every organization needs a supply of trained, qualified personnel. Unions, employee associations and the availability of certain classes of employees can influence the organization's labour market. Labour market forces affecting organizations right now include:

Labour market
The people available for hire by the organization.

1 the growing need for computer-literate knowledge workers

2 the necessity for continuous investment in human resources through recruitment, education, and training to meet the competitive demands of the borderless world

3 the effects of international trading blocs, automation, outsourcing and shifting facility location upon labour dislocations, creating unused labour pools in some areas and labour shortages in others

---

 INNOVATIVE WAY

Nortel Networks

The external environment for Nortel Networks is illustrated in Exhibit 3.2. The Canadian-based company began in 1895 as a manufacturer of telephones and has reinvented itself many times to keep up with changes in the environment. In the late 1990s, the company transformed itself into a major player in wireless technology and equipment for connecting businesses and individuals to the internet. In 1997, the company was about to be run over by rivals such as Cisco Systems that were focused on internet gear. Then-CEO John Roth knew he needed to do something bold to respond to changes in the technological environment. A name change to Nortel Networks symbolized and reinforced the company's new goal of providing unified network solutions to customers worldwide.

One response to the competitive environment was to spend billions to acquire data and voice networking companies, including Bay Networks (which makes internet and data equipment), Cambrian Systems (a hot maker of optical technology), Periphonics (maker of voice-response systems), and Clarify (customer relationship management software). These companies brought Nortel top-notch technology, helping the company snatch customers away from rivals Cisco and Lucent Technologies. In addition, even during rough economic times, Nortel kept spending nearly 20 per cent of its revenues on research and development to keep pace with changing technology.

Internationally, Nortel made impressive inroads in Taiwan, China, Brazil, Mexico, Colombia, Japan and Sweden, among other countries. It also won customers by recognizing the continuing need for traditional equipment and offering hybrid gear that combines old telephone technology with new internet features, allowing companies to transition from the old to the new. Bold new technologies for Nortel include optical systems that move voice and data at the speed of light and third-generation wireless networks (3G), which zap data and video from phone to phone. Nortel is considered a leader in wireless gear and won contracts from Verizon Communications and Orange SA, a unit of France Telecom, to supply equipment that sends phone calls as packets of digital data like that used over the internet.

Companies moving in a Net speed environment risk a hard landing, and when the demand for internet equipment slumped in the early 2000s, Nortel's business was devastated. The company cut more than two-thirds of its workforce and closed dozens of plants and offices. An accounting scandal that led to fraud investigations and senior executive dismissals made things even worse. At one point, Nortel's stock was trading for less than a dollar. By early 2006, though, positive changes in the economic environment, along with a savvy new CEO, put Nortel back on an uphill swing. Analysts predicted that the company would outdo major competitor Lucent in sales growth and other financial metrics. However, as one analyst said, 'It's a tough business', and Nortel's managers have to stay on their toes to help the organization cope in an ever-changing, difficult environment.[33]

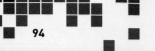

Changes in these various sectors of the general and task environments can create tremendous challenges, especially for organizations operating in complex, rapidly changing industries. Nortel Networks, a Canadian company with multiple US offices, is an example of an organization operating in a highly complex environment.

The Organization–Environment Relationship

Why do organizations care so much about factors in the external environment? The reason is that the environment creates uncertainty for organization managers, and they must respond by designing the organization to adapt to the environment.

Environmental Uncertainty

Organizations must manage environmental uncertainty to be effective. *Uncertainty* means that managers do not have sufficient information about environmental factors to understand and predict environmental needs and changes.[34] As indicated in Exhibit 3.3, environmental characteristics that influence uncertainty are the number of factors that affect the organization and the extent to which those factors change. A large multinational like Nortel Networks has thousands of factors in the external environment creating uncertainty for managers. When external factors change rapidly, the organization experiences high uncertainty; examples are telecommunications and aerospace firms, computer and electronics companies, and e-commerce organizations that sell products and services over the internet. Companies have to make an effort to adapt to the rapid changes in the environment. When an organization deals with only a few external factors and these factors are relatively stable, such as for soft-drink bottlers or food processors, managers experience low uncertainty and can devote less attention to external issues.

TAKE A MOMENT   Are you ready to become a manager in an organization that operates in a highly uncertain environment? Take the New Manager Self-Test on page 107. Learn whether your new-manager's mind seems ready for environmental uncertainty.

Adapting to the Environment

If an organization faces increased uncertainty with respect to competition, customers, suppliers or government regulations managers can use several strategies to adapt to these changes, including boundary-spanning roles, interorganizational partnerships and mergers or joint ventures.

Boundary-Spanning Roles

Boundary-spanning roles
Roles assumed by people and/or departments that link and coordinate the organization with key elements in the external environment.

Departments and boundary-spanning roles link and coordinate the organization with key elements in the external environment. Boundary spanners serve two purposes for the organization: they detect and process information about changes in the

Exhibit 3.2 The External Environment of Nortel

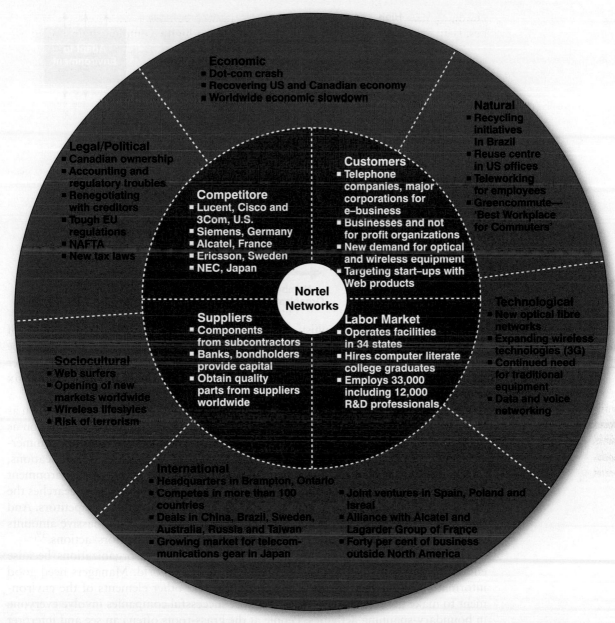

SOURCES: W. C. Symonds, J. B. Levine, N. Gross, and P. Coy, 'High-Tech Star: Northern Telecom Is Challenging Even AT&T', *BusinessWeek* (July 27, 1992): 54–58; I. Austen, 'Hooked on the Net', *Canadian Business* (June 26–July 10, 1998): 95–103; J. Weber with A. Reinhardt and P. Burrows, 'Racing Ahead at Nortel', *BusinessWeek* (November 8, 1999): 93–99; 'Nortel's Waffling Continues: First Job Cuts, Then Product Lines, and Now the CEO', *Telephony* (May 21, 2001): 12; and M. Heinzl, 'Nortel's Profits of 499 Million Exceeds Forecast', *The Wall Street Journal* (January 30, 2004): B4.

environment, and they represent the organization's interests to the environment.[35] Employees in engineering or research and development scan for new technological developments, innovations and raw materials. People in departments such as marketing and purchasing span the boundary to work with customers and suppliers, both face-to-face and through market research. Some organizations are staying in touch with customers through the internet, such as by monitoring gripe sites, communicating with customers on company websites, and contracting with market-research firms that use the Web to monitor rapidly changing marketplace trends.[36] Another recent approach to boundary spanning is the use of *business intelligence*,

Exhibit 3.3 The External Environment and Uncertainty

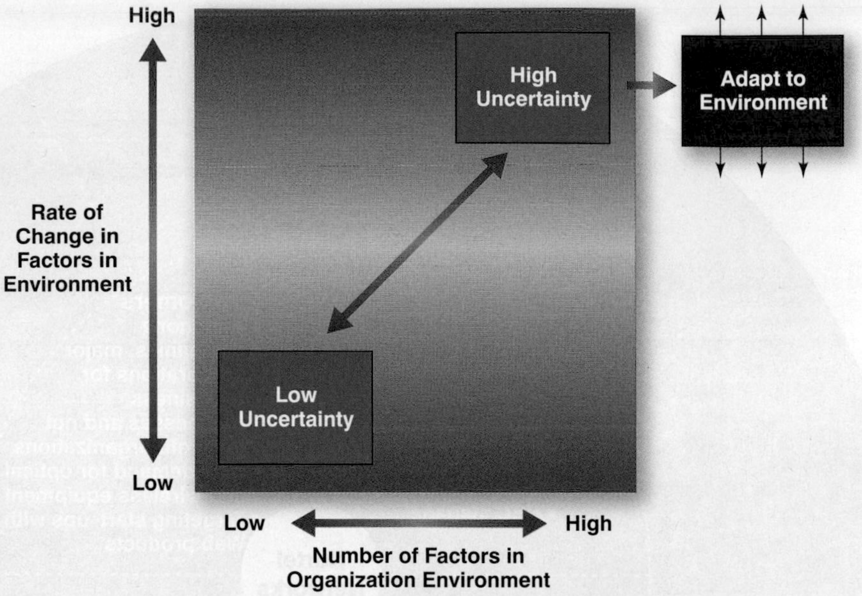

which results from using sophisticated software to search through large amounts of internal and external data to spot patterns, trends and relationships that might be significant. For example, Verizon, the largest American wireless network provider uses business intelligence software to actively monitor customer interactions and fix problems almost immediately.[37]

Business intelligence is related to the growing area of boundary spanning known as *competitive intelligence (CI),* which refers to activities to get as much information as possible about one's rivals. Competitive intelligence specialists use websites, commercial databases, financial reports, market activity, news clippings, trade publications, personal contacts and numerous other sources to scan an organization's environment and spot potential threats or opportunities.[38] Visa has an employee who searches the Web for two hours each day for insights on MasterCard and other competitors. And Harley-Davidson hires an outside research firm to search through massive amounts of data and reveal patterns that help decipher and predict competitors' actions.[39]

Boundary spanning is an increasingly important task in organizations because environmental shifts can happen so quickly in today's world. Managers need good information about their competitors, customers and other elements of the environment to make good decisions. Thus, the most successful companies involve everyone in boundary-spanning activities. People at the grass-roots often can see and interpret significant changes sooner than managers who are more removed from the day-to-day work.[40] However, top executives, too, need to stay in tune with the environment. Tom Stemberg, CEO of Staples, visits a competitor's store once a week and shares what he learns with others on the management team.[41] Perceiving environmental shifts that could impact the organization isn't always easy. Managers must learn to not only interpret the data right in front of them but also to see weak signals on the periphery and answer the question, 'What don't we know that might matter?'[42]

TAKE A MOMENT Read the Ethical Dilemma on page 114 that pertains to competitive intelligence. Do you have the courage to risk your job over the inappropriate use of confidential information?

Interorganizational Partnerships

An increasingly popular strategy for adapting to the environment is to reduce boundaries and increase collaboration with other organizations. North American companies have typically worked alone, competing with one another, but an uncertain and interconnected global environment changed that tendency. Companies are joining together to become more effective and to share scarce resources. Sony, Toshiba and IBM are collaborating to produce a new, tiny computer chip. Supermarket chains Kroger, Albertsons and Safeway banded together to negotiate with labour unions. General Motors teamed up with German automakers DaimlerChrysler AG and BMW AG to develop a hybrid fuel system to compete with Toyota Prius.[43] Head-to-head competition among independent firms is giving way to networks of alliances that compete for business on a global basis. For example, the aerospace industry is controlled by two networks – those of Boeing and Airbus, each of which is made up of more than 100 partner organizations.[44]

Managers shift from an adversarial orientation to a partnership orientation, as summarized in Exhibit 3.4. The new paradigm is based on trust and the ability of partners to work out equitable solutions to conflicts so that everyone profits from the relationship. Managers work to reduce costs and add value to both sides, rather than trying to get all the benefits for their own company. The new model is also characterized by a high level of information sharing, including e-business linkages for automatic ordering, payments, and other transactions. In addition, person-to-person interaction provides corrective feedback and solves problems. People from other companies may be onsite or participate in virtual teams to enable close coordination. Partners are frequently involved in one another's product design and production, and they are committed for the long term. It is not unusual for business partners to help one another, even outside of what is specified in the contract.[45]

Mergers and Joint Ventures

A step beyond strategic partnerships is for companies to become involved in mergers or joint ventures to reduce environmental uncertainty. A frenzy of merger and acquisition activity internationally in recent years is an attempt by organizations to cope

Merger
The combining of two or more organizations into one.

Exhibit 3.4 The Shift to a Partnership Paradigm

From Adversarial Orientation $\longrightarrow$	To Partnership Orientation
• Suspicion, competition, arm's length	• Trust, value added to both sides
• Price, efficiency, own profits	• Equity, fair dealing, everyone profits
• Information and feedback limited	• E-business links to share information and conduct digital transactions
• Lawsuits to resolve conflict	• Close coordination; virtual teams and people onsite
• Minimal involvement and up-front investment	• Involvement in partner's product design and production
• Short-term contracts	• Long-term contracts
• Contracts limit the relationship	• Business assistance goes beyond the contract

CONCEPT CONNECTION Equality stands at the heart of Japanese automaker Honda's corporate culture, and visible manifestations of the cultural values are everywhere. For example, at facilities such as this automobile manufacturing plant in most of the locations internationally, there are open offices, no assigned parking spaces, and the 4500 employees, called *associates,* all eat in the same cafeteria and call each other by their first names. Everyone, from the president on down, comes to work, walks into the locker room and changes into a gleaming white two-piece uniform inscribed with the Honda insignia. It's no accident that it's hard to tell the managers from the front-line workers.

Story
A narrative based on true events and repeated frequently and shared among organizational employees.

Hero
A figure who exemplifies the deeds, character and attributes of a strong corporate culture.

For example, managers at a New York-based start-up that provides internet solutions to local television broadcasters wanted a way to symbolize the company's unofficial mantra of 'drilling down to solve problems'. They bought a dented old drill for $2 and dubbed it 'The Team Drill'. Each month, the drill is presented to a different employee in recognition of exceptional work, and the employee personalizes the drill in some way before passing it on to the next winner.[54]

Symbols often include logos, buildings, office layout, cars and job titles, but may also include specific terminology and language used within the company. At Motorola in the 1980s, Chairman Bob Galvin changed the order of topics at monthly executive meetings. The first two hours of every meeting were spent reviewing quality improvement results. Financial results were last on the agenda. If Bob needed to leave early, he never missed the improvement results, but would skip the financial. This sent an important message regarding first and second priorities.

At IBM, resolving the ten most significant recurring complaints received in a year became part of the following year's business planning process. The goal was to ensure that these problems were eliminated forever. Customer issues received repeated visibility and discussion throughout the year, reinforcing the organization's value of customer service.

Stories

A **story** is a narrative based on true events and is repeated frequently and shared among organizational employees. Stories are told to new employees to keep the organization's primary values alive. One of Nordstrom's primary means of emphasizing the importance of customer service is through corporate storytelling. An example is the story about a sales representative who took back a customer's two-year-old blouse with no questions asked.[55] A frequently told story at UPS concerns an employee who, without authorization, ordered an extra Boeing 737 to ensure timely delivery of a load of Christmas packages that had been left behind in the holiday rush. As the story goes, rather than punishing the worker, UPS rewarded his initiative. By telling this story, UPS workers communicate that the company stands behind its commitment to worker autonomy and customer service.[56]

Heroes

A **hero** is a figure who exemplifies the deeds, character, and attributes of a strong culture. Heroes are role models for employees to follow. Sometimes heroes are real, such as the female security supervisor who once challenged IBM's chairman because he wasn't carrying the appropriate clearance identification to enter a security area.[57] Other times they are symbolic, such as the mythical sales representative at Robinson Jewellers who delivered a wedding ring directly to the church because the ring had been ordered late. The deeds of heroes are out of the ordinary, but not so far out as to be unattainable by other employees. Heroes show how to do the right thing in the organization. Companies with strong cultures take advantage of achievements to define heroes who uphold key values.

 # INNOVATIVE WAY

Toyota

Prior to a major global recall crisis in 2010, Toyota Motor Corporation, an automotive powerhouse, was the most profitable automaker in the world. Known for award-winning reliability and quality, Toyota led the industry in manufacturing and customer service. Toyota is also a leader and innovator in hybrid technology. Toyota offers six Toyota and Lexus hybrid vehicles in the US, where it has sold more than 500 000 hybrids, surpassing the rest of the industry combined.[58]

What made this company so successful prior to the recall crisis? For Toyota, the answer was a strong corporate culture based on 'The Toyota Way'. A popular story of Toyota's founder Kiichiro Toyoda demonstrates his commitment to the culture during the early days of the company's history. Toyoda visited a plant and found a worker scratching his head and muttering about how his grinding machine would not run. Toyoda rolled up his sleeves and thrust his hands into the machine's oil pan. He came up with two handfuls of sludge and threw them to the floor. 'How can you expect to do your job without getting your hands dirty', he exclaimed. This was the origin of one of the key elements of Toyota's culture: *genchi genbutsu*, meaning 'go and see'. To Toyota employees, this means go and seek out facts and information that help you make good decisions – even if it means rolling up your sleeves and getting dirty.[59] The recall crisis, however, has led to questioning of this approach, with some commentators claiming the strong culture stifled concerns at the start of the crisis.

At 3M Corporation, top managers keep alive the heroes who developed projects that were killed by top management. One hero was a vice president who was fired earlier in his career for persisting with a new product even after his boss had told him, 'That's a stupid idea. Stop!' After the worker was fired, he would not leave. He stayed in an unused office, working without a salary on the new product idea. Eventually he was rehired, the idea succeeded, and he was promoted to vice president. The lesson of this hero as a major element in 3M's culture is to persist at what you believe in.[60]

Slogans

A **slogan** is a phrase or sentence that succinctly expresses a key corporate value. Many companies use a slogan or saying to convey special meaning to employees. The Ritz-Carlton adopted the slogan, 'Ladies and gentlemen taking care of ladies and gentlemen' to demonstrate its cultural commitment to take care of both employees and customers. 'We're in the service business, and service comes only from people. Our promise is to take care of them, and provide a happy place for them to work', said General Manager Mark DeCocinis, who manages the Portman Hotel in Shanghai, recipient of the 'Best Employer in Asia' for three consecutive years. Cultural values can also be discerned in written public statements, such as corporate mission statements or other formal statements that express the core values of the organization. The mission statement for Hallmark Cards, for example, emphasizes values of excellence, ethical and moral conduct in all relationships, business innovation and corporate social responsibility.[61]

Slogan
A phrase or sentence that succinctly expresses a key corporate value.

Ceremonies

A **ceremony** is a planned activity at a special event that is conducted for the benefit of an audience. Managers hold ceremonies to provide dramatic examples of company

Ceremony
A planned activity at a special event that is conducted for the benefit of an audience.

Exhibit 3.8 Combining Culture and Performance

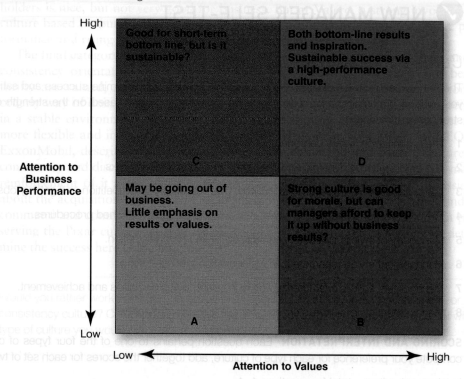

SOURCE: Adapted from Jeff Rosenthal and Mary Ann Masarech, 'High-Performance Cultures: How Values Can Drive Business Results', *Journal of Organizational Excellence* (Spring 2003): 3–18.

how well they toe the values line. The problem is that top executives lost sight of the business performance side of the issue; thus, when Levi jeans began losing market share to new, hip rivals, the company was unable to adapt quickly to the changing environment.[76]

Quadrant C represents organizations that are focused primarily on bottom-line results and pay little attention to organizational values. This approach may be profitable in the short run, but the success is difficult to sustain over the long term because the 'glue' that holds the organization together – that is, shared cultural values – is missing. Think about the numerous get-rich-quick goals of dot-com entrepreneurs. Thousands of companies that sprang up in the late 1990s were aimed primarily at fast growth and quick profits, with little effort to build a solid organization based on long-term mission and values. When the crash came, these companies failed. Those that survived were typically companies with strong cultural values that helped them weather the storm. For example, both eBay and Amazon.com managers paid careful attention to organizational culture, as did smaller e-commerce companies like Canada's Mediagrif Interactive Technologies, an online B2B brokerage that allows businesses to meet online and trade their goods.[77]

Finally, companies in Quadrant D put high emphasis on both culture and solid business performance as drivers of organizational success. Managers in these organizations align values with the company's day-to-day operations – hiring practices, performance management, budgeting, criteria for promotions and rewards, and so forth. A 2004 study of corporate values by Booz Allen Hamilton and the Aspen Institute found that managers in companies that report superior financial results typically put a high emphasis on values and link them directly to the way they run the organization.[78] A good example is the fast-growing Umpqua Bank, which expanded from 11 branches and $140 million in assets in 1994 to 92 branches and $5 billion in assets nine years later. At Umpqua, every element of the culture focuses on serving customers, and every aspect of operations reflects the cultural values. Consider training programmes. To avoid the 'it's not my job' attitude that infects many banks, managers devised the 'universal associate' programme, which trains every bank staffer in every task, so that a teller can take a mortgage application and a loan officer can process your deposit account. Employees are empowered to make their own decisions about how to satisfy customers, and branches have free rein to devise unique ways to coddle the clientele in their particular location. Umpqua also carefully measures and rewards the cultural values it wants to maintain. The bank's executive vice president of cultural enhancement devised a software program that measures how cultural values are connected to performance, which the bank calls 'return on quality' (ROQ). The ROQ scores for each branch and department are posted every month, and they serve as the basis for determining incentives and rewards.[79]

Quadrant D organizations represent the high-performance culture, a culture that:

1 is based on a solid organizational mission or purpose

2 embodies shared adaptive values that guide decisions and business practices

3 encourages individual employee ownership of both bottom-line results and the organization's cultural backbone[80]

In Chapter 2 the Innovative Way box describes the culture at Oticon, where the company's abolition of traditional boundaries has contributed to amazing business success.

One of the most important things managers do is create and influence organizational culture to meet strategic goals, because culture has a significant impact on performance. In *Corporate Culture and Performance*, Kotter and Heskett provided evidence that companies that intentionally managed cultural values outperformed similar companies that did not. Recent research validated that some elements of corporate culture are positively correlated with higher financial performance.[81] A good example is Caterpillar Inc. Caterpillar developed a Cultural Assessment Process (CAP) to measure and manage how effectively the culture contributes to organizational effectiveness. The assessment gave top executives hard data documenting millions of dollars in savings attributed directly to cultural factors.[82]

> **High-performance culture**
> A culture based on a solid organizational mission or purpose that uses shared adaptive values to guide decisions and business practices and to encourage individual employee ownership of both bottom-line results and the organization's cultural backbone.

TAKE A MOMENT

Even as a new manager you can manage for high performance by creating an adaptive culture and tying cultural values to the accomplishment of business results. Act as a cultural leader by communicating the desired values and outcomes and then modelling them in your daily behaviour and decisions.

A cultural leader defines and uses signals and symbols to influence corporate culture. Cultural leaders influence culture in two key areas:

1 *The cultural leader articulates a vision for the organizational culture that employees can believe in.* The leader defines and communicates central values that employees believe in and will rally around. Values are tied to a clear and compelling mission, or core purpose.

> **Cultural leader**
> A manager who uses signals and symbols to influence corporate culture.

A MANAGER'S ESSENTIALS: WHAT HAVE WE LEARNED?

- The organizational environment includes all elements existing outside the organization's boundaries that have the potential to affect the organization. Events in the external environment are considered important influences on organizational behaviour and performance. The external environment consists of two layers: the task environment and the general environment. The task environment includes customers, competitors, suppliers and the labour market. The general environment includes technological, sociocultural, economic, legal-political, international and natural dimensions. Management techniques for helping the organization adapt to the environment include boundary-spanning roles, interorganizational partnerships, and mergers and joint ventures.

- The organization also has an internal environment, which includes the elements within the organization's boundaries. A major internal element for helping organizations adapt to the environment is culture. Corporate culture is an important part of the internal organizational environment and includes the key values, beliefs, understandings and norms that organization members share. Organizational activities that illustrate corporate culture include symbols, stories, heroes, slogans and ceremonies. For the organization to be effective, corporate culture should be aligned with organizational strategy and the needs of the external environment.

- Four types of culture are adaptability, achievement, involvement and consistency. Strong cultures are effective when they enable an organization to meet strategic goals and adapt to changes in the external environment.

- Culture is important because it can have a significant impact on organizational performance. Managers emphasize both values and business results to create a high-performance culture, enabling the organization to achieve solid business performance through the actions of motivated employees who are aligned with the mission and goals of the company.

- Managers create and sustain adaptive high-performance cultures through cultural leadership. They define and articulate important values that are tied to a clear and compelling mission, and they widely communicate and uphold the values through their words and particularly their actions. Work procedures, budgeting, decision-making, reward systems and other day-to-day activities are aligned with the cultural values.

One problem for Microsoft, described in the chapter opening, is that the culture has become out of alignment with its environment. Years of success led to complacency and even resistance to changes in key sectors of the environment. The company's adaptability culture did not stay aggressive. The focus on protecting Microsoft's dominance in PC software caused the company to miss two of the hottest technology advances, internet search and downloading music. Now, its PC software business, which Microsoft still relies on for 80 per cent of its sales and 140 per cent of its profits, is under attack. Microsoft CEO Steven Ballmer is trying various structural alternatives and management changes to beef up boundary spanning and get employees more focused on customers and new trends in the shifting external environment. Microsoft has more than a dozen new products scheduled for release, which Ballmer believes will keep the company on top. However, most of those products are considered catch-up, while younger, more adaptable companies are already moving to the next level of new products. Microsoft is a large and powerful company, but it may have reached a midlife crisis and likely will need a cultural adjustment to stay in tune with changes in key environmental sectors. Managers can use symbols, stories, heroes, slogans and cultural leadership to engage adaptable values that will help Microsoft move fast in response to new opportunities.[90]

DISCUSSION QUESTIONS

1 What can you do now as a student – both inside and outside the classroom – to train yourself to be a more effective manager in an increasingly global business environment?

2 Would the task environment for a mobile phone company contain the same elements as that for a government health care provider? Discuss.

3 What do you think are the most important forces in the external environment creating uncertainty for organizations today? Do the forces you identified typically arise in the task environment or the general environment?

4 Contemporary best-selling management books often argue that customers are the most important element in the external environment. Do you agree? In what company situations might this statement be untrue?

5 Why do you think many managers are surprised by environmental changes and unable to help their organizations adapt? Can a manager ever be prepared for an environmental change as dramatic as that experienced by airlines in the United States following the September 11, 2001 terrorist attacks in New York and Washington?

6 Why are interorganizational partnerships so important for today's companies? What elements in the current environment might contribute to either an increase or a decrease in interorganizational collaboration? Discuss.

7 Consider the chairs you have seen in an office. How does the assistant's chair, the manager's chair and executive's chair differ? What do the differences mean?

8 Why are symbols important to a corporate culture? Do stories, heroes, slogans and ceremonies have symbolic value? Discuss.

9 Both China and India are rising economic powers. How might your approach to doing business with tightly government controlled China be different from your approach to doing business with India, the world's most populous democracy? In which country would you expect to encounter the most rules? The most bureaucracy? Why?

10 The US based General Electric is famous for firing the lowest-performing 10 per cent of its managers each year. With its strict no-layoff policy, Oticon, the Danish hearing-aid manufacturer believes people need to feel secure in their jobs to perform their best. Yet both are high-performing companies. How do you account for the success of such opposite philosophies?

11 Many companies are 'going green' or adopting more environmentally friendly business strategies. What do they hope to gain? Will they be successful?

12 As public sector organizations seek to become more 'business-like' to what extent do they need to gain a better understanding of their 'customers' and external environment? How might this impact on the internal culture of the organization?

MANAGEMENT IN PRACTICE: EXPERIENTIAL EXERCISE

Working in an Adaptive Culture

Think of a specific full-time job you have held. Please answer the following questions according to your perception of the *managers above you* in that job. Circle a number on the 1–5 scale based on the extent to which you agree with each statement about the managers above you:

5 Strongly agree

4 Agree

3 Neither agree nor disagree

2 Disagree

1 Strongly disagree

1 Good ideas got serious consideration from management above me.

1 2 3 4 5

Questions

1 What environmental factors have helped to create the situation Melanie Schmidt faces? What factors does Melanie need to consider when deciding on her course of action?

2 Analyse Westcode's culture. In addition to the expressed cultural values and beliefs, what other subconscious values and beliefs do you detect?

Are conflicting values present? When values are in conflict, how would you decide which ones take precedence?

3 Assume you are Melanie. What are the first two action steps you would take to handle this situation? How would your role as a cultural leader influence your decision? What message will your solution send to the other managers and rank-and-file employees?

ENDNOTES

1. Robert A. Guth and Kevin J. Delaney, 'Default Lines; Pressuring Microsoft, PC Makers Team Up with Software Rivals', *The Wall Street Journal* (February 7, 2006): A1, A25. Reuters (2009) 'HP Launches ProBook with Linux Pre-Installed', Datamation, [online] available from: http://itmanagement.earthweb.com/osrc/article.php/3817591/HP-Launches-ProBook-with-Linux-Pre-Installed.htm (accessed February 18, 2010).

2. The self-test questions are based on ideas from R. L. Daft and R. M. Lengel, *Fusion Leadership* (San Francisco: Berrett Koehler, 2000): Chapter 4; B. Bass and B. Avolio, *Multifactor Leadership Questionnaire,* 2nd ed. (Menlo Park, CA: Mind Garden, Inc., 2004); and Karl E. Weick and Kathleen M. Sutcliffe, *Managing the Unexpected: Assuring High Performance in an Age of Complexity* (San Francisco: Jossey-Bass, 2001).

3. Betsy Morris, 'The Accidental CEO', *Fortune* (June 23, 2003): 58–67; Pamela L. Moore, 'She's Here to Fix the Xerox', *BusinessWeek* (August 6, 2001): 47–48; and Ann Harrington and Petra Bartosiewicz, 'The 50 Most Powerful Women in Business: Who's Up? Who's Down?', *Fortune* (October 18, 2004): 181–188; Ann Carns, 'Point Taken; Hit Hard by Imports, American Pencil Icon Tries to Get a Grip', *The Wall Street Journal* (November 24, 1999): A1, A6.

4. Christopher Palmeri, 'What Went Wrong at Mattel' *BusinessWeek Online*, August 14, 2007, http://www.businessweek.com/bwdaily/dnflash/content/aug2007/db20070814_154726_page_2.htm (accessed February 5, 2008).

5. David Barboza and Louise Story, 'Dancing Elmo Smackdown', *The New York Times Online*, July 26, 2007, http://www.nytimes.com/2007/07/26/business/26toy.html?_r=1&scp=1&sq=dancing+elmo+smackdown&st=nyt&oref=slogin (accessed February 5, 2008).

6. This section is based on Richard L. Daft, *Organization Theory and Design*, 8th ed. (Cincinnati, OH: South-Western, 2004): 136–140.

7. L. J. Bourgeois, 'Strategy and Environment: A Conceptual Integration', *Academy of Management Review 5* (1980): 25–39.

8. Pete Engardio, 'A New World Economy', *BusinessWeek* (August 22–29, 2005): 52–58.

9. Robert Rosen, with Patricia Digh, Marshall Singer, and Carl Phillips, *Global Literacies: Lessons on Business Leadership and National Cultures* (New York: Simon and Schuster, 2000).

10. Engardio, 'A New World Economy'.

11. Cliff Edwards, 'Wherever You Go, You're On the Job', *BusinessWeek* (June 20, 2005): 87–90.

12. Stephen Baker and Adam Astor, 'The Business of Nanotech', *BusinessWeek* (February 14, 2005): 64–71.

13. William B. Johnston, 'Global Work Force 2000: The New World Labor Market', *Harvard Business Review* (March–April 1991): 115–127.

14. US Census Bureau statistics reported in 'Minorities Should Be Very Close to Majority by 2050, Census Projection Says', AP Story in *Johnson City Press* (March 18, 2004): 5A; and Peter Coy, 'The Creative Economy', *BusinessWeek* (August 28, 2000): 76–82.

15. Peter Coy, 'Old. Smart. Productive', *BusinessWeek* (June 27, 2005): 78–86; Danielle Sacks, 'Scenes from the Culture Clash', *Fast Company* (January–February 2006): 73–77; and Ellyn Spragins, 'The Talent Pool', *FSB* (October 2005): 93–102.

16. US Census, *www.census.gov/.*

17. Michelle Conlin, 'UnMarried America', *BusinessWeek* (October 20, 2003): 106–116.

18. Sebastian Moffett, 'Senior Moment: Fast-Aging Japan Keeps Its Elders on the Job Longer', *The Wall Street Journal* (June 15, 2005): A1.

19. Julie Dunn, 'Restaurant Chains, Too, Watch Their Carbs', *The New York Times* (January 4, 2004); Brian Grow with Gerry Khermouch, 'The Low-Carb Food Fight Ahead', *BusinessWeek* (December 22, 2003): 48; and Laura Crimaldi, 'Girl Scout Numbers Drop', *Boston Herald* (March 11, 2005): 7.

20. Samuel Loewenberg, 'Europe Gets Tougher on US Companies', *The New York Times* (April 20, 2003): Section 3, 6.

21. Jeremy Caplan, 'Paper War', *Time* (January 2006): A11.

22. Linda Himelstein and Laura Zinn, with Maria Mallory, John Carey, Richard S. Dunham, and Joan O. C. Hamilton, 'Tobacco: Does It Have a Future?', *BusinessWeek* (July 4, 1994): 24–29; Bob Ortega, 'Aging Activists Turn, Turn, Turn Attention to Wal-Mart Protests', *The Wall Street Journal* (October 11, 1994): A1, A8.

23. Nick Mathiason, 'Tesco faces attack over carbon footprint', *Observer* (September 9, 2007) http://observer.guardian.co.uk/business/story/0,,2165058,00.html.

24. Etzion, Dror, 'Research on Organizations and the Natural Environment', *Journal of Management* 33 (August 2007): 637–654.

25. Bruce Horovitz, 'Whole Foods Sacks Plastic Bags', *USA Today*, January 22, 2008.

26. Stuart Birch, 'Now Companies Are Going Green Right from the Start', *The Times,* Green Motoring Focus Report 7, January 25, 2008.

27. Matthew L. Wald, 'What's Kind to Nature Can be Kind to Profits', *The New York Times*, May 17, 2006, http://www.nytimes.com/2006/05/17/business/businessspecial2/17giant.html?scp=1&sq=What%27s+Kind+to+Nature+Can+Be+Kind+to+Profits&st=nyt (accessed January 30, 2008).

28. Jessi Hempel, 'The MySpace Generation', *BusinessWeek* (December 12, 2005): 86–94.

29. John Simons, 'Stop Moaning About Gripe Sites and Log On', *Fortune* (April 2, 2001): 181–182.

30. Rick Brooks, 'Home Depot Turns Copycat in Its Efforts to Stoke New Growth', *The Wall Street Journal* (November 21, 2000): A1; Dan Sewell, 'Home Depot, Lowe's Building Up Competition', *Lexington Herald-Leader*: Business Profile supplement (December 8, 1997): 3.

31. Julia Angwin and Motoko Rich, 'Inn Fighting: Big Hotel Chains Are Striking Back Against Web Sites', *The Wall Street Journal* (March 14, 2003): A1; Paul Glader, 'Steel-Price Rise Crimps Profits, Adds Uncertainty', *The Wall Street Journal* (February 23, 2004): A1.

32. John R. Wilke and Kathy Chen, 'Planned Economy; As China's Trade Clout Grows, So Do Price-Fixing Accusations', *The Wall Street Journal* (February 10, 2006): A1.

33. Olga Kharif, 'Nortes's New Lease on Life', *BusinessWeek Online* (January 26, 2006); Roger O. Crockett, 'Nortel: Desperately Seeking Credibility', *BusinessWeek* (January 17, 2005): 60–61; Bernard Simon, 'A Bright New Day for the Telecom Industry, If the Public Will Go Along', *The New York Times* (January 12, 2004): C3; Mark Heinzl, 'Nortel's Profit of $499 Million Exceeds Forecast', *The Wall Street Journal* (January 30, 2004): B4; Joseph Weber with Andy Reinhardt and Peter Burrows, 'Racing Ahead at Nortel', *BusinessWeek* (November 8, 1999): 93–99; Ian Austen, 'Hooked on the Net', *Canadian Business* (June 26–July 10, 1998): 95–103; 'Nortel's Waffling Continues; First Job Cuts, Then Product Lines, and Now the CEO. What's Next?', *Telephony* (May 21, 2001): 12.

34. Robert B. Duncan, 'Characteristics of Organizational Environment and Perceived Environmental Uncertainty', *Administrative Science Quarterly* 17 (1972): 313–327; and Daft, *Organization Theory and Design.*

35. David B. Jemison, 'The Importance of Boundary Spanning Roles in Strategic Decision-Making', *Journal of Management Studies* 21 (1984): 131–152; and Marc J. Dollinger, 'Environmental Boundary Spanning and Information Processing Effects on Organizational Performance', *Academy of Management Journal* 27 (1984): 351–368.

36. Sarah Moore, 'On Your Markets', *Working Woman* (February 2001): 26; and John Simons, 'Stop Moaning about Gripe Sites and Log On', *Fortune* (April 2, 2001): 181–182.

37. Tom Duffy, 'Spying the Holy Grail', *Microsoft Executive Circle* (Winter 2004): 38–39.

38. Gary Abramson, 'All Along the Watchtower'. *CIO Enterprise* (July 15, 1999): 24–34.

39. Girard, 'Snooping on a Shoestring', *Business 2.0* (May 2003): 64–66.

40. Edwin M. Epstein, 'How to Learn from the Environment about the Environment – A Prerequisite for Organizational Well-Being', *Journal of General Management* 29, no. 1 (Autumn 2003): 68–80.

41. Mark McNeilly, 'Gathering Information for Strategic Decisions, Routinely', *Strategy & Leadership* 30, no 5 (2002): 29–34.

42. Day and Schoemaker, 'Scanning the Periphery'.

43. A discussion of the Sony–Toshiba–IBM alliance was heard by the author on NPR's *Morning Edition*; information on Kroger, Albertson's, and Safeway from an Associated Press story, 'Strike Increases Pressure on Safeway CEO', in *Johnson City Press* (February 1, 2004): 7D; Norihiko Shirouzu and Jathon Sapsford, 'Power Struggle; As Hybrid Cars Gain Traction, Industry Battles Over Designs', *The Wall Street Journal* (October 19, 2005): A1.

44. Lynn A. Isabella, 'Managing an Alliance Is Nothing Like Business as Usual', *Organizational Dynamics* 31, no. 1 (2002): 47–59; Cyrus F. Freidheim, Jr. *The Trillion-Dollar Enterprise: How the Alliance Revolution Will Transform Global Business* (New York: Perseus Books, 1998).

45. Stephan M. Wagner and Roman Boutellier, 'Capabilities for Managing a Portfolio of Supplier Relationships', *Business Horizons* (November–December 2002): 79–88; Peter Smith Ring and Andrew H. Van de Ven, 'Developmental Processes of Corporate Interorganizational Relationships', *Academy of Management Review* 19 (1994): 90–118; Myron Magnet, 'The New Golden Rule of Business', *Fortune* (February 21, 1994): 60–64; and Peter Grittner, 'Four Elements of Successful Sourcing Strategies', *Management Review* (October 1996): 41–45

46. Richard L. Daft, 'After the Deal: The Art of Fusing Diverse Corporate Cultures into One', paper presented at the Conference on International Corporate Restructuring, Korea University, Seoul, Korea Institute of Business Research and Education, (June 16, 1998).

47. Patricia Sellers, 'The Business of Being Oprah', *Fortune* (April 1, 2002): 50–64

48. Warren St. John, 'Barnes & Noble's Epiphany', *Wired* (June 1999): 132–144; Ron Grover and Richard Siklos, 'When Old Foes Need Each Other', *BusinessWeek* (October 25, 1999): 114, 118.

49. James E. Svatko, 'Joint Ventures', *Small Business Reports* (December 1988): 65–70; and Joshua Hyatt, 'The Partnership Route', *Inc.* (December 1988): 145–148.

50. Yoash Wiener, 'Forms of Value Systems: A Focus on Organizational Effectiveness and Culture Change and Maintenance', *Academy of Management Review* 13 (1988): 534–545; V. Lynne Meek, 'Organizational Culture: Origins and Weaknesses', *Organization Studies* 9 (1988): 453–473; John J. Sherwood, 'Creating Work Cultures with Competitive Advantage', *Organizational Dynamics* (Winter 1988): 5–27; and Andrew D. Brown and Ken Starkey, 'The Effect of Organizational Culture on Communication and Information', *Journal of Management Studies* 31, no. 6 (November 1994): 807–828.

51. Joanne Martin, *Organizational Culture: Mapping the Terrain* (Thousand Oaks, CA: Sage Publications, 2002); Ralph H. Kilmann, Mary J. Saxton, and Roy Serpa, 'Issues in Understanding and Changing Culture', *California Management Review* 28 (Winter 1986): 87–94; and Linda Smircich, 'Concepts of Culture and Organizational Analysis', *Administrative Science Quarterly* 28 (1983): 339–358.

52. Based on Edgar H. Schein, *Organizational Culture and Leadership*, 2nd ed. (San Francisco: Jossey-Bass, 1992): 3–27.

53. Michael G. Pratt and Anat Rafaeli, 'Symbols as a Language of Organizational Relationships', *Research in Organizational Behaviour* 23 (2001): 93–132.

54. Christine Canabou, 'Here's the Drill', *Fast Company* (February 2001): 58.

55. Alex Frangos, 'In Office Mock-Up, Real Workers Put Layout Ideas to Test', *The Wall Street Journal* (December 1, 2004).

56. Patrick M. Lencioni, 'Make Your Values Mean Something', *Harvard Business Review* (July 2002): 113–117.

57. Joanne Martin, *Organizational Culture*: 71–72.

58. Robert E. Quinn and Gretchen M. Spreitzer, 'The Road to Empowerment: Seven Questions Every Leader Should Consider', *Organizational Dynamics* (Autumn 1997): 37–49.

59. Toyota Web site, http://www.toyota.com (accessed February 12, 2008); Jarnagin and Slocum, 'Creating Corporate Cultures through Mythopoetic Leadership'.

60. Terrence E. Deal and Allan A. Kennedy, *Corporate Cultures: The Rites and Rituals of Corporate Life* (Reading, MA: Addison-Wesley, 1982).

61. Patricia Jones and Larry Kahaner, *Say It and Live It: 50 Corporate Mission Statements That Hit the Mark* (New York: Currency Doubleday, 1995).

62. Harrison M. Trice and Janice M. Beyer, 'Studying Organizational Cultures Through Rites and Ceremonials', *Academy of Management Review* 9 (1984): 653–669.

63. Brent Schlender, 'Wal-Mart's $288 Billion Meeting', *Fortune* (April 18, 2005): 90–106.

64. Alan Farnham, 'Mary Kay's Lessons in Leadership', *Fortune* (September 20, 1993): 68–77.

65. Jennifer A. Chatman and Karen A. Jehn, 'Assessing the Relationship Between Industry Characteristics and Organizational Culture: How Different Can You Be?', *Academy of Management Journal* 37, no. 3 (1994): 522–553.

66. John P. Kotter and James L. Heskett, *Corporate Culture and Performance* (New York: The Free Press, 1992).

67. This discussion is based on Paul McDonald and Jeffrey Gandz, 'Getting Value from Shared Values', *Organizational Dynamics* 21, no. 3 (Winter 1992): 64–76; Daniel R. Denison and Aneil K. Mishra, 'Toward a Theory of Organizational Culture and Effectiveness', *Organization Science* 6, no. 2 (March–April 1995): 204–223; and Richard L. Daft, *The Leadership Experience,* 3rd ed. (Cincinnati, OH: South-Western, 2005): 570–573.

68. Lucas Conley, 'Rinse and Repeat', *Fast Company* (July 2005): 76–77.

69. Robert Hooijberg and Frank Petrock, 'On Cultural Change: Using the Competing Values Framework to Help Leaders Execute a Transformational Strategy', *Human Resource Management* 32, no. 1 (1993): 29–50.

70. Lencioni, 'Make Your Values Mean Something'; and Melanie Warner, 'Confessions of a Control Freak', *Fortune* (September 4, 2000): 130–140.; Janet Guyon, 'The Soul of a

Moneymaking Machine', *Fortune* (October 3, 2005): 113–120.; Rekha Balu, 'Pacific Edge Projects Itself', *Fast Company* (October 2000): 371–381.

71. Jeffrey Pfeffer, *The Human Equation: Building Profits by Putting People First* (Boston: Harvard Business School Press, 1998).

72. Jeremy Kahn, 'What Makes a Company Great?', *Fortune* (October 26, 1998): 218; James C. Collins and Jerry I. Porras, *Built to Last: Successful Habits of Visionary Companies* (New York: HarperCollins, 1994); and James C. Collins, 'Change Is Good – But First Know What Should Never Change', *Fortune* (May 29, 1995): 141.

73. Wahl, 'Culture Shock'.

74. Jennifer A. Chatman and Sandra Eunyoung Cha, 'Leading by Leveraging Culture', *California Management Review* 45, no. 4 (Summer 2003): 20–34.

75. This section is based on Jeff Rosenthal and Mary Ann Masarech, 'High Peformance Cultures: How Values Can Drive Business Results', *Journal of Organizational Excellence* (Spring 2003): 3–18.

76. Rosenthal and Masarech, 'High-Performance Cultures'.

77. Katherine Mieszkowski, 'Community Standards', *Fast Company* (September 2000): 368; Rosabeth Moss Kanter, 'A More Perfect Union', *Inc.* (February 2001): 92–98; Raizel Robin, 'Net Gains' segment of 'E-Biz That Works', *Canadian Business* (October 14–October 26, 2003): 107.

78. Reggie Van Lee, Lisa Fabish, and Nancy McGaw, 'The Value of Corporate Values: A Booz Allen Hamilton/Aspen Institute Survey', *Strategy + Business*, 39 (Spring 2005): 52–65.

79. Lucas Conley, 'Cultural Phenomenon', *Fast Company* (April 2005): 76–77.

80. Rosenthal and Masarech, 'High-Performance Cultures'.

81. John P. Kotter and James L. Heskett, *Corporate Culture and Performance* (New York: The Free Press, 1992); Eric Flamholtz and Rangapriya Kannan-Narasimhan, 'Differential Impact of Cultural Elements on Financial Performance', *European Management Journal* 23, no. 1 (2005): 50–64. Also see J. M. Kouzes and B. Z. Posner, *The Leadership Challenge: How to Keep Getting Extraordinary Things Done in Organizations,* 3rd ed. (San Francisco: Jossey-Bass, 2002).

82. Micah R. Kee, 'Corporate Culture Makes a Fiscal Difference', *Industrial Management* (November–December 2003): 16–20.

83. *Business Week* (2007) 'No Cubicle Culture', http://www.businessweek.com/magazine/content/07_34/b4047412.htm?chan=search; www.oticon.nl; http://www.job.oticon.com/eprise/main/Oticon/com/SEC_AboutUs/_Index

84. Jenny C. McCune, 'Exporting Corporate Culture', *Management Review* (December 1999): 52–56.

85. Lencioni, 'Make Your Values Mean Something'.

86. Andrew Wahl, 'Culture Shock', *Canadian Business* (October 10–23, 2005): 115–116; and Calvin Leung, Michelle Magnan, and Andrew Wahl, 'People Power', *Canadian Business* (October 10–23, 2005): 125–126.

87. Guyon, 'The Soul of a Moneymaking Machine' and Geoff Colvin, 'The 100 Best Companies to Work For 2006', *Fortune* (January 23, 2006).

88. Buth and Delaney, 'Default Lines' Victoria Murphy, 'Microsoft's Midlife Crisis', *Forbes* (October 3, 2005): 88; Jonathan Krim, 'Microsoft Is Losing Some of Its Elbow Room; As Software King's Growth Slows, Rivals Stake Out Their Own Territory', *The Washington Post* (December 22,

2005): D1; and Jon Birger and David Stires, 'The Toughest Jobs in Business: 10 on the Spot', *Fortune* (February 20, 2006): 81–88.

89. Fiona Wilson (1999) 'Organizational Culture and Control', *Organizational Behaviour*, p. 101; Grint, K. (1991) *The Sociology of Work*: An Introduction, Cambridge: Polity; Jenkins, R. (1985) 'Black Workers in the Labour Market: The Price of Recession', in B. Roberts, R. Finnegan and D. Gallie (eds.), *New Approaches to Economic Life*. Manchester: Manchester University Press.

90. Jenkins, R. (1988) 'Discrimination and Equal Opportunity in Employment: Ethnicity and "Race" in the United Kingdom', in D. Gallie (ed.), *Employment in Britain* (Oxford: Blackwell); *Personnel Today*, 31 January 1995; *Guardian*, 3 June 1997; *Independent*, 13 November 1997, p. 22.

© JERRY HORBERT/SHUTTERSTOCK

CHAPTER OUTLINE

LEARNING OBJECTIVES

After reading this chapter, you should be able to:

1   Describe the emerging borderless world and some issues of particular concern for today's managers.

2   Understand market entry strategies that businesses use to develop foreign markets.

3   Define international management and explain how it differs from the management of domestic business operations.

4   Indicate how dissimilarities in the economic, sociocultural and legal-political environments throughout the world can affect business operations.

5   Describe how regional trading alliances are reshaping the international business environment.

6   Understand the key characteristics of a multinational corporation.

7   Explain cultural intelligence and why it is necessary for managers working in foreign countries.

CHAPTER 4

MANAGING IN A GLOBAL ENVIRONMENT

Manager's Challenge

The year was 1984. Sitting in his college room, Michael Dell had a powerful insight: Why not sell personal computers directly to consumers rather than going through distributors or retailers? Dell Computer Corporation was born, and the computer industry was revolutionized. Now, Dell is striving to apply its ultra-efficient processes to shake up the Chinese computer industry the same way it did in the US and Europe. But things are proving difficult, with the company encountering problems ranging from language barriers and cultural resistance to tough competition from Lenovo, a Chinese firm that is quickly becoming a global player in PCs and services. Even the term *direct sales* was a problem for Dell, translating into a Chinese term most often used to describe illegal pyramid marketing schemes. The language problem was solved, but by sticking to its direct sales model, Dell is losing Chinese customers who typically want to see and touch products before they buy. Lenovo, with 4800 retail outlets, has long been the market leader in China and is now making a global push with the purchase of IBM's PC unit. Dell recently lost its most experienced Asia-Pacific executive when Lenovo snared Dell's Asia chief Bill Amelio as its new CEO. Amelio and Lenovo chairman Yang Yuanqing vowed that Lenovo wouldn't concede the Asia market to Dell. Moreover, Lenovo managers are now aiming to compete with Dell in its established markets as well. They invested $60 million to become China's first Olympic sponsor and provider of computers to the Beijing Summer Olympics in 2008. 'It's a coming-out party to say, "Here's Lenovo; we're a global brand and we're here to stay",' said Amelio.[1]

Dell's core US and European markets are saturated, and its biggest potential for growth lies in emerging markets such as China. But managers at Dell are learning, as other multinational companies have, that they may have to adjust how the company operates to succeed in a new country or region. Wal-Mart, for example, has faced significant challenges in Germany, where the giant US firm is still a secondary player

Managing in a Global Environment: Are You Ready to Work Internationally?[2]

Are you ready to negotiate a sales contract with someone from another country? Companies large and small deal on a global basis. To what extent are you guilty of the behaviours below? Answer each item as Mostly True or Mostly False for you.

Are you typically:	Mostly True	Mostly False
1 Impatient? Do you have a short attention span? Do you want to keep moving to the next topic?	☐	☐
2 A poor listener? Are you uncomfortable with silence? Does your mind think about what you want to say next?	☐	☐
3 Argumentative? Do you enjoy arguing for its own sake?	☐	☐
4 Unfamiliar with cultural specifics in other countries? Do you have limited experience in other countries?	☐	☐
5 Short-term oriented? Do you place more emphasis on the short-term than on the long-term in your thinking and planning?	☐	☐
6 'All business'? Do you think that it is a waste of time getting to know someone personally before discussing business?	☐	☐
7 Legalistic to win your point? Do you hold others to an agreement regardless of changing circumstances?	☐	☐
8 Thinking 'win/lose' when negotiating? Do you usually try to win a negotiation at the other's expense?	☐	☐

SCORING AND INTERPRETATION Many managers often display cross-cultural ignorance during business negotiations compared to counterparts in other countries. For instance American negotiating habits can be disturbing, such as emphasizing areas of disagreement over agreement, spending little time understanding the views and interests of the other side, and adopting an adversarial attitude. Americans often like to leave a negotiation thinking they won, which can be embarrassing to the other side. For this quiz, a low score shows better international presence. If you answered 'Mostly True' to three or fewer questions, then consider yourself ready to assist with an international negotiation. If you scored six or more 'Mostly True' responses, it is time to learn more about other national cultures before participating in international business deals. Try to develop greater focus on other people's needs and an appreciation for different viewpoints. Be open to compromise and develop empathy for people who are different from you.

Do you think if you stay in your hometown as a manager you won't have to interact with people from other cultures? Think again. Many people who grew up in small towns with little diversity fail to appreciate the importance of cross-cultural skills. Yet in today's world, every manager needs to think globally. Rapid advances in technology and communications have made the international dimension an increasingly important part of the external environment discussed in Chapter 3. The future of our businesses and our societies is being shaped by global rather than local relationships.

A global mind-set and international experience are fast becoming prerequisites for managerial success. Many companies such as Carrefour, BP, Coca-Cola, HSBC, Nokia, Toyota and Siemens have learned that the greatest potential for growth lies overseas. In addition, the demand for raw materials such as steel, aluminium, cement and copper has slowed in the developed countries in the West, but is booming in countries such as China, India and Brazil.[3] For online companies, too, such as Amazon, Yahoo!, eBay and Google, going global is a key to growth. The number of residential internet subscribers in China is growing significantly faster than that of the US. Western Europe and Japan together account for a huge share of the world's e-commerce revenue.[4]

Do you believe Dell can duplicate its US and European success in China? How do you think Lenovo will fare as it tries to become a global brand? If you were a manager at Dell, what recommendations would you have for Dell managers as they go head-to-head with Lenovo for control of the world's fastest-growing market?

TAKE A MOMENT

---

after ten years' effort. The German market is dominated by local retail chains who cater to local tastes and are familiar with tough union rules and labour laws in that country. Wal-Mart also struggled in South America and Japan, partly because of managers' tendency for doing things the Wal-Mart way without adequately considering local customs.

However, this is not just an issue for large US Corporations looking to operate globally. The leading UK supermarket group Tesco has attempted, with mixed success, to expand into the lucrative US market through its 'Fresh and Easy' stores. It had announced plans to build a network of a thousand outlets, with a focus on basic facilities selling fresh food and ready meals at low prices, but has called a temporary halt after opening only 60 stores amid claims that it had failed to cater correctly for local food tastes and shopping habits. In fact few retailers have ever successfully broken into a mature grocery market in a developed country. For instance, Carrefour, Marks & Spencer and Sainsbury's have all previously attempted unsuccessfully to penetrate the US retail market to any significant extent.

The environment for today's organizations has therefore become extremely competitive and highly complex. Less-developed countries are challenging mature countries in a number of industries. China is the world's largest maker of consumer electronics and is rapidly and expertly moving into biotechnology, computer manufacturing, and semiconductors. At least 19 advanced new semiconductor plants are in or nearing operation in China.[5] The pace of innovation in India is startling in industries as diverse as precision manufacturing, health care and pharmaceuticals, and some observers see the beginnings of hypercompetitive multinationals in that country.[6]

This chapter introduces basic concepts about the global environment and international management. First, we consider the difficulty managers have operating in an increasingly borderless world. We then touch on various types of strategies and techniques for entering foreign markets and address the economic, legal-political and sociocultural challenges companies encounter within the global business environment. The chapter also describes multinational corporations, looks at the impact of trade agreements, and considers the globalization backlash. The final section of the chapter talks about some of the challenges managers face when working cross-culturally.

A Borderless World

A manager's reality is that isolation from international forces is no longer possible.

Business has also become a unified, global field as trade barriers fall, communication becomes faster and cheaper, and consumer tastes in everything from clothing to cellular phones converge. Thomas Middelhoff of Germany's Bertelsmann AG, which purchased US publisher Random House, put it this way: 'There are no German and American companies. There are only successful and unsuccessful companies'.[7] The difficulties and risks of a borderless world are matched by benefits and opportunities.

Today, even small companies can locate different parts of the organization wherever it makes the most business sense. Virtual connections enable close, rapid coordination among people working in different parts of the world, so it is no longer necessary to keep everything in one place. Organizations can go wherever they want to find the lowest costs or the best brain-power. Samsung, the Korean electronics giant, moved its semiconductor-making facilities to Silicon Valley to be closer to the best scientific brains in the industry. Canada's Nortel Networks selected a location in the southwest of England as its world manufacturing centre for a new fixed-access radio product, while the US owned DuPont shifted its electronic operations headquarters to Japan. Many companies outsource certain functions to contractors in other countries as easily as if the contractor were located right next door.[8]

CONCEPT CONNECTION Today's companies compete in a *borderless world*. Procter & Gamble sales in Southeast Asia make up a rapidly growing percentage of the company's worldwide sales. These shoppers are purchasing P&G's disposal nappy products, Pampers, in Malaysia. However, in turn this can raise other issues such as the environmental debate over the biodegradability and safe disposal of such products

---

TAKE A MOMENT   As a new manager, learn to 'think globally'. Take an interest in international people and issues. Don't hinder your own or your company's success by thinking only in terms of domestic issues, competitors and markets. Expand your thinking by reading and networking broadly.

A borderless world means consumers can no longer tell from which country they're buying. US-based Ford Motor Company owns Sweden's Volvo, while the iconic American beer Miller is owned by a South African company. Toyota is a Japanese corporation, but it has manufactured more than ten million vehicles in North American factories. The technology behind Intel's Centrino wireless components was born in a lab in Haifa, Israel, and Chinese researchers designed the microprocessors that control the pitch of the blade on General Electric's giant wind turbines.[9]

For managers who think globally, the whole world is a source of ideas, resources, information, employees, and customers. Managers can move their companies into the international arena on a variety of levels. The process of globalization typically passes through four distinct stages, as illustrated in Exhibit 4.1.

1 In the *domestic stage*, market potential is limited to the home country, with all production and marketing facilities located at home. Managers may be aware of the global environment and may want to consider foreign involvement.

Exhibit 4.1 Four Stages of Globalization

	1. Domestic	2. International	3. Multinational	4. Global
Strategic Orientation	Domestically oriented	Export-oriented, multidomestic	Multinational	Global
Stage of Development	Initial foreign involvement	Competitive positioning	Explosion of international operations	Global
Cultural Sensitivity	Of little importance	Very important	Somewhat important	Critically important
Manager Assumptions	'One best way'	'Many good ways'	'The least-cost way'	'Many good ways'

SOURCE: Based on Nancy J. Adler, *International Dimensions of Organizational Behaviour*, 4th ed. (Cincinnati, OH: South-Western, 2002), pp. 8–9.

2 In the *international stage*, exports increase, and the company usually adopts a *multidomestic* approach, meaning that competition is handled for each country independently. Product design, marketing and advertising are adapted to the specific needs of each country, requiring a high level of sensitivity to local values and interests. Typically, these companies use an international division to deal with the marketing of products in several countries individually.

3 In the *multinational stage*, the company has marketing and production facilities located in many countries, with more than one-third of its sales outside the home country. These companies adopt a *globalization* approach, meaning they focus on delivering a similar product to multiple countries. Product design, marketing and advertising strategies are standardized throughout the world.

4 Finally, the *global* (or *stateless*) *stage* of corporate international development transcends any single home country. These corporations operate in true global fashion, making sales and acquiring resources in whatever country offers the best opportunities and lowest cost. At this stage, ownership, control and top management tend to be dispersed among several nationalities.[10]

Today, the number of global or stateless corporations is increasing and the awareness of national borders decreasing, as reflected in the frequency of foreign participation at the top management level. Consider what's happening in the corner office of corporate America, where 14 of the *Fortune* 100 companies are now run by foreign-born CEOs. For instance, in 2007 PepsiCo appointed Indra Nooyi, an Indian born woman, as its CEO. Nooyi grew up in Chennai (formerly Madras), and after graduating from the Indian Institute of Management in Calcutta, and the Yale School of Management, gained experience at Boston Consulting Group and Motorola before joining PepsiCo in 1994 and then rising through the ranks to the CEO position. One of her first actions as CEO has been to reorganize PepsiCo to make it less fixated on the US and to broaden the management structure, including promoting an Italian native, Massimo d'Amore, as head of the US soft drinks division. Similarly, Citigroup appointed India-born Vikram S. Pandit as its CEO. Alcoa's top leader was born in Morocco, and Dow Chemical is headed by a native Australian.[11]

The trend is seen in other countries as well. Wales-born Howard Stringer was named Sony's first non-Japanese CEO in 2004, and Nancy McKinstry is the first

American to head Dutch publisher Wolters Kluwer. Similarly, Glaxo-Smith Kline, the large British pharmaceutical company, until very recently had Jean-Pierre Garnier, a Frenchman, as CEO, while Henry McKinnell, CEO of Pfizer, prepared for the job by spending 14 years working for the company in Iran, Japan and Hong Kong.[12] Increasingly, managers at lower levels are also expected to know a second or third language and have international experience.

Getting Started Internationally

Market entry strategy
An organizational strategy for entering a foreign market.

Organizations have a couple of ways to become involved internationally. One is to seek cheaper sources of materials or labour offshore, which is called *offshoring* or *global outsourcing*. Another is to develop markets for finished products outside their home countries, which may include exporting, licensing and direct investing. These market entry strategies represent alternative ways to sell products and services in foreign markets. Most firms begin with exporting and work up to direct investment. Exhibit 4.2 shows the strategies companies can use to enter foreign markets.

Exporting

Exporting
An entry strategy in which the organization maintains its production facilities within its home country and transfers its products for sale in foreign countries.

With exporting, the corporation maintains its production facilities within the home nation and transfers its products for sale in foreign countries.[13] Exporting enables a company to market its products in other countries at modest resource cost and with limited risk. Exporting does entail numerous problems based on physical distances, government regulations, foreign currencies, and cultural differences, but it is less expensive than committing the firm's own capital to building plants in host countries. For example, at Cornish Stairways', who's spiral staircases grace the homes of the rich and famous in the UK, despite a growing international reputation, only around 10 per cent of the company's turnover is achieved through exports. Prompted by a number of lucrative Middle Eastern contracts, gained via recommendation, Cornish Stairways began to think seriously about developing an export strategy. They found

Exhibit 4.2 Strategies for Entering International Markets

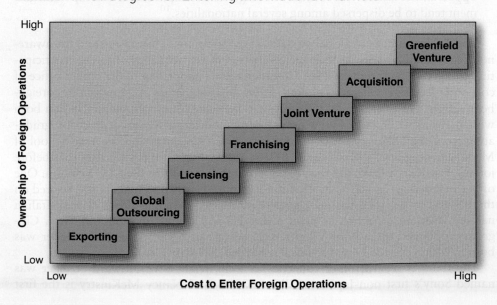

that it was better in many cases for Cornish Stairways to provide the design expertise and then for the product to be made and fitted in Dubai.

Many small- to medium-sized companies are benefiting from increased exporting. Henry Estate, a winery in Umpqua, Oregon, exports quality wines to Canada, Japan and the UK and has recently begun exporting to China to tap into the 1.3 billion potential wine drinkers in that country. Similarly K-Pumps, the UK's largest supplier of refurbished equipment for the brewing industry, which until recently derived all its revenue for its domestic market is now successfully exporting to customers in Sweden, Norway and Finland, with plans to move next into Spain.[14]

A form of exporting to less-developed countries is called countertrade, which is the barter of products for products rather than the sale of products for currency. Many less-developed countries have products to exchange but have no foreign currency. An estimated 20 per cent of world trade is countertrade.

Outsourcing

Global outsourcing, also called *offshoring*, means engaging in the international division of labour so that work activities can be done in countries with the cheapest sources of labour and supplies. Millions of low-level jobs such as textile manufacturing, call centre operations and credit card processing have been outsourced to low-wage countries in recent years. For instance, Burberry, the British luxury brand, closed its factory in South Wales in 2007, transferring production to China. The commercial reality was that Burberry's polo shirts cost £12 to produce in Wales, and only £4 in the Far East. Similarly *The Economist* (on February 25, 2006) reported that '15 years ago, almost 90 per cent of Benetton's colourful clothes were produced in its home market. Today, Italian makers supply less than 30 per cent, and this will fall to 10 per cent over the next few years'. Dyson, the UK company which pioneered the 'bagless' vacuum cleaner, similarly moved its manufacturing to Malaysia lowering its cost base so that the extra profitability now allowed them to employ more scientists and researchers at the headquarters in Malmesbury than they used to employ blue-collar workers making vacuum cleaners.

The internet and plunging telecommunications costs are enabling companies to outsource more and higher-level work as well. Netgear, a Santa Clara, California-based company, makes networking equipment that is designed and marketed in the US, engineered in Taiwan, and manufactured in China, helping the small company take advantage of the efficiencies it can gain in three different countries.[15] British banks such as Barclays have transferred back-office operations to companies in China and India, as well. However this is not always successful. For instance, in 2007 Lloyds TSB announced a major policy U-turn by allowing customers to telephone their branches and shutting down its call centres in India. This appears to be part of a trend with Powergen, Esure and Aviva having also recently reverted back to UK operations.

The most recent trend is outsourcing core processes, which Joe McGrath, CEO of Unisys, refers to as the 'natural next phase of the offshoring movement'.[16] After the Sarbanes–Oxley Act went into effect, Unisys had a hard time finding enough internal auditors in the US, so managers outsourced their core auditing practice to China. Large pharmaceutical companies farm out much of their early-stage chemistry research to cheaper labs in China and India.[17] Many organizations are even outsourcing aspects of innovation. One survey found that 65 per cent of companies reported that part of

Countertrade
The barter of products for other products rather than their sale for currency.

Global outsourcing
Engaging in the international division of labour so as to obtain the cheapest sources of labour and supplies regardless of country; also called *offshoring*.

© STEWART GOLDSTEIN/ALAMY

CONCEPT CONNECTION
After rapid expansion in the UK, Hotel Chocolat is going global with new stores in Boston and Bahrain – bringing gourmet chocolate to an increasingly diverse international luxury goods market. In 2006 founders Angus Thirlwell and Peter Harris took the rare step of setting up their own cocoa estate in St Lucia, the Rabot Estate, which now exports record amounts of cocoa processed by the company's chocolate factories, including one at Huntingdon, UK, for their global chain of outlets.

their research and development takes place overseas. Both Microsoft and General Electric have research centres in China, and IBM has established an R&D centre in India.[18]

Licensing

Licensing
An entry strategy in which an organization in one country makes certain resources available to companies in another to participate in the production and sale of its products abroad.

The next stage in pursuing international markets is licensing. With **licensing**, a corporation (the licensor) in one country makes certain resources available to companies in another country (the licensee). These resources include technology, managerial skills and/or patent and trademark rights. They enable the licensee to produce and market a product similar to what the licensor has been producing. Heineken, the Dutch brewing giant, which has been called the world's first truly global brand of beer, usually begins by exporting to help boost familiarity with its product; if the market looks enticing enough, Heineken then licenses its brands to a local brewer. It currently has links to 115 breweries in 66 countries including 16 in Africa and the Middle East. Licensing offers a business firm relatively easy access to international markets at low cost, but it limits the company's participation in and control over the development of those markets.

Franchising
A form of licensing in which an organization provides its foreign franchisees with a complete package of materials and services.

One special form of licensing is **franchising**, which occurs when a franchisee buys a complete package of materials and services, including equipment, products, product ingredients, trademark and trade name rights, managerial advice, and a standardized operating system. Whereas with licensing, a licensee generally keeps its own company name, autonomy and operating systems, a franchise takes the name and systems of the franchisor. The fast-food chains are some of the best-known franchisors. KFC, Burger King, Wendy's, and McDonald's outlets are found in almost every large city in the world. The story is often told of the Japanese child visiting Los Angeles who excitedly pointed out to his parents, 'They have McDonald's in America.'

Direct Investing

Direct investing
An entry strategy in which the organization is involved in managing its production facilities in a foreign country.

A higher level of involvement in international trade is direct investment in facilities in a foreign country. **Direct investing** means that the company is involved in managing the productive assets, which distinguishes it from other entry strategies that permit less managerial control. French supermarket group Carrefour wasn't the first foreign retailer in mainland China to open a hypermarket. But since Carrefour opened its first store, in 1995, it has become the largest. China is now Carrefour's fifth-largest market, and the company expects its sales in China to go on growing by 25 per cent to 30 per cent annually over the next five years.

Joint venture
A variation of direct investment in which an organization shares costs and risks with another firm to build a manufacturing facility, develop new products or set up a sales and distribution network.

Currently, the most popular type of direct investment is to engage in strategic alliances and partnerships. In a **joint venture**, a company shares costs and risks with another firm, typically in the host country, to develop new products, build a manufacturing facility, or set up a sales and distribution network.[19] A partnership is often the fastest, cheapest and least risky way to get into the global game. For example, Auburn Farms, a Sacramento, California, manufacturer of all-natural snack foods, formed a joint venture with South Africa's Beacon Sweets & Chocolates.[20] In India, where government regulations prohibit direct foreign investment in the retail sector, Tesco plans to open wholesale grocery stores in India supplying hypermarkets owned by Indian conglomerate Tata Group. The supermarket giant is to invest £60 million over two years to help develop its wholesale business. According to Tesco, the joint venture will allow it to complement its existing businesses in China and the US, while Marks & Spencer has entered into a joint venture with Reliance Retail of India in the hope of establishing their brand in India.

Internet companies have also used joint ventures as a way to expand. AOL created a joint venture with Venezuela's Cisneros Group to smooth its entry into Latin America.[21] In addition to joint ventures, the complexity of today's global business environment is causing managers at many companies to develop alliance networks, which refer to collections of partnerships with various other firms, often across international boundaries.[22] These alliance networks help companies reduce costs, enhance their competitive position in the international environment, and increase knowledge on a global scale.

The other choice is to have a **wholly owned foreign affiliate**, over which the company has complete control. Direct *acquisition* of an affiliate may provide cost savings over exporting by shortening distribution channels and reducing storage and transportation costs. Local managers also have heightened awareness of economic, cultural and political conditions. Home Depot purchased the number two home-improvement retailer in Mexico, Home Mart, and turned it into today's leading chain with 50 stores. Philip Morris recently acquired Indonesia's third largest cigarette maker to tap into the lucrative Asian cigarette market.[23]

The most costly and risky direct investment is called a **greenfield venture**, which means a company builds a subsidiary from scratch in a foreign country. The advantage is that the subsidiary is exactly what the company wants and has the potential to be highly profitable. The disadvantage is that the company has to acquire all market knowledge, materials, people and know-how in a different culture, and mistakes are possible. An example of a greenfield venture is the Nissan plant in Sunderland, UK. The plant represents the first car factory ever built in Sunderland, where the Japanese company had to rely on an untested and largely inexperienced workforce who had previously worked in the locally declining steel and ship-building industries. The logistical and cultural hurdles were enormous but it has proved to be a real success and is now the largest car plant in the UK and the most productive in Europe The US auto parts maker Delphi is taking a similar leap by building a $40 million, 200 000-square-foot car electronics parts plant in Suzhou, China.[24]

China Inc

Many companies today are going straight to China or India as a first step into international business. Business in both countries is booming, and US and European companies are taking advantage of opportunities for all of the tactics we've discussed in this section: exporting, outsourcing, licensing and direct investment. Foreign companies are investing more in business in China than they are spending anywhere else in the world.[25] In addition, multinationals based in the US and Europe manufacture more and more products in China using design, software and services from India. This trend prompted one business writer to coin the term *Chindia* to reflect the combined power of the two countries in the international dimension.[26]

Outsourcing is perhaps the most widespread approach to international involvement in China and India. China manufactures an ever-growing percentage of the industrial and consumer products sold in the US – and in other countries as well. China produces more clothes, shoes, toys, television sets,

Wholly owned foreign affiliate
A foreign subsidiary over which an organization has complete control.

Greenfield venture
The most risky type of direct investment, whereby a company builds a subsidiary from scratch in a foreign country.

© ADRIAN BRADSHAW/CORBIS

CONCEPT CONNECTION Wal-Mart had $90.6 billion in international sales for the fiscal year ending January 2008 and operates more than 3000 stores overseas, including this one which opened in Beijing in 2005. But the world's largest retailer isn't stopping there. Managers plan to increase the international division's share of total sales and earnings through a direct investment market entry strategy that includes joint ventures, acquisitions and greenfield ventures. Wal-Mart is currently moving strongly into India, recently announcing a joint venture with Bharti Enterprises to establish Bharti Wal-Mart Private Limited, for wholesale cash-and-carry and back-end supply chain management operations in that country.

DVD players and cell phones than any other country. Furniture and cabinetmakers have also shifted much of their production to that country in recent years, and manufacturers in China are moving into higher-ticket items such as automobiles, computers and airplane parts.

China can manufacture almost any product at a much lower cost than Western manufacturers. Despite the advantages, however, companies are finding that operating smoothly in China isn't automatic. Mattel learned the hard way after having to recall millions of Chinese-made toys tainted with lead paint, as mentioned in Chapter 3, hurting the company financially and damaging its reputation. If a company like Mattel that has been operating in China since the late 1950s can run into trouble, think of the uncertainty newcomers must face.[27]

Many large organizations are developing joint ventures or building subsidiaries in China. Toyota Motors was one of the earliest firms to open a plant in China.

Toyota Motors

Toyota Motors has forged two joint ventures in China, with First Auto Works and Guangzhou Auto. In 2006 it announced local production of the Prius, priced around $36 000 in what would be China's first hybrid car. Despite exporting cars to the mainland since the 1960s, Toyota's market share is only 3.5 per cent in China, compared to 13 per cent in the US and more than 40 per cent at home in Japan. Market leader General Motors sell more than 650 000 vehicles in China a year, while second-placed Volkswagen, with sales of over 500 000, is also way ahead of Toyota's 179 000 units in 2005. For a number of years Toyota struggled with everything from poor travel conditions to bureaucratic controls on product lines. But don't expect Toyota to be lagging behind for too long. Just as Toyota has grown rapidly in the US over the past decade, it's now gearing up for rapid expansion in China.

Leading Toyota's rapid expansion in China is Yoshimi Inaba, who splits his time equally between Tokyo, Toyota City and China. Inaba sees working with two local partners as essential to its growth strategy. First Auto Works (FAW) and Guanggzhou Automotive (GA) have totally separate franchises and sales networks under the name Toyota, while Toyota also markets Lexus separately as an 100 per cent self-owned operation. By nurturing partnerships with local companies, Toyota is able to reduce its risks, minimize capital costs and gain a marketing edge. In China, where relationships are paramount, the connection with both FAW and GA provides invaluable help to Toyota in working through red tape, avoiding cultural blunders, and gaining access to China's markets.

Toyota has actually found that selling cars in China is very similar to that in the US. It is predominantly commission-based dealership sales, supported by a very small fixed salary. That is very different from Japan or even Europe, and underpins the whole dealer network. However the dealers tended to be much younger although they have pretty much the same entrepreneurial mentality as US dealers.

What about Chinese Consumers? How do they Compare with Other Markets?

About 85 per cent are new, first-time buyers, whether they're young or old. There is also a strong element of status or lifestyle expressed by the cars people buy. Given that China is a very young market relative to the US or Japan, Toyota have had to tune their marketing approach to a younger generation of people. They also try to promote more customer test-driving experiences – it's more about personal experiences rather than just image.

Who will be the Biggest Rivals for Toyota in China?

Inaba is very confident that Toyota can succeed in China. 'We're a minor player in the China market, with a 3.5 per cent share, but we're one of the few manufacturers where demand exceeds supply. Even though we see big potential for growth, we will make sure we're not in a position of overcapacity. That will be a very key element. And as long as you retain the quality, treat dealers as partners and avoid oversupply, the results will come. The race for the Chinese market is just around the first corner.' China is a sizeable car market, and large overseas manufacturers such as BMW and General Motors have visible presences. However, local Chinese manufacturers such as Geely or Chery, as well as Hyundai [of Korea] are also expanding quickly.[28]

India

India, for its part, is a rising power in software design, services and precision engineering. Nearly 50 per cent of microchip engineering for Conexant Systems is done in India.[29] The California company makes the intricate brains behind internet access for home computers and satellite-connection set-top boxes for televisions. Google sees India as the perfect place for finding the next set of ideas to keep the company on the cutting edge in global information services.

Google isn't the only company to see India as a major source of technological talent. Yahoo employs about 900 engineers at a research centre in India, and IBM has become the country's largest foreign employer with more than 50 000 people employed there.

 INNOVATIVE WAY

Google

Google didn't go to India for cheap labour. It went there for technological talent. When the company wanted to open a new R&D centre, it chose Bangalore, partly because many of the Indian engineers working at Google's California headquarters wanted to return home and participate in India's growth. Managers knew Google would have a hard time finding the technological brainpower the company needed in the US alone. The company also has a larger facility in Hyderabad and two smaller offices in Mumbai and Delhi.

In addition to its hopes for India as a hotbed of innovation, Google also sees India as a vast potential market. The country's online advertising industry is miniscule today but projected to grow rapidly. Managers also believe that people in India are perfectly suited to help Google develop products for emerging markets where billions of people aren't yet on the internet. 'The fact that they come from this culture, the fact that they've seen the population of the world that's not on the internet ... puts them in a fairly unique position to transcend both worlds and be creative about emerging-world products', says Prasad Ram who heads the Bangalore research centre.

For one thing, Indian engineers know that developing markets have different priorities. For most people in developed countries like the US, internet use is about lifestyle, but for those in developing nations such as India and China, it's about *livelihood*. They want to know how the internet can help them generate income, improve their communities, and further their own and the country's economic development. That entrepreneurial spirit is a perfect fit for Google, where the guiding philosophy is to take risks and be aggressive in finding new applications to serve new markets.[30]

The International Business Environment

International management
The management of business operations conducted in more than one country.

International management is the management of business operations conducted in more than one country. The fundamental tasks of business management – including the financing, production, and distribution of products and services – do not change in any substantive way when a firm is transacting business across international borders. The basic management functions of planning, organizing, leading and controlling are the same whether a company operates domestically or internationally. However, managers will experience greater difficulties and risks when performing these management functions on an international scale. Consider the following blunders:

- When setting up the operations in Europe, the Walt Disney Company extended its domestic policy of serving no alcohol in its parks in California, Florida, and Tokyo to France. This caused astonishment and rebellion in France where a glass of wine for lunch is a given. After widespread protest that Disney were being insensitive to French culture, the Company had to change its policy and allowed wine and beer in the Paris theme park. Disney's American managers also required English to be spoken at all meetings and Disney's appearance code for members of staff, which listed regulations and limitations for the use of make up, facial hair, tattoos and jewellery. French labour unions mounted protests against the appearance code, which they saw as 'an attack on individual liberty'. [31]
- It took McDonald's more than a year to figure out that Hindus in India do not eat beef. The company's sales took off only after McDonald's started making burgers sold in India out of lamb. [32]
- In Africa, the labels on bottles show pictures of what is inside so illiterate shoppers can know what they're buying. When a baby-food company showed a picture of an infant on its label, the product didn't sell very well. [33]
- United Airlines discovered that even colours can doom a product. The airline handed out white carnations when it started flying from Hong Kong, only to discover that, to many Asians, such flowers represent death and bad luck. [34]

Some of these examples might seem humorous, but there's nothing funny about them to managers trying to operate in a highly competitive global environment. What should managers of emerging global companies look for to avoid obvious international mistakes? When they are comparing one country with another, the economic, legal-political and sociocultural sectors present the greatest difficulties. Key factors to understand in the international environment are summarized in Exhibit 4.3.

The Economic Environment

The economic environment represents the economic conditions in the country where the international organization operates. This part of the environment includes such factors as economic development, resource and product markets, and exchange rates, each of which is discussed in the following sections. In addition, factors such as inflation, interest rates and economic growth are also part of the international economic environment.

Economic Development

Economic development differs widely among the countries and regions of the world. Countries can be categorized as either *developing* or *developed*. Developing countries are referred to as *less-developed countries (LDCs)*. The criterion traditionally

Exhibit 4.3 Key Factors in the International Environment

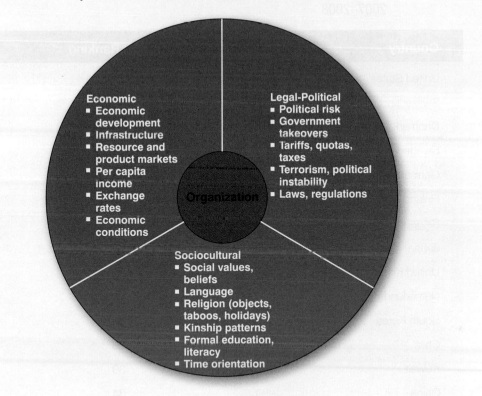

used to classify countries as developed or developing is *per capita income*, which is the income generated by the nation's production of goods and services divided by total population. The developing countries have low *per capita* incomes. Less-developed countries generally are located in Asia, Africa and South America. Developed countries are generally located in North America, Europe and Japan. Most international business firms are headquartered in the wealthier, economically advanced countries, but smart managers are investing heavily in Asia, Eastern Europe, Latin America and Africa.[35] These companies face risks and challenges today, but they stand to reap huge benefits in the future.

Each year, the World Economic Forum analyzes data to gauge how companies are doing in the economic development race and releases its Global Competitiveness Report, which tallies 113 factors that contribute to an economy's competitiveness.[36] The report considers both hard data and perceptions of business leaders around the world and considers government policies, institutions, market size, the sophistication of financial markets, and other factors that drive productivity and thus enable sustained economic growth. Exhibit 4.4 shows the top ten countries in the overall ranking, along with several other countries for comparison. Note that highly developed countries rank higher in the competitiveness index. One important factor in gauging competitiveness is the country's infrastructure, that is, the physical facilities such as highways, airports, utilities and telephone lines that support economic activities. Companies operating in emerging countries must often contend with lower levels of technology and poor logistical, distribution and communication infrastructure. This though can also produce opportunities. For example, Vodafone has found that tough market conditions in Europe have been offset by the performance in emerging markets, which saw sales grow by 40 per cent to £4.3 billion. The largest growth was in Egypt where revenues grew by 33 per cent.

Infrastructure
A country's physical facilities that support economic activities.

Exhibit 4.4 World Economic Forum Global Competitiveness Index 2007–2008

Country	Overall Ranking
United States	1
Switzerland	2
Denmark	3
Sweden	4
Germany	5
Finland	6
Singapore	7
Japan	8
United Kingdom	9
Netherlands	10
South Korea	11
Chile	26
Kuwait	30
China	34
Lithuania	38
South Africa	44
India	48

SOURCE: The Global Competitiveness Report 2007–08, World Economic Forum, http://www.gcr.weforum.org (accessed April 30, 2008).

Resource and Product Markets

When operating in another country, company managers must evaluate the market demand for their products. If market demand is high, managers may choose to export products to that country. To develop plants, however, resource markets for providing needed raw materials and labour must also be available. For example, the greatest challenge for McDonald's, which sells Big Macs on every continent except Antarctica, is to obtain supplies of everything from potatoes to hamburger buns to plastic straws. At McDonald's in Cracow, the burgers come from a Polish plant, partly owned by Chicago-based OSI Industries; the onions come from Fresno, California; the buns come from a production and distribution centre near Moscow; and the potatoes come from a plant in Aldrup, Germany.[37]

Exchange Rates

Exchange rate is the rate at which one country's currency is exchanged for another country's. Volatility in exchange rates is a major concern for companies doing business internationally.[38] Changes in the exchange rate can have major implications for the profitability of international operations that exchange millions of dollars into other currencies every day.[39] For example, assume that the British pound is exchanged for €1.2. If the pound increases in value to €1.3, British goods will be more expensive in France because it will take more euros to buy a pound's worth of UK goods. It will be more difficult to export UK goods to France, and profits will be slim. If the pound drops to a value of €1.1, by contrast, UK goods will be cheaper in France and can be exported at a profit.

The Legal-Political Environment

Businesses must deal with unfamiliar political systems when they go international, as well as with more government supervision and regulation. Government officials and the general public often view foreign companies as outsiders or even intruders and are suspicious of their impact on economic independence and political sovereignty.

Political risk is defined as the risk of loss of assets, earning power or managerial control due to politically-based events or actions by host governments.[40] One example is a new government effort in Russia to tighten financial monitoring. Critics charge that tax authorities demand confidential client information without a legal basis and vary their interpretation of Russian law as it pleases them. PricewaterhouseCoopers has had its Moscow offices raided and was ordered to pay $15 million in back taxes that the firm said it didn't owe.[41] Political risk also includes government takeovers of property and acts of violence directed against a firm's properties or employees. In Mexico, for example, business executives and their families are prime targets for gangs of kidnappers, many of which are reportedly led by state and local police. Estimates are that big companies in Mexico typically spend between 5 and 15 per cent of their annual budgets on security,[42] and organizations in other countries face similar security issues.

Some companies buy political risk insurance, and risk management has emerged as a critical element of management strategy for multinational organizations.[43] To reduce uncertainty, companies sometimes rely on the *Index of Economic Freedom*, which ranks countries according to the impact political intervention has on business decisions, and the *Corruption Perception Index*, which assesses 91 countries according to the level of perceived corruption in government and public administration.[44]

Another frequently cited problem for international companies is **political instability**, which includes riots, revolutions, civil disorders and frequent changes in government. In recent decades, civil wars and large-scale violence occurred in the Ukraine, Indonesia, Thailand, Sri Lanka (Ceylon) and Myanmar (Burma). China is highly vulnerable to periods of widespread public unrest due to the shifting political climate. For instance, nationalist protests against the French supermarket chain Carrefour spread across China in April 2008, with thousands demonstrating outside stores over the West's stance on Tibet. Carrefour appeared to take the blame for France as a whole after a protester in Paris tried to snatch the Olympic flame from a paralympian during the relay, and because of a rumour that the supermarket had donated money to the Dalai Lama. Carrefour denied that it has ever given money to any political or religious cause.[45]

© JOHN VAN HASSELT/SYGMA/CORBIS

CONCEPT CONNECTION While working as a New York investment banker, Bangladesh native Iqbal Quadir realized that connectivity equals productivity. He also knew his impoverished homeland was one of the least connected places on earth. That prompted him to collaborate with countryman Muhammad Yunus, Grameen Bank founder and 2006 Nobel Peace Prize winner, to create Village Phone. Entrepreneurs, mostly women, use Grameen Bank microloans to purchase cell phones. 'Telephone ladies', such as Monwara Begum pictured here, then earn the money to repay the debt by providing phone service to fellow villagers. Village Phone results in thousands of new small businesses, as well as an improved communication infrastructure that makes a wide range of economic development possible.

Political risk
A company's risk of loss of assets, earning power or managerial control due to politically based events or actions by host governments.

Political instability
Events such as riots, revolutions or government upheavals that affect the operations of an international company.

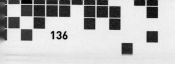

© LOUIE PSIHOYOS/CORBIS

CONCEPT CONNECTION Despite the political risk, political instability and the local laws and regulations of countries such as Morocco, the Coca-Cola Company earns about 80 per cent of its profits from markets outside North America. The soft-drink company suffered in global markets after complaints of tainted products from Belgium bottling plants. Managers are busily trying to rebuild relationships because of the importance of international sales.

The Middle East remains an area of extreme instability as the US and its allies pursues a difficult and protracted reconstruction following the Iraqi war. US firms or companies linked to the US often are subject to major threats in countries characterized by political instability. For example, on the first Muslim holy day after the US began bombings in Afghanistan, thousands of demonstrators in Pakistan set fire to a KFC restaurant as a symbol of America.[46]

Differing laws and regulations also make doing business a true challenge for international firms. Host governments have myriad laws concerning libel statutes, consumer protection, information and labelling, employment and safety, and wages. International companies must learn these rules and regulations and abide by them. In addition, the internet increases the impact of foreign laws on companies because it expands the potential for doing business on a global basis. First Net Card, started in 1999 to provide credit for online transactions to anyone in the world, found the complication of dealing with international credit and banking laws mind-boggling. After two years and a mountain of legal research, the company was licensed to provide credit only in the US, Canada and Britain.[47]

The SocioCultural Environment

A nation's culture includes the shared knowledge, beliefs and values, as well as the common modes of behaviour and ways of thinking among members of a society. Cultural factors can be more perplexing than political and economic factors when working or living in a foreign country.

Social Values

Many managers fail to realize that the values and behaviours that typically govern how business is done in their home market don't translate to the rest of the world. One way managers can get a handle on local cultures is to understand differences in social values.

Hofstede's Value Dimensions In research that included 116 000 IBM employees in 40 countries, Geert Hofstede identified four dimensions of national value systems that influence organizational and employee working relationships.[48] Examples of how countries rate on the four dimensions are shown in Exhibit 4.5.

Power distance
The degree to which people accept inequality in power among institutions, organizations and people.

Uncertainty avoidance
A value characterized by people's intolerance for uncertainty and ambiguity and resulting support for beliefs that promise certainty and conformity.

Individualism
A preference for a loosely knit social framework in which individuals are expected to take care of themselves.

1 *Power distance.* High power distance means that people accept inequality in power among institutions, organizations and people. Low power distance means that people expect equality in power. Countries that value high power distance are Malaysia, the Philippines and Panama. Countries that value low power distance are Denmark, Austria and Israel.

2 *Uncertainty avoidance.* High uncertainty avoidance means that members of a society feel uncomfortable with uncertainty and ambiguity and thus support beliefs that promise certainty and conformity. Low uncertainty avoidance means that people have high tolerance for the unstructured, the unclear and the unpredictable. High uncertainty avoidance countries include Greece, Portugal and Uruguay. Countries with low uncertainty avoidance values are Singapore and Jamaica.

3 *Individualism and collectivism.* Individualism reflects a value for a loosely knit social framework in which individuals are expected to take care of themselves.

Exhibit 4.5 Rank Orderings of Ten Countries along Four Dimensions of National Value Systems

Country	Power Distance[a]	Uncertainty Avoidance[b]	Individualism[c]	Masculinity[d]
Australia	7	7	2	5
Costa Rica	8 (tie)	2 (tie)	10	9
France	3	2 (tie)	4	7
West Germany	8 (tie)	5	5	3
India	2	9	6	6
Japan	5	1	7	1
Mexico	1	4	8	2
Sweden	10	10	3	10
Thailand	4	6	9	8
United States	6	8	1	4

a = highest power distance   b = highest uncertainty avoidance
10 = lowest power distance   10 = lowest uncertainty avoidance
c = highest individualism   d = highest masculinity
10 = lowest individualism   10 = lowest masculinity

SOURCE: Dorothy Marcic, *Organizational Behaviour and Cases*, 4th ed. (St. Paul, MN: West, 1995). Based on two books by Geert Hofstede: *Culture's Consequences* (London: Sage Publications, 1984) and *Cultures and Organizations: Software of the Mind* (New York: McGraw-Hill, 1991).

Collectivism means a preference for a tightly knit social framework in which individuals look after one another and organizations protect their members' interests. Countries with individualist values include the US, Canada, Great Britain and Australia. Countries with collectivist values are Guatemala, Ecuador and China.

4 *Masculinity/femininity.* Masculinity stands for preference for achievement, heroism, assertiveness, work centrality (with resultant high stress) and material success. Femininity reflects the values of relationships, cooperation, group decision-making and quality of life. Societies with strong masculine values are Japan, Austria, Mexico and Germany. Countries with feminine values are Sweden, Norway, Denmark and France. Both men and women subscribe to the dominant value in masculine and feminine cultures.

Hofstede and his colleagues later identified a fifth dimension, long-term orientation versus short-term orientation. The long-term orientation, found in China and other Asian countries, includes a greater concern for the future and highly values thrift and perseverance. A short-term orientation, found in Russia and West Africa, is more concerned with the past and the present and places a high value on tradition and meeting social obligations.[49] Researchers continue to explore and expand on Hofstede's findings. For example, in the last 25 years, more than 1400 articles and numerous books were published on individualism and collectivism alone.[50]

Collectivism
A preference for a tightly knit social framework in which individuals look after one another and organizations protect their members' interests.

Masculinity
A cultural preference for achievement, heroism, assertiveness, work centrality and material success.

Femininity
A cultural preference for relationships, cooperation, group decision-making and quality of life.

Long-term orientation
A greater concern for the future and high value on thrift and perseverance.

Short-term orientation
A concern with the past and present and a high value on meeting social obligations.

c. Saudi Arabia

d. China

e. United States

8 In many Asian cultures, a direct order such as 'Get me the Amex report' is most likely to be given by:

a. Senior management to most subordinates

b. A junior employee to a peer

c. Senior management only to very junior employees

d. Junior employees to outsiders

e. None of the above

9 In the United States, scratching one's head usually means that the person is confused or sceptical. In Russia, it means:

a. 'You're crazy!'

b. 'I am listening carefully'

c. 'I want to get to know you better'

d. 'I'm confused or sceptical'

e. None of the above

10 A polite way to give your business card to a Japanese businessperson is:

a. Casually, after several hours of getting to know the person

b. When first meeting, presenting your card with both hands

c. At the very end of the first meeting

d. Casually during the meeting, with the information down to show humility

e. Never; it is considered rude in Japan to give business cards

SOURCES Steven L. McShane and Mary Ann Von Glinow, *Organizational Behaviour: Emerging Realities for the Workplace Revolution,* 3rd ed. (New York: McGraw-Hill/Irwin, 2004); 'Cross-Cultural Communication Game', developed by Steven L. McShane, based on material in R. Axtell, *Gestures: The Do's and Taboos of Body Language Around the World* (New York: Wiley, 1991); R. Mead, *Cross-Cultural Management Communication* (Chichester, UK: Wiley, 1990), chapter 7; and J. V. Thill and C. L. Bovée, *Excellence in Business Communication* (New York: McGraw-Hill, 1995), chapter 17.

Answers

1. e; 2. d; 3. d; 4. b; 5. c; 6. d; 7. c; 8. c; 9. d; 10. b

Exhibit 4.6 gives examples of how some countries rank on several of the GLOBE dimensions. These dimensions give managers an added tool for identifying and managing cultural differences. Although Hofstede's dimensions are still valid, the GLOBE research provides a more comprehensive view of cultural similarities and differences.

Social values greatly influence organizational functioning and management styles. Consider the difficulty that managers encountered when implementing self-directed work teams in Mexico. As shown in Exhibit 4.5, Mexico is characterized by very high power distance and a relatively low tolerance for uncertainty, characteristics that often conflict with the American concept of teamwork, which emphasizes shared power and authority, with team members working on a variety of problems without formal guidelines, rules and structure. Many workers in Mexico, as well as in France and Mediterranean countries, expect organizations to be hierarchical. In Russia, people are good at working in groups and like competing as a team rather than on an individual basis. Organizations in Germany and other central European countries typically strive to be impersonal, well-oiled machines. Effective management styles differ in each country, depending on cultural characteristics.[52]

Exhibit 4.6 Examples of Country Rankings on Selected GLOBE Value Dimensions

Dimension	Low	Medium	High
Assertiveness	Sweden	Egypt	Spain
	Switzerland	Iceland	United States
	Japan	France	Germany (former East)
Future Orientation	Russia	Slovenia	Denmark
	Italy	Australia	Canada
	Kuwait	India	Singapore
Gender Differentiation	Sweden	Italy	South Korea
	Denmark	Brazil	Egypt
	Poland	Netherlands	China
Performance Orientation	Russia	Israel	United States
	Greece	England	Taiwan
	Venezuela	Japan	Hong Kong
Humane Orientation	Germany	New Zealand	Indonesia
	France	Sweden	Egypt
	Singapore	United States	Iceland

SOURCE: Mansour Javidan and Robert J. House, 'Cultural Acumen for the Global Manager: Lessons from Project GLOBE', *Organizational Dynamics* 29, no. 4 (2001): 289–305.

TAKE A MOMENT

As a new manager, remember that understanding national culture is as important as paying attention to economic and political matters when working in or with a foreign country. Prepare yourself by studying how the foreign country's social and cultural values compare to your own country. Avoid an ethnocentric attitude and recognize how the ethnocentrism of others may affect your perspective or work attitudes.

Communication Differences

People from some cultures tend to pay more attention to the social context (social setting, nonverbal behaviour, social status) of their verbal communication than Americans do. For example, American managers working in China have discovered that social context is considerably more important in that culture, and they need to learn to suppress their impatience and devote the time necessary to establish personal and social relationships.

Exhibit 4.7 indicates how the emphasis on social context varies among countries. In a **high-context culture**, people are sensitive to circumstances surrounding social exchanges. People use communication primarily to build personal social relationships; meaning is derived from context – setting, status and non-verbal behaviour – more than from explicit words; relationships and trust are more important than business; and the welfare and harmony of the group are valued. In a **low-context culture**, people use communication primarily to exchange facts and information; meaning is derived primarily from words; business transactions are more important than building relationships and trust; and individual welfare and achievement are more important than the group.[53]

High-context culture
A culture in which communication is used to enhance personal relationships.

Low-context culture
A culture in which communication is used to exchange facts and information.

GATT and the World Trade Organization

The General Agreement on Tariffs and Trade (GATT), signed by 23 nations in 1947, started as a set of rules to ensure non-discrimination, clear procedures, the negotiation of disputes, and the participation of lesser-developed countries in international trade.[56] GATT sponsored eight rounds of international trade negotiations aimed at reducing trade restrictions. The 1986 to 1994 Uruguay Round (the first to be named for a developing country) involved 125 countries and cut more tariffs than ever before. In addition to lowering tariffs 30 per cent from the previous level, it boldly moved the world closer to global free trade by calling for the establishment of the World Trade Organization (WTO).

The WTO represents the maturation of GATT into a permanent global institution that can monitor international trade and has legal authority to arbitrate disputes on some 400 trade issues. As of July 2007, 151 countries, including China (but not Russia), were members of the WTO. As of 2009, 153 countries, representing more than 95 per cent of total world trade, and including China (but not Russia), were members of the WTO. As a permanent membership organization, the WTO is bringing greater trade liberalization in goods, information, technological developments and services; stronger enforcement of rules and regulations; and greater power to resolve disputes among trading partners.

European Union

An alliance begun in 1957 to improve economic and social conditions among its members, the European Economic Community has evolved into the 27-nation European Union (EU) illustrated in Exhibit 4.8. The biggest expansion came in 2004, when the EU welcomed ten new members from southern and eastern Europe.[57]

The goal of the EU is to create a powerful single market system for Europe's millions of consumers, allowing people, goods and services to move freely. The increased competition and economies of scale within Europe enable companies to grow large and efficient, becoming more competitive in the US and other world markets. Some observers fear that the EU will become a trade barrier, creating a *fortress Europe* that will be difficult to penetrate by companies in other nations.

Euro
A single European currency that replaced the currencies of 15 European nations.

Another aspect of significance to countries operating globally is the introduction of the euro. Sixteen Member States of the EU have adopted the euro, a single European currency that replaced national currencies in Austria, Belgium, Cyprus, Finland, France, Germany, Greece, Ireland, Italy, Luxembourg, Malta, the Netherlands, Portugal, Slovakia, Slovenia and Spain. However, the UK, Sweden and Denmark have so far decided not to adopt the euro.

Consequently, as of 2009 the euro is used daily by some 329 million Europeans, while a further 175 million people worldwide use currencies which are pegged to the euro, including more than 150 million people in Africa. Several other EU countries are using the euro under formal agreements, although they haven't yet met all the conditions to officially adopt the single currency.[58] The implications of a single European currency are therefore enormous, within as well as outside Europe. Because it potentially replaces up to 27 European domestic currencies, the euro will affect legal contracts, financial management, sales and marketing tactics, manufacturing, distribution, payroll, pensions, training, taxes, and information management systems. Every corporation that does business in or with EU countries will feel the impact.[59]

North American Free Trade Agreement (NAFTA)

The North American Free Trade Agreement (NAFTA), which went into effect on January 1, 1994, merged the US, Canada and Mexico into the world's largest trading

Exhibit 4.8 The Nations of the European Union

bloc with more than 421 million consumers. Intended to spur growth and investment, increase exports and expand jobs in all three nations, NAFTA broke down tariffs and trade restrictions over a 15-year-period in a number of key areas. Thus, by 2008, virtually all US industrial exports into Canada and Mexico were duty-free.

Over the first decade of NAFTA, US trade with Mexico increased more than threefold, while trade with Canada also rose dramatically.[60] Significantly, NAFTA spurred the entry of small businesses into the global arena. Jeff Victor, general manager of Treatment Products, Ltd, which makes car cleaners and waxes, credits NAFTA for his surging export volume. Prior to the pact, Mexican tariffs as high as 20 per cent made it impossible for the Chicago-based company to expand its presence south of the border.[61]

However, opinions over the benefits of NAFTA appear to be as divided as they were when talks began, with some people calling it a spectacular success and others referring to it as a dismal failure.[62] Although NAFTA has not lived up to its grand expectations, experts stress that it increased trade, investment and income and continues to enable companies in all three countries to compete more effectively with rival Asian and European firms.[63]

Other Trade Alliances

The creation of trading blocs is an increasingly important aspect of international business. The Association of Southeast Asian Nations (ASEAN) is a trading alliance of ten Southeast Asian nations, including Cambodia, Vietnam, Singapore, Malaysia, Indonesia, Thailand and the Philippines. This region will likely be one of the fastest-growing economic regions of the world, and the ASEAN could eventually be as powerful as the European Union and NAFTA.

A free trade bloc known as Mercosur encompasses Argentina, Brazil, Bolivia, Chile, Columbia, Ecuador, Paraguay, Peru and Uruguay. The Central America Free Trade Agreement (CAFTA), which rolled out in 2006, lowers tariffs and eases regulations between the US, the Dominican Republic, Guatemala, Honduras, Nicaragua and El Salvador, with Costa Rica pending. And more than 30 countries in the Americas are negotiating to establish a hemisphere-wide trade agreement, the Free Trade Area of the Americas (FTAA). These agreements entail a new future for international companies, and both corporations and managers will be affected by these important trends.

The Globalization Backlash

As the world becomes increasingly interconnected, a backlash over globalization is occurring. In a *Fortune* magazine poll, 68 per cent of Americans say other countries benefit the most from free trade. The sentiment is reflected in other countries such as Germany, France and even India. 'For some reason, everyone thinks they are the loser', said former US trade representative Mickey Kantor.[64]

The primary concern is the loss of jobs as companies expand their offshoring activities by exporting more and more work overseas. Consider, for example, that Boeing uses aeronautical specialists in Russia to design luggage bins and wing parts for planes. They make about $650 a month, compared to a counterpart in the US making $6000.[65] The transfer of jobs such as making shoes, clothing and toys began two decades ago. Today, services and knowledge work are rapidly moving to developing countries. A 2004 study by analyst group Forrester Research concluded that more than one million jobs in Europe will move offshore by 2015. Principal analyst Andrew Parker, says that the UK will lead the migration. 'As European firms – especially in the UK – ramp up their spending with offshore service providers in countries like India', he says, 'they will increasingly displace substantial numbers of employees from their current roles'. According to the report, by 2015, the number of jobs being exported overseas annually will increase to 760 000, suggesting that 3 per cent of all UK jobs will be outsourced offshore every year.

Following the UK will be Germany, France, the Netherlands and Italy. Countries such as Ireland, Greece and Portugal face far lower employment impacts from the trend since companies in these countries show a far lower tendency to adopt offshore outsourcing as a budget option. Also, in many respects such countries act as low-cost IT and service locations in their own right.[66]

Many American shoppers say they'd be willing to pay higher prices to keep down foreign competition. President Barack Obama tapped into strong sentiments when he declared, 'People don't want a cheaper T-shirt if they're losing a job in the process.'[67]

Business leaders, meanwhile, insist that economic benefits flow back to the outsourcing economy in the form of lower

CONCEPT CONNECTION Protesters shout slogans during a demonstration against the World Trade Organization outside a hotel in Jakarta, Indonesia, February 2007. Hundreds of activists held a demonstration to protest the visit of WTO director general Pascal Lamy and to urge the Indonesian government not to waiver on its stance favouring product exemptions. With increased globalization has come a globalization backlash, with most groups thinking other groups and countries benefit more from international trade.

© MICHAEL GOTTSCHALK/GETTY IMAGES

prices, expanded markets and increased profits that can fund innovation.[68] Some American companies are clearly benefiting from free trade. When Kalexsyn, a small chemistry research company in Kalamazoo, Michigan, couldn't get contracts with major US pharmaceutical companies that were sending work to India and China, the owners found that European companies were eager to outsource chemical research to the US.[69] US exports grew 12 per cent in 2006, based partly on the need for equipment and supplies for building infrastructure in place such as China, Brazil and India.[70] In the end, it is not whether globalization is good or bad, but how business and government managers can work together to ensure that the advantages of a global world are fully and fairly shared.[71]

Multinational Corporations

The size and volume of international businesses are so large that they are hard to comprehend. For example, the value added (the sum of total wages, pre-tax profits, and depreciation and amortization) of ExxonMobil is comparable to the gross national product (GNP) of the Czech Republic. The value added of Wal-Mart is comparable to the size of Peru's GNP, and that of Toyota to the GNP of Kuwait.[72]

As discussed earlier in this chapter, a large volume of international business is being carried out in a seemingly borderless world by large international businesses that can be thought of as *global corporations, stateless corporations* or *transnational corporations*. In the business world, these large international firms typically are called *multinational corporations (MNCs)*, which have been the subject of enormous attention. MNCs can move a wealth of assets from country to country and influence national economies, politics, and cultures.

Although the term has no precise definition, a multinational corporation (MNC) typically receives more than 25 per cent of its total sales revenues from operations outside the parent's home country. A recent report indicates that by 2007 as much 42 per cent of the global sales of US manufacturing multinationals came from sales by their foreign affiliates.[73] MNCs also have the following distinctive managerial characteristics:

1 An MNC is managed as an integrated worldwide business system in which foreign affiliates act in close alliance and cooperation with one another. Capital, technology and people are transferred among country affiliates. The MNC can acquire materials and manufacture parts wherever in the world it is most advantageous to do so.

2 An MNC is ultimately controlled by a single management authority that makes key strategic decisions relating to the parent and all affiliates. Although some headquarters are *binational*, such as the Royal Dutch/Shell Group, some centralization of management is required to maintain worldwide integration and profit maximization for the enterprise as a whole.

3 MNC top managers are presumed to exercise a global perspective. They regard the entire world as one market for strategic decisions, resource acquisition, and location of production, advertising and marketing efficiency.

Multinational corporation (MNC)
An organization that receives more than 25 per cent of its total sales revenues from operations outside the parent company's home country; also called global corporation or *transnational corporation*.

© DAVID PEARSON/ALAMY

CONCEPT CONNECTION The new McItaly Burger served at this McDonald's in Milan, Italy, represents how this multinational corporation changed its business model by decentralizing its operations. When McDonald's initiated international units, it copied what it did and sold in the US. Today, though, the fast-food giant seeks local managers who understand the culture and laws of each country. As illustrated in the photograph, McDonald's country managers have the freedom to use different furnishings and develop new products to suit local tastes.

© CANCAN CHU/GETTY IMAGES

CONCEPT CONNECTION International markets provide many opportunities but are also fraught with difficulty. Dell Inc., described at the beginning of this chapter, has enjoyed significant success translating its direct-sales business model to other countries. However, Dell was unprepared for the difficulties it is facing in China and is outgunned at the moment by Lenovo, which has a 20.4 per cent market share in Asia and 4800 retail outlets in China alone.

In a few cases, the MNC management philosophy may differ from that just described. For example, some researchers have distinguished among *ethnocentric companies*, which place emphasis on their home countries, *polycentric companies*, which are oriented toward the markets of individual foreign host countries, and *geocentric companies*, which are truly world oriented and favour no specific country.[74] The truly global companies that transcend national boundaries are growing in number. These companies no longer see themselves as British, American, Chinese or German; they operate globally and serve a global market.

As discussed in Chapter 1, some observers believe Lenovo could eventually challenge Dell's lead on a global basis, which illustrates the growing power of Chinese companies in international business. Behind the scenes, Lenovo is scrambling to cut its costs to match Dell's efficiency and has begun dealing with large customers directly rather than through distributors. For its part, Dell has stuck to its direct sales model and is going it alone in China, whereas other computer manufacturers have forged joint ventures with local companies. Dell's strategy has been fairly successful as the company focuses on large business and government customers in major cities. However, observers believe that as Dell starts courting consumers and businesses in smaller cities, where demand is growing faster, it will run into more trouble competing with Lenovo.

Direct sales in China are currently a problem because few Chinese customers use credit cards, for example. Dell is loath to break with its successful model, but somehow establishing 'a presence on the street' through kiosks or retailers, or perhaps by partnering with a local company, may be necessary for Dell to compete successfully with the home-town leader in this new market.

Managing in a Global Environment

New managers who want their careers to move forward recognize the importance of global experience.[75] But working in a foreign country can present tremendous personal and organizational challenges. A clue to the complexity of working internationally comes from a study of the factors that contribute to global manager failures. Based on extensive interviews with global managers, researchers found that personal traits, the specific cultural context or management mistakes made by the organization could all contribute to failure in an international assignment.[76]

TAKE A MOMENT   Before reading the next section, find out your CQ (cultural intelligence) by answering the questions in the New Manager Self-Test on page 151. Your answers will indicate your level of cultural intelligence and help you relate to the concepts that follow. As a new manager, begin soon to develop cultural intelligence so you can work effectively with people from other countries.

Developing Cultural Intelligence

Managers will be most successful in foreign assignments if they are culturally flexible and able to adapt easily to new situations and ways of doing things. In other words, managers working internationally need cultural intelligence.

Cultural intelligence (CQ) refers to a person's ability to use reasoning and observation skills to interpret unfamiliar gestures and situations and devise appropriate behavioural responses.[77]

It is important for a manager working in a foreign country to study the language and learn as much as possible about local norms, customs, beliefs and taboos. However, that information alone cannot prepare the manager for every conceivable situation. Developing a high level of CQ enables a person to interpret unfamiliar situations and adapt quickly. Rather than a list of global 'dos and don'ts', CQ is a practical learning approach that enables a person to ferret out clues to a culture's shared understandings and respond to new situations in culturally appropriate ways. Consider what Pat McGovern does whenever he travels to a foreign country. McGovern is the founder and CEO of IDG, a technology publishing and research firm in Massachusetts that owns magazines such as *CIO* and *Computerworld*. IDG operates in 85 countries and gets 80 per cent of profits from outside the US. When McGovern goes to country for the first time, he spends the weekend just wandering around observing people. By watching how people in a foreign country behave, McGovern says he gets a sense of the culture – how fast people walk, how much they gesture, what they wear, how the treat one another.[78] McGovern believes you can be in sync anywhere if you pay attention.

Cultural intelligence includes three components that work together: cognitive, emotional, and physical.[79] The cognitive component involves a person's observational and learning skills and the ability to pick up on clues to understanding. The emotional aspect concerns one's self-confidence and self-motivation. A manager has to believe in his or her ability to understand and assimilate into a different culture. Difficulties and setbacks are triggers to work harder, not a cause to give up. Working in a foreign environment is stressful, and most managers in foreign assignments face a period of homesickness, loneliness and culture shock as a result of being suddenly immersed in a culture with completely different languages, foods, values, beliefs and ways of doing things. **Culture shock** refers to the frustration and anxiety that result from constantly being subjected to strange and unfamiliar cues about what to do and how to do it. A person with high CQ is able to move quickly through this initial period of culture shock.

The third component of CQ, the physical, refers to a person's ability to shift his or her speech patterns, expressions and body language to be in tune with people from a different culture. Most managers aren't equally strong in all three areas, but maximizing cultural intelligence requires that they draw upon all three facets. In a sense, CQ requires that the head, heart and body work in concert.

High CQ also requires that a manager be open and receptive to new ideas and approaches. One study found that people who adapt to global management most easily are those who have grown up learning how to understand, empathize and work with others who are different from themselves. For example, Singaporeans consistently hear English and Chinese spoken side by side. The Dutch have to learn English, German and French, as well as Dutch, to interact and trade with their economically dominant neighbours. English Canadians must not only be well-versed in American culture and politics, but they also have to consider the views and ideas of French Canadians, who, in turn, must learn to think like North Americans, members of a global French community, Canadians, and Quebecois.[80] People in the UK or US who have grown up without this kind of language and cultural diversity typically have more difficulties with foreign assignments, but willing managers from any country can learn to open their minds and appreciate other viewpoints.

Cultural intelligence (CQ)
A person's ability to use reasoning and observation skills to interpret unfamiliar gestures and situations and devise appropriate behavioural responses.

Culture shock
Feelings of confusion, disorientation, and anxiety that result from being immersed in a foreign culture.

Managing Cross-Culturally

Which two of the following three items go together: a panda, a banana and a monkey? If you said a monkey and a banana, you answered like a majority of Asians; if you said a panda and a monkey, you answered like a majority of people in Western Europe and the US. Where Westerners see distinct categories (animals), Asians see relationships (monkeys eat bananas).[81] Although this test is not definitive, it serves to illustrate an important fact for managers. The cultural differences in how people think and see the world affect working relationships. To be effective on an international level, managers need to interpret the culture of the country and organization in which they are working and develop the sensitivity required to avoid making costly cultural blunders.[82]

In addition to developing cultural intelligence, managers can prepare for foreign assignments by understanding how the country differs in terms of the Hofstede and GLOBE social values discussed earlier in this chapter. These values greatly influence how a manager should interact with subordinates and colleagues in the new assignment. For example, the US scores extremely high on individualism, and a US manager working in a country such as Japan, which scores high on collectivism, will have to modify his or her approach to leading and controlling to be successful. The following examples are broad generalizations, but they give some clues to how expatriate managers can be more successful. **Expatriates** are employees who live and work in a country other than their own.

Expatriates
Employees who live and work in a country other than their own.

Human Resources

Not every manager will thrive in an international assignment, and careful screening, selection, and training of employees to serve overseas increase the potential for corporate global success. Human resource managers consider global skills in the selection process. In addition, expatriates receive cross-cultural training that develops language skills and provides cultural and historical orientation.[83] Equally important is honest self-analysis by overseas candidates and their families. Before seeking or accepting an assignment in another country, a candidate should ask himself or herself such questions as the following:

■ Can you initiate social contacts in a foreign culture?
■ Can you adjust well to different environments and changes in personal comfort or quality of living, such as the lack of television, limited hot water, varied cuisine and national phone strikes?
■ Can you manage your future re-entry into the job market by networking and maintaining contacts in your home country?[84]

Employees working overseas must adjust to all of these conditions. In addition, managers going global often find that their management styles need adjustment to succeed in a country other than their native one.

TAKE A MOMENT   Complete the Experiential Exercise on pages 154 that pertains to your global management potential. How well do your knowledge and preferences reflect a global perspective?

Leading

In relationship-oriented societies that rank high on collectivism, such as those in Asia, the Arab world and Latin America, leaders typically use a warm, personalized approach with employees. One of the greatest difficulties US or UK leaders

NEW MANAGER SELF-TEST

Are You Culturally Intelligent?

The job of a manager demands a lot, and before long your activities will include situations that will test your knowledge and capacity for dealing with people from other national cultures. Are you ready? To find out, think about your experiences in other countries or with people from other countries. To what extent does each of the following statements characterize your behaviour? Please answer each of the following items as Mostly True or Mostly False for you.

	Mostly True	Mostly False
1 I plan how I'm going to relate to people from a different culture before I meet them.	☐	☐
2 I understand the religious beliefs of other cultures.	☐	☐
3 I understand the rules for nonverbal behaviour in other cultures.	☐	☐
4 I seek out opportunities to interact with people from different cultures.	☐	☐
5 I can handle the stresses of living in a different culture with relative ease.	☐	☐
6 I am confident that I can befriend locals in a culture that is unfamiliar to me.	☐	☐
7 I change my speech style (e.g. accent, tone) when a cross-cultural interaction requires it.	☐	☐
8 I alter my facial expressions and gestures as needed to facilitate a cross-culture interaction.	☐	☐
9 I am quick to change the way I behave when a cross-culture encounter seems to require it.	☐	☐

SCORING AND INTERPRETATION Each question pertains to some aspect of cultural intelligence. Questions 1–3 pertain to the head (*cognitive CQ* subscale), questions 4–6 to the heart (*emotional CQ* subscale), and questions 7–9 to behaviour (*physical CQ* subscale). If you have sufficient international experience and CQ to have answered 'Mostly True' to two of three questions for each subscale or six of nine for all the questions, then consider yourself at a high level of CQ for a new manager. If you scored one or fewer 'Mostly True' on each subscale or three or fewer for all nine questions, it is time to learn more about other national cultures. Hone your observational skills and learn to pick up on clues about how people from a different country respond to various situations.

SOURCES Based on P. Christopher Earley and Elaine Mosakowski, 'Cultural Intelligence', *Harvard Business Review* (October 2004): 139–146; and Soon Ang, Lynn Van Dyne, Christine Koh, K. Yee Ng, Klaus J. Templer, Cheryl Tay, and N. Anand Chandrasekar, 'Cultural Intelligence: Its Measurement and Effects on Cultural Judgment and Decision-Making, Cultural Adaptation and Task Performance', *Management and Organization Review* 3 (2007): 335–371.

encounter in doing business in China, for example, is failing to recognize that to the Chinese any relationship is a personal relationship.[85] Managers are expected to have periodic social visits with workers, inquiring about morale and health. Leaders should be especially careful about how and in what context they criticize others.

To Asians, Africans, Arabs, and Latin Americans, the loss of self-respect brings dishonour to themselves and their families. The principle of *saving face* is highly important in some cultures.

Decision-making

In the United Kingdom, mid-level managers may discuss a problem and give the boss a recommendation. On the other hand, managers in Iran, which reflects South Asian cultural values, expect the boss to make a decision and issue specific instructions.[86] In Mexico, employees often don't understand participatory decision-making. Mexico ranks extremely high on power distance, and many workers expect managers to exercise their power in making decisions and issuing orders. American managers working in Mexico have been advised to rarely explain a decision, lest workers perceive this as a sign of weakness.[87] In contrast, managers in many Arab and African nations are expected to use consultative decision-making in the extreme.

Motivating

Motivation must fit the incentives within the culture. Recent data from Towers Perrin give some insight into what motivates people in different countries based on what potential employees say they want most from the company. In the US, competitive base pay is considered most important, whereas prospective employees in Brazil look for career opportunities. In China, people want chances to learn, and employees in Spain put work-life balance at the top of their list.[88] Another study also found that intrinsic factors such as challenge, recognition and the work itself are less effective in countries that value high power distance. It may be that workers in these cultures perceive manager recognition and support as manipulative and therefore demotivating.[89] A high value for collectivism in Japan means that employees are motivated in groups. An individual bonus for a high performer would be considered humiliating, but a reward for the team could be highly motivating. Managers in Latin America, Africa and the Middle East can improve motivation by showing respect for employees as individuals with needs and interests outside of work.[90]

Controlling

When things go wrong, managers in foreign countries often are unable to get rid of employees who do not work out. Consider the following research finding: when asked what to do about an employee whose work had been sub-standard for a year after 15 years of exemplary performance, 75 per cent of Americans and Canadians said fire her; only 20 per cent of Singaporeans and Koreans chose that solution.[91] In Europe, Mexico and Indonesia, as well, to hire and fire based on performance seems unnaturally brutal. In addition, workers in some countries are protected by strong labour laws and union rules.

Managers also have to learn not to control the wrong things. A Sears manager in Hong Kong insisted that employees come to work on time instead of 15 minutes late. The employees did exactly as they were told, but they also left on time instead of working into the evening as they had previously. A lot of work was left unfinished. The manager eventually told the employees to go back to their old ways. His attempt at control had a negative effect.

A MANAGER'S ESSENTIALS: WHAT HAVE WE LEARNED?

- Successful companies are expanding their business overseas and successfully competing with foreign companies on their home turf. International markets provide many opportunities but are also fraught with difficulty.

- Major alternatives for entering foreign markets are outsourcing exporting, licensing, and direct investing through joint ventures or wholly owned subsidiaries.

- Business in the global arena involves special risks and difficulties because of complicated economic, legal-political and sociocultural forces. Moreover, the global environment changes rapidly, as illustrated by the emergence of the World Trade Organization, the European Union, ASEAN, and the North American Free Trade Agreement.

- The expansion of free-trade policies has sparked a globalization backlash among people who are fearful of losing their jobs and economic security.

- Much of the growth in international business has been carried out by large businesses called multinational corporations (MNC). These large companies exist in an almost borderless world, encouraging the free flow of ideas, products, manufacturing and marketing among countries to achieve the greatest efficiencies.

- Managers in MNCs as well as those in much smaller companies doing business internationally face many challenges and must develop a high level of cultural intelligence (CQ) to be successful. CQ, which involves a cognitive component (head), an emotional component (heart) and a physical component (body), helps managers interpret unfamiliar situations and devise culturally appropriate responses.

- Social and cultural values differ widely across cultures and influence appropriate patterns of leadership, decision-making, motivation, and managerial control.

DISCUSSION QUESTIONS

1 What specifically would the experience of living and working in another country contribute to your skills and effectiveness as a manager in your own country?

2 What might be some long-term ramifications of the war in Iraq for UK and/or French managers and companies operating internationally?

3 What do you think is your strongest component of cultural intelligence? Your weakest? How would you go about shoring up your weaknesses?

4 What steps could a company take to avoid making product design and marketing mistakes when introducing new products into India? How would you go about hiring a plant manager for a facility you are planning to build in India?

5 Compare the advantages associated with the foreign-market entry strategies of exporting, outsourcing, licensing and wholly owned subsidiaries. What information would you need to collect and what factors would you consider when selecting a strategy?

6 Should a multinational corporation operate as a tightly integrated, worldwide business system, or would it be more effective to let each national subsidiary operate autonomously?

7 How might the globalization backlash affect you as a future manager or the company for which you work?

8 A Russian and a Swedish company are competing to take over a large factory in the Czech Republic. One delegation tours the facility and asks questions about how the plant might be run more efficiently. The other delegation focuses on ways to improve working conditions and produce a better product. Which delegation do you think is more likely to succeed with the plant? Why? What information would you want to collect to decide whether to acquire the plant for your company?

9 Which style of communicating do you think would be most beneficial to the long-term success of a British company operating internationally – high-context or low-context communications? Why?

10 How might the social value of low versus high power distance influence how you would lead and motivate employees? What about the value of low versus high performance orientation?

11 How do you think trade alliances such as NAFTA, the EU, and ASEAN might affect you as a future manager?

MANAGEMENT IN PRACTICE: EXPERIENTIAL EXERCISE

Rate Your Global Management Potential

A global environment requires that managers learn to deal effectively with people and ideas from a variety of cultures. How well-prepared are you to be a global manager? Read the following statements and circle the number on the response scale that most closely reflects how well the statement describes you.

Good   10 9 8 7 6 5 4 3 2 1 Poor
Description   Description

1 I reach out to people from different cultures.

10 9 8 7 6 5 4 3 2 1

2 I frequently attend seminars and lectures about other cultures or international topics.

10 9 8 7 6 5 4 3 2 1

3 I believe female expatriates can be equally as effective as male expatriates.

10 9 8 7 6 5 4 3 2 1

4 I have a basic knowledge about several countries in addition to my native country.

10 9 8 7 6 5 4 3 2 1

5 I have good listening and empathy skills.

10 9 8 7 6 5 4 3 2 1

6 I have spent more than two weeks travelling or working in another country.

10 9 8 7 6 5 4 3 2 1

7 I easily adapt to the different work ethics of students from other cultures when we are involved in a team project.

10 9 8 7 6 5 4 3 2 1

8 I can speak a foreign language.

10 9 8 7 6 5 4 3 2 1

9 I know which countries tend to cluster into similar sociocultural and economic groupings.

10 9 8 7 6 5 4 3 2 1

10 I feel capable of assessing different cultures on the basis of power distance, uncertainty avoidance, individualism, and masculinity.

10 9 8 7 6 5 4 3 2 1

Total Score: _____

Scoring and Interpretation

Add up the total points for the ten questions. If you scored 81–100 points, you have a great capacity for developing good global management skills. A score of 61–80 points indicates that you have potential but may lack skills in certain areas, such as language or foreign experience. A score of 60 or less means you need to do some serious work to improve your potential for global management. Regardless of your total score, go back over each item and make a plan of action to increase scores of less than five on any question.

SOURCE Based in part on 'How Well Do You Exhibit Good Inter-cultural Management Skills?', in John W. Newstrom and Keith Davis, *Organizational Behaviour: Human Behaviour at Work* (Boston, MA: McGraw-Hill Irwin, 2002), pp. 415–416.

MANAGEMENT IN PRACTICE: ETHICAL DILEMMA

AH Biotech

Dr Abraham Hassan knew he couldn't put off the decision any longer. AH Biotech, the pharmaceutical company started up by this psychiatrist-turned-entrepreneur, had developed a novel drug that seemed to promise long-term relief from panic attacks. If it gained FDA approval, it would be the company's first product. It was now time for large-scale clinical trials. But where should AH Biotech conduct those tests?

David Berger, who headed up research and development, was certain he already knew the answer to that question: Albania. 'Look, doing these trials in Albania will be quicker, easier and a lot cheaper than doing them in the EU or the States', he pointed out. 'What's not to like'?

Dr Hassan had to concede Berger's arguments were sound. If they did trials in the EU or US, AH Biotech would spend considerable time and money advertising for patients and then finding physicians who'd be willing to serve as clinical trial investigators. Rounding up doctors prepared to take on that job was getting increasingly difficult. They just didn't want to take time out of their busy practices to do the testing, not to mention all the recordkeeping such a study entailed.

In Albania, it was an entirely different story. It was one of the poorest Eastern European countries, if not *the* poorest, with a just barely functioning health-care system. Albanian physicians and patients would practically arrive at AH Biotech's doorstep asking to take part. Physicians there could earn much better money as clinical investigators for a pharmaceutical company than they could actually practicing medicine, and patients saw signing up as test subjects as their best chance for receiving any treatment at all, let alone cutting-edge Western medicine. All of these factors meant that the company could count on realizing at least a 25 per cent savings, maybe more, by running the tests overseas.

What's not to like? As the Egyptian-born CEO of a start-up biotech company with investors and employees hoping for its first marketable drug, there was absolutely nothing not to like. It was when he thought like a US-trained physician that he felt qualms. If he used US or EU test subjects, he knew they'd probably continue to receive the drug until it was approved. At that point, most would have insurance or government provision that covered most of the cost of their prescriptions. But he already knew it wasn't going to make any sense to market the drug in a poor country like Albania, so when the study was over, he'd have to cut off treatment. Sure, he conceded, panic attacks weren't usually fatal. But he knew how debilitating these sudden bouts of feeling completely terrified were – the pounding heart, chest pain, choking sensation and nausea. The severity and unpredictability of these attacks often made a normal life all but impossible. How could he offer people dramatic relief and then snatch it away?

What Would You Do?

1 Do the clinical trials in Albania. You'll be able to bring the drug to market faster and cheaper, which will be good for AH Biotech's employees and investors and good for the millions of people who suffer from anxiety attacks.

2 Do the clinical trials in the European Union or US. Even though it will certainly be more expensive and time-consuming, you'll feel as if you're living up to the part of the Hippocratic Oath that instructed you to 'prescribe regimens for the good of my patients according to my ability and my judgement and never do harm to anyone'.

3 Do the clinical trials in Albania, and if the drug is approved, use part of the profits to set up a compassionate use programme in Albania, even though setting up a distribution system and training doctors to administer the drug, monitor patients for adverse effects and track results will entail considerable expense.

SOURCES Based on Gina Kolata, 'Companies Facing Ethical Issue as Drugs Are Tested Overseas', *The New York Times*, March 5, 2004; and Julie Schmit, 'Costs, Regulations Move More Drug Tests Outside USA', *USA Today*, June 16, 2005, http://www.usatoday.com/money/industries/health/drugs/2005-05-16-drug-trials-usat_x.htm.

31. Anthony, Robert (1993). *Euro Disney: The First 100 Days*, Harvard Business School, ASIN B0006R2N8Y-1.

32. Jim Holt, 'Gone Global?', *Management Review* (March 2000): 13.

33. Ibid.

34. 'Slogans Often Lose Something in Translation', *The New Mexican*, July 3, 1994.

35. Louis S. Richman, 'Global Growth Is on a Tear', in *International Business 97/98, Annual Editions*, ed. Fred Maidment (Guilford, CT: Dushkin Publishing Group, 1997), p. 6–11.

36. 'The Global Competitiveness Report 2007–2008', World Economic Forum, www.gcr.weforum.org (accessed April 30, 2008).

37. Andrew E. Serwer, 'McDonald's Conquers the World', *Fortune* (October 17, 1994): 103–116.

38. David W. Conklin, 'Analyzing and Managing Country Risks', *Ivey Business Journal* (January–February 2002): 37–41.

39. Bruce Kogut, 'Designing Global Strategies: Profiting from Operational Flexibility', *Sloan Management Review* 27 (Fall 1985): 27–38.

40. Ian Bremmer, 'Managing Risk in an Unstable World', *Harvard Business Review* (June 2005): 51–60; and Mark Fitzpatrick, 'The Definition and Assessment of Political Risk in International Business: A Review of the Literature', *Academy of Management Review* 8 (1983): 249–254.

41. Jason Bush, 'Business in Russia Just Got Riskier', *BusinessWeek* (April 23, 2007): 43.

42. Kevin Sullivan, 'Kidnapping Is Growth Industry in Mexico; Businessmen Targeted in Climate of Routine Ransoms, Police Corruption', *The Washington Post*, September 17, 2002.

43. Conklin, 'Analyzing and Managing Country Risks'; Nicolas Checa, John Maguire, and Jonathan Barney, 'The New World Disorder', *Harvard Business Review* (August 2003): 71–79; Jennifer Pellet, 'Top 10 Enterprise Risks: What Potential Threats Keep CEOs Up at Night? (Roundtable)', *Chief Executive* (October–November 2007): 48–53.

44. See Conklin, 'Analyzing and Managing Country Risks'.

45. French supermarket Carrefour faces wrath of Chinese protesters, *The Times*, April 21, 2008.

46. O'Keefe, 'Global Brands'.

47. Barbara Whitaker, 'The Web Makes Going Global Easy, Until You Try to Do It', *The New York Times*, September 2000.

48. Geert Hofstede, 'The Interaction between National and Organizational Value Systems', *Journal of Management Studies* 22 (1985): 347–357; and Geert Hofstede, 'The Cultural Relativity of the Quality of Life Concept', *Academy of Management Review* 9 (1984): 389–398.

49. Geert Hofstede, 'Cultural Constraints in Management Theory', *Academy of Management Executive* 7 (1993): 81–94; and G. Hofstede and M. H. Bond, 'The Confucian Connection: From Cultural Roots to Economic Growth', *Organizational Dynamics* 16 (1988): 4–21.

50. For an overview of the research and publications related to Hofstede's dimensions, see 'Retrospective: *Culture's Consequences*', a collection of articles focusing on Hofstede's work, in *The Academy of Management Executive* 18, no. 1 (February 2004): 72–93. See also Michele J. Gelfand, D. P. S. Bhawuk, Lisa H. Nishii, and David J. Bechtold, 'Individualism and Collectivism', in *Culture, Leadership and Organizations: The Globe Study of 62 Societies*, ed. R. J. House, P. J. Hanges, M. Javidan, and P. Dorfman (Thousand Oaks, CA: Sage, 2004).

51. Robert J. House, Paul J. Hanges, Mansour Javidan, and Peter W. Dorfman, eds., *Culture, Leadership, and Organizations: The GLOBE Study of 62 Societies* (Thousand Oaks, CA: Sage Publications, 2004); M. Javidan and R. J. House, 'Cultural Acumen for the Global Manager: Lessons from Project GLOBE', *Organizational Dynamics* 29, no. 4 (2001): 289–305; and R. J. House, M. Javidan, Paul Hanges and Peter Dorfman, 'Understanding Cultures and Implicit Leadership Theories Across the Globe: An Introduction to Project GLOBE', *Journal of World Business* 37 (2002): 3–10.

52. Chantell E. Nicholls, Henry W. Lane, and Mauricio Brehm Brechu, 'Taking Self-Managed Teams to Mexico', *Academy of Management Executive* 13, no. 2 (1999): 15–27; Carl F. Fey and Daniel R. Denison, 'Organizational Culture and Effectiveness: Can American Theory Be Applied in Russia?', *Organization Science* 14, no. 6 (November–December 2003): 686–706; Ellen F. Jackofsky, John W. Slocum, Jr. and Sara J. McQuaid, 'Cultural Values and the CEO: Alluring Companions?', *Academy of Management Executive* 2 (1988): 39–49.

53. J. Kennedy and A. Everest, 'Put Diversity in Context', *Personnel Journal* (September 1991): 50–54.

54. Terence Jackson, 'The Management of People Across Cultures: Valuing People Differently', *Human Resource Management* 41, no. 4 (Winter 2002): 455–475.

55. Elizabeth Esfahani, 'Thinking Locally, Succeeding Globally', *Business 2.0* (December 2005): 96–98.

56. This discussion is based on 'For Richer, for Poorer', *The Economist* (December 1993): 66; Richard Harmsen, 'The Uruguay Round: A Boon for the World Economy', *Finance & Development* (March 1995): 24–26; Salil S. Pitroda, 'From GATT to WTO: The Institutionalization of World Trade', *Harvard International Review* (Spring 1995): 46–47, 66–67; and World Trade Organization, www.wto.org (accessed February 11, 2008).

57. 'The History of the European Union', www.europa.eu.int/abc/history/index_en.htm (accessed February 11, 2008).

58. European Commission Economic and Financial Affairs, Website, http://ec.europa.eu/economy_finance/the_euro/index_en.htm?cs_mid=2946 (accessed August 8, 2008).

59. Lynda Radosevich, 'New Money', *CIO Enterprise*, section 2 (April 15, 1998): 54–58.

60. Tapan Munroe, 'NAFTA Still a Work in Progress', *Knight Ridder/Tribune News Service* (January 9, 2004), p. 1; and J. S. McClenahan, 'NAFTA Works', *IW* (January 10, 2000): 5–6.

61. Amy Barrett, 'It's a Small (Business) World', *BusinessWeek* (April 17, 1995): 96–101.

62. Eric Alterman, 'A Spectacular Success?', *The Nation* (February 2, 2004): 10; Jeff Faux, 'NAFTA at 10: Where Do We Go From Here?', *The Nation* (February 2, 2004): 11; Geri Smith and Cristina Lindblad, 'Mexico: Was NAFTA Worth It? A Tale of What Free Trade Can and Cannot Do', *BusinessWeek* (December 22, 2003): 66; Jeffrey Sparshott, 'NAFTA Gets Mixed Reviews', *The Washington Times*, December 18, 2003; and Munroe, 'NAFTA Is Still Work in Progress'.

63. Munroe, 'NAFTA Is Still Work in Progress'; Jeffrey Sparshott, 'NAFTA Gets Mixed Reviews', *The Washington Times*, December 18, 2003; Amy Borrus, 'A Free-Trade Milestone, with Many More Miles to Go', *BusinessWeek* (August 24, 1992): 30–31.

64. Nina Easton, 'Make the World Go Away', *Fortune* (February 4, 2008): 105–108.

65. Pete Engardio, Aaron Bernstein, and Manjeet Kripalani, 'Is Your Job Next?', *BusinessWeek* (February 3, 2003): 50–60.

66. Jyoti Thottam, 'Is Your Job Going Abroad?', *Time* (March 1, 2004): 26–36. Andrew Parker, with David Metcalfe, Sonoko Takahashi, Two-Speed Europe: Why 1 Million Jobs Will Move Offshore, 2004, available at http://www.forrester.com/Research/Document/Excerpt/0,7211,35212,00.html.

67. Easton, 'Make the World Go Away'.

68. Michael Schroeder and Timothy Aeppel, 'Skilled Workers Sway Politicians with Fervor Against Free Trade', *The Wall Street Journal*, December 10, 2003.

69. Alison Stein Wellner, 'Turning the Tables', *Inc. Magazine* (May 2006): 55–59.

70. Easton, 'Make the World Go Away'.

71. William J. Holstein, 'Haves and Have-Nots of Globalization', *The New York Times*, July 8, 2007.

72. World Bank and *Fortune* magazine, as reported in Paul DeGrauwe, University of Leuven and Belgian Senate, and Filip Camerman, Belgian Senate, 'How Big are the Big Multinational Companies?', unpublished paper (2002).

73. Reported in Thomas J. Duesterberg, 'Exporting Offers a Global Advantage', *Industry Week* (May 2007): 13.

74. Howard V. Perlmutter, 'The Tortuous Evolution of the Multinational Corporation', *Columbia Journal of World Business* (January–February 1969): 9–18; and Youram Wind, Susan P. Douglas, and Howard V. Perlmutter, 'Guidelines for Developing International Marketing Strategies', *Journal of Marketing* (April 1973): 14–23.

75. Christopher Bartlett, *Managing Across Borders*, 2nd ed. (Boston: Harvard Business School Press, 1998); and quote from Buss, 'World Class'.

76. Morgan W. McCall Jr. and George P. Hollenbeck, 'Global Fatalities: When International Executives Derail', *Ivey Business Journal* (May–June 2002): 75–78.

77. The discussion of cultural intelligence is based on P. Christopher Earley and Elaine Mosakowski, 'Cultural Intelligence', *Harvard Business Review* (October 2004): 139; Ilan Alon and James M. Higgins, 'Global Leadership Success Through Emotional and Cultural Intelligence', *Business Horizons* 48 (2005): 501–512; P. C. Earley and Soon Ang,

Cultural Intelligence: Individual Actions Across Cultures (Stanford, CA: Stanford Business Books); and David C. Thomas and Kerr Inkson, *Cultural Intelligence* (San Francisco: Berrett-Koehler, 2004).

78. Pat McGovern, 'How to Be a Local, Anywhere', *Inc. Magazine* (April 2007): 113–114.

79. These components are from Earley and Mosakowski, 'Cultural Intelligence'.

80. Karl Moore, 'Great Global Managers', *Across the Board* (May–June 2003): 40–43.

81. Richard E. Nisbett, *The Geography of Thought: How Asians and Westerners Think Differently ... and Why* (New York: The Free Press, 2003), reported in Sharon Begley, 'East vs. West: One Sees the Big Picture, The Other Is Focused', *The Wall Street Journal*, March 28, 2003.

82. Robert T. Moran and John R. Riesenberger, *The Global Challenge* (London: McGraw-Hill, 1994), pp. 251–262.

83. Joann S. Lublin, 'Companies Use Cross-Cultural Training to Help Their Employees Adjust Abroad', *The Wall Street Journal*, August 4, 1992.

84. Gilbert Fuchsberg, 'As Costs of Overseas Assignments Climb, Firms Select Expatriates More Carefully', *The Wall Street Journal*, January 9, 1992.

85. Valerie Frazee, 'Keeping Up on Chinese Culture', *Global Workforce* (October 1996): 16–17; and Jack Scarborough, 'Comparing Chinese and Western Cultural Roots: Why "East Is East and ..."', *Business Horizons* (November–December 1998): 15–24.

86. Mansour Javidan and Ali Dastmalchian, 'Culture and Leadership in Iran: The Land of Individual Achievers, Strong Family Ties, and Powerful Elite', *Academy of Management Executive* 17, no. 4 (2003): 127–142.

87. Randall S. Schuler, Susan E. Jackson, Ellen Jackofsky, and John W. Slocum, Jr., 'Managing Human Resources in Mexico: A Cultural Understanding', *Business Horizons* (May–June 1996): 55–61.

88. Towers Perrin data reported in 'Workers Want ...' sidebar in Peter Coy, 'Cog or Co-Worker?', *Business-Week* (August 20 and 27, 2007): 58–60.

89. Xu Huang and Evert Van De Vliert, 'Where Intrinsic Job Satisfaction Fails to Work: National Moderators of Intrinsic Motivation', *Journal of Organizational Behaviour* 24 (2003): 159–179.

90. Shari Caudron, 'Lessons from HR Overseas', *Personnel Journal* (February 1995): 88.

91. Reported in Begley, 'East vs. West'.

CHAPTER OUTLINE

© EYEIDEA/ISTOCK

LEARNING OBJECTIVES

After reading this chapter, you should be able to:

1 Define ethics and explain how ethical behaviour relates to behaviour governed by law and free choice.

2 Explain the utilitarian, individualism, moral-rights and justice approaches for evaluating ethical behaviour.

3 Describe the factors that shape a manager's ethical decision-making.

4 Identify important stakeholders for an organization and discuss how managers balance the interests of various stakeholders.

5 Explain the bottom-of-the-pyramid concept and some of the innovative strategies companies are using.

6 Understand the philosophy of sustainability and why organizations are embracing it.

7 Define corporate social responsibility and how to evaluate it along economic, legal, ethical, and discretionary criteria.

8 Discuss how ethical organizations are created through ethical leadership and organizational structures and systems.

CHAPTER 5

MANAGING ETHICS AND SOCIAL RESPONSIBILITY

What does courage have to do with a chapter on ethics? Unfortunately, many managers slide into unethical or illegal behaviour simply because they don't have the courage to stand up and do the right thing. Remember the scandal at WorldCom? This small long-distance company became a dazzling star during the late 1990s telecom boom. Just as quickly, it all came crashing down as one executive after another was hauled away on conspiracy and securities fraud charges. For controller David Myers, it was one small step that put him on a slippery slope. When CEO Bernard Ebbers and Chief Financial Officer Scott Sullivan asked Myers to reclassify some expenses that would boost the company's earnings for the quarter, Myers admits that he 'didn't think it was the right thing to do', but he didn't want to oppose his superiors. After that first mistake, Myers had to keep making – and asking his subordinates to make – increasingly irregular adjustments to try to get things back on track.[1] Myers, as well as accountants Buford Yates, Betty Vinson and Troy Normand, who acted on his orders, all expressed misgivings but continued to make increasingly irregular adjustments over the course of six quarters, clinging to a hope that each would be the last.

Top executives persuaded these managers, who were all known as hardworking, dedicated employees, that their gimmicks would help pull WorldCom out of its troubles and get everything back to normal. The lower-level managers rationalized that if Myers and the chief financial officer thought the transfers and other gimmicks were all right, they didn't have the right to question it. When WorldCom's problems exploded into public view, Myers, Yates, Normand and Vinson found themselves in the middle of one of the largest financial fraud cases in corporate history. All eventually pleaded guilty to conspiracy and securities fraud, and some were awarded prison sentences.[2]

These managers were not unscrupulous people. All had misgivings about what they were doing, but they continued to go along with their superiors' requests. It's a reminder that all of our ethical decisions are made within the context of interactions

Managing Ethics and Social Responsibility: Will You Be a Courageous Manager?

It probably won't happen right away, but soon enough in your duties as a new manager you will be confronted with a situation that will test the strength of your moral beliefs or your sense of justice or fair play. Are you ready? To find out, think about times when you were part of a student or work group. To what extent does each of the following statements characterize your behaviour? Please answer each of the following items as Mostly True or Mostly False for you.

		Mostly True	Mostly False
1	I risked substantial personal loss to achieve the vision.	☐	☐
2	I took personal risks to defend my beliefs.	☐	☐
3	I would say no to inappropriate things even if I had a lot to lose.	☐	☐
4	My significant actions were linked to higher values.	☐	☐
5	I easily acted against the opinions and approval of others.	☐	☐
6	I quickly told people the truth as I saw it, even when it was negative.	☐	☐
7	I spoke out against group or organizational injustice.	☐	☐
8	I acted according to my conscience even if I would lose stature.	☐	☐

SCORING AND INTERPRETATION Each of these questions pertains to some aspect of displaying courage in a group situation, which often reflects a person's level of moral development. Count the number of checks for Mostly True. If you scored five or more, congratulations! That behaviour would enable you to become a courageous manager about moral issues. A score below four indicates that you may avoid difficult issues or have not been in situations that challenged your moral courage.

Study the specific questions for which you scored Mostly True and Mostly False to learn more about your specific strengths and weaknesses. Think about what influences your moral behaviour and decisions, such as need for success or approval. Study the behaviour of others you consider to be moral individuals. How might you increase your courage as a new manager?

with other people. The social networks within an organization play an important role in guiding people's actions. For most of us, doing something we know is wrong becomes easier when 'everyone else is doing it'. In organizations, the norms and values of the team, department or organization as a whole have a profound influence on ethical behaviour. Research verifies that these values strongly influence employee actions and decision-making.

In particular, corporate culture, as described in Chapter 3, lets employees know what beliefs and behaviours the company supports and those it will not tolerate. If unethical behaviour is tolerated or even encouraged, it becomes routine. In many companies, employees believe that if they do not go along, their jobs will be in jeopardy or they will not fit in.

WorldCom is one of many examples of widespread moral lapses and corporate financial scandals that have brought the topic of ethics to the forefront. The pervasiveness of ethical lapses in the early 2000s was astounding. Once-respected firms such as Enron, Arthur Andersen, Tyco, and Madoff Securities in the US, and Parmalat, Royal Ahold, and Skandia in Europe, have became synonymous with greed, deceit and financial chicanery.[3]

So it is perhaps not surprising that an Ipsos-Mori 2006 survey in UK found that only 31 per cent of the general public trusted business leaders.[4] The sentiment is echoed in other countries as well. Recent investigations of dozens of top executives in Germany for tax evasion, bribery and other forms of corruption have destroyed the high level of public trust business leaders there once enjoyed, with just 15 per cent of respondents now saying business leaders are trustworthy.[5]

This chapter expands on the ideas about environment, corporate culture, and the international environment discussed in Chapters 3 and 4. We first focus on the topic of ethical values, which builds on the idea of corporate culture. We examine fundamental approaches that can help managers think through difficult ethical issues, and we look at factors that influence how managers make ethical choices. Understanding these ideas will help you build a solid foundation on which to base future decision-making. We also examine organizational relationships to the external environment as reflected in corporate social responsibility. The final section of the chapter describes how managers build an ethical organization using codes of ethics and other organizational policies, structures and systems.

Manager's Challenge

Today, we find many Corporations around the globe rushing to adopt stringent codes of ethics, strengthen ethical and legal safeguards, and develop socially responsible policies. For instance, after BP reported in 2005 that it had sacked 252 people for 'unethical behaviour', a 50 per cent rise on the previous year, it quickly established a new corporate social responsibility team to govern legal compliance and business ethics as well as enforce a company wide code of conduct.[6]

Many companies are adopting new tougher zero-tolerance policies that hold their employees to lofty standards of business and personal behaviour. However, sometimes managers themselves can be slow to adapt to this new environment. For instance, when Eric Corrigan and Thomas Chen were called to their boss's office at Bank of America in March 2005, they were expecting congratulations for a job well done. In the previous year, both had received praise and generous bonuses for their work as successful and respected investment bankers. Acting on a tip from Thomas Heath who worked at JPMorgan Chase & Co. while they were interviewing him for a job at Bank of America, they were told that JPMorgan was working for Hibernia Corp, Louisiana's biggest bank, in its planned $5.3 billion takeover by Capital One Financial Corporation. Heath shouldn't have broken the confidence of his client, or his then employer. Once he did, though, Corrigan and Chen did what many investment bankers would do – they went after a piece of the action. That kind of aggressive move to secure an edge is what made their careers – and helped put Bank of America on the map. Thus we find the two reaching the executive suite prepared for accolades. A few minutes later, the stunned bankers are hearing that they've been fired. Pressed for clarification, their boss admits they've broken no regulations, and Corrigan and Chen argue that their actions were simply part of the way all bankers do business.

It seems that Corrigan and Chen had failed to perceive the change in business culture and expectations at the Bank, as the boom of the late 1990s gave way to the bust of the early 2000s. They both now need to consider that their careers are so badly damaged, that they will most probably never work on Wall Street again.[7]

TAKE A MOMENT

As a potential manager, what do you think Eric Corrigan and Thomas Chen did wrong? If you were Corrigan and Chen's boss, would you reconsider your judgement or stick to your decision to fire them? What would you do about Thomas Heath?

The situation at Bank of America illustrates how difficult ethical issues can be and symbolizes the growing importance of discussing ethics and social responsibility. Managers often face situations in which it is difficult to determine what is right. Ethics has always been a concern for managers. However, recent widespread moral lapses and corporate financial scandals bring the topic to the forefront and pressure managers in both large and small companies to put ethics near the top of their priorities list. Bank of America is certainly not alone in taking a stronger stand against ethical lapses that would once have been considered 'the standard way of doing business'.[8]

However, positive news can be found too. After catastrophic floods hit Bangladesh in November 2007, the logistics giant TNT's emergency response team was on full alert. At its headquarters in Amsterdam, TNT keeps 50 people on permanent stand-by ready to intervene following natural disasters anywhere in the world at 48 hours notice. This is part of its five-year old partnership with World Food Programme (WFP), the UN agency that fights hunger. The TNT team has attended more than two dozen emergencies including the Asian tsunami in 2004. In addition TNT staff often do short stints on secondment to WFP projects, as well as voluntarily raising £2.5 million donations for the programme in 2007. For TNT this partnership is a good fit, because hunger is, at least in part, a logistics problem.[9] Indeed it is not just large corporations that are getting involved in social initiatives. In 2006, Tanya Goodin, founder of the British software-development company Tamar, took her entire staff of 40 to Guguletu township in Cape Town for a week to build classrooms, a playground and a basketball court at a local school. Goodin, a mother of two, said that the idea of doing something for children came to her after a near-fatal car crash, when she realized that she didn't want to feel that all she had done with her life was create wealth.[10] A number of companies have also begun to look at remuneration packages, tying managers' pay to ethical factors such as how well they treat employees or how effectively they live up to the stated corporate values.

What is Managerial Ethics?

Ethics
The code of moral principles and values that governs the behaviours of a person or group with respect to what is right or wrong.

Ethics is difficult to define in a precise way. In a general sense, ethics is the code of moral principles and values that governs the behaviours of a person or group with respect to what is right or wrong. Ethics sets standards as to what is good or bad in conduct and decision-making.[11] An ethical issue is present in a situation when the actions of a person or organization may harm or benefit others.[12] Yet ethical issues can sometimes be exceedingly complex. People in organizations may hold widely divergent views about the most ethically appropriate or inappropriate actions related to a situation.[13] Managers often face situations in which it is difficult to determine what is right. In addition, they might be torn between their misgivings and their sense of duty to their bosses and the organization. Sometimes, managers want to take a stand but don't have the backbone to go against others, bring unfavourable attention to themselves, or risk their jobs.

Ethics can be more clearly understood when compared with behaviours governed by law and by free choice. Exhibit 5.1 illustrates that human behaviour falls into three categories. The first is codified law, in which values and standards are written into the legal system and enforceable in the courts. In this area, lawmakers set rules that people and corporations must follow in a certain way, such as obtaining licences for cars or paying corporate taxes. The courts alleged that executives at companies such as WorldCom, Enron and Parmalat broke the law, for example, by manipulating financial results, such as using off-balance-sheet partnerships to improperly create income and hide debt. The domain of free choice is at the opposite end of the scale and pertains to behaviour about which the law has no say and for which an individual or organization enjoys complete freedom. A manager's choice of where to eat lunch or a music company's choice of the number of CDs to release is an example of free choice.

Between these domains lies the area of ethics. This domain has no specific laws, yet it does have standards of conduct based on shared principles and values about moral conduct that guide an individual or company. Executives at Enron, for example, did not break any specific laws by encouraging employees to buy more shares of stock even when they believed the company was in financial trouble and the price of the shares was likely to decline. However, this behaviour was a clear violation of the executives' ethical responsibilities to employees.[14] These managers were acting based on their own interests rather than their duties to employees and other stakeholders.

Many companies and individuals get into trouble with the simplified view that choices are governed by either law or free choice. This view leads people to mistakenly assume that if it's not illegal, it must be ethical, as if there were no third domain.[15] A better option is to recognize the domain of ethics and accept moral values as a powerful force for good that can regulate behaviours both inside and outside organizations.

Laura Nash defines business ethics as, 'The study of how personal moral norms apply to the activities and goals of a commercial enterprise. It is not a separate moral standard, but the study of how the business context poses its own unique problems for the moral person who acts as agent of the system.'[16] This definition focuses on the person as moral agent. As a new manager, be prepared to build or enforce an ethical culture in your area of responsibility. Remember that managers make decisions within the norms of their interactions with others. Make sure your values and the organization's values support and encourage doing the right thing. Finally remember Joanna Ciulla's[17] advice that 'the really creative part of business ethics is discovering ways to do what is morally right and socially responsible without ruining your career and company'.

Exhibit 5.1 Three Domains of Human Action

Ethical Dilemmas: What Would You Do?

Ethical dilemma
A situation that arises when all alternative choices or behaviours are deemed undesirable because of potentially negative consequences, making it difficult to distinguish right from wrong.

Ethics is always about making decisions, and some issues are difficult to resolve. Because ethical standards are not codified, disagreements and dilemmas about proper behaviour often occur. An **ethical dilemma** arises in a situation concerning right or wrong when values are in conflict.[18] Right and wrong cannot be clearly identified.

The individual who must make an ethical choice in an organization is the *moral agent*.[19] Here are some dilemmas that a manager in an organization might face. Think about how you would handle them:

1 Your company requires a money laundering screening for all new customers, which takes approximately 24 hours from the time an order is placed. You can close a lucrative deal with a potential long-term customer if you agree to ship the products overnight, even though that means the required money laundering screening will have to be done after the fact.[20]

2 As a sales manager for a major pharmaceuticals company, you've been asked to promote a new drug that costs £1500 per dose. You've read the reports saying the drug is only 1 per cent more effective than an alternate drug that costs less than £400 per dose. Your head of sales wants you to aggressively promote the £1500-per-dose drug. He reminds you that, if you don't, lives could be lost that might have been saved with that 1 per cent increase in the drug's effectiveness. Can you in good conscience promote the £1500 per-dose drug rather than the £400 per-dose alternative?

CONCEPT CONNECTION The Anglo-South African Insurance Giant, Old Mutual PLC shows its commitment to ethics through its corporate code of conduct: 'As a Group we should maintain the highest ethical standards in carrying out our business activities. Our reputation is one of our most important assets. Maintaining the trust and confidence of all those whom we deal with is accordingly one of our most vital responsibilities, so in all of our operations our set of core values must be used to guide and direct the way we do business'.[23] Among those core values is treating others as you would wish to be treated yourself.

Treating others the way you want to be treated is one approach to making ethically-responsible decisions and handling ethical dilemmas. However, insurance companies often have to rely on a utilitarian approach to ethical decision-making that considers how to provide the greatest good to the greatest number of policyholders.

3 Your company is hoping to build a new overseas manufacturing plant. You could save about £3 million by not installing standard pollution control equipment that is required in the European Union. The plant will employ many local workers in a poor country where jobs are scarce. Your research shows that pollutants from the factory could potentially damage the local fishing industry. Yet building the factory with the pollution control equipment will likely make the plant too expensive to build.[21]

4 You have been collaborating with a fellow manager on an important project. One afternoon, you walk into his office a bit earlier than scheduled and see sexually explicit images on his computer monitor. The company has a zero-tolerance sexual harassment policy, as well as strict guidelines regarding personal use of the internet. However, your colleague was in his own office and not bothering anyone else.[22]

5 You are the accounting manager of a division that is £15 000 below profit targets. Approximately £20 000 of office supplies were delivered on December 21. The accounting rule is to pay expenses when incurred. The division general manager asks you not to record the invoice until February.

These kinds of dilemmas and issues fall squarely in the domain of ethics. How would you handle each of the above situations? Now consider the following hypothetical dilemma, which scientists are using to study human morality.[24]

■ A runaway train engine is heading down the tracks toward five unsuspecting people. You're standing near a switch that will divert the engine onto a siding, but there is a single workman on the siding who cannot be warned in time to escape and will almost certainly be killed. Would you throw the switch?

■ Now, what if the workman is standing on a bridge over the tracks and you have to push him off the bridge to try and stop the engine with his body in order to save the five unsuspecting people? (Assume his body is large enough to stop the engine and yours is not.) Would you push the man, even though he will almost certainly be killed?

These dilemmas show how complex questions of ethics and morality can some-times be. In *Time* magazine's readers' poll, 97 per cent of respondents said they could throw the switch (which would almost certainly lead to the death of the work-man), but only 42 per cent said they could actually push the man to his death.[25]

Criteria for Ethical Decision-making

Most ethical dilemmas involve a conflict between the needs of the part and the whole – the individual versus the organization or the organization versus society as a whole. For example, should a company perform surveillance on managers' non-workplace conduct, such as implementing random mandatory alcohol and drug testing for employees, which might benefit the organization as a whole but reduce the individ-ual freedom of employees? Or should products that fail to meet tough regulatory standards be exported to other countries where government standards are lower, benefiting the company but potentially harming world citizens? Sometimes ethical decisions entail a conflict between two groups. For example, should the potential for local health problems resulting from a company's pollution take precedence over the jobs it creates as the town's leading employer?

Managers faced with these kinds of tough ethical choices often benefit from a normative strategy – one based on norms and values – to guide their decision-making. Normative ethics uses several approaches to describe values for guiding ethical decision-making. Four of these approaches that are relevant to managers are the utilitarian approach, individualism approach, moral-rights approach and Justice approach.[26]

Utilitarian Approach

The utilitarian approach, espoused by the nineteenth-century philosophers Jeremy Bentham and John Stuart Mill, holds that moral behaviour produces the greatest good for the greatest number. Under this approach, a decision-maker is expected to consider the effect of each decision alternative on all parties and select the one that optimizes the benefits for the greatest number of people. In the runaway engine di-lemma above, for instance, the utilitarian approach would hold that it would be moral to push one person to his death in order to save five. In organizations, because actual computations can be complex, simplifying them is considered appropriate. For example, a simple economic frame of reference could be used by calculating monetary costs and monetary benefits. The utilitarian ethic is cited as the basis for the recent trend among companies to monitor employee use of the internet and police personal habits such as alcohol and tobacco consumption, or excessive gambling, because such behaviour affects the entire workplace.[27]

Utilitarian approach
The ethical concept that moral behaviours produce the greatest good for the greatest number.

INNOVATIVE WAY

National Health Service Denies Kidney Cancer Drugs to Patients

The National Institute for Health and Clinical Excellence (NICE) controversially ruled in August 2008 that patients with advanced kidney cancer would be denied four treatments on the National Health Service (NHS) in England and Wales. NICE is the government's drugs advisory body. It ruled that the drugs – bevacizumab, sorafenib, sunitinib and temsirolimus – do not offer 'value for money'. The drugs are routinely available in the US and in the rest of Europe. More than 7000 people are diagnosed with kidney cancer annually in the UK, and of these, around 1700 patients will be diagnosed with advanced cancer. Although the drugs are not able to cure renal cell carcinoma or cancer that has spread from the initial tumour, they are able to extend life by five to six months. NICE's main criterion for assessing drugs is whether they offer 'value for money' and are 'cost-effective'. Extending a patient's life by six

months was deemed to be uneconomical. Professor Peter Littlejohns of NICE said: 'The decisions NICE has to make are some of the hardest in public life. NHS resources are not limitless and NICE has to decide what treatments represent best value to the patient as well as the NHS. Although these treatments are clinically effective, regrettably, the cost to the NHS is such that they are not a cost-effective use of NHS resources … If these treatments were provided on the NHS 'other patients would lose out on treatments that are both clinically and cost effective.'[28]

By emphasizing the potential costs to many over the benefits to a few, given the finite resources available within the NHS, the NICE decision reflects a approach based in the utilitarian ethic. However, it contradicted the position of NICE's own citizen's council, which had recommended funding the drug treatment having concluded that individuals in 'desperate and exceptional circumstances' should sometimes receive greater help than can be justified by a 'purely utilitarian approach'.

The utilitarian ethic can be used to partly explain decisions within the UK National Health Service (NHS) on whether or not to fund certain medical treatments from it central budget.

Individualism Approach

Individualism approach
The ethical concept that acts are moral when they promote the individual's best long-term interests.

The **individualism approach** contends that acts are moral when they promote the individual's best long-term interests. Individual self-direction is paramount, and external forces that restrict self-direction should be severely limited.[29] Individuals calculate the best long-term advantage to themselves as a measure of a decision's goodness. The action that is intended to produce a greater ratio of good to bad for the individual compared with other alternatives is the right one to perform. In theory, with everyone pursuing self-direction, the greater good is ultimately served because people learn to accommodate each other in their own long-term interest. Individualism is believed to lead to honesty and integrity because that works best in the long run. Lying and cheating for immediate self-interest just causes business associates to lie and cheat in return. Thus, individualism ultimately leads to behaviour toward others that fits standards of behaviour people want toward themselves.[30]

One value of understanding this approach is to recognize short-term variations if they are proposed. People might argue for short-term self-interest based on individualism, but that misses the point. Because individualism is easily misinterpreted to support immediate self-gain, it is not popular in the highly organized and group-oriented society of today. Dozens of disgraced top executives from WorldCom, Enron, Tyco,

Parmalat and other companies demonstrate the flaws of the individualism approach. This approach is closest to the domain of free choice described in Exhibit 5.1.

Moral-rights Approach

The moral-rights approach asserts that human beings have fundamental rights and liberties that cannot be taken away by an individual's decision. Thus, an ethically correct decision is one that best maintains the rights of those affected by it.

Six moral rights should be considered during decision-making:

1 *The right of free consent.* Individuals are to be treated only as they knowingly and freely consent to be treated.

2 *The right to privacy.* Individuals can choose to do as they please away from work and have control of information about their private life.

3 *The right of freedom of conscience.* Individuals may refrain from carrying out any order that violates their moral or religious norms.

4 *The right of free speech.* Individuals may criticize truthfully the ethics or legality of actions of others.

5 *The right to due process.* Individuals have a right to an impartial hearing and fair treatment.

6 *The right to life and safety.* Individuals have a right to live without endangerment or violation of their health and safety.

To make ethical decisions, managers need to avoid interfering with the fundamental rights of others. For instance, NICE's decision discussed above not to fund new drug treatment for kidney cancer, might be construed by some people to violate the right to life. A decision to eavesdrop on employees violates the right to privacy. A decision to monitor employees' non-work activities violates the right to privacy. Sexual harassment is unethical because it violates the right to freedom of conscience. The right of free speech would support whistle-blowers who call attention to illegal or inappropriate actions within a company.

> **Moral-rights approach**
> The ethical concept that moral decisions are those that best maintain the rights of those people affected by them.

> **Justice approach**
> The ethical concept that moral decisions must be based on standards of equity, fairness and impartiality.

TAKE A MOMENT

Turn to the section on Ethical Dilemmas on page 166 and select two. First apply the utilitarian approach to reach a decision in each situation, and then apply the moral-rights approach. Did you reach the same or different conclusions? As a new manager, do you think one approach is generally better for managers to use?

Justice Approach

The justice approach holds that moral decisions must be based on standards of equity, fairness and impartiality. Three types of justice are of concern to managers. Distributive justice requires that different treatment of people not be based on arbitrary characteristics. Individuals who are similar in ways relevant to a decision should be treated similarly. Thus, men and women should not receive different salaries if they are performing the same job. However, people who differ in a substantive way, such as job skills or job responsibility, can be treated differently in proportion to the differences in skills or responsibility among them. This difference should have a clear relationship to organizational goals and tasks.

> **Distributive justice**
> The concept that different treatment of people should not be based on arbitrary characteristics. In the case of substantive differences, people should be treated differently in proportion to the differences among them.

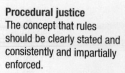

Procedural justice
The concept that rules should be clearly stated and consistently and impartially enforced.

Compensatory justice
The concept that individuals should be compensated for the cost of their injuries by the party responsible and also that individuals should not be held responsible for matters over which they have no control.

Procedural justice requires that rules be administered fairly. Rules should be clearly stated and consistently and impartially enforced.

Compensatory justice argues that individuals should be compensated for the cost of their injuries by the party responsible. Moreover, individuals should not be held responsible for matters over which they have no control.

The justice approach is closest to the thinking underlying the domain of law in Exhibit 5.1 because it assumes that justice is applied through rules and regulations. This theory does not require complex calculations such as those demanded by a utilitarian approach, nor does it justify self-interest as the individualism approach does. Managers are expected to define attributes on which different treatment of employees is acceptable. Questions such as how minority workers should be compensated for past discrimination are extremely difficult. However, this approach justifies the ethical behaviour of efforts to correct past wrongs, play fair under the rules, and insist on job-relevant differences as the basis for different levels of pay or promotion opportunities. Most of the laws guiding human resource management (Chapter 11) are based on the justice approach.

Understanding these various approaches is only a first step. Managers still have to consider how to apply them. The approaches offer general principles that managers can recognize as useful in making ethical decisions.

Manager's Ethical Choices

A number of factors influence a manager's ability to make ethical decisions. Individuals bring specific personality and behavioural traits to the job. Personal needs, family influence and religious background all shape a manager's value system. Specific personality characteristics, such as ego strength, self-confidence and a strong sense of independence, may enable managers to make ethical choices despite personal risks.

One important personal trait is the stage of moral development.[31] A simplified version of one model of personal moral development is shown in Exhibit 5.2.

Exhibit 5.2 Three Levels of Personal Moral Development

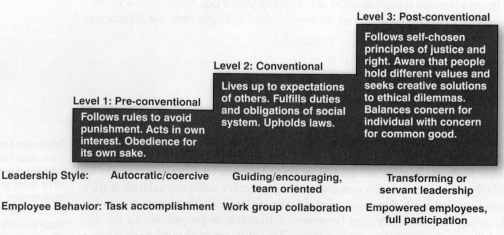

Level 1: Pre-conventional
Follows rules to avoid punishment. Acts in own interest. Obedience for its own sake.

Level 2: Conventional
Lives up to expectations of others. Fulfills duties and obligations of social system. Upholds laws.

Level 3: Post-conventional
Follows self-chosen principles of justice and right. Aware that people hold different values and seeks creative solutions to ethical dilemmas. Balances concern for individual with concern for common good.

| Leadership Style: | Autocratic/coercive | Guiding/encouraging, team oriented | Transforming or servant leadership |
| Employee Behavior: | Task accomplishment | Work group collaboration | Empowered employees, full participation |

SOURCES: Based on L. Kohlberg, 'Moral Stages and Moralization: The Cognitive-Developmental Approach', in *Moral Development and Behaviour: Theory, Research, and Social Issues*, ed. T. Lickona (New York: Holt, Rinehart, and Winston, 1976), pp. 31–53; and Jill W. Graham, 'Leadership, Moral Development and Citizenship Behaviour', *Business Ethics Quarterly* 5, no. 1 (January 1995): 43–54.

At the *preconventional level*, individuals are concerned with external rewards and punishments and obey authority to avoid detrimental personal consequences. In an organizational context, this level may be associated with managers who use an autocratic or coercive leadership style, with employees oriented toward dependable accomplishment of specific tasks.

At level two, called the *conventional level*, people learn to conform to the expectations of good behaviour as defined by colleagues, family, friends, and society. Meeting social and interpersonal obligations is important. Work group collaboration is the preferred manner for accomplishment of organizational goals, and managers use a leadership style that encourages interpersonal relationships and cooperation.

At the *post-conventional*, or *principled* level, individuals are guided by an internal set of values based on universal principles of justice and right and will even disobey rules or laws that violate these principles. Internal values become more important than the expectations of significant others. This chapter's Manager's Shoptalk gives some tips for how post-conventional managers can effectively challenge their superiors concerning questionable ethical matters. One example of the post-conventional or principled approach comes from World War II. When the *USS Indianapolis* sank after being torpedoed, one Navy pilot disobeyed orders and risked his life to save men who were being picked off by sharks. The pilot was operating from the highest level of moral development in attempting the rescue despite a direct order from superiors. When managers operate from this highest level of development, they use transformative or servant leadership, focusing on the needs of followers and encouraging others to think for themselves and to engage in higher levels of moral reasoning. Employees are empowered and given opportunities for constructive participation in governance of the organization.

The great majority of managers operate at level two, meaning their ethical thought and behaviour is greatly influenced by their superiors, colleagues, and other significant people in the organization or industry. A few have not advanced beyond level one. Only about 20 per cent of US managers reach the level-three post-conventional stage of moral development. People at level three are able to act in an independent, ethical manner regardless of expectations from others inside or outside the organization. Managers at level three of moral development will make ethical decisions whatever the organizational consequences for them.

Globalization makes ethical issues even more complicated for today's managers.[33] For example, although tolerance for bribery is waning, bribes are still considered a normal part of doing business in many foreign countries. Transparency International, an international organization that monitors corruption, publishes an annual report ranking 30 leading exporting countries based on the propensity of international businesses to offer bribes. Exhibit 5.3 shows results of the organization's most recent available report. Emerging export powers rank the worst, with India showing the greatest propensity for bribery

© JEFF MORGAN HAY ON WYE/ALAMY

CONCEPT CONNECTION Bob Geldof had chart-topping success with The Boomtown Rats, co-wrote one of the best-selling singles of all time, and with his Live Aid and Live 8 concerts has organized some of the most-watched events ever screened on television. Yet Geldof is motivated not by a personal desire for influence, power or money, but by the results of mobilizing huge charitable movements, particularly regarding the alleviation of poverty in Africa. Like other post-conventional individuals he's also not afraid to ignore social rules to get these results, as illustrated by his infamous use of strong language to demand charitable donations at many of his events.

© PAUL HAWTHORNE/GETTY IMAGES

CONCEPT CONNECTION One interesting study indicates that most researchers fail to account for the different ways in which women view social reality and develop psychologically and have thus consistently classified women as being stuck at lower levels of development. Researcher Carol Gilligan (left) suggested that the moral domain be enlarged to include responsibility and care in relationships. Women may, in general, perceive moral complexities more astutely than men and make moral decisions based not on a set of absolute rights and wrongs but on principles of not causing harm to others.[32]

TAKE A MOMENT Review your responses to the questions at the beginning of this chapter, which will give you some insight into your own level of manager courage, which is related to moral development. As a new manager, strive for a high level of personal moral development. You can test yours by completing the New Manager Self-Test on page 174.

 MANAGER'S SHOPTALK

How to Challenge the Boss on Ethical Issues

Many of today's top executives put a renewed emphasis on ethics in light of serious ethical lapses that tarnished the reputations and hurt the performance of previously respected and successful companies. Yet keeping an organization in ethical line is an ongoing challenge, and it requires that people at all levels be willing to stand up for what they think is right. Challenging the boss or other senior leaders on potentially unethical behaviour is particularly unnerving for most people. Here are some tips for talking to the boss about an ethically questionable decision or action. Following these guidelines can increase the odds that you'll be heard and your opinions will be seriously considered.

- **Do your research.** Marshall any facts and figures that support your position on the issue at hand, and develop an alternative policy or course of action that you can suggest at the appropriate time. Prepare succinct answers to any questions you anticipate being asked about your plan.

- **Begin the meeting by giving your boss the floor.** Make sure you really do understand what the decision or policy is and the reasons behind it. Ask open-ended questions, and listen actively, showing through both your responses and your body language that you're seriously listening and trying to understand the other person's position. In particular, seek out information about what the senior manager sees as the decision or policy's benefits as well as any potential downsides. It'll give you information you can use later to highlight how your plan can produce similar benefits while avoiding the potential disadvantages.

- **Pay attention to your word choice and demeanour.** No matter how strongly you feel about the matter, don't rant and rave about it. You're more likely to be heard if you remain calm, objective and professional. Try to disagree without making it personal. Avoid phrases such as 'you're wrong', 'you can't', 'you should', or 'how could you?' to prevent triggering the other person's automatic defence mechanisms.

- **Take care how you suggest your alternative solution.** You can introduce your plan with phrases such as 'here's another way to look at this' or 'what would you think about . . . ?' Check for your superior's reactions both by explicitly asking for feedback and being sensitive to body language clues. Point out the potential negative consequences of implementing decisions that might be construed as unethical by customers, shareholders, suppliers or the public.

- **Be patient.** Don't demand a resolution on the spot. During your conversation, you may realize that your plan needs some work, or your boss might just need time to digest the information and opinions you've presented. It's often a good idea to ask for a follow-up meeting.

If the decision or action being considered is clearly unethical or potentially illegal, and this meeting doesn't provide a quick resolution, you might need to take your concerns to higher levels, or even blow the whistle to someone outside the organization who can make sure the organization stays in line. However, most managers don't want to take actions that will harm the organization, its people or the community. In many cases, questionable ethical issues can be resolved by open and honest communication. That, however, requires that people have the courage – and develop the skills – to confront their superiors in a calm and rational way.

SOURCES Kevin Daley, 'How to Disagree: Go Up Against Your Boss or a Senior Executive and Live to Tell the Tale', *T&D* (April 2004); Diane Moore, 'How to Disagree with Your Boss – and Keep Your Job', *Toronto Star*, November 12, 2003; 'How to Disagree with Your Boss', *WikiHow,* http://wiki.ehow.com/Disagree-With-Your-Boss; and 'How to Confront Your Boss Constructively', *The Buzz* (October 23–29, 1996), www.hardatwork.com/Buzz/ten.html.

Exhibit 5.3 The Transparency International Bribe Payers Index

Rank		Score	Rank		Score
1	Switzerland	7.81	16	Portugal	6.47
2	Sweden	7.62	17	Mexico	6.45
3	Australia	7.59	18	Hong Kong	6.01
4	Austria	7.50	18 (tie)	Israel	6.01
5	Canada	7.46	20	Italy	5.94
6	United Kingdom	7.39	21	South Korea	5.83
7	Germany	7.34	22	Saudi Arabia	5.75
8	Netherlands	7.28	23	Brazil	5.65
9	Belgium	7.22	24	South Africa	5.61
9 (tie)	United States	7.22	25	Malaysia	5.59
11	Japan	7.10	26	Taiwan	5.41
12	Singapore	6.78	27	Turkey	5.23
13	Spain	6.63	28	Russia	5.16
14	UAE	6.62	29	China	4.94
15	France	6.50	30	India	4.62

SOURCES: Transparency International, *www.transparency.org/policy_research/surveys_indices/bpi/bpi 2006* (accessed February 18, 2008).

and China, which has become the world's fourth largest exporter, almost as bad. However, multinational firms in the US, Japan, France and Spain also reveal a relatively high propensity to pay bribes overseas.

These are difficult issues for managers to resolve. Companies that don't oil the wheels of contract negotiations in foreign countries can put themselves at a competitive disadvantage, yet managers walk a fine line when doing deals overseas. Although US laws allow certain types of payments, tough federal anti-bribery laws are also in place. Many companies, including Monsanto and IBM, have got into trouble with the US Securities and Exchange Commission, while Mabey & Johnson, a bridge-building firm, became the first major British company to be prosecuted in the UK after admitting paying bribes to win contracts in Ghana, Jamaica and Iraq.[34]

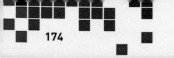

NEW MANAGER SELF-TEST

Self and Others

Leaders differ in how they view human nature and the tactics they use to get things done through others. Answer the questions below based on how you view yourself and others. Think carefully about each question and be honest about what you feel inside. Please answer whether each item below is Mostly True or Mostly False for you.

		Mostly True	Mostly False
1	I prefer not to depend on anyone else to get things done.	☐	☐
2	I appreciate that I am a special person.	☐	☐
3	I help orient new people even though it is not required.	☐	☐
4	I like to be the centre of attention.	☐	☐
5	I am always ready to lend a helping hand to those around me.	☐	☐
6	I tend to see my co-workers as competitors.	☐	☐
7	I am quick to see and point out others' mistakes.	☐	☐
8	I frequently interrupt someone to make my point.	☐	☐
9	I often have to admit that people around me are not very competent.	☐	☐

SCORING AND INTERPRETATION: This scale is about orientation toward self versus others. A high score suggests you could be ego-centred, and may come across to others as something of an idiot. To compute your score, give yourself one point for each Mostly False answer to items 3 and 5, and one point for each Mostly True answer to items 1, 2, 4, 6, 7, 8 and 9. A score of 7 to 9 points suggests a self-oriented person who might take the *individualism approach* to the extreme or function at the *pre-conventional level 1* of moral development (Exhibit 5.2). A score from 4 to 6 points suggests a balance between self and others. A score from 0 to 3 points would indicate an 'other' orientation associated with a *utilitarian* or *moral-rights approach* and *level 2 or level 3 moral development,* suggesting little likelihood of coming across as a jerk.

With some major corporate scandals such as those at Madoff Security or Parmalat, it is difficult to believe what has been claimed, that a large number of other individuals, including employees, suppliers and sub-contractors could have remained ignorant of such large scale fraud over such a long period of time. The values adopted within the organization are highly important, especially when we understand that most people are at the level-two stage of moral development, which means they believe their duty is to fulfil obligations and expectations of others. At Parmalat Calisto Tanzi was a very influential and charismatic entrepreneur and it was difficult for others to question his actions. Similarly, Bernard Madoff was a very respected member of his profession, who deflected outside questioning about his investment strategies by claiming that he was prevented from revealing his trade secrets by client confidentiality. These cases have some echoes of the actions of Robert Maxwell at the Mirror Group some years earlier.[35]

What is Corporate Social Responsibility?

Now let's turn to the issue of corporate social responsibility. In one sense, the concept of social responsibility, like ethics, is easy to understand: it means distinguishing right from wrong and doing right. It means being a good corporate citizen. The formal definition of corporate social responsibility (CSR) is management's obligation to make choices and take actions that will contribute to the welfare and interests of society as well as the organization.[36]

As straightforward as this definition seems, CSR can be a difficult concept to grasp because different people have different beliefs as to which actions improve society's welfare.[37] To make matters worse, social responsibility covers a range of issues, many of which are ambiguous with respect to right or wrong. If a bank deposits the money from a customer into a low-interest account for 90 days, from which it makes a substantial profit, is it being a responsible corporate citizen? How about two companies engaging in intense competition? Is it socially responsible for the stronger corporation to drive the weaker one into bankruptcy or a forced merger?

Or consider companies such as Chiquita, Kmart or Dana Corporation, all of which declared bankruptcy – which is perfectly legal – to avoid mounting financial obligations to suppliers, labour unions or competitors. At Kmart, one of America's biggest supermarket chains, it later emerged that the company loaned one of its executives $30m just before the company filed for bankruptcy. In the UK, after the Farepak disaster in 2006, in which 150 000 customers of the Christmas hamper saving scheme lost their money, the Government claimed to have created an industry standards scheme to protect such consumers in future. Yet thousands of distraught brides were dealt the same blow in August 2008 when UK wedding list business WrapIt crashed into administration. At WrapIt, customers paid money up front, expecting a lavish package of wedding gifts. As with Farepak, when WrapIt went bust it emerged all the money had been spent and there were no gifts to show for it.[39]

Certainly the actions of John Mackay, boss of Whole Foods, now under investigation for his planned acquisition of Wild Oats, a rival chain, raises some ethical concerns. He is alleged to have posted numerous comments online over a number of years under the name 'Rahodeb' praising his firm and criticizing Wild Oats.[40]

These examples contain moral, legal and economic considerations that make socially responsible behaviour hard to define. There is a plethora of academic debate and theories over

Corporate social responsibility
The obligation of an organization's management to make decisions and take actions that will enhance the welfare and interests of society as well as the organization.

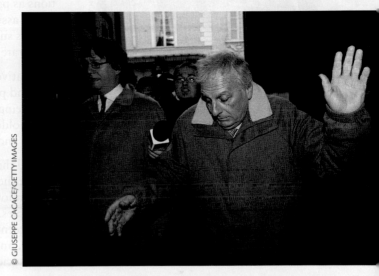

© GIUSEPPE CACACE/GETTY IMAGES

CONCEPT CONNECTION Rarely can ethical or unethical corporate actions be attributed solely to the personal values of a single manager. One notable exception may be the problems at Parmalat in Italy, the third largest manufacturer of European dairy products after the Swiss firm Nestlé and French group Danone. At first sight, Parmalat may seem to be a one-off, albeit with some characteristically Italian features. Unlike the US scandals where managers at Enron, WorldCom and Global Crossing were cooking the books in an attempt to maximize the value of their stock options, Parmalat was about the response of one entrepreneur, Calisto Tanzi, to his deteriorating financial circumstances.[38]

Parmalat represents a 'European Enron', according to Giullo Tremonte, Italy's economy minister, who has calculated that the fraudulent bankruptcy claim by the Italian dairy magnate will cost the national economy the equivalent of €11 billion, or almost 1 per cent of the country's Gross Domestic Product. It appears that for 15 years, Calisto Tanzi himself, aided only by his right-hand man Fausto Tonna, the company's financial director, painstakingly falsified Parmalat's accounts. Le Monde reports that Parmalat's accounts are filled with thousands of virtual operations, such as an imaginary 300 000-ton consignment of powdered milk to Cuba or the fictitious licence for the Santal brand of fruit juices in the US. Bank of America revealed that Bonlat, Parmalat's subsidiary in the Cayman Islands, did not in reality possess a four-billion euro account, as claimed in the company accounts, and that the US bank logo that Parmalat had used on its documents was a fake.

CONCEPT CONNECTION The International Olympic Committee (IOC) must respond to numerous stakeholders, including the 205 National Olympic Committees that make up its membership, the countries and cities at which various Olympic events will be held, the business community that will cater to attendees, numerous sponsors, media organizations, the participating athletes, and an international public that has varying and conflicting interests. The symbolic running of the torch for the 2008 Olympics was plagued by protests over China's alleged human rights violations. This photo shows protesters marching while the torch relay takes place.

what actually constitutes corporate social responsibility. A widely accepted categorization by Garriga and Mele[41] summarizes these within four general categories:

1 Instrumental theories which focus on profit maximization, and therefore consider CSR simply in terms of impact on profit maximization. This approach is most closely associated with Milton Friedman (1970), but would also include more recent strategic literature such as Porter and Kramer.[42]

2 Political theories which ascribe responsibilities to organizations as part of the social contract or 'licence to operate' that it assumes exists between business and society. Supporters such as Crane and Matten[43] put an emphasis on corporate citizenship.

3 Integrative theories which suggest that the long-term success and profitability of organizations is closely allied to the well-being of society. This would include literature on stakeholder management such as Mitchell *et al.*, and Goodpaster and Matthews.[44]

4 Ethical theories which apply ethics on organizations and deduct the responsibility of firms from universal and/or conventional norms and values and fundamental moral principles. This normative approach can be seen in Evan and Freeman,[45] as well as more recent literature on sustainability, and focuses on the right thing to do to achieve a good society.

Many firms, such as Burberry, Enterprise plc, Marks & Spencer, and Zurich now prefer to refer to the broader term Corporate Responsibility, rather than Corporate Social Responsibility, which they feel has become slightly restrictive and tainted by some of the earlier debates over meaning.

Organizational Stakeholders

One reason for the difficulty understanding and applying CSR is that managers must confront the question, 'Responsibility to whom?' Recall from Chapter 3 that the organization's environment consists of several sectors in both the task and general environment. From a social responsibility perspective, enlightened organizations view the internal and external environment as a variety of stakeholders.

Stakeholder
Any group within or outside the organization that has a stake in the organization's performance.

A stakeholder is any individual or group within or outside the organization that has a stake in the organization's performance. Each stakeholder has a different criterion of responsiveness because it has a different interest in the organization, and differing levels of power to influence the decisions and actions of the company.[46] For example, Wal-Mart uses aggressive bargaining tactics with suppliers so that it is able to provide low prices for customers. Some stakeholders see this type of corporate behaviour as responsible because it benefits customers and forces suppliers to be more efficient. Others, however, argue that the aggressive tactics are unethical and socially irresponsible because they force manufacturers to lay off workers, close factories, and outsource from low-wage countries. One supplier said clothing is being sold so cheaply at Wal-Mart that many US companies could not compete even if they paid their employees nothing.[47]

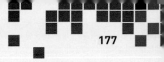

INNOVATIVE WAY

Monsanto

Over the past decade or so, Monsanto has been transformed from a chemicals firm into a biotechnology company. The organization's vast array of stakeholders around the world includes customers, investors, suppliers, partners, health and agricultural organizations, regulatory agencies, research institutes, and governments.

Monsanto experienced some big problems in recent years because of its failure to satisfy various stakeholder groups. For example, the company's genetic seed business has been the target of controversy and protest. Small farmers were concerned about new dependencies that might arise for them with using the new seeds. European consumers rebelled against a perceived imposition of unlabeled, genetically modified food ingredients. Research institutes and other organizations took offence at what they perceived as Monsanto's arrogant approach to the new business. Activist groups accused the company of creating

'Frankenstein foods'. To make matters even worse, in seeking to sell genetically modified seeds in Indonesia, managers allegedly bribed government officials, which got Monsanto into hot water with the SEC.

In light of these stakeholder issues, CEO Hendrik Verfaillie offered an apology to some stakeholders at a *Farm Journal* Conference in Washington, D.C., saying that Monsanto 'was so blinded by its enthusiasm for this great new technology that it missed the concerns the technology raised for many people'. Verfaillie also announced a five-part pledge that aims to restore positive stakeholder relationships. Each of the five commitments requires an ongoing dialogue between Monsanto managers and various stakeholder constituencies. The company paid $1.5 million to settle the SEC charges and is voluntarily co-operating with regulatory investigators. Monsanto managers understand the importance of effectively managing critical stakeholder relationships.[48]

The organization's performance affects stakeholders, but stakeholders can also have a tremendous effect on the organization's performance and success. Consider the case of Monsanto, a leading competitor in the life sciences industry.

Exhibit 5.4 illustrates important stakeholders for Monsanto. Most organizations are similarly influenced by a variety of stakeholder groups. Investors and shareholders, employees, customers and suppliers are considered primary stakeholders, without whom the organization cannot survive. Investors, shareholders and suppliers' interests are served by managerial efficiency – that is, use of resources to achieve profits. Employees expect work satisfaction, pay and good supervision. Customers are concerned with decisions about the quality, safety and availability of goods and services. When any primary stakeholder group becomes seriously dissatisfied, the organization's viability is threatened.[49]

Other important stakeholders are the government and the community, which have become increasingly important in recent years. Most corporations exist only under the proper charter and licences and operate within the limits of safety laws, environmental protection requirements, antitrust regulations, anti-bribery legislation, and other laws and regulations in the government sector. The community includes local government, the natural and physical environments, and the quality of life provided for residents. Special interest groups, still another stakeholder, may include trade associations, political action committees, professional associations and consumerists.

Monsanto's situation neatly illustrates how for multinational companies operating on a global basis, apparently similar stakeholder groups such as farmers, government or consumers actually differ across the globe. While Europeans have rejected genetically modified crops, it is very different in Asia and Latin America. By 2006, genetically modified crops were grown on more than 100 million hectares in 22 countries, with farmers in China and India clamouring for more. The driver for this has expansion has been demographics, and rising food prices. Land has become

Exhibit 5.4 Major Stakeholders Relevant to Monsanto Company

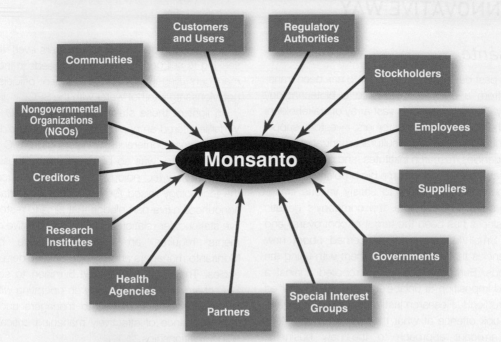

SOURCES: Based on information in D. Wheeler, B. Colbert, and R. E. Freeman, 'Focusing on Value: Reconciling Corporate Social Responsibility, Sustainability, and a Stakeholder Approach in a Networked World', *Journal of General Management* 28, no. 3 (Spring 2003): 1–28; and J. E. Post, L. E. Preston, and S. Sachs, 'Managing the Extended Enterprise: The New Stakeholder View', *California Management Review* 45, no. 1 (Fall 2002): 6–28.

scarce as cities expand and companies such as Monsanto and Syngenta, its Swiss rival, make plants that produce bigger yields at lower costs, repel predatory bugs, use less herbicide in a world that needs to feed an extra three billion people by 2050.

These companies certainly appear to have won the commercial argument globally if not in Europe, and have profited hugely. Syngenta's share price surged by 50 per cent last year, while Monsanto's grew by 140 per cent and the American company revealed that its sales of seeds had risen by 23 per cent in 2008 because of soaring demand in Latin America. An astonishing achievement for a business that was almost on its knees in 2002, accused of poisoning the world for profit.[50]

Socially responsible organizations consider the effects of their actions on all stakeholder groups. Some large businesses with the resources needed to serve developing countries are extending their field of stakeholders by serving the *bottom of the pyramid*.

The Bottom of the Pyramid

Bottom of the pyramid concept
The idea that large corporations can both alleviate social problems and make a profit by selling goods and services to the world's poorest people.

The **bottom of the pyramid (BOP)** concept, sometimes called *base of the pyramid*, proposes that corporations can alleviate poverty and other social ills, as well as make significant profits, by selling to the world's poorest people. The term *bottom of the pyramid* refers to the more than four billion people who make up the lowest level of the world's economic 'pyramid' as defined by per capita income. These people earn less than US$1500 a year, with about one-fourth of them earning less than a dollar a day.[51] Traditionally, these people haven't been served by most large businesses because products and services are too expensive, inaccessible and not suited to their needs. A number of leading companies are changing that by adopting BOP business models geared to serving the poorest of the world's consumers.

💡 INNOVATIVE WAY

Unilever/Hindustan Lever

The World Health Organization estimates that diarrhoea-related illnesses kill more than 1.8 million people a year. One way to prevent the spread of these diseases is better hand-washing, and marketing managers for Lifebuoy soap are trying to make sure people know that fact.

British soap maker Lever Brothers (now the global organization Unilever) introduced Lifebuoy to India more than a century ago, promoting it as the enemy of dirt and disease. The basic approach today is the same. Several years ago, the company's India subsidiary,

Hindustan Lever Limited, introduced a campaign called *Swasthya Chetna* (Glowing Health), sending Lifebuoy teams into rural villages with a 'glo-germ kit' to show people that even clean-looking hands can carry dangerous germs – and that soap-washed hands don't.

Sales of Lifebuoy have risen sharply since the campaign, aided by the introduction of a smaller-size bar that costs five rupees (about 12 cents). Just as importantly, says Hindustan Lever's chairman Harish Manwani, the campaign has reached around 80 million of the rural poor with education about how to prevent needless deaths.[52]

The BOP motive is two-fold. Of course, companies are in business with a goal to make money, and managers see a vast untapped market in emerging economies. However, another goal is to play a pivotal role in addressing global poverty and other problems such as environmental destruction, social decay and political instability in the developing world. Although the BOP concept has gained significant attention only recently, the basic idea is nothing new. Here's an example of a company that has been practising bottom of the pyramid activities for more than a hundred years.

Marketing manager Punit Misra, who oversees the Lifebuoy brand, emphasizes that 'profitable responsibility' is essential for companies to have a true impact on solving the world's problems. 'If it's not really self-sustaining, somewhere along the line it will drop off', Misra says.[53] Other proponents of bottom-of-the pyramid thinking agree that BOP works because it ties social responsibility directly into the heart of the company. Businesses contribute to lasting change when the profit motive goes hand-in-hand with the desire to make a contribution to humankind. For instance, Marks & Spencer launched Oxfam clothes exchange in order to encourage customers to recycle their old clothes. The aim is to both support the humanitarian work of the charity Oxfam in developing countries, as well as reduce the amount of clothes, currently one million tonnes, being sent to landfill sites in Britain.[54]

Beyond maintaining high ethical standards, top managers at a growing number of companies recognize how to target their social responsibility efforts in ways that also benefit the business. More than 3000 products now bear the Fairtrade logo introduced in Chapter 3, and supermarkets such as Sainsbury, Tesco and Marks & Spencer are keen to promote their fairtrade credentials. One farmers' cooperative to benefit from fairtrade is Kuapa Kokoo in Ghana. Launched in 1993, the co-op now represents the interests of 45 000 cocoa farmers and as well as guaranteeing a good price for the cocoa beans, it has used its Fairtrade premium to fund a large number of community-based educational, employment, financial and health projects.

Starbucks claims to build social responsibility into its business model by paying hourly employees above minimum wage, buying fair-trade coffee, and negotiating long-term contracts with coffee growers who farm in environmentally friendly ways. These efforts make good business sense at the same time they build the image of these companies as good corporate citizens. Walk into Starbucks and the Fairtrade logo is prominent throughout the store, although only filter coffee, one of Starbucks least popular lines, actually uses the ethically sourced beans. Recently, Starbucks has entered into a partnership with Product Red, the global organization fronted by the rock star Bono, which funds AIDS programmes in Africa. Starbucks will donate £3 from every Product Red tumbler sold and 5p every time a customer uses a Product Red card to purchase coffee. Product Red has previously formed partnerships with companies such as Apple, Converse and Dell to create limited edition products and donate a percentage of the revenue to fund programmes in Africa that provide support and medicine for people affected by HIV. Product Red is a reasonably successful initiative raising more than $130m in three years, though critics claim that there is a significant difference between this 'cause branding' approach and what is generally understood as corporate social responsibility. The latter is about companies managing their business processes to produce positive outcomes; or at least not to produce negative outcomes for society, whilst this approach is more about encouraging consumers to change their brand choices. It is more a question of where to shop rather than how to shop.

Social Enterprises

Cafédirect, the Big Issue and Jamie Oliver's Fifteen are social enterprises – businesses that make money and plough it back into social or environmental goals. They are all fully fledged companies and not just organizations that rely on donations. As Penny Newman, chief executive of Cafédirect, said: 'Social enterprise is first and foremost an intrinsically sensible business model. But secondly, from a personal perspective, I can't imagine a job that could be more enjoyable'.[55]

It is estimated that only a quarter of people in Britain are aware of social enterprises, yet there are about 55 000 such organizations. They range from the large, famous companies such as the Co-Operative Group, to smaller, lesser-known organizations such as the Oxo Tower restaurant and Gabriel's Wharf, which were built by a company founded by local people to regenerate their area. According to recent government figures, social enterprises account for 5 per cent of all businesses and contribute £8.4 billion a year to the UK economy – almost 1 per cent of annual GDP.

Another example is HCT Group, a social enterprise founded in 1982, which aims to make public transport available for all. Structured as a holding company, HCT is expected to turn over £15.5 million this year – a jump of more than 50 per cent in the past two years – and has commercial activities that include four red bus routes in London and yellow school bus routes in Yorkshire. The company, which employs more than 400 people, competes with the likes of Stagecoach to get these contracts. The surplus generated from these operations is ploughed back into the group's community transport services division, which includes ScootAbility, an electric wheel-chair-hire service in Camden, London. The money is also used for the group's training division, which aims to help mainly unemployed people get jobs in the transport sector as bus drivers and passenger assistants. It also teaches people with learning difficulties how to use public transport to boost their independence.

The Ethic of Sustainability and the Natural Environment

Sustainability
Economic development that generates wealth and meets the needs of the current population while preserving the environment for the needs of future generations.

Corporations involved in bottom-of-the-pyramid activities, as well as a number of other companies around the world, are also embracing a revolutionary idea called *sustainability* or *sustainable development*. Sustainability refers to economic development that generates wealth and meets the needs of the current generation while saving the environment so future generations can meet their needs as well.[56] With a philosophy of sustainability, managers weave environmental and social concerns

Exhibit 5.5 The Shades of Corporate Green

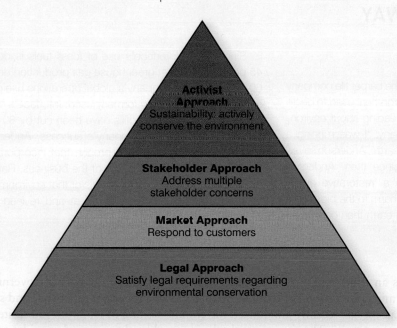

Activist Approach
Sustainability: actively conserve the environment

Stakeholder Approach
Address multiple stakeholder concerns

Market Approach
Respond to customers

Legal Approach
Satisfy legal requirements regarding environmental conservation

SOURCES: Based on R. E. Freeman, J. Pierce, and R. Dodd, *Shades of Green: Ethics and the Environment* (New York: Oxford University Press, 1995).

into every strategic decision, revise policies and procedures to support sustainability efforts, and measure their progress toward sustainability goals.

One model uses the phrase *shades of green* to evaluate a company's commitment to environmental responsibility. The various shades, which represent a company's approach to addressing environmental concerns, are illustrated in Exhibit 5.5. With a *legal approach*, the organization does just what is necessary to satisfy legal requirements. In general, managers and the company show little concern for environmental issues.

The next shade, the *market approach*, represents a growing awareness of and sensitivity to environmental concerns, primarily to satisfy customers. A company might provide environmentally friendly products because customers want them, for instance, not necessarily because of strong management commitment to the environment. For instance, Toyota has built a competitive advantage from the environmental benefits of its hybrid technology in its Prius hybrid car range.

A further step is to respond to multiple demands from the environment. The *stakeholder approach* means that companies attempt to answer the environmental concerns of various stakeholder groups, such as customers, the local community, business partners and special interest groups. For Instance RWE npower – the German utility giant – teamed up with the environmental pressure group Greenpeace to promote Juice, a renewable energy product, to thousands of consumers in the UK as a clean energy option. Not everyone though agrees with Greenpeace partnering with npower. The World Wildlife Fund, for example, refuses to work in any way with RWE because it burns coal in power stations and operates nuclear facilities. Other critics say such partnerships do not create lasting change.

Finally, at the highest level of green, organizations take an *activist approach* to environmental issues by actively searching for ways to conserve the Earth's resources. A growing number of companies around the world are embracing a revolutionary idea called *sustainability* or *sustainable development*. Alcatel Lucent are a company that are investing heavily in they sustainability agenda. They have signed the United Nations' Caring for Climate initiative which is designed to 'advance practical solutions and shape both public opinion and public policy, raising awareness that climate

💡 INNOVATIVE WAY

Interface

For Ray Anderson, who founded the carpet tile company Interface, the approach to the environment used to be 'to follow the law'. Then he started reading about environmental issues and had an epiphany: 'I was running a company that was plundering the earth', Anderson says.

How things have changed since then. Anderson challenged Interface to become a 'restorative enterprise', an operation that does no harm to the biosphere and that takes nothing out of the earth than cannot be recycled or quickly regenerated.

Since 1994, Interface's use of fossil fuels is down 45 per cent, with net greenhouse gas production down 60 per cent. The company's global operations use only one-third the water they formerly used. Interface's contributions to garbage landfills have been cut by 80 per cent. One key to the company's success, Anderson says, is a comprehensive approach that incorporates sustainability into every aspect of the business. Rather than going green by tacking on this or that environmental programme, managers looked at and revised the whole system.

change is an issue requiring urgent and extensive action on the part of governments, business and citizens in order to avoid serious damage to global prosperity and safety'. Alcatel Lucent has recently announced the commissioning of its 200th radio site powered by solar energy. The site is completely powered by the sun, and provides telecom services to remote communities on the remote Senegalese island of Bettenty and the surrounding Saloum islands that previously had no access to wireless communications services.[57]

One of the most ardent, and perhaps unlikely, advocates of sustainability is a carpet manufacturer.

Ray Anderson's mission is a lot easier than it used to be. Even companies that have typically paid little attention to the green movement are grappling with issues related to sustainability, partly because of the growing clout of environmentalists. Even Wal-Mart is paying attention. The company teamed up with Conservation International to help develop ways to cut energy consumption, switch to renewable power, and sell millions of energy-efficient fluorescent bulbs.[58] Sustainability argues that organizations can find innovative ways to create wealth at the same time they are preserving natural resources. General Mills used to pay to have oat hulls from its cereal production process hauled to the landfill. Now customers compete to buy the company's solid waste to be burned as fuel. GM earns more money from recycling than it once spent on disposal.[59]

CONCEPT CONNECTION Alcoa Inc.'s 'Taking Action' initiative involves Alcoa employees visiting schools to talk to students about natural resources and sustainability. This annual employee volunteer programme represents only one facet of the company's commitment to sustainable development. Alcoa's *2020 Strategic Framework for Sustainability* spells out goals for integrating sustainability principles into its ongoing operations and establishes specific benchmarks. The World Economic Forum named Alcoa one of the world's most sustainable corporations, and in recognition of its 80 per cent reduction of greenhouse gas per fluorocarbon, *BusinessWeek* and The Climate Group cited the world's leading aluminium producer as a top 'green' company of the decade.

Evaluating Corporate Social Responsibility

A model for evaluating corporate social performance is presented in Exhibit 5.6. The model indicates that total corporate social responsibility can be subdivided into four primary criteria: economic, legal, ethical and discretionary responsibilities.[60] These four criteria fit together to form the whole of a company's social responsiveness.

Exhibit 5.6 Criteria of Corporate Social Performance

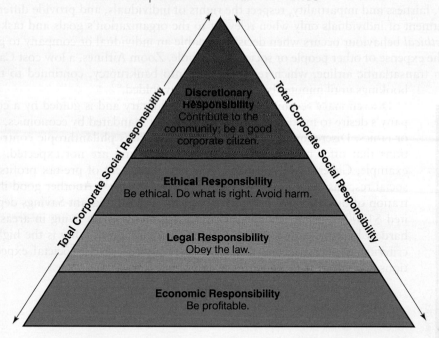

Total Corporate Social Responsibility

Discretionary Responsibility
Contribute to the community; be a good corporate citizen.

Ethical Responsibility
Be ethical. Do what is right. Avoid harm.

Legal Responsibility
Obey the law.

Economic Responsibility
Be profitable.

SOURCES: Based on Archie B. Carroll, 'A Three-Dimensional Conceptual Model of Corporate Performance', *Academy of Management Review* 4 (1979): 499; A. B. Carroll, 'The Pyramid of Corporate Social Responsibility: Toward the Moral Management of Corporate Stakeholders', *Business Horizons* 34 (July–August 1991): 42; and Mark S. Schwartz and Archie B. Carroll, 'Corporate Social Responsibility: A Three-Domain Approach', *Business Ethics Quarterly* 13, no. 4 (2003): 503–530.

The first criterion of social responsibility is *economic responsibility*. The business institution is, above all, the basic economic unit of society. Its responsibility is to produce the goods and services that society wants and to maximize profits for its owners and shareholders. Economic responsibility, carried to the extreme, is called the *profit-maximizing view*, advocated by Nobel economist Milton Friedman. This view argues that the corporation should be operated on a profit-oriented basis, with its sole mission to increase its profits as long as it stays within the rules of the game.[61] The purely profit-maximizing view is no longer considered an adequate criterion of performance in Canada, the US, and Europe. This approach means that economic gain is the only social responsibility and can lead companies into trouble.

Legal responsibility defines what society deems as important with respect to appropriate corporate behaviour.[62] That is, businesses are expected to fulfil their economic goals within the framework of legal requirements imposed by local town councils, state legislators, and federal regulatory agencies.

Examples of illegal acts by corporations include corporate fraud, intentionally selling defective goods, performing unnecessary repairs or procedures, deliberately misleading consumers, and billing clients for work not done. Organizations that knowingly break the law are poor performers in this category. For example, Dow Chemical was fined $2 million for violating an agreement to halt false safety claims about its pesticide products. Prudential Insurance also came under fire for misleading consumers about variable life insurance policies.[63] In 2004 Royal Dutch Shell paid fines of £83 million to settle action over its deliberate overestimation of its oil reserves in its accounts.

Ethical responsibility includes behaviours that are not necessarily codified into law and may not serve the corporation's direct economic interests. As described

---

Read the Ethical Dilemma on page 192 that pertains to legal and ethical responsibilities. How important is it to you to protect the natural environment?

TAKE A MOMENT

Discretionary responsibility
Organizational responsibility that is voluntary and guided by the organization's desire to make social contributions not mandated by economics, law or ethics.

© MICHAEL NAGLE/GETTY IMAGES

CONCEPT CONNECTION
The fall of financial services icon Bear Stearns grabbed the headlines, but numerous mortgage companies were declaring bankruptcy at the same time. When looking for who failed to meet their economic and ethical responsibilities in the mortgage industry meltdown, there is plenty of blame to go around. Some mortgage brokers and companies had lenient lending policies and offered exotic mortgage types that borrowers did not fully understand. Some homebuyers and real estate investors over-extended in their purchasing. Some financial institutions bundled mortgages into investment securities. The resulting large number of foreclosed mortgages left empty houses, failed companies and devastated families that will negatively impact some communities for years.

earlier in this chapter, to be *ethical*, organization decision-makers should act with equity, fairness and impartiality, respect the rights of individuals, and provide different treatment of individuals only when relevant to the organization's goals and tasks.[64] *Unethical* behaviour occurs when decisions enable an individual or company to gain at the expense of other people or society as a whole. Zoom Airlines, a low cost Canadian transatlantic airline, which recently went into bankruptcy, continued to take bookings until minutes before the company folded.[65]

Discretionary responsibility is purely voluntary and is guided by a company's desire to make social contributions not mandated by economics, law or ethics. Discretionary activities include generous philanthropic contributions that offer no pay-back to the company and are not expected. For example, General Mills spends more than 5 per cent of pre-tax profits on social responsibility initiatives and charitable giving.[66] Another good illustration of discretionary behaviour occurred when Emigrant Savings deposited $1000 into the accounts of nearly 1000 customers living in areas hit hardest by Hurricane Katrina.[67] Discretionary responsibility is the highest criterion of social responsibility because it goes beyond societal expectations to contribute to the community's welfare.

Managing Company Ethics and Social Responsibility

An expert on the topic of ethics said, 'Management is responsible for creating and sustaining conditions in which people are likely to behave themselves'.[68] Exhibit 5.7 illustrates ways in which managers create and support an ethical organization. One of the most important steps managers can take is to practice ethical leadership. *Ethical leadership* means that managers are honest and trustworthy, fair in their dealings with employees and customers, and behave ethically in both their personal and professional lives. Managers and first-line supervisors are important role models for ethical behaviour, and they strongly influence the ethical climate in the organization by adhering to high ethical standards in their own behaviour and decisions. Moreover, managers are proactive in influencing employees to embody and reflect ethical values.[69]

Managers can also implement organizational mechanisms to help employees and the company stay on an ethical footing. Some of the primary ones are codes of ethics, ethical structures and measures to protect It is often easier for small companies to actively promote social entrepreneurship. Many organizations, such as The Body Shop, Green & Black's, and Ben & Jerry's, which have been at the forefront of promoting ethical campaigns as an integral part of their business model, have found it hard to remain independent once they have grown to a size where they wish to attract outside investment and list on the stock market. All three are now part of large conglomerates – Body Shop was acquired by L'Oréal, Green & Black by Cadbury, and Ben and Jerry by Unilever.[70] However, a plethora of new, small companies have started up based on ethical trading. For instance, Belu is the UK's only 100 per cent charity-owned non-profit bottled-water brand. It uses 100 per cent recyclable, biodegradable corn-based bottles as well as glass ones. It was launched in 2004, and owner Reed Paget pays himself an annual salary of only £10 000. The company has ten employees and produces an annual turnover of £5 million.

Exhibit 5.7 Building an Ethical Organization

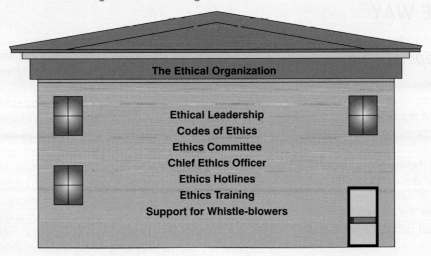

The Ethical Organization

Ethical Leadership
Codes of Ethics
Ethics Committee
Chief Ethics Officer
Ethics Hotlines
Ethics Training
Support for Whistle-blowers

SOURCES: Adapted from Linda Klebe Treviño, Laura Pincus Hartman and Michael Brown, 'Moral Person and Moral Manager', *California Management Review* 42, no. 4 (Summer 2000): 128–142.

The company has ploughed 100 per cent of its net profits to date, £279 000, into clean-water projects in India and Mali, and to reducing river pollution in the UK.[71]

Code of Ethics

A **code of ethics** is a formal statement of the company's values concerning ethics and social issues; it communicates to employees what the company stands for. Codes of ethics tend to exist in two types: principle-based statements and policy-based statements. *Principle-based statements* are designed to affect corporate culture; they define fundamental values and contain general language about company responsibilities, quality of products and treatment of employees. General statements of principle are often called *corporate credos*. One good example is Johnson & Johnson's 'The Credo'.

Code of ethics
A formal statement of the organization's values regarding ethics and social issues.

Do an internet search for Johnson & Johnson's Credo, which is available in 36 languages. For more than 00 years, the Credo has guided Johnson & Johnson's managers in making decisions that honour the company's responsibilities to employees, customers, the community and stockholders.

TAKE A MOMENT

Policy-based statements generally outline the procedures to be used in specific ethical situations. These situations include marketing practices, conflicts of interest, observance of laws, proprietary information, political gifts and equal opportunities. Examples of policy-based statements are Boeing's 'Business Conduct Guidelines', Chemical Bank's 'Code of Ethics', GTE's 'Code of Business Ethics' and Royal Dutch Shell's 'Code of Ethics'.[72]

Codes of ethics state the values or behaviours expected and those that will not be tolerated. A survey of *Fortune* 1000 companies found that 98 per cent address issues of ethics and business conduct in formal corporate documents, and 78 per cent of those have separate codes of ethics that are widely distributed.[73] When top management supports and enforces these codes, including rewards for compliance and discipline for violation, ethics codes can boost a company's ethical climate.[74]

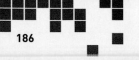

INNOVATIVE WAY

Guardian Newspaper Group

In recent years, charges of plagiarism and other ethical violations cast a spotlight on newspaper publishers and other media outlets. As a result, many companies put renewed emphasis on journalistic standards of integrity.

Executives at Guardian Newspapers, hope the company's clear and comprehensive code of ethics will reinforce the public's trust as well as prevent ethical misconduct. This excerpt from the opening sections of the code outlines some broad provisions for what the company stands for.

The most important currency of the Guardian is trust. This is as true today as when CP Scott marked the centenary of the founding of the paper with his famous essay on journalism in 1921. The purpose of this code is, above all, to protect and foster the bond of trust between the paper and its readers, and therefore to protect the integrity of the paper and of the editorial content it carries. As a set of guidelines, this will not form part of a journalist's contract of employment, nor will it form part, for either editorial management or journalists, of disciplinary, promotional or recruitment procedures. However, by observing the code, journalists working for the Guardian will be protecting not only the paper but also the independence, standing and reputation of themselves and their colleagues. It is important that freelances working for the Guardian also abide by these guidelines while on assignment for the paper.

The Guardian's code of ethics also includes statements on professional practice, setting out guidelines on issues such as anonymous sources and quotes, children, fairness, language, libel and contempt laws, photographs, plagiarism, privacy and subterfuge, as well as on personal behaviour and conflict of interest issue, such as confidential information, declarations of interest, freelance work, relationships, and accepting gifts and favours. In addition, The Guardian's code incorporates the Press Complaints Commission (PCC) Code of Practice which was framed by the UK newspaper and periodical industry and ratified by the PCC in 1999. This code sets out the benchmark for the press to maintain the highest professional and ethical standards. It both protects the rights of the individual and upholds the public's right to know. The code is the cornerstone of the system of self-regulation in the UK newspaper industry.[75]

By giving people some guidelines for confronting ethical questions and promising protection from recriminations for people who report wrongdoing, the Guardian's code of ethics gives all employees the responsibility and the right to maintain the organization's ethical climate.

The editorial code of ethics for the UK's Guardian Newspaper Group gives employees some guidelines for dealing with ethical questions.

Ethical Structures

Ethical structures represent the various systems, positions and programmes a company can undertake to implement ethical behaviour. One of the newest positions in organizations is the *chief accounting officer*, a response to widespread financial wrongdoing in recent years. These high-level executives handle reporting and compliance, ensure due diligence and work with outside auditors.[76] An ethics or corporate responsibility committee is a group of executives appointed to oversee company ethics. The committee provides rulings on questionable ethical issues and assumes responsibility for disciplining wrongdoers. Motorola's Ethics Compliance Committee, for instance, is charged with interpreting, clarifying and communicating the company's code of ethics and with adjudicating suspected code violations.

Many companies set up ethics offices with full-time staff to ensure that ethical standards are an integral part of company operations. These offices are

Ethics or corporate responsibility committee
A group of executives assigned to oversee the organization's ethics by ruling on questionable issues and disciplining violators.

headed by a **chief ethics officer**, a company executive who oversees all aspects of ethics and legal compliance, including establishing and broadly communicating standards, ethics training, dealing with exceptions or problems, and advising senior managers in the ethical and compliance aspects of decisions.[77] The title of *chief ethics officer* was almost unheard of a decade ago, but highly publicized ethical and legal problems in recent years sparked a growing demand for these ethics specialists.

Chief ethics officer
A company executive who oversees ethics and legal compliance.

Complete the Experiential Exercise on page 191 that pertains to ethical work environments. With what level of ethical climate are you most comfortable? As a manager, how might you improve the ethical climate of a department for which you are responsible?

TAKE A MOMENT

Ethics training programmes also help employees deal with ethical questions and translate the values stated in a code of ethics into everyday behaviour.[78] Training programmes are an important supplement to a written code of ethics. General Electric implemented a strong compliance and ethics training programme for all 320 000 employees worldwide. Much of the training is conducted online, with employees able to test themselves on how they would handle thorny ethical issues. In addition, small group meetings give people a chance to ask questions and discuss ethical dilemmas or questionable actions. Every quarter, each of GE's business units reports to headquarters the percentage of division employees who completed training sessions and the percentage that have read and signed off on the company's ethics guide, 'Spirit and Letter'.[79] A strong ethics programme is important, but it is no guarantee against lapses. Enron could boast of a well-developed ethics programme, for example, but managers failed to live up to it. Enron's problems sent a warning to other managers and organizations. It is not enough to *have* an impressive ethics programme. The ethics programme must be merged with day-to-day operations, encouraging ethical decisions throughout the company.

Ethics training
Training programmes to help employees deal with ethical questions and values.

Whistle-blowing

Employee disclosure of illegal, immoral, or illegitimate practices on the employer's part is called **whistle-blowing**.[80] No organization can rely exclusively on codes of conduct and ethical structures to prevent all unethical behaviour. Holding organizations accountable depends to some degree on individuals who are willing to blow the whistle if they detect illegal, dangerous or unethical activities. Whistle-blowers often report wrongdoing to outsiders, such as regulatory agencies, politicians or newspaper reporters. Some firms have instituted innovative programmes and confidential hotlines to encourage and support internal whistle-blowing. For this practice to be an effective ethical safeguard, however, companies must view whistle-blowing as a benefit to the company and make dedicated efforts to protect whistle-blowers.[81] Pricewaterhouse Coopers conducted a Global Economic Crime survey and reported that the two most effective investments in ethics programmes are internal auditing and support of whistle-blowers.[82]

Without effective protective measures, whistle-blowers suffer. Whistle-blowing has become widespread, but it is still risky for employees, who can lose their jobs,

Whistle-blowing
The disclosure by an employee of illegal, immoral or illegitimate practices by the organization.

be ostracized by co-workers or be transferred to lower-level positions. Consider what happened when Karen Reissmann, a Manchester nurse, spoke out publicly about her employers, Manchester Mental Health and Social Care trust. Reissmann, a community psychiatric nurse was sacked on four counts of gross misconduct. The trust found that she had brought the trust into disrepute by criticising, in an interview given to a Manchester-based social enterprise magazine, the transfer of NHS work to a voluntary organization. The other three charges were for telling people that she was suspended, protesting her innocence and allowing the press to print information about her case. A fifth charge of misusing time was dropped. The trust did not think Reissmann was a bad nurse, however. On the day she was suspended last year, she received a letter confirming her promotion to senior nurse practitioner.[83]

Many managers still look on whistle-blowers as disgruntled employees who aren't good team players. Yet to maintain high ethical standards, organizations need people who are willing to point out wrongdoing. Managers can be trained to view whistle-blowing as a benefit rather than a threat, and systems can be set up to effectively protect employees who report illegal or unethical activities.

CONCEPT CONNECTION When American Airlines and Southwest Airlines were allowed to continue flying planes that Federal Aviation Administration inspectors thought needed repairs, some inspectors were allegedly threatened or punished to keep them quiet. The resulting whistle-blower complaints of the FAA inspectors faulted the cosy relationship between the FAA and the airline companies. Ultimately, the FAA grounded American and Southwest fleets of MD-80s for the mandated maintenance and repairs. American Airlines CEO Gerald Arpey said he believed that 'the safety of our MD-80 fleet was never at issue'.

The Business Case for Ethics and Social Responsibility

Most managers now realize that paying attention to ethics and social responsibility is as important a business issue as paying attention to costs, profits and growth. Across the developed economies, varied stakeholders are increasingly pushing new reporting initiatives connected to the sustainability movement that emphasize *the triple bottom line* of economic, social and environmental performance.

Naturally, the relationship of a corporation's ethics and social responsibility to its financial performance concerns both managers and management scholars and has generated a lively debate.[84] One concern of managers is whether good citizenship will hurt performance – after all, ethics programmes and social responsibility cost money. A number of studies, undertaken to determine whether heightened ethical and social responsiveness increases or decreases financial performance, provided varying results but generally found a

TAKE A MOMENT   Strive to be an ethical leader by adhering to high standards in your personal and professional behaviour. As a new manager, use tools such as codes of ethics, ethics training programmes, and ethics offices to promote ethical behaviour in your unit and help people resolve ethical dilemmas. Treasure whistle-blowers who have the courage to point out wrongdoing, and set up organizational systems to protect them.

positive relationship between social responsibility and financial performance.[85] For example, a study of the financial performance of large US corporations considered 'best corporate citizens' found that they enjoy both superior reputations and superior financial performance.[86] Although results from these studies are not proof, they do provide an indication that use of resources for ethics and social responsibility does not hurt companies.[87] Moreover, one survey found that 70 per cent of global CEOs believe corporate social responsibility is vital to their companies' profitability.[88]

Companies are also making an effort to measure the nonfinancial factors that create value. Researchers find, for example, that people prefer to work for companies that demonstrate a high level of ethics and social responsibility; thus, these organizations can attract and retain high-quality employees.[89] Customers pay attention too. A study by Walker Research indicates that, price and quality being equal, two-thirds of customers say they would switch brands to do business with a company that is ethical and socially responsible.[90] Enlightened companies realize that integrity and trust are essential elements in sustaining successful and profitable business relationships with an increasingly connected web of employees, customers, suppliers and partners. Although doing the right thing might not always be profitable in the short run, many managers believe it can provide a competitive advantage by developing a level of trust that money can't buy.

 INNOVATIVE WAY

Unión Fenosa

One organization in Spain, Unión Fenosa, pioneered the concept of corporate social responsibility as a business issue. Unión Fenosa is a large Spanish business group that does business in three major industries: energy, consulting services and telecommunications. The company's approach to corporate social responsibility – called 'complicity with the environment' – emerged during the 1980s when Unión Fenosa was building power stations in isolated areas and providing consulting services to other companies moving into developing countries.

Former head engineer José Luis Castro recalls that the company had to essentially build an entire community around a developing power station to serve the personal and social needs of engineers, technicians, local workers and their families. From the beginning, productivity and progress in business was seen to go hand-in-hand with the well-being of the community.

Thus began Unión Fenosa's concept of 'complicity with the environment' as a key to business success. The company sees its success as inextricably tied to the well-being of not only shareholders but also workers, suppliers and the immediate environment in which the company is working.

Although some degree of altruism influences Unión Fenosa's philanthropy, top leaders emphasize that it's really a business issue: the survival of the company is based on its ability to involve itself with the local community in a way that makes money for the company at the same time it makes the community better than it was before.[91]

Unión Fenosa executives believe that a concern with *social sustainability* is essential for a company to remain competitive and successful. Social sustainability refers to interacting with the community in which a company does business in a way that makes money for the company but also improves the long-term well-being of the community.

A MANAGER'S ESSENTIALS: WHAT HAVE WE LEARNED?

■ Ethics is the code of moral principles that governs behaviour with respect to what is right or wrong. An ethical issue is present in any situation when the actions of an individual or organization may harm or benefit others. Ethical decisions and behaviour are typically guided by a value system. Four value-based approaches that serve as criteria for ethical decision-making are utilitarian, individualism, moral-rights and justice.

■ For an individual manager, the ability to make ethical choices depends partly on whether the person is at a preconventional, conventional or post-conventional level of moral development.

■ Corporate social responsibility concerns a company's values toward society. The model for evaluating social performance uses four criteria: economic, legal, ethical and discretionary.

■ The question of how an organization can be a good corporate citizen is complicated because organizations respond to many different stakeholders, including customers, employees, stockholders and suppliers. Some organizations are extending their field of stakeholders through bottom-of-the-pyramid business activities.

■ One social issue of growing concern is responsibility to the natural environment. The philosophy of sustainability emphasizes economic development that meets the needs of today while preserving resources for the future.

■ Managers can help organizations be ethical and socially responsible by practising ethical leadership and using mechanisms such as codes of ethics, ethics committees, chief ethics officers, training programmes and procedures to protect whistle-blowers. After years of scandal, many managers are recognizing that managing ethics and social responsibility is just as important as paying attention to costs, profits and growth. Companies that are ethical and socially responsible perform as well as – and often better than – those that are not socially responsible.

DISCUSSION QUESTIONS

1 Dr Martin Luther King, Jr., said, 'As long as there is poverty in the world, I can never be rich. . . . As long as diseases are rampant, I can never be healthy. . . . I can never be what I ought to be until you are what you ought to be.' Discuss this quote with respect to the material in this chapter. Would this idea be true for companies, too?

2 Environmentalists are trying to pass laws for oil spills that would remove all liability limits for the oil companies. This change would punish corporations financially. Is this approach the best way to influence companies to be socially responsible?

3 Imagine yourself in a situation of being encouraged by colleagues to inflate your expense account. What factors do you think would influence your choice? Explain.

4 Is it socially responsible for organizations to undertake political activity or join with others in a trade association to influence the government? Discuss.

5 Was it ethical during the 1990s for car manufacturers to attempt to accommodate an ever-increasing consumer appetite for SUVs with their low fuel efficiency? Was it good business?

6 A noted business executive said, 'A company's first obligation is to be profitable. Unprofitable enterprises can't afford to be socially responsible.' Do you agree? How does this idea relate to the bottom-of-the-pyramid concept?

7 Do you believe it is ethical for companies to compile portfolios of personal information about their website visitors without informing them? What about organizations monitoring their employees' email? Discuss.

8 Which do you think would be more effective for shaping long-term ethical behaviour in an organization: a written code of ethics combined with ethics training or strong ethical leadership? Which would have more impact on you? Why?

9 'Proactive corporations will tend to move towards a strategic Corporate Social Responsibility (CSR) perspective, leveraging CSR to more efficiently or effectively create and renew competitive advantage'

   Critically consider the statement above. To what extent do you agree with this view? Justify your conclusion. If organizations pursue CSR policies from strategic rather than ethical motives does this really matter?

10 Do you think bottom-of-the-pyramid business practices can really have a positive effect on poverty and social problems in the developing world? Discuss.

11 A recent survey showed differences in managerial priorities across countries. For example, Japanese firms feel that if they are going through a tough period financially, keeping their employees on the job is much more important than maintaining dividends to shareholders. Specifically, only 3 per cent of Japanese managers said companies should maintain dividend payments to shareholders even if it means the company has to lay off workers, compared with 41 per cent in Germany, 40 per cent in France, and 89 per cent in both the US and the UK.

   Is it appropriate for management to define some stakeholders as more important than others? Should all stakeholders be considered equal?

12 Do you think a social entrepreneur can run a profitable business with a primary goal of improving society? Discuss.

MANAGEMENT IN PRACTICE: EXPERIENTIAL EXERCISE

Ethical Work Climates

Think of an organization for which you were employed. Answer the following questions twice: the first time, circle the number that best describes the way things actually were. The second time, answer the questions based on your beliefs about the ideal level to meet the needs of both individuals and the organization.

Disagree 1   2   3   4   5   Agree

1 What was best for everyone in the company was the major consideration there.

   1   2   3   4   5

2 Our major concern was always what was best for the other person.

   1   2   3   4   5

3 People were expected to comply with the law and professional standards over and above other considerations.

   1   2   3   4   5

4 In the company, the first consideration was whether a decision violated any law.

   1   2   3   4   5

5 It was very important to follow the company's rules and procedures there.

   1   2   3   4   5

6 People in the company strictly obeyed the company policies.

   1   2   3   4   5

7 In the company, people were mostly out for themselves.

   1   2   3   4   5

8 People were expected to do anything to further the company's interests, regardless of the consequences.

   1   2   3   4   5

9 In the company, people were guided by their own personal ethics.

   1   2   3   4   5

10 Each person in the company decided for himself or herself what was right and wrong.

   1   2   3   4   5

Scoring and Interpretation

Subtract each of your scores for questions 7 and 8 from the number 6. Then, add up your score for all 10 questions: Actual = _____. Ideal = _____. These questions measure the dimensions of an organization's ethical climate. Questions 1 and 2 measure caring for people, questions 3 and 4 measure lawfulness, questions 5 and 6 measure adherence to rules, questions 7 and 8 measure emphasis on financial and company performance, and questions 9 and 10 measure individual independence. A total score above 40 indicates a highly positive ethical climate. A score from 30 to 40 indicates above-average ethical climate. A score from 20 to 30 indicates a below-average ethical climate, and a score below 20 indicates a poor ethical climate. How far from your ideal score was the actual score for your organization? What does that difference mean to you?

Go back over the questions and think about changes that you could have made to improve the ethical climate in the organization. Discuss with other students what you could do as a manager to improve ethics in future companies for which you work.

SOURCE Based on Bart Victor and John B. Cullen, 'The Organizational Bases of Ethical Work Climates', *Administrative Science Quarterly* 33 (1988): 101–125.

MANAGEMENT IN PRACTICE: ETHICAL DILEMMA

Should We Go beyond the Law?

Nathan Randerson stared out his office window at the lazy curves and lush, green, flower-lined banks of the Dutch Valley River. He'd grown up near here, and he envisioned the day his children would enjoy the river as he had as a child. But now his own company might make that a risky proposition.

Nathan is a key product developer at Chem-Tech Corporation, an industry leader. Despite its competitive position, Chem-Tech experienced several quarters of dismal financial performance. Nathan and his team developed a new lubricant product that the company sees as the turning point in its declining fortunes. Top executives are thrilled that they can produce the new product at a significant cost savings because of recent changes in environmental regulations. Regulatory agencies loosened requirements on reducing and recycling wastes, which means Chem-Tech can now release waste directly into the Dutch Valley River.

Nathan is as eager as anyone to see Chem-Tech survive this economic downturn, but he doesn't think this route is the way to do it. He expressed his opposition regarding the waste dumping to both the plant manager and his direct supervisor, Martin Feldman. Martin has always supported Nathan, but this time was different. The plant manager, too, turned a deaf ear. 'We're meeting government standards', he'd said. 'It's up to them to protect the water. It's up to us to make a profit and stay in business.'

Frustrated and confused, Nathan turned away from the window, his prime office view mocking his inability to protect the river he loved. He knew the director of manufacturing was visiting the plant next week. Maybe if he talked with her, she would agree that the decision to dump waste materials in the river was ethically and socially irresponsible. But if she didn't, he would be skating on thin ice. His supervisor had already accused him of not being a team player. Maybe he should just be a passive bystander – after all, the company isn't breaking any laws.

What Would You Do?

1 Talk to the director of manufacturing and emphasize the responsibility Chem-Tech has as an industry leader to set an example. Present her with a recommendation that Chem-Tech participate in voluntary pollution reduction as a marketing tool, positioning itself as the environmentally friendly choice.

2 Mind your own business and just do your job. The company isn't breaking any laws, and if Chem-Tech's economic situation doesn't improve, a lot of people will be thrown out of work.

3 Call the local environmental advocacy group and get them to stage a protest of the company.

SOURCE Adapted from Janet Q. Evans, 'What Do You Do: What If Polluting Is Legal?', *Business Ethics* (Fall 2002): 20.

CASE FOR CRITICAL ANALYSIS 5.1

The Python Motor Company has developed a new family motor that will out-perform other competitor cars currently on the market. The firm's marketing research has indicated that there will be a very strong market demand for the product if it is priced at roughly £15 000.

Python's research and development department have developed two designs of the product. Version 1 would retail for about £14 000. Version 2 includes a range of additional safety features but would push the price up to £20 000. The firm's research indicated that Version 1 is a virtually perfect product, with one exception: confidential tests have shown that after normal use over two or three years, there is a 1:50 000 possibility that the car could suffer an electrical fire. In certain circumstances, this may happen so quickly that the occupants of the car may be unable to escape, although the possibility of this extreme case could be as high as 1:1 000 000. Version 2, which is much more robust, will last much longer and has shown no evidence of this problem.

Peter Smith, Python's Managing Director, has asked his R & D team to find a solution to the problem. They have suggested some design changes that includes using higher quality electrical equipment. This would likely reduce the probability of anyone suffering an electrical fire to 1:500 000. However these design changes would increase the cost of producing Version 1 considerably, so that it would then need to be priced at a minimum of £17 500. His sales force is worried that it will not sell at that price.

Peter is also aware from his sales force that the main competitor, Adder Motors, is also well advanced with plans to launch a new model. Their product sounds very similar to Python's Version 1, including its price. The market rumours are that it also suffers from potential electrical faults, but that the rival company is proceeding with production anyway.

Peter needs to review his options. If he makes the decision quickly, he can still beat his rival to market with the product. If he launches his product (Version 1) first, without modification, there is a high probability that Python can capture a significant part of the market though a first mover advantage, and get out of its current sales slump. But he is also aware that normal use of the product over 3–5 years might well lead to future legal claims, if people suffer injury through design faults in the cars, while there is a remote yet real possibility that someone might even die.

On the other hand, if Python launches the modified Version 1 or even Version 2, sales are likely to be unacceptably low. The rival company, Adder Ltd., would introduce its own version within 6–12 months time, and capture the bulk of the market.

Peter has considered developing an advertising campaign that might change the nature of market demand, by calling attention to the risks associated with the cheaper models. However, his lawyers have warned that Python might then be subjected to an expensive legal case from Adder, disputing the claims, and claiming substantial compensation. His Marketing Manager has also told him that the Advertising Standards Authority (ASA) actually prohibit such types of advertising anyway. Peter concluded that this was therefore not a viable option.

The Marketing Manager is convinced that the launch should still go ahead. Python need a competitively priced model, and in her opinion all products of this nature carry some risks. The car design has been authorized by government testers who have not discovered the electrical fault, and are not aware of the company's own research findings. She believes strongly in the doctrine of *caveat emptor*. However, the Deputy Marketing Manager who has recently graduated from the Leicester Business School at De Montfort University is less certain. He believes that the company has a moral duty to take action and shouldn't launch a product that it believes may be unsafe. He also believes that in the longer-term the company will benefit from adopting a clear policy of corporate social responsibility.

Before making a final decision, Peter decided to consult his Operations Director. He learned, that in his opinion, if they didn't shortly introduce the new model, and at the lower price, then Python would have to lay off at least 4000 of its 6000 production workers.

Peter finally consulted his Finance Director, who was equally pessimistic about the financial prospects of the company. Given the current sales slump, he advised that the expense already spent in developing the product, if it was now abandoned, could lead the company into bankruptcy or at least being taken over, within the next two years. He urged Peter to go ahead with the launch of lower priced Version 1 pointing out that their rival company was willing to do so. He also suggested that they could shred all the research information that suggested that the design could be faulty, so that in the event of future claims they could plead innocence, and pass the liability and costs on to their public liability insurers. The short-term financial pressures must override longer-term considerations of reputation or ethics in this instance.

Questions

1   What are the dilemmas in this case? What are the main ethical and legal issues involved? Is it ever possible in circumstances such as these to achieve an equitable balance of the various stakeholder interests? What course of action would you advise Peter to take in this instance? Justify your decision.

2   If you were advising the Deputy Marketing Manager, who is morally opposed to ignoring the problem, what would you recommend that they do if the company went ahead with the launch of the new product? Should they become a whistleblower? What are the likely results of being a whistleblower in these circumstances? What legal protection might they have?

3   Would the dilemma have been different if the design fault became apparent after and not before the product was launched? How would you deal with the issue then?

(This case is purely hypothetical, and is based on a scenario set out in *Business Ethics* by Farrell & Farrell (1997), Houghton Muffin.)

ENDNOTES

1. This example comes from Susan Pulliam, 'Crossing the Line; At Center of Fraud, WorldCom Official Sees Life Unravel', *The Wall Street Journal*, March 24, 2005; and S. Pulliam, 'Over the Line: A Staffer Ordered to Commit Fraud Balked, Then Caved', *The Wall Street Journal*, (June 23, 2003).

2. BBC. WorldCom: Wall Street Scandal available at: http://news.bbc.co.uk/1/hi/business/2077838.stm

3. *Financial Times*, 'Skandia sues ex-executives over bonuses', December 31, 2003; BBC, Madoff millions vanish into thin air http://news.bbc.co.uk/1/hi/business/7783386.stm

4. Ipsos-Mori report available at http://www.ipsos-mori.com/researchpublications/researcharchive.aspx?page=3&keyword=health5 Mike Esterl, 'Executive Derision: In Germany, Scandals Tarnish Business Elite', *The Wall Street Journal*, (March 4, 2008).

5. Mike Esterl, "Executive Decision: In Germany, Scandals Tarnish Business Elite", *The Wall Street Journal*, (March 4, 2008).

6. Daily Edit, Rise in emissions and unethical behaviour tarnish BP's image, available at http://www.edie.net/news/news_story.asp?id=9797

7. John R. Emshwiller and Alexei Barrionuevo, 'US Prosecutors File Indictment Against Skilling', *The Wall Street Journal*, February 20, 2004.

8. Landon Thomas, Jr. 'On Wall Street, A Rise in Dismissals Over Ethics', *The New York Times* (March 29, 2005), www.nytimes.com

9. Leveraging Logistics Partnerships 'Lessons from humanitarian organizations', http://publishing.eur.nl/ir/repub/asset/14519/EPS2008153LIS9058921864Samii.pdf

10. Tamar website available at http://www.tamar.com/servlet.cgi?page_id=287

11. Gordon F. Shea, *Practical Ethics* (New York: American Management Association, 1988); and Linda K. Treviño, 'Ethical Decision Making in Organizations; A Person-Situation Interactionist Model', *Academy of Management Review* 11 (1986): 601–617.

12. Thomas M. Jones, 'Ethical Decision Making by Individuals in Organizations: An Issue-Contingent Model', *Academy of Management Review* 16(1991): 366–395.

13. Shelby D. Hunt and Jared M. Hansen, 'Understanding Ethical Diversity in Organizations', *Organizational Dynamics* 36, no. 2 (2007): 202–216.

14. See Clinton W. McLemore, *Street-Smart Ethics: Succeeding in Business Without Selling Your Soul* (Louisville, KY: Westminster John Knox Press, 2003), for a cogent discussion of some ethical and legal issues associated with Enron's collapse.

15. Rushworth M. Kidder, 'The Three Great Domains of Human Action', *Christian Science Monitor*, January 30, 1990.

16. Laura Nash *Good intentions aside: a manager's guide to resolving ethical problems* (Boston: Harvard Business School Press, 1990).

17. J. Ciulla *Ethics, The Heart of Leadership* (Santa Barbara, CA: Praeger publishers: 1998).

18. Linda K. Treviño and Katherine A. Nelson, *Managing Business Ethics: Straight Talk About How to Do It Right* (New York: John Wiley & Sons, Inc., 1995), p. 4.

19. Jones, 'Ethical Decision Making by Individuals in Organizations'.

20. Based on a question from a General Electric employee ethics guide, reported in Kathryn Kranhold, 'US Firms Raise Ethics Focus', *The Wall Street Journal*, November 28, 2005.

21. Based on information in Constance E. Bagley, 'The Ethical Leader's Decision Tree', *Harvard Business Review* (February 2003): 18–19.

22. Based on information in Vadim Liberman, 'Scoring on the Job', *Across the Board* (November–December 2003): 46–50.

23. Old Mutual webpage http://www.oldmutualfunds.co.uk/home.aspx

24. From Jeffrey Kluger, 'What Makes Us Moral?', *Time* (December 3, 2007): 54–60.

25. 'The Morality Quiz', at http://www.time.com/morality (accessed February 19, 2008).

26. This discussion is based on Gerald F. Cavanagh, Dennis J. Moberg, and Manuel Velasquez, 'The Ethics of Organizational Politics', *Academy of Management Review* 6 (1981): 363–374; Justin G. Longenecker, Joseph A. McKinney, and Carlos W. Moore, 'Egoism and Independence: Entrepreneurial Ethics', *Organizational Dynamics* (Winter 1988): 64–72; Carolyn Wiley, 'The ABCs of Business Ethics: Definitions, Philosophies, and Implementation', *IM* (February 1995): 22–27; and Mark Mallinger, 'Decisive Decision Making: An Exercise Using Ethical Frameworks', *Journal of Management Education* (August 1997): 411–417.

27. Michael J. McCarthy, 'Now the Boss Knows Where You're Clicking', and 'Virtual Morality: A New Workplace Quandary', *The Wall Street Journal*, October 21, 1999; and Jeffrey L. Seglin, 'Who's Snooping on You?', *Business 2.0* (August 8, 2000): 202–203.

28. *The Times*, August 7, 2008 £35,000-a-year kidney cancer drugs too costly for NHS http://www.timesonline.co.uk/tol/life_and_style/health/article4474425.ece

29. John Kekes, 'Self-Direction: The Core of Ethical Individualism', in *Organizations and Ethical Individualism*, ed. Konstanian Kolenda (New York: Praeger, 1988), pp. 1–18.

30. Tad Tulega, *Beyond the Bottom Line* (New York: Penguin Books, 1987).

31. L. Kohlberg, 'Moral Stages and Moralization: The Cognitive-Developmental Approach', in *Moral Development and Behaviour: Theory, Research, and Social Issues,* ed. T. Lickona (New York: Holt, Rinehart & Winston, 1976), pp. 31–83; L. Kohlberg, 'Stage and Sequence: The Cognitive-Developmental Approach to Socialization', in *Handbook of Socialization Theory and Research*, ed. D. A. Goslin (Chicago: Rand Mc-Nally, 1969); Linda K. Treviño, Gary R. Weaver, and Scott J. Reynolds, 'Behavioural Ethics in Organizations: A Review', *Journal of Management* 32, no. 6 (December 2006): 951–990; and Jill W. Graham, 'Leadership, Moral Development, and Citizenship Behaviour', *Business Ethics Quarterly* 5, no. 1 (January 1995): 43–54.

32. Carol Gilligan, *In a Different Voice: Psychological Theory and Women's Development* (Cambridge, MA: Harvard University Press, 1982).

33. See Thomas Donaldson and Thomas W. Dunfee, 'When Ethics Travel: The Promise and Peril of Global Business Ethics', *California Management Review* 41, No. 4 (Summer 1999): 45–63.

34. *The Guardian*, Corrupt firm's work found to be defective, (August 8, 2009) p. 13.

35. Transparency International, 'The BPI 2006 – The Ranking', www.transparency.org/policy_research/surveys_indices/bpi/bpi_2006 (accessed February 18, 2007).

36. Eugene W. Szwajkowski, 'The Myths and Realities of Research on Organizational Misconduct', in *Research in Corporate Social Performance and Policy*, ed. James E. Post (Greenwich, CT: JAI Press, 1986), 9: 103–122; and Keith Davis, William C. Frederick, and Robert L. Blostrom, *Business and Society: Concepts and Policy Issues* (New York: McGraw-Hill, 1979).

37. Douglas S. Sherwin, 'The Ethical Roots of the Business System', *Harvard Business Review* 61 (November–December 1983): 183–192.

38. Parmalat Special Report Guardian at http://www.guardian.co.uk/parmalat/0,14141,1114024,00.html

39. Louisa Wood, 'Pipe down affluent newlyweds – you're not Wrapit's only victim', *The Guardian*, August 11, 2008, http://www.guardian.co.uk/theguardian/2008/aug/11/planningyourwedding.consumeraffairs

40. 'Not so Wholesome Activity at Whole Foods Market', http://www.naturalchoices.co.uk/Not-so-Wholesome-activity-at-Whole?id_mot=1 (accessed July 16, 2007).

41. Garriga and Mele 'Corporate Social Responsibility Theories: Mapping the Territory', *Journal of Business Ethics*, 53 (2004): 51–71.

42. Porter, M & Kramer (2006) Strategy and Society: The link between Competitive Advantage and Corporate Social Responsibility, *Harvard Business Review*, December 2006.

43. Crane, Andrew & Matten Dirk, Business Ethics: Managing Corporate Citizenship and Sustainability in the Age of Globalization.

44. R.K. Mitchell, B.R. Agle and D.J. Wood, 'Toward a theory of stakeholder identification and salience: defining the principle of who and what really counts', *Academy of Management Review*, 22 No. 4, (1997); and Kenneth Goodpaster and John Mathews 'Can a Corporation Have a conscience?', *Harvard Business Review*, 60 (10) (1982): 132–141.

45. Evan, W.M., Freeman, R.F. (1993), "A stakeholder theory of the modern corporation: Katian capitalism", in Donaldson, T., Werhane, P.H. (Eds), *Ethical Issues in Business*, Prentice Hall, Englewood Cliffs, NJ, pp. 166–71.

46. Nancy C. Roberts and Paula J. King, 'The Stakeholder Audit Goes Public', *Organizational Dynamics* (Winter 1989): 63–79; Thomas Donaldson and Lee E. Preston, 'The Stakeholder Theory of the Corporation: Concepts, Evidence, and Implications', *Academy of Management Review* 20, no. 1 (1995): 65–91; and Jeffrey S. Harrison and Caron H. St. John, 'Managing and Partnering with External Stakeholders', *Academy of Management Executive* 10, no. 2 (1996): 46–60.

47. Clay Chandler, 'The Great Wal-Mart of China', *Fortune* (July 25, 2005): 104–116; and Charles Fishman, 'The Wal-Mart You Don't Know – Why Low Prices Have a High Cost', *Fast Company* (December 2003): 68–80.

48. David Wheeler, Barry Colbert, and R. Edward Freeman, 'Focusing on Value: Reconciling Corporate Social Responsibility, Sustainability, and a Stakeholder Approach in a Networked World', *Journal of General Management* 28, no. 3 (Spring 2003): 1–28; James E. Post, Lee E. Preston, and Sybille Sachs, 'Managing the Extended Enterprise: The New Stakeholder View', *California Management Review* 45, no. 1 (Fall 2002): 6–28; and Peter Fritsch and Timothy Mapes, 'Seed Money; In Indonesia, A Tangle of Bribes Creates Trouble for Monsanto', *The Wall Street Journal*, April 5, 2005.

49. Max B. E. Clarkson, 'A Stakeholder Framework for Analyzing and Evaluating Corporate Social Performance', *Academy of Management Review* 20, no. 1 (1995): 92–117.

50. *The Times*, January 9, 2008, Frankenstein foods are not monsters, http://business.timesonline.co.uk/tol/business/columnists/article3155919.ece

51. C. K. Prahalad and S. L. Hart, 'The Fortune at the Bottom of the Pyramid', *Strategy + Business* 26 (2006): 54–67.

52. Rob Walker, 'Cleaning Up', *New York Times Magazine* (June 10, 2007): 20.

53. Ibid.

54. Values into Community Action annual report 2007/08 http://www.allenovery.com/AOWeb/binaries/50656.pdf

55. *The Guardian*, 'How capitalism got a conscience', July 25 2007, http://www.guardian.co.uk/business/2007/jul/25/voluntarysector.greenbusiness

56. This definition is based on Marc J. Epstein and Marie-Josée Roy, 'Improving Sustainability Performance: Specifying, Implementing and Measuring Key Principles', *Journal of General Management* 29, no. 1 (Autumn 2003): 15–31, World Commission on Economic Development, *Our Common Future* (Oxford: Oxford University Press, 1987): and Marc Gunther, 'Tree Huggers, Soy Lovers, and Profits', *Fortune* (June 23, 2003): 98–104.

57. Alcatel-Lucent installs its 200th solar-powered radio site http://www.babiz.co.uk/news.jsp?path=view&ID=315508 22949d6cc18c9d922c126c6b13&icode=13

58. John Carey, 'Hugging the Tree Huggers'.

59. Mark Borden, Jeff Chu, Charles Fishman, Michael A. Prospero, and Danielle Sacks, '50 Ways to Green Your Business', *Fast Company* (November, 2007).

60. Mark S. Schwartz and Archie B. Carroll, 'Corporate Social Responsibility: A Three-Domain Approach', *Business Ethics Quarterly* 13, no. 4 (2003): 503–530; and Archie B. Carroll, 'A Three-Dimensional Conceptual Model of Corporate Performance', *Academy of Management Review* 4 (1979): 497–505. For a discussion of various models for evaluating corporate social performance, also see Diane L. Swanson, 'Addressing a Theoretical Problem by Reorienting the Corporate Social Performance Model', *Academy of Management Review* 20, no. 1 (1995): 43–64.

61. Milton Friedman, *Capitalism and Freedom* (Chicago: University of Chicago Press, 1962), p. 133; and Milton Friedman and Rose Friedman, *Free to Choose* (New York: Harcourt Brace Jovanovich, 1979).

62. Eugene W. Szwajkowski, 'Organizational Illegality: Theoretical Integration and Illustrative Application', *Academy of Management Review* 10 (1985): 558–567.

63. Reported in Ronald W. Clement, 'Just How Unethical is American Business?', *Business Horizons* 49 (2006): 313–327.

64. David J. Fritzsche and Helmut Becker, 'Linking Management Behaviour to Ethical Philosophy – An Empirical Investigation', *Academy of Management Journal* 27 (1984): 165–175.

65. BBC, 'Zoom Airlines suspend all flights', August 28, 2008, http://news.bbc.co.uk/1/hi/business/7586654.stm

66. O'Sullivan, 'Virtue Rewarded'.

67. Katie Hafner and Claudi H. Deutsch, 'When Good Will Is Also Good Business', *The New York Times*, September 14, 2005, www.nytimes.com.

68. Saul W. Gellerman, 'Managing Ethics from the Top Down', *Sloan Management Review* (Winter 1989): 73–79.

69. Michael E. Brown and Linda K. Treviño, 'Ethical Leadership: A Review and Future Directions', *The Leadership Quarterly* 17 (2006): 595–616; Gary R. Weaver, Linda Klebe Treviño, and Bradley Agle, '"Somebody I Look Up To": Ethical Role Models in Organizations', *Organizational Dynamics* 34, no. 4 (2005): 313–330; and L. K. Treviño, G. R. Weaver, David G. Gibson, and Barbara Ley Toffler, 'Managing Ethics and Legal Compliance: What Works and What Hurts?', *California Management Review* 41, no. 2 (Winter 1999): 131–151.

70. *The Times*, April 8, 2009, 'Foodie sell-offs do not mean a sell-out', http://www.timesonline.co.uk/tol/comment/columnists/guest_contributors/article6054941.ece

71. *Sunday Times*, April 1, 2007, 'Do the right-on thing', http://www.timesonline.co.uk/tol/news/uk/article1581109.ece

72. Ibid.

73. Treviño *et al.*, 'Managing Ethics and Legal Compliance'.

74. Carolyn Wiley, 'The ABC's of Business Ethics: Definitions, Philosophies, and Implementation', *IM* (January–February 1995): 22–27; Joseph L. Badaracco and Allen P. Webb, 'Business Ethics: A View from the Trenches', *California Management Review* 37, no. 2 (Winter 1995): 8–28; and Ronald B. Morgan, 'Self- and Co-Worker Perceptions of Ethics and Their Relationships to Leadership and Salary', *Academy of Management Journal* 36, no. 1 (February 1993): 200–214.

75. Guidelines, The Guardian's Editorial Code, Updated April 2007, http://image.guardian.co.uk/sys-files/Guardian/documents/2007/06/14/EditorialCode2007.pdf

76. Cheryl Rosen, 'A Measure of Success? Ethics after Enron', *Business Ethics* (Summer 2006): 22–26.

77. Alan Yuspeh, 'Do the Right Thing', *CIO* (August 1, 2000): 56–58.

78. Beverly Geber, 'The Right and Wrong of Ethics Offices', *Training* (October 1995): 102–118.

79. Kranhold, 'US Firms Raise Ethics Focus' and 'Our Actions: GE 2005 Citizenship Report', General Electric Company, 2005.

80. Marcia Parmarlee Miceli and Janet P. Near, 'The Relationship among Beliefs, Organizational Positions, and Whistle-Blowing Status: A Discriminant Analysis', *Academy of Management Journal* 27 (1984): 687–705.

81. Eugene Garaventa, '*An Enemy of the People* by Henrik Ibsen: The Politics of Whistle-Blowing', *Journal of Management Inquiry* 3, no. 4 (December 1994): 369–374; Marcia P. Miceli

and Janet P. Near, 'Whistleblowing: Reaping the Benefits', *Academy of Management Executive* 8, no. 3 (1994): 65–74.

82. Reported in Rosen, 'A Measure of Success? Ethics after Enron'.

83. Kim Pilling, 'Nurse who spoke out settles with NHS trust', *The Independent*, 28 January 2009, http://www.indep endent.co.uk/life-style/health-and-families/health-news/nurse who-spoke-out-settles-with-nhs-trust-1518567.html

84. Homer H. Johnson, 'Does It Pay to Be Good? Social Responsibility and Financial Performance', *Business Horizons* (November–December 2003): 34–40; Jennifer J. Griffin and John F. Mahon, 'The Corporate Social Performance and Corporate Financial Performance Debate: Twenty-Five Years of Incomparable Research', *Business and Society* 36, no. 1 (March 1997): 5–31; Bernadette M. Ruf, Krishnamurty Muralidar, Robert M. Brown, Jay J. Janney and Karen Paul, 'An Empirical Investigation of the Relationship between Change in Corporate Social Performance and Financial Performance: A Stakeholder Theory Perspective', *Journal of Business Ethics* 32, no. 2 (July 2001): 143; Philip L. Cochran and Robert A. Wood, 'Corporate Social Responsibility and Financial Performance', *Academy of Management Journal* 27 (1984): 42–56.

85. Paul C. Godfrey, 'The Relationship Between Corporate Philanthropy and Shareholder Wealth: A Risk Management Perspective', *Academy of Management Review* 30, no. 4 (2005): 777–798; Oliver Falck and Stephan Heblich, 'Corporate Social Responsibility: Doing Well by Doing Good',

Business Horizons 50 (2007): 247–254; J. A. Pearce II and J. P. Doh, 'The High Impact of Collaborative Social Initiatives'; Curtis C. Verschoor and Elizabeth A. Murphy, 'The Financial Performance of Large US Firms and Those with Global Prominence: How Do the Best Corporate Citizens Rate?', *Business and Society Review* 107, no. 3 (Fall 2002): 371–381; Johnson, 'Does It Pay to Be Good?'; Dale Kurschner, '5 Ways Ethical Business Creates Fatter Profits', *Business Ethics* (March–April 1996): 20–23. Also see studies reported in Lori Ioannou, 'Corporate America's Social Conscience', *Fortune* (May 26, 2003): S1–S10.

86. Verschoor and Murphy, 'The Financial Performance of Large US Firms'.

87. Jean B. McGuire, Alison Sundgren and Thomas Schneeweis, 'Corporate Social Responsibility and Firm Financial Performance,' *Academy of Management Journal* 31 (1988): 854–872; and Falck and Heblich, 'Corporate Social Responsibility: Doing Well by Doing Good'.

88. Vogel, 'Is There a Market for Virtue?'.

89. Daniel W. Greening and Daniel B. Turban, 'Corporate Social Performance as a Competitive Advantage in Attracting a Quality Workforce', *Business and Society* 39, no. 3 (September 2000): 254; and O'Sullivan, 'Virtue Rewarded'.

90. 'The Socially Correct Corporate Business', in Leslie Holstrom and Simon Brady, 'The Changing Face of Global Business', *Fortune* (July 24, 2000): S1–S38.

91. Union Fenosa http://www.csreurope.org/solutions.php?action=show_solution&solution_id=611

CHAPTER OUTLINE

© NETRUN78/SHUTTERSTOCK

LEARNING OBJECTIVES

After reading this chapter, you should be able to:

1   Describe the importance of entrepreneurship to the world
     economy.

2   Define the personality characteristics of a typical entrepreneur.

3   Explain social entrepreneurship as a vital part of today's small
     business environment.

4   Outline the planning necessary to launch an entrepreneurial
     start-up.

5   Describe the five stages of growth for an entrepreneurial
     company.

6   Explain how the management functions of planning,
     organizing, leading and controlling apply to a growing
     entrepreneurial company.

CHAPTER 6

MANAGING SMALL BUSINESS START-UPS

Manager's Challenge

Stella Ogiale is facing a dilemma. After being out of the workforce for years, she finds herself in need of a job. Ogiale moved to the US from Nigeria as a teenager to attend college. After earning a masters degree in public administration and finance, she began working in Washington, DC, where she fell in love, got married and put her career on hold to have children. Now, years later, after a separation from her husband, Ogiale needs to go back to work. The only problem is, Ogiale doesn't want a regular 9–5 job that will interfere with caring for her three young children, especially her son Chester, who was born with autism. In 1996, while working nights part-time at UPS, Ogiale thinks about her determination to keep Chester at home rather than putting him in an institution, and she has an idea. What if she could bring all the amenities of an institution – medical supplies, pharmaceuticals, and specialized physicians and caregivers – to mentally and physically disabled patients at home? Research shows her that starting a home health care business is fraught with challenges. Payments are low, workers are hard to find and keep, and government regulations are overwhelming. Yet Ogiale also sees that the elderly population in the US is growing and some states are beginning to search for alternatives to costly nursing home care. She borrows $500 from her sister and uses some birthday money to start Chesterfield Health Services, naming it after her son. Then reality sets in. Ogiale knows she has a good idea, but she also knows she's facing tremendous hurdles.[1]

What advice would you give Stella Ogiale about getting her new company started? Do you think one person with a good idea can create a successful company in a high-risk business like home health care?

TAKE A MOMENT

Do You Think Like an Entrepreneur?[2]

An entrepreneur faces many demands. Do you have the proclivity to start and build your own business? To find out, consider the extent to which each of the following statements characterizes your behaviour. Please answer each of the following items as Mostly True or Mostly False for you.

		Mostly True	Mostly False
1	Give me a little information and I can come up with a lot of ideas.	☐	☐
2	I like pressure in order to focus.	☐	☐
3	I don't easily get frustrated when things don't go my way.	☐	☐
4	I identify how resources can be recombined to produce novel outcomes.	☐	☐
5	I enjoy competing against the clock to meet deadlines.	☐	☐
6	People in my life have to accept that nothing is more important than the achievement of my school, my sport or my career goals.	☐	☐
7	I serve as a role model for creativity.	☐	☐
8	I think 'on my feet' when carrying out tasks.	☐	☐
9	I am determined and action-oriented.	☐	☐

SCORING AND INTERPRETATION Each question pertains to some aspect of improvization, which is a correlate of entrepreneurial intentions. Entrepreneurial improvization consists of three elements. Questions 1, 4 and 7 pertain to creativity/ingenuity, the ability to produce novel solutions under constrained conditions. Questions 2, 5 and 8 pertain to working under pressure/stress, the ability to excel under pressure-filled circumstances. Questions 3, 6 and 9 pertain to action/persistence, the determination to achieve goals and solve problems in the moment. If you answered 'Mostly True' to at least two of three questions for each subscale or six of nine for all the questions, then consider yourself an entrepreneur in the making, with the potential to manage your own business. If you scored one or fewer 'Mostly True' on each subscale or three or fewer for all nine questions, you might want to consider becoming a manager by working for someone else.

Many people dream of starting their own business. Some, like Stella Ogiale, decide to start a business because they're inspired by a great idea or want the flexibility that comes from being self-employed. Others decide to go into business for themselves after they get fired or find their opportunities limited in big companies. Interest in entrepreneurship and small business is at an all-time high. At university and college campuses across the world, ambitious courses, programmes and centres teach the fundamentals of starting a small business. Entrepreneurs have access to business incubators, support networks and online training courses. The enormous growth of franchising gives beginners an escorted route into a new business. In addition, the internet opens new avenues for small business formation.

Today, the fastest growing segment of small business in both the US and Canada is in one-owner operations, sole-trader or *sole proprietorships*.[3] Sole proprietorships in the US grew about 4 per cent in 2002 alone, the most recent year with statistics available, to 17.6 million. Their combined revenues increased 5.5 per cent to $770 billion.[4] In the UK in the same period self-employment increased by 8.9 per cent. (UK National Statistics) After the crash of the dot-com boom, many of these entrepreneurs are finding opportunities in low-tech businesses such as landscaping, child care and janitorial services. Overall, since the 1970s, the number of businesses in the world economy has been growing faster than the labour force.[5]

© DAVID LEVENSON/GETTY IMAGES

What is Entrepreneurship?

Entrepreneurship is the dynamic process of creating incremental wealth. The wealth is created by individuals who assume the major risks in terms of equity, time and/or career commitment or provide value for some product or service. The product or service may or may not be new or unique, but value must somehow be infused by the entrepreneur by receiving and locating the necessary skills and resources.

Entrepreneurship is also the process of initiating a business venture, organizing the necessary resources and assuming the associated risks and rewards.[6] An **entrepreneur** is someone who engages in entrepreneurship. An entrepreneur recognizes a viable idea for a business product or service and carries it out by finding and assembling the necessary resources – money, people, machinery, location – to undertake the business venture. Entrepreneurs also assume the risks and reap the rewards of the business. They assume the financial and legal risks of ownership and receive the business's profits.

A good example of entrepreneurship is Anita Roddick, who opened her first Body Shop in 1976 despite not having any business experience, The reason she chose cosmetics is because of her travels – she learnt right from the grass roots as to what people should put into their body, it was just taking that knowledge into the business. Anita only had 19 products, but by selling them in five different sizes she was able to fill up the shelves in the store. Body Shop growth came through a franchising model. In 1984 the company went public, and at its height The Body Shop was worth £700 million. However, following an expansion programme that failed to meet expectations and a fall in profits, Anita stepped down as chief executive in 1998 and acted as a consultant until her death in 2007, as well as running her own publishing firm. Despite some initial problems when Anita's successors took over, the Body Shop continues to be profitable, with over 2000 stores in 12 time zones worldwide.

Successful entrepreneurs have many different motivations, and they measure rewards in different ways. One study classified small business owners in five different categories, as illustrated in Exhibit 6.1. Some people are *idealists*, who like the idea of working on something that is new, creative or personally meaningful. *Optimizers* are rewarded by the personal satisfaction of being business owners. Entrepreneurs in the *sustainer* category like the chance to balance work and personal life and often don't want the business to grow too large, while *hard workers* enjoy putting in the long hours and dedication to build a larger, more profitable business. The *juggler* category includes entrepreneurs who like the chance a small business gives them to

CONCEPT CONNECTION To an economist, an entrepreneur is one who brings resources, labour, materials and other assets into combinations that make their value greater than before, and also one who introduces changes, innovations and a new order.

To a psychologist, such a person is typically driven by certain forces the needs to obtain or attain something, to experiment, to accomplish or perhaps to escape the authority of others.

To one businessman, an entrepreneur appears as a threat, an aggressive competitor, whereas to another person the same entrepreneur may be an ally, a source of supply, a customer or someone who creates wealth for others, as well as finds better ways to utilize resources, reduce waste and produce jobs others are glad to get.

Anita Roddick (discussed in the text) is pictured here with some of her products.

Entrepreneurship
The process of initiating a business venture, organizing the necessary resources and assuming the associated risks and rewards.

Entrepreneur
Someone who recognizes a viable idea for a business product or service and carries it out.

Exhibit 6.1 Five Types of Small Business Owners

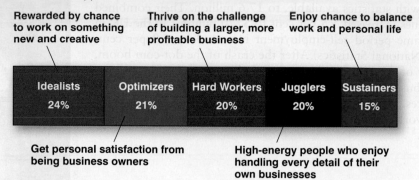

SOURCE: Study conducted by Yankelovich Partners, reported in Mark Henricks, 'Type-Cast', *Entrepreneur* (March 2000): 14–16.

handle everything themselves. These high-energy people thrive on the pressure of paying bills, meeting deadlines and making payroll.[7]

Sometimes people start new businesses when they lose their jobs due to corporate downsizing. The major layoffs in the early 2000s provided just the push some latent entrepreneurs needed to strike out on their own. Some experts think an economic downturn is actually the best time to start a business. For one thing, a downturn opens up lots of opportunities because people are looking for lower costs and better ways of doing things. The economic climate also enables the new business to hire good people, forces the entrepreneur to keep costs in line, and provides the time needed to build something of lasting value rather than struggling to keep pace with rapid growth.[8]

Many people also regard entrepreneurship as a better use of their time, talent and energy. Women and minorities, who have sometimes found their opportunities limited in the corporate world, are often seeing entrepreneurship as the only way to go. Hispanic and African American entrepreneurship is on the rise. The National Federation of Women Business Owners reports that Hispanic women are starting companies in the US at four times the national growth rate. 'The [corporate] work environment is not friendly to Latinas', says Alma Morales Fiojas, CEO of Mana, a National Latina Organization. 'Sometimes the best avenue … is to go into your own business, where there is more flexibility and you can accomplish more.'[9]

TAKE A MOMENT   Are you interested in becoming a new manager by starting your own business?

Entrepreneurship and the Environment

Not so long ago, scholars and policy makers were worrying about the potential of small business to survive. The turbulence in the technology sector and the demise of many dot-com start-ups heightened concerns about whether small companies can compete with big business. However, entrepreneurship and small business, including high-tech start-ups, are vital, dynamic and increasingly important parts of the world economy.

These firms account for a tremendous portion of the goods and services provided. Entrepreneurship in other countries is also booming. The list of the most entrepreneurial countries, shown in Exhibit 6.2, is intriguing. A project monitoring entrepreneurial activity around the world reports that an estimated 25 per cent of adults age 18 to 64 in Venezuela are either starting up or managing new enterprises. The percentage in

Exhibit 6.2 The World's Most Entrepreneurial Countries

Country	Percentage of Individuals Age 18 to 64 Active in Starting or Managing a New Business, 2005
Venezuela	25.00
Thailand	20.70
New Zealand	17.60
Jamaica	17.00
China	13.70
United States	12.40
Brazil	11.30
Chile	11.10
Australia	10.90
Iceland	10.70
Argentina	9.50
Canada	9.30
Singapore	7.20
Latvia	6.60
Croatia	6.10
Average of countries surveyed	8.40

SOURCE: Permission to reproduce a figure from the GEM 2005 Global Report, which appears here, has been kindly granted by the copyright holders. The GEM is an international consortium and this report has been produced from data collected in, and received from, 37 countries in 2008. Our thanks go to the authors, national teams, researchers, funding bodies and other contributors who have made this possible.

Thailand is 20.7 per cent, and in Jamaica 17 per cent. China and New Zealand also show higher rates of entrepreneurial activity than the US rate of 12.4 per cent.[10] Japan, which shows a low rate of only 2.2 per cent, is attempting to spur entrepreneurial activity with a new law that makes it possible to start a business with capital of just 1 yen.[11] Structural reforms in Russia spurred a jump in small business formation in that country, and one economic study predicts a doubling of small business as a part of Russia's gross domestic product between the years of 2004 and 2009.[12]

Entrepreneurship Today

Small business is such a dynamic part of today's economy for a number of reasons, including economic changes, globalization and increased competition, advancing technology, and new market niches.[13]

Global Entrepreneurial Activity[14]

Global Entrepreneurial Activity is monitored by the GEM (Global Entrepreneurship Monitor), a not-for-profit academic research consortium with headquarters in London Business School that has as its goal making high-quality international research

Exhibit 6.3 Stages of Entrepreneurial Activity

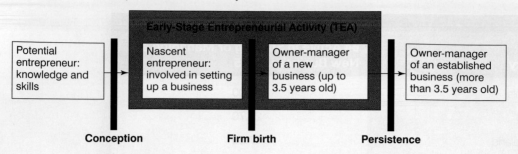

SOURCE: Permission to reproduce figures from the GEM 2007 Global Report, which appear here, has been kindly granted by the copyright holders - www.gemconsortium.org

data on entrepreneurial activity readily available for wider audience. GEM views entrepreneurship as a process and considers people in entrepreneurial activity in different phases: from the very early phase when the business is in gestation to the established phase and possibly discontinuation of the business. In GEM's 2007 Executive Report it identifies the stages of entrepreneurial activity shown in Exhibit 6.3.

When evaluating the Total Entrepreneurial Activity (TEA) GEM divides the countries under investigation into the following types:

- high income countries, represented by the US, Israel, Iceland and Canada, exhibit the highest adult-population prevalence rates of high-growth expectation entrepreneurship;
- middle and low income countries, represented by Russia, India, Turkey and Peru, with China indicating the highest rate of EA, followed by Argentina.

High-income countries tend to have a higher ratio of high-growth expectation entrepreneurship to overall entrepreneurship, or relative prevalence of high-growth expectation entrepreneurship, than middle- and low-income countries. The highest relative prevalence of high expectation entrepreneurship is found in Singapore and Israel (high-income countries) and Russia and China (middle- and low-income countries).

The GEM results point to high and decreasing rates of early-stage entrepreneurial activity in Latin American countries. Some middle- and low-income countries in Eastern Europe and Central Asia, however, have relatively low levels of early-stage entrepreneurial activity. Among middle- and low-income countries, Thailand (26.9 per cent), Peru (25.9 per cent) and Colombia (22.7 per cent) had the highest rates of early-stage entrepreneurial activity. Lowest rates were found in Russia (2.7 per cent), Romania (4.0 per cent) and Latvia (4.5 per cent).

The GEM results point to high and decreasing rates of early-stage entrepreneurial activity in Latin American countries. Some middle- and low-income countries in Eastern Europe and Central Asia, however, have relatively low levels of early-stage entrepreneurial activity. Among middle- and low-income countries, Thailand (26.9 per cent), Peru (25.9 per cent) and Colombia (22.7 per cent) had the highest rates of early-stage entrepreneurial activity. Lowest rates were found in Russia (2.7 per cent), Romania (4.0 per cent) and Latvia (4.5 per cent).

Although characteristics of entrepreneurial activity differ across countries, the importance of entrepreneurship for economic development is widely acknowledged. While scientific evidence for this relationship has been accumulating, national, international and regional institutions have become more and more explicit in their efforts to create an entrepreneurial society. Earlier GEM reports demonstrated a systematic, U-shaped relationship between a country's level of economic development and its level and type of entrepreneurial activity.

Exhibit 6.4 Early Stage Entrepreneurial Activity Rates and Per Capita GDP, 2007

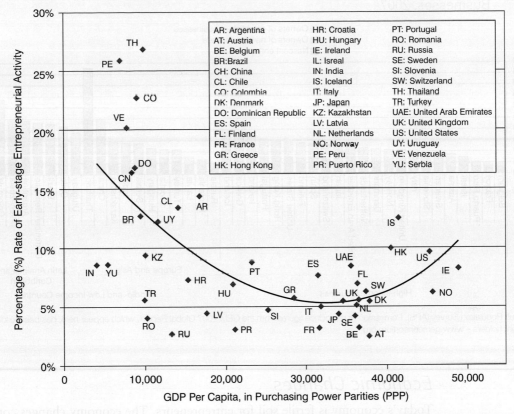

SOURCE: Permission to reproduce figures from the GEM 2007 Global Report, which appear here, has been kindly granted by the copyright holders - www.gemconsortium.org

Exhibit 6.4 illustrates this U-shaped relationship between per capita GDP-levels and early-stage entrepreneurial activity. Early-stage entrepreneurial activity rates in 2007 are derived from the annual GEM Adult Population Surveys (APS) administered to representative samples of the national adult population in 42 countries. The measure is described in more detail in the introduction. The U-shaped relationship between *per capita* GDP-levels and early stage entrepreneurial activity has been consistent over the years.

In countries with low levels of *per capita* income, the national economy is characterized by the prevalence of many very small businesses. As *per capita* income increases, industrialization and economies of scale allow larger and established firms to satisfy the increasing demand of growing markets and to increase their relative role in the economy. An important factor for achieving growth is the presence of macroeconomic and political stability, which is reflected by the development of strong institutions. The increase in the role of large firms may be accompanied by a reduction in the number of new businesses, since a growing number of people find stable employment in large industrial plants.

The percentage of a population engaged in setting up or running their own businesses is another way of gauging a country's entrepreneurial activity. Exhibit 6.5 describes the share of each of the three main stages of owner-managed business engagement as identified by GEM. Latin American and Caribbean countries, China and Thailand stand out from the rest on this measure. Also, the share of early-stage entrepreneurial activity (nascent entrepreneurs and new business owners) is significantly larger in Latin American countries than in high-income European countries.

Exhibit 6.5 Share of Population that is in Different Stages of Engagement in Owner-Managed Businesses, 2007

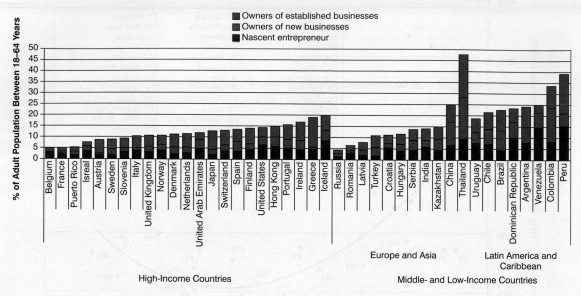

SOURCE: Adult Population Survey (APS). Permission to reproduce figures from the GEM 2007 Global Report, which appear here, has been kindly granted by the copyright holders – www.gemconsortium.org

Economic Changes

Today's economy is fertile soil for entrepreneurs. The economy changes constantly, providing opportunities for new businesses. The demand for services is booming, and 97 per cent of service firms are small, with fewer than 100 employees. Landscaping, for example, is one of the fastest growing small businesses, spurred by a surge in housing and office construction.[15] The trend toward outsourcing work to companies that can do it cheaper has also given entrepreneurs new openings.

Globalization and Increased Competition

Even the largest of companies can no longer dominate their industry in a fast-changing global marketplace. Globalization demands entrepreneurial behaviour and gives an advantage to the flexibility and fast response that small business can offer rather than to huge companies with economies of scale. Rather than being hurt by the globalization of today's business world, many entrepreneurs are finding new opportunities. Stefanie Heiter started a four-person consulting business called HeiterConnect that helps global managers communicate, collaborate and motivate across borders.[16] Bill Weiller bought a nearly bankrupt company called Purafil, which was then focused exclusively on making air filters for US pulp and paper factories, and transformed it into a global powerhouse. Purafil now sells filters in 11 industries to companies in 50 countries and 60 per cent of Purafil's revenues come from overseas.[17]

Technology

Rapid advances and dropping prices in computer technology spawned whole new industries, as well as entirely new methods of producing goods and delivering services. Unlike technological progress of the past, these advances are within the reach of companies of all sizes. The explosive growth of the internet created tremendous opportunities for entrepreneurs. For every story of a failed dot-com business, numerous other small companies are successfully using the Web to sell products and services, to improve productivity, communications and customer service, or to obtain information and market their services. Larry Page and Sergey Brin, the co-founders of Google have utilized their skills in IT and established a company which is able to solve one of computing's biggest challenges: retrieving relevant information from a massive set of data.[18]

Other technological advances also provide opportunities for small business. Biotechnology, aided by recent work in genomics, is a growing field for small businesses. Five Prime Therapeutics, for example, developed a protein-screening process that can accelerate the development of hit drugs for diseases such as cancer, Type 2 diabetes and rheumatoid arthritis.[19] Research into microelectromechanical systems (MEMS), tiny machines used in numerous applications from biotechnology and telecommunications to the auto industry, is being conducted primarily by small companies: Oki, DENSO in Japan, MEMSIC in China, Freescale and Kionix in the US and Sonion MEMS in Europe.

© REUTERS/CORBIS

CONCEPT CONNECTION U2 lead singer Bono is a classic example of an idealist entrepreneur. He started a fashion company, Edun (yes, that's *nude* spelled backwards) to reflect his strong commitment to social causes. The for-profit Dublin-based company's high-end apparel is made in locally run African, South American and Indian factories that use fair labour practices and, whenever possible, organic materials. Bono believes fostering increased participation in world trade is the best way to help developing nations. He is shown here talking with dancing a Ghanaian woman involved in a microfinance programme. The microfinance industry gives tiny loans for people in developing nations to start small businesses.

New Opportunities and Market Niches

Today's entrepreneurs are taking advantage of the opportunity to meet changing needs in the marketplace. Tapping into the growing *sustainability* movement, for example, Ron Warnecke founded Nitro-Cision, a company that mops up radioactive and industrial waste without the use of chemicals.[20] Stampp Corbin spotted an opportunity in the growing need for companies to dispose of outdated equipment such as personal computers, printers and servers. His company, RetroBox, wipes the machines clean of all data, refurbishes and sells any that are still useful, and makes sure others are disposed of safely. With organizations continually upgrading, Corbin's business grows each year, with revenue climbing to $14 million in 2004.[21]

Definition of Small Business

The full definition of *small business* used by the US Small Business Administration (SBA) is detailed and complex, including 37 different benchmarks that define 1151 industries and 13 sub-industries across the US. In general, a small business is considered to be 'one that is independently owned and operated and which is not dominant in its field of operation'.[23] Exhibit 6.6 gives a few examples of how the SBA defines small business for a sample of industries.

However, the definition of small business is currently under revision in response to concerns from small business owners. After nationwide public hearings in 2005, the SBA determined that standards should be changed in light of shifting economic and industry conditions. Redefining small business size standards is a daunting task, but SBA leaders agree that the standards need to be more flexible in today's world. The SBA's definition has been revised a number of times over the years to reflect changing economic conditions.[24]

Exhibit 6.6 also illustrates general categories of businesses most entrepreneurs start: retail, manufacturing and service. Additional categories of small businesses are construction, hospitality, communications, finance and real estate.

Exhibit 6.6 Examples of SBA Definitions of Small Businesses

Manufacturing	
Soft-drink manufacturing	Number of employees does not exceed 500
Electronic computer manufacturing	Number of employees does not exceed 1000
Prerecorded CD, tape and record producing	Number of employees does not exceed 750

Retail (Store and Nonstore)	
Sporting goods stores	Average annual receipts do not exceed $6.0 million
Electronic auctions	Average annual receipts do not exceed $21.0 million
Vending machine operators	Average annual receipts do not exceed $6.0 million

Miscellaneous Internet Services	
Internet service providers	Average annual receipts do not exceed $21.0 million
Web search portals	Average annual receipts do not exceed $6.0 million
Internet publishing and broadcasting	Number of employees does not exceed 500

© RON WURZER/MICROSOFT VIA GETTY IMAGES

CONCEPT CONNECTION Team Germany survived fierce competition to become a finalist in Microsoft's 2006 Imagine Cup, an annual student technology competition. Here, two team members, Piotr Wendt and Mark Thomé, demonstrate to Microsoft chairperson Bill Gates their navigation system for the disabled, which is powered by software they developed. Team Germany's invention earned them the right to participate in the Innovation Accelerator, an intensive two-week workshop co-sponsored by Microsoft and BT. The workshop's goal is to give students the business training they need to translate their technological advances into commercial ventures.

Impact of Entrepreneurial Companies

The impact of entrepreneurial companies on the world economy is astonishing. Inspired by the growth of companies such as eBay, Google and Amazon.com, entrepreneurs are still flocking to the Internet to start new businesses. In addition, demographic and lifestyle trends create new opportunities in areas such as environmental services, lawn care, computer maintenance, children's markets, fitness and home health care. Entrepreneurship and small business is an engine for job creation and innovation in many countries around the world.

Job Creation

Researchers disagree over what percentage of new jobs is created by small business. Research indicates that the *age* of a company, more than its size, determines the number of jobs it creates. That is, virtually *all* new jobs in recent years have come from new companies, which include not only small companies but also new branches of huge, multinational organizations.[25] However, small companies still are thought to create a large percentage of new jobs in the US. The SBA reports that small businesses create 65 per cent or more of America's new jobs. Jobs created by small businesses give the US an economic vitality no other country can claim. However, as we discussed earlier, other countries are also finding new ways to encourage entrepreneurial economic activity.

TAKE A MOMENT

As an aspiring entrepreneur, can you see a market niche that is not being met by an existing organization? How do you feel about organizing the necessary resources and taking the risks to start a company to serve that niche?

 INNOVATIVE WAY

GreenThumb Lawn Treatment Service[22]

It's not an easy step to make, from an office in the back of a Sierra armed with only a bucket of lawn fertiliser, to being the CEO of a business with a £50 million turnover. And you may have thought that along the path to success Stephen Waring, founder of GreenThumb Lawn Treatment Service, may have lost his sense of wonder about the miracle of making grass grow. But it's not the case. He still has it, but mainly he wonders why householders waste their weekends trekking into garden centres to buy feed and weed killer, and even more time walking up and down their own patches of lawn, applying it.

He has built his present success on offering an easy alternative to lawn feed and weed killer, letting franchised teams across the UK do the hard work. They visit more than 400,000 lawns every couple of months to carry out individually tailored lawn treatments through the year. Importantly, they visit during the week, leaving weekends free for householders to sit back and enjoy relaxing in the garden. Stephen, determined to be a success, realized that with an estimated 20 million UK lawns, there was a huge untapped

market. He researched the idea and set up GreenThumb UK, tailoring the concept to meet the needs of the British market and climate.

The company, now based in Denbighshire, north Wales, grew steadily, with Stephen taking on staff to help him deliver the service across north Wales and northwest England. He adds: 'The biggest obstacle in getting the business up and running was probably creating the marketplace, and educating people to recognize what we were offering. It was literally inventing an industry.' Then, eleven years ago, as the present wave of garden care took off, Stephen took the next big step in his business career. He decided that to spread across the whole of the UK more quickly, he wanted to expand through franchising. Some of the first franchisees were the crews that had been working alongside him.

Now the company is growing again, with over 200 branches carrying out over 2 million lawn treatments every year. His no-scorch fertiliser has been patented, and they have introduced other new products. And within the next five years Stephen expects to have a fleet of more than 1,500 GreenThumb vans on the road and provide jobs for over 2,000 people, treating more than one million lawns each year.

Innovation

According to Cognetics, Inc., a research firm run by David Birch that traces the employment and sales records of some nine million companies, new and smaller firms have been responsible for 55 per cent of the innovations in 362 different industries and 95 per cent of all radical innovations. In addition, fast-growing businesses, which Birch calls *gazelles*, produce twice as many product innovations per employee as do larger firms. Consulting firm CHI Research, which tracks innovation in both small and large firms, found that among 1270 'highly innovative' firms, the number of small businesses rose from 33 per cent in 2000 to 40 per cent in 2002. Small firms that file for patents typically produce 13 to 14 times more patents per employee than large patenting firms.[26]

Among the notable products for which small businesses can be credited are Dyson Hoover, Yo-Yo, WD-40, the jet engine and the shopping cart. Virtually every new business represents an innovation of some sort, whether a new product or service, how the product is delivered, or how it is made.[27] Samantha Fountain started a company called Shewee to make and sell a moulded plastic funnel that provides women with a simple, private and hygienic method of urinating without removing their clothes, while standing or sitting.

💡 INNOVATIVE WAY

Shewee[28]

At just seven inches long and weighing less than a mobile phone, the Shewee is small enough to fit into even the most crammed of handbags. This portable plastic device could well be the solution to that rare occasion when women wish they could be men, as the Shewee enables them to urinate standing up, without the hassle of having to remove their clothing in the process.

A few years ago Sam Fountain, the brainchild behind the Shewee, was working as a PA to the director of a city consultancy firm. To many this might have seemed like a promising career, but then not many people are award winning product designers by their early twenties. The idea first came to Sam when she was writing her dissertation at university on how to improve the facilities in public toilets, something that she believes is a concern for most women.

The idea won Sam the Dyson Product Design Award in 1999, which included a six-month placement with James Dyson himself, helping to design a robotic vacuum cleaner. This opportunity gave her the chance to work with plastic manufacturers, and increased her determination to make the design a success.

The obstacles along the way ranged from developing a business plan to make the 'idea and prototype' into a realistic business, sourcing financing for this while at the same time talking to manufactures and marketing companies.

To source the financing Sam decided to make Shewee a limited company and sell shares. The value of the company was determined by the business plan. Sam kept 51 per cent of the shares and sold the other 49 per cent to individuals; some of whom are family friends and others friends of friends or previous work colleagues. The selling of these shares was done in three tranches, the shares rising in value for new buyers in each tranche. It was done like this so that original investors purchased more shares at each stage as they could see Shewee Ltd growing successfully.

She says that having her own business has undoubtedly been exciting, but the challenge has brought with it new responsibilities. 'It's not like a normal day job, where I could just resign if I didn't enjoy it anymore. I have a dozen or so investors depending on me to make the idea profitable, and that is quite daunting.'

'I now know what is involved in running my own business, and am confident I could turn my hand to something else if need be. People have approached me with other ideas that could be looked at in the future, but for now I want to concentrate on my Shewee.'

It seems that women are now taking the case for equality one step further. With her appearance on BBC2's *Dragon's Den*, recently winning the Silver Award for the British Female Inventor, and Innovator awards and sales to the NHS and the active woman growing monthly, you can be sure we will be hearing a lot more of Sam and her Shewee in the near future.

Who are Entrepreneurs?

The heroes of business – Henry Ford, Steve Jobs, Richard Branson, Sam Walton, Bill Gates, Pedro Flores, Michael Dell, Li Ka Shing, Larry Page and Sergey Brin – are almost always entrepreneurs. Entrepreneurs start with a vision. Often they are unhappy with their current jobs and see an opportunity to bring together the resources needed for a new venture. How ever, the image of entrepreneurs as bold pioneers probably is overly romantic. A survey of the CEOs of the nation's fastest-growing small firms found that these entrepreneurs could be best characterized as hardworking and practical, with great familiarity with their market and industry.[29] For example, Nancy Rodriguez was a veteran R&D manager at Swift Foods before she started Food Marketing Support Services. Rodriguez started the firm in the mid-1980s when Swift and other big food companies were cutting staff and R&D budgets. Large companies can now take a rough new product idea to Food Marketing, which fully develops the concept, creates prototypes, does taste-testing, and so forth. American Pop Corn, which makes Jolly Time Pop Corn, allocated 100 per cent of its new-product development dollars to the 20-person firm, which does about $5 million in business a year.[30]

© BOB HANDELMAN/GETTY IMAGES

CONCEPT CONNECTION Who hasn't felt trapped in a bad date or an endless meeting? BeVocal, a company that designs voice-activated software for the telecommunications market, used its talent for innovation to capitalize on a new opportunity. Thanks to BeVocal software, Cingular and Virgin Mobile customers can arrange to be called with a pre-recorded emergency message if they find themselves in a tedious social situation. In the case of Virgin Mobile, it is company founder Richard Branson who feeds excuses that the customer can use to make a graceful getaway.

Diversity of Entrepreneurs

Entrepreneurs often have backgrounds and demographic characteristics that distinguish them from other people. Entrepreneurs are more likely to be the first-born within their families, and their parents are more likely to have been entrepreneurs. Children of immigrants also are more likely to be entrepreneurs.[31] Consider Hector Barreto Jr., whose parents were both Mexican immigrants and ran several successful businesses in Kansas City, Missouri, including a restaurant, an import-export business and a construction firm. After a four-year stint as an area manager for Miller Brewing Company, Hector moved to California and started Barreto Financial Services. Later, he started another firm to provide technical assistance to small businesses. Barreto's next step was into the head office of the Small Business Administration, where he became the first entrepreneur to lead the government agency.[32]

Entrepreneurship offers opportunities for individuals who may feel blocked in established corporations. Women-owned and minority-owned businesses may be the emerging growth companies of the next decade. In 2005, women owned 6.5 million US businesses that generated $950.6 billion in revenues and employed more than seven million workers. In Canada as well, women entrepreneurs are thriving. Since 1989, the rate of small businesses started by women in Canada grew 60 per cent faster than the growth in the number of small businesses started by men.[33] Statistics for minorities in the US are also impressive, with minorities owning 4.1 million firms that generated $694 billion in revenues and employed 4.8 million people.[34] The number of new firms launched by minorities is growing about 17 per cent a year, with African American businesses growing at a rate of about 26 per cent a year. African American males between the ages of 25 and 35 start more businesses than any other group in the country. Moreover, the face of entrepreneurship for the future will be increasingly diverse. When Junior Achievement (an organization that educates

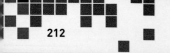

Exhibit 6.7 A Glimpse of Tomorrow's Entrepreneurs

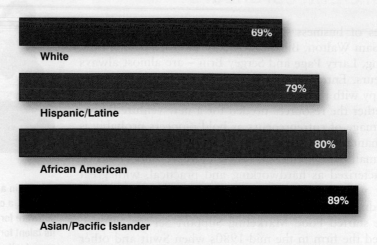

White — 69%

Hispanic/Latine — 79%

African American — 80%

Asian/Pacific Islander — 89%

Percentage of teenagers polled by Junior Achievement who said they want to start their own business

SOURCE: Junior Achievement Survey results reported in Cora Daniels, 'Minority Rule', *FSB* (December 2003–January 2004): 65–66.

young people about business) conducted a poll of teenagers ages 13 to 18, it found a much greater interest among minorities than whites in starting a business, as shown in Exhibit 6.7.[35]

Personality Traits

A number of studies investigated the personality characteristics of entrepreneurs and how they differ from successful managers in established organizations. Some suggest that entrepreneurs in general want something different from life than do traditional managers. Entrepreneurs seem to place high importance on being free to achieve and maximize their potential. Some 40 traits are identified as associated with entrepreneurship, but six have special importance.[36] These characteristics are illustrated in Exhibit 6.8.

Internal Locus of Control

The task of starting and running a new business requires the belief that you can make things come out the way you want. The entrepreneur not only has a vision but also must be able to plan to achieve that vision and believe it will happen. An

Exhibit 6.8 Characteristics of Entrepreneurs

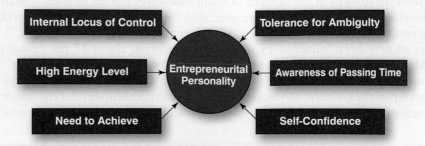

Internal Locus of Control — Tolerance for Ambiguity — High Energy Level — **Entrepreneurial Personality** — Awareness of Passing Time — Need to Achieve — Self-Confidence

SOURCE: Adapted from Charles R. Kuehl and Peggy A. Lambing, *Small Business: Planning and Management* (Ft.Worth: The Dryden Press, 1994): 45.

internal locus of control is the belief by individuals that their future is within their control and that external forces have little influence. For entrepreneurs, reaching the future is seen as being in the hands of the individual. Many people, however, feel that the world is highly uncertain and that they are unable to make things come out the way they want. An **external locus of control** is the belief by individuals that their future is not within their control but rather is influenced by external forces. Entrepreneurs are individuals who are convinced they can make the difference between success and failure; hence, they are motivated to take the steps needed to achieve the goal of setting up and running a new business.

Internal locus of control
The belief by individuals that their future is within their control and that external forces have little influence.

External locus of control
The belief by individuals that their future is not within their control but rather is influenced by external forces.

High Energy Level

A business start-up requires great effort. Most entrepreneurs report struggle and hardship. They persist and work incredibly hard despite traumas and obstacles. A survey of business owners reported that half worked 60 hours or more per week. Another reported that entrepreneurs worked long hours, but that beyond 70 hours little benefit was gained. The data in Exhibit 6.9 show findings from a survey conducted by the National Federation of Independent Business. New business owners work long hours, with only 23 per cent working fewer than 50 hours, which is close to a normal working week for managers in established businesses.

Need to Achieve

Another human quality closely linked to entrepreneurship is the **need to achieve**, which means that people are motivated to excel and pick situations in which success is likely.[37] People who have high achievement needs like to set their own goals, which are moderately difficult. Easy goals present no challenge; unrealistically difficult goals cannot be achieved. Intermediate goals are challenging and provide great satisfaction when achieved. High achievers also like to pursue goals for which they can obtain feedback about their success.

Need to achieve
A human quality linked to entrepreneurship in which people are motivated to excel and pick situations in which success is likely.

Self-Confidence

People who start and run a business must act decisively. They need confidence about their ability to master the day-to-day tasks of the business. They must feel sure about their ability to win customers, handle the technical details and keep the business moving. Entrepreneurs also have a general feeling of confidence that they can deal with anything in the future; complex, unanticipated problems can be handled as they arise.

Exhibit 6.9 Reported Hours per Week Worked by Owners of New Businesses

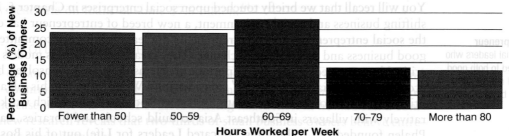

SOURCE: National Federation of Independent Business. Reported in Mark Robichaux, 'Business First, Family Second', *The Wall Street Journal* (May 12, 1989): B1.

classroom. The remaining 67 per cent were firmly of the view that they cannot be taught. While many respondents to the survey said general business skills such as sales and marketing, time management and effective negotiation can be taught, most believed that entrepreneurial traits – like risk-taking, focus and sacrifice – are inherent.

One respondent said: 'I think there are natural entrepreneurs and they have certain traits that are inherent and cannot be acquired. I think it is also possible to acquire business skills and become business savvy but this is separate from being an entrepreneur.' Another commented: 'An entrepreneur is born with an ability to takes risks, make money and think out of the box. It cannot be taught – you are born with it and very few get there.'

Dan Martin, chairman of UK Business Forums, said: 'It is clear from our survey that entrepreneurs are firmly of the belief that while the basic of business can be taught in the classroom, when it actually comes to being a proper entrepreneur, these are skills which are natural and cannot be learnt from text books. .... The number of hugely successful company founders who left school early but went on to make millions suggests our members may be right. The vast amount of enterprise courses on offer may produce many so-called business experts but it looks like we're not going to find the next generation of risk-taking entrepreneurs in the classroom.'

Do you agree with this statement? Can anyone be entrepreneurial or do you have to be born with the key entrepreneurial traits?

Launching an Entrepreneurial Start-Up

Whether one starts a socially oriented company or a traditional for-profit small business, the first step in pursuing an entrepreneurial dream is to come up with a viable idea and then plan like crazy. Once someone has a new idea in mind, a business plan must be drawn and decisions must be made about legal structure, financing and basic tactics, such as whether to start the business from scratch and whether to pursue international opportunities from the start.

Starting with the Idea

To some people, the idea for a new business is the easy part. They do not even consider entrepreneurship until they are inspired by an exciting idea. Other people decide they want to run their own business and set about looking for an idea or opportunity. Exhibit 6.10 shows the most important reasons that people start a new business and the source of new business ideas. Note that 37 per cent of business founders got their idea from an in-depth understanding of the industry, primarily because of past job experience. Interestingly, almost as many – 36 per cent – spotted a market niche that wasn't being filled.[45]

The trick for entrepreneurs is to blend their own skills and experience with a need in the marketplace. Acting strictly on one's own skills may produce something no one wants to buy. On the other hand, finding a market niche that one does not have the ability to fill doesn't work either. Both personal skill and market need typically must be present.

Writing the Business Plan

Business plan
A document specifying the business details prepared by an entrepreneur prior to opening a new business.

Once an entrepreneur is inspired by a new business idea, careful planning is crucial. A **business plan** is a document specifying the business details prepared by an

Exhibit 6.10 Sources of Entrepreneurial Motivation and New-Business Ideas

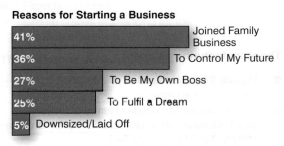

Reasons for Starting a Business

41%	Joined Family Business
36%	To Control My Future
27%	To Be My Own Boss
25%	To Fulfil a Dream
5%	Downsized/Laid Off

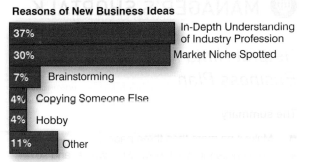

Reasons of New Business Ideas

37%	In-Depth Understanding of Industry Profession
30%	Market Niche Spotted
7%	Brainstorming
4%	Copying Someone Else
4%	Hobby
11%	Other

SOURCE: 'The Rewards', *Inc.* (May 29, 2001): 60–61; and Leslie Brokaw, 'How to Start an *Inc.* 500 Company', *Inc.* 500 (1994): 51–66.

entrepreneur prior to opening a new business. Planning forces the entrepreneur to carefully think through the issues and problems associated with starting and developing the business. Most entrepreneurs have to borrow money, and a business plan is absolutely critical for persuading lenders and investors to participate in the business. Studies show that small businesses with a carefully thought-out, written business plan are much more likely to succeed than those without one.[46] To attract the interest of venture capitalists or other potential investors, the entrepreneur should keep the plan crisp and compelling.

The details of a business plan may vary, but successful business plans generally share several characteristics:[47]

- Demonstrate a clear, compelling vision that creates an air of excitement.
- Provide clear and realistic financial projections.
- Profile potential customers and the target market.
- Include detailed information about the industry and competitors.
- Provide evidence of an effective entrepreneurial management team.
- Pay attention to good formatting and clear writing.
- Keep the plan short – no more than 50 pages.
- Highlight critical risks that may threaten business success.
- Spell out the sources and uses of start-up funds and operating funds.
- Capture the reader's interest with a killer summary.

The business plan should indicate where the product or service fits into the overall industry and should draw on concepts that will be discussed throughout this book. For example, Chapter 8 will describe competitive strategies that entrepreneurs can use. Detailed suggestions for writing a business plan are provided in the Manager's Shoptalk box.

Choosing a Legal Structure

Before entrepreneurs begin a business, and perhaps again as it expands, they must choose an appropriate legal structure for the company. The three basic choices are proprietorship, partnership or corporation.

CONCEPT CONNECTION Social entrepreneurs Eric Schwarz and Ned Rimer created Citizen Schools to reach out to middle school children, pictured here, with after-school programmes that include hands-on apprenticeships taught by volunteer professionals. The apprentices create actual products, ranging from solar cars to well-managed stock portfolios. The goal is to give students the skills and motivation to do well in their academic and personal lives. One reason the organization is so successful is that it is run on solid business principles, with a well-honed strategy and growth plan that includes concrete objectives and specific performance measures.

© BILL MCCARTY/CITIZEN SCHOOLS

Obtaining Finance

Most entrepreneurs are particularly concerned with financing the business. A few types of businesses can still be started with a few thousand dollars, but starting a business usually requires coming up with a significant amount of initial funding. An investment is required to acquire labour and raw materials and perhaps a building and equipment. High-tech businesses, for example, typically need from $50 000 to $500 000 just to get through the first six months, even with the founder drawing no salary.[49] Forrester Research estimates that the total cost to get a business up and running on the internet ranges from $2 million to $40 million.[50]

Many entrepreneurs rely on their own resources for initial funding, but they often have to mortgage their homes, depend on credit cards, borrow money from a bank, or give part of the business to a venture capitalist.[51] The financing decision initially involves two options – whether to obtain loans that must be repaid (debt financing) or whether to share ownership (equity financing).

Debt Financing

Borrowing money that has to be repaid at a later date in order to start a business is referred to as **debt financing**. One common source of debt financing for a start-up is to borrow from family and friends. Increasingly, entrepreneurs are using their personal credit cards as a form of debt financing. Another common source is a bank loan. Banks provide some 25 per cent of all financing for small business. Sometimes entrepreneurs can obtain money from a finance company, wealthy individuals or potential customers. A typical source of funds for businesses with high potential is through **angel financing**. Angels are wealthy individuals, typically with business experience and contacts, who believe in the idea for the start-up and are willing to invest their personal funds to help the business get started. Significantly, angels also provide advice and assistance as the entrepreneur is developing the company. The entrepreneur wants angels who can make business contacts, help find talented employees, and serve as all-around advisors.

Another form of loan financing is provided by the Small Business Administration (SBA). Staples, which started with one office supply store in Brighton, Massachusetts, in 1986, got its start toward rapid growth with the assistance of SBA financing. Today, Staples is the country's largest operator of office superstores, with more than 1500 stores and 58 000 employees worldwide.[52] The SBA is especially helpful for people without substantial assets, providing an opportunity for single parents, minority group members and others with a good idea but who might be considered high-risk by a traditional bank. The percentage of SBA loans to women, Hispanics, African Americans and Asian Americans increased significantly in recent years.[53]

Equity Financing

Any money invested by owners or by those who purchase stock in a corporation is considered equity funds. **Equity financing** consists of funds that are invested in exchange for ownership in the company.

A **venture capital firm** is a group of companies or individuals that invests money in new or expanding businesses for ownership and potential profits. This form of

CONCEPT CONNECTION
Entrepreneurs Roberto Monti and his wife Maria Guerrizio, founders of Milan-based fashion house Piazza Sempione, knew exactly where they wanted the company to go. After getting Piazza Sempione established, they wanted to open more stand-alone stores, expand into handbags and shoes, and go global. But that required an infusion of cash. The partners at L Capital, a private equity firm, were so impressed by the entrepreneurs' solid business plan that they acquired a majority stake in the company. That gave Piazza Sempione both the funds and the strategic expertise needed to take it to the next level.

Debt financing
Borrowing money that has to be repaid at a later date in order to start a business.

Angel financing
Financing provided by a wealthy individual who believes in the idea for a start-up and provides personal funds and advice to help the business get started.

capital is a potential for businesses with high earning and growth possibilities. Venture capitalists are particularly interested in high-tech businesses such as biotechnology, innovative online ventures or telecommunications because they have the potential for high rates of return on investment.[54] The venture capital firm Lighthouse Capital Partners, for example, provided some of the early funding for Netflix, the online DVD rental service.[55] Venture capitalists also usually provide assistance, advice and information to help the entrepreneur prosper. A growing number of minority-owned venture capital firms, such as Provender Capital, founded by African American entrepreneur Fred Terrell, are ensuring that minorities have a fair shot at acquiring equity financing.[56]

Equity financing
Financing that consists of funds that are invested in exchange for ownership in the company.

Venture capital firm
A group of companies or individuals that invests money in new or expanding businesses for ownership and potential profits.

Go to the Ethical Dilemma on page 230 that pertains to raising funds for high-tech start-ups.   TAKE A MOMENT

Tactics for Becoming a Business Owner

Aspiring entrepreneurs can become business owners in several different ways. They can start a new business from scratch, buy an existing business or start a franchise. Another popular entrepreneurial tactic is to participate in a business incubator.

Start a New Business

One of the most common ways to become an entrepreneur is to start a new business from scratch. This approach is exciting because the entrepreneur sees a need for a product or service that has not been filled before and then sees the idea or dream become a reality. Ray Petro invested his $50 000 life savings and took out a $25 000 loan to launch Ray's Mountain Bike Indoor Park after learning from other mountain biking enthusiasts of their frustration with not being able to ride during the winter months. Taryn Rose started her shoe company, Taryn Rose International, after searching for stylish shoes that wouldn't destroy her feet while working long hours as an orthopaedic surgeon.[57] The advantage of starting a business is the ability to develop and design the business in the entrepreneur's own way. The entrepreneur is solely responsible for its success. A potential disadvantage is the long time it can take to get the business off the ground and make it profitable. The uphill battle is caused by the lack of established clientele and the many mistakes made by someone new to the business. Moreover, no matter how much planning is done, a start-up is risky, with no guarantee that the new idea will work. Some entrepreneurs, especially in high-risk industries, develop partnerships with established companies that can help the new company get established and grow. Others use the technique of outsourcing – having some activities handled by outside contractors – to minimize the costs and risks of doing everything in-house.[58] For example, Philip Chigos and Mary Domenico are building their children's pyjama business from the basement of their two-bedroom apartment, using manufacturers in China and Mexico to produce the goods and partnering with a local firm to receive shipments, handle quality control and distribute finished products.[59]

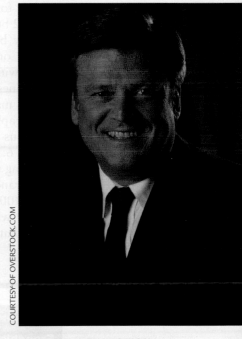

COURTESY OF OVERSTOCK.COM

CONCEPT CONNECTION Finding financing can be difficult for entrepreneurs. For example, over 50 venture capital firms turned down Patrick Byrne when he was trying to start Overstock.com, a retail liquidation, Web-based business. Motivated in part by his desire to be his own boss, Byrne started the company anyway after liquidating most of his personal assets. Still, the challenges and risks do not stop there. According to the Small Business Administration, only half of all new employer firms survive beyond four years.

Buy an Existing Business

Because of the long start-up time and the inevitable mistakes, some entrepreneurs prefer to reduce risk by purchasing an existing business. This direction offers the advantage of a shorter time to get started and an existing track record. The entrepreneur may get a bargain price if the owner wishes to retire or has other family considerations. Moreover, a new business may overwhelm an entrepreneur with the amount of work to be done and procedures to be determined. An established business already has filing systems, a payroll tax system, and other operating procedures. Potential disadvantages are the need to pay for goodwill that the owner believes exists and the possible existence of ill will toward the business. In addition, the company may have bad habits and procedures or outdated technology, which may be why the business is for sale.

Buy a Franchise

Franchising is perhaps the most rapidly growing path to entrepreneurship. The International Franchise Association reports that the country's 320 000 franchise outlets account for about $1 trillion in annual sales.[60] According to some estimates, 1 out of every 12 businesses in the US is franchised, and a franchise opens every eight minutes of every business day.[61] Franchising is an arrangement by which the owner of a product or service allows others to purchase the right to distribute the product or service with help from the owner. The franchisee invests his or her money and owns the business but does not have to develop a new product, create a new company, or test the market. Franchises exist for weight-loss clinics, pet-sitting services, sports photography, bakeries, janitorial services, car repair shops, estate agents and numerous other types of businesses, in addition to the traditional fast-food outlets. Exhibit 6.11 lists five franchise concepts that have been popular in recent years, according to *The Wall Street Journal*. The exhibit lists the type of business, the number of franchisees as of late 2003, and the initial costs. Initial franchise fees can range from $1000 to $250 000, and that doesn't count the other start-up costs the entrepreneur will have to cover. A study by an economics professor several years ago found that the typical franchise costs $94 886 to open.[62] For a casual restaurant

Franchising
An arrangement by which the owner of a product or service allows others to purchase the right to distribute the product or service with help from the owner.

Exhibit 6.11 Five Hot Franchise Concepts for Today

Franchise	Type of Business	Numbers of Outlets	Initial Costs
Curves for Women	Exercise, weight loss centres	5646	$30 625, not including real estate
Cruise Planners	Selling ocean cruises	389	$2095–$18 600
Buffalo Wild Wings Grill & Bar	Sports bar	145	$969 500+
Jani-King	Building cleaning, maintenance	7843	$11 300–$34 100
Comfort Keepers	Nonmedical home care for seniors	386	$39 700–$65 100

SOURCE: Richard Gibson, 'Small Business (A Special Report); Where the Buzz Is: Five of the Hottest Franchise Concepts Out There – and Their Chances of Becoming the Next Big Thing', *The Wall Street Journal* (December 15, 2003): R7.

Exhibit 6.12 Sample Questions for Choosing a Franchise

Questions about the Entrepreneur	Questions about the Franchisor	Before Signing on the Dotted Line
1. Will I enjoy the day-to-day work of the business?	1. What assistance does the company provide in terms of selection of location, setup costs and securing credit; day-to-day technical assistance; marketing; and ongoing training and development?	1. Do I understand the risks associated with this business, and am I willing to assume them?
2. Do my background, experience and goals make this opportunity a good choice for me?	2. How long does it take the typical franchise owner to start making a profit?	2. Have I had an advisor review the disclosure documents and franchise agreement?
3. Am I willing to work within the rules and guidelines established by the franchisor?	3. How many franchises changed ownership within the past year, and why?	3. Do I understand the contract?

SOURCE: Based on Thomas Love, 'The Perfect Franchisee', *Nation's Business* (April 1998): 59–65; and Roberta Maynard, 'Choosing a Franchise', *Nation's Business* (October 1996): 56–63.

such as Buffalo Wild Wings Grill & Bar, listed in the exhibit, the cost is much higher, $969 500 and up, depending on the restaurant location.

The powerful advantage of a franchise is that management help is provided by the owner. For example, Subway, the second fastest growing franchise in the country, does not want a franchisee to fail. Subway has regional development agents who do the research to find good locations for Subway's sandwich outlets. The Subway franchisor also provides two weeks of training at company headquarters and ongoing operational and marketing support.[63] Franchisors provide an established name and national advertising to stimulate demand for the product or service. Potential disadvantages are the lack of control that occurs when franchisors want every business managed in exactly the same way. In some cases, franchisors require that franchise owners use certain contractors or suppliers that might cost more than others would. In addition, franchises can be expensive, and the high start-up costs are followed with monthly payments to the franchisor that can run from 2 per cent to 15 per cent of gross sales.[64]

Entrepreneurs who are considering buying a franchise should investigate the company thoroughly. The prospective franchisee is legally entitled to a copy of franchisor disclosure statements, which include information on 20 topics, including litigation and bankruptcy history, identities of the directors and executive officers, financial information, identification of any products the franchisee is required to buy, and from whom those purchases must be made. The entrepreneur also should talk with as many franchise owners as possible, because they are among the best sources of information about how the company really operates.[65] Exhibit 6.12 lists some specific questions entrepreneurs should ask about themselves and the company when considering buying a franchise. Answering such questions can improve the chances for a successful career as a franchisee.

TAKE A MOMENT   As a new manager considering entrepreneurship, think about whether you want to start a business from scratch, buy an existing business, or open a franchise. You will want to evaluate the advantages and disadvantages of each, and talk with other entrepreneurs for advice. Consider joining a business incubator to benefit from the knowledge and expertise of a mentor.

Participate in a Business Incubator

Business incubator
An innovation that provides shared office space, management support services, and management advice to entrepreneurs

An attractive option for entrepreneurs who want to start a business from scratch is to join a business incubator. A **business incubator** typically provides shared office space, management support services, and management and legal advice to entrepreneurs. Incubators also give entrepreneurs a chance to share information with one another about local business, financial aid and market opportunities. A recent innovation is the *virtual incubator*, which does not require that people set up on-site. These virtual organizations connect entrepreneurs with a wide range of experts and mentors and offer lower overhead and cost savings for cash-strapped small business owners. Christie Stone, co-founder of Ticobeans, a coffee distributor in New Orleans, likes the virtual approach because it gives her access to top-notch advice while allowing her to keep her office near her inventory.[66]

The concept of business incubators arose about two decades ago to nurture start-up companies. Business incubators have become a significant segment of the small business economy, with approximately 1100 in operation in the US in 2005.[67] During the dot-com boom, a tremendous jump in the number of for-profit incubators ended as many of them went out of business when the tech economy crashed.[68] The incubators that are thriving are primarily not-for-profits and those that cater to niches or focus on helping women or minority entrepreneurs. These incubators include those run by government agencies and universities to boost the viability of small business and spur job creation.[69] The great value of an incubator is the expertise of a mentor, who serves as advisor, role model, and cheerleader, and ready access to a team of lawyers, accountants and other advisors. Incubators also give budding entrepreneurs a chance to network and learn from one another.[70] Incubators are an important part of the international entrepreneurial landscape, as well. For example, Harmony is a global network support system for business incubators. Harmony was started in 1998 – with partners in Germany, France, Spain, Finland, Switzerland, Australia, Japan and the US – to provide training and support for both new and established incubators worldwide, enabling them to better serve clients and improve the success of small businesses.[71]

Managing a Growing Business

Once an entrepreneurial business is up and running, how does the owner manage it? Often the traits of self-confidence, creativity, and internal locus of control lead to financial and personal grief as the enterprise grows. A hands-on entrepreneur who gave birth to the organization loves perfecting every detail. But after the start-up, continued growth requires a shift in management style. Those who fail to adjust to a growing business can be the cause of the problems rather than the solution.[72] In this section, we look at the stages through which entrepreneurial companies move and then consider how managers should carry out their planning, organizing, leading and controlling.

Exhibit 6.13 Five Stages of Growth for an Entrepreneurial Company

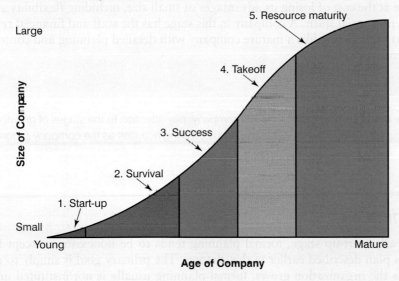

SOURCE: Based on Neil C. Churchill and Virginia L. Lewis, 'The Five Stages of Small Business Growth', *Harvard Business Review* (May–June 1993): 30–50.

Stages of Growth

Entrepreneurial businesses go through distinct stages of growth, with each stage requiring different management skills. The five stages are illustrated in Exhibit 6.13.

1 *Start-up*. In this stage, the main problems are producing the product or service and obtaining customers. Several key issues facing managers are: Can we get enough customers? Will we survive? Do we have enough money? Burt's Bees was in the start-up stage when Roxanne Quimby was hand-making candles and personal care products from the beeswax of Burt Shavitz's bees and selling them at craft fairs in Maine.

2 *Survival*. At this stage, the business demonstrates that it is a workable business entity. It produces a product or service and has sufficient customers. Concerns here involve with finances – generating sufficient cash flow to run the business and making sure revenues exceed expenses. The organization will grow in size and profitability during this period. Burt's Bees reached $3 million in sales by 1993, and Quimby moved the business from Maine to North Carolina to take advantage of state policies that helped her keep costs in line.

3 *Success*. At this point, the company is solidly based and profitable. Systems and procedures are in place to allow the owner to slow down if desired. The owner can stay involved or consider turning the business over to professional managers. Quimby chose to stay closely involved with Burt's Bees, admitting that she's a bit of a control freak about the business.

4 *Takeoff*. Here the key problem is how to grow rapidly and finance that growth. The owner must learn to delegate, and the company must find sufficient capital to invest in major growth. This period is pivotal in an entrepreneurial company's life. Properly managed, the company can become a big business. However, another problem for companies at this stage is how to maintain the advantages of 'smallness' as the company grows. In 2003, Quimby sold 80 per cent of Burt's Bees to AEA Investors, a private equity firm, for more than $175 million. She continued as CEO and focuses on continuing to grow the business.

5 *Resource maturity.* At this stage, the company's substantial financial gains may come at the cost of losing its advantages of small size, including flexibility and the entrepreneurial spirit. A company in this stage has the staff and financial resources to begin acting like a mature company with detailed planning and control systems.

TAKE A MOMENT   As a new manager in an entrepreneurial company, pay attention to the stages of growth, and adapt your planning, organizing, leading and controlling activities as the company progresses.

Planning

In the early start-up stage, formal planning tends to be nonexistent except for the business plan described earlier in this chapter. The primary goal is simply to remain alive. As the organization grows, formal planning usually is not instituted until the success stage. Recall from Chapter 1 that planning means defining goals and deciding on the tasks and use of resources needed to attain them. Chapters 7, 8, and 9 will describe how entrepreneurs can define goals and implement strategies and plans to meet them. It is important that entrepreneurs view their original business plan as a living document that evolves as the company grows or the market changes.

One planning concern for today's small businesses is the need to be Web-savvy. For many small companies today, their Web operations are just as critical as traditional warehouse management or customer service operations. The growing importance of e-business means entrepreneurs have to plan and allocate resources for internet operations from the beginning and grow those plans as the company grows. Of the small companies that have websites, more than half say the site has broken even or paid for itself in greater efficiency, improved customer relationships, or increased business.[73]

Organizing

In the first two stages of growth, the organization's structure is typically informal with all employees reporting to the owner. At about stage 3 – success – functional managers often are hired to take over duties performed by the owner. A functional organization structure will begin to evolve with managers in charge of finance, manufacturing and marketing. Another organizational approach is to use outsourcing, as described earlier. Method, a company launched by two 20-something entrepreneurs to develop a line of non-toxic cleaning products in fresh scents and stylish packaging, contracted with an industrial designer for the unique dish soap bottle and uses contract manufacturers in every region of the country to rapidly make products and get them to stores.[74]

During the latter stages of entrepreneurial growth, managers must learn to delegate and decentralize authority. If the business has multiple product lines, the owner may consider creating teams or divisions responsible for each line. The organization must hire competent managers and have sufficient management talent to handle fast growth and eliminate problems caused by increasing size. As an organization grows, it might also be characterized by greater use of rules, procedures, and written job descriptions. For example, Tara Cronbaugh started a small coffee-house in a college town, but its success quickly led to the opening of three additional houses. With the rapid growth, Cronbaugh found that she needed a way to ensure consistency across operations. She put together an operations manual with detailed rules, procedures, and job descriptions so managers and employees at each coffee-house would be following the same pattern.[75] Chapters 10 through 13 will discuss organizing in detail.

Leading

The driving force in the early stages of development is the leader's vision. This vision, combined with the leader's personality, shapes corporate culture. The leader can signal cultural values of service, efficiency, quality or ethics. Often entrepreneurs do not have good people skills but do have excellent task skills in either manufacturing or marketing. By the success stage of growth, the owner must either learn to motivate employees or bring in managers who can. Rapid takeoff is not likely to happen without employee cooperation. Stepping from the self-absorption of the early days of a company to the more active communication necessary for growth can be tricky for entrepreneurs. Stan and Bob Lee built a successful business making spare parts for the corrugated box industry, but as the company grew, the two entrepreneurs had trouble shifting to more active leadership and communication. One consultant joked that the two seemed to fear that sales might actually increase if they listened to their staff.[76] The president of Foreign Candy Company of Hull, Iowa, saw his company grow rapidly when he concentrated more on employee needs and less on financial results. He made an effort to communicate with employees, conducted surveys to learn how they were feeling about the company, and found ways to involve them in decision-making. His shift in leadership style allowed the company to enter the takeoff stage with the right corporate culture and employee attitudes to sustain rapid growth.

Leadership also is important because many small firms have a hard time hiring qualified employees. Labour shortages often hurt small firms that grow rapidly. A healthy corporate culture can help attract and retain good people.[77] You will learn more about leadership in Chapters 14 through 18.

CONCEPT CONNECTION In 2005, Spanish Internet radio broadcaster Batanga.com concluded a merger agreement that propelled it into the take-off stage of growth. The Greensboro, North Carolina, company joined forces with Planeta Networks of Miami, a broadband platform supplier, to form Hispanic Media, Inc. 'Both companies had turned a corner and we were both looking for ways to expand,' explained Batanga co-founder and CEO Troy McConnell, pictured here. Hispanic Media, Inc. is well positioned to attract more advertising dollars than Batanga could on its own and to appeal to new markets, such as launching a new auto channel that features both text and broadband video.

Controlling

Financial control is important in each stage of the entrepreneurial firm's growth. In the initial stages, control is exercised by simple accounting records and by personal supervision. By stage 3 – success – operational budgets are in place, and the owner should start implementing more structured control systems. During the takeoff stage, the company will need to make greater use of budgets and standard cost systems and use computer systems to provide statistical reports. These control techniques will become more sophisticated during the resource maturity stage.

As Amazon.com grew and expanded internationally, for example, entrepreneur and CEO Jeff Bezos needed increasingly sophisticated control mechanisms. Bezos hired a computer systems expert to develop a system to track and control all of the company's operations.[78] Control will be discussed further in Chapters 19 through 21.

A MANAGER'S ESSENTIALS: WHAT HAVE WE LEARNED?

- This chapter discussed organizational planning, which involves defining goals and developing plans with which to achieve them.

- An organization exists for a single, overriding purpose known as its *mission* – the basis for strategic goals and plans. Goals within the organization begin with strategic goals followed by tactical and operational goals. Plans are defined similarly, with strategic, tactical and operational plans used to achieve the goals. Managers can use strategy maps to clearly align goals and communicate them throughout the organization.

- Managers formulate goals that are specific and measurable, cover key result areas, are challenging but realistic, have a defined time period, and are linked to rewards.

- The chapter described several types of operational plans, including management by objectives, single-use and standing plans and contingency plans. Two extensions of contingency planning are scenario building and crisis planning. Scenarios are alternative vivid pictures of what the future might be like. They provide a framework for managers to cope with unexpected or unpredictable events. Crisis planning involves the stages of prevention and preparation.

- In the past, planning was almost always done entirely by top managers, consultants, or central planning departments. During turbulent times, planning is decentralized and people throughout the organization are involved in establishing dynamic plans that can meet rapidly changing needs in the environment.

- Some guidelines for high-performance planning in a turbulent environment include setting stretch goals for excellence, using performance dashboards and organizing intelligence teams.

DISCUSSION QUESTIONS

1 Are entrepreneurs born or made? Why? Illustrate with examples.

2 Over the past 20 years, entrepreneurship has been the fastest-growing course of study on campuses throughout the country. However, debate continues about whether you can teach someone to be an entrepreneur. Do you think entrepreneurship can be taught? Why or why not?

3 Why would small business ownership have great appeal to immigrants, women and minorities?

4 Consider the six personality characteristics of entrepreneurs. Which two traits do you think are most like those of managers in large companies? Which two are least like those of managers in large companies?

5 How would you go about deciding whether you wanted to start a business from scratch, buy an existing business, or buy into a franchise? What information would you collect and analyze?

6 If you were to start a new business, would you have to search for an idea, or do you already have an idea to try? Explain.

7 Many entrepreneurs say they did little planning, perhaps scratching notes on a legal pad. How is it possible for them to succeed?

8 What personal skills do you need to keep your financial backers feeling confident in your new business? Which skills are most useful when you're dealing with more informal sources such as family and friends versus receiving funds from stockholders, a bank, or a venture capital firm? Would these considerations affect your financing strategy?

9 Many people who are successful at the start-up stage of a business are not the right people to carry the venture forward. How do you decide whether you're better suited to be a serial entrepreneur (start the business and then move on to start another) or whether you can guide the venture as it grows and matures?

10 How does starting a high-tech business such as an Internet company differ from starting a small business such as a local car repair shop or delicatessen? What is the role of alliances and partnerships in online versus traditional small businesses?

11 Do you think entrepreneurs who launched a new business after deciding to leave a job on their own versus those who have been forced to leave a job as a result of downsizing are likely to have different traits? Which group is more likely to succeed? Why?

MANAGEMENT IN PRACTICE: EXPERIENTIAL EXERCISE

What's Your Entrepreneurial IQ?

Rate yourself on the following 15 behaviours and characteristics, according to the following scale.

1 = Strongly disagree

2 = Disagree

3 = Agree

4 = Strongly agree

1 I am able to translate ideas into concrete tasks and outcomes.

1   2   3   4

2 When I am interested in a project, I tend to need less sleep.

1   2   3   4

3 I am willing to make sacrifices to gain long-term rewards.

1   2   3   4

4 Growing up, I was more of a risk-taker than a cautious child.

1   2   3   4

5 I often see trends, connections, and patterns that are not obvious to others.

1   2   3   4

6 I have always enjoyed spending much of my time alone.

1   2   3   4

7 I have a reputation for being stubborn.

1   2   3   4

8 I prefer working with a difficult but highly competent person to working with someone who is congenial but less competent.

1   2   3   4

9 As a child, I had a paper round, lemonade stand or other small enterprise.

1   2   3   4

10 I usually keep New Year's resolutions.

1   2   3   4

11 I'm not easily discouraged, and I persist when faced with major obstacles.

1   2   3   4

12 I recover quickly from emotional setbacks.

1   2   3   4

13 I would be willing to dip deeply into my 'nest egg' – and possibly lose all I had saved – to go it alone.

1   2   3   4

14 I get tired of the same routine day in and day out.

1   2   3   4

15 When I want something, I keep the goal clearly in mind.

1   2   3   4

Scoring and Interpretation

Total your score for the 15 items. If you tallied 50–60 points, you have a strong entrepreneurial IQ. A score of 30–50 indicates good entrepreneurial possibilities. Your chances of starting a successful entrepreneurial business are good if you have the desire and motivation. If you scored below 30, you probably do not have much entrepreneurial potential.

Go back over each question, thinking about changes you might make to become more or less entrepreneurial, depending on your career interests.

2005): www.nytimes.com; and 'CIBC Report Predicts Canada Will Be Home to One Million Women Entrepreneurs By 2010', *Canada NewsWire* (June 28, 2005): 1.

4. Olson, 'They May Be Mundane, But Low-Tech Businesses Are Booming'.

5. John Case, 'Where We Are Now', *Inc.* (May 29, 2001): 18–19.

6. Donald F. Kuratko and Richard M. Hodgetts, *Entrepreneurship: A Contemporary Approach*, 4th ed. (Fort Worth: The Dryden Press, 1998): 30.

7. Study conducted by Yankelovich Partners, reported in Mark Henricks, 'Type-Cast', *Entrepreneur* (March 2000): 14–16.

8. Norm Brodsky, 'Street Smarts: Opportunity Knocks', *Inc.* (February 2002): 44–46; and Hilary Stout, 'Start Low', *The Wall Street Journal* (May 14, 2001): R8.

9. Kathleen Collins, '¡La Vida Próspera! Latin-Owned Businesses Explode', *Working Woman* (October 2000): 13.

10. Global Entrepreneurship Monitor, 'Table 2: Prevalence Rates of Entrepreneurial Activity Across Countries, 2005' *2005 GEM Tables and Figures*, Babson College and the London Business School, (March 14, 2006): www.gemconsortium.org/category_list.asp.

11. 'One-Yen Wonders', *The Economist* (June 28, 2003): 66.

12. Ovetta Wiggins, 'Report: Small Business Set to Double By 2009', *The Moscow Times*, as reported on The America's Intelligence Wire, (March 2, 2004): www.themoscowtimes.com.

13. This section based on John Case, 'The Wonderland Economy', *The State of Small Business* (1995): 14–29; and Richard L. Daft, *Management*, 3rd ed. (Fort Worth, Texas: The Dryden Press, 1992).

14. Permission to reproduce material from the GEM 2007 Global Report, which appear here, has been kindly granted by the copyright holders. The GEM is an international consortium and this report has been produced from data collected in, and received from, 42 countries in 2008. Our thanks go to the authors, national teams, researchers, funding bodies and other contributors who have made this possible.

15. 'Number of Small Businesses Continues to Grow; Nevada, Georgia Lead the Way', *The Network Journal* (March–April 2005): 54.

16. Alessandra Bianchi, 'Erasing Borders', in Joshua Hyatt, 'Small and Global', *FSB* (June 2004): 44–45.

17. Julia Boorstin, 'Exporting Cleaner Air', in Joshua Hyatt, 'Small and Global', *FSB* (June 2004): 44–45.

18. Google inc. online www.google.com

19. Brian Caulfield *et al.*, '12 Hot Startups', *Business 2.0* (January–February 2004): 93–97.

20. Caulfield *et al.*, '12 Hot Startups'.

21. Christine Y. Chen, 'The E-Recycler', *FSB* (May 2005): 93–94.

22. GreenThumb Lawn Treatment Service online at www.greenthumb.co.uk

23. www.sba.gov.

24. Thuy-Doan Le Bee, 'How Small Is Small? SBA Holds Hearings to Decide', *The Sacramento Bee* (June 29, 2005): D2.

25. Barbara Benham, 'Big Government, Small Business', *Working Woman* (February 2001): 24.

26. Ian Mount, 'The Return of the Lone Inventor', *FSB* (March 2005): 18; Office of Advocacy, US Small Business Administration, www.sba.gov/advo.

27. Kuratko and Hodgetts, *Entrepreneurship: A Contemporary Approach*, 4th ed. (Fort Worth: The Dryden Press, 1998): 11; and '100 Ideas for New Businesses', *Venture* (November 1988): 35–74.

28. Adapted from 'My story' by Sam Fountain, www.shewee.com.

29. John Case, 'The Origins of Entrepreneurship', *Inc.* (June 1989): 51–53.

30. Greco and Grant, 'Innovation, Part III: Creation Nation'.

31. Robert D. Hisrich, 'Entrepreneurship-Intrapreneurship', *American Psychologist* (February 1990): 209–222.

32. Olson, 'From One Business to 23 Million'.

33. www.sba.gov; 'CIBC Report Predicts Canada Will Be Home to One Million Women Entrepreneurs by 2010', *Canada NewsWire* (June 28, 2005): 1.

34. www.sba.gov.

35. Statistics reported in Cora Daniels, 'Minority Rule', *FSB* (December 2003–January 2004): 65–66; Elizabeth Olson, 'New Help for the Black Entrepreneur', *The New York Times* (December 23, 2004): C6; and David J. Dent, 'The Next Black Power Movement', *FSB* (May 2003): 10–13.

36. This discussion is based on Charles R. Kuehl and Peggy A. Lambing, *Small Business: Planning and Management*, 3rd ed. (Ft. Wort: The Dryden Press, 1994).

37. David C. McClelland, *The Achieving Society* (New York: Van Nostrand, 1961).

38. Paulette Thomas, 'Entrepreneurs' Biggest Problems – and How They Solve Them', *The Wall Street Journal* (March 17, 2003): R1.

39. Definition based on Albert R. Hunt, 'Social Entrepreneurs: Compassionate and Tough-Minded', *The Wall Street Journal* (July 13, 2000): A27; David Puttnam, 'Hearts Before Pockets', *The New Statesman* (February 9, 2004): 26; and Christian Seelos and Johanna Mair, 'Social Entrepreneurship: Creating New Business Models to Serve the Poor', *Business Horizons* 48 (2005): 241–246.

40. Cheryl Dahle, 'Filling the Void: The 2006 Social Capitalist Award Winners', *Fast Company* (January–February 2006): 50–61.

41. Putnam, 'Hearts Before Pockets'.

42. Cheryl Dahle, 'The Change Masters', *Fast Company* (January 2005): 47–58; David Bornstein, *How to Change the World: Social Entrepreneurs and the Power of New Ideas* (Oxford and New York: Oxford University Press, 2004).

43. Brian Dumaine, 'See Me, Hear Me', segment in 'Two Ways to Help the Third World', *Fortune* (October 27, 2003): 187–196.

44. Dahle, 'Filling the Void'; and Cheryl Dahle, 'Social Capitalists: The Top 20 Groups That Are Changing the World', *Fast Company* (January 2004): 45–57.

45. Leslie Brokaw, 'How to Start an Inc. 500 Company', *Inc. 500* (1994): 51–65.

46. Paul Reynolds, 'The Truth about Start-Ups', *Inc.* (February 1995): 23; Brian O'Reilly, 'The New Face of Small Businesses', *Fortune* (May 2, 1994) 82–88.

47. Based on Ellyn E. Spragins, 'How to Write a Business Plan That Will Get You in the Door', *Small Business Success*

(Inc. 2001); Linda Elkins, 'Tips for Preparing a Business Plan', *Nation's Business* (June 1996): 60R–61R; Carolyn M. Brown, 'The Do's and Don'ts of Writing a Winning Business Plan', *Black Enterprise* (April 1996): 114–116; and Kuratko and Hodgetts, *Entrepreneurship,* 295–397. For a clear, thorough step-by-step guide to writing an effective business plan, see Linda Pinson and Jerry Jinnett, *Anatomy of a Business Plan,* 5th ed. (Virginia Beach, VA: Dearborn, 2001).

48. The Inc. Faxpoll, *Inc.* (February 1992): 24.
49. MacVicar, 'Ten Steps to a High-Tech Start-Up'.
50. Reported in H. M. Dietel, P. J. Dietel and K. Steinbuhler, *e-Business and e-Commerce for Managers* (Upper Saddle River, NJ: Prentice Hall, 2001): 58.
51. 'Venture Capitalists' Criteria', *Management Review* (November 1985): 7–8.
52. 'Staples Makes Big Business from Helping Small Businesses', *SBA Success Stories, www.sba.gov/successstories. html* (accessed on March 12, 2004).
53. Olson, 'From One Business to 23 Million'.
54. 'Where the Venture Money Is Going', *Business 2.0* (January–February 2004): 98.
55. Gary Rivlin, 'Does the Kid Stay in the Picture?', *The New York Times* (February 22, 2005): E1, E8.
56. Dent, 'The Next Black Power Movement'.
57. Kristen Hampshire, 'Roll With It', *FSB* (November 2005): 108–112; Jennifer Maxwell profile in Betsy Wiesendanger, 'Labours of Love',' *Working Woman* (May 1999): 43–56; Jena McGregor, Taryn Rose profile in '25 Top Women Business Builders',' *Fast Company* (May 2005): 67–75.
58. Wendy Lea, 'Dancing With a Partner', *Fast Company* (March 2000): 159–161.
59. Matt Richtel, 'Outsourced All the Way', *The New York Times* (June 21, 2005): www.nytimes.com.
60. Reported in Sheryl Nance-Nash, 'More Are Betting the Franchise', *The New York Times* (February 29, 2004): Section 14 LI, 6.
61. Echo Montgomery Garrett, 'The Twenty-First-Century Franchise', *Inc.* (January 1995): 79–88; Lisa Benavides, 'Linking Up with a Chain', *The Tennessean* (April 6, 1999): 1E.
62. Henry Weil, 'Business in a Box', *Working Woman* (September 1999): 59–64.
63. Quinne Bryant, 'Who Owns 20+ Subway Franchises?', *The Business Journal of Tri-Cities Tennessee/Virginia* (August 2003): 42–43.
64. For a current discussion of the risks and disadvantages of owning a franchise, see Anne Fisher, 'Risk Reward', *FSB* (December 2005–January 2006): 44.
65. Anne Field, 'Your Ticket to a New Career? Franchising Can Put Your Skills to Work in Your Own Business', in *Business Week Investor: Small Business* section, *BusinessWeek* (May 12, 2003): 100+: and Roberta Maynard, 'Choosing a Franchise', *Nation's Business* (October 1996): 56–63.
66. Darren Dahl, 'Getting Started: Percolating Profits'. *Inc.* (February 2005): 38.
67. Ibid.
68. Reported in Dahl, 'Getting Started: Percolating Profits'.
69. Harvard Business School, reported in Kimberly Weisul, 'Incubators Lay an Egg', *BusinessWeek Frontier* (October 9, 2000): F14.
70. Oringel, 'Sowing Success'.
71. Peter Balan, University of South Australia, 'Harmony: A Global Network Support System for Incubators', and 'Harmony: A Network System to Support Innovation Commercialisation', http://business2.unisa.edu.au/cde/docs/HarmonyOverviewAndBenefits%2025Feb02.pdf.
72. Carrie Dolan, 'Entrepreneurs Often Fail as Managers', *The Wall Street Journal* (May 15, 1989): B1.
73. Mannes, 'Don't Give Up on the Web'.
74. Finn, 'Selling Cool in a Bottle'.
75. Amanda Walmac, 'Full of Beans', *Working Woman* (February 1999): 38–40.
76. Ron Stodghill, 'Boxed Out', *FSB* (April 2005): 69–72.
77. Udayan Gupta and Jeffery A. Tannenbaum, 'Labour Shortages Force Changes at Small Firms', *The Wall Street Journal* (May 22, 1989): B1, B2; 'Harnessing Employee Productivity', *Small Business Report* (November 1987): 46–49; and Molly Kilmas, 'How to Recruit a Smart Team', *Nation's Business* (May 1995): 26–27.
78. Saul Hansell, 'Listen Up! It's Time for a Profit: A Front Row Seat as Amazon Gets Serious', *The New York Times* (May 20, 2001): Section 3, 1.

Questions

1 How important is it to IKEA's international success that it's corporate culture should be adapted to suit the country or region where it is opening a new store? Explain.

2 Discuss the need for IKEA's management to understand a country's sociocultural environment prior to opening a store in that country.

3 Identify who IKEA's organizational stakeholders might be in one of its Middle Eastern stores? Are these stakeholders liable to be different from those in a European store? If so, how do these stakeholders differ?

SOURCES 'IKEA Accused of Flat pack Sexism', (2005), Times Online at: http://www.limesonline.co.uk/tol/news/world/article 424328.ece; 'IKEA's Globalization Strategies and its Foray in China', (2005), Online at: http://www.icmrindia.org/casestudie s/catalogue/Business%20Strategy/IKEA%20Globalization%20Str ategies-Foray%20in%20China-Intro2.htm; 'IKEA launches own-brand hijab for Muslim staff', (2005), Free Press Release, Online at: http://www.free-press-release.com/news/200508/11245903 44.html; 'IKEA's First Japanese Store Managers', William J. Ross (2008), Swedish Chamber of Commerce and Industry in Japan; 'IKEA Kuwait welcomes festive season with "Ramadan Surprises"' (2008), Arabian Business.Com, online at: http://www.arabianbusiness.com/press_releases/detail/27333

PART 3

PLANNING

Planning does not require perfection, but the better the plan, the more predictable the outcome.

The *Millennium Dome,* was the original name of the building, used to house the **Millennium Experience,** a major exhibition celebrating the beginning of the third millennium. Designed by the architect Richard Rogers, and located on the Greenwich Peninsula in south-east London, England, the exhibition opened to the public on 1 January 2000 and ran until 31 December 2000. However, the project and exhibition was the subject of considerable political controversy as it failed to attract the number of visitors anticipated, leading to recurring financial problems.

The structure of the Dome is the largest of its type in the world and has gained iconic status. Externally it appears as a large white marquee with twelve 100m-high yellow support towers, one for each month of the year, or each hour of the clock face, representing the role played by Greenwich Mean Time. In plan view it is circular, 365m in diameter – one metre for each day of the year – with scalloped edges. It has become one of the United Kingdom's most recognisable landmarks, and can easily be seen on aerial photographs of London

Originally the Dome project was conceived as quite small scale, but the incoming Labour government elected in 1997, greatly expanded the size, scope and funding of the project. It also significantly increased expectations of what would be delivered. Just before its opening, Prime Minister Blair claimed the Dome would be "a triumph of confidence over cynicism, boldness over blandness, excellence over mediocrity".

The press though largely reported the project to have been a flop: badly thought-out, badly executed, and leaving the government with the embarrassing question of what to do with it afterwards. A key problem was that the financial predictions were based on an unrealistically high forecast of 12 milion visitors, against an actual realised number of 6.5 million visitors, resulting in a €204 million revenue shortfall against original estimates.

However, unlike the negative opinion of the press, visitor feedback was extremely positive. The Dome was in fact the most popular UK tourist attraction in 2000, ahead of both the London Eye, and Alton Towers, which had been first in 1999.

Following the closure of the Millennium Experience at the end of 2000, the Dome remained closed for most of the next 6 years, with many ideas for re-development failing to go forward. Eventually, on May 31st 2005, the dome was publicly renamed as The O_2, in a €6 million-per-year deal with telecommunications company O_2 plc, a subsidiary of Telefónica O_2. This signalled a major redevelopment of the site which retained little beyond the shell of the dome, and marked the Dome's transition into an entertainment district including an indoor arena, a music club, a cinema, an exhibition space and bars and restaurants. This redevelopment cost £600 million, and the resulting venue opened to the public on 24 June 2007, with a concert by rock band Bon Jovi.

As in management, an architectural plan must have a goal and strategy formulation before crews and equipment can be hired and scheduled. The story of the Millennium Dome is an example of what happens when plans have errors. The building itself was spectacular and iconic, but despite the success of being the largest visitor attraction in UK in 2000, the overall project suffered from poor budget forecasting and controls, as well as having no realistic plans in place for what would happen to the site once the main exhibition had closed.

Goal setting, planning, strategy formulation and implementation are ongoing for any company, large or small. No company can expect to devise the perfect plan, and while planning doesn't have to be perfect, it does have to be done. Thankfully, even when planning results in unexpected or less than optimal results, usually the only mistake that cannot be rectified is not planning at all.

© NIKADA/ISTOCK

LEARNING OBJECTIVES

After reading this chapter, you should be able to:

1 Define goals and plans and explain the relationship between them.

2 Explain the concept of organizational mission and how it influences goal setting and planning.

3 Describe the types of goals an organization should have and how managers use strategy maps to align goals.

4 Define the characteristics of effective goals.

5 Describe the four essential steps in the management by objectives (MBO) process.

6 Explain the difference between single-use plans and standing plans.

7 Describe and explain the importance of contingency planning, scenario building and crisis planning in today's environment.

8 Summarize the guidelines for high-performance planning in a fast-changing environment.

CHAPTER 7

MANAGERIAL PLANNING AND GOAL SETTING

One of the primary responsibilities of managers is to decide where the organization should go in the future and how to get it there. In some organizations, typically small ones, planning is informal. In others, managers follow a well-defined planning framework. The company establishes a basic mission and periodically develops formal goals and plans for carrying it out. Large organizations such as Royal Dutch Shell, and IBM, as well as many public bodies, such as local councils or the police service, undertake a strategic planning exercise each year – reviewing their missions, goals and plans to meet environmental changes or the expectations of important stakeholders such as the community, owners or customers.

Of the four management functions – planning, organizing, leading and controlling – described in Chapter 1, planning is considered the most fundamental. Everything else stems from planning. Yet planning also is the most controversial management function. How do managers plan for the future in a constantly changing environment? The economic, political, and social turmoil of recent years has sparked a renewed interest in organizational planning, particularly planning for unexpected problems and events. Yet planning cannot read an uncertain future, neither can it tame a turbulent environment. The 19th century German military strategist, Field Marshall Helmuth von Moltke, wrote that 'No battle plan survives contact with the enemy.' His point was that once the battle starts, the plan you devised beforehand will invariably have to change.[1] Does that mean it's useless to make plans? Of course not. No plan can be perfect, but without plans and goals, organizations and employees flounder. However, good managers understand that plans should grow and change to meet new conditions. And as the legendary South African golfer Gary Player once claimed, 'The more I practise, the luckier I get', which in planning terms might be interpreted as the more effort a company puts into its planning the more chance it has of getting it right.

Does goal setting fit your management style?

Are you a good planner? Do you set goals and identify ways to accomplish them? This questionnaire will help you understand how your work habits fit with making plans and setting goals. Answer the following questions as they apply to your work or study habits. Please indicate whether each item is Mostly True or Mostly False for you.

		Mostly True	Mostly False
1	I have clear, specific goals in several areas of my life.	☐	☐
2	I have a definite outcome in life I want to achieve.	☐	☐
3	I prefer general to specific goals.	☐	☐
4	I work better without specific deadlines.	☐	☐
5	I set aside time each day or week to plan my work.	☐	☐
6	I am clear about the measures that indicate when I have achieved a goal.	☐	☐
7	I work better when I set more challenging goals for myself.	☐	☐
8	I help other people clarify and define their goals.	☐	☐

SCORING AND INTERPRETATION Give yourself one point for each item you marked as Mostly True except items 3 and 4. For items 3 and 4 give yourself one point for each one you marked Mostly False. A score of five or higher suggests a positive level of goal-setting behaviour and good preparation for a new manager role in an organization. If you scored four or less you might want to evaluate and begin to change your goal-setting behaviour. An important part of a new manager's job is setting goals, measuring results and reviewing progress for the department and subordinates.

These questions indicate the extent to which you have already adopted the disciplined use of goals in your life and work. But if you scored low, don't despair. Goal setting can be learned. Most organizations have goal setting and review systems that new managers use. Not everyone thrives under a disciplined goal-setting system, but as a new manager, setting goals and assessing results are tools that will enhance your impact. Research indicates that setting clear, specific and challenging goals in key areas will produce better performance.

Manager's Challenge

Nancy Sorrells isn't easily scared, but the challenges in her new job have her worried. Something is definitely wrong at the Marriott Hotel where Sorrells has recently been hired as general manager. But it's not easy to tell exactly what that *something* is. Despite the fact that the hotel was only four years old and close to a major airport, it had trouble maintaining steady business at premium room rates. The hotel was running nearly £2.0 million behind budget on revenue, and inspections showed numerous deficiencies in all areas. Moreover, employees seemed lackadaisical and unmotivated to improve things. To make matters worse, Sorrells had been hired to

replace a manager who was much loved by the staff, and the resentment of employees was palpable. The fact that she had previously managed a Holiday Inn, a lesser brand in the hotel pecking order, didn't help her status either. Sorrells began working through the hotel person-by-person, looking for those who would support her vision for turning the hotel around. Although she gained some cooperation, performance didn't seem to improve. In exasperation, one veteran department head finally blurted, 'I'd like to follow you, but I don't know where you're going.'[2]

If you were in Nancy Sorrell's position, what would be your first step to turn things around at the hotel? How would you get everyone moving in the same direction and enable them to achieve high performance?

TAKE A MOMENT

One of the primary responsibilities of managers is to decide where the organization should go in the future and how to get it there. Without clear goals and plans, employees cannot perform up to their potential and the organization flounders.

In this chapter, we explore the process of planning and consider how managers develop effective plans. Special attention is given to goal setting, for that is where planning starts. Then, we discuss the various types of plans that managers use to help the organization achieve those goals. We also take a look at planning approaches that help managers deal with uncertainty, such as contingency planning, scenario building and crisis planning. Finally, we examine new approaches to planning that emphasize the involvement of employees, and sometimes other stakeholders, in strategic thinking and execution. Chapter 8 will look at strategic planning in depth and examine a number of strategic options managers can use in a competitive environment. In Chapter 9, we look at management decision-making. Proper decision-making techniques are crucial to selecting the organization's goals, plans, and strategic options.

Overview of Goals and Plans

A **goal** is a desired future state that the organization attempts to realize.[3] Goals are important because organizations exist for a purpose, and goals define and state that purpose. A **plan** is a blueprint for goal achievement and specifies the necessary resource allocations, schedules, tasks and other actions. Goals specify future ends; plans specify today's means. The concept of **planning** usually incorporates both ideas; it means determining the organization's goals and defining the means for achieving them.[4]

The structure of the Dome is the largest of its type in the world and has gained iconic status. Externally it appears as a large white marquee with 12 100 metre-high yellow support towers, one for each month of the year, or each hour of the clock face, representing the role played by Greenwich Mean Time. In plain view it is circular, 365m in diameter – 1 metre for each day of the year – with scalloped edges. It has become one of the UK's most recognizable landmarks, and can easily be seen on aerial photographs of London.

Originally the Dome project was conceived as quite small scale, but the incoming Labour government elected in 1997, greatly expanded the size, scope and funding of the project. It also significantly increased expectations of what would be delivered. Just before its opening, Prime Minister Blair claimed the Dome would be 'a triumph of confidence over cynicism, boldness over blandness, excellence over mediocrity.'[5]

The press though largely reported the project as a flop: badly thought-out, badly executed and leaving the Government with the embarrassing question of what to do

Goal
A desired future state that the organization attempts to realize.

Plan
A blueprint specifying the resource allocations, schedules, and other actions necessary for attaining goals.

Planning
The act of determining the organization's goals and the means for achieving them.

CONCEPT CONNECTION The Co-operative Bank states that customer's money will never be used to support regimes that abuse human rights, and that 'it will always be invested according to sound environmental principles'. Consequently it has produced an Ecological Mission Statement which states that it will continue to develop the business taking into account the impact its activities have on the environment and society at large. This states that: 'The nature of our activities are such that our indirect impact by being selective in terms of the provision of finance and banking arrangements is more ecologically significant than the direct impact of our trading operations. However, we undertake to continually assess all our activities and implement a programme of ecological improvement based on the pursuit of the following four scientific principles:

1 Nature cannot withstand a progressive build-up of waste derived from the Earth's crust.
2 Nature cannot withstand a progressive build-up of society's waste, particularly artificial persistent substances which it cannot degrade into harmless materials.
3 The productive area of nature must not be diminished in quality (diversity) or quantity (volume) and must be enabled to grow.
4 Society must utilize energy and resources in a sustainable, equitable and efficient manner.

'We consider that the pursuit of these principles constitutes a path of ecological excellence and will secure future prosperity for society by sustainable economic activity.'

'The Co-operative Bank will not only pursue the above path itself, but endeavour to help and encourage all its stakeholders to do likewise.'[11]

the company money, in order to meet the targets. The fast-growing retailer's unwritten mantra of 'Take the deal' means that salespeople are trained to take any profitable deal, even at razor-thin margins, to meet daily sales targets.[10]

■ *Rationale for decisions.* Through goal setting and planning, managers clarify what the organization is trying to accomplish. They can make decisions to ensure that internal policies, roles, performance, structure, products and expenditures will be made in accordance with desired outcomes. Decisions throughout the organization will be in alignment with the plan.

■ *Standard of performance.* Because goals define desired outcomes for the organization, they also serve as performance criteria. They provide a standard of assessment. If an organization wishes to grow by 15 per cent, and actual growth is 17 per cent, managers will have exceeded their prescribed standard.

Interestingly, following the recent global financial turmoil the Co-operative Bank, along with other 'ethical' banks such as Triodos Bank, and the Ecology Building Society, appear to have been better placed to weather the 'credit crunch' in the world's financial markets, thanks to 'a historically prudent approach to lending and a strong reputation for trust'.

The Organizational Planning Process

The overall planning process, illustrated in Exhibit 7.2, prevents managers from thinking merely in terms of day-to-day activities. The process begins when managers develop the overall plan for the organization by clearly defining mission and strategic (company-level) goals. Second, they translate the plan into action, which includes defining tactical plans and objectives, developing a strategic map to align goals, formulating contingency and scenario plans, and identifying intelligence teams to analyze major competitive issues. Third, managers lay out the operational factors needed to achieve goals. This involves devising operational goals and plans, selecting the measures and targets that will be used to determine if things are on track, and identifying stretch goals and crisis plans that might need to be put into action. Tools for executing the plan include management by objectives, performance dashboards, single-use

Exhibit 7.2 The Organizational Planning process

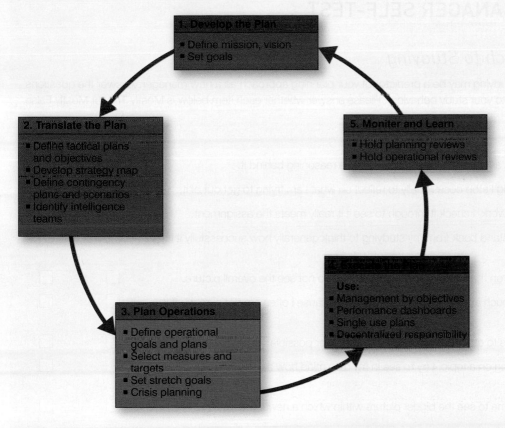

SOURCE: Based on Robert S. Kaplan and David P. Norton, 'Mastering the Management System', *Harvard Business Review* (January 2008): 63–77.

plans and decentralized responsibility. Finally, managers periodically review plans to learn from results and shift plans as needed, starting a new planning cycle.

As a new manager, what approach will you take to goal setting and planning? Complete the New Manager Self-Test on page 250 to get some insight into your planning approach from the way you study as a student.

TAKE A MOMENT

Goals in Organizations

Setting goals starts with top managers. The overall planning process begins with a mission statement and goals for the organization as a whole.

Organizational Mission

At the top of the goal hierarchy is the **mission** – the organization's reason for existence. The mission describes the organization's values, aspirations and reason for being. A well-defined mission is the basis for development of all subsequent goals and plans. Without a clear mission, goals and plans may be developed haphazardly and not take the organization in the direction it needs to go.

Mission
The organization's reason for existence.

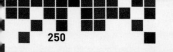

 NEW MANAGER SELF-TEST

Your Approach to Studying

Your approach to studying may be a predictor of your planning approach as a new manager. Answer the questions below as they apply to your study behaviour. Please answer whether each item below is Mostly True or Mostly False for you.

		Mostly True	Mostly False
1	Before I tackle an assignment, I try to work out the reasoning behind it.	☐	☐
2	When I am reading I stop occasionally to reflect on what I am trying to get out of it.	☐	☐
3	When I finish my work, I check it through to see if it really meets the assignment.	☐	☐
4	Now and then, I stand back from my studying to think generally how successfully it is going.	☐	☐
5	I frequently focus on the facts and details because I do not see the overall picture.	☐	☐
6	I write down as much as possible during lectures, because I often am not sure what is really important.	☐	☐
7	I try to relate ideas to other topics or courses whenever possible.	☐	☐
8	When I am working on a topic, I try to see in my own mind how all the ideas fit together.	☐	☐
9	It is important to me to see the bigger picture within which a new concept fits.	☐	☐

SCORING AND INTERPRETATION Give yourself one point for each item you marked as Mostly True except items 5 and 6. For items 5 and 6 give yourself one point for each one you marked Mostly False. An important part of a new manager's job is to plan ahead, which involves grasping the bigger picture. The items above measure *meta-cognitive awareness,* which means to step back and see the bigger picture of one's own learning activities. This same approach enables a manager to step back and see the big picture required for effective planning, monitoring, and evaluating an organization. If you scored three or fewer points you may be caught up in the details of current activities. A score of seven or above suggests that you see yourself in a bigger picture, which is an approach to studying that very well may reflect a successful planning aptitude.

SOURCE Adapted from Kristin Backhaus and Joshua P. Liff, 'Cognitive Styles and Approaches to Studying in Management Education', *Journal of Management Education* 31 (August 2007): 445–466; and A. Duff, 'Learning Styles Measurement: The Revised Approaches to Studying Inventory', *Bristol Business School Teaching and Research Review* 3 (2000).

Mission statement
A broadly stated definition of the organization's basic business scope and operations that distinguishes it from similar types of organizations.

The formal **mission statement** is a broadly stated definition of purpose that distinguishes the organization from others of a similar type. A well-designed mission statement can enhance employee motivation and organizational performance.[12] The content of a mission statement often focuses on the market and customers and identifies desired fields of endeavour. Some mission statements describe company characteristics such as corporate values, product quality, location of facilities and attitude toward employees. The mission statement of Volvo Group is shown in Exhibit 7.3. Such short, straightforward mission statements describe basic business activities and purposes as well as the values that guide the company. Another example of this type of mission statement is that of easyJet.

easyJet's mission is 'To provide our customers with safe, good value, point-to-point air services. To effect and to offer a consistent and reliable product and fares appealing to leisure and business markets on a range of European routes. To achieve this we will develop our people and establish lasting relationships with our suppliers.'

Because of mission statements such as those of Volvo Group and easy-Jet, employees as well as customers, suppliers, and stockholders know the company's stated purpose and values.

Goals and Plans

Strategic goals, sometimes called *official goals*, are broad statements describing where the organization wants to be in the future. These goals pertain to the organization as a whole rather than to specific divisions or departments. For example, RWE, the German energy company, has a strategic goal to greatly expand its renewables activities.

Strategic plans define the action steps by which the company intends to attain strategic goals. The strategic plan is the blueprint that defines the organizational activities and resource allocations – in the form of cash, personnel, space and facilities – required for meeting these targets. Strategic planning tends to be long term and may define organizational action steps from two to five years in the future. The purpose of strategic plans is to turn organizational goals into realities within that time period. For example, in order to meet its strategic goal outlined above, RWE intends to invest at least €1 billion per year from 2008 onwards on the planning, construction and operation of plants for renewable power generation and energy recovery. 'Our clear focus lies on both onshore and offshore wind power projects in Europe. But we will also grow in the field of hydropower and biomass,' states Professor Dr Fritz Vahrenholt.[13] In addition, RWE will intensively pursue activities in the area of solar and geothermal power, along with wave and tidal power plants.

For another example, consider the new strategic goals and plans at Borders, the number two book retailer in the US.

The Borders CEO knows that achieving the goal 'won't be a slam dunk', but he sees it as the best way to keep Borders relevant in the book retailing industry. The new strategic goals and plans, he believes, will revive the company by enabling Borders to provide greater benefits to customers and partner with a variety of companies for innovative projects.

After strategic goals are formulated, the next step is defining **tactical goals**, which are the results that major divisions and departments within

© ORKNEYPICS/ALAMY

CONCEPT CONNECTION RWE has set itself a strategic goal of having renewable energy projects with a volume of 10,000 megawatts in operation by 2020, by investing €1 billion each year in projects such as the Causeymire Wind Farm in the photograph. A major new offshore wind farm, situated five miles off the north Wales coast, opened in December 2009 and powers the equivalent of 61,000 households per year, saving several tens of thousands of tonnes of carbon emissions.

Exhibit 7.3 Mission statement for Volvo group

Volvo Group Mission Statement

By creating value for our customers, we create value for our shareholders.

We use our expertise to create transport-related products and services of superior quality, safety and environmental care for demanding customers in selected segments.

We work with energy, passion and respect for the individual.

SOURCE: AB Volvo.
Reprinted with permission.

 INNOVATIVE WAY

Borders Group Inc.

It's a tough environment for booksellers today. A sluggish book market, combined with competition from discounters, has put tremendous pressure on traditional book retailers to find the right approach to keep growing and thriving.

Borders Group revolutionized bookselling in the 1990s by building huge superstores, and managers stayed with the strategic goals of building more bricks-and-mortar stores even after the internet changed the rules of the game. A partnership with Amazon was the extent of Borders' online selling. Now, managers are realizing the bricks-and-mortar approach no longer works. Online book sales are soaring, while sales at US bookstores have sagged. Recently named CEO George Jones announced a new strategic goal of making Borders a force in online bookselling.

To achieve the goal, Borders is ending its alliance with Amazon and opening its own branded e-commerce site, giving Borders Rewards members the chance to earn benefits online, which they weren't able to do through Amazon. The plan also calls for closing some of its US stores, including nearly half of the smaller Waldenbooks outlets. In addition, in September 2009, following the lead of its main US high street competitor Barnes & Noble, the chain discontinued its free-based wireless service provided by T-Mobile and began implementing a free wifi network provided by Verizon. Borders Managers are also giving up on the idea of expanding the book superstore concept internationally, selling off or franchising most of Borders overseas stores, with the UK subsidary being sold to private equity group Risk Capital Partner in early 2009. Borders in the UK and Ireland has subsequently gone into administration, perhaps justifying the US company's earlier strategic decision to sell it.[14]

Strategic goals
Broad statements of where the organization wants to be in the future; pertain to the organization as a whole rather than to specific divisions or departments.

Strategic plans
The action steps by which an organization intends to attain strategic goals.

Tactical goals
Goals that define the outcomes that major divisions and departments must achieve for the organization to reach its overall goals.

Tactical plans
Plans designed to help execute major strategic plans and to accomplish a specific part of the company's strategy.

Operational goals
Specific, measurable results expected from departments, work groups, and individuals within the organization.

the organization intend to achieve. These goals apply to middle management and describe what major subunits must do for the organization to achieve its overall goals.

Tactical plans are designed to help execute the major strategic plans and to accomplish a specific part of the company's strategy.[15] Tactical plans typically have a shorter time horizon than strategic plans – over the next year or so. The word *tactical* originally comes from the military. In a business or non-profit organization, tactical plans define what major departments and organizational subunits will do to implement the organization's strategic plan. For example, the overall strategic plan of a large florist might involve becoming the number one telephone and internet-based purveyor of flowers, which requires high-volume sales during peak seasons such as Valentine's Day and Mother's Day. Human resource managers will develop tactical plans to ensure that the company has the dedicated order takers and customer service representatives it needs during these critical periods. Tactical plans might include cross-training employees so they can switch to different jobs as departmental needs change, allowing order takers to transfer to jobs at headquarters during off-peak times to prevent burnout, and using regular order takers to train and supervise temporary workers during peak seasons.[16] These actions help top managers implement their overall strategic plan. Normally, it is the middle manager's job to take the broad strategic plan and identify specific tactical plans.

The results expected from departments, work groups, and individuals are the **operational goals**. They are precise and measurable. 'Process 150 sales applications each week', 'achieve 90 per cent of deliveries on time', 'reduce overtime by 10 per cent next month' and 'develop two new online courses in accounting', are examples of operational goals. Managers at Hewlett Packard (HP) set a goal to double the company's global purchases of renewable power from under 4 per cent in 2008 to 8 per cent by 2012. This is in addition to HP's goal to reduce energy consumption and the resulting greenhouse gas emissions from HP-owned and HP-leased facilities worldwide to 16 per cent below 2005 levels by 2010.[17]

Operational plans are developed at the lower levels of the organization to specify action steps toward achieving operational goals and to support tactical plans. The operational plan is the department manager's tool for daily and weekly operations. Goals are stated in quantitative terms, and the department plan describes how goals will be achieved. Operational planning specifies plans for department managers, supervisors, and individual employees. Schedules are an important component of operational planning. Schedules define precise time frames for the completion of each operational goal required for the organization's tactical and strategic goals. Operational planning also must be coordinated with the budget, because resources must be allocated for desired activities.

© ANDREW MILLIGAN-POOL-GETTY IMAGES

www.alexander-dennis.com

Aligning Goals with Strategy Maps

Effectively designed organizational goals are aligned; that is, they are consistent and mutually supportive so that the achievement of goals at low levels permits the attainment of high-level goals. Organizational performance is an outcome of how well these interdependent elements are aligned, so that individuals, teams, departments, and so forth are working in concert to attain specific goals that ultimately help the organization achieve high performance and fulfil its mission.[19]

An increasingly popular technique for achieving *goal alignment* is the strategy map. A **strategy map** is a visual representation of the key drivers of an organization's success and shows how specific goals and plans in each area are linked.[20] The strategy map provides a powerful way for managers to see the cause-and-effect relationships among goals and plans. The simplified strategy map in Exhibit 7.4 illustrates four key areas that contribute to a firm's long-term success – learning and growth, internal processes, customer service and financial performance – and how the various goals and plans in each area link to the other areas. The idea is that learning and growth goals serve as a foundation to help achieve goals for excellent internal business processes. Meeting business process goals, in turn, enables the organization to meet goals for customer service and satisfaction, which helps the organization achieve its financial goals and optimize its value to all stakeholders.

In the strategy map shown in Exhibit 7.4, the organization has learning and growth goals that include developing employees, enabling continuous learning and knowledge sharing, and building a culture of innovation. Achieving these will help the organization build internal business processes that promote good relationships with suppliers and partners, improve the quality and flexibility of operations, and excel at developing innovative products and services. Accomplishing internal process

CONCEPT CONNECTION In 2004, the UKs biggest bus builder Alexander Dennis Ltd was in administration and facing bankruptcy. Its strategic goal was clear: growth. But, its expansion had gone awry. Undeterred, a consortium of the UK's brightest business minds including Sir David Murray, Angus Grossart, Brian Souter and Ann Gloag stepped in. If they had not, it is very likely that the company's operations would have permanently closed down. Together they formulated a new strategic plan, in which the company responded to the drive for more environmentally friendly public transport by building engines that deliver fuel savings and are slash carbon emissions. This gave the company a real competitive edge, and by 2007, Alexander Dennis was posting pre-tax profits of £10.5 million, up 163 per cent on the previous year on turnover up 14.3 per cent to £171.8 million.[18]

Operational plans
Plans developed at the organization's lower levels that specify action steps toward achieving operational goals and that support tactical planning activities.

Strategy map
A visual representation of the key drivers of an organization's success, showing the cause-and-effect relationships among goals and plans.

Go to the Experiential Exercise on page 268 that pertains to developing action plans for accomplishing strategic goals.

TAKE A MOMENT

Exhibit 7.4 A Strategy Map for Aligning Goals

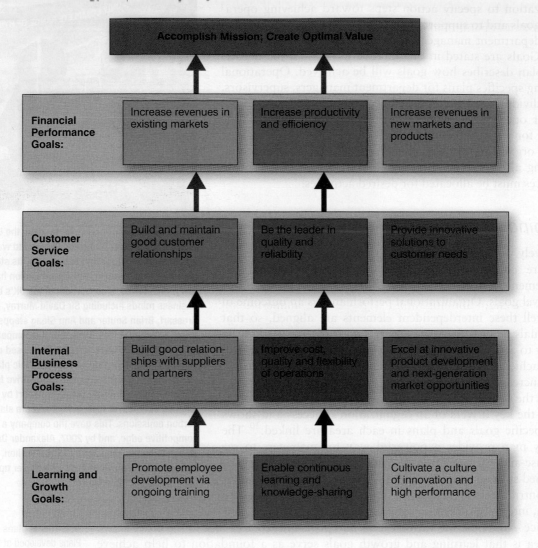

Accomplish Mission; Create Optimal Value

Financial Performance Goals:
- Increase revenues in existing markets
- Increase productivity and efficiency
- Increase revenues in new markets and products

Customer Service Goals:
- Build and maintain good customer relationships
- Be the leader in quality and reliability
- Provide innovative solutions to customer needs

Internal Business Process Goals:
- Build good relationships with suppliers and partners
- Improve cost, quality and flexibility of operations
- Excel at innovative product development and next-generation market opportunities

Learning and Growth Goals:
- Promote employee development via ongoing training
- Enable continuous learning and knowledge-sharing
- Cultivate a culture of innovation and high performance

SOURCE: Based on Robert S. Kaplan and David P. Norton, 'Mastering the Management System', *Harvard Business Review* (January 2008): 63–77; and R. S. Kaplan and D. P. Norton, 'Having Trouble with Your Strategy? Then Map It', *Harvard Business Review* (September–October 2000): 167–176.

goals, in turn, enables the organization to maintain strong relationships with customers, be a leader in quality and reliability, and provide innovation solutions to emerging customer needs. At the top of the strategy map, the accomplishment of these lower-level goals helps the organization increase revenues in existing markets, increase productivity and efficiency, and grow through selling new products and services and serving new markets segments.

In a real-life organization, the strategy map would typically be more complex and would state concrete, specific goals relevant to the particular business. However, the generic map in Exhibit 7.4 gives an idea of how managers can map goals and plans so that they are mutually supportive. The strategy map is also a good way to communicate goals, because everyone in the organization can see what part they play in helping the organization accomplish its mission.

Operational Planning

Managers use operational goals to direct employees and resources toward achieving specific outcomes that enable the organization to perform efficiently and effectively. One consideration is how to establish effective goals. Then managers use a number of planning approaches, including management by objectives, single-use plans and standing plans.

Criteria for Effective Goals

Research has identified certain factors, listed in Exhibit 7.5, that characterize effective goals. First and foremost, goals need to be *specific and measurable*. When possible, operational goals should be expressed in quantitative terms, such as increasing profits by 2 per cent, having zero incomplete sales order forms, or increasing average teacher effectiveness ratings from 3.5 to 3.7. Not all goals can be expressed in numerical terms, but vague goals have little motivating power for employees. By necessity, goals are qualitative as well as quantitative. The important point is that the goals be precisely defined and allow for measurable progress. Effective goals also have a *defined time period* that specifies the date on which goal attainment will be measured. School administrators might set a deadline for improving teacher effectiveness ratings, for instance, at the end of the 2009 school term. When a goal involves a two- to three-year time horizon, setting specific dates for achieving parts of it is a good way to keep people on track toward the goal.

Goals should *cover key result areas*. Goals cannot be set for every aspect of employee behaviour or organizational performance; if they were, their sheer number would render them meaningless. Instead, managers establish goals based on the idea of *choice and clarity*. A few carefully chosen, clear, and direct goals can more powerfully focus organizational attention, energy, and resources.[21] Managers should set goals that are *challenging but realistic*. When goals are unrealistic, they set employees up for failure and lead to a decrease in employee morale. However, if goals are too easy, employees may not feel motivated. Goals should also be *linked to rewards*. The ultimate impact of goals depends on the extent to which salary increases, promotions, and awards are based on goal achievement. Employees pay attention to what gets noticed and rewarded in the organization.[22]

Many organizations sometimes refer to the criteria used to set effective goals by the acronym SMART – specific, measurable, agreed upon, realistic and time-based.

SMART has a number of slightly different variations, which can be used to provide a more comprehensive definition for goal setting:

Exhibit 7.5 Characteristics of Effective Goal Setting

Goal Characteristics
- Specific and measurable
- Defined time period
- Cover key result areas
- Challenging but realistic
- Linked to rewards

S – specific, significant, stretching

M – measurable, meaningful, motivational

A – agreed upon, attainable, achievable, acceptable, action-oriented

R – realistic, relevant, reasonable, rewarding, results-oriented

T – time-based, timely, tangible, trackable

TAKE A MOMENT

As a new manager, establish operational goals that are in alignment with the tactical and strategic goals set at higher levels in the organization. Make goals specific, measurable and challenging, but realistic. Remember that a few carefully chosen goals are powerful for directing employee energy and motivation. Reward people when they meet goals.

Management by Objectives

Described by famed management scholar Peter Drucker in his 1954 book, *The Practice of Management*, management by objectives has remained a popular and compelling method for defining goals and monitoring progress toward achieving them. Management by objectives (MBO) is a system whereby managers and employees define goals for every department, project, and person and use them to monitor subsequent performance.[23] A model of the essential steps of the MBO system is presented in Exhibit 7.6. Four major activities make MBO successful:[24]

Management by objectives (MBO)
A method of management whereby managers and employees define goals for every department, project, and person and use them to monitor subsequent performance.

1 *Set goals.* Setting goals involves employees at all levels and looks beyond day-to-day activities to answer the question 'What are we trying to accomplish'? Managers heed the criteria of effective goals described in the previous section and make sure to assign responsibility for goal accomplishment. However, goals should be jointly derived. Mutual agreement between employee and supervisor creates the strongest commitment to achieving goals. In the case of teams, all team members may participate in setting goals.

Exhibit 7.6 Model of MBO Process

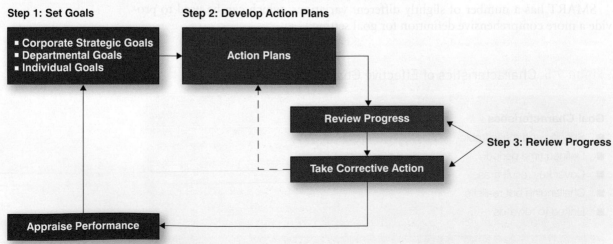

 INNOVATIVE WAY

Siemens

Siemens of Germany, which makes everything from mobile phones to gas-turbine generators to light bulbs, has always had great engineers bent on producing products of the highest quality. But in recent years, managers have learned that competing with the likes of US-based General Electric and Korea's Samsung takes more than quality – it also requires speed to market, relentless innovation, and ruthless attention to costs. Within two years, Siemens' profits sank by two-thirds and company shares fell even faster. CEO Heinrich von Pierer developed a plan for getting Siemens back on track, with a specific goal (MBO step 1) of strengthening the overall business to be in financial shape for listing on a US stock exchange within three years.

Managers developed an action plan (MBO step 2) that included: (1) cutting the time it takes to develop and produce new products; (2) selling or closing poor-performing units and strengthening remaining businesses through acquisitions to achieve world leadership; (3) setting tough profit targets for managers and tying pay

to performance; and (4) converting accounting practices to report results according to US accounting standards. Managers of the various business divisions then developed action plans for employees in their own units. Progress was reviewed (MBO step 3) at quarterly meetings where managers from the 14 business units reported on their advancements directly to von Pierer.

Managers were required to explain if benchmarks weren't met and how shortcomings would be corrected. At the end of each year of the turnaround plan, an overall performance appraisal was held for each business and the corporation as a whole (MBO step 4). Managers who met goals were rewarded; those who had consistently failed to meet them were let go, with the poorest performers going first. Since the plan was implemented, Siemens dramatically improved its speed and overall financial performance. The MBO system helped to energize manager and employee actions companywide toward goals deemed critical by top management.[25]

2 *Develop action plans.* An *action plan* defines the course of action needed to achieve the stated goals. Action plans are made for both individuals and departments.

3 *Review progress.* A periodic progress review is important to ensure that action plans are working. These reviews can occur informally between managers and subordinates, where the organization may wish to conduct three-, six- or nine-month reviews during the year. This periodic check-up allows managers and employees to see whether they are on target or whether corrective action is needed. Managers and employees should not be locked into predefined behaviour and must be willing to take whatever steps are necessary to produce meaningful results. The point of MBO is to achieve goals. The action plan can be changed whenever goals are not being met.

4 *Appraise overall performance.* The final step in MBO is to carefully evaluate whether annual goals have been achieved for both individuals and departments. Success or failure to achieve goals can become part of the performance appraisal system and the designation of salary increases and other rewards. The appraisal of departmental and overall corporate performance shapes goals for the next year. The MBO cycle repeats itself on an annual basis.

The specific application of MBO must fit the needs of each company. For example, Siemens used MBO to improve its overall financial performance.

Many companies, including Intel, Black & Decker, and DuPont, have adopted MBO, and most managers think MBO is an effective management tool.[26] Managers believe they are better oriented toward goal achievement when MBO is used. In

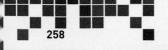

Exhibit 7.7 MBO Benefits and Problems

Benefits of MBO	Problems with MBO
1. Manager and employee efforts are focused on activities that will lead to goal attainment.	1. Constant change prevents MBO from taking hold.
2. Performance can be improved at all company levels.	2. An environment of poor employer–employee relations reduces MBO effectiveness.
3. Employees are motivated.	3. Strategic goals may be displaced by operational goals.
4. Departmental and individual goals are aligned with company goals.	4. Mechanistic organizations and values that discourage participation can harm the MBO process.
	5. Too much paperwork saps MBO energy.

recent years, the US Congress required that federal agencies use a type of MBO system to focus government employees on achieving specific outcomes.[27] Like any system, MBO achieves benefits when used properly but results in problems when used improperly. Benefits and problems are summarized in Exhibit 7.7.

The benefits of the MBO process can be many. Corporate goals are more likely to be achieved when they focus manager and employee efforts. Using a performance measurement system, such as MBO, helps employees see how their jobs and performance contribute to the business, giving them a sense of ownership and commitment.[28] Performance is improved when employees are committed to attaining the goal, are motivated because they help decide what is expected, and are free to be resourceful. Goals at lower levels are aligned with and enable the attainment of goals at top management levels.

Problems with MBO occur when the company faces rapid change. The environment and internal activities must have some stability for performance to be measured and compared against goals. Setting new goals every few months allows no time for action plans and appraisal to take effect. Also, poor employer–employee relations reduce effectiveness because of an element of distrust that may be present between managers and workers. Sometimes goal 'displacement' occurs if employees focus exclusively on their operational goals to the detriment of other teams or departments. Overemphasis on operational goals can harm the attainment of overall goals. Another problem arises in mechanistic organizations characterized by rigidly defined tasks and rules that may not be compatible with MBO's emphasis on mutual determination of goals by employee and supervisor. In addition, when participation is discouraged, employees will lack the training and values to jointly set goals with employers. Finally, if MBO becomes a process of filling out annual paperwork rather than energizing employees to achieve goals, it becomes an empty exercise. Once the paperwork is completed, employees forget about the goals, perhaps even resenting the paperwork in the first place.

Single-use plans
Plans that are developed to achieve a set of goals that are unlikely to be repeated in the future.

Standing plans
Ongoing plans that are used to provide guidance for tasks performed repeatedly within the organization

Single-Use and Standing Plans

Single-use plans are developed to achieve a set of goals that are not likely to be repeated in the future. **Standing plans** are ongoing plans that provide guidance for tasks or situations that occur repeatedly within the organization. Exhibit 7.8 outlines

Exhibit 7.8 Major types of single use and standing plans

Single-Use Plans	Standing Plans
Program ■ Plans for attaining a one-time organizational goal ■ Major undertaking that may take several years to complete ■ Large in scope; may be associated with several projects **Examples:** Building a new headquarters Converting all paper files to digital	**Policy** ■ Broad in scope – general guide to action ■ Based on organization's overall goals/strategic plan ■ Defines boundaries within which to make decisions **Examples:** Sexual harassment policies Internet and email usage policies
Project ■ Also a set of plans for attaining a one-time goal ■ Smaller in scope and complexity than a programme; shorter in horizon ■ Often one part of a larger programme **Examples:** Renovating the office Setting up a company intranet	**Rule** ■ Narrow in scope ■ Describes how a specific action is to be performed ■ May apply to specific setting **Examples:** No eating rule in areas of company where employees are visible to the public **Procedure** ■ Sometimes called a standard operating procedure ■ Defines a precise series of steps to attain certain goals **Examples:** Procedures for issuing refunds Procedures for handling employee grievances

the major types of single-use and standing plans. Single-use plans typically include both programmes and projects. The primary standing plans are organizational policies, rules and procedures. Standing plans generally pertain to such matters as employee illness, absences, smoking, discipline, hiring and dismissal. Many companies are discovering a need to develop standing plans regarding the use of email, as discussed in the Manager's Shoptalk box.

Planning for a Turbulent Environment

As increasing turbulence and uncertainty shake the business world, managers have turned to innovative planning approaches that help brace the organization for unexpected – even unimaginable – events. Three critical planning methods are contingency planning, building scenarios and crisis planning.

Contingency Planning

When organizations are operating in a highly uncertain environment or dealing with long time horizons, sometimes planning can seem like a waste of time. Indeed, inflexible plans may hinder rather than help an organization's performance in the face of

MANAGER'S SHOPTALK

Regulating Email in the Workplace

Email is estimated to grow by 40 per cent each year, commanding more and more of employees' working hours. According to the UK Office for National Statistics employees spend, on average, two hours a day on email – assessing, managing and responding to messages. This equates to 11 working weeks for every user and translates into millions of pounds for organizations, without even taking into account the cost of lost productivity due to email misuse.

Top executives around the globe are discovering that casual email messages can come back to haunt them – in court. The American Management Association (AMA) surveyed 1100 companies and found that 14 per cent of them had been ordered to disclose email messages. Eight brokerage firms were fined $8 million for not keeping and producing email in accordance with SEC guidelines. Some companies have had to pay millions to settle sexual harassment lawsuits arising from inappropriate emails. In addition, there are numerous examples of cringe-worthy personal emails being dispatched around the world and rapidly making the headlines, such as Lucy Gao, an intern at Citibank, London, whose 21st birthday invitation to the Ritz was circulated around the City and incited ridicule from her colleagues and peers.[29]

As with any powerful tool, email has the potential to be hazardous, backfiring not only on the employee but on the organization as well. One study found that 'potentially dangerous or non-productive' messages account for fully 31 per cent of all company email. Experts say a formal written policy is the best way for companies to protect themselves, and they offer some tips for managers on developing effective policies governing the use of email.

- *Make clear that all email and its contents are the property of the company.* Many experts recommend warning employees that the company reserves the right to read any messages transmitted over its system. 'Employees need to understand that a company can access employees' email at any time without advance notice or consent', says lawyer Pam Reeves. This rule helps to discourage frivolous emails or those that might be considered crude and offensive. However, a recent court case, *Copland v United Kingdom* (2007) decided an employer had breached the European Human Rights Act by secretly monitoring an employee's emails without her knowledge. The European Court of Human Rights ruled that the surveillance without her knowledge 'amounted to an interference with her right to a private life'.[30]

- *Tie the policy to the company's sexual harassment policy or other policies governing employee behaviour on the job.* Starwood Hotel and Resorts ousted its CEO after an investigation uncovered emails that seem to substantiate claims that he made sexual advances to female employees. In almost all sexual harassment cases, judges have ruled that the use of email is considered part of the workplace environment.

- *Establish clear guidelines on matters such as the use of email for jokes and other nonwork-related communications, the sending of confidential messages, and how to handle junk email.* At Prudential Insurance, for example, employees are prohibited from using company email to share jokes, photographs, or any kind of non-business information.

- *Establish guidelines for deleting or retaining messages.* Retention periods of 30 to 90 days for routine messages are typical. Most organizations also set up a centralized archive for retaining essential email messages.

- *Consider having policies pop up on users' screens when they log on.* It is especially important to remind employees that email belongs to the employer and may be monitored.

The field of computer forensics is booming, and even deleted emails can usually be tracked down. An effective policy is the best step companies can take to manage the potential risks of email abuse.

SOURCES 'E-Mail: The DNA of Office Crimes', *Electric Perspectives* 28, no. 5 (September–October 2003): 4; Marcia Stepanek with Steve Hamm, 'When the Devil Is in the E-mails', *BusinessWeek* (June 8, 1998): 72–74; Joseph McCafferty, 'The Phantom Menace', *CFO* (June 1999): 89–91; 'Many Company Internet and E-mail Policies Are Worth Revising', *The Kiplinger Letter* (February 21, 2003): 1; and Carol Hymowitz, 'Personal Boundaries Shrink as Companies Punish Bad Behavior', *The Wall Street Journal*, June 18, 2007.

rapid technological, social, economic, or other environmental change. In these cases, managers can develop multiple future alternatives to help them form more adaptive plans.

Contingency plans define company responses to be taken in the case of emergencies, setbacks, or unexpected conditions. To develop contingency plans, managers identify important factors in the environment, such as possible economic downturns, declining markets, increases in cost of supplies, new technological developments, or safety accidents. Managers then forecast a range of alternative responses to the most likely high-impact contingencies, focusing on the worst case.[31] For example, if sales fall 20 per cent and prices drop 8 per cent, what will the company do? Managers can develop contingency plans that might include layoffs, emergency budgets, new sales efforts, or new markets. A real-life example comes from FedEx, which has to cope with some kind of unexpected disruption to its service somewhere in the world on a daily basis. In one recent year alone, managers activated contingency plans related to more than two dozen tropical storms, an air traffic controller strike in France and a blackout in Los Angeles. The company also has contingency plans in place for events such as labour strikes, social upheavals in foreign countries or incidents of terrorism.[32]

Building Scenarios

An extension of contingency planning is a forecasting technique known as scenario building.[33] **Scenario building** involves looking at current trends and discontinuities and visualizing future possibilities. Rather than looking only at history and thinking about what has been, managers think about what *could be*. The events that cause the most damage to companies are those that no one even conceived of, such as the collapse of the World Trade Center towers in New York due to terrorist attack. Managers can't predict the future, but they can rehearse a framework within which future events can be managed. With scenario building, a broad base of managers mentally rehearses different scenarios based on anticipating varied changes that could affect the organization. Scenarios are like stories that offer alternative vivid pictures of what the future will be like and how managers will respond. Typically, two to five scenarios are developed for each set of factors, ranging from the most optimistic to the most pessimistic view.[34] Scenario building forces managers to mentally rehearse what they would do if their best-laid plans collapse.

Royal Dutch/Shell has long used scenario building to help managers navigate the instability and uncertainty of the oil industry. A classic example is the scenario Shell managers rehearsed in 1970 that focused on an imagined accident in Saudi Arabia that severed an oil pipeline, which in turn decreased supply. The market reacted by increasing oil prices, which allowed OPEC nations to pump less oil and make more money. This story caused managers to re-examine the standard assumptions about oil price and supply and imagine what would happen and how they would respond if OPEC increased prices. Nothing in the exercise told Shell managers to expect an embargo, but by rehearsing this scenario, they were much more prepared than the competition when OPEC announced its first oil embargo in October 1973. The company's speedy response to a massive shift in the environment enabled Shell to move in two years' from being the world's eighth largest oil company to being number two.[35]

CONCEPT CONNECTION A desert flare marks the area where geologists discovered Libya's rich Zilten oilfield in the 1950s. At their peak in 1970, Libyan oil fields operated by Occidental Petroleum were producing 660 000 barrels a day, more than the company's total oil production in 2003. Today, with economic sanctions against Libya lifted by the US Government, big oil companies like Occidental, Chevron Texaco, and Exxon Mobil are again ready to do business with Libya's National Oil Corporation. Yet, the current environment of terrorist threats and general uncertainty means managers have to be prepared for whatever might happen. They are busy developing contingency plans to define how their companies will respond in case of unexpected setbacks associated with renewed Libyan operations. Companies are willing to take the risks because the potential rewards are huge.

Contingency plans
Plans that define company responses to specific situations, such as emergencies, setbacks or unexpected conditions.

Scenario building
Looking at trends and discontinuities and imagining possible alternative futures to build a framework within which unexpected future events can be managed.

TAKE A MOMENT As a new manager, get in the mind-set of scenario planning. Go to http://www.shell.com/
scenarios, where Shell Oil publishes the outline of its annual scenario planning exercise. You
might also want to do an internet search and type in 'national intelligence agency scenarios' to
find links to reports of global trends and scenario planning done by various organizations.

Try also the Swedish National Defence Research Agency (www.foi.se/) which has
used a form of scenario planning called morphological analysis successfully to help
fire services plan resources for dealing with chemical incidents, as well as improving
the efficiency of the Swedish postal services and energy industry

Crisis Planning

Surveys of companies' use of management techniques reveal that the use of contingency
and scenario planning surged after the September 11, 2001 terrorist attacks in the US
and has remained high ever since, reflecting a growing emphasis on managing uncertainty.[36] Some firms also engage in *crisis planning* to enable them to cope with unexpected events that are so sudden and devastating that they have the potential to destroy
the organization if managers aren't prepared with a quick and appropriate response.

Crises have become integral features of organizations in today's world. Consider
events such as that facing Coca-Cola in Belgium in mid-1999, when a number of
people, mostly school children, fell ill after consuming its products and the entire inventory of Coca-Cola's products in Belgium was banned from sale. Coca-Cola had
to recall about 30 million cans and bottles, the largest ever product recall in its 113-
year history. Similarly, managers at Eurotunnel, operator of the Channel Tunnel,
have had to cope in September 2008 with the sudden closure and repair of the tunnel
after a serious fire, and more recently in December 2009 when five London-bound
trains failed inside the tunnel, because of an electrical fault caused by the transition
from the cold air in France, the coldest night for eight years, to very warm tempera-
tures inside the tunnel, trapping 2000 passengers in the tunnel overnight. Although
crises may vary, a carefully thought-out and coordinated plan can be used to
respond to any disaster. In addition, crisis planning reduces the incidence of trouble,
much like putting a good lock on a door reduces burglaries.[37] Exhibit 7.9 outlines
two essential stages of crisis planning.[38]

- *Crisis prevention.* The *crisis prevention* stage involves activities managers undertake to try to prevent crises from occurring and to detect warning signs of potential crises. A critical part of the prevention stage is building open, trusting
  relationships with key stakeholders such as employees, customers, suppliers,
  governments, unions and the community. By developing favourable relationships, managers can often prevent crises from happening and respond more
  effectively to those that cannot be avoided. For example, organizations that have
  open, trusting relationships with employees and unions may avoid crippling
  labour strikes. When Coca-Cola suffered its crisis in Belgium referred to above,
  it was because it failed to respond quickly to reports of 'foul-smelling' Coke in
  Belgium. A former CEO observed that every problem the company has faced in
  recent years 'can be traced to a singular cause: we neglected our relationships'.[39]

- *Crisis preparation.* The *crisis preparation* stage includes all the detailed planning
  to handle a crisis when it occurs. Three steps in the preparation stage are: (1) des-
  ignating a crisis management team and spokesperson, (2) creating a detailed crisis management plan and (3) setting up an effective communications system. The
  crisis management team, for example, is a cross-functional group of people who

Exhibit 7.9 Essential stages of crisis planning

> **Crisis Planning Prevention**
> - Build relationships.
> - Detect signals from environment.
>
> **Preparation**
> - Designate crisis management team and spokesperson.
> - Create detailed crisis management plan.
> - Set up effective communications system.

SOURCE: Based on information in W. Timothy Coombs, *Ongoing Crisis Communication: Planning, Managing, and Responding* (Thousand Oaks, CA: Sage Publications, 1999).

are designated to swing into action if a crisis occurs. The organization should also designate a spokesperson who will be the voice of the company during the crisis.[40] The crisis management plan (CMP) is a detailed, written plan that specifies the steps to be taken, and by whom, if a crisis occurs. The CMP should include the steps for dealing with various types of crises, such as natural disasters like fires or earthquakes, normal accidents like economic crises or industrial accidents, and abnormal events such as product tampering or acts of terrorism.[41] A key point is that a crisis management plan should be a living, changing document that is regularly reviewed, practised and updated as needed. Done well, managing a crisis situation can actually help an organization improve its reputation, such as the example of Virgin Train's given in chapter1. Done badly, it can prove very costly. Maclaren, which has sold millions of children's fold-up pushchairs in the UK since it began trading in 1967, has recently been heavily criticized for its initial decision to issue a product recall only in the US after 12 children lost their fingertips because of an uncovered hinge. Complaints from British families, where there had also been similar injuries, that they were not being treated equally, quickly prompted the company to issue parents in the UK with protective hinge covers to try to limit the potential negative publicity.

Planning for High Performance

The purpose of planning and goal setting is to help the organization achieve high performance. The process of planning is changing to be more in tune with today's environment and the shifting attitudes of employees. Traditionally, strategy and planning have been the domain of top managers. Today, however, managers involve people throughout the organization, which can spur higher performance because people understand the goals and plans and buy into them.

Traditional Approaches to Planning

Traditionally, corporate planning has been done entirely by top executives, by consulting firms, or, most commonly, by central planning departments. **Central planning departments** are groups of planning specialists who report directly to the CEO or president. This approach was popular during the 1970s. Planning specialists were hired to gather data and develop detailed strategic plans for the corporation as a whole. This planning approach was top down because goals and plans were assigned to major divisions and departments from the planning department after approval by the president.

Central planning department
A group of planning specialists who develop plans for the organization as a whole and its major divisions and departments and typically report directly to the president or CEO.

TAKE A MOMENT   Go to the Ethical Dilemma on page 269 that pertains to potential problems with high performance planning.

Decentralized planning
Managers work with planning experts to develop their own goals and plans.

Stretch goal
A reasonable yet highly ambitious, compelling goal that energizes people and inspires excellence.

This approach worked well in many applications and is still popular with some companies. However, formal planning increasingly is being criticized as inappropriate for today's fast-paced environment. Central planning departments may be out of touch with the constantly changing realities faced by front-line managers and employees, which may leave people struggling to follow a plan that no longer fits the environment and customer needs. In addition, formal plans dictated by top managers and central planning departments can inhibit employee innovation and learning.

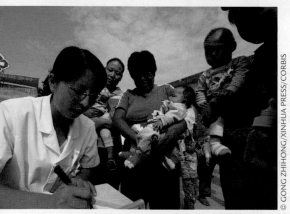

CONCEPT CONNECTION In 2008 there were serious health problems in China arising from milk powder laced with the industrial chemical melamine which led to nearly 13 000 Chinese infants being admitted to hospital, with at least four deaths and over a hundred more in a serious condition with kidney stones and agonizing complications. This forced the Chinese Government to trigger crisis management plans to contain the public health menace. Producers were forced to recall milk powder products, supermarkets swept shelves clear of related products, and the Government began investigations to discover what had caused the problems. Various groups also proposed future prevention measures. Some advocated more stringent government regulation, while others argued for producers doing more product testing and a better job of tracking produce from field to table.

Outside mainland China, supermarkets in Hong Kong quickly pulled Nestlé's milk powder from the shelves amid media reports that the territory's government had found a sample that contained melamine, something denied by Nestlé. Meanwhile Holland's Friesland Foods, which sold Chinese-supplied milk in the Far East under the Dutch Lady label, had to withdraw products from Singapore, Hong Kong and Macau after a strawberry flavoured milk shake tested positive.[42]

High-Performance Approaches to Planning

A fresh approach to planning is to involve everyone in the organization, and sometimes outside stakeholders as well, in the planning process. The evolution to a new approach began with a shift to **decentralized planning**, which means that planning experts work with managers in major divisions or departments to develop their own goals and plans. Managers throughout the company come up with their own creative solutions to problems and become more committed to following through on the plans. As the environment became even more volatile, top executives saw the benefits of pushing decentralized planning even further, by having planning experts work directly with line managers and front-line employees to develop dynamic plans that meet fast-changing needs.

In a complex and competitive business environment, strategic thinking and execution become the expectation of every employee.[43] Planning comes alive when employees are involved in setting goals and determining the means to reach them. Here are some guidelines for planning in the new workplace.

Set Stretch Goals for Excellence

Stretch goals are reasonable yet highly ambitious goals that are so clear, compelling and imaginative that they fire up employees and engender excellence. Stretch goals are typically so far beyond the current levels that people have to be innovative to find ways to reach them. An extension of the stretch goal is the *big hairy audacious goal* or *BHAG*. The phrase was first proposed by James Collins and Jerry Porras in their 1996 article entitled 'Building Your Company's Vision'.[44] Since then, it has evolved to a term used to describe any goal that is so big, inspiring and outside the prevailing paradigm that it hits people in the gut and shifts their thinking. At the same time, however, goals must be seen as achievable or employees will be discouraged and demotivated.[45]

Stretch goals and BHAGs have become extremely important because things move fast. A company that focuses on gradual, incremental improvements in products, processes or systems will get left behind. Managers can use these goals to compel employees to think in new ways that can lead to bold, innovative breakthroughs. Motorola used stretch goals to achieve *Six Sigma* quality, which has now become the standard for numerous companies. Managers first set a goal of a tenfold increase in quality over a two-year period. After this goal was met, they set a new stretch goal of a hundredfold improvement over a four-year period.[46]

© MTP/ALAMY

CONCEPT CONNECTION Netflix is trying to meet a stretch goal of improving its internet movie recommendation system ('people who liked this movie also rented...') by 10 per cent. In October 2006, the company invited the biggest math brains in the world to compete for a $1 million prize to reach that goal. In the first year, more than 2500 teams from a dozen countries submitted entries. At the one-year anniversary, a team of AT&T researchers (Chris Volinsky, Yehuda Koren and Bob Bell) won a $50 000 progress award for improving the system by 8.43 per cent. Some speculate that a 10 per cent improvement is unobtainable. By May 2008, the team had reached a 9.15 per cent improvement of the system.

Use Performance Dashboards

People need a way to see how plans are progressing and gauge their progress toward achieving goals. Companies began using *business performance dashboards* as a way for executives to keep track of key performance metrics, such as sales in relation to targets, number of products on back order, or percentage of customer service calls resolved within specified time periods. Today, dashboards are evolving into organization-wide systems that help align and track goals across the enterprise. Exhibit 7.10 shows a business performance dashboard from Celequest that can deliver real-time key performance metrics to any employee's desktop. The true power of dashboards comes from applying them throughout the company, even on the factory floor, so that all employees can track progress toward goals, see when things are falling short, and find innovative ways to get back on course toward reaching the specified targets. At Little Earth, which sells eco-fashion products, the CEO Jerry Driggs uses dashboards to manage production, sales, and financial operations. 'Once you see it is so intuitive, you wonder how we ran the business before', says Driggs. In fact, before adopting its dashboard technology the company had no real system to measure its production requirements or level of raw materials, much of which came from China, it took about six weeks to make and ship a handbag. And Little Earth constantly struggled with cash problems because Driggs would often buy more supplies than he needed. 'You used to see dollars sitting on the shelves', he says. Now, using NetSuite, Driggs can monitor his purchase orders and inventory levels, and the system even alerts him when he is running low on closures and other parts. The result: Little Earth has slashed its shipping time to three days. 'All of those things that used to drive us crazy are literally at our fingertips', says Driggs.[47] Some dashboard systems also incorporate software that lets users perform what-if scenarios to evaluate the impact of various alternatives for meeting goals.

As a new manager, involve others in planning and goal setting to enhance commitment and performance. Set stretch goals to encourage innovation and excellence. Make use of business performance dashboards to help people track progress toward goals, and deploy intelligence teams to analyze major competitive issues.

TAKE A MOMENT

Exhibit 7.10 A Performance Dashboard for Planning

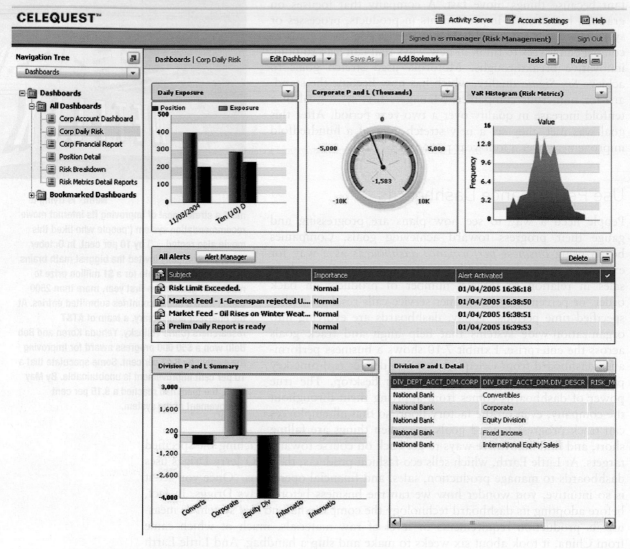

Deploy Intelligence Teams

Intelligence team
A cross-functional group of managers and employees who work together to gain a deep understanding of a specific competitive issue and offer insight and recommendations for planning.

Anticipating and managing uncertainty and turbulence in the environment is a crucial part of planning, which means managers need good intelligence to make informed choices about goals and plans. A growing number of leading companies are using intelligence teams to manage this challenge. An **intelligence team** is a cross-functional group of managers and employees, usually led by a competitive intelligence professional, who work together to gain a deep understanding of a specific business issue, with the aim of presenting insights, possibilities, and recommendations about goals and plans related to that issue.[48] Intelligence teams are useful when the organization confronts a major intelligence challenge. For example, consider a large financial services firm that learns that an even-larger rival is potentially moving to compete directly with one of its major profit-generating businesses. Top managers might form an intelligence team to identify when and how this might happen and how it might affect the organization. Intelligence teams can provide insights that enable managers to make more informed decisions about goals, as well as to devise contingency plans and scenarios related to major strategic issues.

A MANAGER'S ESSENTIALS: WHAT HAVE WE LEARNED?

- This chapter discussed organizational planning, which involves defining goals and developing plans with which to achieve them.

- An organization exists for a single, overriding purpose known as its *mission* – the basis for strategic goals and plans. Goals within the organization begin with strategic goals followed by tactical and operational goals. Plans are defined similarly, with strategic, tactical and operational plans used to achieve the goals. Managers can use strategy maps to clearly align goals and communicate them throughout the organization.

- Managers formulate goals that are specific and measurable, cover key result areas, are challenging but realistic, have a defined time period and are linked to rewards.

- The chapter described several types of operational plans, including management by objectives, single-use and standing plans, and contingency plans. Two extensions of contingency planning are scenario building and crisis planning. Scenarios are alternative vivid pictures of what the future might be like. They provide a framework for managers to cope with unexpected or unpredictable events. Crisis planning involves the stages of prevention and preparation.

- In the past, planning was almost always done entirely by top managers, consultants or central planning departments. During turbulent times, planning is decentralized and people throughout the organization are involved in establishing dynamic plans that can meet rapidly changing needs in the environment.

- Some guidelines for high-performance planning in a turbulent environment include setting stretch goals for excellence, using performance dashboards, and organizing intelligence teams.

Nancy Sorrells, the general manager at the Marriott Hotel described in the chapter opening, realized that if people didn't know where they were going, they didn't have any idea how to get there. She needed to get everyone aligned with the hotel's mission before she could expect them to establish and meet high performance goals. Sorrells held meetings with department heads and employees throughout the hotel to talk about the five aspects of the hotel's mission: creating a great experience for guests; creating a great work experience for employees; the profitability of the hotel; quality inside the hotel; and growth of the company. She worked with department heads to set departmental goals and asked them to set clear, measurable goals for employees that fell in line with the five elements of the mission. She reminded everyone that even the slightest ambiguity in the goals could throw people off course. Some department heads resisted and either found other jobs or were let go. Most were inspired by her vision to turn the hotel around and were glad to have a clear focus for what they should be doing. They started with basic employee performance goals such as getting to work on time and taking care of the basics. Each staff meeting, higher goals were set, and guests started noticing and commenting on the improvements. Employees now knew what was expected of them, so they were able to succeed. People began taking more pride in their work, and motivation and performance improved. Sorrells insisted the attention to detail in every department extend to creating a good work experience for employees. She established goals related to employee satisfaction, including the quality of the food, the cleanliness and comfort of the break area and employee restrooms, and so forth. People saw that Sorrells was deeply committed to the mission and to the success of the team. After nine months, basic inspection scores had increased from 59 out of 100 to 95 out of 100. In WHI's annual survey of employee motivation at the company's 31 hotels, the Sorrell's Marriott moved from 25th place to 6th place. The financial picture brightened as well, with sales going from £2.0 million behind budget to £350 000 ahead of budget. By establishing clear, focused, and measurable goals aligned with the mission and vision, Sorrells turned the hotel around and made life better for its employees.[49]

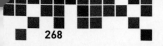

DISCUSSION QUESTIONS

1 Write a brief mission statement for a local business with which you are familiar. How might having a clear, written mission statement benefit a small organization?

2 What strategic plans could the college or university at which you are taking this management course adopt to compete for students in the marketplace? Would these plans depend on the school's goals?

3 One of the benefits of a strategy map is that goals and how they are linked can be clearly communicated to everyone in the organization. Does a minimum wage maintenance worker in a hospital really need to understand any goals beyond keeping the place clean? Discuss.

4 Assume Arkle Airways has more customer complaints due to late flights and mishandled baggage than any other major carrier. If you were an operations manager at Arkle Airways, how might you use MBO to solve these problems? Could scenario planning be useful for airline managers who want planes to run on time? Discuss.

5 A new business venture must develop a comprehensive business plan to borrow money to get started. Companies such as Virgin, FedEx, and Nike say they did not follow the original plan closely. Does that mean that developing the plan was a waste of time for these eventually successful companies?

6 How do you think planning in today's organizations compares to planning 25 years ago?

Do you think planning becomes more important or less important in a world where everything is changing fast and crises are a regular part of organizational life? Why?

7 ABC University decides to: (1) raise its admission standards and (2) initiate a business fair to which it invites local residents and companies. What types of plans might it use to carry out these two activities?

8 Why would an organization want to use an intelligence team? Discuss.

9 Some people say an organization could never be 'prepared' for a disaster such as the massacre at Virginia Tech, which left 33 people dead. If so, then what's the point of crisis planning?

10 Come up with a BHAG for some aspect of your own life. How do you determine whether it makes sense to pursue a big hairy audacious goal?

11 Performance dashboards are still in their infancy, and the size and scope of implementation remains relatively small. To what extent do you think this will change as organizations gain more experience with these systems?

12 If you were a top manager of a medium-sized estate agency, would you use MBO? If so, give examples of goals you might set for managers and sales agents.

MANAGEMENT IN PRACTICE: EXPERIENTIAL EXERCISE

Business School Ranking

The dean of the business school at a major university in your area has contacted students in your class to develop a plan for improving its national ranking among business schools. The school recently dropped ten places in the rankings, and the dean wants to restore the school's perceived lustre. The dean provided the following list of variables on which the national ranking is based:

- Written assessment by deans from peer institutions on a scale of 1 to 5.
- Written assessment by recruiters on a scale of 1 to 5.
- Average entry grades of incoming students.
- Acceptance rate of student applications (a lower percentage is better).
- Average starting salary of the school's most recent graduates.

- Percentage of graduates employed on the date of graduation.
- Percentage of graduates employed three months after graduation.
- Written assessment of 'satisfaction' from graduating students on a scale of 1 to 5.
- Degree classifications awarded to students.

The business school has a goal of improving its ranking by ten places in two years. Brainstorm ideas and develop a ten-point action plan that will list the steps the dean can take to achieve this goal. To develop the plan, think carefully about actions the school might take to improve its ranking on any or all of the measured variables listed above.

After writing down your ideas, meet in small groups of three or four students to share ideas and select the most helpful action steps that will be part of the action plan recommended to the business school dean.

MANAGEMENT IN PRACTICE: ETHICAL DILEMMA

Inspire Learning Corporation

When the idea first occurred to her, it seemed like such a win-win situation. Now she wasn't so sure.

Marge Brygay was a hard-working sales rep for Inspire Learning Corporation, a company intent on becoming the top educational software provider in five years. That newly adopted strategic goal translated into an ambitious million-pound sales target for each of Inspire's sales reps. At the beginning of the fiscal year, her share of the sales department's operational goal seemed entirely reasonable to Marge. She believed in Inspire's products. The company had developed innovative, highly regarded maths, language, science and social studies programs for the under 12 market. What set the software apart was a foundation in truly cutting-edge research. Marge had seen for herself how Inspire programs could engage whole classrooms of normally unmotivated kids; the significant rise in test scores on those increasingly important standardized tests bore out her subjective impressions.

But now, just days before the end of the year, Marge's sales were £1000 short of her million-pound goal. The sale that would have put her comfortably over the top fell through due to last-minute cuts in one large school system's budget. At first, she was nearly overwhelmed with frustration, but then it occurred to her that if she contributed £1000 to Central High, the inner-city high school in her territory probably most in need of what she had for sale, they could purchase the software and put her over the top.

Her scheme would certainly benefit Central High students. Achieving her sales goal would make Inspire happy, and it wouldn't do her any harm, either professionally or financially. Making the goal would earn her a £10 000 bonus that would come in handy when the time came to write out that first tuition cheque for her oldest child, who had just been accepted to a well-known university.

Initially, it seemed like the perfect solution all the way around. The more she thought about it, however, the more it didn't quite sit well with her conscience. Time was running out. She needed to decide what to do.

What Would You Do?

1 Donate the £1000 to Central High, and consider the £10 000 bonus a good return on your gift.

2 Accept the fact you didn't quite make your sales goal this year. Figure out ways to work smarter next year to increase the odds of achieving your target.

3 Don't make the donation, but investigate whether any other ways were available to help Central High raise the funds that would allow them to purchase the much-needed educational software.

4 Something else?

SOURCE Based on Shel Horowitz, 'Should Mary Buy Her Own Bonus?', *Business Ethics* (Summer 2005): 34.

CASE FOR CRITICAL ANALYSIS

Victoria Hotels

Consultant Peter Lee strode into the conference room in Bill Brown's wake. Bill, the Chairman of Victoria Hotels, had hired Peter to help the hotel company's management team with their strategic planning. Wasting no time, Bill introduced Peter to human resources director Karen Rees, marketing head Tony Jackson, hotel operations chief Dave Rowbotham, and accountant Arthur Mears. Already written in large block letters on a flipchart at the front of the room was the company's ten-year-old mission statement: 'Victoria Hotels strives to exceed the expectations of our guests by providing excellent value in well-run hotels located off the beaten track. In this way, we will meet our profit, quality, and growth goals.'

Peter, of course, had digested all of the background materials the Chairman had sent him, so he knew the company currently owned 21 properties: the original ten Victoria Hotels and two Albert Inns, plus eight hotels in Ireland, and a property in France, acquired since Bill assumed the Chairmanship five years ago. Peter was also well aware that even though Victoria Hotels was a reasonably profitable company, Bill wasn't satisfied.

The consultant started the ball rolling by asking each person in the room to describe his or her vision for domestic operations over the next ten years. How many hotels should Victoria Hotels own? Where should they be located, and what should the target market be? As the managers shared their views, Keith summarized their answers on the flip chart.

The consultant wasn't at all surprised that Bill's goals were the most ambitious. He advocated for an intermediate goal of adding 27 properties in five years and a long-term goal of 50 in ten years. The other managers didn't come close, calling for only 15 hotels to be added in five years and no more than 20 over a decade. The Victoria Hotels senior managers just sat and stared at the figures.

Keith asked for reactions. After an uncomfortable silence, Dave was the first to jump into the fray. 'We can't build something like five hotels a year. We would outpace our income. And we couldn't run them, certainly not given our current staffing. I don't see how we could afford to hire the people we'd need.' Arthur nodded in agreement.

'You know, we've always concentrated on medium-priced hotels in smaller towns where we don't have much competition', pointed out Tony.

Karen jumped in. 'Well, do we need to think about moving to bigger towns now, like maybe Bristol? We've got one property in the West Country already. Maybe we should look into building another one there'.

'Why stick so close to home?', asked Bill. 'You know, we're already looking at the possibility of going to Bristol. But why stop there? We've got an interesting opportunity out in Glasgow, and we might have another one in London.'

Peter was beginning to fully appreciate the breadth and depth of the job he had on his hands. He looked at the mission statement, reviewed the list of current properties, and realized as he listened to the managers that nothing really matched up. So, now what should he do?

Questions

1 What are the causes of the confusion confronting Peter Lee? Is Victoria Hotels ready to formulate a strategic plan? Why or why not?

2 If you were Peter, what questions would you ask the managers? What steps would you recommend in your effort to help Victoria Hotels successfully formulate strategic goals and plans?

3 If you were Bill Brown, what might you have done differently during your tenure as Victoria Hotel's chairman?

SOURCE Adapted from and based on a case provided by James Higgins.

ENDNOTES

1. Quote at http://militaryhistory.about.com/od/1800sarmy biographies/p/vonmoltke.htm.

2. Wagner, 'Fixing a 'Sneaky-Broke' Hotel', *Gallup Management Journal* (October 13, 2005), http://www.gmj.gallup. com.

3. Amitai Etzioni, *Modern Organizations* (Englewood Cliffs, NJ: Prentice Hall, 1984), p. 6.

4. Ibid.

5. Max D. Richards, *Setting Strategic Goals and Objectives*, 2nd ed. (St. Paul, MN: West, 1986).

6. Millennium Dome http://www.london-architecture.info/ LO-019.htm.

7. C. Chet Miller and Laura B. Cardinal, 'Strategic Planning and Firm Performance: A Synthesis of More Than Two Decades of Research', *Academy of Management Journal* 37, no. 6 (1994): 1649–1685.

8. This discussion is based on Richard L. Daft and Richard M. Steers, *Organizations: A Micro/Macro Approach* (Glenview, IL: Scott, Foresman, 1986), pp. 319–321; Herbert A. Simon, 'On the Concept of Organizational Goals', *Administrative Science Quarterly* 9 (1964): 1–22; and Charles B. Saunders and Francis D. Tuggel, 'Corporate Goals', *Journal of General Management* 5 (1980): 3–13.

9. Marc Gunther, 'Tree Huggers, Soy Lovers, and Profits', *Fortune* (June 23, 2003): 98–104.

10. Paul Sloan, 'The Sales Force That Rocks', *Business 2.0* (July 2005): 102–107.

11. Co-Operative Ethical Mission statement available at http://www.co-operativebank.co.uk/partnership1997/ 97_ecology. html.

12. Mary Klemm, Stuart Sanderson and George Luffman, 'Mission Statements: Selling Corporate Values to Employees', *Long-Range Planning* 24, no. 3 (1991): 73–78; John A. Pearce II and Fred David, 'Corporate Mission Statements: The Bottom Line', *Academy of Management Executive* (1987): 109–116; Jerome H. Want, 'Corporate Mission: The Intangible Contributor to Performance', *Management Review* (August 1986): 46–50; and Forest R. David and Fred R. David, 'It's Time to Redraft Your Mission Statement', *Journal of Business Strategy* (January–February 2003): 11–14.

13. RWE at http://www.google.co.uk/search?hl=en&q=RWE+ grow+Prof.+Dr.+Fritz+Vahrenholt&btnG=Search&meta=

14. Jeffrey A. Trachtenberg, 'Borders Business Plan Gets a Rewrite; It Will Reopen website, Give Up Most Stores Abroad, Close Many Waldenbooks', *Wall Street Journal*, March 22, 2007, B1. Copyright 2007 by Dow Jones & Company, Inc. Reproduced with permission of Dow Jones & Company, Inc. in the format Textbook via Copyright Clearance Center.

15. Paul Meising and Joseph Wolfe, 'The Art and Science of Planning at the Business Unit Level', *Management Science* 31 (1985): 773–781.

16. Based in part on information about 1-800-Flowers, in Jenny C. McCune, 'On the Train Gang', *Management Review* (October 1994): 57–60.

17. http://www.hp.com/hpinfo/globalcitizenship/07gcreport/ operations.html.

18. http://www.google.co.uk/search?hl=en&q=Alexander+De nnis+Ltd&btnG=Search&meta=

19. Geary A. Rummler and Kimberly Morrill, 'The Results Chain', *TD* (February 2005): 27–35; and John C. Crotts, Duncan R. Dickson and Robert C. Ford, 'Aligning Organizational Processes with Mission: The Case of Service Excellence', *Academy of Management Executive* 19, no. 3 (August 2005): 54–68.

20. This discussion is based on Robert S. Kaplan and David P. Norton, 'Mastering the Management System', *Harvard Business Review* (January 2008): 63–77; and Robert S. Kaplan and David P. Norton, 'Having Trouble with Your Strategy? Then Map It', *Harvard Business Review* (September–October 2000): 167–176.

21. Sayan Chatterjee, 'Core Objectives: Clarity in Designing Strategy', *California Management Review* 47, no. 2 (Winter 2005): 33–49.

22. Edwin A. Locke, Gary P. Latham and Miriam Erez, 'The Determinants of Goal Commitment', *Academy of Management Review* 13 (1988): 23–39.

23. Peter F. Drucker, *The Practice of Management* (New York: Harper & Row, 1954); George S. Odiorne, 'MBO: A Backward Glance', *Business Horizons* 21 (October 1978): 14–24.

24. Jan P. Muczyk and Bernard C. Reimann, 'MBO as a Complement to Effective Leadership', *The Academy of Management Executive* 3 (1989): 131–138; and W. Giegold, *Objective Setting and the MBO Process*, vol. 2 (New York: McGraw-Hill, 1978).

25. Jack Ewing, 'Siemens Climbs Back', *Business Week* (June 5, 2000): 79–82.

26. John Ivancevich, J. Timothy McMahon, J. William Streidl and Andrew D. Szilagyi, 'Goal Setting: The Tenneco Approach to Personnel Development and Management Effectiveness', *Organizational Dynamics* (Winter 1978): 48–80.

27. Brigitte W. Schay, Mary Ellen Beach, Jacqueline A. Caldwell and Christelle LaPolice, 'Using Standardized Outcome Measures in the Federal Government', *Human Resource Management* 41, no. 3 (Fall 2002): 355–368.

28. Eileen M. Van Aken and Garry D. Coleman, 'Building Better Measurement', *Industrial Management* (July–August 2002): 28–33.

29. *Daily Mail*, 'Embarrassed city girl apologies as party email goes around the globe', August 25, 2006, http://www. dailymail.co.uk/news/article-402244/Embarrassed-city-girl-apologies-party-email-goes-globe.html.

30. *The Times*, 'Employee's privacy breached by employer's monitoring', April 24, 2007 http://business.timesonline.co. uk/tol/business/law/reports/article1695516.ece.

31. Curtis W. Roney, 'Planning for Strategic Contingencies', *Business Horizons* (March–April 2003): 35–42; and 'Corporate Planning: Drafting a Blueprint for Success', *Small Business Report* (August 1987): 40–44.

32. Ellen Florian Kratz, 'For FedEx, It Was Time to Deliver', *Fortune* (October 3, 2005): 83–84.

33. This section is based on Steven Schnaars and Paschalina Ziamou, 'The Essentials of Scenario Writing', *Business Horizons* (July–August 2001): 25–31; and Audrey Schriefer and

Michael Sales, 'Creating Strategic Advantage with Dynamic Scenarios', *Strategy & Leadership* 34, no. 3 (2006): 31–42; Geoffrey Colvin, 'An Executive Risk Handbook', *Fortune* (October 3, 2005): 69–70; and Syed H. Akhter, 'Strategic Planning, Hypercompetition, and Knowledge Management', *Business Horizons* (January–February 2003): 19–24.

34. Peter Cornelius, Alexander Van de Putte, and Mattia Romani, 'Three Decades of Scenario Planning in Shell', *California Management Review* 48, no. 1 (Fall 2005); and Schnaars and Ziamou, 'The Essentials of Scenario Writing'.

35. Colvin, 'An Executive Risk Handbook'; and Ian Wylie, 'There Is No Alternative To … ', *Fast Company* (July 2002): 106–110.

36. Bain & Company Management Tools and Trends Survey, reported in Darrell Rigby and Barbara Bilodeau, 'A Narrowing Focus on Preparedness', *Harvard Business Review* (July–August 2007): 21–22.

37. Ian Mitroff with Gus Anagnos, *Managing Crises Before They Happen* (New York: AMACOM, 2001); Ian Mitroff and Murat C. Alpaslan, 'Preparing for Evil', *Harvard Business Review* (April 2003): 109–115.

38. This discussion is based largely on W. Timothy Coombs, *Ongoing Crisis Communication: Planning, Managing, and Responding* (Thousand Oaks, CA: Sage Publications, 1999).

39. Ian I. Mitroff, 'Crisis Leadership', *Executive Excellence* (August 2001): 19; Andy Bowen, 'Crisis Procedures that Stand the Test of Time', *Public Relations Tactics* (August 2001): 16.

40. Christine Pearson, 'A Blueprint for Crisis Management', *Ivey Business Journal* (January–February 2002): 69–73.

41. See Ian I. Mitroff and Murat C. Alpaslan: 2003, 'Preparing for Evil', *Harvard Business Review* 81 no. 4 (2003): 109–115. Outlining the many different kinds of crises organizations may face.

42. BBC, Anger over China milk scandal, 17 September 2008, http://news.bbc.co.uk/1/hi/world/asia-pacific/7620382.stm.

43. Harari, 'Good News/Bad News about Strategy'.

44. James C. Collins and Jerry I. Porras, 'Building Your Company's Vision', *Harvard Business Review* (September–October 1996): 65–77.

45. Steven Kerr and Steffan Landauer, 'Using Stretch Goals to Promote Organizational Effectiveness and Personal Growth: General Electric and Goldman Sachs', *Academy of Management Executive* 18, no. 4 (November 2004): 134–138.

46. See Kenneth R. Thompson, Wayne A. Hockwarter and Nicholas J. Mathys, 'Stretch Targets: What Makes Them Effective?', *Academy of Management Executive* 11, no. 3 (August 1997): 48.

47. *Business Week* Giving The Boss The Big Picture, February 13, 2006 http://www.businessweek.com/magazine/content/06_07/b3971083.htm.

48. This section is based on Liam Fahey and Jan Herring, 'Intelligence Teams', *Strategy & Leadership* 35, no. 1 (2007): 13–20.

49. Wagner, 'Fixing a "Sneaky-Broke" Hotel'.

After reading this chapter, you should be able to ...

Define the components of strategic management and discuss the levels of strategy.

Describe the strategic management process and SWOT analysis.

Explain corporate-level strategies and explain the BCG matrix, portfolio, and diversification approaches.

Discuss Porter's competitive forces and strategies.

Discuss new trends in strategy, including innovation from within and strategic partnerships.

Examine the organizational dimensions used for strategy execution.

© endopack/iStock

LEARNING OBJECTIVES

After reading this chapter, you should be able to:

1   Define the components of strategic management and discuss the levels of strategy.

2   Describe the strategic management process and SWOT analysis.

3   Explain corporate-level strategies and explain the BCG matrix, portfolio, and diversification, approaches.

4   Understand Porter's competitive forces and strategies.

5   Discuss new trends in strategy, including innovation from within and strategic partnerships.

6   Examine the organizational dimensions used for strategy execution.

CHAPTER 8

STRATEGY FORMULATION AND IMPLEMENTATION

How important is strategic management? It largely determines which organizations succeed and which ones struggle. How did Primark overtake Matalan as the UK's biggest 'value fashion' retailer, or Hewlett-Packard gain an impressive lead over Dell in personal computer sales? A big part of the reason is the strategies managers chose and how effectively they were executed.

Manager's Challenge

In April 2008, Primark announced that half-year takings rose 25 per cent to £899 million as hard-pressed shoppers sought out bargains on its racks. The increase gives Primark a 10 per cent share of UK clothing sales by volume, making it the UK's second biggest clothing retailer. It has overtaken Asda's George label and is now catching up on Marks & Spencer, which has a 12 per cent market share. Today, of every £10 spent on clothes in Britain, £1 now goes to Primark. That is a long way from the first store in Ireland, opened in 1969 by the man who still runs the business, Arthur Ryan.

So how has Primark, part of Associated British Foods (ABF) which owns brands such as Silver Spoon sugar, Twinings tea and Kingsmill bread, managed to flourish, while more established rivals such as Allders and Littlewoods have folded, and others such as Bhs and Matalan have struggled?

Primark's success is based on its ability to capture the latest catwalk trends and deliver cut-price versions within a matter of weeks. It has targeted the fashion conscious under-35s market segment with the slogan 'Look good pay less'. It offers fashionable clothes at very competitive prices (for example, jeans for £4) and reasonable quality – in other words, a classic value for money strategy. In competitive strategy terms, Primark is pursuing a 'focus cost leadership' strategy.

What is Your Strategy Strength?[1]

As a new manager, what are your strengths concerning strategy formulation and implementation? To find out, think about how *you handle challenges and issues* in your school or job. Then mark (a) or (b) for each of the following items, depending on which is more descriptive of your behaviour. There are no right or wrong answers. Respond to each item as it best describes how you respond to work situations.

1 When keeping records, I tend to:

_____ **a**   Be careful about documentation.

_____ **b**   Be haphazard about documentation.

2 If I run a group or a project, I:

_____ **a**   Have the general idea and let others figure out how to do the tasks.

_____ **b**   Try to figure out specific goals, timelines, and expected outcomes.

3 My thinking style could be more accurately described as:

_____ **a**   Linear thinker, going from A to B to C.

_____ **b**   Thinking like a grasshopper, hopping from one idea to another.

4 In my office or home things are:

_____ **a**   Here and there in various piles.

_____ **b**   Laid out neatly or at least in reasonable order.

5 I take pride in developing:

_____ **a**   Ways to overcome a barrier to a solution.

_____ **b**   New hypotheses about the underlying cause of a problem.

6 I can best help strategy by encouraging:

_____ **a**   Openness to a wide range of assumptions and ideas.

_____ **b**   Thoroughness when implementing new ideas.

7 One of my strengths is:

_____ **a**   Commitment to making things work.

_____ **b**   Commitment to a dream for the future.

8 I am most effective when I emphasize:

_____ **a**   Inventing original solutions.

_____ **b**   Making practical improvements.

SCORING AND INTERPRETATION Managers have differing strengths and capabilities when it comes to formulating and implementing strategy. Here's how to determine yours. For *Strategic Formulator* strength, score one point for each (a) answer marked for questions 2, 4, 6 and 8, and for each (b) answer marked for questions 1, 3, 5 and 7. For *Strategic Implementer* strength, score one point for each (b) answer marked for questions 2, 4, 6 and 8, and for each (a) answer marked for questions 1, 3, 5 and 7. Which of your two scores is higher and by how much? The higher score indicates your strategy strength.

Formulator and Implementer are two important ways new managers bring value to strategic management. New managers with implementer strengths tend to work within the situation and improve it by making it more efficient and reliable. Leaders with the formulator strength push toward out-of-the-box strategies and like to seek dramatic breakthroughs. Both styles are essential to strategic management. Strategic formulators often use their skills in creating whole new strategies, and strategic implementers often work with strategic improvements and implementation.

If the difference between your two scores is two or less, you have a balanced formulator/implementer style and work well in both arenas. If the difference is four or five points, you have a moderately strong style and probably work best in the area of your strength. And if the difference is seven or eight points, you have a distinctive strength and almost certainly would want to work in the area of your strength rather than in the opposite domain.

Firms selling a 'no-frills' product, such as easyJet or SouthWest airlines are usually attempting a cost leadership strategy. The 'focus' part of Primark's strategy is the specific customer segment it focuses on, i.e., the under-35s. It is not attempting to sell to everybody. It has selected a particular customer segment, just as the '18–30' holiday company has selected a clear market segment based on age group within the leisure industry. For Primark, having a very clear market positioning at the cheap end of the market, helps it avoid some of the 'stuck-in the-middle' positioning problems faced by other competitors such as Marks & Spencer or Bhs.

Some of Primark's strongest successful competitors are TK Maxx and George at Asda. However, although all three are in the 'value' segment and therefore have similar market positioning, the other two have different strategies to that of Primark. TK Maxx sells heavily-discounted prestige brands and George at Asda has created its own private-label brand mostly at out-of town stores. Primark is a high street retailer which has a family of brands and focuses much more on buying, logistics and supply chain management rather than branding.

The story of Primark and Matalan illustrates the importance of strategic planning. Managers at Primark formulated and implemented strategies that made the chain the player to beat in 'value fashion' retailing, while Matalan managers failed to respond to increased competition and changing customer expectations. Top managers are now analyzing the situation and considering strategies that can ignite growth and revive the company, include a major re-fit of the Matalan stores.[2]

 INNOVATIVE WAY

Primark and Matalan Story

How did managers at Primark formulate and implement strategies that helped the company overtake a large, established value chain such as Matalan? In 1998, Matalan had a share of the 'value' market twice that of Primark. In Verdict's latest report, those positions have been reversed: Primark now controls nearly 18.5 per cent of the market, compared with Matalan's 9.8 per cent.[3]

In the 1990s large-scale operators, such as Matalan, began a seismic realignment in fashion retailing, offering cheap clothing, and keeping costs low through operating from large warehouse type stores in secondary out-of-town locations and retail parks. Primark,

recognizing a shift in attitudes to value segment 'fashion' since 2000, however hit on a winning formula of operating instead from more prime high-street and up-market sites. Primark spends virtually nothing on advertising, but hasn't needed to since the fashion world 'discovered' Primark a couple of years ago. This has generated millions of pounds of free publicity in newspaper and magazine fashion spreads such as *Vogue* that enthuse about its rock bottom prices and the speed with which what they call 'Pradamark' replicates catwalk trends.

If you were the new CEO of Matalan, what strategies might you adopt to help the company regain a competitive edge?

Every company is concerned with strategy. Apple has succeeded in recent years with a strategy of fierce product innovation. In one year alone, three major new products – the iPhone, iPod Touch and Leopard OS – led to triple-digit revenue growth for the once-struggling maker of computers.[4] Ocado the UK-based home-shopping food delivery service has grown sales by 25 per cent a year since its launch in 2002, recently notching up £1 billion of sales. Ocado, has taken strategic advantage of the growth in online shopping, and continues to target further substantial future growth as the MySpace generation grow up.[5] McDonald's devised a new strategy of downsizing its menu items and adding healthier products in response to changes in the environment. Super-sized French fries and soft drinks were eliminated in favour of fresh salads and low-fat items to counter public accusations that McDonald's was responsible for Americans' growing waistlines. Now the fast-food icon is expanding to include specialty coffee drinks and smoothies to try to lure more teenagers and young adults.[6]

Strategic blunders can hurt a company. For example, Kodak stumbled by failing to plan for the rapid rise of digital photography, assuming sales of film and paper would stay strong for years to come. Between 2001 and 2005, Kodak's earnings dropped about 60 per cent as interest in film photography tanked.[7] Toymaker Mattel has similarly suffered in recent years, this time by losing sight of its core business and trying to compete as a maker of computer games.

Managers at McDonald's, Ocado, Kodak, Mattel and Apple are all involved in strategic management. They are trying to find ways to respond to competitors, cope with difficult environmental changes, meet changing customer needs, and effectively use available resources. Strategic management has taken on greater importance in today's environment because managers are responsible for positioning their organizations for success in a world that is constantly changing. Today's top companies thrive by changing the rules of an industry to their advantage or by creating entirely new industries.[8] For example, Lindsay Owens-Jones, when running L'Oréal's US division in the early 1980s, was told by colleagues that European brands such as Lancôme could never compete with established US brands. Owens-Jones refused to accept that, and his strategic decisions changed the whole face of US cosmetics counters. Today, as CEO, Owens-Jones is aggressively promoting L'Oréal's brands globally, gaining huge market share in Asia, Africa and other parts of the world.[9]

Kim and Mauborgne (2005) have introduced the concept of *Blue ocean Strategies*.[10] They argue that tomorrow's leading companies will succeed not by battling competitors in existing market segments but by creating 'blue oceans' of untapped market demand. Effectively this is creating new markets. **Blue ocean strategy** is based on the view that market boundaries and industry structure are not given and can be reconstructed by the actions and beliefs of industry players.

For instance, Cirque du Soleil has revolutionized the concept of a modern circus through adopting a *blue ocean strategy*. Each show is a synthesis of circus styles from around the world, with its own central theme and storyline. There is no traditional circus ring and animals are not used in the performance. They draw the audience into the performance through continuous live music, and have attracted new corporate audiences alongside the traditional families. Cirque expanded rapidly through the 1990s and 2000s, going from one show with 73 employees in 1984 to approximately 3500 employees from over 40 countries, with an estimated annual revenue exceeding $600 million. Similarly Nintendo has used the Wii to extend the traditional gaming market, from a niche enjoyed predominantly by males in 15–30 range, to something that also appeals to the whole family.[11]

Chapter 7 provided an overview of the types of goals and plans that organizations use. In this chapter, we will explore strategic management, which is one specific type

Blue ocean strategy is a creative battle where the players of a particular segment don't compete with each other remaining in the same market space; instead explore, create and acquire new market spaces by dealing with new demand.

of planning. First, we define the components of strategic management and discuss the purposes and levels of strategy. Then, we examine several models of strategy formulation at the corporate and business levels. Finally, we discuss the tools managers use to execute their strategic plans.

Thinking Strategically

What does it mean to think strategically? Strategic thinking means to take the long-term view and to see the big picture, including the organization and the competitive environment, and consider how they fit together. Strategic thinking is important for both businesses and non-profit organizations. In for-profit firms, strategic planning typically pertains to competitive actions in the marketplace. In non-profit organizations such as the Red Cross or The Salvation Army, strategic planning pertains to events in the external environment.

Research has shown that strategic thinking and planning positively affect a firm's performance and financial success. Most managers are aware of the importance of strategic planning, as evidenced by a *McKinsey Quarterly* survey, with 51 per cent of responding executives whose companies had no formal strategic planning process saying they were dissatisfied with the company's development of strategy, compared to only 20 per cent of those at companies that had a formal planning process.[12] CEOs at successful companies make strategic thinking and planning a top management priority. For an organization to succeed, the CEO must be actively involved in making the tough choices and trade-offs that define and support strategy.[13] However, senior executives at today's leading companies want middle- and low-level managers to think strategically as well. Understanding the strategy concept and the levels of strategy is an important start toward strategic thinking.

Complete the New Manager Self-Test on page 280 to get some idea about your strategic thinking ability. As a new manager, practise thinking strategically by studying your department's or your organization's environment, market and competitors. Think about what the long-term future might hold and how you think the company can best be positioned to stay competitive.

TAKE A MOMENT

What is Strategic Management?

Strategic management refers to the set of decisions and actions used to formulate and execute strategies that will provide a competitively superior fit between the organization and its environment so as to achieve organizational goals.[14] An alternative definition would be the direction and scope of an organization over the long term, which seeks to achieve competitive advantage in a changing environment, through the correct configuration of resources and competences in order to meet and satisfy relevant stakeholder expectations.[15]

Managers ask questions such as what changes and trends are occurring in the competitive environment? Who are our competitors and what are their strengths and weaknesses? Who are our customers? What products or services should we offer, and how can we offer them most efficiently? What does the future hold for our

Strategic management
The set of decisions and actions used to formulate and implement strategies that will provide a competitively superior fit between the organization and its environment so as to achieve organizational goals.

 NEW MANAGER SELF-TEST

Your Approach to Studying, Part 2

Your approach to studying may reveal whether you have the ability to think strategically. Answer the questions below as they apply to your study behaviour. Please answer whether each item below is Mostly True or Mostly False for you.

		Mostly True	Mostly False
1	One way or another, I manage to obtain whatever books and materials I need for studying.	☐	☐
2	I make sure I find study conditions that let me do my work easily.	☐	☐
3	I put effort into making sure I have the most important details at my fingertips.	☐	☐
4	When I read an article or book, I try to work out for myself what is being said.	☐	☐
5	I know what I want to get out of this course, and I am determined to achieve it.	☐	☐
6	When I am working on a new topic, I try to see in my mind how the ideas fit together.	☐	☐
7	It is important to me to follow the argument and see the reasoning behind something.	☐	☐
8	I look at the evidence carefully and then try to reach my own conclusions about things I am studying.	☐	☐
9	When I am reading, I think how the ideas fit in with previous material.	☐	☐

SCORING AND INTERPRETATION The items above represent a *strategic approach* to studying. Strategy means knowing your desired outcomes, how to acquire factual knowledge, thinking clearly about tactics and cause–effect relationships, and implementing behaviours that will achieve the desired outcomes. Give yourself one point for each item you marked as Mostly True. If you scored three or lower you probably are not using a strategic approach to studying. A score of six or above suggests a strategic approach to studying that will likely translate into strategic management ability as a new manager.

SOURCES Adapted from Kristin Backhaus and Joshua P. Liff, 'Cognitive Styles and Approaches to Studying in Management Education', *Journal of Management Education,* 31 (August 2007): 445–466; and A. Duff, 'Learning Styles Measurement: The Revised Approaches to Studying Inventory', *Bristol Business School Teaching and Research Review,* 3 (2000).

Strategy
The plan of action that prescribes resource allocation and other activities for dealing with the environment, achieving a competitive advantage and attaining organizational goals.

Competitive advantage
What sets the organization apart from others and provides it with a distinctive edge in the marketplace.

industry, and how can we change the rules of the game? Answers to these questions help managers make choices about how to position their organizations in the environment with respect to rival companies.[16] Superior organizational performance is not a matter of luck. It is determined by the choices that managers make.

Purpose of Strategy

The first step in strategic management is to define an explicit **strategy**, which is the plan of action that describes resource allocation and activities for dealing with the environment, achieving a competitive advantage and attaining the organization's goals. **Competitive advantage** refers to what sets the organization apart from others and provides it with a distinctive edge for meeting customer or client needs in the marketplace. The essence of formulating strategy is choosing how the organization will be different.[17] Managers make decisions about whether the company will perform different activities or will execute similar activities differently than its rivals do. Strategy necessarily changes over time to fit environmental conditions, but to remain competitive, companies develop strategies that focus on core competencies, develop synergy and create value for customers.

Exploit Core Competence

A company's **core competence** is something the organization does especially well in comparison to its competitors. A core competence represents a competitive advantage because the company acquires expertise that competitors do not have. A core competence may be in the area of superior research and development, expert technological know-how, process efficiency or exceptional customer service.[18] At VF, a large clothing company that owns Vanity Fair, Nautica, Wrangler and the North Face, strategy focuses on the company's core competencies of operational efficiency and merchandizing know-how. When VF bought the North Face, for example, its distribution systems were so poor that stores were getting ski apparel at the end of winter and camping gear at the end of summer. The company's operating profit margin was minus 35 per cent. Managers at VF revamped the North Face's sourcing, distribution, and financial systems and within five years doubled sales to $500 million and improved profit margins to a healthy 13 per cent.[19] At Honda, the primary core competency is expertise in engines, which permits the company to provide consumers with a wide variety of products that use engines, from lawn mowers to outboard motors to automobiles. At Amazon, it is logistics, which permits the company to provide customers with the benefits of choice, availability, and low prices allied to efficient delivery. Robinson Helicopter succeeds through superior technological know-how for building small, two-seater helicopters used for everything from police patrols in Los Angeles to herding cattle in Australia.[20]

Core competencies also apply to the services sector. For example, fast cycle times are a critical factor in providing customer service in many industries. Sportswear producer and retailer, Benetton, owes much of its success and growth to fast cycle times made possible by the use of information technology.[21] It starts in new product development with a CAD system which automatically translates a new design into a full range of sizes and transmits the patterns to computerized cutting machines to await customer orders. Undyed fabric is stored at demand-scheduled just-in-time (JIT) factories and cut and dyed strictly to order. Retail outlets are also run on a minimum stock JIT basis. Similarly, a key to Primark's success is its speed at turning out designs inspired by the catwalk and red carpet. It takes on average just six weeks for an item to go from concept stage into Primark shops on the high street.

In each case above, leaders identified what their company does especially well and built strategy around it. Sony's decision to specialize in the miniaturization of electronic devices is a good example of a firm selecting a core competency for development. This decision was made years before the Walkman, the portable CD player and portable television sets became popular consumer products.

© CLYNT GARNHAM TECHNOLOGY/ALAMY

CONCEPT CONNECTION
When the BBC needed a new digital format for presenting their weather forecasts, they looked to software providers around the world. But few had in-house meteorological expertise and many were often largely focused on the technicalities of the software itself. Metra Information had the competitive advantage. As a subsidiary of the Meteorological Service of New Zealand, Metra Information developed Weatherscape XT in-house using a team of 3D animation experts, database developers and meteorologists with access to decades of experience in forecasting one of the most complex weather systems in the world. Metra Information won the contract and the software is now used by networks around the world including Sky, CNBC Europe and The Weather Channel.

Core competence
A business activity that an organization does particularly well in comparison to competitors.

Build Synergy

When organizational parts interact to produce a joint effect that is greater than the sum of the parts acting alone, synergy occurs. The organization may attain a special advantage with respect to cost, market power, technology or management skill. When properly managed, synergy can create additional value with existing resources, providing a big boost to the bottom line.[22] Synergy was the motivation for Pepsi to buy Frito-Lay for instance, and for News Corporation to buy MySpace.

Synergy can also be obtained by good relationships between organizations. For example, Brandhouse Beverages (Pty) Ltd is a three-way joint venture in South Africa between Diageo, Heineken and Namibian Breweries Ltd established in 2004. Paul Walsh, believes the companies enjoy significant synergies when marketing and distributing their respective ranges of premium drinks. For instance he believes Diageo's spirits portfolio is a natural fit with the Heineken brand, which is sold as a premium export beer. The deal allows the company's sales force to offer both supermarkets and bars a portfolio of brands combining Heineken and Guinness with Scotch whiskies such as Johnnie Walker, Bells and White Horse. Diageo's other spirits brands such as Smirnoff and Captain Morgan are also be included. The key motivation is to challenge SABMiller in its own domestic market where it has always dominated, British drinks giant Diageo and Dutch brewer Heineken have subsequently agreed to strengthen their ties in South Africa even more by jointly building a brewery there by the end of 2009.

Similarly, the Disney Channel invites magazines such as *Twist*, and *Popstar* to visit the set of shows like 'Hannah Montana' and 'High School Musical', gives reporters access for interviews and photo shoots, and provides brief videos for the magazines to post on their websites. The synergy keeps pre-teen interest booming for both the television shows and the magazines.[23]

Deliver Value

Delivering value to the customer is at the heart of strategy. Value can be defined as the combination of benefits received and costs paid. Managers help their companies create value by devising strategies that exploit core competencies and attain synergy. The Swedish retailer IKEA has become a global cult brand by offering beautiful, functional products at modest cost, thus delivering superior value to customers.[24] To compete with the rising threat from online news, for example, newspapers such as The *Financial Times*, and the *International Herald Tribune* are trying to provide better value by integrating the internet and other technology into their business model. This enables them to offer video stories, interactive reader feedback and blogs, as well as restricted premium content. The *Financial Times* is the first newspaper in the world to be delivered by BlackBerry according to its Editor Andrew Gowers. He said: 'There's a very great potential overlap between the sort of people who own BlackBerrys and the sort of people who read, or should read, the FT. They are on the move; they are probably making decisions about reasonable amounts of money and they need information wherever they are.'[25]

Consider how German owned Aldi has grown into one of the fastest growing most successful grocery chains in the UK with a strategy based on exploiting core competencies, building synergy and providing value to customers.

CONCEPT CONNECTION
Rather than trying to be all things to all pizza lovers, Upper Crust Pizza founder Jordan Tobins aims to grow by doing one thing better than anyone else. That one thing is his Neapolitan-style pizza, prepared here by Antonio Carlos Filho. The Boston-area pizza chain has succeeded with a business-level strategy of focusing on high quality in a limited product line. As Upper Crust fan and former General Electric CEO Jack Welch enthused, 'You could faint just describing the flavour of the sauce, and the crust puts you over the edge.'

 INNOVATIVE WAY

Aldi

Aldi was founded by the Albrecht family in Germany in the 1950s. It is now the market leader in Germany, where 40 per cent of the market is in the hands of discounters. In 1962 brothers Karl and Theo Albrecht fell out over strategy and the business was split into two separate legal entities – Aldi Nord and Aldi Sud – which have expanded across Europe, Australia and the US. The brothers, whose businesses remain on 'friendly' terms, and follow the same business model and strategies, are Germany's richest men.

Aldi made its first foray into overseas markets in 1967, when it purchased the Hofer chain of supermarkets in Austria. The UK business, part of Aldi Sud, started in Birmingham in 1990. The 430-strong chain of discount supermarkets is growing rapidly, pulling in thousands of new customers trying to save a few pounds on their weekly shop. Aldi intends to open a new store every week until it reaches it's 1050 target.

Aldi's business model is based on simplicity and efficiency. The company's motto was 'Top quality at incredibly low prices – guaranteed'. All the elements in Aldi's business model are aimed at keeping costs low, so that the company could fulfil its promise of providing the lowest prices to its customers. Aldi's product strategy is based on carrying a limited variety of fast-moving products. The company specialized in selling staple products like food, beverages and household supplies, which customers shopped for on a regular basis.

Typically, Aldi carries a limited range – just 1000 products compared with the 25 000 in a typical supermarket – but buys in huge numbers and gets top quality. Aldi has obtained synergy by developing good relationships with a handful of core suppliers. Only about 15 brand names, such as Marmite, Tetley teabags and Budweiser, are on the shelves.

Aldi thrives by using its core competency of cost efficiency, which enables the stores to sell goods at prices much lower than major supermarkets rivals. The chain rigorously controls costs and the stores are, well, basic. There is no fancy flooring or fixtures. The lighting is definitely not designed to enhance the products. It is not a sophisticated shopping experience. There is also a range of non-food goods that changes weekly. There are none of the buy-one-get-one-free or half-price promotions offered by rival supermarkets. 'Promotions don't fool the customer. Customers know how much each supermarket costs', says Paul Foley, managing director of Aldi in the UK. He believes the reason for Aldi's success is simple: 'You will save about £30 on a £100 weekly shop.'

The value customers get from Aldi is based not just on low prices, but also on the quality. Foley takes exception to the idea that shoppers 'trade down' to Aldi: 'I don't see it as trading down. There is no trading down in buying the same quality product. You are just trading down in price.' Privately, rival supermarket executives marvel at the quality of Aldi's own label. In the discounter's head office a cabinet displays 50 awards and citations for the quality of various Aldi food products.

Foley is aiming directly at the mid-market: 'The bottom end of the market is not that attractive to us. They don't have much money, they don't travel very far and they are very brand-conscious. The very top of the market – where the amount spent on food is a very small amount of disposable income – is not attractive either. But everything in the middle is fair game.' The utilitarian look of the stores does not seem to be bothering the shoppers. Half Aldi's customers are now in the ABC1 social category – 17 per cent up on a year ago.

The key difference between the discount sector and the big grocers, says Foley, is a focus on costs rather than growing sales. 'I know exactly the tonnage of waste cardboard we produce every week and how much I can sell it for. I know that it takes 22 minutes, with the right kind of machine, to clean the floor of the store. Supermarkets are interested in how much they can sell. I think about how much it costs to sell the product.'

Not all costs are squeezed. 'Graduates start on £45 000. I want the best people and if I don't pay the best they will go and join merchant banks. I need the brightest brains. You can't do it any other way,' says Foley. As a result Aldi is rated the ninth best place for graduates to get a job in the UK in an annual survey by *The Times*. It is ranked higher than Goldman Sachs, Shell and GlaxoSmithKline. Tesco the UK's largest retailer is only 26th.[26]

TAKE A MOMENT   As a new manager, can you identify the core competence of your team or department and identify ways that it can contribute to the overall organization's strategy? Who are your team's or department's customers, and how can you deliver value?

Levels of Strategy

Another aspect of strategic management concerns the organizational level to which strategic issues apply. Strategic managers normally think in terms of three levels of strategy, as illustrated in Exhibit 8.1.[27]

Corporate-level strategy
The level of strategy concerned with the question 'What business are we in?' Pertains to the organization as a whole and the combination of business units and product lines that make it up.

■   *What Business Are We In?* This is the question managers address when they consider corporate-level strategy. **Corporate-level strategy** pertains to the organization as a whole and the combination of business units and product lines that make up the corporate entity. Strategic actions at this level usually relate to the acquisition of new businesses; additions or divestments of business units, plants, or product lines; and joint ventures with other corporations in new areas. An example of corporate-level strategy is Brunswick, which was once associated primarily with billiard tables and bowling gear. CEO George Buckley is transforming Brunswick into the 'Toyota of boating' by selling off unprofitable businesses and buying companies such as Sea Pro, Hatteras and Princecraft to give Brunswick a slice of every boating niche.[28]

Business-level strategy
The level of strategy concerned with the question 'How do we compete?' Pertains to each business unit or product line within the organization.

■   *How Do We Compete?* **Business-level strategy** pertains to each business unit or product line. Strategic decisions at this level concern amount of advertising, direction and extent of research and development, product changes, new-product development, equipment and facilities, and expansion or contraction of product and service lines. Many companies have opened e-commerce units as a part of business-level strategy. For example, Zubka (www.zubka.com) a UK-based online recruitment site, is taking on both traditional and online recruitment firms. Its unique selling point is recommendations: the person putting forward a candidate (often a friend) can get between 6 to 8 per cent of the starting salary. Zubka takes 15 per cent of a successful job applicant's starting salary. By

Exhibit 8.1 Three Levels of Strategy in Organizations

Corporate–Level Strategy: What business are we in?

Corporation

Business–Level Strategy: How do we compete?

Consumer Products Unit   Biotechnology Unit   Media Unit

Functional–Level Strategy: How do we support the business–level strategy?

Finance   R&D   Manufacturing   Marketing

SOURCE: Milton Leontiades, *Strategies for Diversification and Change* (Boston: Little, Brown, 1980): 63; and Dan E. Schendel and Charles W. Hofer, eds., *Strategic Management: A New View of Business Policy and Planning* (Boston: Little, Brown, 1979): 11–14.

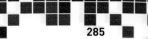

offering incentives for recommendations, the pool of applicants is increased. And by conducting business online, overheads are reduced. Zubka is now expanding its services into Europe and has already established a presence in the Netherlands.[29]

Go to the Ethical Dilemma on page 305 that pertains to business- and functional-level strategy.   **TAKE A MOMENT**

■ *How Do We Support the Business-Level Strategy?* **Functional-level strategy** pertains to the major functional departments within the business unit. Functional strategies involve all of the major functions, including finance, research and development, marketing and manufacturing. The new functional-level strategy for Asda's marketing department, for example, was to feature real-life women, to front its George clothing ads, starting with doctors and nurses, after listening to customers and concluding that it was inappropriate to spend money on celebrity endorsements in the economic climate at the end of 2008.

Another example of functional-level strategy is Procter & Gamble's research and development department, which is taking a new approach to stay competitive in the slow-growing consumer products industry. Instead of developing new products in the lab and then testing them with consumers, researchers are spending hours with customers, watching them do laundry, clean the floor or apply makeup, looking for nuisances that a new product might solve. Then they go into the lab with a goal of addressing the concerns of real-life customers.[30]

Functional-level strategy
The level of strategy concerned with the question 'How do we support the business-level strategy?' Pertains to all of the organization's major departments.

The Strategic Management Process

The overall strategic management process is illustrated in Exhibit 8.2. It begins when executives evaluate their current position with respect to mission, goals and

Exhibit 8.2 The Strategic Management Process

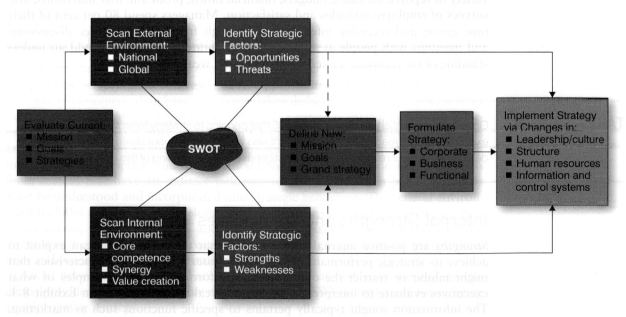

Strategic business unit (SBU)

A division of the organization that has a unique business mission, product line, competitors and markets relative to other SBUs in the same corporation.

Portfolio strategy

The organization's mix of strategic business units and product lines that fit together in such a way as to provide the corporation with synergy and competitive advantage.

Formulating Corporate-Level Strategy

Portfolio Strategy

Individual investors often wish to diversify in an investment portfolio with some high-risk stocks, some low-risk stocks, some growth stocks, and perhaps a few income bonds. In much the same way, corporations like to have a balanced mix of business divisions called **strategic business units (SBUs)**. An SBU has a unique business mission, product line, competitors, and markets relative to other SBUs in the corporation.[33] Executives in charge of the entire corporation generally define an overall strategy and then bring together a portfolio of strategic business units to carry it out. **Portfolio strategy** pertains to the mix of business units and product lines that fit together in a logical way to provide synergy and competitive advantage for the corporation. Managers don't like to become too dependent on one business. For example, at United Technologies Corporation (UTC), the aerospace-related business units have been struggling through one of the worst slumps in history. However, UTC's Otis Elevator division is keeping the corporation's sales and profits strong. Otis has a commanding share of the worldwide market for new elevators and escalators. In addition, the unit provides a steady revenue stream from elevator maintenance, repair, and upgrade. The elevators in the Waldorf-Astoria, for example, were installed in 1931 and have been steadily upgraded by Otis ever since.[34] One useful way to think about portfolio strategy is the BCG matrix.

The BCG Matrix

The BCG (for Boston Consulting Group) matrix is illustrated in Exhibit 8.4. The **BCG matrix** organizes businesses along two dimensions – business growth rate and market share.[35] *Business growth rate* pertains to how rapidly the entire industry is increasing. *Market share* defines whether a business unit has a larger or smaller share than competitors. The combinations of high and low market share and high and low business growth provide four categories for a corporate portfolio.

The *star* has a large market share in a rapidly growing industry. The star is important because it has additional growth potential, and profits should be ploughed into this business as investment for future growth and profits. The star is visible and attractive and will generate profits and a positive cash flow even as the industry matures and market growth slows.

The *cash cow* exists in a mature, slow-growth industry but is a dominant business in the industry, with a large market share. Because heavy investments in advertising and plant expansion are no longer required, the corporation earns a positive cash flow. It can milk the cash cow to invest in other, riskier businesses.

The *question mark* exists in a new, rapidly growing industry, but has only a small market share. The question mark business is risky: it could become a star, or it could fail. The corporation can invest the cash earned from cash cows in question marks with the goal of nurturing them into future stars.

© JACK GUEZ/AFP/GETTY IMAGES

CONCEPT CONNECTION The effects of an oil fire in Iraq were felt thousands of miles away – in the executive suites at companies such as United Airlines and Delta in the US, British Airways and Virgin Atlantic in the UK, and Cathay Pacific, Singapore Airlines and Air China in Asia. The major air carriers, already struggling, were devastated when the price of fuel spiked in the spring and summer of 2008. Uncertainty about oil costs and supplies is a significant external threat to the nation's airlines. Other threats include stiff competition from low-cost carriers and the lingering fear of terrorism.

For instance, Finnair's fuel bill increased by £126.7 million compared to the previous year, as oil reached a record of more than $139 per barrel. This in turn led to a fall in customer demand, as consumers affected by rising food and fuel prices cut back on non-essential travel, so forcing Finnair, the Finnish national carrier, to announce 500 job losses, 5.3 per cent of its workforce, in an attempt to save money. Many other airlines fared even worse, with a number going into liquidation such as Oasis Hong Kong Airlines, US based ATA Airlines and the South African budget airline Nationwide Airlines.

 ## INNOVATIVE WAY

Facebook Inc.

MySpace is still in the lead in online social networking, but Facebook is getting all the attention. The start-up grew rapidly in the first four years after 23-year-old Mark Zuckerberg founded it while still a student at Harvard University. To keep Facebook growing, the young CEO made some strategic decisions that can be understood by looking at the company's strengths, weaknesses, opportunities, and threats.

Facebook's *strengths* include technological know-how and an aggressive and innovative culture. In addition, Facebook has a major partnership with Microsoft, which has invested $240 million, brokers banner ads for the company, and is developing tools that make it easy to create links between Windows applications and Facebook's network. Since Facebook expanded beyond students, membership has boomed, and Facebook is preferred over MySpace by older users and professionals. Work networks on Facebook are exploding. The primary *weakness* is a lack of management expertise to help the company meet the challenges of growing up.

The biggest *threat* to the company is that Facebook is still spending more cash than it is bringing in. In addition, Zuckerberg is gaining a reputation in the industry as an arrogant and standoffish manager, which could hurt Facebook's chances of successful partnerships. *Opportunities* abound to expand the company's operations internationally and to take advantage of Facebook's popularity to introduce features that can command higher web advertising rates and bring in more revenue.

What does SWOT analysis suggest for Facebook? Zuckerberg is trying to capitalize on Facebook's popularity by making it a place for companies to provide services to members. For example, Prosper.com developed a Facebook application for its service that allows members to lend one another money at negotiated interest rates. Non-internet companies such as Red Bull have also developed Facebook applications to reach Facebook's vast customer base. Companies that put applications on the Facebook website can experience a sort of viral popularity as word spreads among millions of members.

To implement the strategy, Zuckerberg is bringing in executives with more strategy experience than himself, such as Chamath Palihapitiya, a former AOL manager, as vice president of product marketing, and Sheryl Sandberg, formerly of Google, as chief operating officer. These managers have the traditional skills Facebook needs to execute the new strategy both in the United States and internationally.[36]

It's too soon to tell if Facebook's strategy is working.[37] Zuckerberg is continuing his efforts to build a more seasoned executive team to keep growing and avoid damaging mistakes as Facebook pursues its strategy.

The *dog* is a poor performer. It has only a small share of a slow-growth market. The dog provides little profit for the corporation and may be targeted for divestment or liquidation if turnaround is not possible.

The circles in Exhibit 8.4 represent the business portfolio for a hypothetical corporation. Circle size represents the relative size of each business in the company's portfolio. Most large organizations, such as General Electric (GE), have businesses in more than one quadrant, thereby representing different market shares and growth rates.

BCG matrix
A concept developed by the Boston Consulting Group that evaluates strategic business units with respect to the dimensions of business growth rate and market share.

Diversification Strategy

The strategy of moving into new lines of business, as GE did by getting into healthcare, finance and alternative forms of energy, is called **diversification**. Other examples of diversification include Apple's entry into the mobile phone business with the iPhone, the move by News Corporation into online social networking with the acquisition of MySpace, and Nestlé's entry into the pet food business with the purchase of Ralston.

Diversification
A strategy of moving into new lines of business.

Exhibit 8.4 The BCG Matrix

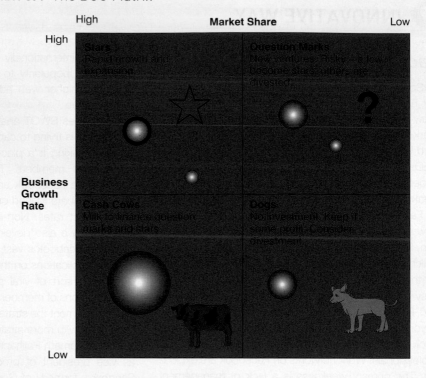

The matrix axes: **Market Share** (High to Low), **Business Growth Rate** (High to Low).

Stars: Rapid growth and expansion

Question Marks: New ventures. Risky — a few become stars, others are divested.

Cash Cows: Milk to finance question marks and stars

Dogs: No investment. Keep if some profit. Consider divestment.

💡 INNOVATIVE WAY

General Electric

General Electric Company, or GE, is a multinational American technology and services conglomerate, and the world's third largest company. Since he took over as General Electric's CEO, Jeff Immelt has been reshuffling the corporation's mix of businesses in a way that he believes will better position GE for the long term. GE is investing heavily in its stars and question marks to ensure that its portfolio will continue to include cash cows in a future that might be very different from today's world.

The most famous cash cows in General Electric's portfolio are the appliance division and lighting, which hold a large share of a stable market and account for a big portion of sales and profits. The GE Security division has star status, and GE is pumping money into development of new products for hot areas such as fire safety, industrial security and homeland security. GE

Healthcare is also a star, and managers are investing research dollars to become a leader in the growing business of biosciences and personalized medicine. Some products under development might not hit the marketplace for a decade but hold the promise of huge returns.

GE's renewable energy business is still a question mark. The company moved into wind and solar power and biogas with acquisitions such as Enron Wind. Managers hope the division can become a star, but the potential demand for renewable energy is uncertain at this point.

GE's consumer finance division is also a question mark. Top executives are currently overhauling the brand image of consumer finance to see whether it will revive the division enough to keep it in the portfolio. If they decide the division is a dog, GE will sell it off as they did the less profitable and slow-growing insurance business.[38]

The purpose of diversification is to expand the firm's business operations to produce new kinds of valuable products and services. When the new business is related to the company's existing business activities, the organization is implementing a strategy of **related diversification**. For example, GE's move into renewable energy and Nestlé's move into pet foods are linked to these firms' existing energy and nutrition businesses. **Unrelated diversification** occurs when an organization expands into a totally new line of business, such as GE's entry into consumer finance or Associated British Food move into the value fashion market with Primark. With unrelated diversification, the company's lines of business aren't explicitly logically associated with one another; therefore, it can be difficult to make the strategy successful. Consequently some companies are giving up on unrelated diversification strategies, selling off unrelated businesses to focus on core areas.

A firm's managers may also pursue diversification opportunities to create value through a strategy of vertical integration. **Vertical integration** means the company expands into businesses that either produce the supplies needed to make products or that distribute and sell those products to customers. For example, E & J Gallo Winery started a new business to make its own wine bottles rather than buying them from a supplier.[39] Gallo could make bottles more cheaply than it could buy them, enabling managers to reduce costs. In addition, the new division enabled the company to distinguish its wines with unique bottle shapes. An example of diversifying to distribute products comes from Apple, which opened retail stores to increase visibility and sell its innovative products to customers. The strategy was a big success. Customers can try the products before they buy and get free help on how to use Macintosh computers, iPods and iPhones, Apple software and accessories like digital cameras.[40]

Related diversification
Moving into a new business that is related to the company's existing business activities.

Unrelated diversification
Expanding into a totally new line of business.

Vertical integration
Expanding into businesses that either produce the supplies needed to make products or that distribute and sell those products.

Formulating Business-Level Strategy

Now we turn to strategy formulation within the strategic business unit, in which the concern is how to compete. A popular and effective model for formulating strategy is Porter's competitive forces and strategies. Michael E. Porter studied a number of business organizations and proposed that business-level strategies are the result of five competitive forces in the company's environment.[41] More recently, Porter examined the impact of the internet on business-level strategy.[42] New web-based technology is influencing industries in both positive and negative ways, and understanding this impact is essential for managers to accurately analyze their competitive environments and design appropriate strategic actions.

Porter's Five Competitive Forces

Exhibit 8.5 illustrates the competitive forces that exist in a company's environment and indicates some ways internet technology is affecting each area. These forces help determine a company's position vis-à-vis competitors in the industry environment.

1 *Potential new entrants.* Capital requirements and economies of scale are examples of two potential barriers to entry that can keep out new competitors. It is far more costly to enter the automobile industry, for instance, than to start a specialized mail-order business. In general, internet technology has made it much easier for new companies to enter an industry by curtailing the need for such organizational elements as an established sales force, physical assets such as buildings and machinery, or access to existing supplier and sales channels.

Exhibit 8.5 Porter's Five Forces Affecting Industry Competition

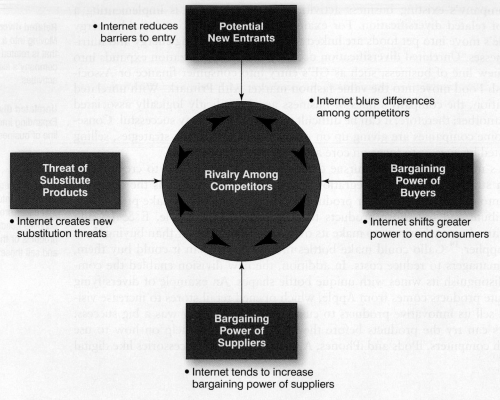

- Internet reduces barriers to entry

Potential New Entrants

- Internet blurs differences among competitors

Threat of Substitute Products

Rivalry Among Competitors

Bargaining Power of Buyers

- Internet creates new substitution threats

- Internet shifts greater power to end consumers

Bargaining Power of Suppliers

- Internet tends to increase bargaining power of suppliers

SOURCE: Based on Michael E. Porter, *Competitive Strategy: Techniques for Analyzing Industries and Competitors* (New York: Free Press, 1980); and Michael E. Porter, 'Strategy and the Internet', *Harvard Business Review* (March 2001): 63–78.

2 *Bargaining power of buyers.* Informed customers become empowered customers. The internet provides easy access to a wide array of information about products, services, and competitors, thereby greatly increasing the bargaining power of end consumers. For example, a customer shopping for a car can gather extensive information about various options, such as wholesale prices for new cars or average value for used vehicles, detailed specifications, repair records, and even whether a used car has ever been involved in an accident.

3 *Bargaining power of suppliers.* The concentration of suppliers and the availability of substitute suppliers are significant factors in determining supplier power. The sole supplier of engines to a manufacturer of small airplanes will have great power, for example. The impact of the internet in this area can be both positive and negative. That is, procurement over the web tends to give a company greater power over suppliers, but the web also gives suppliers access to a greater number of customers, as well as the ability to reach end users. Overall, the internet tends to raise the bargaining power of suppliers.

4 *Threat of substitute products.* The power of alternatives and substitutes for a company's product may be affected by changes in cost or in trends such as increased health consciousness that will deflect buyer loyalty. Companies in the sugar industry suffered from the growth of sugar substitutes; manufacturers of aerosol spray cans lost business as environmentally conscious consumers chose other products. The internet created a greater threat of new substitutes by

enabling new approaches to meeting customer needs. For example, offers of low-cost airline tickets over the internet hurt traditional travel agencies.

5   *Rivalry among competitors.* As illustrated in Exhibit 8.5, rivalry among competitors is influenced by the preceding four forces, as well as by cost and product differentiation. With the levelling force of the internet and information technology, it has become more difficult for many companies to find ways to distinguish themselves from their competitors, which intensifies rivalry. Porter referred to the 'advertising slugfest' when describing the scrambling and jockeying for position that occurs among fierce rivals within an industry. Nintendo and Sony are fighting for control of the video game console industry, British Airways and Virgin Atlantic are competing for the transatlantic airline business, TNT, UPS, DHL and FedEx in the growing China logistics industry, while Pepsi and Coke are still battling it out in the cola wars.

A further example is the fierce rivalry between Anglo-Dutch owned Unilever and US owned Proctor and Gamble in the global Fast Moving Consumer Goods (FMCG). This market, is characterized by products which are sold quickly at relatively low cost. The absolute profit made on FMCG products is relatively small, though they generally sell in large quantities, so the cumulative profit on such products can be large. As a result we experience frequent brand wars across sectors such as washing powders between Unilever's Persil, Omo and Surf versus P&G's Tide, Ariel, Daz and Bold: in soap (Dove, Lux and Pears versus Ivory, Camay and Zest), dental care (Signal and Mentadent against Crest and Oral-B), deodorants (Lynx/Axe and Sure/Rexona versus Old Spice and Secret) and hair care (Timotei versus Wella and Head & Shoulders).

Porter's model has been subject to a number of criticisms.[43] In particular has been the suggestion that the framework could be transformed into a more dynamic model, both at the industry level, and at a more micro transactional level. It's applicability to the non-for-profit and public sectors has also been questioned. Notwithstanding, it still remains a very influential, popular and practical model for understanding the dynamics of a competitive industry sector.

As a new manager, examine the competitive forces that are affecting your organization. What can you do as a lower-level manager to help the firm find or keep its competitive edge through a differentiation, cost-leadership or focus strategy?

TAKE A MOMENT

Competitive Strategies

In finding its competitive edge within these five forces, Porter suggests that a company can adopt one of three strategies: differentiation, cost leadership or focus. The organizational characteristics typically associated with each strategy are summarized in Exhibit 8.6.

Differentiation

The **differentiation** strategy involves an attempt to distinguish the firm's products or services from others in the industry. The organization may use creative advertising, distinctive product features, exceptional service or new technology to achieve a product perceived as unique. Examples of products that have benefited from a

Differentiation
A type of competitive strategy with which the organization seeks to distinguish its products or services from that of competitors.

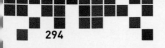

Exhibit 8.6 Organizational Characteristics of Porter's Competitive Strategies

Strategy	Organizational Characteristics
Differentiation	Acts in a flexible, loosely knit way, with strong coordination among departments
	Strong capability in basic rewards
	Creative flair, thinks 'out of the box'
	Strong marketing abilities
	Rewards employee innovation
	Corporate reputation for quality or technological leadership
Cost Leadership	Strong central authority; tight cost controls
	Maintains standard operating procedures
	Easy-to-use manufacturing technologies
	Highly efficient procurement and distribution systems
	Close supervision, finite employee empowerment
Focus	Frequent, detailed control reports
	May use combination of above policies directed at particular strategic target
	Values and rewards flexibility and customer intimacy
	Measures cost of providing service and maintaining customer loyalty
	Pushes empowerment to employees with customer contact

SOURCE: Based on Michael E. Porter, *Competitive Strategy: Techniques for Analyzing Industries and Competitors* (New York: The Free Press: 1980); Michael Treacy and Fred Wiersema, 'How Market Leaders Keep Their Edge', *Fortune* (February 6, 1995): 88–98; and Michael A. Hitt, R. Duane Ireland and Robert E. Hoskisson, *Strategic Management* (St. Paul, MN: West, 1995), pp. 100–113.

differentiation strategy include Harley-Davidson motorcycles, Dyson bagless cleaners and Gore-Tex fabrics, all of which are perceived as distinctive in their markets. Service companies such as Starbucks, Primark, Whole Foods Market, Aldi and IKEA also use a differentiation strategy.

A differentiation strategy can reduce rivalry with competitors if buyers are loyal to a company's brand. Successful differentiation can also reduce the bargaining power of large buyers because other products are less attractive, which also helps the firm fight off threats of substitute products. In addition, differentiation erects entry barriers in the form of customer loyalty that a new entrant into the market would have difficulty overcoming.

Cost Leadership

Cost leadership
A type of competitive strategy with which the organization aggressively seeks efficient facilities, cuts costs and employs tight cost controls to be more efficient than competitors.

With a **cost leadership** strategy, the organization aggressively seeks efficient facilities, pursues cost reductions and uses tight cost controls to produce products more efficiently than competitors. A low-cost position means that the company can undercut competitors' prices and still offer comparable quality and earn a reasonable profit.

For example, Premier Inn and Travelodge are low-priced alternatives to Four Seasons or Marriott, while easyCar is a low-priced alternative to Hertz rent-a-car.

Being a low-cost producer provides a successful strategy to defend against the five competitive forces in Exhibit 8.5. The most efficient, low-cost company is in the best position to succeed in a price war while still making a profit. Likewise, the low-cost producer is protected from powerful customers and suppliers, because customers cannot find lower prices elsewhere, and other buyers would have less slack for price negotiation with suppliers. If substitute products or potential new entrants occur, the low-cost producer is better positioned than higher-cost rivals to prevent loss of market share. The low price acts as a barrier against new entrants and substitute products.[44]

Focus

With a **focus** strategy, the organization concentrates on a specific regional market or buyer group. The company will use either a differentiation or cost leadership approach, but only for a narrow target market. Primark, described earlier, uses a focused cost leadership strategy, putting low-priced 'fashion' onto the high street. One type of organization that relies specifically on a focus strategy is a credit union. A credit union has a 'common bond' which determines who can become a member of the company. The common bond may be for people living or working in the same area, people working for the same employer or people who belong to the same association, such as a church or trade union. For example Kuapa Kokoo Union, refered to earlier in chapter 5, was founded as a credit union in 1993 by a group of cocoa farmers and Twin Trading as a response to the liberalization of the cocoa market in Ghana. Kuapa purchases and markets its members' cocoa beans, and represents 48 854 farmers from 1124 village-level farmer societies.[45]

Managers should think carefully about which strategy will provide their company with its competitive advantage. Gibson Guitar Corporation, famous in the music world for its innovative, high-quality products, found that switching to a low-cost strategy to compete against Japanese rivals such as Yamaha and Ibanez actually hurt the company. When managers realized people wanted Gibson products because of their reputation, not their price, they went back to a differentiation strategy and invested in new technology and marketing.[46] In his studies, Porter found that some businesses did not consciously adopt one of these three strategies and were stuck with no strategic advantage. Without a strategic advantage, businesses earned below-average profits compared with those that used differentiation, cost leadership or focus strategies. Similarly, a five-year study of management practices in hundreds of businesses, referred to as the *Evergreen Project*, found that a clear strategic direction was a key factor that distinguished winners from losers.[47]

Focus
A type of competitive strategy that emphasizes concentration on a specific regional market or buyer group.

© AFP/GETTY IMAGES

CONCEPT CONNECTION The MINI's trademarked term 'Whiptastic Handling' is one of the ways the company distinguishes itself in the automobile industry. MINI, a division of BMW, is thriving with its differentiation strategy. The company trademarked the Whiptastic name to emphasize that driving a MINI Cooper is unlike anything else. Customers seem to agree; sales are zooming.

New Trends in Strategy

Organizations have been in a merger and acquisition frenzy in recent years. Lloyds Bank and HBOS merged, L'Oréal bought The Body Shop, and Disney merged with ABC.

Another example, is the $1.48 billion (£870 million) merger between Ghana's Ashanti Goldfields and South Africa's AngloGold which paved the way for the creation of a new gold mining giant that could compete on a par with world number one Newmont Mining Corporation. Similarly Spain's largest Bank, Banco Santander, has recently taken advantage of problems in the UK mortgage market to acquire Alliance & Leicester, and Bradford & Bingley, to add to its Abbey National brand, to become the Eurozone's largest bank. By increasing its scope and leverage simply by becoming bigger, companies usually increase liquidity and access to the capital markets while broadening the name or brand awareness into an additional geographic market.

Some companies still seek to gain or keep a competitive edge by acquiring new capabilities via mergers and acquisitions. Yet today, a decided shift has also occurred toward enhancing the organization's existing capabilities as the primary means of growing and innovating. Another current trend is using strategic partnerships as an alternative to mergers and acquisitions.

Dynamic capabilities
Leveraging and developing more from the firm's existing assets, capabilities, and core competencies in a way that will provide a sustained competitive advantage.

Innovation from within

The strategic approach referred to as **dynamic capabilities** means that managers focus on leveraging and developing more from the firm's existing assets, capabilities and core competencies in a way that will provide a sustained competitive advantage.[48] Learning, reallocation of existing assets and internal innovation are the route to addressing new challenges in the competitive environment and meeting new customer needs. For example, General Electric, as described earlier, has acquired a number of other companies to enter a variety of diverse businesses. Yet today, the emphasis at GE is not on making deals but rather on stimulating and supporting internal innovation. Instead of spending billions to buy new businesses, CEO Jeff Immelt is investing in internal 'Imagination Breakthrough' projects that will take GE into internally developed new lines of business, new geographic areas or a new customer base. The idea is that getting growth out of existing businesses is cheaper and more effective than trying to buy it from outside.[49]

Another example of dynamic capabilities is IBM, which many analysts had written off as a has-been in the early 1990s. Since then, new top managers have steered the company through a remarkable transformation by capitalizing on IBM's core competence of expert technology by learning new ways to apply it to meet changing customer needs. By leveraging existing capabilities to provide solutions to major customer problems rather than just selling hardware, IBM has moved into businesses as diverse as life sciences, banking and automotive.[50]

COURTESY OF IROBOT

CONCEPT CONNECTION The technology company iRobot is best known for the Roomba – a pet-like robotic vacuum, shown here with a live flesh-and-blood pet. But iRobot also fulfils a more serious purpose of providing military robots that perform dangerous jobs such as clearing caves and sniffing out bombs. The company's dynamic capabilities approach included sending an engineer to Afghanistan for field testing and learning. For its consumer products, iRobot primarily uses internal interdisciplinary teams to incubate ideas. But partnerships feed iRobot's innovation machine, as well, such as when the company partnered with an explosives-sensor company to develop its bomb-sniffing robot.

Strategic Partnerships

Internal innovation doesn't mean companies always go it alone, however. Collaboration with other organizations, sometimes even with competitors, is an important part of how today's successful companies enter new areas of business.

Consider Procter and Gamble (P&G) and Clorox. The companies are fierce rivals in cleaning products and water purification, but both profited by collaborating on a new plastic wrap. P&G researchers invented a wrap that seals tightly only where it is pressed, but P&G didn't have a plastic wrap category. Managers negotiated a strategic partnership with Clorox to market the wrap under the well-established Glad brand name, and Glad Press & Seal became one of the company's most popular products.[51] Therefore while P&G still competes fiercely with Clorox on cleaning products, it co-operates quite happily through a joint venture when it comes to wraps.

The internet is both driving and supporting the move toward partnership thinking. The ability to rapidly and smoothly conduct transactions, communicate information, exchange ideas, and collaborate on complex projects via the internet means that companies such as Citigroup, Dow Chemical and Procter and Gamble have been able to enter entirely new businesses by partnering in business areas that were previously unimaginable.[52]

Global Strategy

Many organizations operate globally and pursue a distinct strategy as the focus of global business. Senior executives try to formulate coherent strategies to provide synergy among worldwide operations for the purpose of fulfilling common goals. Yet managers face a strategic dilemma between the need for global integration and national responsiveness.

The various global strategies are shown in Exhibit 8.7. Recall from Chapter 4 that the first step toward a greater international presence is when companies begin exporting domestically produced products to selected countries. The *export strategy* is shown in the lower left corner of the exhibit. Because the organization is domestically focused, with only a few exports, managers have little need to pay attention to issues of either local responsiveness or global integration. Organizations that pursue further international expansion must decide whether they want each global affiliate to act autonomously or whether activities should be standardized and centralized across countries. This choice leads managers to select a basic strategy alternative such as globalization versus multi-domestic strategy. Some corporations may seek to achieve both global integration and national responsiveness by using a transnational strategy.

Globalization

When an organization chooses a strategy of globalization, it means that product design and advertising strategies are standardized throughout the world.[53] This approach is based on the assumption that a single global market exists for many consumer and industrial products. The theory is that people everywhere want to buy the same products and live the same way. People everywhere want to drink Coca-Cola and eat McDonald's hamburgers.[54] A globalization strategy can help an organization reap efficiencies by standardizing product design and manufacturing, using common suppliers, introducing products around the world faster, coordinating prices, and eliminating overlapping facilities. For example, Gillette Company has large production

Globalization
The standardization of product design and advertising strategies throughout the world.

© ST-IMAGES/ALAMY

CONCEPT CONNECTION AT&T is the exclusive service provider for the iPhone in the US. This strategic partnership with Apple provided AT&T with new, younger customers and a hipper image. Similar exclusive one-carrier deals were agreed in other countries, for example in the UK sales were going through the O2 unit of Telefónica, while in Germany, sales were being offered through Deutsche Telekom's T-Mobile division. AT&T struck the US deal to provide growth in the wireless service market.

Exhibit 8.7 Global Corporate Strategies

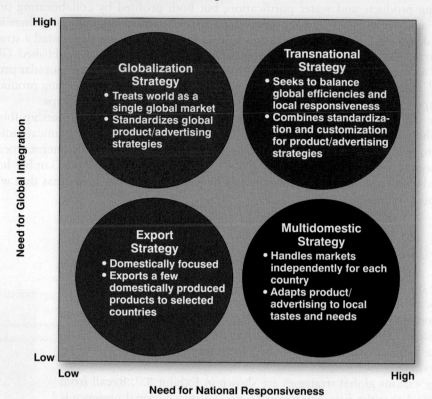

SOURCE: Based on Michael A. Hitt, R. Duane Ireland and Robert E. Hoskisson, *Strategic Management: Competitiveness and Globalization* (St. Paul, MN; West, 1995), p. 239; and Thomas M. Begley and David P. Boyd, 'The Need for a Corporate Global Mindset', *MIT Sloan Management Review* (Winter 2003): 25–32.

facilities that use common suppliers and processes to manufacture products whose technical specifications are standardized around the world.[55]

Globalization enables marketing departments alone to save millions of dollars. One consumer products company reports that, for every country where the same commercial runs, the company saves $1 million to $2 million in production costs alone. More millions have been saved by standardizing the look and packaging of brands.[56]

Multidomestic Strategy

Multidomestic strategy
The modification of product design and advertising strategies to suit the specific needs of individual countries.

When an organization chooses a **multidomestic strategy**, it means that competition in each country is handled independently of industry competition in other countries. Thus, a multinational company is present in many countries, but it encourages marketing, advertising and product design to be modified and adapted to the specific needs of each country.[57] Many companies reject the idea of a single global market. They have found that the French do not drink orange juice for breakfast, that laundry detergent is used to wash dishes in parts of Mexico, and that people in the Middle East prefer toothpaste that tastes spicy. Service companies also have to consider their global strategy carefully. The 7-Eleven convenience store chain uses a multi-domestic strategy because the product mix, advertising approach and payment methods need to be tailored to the preferences, values and government regulations in different parts of the world. For example, in Japan, customers like to use convenience stores to pay utility and other bills. 7-Eleven Japan also set up a way for people to pick up and pay for purchases made over the internet at their local 7-Eleven market.[58]

Transnational Strategy

A **transnational strategy** seeks to achieve both global integration and national responsiveness.[59] A true transnational strategy is difficult to achieve, because one goal requires close global coordination while the other goal requires local flexibility. However, many industries are finding that, although increased competition means they must achieve global efficiency, growing pressure to meet local needs demands national responsiveness.[60] One company that effectively uses a transnational strategy is Caterpillar, Inc., a heavy equipment manufacturer, which has over 300 operations in 40 countries across the world. Caterpillar achieves global efficiencies by designing its products to use many identical components and centralizing manufacturing of components in a few large-scale facilities. However, assembly plants located in each of Caterpillar's major markets add certain product features tailored to meet local needs.[61]

Although most multinational companies want to achieve some degree of global integration to hold costs down, even global products may require some customization to meet government regulations in various countries or some tailoring to fit consumer preferences. In addition, some products are better suited for standardization than others. Most large multinational corporations with diverse products and services will attempt to use a partial multidomestic strategy for some product or service lines and global strategies for others. Coordinating global integration with a responsiveness to the heterogeneity of international markets is a difficult balancing act for managers, but it is increasingly important in today's global business world.

CONCEPT CONNECTION Since first going International in 1971, Mary Kay Inc. has expanded to more than 30 markets on five continents. The company uses a multidomestic strategy that handles competition independently in each country. In China, for example, Mary Kay is working on lotions that incorporate traditional Chinese herbs, and it sells skin whiteners there, not bronzers. As Mary Kay China President Paul Mak (pictured here) explains, Chinese women prize smooth white skin. Managers' efforts in China have paid off. Estimates are that by 2015, more Mary Kay product will be sold in China than in the rest of the world combined.

Transnational strategy
A strategy that combines global coordination to attain efficiency with flexibility to meet specific needs in various countries.

Strategy Execution

The final step in the strategic management process is strategy execution – how strategy is implemented or put into action. Many people argue that execution is the most important, yet the most difficult, part of strategic management.[62] Indeed, many struggling companies may have file drawers full of winning strategies, but managers can't effectively execute them.[63]

No matter how brilliant the formulated strategy, the organization will not benefit if it is not skilfully executed. Strategy execution requires that all aspects of the organization be in congruence with the strategy and that every individual's efforts be coordinated toward accomplishing strategic goals.[64] Strategy execution involves using several tools – parts of the firm that can be adjusted to put strategy into action – as illustrated in Exhibit 8.8. Once a new strategy is selected, it is implemented through changes in leadership, structure, information and control systems, and human resources.[65] The Manager's Shoptalk box gives some further tips for strategy execution.

Leadership

The primary key to successful strategy execution is leadership. *Leadership* is the ability to influence people to adopt the new behaviours needed for putting the strategy

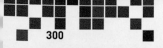

Exhibit 8.8 Tools for Putting Strategy into Action

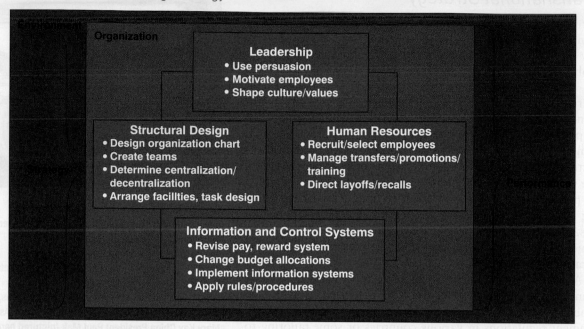

SOURCE: From Galbraith/Kazanjian. *Strategy Implementation*, 2nd ed. © 1986 South-Western, Cengage Learning. Reproduced by permission. www.cengage.com/permissions.

into action. Leaders use persuasion, motivation techniques, and cultural values to support the new strategy. They might make speeches to employees, build coalitions of people who support the new strategic direction, and persuade middle managers to go along with their vision for the company. At IBM, for example, CEO Sam Palmisano used leadership to get people aligned with the strategy of getting IBM intimately involved in revamping and even running customers' business operations. To implement the new approach, he invested tons of money to teach managers at all levels how to lead rather than control their staff. And he talked to people all over the company, appealing to their sense of pride and uniting them behind the new vision and strategy.[66]

Structural Design

Structural design pertains to managers' responsibilities, their degree of authority, and the consolidation of facilities, departments and divisions. Structure also pertains to such matters as centralization versus decentralization and the design of job tasks. Trying to execute a strategy that conflicts with structural design, particularly in relation to managers' authority and responsibility, is a top obstacle to putting strategy into action effectively.[67] Many new strategies require making changes in organizational structure, such as adding or changing positions, reorganizing to teams, redesigning jobs, or shifting managers' responsibility and accountability. At IBM, Palmisano dismantled the executive committee that previously presided over strategic initiatives and replaced it with committees made up of people from all over the company. In addition, the entire firm was reorganized into teams that work directly with customers. As the company moves into a new business such as

 MANAGER'S SHOPTALK

Tips for Effective Strategy Execution

One survey found that only 57 per cent of responding firms reported that managers successfully executed the new strategies they had devised. Strategy gives a company a competitive edge only if it is skillfully executed through the decisions and actions of front-line managers and employees. Here are a few clues for creating an environment and process conducive to effective strategy execution.

1 *Build commitment to the strategy.* People throughout the organization have to buy into the new strategy. Managers make a deliberate and concentrated effort to bring front-line employees into the loop so they understand the new direction and have a chance to participate in decisions about how it will be executed. When Saab managers wanted to shift their strategy, they met with front-line employees and dealers to explain the new direction and ask for suggestions and recommendations on how to put it into action. Clear, measurable goals and rewards that are tied to implementation efforts are also important for gaining commitment.

2 *Devise a clear execution plan.* Too often, managers put forth great effort to formulate a strategy and next to none crafting a game plan for its execution. Without such a plan, managers and staff are likely to lose sight of the new strategy when they return to the everyday demands of their jobs. For successful execution, translate the strategy into a simple, streamlined plan that breaks the implementation process into a series of short-term actions, with a timetable for each step. Make sure the plan spells out who is responsible for what part of the strategy execution, how success will be measured and tracked, and what resources will be required and how they will be allocated.

3 *Pay attention to culture.* Culture drives strategy, and without the appropriate cultural values, employees' behaviour will be out of sync with the company's desired positioning in the marketplaces. For example, Air Canada's CEO made a sincere commitment to making the airline the country's customer service leader. However, employee behaviour didn't change because the old culture values supported doing things the way they had always been done.

4 *Take advantage of employees' knowledge and skills.* Managers need to get to know their employees on a personal basis so they understand how people can contribute to strategy execution. Most people want to be recognized and want to be valuable members of the organization. People throughout the organization have unused talents and skills that might be crucial for the success of a new strategy. In addition, managers can be sure people get training so they are capable of furthering the organization's new direction.

5 *Communicate, communicate, communicate.* Top managers have to continually communicate, through words and actions, their firm commitment to the strategy. In addition, managers have to keep tabs on how things are going, identify problems and keep people informed about the organization's progress. Managers should break down barriers to effective communication across functional and hierarchical boundaries, often bringing customers into the communication loop as well. Information systems should provide accurate and timely information to the people who need it for decision-making.

Executing strategy is a complex job that requires everyone in the company to be aligned with the new direction and working to make it happen. These tips, combined with the information in the text, can help managers meet the challenge of putting strategy into action.

SOURCES Brooke Dobni, 'Creating a Strategy Implementation Environment', *Business Horizons* (March–April 2003): 43–46; Michael K. Allio, 'A Short Practical Guide to Implementing Strategy', *Journal of Business Strategy* (August 2005): 12–21; 'Strategy Execution: Achieving Operational Excellence', *Economist Intelligence Unit* (November 2004); and Thomas W. Porter and Stephen C. Harper, 'Tactical Implementation: The Devil Is in the Details', *Business Horizons* (January–February 2003): 53–60.

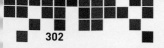
insurance claims processing or supply-chain optimization, IBM assigns SWAT teams to work with a handful of initial clients to learn what customers want and deliver it fast. Practically every job in the giant corporation was redefined to support the new strategy. A recent mission undertaken by the IBM SWAT team was at Banesto, a leading Spanish bank, where a WAP-based extension to the bank's existing e-business solution was delivered in ten days.[68]

Information and Control Systems

Information and control systems include reward systems, pay incentives, budgets for allocating resources, information technology systems, and the organization's rules, policies and procedures. Changes in these systems represent major tools for putting strategy into action.[69] For example, Pizza Hut has made excellent use of sophisticated information technology to support a differentiation strategy of continually innovating with new products. Data from point-of-sale customer transactions goes into a massive data warehouse. Managers can mine the data for competitive intelligence that enables them to predict trends as well as better manage targeted advertising and direct-mail campaigns.[70] Information technology can also be used to support a low-cost strategy, such as Wal-Mart and Tesco have done by accelerating checkout, managing inventory, and controlling distribution.[71] By contrast, in the UK, Woolworths become a byword for empty shelves and poor stock control performed because of weak information and control systems, which contributed to it eventually going into administration.[72]

At General Electric, described earlier in the chapter, CEO Jeff Immelt is tying manager's compensation to their ability to come up with new ideas, demonstrate improved customer service, generate growth and boost sales. For example, 20 per cent of division managers' bonuses is based on how well the business is improving its ability to meet customer needs. Similarly, as we saw in Chapter 7, at Little Earth, which sells eco-fashion products, the CEO Jerry Driggs uses dashboards to manage production, sales and financial operations enabling it to slash it's shipping time to three day. New information technology can also be used to support differentiation strategies, such as by enabling collaborative design of new products or customizing products and services to exact customer specification.

Human Resources

The organization's *human resources* are its employees. The human resource function recruits, selects, trains, transfers, promotes and lays off employees to achieve strategic goals. Longo Toyota of El Monte, California, recruits a highly diverse workforce to create a competitive advantage in selling cars and trucks. The staff speaks more than 30 languages and dialects, which gives Longo a lead because research shows that minorities prefer to buy a vehicle from someone who speaks their language and understands their culture.[73] Training employees is also important because it helps them understand the purpose and importance of a new strategy, overcome resistance, and develop the necessary skills and behaviours to implement the strategy. Southwest supports its low-cost strategy by cross-training employees to perform a variety of functions, minimizing turnover time of planes.[74]

A MANAGER'S ESSENTIALS: WHAT HAVE WE LEARNED?

- This chapter described important concepts of strategic management. Strategic management begins with an evaluation of the organization's current mission, goals and strategy. This evaluation is followed by situation analysis (called SWOT analysis), which examines opportunities and threats in the external environment as well as strengths and weaknesses within the organization. Situation analysis leads to the formulation of explicit strategies, which indicate how the company intends to achieve a competitive advantage. Managers formulate strategies that focus on core competencies, develop synergy and create value.

- Strategy formulation takes place at three levels: corporate, business and functional. Frameworks for corporate strategy include portfolio strategy, the BCG matrix and diversification strategy. An approach to business-level strategy is Porter's competitive forces and strategies. The internet is having a profound impact on the competitive environment, and managers should consider its influence when analyzing the five competitive forces and formulating business strategies. Once business strategies have been formulated, functional strategies for supporting them can be developed.

- New approaches to strategic thought emphasize innovation from within and strategic partnerships rather than acquiring skills and capabilities through mergers and acquisitions.

- Even the most creative strategies have no value if they cannot be translated into action. Execution is the most important and most difficult part of strategy. Managers put strategy into action by aligning all parts of the organization to be in congruence with the new strategy. Four areas that managers focus on for strategy execution are leadership, structural design, information and control systems, and human resources.

- Many organizations also pursue a separate global strategy. Managers can choose to use a globalization strategy, a multi-domestic strategy or a transnational strategy as the focus of global operations.

The earlier discussion on Primark and Matalan indicated how Primark had used superior strategy formulation and implementation to overtake the former leader in the UK value fashion retailing sector. It stayed focused on its core market, and managers implemented a carefully thought out customer-focused strategy. Matalan also stayed with its strategy of locating stores in second-tier shopping centres, but customers were no longer willing to drive the extra mile. Why should they, when Primark stores were located in prime locations along the high street?

John Hargreaves, the founder of Matalan, has now implemented a new strategy to reposition Matalan and generate new growth. He has frozen Matalan's expansion plans and launched a review of its property portfolio. The company will relocate unprofitable stores and could bring in third-party retailers to run concessions in excess store space. Hargreaves is keen to move away from the trend for quickly sourced, catwalk-influenced throwaway clothes that has seen rival discount retailers such as Primark take market share from Matalan. He will do this by reducing the number of clothing lines but increasing the stock of top sellers. In January 2008, Matalan unveiled its latest attempt to woo customers based on the enduring popularity of more mature celebrities such as Antony Worrall Thompson, Ainsley Harriott, Anthea Turner and Laurence Llewelyn-Bowen. The celebrity-branded areas, carrying a selection of the stars' endorsed homeware products, are intended to give the stores a more stylish feel. Business results at Matalan have improved since managers refocused on the core business and began taking careful steps to strategy implementation. However, it remains to be seen whether the company can regain a competitive edge and hold its own against Primark, which continues to change the rules of the game in value fashion retailing. In the past two years, Primark has taken over and reopened 41 former Littlewoods stores and opened a flagship store in Oxford Street. That sold more than one million items in its first ten days of trading. Revenues at Primark jumped 37 per cent from £1.17 billion to £1.6 billion in the year with operating profits up from £166 million to £200 million. The profit margin is a healthy 12.5 per cent. CEO George Weston is particularly pleased by Primark's move into Spain, where it will shortly add more stores to the existing two opened last year. This year Primark has even opened its first outlets in Germany

and Portugal. In the current recession Primark has been able to shrug off complaints from pressure groups, such as War on Want[75] about exploitation of low-waged workers overseas. It remains to be seen whether the low-cost model will need to adapt once the economy moves back out of recession.

DISCUSSION QUESTIONS

1 In 2006, High Street beauty products retailer The Body Shop agreed to be taken over by French cosmetics giant L'Oréal in a deal worth £652 million. Based on your knowledge and experience of the two brands, how would you define the core competencies of the two companies? Do you think the results so far show evidence of the synergy the dealmakers hoped for?

2 How might a corporate management team go about determining whether the company should diversify? What factors should they take into consideration? What kinds of information should they collect?

3 You are a middle-manager helping to implement a new corporate cost-cutting strategy, and you're meeting scepticism, resistance, and in some cases, outright hostility from your subordinates. In what ways might you or the company have been able to avoid this situation? Where do you go from here?

4 Perform a SWOT analysis for the college or university you attend. Do you think university administrators consider the same factors when devising their strategy?

5 Do you think the movement toward strategic partnerships is a passing phenomenon or here to stay? What skills would make a good manager in a partnership with another company? What skills would make a good manager operating in competition with another company?

6 Using Porter's competitive strategies, how would you evaluate the strategies of Amazon, Tesco and BMW Mini?

7 Walt Disney Company has four major strategic business units: movies (including Miramax and Touch-stone), theme parks, consumer products and television (ABC and cable). Place each of these SBUs on the BCG matrix based on your knowledge of them.

8 As an administrator for a medium-sized residential home for elderly residents, offering accommodation, meals and personal care, such as help with bathing and dressing, you and the board of directors have decided to change to a nursing home offering qualified nurses in constant attendance to look after the residents' medical needs as well. How would you go about implementing this strategy?

9 Game maker Electronic Arts was criticized as 'trying to buy innovation' in its bid to acquire Take Two Interactive, known primarily for the game Grand Theft Auto. Does it make sense for EA to offer more than $2 billion to buy Take Two when creating a new video game costs only $20 million? Why would EA ignore internal innovation to choose an acquisition strategy?

10 If you were the CEO of a global company, how might you determine whether a globalization, transnational, or multi-domestic strategy would work best for your enterprise? What factors would influence your decision?

11 Examine how the internet increases the bargaining power of consumers, one of Porter's five competitive forces. To what extent have you felt increased power as a consumer because of the internet? Give examples?

12 How might a corporate management team go about determining whether it should formulate a growth strategy or a stability strategy? What factors should they take into consideration? What kinds of information should they collect?

MANAGEMENT IN PRACTICE: EXPERIENTIAL EXERCISE

Developing Strategy for a Small Business

Instructions: Your instructor may ask you to do this exercise individually or as part of a group. Select a local business with which you (or group members) are familiar. Complete the following activities.

Activity 1 – Perform a SWOT analysis for the business':

Strengths.

Weaknesses.

Opportunities.

Threats.

Activity 2 – Write a statement of the business's current strategy.

Activity 3 – Decide on a goal you would like the business to achieve in two years, and write a statement of proposed strategy for achieving that goal.

Activity 4 – Write a statement describing how the proposed strategy will be implemented.

Activity 5 – What have you learned from this exercise?

MANAGEMENT IN PRACTICE: ETHICAL DILEMMA

The Spitzer Group

Irving Silberstein, marketing director for the Spitzer Group, a growing regional marketing and corporate communications firm, was hard at work on an exciting project. He was designing Spitzer's first word-of-mouth campaign for an important client, a manufacturer of beauty products.

In a matter of just a few years, word-of-mouth advertising campaigns morphed from a small fringe specialty to a mainstream marketing technique embraced by no less than consumer product giant Procter and Gamble (P&G). The basic idea was simple, really. You harnessed the power of existing social networks to sell your products and services. The place to start, Irving knew, was to take a close look at how P&G's in-house unit, Vocal-point, conducted its highly successful campaigns, both for its own products and those of its clients.

Because women were key purchasers of P&G consumer products, Vocalpoint focused on recruiting mothers with extensive social networks, participants known internally by the somewhat awkward term, *connectors*. The Vocalpoint webpage took care to emphasize that participants were members of an 'exclusive' community of moms who exerted significant influence on P&G and other major companies. Vocalpoint not only sent the women new product samples and solicited their opinions, but it

also carefully tailored its pitch to the group's interests and preoccupations so the women would want to tell their friends about a product. For example, it described a new dishwashing foam that was so much fun to use, kids would actually volunteer to clean up the kitchen, music to any mother's ears. P&G then furnished the mothers with coupons to hand out if they wished. It's all voluntary, P&G pointed out. According to a company press release issued shortly before Vocalpoint went national in early 2006, members 'are never obligated to do or say anything'.

One of the things Vocalpoint members weren't obligated to say, Irving knew, was that the women were essentially unpaid participants in a P&G-sponsored marketing programme. When asked about the policy, Vocalpoint CEO Steve Reed replied, 'We have a deeply held belief you don't tell the consumer what to say.' However, sceptical observers speculated that what the company really feared was that the women's credibility might be adversely affected if their Vocal-point affiliation were known. Non-disclosure really amounted to lying for financial gain, Vocalpoint's critics argued, and furthermore the whole campaign shamelessly exploited personal relationships for commercial purposes. Others thought the critics were making mountains out of molehills. P&G wasn't forbidding participants from disclosing their ties to Vocalpoint and P&G. And the fact that they weren't paid meant the women had no vested interest in endorsing the products.

So as Irving designs the word-of-mouth campaign for his agency's client, just how far should he emulate the company that even its detractors acknowledge as a master of the technique?

What Would You Do?

1 Don't require Spitzer 'connectors' to reveal their affiliation with the corporate word-of-mouth marketing campaign. They don't have to recommend a product they don't believe in.

2 Require that Spitzer participants reveal their ties to the corporate marketing programme right up front before they make a recommendation.

3 Instruct Spitzer participants to reveal their participation in the corporate marketing programme only if directly asked by the person they are talking to about the client's products.

SOURCES Robert Berner, 'I Sold It Through the Grapevine', *Business-Week* (May 29, 2006): 32–34; 'Savvy Moms Share Maternal Instincts; Vocalpoint Offers Online Moms the Opportunity to be a Valuable Resource to Their Communities', *Business Wire* (December 6, 2005); and 'Word of Mouth Marketing: To Tell or Not To Tell', *AdRants.com* (May 2006), www.adrants.com/2006/05/word-of-mouth-marketing-to-tell-or-not-to.php.

CASE FOR CRITICAL ANALYSIS 8.1

Associated Newspapers Ltd (ANL) – Metro & London Lite

Newspapers across the world, especially those in large metropolitan areas such as London, are facing tough times. A 2004 report from European Commission (EC) warned that readers are ageing and yet most papers have failed to find profitable online services 'to counter the threat of online news services and erosion of advertising income'. While display advertising has been slow to develop on the internet, the report says nearly all newspapers have recognized the growing competition for classified ads. Online advertising is forecast to grow faster than other forms of advertising, reaching €4.2 billion by 2006. At that level it would command around 15 per cent of all advertising revenue in some countries.

One newspaper group that is better prepared than most to meet this challenge is Associated Newspapers Limited (ANL) the management company for a number of major newspapers including the *Daily Mail*, *Mail on Sunday* and *Evening Standard*, which launched the *Metro* in March 1999 as a free, colour, weekday newspaper for London's commuters. It now has a circulation of over 1.1 million copies across the UK and is the world's largest free newspaper and the fourth biggest newspaper in the UK. The Metro is now available to commuters on their way to work in 16 cities around the UK including London, Manchester, Birmingham, Leeds, Sheffield, Newcastle, Leicester, Derby, Nottingham, Bristol,

Bath, Glasgow and Edinburgh covering a combined area with a population of more than 18 million. The paper's income is derived solely through advertising revenue.

The idea to launch the *Metro* came when top managers decided to try a new business-level strategy: focusing on celebrity news and more local coverage. Today the *Metro* aimed to appeal to younger people, aged 18 to 35, who do not currently read a newspaper, and expect to get their news for free. Steve Auckland, head of free newspapers division, at ANL thinks that only newspapers that have got a clear definition as to what their market is are the ones that will survive. He says: 'That's where *Metro* has been successful, it's a young, urban, travelling audience and it's fulfilling a need for that audience at that place and time. We don't want older readers and we don't want young kids. Online we know we are not going to break the news first but we can be quirkier and get a cult image with that market.'

Coverage of the sports, celebrity and entertainment industry has been bumped up significantly, and stories on serious matters have been scaled back, with managers asking for shorter, to-the-point stories rather than in-depth analyses. The scaled-back national and international coverage also makes room for more local and regional reporting. Steve Auckland, balks at any accusations of 'dumbing down'. 'It actually requires a lot of skill to produce short copy, to write four paragraphs instead of 12 and still capture the essence of a story', he says. 'Our free papers provide young people with something new and different: speedy news and bite-size information, which means they can keep up to speed with a minimum of fuss. That is a good service, and it is good journalism.'

Rupert Murdoch, head of rival newspaper group, News International, admitted in 2005 that the *Metro* was eating into sales of the *Sun*, the largest selling UK daily newspaper, and said he was watching the market with apprehension. Not surprisingly, in September 2006 News International decided to launch a rival free newspaper *thelondonpape*r with a promise to give Londoners a 'fresh perspective' on the news. ANL responded immediately by launching a second free paper called *London Lite* designed to be especially attractive to younger female readers, and features a wide range of lifestyle articles but less news and business news than the main paper.

Auckland and other managers believe the new business-level strategy at ANL has helped them find a profitable niche as the newspaper industry continues to grapple with how to remain relevant in a changing world where people have myriad sources of information and less time for reading in-depth stories in the daily paper.

Questions

1 What would the SWOT analysis look like for this company?

2 What role do you expect the internet to play in the newspaper industry? What are some ways that Associated Newspapers and News International could better use the internet to foster growth and/or increase profitability?

3 Which of Porter's competitive strategies would you recommend that Associated Newspapers follow in future? Why? Which of the strategies do you think would be least likely to succeed?

SOURCE The *Guardian*, 'Associated unveils Metro for women', November 8, 2004, http://www.guardian.co.uk/media/2004/nov/08/associatednewspapers.press and publishing; The *Guardian*, 'Murdoch worried as Metro eats into sales of the Sun', February 3, 2005, http://www. guardian.co.uk/media/2005/feb/03/sun.rupertmurdoch.

ENDNOTES

1. This questionnaire is adapted from Dorothy Marcic and Joe Seltzer, *Organizational Behaviour: Experiences and Cases* (Cincinnati, OH: SouthWestern, 1998), pp. 284–287; and William Miller, *Innovation Styles* (Global Creativity Corporation,1997).

2. The *Guardian*, 'Primark bucks high street trend with rise in sales', July 10, 2009, http://www.guardian.co.uk/business/2009/jul/10/primark-retail, BBC 'Primark sales defy retail gloom', July 9, 2009, http://news.bbc.co.uk/1/hi/business/8141671.stm; *Times*, 'Rich pickings for shoppers in Primark and Burberry' April 22, 2009, http://business.timesonline.co.uk/tol/business/industry_sectors/retailing/article6143980.ece

3. Telegraph online 'Matalan is praying for a chill wind to do good', November 1, 2005, http://www.telegraph.co.uk/finance/2925111/Matalan-is-praying-for-a-chill-wind-to-do-good.html.

4. 'The World's Most Innovative Companies', *Fast Company* (March 2008): 92–118.

5. The *Guardian* 'Ocado plans expansion after delivering first £1bn of sales' July 21, 2008, http://www.guardian.co.uk/business/2008/jul/21/supermarkets.retail?gusrc=rss&feed=business.

6. Janet Adamy, 'McDonald's Takes on a Weakened Starbucks; Food Giant to Install Specialty Coffee Bars', *The Wall Street Journal*, January 7, 2008.

7. Nanette Byrnes and Peter Burrows, 'Where Dell Went Wrong', *Business-Week* (February 19, 2007): 62–63; William M. Bulkeley, 'SofterView; Kodak Sharpens Digital Focus on Its Best Customers: Women', *The Wall Street Journal*, July 6, 2005.

8. Chet Miller and Laura B. Cardinal, 'Strategic Planning and Firm Performance: A Synthesis of More than Two Decades of Research', *Academy of Management Journal* 37, no. 6 (1994): 1649–1665.

9. Richard Tomlinson, 'L'Oréal's Global Makeover', *Fortune* (September 30, 2002): 141–146.

10. W. Chan Kim and Renee Mauborgne, *Blue Ocean Strategy*, (Harvard: Harvard Business Press, 2005). Blue ocean strategy is based on the view that market boundaries and industry structure are not given and can be reconstructed by the actions and beliefs of industry players.

11. Lucy Barratt, The *Guardian*, 'Blue ocean' thinking can create waves, February 2, 2009.

12. Renée Dye and Olivier Sibony, 'How to Improve Strategic Planning', *McKinsey Quarterly*, no. 3 (2007).

13. Keith H. Hammonds, 'Michael Porter's Big Ideas', *Fast Company* (March 2001): 150–156.

14. John E. Prescott, 'Environments as Moderators of the Relationship between Strategy and Performance', *Academy of Management Journal* 29 (1986): 329–346; John A. Pearce II and Richard B. Robinson, Jr., *Strategic*

Management: Strategy, Formulation, and Implementation, 2nd ed. (Homewood, IL: Irwin, 1985); and David J. Teece, 'Economic Analysis and Strategic Management', *California Management Review* 26 (Spring 1984): 87–110.

15. Adapted from Johnson, Scholes and Whittington, *Exploring Corporate Strategy,* 2005.

16. Jack Welch, 'It's All in the Sauce', excerpt from his book, *Winning,* in *Fortune* (April 18, 2005): 138–144; and Constantinos Markides, 'Strategic Innovation', *Sloan Management Review* (Spring 1997): 9–23.

17. Michael E. Porter, 'What Is Strategy?', *Harvard Business Review* (November–December 1996): 61–78.

18. Arthur A. Thompson, Jr. and A. J. Strickland III, *Strategic Management: Concepts and Cases,* 6th ed. (Homewood, IL: Irwin, 1992); and Briance Mascarenhas, Alok Baveja and Mamnoon Jamil, 'Dynamics of Core Competencies in Leading Multinational Companies', *California Management Review* 40, no. 4 (Summer 1998): 117–132.

19. Michael V. Copeland, 'Stitching Together an Apparel Power-house', *Business 2.0* (April 2005): 52–54.

20. Chris Woodyard, 'Big Dreams for Small Choppers Paid Off', *USA Today,* September 11, 2005, http://www.usatoday.com.

21. Joseph L. Bower and Thomas M. Hout. 'Fast-Cycle Capability for Competitive Power' *Harvard Business Review* (November–December 1988): 110–118.

22. Michael Goold and Andrew Campbell, 'Desperately Seeking Synergy', *Harvard Business Review* (September–October 1998): 131–143.

23. Elizabeth Olson, 'OMG! Cute Boys, Kissing Tips and Lots of Pics, As Magazines Find a Niche', *The New York Times,* May 28, 2007.

24. Kerry Capell, 'IKEA: How the Swedish Retailer Became a Global Cult Brand', *BusinessWeek* (November 14, 2005): 96–106.

25. The *Independent,* Andrew Gowers 'Pink'Un goes BlackBerry', 26 September 2005, http://www.independent.co.uk/news/media/andrew-gowers-pink-un-goes-blackberry-508450.html.

26. The *Guardian* 'Aldi's sales soar as it lures wealthier shoppers' January 13, 2009, http://www.guardian.co.uk/business/2009/jan/13/aldi-sales-recession; *Dail Mail,* 'Aldi now UK's fastest-growing food store' http://www.thisismoney.co.uk/markets/article.html?in_article_id=465929&in_page_id=3; *Business Week,* 'The Next Wal-Mart?', April 26, 2004 http://www.businessweek.com/magazine/content/04_17/b3880010.htm.

27. Milton Leontiades, *Strategies for Diversification and Change* (Boston: Little, Brown, 1980), p. 63 and Dan E. Schendel and Charles W. Hofer, eds, *Strategic Management: A New View of Business Policy and Planning* (Boston: Little, Brown, 1979), pp. 11–14.

28. Georgia Flight, 'Powerboating's New Powerhouse', *Business 2.0* (November 2005): 62–67.

29. Zubka website http://www.zubka.com/public.php/what/what_is; The *Guardian,* 'Zubka', July 30, 2007, http://www.guardian.co.uk/technology/2007/jul/30/zubka; 27 *Marketing Week,* 'Procter vs Unilever', May 24, 2007.

30. Alice Dragoon, 'A Travel Guide to Collaboration', *CIO* (November 15, 2004): 68–75.

31. Milton Leontiades, 'The Confusing Words of Business Policy', *Academy of Management Review* 7 (1982): 45–48.

32. Lawrence G. Hrebiniak and William F. Joyce, *Implementing Strategy* (New York: Macmillan, 1984).

33. Frederick W. Gluck, 'A Fresh Look at Strategic Management', *Journal of Business Strategy* 6 (Fall 1985): 4–19.

34. J. Lynn Lunsford, 'Going Up; United Technologies' Formula: A Powerful Lift from Elevators', *The Wall Street Journal,* July 2, 2003.

35. Thompson and Strickland, *Strategic Management;* and William L. Shanklin and John K. Ryans, Jr., 'Is the International Cash Cow Really a Prize Heifer?', *Business Horizons* 24 (1981): 10–16.

36. David Kirkpatrick, 'Facebook's Plan To Hook Up the World', *Fortune* (June 11, 2007): 127–130; Brad Stone, 'Facebook Expands Into MySpace's Territory', *The New York Times,* May 25, 2007; and Vauhini Vara, 'Facebook CEO Seeks Help as Site Suffers Growing Pains', *The Wall Street Journal,* March 5, 2008.

37. Vara, 'Facebook CEO Seeks Help'.

38. Diane Brady, 'The Immelt Revolution', *Business Week* (March 28, 2005): 64–73.

39. Example cited in Gareth R. Jones and Jennifer M. George, *Contemporary Management,* 4th ed. (Boston, MA: McGraw-Hill Irwin, 2006), p. 283.

40. Steve Lohr, 'Apple, a Success at Stores, Bets Big on Fifth Avenue', *The New York Times,* May 19, 2006; and Brent Schlender, 'How Big Can Apple Get?', *Fortune* (February 21, 2005): 66–76.

41. Michael E. Porter, 'The Five Competitive Forces That Shape Strategy', *Harvard Business Review* (January 2008): 79–93; Michael E. Porter, *Competitive Strategy* (New York: Free Press, 1980), pp. 36–46; Danny Miller, 'Relating Porter's Business Strategies to Environment and Structure: Analysis and Performance Implementations', *Academy of Management Journal* 31 (1988): 280–308; and Michael E. Porter, 'From Competitive Advantage to Corporate Strategy', *Harvard Business Review* (May–June 1987): 43–59.

42. Michael E. Porter, 'Strategy and the Internet', *Harvard Business Review* (March 2001): 63–78.

43. Tony Grundy, 'Rethinking and reinventing Michael Porter's five forces model calon', *Strategic Change,* 15 (2006): 213–229.

44. Andrew Park and Peter Burrows, 'Dell, the Conqueror', *BusinessWeek* (September 24, 2001): 92–102; and Thompson and Strickland, *Strategic Management.*

45. Fairtrade Foundation http://www.fairtrade.org.uk/producers/cacao/kuapa_kokoo_union.aspx.

46. Joshua Rosenbaum, 'Guitar Maker Looks for a New Key', *The Wall Street Journal,* February 11, 1998.

47. Nitin Nohria, William Joyce, and Bruce Roberson, 'What Really Works', *Harvard Business Review* (July 2003): 43–52.

48. This discussion is based on J. Bruce Harreld, Charles A. O'Reilly III and Michael L. Tushman, 'Dynamic Capabilities at IBM: Driving Strategy into Action', *California Management Review* 49, no. 4 (2007).

49. Diane Brady, 'The Immelt Revolution', *Business Week* (March 28, 2005): 64–73.

50. Harreld *et al.,* 'Dynamic Capabilities at IBM'.

51. Alice Dragoon, 'A Travel Guide to Collaboration', *CIO* (November 15, 2004): 68–75.

52. Don Tapscott, 'Rethinking Strategy in a Networked World', *Strategy & Business,* no. 24 (Third Quarter 2001): 34–41.

53. Kenichi Ohmae, 'Managing in a Borderless World', *Harvard Business Review* (May–June 1990): 152–161.

54. Theodore Levitt, 'The Globalization of Markets', *Harvard Business Review* (May–June 1983): 92–102.

55. Cesare Mainardi, Martin Salva, and Muir Sanderson, 'Label of Origin: Made on Earth', *strategy + business, no. 15* (Second Quarter, 1999).

56. Joanne Lipman, 'Marketers Turn Sour on Global Sales Pitch Harvard Guru Makes', *The Wall Street Journal*, May 12, 1988.

57. Michael E. Porter, 'Changing Patterns of International Competition', *California Management Review* 28 (Winter 1986): 40.

58. Mohanbir Sawhney and Sumant Mandal, 'What Kind of Global Organization Should You Build?', *Business 2.0* (May 2000): 213.

59. Based on Michael A. Hitt, R. Duane Ireland, and Robert E. Hoskisson, *Strategic Management: Competitiveness and Globalization* (St. Paul, MN: West, 1995), p. 238.

60. Anil K. Gupta and Vijay Govindarajan, 'Converting Global Presence into Global Competitive Advantage', *Academy of Management Executive* 15, no. 2 (2001): 45–56.

61. Thomas S. Bateman and Carl P. Zeithaml, *Management: Function and Strategy*, 2nd ed. (Homewood, IL: Irwin, 1993), p. 231.

62. Lawrence G. Hrebiniak, 'Obstacles to Effective Strategy Implementation', *Organizational Dynamics* 35, no. 1 (2006): 12–31; Eric M. Olson, Stanley F. Slater, and G. Tomas M. Hult, 'The Importance of Structure and Process to Strategy Implementation', *Business Horizons* 48 (2005): 47–54; L. J. Bourgeois III and David R. Brodwin, 'Strategic Implementation: Five Approaches to an Elusive Phenomenon', *Strategic Management Journal* 5 (1984): 241–264; Anil K. Gupta and V. Govindarajan, 'Business Unit Strategy, Managerial Characteristics, and Business Unit Effectiveness at Strategy Implementation', *Academy of Management Journal* (1984): 25–41; and Jeffrey G. Covin,

Dennis P. Slevin and Randall L. Schultz, 'Implementing Strategic Missions: Effective Strategic, Structural, and Tactical Choices', *Journal of Management Studies* 31, no. 4 (1994): 481–505.

63. Based on a statement by Louis Gerstner, quoted in Harreld *et al.*, 'Dynamic Capabilities at IBM'.

64. Olson, Slater, and Hult, 'The Importance of Structure and Process to Strategy Implementation'.

65. Jay R. Galbraith and Robert K. Kazanjian, *Strategy Implementation: Structure, Systems and Process*, 2nd ed. (St. Paul, MN: West, 1986); and Paul C. Nutt, 'Selecting Tactics to Implement Strategic Plans', *Strategic Management Journal* 10 (1989): 145–161.

66. Spencer E. Ante, 'The New Blue', *Business Week* (March 17, 2003): 80–88.

67. Survey results reported in Hrebiniak, 'Obstacles to Effective Strategy Implementation'.

68. Steve Hamm, 'Beyond Blue', *Business Week* (April 18, 2005): 68–76.

69. Gupta and Govindarajan, 'Business Unit Strategy'; and Bourgeois and Brodwin, 'Strategic Implementation'.

70. Obasi Akan, Richard S. Allen, Marilyn M. Helms and Samuel A. Spralls III, 'Critical Tactics for Implementing Porter's Generic Strategies', *Journal of Business Strategy* 27, no. 1 (2006): 43–53.

71. Nitin Nohria, William Joyce and Bruce Roberson, 'What Really Works', *Harvard Business Review* (July 2003): 43–52.

72. The *Guardian* '30000 jobs at risk as Woolworths teeters on the brink', November 22, 2008, http://www.guardian.co.uk/business/2008/nov/22/woolworths-retail-mk-one.

73. Akan *et al.*, 'Critical Tactics for Implementing Porter's Generic Strategies'.

74. Ibid.

75. War on Want, 'Sweatshops' protest hits Primark', June 23, 2008, http://www.waronwant.org/news/press-releases/16133-sweatshops-protest-hits-primark.

CHAPTER OUTLINE

LEARNING OBJECTIVES

After reading this chapter, you should be able to:

1. Explain why decision-making is an important component of good management.

2. Discuss the difference between programmed and non-programmed decisions and the decision characteristics of certainty and uncertainty.

3. Describe the ideal, rational model of decision-making and the political model of decision-making.

4. Consider the process by which managers actually make decisions in the real world.

5. Identify the six steps used in managerial decision-making.

6. Describe four personal decision styles used by managers, and explain the biases that frequently cause managers to make bad decisions.

7. Examine and explain techniques for innovative group decision-making.

CHAPTER 9

MANAGERIAL DECISION-MAKING

Managers often are referred to as *decision-makers*, and every organization grows, prospers, or fails as a result of decisions by its managers. Many manager decisions are strategic, such as whether to build a new factory, move into a new line of business or sell off a division. Yet managers also make decisions about every other aspect of an organization, including structure, control systems, responses to the environment and human resources. Managers scout for problems, make decisions for solving them, and monitor the consequences to see whether additional decisions are required. Good decision-making is a vital part of good management because decisions determine how the organization solves its problems, allocates resources and accomplishes its goals.

Manager's Challenge

Marjorie Yang had to contemplate the biggest decision of her career – perhaps the biggest decision in her company's history. As chairperson and CEO of Esquel Group, a privately owned textile manufacturer based in Hong Kong, that makes clothes for top brands such as Tommy Hilfiger, Hugo Boss, Brooks Brothers, Abercrombie & Fitch, Nike, Lands' End and Muji, and major retailers such as Marks & Spencer, Nordstrom and Jusco, Yang had the ultimate say in whether the company invested $150 million in a brand-new fabric mill that would be the best mill in China and could make Esquel the top shirt maker in the world. Like most textile manufacturers, Esquel was going through a rough period. With the end of US textile quotas in early 2005, world capacity was going up, prices going down, and profit margins squeezed in the middle. Esquel's strategy for years had been to go for top quality, first aiming to achieve Japanese quality in the 1980s and then shooting to reach Italian quality, the best in the world.

Esquel is vertically integrated growing its own high-quality cotton in western China, and Yang figured the new factory could help them make the most of it. With

How Do You Make Decisions?

Most of us make decisions automatically and without realizing that people have diverse decision-making behaviours, which they bring to management positions. Think back to how you make decisions in your personal, student, or work life, especially where other people are involved. Please answer whether each of the following items is Mostly True or Mostly False for you.

		Mostly True	Mostly False
1	I like to decide quickly and move on to the next thing.	☐	☐
2	I would use my authority to make the decision if certain I was right.	☐	☐
3	I appreciate decisiveness.	☐	☐
4	There is usually one correct solution to a problem.	☐	☐
5	I identify everyone who needs to be involved in the decision.	☐	☐
6	I explicitly seek conflicting perspectives.	☐	☐
7	I use discussion strategies to reach a solution.	☐	☐
8	I look for different meanings when faced with a great deal of data.	☐	☐
9	I take time to reason things through and use systematic logic.	☐	☐

SCORING AND INTERPRETATION   All nine items in the list reflect appropriate decision-making behaviour, but items 1–4 are more typical of new managers. Items 5–8 are typical of successful senior manager decision-making. Item 9 is considered part of good decision-making at all levels. If you checked Mostly True for three or four of items 1–4 and 9, consider yourself typical of a new manager. If you checked Mostly True for three or four of items 5–8 and 9, you are using behaviour consistent with top managers. If you checked a similar number of both sets of items, your behaviour is probably flexible and balanced.

New managers typically use a different decision behaviour than seasoned executives. The decision behaviour of a successful CEO may be almost the opposite of a first-level supervisor. The difference is due partly to the types of decisions and partly to learning what works at each level. New managers often start out with a more directive, decisive, command-oriented behaviour and gradually move toward more openness, diversity of viewpoints and interactions with others as they move up the hierarchy.[1]

the end of quotas, she reasoned that more competitors would be investing in the low-quality end of the market; thus, if Esquel could be the first company in China to reach the pinnacle of quality, it would have a huge advantage with higher profit margins and less competition. Yet doing the deal now was risky. At least half of the money would have to be borrowed, and profits were sure to suffer in the short run. Although most of Esquel's top executives agreed that the idea was good, at least half of them believed building the factory now was too risky and that Yang should wait a couple of years until the industry settled down and trends are clearer.[2]

TAKE A MOMENT

If you were Marjorie Yang, how would you have decided whether to wait or move ahead now with the $150 million factory? What decision would you have made and why?

Every organization grows, prospers, or fails as a result of decisions by its managers, and top executives like Marjorie Yang make difficult decisions every day. Although many of their important decisions are strategic, such as Yang's decision whether to build a new factory. Managers also make decisions about every other aspect of an organization, including structure, control systems, responses to the environment and human resources. Managers scout for problems, make decisions for solving them, and monitor the consequences to see whether additional decisions are required. Good decision-making is a vital part of good management, because decisions determine how the organization solves its problems, allocates resources, and accomplishes its goals.

The business world is full of evidence of both good and bad decisions. Apple, which seemed all but dead in the mid-1990s, became the world's most admired company in 2008 based on decisions made by CEO Steve Jobs and other top managers. No longer just a maker of computers, Apple is now in the music player business, the cell phone business, and the retailing business, among others. iTunes is now the second-largest seller of music in the US behind Wal-Mart.[3] Cadillac's sales made a comeback after managers ditched stuffy golf and yachting sponsorships and instead tied in with top Hollywood movies.[4] On the other hand, Decca Records' decision in the 1960s to reject a chance to sign an unknown band from Liverpool named The Beatles because they thought guitar based music was going out of fashion, and Coca-Cola's attempt to change the formula and rebrand it 'New Coke', left their company executives looking as if they didn't know what they were doing. Or consider the decision of Timex managers to replace the classic tag line, 'It takes a licking and keeps on ticking', with the bland 'Life is ticking'. The desire to modernize their company's image led Timex managers to ditch one of the most recognizable advertising slogans in the world in favour of a lame and rather depressing new one.[5] Decision-making is not easy. It must be done amid ever-changing factors, unclear information, and conflicting points of view.

Chapters 7 and 8 described strategic planning. This chapter explores the decision process that underlies strategic planning. Plans and strategies are arrived at through decision-making; the better the decision-making, the better the strategic planning. First, we examine decision characteristics. Then we look at decision-making models and the steps executives should take when making important decisions. The chapter also explores some biases that can cause managers to make bad decisions. Finally, we examine some techniques for innovative group decision-making.

Types of Decisions and Problems

A **decision** is a choice made from available alternatives. For example, an accounting manager's selection among Colin, Tasha, and Carlos for the position of junior auditor is a decision. Many people assume that making a choice is the major part of decision-making, but it is only a part.

Decision-making is the process of identifying problems and opportunities and then resolving them. Decision-making involves effort both before and after the actual choice. Thus, the decision as to whether to select Colin, Tasha or Carlos requires the accounting manager to ascertain whether a new junior auditor is needed, determine the availability of potential job candidates, interview candidates to acquire necessary information, select one candidate, and follow up with the socialization of the new employee into the organization to ensure the decision's success.

Decision
A choice made from available alternatives.

Decision-making
The process of identifying problems and opportunities and then resolving them.

Programmed decision
A decision made in response to a situation that has occurred often enough to enable decision rules to be developed and applied in the future.

Non-programmed decision
A decision made in response to a situation that is unique, is poorly defined and largely unstructured, and has important consequences for the organization.

Programmed and Non-Programmed Decisions

Management decisions typically fall into one of two categories: programmed and non-programmed. **Programmed decisions** involve situations that have occurred often enough to enable decision rules to be developed and applied in the future.[6] Programmed decisions are made in response to recurring organizational problems. The decision to reorder paper and other office supplies when inventories drop to a certain level is a programmed decision. Other programmed decisions concern the types of skills required to fill certain jobs, the reorder point for manufacturing inventory, exception reporting for expenditures 10 per cent or more over budget, and selection of freight routes for product deliveries. Once managers formulate decision rules, subordinates and others can make the decision, freeing managers for other tasks.

TAKE A MOMENT   Go to the Ethical Dilemma on page 335 that pertains to making non-programmed decisions.

© JEWEL SAMAD/AFP/GETTY IMAGES

CONCEPT CONNECTION In the entertainment industry, many organizations are prepared to take a high degree of risk involved in non-programmed decisions For instance, the BBC recognized that employing controversial radio presenters Russell Brand and Jonathon Ross on Radio 2 was inherently risky as they were likely at some stage to say something which would generate adverse publicity for the Corporation, but equally they were likely to attract a younger audience who otherwise wouldn't be interested in the station. However, after a number of listener complaints, the Director-General eventually had to dismiss Brand and suspend Ross for a period of time.[7]

Non-programmed decisions are made in response to situations that are unique, are poorly defined and largely unstructured, and have important consequences for the organization. Many non-programmed decisions involve strategic planning because uncertainty is great and decisions are complex. Decisions to build a new factory, develop a new product or service, enter a new geographical market, or relocate headquarters to another city are all non-programmed decisions. One good example of a non-programmed decision is Exxon-Mobil's decision to form a consortium to drill for oil in Siberia. One of the largest foreign investments in Russia, the consortium committed $4.5 billion before pumping the first barrel and expects a total capital cost of $12 billion-plus. The venture could produce 250 000 barrels a day, about 10 per cent of ExxonMobil's global production. But if things go wrong, the oil giant will take a crippling hit. For instance, it has recently seen its rivals Royal Dutch Shell and BP both experience financial problems after being heavily censured by the Russian Government.

Facing Certainty and Uncertainty

One primary difference between programmed and non-programmed decisions relates to the degree of certainty or uncertainty that managers deal with in making the decision. In a perfect world, managers would have all the information necessary for making decisions. In reality, however, some things are unknowable; thus, some decisions will fail to solve the problem or attain the desired outcome. Managers try to obtain information about decision alternatives that will reduce decision uncertainty. Every decision situation can be organized on a scale according to the availability of information and the possibility of failure. The four positions on the scale are certainty, risk, uncertainty and ambiguity, as illustrated in Exhibit 9.1. Whereas programmed decisions can be made in situations involving certainty, many situations that managers deal with every day involve at least some degree of uncertainty and require non-programmed decision-making.

Exhibit 9.1 Conditions That Affect the Possibility of Decision Failure

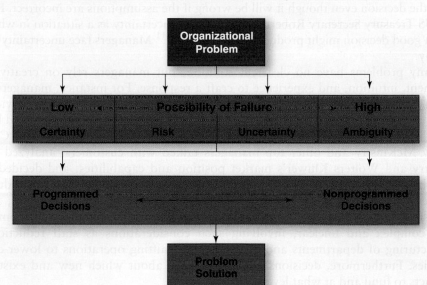

Certainty

Certainty means that all the information the decision-maker needs is fully available.[8] Managers have information on operating conditions, resource costs or constraints, and each course of action and possible outcome. For example, if a company considers a £10 000 investment in new equipment that it knows for certain will yield £4000 in cost savings per year over the next five years, managers can calculate a before-tax rate of return of about 40 per cent. If managers compare this investment with one that will yield only £3000 per year in cost savings, they can confidently select the 40 per cent return. However, few decisions are certain in the real world. Most contain risk or uncertainty.

Risk

Risk means that a decision has clear-cut goals and that good information is available, but the future outcomes associated with each alternative are subject to chance. However, enough information is available to allow the probability of a successful outcome for each alternative to be estimated.[9] Statistical analysis might be used to calculate the probabilities of success or failure. The measure of risk captures the possibility that future events will render the alternative unsuccessful. For example, to make restaurant location decisions, McDonald's can analyze potential customer demographics, traffic patterns, supply logistics, and the local competition and come up with reasonably good forecasts of how successful a restaurant will be in each possible location.[10]

Uncertainty

Uncertainty means that managers know which goals they wish to achieve, but information about alternatives and future events is incomplete. Factors that may affect a decision, such as price, production costs, volume or future interest rates, are difficult

Certainty
The situation in which all the information the decision-maker needs is fully available.

Risk
A situation in which a decision has clear-cut goals and good information is available, but the future outcomes associated with each alternative are subject to chance.

Uncertainty
The situation that occurs when managers know which goals they wish to achieve, but information about alternatives and future events is incomplete.

to analyze and predict. Managers may have to make assumptions from which to forge the decision even though it will be wrong if the assumptions are incorrect. Former US Treasury Secretary Robert Rubin defined uncertainty as a situation in which even a good decision might produce a bad outcome.[11] Managers face uncertainty every day.

Many problems have no clear-cut solution, but managers rely on creativity, judgment, intuition, and experience to craft a response. For instance, managers at Dutch-based company Wolters Kluwer, a leader in online information services, faced uncertainty as they considered ways to spark growth. The company had historically grown through acquisition, but that strategy had reached its limit. CEO Nancy McKinstry and other top managers talked with customers, analyzed the industry and Wolters Kluwer's market position and capabilities, and decided to shift the company toward growing through internal development of new products and services. Wolters Kluwer didn't have a track record in internal growth, and analysts were sceptical. Decisions about how to finance the internal development were complex and unclear, involving such considerations as staff reductions, restructuring of departments and divisions, and shifting operations to lower-cost facilities. Furthermore, decisions had to be made about which new and existing products to fund and at what levels.[12]

TAKE A MOMENT   As a new manager, consider the degree of risk, uncertainty or ambiguity in a specific decision you face. Develop decision rules for programmed decisions and let other people handle the decisions. Save your time and energy for coping with complex, non-programmed decisions.

Ambiguity and Conflict

Ambiguity
A condition in which the goals to be achieved or the problem to be solved is unclear, alternatives are difficult to define and information about outcomes is unavailable.

Ambiguity is by far the most difficult decision situation. Ambiguity means that the goals to be achieved or the problem to be solved is unclear, alternatives are difficult to define and information about outcomes is unavailable.[13] Ambiguity is what students would feel if an instructor created student groups, told each group to complete a project, but gave the groups no topic, direction or guidelines whatsoever. In some situations, managers involved in a decision create ambiguity because they see things differently and disagree about what they want. Managers in different departments often have different priorities and goals for the decision, which can lead to conflicts over decision alternatives.

A highly ambiguous situation can create what is sometimes called a *wicked decision problem*. Wicked decisions are associated with conflicts over goals and decision alternatives, rapidly changing circumstances, fuzzy information, and unclear links among decision elements.[14] Sometimes managers will come up with a 'solution' only to realize that they hadn't clearly defined the real problem to begin with.[15] When managers at Ford Motor Company and Firestone confronted the problem of tyres used on the Ford Explorer coming apart on the road, causing deadly blowouts and rollovers, just defining the problem and whether the tyre itself or the design of the Explorer was at fault was the first hurdle. Information was fuzzy and fast-changing, and managers were in conflict over how to handle the problem. Neither side dealt effectively with this decision situation and the reputations of both companies suffered as a result. Fortunately, most decisions are not characterized by ambiguity. But when they are, managers must conjure up goals and develop reasonable scenarios in the absence of information.

Decision-Making Models

The approach managers use to make decisions usually falls into one of three types – the classical model, the administrative model or the political model. The choice of model depends on the manager's personal preference, whether the decision is programmed or non-programmed, and the degree of uncertainty associated with the decision.

The Ideal, Rational Model

The classical model of decision-making is based on rational economic assumptions and manager beliefs about what ideal decision-making should be. This model has arisen within the management literature because managers are expected to make decisions that are economically sensible and in the organization's best economic interests. The four assumptions underlying this model are as follows:

1 The decision-maker operates to accomplish goals that are known and agreed on. Problems are precisely formulated and defined.

2 The decision-maker strives for conditions of certainty, gathering complete information. All alternatives and the potential results of each are calculated.

3 Criteria for evaluating alternatives are known. The decision-maker selects the alternative that will maximize the economic return to the organization.

4 The decision-maker is rational and uses logic to assign values, order preferences, evaluate alternatives and make the decision that will maximize the attainment of organizational goals.

Classical model
A decision-making model based on the assumption that managers should make logical decisions that will be in the organization's best economic interests.

The classical model of decision-making is considered to be **normative**, which means it defines how a decision-maker *should* make decisions. It does not describe how managers actually make decisions so much as it provides guidelines on how to reach an ideal outcome for the organization. The ideal, rational approach of the classical model is often unattainable by real people in real organizations, but the model has value because it helps decision-makers be more rational and not rely entirely on personal preference in making decisions.

The classical model is most useful when applied to programmed decisions and to decisions characterized by certainty or risk because relevant information is available and probabilities can be calculated. For example, new analytical software programs automate many programmed decisions, such as freezing the account of a customer who has failed to make payments, determining the mobile phone service plan that is most appropriate for a particular customer, or sorting insurance claims so that cases are handled most efficiently.[16] Airlines use automated systems to optimize seat pricing, flight scheduling, and crew assignment decisions. Retailers such as Carrefour, Tesco and Wal-Mart use software programs to analyze sales data and decide when, where, and how much to mark down prices. Many companies use systems that capture information about customers to help managers evaluate risks and make credit decisions.[17]

The growth of quantitative decision techniques that use computers has expanded the use of the classical approach. Quantitative techniques include such things as decision trees, payoff matrices, break-even analysis, linear programming, forecasting and operations research models. Low cost airlines such as easyJet, Ryanair and Southwest use quantitative models to help retain their position as the industry's low-cost leaders.

Normative
An approach that defines how a decision-maker should make decisions and provides guidelines for reaching an ideal outcome for the organization.

⊙ INNOVATIVE WAY

Southwest Airlines

Southwest Airlines is often credited with pioneering the low cost short haul model in the airline industry. It's wacky, people-oriented culture has often been cited as a key factor in the company's success. But managers point out that keeping a hawk's eye on costs is just as much a part of the culture as silliness and fun.

One way managers keep a lid on costs is by applying technology to support decision-making. Consider the use of a new breed of simulation software to help make decisions about the airline's freight operations. BiosGroup, a joint venture between Santa Fe Institute biologist Stuart Kauffman and the consulting firm Cap Gemini Ernst & Young, uses adaptive, agent-based computer modelling to help companies solve complex operations problems. For the Southwest project, the computer simulation model represented individual baggage handlers and other employees; the model was created to see how thousands of individual day-to-day decisions and interactions determined the behaviour of the airline's overall freight operation.

A BiosGroup team spent many hours interviewing all the employees whose jobs related to freight handling. Then, they programmed the computer to simulate the people in the freight house who accepted a customer's package, those who figured out which flight the package should go on, those on the ramp who were loading the planes, and so forth. When the computer ran a simulation of a week's worth of freight operations, various aspects of operations were measured – such as how many times employees had to load and unload cargo or how often freight had to be stored overnight. The simulation indicated that, rather than unloading cargo from incoming flights and putting it on the next direct flight to its destination, Southwest would be better off to just let the freight take the long way around. Paradoxically, this approach turned out to usually get the freight to its destination faster and saved the time and cost of unloading and reloading.

Southwest managers lost no time in implementing the decision to change the freight handling system. By applying technology to find a more efficient way of doing things, Southwest is saving an estimated $10 million over five years.[18]

Administrative model
A decision-making model that describes how managers actually make decisions in situations characterized by non-programmed decisions, uncertainty, and ambiguity.

Descriptive
An approach that describes how managers actually make decisions rather than how they should make decisions according to a theoretical ideal.

Bounded rationality
The concept that people have the time and cognitive ability to process only a limited amount of information on which to base decisions.

Satisficing
To choose the first solution alternative that satisfies minimal decision criteria, regardless of whether better solutions are presumed to exist.

How Managers Actually Make Decisions

Another approach to decision-making, called the **administrative model**, is considered to be **descriptive**, meaning that it describes how managers actually make decisions in complex situations rather than dictating how they *should* make decisions according to a theoretical ideal. The administrative model recognizes the human and environmental limitations that affect the degree to which managers can pursue a rational decision-making process. In difficult situations, such as those characterized by non-programmed decisions, uncertainty and ambiguity, managers are typically unable to make economically rational decisions even if they want to.[19]

Bounded Rationality and Satisficing

The administrative model of decision-making is based on the work of Herbert A. Simon. Simon proposed two concepts that were instrumental in shaping the administrative model: bounded rationality and satisficing. **Bounded rationality** means that people have limits, or boundaries, on how rational they can be. The organization is incredibly complex, and managers have the time and ability to process only a limited amount of information with which to make decisions.[20] Because managers do not have the time or cognitive ability to process complete information about complex decisions, they must satisfice. **Satisficing** means that decision-makers choose the first

As a new manager, choose the right decision approach. Use the classical model when problems are clear-cut, goals are agreed on, and clear information is available. For the classical model, use analytical procedures, including new software programs, to calculate the potential results of each alternative. When goals are vague or conflicting, decision time is limited and information is unclear, use bounded rationality, satisficing and intuition for decision-making.

solution alternative that satisfies minimal decision criteria. Rather than pursuing all alternatives to identify the single solution that will maximize economic returns, managers will opt for the first solution that appears to solve the problem, even if better solutions are presumed to exist. The decision-maker cannot justify the time and expense of obtaining complete information.[21]

Managers sometimes generate alternatives for complex problems only until they find one they believe will work. For example, several years ago, then-CEO William Smithburg of Quaker Oats attempted to thwart takeover attempts but had limited options. He satisficed with a quick decision to acquire Snapple, thinking he could use the debt acquired in the deal to discourage a takeover. The acquisition had the potential to solve the problem at hand; thus, Smithburg looked no further for possibly better alternatives It has subsequently been claimed that the decision to purchase Snapple, which Quaker sold on two years later, cost somewhere between $1–$1.5 billion in lost profits. Smithsburg resigned shortly after the Snapple sale, and PepsiCo then acquired Quaker itself in December 2000.[22]

The administrative model relies on assumptions different from those of the classical model and focuses on organizational factors that influence individual decisions. According to the administrative model:

1 Managers are unaware of problems or opportunities that exist in the organization.

2 Rational procedures are not always used, and, when they are, they are confined to a simplistic view of the problem that does not capture the complexity of real organizational events.

3 Managers' searches for alternatives are limited because of human, information and resource constraints.

4 Most managers settle for a satisficing rather than a maximizing solution, partly because they have limited information and partly because they have only vague criteria for what constitutes a maximizing solution.

Intuition

Another aspect of administrative decision-making is intuition. **Intuition** represents a quick apprehension of a decision situation based on past experience but without conscious thought.[23] Intuitive decision-making is not arbitrary or irrational because it is based on years of practice and hands-on experience that enable managers to quickly identify solutions without going through painstaking computations. In today's fast-paced business environment, intuition plays an increasingly important role in decision-making. A survey of managers conducted by Christian and Timbers found that nearly half of executives say they rely more on intuition than on rational analysis to run their companies.[24]

© ART SHAY/TIME LIFE PICTURES/GETTY IMAGES

CONCEPT CONNECTION
Howard Shultz turned Starbucks into a household name by following his intuition that the leisurely *caffe* model he observed in Italy would work in the US. Ray Kroc, the founder of the McDonald's chain, has said that he followed his instinct when deciding to borrow $2.7 million in 1960, against his lawyer's advice, to buy out the fast-food franchise that he had started. Sir Richard Branson, who's used his Virgin brand to launch everything from a record company to an airline to a soft drink, insists that he's never been guided by mere business logic and analysis. 'I've always done everything by intuition and gut feeling, and almost never used accountants to decide if I should start a new business', he says.[25]

Intuition
The immediate comprehension of a decision situation based on past experience but without conscious thought.

Psychologists and neuroscientists have studied how people make good decisions using their intuition under extreme time pressure and uncertainty.[26] Good intuitive decision-making is based on an ability to recognize patterns at lightning speed. When people have a depth of experience and knowledge in a particular area, the right decision often comes quickly and effortlessly as a recognition of information that has been largely forgotten by the conscious mind. For example, fire-fighters make decisions by recognizing what is typical or abnormal about a fire, based on their experiences. Similarly, in the business world, managers continuously perceive and process information that they may not consciously be aware of, and their base of knowledge and experience helps them make decisions that may be characterized by uncertainty and ambiguity.

However, intuitive decisions don't always work out, and managers should take care to apply intuition under the right circumstances and in the right way rather than considering it a magical way to make important decisions.[27] Managers may walk a fine line between two extremes: on the one hand, making arbitrary decisions without careful study; and on the other, relying obsessively on rational analysis. Richard Branson is quick to acknowledge that launching Virgin Cola to try and compete with Coke and Pepsi suggests that he doesn't always get every decision right. Overall, one approach is not better than the other, and managers need to take a balanced approach by considering both rationality and intuition as important components of effective decision-making.[28]

TAKE A MOMENT   Do you tend to analyze things or rely on gut feelings when it comes to making an important decision? Complete the New Manager Self-Test opposite to find out your predominant approach.

Political Model

The third model of decision-making is useful for making non-programmed decisions when conditions are uncertain, information is limited, and there are manager conflicts about what goals to pursue or what course of action to take. Most organizational decisions involve many managers who are pursuing different goals, and they have to talk with one another to share information and reach an agreement. Managers often engage in coalition building for making complex organizational decisions. A coalition is an informal alliance among managers who support a specific goal. *Coalition building* is the process of forming alliances among managers. In other words, a manager who supports a specific alternative, such as increasing the corporation's growth by acquiring another company, talks informally to other executives and tries to persuade them to support the decision. Without a coalition, a powerful individual or group could derail the decision-making process. Coalition building gives several managers an opportunity to contribute to decision-making, enhancing their commitment to the alternative that is ultimately adopted.[29]

The political model closely resembles the real environment in which most managers and decision-makers operate. For example, interviews with CEOs in high-tech industries found that they strived to use some type of rational process in making decisions, but the way they actually decided things was through a complex interaction with other managers, subordinates, environmental factors and organizational events.[30] Decisions are complex and involve many people, information is often ambiguous, and

Coalition
An informal alliance among managers who support a specific goal.

 NEW MANAGER SELF-TEST

Making Important Decisions

How do you make important personal decisions? To find out, think about a time when you made an important career decision or made a large purchase or investment. To what extent do each of the words below describe how you reached the final decision? Please tick five words below that best describe how you made your final choice.

1	Logic	☐
2	Inner knowing	☐
3	Data	☐
4	Felt sense	☐
5	Facts	☐
6	Instincts	☐
7	Concepts	☐
8	Hunch	☐
9	Reason	☐
10	Feelings	☐

SCORING AND INTERPRETATION The odd-numbered items pertain to a linear decision style and the even-numbered items pertain to a non-linear decision approach. Linear means using logical *rationality* to make decisions; non-linear means to use primarily *intuition* to make decisions. Of the five words you chose, how many represent rationality versus intuition? If all five words are either linear or non-linear, then that is clearly your dominant decision approach. If four words are either linear or non-linear, then that approach would be considered your preference. Rationality approach means a preference for the *rational model* of decision-making as described in the text. Intuition approach suggests a preference for the *satisficing* and *intuition* models.

SOURCE Charles M. Vance, Kevin S. Groves, Yongsun Paik and Herb Kindler, 'Understanding and Measuring Linear-Non-linear Thinking Style for Enhanced Management Education and Professional Practice', *Academy of Management Learning & Education* 6, no. 2 (2007): 167–185.

disagreement and conflict over problems and solutions are normal. The political model begins with four basic assumptions:

1 Organizations are made up of groups with diverse interests, goals, and values. Managers disagree about problem priorities and may not understand or share the goals and interests of other managers.

2 Information is ambiguous and incomplete. The attempt to be rational is limited by the complexity of many problems as well as personal and organizational constraints.

3 Managers do not have the time, resources, or mental capacity to identify all dimensions of the problem and process all relevant information. Managers talk to each other and exchange viewpoints to gather information and reduce ambiguity.

4 Managers engage in the push and pull of debate to decide goals and discuss alternatives. Decisions are the result of bargaining and discussion among coalition members.

Exhibit 9.2 Characteristics of Classical, Administrative and Political Decision-Making Models

Classical Model	Administrative Model	Political Model
Clear-cut problem and goals	Vague problem and goals	Pluralistic; conflicting goals
Condition of certainty	Condition of uncertainty	Condition of uncertainty/ambiguity
Full information about alternatives and their outcomes	Limited information about alternatives and their outcomes	Inconsistent viewpoints; ambiguous information
Rational choice by individual for maximizing outcomes	Satisficing choice for resolving problem using intuition	Bargaining and discussion among coalition members

An example of the political model was when Zhang Ruimin, CEO of the Chinese electronics company, Haier Group, built a coalition to support the development of an industrial park to enable Haier to expand its product range from refrigerators to washing machines, air conditioners and other home appliances. Opposition to the expansion was strong, but Zhang talked with other executives and formed a coalition that supported the move as the best way to position Haier in anticipation of a major expansion in the Chinese domestic market, as well as launch itself internationally. The decision proved to be a turning point, enabling Haier today to have become the world's fourth largest white goods manufacturer.[31]

The key dimensions of the classical, administrative, and political models are listed in Exhibit 9.2. Research into decision-making procedures found rational, classical procedures to be associated with high performance for organizations in stable environments. However, administrative and political decision-making procedures and intuition have been associated with high performance in unstable environments in which decisions must be made rapidly and under more difficult conditions.[32]

TAKE A MOMENT   As a new manager, use your political skills to reach a decision in the midst of disagreement about goals or problem solutions. Talk with other managers or employees and negotiate to gain support for the goal or solution you favour. Learn to compromise and to support others when appropriate.

Decision-Making Steps

Whether a decision is programmed or non-programmed and regardless of managers' choice of the classical, administrative, or political model of decision-making, six steps typically are associated with effective decision processes. These steps are summarized in Exhibit 9.3.

Exhibit 9.3 Six Steps in the Managerial Decision-Making Process

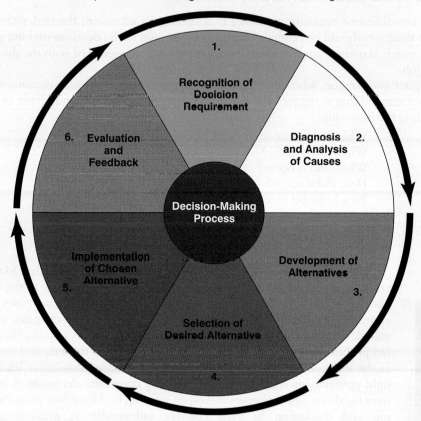

Recognition of Decision Requirement

Managers confront a decision requirement in the form of either a problem or an opportunity. A **problem** occurs when organizational accomplishment is less than established goals. Some aspect of performance is unsatisfactory. An **opportunity** exists when managers see potential accomplishment that exceeds specified current goals. Managers see the possibility of enhancing performance beyond current levels.

Awareness of a problem or opportunity is the first step in the decision sequence and requires surveillance of the internal and external environment for issues that merit executive attention.[33] This process resembles the military concept of gathering intelligence. Managers scan the world around them to determine whether the organization is satisfactorily progressing toward its goals.

Some information comes from periodic financial reports, performance reports, and other sources that are designed to discover problems before they become too serious. Managers also take advantage of informal sources. They talk to other managers, gather opinions on how things are going, and seek advice on which problems should be tackled or which opportunities embraced.[34] Recognizing decision requirements is difficult because it often means integrating bits and pieces of information in novel ways. For example, the failure of Indian intelligence leaders to recognize the imminent terrorist threat prior to the November 2008 attacks on the Oberoi Trident and Taj Mahal Hotels in Mumbai, has been attributed partly to the lack of systems that could help leaders put together myriad snippets of information that pointed to the likelihood of an attack.

Problem
A situation in which organizational accomplishments have failed to meet established goals.

Opportunity
A situation in which managers see potential organizational accomplishments that exceed current goals.

Diagnosis and Analysis of Causes

Diagnosis
The step in the decision-making process in which managers analyze underlying causal factors associated with the decision situation.

Once a problem or opportunity comes to a manager's attention, the understanding of the situation should be refined. Diagnosis is the step in the decision-making process in which managers analyze underlying causal factors associated with the decision situation.

Kepner and Tregoe, who conducted extensive studies of manager decision-making, recommend that managers ask a series of questions to specify underlying causes, including the following:

- What is the state of disequilibrium affecting us?
- When did it occur?
- Where did it occur?
- How did it occur?
- To whom did it occur?
- What is the urgency of the problem?
- What is the interconnectedness of events?
- What result came from which activity?[35]

Such questions help specify what actually happened and why. Managers at Avon are struggling to diagnose the underlying factors in the company's recent troubles. After six straight years of growing sales and earnings, revenues sagged, overhead spiked and the stock price plummeted. CEO Andrea Jung and other top managers are examining the myriad problems facing Avon, tracing the pattern of the decline, and looking at the interconnectedness of issues such as changing consumer interests, tight government regulations in developing countries, decreases in incentives for direct sales representatives, an approach of handling manufacturing and marketing in each country independently, preventing the company from achieving economies of scale, and weak internal communications that allowed problems to go unnoticed.[36]

© LOURENS SMAK/ALAMY

CONCEPT CONNECTION
When Unilever, the Anglo-Dutch blue-chip company, was forced to issue the first profit warning from its Rotterdam headquarters in its 77-year history, senior management immediately set about diagnosing the cause. As the CEO at the time, Patrick Cescau, explained, it was quite simple: excessive growth. "All those targets prevented us from adapting to changing circumstances and a difficult environment." Diagnosing the cause "liberated" the company, allowing managers to reassess their environments and proceed with a shared sense of purpose built around an internal focus on "One Unilever".

Development of Alternatives

The next stage is to generate possible alternative solutions that will respond to the needs of the situation and correct the underlying causes.

For a programmed decision, feasible alternatives are easy to identify and in fact usually are already available within the organization's rules and procedures. Non-programmed decisions, however, require developing new courses of action that will meet the company's needs. For decisions made under conditions of high uncertainty, managers may develop only one or two custom solutions that will satisfice for handling the problem. However, studies find that limiting the search for alternatives is a primary cause of decision failure in organizations.[37]

Decision alternatives can be thought of as tools for reducing the difference between the organization's current and desired performance. For example, to improve sales at fast-food giant McDonald's, executives considered alternatives such as using mystery shoppers and unannounced inspections to improve quality and service, motivating demoralized franchisees to get them to invest in new equipment and programmes, taking R&D out of the test kitchen and encouraging franchisees to help come up with successful new menu items, and closing some stores to avoid cannibalizing its own sales.[38]

Selection of Desired Alternative

Once feasible alternatives are developed, one must be selected. The decision choice is the selection of the most promising of several alternative courses of action. The best alternative is one in which the solution best fits the overall goals and values of the organization and achieves the desired results using the fewest resources.[39] The manager tries to select the choice with the least amount of risk and uncertainty. Because some risk is inherent for most non-programmed decisions, managers try to gauge prospects for success. They might rely on their intuition and experience to estimate whether a given course of action is likely to succeed. Basing choices on overall goals and values can also effectively guide managers' selection of alternatives. Recall from Chapter 3 Valero Energy's decision to keep everyone on the payroll after Hurricane Katrina hit the Gulf Coast, while other refineries shut down and laid off workers. For Valero managers, the choice was easy based on values of putting employees first. Valero's values-based decision-making helped the company zoom from number 23 to number 3 on *Fortune* magazine's list of best companies to work for – and enabled Valero to get back to business weeks faster than competitors.[40]

Choosing among alternatives also depends on managers' personality factors and willingness to accept risk and uncertainty. **Risk propensity** is the willingness to undertake risk with the opportunity of gaining an increased payoff. The level of risk a manager is willing to accept will influence the analysis of cost and benefits to be derived from any decision. Consider the situations in Exhibit 9.4. In each situation, which alternative would you choose? A person with a low risk propensity would tend to take assured moderate returns by going for a tie score, building a domestic plant or pursuing a career as a doctor. A risk taker would go for the victory, build a plant in a foreign country or embark on an acting career.

© SCOTT OLSON/GETTY IMAGES

CONCEPT CONNECTION UPS knows many businesses have a low risk propensity when it comes to matters affecting their cash flow. The company's UPS Capital Insurance division reduces customers' risk of delayed payments through a variety of trade insurance policies. This advertisement for Exchange Collect promises peace of mind for companies dealing with international customers or suppliers. The service works like a secure international COD, with UPS securing payment on behalf of the customer before delivering goods. For UPS customers, the results are improved cash flow and less risk.

Risk propensity
The willingness to undertake risk with the opportunity of gaining an increased payoff.

Exhibit 9.4 Decision Alternatives with Different Levels of Risk

> **For each of the following decisions, which alternative would you choose? Reflect on your answer to these questions and think what this says about your own attitude to risk versus return.**
>
> 1. In the final seconds of a game with the university's traditional rival, the captain of the rugby team may choose a penalty kick which has a 95 per cent chance of producing a tie score, or go for a lineout with a 30 per cent chance of it leading to a try and victory, but sure defeat if it fails.
>
> 2. The CEO of a Canadian company must decide whether to build a new plant within Canada that has a 90 per cent chance of producing a modest return on investment or to build it in a foreign country with an unstable political history. The latter alternative has a 40 per cent chance of failing, but the returns would be enormous if it succeeded.
>
> 3. A student with considerable acting talent must choose a career. She has the opportunity to go on to medical school and become a doctor, a career in which she is 80 per cent likely to succeed. She would rather be an actress but realizes that the opportunity for success is only 20 per cent.

3 People who tend toward a *conceptual style* also like to consider a broad amount of information. However, they are more socially oriented than those with an analytical style and like to talk to others about the problem and possible alternatives for solving it. Managers using a conceptual style consider many broad alternatives, rely on information from both people and systems, and like to solve problems creatively.

4 The *behavioural style* is often the style adopted by managers having a deep concern for others as individuals. Managers using this style like to talk to people one-on-one and understand their feelings about the problem and the effect of a given decision on them. People with a behavioural style usually are concerned with the personal development of others and may make decisions that help others achieve their goals.

TAKE A MOMENT   To learn more about how you rate on these four styles, go to the Experiential Exercise on page 334 that evaluates your personal decision style.

Many managers have a dominant decision style. However, managers frequently use several different styles or a combination of styles in making the varied decisions they confront daily. A manager might use a directive style for deciding on which printing company to use for new business cards, yet shift to a more conceptual style when handling an interdepartmental conflict. The most effective managers are able to shift among styles as needed to meet the situation. Being aware of one's dominant decision style can help a manager avoid making critical mistakes when his or her usual style may be inappropriate to the problem at hand.

© SEAN GALLUP/GETTY IMAGES FOR BURDA MEDIA

CONCEPT CONNECTION Facebook founder Mark Zuckerberg stepped into a hole when he decided to retrofit his site with a feature named Beacon. Beacon was designed to pass information about customer web activity to participating vendors, providing a new source of revenue for Facebook. But when Beacon was implemented, Facebook was slammed with complaints about privacy intrusion and a lawsuit. What caused this poor decision? Based on the wild popularity of his social network site and his rapid rise in the business world, Zuckerberg was probably overly confident about how users would receive Beacon. Facebook management quickly decided to make it easier for customers to opt out of the service.

Why Do Managers Make Bad Decisions?

Managers are faced with a relentless demand for decisions, from solving minor problems to implementing major strategic changes. Even the best manager will make mistakes, but managers can increase their percentage of good decisions by understanding some of the factors that cause people to make bad ones. Most bad decisions are errors in judgement that originate in the human mind's limited capacity and in the natural biases managers display during decision-making. Awareness of the following six biases can help managers make more enlightened choices:[45]

1 *Being influenced by initial impressions.* When considering decisions, the mind often gives disproportionate weight to the first information it receives. These initial impressions, statistics or estimates act as an anchor to our subsequent thoughts and judgements. Anchors can be as simple as a random comment by a colleague or a statistic read in a newspaper. Past events and trends also act as anchors. For example, in business, managers frequently look at the previous year's sales when estimating sales for the coming year. Giving too much weight to the past can lead to poor forecasts and misguided decisions.

2 *Justifying past decisions.* Many managers fall into the trap of making choices that justify their past decisions, even if those decisions no longer seem valid. Consider managers who invest tremendous time and energy into improving the performance of a problem employee whom they now realize should never have been hired in the first place. Another example is when a manager continues to pour money into a failing project, hoping to turn things around. People don't like to make mistakes, so they continue to support a flawed decision in an effort to justify or correct the past.

3 *Seeing what you want to see.* People frequently look for information that supports their existing instinct or point of view and avoid information that contradicts it. This bias affects where managers look for information, as well as how they interpret the information they find. People tend to give too much weight to supporting information and too little to information that conflicts with their established viewpoints. It is important for managers to be honest with themselves about their motives and to examine all the evidence with equal rigour. Having a devil's advocate is also a good way to avoid seeing only what you want to see.

4 *Perpetuating the status quo.* Managers may base decisions on what has worked in the past and fail to explore new options, dig for additional information, or investigate new technologies. For example, DuPont clung to its cash cow, nylon, despite growing evidence in the scientific community that a new product, polyester, was superior for tyre cords. Celanese, a relatively small competitor, blew DuPont out of the water by exploiting this new evidence, quickly capturing 75 per cent of the tyre market.

5 *Being influenced by problem framing.* The decision response of a manager can be influenced by the mere wording of a problem. For example, consider a manager faced with a decision about salvaging the cargo of three barges that sank off the coast of West Africa. If managers are given the option of approving plan A that has a 100 per cent chance of saving the cargo of one of the three barges, worth £200 000, or plan B that has a one-third chance of saving the cargo of all three barges, worth £600 000 and a two-thirds chance of saving nothing, most managers choose option A. The same problem with a negative frame would give managers a choice of selecting plan C that has a 100 per cent chance of losing two of the three cargoes, worth £400 000 or plan D that has a two-thirds chance of losing all three cargoes but a one-third chance of losing no cargo. With this framing, most managers choose option D. Because both problems are identical, the decision choice depends strictly on how the problem is framed.

6 *Overconfidence.* Most people overestimate their ability to predict uncertain outcomes. Before making a decision, managers have unrealistic expectations of their ability to understand the risk and make the right choice. Overconfidence is greatest when answering questions of moderate to extreme difficulty. For example, when people are asked to define quantities about which they have little direct knowledge ('What was Toyota's 2007 revenue'? 'What was the market value of Tesco as of March 14, 2008'?), they overestimate their accuracy. Evidence of overconfidence is illustrated in cases in which subjects were so certain of an answer that they assigned odds of 1000 to 1 of being correct but in fact were correct only about 85 per cent of the time. When uncertainty is high, managers may unrealistically expect that they can successfully predict outcomes and hence select the wrong alternative.

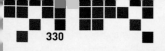

As a new manager, be aware of biases that can cloud your judgement and lead to bad decisions. The Manager's Shoptalk describes a new way of thinking about decision-making that can help you avoid decision traps such as overconfidence, seeing only what you want to see, or justifying past decisions.

Innovative Group Decision-Making

The ability to make fast, widely supported, high-quality decisions on a frequent basis is a critical skill in today's fast-moving organizations.[46] In many industries, the rate of competitive and technological change is so extreme that opportunities are fleeting, clear and complete information is seldom available, and the cost of a slow decision means lost business or even company failure. Do these factors mean managers should make the majority of decisions on their own? No. The rapid pace of the business environment calls for just the opposite – that is, for people throughout the organization to be involved in decision-making and have the information, skills and freedom they need to respond immediately to problems and questions.

Managers do make some decisions as individuals, but decision-makers more often are part of a group. Indeed, major decisions in the business world rarely are made entirely by an individual.

Start with Brainstorming

Brainstorming
A technique that uses a face-to-face group to spontaneously suggest a broad range of alternatives for decision-making.

Brainstorming uses a face-to-face interactive group to spontaneously suggest a wide range of alternatives for decision-making. The keys to effective brainstorming are that people can build on one another's ideas; all ideas are acceptable, no matter how crazy they seem; and criticism and evaluation are not allowed. The goal is to generate as many ideas as possible. Brainstorming has been found to be highly effective for quickly generating a wide range of alternative solutions to a problem, but it does have some drawbacks. For one thing, people in a group often want to conform to what others are saying, a problem sometimes referred to as *groupthink*. Others may be concerned about pleasing the boss or impressing colleagues. In addition, many creative people simply have social inhibitions that limit their participation in a group session or make it difficult to come up with ideas in a group setting. In fact, one study found that when four people are asked to 'brainstorm' individually, they typically come up with twice as many ideas as a group of four brainstorming together.

Electronic brainstorming
Bringing people together in an interactive group over a computer network to suggest alternatives; sometimes called *brainwriting*.

One recent approach, electronic brainstorming, takes advantage of the group approach while overcoming some disadvantages. **Electronic brainstorming**, sometimes called *brainwriting*, brings people together in an interactive group over a computer network.[47] One member writes an idea, another reads it and adds other ideas, and so on. Studies show that electronic brainstorming generates about 40 per cent more ideas than individuals brainstorming alone, and 25 to 200 per cent more ideas than regular brainstorming groups, depending on group size.[48] Why? Because the process is anonymous, the sky's the limit in terms of what people feel free to say. People can write down their ideas immediately, avoiding the possibility that a good idea might slip away while the person is waiting for a chance to speak in a face-to-face group. Social inhibitions and concerns are avoided, which typically allows for a broader range of participation. Another advantage is that electronic brainstorming can potentially be done with groups made up of employees from around the world, further increasing the diversity of alternatives.

 MANAGER'S SHOPTALK

Evidence-Based Management

At a time when decision-making is so important, many managers do not know how to make a good choice among alternatives. Using evidence-based decision-making can help. Evidence-based decision-making simply means a commitment to make more informed and intelligent decisions based on the best available facts and evidence. It means being aware of our biases and seeking and examining evidence with rigor. Managers practice evidence-based decision-making by being careful and thoughtful rather than carelessly relying on assumptions, past experience, rules of thumb or intuition.

Here are some ideas for applying evidence-based decision-making:

- *Demand Evidence.* Educate people throughout the organization to use data and facts to the extent possible to inform their decisions. Many manager problems are uncertain, and hard facts and data aren't available, but by always asking for evidence, managers can avoid relying on faulty assumptions. Managers at one computer company kept blaming the marketing staff for the trouble the company had selling their products in retail stores. Then, members of the senior team posed as mystery shoppers and tried to buy the company's computers. They kept encountering sales clerks that tried to dissuade them from purchasing the firm's products, citing the excessive price, clunky appearance, and poor customer service. Real-world observations told them something that was very different from what they assumed.

- *Practice the Five Whys.* One simple way to get people to think more broadly and deeply about problems rather than going with a superficial understanding and a first response is called the Five Whys. For every problem, managers ask 'Why?' not just once, but five times. The first *why* generally produces a superficial explanation for the problem, and each subsequent *why* probes deeper into the causes of the problem and potential solutions.

- *Do a Post-Mortem.* A technique many companies have adopted from the Army to encourage examination of the evidence and continuous learning is the after-action review. After implementation of any significant decision, managers evaluate what worked, what didn't, and how to do things better. Many problems are solved by trial and error.

- *Balance Decisiveness and Humility.* The best decision-makers have a healthy appreciation for what they don't know. They're always questioning and encouraging others to question their knowledge and assumptions. They foster a culture of inquiry, observation, and experimentation.

SOURCES Based on Jeffrey Pfeffer and Robert I. Sutton, 'Evidence-Based Management', *Harvard Business Review* (January 2006): 62–74; Rosemary Stewart, *Evidence-based Decision Making* (Abingdon, UK: Radcliffe Publishing, 2002); Joshua Klayman, Richard P. Larrick and Chip Heath, 'Organizational Repairs', *Across the Board* (February 2000): 26–31; and Peter Eisler, Blake Morrison and Tom Vanden Brook, 'Strategy That's Making Iraq Safer Was Snubbed for Years', *USA Today*, December 19, 2007.

Engage in Rigorous Debate

An important key to better decision-making is to encourage a rigorous debate of the issue at hand.[49] Good managers recognize that constructive conflict based on divergent points of view can bring a problem into focus, clarify people's ideas, stimulate creative thinking, create a broader understanding of issues and alternatives, and improve decision quality.[50] Chuck Knight, the former CEO of Emerson Electric, always sparked heated debates during strategic planning meetings. Knight believed rigorous debate gave people a clearer picture of the competitive landscape and forced managers to look at all sides of an issue, helping them reach better decisions.[51]

among all the customers; he'll get his act together.' However, when Moses discussed the problem with Carolyn Walter, director of operations, she argued that Carpenter should be dismissed. 'You're under no obligation to keep him just because you said you would', she pointed out. 'This was a major screw-up, and it's perfectly legal to fire someone for absenteeism. Your calls to customers should make it clear that this situation was not a onetime thing. Get rid of him now before things get worse. If you think eating half that £200 000 fee hurts now, just think what could happen if this behaviour continues.'

What Would You Do?

1 Give him a month's notice and terminate. He's known as a good consultant, so he probably won't have any trouble finding a new job, and you'll avoid any further problems associated

with his emotional difficulties and his possible alcohol problem.

2 Let it slide. Missing the appointment is Carpenter's first big mistake. He says he is getting things under control, and you believe he should be given a chance to get himself back on track.

3 Let Carpenter know that you care about what he's going through, but insist that he take a short paid leave and get counselling to deal with his emotional difficulties and evaluate the seriousness of his problems with alcohol. If the alcohol abuse continues, require him to attend a treatment programme or find another job.

SOURCES Based on information in Jeffrey L. Seglin, 'The Savior Complex', *Inc.* (February 1999): 67–69; and Nora Johnson, '"He's Been Beating Me", She Confided', *Business Ethics* (Summer 2001): 21.

CASE FOR CRITICAL ANALYSIS 9.1

Van Heerden Foods

Don Stransky is the new CEO at Van Heerden foods, one of the largest food manufacturers in South Africa, and he knows that he has to make a key decision before the next day's board meeting. He also knows that whatever his decision it will be unpopular with at least some of his senior managers.

Van Heerden Foods had been facing some difficult challenges in recent years. To get things back on track, Don had been evaluating the company by looking at its strengths, weaknesses, opportunities and threats (SWOT).

Van Heerden's greatest *strengths* were undoubtedly its powerful brands and its loyal customers. It also has a strong track record as an innovator, and a well-funded R&D budget. However, its biggest *weaknesses* had been the recent loss of top management talent to competitors and a cultural resistance to change that slowed response to market forces.

Several major *threats* have been building for a couple years. For instance, less-expensive, private-label brands have been successfully stealing market share from its core brands, while a number of overseas manufacturers had been aggressively targeting the South African market. At the same time, local competitors have

been quicker to respond to growing consumer demands for less fattening, more healthful food choices.

The question now was whether Van Heerden, should attempt to exploit an opportunity to acquire JF Foods, a smaller rival. JF Foods was well known for its ability to manufacture quality ready-to-heat, snack foods and comfort foods, which was a growing sector of the market, as well as having a sizeable foothold in the private label market.

Stransky has just heard a credible rumour that one of its main competitors was planning to launch a hostile takeover bid for JF. Coincidentally, Don knew JF well as he had recently been discussing a possible joint venture with them to develop a new premium range of ready meals made from high-quality ingredients, for consumers who want restaurant quality food without leaving the comfort of their own home. The joint venture hadn't worked out, but perhaps by acquiring JF, then Van Heerden's could acquire their core competencies for innovation.

Don, a hard-nosed 45-year-old firmly believed that bigger was better. Although Van Heerden's had been struggling lately, he had agreed to become the CEO because his sixth sense had told him that the company had good growth potential. Until now, he hadn't been entirely sure where that potential lay, but he was a problem-solver by nature with a good track record of successfully spotting new market opportunities. In the past, he had always acted on instinct, which had paid off handsomely.

So far, Don had managed to modestly nudge Van Heerden's revenue growth and increase its market share through aggressive pricing that successfully kept customers from switching to several potential foreign rivals. But those moves inevitably chipped away at the company's healthy profit margins. In any case, he recognized he'd taken the company down that road as far as he could. It was time for a real change in strategy. Instead of concentrating on traditional lines he wanted to transform Van Heerden into a highly flexible, customer focused company, and use the acquisition to develop new organic and healthy low fat products. Such a drastic metamorphosis was going to require a new, service-oriented corporate culture, and some corporate and marketing rebranding he admitted, but it was the only way he could see achieving the growth and profit-ability he envisioned. Acquiring JF looked like a good place to start, but this option would be gone if JF sold out to another firm.

Jennifer Le Roux, services division head, was enthusiastic about both the acquisition and the new strategy. 'Acquiring JF is the chance of a lifetime', she crowed. Not all the senior managers agreed. In particular, CFO Sam Botha advanced arguments against the acquisition that were hard to dismiss. The timing was wrong, he insisted. Van Heerden's recent drop in profitability hadn't escaped the stick market's attention, and the further negative impact on earnings that would result from the JF acquisition wasn't likely to make already wary investors feel any better. But then Sam shocked Don by offering an even more fundamental critique. 'Getting into these new product lines Don. It's what everybody's doing right now. Just look at the number of our competitors who've already taken steps to break into that market. What makes you think we'll come out on top? And when I look at our customers, many of them like what we do just fine. Customers are buying on price in the current economic climate. This is a big investment, with a high risk, and no guaranteed return.'

With such a big decision, Don's head had to agree with Botha's position that was based on his usual CFO thoroughness with number-crunching. But his gut wasn't so sure. Sometimes, he thought, you just have to go with your instincts. And his instincts were champing at the bit to go after JF Foods.

Questions

1 What steps in the decision-making process have Don Stransky and Van Heerdens taken? Which ones have they not completed?

2 Which decision-making style best describes Don's approach: directive, analytical, conceptual or behavioural? Which style best describes Sam Botha's approach?

3 Would you recommend that Van Heerdens attempt to acquire JF? If so, why? If not, what alternatives would you suggest?

SOURCE Adapted from Paul Hemp, 'Growing for Broke', *Harvard Business Review* (September 2002): 27–37.

ENDNOTES

1. See Kenneth R. Brousseau, Michael L. Driver, Gary Hourihan and Rikard Larsson, 'The Seasoned Executive's Decision Making Style', *Harvard Business Review* (February 2006): 110ff, for a discussion of how decision-making behaviour evolves as managers progress in their careers.

2. Cait Murphy, 'Building a new factory' interview with Marjorie Yang in "The Path to Power", *Fortune* (November 14, 2005): 145–156.

3. Betsy Morris, 'What Makes Apple Golden?', *Fortune* (March 17, 2008): 68–74.

4. Michael V. Copeland and Owen Thomas, 'Hits (& Misses)', *Business 2.0* (January–February 2004): 126.

5. Michael V. Copeland, 'Stuck in the Spin Cycle', *Business 2.0* (May 2005): 74–75; Adam Horowitz, Mark Athitakis, Mark Lasswell and Owen Thomas, '101 Dumbest Moments in Business', *Business 2.0* (January–February 2004): 72–81.

6. Herbert A. Simon, *The New Science of Management Decision* (Englewood Cliffs, NJ: Prentice Hall, 1977), p. 47.

7. BBC, 'Brand and Ross suspended by BBC' October 29, 2008, http://news.bbc.co.uk/1/hi/entertainment/7696714.stm.

8. Samuel Eilon, 'Structuring Unstructured Decisions', *Omega* 13 (1985): 369–377; and Max H. Bazerman, *Judgment in Managerial Decision Making* (New York: Wiley, 1986).

9. James G. March and Zur Shapira, 'Managerial Perspectives on Risk and Risk Taking', *Management Science* 33 (1987): 1404–1418; and Inga Skromme Baird and Howard Thomas, 'Toward a Contingency Model of Strategic Risk Taking', *Academy of Management Review* 10 (1985): 230–243.

10. Hugh Courtney, 'Decision-Driven Scenarios for Assessing Four Levels of Uncertainty', *Strategy & Leadership* 31, no. 1 (2003): 14–22.

11. Reported in David Leonhardt, 'This Fed Chief May Yet Get a Honeymoon', *The New York Times*, August 23, 2006.

12. Janet Guyon, 'Changing Direction', Interview with Nancy McKinstry in 'The Path to Power', *Fortune* (November 14, 2005): 145–156.

13. Michael Masuch and Perry LaPotin, 'Beyond Garbage Cans: An AI Model of Organizational Choice', *Administrative Science Quarterly* 34 (1989): 38–67; and Richard L. Daft and Robert H. Lengel, 'Organizational Information Requirements, Media Richness and Structural Design', *Management Science* 32 (1986): 554–571.

14. David M. Schweiger, William R. Sandberg and James W. Ragan, 'Group Approaches for Improving Strategic Decision Making: A Comparative Analysis of Dialectical Inquiry, Devil's Advocacy, and Consensus', *Academy of Management Journal* 29 (1986): 51–71; and Richard O. Mason and Ian I. Mitroff, *Challenging Strategic Planning Assumptions* (New York: Wiley Inter-science, 1981).

15. Michael Pacanowsky, 'Team Tools for Wicked Problems', *Organizational Dynamics* 23, no. 3 (Winter 1995): 36–51.

16. Thomas H. Davenport and Jeanne G. Harris, 'Automated Decision Making Comes of Age', *MIT Sloan Management Review* (Summer 2005): 83–89; and Stacie McCullough, 'On the Front Lines', *CIO* (October 15, 1999): 78–81.

17. Julie Schlosser, 'Markdown Lowdown', *Fortune* (January 12, 2004): 40; Srinivas Bollapragada, Prasanthi Ganti, Mark Osborn, James Quaile and Kannan Ramanathan, 'GE's Energy Rentals Business Automates Its Credit Assessment Process', *Interfaces* 33, no. 5 (September–October 2003): 45–56.

18. Mitchell Waldrop, 'Chaos, Inc.', *Red Herring* (January 2003): 38–40; Andy Serwer, 'Southwest Airlines: The Hottest Thing in the Sky', *Fortune* (March 8, 2004): 86–106; Perry Flint, 'The Darkest Hour', *Air Transport World* (December 2005): 52–53; *Southwest Airlines 2005 Annual Report*, www.southwest.com/investor_relations/swaar05.pdf; and John Heimlich, 'State of the Industry Q&A', Air Transport Association of America, Inc. (April 11, 2006), www.airlines.org/econ/d.aspx?nid=9630.

19. Herbert A. Simon, *The New Science of Management Decision* (New York: Harper & Row, 1960), pp. 5–6; and Amitai Etzioni, 'Humble Decision Making', *Harvard Business Review* (July–August 1989): 122–126.

20. James G. March and Herbert A. Simon, *Organizations* (New York: Wiley, 1958).

21. Herbert A. Simon, *Models of Man* (New York: Wiley, 1957), pp. 196–205; and Herbert A. Simon, *Administrative Behaviour*, 2nd ed. (New York: Free Press, 1957).

22. Paul C. Nutt, 'Expanding the Search for Alternatives During Strategic Decision Making', *Academy of Management Executive* 18, no. 4 (2004): 13–28.

23. Weston H. Agor, 'The Logic of Intuition: How Top Executives Make Important Decisions', *Organizational Dynamics* 14 (Winter 1986): 5–18; and Herbert A. Simon, 'Making Management Decisions: The Role of Intuition and Emotion', *Academy of Management Executive* 1 (1987): 57–64. For a recent review of research, see Erik Dane and Michael G. Pratt, 'Exploring Intuition and Its Role in Managerial Decision Making', *Academy of Management Review* 32, no. 1 (2007): 33–54.

24. Study reported in C. Chet Miller and R. Duane Ireland, 'Intuition in Strategic Decision Making: Friend or Foe in the Fast-Paced 21st Century?', *Academy of Management Executive* 19, no. 1 (2005): 19–30.

25. Richard Branson on taking big leaps http://www.theglobeandmail.com/report-on-business/article722434.ece.

26. See Gary Klein, *Intuition at Work: Why Developing Your Gut Instincts Will Make You Better at What You Do* (New York: Doubleday, 2002); Kurt Matzler, Franz Bailom and Todd A. Mooradian, 'Intuitive Decision Making', *MIT Sloan Management Review* 49, no. 1 (Fall 2007): 13–15; Malcolm Gladwell, *Blink: The Power of Thinking Without Thinking* (New York: Little Brown, 2005); and Sharon Begley, 'Follow Your Intuition: The Unconscious You May Be the Wiser Half', *The Wall Street Journal*, August 30, 2002.

27. Miller and Ireland, 'Intuition in Strategic Decision Making', and Eric Bonabeau, 'Don't Trust Your Gut', *Harvard Business Review* (May 2003): 116ff.

28. Eugene Sadler-Smith and Erella Shefy, 'The Intuitive Executive: Understanding and Applying "Gut Feel" in Decision Making', *Academy of Management Executive* 18, no. 4 (2004): 76–91; Simon, 'Making Management Decisions', and Ann Langley, 'Between "Paralysis by Analysis" and "Extinction by Instinct"', *Sloan Management Review* (Spring 1995): 63–76.

29. William B. Stevenson, Jon L. Pierce and Lyman W. Porter, 'The Concept of 'Coalition' in Organization Theory and Research', *Academy of Management Review* 10 (1985): 256–268.

30. George T. Doran and Jack Gunn, 'Decision Making in High-Tech Firms: Perspectives of Three Executives', *Business Horizons* (November–December 2002): 7–16.

31. Zhang Ruimin, 'Raising Haier', *Harvard Business Review* (Feb 2007).

32. James W. Fredrickson, 'Effects of Decision Motive and Organizational Performance Level on Strategic Decision Processes', *Academy of Management Journal* 28 (1985): 821–843; James W. Fredrickson, 'The Comprehensiveness of Strategic Decision Processes: Extension, Observations, Future Directions', *Academy of Management Journal* 27 (1984): 445–466; James W. Dean, Jr. and Mark P. Sharfman, 'Procedural Rationality in the Strategic Decision-Making Process', *Journal of Management Studies* 30, no. 4 (July 1993): 587–610; Nandini Rajagopalan, Abdul M. A. Rasheed, and Deepak K. Datta, 'Strategic Decision Processes: Critical Review and Future Directions', *Journal of Management* 19, no. 2 (1993): 349–384; and Paul J. H. Schoemaker, 'Strategic Decisions in Organizations: Rational and Behavioural Views', *Journal of Management Studies* 30, no. 1 (January 1993): 107–129.

33. Marjorie A. Lyles and Howard Thomas, 'Strategic Problem Formulation: Biases and Assumptions Embedded in Alternative Decision-Making Models', *Journal of Management Studies* 25 (1988): 131–145; and Susan E. Jackson and Jane E. Dutton, 'Discerning Threats and Opportunities', *Administrative Science Quarterly* 33 (1988): 370–387.

34. Richard L. Daft, Juhani Sormunen and Don Parks, 'Chief Executive Scanning, Environmental Characteristics, and

Company Performance: An Empirical Study', (unpublished manuscript, Texas A&M University, 1988).

35. C. Kepner and B. Tregoe, *The Rational Manager* (New York: McGraw-Hill, 1965).

36. Nanette Byrnes, 'Avon: More Than Cosmetic Changes', *BusinessWeek* (March 12, 2007): 62–63.

37. Paul C. Nutt, 'Expanding the Search for Alternatives During Strategic Decision Making', *Academy of Management Executive* 18, no. 4 (2004): 13–28; and P. C. Nutt, 'Surprising But True: Half the Decisions in Organizations Fail', *Academy of Management Executive* 13, no. 4 (1999): 75–90.

38. Pallavi Gogoi and Michael Arndt, 'Hamburger Hell', *BusinessWeek* (March 3, 2003): 104.

39. Peter Mayer, 'A Surprisingly Simple Way to Make Better Decisions', *Executive Female* (March–April 1995): 13–14; and Ralph L. Keeney, 'Creativity in Decision Making with Value-Focused Thinking', *Sloan Management Review* (Summer 1994): 33–41.

40. Janet Guyon, 'The Soul of a Money-making Machine', *Fortune* (October 3, 2005): 113–120; Robert Levering and Milton Moskowitz, 'And the Winners Are … (The 100 Best Companies to Work For)', *Fortune* (January 23, 2006): 89–108.

41. Mark McNeilly, 'Gathering Information for Strategic Decisions, Routinely', *Strategy & Leadership* 30, no. 5 (2002): 29–34.

42. Ibid.

43. Jenny C. McCune, 'Making Lemonade', *Management Review* (June 1997): 49–53; and Douglas S. Barasch, 'God and Toothpaste', *New York Times*, December 22, 1996.

44. Based on A. J. Rowe, J. D. Boulgaides, and M. R. McGrath, *Managerial Decision Making* (Chicago: Science Research Associates, 1984); and Alan J. Rowe and Richard O. Mason, *Managing with Style: A Guide to Understanding, Assessing, and Improving Your Decision Making* (San Francisco: Jossey-Bass, 1987).

45. This section is based on John S. Hammond, Ralph L. Keeney and Howard Raiffa, *Smart Choices: A Practical Guide to Making Better Decisions* (Boston: Harvard Business School Press, 1999); Max H. Bazerman and Dolly Chugh, 'Decisions Without Blinders', *Harvard Business Review* (January 2006): 88–97; J. S. Hammond, R. L. Keeney and H. Raiffa, 'The Hidden Traps in Decision Making', *Harvard Business Review* (September–October 1998): 47–58; Oren Harari, 'The Thomas Lawson Syndrome', *Management Review* (February 1994): 58–61; Dan Ariely, 'Q&A: Why Good CIOs Make Bad Decisions', *CIO* (May 1, 2003): 83–87; Leigh Buchanan, 'How to Take Risks in a Time of Anxiety', *Inc.* (May 2003): 76–81; and Max H. Bazerman, *Judgment in Managerial Decision Making*, 5th ed. (New York: John Wiley & Sons, 2002).

46. Kathleen M. Eisenhardt, 'Strategy as Strategic Decision Making', *Sloan Management Review* (Spring 1999): 65–72.

47. R. B. Gallupe, W. H. Cooper, M. L. Grise and L. M. Bastianutti, 'Blocking Electronic Brainstorms', *Journal of Applied Psychology* 79 (1994): 77–86; R. B. Gallupe and W. H. Cooper, 'Brainstorming Electronically', *Sloan Management Review* (Fall 1993): 27–36; and Alison Stein Wellner, 'A Perfect Brainstorm', *Inc.* (October 2003): 31–35.

48. Wellner, 'A Perfect Brainstorm'; Gallupe and Cooker, 'Brainstorming Electronically'.

49. Michael A. Roberto, 'Making Difficult Decisions in Turbulent Times', *Ivey Business Journal* (May–June 2003): 1–7.

50. Eisenhardt, 'Strategy as Strategic Decision Making'; and David A. Garvin and Michael A. Roberto, 'What You Don't Know About Making Decisions', *Harvard Business Review* (September 2001): 108–116.

51. Roberto, 'Making Difficult Decisions in Turbulent Times'.

52. David M. Schweiger and William R. Sandberg, 'The Utilization of Individual Capabilities in Group Approaches to Strategic Decision Making', *Strategic Management Journal* 10 (1989): 31–43; and 'The Devil's Advocate', *Small Business Report* (December 1987): 38–41.

53. George T. Doran and Jack Gunn, 'Decision Making in High-Tech Firms: Perspectives of Three Executives', *Business Horizons* (November–December 2002): 7–16.

54. Kathleen Eisenhardt, 'Strategy as Strategic Decision Making', *Sloan Management Review* (1999) 40: 65–72.

55. David A. Garvin and Michael A. Roberto, 'What You Don't Know About Making Decisions', *Harvard Business Review* 79, no. 8 (September 2001): 108–116.

56. Irving L. Janis, *Groupthink: Psychological Studies of Policy Decisions and Fiascoes*, 2nd ed. (Boston: Houghton Mifflin, 1982).

57. Jerry B. Harvey, 'The Abilene Paradox: The Management of Agreement', *Organizational Dynamics* (Summer 1988): 17–43.

58. Hans Wissema, 'Driving Through Red Lights; How Warning Signals Are Missed or Ignored', *Long Range Planning* 35 (2002): 521–539.

59. Ibid.

60. Cait Murphy, 'Building a new factory' interview with Marjorie Yang in 'The Path to Power', *Fortune* (November 14, 2005): 145–156.

CONTINUING CASE
BY ALAN HOGARTH

IKEA
PART THREE: STRATEGIC MISSION IMPOSSIBLE

All major multinational companies have a mission statement and IKEA is no exception. IKEA's mission and main goals are based on its founding values expounded in a booklet by Ingvar Kamprad entitled *Testament of a Furniture Dealer*. This booklet is given to every IKEA employee. The stated values included in the booklet are simplicity, humility and honesty in internal relations among co-workers and in external relations with suppliers and customers; risk-taking and daring to be different. Accordingly, 'IKEA's mission is to offer a wide range of home furnishing items of good design and function, excellent quality and durability, at prices so low that the majority of people can afford to buy them' (IKEA 1994). In essence IKEA aims to attract customers who are looking for quality products at reasonable prices, but who are willing to assemble their furniture themselves and participate in a self-service culture. The typical target customers are young families with a low to middle income.

The basis of IKEA's strategy is a mixture of innovative modular designs, mass produced components and a dedicated supplier network all geared towards serving price conscious customers while still maintaining a to a high standard of goods and workmanship. This strategy relied on IKEA's ability to form exclusive contracts with independent furniture makers and suppliers, to design furniture that could be sold as a kit and assembled in the consumers' home. Other competitive advantages of IKEA's strategy is that the product line is standardized, allowing for a global market and economies of scale.

IKEA's operating strategy is based around facilitating shopping in its stores. IKEA provides catalogues, tape measures, shopping lists and pencils for writing notes and measurements. Car roof racks are available for purchase and IKEA vans are available for rental. Also, the flat pack kits are stacked conveniently on racks allowing the stores to carry a large supply of inventory. These flat pack designs could be picked up by the customers themselves rather than having them wait for the furniture to be delivered. The store layout is also another important firm specific advantage. For example in their stores IKEA staff have erected mock ups of complete rooms. The advantage of this strategy is that it allows the customer to visualize how the furniture may look in their own homes. Basically IKEA's success is based on the relatively simple idea of keeping the cost between manufacturers and customers down.

Another important aspect that has contributed to IKEA's strategic vision is its 'environmentally friendly' policy. As Anders Moberg, President of IKEA said, 'Sustainability is the key word for the future. Our ambition is to work step by carefully thought-out step, and with great respect, towards a business based on sound ecological principles. It is not enough to be friendly toward the environment, we must adapt to it.' However, this was not always IKEA's view. This strategy was encouraged due to pressure from environmental groups in the late 1980s who called for the boycotting of companies using wood products from tropical rain forests. It was recognized that IKEA would have to start altering their business strategy. Due to these pressures IKEA adopted *The Natural Step Framework* as the basis for its environmental policy. After a milestone meeting in 1992 IKEA introduced an Environmental Action Plan which highlighted practical measures for the company to deal with environmental issues. Also at this meeting, it was recognized that IKEA would have to start strategically changing direction. As such IKEA set out to consider the possibility of a line of 'eco range' products. These were to go under the name of 'Eco-Plus' and consist of products that were more environmentally friendly. However, during the development of the Eco-Plus line IKEA management decided to reassess and change this strategy. They considered that the best way that IKEA could better improve the environment was not by producing a few select 'Eco-Plus' products, but that it would be better to concentrate on their existing products and make them more environmentally acceptable. According to an IKEA report, 'The new strategy was not a matter of taking 5 or 15 per cent of the product range and making it environmentally the best. It is taking the whole range and improving it step by step.' IKEA's Environmental Action Plan continues to this day and is being constantly updated to accommodate prevailing environmental issues. In keeping with the IKEA mission, Anders Moberg, wrote, 'Once and for all, IKEA has decided to side with the majority of people: to create a better everyday life. Therefore, it is our responsibility to do what we can to contribute to a better environment.'

At store level all managers are issued with the Environmental Action Plan and once they receive it they are responsible for making local decisions that are relevant to their own stores. Part of this decision-making process, however, involves all staff including co-workers and management. As Edoardo, Customer Services & Marketing Manager, IKEA Italy highlights, 'At IKEA everyone is treated as an individual. A lot of people are involved in the decision-making process. Everyone's opinion is valued. A good manager should solve problems, but only with the help of the entire team.' To be an effective manager at IKEA, encouraging collaborative decision making is essential, but it is not all plain sailing. Edoardo is realistic about this decision-making process when he admits that, 'Of course I can get frustrated with what seems to be rather a lengthy decision-making process, but it is more effective in the long run since everyone is involved.'

Despite IKEA's efforts to implement environmentally friendly policies, from a business perspective IKEA have never been noted for their transparency. As such the public at large and the wider business community have never been fully aware of IKEA's environmental strategy. As Justin Thomas says, 'The paradox is in part due to IKEA's strategy of pursuing environmental and social initiatives with hardly a thought to communicating either goals or results to the public.' However, with its growing globalization policy IKEA has finally recognized the demands faced by multinational companies. 'We would present it this way: A part of Swedish culture is to be humble, and that's also part of our culture, not putting ourselves on a pedestal or patting ourselves on the back', says corporate social responsibility manager John Zurcher. 'But we have also recently realized that many companies are much more transparent and visible about what they do, and we need to be more visible too.'

As part of this new found transparency the company has also highlighted a new set of ambitious goals recently adopted for 2006–2009. These are that all new stores will be built to a certified green building standard. Organic goods, starting with coffee, strawberry jam, blue cheese, tomato sauce, and schnapps, the Swedish aquavit will be phased-in to both IKEA's restaurants and its Swedish produce shops. In the same three-year goal period, the company plans to encourage 10 per cent of its customers around the world to travel to its stores using public transport.

Questions

1 What benefits would IKEA expect to accrue from a well designed Mission Statement? What relevance is such a mission statement to IKEA's strategic goals?

2 Using the IKEA experience as an example, explain what the difference is between strategy formulation and strategy implementation?

3 Given IKEA's approach to decision-making, discuss how electronic brainstorming could aid their managers in gauging employee particpation in the process.

SOURCES IKEA, (2008). 'True Stories', online at: http://www.ikea.com/ms/en_GB/jobs/true_stories/edoardo/index.html. IKEA Case study, 'The Natural Step', online at: http://www.naturalstep.org.nz/downloads/International_Case_Study_pdfs/TNSI_Ikea_Denmark.pdf. Kamprad, I (1976). *'Testament of a Furniture Dealer'*, IKEA internal document. Nattress, B and Altomare, M. (1999).

'IKEA: Nothing Is Impossible', *Journal of Business Administration and Politics*. Owens, Heidi, 'IKEA: the Natural Step Case Study', online at: http://www.naturalstep.ca/en/usa/ikea. Thomas, Justin (2006), 'Ultra-Efficient IKEA has More in Store', *Business and Politics*, online at: http://www.treehugger.com/files/2006/07/post_72.php.

PART 4

ORGANIZING

When approaching a building project, an architect organises at two levels. First, the architect organises the design of the structure in electronic blueprints. These blueprints are the architect's instructions for how the structure is to be built and tracks any changes that are made to the original design. The architect is also interested in the organization of the final structure, which must be clearly integrated in the structure's function.

Organization must do more than simply accommodate function. Organization is inherent in function and when properly implemented leads to fitness and form. When an architect designs a structure, organization underlies how the pieces fit together and give meaning to the form, fit, and function of that structure. How a structure is organised will dictate how people or objects flow through that structure and a good design will inherently accommodate the most natural movement from place to place. A museum must be designed to gently lead visitors through the exhibits, guiding their way at a subconscious level. A restaurant can be elegant or cozy, but the staff must be able to flow easily through the dining area, bringing diners their meals without fear of accidents or collisions.

Managers must organise people, technology, and institutional knowledge to achieve goals as well. Sometimes that means organising a company's internal structures, but it can also mean reorganising a department, region, or entire company in the face of advancing technology, changing markets, or a changing workforce. The manufacturing process is the most obvious application of organising: moving physical objects from point A to point B and performing certain tasks in a certain order. And while abstract yet just as real, managers must also organise ideas, information, and technology which requires innovation and imagination. And finally the manager must be prepared to alter that organization again as needed to accommodate the ever changing world.

CHAPTER OUTLINE

© SHIRONOSOV/ISTOCK

LEARNING OBJECTIVES

After reading this chapter, you should be able to:

1   Discuss the fundamental characteristics of organizing, including such concepts as work specialization, chain of command, span of management and centralization versus decentralization.

2   Describe functional and divisional approaches to structure.

3   Explain the matrix approach to structure and its application to both domestic and international organizations.

4   Describe the contemporary team and virtual network structures and why they are being adopted by organizations.

5   Explain why organizations need coordination across departments and hierarchical levels, and describe mechanisms for achieving coordination.

6   Identify how structure can be used to achieve an organization's strategic goals.

7   Illustrate how organization structure can be designed to fit environmental uncertainty.

8   Define production technology (manufacturing, service and digital) and explain how it influences organization structure.

CHAPTER 10

DESIGNING ADAPTIVE ORGANIZATIONS

Manager's Challenge

The call to Carlos Ghosn came on a blustery March day. Louis Schweitzer, CEO of Renault, was asking Ghosn to take on the biggest challenge of his management career – to lead a turnaround of Japan's Nissan. Renault and Nissan had just agreed to an important strategic alliance, but its success depended on transforming Nissan into a profitable business. Ghosn had succeeded before as a turnaround artist, but Nissan was a whole different story. The once-thriving company had been struggling to turn a profit for eight years. Purchasing and manufacturing costs were high and profit margins notoriously low. The company's debt, even after the Renault investment, amounted to a staggering $11 billion. Product innovation was at a standstill, and the company was trying to compete with ageing and outdated car models. When Ghosn got to Nissan, he found deeper problems, including a culture of blame where no one was willing to accept responsibility for mistakes. One reason, he discovered, was that most Nissan managers did not have clearly defined areas of responsibility and authority. Another impediment was the lack of trust, communication and collaboration across departments. When something went wrong, sales blamed product planning, product planning blamed engineering, engineering blamed sales, sales blamed finance, and on and on – and nothing ever got solved. Ghosn knew he was facing a do-or-die situation: either fix these fundamental problems, or Nissan would die.[1]

What advice would you give Carlos Ghosn about using structural design to help turn Nissan around? What structural changes might solve Nissan's problems with poor coordination and shatter the pervasive culture of blame?

TAKE A MOMENT

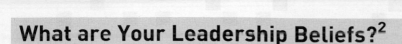

What are Your Leadership Beliefs?[2]

The fit between a new manager and the organization is often based on personal beliefs about the role of leaders. Things work best when organization design matches a new manager's beliefs about his or her leadership role. To understand your leadership beliefs, please answer each item below as Mostly True or Mostly False for you.

Think about the extent to which each statement reflects your beliefs about a leader's role in an organization. Mark as Mostly True the four statements that are *most* true for you, and mark as Mostly False the four that are *least* true for you.

		Mostly True	Mostly False
1	A leader should take charge of the group or organization.	☐	☐
2	The major tasks of a leader are to make and communicate decisions.	☐	☐
3	Group and organization members should be loyal to designated leaders.	☐	☐
4	The responsibility for taking risks lies with the leaders.	☐	☐
5	Leaders should foster member discussions about the future.	☐	☐
6	Successful leaders make everyone's learning their highest priority.	☐	☐
7	An organization needs to be always changing the way it does things to adapt to a changing world.	☐	☐
8	Everyone in an organization should be responsible for accomplishing organizational goals.	☐	☐

SCORING AND INTERPRETATION   Each question pertains to one of two subscales of *leadership beliefs*. Questions 1–4 reflect *position-based* leadership beliefs. This is the belief that the most competent and loyal people are placed in positions of leadership where they assume responsibility and authority for the group or organization. Questions 5–8 reflect *non-hierarchical* leadership beliefs. This belief is that the group or organization faces a complex system of adaptive challenges, and leaders see their job as facilitating the flow of information among members and their full engagement to respond to those challenges. The subscale for which you ticked more items Mostly True may reveal your personal beliefs about position-based versus non-hierarchical leadership. Position-based beliefs typically work for managers in a traditional vertical hierarchy or mechanistic organization. Non-hierarchical beliefs typically work for managers engaged with horizontal organizing or organic organizations, such as managing teams, projects and re-engineering.

The problem confronting Carlos Ghosn at Nissan is largely one of structural design. Ghosn wants to use elements of structure to define authority and responsibility for managers, promote accountability and improve coordination so that Nissan can bring out new products and regain a competitive edge. Every firm wrestles with the problem of how to organize. Reorganization often is necessary to reflect a new strategy, changing market conditions or innovative technology. In recent years, many companies, including American Express, IBM, Microsoft, Hewlett-Packard and Ford Motor Co., have realigned departmental groupings, chains of command

and horizontal coordination mechanisms to attain new strategic goals. Structure is a powerful tool for reaching strategic goals, and a strategy's success often is determined by its fit with organization structure.

Many organizations have found a need to make structural changes that are compatible with use of the internet for e-business, which requires stronger horizontal coordination. Tikkurilla Oy, a Finnish manufacturer of decorative paints and industrial coating, reorganized to increase cross-functional collaboration in connection with the rollout of a new system that links customers, distributors and suppliers over the internet. Ford Motor Company used a horizontal team approach to design and build the Escape Hybrid, bringing the first hybrid SUV to market in record time.[3] Companies are increasingly using outsourcing as a structural option, as the internet has expanded the types of activities firms can farm out to subcontractors. WuXi Pharmatech in Shanghai, China, for example, not only manufactures drugs but does laboratory and drug development work for most of the large pharmaceuticals firms in the US and Europe. Drug makers such as Roche Holding of Switzerland, GlaxoSmithKline of Britain and Eli Lilly of the US are also outsourcing clinical trial work to low-wage countries such as India, a practice that is raising both economic and ethical concerns.[4] Some of today's companies operate as virtual network organizations, limiting themselves to a few core activities and letting outside specialists handle everything else. Each of these organizations is using fundamental concepts of organizing. **Organizing** is the deployment of organizational resources to achieve strategic goals. The deployment of resources is reflected in the organization's division of labour into specific departments and jobs, formal lines of authority, and mechanisms for coordinating diverse organization tasks.

Organizing is important because it follows from strategy – the topic of Part 3. Strategy defines *what* to do; organizing defines *how* to do it. Organization structure is a tool that managers use to harness resources for getting things done. Part 4 explains the variety of organizing principles and concepts used by managers. This chapter covers fundamental concepts that apply to all organizations and departments, including organizing the vertical structure and using mechanisms for horizontal coordination. The chapter also examines how managers tailor the various elements of structural design to the organization's situation. Chapter 11 discusses how organizations can be structured to facilitate innovation and change. Chapters 12 and 13 consider how to utilize human resources to the best advantage within the organization's structure.

© REUTER RAYMOND/SYGMA/CORBIS

CONCEPT CONNECTION Volvo is one of the world's leading heavy truck brands with over nine different business units operating under the umbrella of the main organization. Worldwide, Volvo trucks are known for their driver comfort and safety. In total, about 750 000 Volvo trucks are today in useful service all over the world. For a large organization such as this, organizing is a critical part of good management. The Volvo Group is organized in product-related business areas and supporting business units. This organization permits companies to work closely with their customers and efficiently utilize Group-wide resources.

The business units are organized globally and created to combine expertise in key areas. They have the overall responsibility for product planning and purchasing, and for developing and delivering components, subsystems, services, and service and support to the Group's business areas. The right organizational structure of the Group creates economies of scale in several areas, such as product development, production, parts supply and logistics, as well as in administration and support functions.

Organizing
The deployment of organizational resources to achieve strategic goals.

Organizing the Vertical Structure

The organizing process leads to the creation of organization structure, which defines how tasks are divided and resources deployed. **Organization structure** is defined as (1) the set of formal tasks assigned to individuals and departments; (2) formal reporting relationships, including lines of authority, decision responsibility, number of

Organization structure
The framework in which the organization defines how tasks are divided, resources are deployed and departments are coordinated.

hierarchical levels and span of managers' control; and (3) the design of systems to ensure effective coordination of employees across departments.[5]

The set of formal tasks and formal reporting relationships provides a framework for vertical control of the organization. The characteristics of vertical structure are portrayed in the **organization chart**, which is the visual representation of an organization's structure.

A sample organization chart for a water bottling plant is illustrated in Exhibit 10.1. The plant has four major departments – accounting, human resources, production and marketing. The organization chart delineates the chain of command, indicates departmental tasks and how they fit together, and provides order and logic for the organization. Every employee has an appointed task, line of authority and decision responsibility. The following sections discuss several important features of vertical structure in more detail.

Organization chart
The visual representation of an organization's structure.

Work Specialization

Organizations perform a wide variety of tasks. A fundamental principle is that work can be performed more efficiently if employees are allowed to specialize.[6] Work specialization, sometimes called *division of labour*, is the degree to which organizational tasks are subdivided into separate jobs. Work specialization in Exhibit 10.1 is illustrated by the separation of production tasks into bottling, quality control, and maintenance. Employees within each department perform only the tasks relevant to their specialized function. When work specialization is extensive, employees specialize in a

Work specialization
The degree to which organizational tasks are subdivided into individual jobs; also called division of labour.

Exhibit 10.1 Organization Chart for a Water Bottling Plant

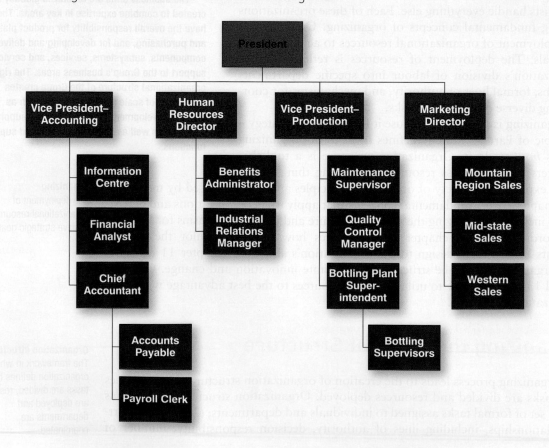

single task. Jobs tend to be small, but they can be performed efficiently. Work specialization is readily visible on an automobile assembly line where each employee performs the same task over and over again. It would not be efficient to have a single employee build the entire automobile, or even perform a large number of unrelated jobs.

Despite the apparent advantages of specialization, many organizations are moving away from this principle. With too much specialization, employees are isolated and do only a single, boring job. Many companies are enlarging jobs to provide greater challenges or assigning teams so that employees can rotate among the several jobs performed by the team.

Chain of Command

The chain of command is an unbroken line of authority that links all persons in an organization and shows who reports to whom. It is associated with two underlying principles. *Unity of command* means that each employee is held accountable to only one supervisor. The *scalar principle* refers to a clearly defined line of authority in the organization that includes all employees. Authority and responsibility for different tasks should be distinct. All persons in the organization should know to whom they report as well as the successive management levels all the way to the top. In Exhibit 10.1, the payroll clerk reports to the chief accountant, who in turn reports to the vice president, who in turn reports to the company president.

> **Chain of command**
> An unbroken line of authority that links all individuals in the organization and specifies who reports to whom.

Authority, Responsibility, and Delegation

The chain of command illustrates the authority structure of the organization. Authority is the formal and legitimate right of a manager to make decisions, issue orders and allocate resources to achieve organizationally desired outcomes. Authority is distinguished by three characteristics:[7]

> **Authority**
> The formal and legitimate right of a manager to make decisions, issue orders and allocate resources to achieve organizationally desired outcomes.

1 *Authority is vested in organizational positions, not people.* Managers have authority because of the positions they hold, and other people in the same positions would have the same authority.

2 *Authority is accepted by subordinates.* Although authority flows top-down through the organization's hierarchy, subordinates comply because they believe that managers have a legitimate right to issue orders. The *acceptance theory of authority* argues that a manager has authority only if subordinates choose to accept his or her commands. If subordinates refuse to obey because the order is outside their zone of acceptance, a manager's authority disappears.[8]

3 *Authority flows down the vertical hierarchy.* Positions at the top of the hierarchy are vested with more formal authority than are positions at the bottom.

Responsibility is the flip side of the authority coin. Responsibility is the duty to perform the task or activity as assigned. Typically, managers are assigned authority commensurate with responsibility. When managers have responsibility for task outcomes but little authority, the job is possible but difficult. They rely on persuasion and luck. When managers have authority exceeding responsibility, they may become tyrants, using authority toward frivolous outcomes.[9]

> **Responsibility**
> The duty to perform the task or activity an employee has been assigned.

Go to the Ethical Dilemma on page 387 that pertains to issues of authority, responsibility and delegation.

TAKE A MOMENT

Accountability
The fact that the people with authority and responsibility are subject to reporting and justifying task outcomes to those above them in the chain of command.

Delegation
The process managers use to transfer authority and responsibility to positions below them in the hierarchy.

Accountability is the mechanism through which authority and responsibility are brought into alignment. Accountability means that the people with authority and responsibility are subject to reporting and justifying task outcomes to those above them in the chain of command.[10] For organizations to function well, everyone needs to know what they are accountable for and accept the responsibility and authority for performing it. Accountability can be built into the organization structure. For example, at Whirlpool, incentive programmes tailored to different hierarchical levels provide strict accountability. Performance of all managers is monitored, and bonus payments are tied to successful outcomes. Another example comes from Caterpillar Inc., which got hammered by new competition in the mid-1980s and reorganized to build in accountability.

Some top managers at Caterpillar had trouble letting go of authority and responsibility in the new structure because they were used to calling all the shots. Another important concept related to authority is delegation.[11] Delegation is the process managers use to transfer authority and responsibility to positions below them in the hierarchy. Most organizations today encourage managers to delegate authority to the lowest possible level to provide maximum flexibility to meet customer needs and adapt to the environment. However, as at Caterpillar, many managers find delegation difficult. Microsoft's chief financial officer John Conners nearly resigned because of CEO Steven Ballmer's inability to delegate. By taking it upon himself to make financial decisions, Ballmer undermined the role of Conners and his team. Ballmer is learning to give up some control and delegate more so that people can do their jobs more effectively.[12] Techniques for effective delegation are discussed in the Manager's Shoptalk box.

INNOVATIVE WAY

Caterpillar Inc.

Caterpillar, which makes large construction equipment, engines, and power systems, had almost total control of its markets until the mid-1980s, when a combination of global recession and runaway inflation opened the door to a host of new competitors, including Japan's Komatsu. The unanticipated surge of competition almost put Cat under, and the company was losing $1 million a day seven days a week in 1983 and 1984.

When George Schaefer took over as CEO, he and other top managers decided to undertake a major transformation to make sure Cat wasn't caught flat-footed again. They started with structure. One major problem Schaefer saw was that the organization didn't have clear accountability. Schaefer pushed authority, responsibility and accountability dramatically downward by reorganizing Caterpillar into several new business divisions that would be judged on divisional

profitability. Business units could now design their own products, develop their own manufacturing processes, and set their own prices rather than getting permission or directives from headquarters. The division managers were strictly accountable for how they used their new decision-making authority. Each division was judged on profitability and return on assets (ROA), and any division that couldn't demonstrate 15 per cent ROA was subject to elimination. The CEO held regular meetings with each division president and kept notes of what they said they would achieve. Then at the next meeting, he would review each manager's performance compared to his or her commitments. The compensation plan was also overhauled to base individual managers' bonuses on meeting divisional plan targets.

Previously, if things went wrong, division managers would blame headquarters. The clear accountability of the new structure forced people to find solutions to their problems rather than assigning blame.[13]

Line and Staff Authority

An important distinction in many organizations is between line authority and staff authority, reflecting whether managers work in line or staff departments in the organization's structure. *Line departments* perform tasks that reflect the organization's primary goal and mission. In a software company, line departments make and sell the product. In an internet-based company, line departments would be those that develop and manage online offerings and sales. *Staff departments* include all those that provide specialized skills in support of line departments. Staff departments have an advisory relationship with line departments and typically include marketing, labour relations, research, accounting and human resources.

Line authority means that people in management positions have formal authority to direct and control immediate subordinates. **Staff authority** is narrower and includes the right to advise, recommend, and counsel in the staff specialists' area of expertise. Staff authority is a communication relationship; staff specialists advise managers in technical areas. For example, the finance department of a manufacturing firm would have staff authority to coordinate with line departments about which accounting forms to use to facilitate equipment purchases and standardize payroll services.

Line authority
A form of authority in which individuals in management positions have the formal power to direct and control immediate subordinates.

Staff authority
A form of authority granted to staff specialists in their area of expertise.

Span of Management

The **span of management** is the number of employees reporting to a supervisor. Sometimes called the *span of control*, this characteristic of structure determines how closely a supervisor can monitor subordinates. Traditional views of organization design recommended a span of management of about seven subordinates per manager. However, many lean organizations today have spans of management as high as 30, 40 and even higher. For example, at Consolidated Diesel's team-based engine assembly plant, the span of management is 100.[14] Research over the past 40 or so years shows that span of management varies widely and that several factors influence the span.[15] Generally, when supervisors must be closely involved with subordinates, the span should be small, and when supervisors need little involvement with subordinates, it can be large. The following factors are associated with less supervisor involvement and thus larger spans of control.

Span of management
The number of employees reporting to a supervisor; also called *span of control*.

1 Work performed by subordinates is stable and routine.

2 Subordinates perform similar work tasks.

3 Subordinates are concentrated in a single location.

4 Subordinates are highly trained and need little direction in performing tasks.

5 Rules and procedures defining task activities are available.

6 Support systems and personnel are available for the manager.

7 Little time is required in non-supervisory activities such as coordination with other departments or planning.

8 Managers' personal preferences and styles favour a large span.

MANAGER'S SHOPTALK

How to Delegate

The attempt by top management to decentralize decision-making often gets bogged down because middle managers are unable to delegate. Managers may cling tightly to their decision-making and task responsibilities. Failure to delegate occurs for a number of reasons: managers are most comfortable making familiar decisions; they feel they will lose personal status by delegating tasks; they believe they can do a better job themselves; or they have an aversion to risk – they will not take a chance on delegating because performance responsibility ultimately rests with them.

Yet decentralization offers an organization many advantages. Decisions are made at the right level, lower-level employees are motivated and employees have the opportunity to develop decision-making skills. Overcoming barriers to delegation in order to gain these advantages is a major challenge. The following approach can help each manager delegate more effectively:

1 *Delegate the whole task.* A manager should delegate an entire task to one person rather than dividing it among several people. This type of delegation gives the individual complete responsibility and increases his or her initiative while giving the manager some control over the results.

2 *Select the right person.* Not all employees have the same capabilities and degree of motivation. Managers must match talent to task if delegation is to be effective. They should identify subordinates who made independent decisions in the past and show a desire for more responsibility.

3 *Ensure that authority equals responsibility.* Merely assigning a task is not effective delegation. Managers often load subordinates with increased responsibility but do not extend their decision-making range. In addition to having responsibility for completing a task, the worker must be given the authority to make decisions about how best to do the job.

4 *Give thorough instruction.* Successful delegation includes information on what, when, why, where, who, and how. The subordinate must clearly understand the task and the expected results. It is a good idea to write down all provisions discussed, including required resources and when and how the results will be reported.

5 *Maintain feedback.* Feedback means keeping open lines of communication with the subordinate to answer questions and provide advice, but without exerting too much control. Open lines of communication make it easier to trust subordinates. Feedback keeps the subordinate on the right track.

6 *Evaluate and reward performance.* Once the task is completed, the manager should evaluate results, not methods. When results do not meet expectations, the manager must assess the consequences. When they do meet expectations, the manager should reward employees for a job well done with praise, financial rewards when appropriate, and delegation of future assignments.

Are You a Positive Delegator?

Positive delegation is the way an organization implements decentralization. Do you help or hinder the decentralization process? If you answer yes to more than three of the following questions, you may have a problem delegating:

- I tend to be a perfectionist.
- My boss expects me to know all the details of my job.
- I don't have the time to explain clearly and concisely how a task should be accomplished.
- I often end up doing tasks myself.
- My subordinates typically are not as committed as I am.
- I get upset when other people don't do the task right.
- I really enjoy doing the details of my job to the best of my ability.
- I like to be in control of task outcomes.

SOURCES Thomas R. Horton 'Delegation and Team Building: No Solo Acts Please', *Management Review* (September 1992): 58–61; Andrew E. Schwartz, 'The Why, What, and to Whom of Delegation', *Management Solutions* (June 1987): 31–38; 'Delegation', *Small Business Report* (June 1986): 38–43; and Russell Wild, 'CloneYourself', *Working Woman* (May 2000): 79–80.

The average span of control used in an organization determines whether the structure is tall or flat. A **tall structure** has an overall narrow span and more hierarchical levels. A **flat structure** has a wide span, is horizontally dispersed and has fewer hierarchical levels.

Having too many hierarchical levels and narrow spans of control is a common structural problem for organizations. The result may be routine decisions that are made too high in the organization, which pulls higher-level executives away from important long-range strategic issues, and it limits the creativity and innovativeness of lower-level managers in solving problems.[16] The trend in recent years has been toward wider spans of control as a way to facilitate delegation.[17] One study of 300 large US corporations found that the average number of division heads reporting directly to the CEO tripled between the years of 1986 and 1999.[18] Exhibit 10.2 illustrates how an international metals company was reorganized. The multilevel set of managers shown in panel *a* was replaced with ten operating managers and nine staff specialists reporting directly to the CEO, as shown in panel *b*. The CEO welcomed this wide span of 19 management subordinates because it fit his style, his management team was top quality and needed little supervision, and they were all located on the same floor of an office building.

Centralization and Decentralization

Centralization and decentralization pertain to the hierarchical level at which decisions are made. **Centralization** means that decision authority is located near the top of the organization. With **decentralization**, decision authority is pushed downward to lower organization levels. Organizations may have to experiment to find the correct hierarchical level at which to make decisions.

In Europe, the US and Canada, the trend over the past 30 years has been toward greater decentralization of organizations. Decentralization is believed to relieve the burden on top managers, make greater use of employees' skills and abilities, ensure that decisions are made close to the action by well-informed people, and permit more rapid response to external changes.

Tall structure
A management structure characterized by an overall narrow span of management and a relatively large number of hierarchical levels.

Flat structure
A management structure characterized by an overall broad span of control and relatively few hierarchical levels.

Centralization
The location of decision authority near top organizational levels.

Decentralization
The location of decision authority near lower organizational levels.

Exhibit 10.2 Reorganization to Increase Span of Management for President of an International Metals Company

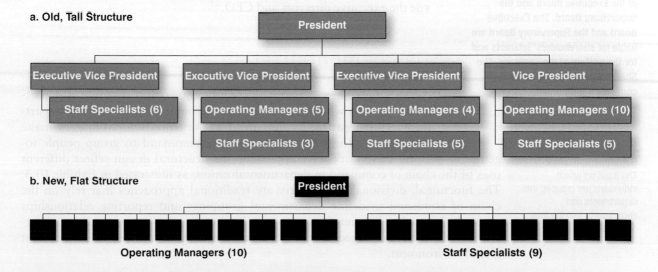

a. Old, Tall Structure

President

Executive Vice President — Staff Specialists (6)

Executive Vice President — Operating Managers (5) — Staff Specialists (3)

Executive Vice President — Operating Managers (4) — Staff Specialists (5)

Vice President — Operating Managers (10) — Staff Specialists (5)

b. New, Flat Structure

President

Operating Managers (10)   Staff Specialists (9)

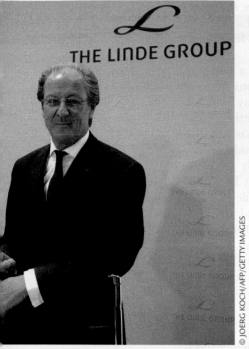

© JOERG KOCH/AFP/GETTY IMAGES

CONCEPT CONNECTION Linde AG, an international company with its registered office in Munich, Germany, is subject to the provisions of the German Stock Corporation Law, the German Codetermination Law and the regulations of the capital market. It is a world leading gases and engineering company with more than 50 000 employees working in around 100 countries worldwide. In the 2007 financial year it achieved sales of € 12.3 billion. The Linde Group has a two-part management and supervisory structure, the two organs of the Executive Board and the Supervisory Board. The Executive Board and the Supervisory Board are liable for shareholders' interests and for the welfare of the company. The Shareholders' Meeting is the company's third organ.

Departmentalization
The basis on which individuals are grouped into departments and departments into the total organization.

However, this trend does not mean that every organization should decentralize all decisions. Managers should diagnose the organizational situation and select the decision-making level that will best meet the organization's needs. Factors that typically influence centralization versus decentralization are as follows:

1 *Greater change and uncertainty in the environment are usually associated with decentralization.* A good example of how decentralization can help cope with rapid change and uncertainty occurred following Hurricane Katrina. A largely decentralized management system empowers people to make rapid on-the-spot decisions. For instance, decentralized decision-making at UPS enabled trucks to keep running on time in New York after the September 2001 terrorist attacks.[19]

2 *The amount of centralization or decentralization should fit the firm's strategy.* For example, Johnson & Johnson gives almost complete authority to its 180 operating companies to develop and market their own products. Decentralization fits the corporate strategy of empowerment that gets each division close to customers so it can speedily adapt to their needs.[20] Taking the opposite approach, Procter & Gamble recentralized some of its operations to take a more focused approach and leverage the giant company's capabilities across business units.[21]

3 *In times of crisis or risk of company failure, authority may be centralized at the top.* When Honda could not get agreement among divisions about new car models, President Nobuhiko Kawamoto made the decision himself.[22]

The Executive Board of Linde AG manages the company and conducts its business. It is bound to the interests of the company and is responsible for achieving sustainable increases in the value of the company. It decides on the strategic direction of the company, obtains the Supervisory Board's approval of this, and ensures that the overall strategy is implemented.

The Supervisory Board is composed of the minimum number of members required by applicable law and its role is to promote shareholders interests through the governance of the company and to hire and supervise the executive directors and CEO.[23]

Departmentalization

Another fundamental characteristic of organization structure is **departmentalization**, which is the basis for grouping positions into departments and departments into the total organization. Managers make choices about how to use the chain of command to group people together to perform their work. Five approaches to structural design reflect different uses of the chain of command in departmentalization, as illustrated in Exhibit 10.3. The functional, divisional, and matrix are traditional approaches that rely on the chain of command to define departmental groupings and reporting relationships along the hierarchy. Two innovative approaches are the use of teams and virtual networks, which have emerged to meet changing organizational needs in a turbulent global environment.

Exhibit 10.3 Five Approaches to Structural Design

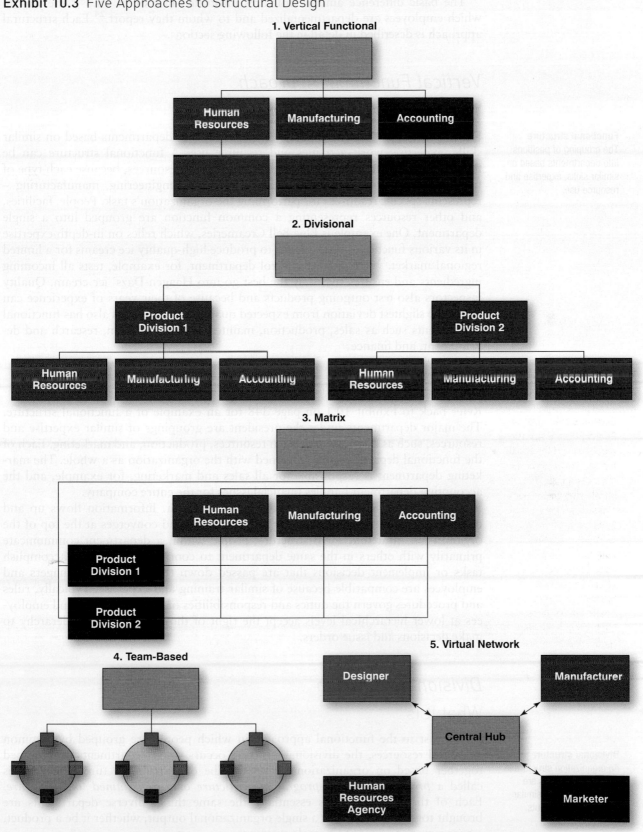

The basic difference among structures illustrated in Exhibit 10.3 is the way in which employees are departmentalized and to whom they report.[24] Each structural approach is described in detail in the following sections.

Vertical Functional Approach

What It Is

Functional structure
The grouping of positions into departments based on similar skills, expertise and resource use.

Functional structure is the grouping of positions into departments based on similar skills, expertise, work activities and resource use. A functional structure can be thought of as departmentalization by organizational resources, because each type of functional activity – accounting, human resources, engineering, manufacturing – represents specific resources for performing the organization's task. People, facilities, and other resources representing a common function are grouped into a single department. One example is Blue Bell Creameries, which relies on in-depth expertise in its various functional departments to produce high-quality ice creams for a limited regional market.[25] The quality control department, for example, tests all incoming ingredients and ensures that only the best go into Häagen-Dazs' ice cream. Quality inspectors also test outgoing products and because of their years of experience can detect the slightest deviation from expected quality. Häagen-Dazs also has functional departments such as sales, production, maintenance, distribution, research and development, and finance.

How It Works

Refer back to Exhibit 10.1 on page 348 for an example of a functional structure. The major departments under the president are groupings of similar expertise and resources, such as accounting, human resources, production, and marketing. Each of the functional departments is concerned with the organization as a whole. The marketing department is responsible for all sales and marketing, for example, and the accounting department handles financial issues for the entire company.

The functional structure is a strong vertical design. Information flows up and down the vertical hierarchy, and the chain of command converges at the top of the organization. In a functional structure, people within a department communicate primarily with others in the same department to coordinate work and accomplish tasks or implement decisions that are passed down the hierarchy. Managers and employees are compatible because of similar training and expertise. Typically, rules and procedures govern the duties and responsibilities of each employee, and employees at lower hierarchical levels accept the right of those higher in the hierarchy to make decisions and issue orders.

Divisional Approach

What It Is

Divisional structure
An organization structure in which departments are grouped based on similar organizational outputs.

In contrast to the functional approach, in which people are grouped by common skills and resources, the **divisional structure** occurs when departments are grouped together based on organizational outputs. The divisional structure is sometimes called a *product structure, programme structure* or *self-contained unit structure*. Each of these terms means essentially the same thing: diverse departments are brought together to produce a single organizational output, whether it be a product, a program, or a service to a single customer.

Most large corporations have separate divisions that perform different tasks, use different technologies, or serve different customers. When a huge organization produces products for different markets, the divisional structure works because each division is an autonomous business. Microsoft has reorganized into three business divisions: Platform Products & Services (which includes Windows and MSN); Business (including Office and Business Solutions products); and Entertainment & Devices (Xbox games, Windows mobile, and Microsoft TV). Each unit is headed by a president who is accountable for the performance of the division, and each contains the functions of a stand-alone company, doing its own product development, sales, marketing, and finance. Facing new competitive threats from Google and makers of the free Linux operating system, top executives initiated the restructuring to help Microsoft be more flexible and nimble in developing and delivering new products. The structure groups together products and services that depend on similar technologies at the same time it will enable more rapid decision-making and less red tape at the giant corporation.[26]

How It Works

Functional and divisional structures are illustrated in Exhibit 10.4. In the divisional structure, divisions are created as self-contained units with separate functional departments for each division. For example, in Exhibit 10.4, each functional department resource needed to produce the product is assigned to each division. Whereas in a functional structure, all engineers are grouped together and work on all products, in a divisional structure separate engineering departments are created within each division. Each department is smaller and focuses on a single product line or customer segment. Departments are duplicated across product lines.

The primary difference between divisional and functional structures is that the chain of command from each function converges lower in the hierarchy. In a divisional structure, differences of opinion among research and development, marketing, manufacturing, and finance would be resolved at the divisional level rather than by the president. Thus, the divisional structure encourages decentralization. Decision-making is pushed down at least one level in the hierarchy, freeing the president and other top managers for strategic planning.

Geographic- or Customer-Based Divisions

An alternative for assigning divisional responsibility is to group company activities by geographic region or customer group. For example, the US Internal Revenue Service shifted to a structure focused on four distinct taxpayer (customer) groups: individuals, small businesses, corporations, and non-profit or government agencies.[27] A global geographic structure is illustrated in Exhibit 10.5. In this structure, all functions in a specific country or region report to the same division manager. The structure focuses company activities on local market conditions. Competitive advantage may come from the production or sale of a product or service adapted to a given country or region. Colgate-Palmolive Company is organized into regional divisions in North America, Europe, Latin America, the Far East and the South Pacific.[28] The structure works for Colgate because personal care products often need to be tailored to cultural values and local customs.

© LIU JIN/AFP/GETTY IMAGES

CONCEPT CONNECTION Beijing Nokia Mobile Telecommunications (BNMT) was the first of Nokia's factories in China to get an ISO 14001 certificate. The cross-functional team lead by Quality Manager Chen Min began its work in 1998 under the quality organization and in June 1999 the factory received the certificate. BNMT is a company committed to using the team-based approach to maintain and grow its market leadership. The company empowers multi-functional teams of employees to develop and launch new consumer products.

Exhibit 10.4 Functional versus Divisional Structures

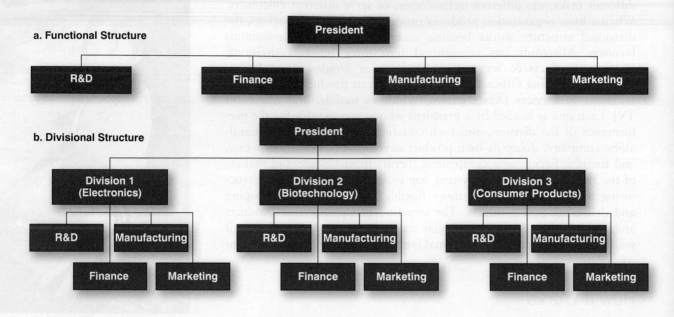

a. Functional Structure

b. Divisional Structure

Exhibit 10.5 Geographic-Based Global Organization Structure

Large non-profit organizations such as the United Way, National Council of YMCAs, Habitat for Humanity International and the Girl Scouts of the USA also frequently use a type of geographical structure, with a central headquarters and semi-autonomous local units. The national organization provides brand recognition, coordinates fund-raising services and handles some shared administrative functions, while day-to-day control and decision-making is decentralized to local or regional units.[29]

Matrix Approach

What It Is

The **matrix approach** combines aspects of both functional and divisional structures simultaneously in the same part of the organization. The matrix structure

Exhibit 10.6 Dual-Authority Structure in a Matrix Organization

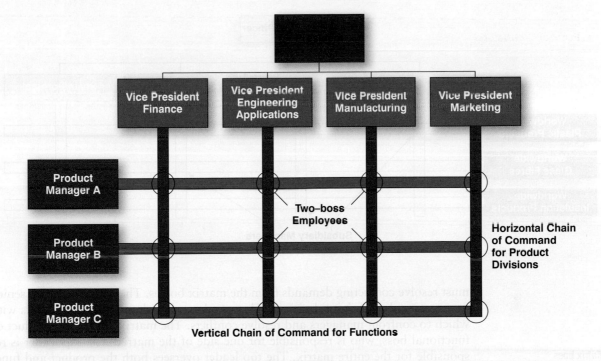

evolved as a way to improve horizontal coordination and information sharing.[30] One unique feature of the matrix is that it has dual lines of authority. In Exhibit 10.6, the functional hierarchy of authority runs vertically, and the divisional hierarchy of authority runs horizontally. The vertical structure provides traditional control within functional departments, and the horizontal structure provides coordination across departments. The matrix structure therefore supports a formal chain of command for both functional (vertical) and divisional (horizontal) relationships. As a result of this dual structure, some employees actually report to two supervisors simultaneously.

How It Works

The dual lines of authority make the matrix unique. To see how the matrix works, consider the global matrix structure illustrated in Exhibit 10.7. The two lines of authority are geographic and product. The geographic boss in Germany coordinates all subsidiaries in Germany, and the plastics products boss coordinates the manufacturing and sale of plastics products around the world. Managers of local subsidiary companies in Germany would report to two superiors, both the country boss and the product boss. The dual authority structure violates the unity-of-command concept described earlier in this chapter but is necessary to give equal emphasis to both functional and divisional lines of authority. Dual lines of authority can be confusing, but after managers learn to use this structure, the matrix provides excellent coordination simultaneously for each geographic region and each product line.

The success of the matrix structure depends on the abilities of people in key matrix roles. **Two-boss employees**, those who report to two supervisors simultaneously,

Matrix approach
An organization structure that utilizes functional and divisional chains of command simultaneously in the same part of the organization.

Two-boss employees
Employees who report to two supervisors simultaneously.

Exhibit 10.7 Global Matrix Structure

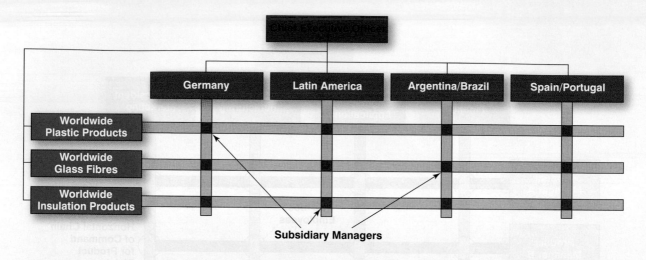

Subsidiary Managers

must resolve conflicting demands from the matrix bosses. They must confront senior managers and reach joint decisions. They need excellent human relations skills with which to confront managers and resolve conflicts. The **matrix boss** is the product or functional boss, who is responsible for one side of the matrix. The top leader is responsible for the entire matrix. The **top leader** oversees both the product and functional chains of command. His or her responsibility is to maintain a power balance between the two sides of the matrix. If disputes arise between them, the problem will be kicked upstairs to the top leader.[31]

At General Motors' Information Systems and Services, CIO Ralph Szygenda created a matrix that helped the unit cut costs and increase effectiveness.

Matrix boss
The product or functional boss, responsible for one side of the matrix.

Top leader
The overseer of both the product and functional chains of command, responsible for the entire matrix.

General Motors Information Systems and Services

When General Motors hired Ralph Szygenda as its first chief information officer in 1996, the company didn't even *have* an information office. Because the entire information technology (IT) function had been spun off to EDS in the early 1990s, GM had no IT staff of its own. Szygenda started with a clean slate and decided to create something unique among corporate IT units – a matrix structure. Szygenda believed the matrix was the best way to cope with the massive IT problems associated with a huge enterprise like GM with several highly autonomous divisions.

Szygenda hired five divisional CIOs to be in charge of information systems and services for the various GM divisions: North America, Europe, Asia-Pacific, Latin America/Africa/Middle East and GM Finance. At the same time, he put in place five process information officers (PIOs) to work horizontally in different processes that crossed divisional lines: product development, supply chain management, production, customer experience and business services. Many Information Systems and Services employees thus report to both a divisional chief information officer and a process information officer (matrix bosses). Szygenda serves as the top leader, in charge of the entire matrix.

Implementing the matrix structure was not without its problems, but employees learned to balance their overlapping responsibilities. Szygenda credits the matrix with helping to cut $1 billion out of GM's IT budget over a seven-year period. General Motors' CEO Rick Waggoner was so impressed by the success of the matrix that he set up global process leaders in other parts of the business, hoping it could help the company reap gains in productivity and manufacturing efficiency.[32]

Team Approach
What It Is

Probably the most widespread trend in departmentalization in recent years has been the implementation of team concepts. The vertical chain of command is a powerful means of control, but passing all decisions up the hierarchy takes too long and keeps responsibility at the top. The team approach gives managers a way to delegate authority, push responsibility to lower levels, and be more flexible and responsive in the competitive global environment. Chapter 18 will discuss teams in detail.

How It Works

One approach to using teams in organizations is through **cross-functional teams**, which consist of employees from various functional departments who are responsible to meet as a team and resolve mutual problems. Team members typically still report to their functional departments, but they also report to the team, one member of whom may be the leader. Cross-functional teams are used to provide needed horizontal coordination to complement an existing divisional or functional structure. A frequent use of cross-functional teams is for change projects, such as new product or service innovation. A cross-functional team of mechanics, flight attendants reservations agents, ramp workers, luggage attendants and aircraft cleaners, for example, collaborated to plan and design a new low-fare airline for British Midland Airways – BMIBaby.

> **Cross-functional teams**
> A group of employees from various functional departments that meet as a team to resolve mutual problems.

The second approach is to use **permanent teams**, groups of employees who are brought together in a way similar to a formal department. Each team brings together employees from all functional areas focused on a specific task or project, such as parts supply and logistics for an automobile plant. Emphasis is on horizontal communication and information sharing because representatives from all functions are coordinating their work and skills to complete a specific organizational task. Authority is pushed down to lower levels, and front-line employees are often given the freedom to make decisions and take action on their own. Team members may share or rotate team leadership. With a **team-based structure**, the entire organization is made up of horizontal teams that coordinate their work and work directly with customers to accomplish the organization's goals. Imagination Ltd., Britain's largest design firm, is based entirely on teamwork. Imagination puts together a diverse team at the beginning of each new project it undertakes, whether it be creating the lighting for Disney cruise ships or redesigning the packaging for Ericsson's cell phone products.[33] Imagination Ltd. has managed to make every project a smooth, seamless experience by building a culture that supports teamwork.

> **Permanent teams**
> A group of participants from several functions who are permanently assigned to solve ongoing problems of common interest.

> **Team-based structure**
> Structure in which the entire organization is made up of horizontal teams that coordinate their activities and work directly with customers to accomplish the organization's goals.

Virtual Network Approach
What It Is

The most recent approach to departmentalization extends the idea of horizontal coordination and collaboration beyond the boundaries of the organization. In a variety of industries, vertically integrated, hierarchical organizations are giving way to

INNOVATIVE WAY

Teams Work at Imagination Ltd

The essence of teamwork is that people contribute self-lessly, putting the good of the whole above their own individual interests. It doesn't always work that way, but London-based Imagination Ltd, Europe's largest independent design and communications agency, seems to have found the secret ingredient to seamless teamwork. According to Adrian Caddy, Imagination's creative director: 'The culture at Imagination is this: you can articulate your ideas without fear.'

Imagination Ltd has made a name for itself by producing award-winning, often highly theatrical programmes. For example, in February 2006, it staged a launch event for the *Harry Potter and the Prisoner of Azkaban* DVD and video by inviting 800 guests to an historic London building where it had recreated four movie sets, among them the Great Hall at the Hogwarts School of Witchcraft and Wizardry. Accomplishing such feats are teams of designers, architects, lighting experts, writers, theatre people, film directors and artists, in addition to IT specialists, marketing experts and other functional specialties. By having employees with a wide range of skills, the company is able to put together a diverse team to provide each client with a new approach to its design problems. Imagination is deliberately non-hierarchical; only four people have formal titles, and on most project teams, no one is really in

charge. Teams meet weekly, and everyone participates in every meeting from the very beginning, so there is no perception that any particular talent is primary – or secondary. Information technology specialists, production people and client-contact personnel are just as much a part of the team as the creative types. In addition, each person is expected to come up with ideas outside his or her area of expertise. The philosophy is that people at Imagination must be willing to *make* all kinds of suggestions and also to *take* all kinds of suggestions. So many ideas get batted around, revised and adapted at the weekly meetings that no one can claim ownership of a particular element of the project. The team also works closely with the client as a source of ideas and inspiration.

Talent and respect help to make the system work. Imagination hires its people carefully, based not only on the quality of their work but also on their open-mindedness and curiosity about the world beyond their functional area of expertise. Then, the company makes sure everyone's work is so closely integrated that people gain an understanding and respect for what others do. 'The integrated approach breeds respect for one another', says writer Chris White. 'When you work alone, or in isolation within your discipline, you can get an overblown sense of your own importance to a project.'

loosely interconnected groups of companies with permeable boundaries.[34] *Outsourcing*, which means farming out certain activities, such as manufacturing or credit processing, has become a significant trend. In addition, partnerships, alliances, and other complex collaborative forms are now a leading approach to accomplishing strategic goals. In the music industry, firms such as Vivendi Universal and Sony have formed networks of alliances with internet service providers, digital retailers, software firms and other companies to bring music to customers in new ways.[35] Some organizations take this networking approach to the extreme to create an innovative structure. The **virtual network structure** means that the firm sub-contracts most of its major functions to separate companies and coordinates their activities from a small headquarters organization.[36] Indian telecom company Bharti Tele-Ventures Ltd, for example, outsources everything except marketing and customer management.[37]

Virtual network structure
An organization structure that disaggregates major functions to separate companies that are brokered by a small headquarters organization.

How It Works

The organization may be viewed as a central hub surrounded by a network of outside specialists, as illustrated in Exhibit 10.8. Rather than being housed under one

Exhibit 10.8 Network Approach to Departmentalization

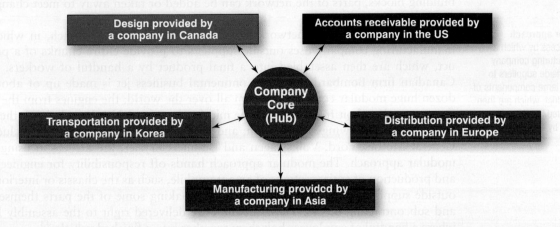

roof, services such as accounting, design, manufacturing and distribution are out-sourced to separate organizations that are connected electronically to the central office.[38] Networked computer systems, collaborative software and the internet enable organizations to exchange data and information so rapidly and smoothly that a loosely connected network of suppliers, manufacturers, assemblers and distributors can look and act like one seamless company.

The idea behind networks is that a company can concentrate on what it does best and contract out other activities to companies with distinctive competence in those specific areas, which enables a company to do more with less.[39] The Birmingham, England-based company, Strida, provides an example of the virtual network approach.

With a network structure such as that used at Strida, it is difficult to answer the question, 'Where is the organization' in traditional terms? The different organizational parts may be spread all over the world. They are drawn together contractually

 INNOVATIVE WAY

Strida

How do two people run an entire company that sells thousands of high-tech folding bicycles all over the world? Steedman Bass and Bill Bennet do it with a virtual network approach that outsources design, manufacturing, customer service, logistics, accounting, and just about everything else to other organizations.

Bass, an avid cyclist, got into the bicycle business when he and his partner Bennet bought the struggling British company Strida, which was having trouble making enough quality bicycles to meet even minimum orders. The partners soon realized why Strida was struggling. The design for the folding bicycle was a clever engineering idea, but it was a manufacturing nightmare. Bass and Bennet immediately turned over production engineering and new product development to an American bicycle designer, still with intentions of building the bikes at the Birmingham factory. However, a large order from Italy sent them looking for other options. Eventually, they transferred all manufacturing to Ming Cycle Company of Taiwan, which builds the bikes with parts sourced from parts manufacturers in Taiwan and mainland China.

Finally, the last piece of the puzzle was to contract with a company in Birmingham that would take over everything else – from marketing to distribution. Bass and Bennet concentrate their energies on managing the partnerships that make the network function smoothly.[40]

and coordinated electronically, creating a new form of organization. Much like building blocks, parts of the network can be added or taken away to meet changing needs.[41]

Modular approach
The process by which a manufacturing company uses outside suppliers to provide large components of the product, which are then assembled into a final product by a few workers.

A similar approach to networking is called the **modular approach**, in which a manufacturing company uses outside suppliers to provide entire chunks of a product, which are then assembled into a final product by a handful of workers. The Canadian firm Bombardier's new Continental business jet is made up of about a dozen huge modular components from all over the world: the engines from the US; the nose and cockpit from Canada; the mid-fuselage from Northern Ireland; the tail from Taiwan; the wings from Japan; and so forth.[42] Automobile plants, including General Motors, Ford, Volkswagen and DaimlerChrysler, are leaders in using the modular approach. The modular approach hands off responsibility for engineering and production of entire sections of an automobile, such as the chassis or interior, to outside suppliers. Suppliers design a module, making some of the parts themselves and subcontracting others. These modules are delivered right to the assembly line, where a handful of employees bolt them together into a finished vehicle.[43]

Advantages and Disadvantages of each Structure

Each of these approaches to departmentalization – functional, divisional, matrix, team and network – has strengths and weaknesses. The major advantages and disadvantages of each are listed in Exhibit 10.9.

Functional Approach

Grouping employees by common task permits economies of scale and efficient resource use. For example, at American Airlines, all information technology (IT) people work in the same, large department. They have the expertise and skills to handle almost any IT problem for the organization. Large, functionally based departments enhance the development of in-depth skills because people work on a variety of related problems and are associated with other experts within their own department. Because the chain of command converges at the top, the functional structure also provides a way to centralize decision-making and provide unified direction from top managers. The primary disadvantages reflect barriers that exist across departments. Because people are separated into distinct departments, communication and coordination across functions are often poor, causing a slow response to environmental changes. Innovation and change require involvement of several departments. Another problem is that decisions involving more than one department may pile up at the top of the organization and be delayed.

Divisional Approach

By dividing employees and resources along divisional lines, the organization will be flexible and responsive to change because each unit is small and tuned in to its environment. By having employees working on a single product line, the concern for customers' needs is high. Coordination across functional departments is better because employees are grouped together in a single location and committed to one product line. Great coordination exists within divisions; however, coordination *across* divisions is often poor. Problems occurred at Hewlett-Packard, for example,

Exhibit 10.9 Structural Advantages and Disadvantages

Structural Approach	Advantages	Disadvantages
Functional	Efficient use of resources; economies of scale	Poor communication across functional departments
	In-depth skill specialisation and development	Slow response to external changes; lagging innovation
	Top manager direction and control	Decisions concentrated at top of hierarchy, creating delay
Divisional	Fast response, flexibility in unstable environment	Duplication of resources across divisions
	Fosters concern for customer needs	Less technical depth and specialisation
	Excellent coordination across functional departments	Poor coordination across divisions
Matrix	More efficient use of resources than single hierarchy	Frustration and confusion from dual chain of command
	Flexibility, adaptability to changing environment	High conflict between two sides of the matrix
	Interdisciplinary cooperation, expertise available to all divisions	Many meetings, more discussion than action
Team	Reduced barriers among departments, increased compromise	Dual loyalties and conflict
	Shorter response time, quicker decisions	Time and resources spent on meetings
	Better morale, enthusiasm from employee involvement	Unplanned decentralisation
Virtual Network	Can draw on expertise worldwide	Lack of control; weak boundaries
	Highly flexible and responsive	Greater demands on managers
	Reduced overhead costs	Employee loyalty weakened

when autonomous divisions went in opposite directions. The software produced in one division did not fit the hardware produced in another. Thus, the divisional structure was realigned to establish adequate coordination across divisions. Another major disadvantage is duplication of resources and the high cost of running separate divisions. Instead of a single research department in which all research people use a single facility, each division may have its own research facility. The organization loses efficiency and economies of scale. In addition, the small size of departments within each division may result in a lack of technical specialization, expertise and training.

Matrix Approach

The matrix structure is controversial because of the dual chain of command. However, the matrix can be highly effective in a complex, rapidly changing environment in which the organization needs to be flexible and adaptable.[44] The conflict and frequent meetings generated by the matrix allow new issues to be raised and resolved. The matrix structure makes efficient use of human resources because specialists can be transferred from one division to another. The major problem is the confusion and frustration caused by the dual chain of command. Matrix bosses and two-boss employees have difficulty with the dual reporting relationships. The matrix structure also can generate high conflict because it pits divisional against functional goals in a domestic structure, or product line versus country goals in a global structure. Rivalry between the two sides of the matrix can be exceedingly difficult for two-boss employees to manage. This problem leads to the third disadvantage: time lost to meetings and discussions devoted to resolving this conflict. Often the matrix structure leads to more discussion than action because different goals and points of view are being addressed. Managers may spend a great deal of time coordinating meetings and assignments, which takes time away from core work activities.[45]

TAKE A MOMENT   As a new manager, understand the advantages and disadvantages of each approach to departmentalization. Recognize how each structure can provide benefits but might not be appropriate for every organization and situation.

Team Approach

The team concept breaks down barriers across departments and improves cooperation. Team members know one another's problems and compromise rather than blindly pursue their own goals. The team concept also enables the organization to more quickly adapt to customer requests and environmental changes and speeds decision-making because decisions need not go to the top of the hierarchy for approval. Another big advantage is the morale boost. Employees are enthusiastic about their involvement in bigger projects rather than narrow departmental tasks. At video games company Ubisoft, for example, each studio is set up so that teams of employees and managers work collaboratively to develop new games. Employees don't make a lot of money, but they're motivated by the freedom they have to propose new ideas and put them into action.[46]

However, the team approach has disadvantages as well. Employees may be enthusiastic about team participation, but they may also experience conflicts and dual loyalties. A cross-functional team may make different demands on members than do their department managers, and members who participate in more than one team must resolve these conflicts. A large amount of time is devoted to meetings, thus increasing coordination time. Unless the organization truly needs teams to coordinate complex projects and adapt to the environment, it will lose production efficiency with them. Finally, the team approach may cause too much decentralization. Senior department managers who traditionally made decisions might feel left out when a team moves ahead on its own. Team members often do not see the big picture of the corporation and may make decisions that are good for their group but bad for the organization as a whole.

Virtual Network Approach

The biggest advantages to a virtual network approach are flexibility and competitiveness on a global scale. The extreme flexibility of a network approach is illustrated by today's 'war on terrorism'. Most experts agree that the primary reason the insurgency is so difficult to fight is that it is a far-flung collection of groups that share a specific mission but are free to act on their own. 'Attack any single part of it, and the rest carries on largely untouched', wrote one journalist after talking with US and Iraqi officials. 'It cannot be decapitated, because the insurgency, for the most part, has no head.'[47] One response is for the US and its allies to organize into networks to quickly change course, put new people in place as needed, and respond to situations and challenges as they emerge.[48]

Today's business organizations can also benefit from a flexible network approach that lets them shift resources and respond quickly. A network organization can draw on resources and expertise worldwide to achieve the best quality and price and can sell its products and services worldwide. Flexibility comes from the ability to hire whatever services are needed, and to change a few months later without constraints from owning plant, equipment, and facilities. The organization can continually redefine itself to fit new product and market opportunities. This structure is perhaps the leanest of all organization forms because little supervision is required. Large teams of staff specialists and administrators are not needed. A network organization may have only two or three levels of hierarchy, compared with ten or more in traditional organizations.[49]

One of the major disadvantages is lack of hands-on control. Managers do not have all operations under one roof and must rely on contracts, coordination, negotiation, and electronic linkages to hold things together. Each partner in the network necessarily acts in its own self-interest. The weak and ambiguous boundaries create higher uncertainty and greater demands on managers for defining shared goals, coordinating activities, managing relationships, and keeping people focused and motivated.[50] Finally, in this type of organization, employee loyalty can weaken. Employees might feel they can be replaced by contract services. A cohesive corporate culture is less likely to develop, and turnover tends to be higher because emotional commitment between organization and employee is weak.

Organizing for Horizontal Coordination

One reason for the growing use of teams and networks is that many companies are recognizing the limits of traditional vertical organization structures in today's fast-shifting environment. In general, the trend is toward breaking down barriers between departments, and many companies are moving toward horizontal structures based on work processes rather than departmental functions.[51] However, regardless of the type of structure, every organization needs mechanisms for horizontal integration and coordination. The structure of an organization is not complete without designing the horizontal as well as the vertical dimensions of structure.[52]

The Need for Coordination

As organizations grow and evolve, two things happen. First, new positions and departments are added to deal with factors in the external environment or with new strategic needs. For example, in recent years most colleges and universities established in-house legal departments to cope with increasing government regulations and a greater threat of lawsuits in today's society. Whereas small schools once relied on outside law firms, legal counsel is now considered crucial to the everyday operation of a college or university.[53] Many organizations establish information technology departments to manage the proliferation of new information systems. As companies add positions and departments to meet changing needs, they grow more complex, with hundreds of positions and departments performing incredibly diverse activities.

Second, senior managers have to find a way to tie all of these departments together. The formal chain of command and the supervision it provides is effective, but it is not enough. The organization needs systems to process information and enable communication among people in different departments and at different levels. Coordination refers to the quality of collaboration across departments. Without coordination, a company's left hand will not act in concert with the right hand, causing problems and conflicts. Coordination is required regardless of whether the organization has a functional, divisional, or team structure. Employees identify with their immediate department or team, taking its interest to heart, and may not want to compromise with other units for the good of the organization as a whole.

Coordination
The quality of collaboration across departments.

Without a major effort at coordination, an organization may be like Chrysler Corporation in the 1980s when Lee Iacocca took over:

'What I found at Chrysler were 35 vice presidents, each with his own turf... I couldn't believe, for example, that the guy running engineering departments wasn't in constant touch with his counterpart in manufacturing. But that's how it was. Everybody worked independently. I took one look at that system and I almost threw up. That's when I knew I was in really deep trouble.

'I'd call in a guy from engineering, and he'd stand there dumbfounded when I'd explain to him that we had a design problem or some other hitch in the engineering-manufacturing relationship. He might have the ability to invent a brilliant piece of engineering that would save us a lot of money. He might come up with a terrific new design. There was only one problem: he didn't know that the manufacturing people couldn't build it. Why? Because he had never talked to them about it. Nobody at Chrysler seemed to understand that interaction among the different functions in a company is absolutely critical. People in engineering and manufacturing almost have to be sleeping together. These guys weren't even flirting!'[54]

If one thing changed at Chrysler (now DaimlerChrysler) in the years before Iacocca retired, it was improved coordination. Cooperation among engineering, marketing, and manufacturing enabled the rapid design and production of the Chrysler PT Cruiser, for example.

The problem of coordination is amplified in the international arena, because organizational units are differentiated not only by goals and work activities but by geographical distance, time differences, cultural values, and perhaps language as well. How can managers ensure that needed coordination will take place in their company, both domestically and globally? Coordination is the outcome of information and cooperation. Managers can design systems and structures to promote horizontal coordination. For example, to support its global strategy, Whirlpool decentralized its operations, giving more authority and responsibility to teams of designers and engineers in developing countries like Brazil, and established outsourcing relationships with manufacturers in China and India.[55] Exhibit 10.10 illustrates the evolution of organizational structures, with a growing emphasis on horizontal coordination. Although the vertical functional structure is effective in stable environments, it does not provide the horizontal coordination needed in times of rapid change. Innovations such as cross-functional teams, task forces, and project managers work within the vertical structure but provide a means to increase horizontal communication and cooperation. The next stage involves re-engineering to structure

Exhibit 10.10 Evolution of Organization Structures

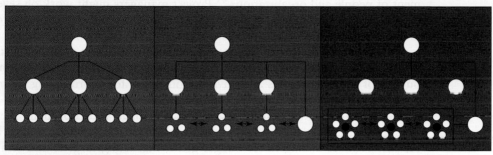

| Traditional Vertical Structure | Cross-Functional Teams and Project Managers | Re-engineering to Horizontal Teams |

the organization into teams working on horizontal processes. The vertical hierarchy is flattened, with perhaps only a few senior executives in traditional support functions such as finance and human resources.

Task Forces, Teams and Project Management

A task force is a temporary team or committee designed to solve a short-term problem involving several departments.[56] Task force members represent their departments and share information that enables coordination. For example, the Shawmut National Corporation created a task force in human resources to consolidate all employment services into a single area. The task force looked at job banks, referral programmes, employment procedures, and applicant tracking systems; found ways to perform these functions for all Shawmut's divisions in one human resource department; and then disbanded.[57] In addition to creating task forces, companies also set up *cross-functional teams*, as described earlier. A cross-functional team furthers horizontal coordination because participants from several departments meet regularly to solve ongoing problems of common interest.[58]

This team is similar to a task force except that it works with continuing rather than temporary problems and might exist for several years. Team members think in terms of working together for the good of the whole rather than just for their own department. For example, top executives at one large consumer products company had to hold frequent marathon meetings to resolve conflicts among functional units. Functional managers were focused on achieving departmental goals and were engaged in little communication across units. Resolving the conflicts that arose was time-consuming and arduous for everyone involved. Establishing a cross-functional team solved the problem by ensuring regular horizontal communication and cooperation regarding common issues and problems.[59]

Companies also use project managers to increase coordination between functional departments. A project manager is a person who is responsible for coordinating the activities of several departments for the completion of a specific project.[60] Project managers are critical today because many organizations are continually reinventing themselves,

Task force
A temporary team or committee formed to solve a specific short-term problem involving several departments.

Project manager
A person responsible for coordinating the activities of several departments on a full-time basis for the completion of a specific project.

© P. COX/ALAMY

CONCEPT CONNECTION After weeks of intense criticism following a global recall of several automobile models, including the iQ in the photograph, Toyota setup a global quality-control task force headed by the company's president, Akio Toyoda. Only a cross-functional team could address the wide-ranging crisis facing the company.

creating flexible structures, and working on projects with an ever-changing assortment of people and organizations.[61] Project managers might work on several different projects at one time and might have to move in and out of new projects at a moment's notice.

The distinctive feature of the project manager position is that the person is not a member of one of the departments being coordinated. Project managers are located outside of the departments and have responsibility for coordinating several departments to achieve desired project outcomes. For example, General Mills, Procter & Gamble, and General Foods all use product managers to coordinate their product lines. A manager is assigned to each line, such as Cheerios, Bisquick and Hamburger Helper. Product managers set budget goals, marketing targets, and strategies and obtain the cooperation from advertising, production and sales personnel needed for implementing product strategy.

TAKE A MOMENT   As a new manager, be a team or task force member who reaches out to facilitate horizontal coordination. Don't limit yourself to your own function. Share information across departmental boundaries to improve horizontal communication and understanding. Build your people skills to influence and persuade as an effective project manager.

In some organizations, project managers are included on the organization chart, as illustrated in Exhibit 10.11. The project manager is drawn to one side of the chart to indicate authority over the project but not over the people assigned to it. Dashed lines to the project manager indicate responsibility for coordination and communication with assigned team members, but department managers retain line authority over functional employees.

Project managers might also have titles such as product manager, integrator, programme manager or process owner. Project managers need excellent people skills. They use expertise and persuasion to achieve coordination among various departments, and their jobs involve getting people together, listening, building trust, confronting problems, and resolving conflicts and disputes in the best interest of the project and the organization. Consider the role of CITI Project Management Consultancy within Eurostar's new project community development initiative.

Exhibit 10.11 Example of Project Manager Relationships to Other Departments

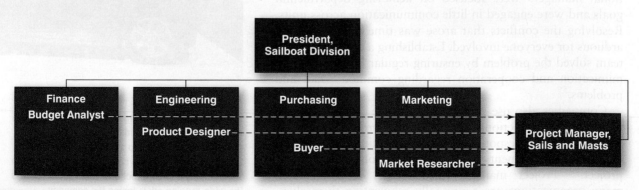

◯ INNOVATIVE WAY

Eurostar[62]

With revenues rising, reliability increasing and travel time falling, Eurostar has transformed the travel market between London and Paris-Brussels. Eurostar's continuing success means that it must gear itself up for change. A new organizational structure had to be in place that focused on the governance and execution of projects. Its business purpose is to make the company more responsive, able to translate strategic and operational imperatives more quickly and more predictably into operational reality.

To ensure that the project community could meet the challenges that he and the marketplace are setting, Richard asked CITI project management consultancy to support his management team. He needed to put in place the components of an integrated portfolio management approach. CITI's starting point was to determine the number and types of projects Eurostar had planned over the next four years. In parallel they profiled all Eurostar's *project managers*. They also ran a number of project health checks to identify common issues and

points of concern. From this analysis five strands of work were woven together into a mutually reinforcing programme of change. Senior managers became involved with seminars and workshops in which the issues and accountabilities associated with the governance of a portfolio and the sponsorship of individual projects were thrashed out and clear lines of responsibility drawn.

The impact of the programme was evident after just nine months. Project governance is in place and working. There is a perceptible 'professionalization' within the project management community. The focus on performance and delivery has sharpened, and the status and influence of the project management office continues to grow. There remains much to do but, leading from the front, Richard has engaged all levels of the business and rapid progress is ensured, and as he says himself: 'The future is looking much brighter for Eurostar as it prepares to celebrate its 10th anniversary, and its demands on its project community continues to grow, and they are now responsive and a genuine asset.'

Re-engineering

Re-engineering, sometimes called *business process re-engineering*, is the radical redesign of business processes to achieve dramatic improvements in cost, quality, service, and speed.[63] Because the focus of re-engineering is on process rather than function, re-engineering generally leads to a shift away from a strong vertical structure to one emphasizing stronger horizontal coordination and greater flexibility in responding to changes in the environment.

Re-engineering changes the way managers think about how work is done in their organizations. Rather than focusing on narrow jobs structured into distinct, functional departments, they emphasise core processes that cut horizontally across the company and involve teams of employees working to provide value directly to customers.[64] A **process** is an organized group of related tasks and activities that work together to transform inputs into outputs and create value. Common examples of processes include new product development, order fulfilment and customer service.[65]

Re-engineering frequently involves a shift to a horizontal team-based structure, as described earlier in this chapter. All the people who work on a particular process have easy access to one another so they can easily communicate and coordinate their efforts, share knowledge and provide value directly to customers.[66] For example, re-engineering at Texas Instruments led to the formation of product development teams that became the fundamental organizational unit. Each team is made up of

Re-engineering
The radical redesign of business processes to achieve dramatic improvements in cost, quality, service, and speed.

Process
An organized group of related tasks and activities that work together to transform inputs into outputs and create value.

business processes can be mind-boggling. AT&T's Network Systems division started with a list of 130 processes and then began working to pare them down to 13 core ones.[69] Organizations often have difficulty realigning power relationships and management processes to support work redesign, and thus do not reap the intended benefits of re-engineering. According to some estimates, 70 per cent of re-engineering efforts fail to reach their intended goals.[70] Because re-engineering is expensive, time consuming, and usually painful, it seems best suited to companies that are facing serious competitive threats.

Factors Shaping Structure

Despite the trend toward horizontal design, vertical hierarchies continue to thrive because they often provide important benefits for organizations.[71] How do managers know whether to design a structure that emphasises the formal, vertical hierarchy or one with an emphasis on horizontal communication and collaboration? The answer lies in the contingency factors that influence organization structure. Research on organization design shows that structure depends on a variety of *contingencies*, as defined in Chapter 2. The right structure is designed to 'fit' the contingency factors of strategy, environment, and production technology, as illustrated in Exhibit 10.13. These three areas are changing quite dramatically for most organizations, creating a need for stronger horizontal coordination.

Structure follows Strategy

In Chapter 8, we discussed several strategies that business firms can adopt. Two strategies proposed by Porter are differentiation and cost leadership.[72] With a differentiation strategy, the organization attempts to develop innovative products unique to the market. With a cost leadership strategy, the organization strives for internal efficiency. The strategies of cost leadership versus differentiation typically require different structural approaches. A recent study demonstrated that business performance is strongly influenced by how well the company's structure is aligned with its strategic intent, so managers strive to pick strategies and structures that are congruent.[73]

Exhibit 10.14 shows a simplified continuum that illustrates how structural approaches are associated with strategic goals. The pure functional structure is appropriate for achieving internal efficiency goals. The vertical functional structure uses task specialization and a strict chain of command to gain efficient use of

Exhibit 10.13 Contingency Factors that Influence Organization Structure

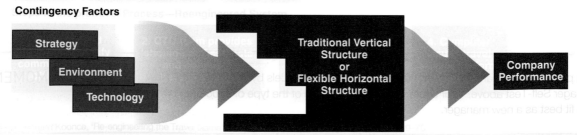

Contingency Factors

Strategy

Environment

Technology

Traditional Vertical Structure
or
Flexible Horizontal Structure

Company Performance

Exhibit 10.14 Relationship of Strategic Goals to Structural Approach

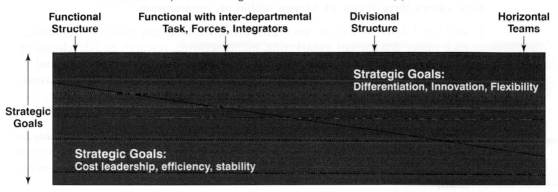

| Functional Structure | Functional with inter-departmental Task, Forces, Integrators | Divisional Structure | Horizontal Teams |

Strategic Goals

Strategic Goals:
Differentiation, Innovation, Flexibility

Strategic Goals:
Cost leadership, efficiency, stability

scarce resources, but it does not enable the organization to be flexible or innovative. In contrast, horizontal teams are appropriate when the primary goal is innovation and flexibility. Each team is small, is able to be responsive, and has the people and resources necessary for performing its task. The flexible horizontal structure enables organizations to differentiate themselves and respond quickly to the demands of a shifting environment but at the expense of efficient resource use. New strategies also shape structure in government organizations. Under financial pressure to cut costs and political pressure to keep customers happy, Departments of Motor Vehicles are farming out DMV business whenever possible by building strong partnerships with other companies. For example, in most states, auto dealers register new cars on site when they are sold.[74]

Exhibit 10.14 also illustrates how other forms of structure represent intermediate steps on the organization's path to efficiency or innovation. The functional structure with cross-functional teams and project managers provides greater coordination and flexibility than the pure functional structure. The divisional structure promotes differentiation because each division can focus on specific products and customers, although divisions tend to be larger and less flexible than small teams. Exhibit 10.14 does not include all possible structures, but it illustrates how structures can be used to facilitate the strategic goals of cost leadership or differentiation.

Structure Reflects the Environment

In Chapter 3, we discussed the nature of environmental uncertainty. Environmental uncertainty means decision-makers have difficulty acquiring good information and predicting external changes. Uncertainty occurs when the

© BRUNO VINCENT/GETTY IMAGES

CONCEPT CONNECTION The Metropolitan Police Service is a large organization with a complex command structure that reflects the diverse range of tasks it is expected to undertake. Following a recent restructuring, most of the day-to-day policing of London is the responsibility of 33 borough operational command units (BOCUs). In addition to policing London's streets, the Met has various specialist units dedicated to reducing all aspects of serious and specialist crime: Specialist Crime Directorate place a renewed emphasis on working collaboratively with communities, boroughs and partners to identify effective solutions to serious crime problems; Specialist Operation Groups deal with tasks such as intelligence, security, protection of politicians, embassies and royalty, and the investigation of certain categories of serious crimes, including racial and violent crime and terrorism. An organization the size of the Metropolitan Police Service could not function without various management, administration and support functions. For this reason the Met has thousands of staff, including police officers as well as civilians, who work behind the scenes to ensure that the front line units can do their job. The Met police adapts to the high-stakes in an uncertain environment surrounding the ever increasing London population by shifting from a mechanistic to an organic system that allows for flexibility and rapid response.

© KIM KULISH/CORBIS

Structure Fits the Technology

Technology includes the knowledge, tools, techniques, and activities used to transform organizational inputs into outputs.[81] Technology includes machinery, employee skills and work procedures. A useful way to think about technology is as production activities. The production activities may be to produce steel castings, television programmes or computer software. Technologies vary between manufacturing and service organizations. In addition, new digital technology has an impact on structure.

CONCEPT CONNECTION Employees at ConocoPhillips' Los Angeles, California, petroleum refinery at Wilmington use continuous process production to supply refined products to markets in California, Nevada and Arizona. This sophisticated type of technology is typically associated with a small span of control, a high degree of horizontal communication, and a flexible structure to handle the complexities that arise. The ConocoPhillips global refining network has a crude oil processing capacity of 2.6 million barrels per day, including 2.2 million in the United States.

Woodward's Manufacturing Technology

The most influential research into the relationship between manufacturing technology and organization structure was conducted by Joan Woodward, a British industrial sociologist.[82] She gathered data from 100 British firms to determine whether basic structural characteristics, such as administrative overhead, span of control, and centralization were different across firms. She found that manufacturing firms could be categorized according to three basic types of production technology:

Small-batch production
A type of technology that involves the production of goods in batches of one or a few products designed to customer specification.

1   *Small-batch and unit production.* **Small-batch production** firms produce goods in batches of one or a few products designed to customer specification. Each customer orders a unique product. This technology also is used to make large, one-of-a-kind products, such as computer-controlled machines. Small-batch manufacturing is close to traditional skilled-craft work, because human beings are a large part of the process. Examples of items produced through small-batch manufacturing include custom clothing, special-order machine tools, space capsules, satellites, and submarines.

Mass production
A type of technology characterized by the production of a large volume of products with the same specifications.

2   *Large-batch and mass production.* **Mass production** technology is distinguished by standardized production runs. A large volume of products is produced, and all customers receive the same product. Standard products go into inventory for sale as customers need them. This technology makes greater use of machines than does small-batch production. Machines are designed to do most of the physical work, and employees complement the machinery. Examples of mass production are automobile assembly lines and the large-batch techniques used to produce tobacco products and textiles.

Continuous process production
A type of technology involving mechanization of the entire work flow and non-stop production.

3   *Continuous process production.* In **continuous process production**, the entire work flow is mechanized in a sophisticated and complex form of production technology. Because the process runs continuously, it has no starting and stopping. Human operators are not part of actual production because machinery does all of the work. Human operators simply read dials, fix machines that break down and manage the production process. Examples of continuous process technologies are chemical plants, distilleries, petroleum refineries and nuclear power plants.

Technical complexity
The degree to which complex machinery is involved in the production process to the exclusion of people.

The difference among the three manufacturing technologies is called **technical complexity**. Technical complexity is the degree to which machinery is involved in the

Exhibit 10.16 Relationship Between Manufacturing Technology and Organization Structure

	Manufacturing Technology		
	Small Batch	**Mass Production**	**Continuous Process**
Technical Complexity of Production Technology:	Low	Medium	High
Organization Structure:			
Centralization	Low	High	Low
Top administrator ratio	Low	Medium	High
Indirect/direct labour ratio	1/9	1/4	1/1
Supervisor span of control	23	48	15
Communication:			
Written (vertical)	Low	High	Low
Verbal (horizontal)	High	Low	High
Overall structure	Organic	Mechanistic	Organic

SOURCE: Based on Joan Woodward, *Industrial Organizations: Theory and Practice* (London: Oxford University Press, 1965).

production to the exclusion of people. With a complex technology, employees are hardly needed except to monitor the machines.

The structural characteristics associated with each type of manufacturing technology are illustrated in Exhibit 10.16. Note that centralization is high for mass production technology and low for continuous process. Unlike small-batch and continuous process production, standardized mass-production machinery requires centralized decision-making and well-defined rules and procedures. The administrative ratio and the percentage of indirect labour required also increase with technological complexity. Because the production process is non-routine, closer supervision is needed. More indirect labour in the form of maintenance people is required because of the machinery's complexity; thus, the indirect/direct labour ratio is high. Span of control for first-line supervisors is greatest for mass production. On an assembly line, jobs are so routinized that a supervisor can handle an average of 48 employees. The number of employees per supervisor in small-batch and continuous process production is lower because closer supervision is needed. Overall, small-batch and continuous process firms have somewhat loose, flexible structures (organic), and mass production firms have tight vertical structures (mechanistic).

The important conclusion about manufacturing technology was described by Woodward as follows: 'Different technologies impose different kinds of demands on individuals and organizations, and these demands have to be met through an appropriate structure'.[83] Woodward found that the relationship between structure and technology was directly related to company performance. Low-performing firms tended to deviate from the preferred structural form, often adopting a structure appropriate for another type of technology. High-performing organizations had characteristics similar to those listed in Exhibit 10.16.

Service Technology

Service organizations are increasingly important in North America. For the past two decades, more people have been employed in service organizations than in manufacturing firms. Examples of service organizations include consulting companies, law firms, brokerage houses, airlines, hotels, advertising companies, amusement parks and educational organizations. In addition, service technology characterizes many departments in large corporations, even manufacturing firms. In a manufacturing company such as Ford Motor Company, the legal, human resources, finance and market research departments all provide service. Thus, the structure and design of these departments reflect their own service technology rather than the manufacturing plant's technology. **Service technology** can be defined as follows:

> **Service technology**
> Technology characterized by intangible outputs and direct contact between employees and customers.

1 *Intangible output.* The output of a service firm is intangible. Services are perishable and, unlike physical products, cannot be stored in inventory. The service is either consumed immediately or lost forever. Manufactured products are produced at one point in time and can be stored until sold at another time.

2 *Direct contact with customers.* Employees and customers interact directly to provide and purchase the service. Production and consumption are simultaneous. Service firm employees have direct contact with customers. In a manufacturing firm, technical employees are separated from customers, and hence no direct interactions occur.[84]

TAKE A MOMENT   As a new manager, recognize how structure fits the contingency factors of strategy, environment and technology. Design the right mix of structural characteristics to fit the contingency factors.

One distinct feature of service technology that directly influences structure is the need for employees to be close to the customer.[85] Structural characteristics are similar to those for continuous manufacturing technology, shown in Exhibit 10.16. Service firms tend to be flexible, informal and decentralized. Horizontal communication is high because employees must share information and resources to serve customers and solve problems. Services also are dispersed; hence each unit is often small and located geographically close to customers. For example, banks, hotels, fast-food franchises, and doctors' offices disperse their facilities into regional and local offices to provide faster and better service to customers.

Some services can be broken down into explicit steps, so that employees can follow set rules and procedures. For example, McDonald's has standard procedures for serving customers and Marriott has standard procedures for cleaning hotel rooms. When services can be standardized, a tight centralized structure can be effective, but service firms in general tend to be more organic, flexible and decentralized.

> **Digital technology**
> Technology characterized by use of the internet and other digital processes to conduct or support business operations.

Digital Technology

Digital technology is characterized by use of the internet and other digital processes to conduct or support business online. E-commerce organizations such as Amazon. com, which sells books and other products to consumers over the internet; eBay, an online auction site; Google, an internet search engine; and Priceline.com, which allows consumers to name their own prices and then negotiates electronically with its partner organizations on behalf of the consumer, are all examples of firms based on digital technology. In addition, large companies such as General Electric, Dell Inc. and Ford Motor Company are involved in business-to-business commerce, using digital technology to conduct transactions with suppliers and partners.

Like service firms, organizations based on digital technology tend to be flexible and decentralized. Horizontal communication and collaboration are typically high, and these companies may frequently be involved in virtual network arrangements. Digital technology is driving the move toward horizontal forms that link customers, suppliers and partners into the organizational network, with everyone working together as if they were one organization. People may use electronic connections to link themselves together into teams. For example, an employee may send an email to people both within and outside the organization who can help with a particular customer problem and quickly form a virtual team to develop a solution.[86] In other words, digital technology encourages *boundarylessness*, where information and work activities flow freely among various organizational participants. Centralization is low, and employees are empowered to work in teams to meet fast-changing needs. Verbal and electronic communication is high, both up and down as well as across the organization, because up-to-the minute information is essential. In the digital world, advantage comes from seeing first and moving fastest, which requires extraordinary openness and flexibility.[87]

Changing Organizational Design

A common response to solving efficiency problem within an organization is to remove essentially 'structural' constraints to equitable and efficient resource use, and assure a supportive management culture.

Lack of organizational congruence may arise for many reasons. For example, it may arise because there has been no recognition of the need to complement separation of functions with organizational change. It may arise from the failure to establish structures that have been approved by the management but not created in practice.

It may arise from the creeping duplication that may occur when a new structure is established and an existing one with similar responsibilities is not removed or 'retooled'. It may arise when reporting channels between organizational departments are not altered to fit new lines of authority and accountability.

Assuming that actors have clearly defined functions and responsibilities and the means to carry them out, one would be interested in the following things:

- The extent to which organizational arrangements minimize overlap, undesirable duplication or fragmentation.
- Whether any intended separation or integration of functions and responsibilities is reflected in organizational arrangements.
- Whether clear and operational lines of communication and reporting exist. For example, do organizational linkages facilitate exchange of information and communication, e.g. between people responsible for capital and recurrent budgeting; between people identifying needs and those planning resources; between people financing and providing services; between projects?

Part of the effectiveness of organizational design can be determined by the management culture within the system and the management's credibility in the eyes of employees. This was discussed in Chapter 3 on culture.

A MANAGER'S ESSENTIALS: WHAT HAVE WE LEARNED?

- Fundamental characteristics of organization structure include work specialization, chain of command, authority and responsibility, span of management, and centralization and decentralization. These dimensions represent the vertical hierarchy and define how authority and responsibility are distributed.

- Another major concept is departmentalization, which describes how organization employees are grouped. Three traditional approaches are functional, divisional and matrix; contemporary approaches are team and virtual network structures. The functional approach groups employees by common skills and tasks. The opposite structure is divisional, which groups people by organizational output such that each division has a mix of functional skills and tasks. The matrix structure uses two chains of command simultaneously, and some employees have two bosses. The team approach uses permanent teams and cross-functional teams to achieve better coordination and employee commitment than is possible with a purely functional structure. The network approach means that a firm concentrates on what it does best and subcontracts other functions to separate organizations that are connected to the headquarters electronically.

- Each organization form has advantages and disadvantages and can be used by managers to meet the needs of the competitive situation. In addition, managers adjust elements of the vertical structure, such as the degree of centralization or decentralization, to meet changing needs.

- As organizations grow, they add new departments, functions, and hierarchical levels. A major problem for management is how to tie the whole organization together. Horizontal coordination mechanisms provide coordination across departments and include re-engineering, task forces, project managers and horizontal teams.

- The correct structural approach is influenced by the firm's strategic goals. When a firm's strategy is to differentiate its products or services, an organic flexible structure using teams, decentralization and empowered employees is appropriate. A mechanistic structure is appropriate for a low-cost strategy, which typically occurs in a stable environment. The structure needs to be looser and more flexible when environmental uncertainty is high.

Returning to the opening example, Carlos Ghosn used structural changes to help revive Nissan and restore its competitive position in the auto industry. Today, Nissan is on a roll, with hot new car and truck models that customers want. The company has the highest profit margins of any major automaker, and racked up record earnings of $4.8 billion in 2004, a year when most other auto manufacturers were reeling from losses. One of Ghosn's first steps was to clarify managers' areas of responsibility and authority and implement mechanisms to ensure accountability. Positions were redesigned so that managers who previously acted as advisors had direct line authority and a clear understanding of how they were expected to contribute to the organization. The compensation and advancement systems were also revised. The major structural change Ghosn made was to create nine cross-functional management teams that would determine a detailed turnaround plan for the organization. Ghosn believed the team approach was the best way to get managers to see beyond the functional and regional boundaries that were hampering collaboration and new product development. Each team was made up of managers from various functional areas. For example, the purchasing team consisted of members from purchasing, engineering, manufacturing, and finance. Within three months, the teams had created a detailed blueprint for Nissan's turnaround. Within three years, implementation of various aspects of the plan had returned Nissan to profitability. The cross-functional teams continue as an integral part of Nissan's management structure, helping ensure continued horizontal communication and collaboration to help the company compete in the turbulent auto industry.[88]

DISCUSSION QUESTIONS

1 Sandra Holt, manager of Electronics Assembly, asked Hector Cruz, her senior technician, to handle things in the department while Sandra worked on the budget. She needed peace and quiet for at least a week to complete her figures. After ten days, Sandra discovered that Hector had hired a senior secretary, not realizing that Sandra had promised interviews to two other people. Evaluate Sandra's approach to delegation.

2 Many experts note that organizations have been making greater use of teams in recent years. What factors might account for this trend?

3 An organizational consultant was heard to say, 'Some aspect of functional structure appears in every organization.' Do you agree? Explain.

4 The divisional structure is often considered almost the opposite of a functional structure. Do you agree? Briefly explain the major differences in these two approaches to departmentalization.

5 Some people argue that the matrix structure should be adopted only as a last resort because the dual chains of command can create more problems than they solve. Discuss. Do you agree or disagree? Why?

6 What is the virtual network approach to structure? Is the use of authority and responsibility different compared with other forms of departmentalization? Explain.

7 The Hay Group published a report that some managers have personalities suited to horizontal relationships such as project management that achieve results with little formal authority. Other managers are more suited to operating roles with much formal authority in a vertical structure. In what type of structure – functional, matrix, team, or virtual network – would you feel most comfortable managing? Which structure would be the most challenging for you? Give your reasons.

8 Experts say that organizations are becoming increasingly decentralized, with authority, decision-making responsibility and accountability being pushed farther down into the organization. How will this trend affect what will be asked of you as a new manager?

9 The chapter suggested that structure should be designed to fit strategy. Some theorists argue that strategy should be designed to fit the organization's structure. With which theory do you agree? Explain.

10 Carnival Cruise Lines provides pleasure cruises to the masses. Carnival has several ships and works on high volume/low price rather than offering luxury cruises. What would you predict about the organization structure of a Carnival Cruise ship compared with a company that had smaller ships for wealthy customers? Discuss why an organization in an uncertain environment requires more horizontal relationships than one in a certain environment.

11 What is the difference between manufacturing and service technology? How would you classify a university, a local discount store, a nursery school? How would you expect the structure of a service organization to differ from that of a manufacturing organization?

12 What impact does the growing use of digital technology have on organizational structure? Would you expect the structure of an internet-based organization such as eBay, which operates almost entirely online, to be different from a bricks-and-mortar company such as General Electric that uses the internet for business-to-business transactions with vendors? Why or why not?

MANAGEMENT IN PRACTICE: EXPERIENTIAL EXERCISE

Organic Versus Mechanistic Organization Structure

Interview an employee at your university, such as a department head or secretary. Have the employee answer the following 13 questions about his or her job and organizational conditions. Then, answer the same set of questions for a job you have held.

Disagree Strongly 1   2   3   4   5   Agree Strongly

1 Your work would be considered routine.

1   2   3   4   5

2 A clearly known way is established to do the major tasks you encounter.

1   2   3   4   5

3 Your work has high variety and frequent exceptions.

1   2   3   4   5

4 Communications from above consist of information and advice rather than instructions and directions.

1   2   3   4   5

5 You have the support of peers and your supervisor to do your job well.

1   2   3   4   5

6 You seldom exchange ideas or information with people doing other kinds of jobs.

1   2   3   4   5

7 Decisions relevant to your work are made above you and passed down.

1   2   3   4   5

8 People at your level frequently have to figure out for themselves what their jobs are for the day.

1   2   3   4   5

9 Lines of authority are clear and precisely defined.

1   2   3   4   5

10 Leadership tends to be democratic rather than autocratic in style.

1   2   3   4   5

11 Job descriptions are written and up-to-date for each job.

1   2   3   4   5

12 People understand each other's jobs and often do different tasks.

1   2   3   4   5

13 A manual of policies and procedures is available to use when a problem arises.

1   2   3   4   5

Scoring and Interpretation

To obtain the total score, subtract the scores for questions 1, 2, 6, 7, 9, 11 and 13 from the number 6 and total the adjusted scores.

Total Score, Employee: _____

Total Score, You: _____

Compare the total score for a place you have worked to the score of the university employee you interviewed. A total score of 52 or above suggests that you or the other respondent is working in an organic organization. The score reflects a loose, flexible structure that is often associated with uncertain environments and small-batch or service technology. People working in this structure feel empowered. Many organizations today are moving in the direction of flexible structures and empowerment.

A score of 26 or below suggests a mechanistic structure. This structure utilizes traditional control and functional specialization, which often occurs in a certain environment, a stable organization, and routine or mass-production technology. People in this structure may feel controlled and constrained.

Discuss the pros and cons of organic versus mechanistic structure. Does the structure of the employee you interviewed fit the nature of the organization's environment, strategic goals and technology? How about the structure for your own workplace? How might you redesign the structure to make the work organization more effective?

MANAGEMENT IN PRACTICE: ETHICAL DILEMMA

A Matter of Delegation

Tom Harrington loved his job as an assistant quality-control officer for Rockingham Toys. After six months of unemployment, he was anxious to make a good impression on his boss, Frank Golopolus. One of his new responsibilities was ensuring that new product lines met the safety guidelines. Rockingham had made several manufacturing changes over the past year. Golopolus and the rest of the quality-control team had been working 60-hour weeks to troubleshoot the new production process.

Harrington was aware of numerous changes in product safety guidelines that he knew would impact the new Rockingham toys. Golopolus was also aware of the guidelines, but he was taking no action to implement them. Harrington wasn't sure whether his boss expected him to implement the new procedures. The ultimate responsibility was his boss's, and Harrington was concerned about moving ahead on his own. To cover for his boss, he continued to avoid the questions he received from the factory floor, but he was beginning to wonder whether Rockingham would have time to make changes with the Christmas season rapidly approaching.

Harrington felt loyalty to Golopolus for giving him a job and didn't want to alienate him by interfering. However, he was beginning to worry what might happen if he didn't act. Rockingham had a fine product safety reputation and was rarely challenged on matters of quality. Should he question Golopolus about implementing the new safety guidelines?

What Would You Do?

1 Prepare a memo to Golopolus, summarizing the new safety guidelines that affect the Rockingham product line and requesting his authorization for implementation.

2 Mind your own business. Golopolus hasn't said anything about the new guidelines and you don't want to overstep your authority. You've been unemployed and need this job.

3 Send copies of the reports anonymously to the operations manager, who is Golopolus's boss.

SOURCE Based on Doug Wallace, 'The Man Who Knew Too Much', *Business Ethics*, 2 (March–April 1993): 7–8.

CASE FOR CRITICAL ANALYSIS 10.1

Lloyds TSB

Marshall Pinkard, president and CEO of Lloyds TSB, a high-street UK national commercial and consumer retail bank, clicked on an email from Ayishia Coles. Ayishia was the bright, hard-working, self-confident woman who'd recently come onboard as the bank's executive vice president and chief information officer. The fact that the person in Coles' position in the company's traditional vertical organization now reported directly to him and was a full-fledged member of the executive committee reflected Lloyds TSB's recognition of just how important information technology was to all aspects of its increasingly competitive business. The successful, leading-edge banks were the ones using information technology not only to operate efficiently, but also to help them focus more effectively on customer needs. Marshall settled back to read what he expected would be a report on how she was settling in. He was sadly mistaken.

After a few months on the job, Ayishia Coles was frustrated. What she needed from him, she wrote, was a clear statement of her responsibilities and authority. The way Ayishia saw it, the relationship between information technology and the bank's other business units was muddled, often causing considerable confusion, friction and inefficiency. Typically someone from retail banking or marketing, for example, came to her department with a poorly defined problem, such as how to link up cheque account records with investment records, and

© OOYOO/ISTOCK

LEARNING OBJECTIVES

After reading this chapter, you should be able to:

1   Define organizational change and explain the forces driving innovation and change in today's organizations.

2   Identify the three innovation strategies managers implement for changing products and technologies.

3   Explain the value of creativity, idea incubators, horizontal linkages, open innovation, idea champions and new-venture teams for innovation.

4   Discuss why changes in people and culture are critical to any change process.

5   Define organization development (OD) and large group interventions.

6   Explain the OD stages of unfreezing, changing and refreezing.

7   Identify sources of resistance to change.

8   Explain force-field analysis and other implementation tactics that can be used to overcome resistance.

CHAPTER 11

MANAGING CHANGE AND INNOVATION

Glance through recent back issues of just about any business magazine and you will see them: *Wired* magazine's 'Wired 40' list of the most innovative companies. *Fast Company*'s 'Fast 50 World's Most Innovative Companies'. *Business Week*'s 'Twenty Five Most Innovative Companies in the World'. Everyone's talking about innovation and extolling the virtues of companies that do it right. Innovation is at the top of everyone's priority list today, but managing innovation and change has always been an important management capability. If organizations don't successfully change and innovate, they die. Consider that just 71 of the companies on *Fortune* magazine's first list of America's 500 largest corporations, compiled in 1955, survived the next half-century.[1]

Manager's Challenge

Samsung Electronics began selling black and white televisions in Korea in the early 1970s and soon expanded its product line and extended its markets around the world. But when Samsung chairman Kun-Hee Lee visited a Los Angeles retailer two decades later, he had a painful experience. While customers inspected and admired the cutting edge equipment from companies such as Sony, Nokia and Motorola, Samsung's products sat gathering dust on back shelves, ignored even by the sales clerks. It was a wake-up call to Lee, who realized that US consumers had come to regard Samsung products as cheap, low-quality knockoffs, suitable only for the bargain bin. Back home in Korea, things weren't looking so bright either. To celebrate the growing success of Samsung Group, the electronics firm's parent company, Lee had given Samsung mobile phones to friends and colleagues. Within days he began receiving complaints that the phones were defective. Humiliated, Lee issued an order that $50 million worth of inventory from the company's Gumi factory be piled in a heap in the courtyard and destroyed. Top managers and employees watched as workers smashed phones, fax machines and other products under a banner

Exhibit 11.1 The World's Most Innovative Companies

Rank	Company	Headquarters In:	Most Known For:
1	Apple	United States	New Products
2	Google	United States	Customer Experience
3	Toyota Motor Co.	Japan	Work Processes
4	General Electric	United States	Work Processes
5	Microsoft	United States	New Products
6	Tata Group	India	New Products
7	Nintendo	Japan	New Products
8	Procter & Gamble	United States	Work Processes
9	Sony	Japan	New Products
10	Nokia	Finland	New Products

SOURCE: 'The World's 50 Most Innovative Companies', *BusinessWeek* (April 28, 2008), http://bwnt.businessweek.com/interactive_reports/innovative_companies/ (accessed May 6, 2008).

embrace many types of change. Businesses must develop improved production technologies, create new products and services desired in the marketplace, implement new administrative systems and upgrade employees' skills. Companies such as General Motors, Sony and Microsoft which have previously been seen as market leaders have found themselves under pressure from more nimble and innovative rivals such as Toyota, Apple and Google who implement all of these changes and more.

Today's successful companies are continually innovating. For example, Johnson & Johnson Pharmaceuticals uses biosimulation software from Entelos that compiles all known information about a disease such as diabetes or asthma and runs extensive virtual tests of new drug candidates. With a new-drug failure rate of 50 per cent even at the last stage of clinical trials, the process helps scientists cut the time and expense of early testing and focus their efforts on the most promising prospects. Telephone companies such as Vodafone and T-mobile are investing in technology to push deeper into the television and broadband markets. Car manufacturers such as DaimlerChrysler, Toyota and Honda are perfecting fuel-cell power systems that could make today's internal combustion engine as obsolete as the steam locomotive.[9] Computer companies are developing computers that are smart enough to configure themselves, balance huge workloads, and know how to anticipate and fix problems before they happen.[10] Organizations that change successfully are both profitable and admired.[11]

However, multinationals also need to recognize that different markets around the world are at different stages of development. For Tata Motors this means developing small, lightweight, cheap motors such as the Nano for the domestic Indian market, while building large four-wheel drives and luxury saloons, such as Land Rover and Jaguar for the British market. However, these differences mean that there is little opportunity for transfer of technology or jobs between these markets for Tata to exploit in the short to medium term.

If the 1990s innovation was all about technology and control of quality and cost, then today it's more about taking corporate organizations built for efficiency and rewiring them for creativity and growth.

Organizational change is defined as the adoption of a new idea or behaviour by an organization.[12] Many organizations struggle with changing successfully. In some cases, employees don't have the desire or motivation to come up with new ideas, or their ideas never get heard by managers who could put them into practice. In other cases, managers learn about good ideas but have trouble getting cooperation from employees for implementation. Successful change requires that organizations be capable of both creating and implementing ideas, which means the organization must learn to be *ambidextrous*.[13]

An ambidextrous approach means incorporating structures and processes that are appropriate for both the creative impulse and for the systematic implementation of innovations. For example, a loose, flexible structure and greater employee freedom are excellent for the creation and initiation of ideas; however, these same conditions often make it difficult to implement a change because employees are less likely to comply. Or, as one scholar put it, companies 'that are healthy enough to consider innovation are also hearty enough to resist change'.[14] With an ambidextrous approach, managers encourage flexibility and freedom to innovate and propose new ideas with creative departments, venture teams and other mechanisms we will discuss in this chapter, but they use a more rigid, centralized and standardized approach for implementing innovations. In the following section, we discuss technology and product changes, which typically rely on new ideas that bubble up from lower levels of the organization.

CONCEPT CONNECTION Rebecca Adlington, who by winning two gold medals at Beijing became Great Britain's most successful Olympic swimmer in 100 years, wears the new Speedo LZR Racer one-piece suit. Olympic swimmers wearing the LZR Racer broke 25 world records. Speedo's 'world's-fastest-swimsuit' innovation was developed with help from NASA scientists. The seams of the suit are ultrasonically sealed and wind-tunnel tested for surface drag. Each athlete gets a 3-D body scan to create a suit with core support in critical areas to make swimmers more streamlined. Adlington also won out of the pool too by becoming the new British face of Speedo following the 2008 games.

Organizational change
The adoption of a new idea or behaviour by an organization.

Ambidextrous approach
Incorporating structures and processes that are appropriate for both the creative impulse and for the systematic implementation of innovations.

Product change
A change in the organization's product or service outputs.

Changing Things: New Products and Technologies

Introducing new products and technologies is a vital area for innovation. A product change is a change in the organization's product or service outputs. Product and service innovation is the primary way in which organizations adapt to changes in markets, technology, and competition.[15] Examples of new products include Apple's iPhone 3G and iPod Shuffle, the MacBook Pro and MacBook Air, HP TouchSmart Desktop, TMobile's GI Google phone, HEC Android Mobile Phone and Subaru's B9Tribeca. When Toyota introduced the hybrid Prius model into the US market in 2001, rivals said the technology would never catch on. Today, GM and Ford are also producing their own gas-electric hybrid vehicles, while Toyota has secured more than 1000 hybrid related patents and expects to be selling a million hybrid vehicles a year within the next five years.[16] Similarly, the introduction of online filing of tax returns by various governments around the world is an example of a new service innovation within the public sector. Product changes are related to changes in the technology of the organization. A technology change is a change in the organization's production process – how the organization does its work. Technology changes are designed to make the production of a product or service more efficient. The adoption of automatic sorting machines by the Royal Mail is one example of a

Technology change
A change that pertains to the organization's production process.

© STEVE LINDRIDGE/ALAMY

Exhibit 11.2 Three Innovative Strategies for New Products and Technologies

SOURCE: Based on Patrick Reinmoeller and Nicole van Baardwijk, 'The Link Between Diversity and Resilience', *MIT Sloan Management Review* (Summer 2005): 61–65.

technology change. At Hasbro, the toy manufacturer, an example of technological innovation is increasing product extension of its toy brands such as Transformers, GI Joe and Littlest Pet Shop into new media, ranging from video-games, films and the internet.

Three critical innovation strategies for changing products and technologies are illustrated in Exhibit 11.2.[17] The first strategy, *exploration*, involves designing the organization to encourage creativity and the initiation of new ideas. The strategy of *cooperation* refers to creating conditions and systems to facilitate internal and external coordination and knowledge sharing. Finally, *entrepreneurship* means that managers put in place processes and structures to ensure that new ideas are carried forward for acceptance and implementation.

Exploration

Exploration is the stage where ideas for new products and technologies are born. Managers design the organization for exploration by establishing conditions that encourage creativity and allow new ideas to spring forth. Creativity, which refers to the generation of novel ideas that might meet perceived needs or respond to opportunities for the organization, is the essential first step in innovation.[18] People noted for their creativity include Edwin Land, who invented the Polaroid camera, Kozo Ohsone who designed the Sony Walkman, James Dyson who invented the bagless vacuum cleaner, as well as Swiss engineer George de Mestral, who created Velcro after noticing the tiny hooks on the burrs caught on his wool socks. These people saw unique and creative opportunities in a familiar situation.

Characteristics of highly creative people are illustrated in the left-hand column of Exhibit 11.3. Creative people often are known for originality, open-mindedness, curiosity, a focused approach to problem solving, persistence, a relaxed and playful attitude, and receptivity to new ideas.[19] Creativity can also be designed into organizations. Companies or departments within companies can be organized to be creative and initiate ideas for change. Most companies want more highly creative employees and often seek to hire creative individuals. However, the individual is only part of the story, and each of us has some potential for creativity. Managers are responsible for creating a work environment that allows creativity to flourish.

The characteristics of creative organizations correspond to those of individuals, as illustrated in the right-hand column of Exhibit 11.3. Creative organizations are loosely structured. People find themselves in a situation of ambiguity, assignments are vague, territories overlap, tasks are loosely defined, and much work is done through teams. Managers in creative companies embrace risk and experimentation. They involve employees in a varied range of projects, so that people are not stuck in the rhythm of routine jobs, and they drive out the fear of making mistakes that can inhibit creative thinking.[20] Creative organizations have an internal culture of playfulness, freedom, challenge and grass-roots participation.[21] To keep creativity alive at

Creativity
The generation of novel ideas that might meet perceived needs or offer opportunities for the organization.

Exhibit 11.3 Characteristics of Creative People and Organizations

The Creative Individual	The Creative Organization or Department
1. Conceptual fluency Open-mindedness	1. Open channels of communication Contact with outside sources Overlapping territories; cross-pollination of ideas across disciplines Suggestion systems, brainstorming, freewheeling discussions
2. Originality	2. Assigning nonspecialists to problems Eccentricity allowed Hiring outside your comfort zone
3. Less authority Independence Self-confidence	3. Decentralization, loosely defined positions, loose control Acceptance of mistakes; rewarding risk-taking People encouraged to challenge their bosses
4. Playfulness Undisciplined exploration Curiosity	4. Freedom to choose and pursue problems Not a tight ship, playful culture, doing the impractical Freedom to discuss ideas; long time horizon
5. Persistence Commitment Focused approach	5. Resources allocated to creative personnel and projects without immediate payoff Reward system encourages innovation Absolution of peripheral responsibilities

SOURCE: Based on Gary A. Steiner, ed., *The Creative Organization* (Chicago: University of Chicago Press, 1965): 16–18; Rosabeth Moss Kanter, 'The Middle Manager as Innovator', *Harvard Business Review* (July–August 1982): 104–105; James Brian Quinn, 'Managing Innovation: Controlled Chaos', *Harvard Business Review* (May–June 1985): 73–84; Robert I. Sutton, 'The Weird Rules of Creativity', *Harvard Business Review* (September 2001): 94–103; and Bridget Finn, 'Playbook: Brainstorming for Better Brainstorming', *Business 2.0* (April 2005), 109–114.

Google, managers let people spend 20 per cent of their time working on any project they choose. People who interview for a job at the company are often asked, 'If you could change the world using Google's resources, what would you build?' Google's managers instil a sense of creative fearlessness, which is part of the reason Google shows up at the top of numerous lists of most innovative companies.[22]

TAKE A MOMENT

As a new manager, you can inspire people to be more creative by giving them opportunities to explore ideas outside their regular jobs and encouraging them to experiment and take risks. Be open-minded and willing to listen to 'crazy ideas', and let people know it's okay to make mistakes.

Another popular way to encourage new ideas within the organization is the **idea incubator**. An idea incubator provides a safe harbour where ideas from employees throughout the company can be developed without interference from company bureaucracy or politics.[23] The great value of an internal incubator is that an employee with a good idea has specific place to go to develop it, rather than having to shop the

Idea incubator
An in-house programme that provides a safe harbour where ideas from employees throughout the organization can be developed without interference from company bureaucracy or politics.

© PAUL HARDY/CORBIS

CONCEPT CONNECTION Innovative companies such as Intuit, which controls 80 per cent of the consumer tax-preparation software market, want everyone to continually be coming up with new ideas. Managers hold free-association team sessions at least once a week, where everyone can proposed all sorts of off-the-wall ideas for discussion without any embarrassment or fear. Founder Scott Cook and CEO Steve Bennett, shown here, encourage creativity during the exploration phase by embracing failure as readily as they do success. 'I've had my share of really bad ideas', Cook admits. Yet failure can have hidden possibilities. Sticky notes, such as those shown here on Intuit's board, were invented at 3M Corporation based on a failed product – a not-very-sticky adhesive that resulted from a chemist's attempts to create a superglue. Post-it Notes became one of the best-selling office products ever. Jim Read, president of the Read Corporation, says, 'When my employees make mistakes trying to improve something, I give them a round of applause. No mistakes mean no new products. If they ever become afraid to make one, my company is doomed.'[27]

idea all over the company and hope someone pays attention. Companies as diverse as Boeing, Adobe Systems, Cisco, United Parcel Service and Symantec are using incubators to quickly produce products and services related to the company's core business.[24]

Cooperation

Another important aspect of innovation is providing mechanisms for both internal and external coordination. Ideas for product and technology innovations typically originate at lower levels of the organization and need to flow horizontally across departments. In addition, people and organizations outside the firm can be rich sources of innovative ideas. Lack of innovation is widely recognized as one of the biggest problems facing today's businesses. Consider that 72 per cent of top executives surveyed by *Business Week* and the Boston Consulting Group reported that innovation is a top priority, yet almost half said they are dissatisfied with their results in that area.[25] Thus, many companies are undergoing a transformation in the way they find and use new ideas, focusing on improving both internal and external coordination.

Internal Coordination

Successful innovation requires expertise from several departments simultaneously, and failed innovation is often the result of failed cooperation.[26] Consider the partner at a large accounting firm who was leading a team of 50 experts to develop new services. After a year of effort, they'd come up with few ideas, and the ones they had produced weren't successful. What went wrong? The leader had divided the team into three separate groups, so that researchers would come up with ideas, then hand them off to technical specialists, who in turn passed them along to marketers. Because the groups were working in isolation, much time and energy was spent on ideas that didn't meet technical specialists' criteria or that the marketers knew wouldn't work commercially.[28]

TAKE A MOMENT   Go to the Experiential Exercise on page 420 that pertains to creativity in organizations.

Companies that successfully innovate usually have the following characteristics:

1 People in marketing have a good understanding of customer needs.

2 Technical specialists are aware of recent technological developments and make effective use of new technology.

3 Members from key departments – research, manufacturing, marketing – cooperate in the development of the new product or service.[29]

One approach to successful innovation is called the **horizontal linkage model**, which is illustrated in the centre circle of Exhibit 11.4.[30] The model shows that the research, manufacturing, and sales and marketing departments within an organization simultaneously contribute to new products and technologies. People from these departments meet frequently in teams and task forces to share ideas and solve problems. Research people inform marketing of new technical developments to learn whether they will be useful to customers. Marketing people pass customer complaints to research to use in the design of new products and to manufacturing people to develop new ideas for improving production speed and quality. Manufacturing informs other departments whether a product idea can be manufactured within cost limits.

The Swedish owned appliance maker Electrolux was struggling with spiralling costs and shrinking market share until CEO Hans Straberg introduced a new approach to product development that has designers, engineers, marketers, and production people working side-by-side to come up with hot new products such as the Pronto cordless stick vacuum, which gained a 50 per cent market share in Europe within two years. 'We never used to create new products together', says engineer Giuseppe Frucco. 'The designers would come up with something and then tell us to build it.' The new horizontal approach saves both time and money at Electrolux by avoiding the technical glitches that crop up as a new design moves through the development process.[31]

The horizontal linkage model is increasingly important in today's high-pressure business environment that requires rapidly developing and commercializing products and services. This kind of teamwork is similar to a rugby match wherein players run together, passing the ball back and forth as they move downfield.[32] Speed is emerging as a pivotal strategic weapon in the global marketplace for a wide variety of industries.[33] Some companies use fast-cycle teams to deliver products and services faster than competitors, giving them a significant strategic advantage. A **fast-cycle team** is a multifunctional, and sometimes multinational, team that works under stringent timelines and is provided with high levels of resources and empowerment to

Horizontal linkage model
An approach to product change that emphasizes shared development of innovations among several departments.

Fast-Cycle team
A multi-functional team that is provided with high levels of resources and empowerment to accomplish an accelerated product development project.

Exhibit 11.4 Coordination Model for Innovation

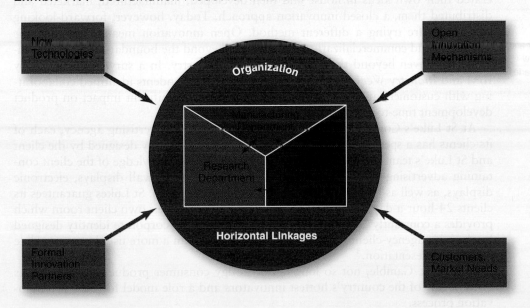

accomplish an accelerated product development project.[34] Stockholm's H&M (Hennes & Mauritz) has become a successful fashion retailer through its ability to spot trends and design, manufacture and rush items into stores in as little as three weeks, for instance a clothing collection designed by Sonia Rykiel and shoes designed by Jimmi Choo for H & M have become an instant hit in the UK in 2009/10. Nissan has cut the time it takes to get a new car to market from 21 months to about ten.

TAKE A MOMENT　Even as a new manager, you can make sure people are communicating and cooperating across organizational boundaries. Implement mechanisms to help your team or department members stay in touch with what's happening in other departments and in the marketplace.

External Coordination

Exhibit 11.4 also illustrates that organizations look outside their boundaries to find and develop new ideas. Engineers and researchers stay aware of new technological developments. Marketing personnel pay attention to shifting market conditions and customer needs. Some organizations build formal strategic partnerships such as alliances and joint ventures to improve innovation success. For example, many leading mobile phone makers work with outsourcing partner Cellon International to take a new phone model from design to market in five months. Cellon, with design and development centres in the US, Canada, China, Korea and France keeps a half-dozen basic designs that it can quickly customize for a particular client. Then, the company works with local manufacturers to rapidly move designs into production. People want hot new phones, and the life cycle of a mobile phone model is about nine months. Companies can't afford the 12 to 18 months it typically takes to develop a new model from scratch.

Today's most successful companies are including customers, strategic partners, suppliers, and other outsiders directly in the product and service development process. One of the hottest trends is *open innovation*.[35] In the past, most businesses generated their own ideas in house and then developed, manufactured, marketed and distributed them, a closed innovation approach. Today, however, forward-looking companies are trying a different method. **Open innovation** means extending the search for and commercialization of new ideas beyond the boundaries of the organization and even beyond the boundaries of the industry. In a survey conducted by IBM and *Industry Week* magazine, 40 per cent of respondents identified collaborating with customers and suppliers as having the most significant impact on product development time-to-market.[36]

At St Luke's Communications, a very successful UK advertising agency, each of its clients has a specific room in the agency's building. Jointly designed by the client and St Luke's team the room is filled with the collective knowledge of the client containing advertising campaigns, and products presented in wall displays, electronic displays, as well as in the furniture and colours in the room. St Lukes guarantees its clients 24-hour-a-day, seven-day-a-week access to enter their own client room which provides a constantly changing yet tangible access to the corporate identity designed by the joint agency-client team in a more vivid way than a more usual paper or slide campaign presentation.[37]

Procter & Gamble, not so long ago a stodgy consumer products company, has become one of the country's hottest innovators and a role model for the open innovation process.

Open innovation
Extending the search for and commercialization of new ideas beyond the boundaries of the organization.

In line with the new way of thinking we discussed in Chapter 1, which sees partnership and collaboration as more important than independence and competition, the boundaries between an organization and its environment are becoming porous, as illustrated by the P&G examples. Through open innovation, ideas flow back and forth among different people and companies that engage in partnerships, joint ventures, licensing agreements and other alliances.

In Africa, Vodafone has launched the M-Pesa payment system which provides a method of transferring cash that bypasses the need for banks and specialist money transfer services. The system was originally designed to help Kenyans overcome the huge distances that they would otherwise have to travel to money transfer agencies, and was originally aimed at workers who had moved to the city but wanted to send money back to their family in the rural areas. It was not an obvious development for Vodafone but they saw an opportunity after consultation with customers to meet a gap in the local market by using its existing expertise and infrastructure to launch the service. In 18 months, four million users have signed up to the service, and the service has now been extended to Tanzania and Afghanistan.[38]

Nokia has used a similar approach in China, India and Nepal to understand how people on low incomes use mobile

© JOHN MACDOUGALL/AFP/GETTY IMAGES

CONCEPT CONNECTION Google co-founders Larry Page (left) and Sergey Brin (right) take the stage during the September 2008 unveiling of the HTC G1 phone by T-Mobile, the first mobile phone to run on Google's Android software. Using an open innovation approach, Google issued a call for anyone to develop new software applications for its open-platform Android. The company's Developer Challenge will award a total of $10 million for the best new applications.

 ## INNOVATIVE WAY

Procter & Gamble (P&G)

The SwifferVac. Crest Spin Brush. Mr Clean Magic Eraser. Valentino Rock 'n Rose Eau de Parfum. Olay Regenerist. These are some of Procter & Gamble's best-selling products – and all of them were developed in whole or in part by someone outside of P&G. The technology for the Mr Clean Magic Eraser was originally developed by Germany's BASF for sound-proofing and insulation in the construction and automotive industries. The Crest Spin Brush was invented by a small entrepreneurial firm in Cleveland.

Procter & Gamble CEO A. G. Lafley set a goal to get 50 per cent of the company's innovation from outside the organization, up from about 35 per cent in 2004 and only 10 per cent in 2000. The company's top executives estimated that for every P&G researcher there were 200 scientists elsewhere who were just as good, so why not tap into that vast pool of creativity and talent? P&G developed a detailed, well-organized process for open innovation with its Connect and

Develop strategy, which taps into networks of inventors, scientists, academics, partners and suppliers to embrace the collective brains of the world. When P&G wanted to make snacks more fun by printing trivia questions, animal facts, jokes and cartoon characters on its Pringles potato crisps, it drew up a technology brief defining the problem and circulated it throughout the global network. It turned out that a small bakery in Bologna, Italy, had an ink-jet method for printing edible images on cakes that P&G was able to adapt for use on the potato crisps. The innovation of Pringles Prints helped P&G's North America Pringles division achieve double-digit growth for the next two years.

But P&G doesn't just look for extensions of its current product categories. An important part of its open innovation process is networking with external scientists in totally new areas that could lead to totally new businesses. For instance, who would have thought that the company that brings us Tide and Pampers could rival beauty titan Channel in premium fragrance sales?[39]

phones. As a result they developed an icon-based menu consisting of pictures rather than letters and numbers which allowed semiliterate villagers to use the phones. Also by listening to customers in poorer countries, Nokia learned that phones had to be more durable, since they're often the most expensive item these customers will buy. To function in a tropical climate, Nokia made the phones more moisture-resistant. It even used special screens that are more legible in bright sunlight.[40]

Crowdsourcing

Crowdsourcing refers to an emerging business trend in which companies get unpaid or low-paid amateurs to design products, create content, even tackle corporate R&D problems in their spare time. It has been more formally defined by Jeff Howe as the act of a company or institution taking a function once performed by employees and outsourcing it to an undefined (and generally large) network of people in the form of an open call. This can take the form of peer-production (when the job is performed collaboratively), but is also often undertaken by sole individuals. The crucial prerequisite is the use of the open call format and the large network of potential labourers.

Similarly, SitePoint, an Australian media company enables clients to hold 'contests' to gain access to the creative talents of the global design community. A company looking for a new design, be it a logo, website or stationery, describes what they are looking for, and after a prize amount and an end-date have been set, designers start submitting their work for all to see. Once the contest holder sees a design they like, they can award the prize to buy the design. Designers retain all rights to their submitted work until they've been awarded the prize on offer and have been paid in full.

While many established designers protest that this type of 'speculative' work is devaluing their profession, others see crowdsourcing as a valid and cost-effective option for small businesses or organizations who can't (yet) afford to hire a traditional branding agency or graphic design firm. Meanwhile, designers from across the world can tap into a much larger market for their services, while building their portfolio, honing their skills and presenting to real clients.

Crowdsourcing has started to be adopted in other areas as well. The *Guardian* newspaper is using crowdsourcing as part of a three-year development project in the Ugandan village of Katine. It carries stories from its reporters, interacting with its residents, and allowing them to share their stories through videos and blogs on the newspapers website. In addition, the *Guardian* has managed to draw readers from around the world in its effort to enhance livelihoods in rural Africa. People from all walks of life are contributing their time and expertise to address the issues involved, be it economists providing their input to the microfinance debate, or education professionals offering insights to repair the broken school system. A recurring theme in crowdsourcing experiments is tapping into audience expertise, and this is especially true in areas where journalists traditionally have

COURTESY OF THREADLESS.COM

CONCEPT CONNECTION Threadless a Chicago-based T-shirt maker has a design process that consists entirely of an online contest. Each week the company receives hundreds of submissions from amateur and professional artists. Threadless posts these to its website, where anyone who signs up may give each shirt a score. The four to six highest-rated designs each week are put into production, but only after enough customers have pre-ordered the design to ensure it won't be a money-loser. Each week's winners get $2000 in cash and prizes, but the real motivation is the chance to have their work seen and potentially worn in public. Threadless puts the designer's name on the label of each shirt. For designers, it's a creative outlet. For customers, it's a wider range of choices. From Threadless' point of view, the company doesn't have to hire a design staff, and only commits financially to shirts with proven, pre-ordered, appeal.[41]

little experience, such as science and business. It is this 'audience participation' that enabled the new Amref office in Katine to become fuelled by solar power. After reading the website Nick Sireau, the director of Solar Aid, contacted the project to offer his expertise in helping Amref deliver renewable energy to the region. With the additional help of a donation from the band Maroon 5, solar power soon replaced the noisy, expensive-to-fuel generators that were previously in place.

Entrepreneurship

The third aspect of product and technology innovation is creating mechanisms to make sure new ideas are carried forward, accepted, and implemented. Managers can directly influence whether entrepreneurship flourishes in the organization by expressing support of entrepreneurial activities, giving employees a degree of autonomy, and rewarding learning and risk-taking.[42] One important matter is fostering idea champions. The formal definition of an **idea champion** is a person who sees the need for and champions productive change within the organization. In 1978, Sony co-founder Masaru Ibuka asked his R&D people to design a lightweight portable playback device so he could listen to music on plane trips. The result was the prototype Walkman. CEO Akio Morita recognized its huge potential, but at that time Sony was in financial trouble and most of its directors wanted to concentrate on TVs and video products. Morita's vision and determination prevailed and the Walkman hit the market a mere four months later and became a phenomenon.

Remember, change does not occur by itself. Personal energy and effort are required to successfully promote a new idea. When Texas Instruments studied 50 of its new-product introductions, a surprising fact emerged: without exception, every new product that failed lacked a zealous champion. In contrast, most of the new products that succeeded had a champion. Managers made an immediate decision: no new product would be approved unless someone championed it. Research confirms that successful new ideas are generally those that are backed by someone who believes in the idea wholeheartedly and is determined to convince others of its value.[43]

Sometimes a new idea is rejected by management, but champions are passionately committed to a new product or idea despite rejection by others. For example, Ron Hickman had the idea for a portable workbench in 1961 and spent many years trying to interest manufacturers without success. They all told him: 'It'll never sell.' He eventually succeeded by manufacturing and selling it himself by mail order. That provided concrete proof that there was good demand for the product, and he was then able to win a licensing agreement with Black and Decker. Four decades and around £25million sales later, it's still the world's leading DIY aid. Similarly, Robert Vincent was fired twice by two different division managers at a semiconductor company. Both times, he convinced the president and chairman of the board to reinstate him to continue working on his idea for an airbag sensor that measures acceleration and deceleration. He couldn't get approval for research funding, so Vincent pushed to complete another project in half the time and used the savings to support the new product development.[44]

Championing an idea successfully requires roles in organizations, as illustrated in Exhibit 11.5. Sometimes a single person may play two or more of these roles, but successful innovation in most companies involves an interplay of different people, each adopting one role. The *inventor* comes up with a new idea and understands its technical value but has neither the ability nor the interest to promote it for acceptance within the organization. The *champion* believes in the idea, confronts the

Idea champion
A person who sees the need for and champions productive change within the organization.

function as a team. An OD expert can work with team members to increase their communication skills, facilitate their ability to confront one another, and help them accept common goals.

2 *Survey-feedback activities.* **Survey feedback** begins with a questionnaire distributed to employees on values, climate, participation, leadership, and group cohesion within their organization. After the survey is completed, an OD consultant meets with groups of employees to provide feedback about their responses and the problems identified. Employees are engaged in problem solving based on the data.

3 *Large-group interventions.* In recent years, the need for bringing about fundamental organizational change in today's complex, fast-changing world prompted a growing interest in applications of OD techniques to large group settings.[62] The **large-group intervention** approach brings together participants from all parts of the organization – often including key stakeholders from outside the organization as well – to discuss problems or opportunities and plan for change. A large-group intervention might involve 50 to 500 people and last several days. The idea is to include everyone who has a stake in the change, gather perspectives from all parts of the system, and enable people to create a collective future through sustained, guided dialogue.

Large-group interventions reflect a significant shift in the approach to organizational change from earlier OD concepts and approaches. Exhibit 11.6 lists the primary differences between the traditional OD model and the large-scale intervention model of organizational change.[63] In the newer approach, the focus is on the entire system, which takes into account the organization's interaction with its environment. The source of information for discussion is expanded to include customers, suppliers, community members, even competitors, and this information is shared widely so that everyone has the same picture of the organization and its environment. The acceleration of change when the entire system is involved can be remarkable. In addition, learning occurs across all parts of the organization simultaneously, rather than in individuals, small groups, or business units. The result is that the large-group approach offers greater possibilities for fundamental, radical transformation of the entire culture, whereas the traditional approach creates incremental change in a few

Survey feedback
A type of OD intervention in which questionnaires on organizational climate and other factors are distributed among employees and their results reported back to them by a change agent.

Large-group intervention
An approach that brings together participants from all parts of the organization (and may include key outside stakeholders as well) to discuss problems or opportunities and plan for major change.

Exhibit 11.6 OD Approaches to Culture Change

	Traditional Organization Development Model	**Large-Group Intervention Model**
Focus for action:	Specific problem or group	Entire system
Information Source:	Organization	Organization and environment
Distribution:	Limited	Widley shared
Time frame:	Gradual	Fast
Learning:	Individual, small group	Whole organization
Change process:	Incremental change	Rapid transformation

SOURCE: Adapted from Barbara Benedict Bunker and Billie T. Alban, 'Conclusion: What Makes Large Group Interventions Effective', *Journal of Applied Behavioural Science* 28, no. 4 (December 1992): 579–591.

INNOVATIVE WAY

General Electric's Work-Out

GE's Work-Out began in large-scale off-site meetings facilitated by a combination of top leaders, outside consultants and human resources specialists. In each business unit, the basic pattern was the same. Hourly and salaried workers came together from many different parts of the organization in an informal three-day meeting to discuss and solve problems. Gradually, the Work-Out events began to include external stakeholders such as suppliers and customers as well as employees. Today, Work-Out is not an event, but a process of how work is done and problems are solved at GE.

The format for Work-Out includes seven steps:

1 Choose a work process or problem for discussion.

2 Select an appropriate cross-functional team, to include external stakeholders.

3 Assign a 'champion' to follow through on recommendations.

4 Meet for several days and come up with recommendations to improve processes or solve problems.

5 Meet with leaders, who are asked to respond to recommendations on the spot.

6 Hold additional meetings as needed to implement the recommendations.

7 Start the process all over again with a new process or problem.

GE's Work-Out process forces a rapid analysis of ideas, the creation of solutions, and the development of a plan for implementation. Over time, this large-group process creates an organizational culture where ideas are rapidly translated into action and positive business results.[64]

---

individuals or small groups at a time. General Electric's Work-Out Programme provides an excellent example of the large-group intervention approach.

Large-group interventions represent a significant shift in the way leaders think about change and reflect an increasing awareness of the importance of dealing with the entire system, including external stakeholders, in any significant change effort.

As a new manager, look for and implement training opportunities that can help people shift their attitudes, beliefs and behaviours toward what is needed for team, department and organization success. Use organization development consultants and techniques such as team building, survey feedback and large-group intervention for widespread change.

TAKE A MOMENT

OD Steps

Organization development experts acknowledge that changes in corporate culture and human behaviour are tough to accomplish and require major effort. The theory underlying OD proposes three distinct stages for achieving behavioural and attitudinal change: (1) unfreezing, (2) changing and (3) refreezing.[65]

The first stage, **unfreezing**, means that people throughout the organization are made aware of problems and the need for change. This stage creates the motivation

Unfreezing
The stage of organization development in which participants are made aware of problems to increase their willingness to change their behaviour.

for people to change their attitudes and behaviours. Unfreezing may begin when managers present information that shows discrepancies between desired behaviours or performance and the current state of affairs. In addition, managers need to establish a sense of urgency to unfreeze people and create an openness and willingness to change. The unfreezing stage is often associated with *diagnosis*, which uses an outside expert called a *change agent*. The **change agent** is an OD specialist who performs a systematic diagnosis of the organization and identifies work-related problems. He or she gathers and analyzes data through personal interviews, questionnaires, and observations of meetings. The diagnosis helps determine the extent of organizational problems and helps unfreeze managers by making them aware of problems in their behaviour.

The second stage, **changing**, occurs when individuals experiment with new behaviour and learn new skills to be used in the workplace. This process is sometimes known as intervention, during which the change agent implements a specific plan for training managers and employees. The changing stage might involve a number of specific steps.[66] For example, managers put together a coalition of people with the will and power to guide the change, create a vision for change that everyone can believe in, and widely communicate the vision and plans for change throughout the company. In addition, successful change involves using emotion as well as logic to persuade people and empowering employees to act on the plan and accomplish the desired changes.

The third stage, **refreezing**, occurs when individuals acquire new attitudes or values and are rewarded for them by the organization. The impact of new behaviours is evaluated and reinforced. The change agent supplies new data that show positive changes in performance. Managers may provide updated data to employees that demonstrate positive changes in individual and organizational performance. Top executives celebrate successes and reward positive behavioural changes. At this stage, changes are institutionalized in the organizational culture, so that employees begin to view the changes as a normal, integral part of how the organization operates. Employees may also participate in refresher courses to maintain and reinforce the new behaviours.

Change agent
An OD specialist who contracts with an organization to facilitate change.

Changing
The intervention stage of organization development in which individuals experiment with new workplace behaviour.

Refreezing
The reinforcement stage of organization development in which individuals acquire a desired new skill or attitude and are rewarded for it by the organization.

Implementing Change

The final step to be managed in the change process is *implementation*. A new, creative idea will not benefit the organization until it is in place and being fully used. Executives at companies around the world are investing heavily in change and innovation projects, but many of them say they aren't very happy with their results.[67] One frustration for managers is that employees often seem to resist change for no apparent reason. To effectively manage the implementation process, managers should be aware of the reasons people resist change and use techniques to enlist employee cooperation. Major, corporate-wide changes can be particularly challenging, as discussed in the Manager's Shoptalk box.

image credit (rotated): © JEFF MORGAN SOCIAL ISSUES/ALAMY

CONCEPT CONNECTION Fear of job loss is one of the biggest reasons for resistance to change. Managers at Burberry decided the company needed to outsource some of its manufacturing, shifting production of its polo shirts to China, Poland, Portugal and Spain. Unfortunately, these changes would lead to plant closure in South Wales, provoking global protests, a benefit concert, and vociferous complaints for the workers from celebrities such as Sir Tom Jones, Bryn Terfel and Emma Thompson.[69]

Need for Change

Many people are not willing to change unless they perceive a problem or a crisis. However, many problems are subtle, so managers have to recognize and then make others aware of the need for change.[68]

One way managers sense a need for change is through the appearance of a performance gap – a disparity between existing and desired performance levels. They then try to create a sense of urgency so that others in the organization will recognize and understand the need for change (similar to the OD concept of *unfreezing*). Recall from Chapter 8 the discussion of SWOT analysis. Managers are responsible for monitoring threats and opportunities in the external environment as well as strengths and weaknesses within the organization to determine whether a need for change exists. Big problems are easy to spot, but sensitive monitoring systems are needed to detect gradual changes that can fool managers into thinking their company is doing fine. An organization may be in greater danger when the environment changes slowly, because managers may fail to trigger an organizational response.

Performance gap
A disparity between existing and desired performance levels.

Resistance to Change

Getting others to understand the need for change is the first step in implementation. Yet most changes will encounter some degree of resistance. Idea champions often discover that other employees are unenthusiastic about their new ideas. Members of a new-venture group may be surprised when managers in the regular organization do not support or approve their innovations. Managers and employees not involved in an innovation often seem to prefer the status quo. People resist change for several reasons, and understanding them can help managers implement change more effectively.

Infosys Technologies Ltd, the Bangalore-based information technology services company takes a direct approach to making sure management stays involved in the innovation process. Chairman and 'chief mentor' N.R. Narayana Murthy introduced the company's 'voice of youth' programme seven years ago. Each year the company selects nine top-performing employees – each under 30 – to participate in its eight-yearly senior management council meetings, presenting and discussing their ideas with the top leadership team. 'We believe these young ideas need the senior-most attention for them to be identified and fostered', says Sanjay Purohit, associate vice-president and head of corporate planning. Infosys CEO Nandan M. Nilekani concurs: 'If an organization becomes too hierarchical, ideas that bubble up from younger people [aren't going to be heard].'[70]

Self-interest

People typically resist a change they believe conflicts with their self-interests. A proposed change in job design, structure, or technology may lead to an increase in employees' workload, for example, or a real or perceived loss of power, prestige, pay or benefits. The fear of personal loss is perhaps the biggest obstacle to organizational change.[71] For example, when FedEx first expanded into ground transportation to be more competitive with UPS, the company's express air service employees felt threatened. Managers smoothly implemented the change by being aware of this possibility and taking steps to alleviate the concerns. Similarly, when FedEx acquired Kinko in 2004, managers recognized that the self-interest of Kinko's employees could trigger some resistance to changes in the organization. However, they struggled to overcome this resistance, and the acquisition though proved problematic, with Kinko unit's profits falling from more than $100 million in 2004 to $45 million in 2007. By 2008, FedEx had announced an $890 million write-off on the purchase and named the third CEO to head Kinko's in four years. And now FedEx is dropping the Kinko's brand. The chain will in future be called FedEx Office.

Lack of Understanding and Trust

Employees often distrust the intentions behind a change or do not understand the intended purpose of a change. If previous working relationships with an idea champion have been negative, resistance may occur. One manager had a habit of initiating a change in the financial reporting system about every 12 months and then losing interest and not following through. After the third time, employees no longer went along with the change because they did not trust the manager's intention to follow through to their benefit.

Uncertainty

Uncertainty is the lack of information about future events. It represents a fear of the unknown. Uncertainty is especially threatening for employees who have a low tolerance for change and fear anything out of the ordinary. They do not know how a change will affect them and worry about whether they will be able to meet the demands of a new procedure or technology.[72] For example, union leaders at an American auto manufacturer resisted the introduction of employee participation programmes. They were uncertain about how the programme would affect their status and thus initially opposed it.

Different Assessments and Goals

Another reason for resistance to change is that people who will be affected by an innovation may assess the situation differently from an idea champion or new-venture group. Critics frequently voice legitimate disagreements over the proposed benefits of a change. Managers in each department pursue different goals, and an innovation may detract from performance and goal achievement for some departments. For example, if marketing gets the new product it wants for customers, the cost of manufacturing may increase, and the manufacturing superintendent thus will resist. Resistance may call attention to problems with the innovation. At a consumer products company, middle managers resisted the introduction of a new employee programme that turned out to be a bad idea. The managers truly believed that the programme would do more harm than good.[73]

These reasons for resistance are legitimate in the eyes of employees affected by the change. The best procedure for managers is not to ignore resistance but to diagnose the reasons and design strategies to gain acceptance by users.[74] Strategies for overcoming resistance to change typically involve two approaches: the analysis of resistance through the force-field technique and the use of selective implementation tactics to overcome resistance.

Force-Field Analysis

Force-field analysis
The process of determining which forces drive and which resist a proposed change.

Force-field analysis grew from the work of Kurt Lewin, who proposed that change was a result of the competition between *driving* and *restraining forces*.[75] Driving forces can be thought of as problems or opportunities that provide motivation for change within the organization. Restraining forces are the various barriers to change, such as a lack of resources, resistance from middle managers or inadequate employee skills. When a change is introduced, management should analyze both the forces that drive change (problems and opportunities) as well as the forces that resist it (barriers to change). By selectively removing forces that restrain change, the driving forces will be strong enough to enable implementation, as illustrated by the move from A to B

 MANAGER'S SHOPTALK

Making Change Stick

Employees are not always receptive to change. A combination of factors can lead to rejection of, or even outright rebellion against, management's 'new and better ideas'.

Lands' End Inc. began as a small US mail-order business specializing in sailing gear. Employees enjoyed the family-like atmosphere and uncomplicated work environment. By the mid-1990s, the company had grown into a $1 billion direct marketing company of casual clothing, accessories, footwear and home products, with overseas outlets in Japan, Germany and the UK. Consider what happened when managers at Lands' End Inc. tried to implement a sweeping overhaul incorporating many of today's management trends – team-working, pension plan changes, peer reviews and the elimination of guards and time clocks. Despite managers' best efforts, employees balked. They had liked the old family-like atmosphere and uncomplicated work environment, and they considered the new requirement for regular meetings a nuisance. 'We spent so much time in meetings that we were getting away from the basic stuff of taking care of business', says one employee. Even a much-ballyhooed new mission statement seemed 'pushy'. One long-time employee complained, 'We don't need anything hanging over our heads telling us to do something we're already doing.'

Confusion and frustration reigned at Lands' End and was reflected in an earnings drop of 17 per cent. Eventually, a new CEO initiated a return to the familiar 'Lands' End Way' of doing things. Teams were disbanded, and many of the once-promising initiatives were shelved as workers embraced what was familiar.

The inability of people to adapt to change is not new. Neither is the failure of management to sufficiently lay the groundwork to prepare employees for change. Harvard professor John P. Kotter established an eight-step plan for implementing change that can provide a greater potential for successful transformation of a company:

1 Establish a sense of urgency through careful examination of the market and identification of opportunities and potential crises.

2 Form a powerful coalition of managers able to lead the change.

3 Create a vision to direct the change and the strategies for achieving that vision.

4 Communicate the vision throughout the organization.

5 Empower others to act on the vision by removing barriers, changing systems, and encouraging risk taking.

6 Plan for and celebrate visible, short-term performance improvements.

7 Consolidate improvements, reassess changes, and make necessary adjustments in the new programmes.

8 Articulate the relationship between new behaviours and organizational success.

Major change efforts can be messy and full of surprises, but following these guidelines can break down resistance and mean the difference between success and failure.

SOURCES Gregory A. Patterson, 'Lands' End Kicks Out Modern New Managers, Rejecting a Makeover', *The Wall Street Journal*, April 3, 1995; and John P. Kotter, 'Leading Changes: Why Transformation Efforts Fail', *Harvard Business Review* (March–April 1995): 59–67.

in Exhibit 11.7. As barriers are reduced or removed, behaviour will shift to incorporate the desired changes.

Just-in-time (JIT) inventory control systems schedule materials to arrive at a company just as they are needed on the production line. In an Ohio manufacturing company, management's analysis showed that the driving forces (opportunities) associated with the implementation of JIT were: (1) the large cost savings from

Exhibit 11.7 Using Force-Field Analysis to Change from Traditional to Just-in-Time Inventory System

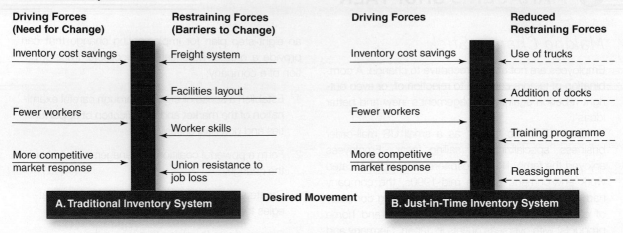

reduced inventories, (2) savings from needing fewer workers to handle the inventory, and (3) a quicker, more competitive market response for the company. Restraining forces (barriers) discovered by managers were: (1) a freight system that was too slow to deliver inventory on time, (2) a facility layout that emphasized inventory maintenance over new deliveries, (3) worker skills inappropriate for handling rapid inventory deployment and (4) union resistance to loss of jobs. The driving forces were not sufficient to overcome the restraining forces.

To shift the behaviour to JIT, managers attacked the barriers. An analysis of the freight system showed that delivery by truck provided the flexibility and quickness needed to schedule inventory arrival at a specific time each day. The problem with facility layout was met by adding four new loading docks. Inappropriate worker skills were attacked with a training programme to instruct workers in JIT methods and in assembling products with uninspected parts. Union resistance was overcome by agreeing to reassign workers no longer needed for maintaining inventory to jobs in another plant. With the restraining forces reduced, the driving forces were sufficient to allow the JIT system to be implemented.

TAKE A MOMENT   As a new manager, recognize that people often have legitimate and rational reasons for resisting change. Don't try to bulldoze a change through a wall of resistance. Use force-field analysis to evaluate the forces that are driving a change and those that are restraining it. Try communication and education, participation and negotiation to melt resistance, and be sure to enlist the support of top-level managers. Use coercion to implement a change only when absolutely necessary.

Implementation Tactics

The other approach to managing implementation is to adopt specific tactics to overcome resistance. Researchers have studied various methods for dealing with resistance to change. The following five tactics, summarized in Exhibit 11.8, have proven successful.[76]

Exhibit 11.8 Tactics for Overcoming Resistance to Change

Approach	When to Use
Communication, education	• Change is technical. • Users need accurate information and analysis to understand change.
Participation	• Users need to feel involved. • Design requires information from others. • Users have power to resist.
Negotiation	• Group has power over implementation. • Group will lose out in the change.
Coercion	• A crisis exists. • Initiators clearly have power. • Other implementation techniques have failed.
Top management support	• Change involves multiple departments or reallocation of resources. • Users doubt legitimacy of change.

SOURCE: Based on J.P. Kotter and L.A. Schlesinger, 'Choosing Strategies for Change', *Harvard Business Review* 57 (March–April 1979): 106–114.

Communication and Education

Communication and *education* are used when solid information about the change is needed by users and others who may resist implementation. Education is especially important when the change involves new technical knowledge or users are unfamiliar with the idea. Canadian Airlines International spent a year and a half preparing and training employees before changing its entire reservations, airport, cargo, and financial systems as part of a new 'Service Quality' strategy. Smooth implementation resulted from this intensive training and communications effort, which involved 50 000 tasks, 12 000 people, and 26 classrooms around the world.[77] Managers should also remember that implementing change requires speaking to people's hearts (touching their feelings) as well as to their minds (communicating facts). Emotion is a key component in persuading and influencing others. People are much more likely to change their behaviour when they both understand the rational reasons for doing so and see a picture of change that influences their feelings.[78]

Participation

Participation involves users and potential resisters in designing the change. This approach is time consuming, but it pays off because users understand and become committed to the change. At Learning Point Associates, which needed to change dramatically to meet new challenges, the change team drew up a comprehensive road map for transformation but had trouble getting the support of most managers. The managers argued that they hadn't been consulted about the plans and didn't feel compelled to participate in implementing them.[79] Research studies have shown that proactively engaging front-line employees in upfront planning and decision-making about changes that affect their work results in much smoother implementation.[80] Participation also helps managers determine potential problems and understand the differences in perceptions of change among employees.

Negotiation

Negotiation is a more formal means of achieving cooperation. *Negotiation* uses formal bargaining to win acceptance and approval of a desired change. For example, if the marketing department fears losing power if a new management structure is implemented, top managers may negotiate with marketing to reach a resolution. Companies that have strong unions frequently must formally negotiate change with the unions. The change may become part of the union contract reflecting the agreement of both parties.

Coercion

Coercion means that managers use formal power to force employees to change. Resisters are told to accept the change or lose rewards or even their jobs. In most cases, this approach should not be used because employees feel like victims, are angry at change managers, and may even sabotage the changes. However, coercion may be necessary in crisis situations when a rapid response is urgent. For example, a number of top managers at Coca-Cola had to be reassigned or let go after they refused to go along with a new CEO's changes for revitalizing the sluggish corporation.[81]

Top Management Support

The visible support of top management also helps overcome resistance to change. *Top management support* symbolizes to all employees that the change is important for the organization. One survey found that 80 per cent of companies that are successful innovators have top executives who frequently reinforce the importance of innovation both verbally and symbolically.[82] Top management support is especially important when a change involves multiple departments or when resources are being reallocated among departments. Without top management support, changes can get bogged down in squabbling among departments. Moreover, when change agents fail to enlist the support of top executives, these leaders can inadvertently undercut the change project by issuing contradictory orders.

Managers can soften resistance and facilitate change and innovation by using smart techniques. At Remploy Ltd., needed changes were at first frightening and confusing to Remploy's workers, 90 per cent of whom have some sort of disability. However, by communicating with employees, providing training, and closely involving them in the change process, managers were able to smoothly implement the new procedures and work methods. As machinist Helen Galloway put it, 'Change is frightening, but because we all have a say, we feel more confident making those changes.'[83]

A MANAGER'S ESSENTIALS: WHAT HAVE WE LEARNED?

- Change is inevitable in organizations, and successful innovation is vital to the health of companies in all industries. This chapter discussed the techniques available for managing the change process. Two key aspects of change in organizations are changing products and technologies and changing people and culture.

- Three essential innovation strategies for changing products and technologies are exploration, cooperation and entrepreneurship. Exploration involves designing the organization to promote creativity, imagination and idea generation. Cooperation requires mechanisms for internal coordination, such as horizontal linkages across departments, and mechanisms for connecting with external parties. One popular approach is open innovation, which extends the search for and commercialization of ideas beyond the boundaries of the organization. Entrepreneurship includes encouraging idea champions and establishing new-venture teams, skunkworks and new-venture funds.

■ People and culture changes pertain to the skills, behaviours, and attitudes of employees. Training and organization development are important approaches to changing people's mind-sets and corporate culture. The OD process entails three steps: unfreezing (diagnosis of the problem), the actual change (intervention) and refreezing (reinforcement of new attitudes and behaviours). Popular OD techniques include team building, survey feedback, and large-group interventions.

■ Implementation of change first requires that people see a need for change. Managers should be prepared to encounter resistance. Some typical reasons for resistance include self-interest, lack of trust, uncertainty and conflicting goals. Force-field analysis is one technique for diagnosing barriers, which often can be removed. Managers can also draw on the implementation tactics of communication, participation, negotiation, coercion or top management support.

Samsung Electronics, described in the chapter opening, has become a hotbed of technology and product change and is the global leader in eight consumer electronics categories. The consulting firm Interbrand calculates that in 2006 Samsung was the world's most valuable electronics brand. Between the years of 2000 and 2005, the company won more awards from the Industrial Design Society of America than any other firm on the planet. One step executives took to create a new mind-set that values creativity, cooperation and innovation over imitation and internal competition was to set up the Innovative Design Lab (IDS), where designers, engineers, marketers and managers from various disciplines took a year-long series of courses aimed at fostering a collaborative environment. The courses also gave people the skills and confidence to risk thinking differently. At the IDS, designers are trained in how to better champion their ideas. Cross-discipline teams study consumers and create what-if scenarios about the world's future buying patterns. Samsung stimulates creativity with the Global Design Workshop, which sends employees to the world's great art and design centres. Designers get Wednesday afternoons off to explore for ideas outside the office. Although managers admit it seemed like slow-going at first, over time these efforts transformed the culture at Samsung. The company also reflects the horizontal model. In the Value Innovation Program (VIP) Center, cross-functional product teams work on problems and cutting-edge ideas without the interruption of phone calls, annoying administrative tasks, or other day-to-day matters that distract people from the project. In a major shift from the past, Samsung is also involved in collaborative relationships with other organizations, such as a partnership with XM Satellite Radio to produce the first portable satellite radio combined with a digital music player. 'We cannot live without change', says Samsung Vice Chairman Jong-Yong Yun. 'The race for survival in this world is not to the strongest, but to the most adaptive.'[84]

DISCUSSION QUESTIONS

1 Times of shared crisis, such as the September 11, 2001, terrorist attack on the World Trade Center or the Gulf Coast hurricanes in 2005, can induce many companies that have been bitter rivals to put their competitive spirit aside and focus on cooperation and courtesy. Do you believe this type of change will be a lasting one? Discuss.

2 A manager of an international chemical company said that few new products in her company were successful. What would you advise the manager to do to help increase the company's success rate?

3 As a manager, how would you deal with resistance to change when you suspect employees' fears of job loss are well founded?

4 How might businesses use the internet to identify untapped customer needs through open innovation? What do you see as the major advantages and disadvantages of the open innovation approach?

5 If you were head of a police department in a mid-sized city, which techniques do you think would be more effective for implementing changes in patrol car officers' daily routines to stop more drivers who are committing traffic offences such as speeding: communication and education, or proactively engaging them through participation?

6 Analyze the driving and restraining forces of a change you would like to make in your life. Do you believe understanding force-field analysis can help you more effectively implement a significant change in your own behaviour?

7 Which role or roles – the inventor, champion, sponsor, or critic – would you most like to play in the innovation process? Why do you think idea champions are so essential to the initiation of change? Could they be equally important for implementation?

8 You are a manager, and you believe the expense reimbursement system for salespeople is far too slow, taking weeks instead of days. How would you go about convincing other managers that this problem needs to be addressed?

9 Do the underlying values of organization development differ from assumptions associated with other types of change? Discuss.

10 How do large-group interventions differ from OD techniques such as team building and survey feedback?

11 What is meant by the terms *internal* and *external forces for change*? Which forces do you think are causes of change in a university? In a pharmaceuticals firm? In a fashion retailer?

MANAGEMENT IN PRACTICE: EXPERIENTIAL EXERCISE

Is Your Company Creative?

An effective way to assess the creative climate of an organization for which you have worked is to fill out the following questionnaire. Answer each question based on your work experience in that firm. Discuss the results with members of your group, and talk about whether changing the firm along the dimensions in the questions would make it more creative.

Instructions

Answer each of the following questions using the five-point scale (*Note:* No rating of 4 is used):

0 We never do this.

1 We rarely do this.

2 We sometimes do this.

3 We frequently do this.

5 We always do this.

1 We are encouraged to seek help anywhere inside or outside the organization with new ideas for our work unit.

   0 1 2 3 5

2 Assistance is provided to develop ideas into proposals for management review.

   0 1 2 3 5

3 Our performance reviews encourage risky, creative efforts, ideas, and actions.

   0 1 2 3 5

4 We are encouraged to fill our minds with new information by attending professional meetings and trade fairs, visiting customers, and so on.

   0 1 2 3 5

5 Our meetings are designed to allow people to freewheel, brainstorm, and generate ideas.

0 1 2 3 5

6 All members contribute ideas during meetings.

0 1 2 3 5

7 Meetings often involve much spontaneity and humor.

0 1 2 3 5

8 We discuss how company structure and our actions help or spoil creativity within our work unit.

0 1 2 3 5

9 During meetings, the chair is rotated among members.

0 1 2 3 5

10 Everyone in the work unit receives training in creativity techniques and maintaining a creative climate.

0 1 2 3 5

Scoring and Interpretation

Add your total score for all ten questions: _____

To measure how effectively your organization fosters creativity, use the following scale: Highly effective: 35–50 Moderately effective: 20–34 Moderately ineffective: 10–19 Ineffective: 0–9

SOURCE Adapted from Edward Glassman, *Creativity Handbook: Idea Triggers and Sparks That Work* (Chapel Hill, NC: LCS Press, 1990). Used by permission.

MANAGEMENT IN PRACTICE: ETHICAL DILEMMA

Off the Hook T-Shirts

Last year, when Ai-Lan Nguyen told her friend Greg Barnwell that Off the Hook T-Shirts, was going to experiment with crowdsourcing, he warned her she wouldn't like the results. Now, as she was about to walk into a meeting called to decide whether to adopt this new business model, she was afraid her friend had been right.

Crowdsourcing uses the internet to invite anyone, professionals and amateurs alike, to perform tasks such as product design that employees usually perform. In exchange, contributors receive recognition – but little or no pay. Ai-Lan, as head of operations for Off the Hook, a company specializing in witty T-shirts aimed at young adults, upheld the values of founder Chris Woodhouse, who like Ai-Lan was a graphic artist. Before he sold the company, the founder always insisted that T-shirts be well designed by top-notch graphic artists to make sure each screen print was a work of art. Those graphic artists reported to Ai-Lan.

During the past 18 months, Off the Hook's sales stagnated for the first time in its history. The crowdsourcing experiment was the latest in a series of attempts to jump-start sales growth. Last spring, Off the Hook issued its first open call for T-shirt designs and then posted the entries on the web so people could vote for their favourites. The top five vote getters were handed over to the in-hose designers, who tweaked the submissions until they met the company's usual quality standards.

When CEO Rob Taylor first announced the company's foray into crowdsourcing, Ai-Lan found herself reassuring the designers that their positions were not in jeopardy. Now Ai-Lan was all but certain she would have to go back on her word. Not only had the crowdsourced tees sold well, but Rob had put a handful of winning designs directly into production, bypassing the design department altogether. Customers didn't notice the difference.

Ai-Lan concluded that Rob was ready to adopt some form of the web-based crowdsourcing because it made T-shirt design more responsive to consumer desires. Practically speaking, it reduced the uncertainty that surrounded new designs, and it dramatically lowered costs. The people who won the competitions were delighted with the exposure it gave them.

However, when Ai-Lan looked at the crowdsourced shirts with her graphic artist's eye, she felt that the designs were competent, but none achieved the aesthetic standards attained by her in-house designers. Crowdsourcing essentially replaced training and expertise with public opinion. That made the artist in her uncomfortable.

More distressing, it was beginning to look as if Greg had been right when he'd told her that his

© SVLUMAGRAPHICA/SHUTTERSTOCK

LEARNING OBJECTIVES

After reading this chapter, you should be able to:

1   Define operations management and describe its application
     within manufacturing and service organizations.

2   Discuss the role of operations management strategy in the
     company's overall competitive strategy.

3   Explain today's partnership approach to supply chain
     management.

4   Summarize considerations in designing an operations
     systems, including product and service design, facilities layout,
     and capacity planning.

5   Explain why small inventories are preferred by most
     organizations and describe just-in-time inventory
     management.

6   Discuss new technologies used for manufacturing and service
     operations, and explain what is meant by lean manufacturing.

7   Define productivity and explain why and how managers seeks
     to improve it.

CHAPTER 12

MANAGING HUMAN RESOURCES

Manager's Challenge

Every hour or so throughout the night, big brown trucks back into the bays at UPS's distribution centre in Lagos, Nigeria, where part-time workers load, unload and sort packages at a rate of 1200 boxes an hour. A typical employee handles a box every three seconds. The packages don't stop until the shift is over, which allows little time for friendly banter and chitchat, even if you could hear over the din of the belts and ramps that carry packages through the cavernous 270,000-square-foot warehouse. It's not the easiest job in the world, and many people don't stick around for long. When Okogbua Okechukwu started his work in Lagos as the new district manager, the attrition rate of part-time workers, who account for half of Lagos's workforce, was 50 per cent a year. With people deserting at that rate, hiring and training costs were through the roof, not to mention the slowdown in operations caused by continually training new workers. Something had to be done to bring in the right employees and make them want to stay longer than a few weeks.

How would you address this enormous human resources challenge? What changes in recruiting, hiring, training, and other human resource practices can help to solve Okogbua Okechukwu's problem in Lagos?　　　　　　　　　　　　　　　**TAKE A MOMENT**

The situation at UPS's Lagos distribution centre provides a dramatic example of the challenges managers face every day. Hiring and retaining quality employees is one of the most urgent concerns of today's managers.[1] The people who make up an organization give the company its primary source of competitive advantage and human resource management plays a key role in finding and developing the organization's

and goals with the correct approach to managing the firm's human capital.[12] Current strategic issues of particular concern to managers include the following:

- Right people to become more competitive on a global basis.
- Right people for improving quality, innovation and customer service.
- Right people to retain during mergers and acquisitions.
- Right people to apply new information technology for e-business.

All of these strategic decisions determine a company's need for skills and employees.

TAKE A MOMENT Go to the Experiential Exercise on page 466 that pertains to your potential for strategic human resource management.

This chapter examines the three primary goals of HRM as illustrated in Exhibit 12.1. HRM activities and goals do not take place inside a vacuum but within the context of issues and factors affecting the entire organization, such as globalization, changing technology and the shift to knowledge work, a growing need for rapid innovation, quick shifts in markets and the external environment, societal trends, government regulations, and changes in the organization's culture, structure, strategy and goals.

The three broad HRM activities outlined in Exhibit 12.1 are to attract an effective workforce, develop the workforce to its potential, and maintain the workforce over the long term.[13] Achieving these goals requires skills in planning, recruiting, training, performance appraisal, wage and salary administration, benefit programmes and even termination. Each of the activities in Exhibit 12.1 will be discussed in this chapter.

Exhibit 12.1 Strategic human resource management

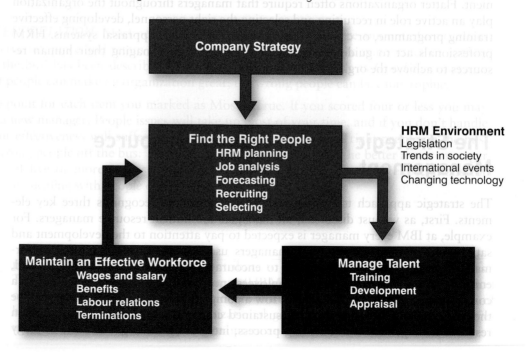

Company Strategy

Find the Right People
HRM planning
Job analysis
Forecasting
Recruiting
Selecting

HRM Environment
Legislation
Trends in society
International events
Changing technology

Maintain an Effective Workforce
Wages and salary
Benefits
Labour relations
Terminations

Manage Talent
Training
Development
Appraisal

Environmental Influences on HRM

'Our strength is the quality of our people.'
'Our people are our most important resource.'

These often-repeated statements by executives emphasize the importance of HRM. Human resource managers must find, recruit, train, nurture and retain the best people.[14] Without the right people, the brightest idea or management trend – whether virtual teams, e-business or flexible compensation – is doomed to failure. In addition, when employees don't feel valued, usually they are not willing to give their best to the company and often leave to find a more supportive work environment. For these reasons, it is important that human resource executives are involved in competitive strategy. Human resource managers also interpret legislation and respond to the changing nature of careers and work relationships.

Competitive Strategy

HRM contributes directly to the bottom line, because it is the organization's human assets – its people – that meet or fail to meet strategic goals. To keep companies competitive, HRM is changing in three primary ways: focusing on building human capital, developing global HR strategies and using information technology.

Building Human Capital

Today, more than ever, strategic decisions are related to human resource considerations. In many companies, especially those that rely more on employee information, creativity, knowledge, and service rather than on production machinery, success depends on the ability to manage human capital.[15] Human capital refers to the economic value of the combined knowledge, experience, skills, and capabilities of employees.[16] To build human capital, HRM develops strategies for finding the best talent, enhancing their skills and knowledge with training programmes and opportunities for personal and professional development, and providing compensation and benefits that enhance the sharing of knowledge and appropriately reward people for their contributions to the organization. A number of organizations that recognize the strategic role of HRM in getting employees mobilized to meet goals are Royal Dutch Shell, LG, William Morrison, International Paper and RSPCA.[17]

All these organisations have a clear strategy focused on developing their employees from the time when they join the organisation through the rites of passage, integration and enhancement. These have different meanings for individual organisations, but will be aligned to the cultural values and norms of not only the organisation but the national culture too.

A good example of an organisation that developed a very strong rite of passage is RSPCA (The Royal Society for the Prevention of Cruelty to Animals, the leading animal welfare charity in the UK). RSPCA uses a six-month training programme in order to identify the people, as potential employees. In those six months the candidates learn how to take care of animals and to undertake animal rescues. A clear requirement for employees is to be in good physical condition and be able to swim 50m fully clothed. This way RSPCA can guarantee the staff's abilities meet their needs. In addition, RSPCA runs training in enhancing social skills amongst its staff whose job to be the interface between the owners of animals and the organisation.

In South Korea, cultural values are well integrated in the organisation like LG Electronics, is a world-class electronics/telecommunication giant. Loyalties to family

Human capital
The economic value of the knowledge, experience, skills and capabilities of employees.

and friends are strong in a society like South Korea and recruitment is done mainly from extended family and friends. This organisation has a predefined formula for talented people they seek, and they call them "Right people. In order to be "Right" a person has to be passionate about winning, be proactive and possess professional skills, like global awareness, technical knowledge. The people who are determined to succeed can fit in well within the LG culture. In return for passion for work and professionalism LG helps its employees achieve financial security and a better quality of life.

Another example of an organisation involved in building and developing its human capital is Morrison's supermarket, which uses profit sharing scheme for higher level employees as a rite of integration and development of commitment and loyalty. This enables an organisation to develop common values and beliefs amongst managers, and this steers those involved to work towards the same target. An Employee of the month award at Morrison's works as a rite of enhancement, and takes place at all stores and hence motivates people at all levels. However, it has not always been easy for this supermarket. When in 2003 Morrisons, well known in the UK for its "Northern" values bought Safeway supermarket chain with more "Southern" values, a lot of training and development programmes were needed in order to integrate the new organisation under the Morrisons umbrella. Morrisons wanted to transfer their values to the Safeway staff in order to develop them into "a lean, sales driven team". Further training was offered to overcome the cultural differences. Sir Ken Morrison (CEO at that time) stated that enhanced performance was seen when Safeway staff altered their sales strategy in order to integrate with that of Morrisons.

A further example of building human capital can be seen at Royal Dutch Shell, an Anglo-Dutch global group of energy and petrochemical companies. The company says that their people are central to the delivery of their strategy and that employees are involved in the planning and direction of their own work. An initiative, 'grow your own timber', is a good example of how Shell puts their philosophy into practice. When the graduates are employed straight out of university, they are provided with training around technical, professional and managerial development and then every few years are rotated and moved to a new role or assignment. This leads to employees feeling secure and appreciated by the organisation. Working in international environments or abroad gives their staff new insights and knowledge. Royal Dutch Shell has a great focus on developing individual skills and capabilities amongst their people, and when an employee moves from one assignment to another, they would be ranked by their line manager against set criteria on their performance, which is adapted across all global Shell sites. Their competitive salaries reflect the market conditions of the country where employees are based and the high level of skill and experience required. Shell recognize and reward individual achievements through performance-related pay and bonuses.

The last example in this section, International Paper, a major player in Pulp and Paper Industry in the world from USA has recognised the need to develop leadership training programmes in foreign countries to ensure they are able to have well prepared employees. For instance in China International Paper develops effective leaders through their in-house Institute of Leadership which is an interactive place of growth and change, where the leaders develop critical skills, which results in engaged employees. In Russia, another area of growth, International Paper provides a robust leadership development programme which recognizes the leadership qualities amongst employees and allows rewarding these individuals through promotion. However, this potentially implies only to certain key employees.

Another concern related to human capital for HRM managers is building *social capital*, which refers to the quality of interactions among employees and whether they share a common perspective. In organizations with a high degree of social capital, for example, relationships are based on honesty, trust and respect, and people cooperate smoothly to achieve shared goals and outcomes.[18]

A simple framework to illustrate the importance of human capital for business results has been designed by Accenture, see Exhibit 12.2, to evaluate human capital processes, and for example illustrate how a company may be able to shift to a new strategy requiring stronger customer focus and greater individual employee accountability. The idea is to show how investments in human capital contribute to stronger organizational performance and better financial results. The framework begins at the bottom (Level 4) by assessing internal processes such as workforce planning, career development, learning management, and so forth. Managers use these activities to increase human capital capabilities (Level 3), such as employee engagement or workforce adaptability. Enhanced capabilities, in turn, drive higher performance in key areas such as innovation or customer satisfaction (Level 2). Finally, improvements in key performance areas lead to improved business results.

Exhibit 12.2 The role and value of human capital investments

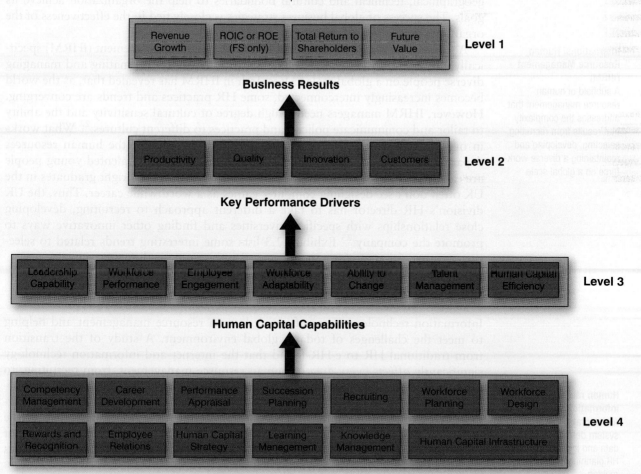

SOURCE: Susan Cantrell, James M. Benton, Terry Laudal, and Robert J. Thomas, 'Measuring the Value of Human capital Investments: The SAP Case', *Strategy & Leadership* 34, no. 2 (2006): 43–52. Copyright 2006 by Emerald Group Publishing Limited. Reproduced with permission of Emerald Group Publishing Limited in the format Textbook via Copyright Clearance Center.

Globalization

An issue of significant concern for today's organizations is competing on a global basis, which brings tremendous new challenges for human resource management. Most companies are still in the early stages of developing effective HRM policies, structures, and services that respond to the current reality of globalization.[19] In a study of more than 200 global companies, including Eli Lilly, PPG Industries and UPS, managers reported that the biggest challenge for HRM is leadership development and training for the international arena. In addition, HRM is responsible for recruitment, training and performance management of employees who might have to work across geographical, technical and cultural boundaries to help the organization achieve its goals. The success of global business strategies is closely tied to the effectiveness of the organization's global HR strategies.[20]

International Human Resource Management (IHRM)
A subfield of human resource management that addresses the complexity that results from recruiting, selecting, developing and maintaining a diverse workforce on a global scale.

A subfield known as **International Human Resource Management (IHRM)** specifically addresses the added complexity that results from coordinating and managing diverse people on a global scale.[21] Research in IHRM has revealed that, as the world becomes increasingly interconnected, some HR practices and trends are converging. However, IHRM managers need a high degree of cultural sensitivity and the ability to tailor and communicate policies and practices to different cultures.[22] What works in one country may not translate well to another. Consider the human resources department at the UK division of Electronic Arts. In the US, talented young people are eager to work for companies such as Electronic Arts, but bright graduates in the UK often don't see designing computer games as a worthwhile career. Thus, the UK division's HR director has to take a different approach to recruiting, developing close relationships with specific universities and finding other innovative ways to promote the company.[23] Exhibit 12.3 lists some interesting trends related to selection, compensation, performance appraisal and training in different countries.

Information Technology

Information technology is transforming human resource management and helping to meet the challenges of today's global environment. A study of the transition from traditional HR to e-HR found that the internet and information technology significantly affects every area of human resource management, from recruiting, to training and career development, to retention strategies.[24] A **human resource information system** is an integrated computer system designed to provide data and information used in HR planning and decision-making. The most basic use is the automation of administrative duties such as handling pay, benefits and retirement plans, which is convenient for employees and can lead to significant cost savings for the organization.

Human resource information system
An integrated computer system designed to provide data and information used in HR planning and decision-making.

Some organizations are coming close to a paperless HRM system, which not only saves time and money but also frees staff from mundane chores so they can focus on important strategic issues, such as how to effectively evaluate and compensate virtual workers or how to meet the challenge of a predicted skilled labour shortage.[25]

Exhibit 12.3 Some Trends in International Human Resource Management

Selection	■ In Japan, HR managers focus on a job applicant's potential and his or her ability to get along with others. Less emphasis is placed on job-related skills and experience.
	■ Employment tests are considered a crucial part of the selection process in Korea, whereas in Taiwan, the job interview is considered the most important criterion for selection.
Compensation	■ Seniority-based pay is used to a greater extent in Asian and Latin countries.
	■ China and Taiwan have surprisingly high use of pay incentives, and are moving toward more incentives based on individual rather than group performance.
Performance Appraisal	■ Across ten countries surveyed, managers consider recognizing subordinates' accomplishments, evaluating their goal achievement, planning their development, and improving their performance to be the most important reasons for performance appraisals.
Training	■ In Mexico, managers consider training and development a reward to employees for good performance.
	■ HR managers in Korea incorporate team-building into nearly all training and development practices.

SOURCE: Mary Ann Von Glinow, Ellen A. Drost and Mary B. Teagarden, 'Converging on IHRM Best Practices: Lessons Learned from a Globally Distributed Consortium on Theory and Practice', *Human Resource Management* 41, no. 1 (Spring 2002): 123–140.

Consider that annual labour force growth is expected to slow to 0.2 per cent by 2020 and stay there for decades.[26] By simplifying the task of analysing vast amounts of data, human resource information systems can dramatically improve the effectiveness of long-term planning to meet this and other HR challenges.

HRM Legislation

Over the past 40 years, a number of laws and directives have been passed to globally ensure equal employment opportunity (EEO). Some of the most significant UK legislation and executive orders are summarized in Exhibit 12.4. The point of the laws is to stop discriminatory practices that are unfair to specific groups and to define enforcement agencies for these laws. EEO legislation attempts to balance the pay given to men and women; provide employment opportunities without regard to race, religion, national origin and gender; ensure fair treatment for employees of all ages; and avoid discrimination against disabled individuals.

Discrimination occurs when some applicants are hired or promoted based on criteria that are not job relevant. For example, refusing to hire a retired or ethnic applicant for a job he or she is qualified to fill or paying a woman a lower wage than a man for the same work are discriminatory acts. When discrimination is found, remedies include providing back pay and taking affirmative action. **Affirmative action** requires that an employer take positive steps to guarantee equal employment opportunities for people within protected groups. An affirmative action plan is a formal document that can be reviewed by employees and enforcement agencies. The goal of

Discrimination
The hiring or promoting of applicants based on criteria that are not job relevant.

Affirmative action
A policy requiring employers to take positive steps to guarantee equal employment opportunities for people within protected groups.

Exhibit 12.4 Major UK Laws Related to Human Resource Management

Law	Year	Provisions
Equal Opportunity/Discrimination Laws		
Sex Discrimination Act	1975	Outlaws discrimination on the grounds of sex, marriage and gender reassignment. UK law relating to sex discrimination has been influenced by a number of EU directives including the **Equal Pay Directive 1975 (75/117)** and the **Equal Treatment Directive 1976 (76/207, as amended by 2002/73)**. Moreover, the principle of equal pay is enshrined in the Treaty of Rome itself (article 141). Seven EU sex equality directives have been combined into one, 2006/54, and implemented by member states by 15 August 2008.
The Race Relations Act	1976 amended by the Race Relations Amendment Act 2000	Outlaws discrimination on racial grounds. Racial grounds are defined as colour, race, nationality, ethnic or national origins. **The EU's race directive of 2000 (2000/43)** has a principle of equal treatment irrespective of race or ethnic origin. A **general framework directive (2000/78)** aims to eliminate inequalities based on religion, belief, disability, age and sexual orientation.
The Trade Union and Labour Relations (Consolidation) Act	1992 [ss 137, 146 and 152–3]	Deals with discrimination related to union membership or activity, or non-membership.
The Disability Discrimination Acts	1995 and 2005	Deal with discrimination against disabled people.
The Protection from Harassment Act	1997	A general piece of legislation which protects people against harassment, whatever the grounds
The Part-time Workers Regulations	2000	Regulation 5(1): 'A part-time worker has the right not to be treated by his employer less favourably than the employer treats a comparable full-time worker. . .'
The Employment Act and the Fixed-term Employees Regulations	2002	Attempts to protect employees on fixed term contracts from suffering inferior treatment to those who are on permanent contracts.
The Religion or Belief Regulations	2003	Protects people from discrimination due to their religion or belief. Religion or belief is defined as 'any religion, religious belief, or similar philosophical belief'.
The Sexual Orientation Regulations	2003	Outlaws discrimination on the grounds of sexual orientation. Sexual orientation is defined in regulation 2(1): 'a sexual orientation towards persons of the same sex; persons of the opposite sex; or persons of the same sex and of the opposite sex'. The regulations do not deal with specific forms of sexual practice or conduct.
The Employment Equality (Age) Regulations	2006	Give effect to the **EU Equal Treatment Framework Directive (2000/78)** as regards age.

Law	Year	Provisions
Compensation/Benefits Laws		
Employers' Liability (Compulsory Insurance) Act	1969	All employers in the UK who have a workforce of more than three individuals, are obliged to take out employers' liability insurance cover. It is possible for workers to claim compensation directly from their employers' compulsory liability insurance if they suffer an accident related injury in the workplace or whilst carrying out their duties. Such claims can be made under no win no fee arrangements with specialist lawyers.
The Equal Pay Act	1970	Makes it unlawful for employers to discriminate between men and women in their pay and conditions where they are doing the same or similar work; work rated as equivalent; or work of equal value. The Act applies to both men and women but does not give anyone the right to claim equal pay with a person of the same sex – any comparison must be with a person of the opposite sex. European law has extended the concept of equal pay to include redundancy payments, travel concessions, employers' pension contributions and occupational pension benefits. This means that even though a man and a woman are receiving the same basic rate of pay there may still be a breach of the principle of equal pay because other benefits (such as a company car, private health care etc.) are not provided on an equal basis. **The Equal Pay Act** applies to pay or benefits provided by the contract of employment. **The Sex Discrimination Act** covers non-contractual arrangements including benefits such as access to a workplace nursery or travel concessions.
Health/Safety Laws		
Health and Safety at Work etc. Act	1974	Defines the fundamental structure and authority for the encouragement, regulation and enforcement of workplace health, safety and welfare within the UK. The **Act** defines general duties on employers, employees, contractors, suppliers of goods and substances for use at work, persons in control of work premises, and those who manage and maintain them, and persons in general.

organizational affirmative action is to reduce or eliminate internal inequities among affected employee groups.

Failure to comply with equal employment opportunity legislation can result in substantial fines and penalties for employers. Claims for discriminatory practices can cover a broad range of employee complaints. One issue of growing concern is *sexual harassment,* which is also a violation in the UK of the Employment Equality (Sex Discrimination) Regulations 2005 and Title VII of the Civil Rights Act in the US. The EEOC guidelines specify that behaviour such as unwelcome advances, requests for sexual favours, and other verbal and physical conduct of a sexual nature becomes sexual harassment when submission to the conduct is tied to continued employment or advancement or when the behaviour creates an intimidating,

hostile, or offensive work environment.[27] Similar legislation applies across the European Union. Sexual harassment will be discussed in more detail in Chapter 13.

Exhibit 12.4 also lists the major laws related to compensation and benefits, and health and safety issues. The scope of human resource legislation is constantly increasing. The working rights and conditions of women, minorities, older employees and the disabled will probably receive increasing legislative attention in the future.

The Changing Nature of Careers

Another current issue is the changing nature of careers. HRM can benefit employees and organizations by responding to recent changes in the relationship between employers and employees and new ways of working such as telecommuting, job sharing, outsourcing and virtual teams.

The Changing Social Contract

In the old social contract between organization and employee, the employee could contribute ability, education, loyalty and commitment and expect in return that the company would provide wages and benefits, work, advancement and training throughout the employee's working life. But volatile changes in the environment have disrupted this contract. As many organizations downsized, significant numbers of employees were eliminated. Employees who are left may feel little stability. In a fast-moving company, a person is hired and assigned to a project. The project changes over time, as do the person's tasks. Then the person is assigned to another project and then to still another. These new projects require working with different groups and leaders and schedules, and people may be working in a virtual environment, where they rarely see their colleagues face-to-face.[28] Careers no longer progress up a vertical hierarchy but move across jobs horizontally. In many of today's companies, everyone is expected to be a self-motivated worker, with excellent interpersonal relationships, who is continuously acquiring new skills.

Exhibit 12.5 lists some elements of the new social contract. The new contract is based on the concept of employability rather than lifetime employment. Individuals manage their own careers; the organization no longer takes care of them or guarantees employment. Companies agree to pay somewhat higher wages and invest in creative training and development opportunities so that people will be more employable when the company no longer needs their services. Employees take more responsibility and control in their jobs, becoming partners in business improvement rather than cogs in a machine. In return, the organization provides challenging work assignments as well as information and resources to enable people continually to learn new skills. The new contract can provide many opportunities for employees to be more involved and express new aspects of themselves.

However, many employees are not prepared for new levels of cooperation or responsibility on the job. In addition, some companies take the new approach as an excuse to treat employees as economic factors to be used when needed and then let go. This attitude leads to a decline in morale and commitment in organizations, as well as a decline in performance. Studies in the US and China found lower employee and firm performance and decreased commitment in companies where the interaction between employer and employee is treated as a contract-like economic exchange rather than a genuine human and social relationship.[29] In general, it is harder than it

Exhibit 12.5 The Changing Social Contract

	New Contract	Old Contract
Employee	■ Employability, personal responsibility ■ Partner in business improvement ■ Learning	■ Job security ■ A cog in the machine ■ Knowing
Employer	■ Continuous learning, lateral career movement, incentive compensation ■ Creative development opportunities ■ Challenging assignments ■ Information and resources	■ Traditional compensation package ■ Standard training programmes ■ Routine jobs ■ Limited information

SOURCES: Based on Louisa Wah, 'The New Workplace Paradox', *Management Review* (January 1998): 7; and Douglas T. Hall and Jonathan E. Moss, 'The New Protean Career Contract: Helping Organizations and Employees Adapt', *Organizational Dynamics* (Winter 1998): 22–37.

was in the past to gain an employee's full commitment and enthusiasm. One study found that even though most workers feel they are contributing to their companies' success, they are increasingly sceptical that their hard work is being fully recognized and appreciated.[30] Some companies find it hard to keep good workers because of diminished employee trust. An important challenge for HRM is revising performance evaluation, training, compensation and reward practices to be compatible with the new social contract. In addition, smart organizations contribute to employees' long-term success by offering extensive professional training and development opportunities, career information and assessment, and career coaching.[31] These programmes help to preserve trust and enhance the organization's social capital. Even when employees are let go or voluntarily leave, they often maintain feelings of goodwill toward the company.

As a new manager, appreciate the opportunities that are offered by the new social contract. Allow people to make genuine contributions of their talents to the organization, and provide them with challenging work and opportunities to learn new skills they can transfer to other jobs in the future.

TAKE A MOMENT

HR Issues in the New Workplace

The rapid change and turbulence in today's business environment bring significant new challenges for human resource management. Some important current issues are becoming an employer of choice, responding to the increasing use of teams and project management, addressing the needs of temporary employees and virtual workers, acknowledging growing employee demands for a work/life balance, and humanely managing downsizing.

CONCEPT CONNECTION It is technology – such as laptops, home computers and broadband – that makes telecommuting possible. But it's social and cultural trends that make its continuing growth probable. For example, many employees believe telecommuting makes it easier to achieve a work/life balance, whereas employers find the new arrangement expands their labour pool and cuts overhead expenses. The federal government has encouraged the practice as well because fewer commuters means improved air quality and reduced energy consumption. So managers will continue to find themselves dealing with the issues telecommuting raises: just how do you select, train, monitor and reward employees you very rarely see?

Becoming an Employer of Choice or Investment in People

The old social contract may be broken for good, but today's best companies recognize the importance of treating people fairly and thinking for the long term rather than looking for quick fixes based on an economic exchange relationship with employees. An *employer of choice* is a company that is highly attractive to potential employees because of human resources practices that focus not just on tangible benefits such as pay and profit sharing, but also on intangibles (such as work/life balance, a trust-based work climate and a healthy corporate culture), and that embraces a long-term view to solving immediate problems.[32] With the Chartered Institute of Personnel and Development (CIPD) in the UK previously suggesting that on average only a third of British staff are fully engaged at work, it's clear that many organizations have a long way to go if they are to head off the damage disengagement inflicts. So it is encouraging that the value of being accredited as a *Best Company* – which rates workplace performance and best practice – continues to climb.

To engage people and spur high commitment and performance, an employer of choice chooses a carefully balanced set of HR strategies, policies and practices that are tailored to the organization's own unique goals and needs. Motek Software, for example, has a strict 9a.m. to 5p.m. policy and gives employees a full month of vacation each year. Founder and CEO Ann Price wants the best and brightest IT workers, and she doesn't want them to burn out and leave after a couple of years. The IT recruitment consulting firm Huxley Associates, on the other hand, doesn't expect people to stay more than a couple of years. People work long hours, but Huxley Associates keeps them motivated and builds social capital by offering plenty of training and career development opportunities.

Teams and Projects

The advent of *teams* and *project management* is a major trend in today's workplace. People who used to work alone on the shop floor, in the advertising department or in middle management are now thrown into teams and succeed as part of a group. Each member of the team acts like a manager, becoming responsible for quality standards, scheduling and even hiring and firing other team members. With the emphasis on projects, the distinctions between job categories and descriptions are collapsing. Many of today's workers straddle functional and departmental boundaries and handle multiple tasks and responsibilities.[33]

Temporary Employees

In the opening years of the twenty-first century, the largest employer in the US and internationally was a temporary employment agency, Manpower Inc.[34] Temporary agencies grew rapidly during the 1990s and early 2000s, and millions of employees today are in temporary firm placements. People in these temporary jobs do everything from data entry, to project management, to becoming the interim CEO.

Although in the past, most temporary workers were in clerical and manufacturing positions, in recent years demand has grown for professionals, particularly financial analysts, interim managers, information technology specialists, accountants, product managers and operations experts.[35] **Contingent (temporary) workers** are people who work for an organization, but not on a permanent or full-time basis. These workers include temporary placements, contracted professionals, leased employees or part-time workers. One estimate is that contingent workers make up at least 25 per cent of the US workforce.[36] The use of temporary workers means reduced payroll and benefit costs, as well as increased flexibility for both employers and employees.

Contingent workers
People who work for an organization, but not on a permanent or full-time basis, including temporary placements, contracted professionals or leased employees.

Technology

Related trends are virtual teams and telecommuting. Some **virtual teams** are made up entirely of people who are hired on a project-by-project basis. Team members are geographically or organizationally dispersed and rarely meet face-to-face, doing their work instead through advanced information technologies and collaborative software. **Telecommuting** means using computers and telecommunications equipment to do work without going to an office. TeleService Resources has more than 25 telephone agents who work entirely from home, using state-of-the-art call-centre technology that provides seamless interaction with TSR's Dallas–Fort Worth call centre.[37] Millions of people in the US and Europe telecommute on a regular or occasional basis.[38] Wireless internet devices, laptops, cell phones and fax machines make it possible for people to work just about anywhere. A growing aspect of this phenomenon is called *extreme telecommuting,* which means that people live and work in countries far away from the organization's physical location. For example, Paolo Concini works from his home in Bali, Indonesia, even though his company's offices are located in China and Europe.[39]

Virtual team
A team made up of members who are geographically or organizationally dispersed, rarely meet face-to-face and do their work using advanced information technologies.

Telecommuting
Using computers and telecommunications equipment to perform work from home or another remote location.

Work/Life Balance

Telecommuting is one way organizations are helping employees lead more balanced lives. By working part of the time from home, for example, parents can avoid some of the conflicts they often feel in coordinating their work and family responsibilities. *Flexible scheduling* for regular employees is also important in today's workplace. When and where an employee does the job is becoming less important. In addition, broad work/life balance initiatives play a critical role in retention strategy, partly in response to the shift in expectations among young employees.[40] Generation Y workers are a fast-growing segment of the workforce. Typically, Gen Y employees work smart and work hard on the job, but they refuse to let work be their whole life. Unlike their parents, who placed a high priority on career, Gen Y workers expect the job to accommodate their personal lives.[41]

Many managers recognize that individuals may have personal needs that require special attention. Some HR responses include benefits such as on-site gym facilities and childcare, assistance with arranging child- and elder-care, and paid leave or sabbaticals.

Downsizing

In some cases, organizations have more people than they need and have to let some employees go. **Downsizing,** which refers to an intentional, planned reduction in the size of a company's workforce, is a reality for many of today's companies. In the first

Downsizing
Intentional, planned reduction in the size of a company's workforce.

© VARIO IMAGES GMBH & CO.KG/ALAMY

CONCEPT CONNECTION The Audi plant in Ingolstadt is not only home to the Group head office of AUDI AG, it is also the company's largest production facility. The Audi A3, A3 Sportback, Audi S4, Audi A4 and Audi A4 Avant models are all currently built at the Ingolstadt plant. The TT Coupé and the TT Roadster bodies are also built and painted here. The plant attracts people from all over the world, with employees from 72 countries currently working at Audi. At the beginning of the year, the number of employees totalled 31,337, 19,995 of whom were blue-collar workers, 9903 white-collar staff and 1439 apprentices.

The workforce at the Neckarsulm plant, the second mainstay of the Audi brand in Germany, is also made up of people of many nationalities, with a total of 48 countries being represented here. With 13,633 employees (as at the end of 2005), Audi is the largest employer in the Heilbronn-Franconia region. Some 10,348 blue-collar workers, 2488 white-collar staff and 797 apprentices work at the Neckarsulm plant.

Matching model
An employee selection approach in which the organization and the applicant attempt to match each other's needs, interests and values.

three years of the twenty-first century, for example, employers cut some 2.7 million jobs.[42] Some researchers found that massive downsizing often failed to achieve the intended benefits and in some cases significantly harmed the organization.[43] Unless HRM departments effectively and humanely manage the downsizing process, layoffs can lead to decreased morale and performance. Managers can smooth the downsizing process by regularly communicating with employees and providing them with as much information as possible, providing assistance to workers who will lose their jobs, and using training and development to help address the emotional needs of remaining employees and enable them to cope with new or additional responsibilities.[44]

Both of the locations of the main manufacturing Audi plants have a tremendous advantage, enabling Audi to attract an effective workforce, mostly second- and third-generation engineers who have followed parents' and grandparents' footsteps. These employees have a can-do attitude and an owner's mindset that matches perfectly with Audi's emphasis on individual initiative, ingenuity and responsibility. Audi truly values its employees as it always invests in individuals who can help it achieve its ambitious plans 'Vorsprung durch Technik'. These various issues present many challenges for organizations and human resource management, such as new ways of recruiting and compensation that address the interests and needs of contingent and virtual workers, new training methods that help people work cross-functionally, or new ways to retain valuable employees. All of these concerns are taken into consideration as human resource managers work toward the three primary HR goals described earlier: attracting, developing and maintaining an effective workforce.

Attracting an Effective Workforce

The first goal of HRM is to attract individuals who show signs of becoming valued, productive and satisfied employees. The first step in attracting an effective workforce involves human resource planning, in which managers or HRM professionals predict the need for new employees based on the types of vacancies that exist, as illustrated in Exhibit 12.6. The second step is to use recruiting procedures to communicate with potential applicants. The third step is to select from the applicants those persons believed to be the best potential contributors to the organization. Finally, the new employee is welcomed into the organization.

Underlying the organization's effort to attract employees is a matching model. With the **matching model**, the organization and the individual attempt to match the needs, interests, and values that they offer each other.[45] HRM professionals attempt to identify a correct match. For example, a small software developer might require long hours from creative, technically skilled employees. In return, it can offer freedom from bureaucracy, tolerance of idiosyncrasies and potentially high pay. A large manufacturer can offer employment security and stability, but it might have more rules and regulations and require greater skills for 'getting approval from the higher-ups'. The individual who would thrive working for the software developer might feel

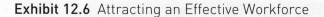

Exhibit 12.6 Attracting an Effective Workforce

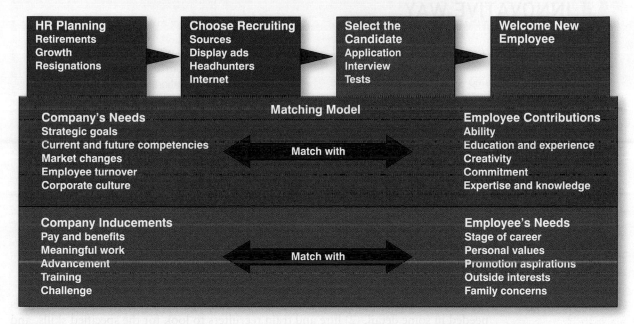

stymied and unhappy working for a large manufacturer. Both the company and the employee are interested in finding a good match. A new approach, called *job sculpting*, attempts to match people to jobs that enable them to fulfil deeply embedded life interests.[46] This matching effort often requires that HR managers play detective to find out what really makes a person happy. The idea is that people can fulfil deep-seated needs and interests on the job, which will induce them to stay with the organization.

Human Resource Planning

Human resource planning is the forecasting of human resource needs and the projected matching of individuals with expected vacancies. Human resource planning begins with several questions:

- What new technologies are emerging, and how will these affect the work system?
- What is the volume of the business likely to be in the next 5–10 years?
- What is the turnover rate, and how much, if any, is avoidable?

The responses to these questions are used to formulate specific questions pertaining to HR activities, such as the following:

- How many senior managers will we need during this time period?
- What types of engineers will we need, and how many?
- Are persons with adequate computer skills available for meeting our projected needs?
- How many administrative personnel – technicians, IT specialists – will we need to support the additional managers and engineers?
- Can we use temporary, contingent or virtual workers to handle some tasks?[47]

Answers to these questions help define the direction for the organization's HRM strategy. For example, if forecasting suggests a strong upcoming need for more

Human resource planning
The forecasting of human resource needs and the projected matching of individuals with expected job vacancies.

INNOVATIVE WAY

Tennessee Valley Authority (TVA)

TVA created an eight-step plan that assesses future HR needs and formulates actions to meet those needs. The first step is laying the groundwork for later implementation of the programme by creating planning and oversight teams within each business unit. Step two involves assessing processes and functions that can be benchmarked. Step three involves projecting the skills and employee numbers (demand data) that will be necessary to reach goals within each business unit. Once these numbers are in place, step four involves projecting the current employee numbers (supply data)

over the planning horizon without new hires and taking into consideration the normal attrition of staff through death, retirement, resignation, and so forth. Comparison of the difference between supply and demand (step five) gives the future gap, or surplus situation. This knowledge enables HR to develop strategies and operational plans (step six). Step seven involves communicating the action plan to employees. The final step is periodically to evaluate and update the plan as the organization's needs change. When TVA faces a demand for additional employees, this process enables the company to recruit workers with the skills needed to help meet organizational goals.[48]

technically trained individuals, the organization can (1) define the jobs and skills needed in some detail, (2) hire and train recruiters to look for the specified skills, and (3) provide new training for existing employees. By anticipating future human resource needs, the organization can prepare itself to meet competitive challenges more effectively than organizations that react to problems only as they arise.

A number of organizations have developed their own human resource planning approaches. IBM looks at trends in information technology to try to gauge what its clients' needs might be in the future, then builds a plan for finding people with the right skills to meet those needs. Recently, for example, the company has built up its roster of people with skills in areas such as open software standards, grid computing and autonomic computing.[49]

Recruiting

Recruiting
The activities or practices that define the desired characteristics of applicants for specific jobs.

Recruiting is defined as 'activities or practices that define the characteristics of applicants to whom selection procedures are ultimately applied'.[50] Today, recruiting is sometimes referred to as *talent acquisition* to reflect the importance of the human factor in the organization's success.[51] Although we frequently think of campus recruiting as a typical recruiting activity, many organizations use *internal recruiting,* or *promote-from-within* policies, to fill their high-level positions.[52] At oil field services company Schlumberger, Ltd., for example, current employees are given preference when a position opens. With 84,000 people of more than 140 nationalities working in approximately 80 countries, the company can identify potential career opportunities in North American, European, CIS, African, Middle Eastern or Asian branches. Some 80 per cent of top managers have been moved up the ranks based on the promote-from-within philosophy; many of them started fresh out of school as field engineers.[53] Internal recruiting has several advantages: it is less costly than an external search, and it generates higher employee commitment, development and satisfaction because it offers opportunities for career advancement to employees rather than outsiders.

Frequently, however, *external recruiting* – recruiting newcomers from outside the organization – is advantageous. Applicants are provided by a variety of outside sources including advertising, state employment services, online recruiting services, private employment agencies *(headhunters)*, job fairs and employee referrals.

Assessing Organizational Needs

An important step in recruiting is to get a clear picture of what kinds of people the organization needs. Basic building blocks of human resource management include job analysis, job descriptions and job specifications. Job analysis is a systematic process of gathering and interpreting information about the essential duties, tasks and responsibilities of a job, as well as about the context within which the job is performed.[54] To perform job analysis, managers or specialists ask about work activities and work flow, the degree of supervision given and received in the job, knowledge and skills needed, performance standards, working conditions, and so forth. The manager then prepares a written job description, which is a clear and concise summary of the specific tasks, duties and responsibilities, and a job specification, which outlines the knowledge, skills, education, physical abilities and other characteristics needed to adequately perform the job.

Job analysis helps organizations recruit the right kind of people and match them to appropriate jobs. For example, to enhance internal recruiting, Sara Lee Corporation identified six functional areas and 24 significant skills that it wants its finance executives to develop, as illustrated in Exhibit 12.7. Managers are tracked on their development and moved into other positions to help them acquire the needed skills.[55] New software programs and web-based, on-demand subscription services are aiding today's companies in more efficiently and effectively recruiting and matching the right candidates with the right jobs.

Realistic Job Previews

Job analysis also helps enhance recruiting effectiveness by enabling the creation of realistic job previews. A realistic job preview (RJP) gives applicants all pertinent and realistic information – positive and negative – about the job and the organization.[56]

Job analysis
The systematic process of gathering and interpreting information about the essential duties, tasks and responsibilities of a job.

Job description
A concise summary of the specific tasks and responsibilities of a particular job.

Job specification
An outline of the knowledge, skills, education and physical abilities needed to adequately perform a job.

Realistic job preview
A recruiting approach that gives applicants all pertinent and realistic information about the job and the organization.

Exhibit 12.7 Sara Lee's Required Skills for Finance Executives

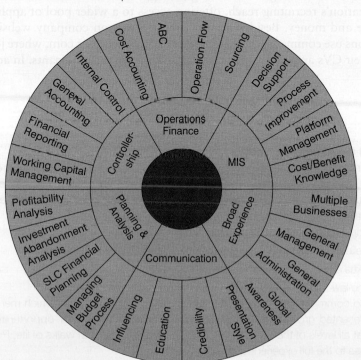

SOURCE: Victoria Griffith, 'When Only Internal Expertise Will Do', *CFO* (October 1998): 95–96, 102.

© NETPICS/ALAMY

CONCEPT CONNECTION

E-cruiting has grown exponentially in recent years with a 2008 CIPD survey revealing 75% of British organizations using their own website for recruiting. Originating in 1994, Monster has been at the forefront of this online growth with, by 2010, 4,200 employees operating in 36 countries. Earning commission from employers is now only part of Monster's strategy, with a massive job contacts database providing rich opportunities for everything from online jobs fairs to data mining analyses of specific roles and industries.

RJPs enhance employee satisfaction and reduce turnover, because they facilitate matching individuals, jobs and organizations. Individuals have a better basis on which to determine their suitability to the organization and 'self-select' into or out of positions based on full information.

Legal Considerations

Organizations must ensure that their recruiting practices conform to the law. As discussed earlier in this chapter, equal employment opportunity (EEO) laws stipulate that recruiting and hiring decisions cannot discriminate on the basis of race, national origin, religion or gender. The Disabilities Act underscored the need for well-written job descriptions and specifications that accurately reflect the mental and physical dimensions of jobs, so that people with disabilities will not be discriminated against. *Affirmative action* refers to the use of goals, timetables or other methods in recruiting to promote the hiring, development and retention of *protected groups* – persons historically under-represented in the workplace. For example, a city might establish a goal of recruiting one black fire-fighter for every white fire-fighter until the proportion of black fire-fighters is commensurate with the black population in the community.

Most large companies try to comply with affirmative action and EEO guidelines. Prudential Insurance Company's policy is presented in Exhibit 12.8. Prudential actively recruits employees and takes affirmative action steps to recruit individuals from all walks of life.

E-cruiting

One of the fastest-growing approaches to recruiting is use of the internet for recruiting, or *e-cruiting*.[57] Recruiting job applicants online dramatically extends the organization's recruiting reach, offering access to a wider pool of applicants and saving time and money. Besides posting job openings on company websites, many organizations use commercial recruiting sites such as Monster.com, where job seekers can post their CVs and companies can search for qualified applicants. In addition, as

Exhibit 12.8 Prudential's Corporate Recruiting Policy

An Equal Opportunity Employer

Prudential recruits, hires, trains, promotes, and compensates individuals without regard to race, color, religion or creed, age, sex, marital status, national origin, ancestry, liability for service in the armed forces of the United States, status as a special disabled veteran or veteran of the Vietnam era, or physical or mental handicap.

This is official company policy because:

■   we believe it is right

■   it makes good business sense

■   it is the law

We are also committed to an ongoing program of affirmative action in which members of under-represented groups are actively sought out and employed for opportunities in all parts and at all levels of the company. In employing people from all walks of life, Prudential gains access to the full experience of our diverse society.

competition for high-quality employees heats up, new online companies, such as TopJob, Moster, Jobster and JobThread, emerge to help companies search for 'passive candidates', people who aren't looking for jobs but might be the best fit for a company's opening. Expedia calls it 'anti-in-box recruiting'. Instead of waiting until it has job openings, it uses online recruitment agencies to build up a ready supply of passive prospects who have the skills and experience the company might need.[58]

Companies as diverse as Deloitte Touche Tohmatsu, Cisco Systems, John Lewis, L'Oréal and Tesco use the Web for recruiting. Organizations have not given up their traditional recruiting strategies, but the Internet gives HR managers new tools for searching the world to find the best available talent.

Other Recent Approaches to Recruiting

Organizations are finding other ways to enhance their recruiting success. One highly effective approach is getting referrals from current employees. A company's employees often know of someone who would be qualified for a position and fit in with the organization's culture. Many organizations offer cash awards to employees who submit names of people who subsequently accept employment, because referral by current employees is one of the cheapest and most reliable methods of external recruiting.[59] At many of today's top companies, managers emphasize that recruiting is part of everyone's job. Here's how Africon finds quality employees:

Having employees assist with recruiting has the added bonus of providing potential candidates with a realistic job preview. At the Container Store, employees share with customers what it's like to work for the company. They want people to know the positive and potentially negative aspects of the job, because it's important to get people who will fit in.

Some companies turn to non-traditional sources to find dedicated employees, particularly in a tight labour market. For example, when Walker Harris couldn't find workers for his ice company on the west side of Chicago, Harris Ice, he began hiring former prison inmates, many of whom have turned out to be reliable, loyal employees.[60] Manufacturer Dee Zee, which makes aluminium truck accessories in a factory in Des Moines, Iowa, found a source of hard-working employees among refugees from Bosnia, Vietnam and Kosovo.[61] Since 1998, Bank of America has hired and trained more than 3000 former welfare recipients in positions that offer the potential for promotions and long-term careers. Numerous companies recruit older workers, who typically have lower turnover rates, especially for part-time jobs. The Home Depot offers 'snowbird specials' – winter work in Florida and summers in Maine.[62] Recruiting on a global basis is on the rise as well. Non-fee-paying schools are recruiting teachers from overseas. High-tech companies are looking for qualified workers in foreign countries because they cannot find people with the right skills in the US.[63]

Test your own preparation as a new manager for recruiting and selecting the right people on your team. Go to the New Manager Self-Test on page 451.

TAKE A MOMENT

Selecting

The next step for managers is to select desired employees from the pool of recruited applicants. In the **selection** process, employers assess applicants' characteristics in an attempt to determine the 'fit' between the job and applicant characteristics. Several

Selection
The process of determining the skills, abilities and other attributes a person needs to perform a particular job.

💡 INNOVATIVE WAY

Africon

Africon is ranked the Number 1 consulting engineering firm in South Africa, as well as one of the Top 200 International Design Firms worldwide. Established more than half a century ago, the firm has grown into a multinational player in the arena of infrastructure design and management, with an enviable track record spanning a wide range of engineering disciplines, from asset and facility management, civil engineering, construction supervision and electrical and power system engineering to mining engineering, project management, structural engineering, traffic engineering and water engineering.

The firm has an extensive office network encompassing 17 offices throughout South Africa, 11 offices in Portuguese- and English-speaking African countries, and a further two offices in the Middle East. Its staff complement comprises more than 1500 dedicated and competent individuals, including more than 1000 engineers and other professionals.

Part of that success is due to the popular track record Africon has on project completion, e.g. the R-1000 traffic study for the Dubai Municipality; the construction of a new Central Terminal Building at OR Tambo International Airport in Johannesburg; the Nova Vida Housing Development in Luanda, Angola; the Rabat Corniche mixed-use property development in Rabat, Morocco; the 45,000-seat Peter Mokaba sports stadium, which is being constructed in the Limpopo Province as part of the preparations for the 2010 Soccer World Cup; and the Moatize Coal project in Mozambique. But another, perhaps even greater, element is Africon's approach to recruiting, which turns the company's best stakeholders into loyal, top-performing employees.

The in-company head-hunting approach has been so successful that approximately a third of the company's workers come from employee referrals. In an industry where most companies are running classified ads or recruiting through recruitment consultants every week or two for new staff, Africon often goes six to eight months without placing a single help-wanted ad. However, this does not mean that they do not use partners for recruitment. Every year they participate in recruitment events like 'Careers in Africa', which bring a healthy flow of applicants.

Employment test
A written or computer-based test designed to measure a particular attribute such as intelligence or aptitude.

Validity
The relationship between an applicant's score on a selection device and his or her future job performance.

Application form
A device for collecting information about an applicant's education, previous job experience and other background characteristics.

selection devices are used for assessing applicant qualifications. The most frequently used are the application form, interview, **employment test**, and assessment centre. Studies indicate that the greater the skill requirements and work demands of an open position, the greater the number and variety of selection tools the organization will use.[64] Human resource professionals may use a combination of devices to obtain a valid prediction of employee job performance. **Validity** refers to the relationship between one's score on a selection device and one's future job performance. A valid selection procedure will provide high scores that correspond to subsequent high job performance.

Application Form

The **application form** is used to collect information about the applicant's education, previous job experience, and other background characteristics. Research in the life insurance industry shows that biographical information inventories can validly predict future job success.[65]

One pitfall to be avoided is the inclusion of questions that are irrelevant to job success. In line with affirmative action, the application form should not ask questions that will create an adverse impact on protected groups unless the questions are clearly related to the job.[66] For example, employers should not ask whether the applicant rents or owns his or her own home because (1) an applicant's response might adversely affect his or her chances at the job, (2) minorities and women may be less likely to own a home, and (3) home ownership is probably unrelated to job

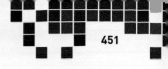

 NEW MANAGER SELF-TEST

What is Your HR Work Orientation?

As new manager, what is your orientation concerning day-to-day work issues? To find out, think about your preferences for the questions below. Circle a or b for each item depending on which one is accurate for you. There are no right or wrong answers.

1 The work elements I prefer are

_____ **a** Administrative

_____ **b** Conceptualizing

2 The work elements I prefer are

_____ **a** Creative

_____ **b** Organizing

3 My mode of living is

_____ **a** Conventional

_____ **b** Original

4 Which is more important to you?

_____ **a** How something looks (form)

_____ **b** How well it works (function)

5 I like to work with

_____ **a** A practical person

_____ **b** An idea person

6 I am more

_____ **a** Idealistic

_____ **b** Realistic

7 For weekend activities, I prefer to

_____ **a** Plan in advance

_____ **b** Be free to do what I want

8 A daily work routine for me is

_____ **a** Painful

_____ **b** Comfortable

SCORING AND INTERPRETATION The HR department typically is responsible for monitoring compliance with federal laws, and it provides detailed and specific employee procedures and records for an organization. Every new manager is involved in HR activities for his or her direct reports, which involves systematic record keeping, awareness of applicable laws, and follow through. For your HR work orientation, score one point for each 'a' answer circled for questions 1, 3, 5, 7 and one point for each 'b' answer circled for questions 2, 4, 6, 8.

New managers with a high score (**7** or **8**) for HR work orientation tend to be practical, organized, good at record keeping and meet commitments on time. New managers with a low score (**1** or **2**) on HR work orientation tend to be more free-spirited, creative and conceptual. These managers tend to think out-of-the-box and may dislike the organization, routine and legal record keeping required for efficient HR management. If your score is midrange (**3** to **6**), you may do well with HR work if you put your mind to it, but HR may not be your area of greatest strength.

performance. By contrast, the CPA exam is relevant to job performance in a CPA firm; thus, it is appropriate to ask whether an applicant for employment has passed the CPA exam, even if only one-half of all female or minority applicants have done so versus nine-tenths of male applicants.

Interview

The *interview* serves as a two-way communication channel that allows both the organization and the applicant to collect information that would otherwise be difficult to obtain. This selection technique is used in almost every job category in nearly every organization. It is another area where the organization can get into legal trouble if the interviewer asks questions that violate EEO guidelines. Exhibit 12.9 lists some examples of appropriate and inappropriate interview questions.

Although widely used, the interview is not generally a valid predictor of job performance. Studies of interviewing suggest that people tend to make snap judgements

Exhibit 12.9 Employment Applications and Interviews: What Can You Ask?

Category	Okay to Ask	Inappropriate or Illegal to Ask
National origin	■ The applicant's name ■ If applicant has ever worked under a different name	■ The origin of applicant's name ■ Applicant's ancestry/ethnicity
Race	■ Nothing	■ Race or colour of skin
Disabilities	■ Whether applicant has any disabilities that might inhibit performance of job	■ If applicant has any physical or mental defects ■ If applicant has ever filed workers' compensation claim
Age	■ If applicant is over 18	■ Applicant's age ■ When applicant left full-time education
Religion	■ Nothing	■ Applicant's religious affiliation ■ What religious holidays applicant observes
Criminal record	■ If applicant has ever been convicted of a crime	■ If applicant has ever been arrested
Marital/family status	■ Nothing	■ Marital status, number of children or planned children ■ Childcare arrangements
Education and experience	■ Where applicant went to school ■ Prior work experience	■ When applicant graduated ■ Hobbies
Citizenship	■ If applicant has a legal right to work in the country	■ If applicant is a citizen of another country

SOURCES: Based on 'Appropriate and Inappropriate Interview Questions', in George Bohlander, Scott Snell and Arthur Sherman, *Managing Human Resources*, 12th ed. (Cincinnati, OH: South-Western, 2001): 207; and 'Guidelines to Lawful and Unlawful Preemployment Inquiries', Appendix E, in Robert L. Mathis and John H. Jackson, *Human Resource Management*, 2nd ed. (Cincinnati, OH: South-Western, 2002), 189–190.

of others within the first few seconds of meeting them and only rarely change their opinions based on anything that occurs in the interview.[67] However, the interview as a selection tool has high *face validity*. That is, it seems valid to employers, and managers prefer to hire someone only after they have been through some form of interview, preferably face-to-face. The Manager's Shoptalk offers some tips for effective interviewing and provides a humourous look at some interview blunders.

Today's organizations are trying different approaches to overcome the limitations of the interview. Some put candidates through a series of interviews, each one conducted by a different person and each one probing a different aspect of the candidate. At Microsoft, for example, interviewers include HRM professionals, managers of the appropriate functional department, peers and people outside the department who are well grounded in the corporate culture.[68] Other companies, including universities in Europe and Asia use *panel interviews*, in which the candidate meets with several interviewers who take turns asking questions, to increase interview validity.[69] For the graduate management positions, companies tend to use group interviews, in which as many as ten candidates are asked to make a pitch for a product that solves a particular organization challenge. This approach gives managers a chance to see how people function as part of a team.[70]

Some organizations also supplement traditional interviewing information with *computer-based interviews*. This type of interview typically requires a candidate to answer a series of multiple-choice questions tailored to the specific job. The answers are compared to an ideal profile or to a profile developed on the basis of other candidates. Companies such as Pinkerton Security, Coopers & Lybrand, and Pic n' Pay Shoe Stores found computer-based interviews to be valuable for searching out information regarding the applicant's honesty, work attitude, drug history, candour, dependability and self-motivation.[71]

TAKE A MOMENT

As a new manager, get the right people in the right jobs by assessing your team's or department's needs, offering realistic job previews, using a variety of recruiting methods, and striving to match the needs and interests of the individual to those of the organization. It is typically wise to use a variety of selection tools. For lower-skilled jobs, an application and brief interview might be enough, but higher-skilled jobs call for a combination of interviews, aptitude and skills tests, and assessment exercises.

Employment Test

The majority of Multi-National Companies use *psychometric tests* that measure attributes like intelligence, aptitude and personality. They provide a potential employer with an insight into how well an applicant works with other people, how well an applicant handles stress, and whether an applicant is able to cope with the intellectual demands of the job. Most of the established psychometric tests used in recruitment and selection make no attempt to analyze emotional or psychological stability. However, in recent years there has been rapid growth (particularly in the US) of tests that claim to measure your integrity or honesty and your predisposition to anger. These tests have attracted a lot of controversy, because of questions about their validity, but their popularity with employers has continued to increase.

 MANAGER'S SHOPTALK

The Right Way to Interview a Job Applicant

A so-so interview usually nets a so-so employee. Many hiring mistakes can be prevented during the interview. The following techniques will ensure a successful interview:

1 *Know what you want.* Before the interview, prepare questions based on your knowledge of the job to be filled.

2 *Prepare a road map.* Develop questions that will reveal whether the candidate has the correct background and qualifications. The questions should focus on previous experiences that are relevant to the current job.

3 *Use open-ended questions in which the right answer is not obvious.* Ask the applicant to give specific examples of previous work experiences. For example, don't ask, 'Are you a hard worker'? or 'Tell me about yourself'. Instead ask, 'Can you give me examples from your previous work history that reflect your level of motivation?' or 'How did you go about getting your current job?'.

4 *Do not ask questions that are irrelevant to the job.* This caution is particularly important when the irrelevant questions might adversely affect minorities or women.

5 *Listen; don't talk.* You should spend most of the interview listening. If you talk too much, the focus will shift to you, and you might miss important cues. One expert actually recommends stating all your questions right at the beginning of the interview. This approach forces you to sit back and listen and also gives you a chance to watch a candidate's behaviour and body language.

6 *Allow enough time so that the interview will not be rushed.* Leave time for the candidate to ask questions about the job. The types of questions the candidate asks can be an important clue to his or her interest in the job.

7 *Avoid reliance on your memory.* Request the applicant's permission to take notes; then do so unobtrusively during the interview or immediately after.

Even a well-planned interview may be disrupted by the unexpected. Here are some of the unusual things that have happened during job interviews, based on surveys of vice presidents and human resource directors at major US corporations:

- The applicant announced she hadn't had lunch and proceeded to eat a burger and chips in the interviewer's office.
- When asked if he had any questions about the job, the candidate answered, 'Can I get an advance on my first month's salary?'.
- The applicant chewed bubble gum and constantly blew bubbles.
- The job candidate said the main thing he was looking for in a job was a quiet place where no one would bother him.
- The job applicant challenged the interviewer to arm wrestle.
- The applicant dozed off and started snoring during the interview.
- When asked how she would handle a difficult situation, the candidate replied, 'I'd let you do it.'

SOURCES James M. Jenks and Brian L. P. Zevnik, 'ABCs of Job Interviewing', *Harvard Business Review* (July–August 1989): 38–42; Dr. Pierre Mornell, 'Zero Defect Hiring', *Inc.* (March 1998): 75–83; Martha H. Peak, 'What Color Is Your Bumbershoot?' *Management Review* (October 1989): 63; and Meridith Levinson, 'How to Hire So You Don't Have to Fire', *CIO* (March 1, 2004): 72–80.

Psychometric testing is now used by over 80 per cent of the Fortune 500 companies in the US and by over 75 per cent of the *Times* Top 100 companies in the UK. Information technology companies, financial institutions, management consultancies, local authorities, the civil service, police forces, fire services and the armed forces all make extensive use of use psychometric testing, as shown in Exhibit 12.10 on the next page.[72]

Exhibit 12.10 Percentage of companies using psychometric testing

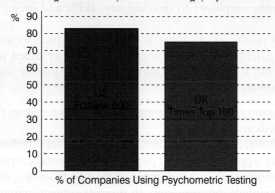

Assessment Centres

First developed by psychologists at AT&T, assessment centres are used to select individuals with high potential for managerial careers by such organizations as IBM, General Electric and others.[73] **Assessment centres** present a series of managerial situations to groups of applicants over, say, a two- or three-day period. One technique is the *in-basket simulation*, which requires the applicant to play the role of a manager who must decide how to respond to ten memos in his or her in-basket within a two-hour period. Panels of two or three trained judges observe the applicant's decisions and assess the extent to which they reflect interpersonal, communication, and problem-solving skills.

Assessment centres have proven to be valid predictors of managerial success, and some organizations now use them for hiring front-line workers as well. Mercury Communications in England uses an assessment centre to select customer assistants. Applicants participate in simulated exercises with customers and in various other exercises designed to assess their listening skills, customer sensitivity and ability to cope under pressure.[74]

Assessment centre
A technique for selecting individuals with high managerial potential based on their performance on a series of simulated managerial tasks.

Developing an Effective Workforce

Following selection, the next goal of HRM is to develop employees into an effective workforce. Development includes training and performance appraisal.

Training and Development

Training and development represent a planned effort by an organization to facilitate employees' learning of job-related skills and behaviours.[75] The training budget of IBM alone in 2005 was $750 million.[76] The most common method of training is on-the-job training. In **on-the-job training (OJT)**, an experienced employee is asked to take a new employee 'under his or her wing' and show the newcomer how to perform job duties. OJT has many advantages, such as minimal out-of-pocket costs for training facilities, materials or instructor fees and easy transfer of learning back to the job. When implemented well, OJT is considered the fastest and most effective means of facilitating learning in the workplace.[77] One type of on-the-job training involves moving people to various types of jobs within the organization, where they work with experienced employees to learn different tasks. This *cross-training* may

On-the-job training (OJT)
A type of training in which an experienced employee 'adopts' a new employee to teach him or her how to perform job duties.

place an employee in a new position for as short a time as a few hours or for as long as a year, enabling the employee to develop new skills and giving the organization greater flexibility.

Another type of on-the-job training is *mentoring*, which means a more experienced employee is paired with a newcomer or a less-experienced worker to provide guidance, support and learning opportunities. Other frequently used training methods include the following:

- *Orientation training*, in which newcomers are introduced to the organization's culture, standards and goals.
- *Classroom training*, including lectures, films, audiovisual techniques and simulations – makes up approximately 70 per cent of all formal corporate training.[78]
- *Self-directed learning*, also called programmed instruction, which involves the use of books, manuals, or computers to provide subject matter in highly organized and logical sequences that require employees to answer a series of questions about the material.
- *Computer-based training*, sometimes called *e-training*, including computer-assisted instruction, Web-based training, and teletraining. As with self-directed learning, the employee works at his or her own pace and instruction is individualized, but as the training programme is interactive and more complex, non-structured information can be communicated. E-training has soared in recent years because it offers cost savings to organizations and allows people to learn at their own pace.[79]

Exhibit 12.11 shows the most frequently used types and methods of training in today's organizations.

Corporate university
An in-house training and education facility that offers broad-based learning opportunities for employees.

Corporate Universities

A recent popular approach to training and development is the corporate university. A **corporate university** is an in-house training and education facility that offers broad-based learning opportunities for employees – and frequently for customers, suppliers and strategic partners as well – throughout their careers.[80] One well-known corporate university is Hamburger University, McDonald's worldwide training centre, which has been in existence for more than 40 years. Numerous other companies, including IBM, FedEx, General Electric, Intel, Harley-Davidson and Capital One, pump millions of dollars into corporate universities to continually build human capital.[81] Employees at Caterpillar attend courses at Caterpillar University, which combines e-training, classroom session and hands-on training activities. Although corporate universities have extended their reach with new technology that enables distance learning via videoconferencing and online education, most emphasize the importance of classroom interaction.[82]

© STOCKBYTE/GETTY IMAGES

CONCEPT CONNECTION 'We don't do training,' says Equifax senior vice president and chief learning officer Lynn Slavenski. 'We do change.' Slavenski oversaw the establishment of Equifax University for the consumer credit reporting company. What distinguishes corporate universities from most old-style training programmes is that the courses – from classes teaching a specific technical skill to corporate-run MBA programmes – are intentionally designed to foster the changes needed to achieve the organization's strategy. It's clearly an idea whose time has come. In 1993, there were just 400 in-house corporate universities. By 2005, that number increased fivefold, and observers predict it will reach 3700 by 2010.

Promotion from Within

Another way to further employee development is through promotion from within, which helps companies retain valuable people. This provides challenging assignments, prescribes new responsibilities and helps employees grow by expanding and developing their abilities. The Peebles Hydro Hotel in Scotland

Exhibit 12.11 Types and Methods of Training

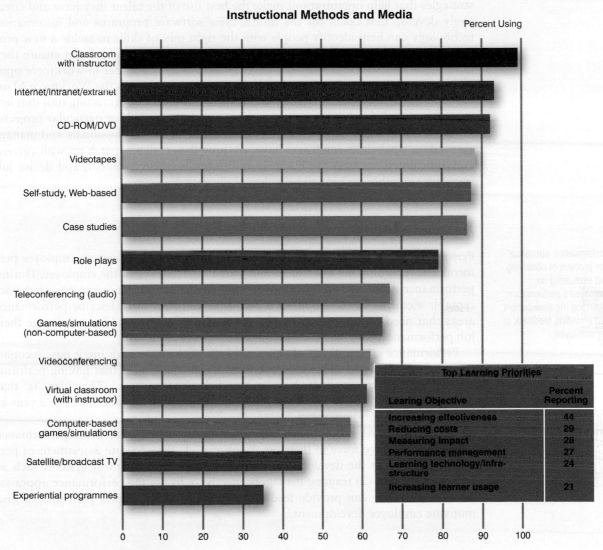

Instructional Methods and Media

Percent Using

Top Learning Priorities

Learing Objective	Percent Reporting
Increasing effectiveness	44
Reducing costs	29
Measuring impact	28
Performance management	27
Learning technology/infrastructure	24
Increasing learner usage	21

SOURCES: Methods data from Tammy Galvin, '2003 Industry Report', *Training* (October 2003): 21+, Reprinted with permission from the October 2003 issue of *Training* magazine, Copyright 2003, Bill Communications, Minneapolis, Minn. All rights reserved. Not for resale. Types data from Holly Dolezalek, '2005 Industry Report', *Training* (December 2005): 14–28.

is passionate about promoting from within as a way to retain good people and give them opportunities for growth. A maid has been promoted to head housekeeper, a wine waitress to restaurant head, and a student worker to deputy manager. The hotel also provides constant training in all areas. These techniques, combined with a commitment to job flexibility, have helped the hotel retain high-quality workers at a time when others in the tourism and hospitality industry are suffering from a shortage of skilled labour. Staff members with ten, 15, or even 20 years of service aren't uncommon at Hydro.[83]

Workforce Optimization

A related approach is **workforce optimization**, which can be defined as putting the right person in the right place at the right time.[84] With today's emphasis on

Workforce optimization
Implementing strategies to put the right people in the right jobs, make the best use of employee talent and skills, and develop human capital for the future.

managing and building human capital, HR professionals are pursuing a range of strategies that help organizations make the best use of the talent they have and effectively develop that talent for the future. New software programs and information technology can help identify people with the right mix of skills to tackle a new project, for example, as well as pinpoint where to move staff internally to ensure they have opportunities for growth and development. IBM is a leader in workforce optimization with a technology-based staff-deployment tool it calls the Workforce Management Initiative. One use of the system is a sort of in-house recruiting tool that lets managers search for employees with the precise skills needed for particular projects. However, the system's greatest impact is that it helps HR professionals and managers analyse what skills employees have, see how those talents match up with current and anticipated needs in the business and technology environment, and devise job transfers and other training to help close skills-gaps.[85]

Performance Appraisal

Performance appraisal
The process of observing and evaluating an employee's performance, recording the assessment and providing feedback to the employee.

Performance appraisal comprises the steps of observing and assessing employee performance, recording the assessment and providing feedback to the employee. During performance appraisal, skilful managers give feedback and praise concerning the acceptable elements of the employee's performance. They also describe performance areas that need improvement. Employees can use this information to change their job performance.

Performance appraisal can also reward high performers with merit pay, recognition and other rewards. However, the most recent thinking is that linking performance appraisal to rewards has unintended consequences. The idea is that performance appraisal should be ongoing, not something that is done once a year as part of a consideration of raises.

Generally, HRM professionals concentrate on two things to make performance appraisal a positive force in their organizations: (1) the accurate assessment of performance through the development and application of assessment systems such as rating scales, and (2) training managers effectively to use the performance appraisal interview, so they can provide feedback that will reinforce good performance and motivate employee development.

Assessing Performance Accurately

To obtain an accurate performance rating, managers acknowledge that jobs are multidimensional and performance thus may be multidimensional as well. For example, a sports broadcaster might perform well on the job-knowledge dimension; that is, she or he might be able to report facts and figures about the players and describe which rule applies when there is a questionable play on the field. But the same broadcaster might not perform as well on another dimension, such as communication. The person might be unable to express the information in a colourful way that interests the audience or might interrupt the other broadcasters.

For performance to be rated accurately, the appraisal system should require the rater to assess each relevant performance dimension. A multidimensional form increases the usefulness of the performance appraisal and facilitates employee growth and development.

360-degree feedback
A process that uses multiple raters, including self-rating, to appraise employee performance and guide development.

A recent trend in performance appraisal is called **360-degree feedback**, a process that uses multiple raters, including self-rating, as a way to increase awareness of strengths and weaknesses and guide employee development. Members of the appraisal group may include supervisors, coworkers and customers, as well as the individual, thus providing appraisal of the employee from a variety of perspectives. One study found that 26 per cent of companies used some type of multirater performance appraisal.[86]

Another alternative performance-evaluation method is the *performance review ranking system*.[87] This method grew quite popular over the past several years, with as many as one third of US corporations using some type of forced ranking system.[88] However, because these systems essentially evaluate employees by pitting them against one another, the method is increasingly coming under fire. As most commonly used, a manager evaluates his or her direct reports relative to one another and categorizes each on a scale, such as A = outstanding performance, B = high-middle performance or C = in need of improvement. Most companies routinely fire those managers falling in the bottom 10 per cent of the ranking. Proponents say the technique provides an effective way to assess performance and offer guidance for employee development. But critics of these systems, sometimes called *rank and yank*, argue that they are based on subjective judgements, produce skewed results, and discriminate against employees who are 'different' from the mainstream. A class-action lawsuit charges that Ford's ranking system discriminates against older managers. Use of the system has also triggered employee lawsuits at Conoco and Microsoft, and employment lawyers warn that other suits will follow.[89]

In addition, critics warn that ranking systems significantly hinder collaboration and risk taking, which are increasingly important for today's companies striving for innovation. One recent study found that forced rankings that include firing the bottom 5 or 10 per cent can lead to a dramatic improvement in organizational performance in the short term, but the benefits dissipate over several years as people become focused on competing with one another rather than improving the business.[90] Many companies, including General Electric, the most famous advocate of forced rankings in recent years, are building more flexibility into the performance review ranking system, and some are abandoning it altogether.[91] Despite these concerns, the appropriate use of performance ranking has been useful for many companies, especially as a short-term way to improve performance. A variation of the system is helping UK supermarket chain Sainsbury's retain quality workers in fairly turbulent market conditions.

Performance Evaluation Errors

Although we would like to believe that every manager assesses employees' performance in a careful and bias-free manner, researchers have identified several rating problems.[93] One of the most dangerous is stereotyping, which occurs when a rater places an employee into a class or category based on one or a few traits or characteristics – for example, stereotyping an older worker as slower and more difficult to train. Another rating error is the halo effect, in which a manager gives an employee the same rating on all dimensions even if his or her performance is good on some dimensions and poor on others.

One approach to overcome performance evaluation errors is to use a behaviour-based rating technique, such as the behaviourally anchored rating scale. The behaviourally anchored rating scale (BARS) is developed from critical incidents pertaining to job performance. Each job performance scale is anchored with specific behavioural statements that describe varying degrees of performance. By relating employee performance to specific incidents, raters can more accurately evaluate an employee's performance.[94]

Exhibit 12.12 illustrates the BARS method for evaluating a production line supervisor. The production supervisor's job can be broken down into several dimensions, such as equipment maintenance, employee training or work scheduling. A

Stereotyping
Placing an employee into a class or category based on one or a few traits or characteristics.

Halo effect
A type of rating error that occurs when an employee receives the same rating on all dimensions regardless of his or her performance on individual ones.

Behaviourally anchored rating scale (BARS)
A rating technique that relates an employee's performance to specific job-related incidents.

reward the type of learning behaviour needed for the organization to adapt and survive in today's environment. In addition, these systems reinforce an emphasis on organizational hierarchy and centralized decision-making and control, which are inconsistent with the growing emphasis on employee participation and increased responsibility.[98]

Skill-based pay systems are becoming increasingly popular in both large and small companies, including Welland Valley Feeds in Market Harborough, UK and Orijen-part of Champion Pet Foods in Canada. Employees with higher skill levels receive higher pay than those with lower skill levels. Located in the heart of Alberta's prairie farmlands, Orijen is a reputable producer of high quality dog and cat foods that are exported worldwide since 1975. At Orijen pet food plant, for example, employees might start at something like $8.75 per hour but reach a top hourly rate of $14.50 when they master a series of skills.[99] Also called *competency-based pay,* skill-based pay systems encourage employees to develop their skills and competencies, thus making them more valuable to the organization as well as more employable if they leave their current jobs.

Compensation Equity

Whether the organization uses job-based pay or skill-based pay, good managers strive to maintain a sense of fairness and equity within the pay structure and thereby fortify employee morale. **Job evaluation** refers to the process of determining the value or worth of jobs within an organization through an examination of job content. Job evaluation techniques enable managers to compare similar and dissimilar jobs and to determine internally equitable pay rates – that is, pay rates that employees believe are fair compared with those for other jobs in the organization.

Organizations also want to make sure their pay rates are fair compared to other companies. HRM managers may obtain **wage and salary surveys** that show what other organizations pay incumbents in jobs that match a sample of 'key' jobs selected by the organization.

Pay-for-performance

Many of today's organizations develop compensation plans based on a *pay-for-performance standard* to raise productivity and cut labour costs in a competitive global environment. **Pay-for-performance**, also called *incentive pay*, means tying at least part of compensation to employee effort and performance, whether it be through merit-based pay, bonuses, team incentives, or various gain-sharing or profit-sharing plans. Data show that, while growth in base wages is slowing in many industries, the use of pay-for-performance has steadily increased since the early 1990s, with approximately 70 per cent of companies now offering some form of incentive pay.[100] President Bush called for implementing performance-based pay in agencies of the federal government. The seniority-based pay system used by most federal agencies has come under intense scrutiny in recent years, with critics arguing that it creates an environment where poor performers tend to stay and the best and brightest leave out of frustration. A survey conducted by the Office of Personnel Management found that only one in four federal employees believe adequate steps are taken to deal with poor performers, and only two in five think strong performers are appropriately recognized and rewarded.[101]

With pay-for-performance, incentives are aligned with the behaviours needed to help the organization achieve its strategic goals. Employees have an incentive to make the company more efficient and profitable because if goals are not met, no bonuses are paid.

Job evaluation
The process of determining the value of jobs within an organization through an examination of job content.

Wage and salary surveys
Surveys that show what other organizations pay incumbents in jobs that match a sample of 'key' jobs selected by the organization.

Pay-for-performance
Incentive pay that ties at least part of compensation to employee effort and performance.

Benefits

The best human resource managers know that a compensation package requires more than money. Although wage/salary is an important component, it is only a part. Equally important are the benefits offered by the organization. Benefits make up 40 per cent of labour costs.[102]

In the US, some benefits are required by law, such as Social Security, unemployment compensation and workers' compensation. In addition, companies with 50 or more employees are required by the Family and Medical Leave Act to give up to 12 weeks of unpaid leave for such things as the birth or adoption of a child, the serious illness of a spouse or family member, or an employee's serious illness. Other types of benefits, such as health insurance, vacations and such things as on-site day-care or fitness centres are not required by law but are provided by organizations to maintain an effective workforce.

One reason benefits make up such a large portion of the compensation package is that health care costs continue to increase. Many organizations are requiring that employees absorb a greater share of the cost of medical benefits, such as through higher co-payments and deductibles. Microsoft, for example, recently sliced health care benefits by requiring a higher co-pay on prescription drugs.[103]

Computerization cuts the time and expense of administering benefits programmes tremendously. At many companies, such as Wells Fargo and LG&E Energy, employees access their benefits package through an intranet, creating a 'self-service' benefits administration.[104] This access also enables employees to change their benefits selections easily. Today's organizations realize that the 'one-size-fits-all' benefits package is no longer appropriate, so they frequently offer *cafeteria-plan benefits packages* that allow employees to select the benefits of greatest value to them.[105] Other companies use surveys to determine which combination of fixed benefits is most desirable. The benefits packages provided by large companies attempt to meet the needs of all employees.

Termination

Despite the best efforts of line managers and HRM professionals, the organization will lose employees. Some will retire, others will depart voluntarily for other jobs, and still others will be forced out through mergers and cutbacks or for poor performance.

Even as a new manager, play a role in how people are compensated. Consider skill-based pay systems and incentive pay to encourage high performers. Don't be dismayed if some people have to be let go. If people have to be laid off or fired, do it humanely. Go to the Ethical Dilemma on page 467 that pertains to termination of employees for poor performance.

TAKE A MOMENT

The value of termination for maintaining an effective workforce is twofold. First, employees who are poor performers can be dismissed. Productive employees often resent disruptive, low-performing employees who are allowed to stay with the company and receive pay and benefits comparable to theirs. Second, employers can use exit interviews as a valuable HR tool, regardless of whether the employee leaves voluntarily or is forced out. An **exit interview** is an interview conducted with departing employees to determine why they are leaving. The value of the exit interview is to provide an inexpensive way to learn about pockets of dissatisfaction within the

Exit interview
An interview conducted with departing employees to determine the reasons for their termination.

105. Robert S. Catapano-Friedman, 'Cafeteria Plans: New Menu for the '90s', *Management Review* (November 1991): 25–29.

106. Byrnes, 'Star Search'.

107. Mike Brewster, 'No Exit', *Fast Company* (April 2005): 93.

108. Yvette Debow, 'GE: Easing the Pain of Layoffs', *Management Review* (September 1997): 15–18.

109. Hammonds, 'Handle with Care'; and Branham, 'Becoming an Employer of Choice'.

CHAPTER OUTLINE

© RONTECH 2000/ISTOCK

LEARNING OBJECTIVES

After reading this chapter, you should be able to:

1   Understand the pervasive demographic changes occurring in the domestic and global marketplace and how corporations are responding.

2   Understand how the definition of diversity has grown to recognize a broad spectrum of differences among employees, and appreciate the dividends of a diverse workforce.

3   Recognize the complex attitudes, opinions and issues that employees bring to the workplace, including prejudice, discrimination, stereotypes and ethnocentrism.

4   Recognize the factors that affect women's opportunities, including the glass ceiling, the opt-out trend and the female advantage.

5   Explain the five steps in developing cultural competence in the workplace.

6   Describe how diversity initiatives and training programmes help create a climate that values diversity.

7   Understand how multicultural teams and employee network groups help organizations respond to the rapidly changing and complex workplace.

CHAPTER 13

MANAGING DIVERSITY

In the UK and beyond, diversity in the population, the workforce and the market-place is a fact of life that no manager can afford to ignore. Globalization, broader access to education, economic development and progressive recruitment policies are just some of the profound shifts driving an increasingly diverse yet more inclusive business landscape. Managing diversity today entails recruiting, training, valuing and maximizing the potential of people who reflect the broad spectrum of society in all areas– gender, race, age, disability, ethnicity, religion, sexual orientation, educa-tion and economic level. Managers in other countries are similarly struggling with diversity issues. Japanese companies, for example, face mounting criticism about the scarcity of women in management positions. In Japan, women make up 41 per cent of the workforce but occupy less than 3 per cent of high-level management posi-tions.[1] In the US, sweeping demographic changes in the US population have trans-formed today's society, creating a cultural mosaic of diverse people. The nation's minority population, for example, is now 100.7 million, making about one in three US residents a minority. Roughly 32 million people speak Spanish at home, and nearly half of these people say they don't speak English very well, according to Cen-sus Bureau figures.[2]

These demographic shifts, among others, are prompting many companies to take notice because these trends open up new markets. To capitalize on those opportuni-ties, organizations have recognized that their workplaces need to reflect the diversity in the marketplace.

Forward-thinking organizations agree and are taking steps to attract and retain a workforce that reflects the cultural diversity of the population. They take seriously the fact that there is a link between the diversity of the workforce and financial success in the marketplace. Top managers say their companies value diversity for a number of reasons, such as: to give the organization access to a broader range of opin-ions and viewpoints, to spur greater creativity and innovation, to reflect an increas-ingly diverse customer base, to obtain the best talent in a competitive environment, and to more effectively compete in a global marketplace.[3] A recent study of diversity management in the UK, Scandinavia and Continental Europe found managers

Do You Know Your Biases?[4]

As a new manager, your day-to-day behaviour will send signals about your biases and values. Some personal biases are active and well known to yourself and others. Other biases are more subtle, and the following questions may provide some hints about where you are biased and don't know it. Answer whether each item is Mostly True or Mostly False for you.

		Mostly True	Mostly False
1	I prefer to be in work teams with people who think like me.	☐	☐
2	I have avoided talking about culture differences with people I met from different cultures because I didn't want to say the wrong thing.	☐	☐
3	My mind has jumped to a conclusion without first hearing all sides of a story.	☐	☐
4	The first thing I notice about people is the physical characteristics that make them different from the norm.	☐	☐
5	Before I hire someone, I have a picture in mind of what they should look like.	☐	☐
6	I typically ignore films, magazines and TV programmes that are targeted toward groups and values that are different from mine.	☐	☐
7	When someone makes a bigoted remark or joke, I don't confront them about it.	☐	☐
8	I prefer to not discuss sensitive topics such as race, age, gender, sexuality or religion at work.	☐	☐
9	There are people I like but would feel uncomfortable inviting to be with my family or close friends.	☐	☐

SCORING AND INTERPRETATION Give yourself one point for each item you marked as Mostly True. The ideal score is zero, but few people reach the ideal. Each question reflects an element of 'passive bias', which can cause people different from you to feel ignored or disrespected by you. Passive bias may be more insidious than active discrimination because it excludes people from opportunities for expression and interaction. If you scored 5 or more, you should take a careful look at how you think and act toward people different from yourself. The sooner you learn to actively include diverse views and people, the better new manager you will be.

reporting similar motives, as well as a desire to enhance the company's image and to improve employee satisfaction.[5] In a survey by the Society for Human Resource Management and *Fortune* magazine, more than 70 per cent of human resources executives indicated that diversity has enhanced their organizations' recruitment efforts and improved the overall corporate culture.[6]

To be successful, these organizations are hiring workers who share the same cultural background as the customers they are trying to reach. Avon, for example, turned around its inner-city markets in the US by putting African-American and Hispanic managers in charge of marketing to these populations.[7] Consider the consulting firm McKinsey & Co. In the 1970s, most consultants were American, but by the turn of the century, McKinsey's chief partner was a foreign national (Rajat Gupta from India), only 40 per cent of consultants were American, and the firm's foreign-born consultants came from 40 different countries.[8] Many other consultancy companies reflect a similar mix of native and foreign-born managers. For instance, Accenture, employs more than 186000 people in 52 countries, including over 35000 Indian and 8000 Chinese employees.

Today's organizations recognize that diversity is no longer just the right thing to do; it is a business imperative and perhaps the single most important factor of the twenty-first century for organization performance.[9] Companies that ignore diversity will have a hard time competing in a multicultural global environment. As Ted Childs, director of diversity at IBM, put it, 'Diversity is the bridge between the workplace and the marketplace.'[10] The global corporations listed in Exhibit 13.1 have been recognized in the US as leaders in corporate diversity. They have made diversity a top priority and have taken steps toward creating a corporate culture that values equality and reflects today's multicultural consumer base.

In this chapter, we explore why demographic changes in local and global market place have prompted companies to place high value on creating a diverse workforce. The chapter considers the advantages of a diverse workforce and the challenges in managing one. We look at the myriad complex issues that face managers and employees in a diverse workplace, including prejudice, stereotypes, discrimination and ethnocentrism. Factors that specifically affect women – the glass ceiling, the opt-out trend and the female advantage – are also considered. After a review of the steps toward cultural competence, the chapter concludes by presenting an overview of initiatives taken by corporations to create an environment that welcomes and values a broad spectrum of diversity among its employees.

Exhibit 13.1 Leaders in Corporate Diversity

Allstate	Marriott International
American Express	Merrill Lynch
Bank of America	Pepsi Bottling Group
Bausch & Lomb	Pricewaterhouse Coopers
Citigroup	Procter & Gamble
Consolidated Edison Company of New York	Starwood Resorts
Daimler Chrysler	The Coca-Cola Company
Deloitte & Touche USA	UPS
Eastman Kodak	Verizon
Ernst & Young	Wachovia
FedEx	Wells Fargo
IBM	Xerox
JP Morgan Chase	

SOURCE: Susan Caminiti, 'The Diversity Factor', *Fortune* (October 29, 2007): 95–105.

Manager's Challenge

Part of the cosmetics giant L'Oréal was found guilty in July 2007 of racial discrimination after it sought to exclude non-white women from promoting its shampoo. In a landmark case, the Garnier division of the beauty empire, along with a recruitment agency it employed, were fined €30 000 each after they recruited women on the basis of race. The historic ruling – the first time a major company has been found guilty of systematic race discrimination in France – saw a senior figure at the agency given a three-month suspended prison sentence.

The French campaign group SOS Racisme brought the case against L'Oréal, the world's largest cosmetics firm, over the campaign in 2000. Garnier France sought saleswomen to demonstrate the shampoo line Fructis Style in supermarkets outside Paris. They sought young women to hand out samples and discuss hairstyling with shoppers.

In July 2000, a fax detailing the profile of hostesses sought by L'Oréal stipulated women should be 18 to 22, size 38–42 (UK size 10–14) and 'BBR', the initials for bleu, blanc, rouge, the colours of the French flag. Prosecutors argued that BBR, a shorthand used by the far right, was also a well-known code among employers to mean 'white' French people and not those of north African, African and Asian backgrounds.

Christine Cassan, a former employee at Districom, a communications firm acting for Garnier, told the court her clients' demanded white hostesses. She said that when she had gone ahead and presented candidates 'of colour' a superior in her own company had said she had 'had enough of Christine and her Arabs'.

One woman working in the recruitment firm involved said foreign-sounding names or photos showing a candidate was of Moroccan, Algerian, Tunisian or other African origin would ensure candidates were eliminated. Another said: 'I once had a good woman candidate but she was non-white. I had to ask someone to pretend that our list was full. It was hard.' In a normal sample of women recruited for similar sales work, around 40 per cent would be non-white. For the Fructis project, less than 4 per cent were of 'non-European' origin.

SOS Racisme said hundreds of jobs had been subject to discrimination in the case. Garnier and the recruitment company were initially acquitted last year, but the appeal court overturned the ruling. Anti-racism campaigners in France hailed the ruling. They claim that racial discrimination in employment is a huge problem in France with a recent survey finding three out of four firms preferred white workers. President Nicolas Sarkozy's justice minister, Rachida Dati, the first woman of north African origin to hold a ministerial post, has ruled that special departments in prosecutors' offices should be set up to deal with race discrimination.[11] Managers are struggling with how to mend L'Oréal s damaged reputation and prove the company's commitment to treating all customers and employees fairly and respectfully.

TAKE A MOMENT   If you were a top manager at L'Oréal what steps would you take to solve this problem? What changes can make L'Oréal a cosmetic company where everyone feels valued and respected?

L'Oréal isn't the only company that has faced difficulties with issues of diversity. In recent years, high-profile racial, gender, age or disability discrimination lawsuits have been filed against the likes Texaco, National Air Traffic Service (NATS), Wal-Mart, Royal Bank of Scotland (RBS) Coca-Cola and Boeing. Mitsubishi is still reeling from a sexual harassment lawsuit charging that managers ignored complaints that women were regularly groped on the factory floor and made to endure crude jokes and lewd photographs.[12]

The Changing Workplace

When Brenda Thomson, the director of diversity and leadership education at the Las Vegas MGM Mirage, steps into one of the company's hotel lobbies, she closes her eyes and listens. 'It's amazing all the different languages I can hear just standing in the lobbies of any of our hotels,' she says. 'Our guests come from all over the world, and it really makes us realize the importance of reflecting that diversity in our workplace.'[13] The diversity Thomson sees in the lobbies of the MGM Mirage hotels is a small reflection of the cultural diversity seen in the larger domestic and global workplaces.

Diversity in the Workplace

In the UK, today's companies reflect the country's image as a melting pot, but with a difference. In the past, the UK was a place where people of different national origins, ethnicities, races, and religions came together and blended to resemble one another. Opportunities for advancement were limited to those workers who easily fit into the mainstream of the larger culture. Some immigrants chose desperate measures to fit in, such as abandoning their native languages, changing their last names, and sacrificing their own unique cultures. In essence, everyone in workplace organizations was encouraged to share similar beliefs, values and lifestyles despite differences in gender, race and ethnicity.[14]

Now organizations recognize that everyone is not the same and that the differences people bring to the workplace are valuable.[15] Rather than expecting all employees to adopt similar attitudes and values, managers are learning that these differences enable their companies to compete globally and to tap into rich sources of new talent. Although diversity in Europe and North America has been a reality for some time, genuine efforts to accept and *manage* diverse people began only in recent years.

Diversity has become a key topic, in part because of the vast changes occurring in today's workplace and consumer base. The average worker is older now, and many more women, people of colour and immigrants are seeking job and advancement opportunities. The following statistics illustrate some of the changes reshaping the workplace.

- **Ageing workforce.** The average worker in many developed countries is older now, as the so-called baby boomers continue to affect the workplace as this massive group of workers progresses through its life stages.[16] This trend is compounded by a falling population in some countries. Japan and Russia are expected to experience significant population falls, with Japan's population expected to slip from 127 million in 2000 to 103 million in 2050. The corresponding data for Russia show an even more severe relative fall – from 147 million in 2000 to 108 million in 2050.

  Generational diversity is a key concern for managers in many of today's companies, with four generations working side-by-side, each with a different mindset and different expectations.

  Many people are opting to stay in the workforce long past retirement age, giving managers opportunities to enhance workforce diversity by incorporating older employees. B&Q is the largest DIY retailer in Europe and China and is

© DAVID BAGNALL/ALAMY

CONCEPT CONNECTION Since 1989, when B&Q opened its Macclesfield store staffed entirely with workers over the age of 50, research has confirmed that this approach has had a direct and positive impact on customer service. At B&Q a quarter of the workforce is over 50, with a similar number under 25. To meet the needs for flexibility from these groups, B&Q has introduced term-time contracts for grandparents, an online job share register, and the facility for older workers to reduce their hours and draw final-salary pensions at same time.

well known for its pioneering work in the employment of older workers. B&Q is committed to eliminating all forms of discrimination and to promoting equality of opportunity in all employment practices to ensure that employees are treated no less favourably on the grounds of age, gender, marital or civil partnership status, colour, ethnic or national origin, culture, religion, religious belief or similar philosophical belief, disability, political affiliation, gender identity, gender reassignment or sexual orientation.

B&Q have operated without a retirement age for many years and offer the same benefits and training/promotion opportunities to everyone, whatever age they are, and were founder members of the Employers Forum on Age. The policy has given B&Q greater flexibility for experienced workers to serve as teachers to younger colleagues, and a workplace culture that increased pride in the work for employees of all ages.

B&Q was presented with the 2007 Gallup Great Workplace Award which recognizes 12 companies for having the world's most engaged and productive workforces.

■ *Other changes in demographics.* More women, ethnic minorities and immigrants are seeking job and advancement opportunities. The UN currently expects the world's population will reach 8.0 billion in 2025 and 9.2 billion in 2050 compared with 6.1 billion in 2000, and just 2.5 billion in 1950.

In the half century from 2000 to 2050, population is expected to increase by 3.1 billion – around 50 per cent – most of which will be accounted for rises in Africa (1.2 billion) and Asia (1.6 billion). A further 600 million of the increase is accounted for by India, the population of which is expected to overtake China's by 2025. In the US the greatest increase in employment will occur with Asians and Hispanics. In fact, the number of Hispanics in the workforce will increase by 6 million between 2006 and 2016, with 27 million Hispanics in the workforce by 2016.[17]

■ *Minority purchasing power.* Exhibit 13.2 shows the growth in employment among different racial and ethnic groups in the US. Hispanics, African-Americans and Asian Americans which together represent $1.5 trillion in annual purchasing power.[18]

■ *Growth in foreign-born population.* In UK, the 2001 census showed 7.9 per cent of the UK belonged to a minority ethnic group, with the figure rising to 29 per cent in London. Not only have most ethnic minority groups mushroomed since then, the enlargement of the EU has also resulted in tens of thousands of Eastern European migrants entering the country. More than 300 languages are now spoken in London alone, according to the Office for National Statistics, and one in five small businesses are owned or managed by members of ethnic minority communities.[19]

Similarly, during the 1990s, the foreign-born population of the US nearly doubled, and immigrants now number more than 37.5 million, meaning that almost one in eight people living in the US was born in another country, the highest percentage since the 1920s.[20]

Exhibit 13.2 Growth in Employment from 2006 to 2016 by Group

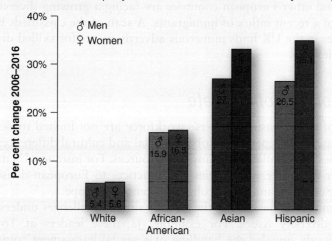

SOURCE: Bureau of Labour Statistics.

So far, the ability of organizations to manage diversity has not kept pace with these demographic trends, thus creating a number of significant challenges for minority workers and women. The pay gap between white men and every other group still exists This inequality shapes perceptions about who can assume leadership roles. Companies that truly value diversity will recognize pay inequality and discrimination in the workplace and make progress toward eliminating them.

However, many managers are ill-prepared to handle diversity issues. Many managers around the world grow up and are educated in racially unmixed neighbourhoods and consequently have had little exposure to people substantially different from themselves. The challenge is particularly great when working with people from other countries and cultures. One recent challenge at IBM involved a new immigrant, a Muslim woman who was required to have a photo taken for a company identification badge. She protested that her religious beliefs required that, as a married woman, she wear a veil and not expose her face to men in public. A typical Western manager, schooled in traditional management training, might insist that she have the photo taken or leave her employment. Fortunately, IBM has a well-developed diversity programme and managers worked out a satisfactory compromise.[21] Consider some other mistakes that managers could easily make:[22]

- To reward a Vietnamese employee's high performance, her manager promoted her, placing her at the same level as her husband, who also worked at the factory. Rather than being pleased, the worker became upset and declined the promotion because Vietnamese husbands are expected to have a higher status than their wives.

- A manager, having learned that a friendly pat on the arm or back would make workers feel good, took every chance to touch his subordinates. His Asian employees hated being touched and thus started avoiding him, and several asked for transfers.

- A manager declined a gift offered by a new employee, an immigrant who wanted to show gratitude for her job. He was concerned about ethics and explained the company's policy about not accepting gifts. The employee was so insulted she quit.

These issues related to cultural diversity are difficult and real. For example, the UK and other European countries are facing a growing diversity challenge because of a recent influx of immigrants. A scan of the classifieds in any major newspaper in the UK finds numerous advertisements for skilled diversity management leaders.

Diversity on a Global Scale

Implications of an increasingly diverse workforce are not limited to domestic markets. For organizations operating globally, social and cultural differences may create more difficulties and conflicts than any other sources. For instance, US managers trying to transfer their diversity policies and practices to European divisions haven't considered the complex and social cultural systems in Europe.

Foreign firms doing business in the US face similar challenges understanding and dealing with diversity issues. For example, Japanese leaders at Toyota Motor Company seriously bungled the handling of a sexual harassment complaint in the company's North American division, leading to a lawsuit. When Sayaka Kobayashi sent a letter to Dennis Cuneo, senior vice president of Toyota North America, saying she had endured months of romantic and sexual advances from her boss, Cuneo told her he would discuss the issue with the boss, Hideaki Otaka. However, Cuneo allegedly said that he didn't want to offend the man (a cultural norm), so he planned to say it was Kobayashi's boyfriend who was upset about the overtures. This chapter's Manager's Shoptalk lists some interesting tips for foreign managers working in the US to help them understand and relate to Americans. Do you agree that these statements provide a good introduction to American culture for a non-native?

National cultures are intangible, pervasive and difficult to comprehend. However, it is imperative that managers in organizations learn to understand local cultures and deal with them effectively.[23] Many companies have taken this challenge seriously and have experienced growth in the global marketplace. For example, Honeywell has a growing role in the global marketplace with 118 000 employees operating in more than 100 countries. Today, 54 per cent of its employees work outside the US. Honeywell made the global connection and incorporated diversity as part of its global strategies and believes that diversity provides the energy to fuel its high-performance culture and achieve sustainable competitive advantage.[24] The director of diversity at Kraft General Foods concurs. 'Being global means that our customers are diverse. Our shareholders are diverse. The population which is available to us, our productivity, creativity, innovation, and people who supply us are diverse. There is no way we can run a business effectively without a deep understanding and accommodating all of these elements.'[25]

Communication Differences

As explained in Chapter 4, people from some cultures tend to pay more attention to the social context (social setting, non-verbal behaviour, social status) of their verbal communication than many Europeans do. In a high-context culture (often identified with Asian and Arab countries), people are sensitive to circumstances surrounding social exchanges. People use communication primarily to build personal social relationships; meaning is derived from context – setting, status, non-verbal behaviour – more than from explicit words; relationships and trust are more important than business; and the welfare and harmony of the group are valued. In a low-context culture (often identified with European and American countries), people use communication primarily to exchange facts and information; meaning is derived primarily from words; business transactions are more important than building relationships and trust; and individual welfare and achievement are more important than the group.

The impact of globalization means cultural differences can provide significant challenges for managing diverse organizations, with a 2006 Accenture UK study finding two thirds of businesses that had outsourced some business processes encountering miscommunication issues with their global sourcing operations. Communication, out of all the key management processes, was identified as the top factor (or obstacle) to the successful fulfilment of outsourcing operations. Interestingly, however, organizations where inter-cultural communications training had been introduced experienced less miscommunication issues and boosted productivity by up to 30 per cent, with the freer exchange of information creating efficiencies and cutting process delays.

Beyond cross-cultural boundaries, cultural sub-groups within organizations add greater complexity and, ultimately, illustrate the priority for clear and sensitive communications across all parties, regardless of cultural background. Traditional distinctions of German and Scandinavian firms as low-context and Italian and French as high-context should always be treated with caution within a business world experiencing unprecedented employee migration. While recent research has questioned the empirical basis for the context paradigm, its value rests with alerting managers to the impact culture, at multiple levels, can have on communication and the challenge of diversity skills training for modern organizations.

 MANAGER'S SHOPTALK

A Guide for Expatriate Managers in America or China

Although each person is different, individuals from a specific country typically share certain values and attitudes. See the discussion on Hofstede's Value Dimensions in Chapter 4. Managers planning to move to a foreign country can learn about these broad value patterns to help them adjust to working and living abroad. The following characteristics are often used to help foreign managers understand what Americans and Chinese are like.

1 **Americans are informal.** They tend to treat everyone alike, even when individuals differ significantly in age or social status.

Chinese are very formal. They show high levels of deference to their superiors. Chinese negotiators expect to see high-level representatives at high-level negotiations.

2 **Americans are direct and decisive.** To some foreigners, this behaviour may seem abrupt or even rude. Typically, Americans don't 'beat around the bush', which means they don't talk around things but get right to the point. They quickly define a problem and decide on the course of action they believe is most likely to get the desired results.

Chinese tend to favour indirect communication. Harmonious relationships between business partners is essential. This can take months to establish involving home visits, long dinners

(without simply talking about business). Displays of anger, aggression or frustration at the negotiating table is likely to be counter-productive.

3   ***Americans love facts.*** They value statistics, data and information in any form.

Chinese avoid breaking up complex negotiations into a series of smaller issues, such as price, quantity and delivery, and prefer to think holistically and talk about all the issues at once, skipping back and forth.

4   ***Americans are competitive.*** They like to keep score, whether at work or play. Americans like to win, and they don't tolerate failure well. Some foreigners might think Americans are aggressive or overbearing. For example, Americans are not at all shy about selling themselves. In fact, it's expected.

Chinese are also very competitive, but not at the expense of damaging a person's reputation and social standing which rests on saving face (Mianzi). To cause embarrassment, even unintentionally, can be disastrous for business relations. This leads to a more modest outward persona.

5   ***Americans believe in hard work.*** For many, commitment to work and career comes first. In general, Americans rarely take time off, even if a family member is ill. They don't believe in long vacations – even corporation presidents often take only two weeks, if that.

Chinese are also famous for their work ethic and place high value on endurance. Hard work is the ideal, and the same applies to negotiating. Work is important, and there is a clear overlap between work and home life.

6   ***Americans are independent and individualistic.*** They place a high value on freedom and believe that people can control their own destinies.

Chinese are communal rather than individualistic, with an emphasis on group harmony and cooperation.

7   ***Americans are questioners.*** They ask a lot of questions, even of someone they have just met. Some of these questions may seem pointless (How ya' doin'?) or personal (What kind of work do you do?).

Chinese are also quite out-going and more than happy to mix personal chat with business discussions.

8   ***Americans dislike silence.*** They would rather talk about the weather than deal with silence in a conversation.

Chinese are happy to bide their time. They have a culture of thrift driven by economic hardship, which still manifests itself today. Expect a lot of haggling over terms and prices, and be prepared for long silences!

9   ***Americans value punctuality.*** They keep appointment calendars and live according to schedules and clocks.

Chinese are also very disciplined, although not quite so rigid over schedules. In particular, meetings may well continue beyond planned timings until discussions concluded.

10   ***Americans pay close attention to appearances.*** They take note of designer clothing and good grooming. They may in fact seem obsessed with bathing, eliminating body odours and wearing clean clothes.

Chinese place great attention on social norms and rituals. Premium is placed on social capital within their group of friends, relatives and close associates. The importance of personal connections in concluding contracts cannot be overstressed.

How many of these statements do you agree with? Discuss them with your friends and classmates, including people from different countries and members of different sub-cultural groups where possible.

SOURCES Winston Fletcher, 'The American Way of Work', *Management Today* (August 1, 2005): 46; 'What Are Americans Like'? Exhibit 4–6 in Stephen P. Robbins and Mary Coulter, *Management*, 8th ed. (Upper Saddle River, NJ: Pearson Prentice Hall, 2005), as adapted from M. Ernest, ed., *Predeparture Orientation Handbook: For Foreign Students and Scholars Planning to Study in the United States* (Washington, DC: US Information Agency, Bureau of Cultural Affairs, 1984), p. 103–105; Amanda Bennett, 'American Culture Is Often a Puzzle for Foreign Managers in the US', *The Wall Street Journal*, February 12, 1986; 'Don't Think Our Way's the Only Way', *The Pryor Report* (February 1988): 9; and B. Wattenberg, 'The Attitudes Behind American Exceptionalism', *US News and World Report* (August 7, 1989): 25. *Harvard Business Review* (Oct 2003) – HBR Spotlight: China Tomorrow (pp. 69–99).

Recruiting and Training Employees to Work Overseas

Expatriates are employees who live and work in a country other than their own. Careful screening, selection, and training of employees to serve overseas increase the potential for corporate global success. Human resource managers consider global skills in the selection process. In addition, expatriates receive cross-cultural training that develops language skills and provides cultural and historical orientation.

Equally important is honest self-analysis by overseas candidates and their families. Before seeking or accepting an assignment in another country, a candidate should ask himself or herself questions such as the following:

- Is your spouse interrupting his or her own career path to support your career? Is that acceptable to both of you?
- Is family separation for long periods involved?
- Can you initiate social contacts in a foreign culture?
- Can you adjust well to different environments and changes in personal comfort or quality of living, such as the lack of television, limited hot water, varied cuisine and national phone strikes?
- Can you manage your future re-entry into the job market by networking and maintaining contacts in your home country?

Employees working overseas must adjust to all of these conditions. Managers going global might find that their management styles need adjustment to succeed in a foreign country. One aspect of this adjustment is understanding differences in social and cultural values as identified by the Hofstede research and the GLOBE project described in Chapter 4.

Managing Diversity

Whether operating on a national or global scale, organizations recognize that their consumer base is changing, and they cannot prosper and succeed without a diverse workforce. Let's first explore the expanding definition of *diversity* and consider the dividends of cultivating a diverse workforce.

What is Diversity?

Diversity is defined as all the ways in which people differ.[26] Diversity wasn't always defined this broadly. Decades ago, many companies defined diversity in terms of race, gender, age, lifestyle and disability. That focus helped create awareness, change mind sets and create new opportunities for many. Today, companies are embracing a more inclusive definition of diversity that recognizes a spectrum of differences that influence how employees approach work, interact with each other, derive satisfaction from their work, and define who they are as people in the workplace.[27]

Exhibit 13.3 illustrates the difference between the traditional model and the inclusive model of diversity. The dimensions of diversity shown in the traditional model include inborn differences that are immediately observable and include race, gender, age and physical ability. However, the inclusive model of diversity includes *all* of the ways in which employees differ, including aspects of diversity that can be acquired or changed throughout one's lifetime. These dimensions may have less impact than those included only in the traditional model but nevertheless affect a person's self-definition and worldview and the way the person is viewed by

Diversity
All the ways in which employees differ.

© TONY WEST/ALAMY

CONCEPT CONNECTION
Luxury clothing brand Burberry, where Angela Ahrendts and Stacey Cartwright are Chief Executive and Chief Financial Officer, is one of the rare exceptions to a boardroom landscape that remains overwhelmingly male. A recent 2009 Female FTSE report from the Cranfield School of Management revealed the number of executive directorships in the FTSE 100 index held by women has fallen across 2009. Across Europe the picture is slightly more positive, with a recent survey identifying almost 10% of the top 300 European companies as having women on their boards, yet progress remains slow.

Exhibit 13.3 Traditional vs. Inclusive Models of Diversity

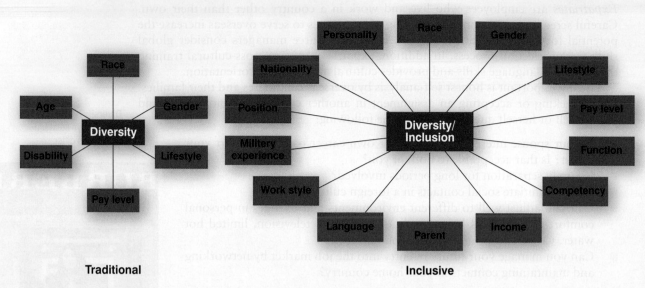

Traditional   Inclusive

SOURCE: Reproduced by permission. Anthony Oshiotse and Richard O'Leary, 'Corning Creates an Inclusive Culture to Drive Technology Innovation and Performance', *Wiley InterScience, Global Business and Organizational Excellence*, 26 no. 3 (March/April 2007): 12.

others. For example, the inclusive model of diversity recognizes people with different spiritual beliefs. As part of its diversity programme, Target addresses issues of faith in its Minneapolis store. Muslim cashiers who object to ringing up pork products due to religious beliefs are allowed to wear gloves, shift to other positions or transfer to other stores.[28]

TAKE A MOMENT   Go to the Ethical Dilemma on pages 508 that pertains to accommodating religious practices in the workplace.

With 35 per cent of its domestic workforce made up of African-Americans, Hispanics, Asian Americans and other minorities, UPS is widely recognized for its commitment to diversity. For the past seven consecutive years, a *Fortune* magazine survey has ranked UPS as one of the '50 Best Companies for Minorities'. In addition, minorities hold 85 senior management positions, with African-Americans filling 52 of those posts, and five of the company's board of directors are African-American.[29] Positive statistics like this help UPS attract and retain a diverse workforce. UPS believes that the diversity reflected in its workforce is the key to its effectiveness.

Yet, a diverse workforce poses unique challenges for managers at UPS and elsewhere. Employees with different backgrounds bring different opinions and ideas. Conflict, anxiety and misunderstandings may increase. Embracing these differences and using them to improve company performance can be challenging. **Managing diversity**, a key management skill in today's global economy, means creating a climate in which the potential advantages of diversity for organizational or group performance are maximized while the potential disadvantages are minimized.[30]

Managing diversity
Creating a climate in which the potential advantages of diversity for organizational or group performance are maximized while the potential disadvantages are minimized.

Exhibit 13.4 Dividends of Workplace Diversity

- Better use of employee talent
- Increased understanding of the marketplace
- Enhanced breadth of understanding in leadership positions
- Increased quality of team problem-solving
- Reduced costs associated with high turnover, absenteeism and lawsuits

SOURCE: Gail Robinson and Kathleen Dechant, 'Building a Business Case for Diversity', *Academy of Management Executive* 11, no. 3 (1997): 22.

Dividends of Workplace Diversity

Corporations that build strong, diverse organizations reap numerous dividends as described below and shown in Exhibit 13.4. The dividends of diversity include the following:

- *Better use of employee talent.* Companies with the best talent are the ones with the best competitive advantage. But attracting a diverse workforce is not enough; companies must also provide career opportunities and advancement for its minority and women employees to retain them.

- *Increased understanding of the marketplace.* The consumer market is becoming increasingly diverse. A diverse workforce is better able to anticipate and respond to changing consumer needs. Ford Motor Company realized it could reach its business objectives only if it created a workforce that reflected the multicultural face of the country. So it assembled a workforce made up of 25 per cent minorities (18.4 per cent are African-American) to foster a culture of inclusion, winning it a spot on *Black Enterprise's* '40 Best Companies for Diversity'.[31]

- *Enhanced breadth of understanding in leadership positions.* Homogeneous top management teams tend to be myopic in their perspectives. According to Niall FitzGerald of Unilever, 'It is important for any business operating in an increasingly complex and rapidly changing environment to deploy a broad range of talents. That provides a breadth of understanding of the world and environment and a fusion of the very best values and different perspectives which make up that world.'[32]

- *Increased quality of team problem solving.* Teams with diverse backgrounds bring different perspectives to a discussion that result in more creative ideas and solutions.[33] Although 85 per cent of Ernst & Young's senior leadership is still male, the company is taking steps to create a more diverse leadership team because it's better for business. 'We know you get better solutions when you put a diverse team at the table. People come from different backgrounds and they have different frames of reference. When you put these people together, you get the best solution for our clients,' says Billie Williamson, director of flexibility and gender equity strategy at Ernst & Young.[34]

- *Reduced costs associated with high turnover, absenteeism, and lawsuits.* Companies that foster a diverse workforce reduce turnover, absenteeism, and the risk of lawsuits. Because family responsibilities contribute to turnover and absenteeism, many companies now offer child-care and elder-care benefits, flexible work arrangements,

© AFP/GETTY IMAGES

CONCEPT CONNECTION With roughly half of its 66 000 employees working outside the US, it's not surprising that American Express is an acknowledged leader in managing global diversity. These East Indian staff members are shown in the company's Delhi offices. American Express developed a training module, 'Valuing Diversity and Practicing Inclusion', for managers throughout the world, but executives let local facilitators customize the tool to fit their cultures. 'We always allow them a period of time to be able to adapt, modify, and customize ... so that it resonates well with employees,' explains Henry Hernandez, Vice President and Chief Diversity Officer.

INNOVATIVE WAY

Tesco

One of the biggest transformations in Tesco's business model has been the company's rise from a relatively small UK supermarket chain to the world's fourth-biggest retailer. Analysts estimate that 65 per cent of future growth will come from overseas, with Tesco making inroads into central Europe, China, Korea and America.

Tesco has now established a Diversity Council designed to allow all staff to meet their full potential regardless of age, gender, disability, ethnicity or sexual orientation. Their diversity strategy aims for a workforce at all levels that mirrors the communities they serve. These priorities reflect those of the countries in which they operate. Tesco focus on employing local people and developing local leaders wherever they operate. Of the 180 000 people employed overseas, fewer than 200 are from the UK business.

Tesco do not discriminate on the basis of ethnic origin and promote understanding of different cultures to help staff work effectively together. In the UK, stores celebrate cultural festivals such as Eid and Diwali alongside traditional British festivals. The managers are provided with a religions toolkit providing information on festivals, diet, fasting and prayer to help them understand and support people from different faiths. In 2007, this toolkit was updated to cover the growing range of cultures and countries that employees and customers come from, including Bangladesh, the Caribbean, China, Ghana, India, Pakistan, Poland and Somalia.

Strong staff retention and the home-grown nature of Tesco management are some of the UK's biggest private-sector employer's key strengths, according to analysts. 'I started with Tesco as a Saturday boy. I became a store manager, then a regional manager and now I'm the retail director and a board member,' said David Potts who, like Sir Terry Leahy, Tesco's Chief Executive, started work as a shelf stacker. As a consequence, Potts believes staff can now expect a career trajectory that can compete with other multinationals. 'We are now a large international company and can offer our employees much more variety and development. You can work for us and go to China or America. You do not need to leave Tesco to advance your career. We also work hard to attract people from all sectors,' he said.

Sukwinder Bassi joined Tesco four years ago after working for B&Q and J Sainsbury. 'I'm now the manager of a large Tesco Extra hypermarket in east London. I chose Tesco over other retailers simply because it's the biggest company with the most opportunity. I'm an ambitious guy and I want to get on,' he said. Bassi's store, at Gallions Reach, has staff from 30 different ethnic backgrounds and is working to introduce more products for the local Asian and Polish communities.

According to Chloe Smith of *The Grocer*, the trade magazine for the sector, Tesco's 'classlessness' and diversity works on the level of both products and employment. She said: 'Tesco has avoided being associated with any one economic group like those who shop at Waitrose or Asda. You can shop in Tesco without feeling that you are making a statement about yourself.'

Management has encouraged the ethos that whatever your background, you can get on. In addition to traditional graduate-training schemes, Tesco has 1000 apprenticeships as well as projects to bring the long-term unemployed back into work.

'We redevelop brownfield sites and in those areas operate schemes for people who have been out of work for a long time – or who have never worked,' said Potts. With more than one fifth of its workforce coming from the over fifties, Tesco is also an important employer of older people. The company has no fixed retirement age and has seen the number of over sixties on the payroll double in the past ten years. Age and experience may bring better customer service but most late-joiners will not at first have seen employment with Tesco as a career. Personnel manager Linda Avis admitted: 'We have a lot of people who join us as a second career. They often think they're coming as a stop-gap to get some money but stay for years and retrain in a new area. We take a significant number of ex-Service people, for example.'

In 2007, Tesco launched the Tesco Women's Network which aims to help female managers and directors progress. Around 150 women from across the Group attended the launch event. They are also in the process of forming a similar network for sexual orientation. Tesco also support flexible hours whenever possible. In the UK this includes family-friendly shifts, maternity leave for full- and part-time workers, paid paternity leave, equal training and development opportunities for full- and part-time workers, childcare vouchers and career breaks.[35]

telecommuting and part-time employment to accommodate employee responsibilities at home. Discrimination lawsuits are also a costly side effect of a discriminatory work environment. A racial harassment suit against Lockheed Martin Corporation cost the company $2.5 million, the largest individual racial-discrimination payment obtained by the Equal Employment Opportunity Commission.[36]

Factors Shaping Personal Bias

To reap the benefits of diversity described above, organizations are seeking managers who will serve as catalysts in the workplace to reduce barriers and eliminate obstacles for disadvantaged people. *Managing diversity*, therefore, has become a sought after management skill. To successfully manage a diverse workgroup and create a positive, productive environment for all employees, managers need to start with an understanding of the complex attitudes, opinions and issues that already exist in the workplace or that employees bring into the workplace. These include several factors that shape personal bias: prejudice, discrimination, stereotypes and ethnocentrism.

Prejudice, Discrimination and Stereotypes

Prejudice is the tendency to view people who are different as being deficient. If someone acts out their prejudicial attitudes toward people who are the targets of their prejudice, discrimination has occurred. Paying a woman less than a man for the same work is gender discrimination. Mistreating people because they have a different ethnicity is ethnic discrimination. Although blatant discrimination is not as widespread as in the past, bias in the workplace often shows up in subtle ways: a lack of choice assignments, the disregard by a subordinate of a minority manager's directions, or the ignoring of comments made by women and minorities at meetings. A survey by Korn Ferry International found that 59 per cent of minority managers surveyed had observed a racially motivated double standard in the delegation of assignments.[37] Minority employees typically feel that they have to put in longer hours and extra effort to achieve the same status as their white colleagues. 'It's not enough to be as good as the next person,' says Bruce Gordon, president of Bell Atlantic's enterprise group. 'We have to be better.'[38]

Many governments have passed legislation to outlaw different types of discrimination, as discussed in Chapter 12. In the UK, these include the following:

- The Equal Pay Act 1970 and Sex Discrimination Act 1975 which outlaws discrimination on the grounds of sex, marriage and gender reassignment.
- The Race Relations Act 1976 amended by the Race Relations Amendment Act 2000 which outlaws discrimination on racial grounds. Racial grounds are defined as colour, race, nationality, ethnic or national origins.
- The Disability Discrimination Acts 1995 and 2005 deal with discrimination against disabled people.
- The Protection from Harassment Act 1997 is a general piece of legislation which protects people against harassment, whatever the grounds.
- The Part-time Workers Regulations 2000. Regulation 5(1): 'A part-time worker has the right not to be treated by his employer less favourably than the employer treats a comparable full-time worker. . .'
- The Religion or Belief Regulations 2003 protects people from discrimination due to their religion or belief. Religion or belief is defined as 'any religion, religious belief, or similar philosophical belief'.

Prejudice
The tendency to view people who are different as being deficient.

Discrimination
When someone acts out their prejudicial attitudes toward people who are the targets of their prejudice.

- The Sexual Orientation Regulations 2003 outlaw discrimination on the grounds of sexual orientation. Sexual orientation is defined in regulation 2(1): 'a sexual orientation towards persons of the same sex; persons of the opposite sex; or persons of the same sex and of the opposite sex'. The regulations do not deal with specific forms of sexual practice or conduct.
- The Employment Equality (Age) Regulations 2006 give effect to the EU Equal Treatment Framework Directive (2000/78) as regards age discrimination.
- The Equality Bill 2009, introduced by the UK Government on 24 April, which when enacted will replace the 116 different pieces of equality legislation in force covering race, age, disability and gender equality, including 35 Acts, 52 Statutory Instruments, 13 Codes of Practice and 16 European Commission Directives. The bill represents more than just legislative housekeeping. It will tackle the pay gap between men and women and is broadening the scope of current age discrimination legislation.

A major component of prejudice is stereotyping, a rigid, exaggerated, irrational belief associated with a particular group of people.[39] To be successful managing diversity, managers need to eliminate harmful stereotypes from their thinking, shedding any biases that negatively affect the workplace. Managers can learn to *value differences* which mean they recognize cultural differences and see the differences with an appreciative attitude. To facilitate this attitude, managers can learn about cultural patterns and typical beliefs of groups to help understand why people act the way they do. It helps to understand the difference between these two ways of thinking, most notably that stereotyping is a barrier to diversity but valuing cultural differences facilitates diversity. These two different ways of thinking are described below and illustrated in Exhibit 13.5.[40]

Stereotype
A rigid, exaggerated, irrational belief associated with a particular group of people.

- *Stereotypes are often based on folklore, media portrayals, and other unreliable sources of information.* In contrast, legitimate cultural differences are backed up by systematic research of real differences.
- *Stereotypes contain negative connotations.* On the other hand, managers who value diversity view differences as potentially positive or neutral. For example, the observation that Asian males are typically less aggressive does not imply they are inferior or superior to white males – it simply means that there is a difference.
- *Stereotypes assume that all members of a group have the same characteristics.* Managers who value diversity recognize that individuals within a group of people may or may not share the same characteristics of the group.

Exhibit 13.5 Difference Between Stereotyping and Valuing Cultural Differences

Stereotyping	Valuing Cultural Differences
Is based on false assumptions, anecdotal evidence or impressions without any direct experience with a group	Views based on cultural differences verified by scientific research methods
Assigns negative traits to members of a group	Views cultural differences as positive or neutral
Assumes that all members of a group have the same characteristics	Does not assume that all individuals within a group have the same characteristics
Example: Suzuko Akoi is an Asian; therefore, she is not aggressive by white, male standards	Example: As a group, Asians tend to be less aggressive than white, male Americans

What judgemental beliefs or attitudes do you have that influence your feelings about people who belong to certain groups? To successfully manage diversity, you will need to shed stereotypes while still appreciating the differences among people.

Not only should managers rid themselves of stereotypical thinking, they should also recognize the stereotype threat that may jeopardize the performance of at-risk employees. Stereotype threat describes the psychological experience of a person who, usually engaged in a task, is aware of a stereotype about his or her identity group suggesting that he or she will not perform well on that task.[41] Suppose you are a member of a minority group presenting complicated market research results to your management team and are anxious about making a good impression. Assume that some members of your audience have a negative stereotype about your identity group. As you ponder this, your anxiety skyrockets and your confidence is shaken. Understandably, your presentation suffers because you are distracted by worries and self-doubt as you invest energy in overcoming the stereotype. The feelings you are experiencing are called *stereotype threat*.

People most affected by stereotype threat are those we consider as disadvantaged in the workplace due to negative stereotypes – racial and ethnic minorities, members of lower socioeconomic classes, women, older people, gay and bisexual men, and people with disabilities. Although anxiety about performing a task may be normal, people with stereotype threat feel an extra scrutiny and worry that their failure will reflect not only on themselves as individuals but on the larger group to which they belong. As pop diva Beyoncé Knowles has said, 'It's like you have something to prove, and you don't want to mess it up and be a negative reflection on black women.'[42]

Stereotype threat
A psychological experience of a person who, usually engaged in a task, is aware of a stereotype about his or her identify group suggesting that he or she will not perform well on that task.

Ethnocentrism

Valuing diversity by recognizing, welcoming, and cultivating differences among people so they can develop their unique talents and be effective organizational members is difficult to achieve. Ethnocentrism can be a roadblock to this type of thinking. Ethnocentrism is the belief that one's own group and subculture are inherently superior to other groups and cultures. Ethnocentrism makes it difficult to value diversity. Viewing one's own culture as the best culture is a natural tendency among most people. Moreover, the business world still tends to reflect the values, behaviours and assumptions based on the experiences of a rather homogeneous, white, middle-class, male workforce. Indeed, most theories of management presume that workers share similar values, beliefs, motivations and attitudes about work and life in general. These theories presume one set of behaviours best helps an organization to be productive and effective and therefore should be adopted by all employees.[43]

Ethnocentric viewpoints and a standard set of cultural practices produce a monoculture, a culture that accepts only one way of doing things and one set of values and beliefs, which can cause problems for minority employees. People of colour, women, gay people, the disabled, the elderly, and other diverse employees may feel undue pressure to conform, may be victims of stereotyping attitudes, and may be presumed deficient because they are different. White, heterosexual men, many of whom do not fit the notion of the 'ideal' employee, may also feel uncomfortable with the monoculture and resent stereotypes that label white males as racists and sexists. Valuing diversity means ensuring that *all* people are given equal opportunities in the workplace.[44]

One organization that is making a firm commitment to break out of monoculture thinking is Hyatt hotels, which has a diversity council made up of employees and managers from different parts of the company and representing different cultural

Ethnocentrism
The belief that one's own group or subculture is inherently superior to other groups or cultures.

Monoculture
A culture that accepts only one way of doing things and one set of values and beliefs.

and ethnic backgrounds. The council meets three times a year to review how well the company is recognizing, developing, and promoting minorities. The hotel splits its diversity initiatives into five parts: commitment, accountability, training, measurement and communication. For managers at Hyatt, 15 per cent of their bonus is dependent on meeting specific diversity goals.[45]

The goal for organizations seeking cultural diversity is pluralism rather than a monoculture and ethno-relativism rather than ethnocentrism. **Ethno-relativism** is the belief that groups and subcultures are inherently equal.

One problem some minority workers feel is they believe they have to become bicultural in order to succeed. **Biculturalism** can be defined as the sociocultural skills and attitudes used by racial minorities as they move back and forth between the dominant culture and their own ethnic or racial culture. Research on differences between whites and blacks has focused on issues of biculturalism and how it affects employees' access to information, level of respect and appreciation, and relation to superiors and subordinates. In general, in Europe and the US non-white feel less accepted in their organizations, perceive themselves to have less discretion on their jobs, receive lower ratings on job performance, experience lower levels of job satisfaction, and reach career plateaus earlier than whites. They find themselves striving to adopt behaviours and attitudes that will help them be successful in the white-dominated corporate world while at the same time maintaining their ties to their own community and culture. For example, in the US Asians who aspire to management positions are often frustrated by the stereotype that they are hardworking but not executive material because they are too quiet and deferential. Assertiveness and pressing your views in a group is seen as a characteristic of leadership in American culture, but Asians typically view this behaviour as inappropriate and immature. Some Asian Americans feel they have a chance for career advancement only by becoming bicultural or abandoning their native cultures altogether.

Pluralism means that an organization accommodates several subcultures. Movement toward pluralism seeks to fully integrate into the organization the employees who otherwise would feel isolated and ignored. To promote pluralism in its corporate headquarters, chefs at Google's corporate cafeteria ensure that its menu accommodates the different tastes of its ethnically diverse workforce.

Ethno-relativism
The belief that groups and subcultures are inherently equal.

Biculturalism
The sociocultural skills and attitudes used by racial minorities as they move back and forth between the dominant culture and their own ethnic or racial culture.

Pluralism
An environment in which the organization accommodates several subcultures, including employees who would otherwise feel isolated and ignored.

 INNOVATIVE WAY

Google

Employees in Google's corporate headquarters come from all corners of the world, but they feel a little closer to home when they see familiar foods from their homeland on the cafeteria menu. With a goal of satisfying a diverse, ethnically varied palate, Google's first food guru and chef Charlie Ayers designed menus that reflected his eclectic tastes yet also met the needs of an increasingly diverse workforce. He created his own dishes, searched all types of restaurants for new recipes, and often got some of his best ideas from foreign-born employees. For example, a Filipino accountant offered a recipe for chicken *adobo,* a popular dish from her native

country. Scattered around the Googleplex are cafés specializing in Southwestern, Italian, California-Mediterranean, and vegetarian cuisines. And because more and more Googlers originally hail from Asia, employees can find sushi at the Japanese-themed Pacific Café or Thai red curry beef at the East Meets West Café.

Google believes food can be a tool for supporting an inclusive workplace. The array of menu options gives people a chance to try new things and learn more about their coworkers. And Google knows that when people need a little comfort and familiarity, nothing takes the edge off of working in a foreign country like eating food that reminds you of home.[46]

Many of today's organizations, like Google, are making conscious efforts to shift from a monoculture perspective to one of pluralism. Others, however, are still hindered by stereotypical thinking. Consider a recent report from the National Bureau of Economic Research, entitled 'Are Greg and Emily More Employable than Lakisha and Jamal'? which shows that employers often unconsciously discriminate against job applicants based solely on the Afrocentric names on their résumé. In interviews prior to the research, most human resource managers surveyed said they expected only a small gap and some expected to find a pattern of reverse discrimination. The results showed instead that white-sounding names got 50 per cent more call-backs than black-sounding names, even when skills and experience were equal.[47] A similar study conducted in France revealed that a job candidate with a North African-sounding name had three times less chance than one with a French-sounding name to get an interview.[48]

Affirmative Action

Affirmative action refers to government-mandated programmes that focus on providing opportunities to women and members of minority groups who previously faced discrimination. It is not the same thing as diversity, but affirmative action has facilitated greater recruitment, retention and promotion of minorities and women in some countries.

Affirmative action policies or positive discrimination have been implemented in a number of countries including the US, Brazil, Canada, India, Malaysia and South Africa to tackle national disadvantages arising from specific historical, overt and institutional discrimination issues in those countries. In many other countries positive discrimination remains unlawful and quotas/selective systems are not generally permitted. In the US affirmative action was developed in response to conditions in the country 40 years ago. Adult white males dominated the workforce, and economic conditions were stable and improving. Because of widespread prejudice and discrimination, legal and social coercion were necessary to allow women, people of colour, immigrants and other minorities to become part of the economic system. Affirmative action is highly controversial today. Some members of non-protected groups argue that affirmative action is no longer needed and that it leads to *reverse discrimination*. Even the intended beneficiaries of affirmative action programmes often disagree as to their value, and some believe these programmes do more harm than good. One reason may be the *stigma of incompetence* that often is associated with affirmative action recruitment. One study found that both working managers and students consistently rated people portrayed as affirmative action employees as less competent and recommended lower salary increases than for those not associated with affirmative action. In addition, people who perceive that they were hired because of affirmative action requirements may demonstrate negative self-perceptions and negative views of the organization, which leads to lower performance and reinforces the opinions of others that they are less competent.

In South Africa, the Employment Equity Act and the Broad Based Black Economic Empowerment Act aim to promote and achieve equality in the workplace, by not only advancing people from designated groups but also specifically dis-advancing the others. By legal definition, the designated groups include all people of colour, white females, people with disabilities and people from rural areas. The term 'black economic empowerment' is somewhat of a misnomer, therefore, because the Acts cover empowerment of any member of the designated groups, regardless of race. In 2008, the High Court in South Africa has ruled that Chinese South Africans are to

Affirmative action
Government-mandated programmes that focus on providing opportunities to women and members of minority groups who previously faced discrimination.

as CEO of Citigroup's Consumer Group after suffering both the death of her mother and a personal life-changing accident in the same year. In evaluating her reasons, Magner said she realized that 'life is about everything, not just the work'.

One school of thought says women don't want corporate power and status in the same way that men do, and clawing one's way up the corporate ladder has become less appealing. Yet critics argue that this view is just another way to blame women themselves for the dearth of female managers at higher levels.[57] Vanessa Castagna, for example, left JC Penney after decades with the company not because she wanted more family or personal time but because she kept getting passed over for top jobs.[58] Although some women are voluntarily leaving the fast track, many more genuinely want to move up the corporate ladder but find their paths blocked. In a surveyed by Catalyst, 55 per cent of executive women said they aspire to senior leadership levels.[59] In addition, a survey of 103 women voluntarily leaving executive jobs in *Fortune* 1000 companies found that corporate culture was cited as the number one reason for leaving.[60] The greatest disadvantages of women leaders stem largely from prejudicial attitudes and a heavily male-oriented corporate culture.[61] Some years ago, when Procter & Gamble asked the female executives it considered 'regretted losses' (that is, high performers the company wanted to retain) why they left their jobs, the most common answer was that they didn't feel valued by the company.[62]

The Female Advantage

Some people think women might actually be better managers, partly because of a more collaborative, less hierarchical, relationship-oriented approach that is in tune with today's global and multicultural environment.[63] As attitudes and values change with changing generations, the qualities women seem to naturally possess may lead to a gradual role reversal in organizations. For example, a stunning gender reversal is taking place in education, with girls outperforming boys at every level. In addition, women of all races and ethnic groups are outpacing men in earning bachelor's and master's degrees.[64]

According to James Gabarino, an author and professor of human development at Cornell University, women are 'better able to deliver in terms of what modern society requires of people – paying attention, abiding by rules, being verbally competent, and dealing with interpersonal relationships in offices'.[65] His observation is supported by the fact that female managers are typically rated higher by subordinates on interpersonal skills as well as on factors such as task behaviour, communication, ability to motivate others, and goal accomplishment.[66] Recent research found a correlation between balanced gender composition in companies (that is, roughly equal male and female representation) and higher organizational performance. Moreover, a study by Catalyst indicates that organizations with the highest percentage of women in top management financially outperform, by about 35 per cent, those with the lowest percentage of women in higher-level jobs.[67]

TAKE A MOMENT   Complete the New Manager Self-Test on page 497 to generate more awareness of gender differences in behaviour.

NEW MANAGER SELF-TEST

Are You Tuned into Gender Differences?

How much do you know about gender differences in behaviour? Answer whether each item below is True or False. Answer all questions before looking at the answers at the bottom of the page.

		True	False
1	Men control the content of conversations, and they work harder to keep conversations going.	☐	☐
2	Women use less personal space than men.	☐	☐
3	A male speaker is listened to more carefully than a female speaker even when they make an identical presentation.	☐	☐
4	In the classroom, male students receive more reprimands and criticism.	☐	☐
5	Men are more likely to interrupt women than to interrupt other men.	☐	☐
6	Female managers communicate with more emotional openness and drama than male managers.	☐	☐
7	Women are more likely to answer questions not addressed to them.	☐	☐
8	In general, men smile more than women do.	☐	☐
9	Both male and female direct reports see female managers as better communicators than male managers.	☐	☐
10	In a classroom, teachers are more likely to give verbal praise to female students.	☐	☐

SCORING AND INTERPRETATION Check your answers below. If you scored seven or more correctly, consider yourself perceptive and observant about gender behaviour. If you scored three or fewer, you may want to tune in to the gender dynamics you are missing.

SOURCE Myra Sadker and Joyce Kaser, *The Communications Gender Gap* (Washington, DC: Mid-Atlantic Center for Sex Equity, 1984).

ANSWERS 1: False (men control content, women work harder); 2: True; 3: True; 4: True; 5: True; 6: False (managers of both sexes communicate about the same way); 7: False; 8: False (women smile more); 9: True; 10: False.

Cultural Competence

A corporate culture, as discussed in Chapter 3, is defined by the values, beliefs, understandings and norms shared by members of the organization. Although some corporate cultures foster diversity, many managers struggle to create a culture that values and nurtures its diverse employees. Managers who have made strategic decisions to foster diversity need a plan that moves a corporate culture toward

Exhibit 13.7 The Most Common Diversity Initiatives: Percentage of *Fortune* 1000 Respondents

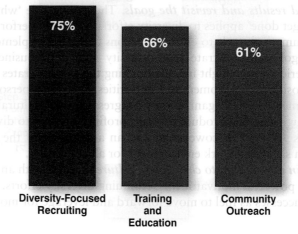

75%	66%	61%
Diversity-Focused Recruiting	Training and Education	Community Outreach

SOURCE: Adapted from data in 'Impact of Diversity Initiatives on the Bottom Line: A SHRM Survey of the *Fortune* 1000', pp; S12–S14, in *Fortune*, special advertising section, 'Keeping Your Edge: Managing a Diverse Corporate Culture', produced in association with the Society for Human Resources Management, http://www.fortune.com/sections.

Mentor
A higher-ranking, senior organizational member who is committed to providing upward mobility and support to a protégé's professional career.

labour markets. Each year Pearson offers a number of places to final year students and graduates from ethnic minority backgrounds a chance to work through the summer in its various companies, the Financial Times, Penguin Books, Edexcel and Pearson Education. Students spend six weeks working on a challenging business related project and gaining valuable skills working for an international media company.[74]

© STEVE RUBIN/THE IMAGE WORKS

Establishing Mentor Relationships

The successful advancement of diverse group members means that organizations must find ways to eliminate the glass ceiling. One of the most successful structures to accomplish this goal is the mentoring relationship. A **mentor** is a higher-ranking organizational member who is committed to providing upward mobility and support to a protégé's professional career. Mentoring provides minorities and women with direct training and inside information on the norms and expectations of the organization. A mentor also acts as a friend or counsellor, enabling the employee to feel more confident and capable. Getting to the top of a big business like BP means travelling a long way from the petrol pump. BP's Mutual Mentoring Programme is designed to remind and refresh senior executives by getting them close to the coalface, pairing them up with junior executives who are typically different to them. As Sarah Murray from the *Financial Times* reports: 'The pairings are designed to foster understanding between people of different genders and backgrounds so, for example, a junior woman might be mentoring a senior man, and executives of different national origins or ethnic backgrounds are often put together.' BP reports that, not only has the programme proved very motivating for both senior and junior staff, but the sharing of understanding is leading to improved communications and decision-making.[75]

CONCEPT CONNECTION Fannie Mae, a major provider of home mortgage funds, was in the news for all the wrong reasons after the US government seized control of it and Freddie Mac to avoid a collapse of the giant firms due to losses from mortgage defaults. Fannie Mae's CEO was ousted and the firm is being restructured, but the company's commitment to workforce diversity remains solid. Fannie Mae offers a structured mentoring programme to enhance individual capabilities and career development. Here the director of legal operations is mentoring two Fannie Mae employees. A partnership with a more experienced employee provides valuable insights and contacts for minorities and women wanting to advance their skills and careers.

One researcher who studied the career progress of high-potential minorities found that those who advance the furthest all share one characteristic – a strong mentor or network of mentors who nurtured their professional development.[76] However, research also indicates that minorities, as well as women, are much less likely than men to develop mentoring relationships.[77] Women and minorities might not seek mentors because they feel that job competency should be enough to succeed, or they might feel uncomfortable seeking out a mentor when most of the senior executives are white males. Women might fear that initiating a mentoring relationship could be misunderstood as a romantic overture, whereas male mentors may think of women as mothers, wives or sisters rather than as executive material. Cross-race mentoring relationships sometimes leave both parties uncomfortable, but the mentoring of minority employees must often be across race because of the low number of minorities in upper-level positions. The few minorities and women who have reached the upper ranks often are overwhelmed with mentoring requests from people like themselves, and they may feel uncomfortable in highly visible minority-minority or female-female mentoring relationships, which isolate them from the white male status quo.

TAKE A MOMENT

Even as a new manager, you may have an opportunity to act as a mentor to a younger or less-experienced minority employee. Use your interpersonal skills to build the person's confidence and help him or her develop valuable contacts. Assist the employee in navigating the office politics and learning the unwritten rules about how things are done in the organization.

The solution is for organizations to overcome some of the barriers to mentor relationships between white males and minorities. When organizations can institutionalize the value of white males actively seeking women and minority protégés, the benefits will mean that women and minorities will be steered into pivotal jobs and positions critical to advancement. Mentoring programmes also are consistent with legislation that increasing encourages the diversification of middle and upper management.

Accommodating Special Needs

Many people have special needs of which top managers may be unaware. For example, if numerous people entering the organization at the lower level are single parents, the company can reassess job scheduling and opportunities for child care. If a substantial labour pool is non-English speaking, training materials and information packets can be provided in another language, or the organization can provide English language classes.

In many families today, both parents work, which means that the company can provide structures to deal with child-care, maternity or paternity leave, flexible work schedules, telecommuting or home-based employment, and perhaps part-time employment or seasonal hours that reflect the school year. The key to attracting and keeping elderly or disabled workers may include long-term care insurance and special health or life insurance benefits. Alternative work scheduling also may be important for these groups of workers. Organizations struggling with generational diversity must find ways to meet the needs of workers at different ages and places in the life cycle.[78] Pitney Bowes created the Life Balance Resources programme to help employees in different generations cope with life cycle issues, such as helping Generation Y workers find their first apartments or cars, assisting Generation X employees in locating child-care or getting home loans, helping baby boomers plan

© TRINITY MIRROR/MIRRORPIX/ALAMY

CONCEPT CONNECTION Bernard Matthews farms seven million turkeys every year in the UK, but has found having a strong brand is not enough when your local employee population is small, there is a limited skill set, severe employee shortages and the firm needs to expand. For Bernard Matthews the solution was to recruit overseas in Portugal, bringing in a significant immigrant workforce to mix and work with existing staff locally. This has led to an increase from 3 per cent to 30 per cent of Portuguese employees. Bernard Matthews responded to the challenge by developing support networks, local English-language training and creating partnerships with the Norfolk Police and the Home Office, as well as a 'fast-tracking' programme at HSBC to ensure bank accounts could be opened quickly. So the challenge of skills shortages was resolved by adopting a diverse workforce and, in response, generated innovative thinking to solve the problems of practical implementation.[82]

Diversity training
Special training designed to educate employees about the importance of diversity, make people aware of their own biases, and teach them skills for communicating and working in a diverse workplace.

for retirement, and aiding older workers in researching insurance and long-term care options.[79]

Another issue for some companies may be that racial/ethnic minorities and immigrants often had fewer educational opportunities than other groups. Some companies work with high schools to provide fundamental skills in literacy and maths, or they provide these programmes within the company to upgrade employees to appropriate educational levels. The movement toward providing educational services for employees can be expected to increase for immigrants and the economically disadvantaged in the years to come.

Providing Diversity Skills Training

Most of today's organizations provide special training, called **diversity training**, to help people identify their own cultural boundaries, prejudices and stereotypes and develop the skills for managing and working in a diverse workplace. By some estimates, about $80 billion has been invested in corporate diversity programmes in the US alone over the past ten years, much of it spent on training.[80] Working or living within a multicultural context requires a person to use interaction skills that transcend the skills typically effective when dealing with others from one's own in-group.[81]

The first step is typically *diversity awareness training* to make employees aware of the assumptions they make and to increase people's sensitivity and openness to those who are different from them. A basic aim of awareness training is to help people recognize that hidden and overt biases direct their thinking about specific individuals and groups. If people can come away from a training session recognizing that they prejudge people and that this tendency needs to be consciously addressed in communications with and treatment of others, an important goal of diversity awareness training has been reached.

The next step is *diversity skills training* to help people learn how to communicate and work effectively in a diverse environment. Rather than just attempting to increase employees' understanding and sensitivity, this training gives people concrete skills they can use in everyday situations, such as how to handle conflict in a constructive manner or how to modify nonverbal communication such as body language and facial expression.[83] Verizon Communications uses an online training tool where managers can tap into various diversity scenarios that might occur in the work-place and see how they can manage them in an appropriate way.[84] In addition to online training, companies may also use classroom sessions, experiential exercises, videotapes or DVDs, and outside consulting firms that help organizations with diversity management issues. Rynes and Rosen have studied the effectiveness of diversity training. They conclude that while only 9 per cent of those going on such courses have a positive view in advance, 75 per cent have positive diversity attitudes after completing the training.[85]

Increasing Awareness of Sexual Harassment

Sexual harassment creates an unhealthy and unproductive work environment. To eliminate it, companies may offer sexual harassment awareness programmes that create awareness of what defines sexual harassment and the legal ramifications of violations. Although psychological closeness between men and women in the workplace may be a positive experience, sexual harassment is not. Sexual harassment is illegal in many countries. As a form of sexual discrimination, sexual harassment in the workplace is a violation of Title VII of the US 1964 Civil Rights Act. In the UK, the Protection from Harassment Act 1997 is a general piece of legislation which protects people against harassment, whatever the grounds, while the Sexual Discrimination Act 1975 includes the legal right not to be sexually harassed at work.

The following list categorizes various forms of sexual harassment as defined by one university:

- **Generalized.** This form involves sexual remarks and actions that are not intended to lead to sexual activity but that are directed toward a coworker based solely on gender and reflect on the entire group.
- **Inappropriate/offensive.** Though not sexually threatening, it causes discomfort in a coworker, whose reaction in avoiding the harasser may limit his or her freedom and ability to function in the workplace.
- **Solicitation with promise of reward.** This action treads a fine line as an attempt to 'purchase' sex, with the potential for criminal prosecution.
- **Coercion with threat of punishment.** The harasser coerces a coworker into sexual activity by using the threat of power (through recommendations, grades, promotions, and so on) to jeopardize the victim's career.
- **Sexual crimes and misdemeanours.** The highest level of sexual harassment, these acts would, if reported to the police, be considered felony crimes and misdemeanours.[86]

Statistics in Canada indicate that between 40 and 70 per cent of women and about 5 per cent of men have been sexually harassed at work.[87] Similarly, around one in three Europeans report witnessing discrimination or harassment in the past year, and 48 per cent think that not enough is being done to fight discrimination. The situation in the UK is just as dire where it is estimated that 50 per cent of women in employment are, or have been, subject to sexual harassment of some form or other.

However, attitudes to sexual harassment can vary across the world. In Russia recently, an advertising executive who sued her boss for sexual harassment lost her case after a judge ruled that employers were obliged to make passes at female staff to ensure the survival of the human race.[88] In Uganda, The State Minister for Works, John Byabagambi has recently condemned employers who sexually harass their employees, noting that there are increasing reports of sexual harassment at workplaces with especially male bosses harassing their female employees In the US, a growing number of men are urging recognition that sexual harassment is not just a woman's problem.[89]

As a new manager, be careful about a romantic relationship in the workplace. In particular, steer clear of such relationships with superiors or subordinates, which is a slippery ethical area. Know what sexual harassment means, and make sure everyone in your team or department understands that sexual harassment is disrespectful and against the law.

TAKE A MOMENT

New Diversity Initiatives

Of the companies responding to a survey by the Society for Human Resource Management 91 per cent believe that diversity initiatives help maintain a competitive advantage. Some specific benefits they cited include improving employee morale, decreasing interpersonal conflict, facilitating progress in new markets, and increasing the organization's creativity.[90] In addition to the ideas already discussed, two new approaches to diversity management – multicultural teams and employee networks – have arisen in response to the rapid change and complexity of the twenty-first-century organization.

Multicultural Teams

Multicultural teams
Teams made up of members from diverse national, racial, ethnic and cultural backgrounds.

Companies have long known that putting together teams made up of members from different functional areas results in better problem solving and decision-making. Now, they are recognizing that **multicultural teams** – teams made up of members from diverse national, racial, ethnic and cultural backgrounds – provide even greater potential for enhanced creativity, innovation and value in today's global marketplace.[91] Research indicates that diverse teams generate more and better alternatives to problems and produce more creative solutions than homogeneous teams.[92] A team made up of people with different perspectives, backgrounds, and cultural values creates a healthy mix of ideas and leads to greater creativity and better decisions.

Some organizations, such as RhonePoulenc Rorer (RPR), based in Collegeville, Pennsylvania, are committed to mixing people from diverse countries and cultures, from the top to the bottom of the organization. There are 15 nationalities represented in RPR's top management teams, including a French CEO, an Austrian head of operations, an American general counsel, an Egyptian head of human resources, and an Italian director of corporate communications.[93] Alison Kay, a partner and diversity champion at Ernst & Young business advisory services, describes how it worked on a pitch to work for a FTSE 100-quoted company. 'We knew we wouldn't win it by offering the same as everyone else,' she says. A team of men and women with a variety of ages, seniority and ethnic backgrounds was assembled. 'We spent days brainstorming. Our different perspectives and experiences brought a real variety of views and ideas. The client liked what we came up with – and we won the contract.'[94]

Despite their many advantages,[95] multicultural teams are more difficult to manage because of the increased potential for miscommunication and misunderstanding. Multicultural teams typically have more difficulty learning to communicate and work together smoothly, but with effective cross-cultural training and good management, teams can learn to work well together.[96] One management team videotaped its meetings so members could see how their body language reflects cultural differences. An American manager remarked, 'I couldn't believe how even my physical movements dominated the table, while Ron [a Filipino American] … actually worked his way off-camera within the first five minutes.'[97]

Employee Network Groups

Employee network groups
Groups based on social identity, such as gender or race, and organized by employees to focus on concerns of employees from that group.

Employee network groups are based on social identity, such as gender or race, and are organized by employees to focus on concerns of employees from that group.[98] Network groups pursue a variety of activities, such as meetings to educate top managers, mentoring programmes, networking events, training sessions and skills seminars, minority intern programmes, and community volunteer activities. These activities give people a chance to meet, interact with and develop social and professional ties to others throughout the organization, which may include key decision-makers. Network groups are a powerful way to reduce social isolation for women and minorities, help these employees be more effective, and enable members to achieve greater career advancement. A recent study confirms that network groups can be important tools for helping organizations retain managerial-level minority employees.[99] 'We have to embrace diversity,' says Ismail Amla of Accenture. 'We just can't recruit the same kind of people any more. We need to talk about changing the way we look for talent. To help us recruit people from different backgrounds and to support staff from ethnic minorities, we've developed networks such as an Asian network, a Chinese network and a women's network. 'We'll point out, for instance, that inviting everyone for a drink after work to talk about things is not appropriate sometimes to Muslims or women with children. It's about behavioural change but also just getting people thinking.'[100]

An important characteristic of successful network groups however is that they are often created informally by employees, not the organization, and membership is voluntary. Employee networks for minorities who have faced barriers to advancement in organizations, including African-Americans, Hispanics, American Indians, Asian Americans, women, gays and lesbians, and disabled employees, show tremendous growth. Even managers who once thought of minority networks as 'gripe groups' are now seeing them as essential to organizational success because they help to retain minority employees, enhance diversity efforts, and spark new ideas that can benefit the organization.[101] At Kraft Foods, networks are considered critical to the success of multicultural teams because they build awareness and acceptance of cultural differences and help people feel more comfortable working together.[102] In general, female and minority employees who participate in a network group feel more pride about their work and are more optimistic about their careers than those who do not have the support of a network.[103]

A MANAGER'S ESSENTIALS: WHAT HAVE WE LEARNED?

■ The domestic and global marketplace is experiencing dramatic demographic changes, including an ageing population and growing immigrant and minority populations. Savvy managers recognize that their workforces should reflect this cultural diversity.

■ Diversity is defined as all the ways in which employees differ. This definition has been broadened in recent years to be more inclusive and recognize a broad spectrum of characteristics including age, religion, physical ability, race, ethnicity, sexual preference, and more. Because of the complexities of managing a diverse workforce, *managing diversity* is a key management skill today.

■ The dividends of diversity are numerous and include better use of employee talent, increased understanding of customers in the marketplace, enhanced breadth of understanding in leadership

positions, increased quality of team problem-solving, and reduced costs associated with high turnover, absenteeism and lawsuits.

■ All employees bring to the workplace opinions and attitudes that affect their ability to treat people equally. Some of these issues include prejudice, discrimination and stereotyping. The performance of minorities and other disadvantaged workers may be affected by a *stereotype threat*, a psychological reaction by employees that is triggered by worry and concern that others may doubt their abilities due to unfair stereotypes. Managers should be aware of the challenges minority employees face and be prepared to handle them, including issues related to ethnocentrism, the glass ceiling, the opt-out trend and the female advantage.

■ When a corporate culture embraces diversity and fosters an environment where all people thrive

10 If someone in your family were homosexual, you would:
   a. View this as a problem and try to change the person to a heterosexual orientation
   b. Accept the person as a homosexual with no change in feelings or treatment
   c. Avoid or reject the person.

11 You react to little children with:
   a. Patience
   b. Annoyance
   c. Sometimes a, sometimes b.

12 Other people's personal habits annoy you:
   a. Often
   b. Not at all
   c. Only if extreme.

13 If you stay in a household run differently from yours (cleanliness, manners, meals and other customs), you:
   a. Adapt readily
   b. Quickly become uncomfortable and irritated
   c. Adjust for a while, but not for long.

14 Which statement do you agree with most?
   a. We should avoid judging others because no one can fully understand the motives of another person
   b. People are responsible for their actions and have to accept the consequences
   c. Both motives and actions are important when considering questions of right and wrong.

Scoring and Interpretation

Circle your score for each of the answers and total the scores:

1 a = 4; b = 0; c = 2

2 a = 4; b = 2; c = 0

3 a = 0; b = 2; c = 4

4 a = 4; b = 2; c = 0

5 a = 4; b = 2; c = 0

6 a = 4; b = 2; c = 0

7 a = 0; b = 4; c = 2

8 a = 0; b = 2; c = 4

9 a = 0; b = 4; c = 2

10 a = 2; b = 0; c = 4

11 a = 0; b = 4; c = 2

12 a = 4; b = 0; c = 2

13 a = 0; b = 4; c = 2

14 a = 0; b = 4; c = 2

Total Score

0–14: If you score 14 or below, you are a very tolerant person and dealing with diversity comes easily to you.

15–28: You are basically a tolerant person and others think of you as tolerant. In general, diversity presents few problems for you; you may be broad-minded in some areas and have less tolerant ideas in other areas of life, such as attitudes toward older people or male–female social roles.

29–42: You are less tolerant than most people and should work on developing greater tolerance of people different from you. Your low tolerance level could affect your business or personal relationships.

43–56: You have a very low tolerance for diversity. The only people you are likely to respect are those with beliefs similar to your own. You reflect a level of intolerance that could cause difficulties in today's multicultural business environment.

SOURCE Adapted from the Tolerance Scale by Maria Heiselman, Naomi Miller, and Bob Schlorman, Northern Kentucky University, 1982. In George Manning, Kent Curtis, and Steve McMillen, *Building Community: The Human Side of Work*, (Cincinnati, OH: Thomson Executive Press, 1996), pp. 272–277.

MANAGEMENT IN PRACTICE: ETHICAL DILEMMA

Anglo-China Computers

Overcoming differences in culture and communication is a major goal of diversity skills training. For Anglo-China Computers, created when Chinese company China Five Star bought out Anglo Computers business, this training is seen as crucial to the company's survival. Anglo-China's chairman, Yang Jingjing, is Chinese; its CEO, Peter Walker, is British; and its chief finance officer, Kishor Patel is

Indian. A little more than 40 per cent of the company's 8000 or so employees work in China, with the rest scattered around the world, mostly in Europe. About half of them can speak fluent English, but no Mandarin, while the other half speak Chinese but with little English.

With such a culturally, geographically and linguistically diverse workforce, Anglo-China has no choice but to implement some serious diversity training. And managers are rising to the challenge, by initiating a wide-ranging worldwide strategy designed to educate its far-flung employees on the cultures, customs and languages of their overseas colleagues. Programmes include Mandarin lessons for European executives and English lessons for managers in China, training sessions on the predominant cultural values of the various countries where Anglo-China operates, and weekly lunchtime cultural understanding seminars exploring issues such as how different cultures regard silence in conversations. A 'knowledge exchange' programme sends employees on short-term overseas assignments so people can learn different perspectives. Anglo-China even has a cross-cultural children's pen-pal programme, for the children of employees to help them learn about one another.

Top executives at Anglo-China consider the diversity of the company to be its biggest competitive advantage. However, they know that to realize Anglo China's full potential, they must find ways to smooth the tensions and stress that diversity can bring and take advantage of differences to create a stronger company.

For instance, there were some problems at the customer service centre in India. The new centre manager, Miss Anita Yu, had recently arrived there, having been promoted from her previous position in Hong Kong. Anita was fluent in English, Mandarin, and Cantonese but did not speak any of the local Indian languages, such as Gujarati or Urdu, spoken by the local workforce.

Anita had several years experience as a manager in Hong Kong, and was very confident in her abilities, but had started to notice since arriving in India that a number of the junior male managers seemed to be uncomfortable about taking instructions from a female manager. Also, although Anita had had a couple of female Hindu friends in Hong Kong, she had never previously come into any contact with Muslims. In arriving in India, she had initially been surprised to discover that there was a sizeable Muslim rather than Hindu workforce at the company,

and that unlike most Western faiths, Islamic religious practices were inextricably woven into everyday life. The previous manager had worked out ways to accommodate Muslim customs, such as allowing women to wear traditional clothing as long as they weren't violating safety standards.

One of the key reasons for Anita's appointment had been an urgent need to increase local productivity, which was far behind that she had been used to in Hong Kong. Anita was therefore intrigued to discover that her Muslim staff needed to perform at least some of the ceremonial washing and prayers they were required to do five times a day during work hours, and that the previous manager had set aside a quiet, clean room where they could observe their 15-minute rituals during their breaks and at sunset.

Anita felt that the Maghrib sunset prayers second shift workers had to perform were disruptive to a smooth workflow. Compared to their midday and afternoon rituals, the Muslim faithful had considerably less leeway as to when they said the sunset prayers, and of course, the sun set at a slightly different time each day. Her initial reaction was that she would like to change the policy, but she was concerned that if she did she risked alienating part of her workforce.

What would You Do?

1 Continue the current policy that leaves it up to the Muslim workers as to when they leave the assembly line to perform their sunset rituals.

2 Try to hire fewer possible Muslim workers so the work line will be efficient on second shift.

3 Ask the Muslim workers to delay their sunset prayers until a regularly scheduled break occurs, pointing out that Anglo-China is primarily a place of business, not a house of worship.

SOURCES Prepared from multiple sources including: Rob Johnson, '30 Muslim Workers Fired for Praying on Job at Dell', *The Tennessean*, March 10, 2005; Anayat Durrani, 'Religious Accommodation for Muslim Employees', *Workforce.com*, www.workforce.com/archive/feature/22/26/98/index.php?ht=muslim%20muslim; US Equal Employment Opportunity Commission, 'Questions and Answers about Employer Responsibilities Concerning the Employment of Muslims, Arabs, South Asians, and Sikhs', www.eeoc.gov/; and US Department of Commerce, Office of Health and Consumer Goods, '2005 Appliance Industry Outlook', *Trade.gov*, http://trade.gov/index.asp.

45. C.J. Prince 'Doing Diversity, The Question Isn't Why to Do it – but How', *Chief Executive* (April 2005).

46. Jim Carlton, 'Dig In', *The Wall Street Journal* (November 14, 2005); Tony DiRomualdo, 'Is Google's Cafeteria a Competitive Weapon?' *Wisconsin Technology Network* (August 30, 2005), http://wistechnology.com/article.php?id=2190; Marc Ramirez, 'Tray Chic: At Work, Cool Cafeterias, Imaginative Menus', *The Seattle Times*, November 21, 2005, http://seattletimes.nwsource.com/html/living/2002634266_cafes21.html?pageid=display-in-thenews.module&pageregion=itnbody.

47. Marianne Bertrand and Sendhil Mullainathan, 'Are Emily and Greg More Employable than Lakisha and Jamal?', National Bureau of Economic Research report, as reported in L. A. Johnson, 'What's in a Name: When Emily Gets the Job Over Lakisha', *The Tennessean*, January 4, 2004.

48. Marie Valla, 'France Seeks Path to Workplace Diversity', *The Wall Street Journal*, January 3, 2007.

49. http://www.timesonline.co.uk/tol/news/world/africa/article4168245.ece (accessed February 17, 2010).

50. Alice H. Eagly and Linda L. Carli, 'Leadership', *Harvard Business Review* (September, 2007): 64.

51. Sheila Wellington, Marcia Brumit Kropf and Paulette R. Gerkovich, 'What's Holding Women Back?', *Harvard Business Review* (June 2003): 18–19.

52. Julie Amparano Lopez, 'Study Says Women Face Glass Walls as Well as Ceilings', *The Wall Street Journal*, March 3, 1992; Ida L. Castro, 'Q: Should Women Be Worried About the Glass Ceiling in the Workplace?', *Insight* (February 10, 1997): 24–27; Debra E. Meyerson and Joyce K. Fletcher, 'A Modest Manifesto for Shattering the Glass Ceiling', *Harvard Business Review* (January–February 2000): 127–136; and Wellington, Brumit Kropf, and Gerkovich, 'What's Holding Women Back?'; Annie Finnigan, 'Different Strokes', *Working Woman* (April 2001): 42–48.

53. Catalyst survey results reported in Jason Forsythe, 'Winning with Diversity', *The New York Times Magazine* (March 28, 2004): 65–72.

54. Cliff Edwards, 'Coming Out in Corporate America', *BusinessWeek* (December 15, 2003): 64–72; Belle Rose Ragins, John M. Cornwell and Janice S. Miller, 'Heterosexism in the Workplace: Do Race and Gender Matter?', *Group & Organization Management* 28, no. 1 (March 2003): 45–74.

55. Sylvia Ann Hewlett and Carolyn Buck Luce, 'Off-Ramps and On- Ramps; Keeping Talented Women on the Road to Success', *Harvard Business Review* (March 2005): 43–54.

56. Belkin, 'The Opt-Out Revolution'.

57. C. J. Prince, 'Media Myths: The Truth About the Opt-Out Hype', *NAFE Magazine* (Second Quarter 2004): 14–18; Patricia Sellers, 'Power: Do Women Really Want It?', *Fortune* (October 13, 2003): 80–100.

58. Jia Lynn Yang, 'Goodbye to All That', *Fortune* (November 14, 2005): 169–170.

59. Sheila Wellington, Marcia Brumit Kropf, and Paulette R. Gerkovich, 'What's Holding Women Back?', *Harvard Business Review* (June 2003): 18–19.

60. The Leader's Edge/Executive Women Research 2002 survey, reported in 'Why Women Leave', *Executive Female* (Summer 2003): 4.

61. Barbara Reinhold, 'Smashing Glass Ceilings: Why Women Still Find It Tough to Advance to the Executive Suite', *Journal of Organizational Excellence* (Summer 2005): 43–55; Des Jardins, 'I Am Woman (I Think)'; and Alice H. Eagly and Linda L. Carli, 'The Female Leadership Advantage: An Evaluation of the Evidence', *The Leadership Quarterly* 14 (2003): 807–834.

62. Claudia H. Deutsch, 'Behind the Exodus of Executive Women: Boredom', *USA Today*, May 2, 2005.

63. Eagly and Carli, 'The Female Leadership Advantage'; Reinhold, 'Smashing Glass Ceilings'; Sally Helgesen, *The Female Advantage: Women's Ways of Leadership* (New York: Doubleday Currency, 1990); Rochelle Sharpe, 'As Leaders, Women Rule: New Studies Find that Female Managers Outshine Their Male Counterparts in Almost Every Measure', *BusinessWeek* (November 20, 2000): 5ff; and Del Jones, '2003: Year of the Woman Among the Fortune 500?' (December 30, 2003): 1B.

64. Tamar Lewin, 'At Colleges, Women Are Leaving Men in the Dust', *The New York Times Online*, July 9, 2006, http://www.nytimes.com/2006/07/09/education/09college.html?_r=1&scp=1&sq=at%20colleges,%20women%20are%20leaving%20men%20in%20the%20dust&st=cse&oref=slogin (accessed March 13, 2008).

65. Quoted in Conlin, 'The New Gender Gap'.

66. Kathryn M. Bartol, David C. Martin and Julie A. Kromkowski, 'Leadership and the Glass Ceiling: Gender and Ethnic Group Influences on Leader Behaviours at Middle and Executive Managerial Levels', *The Journal of Leadership and Organizational Studies* 9, no. 3 (2003): 8–19; Bernard M. Bass and Bruce J. Avolio, 'Shatter the Glass Ceiling: Women May Make Better Managers', *Human Resource Management* 33, no. 4 (Winter 1994): 549–560; and Rochelle Sharpe, 'As Leaders, Women Rule', 75–84.

67. Dwight D. Frink, Robert K. Robinson, Brian Reithel, Michelle M. Arthur, Anthony P. Ammeter, Gerald R. Ferris, David M. Kaplan and Hubert S. Morrisette, 'Gender Demography and Organization Performance: A Two-Study Investigation with Convergence', *Group & Organization Management* 28, no. 1 (March 2003): 127–147; Catalyst research project cited in Reinhold, 'Smashing Glass Ceilings'.

68. Mercedes Martin and Billy Vaughn (2007), *Strategic Diversity & Inclusion Management*, pp. 31–36.

69. Ann M. Morrison, *The New Leaders: Guidelines on Leadership Diversity in America* (San Francisco: Jossey-Bass Publishers, 1992), p. 235.

70. Michael L. Wheeler, 'Diversity: Business Rationale and Strategies', The Conference Board, Report No. 1130-95-RR, 1995, p. 25.

71. Morrison, *'The New Leaders'*.

72. Reported in 'Strength Through Diversity for Bottom-Line Success', *Working Woman* (March 1999).

73. Melanie Trottman, 'A Helping Hand', *The Wall Street Journal*, November 14, 2005; B. Ragins, 'Barriers to Mentoring: The Female Manager's Dilemma', *Human Relations* 42, no. 1 (1989): 1–22; and Belle Rose Ragins, Bickley Townsend, and Mary Mattis, 'Gender Gap in the Executive Suite: CEOs and Female Executives Report on Breaking the Glass Ceiling', *Academy of Management Executive* 12, no. 1 (1998): 28–42.

74. Pearson http://extranet2.pearson.com/diversity/index.cfm?a=13, (accessed February 17, 2010).

75. Sarah Murray, 'Different strokes for different folks: a case study of BP'. *Financial Times, FT Report on Business and Diversity* (May 2004).

76. David A. Thomas, 'The Truth About Mentoring Minorities – Race Matters', *Harvard Business Review* (April 2001): 99–107.

77. Mary Zey, 'A Mentor for All', *Personnel Journal* (January 1988): 46–51.

78. Joanne Sujansky, 'Lead a Multi-Generational Workforce', *The Business Journal of Tri-Cities, Tennessee–Virginia* (February 2004): 21–23.

79. 'Keeping Your Edge: Managing a Diverse Corporate Culture', Special Advertising Section, *Fortune Magazine* (June 3, 2001). S1–S17.

80. Kimberly L. Allers, 'Won't It Be Grand When We Don't Need Diversity Lists?' *Fortune* (August 22, 2005): 101.

81. J. Black and M. Mendenhall, 'Cross-Cultural Training Effectiveness: A Review and a Theoretical Framework for Future Research', *Academy of Management Review* 15 (1990): 113–136.

82. BITC 2004.

83. Laura Egodigwe, 'Back to Class', *The Wall Street Journal*, November 14, 2005.

84. S Rynes and B Rosen, 'A field survey of factors affecting the adoption and perceived success of diversity training', Personnel Psychology 48 (1995): 247–270.

85. Lee Smith, 'Closing the Gap', *Fortune* (November 14, 2005): 211–218.

86. 'Sexual Harassment: Vanderbilt University Policy', (Nashville, TN: Vanderbilt University, 1993).

87. Rachel Thompson, 'Sexual Harassment: It Doesn't Go with the Territory', *Horizons* 15, no. 3 (Winter 2002): 22–26.

88. http://www.telegraph.co.uk/news/worldnews/europe/russia/2470310/Sexual-harrasment-okay-as-it-ensures-humans-breed,-Russian-judge-rules.html (accessed February 17, 2010).

89. Barbara Carton, 'At Jenny Craig, Men Are Ones Who Claim Sex Discrimination', *The Wall Street Journal*, November 29, 1994.

90. 'Impact of Diversity Initiatives on the Bottom Line: A SHRM Survey of the Fortune 1000', (pp. S12–S14), in *Fortune*, 'Keeping Your Edge: Managing a Diverse Corporate Culture', produced in association with the Society for Human Resource Management (June 3, 2001), http://www.fortune.com/sections.

91. Joseph J. Distefano and Martha L. Maznevski, 'Creating Value with Diverse Teams in Global Management', *Organizational Dynamics* 29, no. 1 (Summer 2000): 45–63; and Finnigan, 'Different Strokes'.

92. W. E. Watson, K. Kumar, and L. K. Michaelsen, 'Cultural Diversity's Impact on Interaction Process and Performance: Comparing Homogeneous and Diverse Task Groups', *Academy of Management Journal* 36 (1993): 590–602; G. Robinson and K. Dechant, 'Building a Business Case for Diversity', *Academy of Management Executive* 11, no. 3 (1997): 21–31; and D. A. Thomas and R. J. Ely, 'Making Differences Matter: A New Paradigm for Managing Diversity', *Harvard Business Review* (September–October 1996): 79–90.

93. Marc Hequet, Chris Lee, Michele Picard and David Stamps, 'Teams Get Global', *Training* (December 1996): 16–17.

94. http://business.timesonline.co.uk/tol/business/career_and_jobs/careers_in/article1771546.ece, (accessed 17 February, 2010).

95. See Distefano and Maznevski, 'Creating Value with Diverse Teams', for a discussion of the advantages of multicultural teams.

96. Watson, Kumar and Michaelsen, 'Cultural Diversity's Impact on Interaction Process and Performance'.

97. Distefano and Maznevski, 'Creating Value with Diverse Teams'.

98. This definition and discussion is based on Raymond A. Friedman, 'Employee Network Groups: Self-Help Strategy for Women and Minorities', *Performance Improvement Quarterly* 12, no. 1 (1999): 148–163.

99. Raymond A. Friedman and Brooks Holtom, 'The Effects of Network Groups on Minority Employee Turnover Intentions', *Human Resource Management* 41, no. 4 (Winter 2002): 405–421.

100. Simon Brooke, 'You're welcome to join us: The business case for reflecting a changing society is now self-evident; but putting it into practice needs careful strategy', Sunday Times, May 13, 2007 available online at http://business.timesonline.co.uk/tol/career_and_jobs/careers_in/article1771546.ece (accessed March 3, 2010).

101. Diane Brady and Jena McGregar, 'What Works in Women's Networks', *Business Week* (June 18, 2007): 58.

102. Wasserman, 'A Race for Profits'.

103. Finnigan, 'Different Strokes'.

104. http://www.lemonde.fr/cgi-bin/ACHATS/acheter.cgi?offre=ARCHIVES&type_item=ART_ARCH_30J&objet_id=997620&clef=ARC-TRK-D_01 [French] (accessed February 17, 2010).

105. http://www.loreal.com/_en/_ww/company-l-oreal.aspx (accessed February 17, 2010).

CONTINUING CASE
BY ALAN HOGARTH

IKEA
PART FOUR: PLANNING FOR CHANGE AND DIVERSITY

The organization of any company is one of the most important functions for the management of the company. Organization can take many forms from internal organization of departments or divisions, regional organization and globalization. However, one important element of such organization is that businesses should be adaptable. As such the creation of the organizational structure is seen as one of the major initial activities. Historically, Ingvar Kampard was responsible for IKEA's structure. The following details are from IKEA's own website. The IKEA Group is owned by a foundation, Stichting INGKA Foundation, which is registered in the Netherlands. The foundation owns INGKA Holding B.V. the parent company for all IKEA Group companies – from the industrial group Swedwood to the sales companies that own the stores in the various countries. Inter IKEA Systems B.V., the owner of the IKEA concept and trademark, has franchising agreements with every IKEA store in the world. The IKEA Group is the biggest franchisee of Inter IKEA Systems B.V). The organizational structure diagram is shown in Figure 1.

This corporate structure allows Kamprad to maintain tight control over the operations of Ingka Holding and, because of this, the operation of most IKEA stores worldwide. Also, the Ingka Foundation's five-person executive

Figure 1 How IKEA is Organized

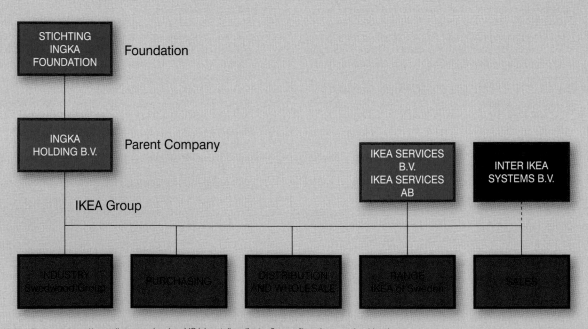

SOURCE: Online at: http://www.ikea.com/ms/en_US/about_ikea/facts_figures/ikea_is_organized.html

committee is chaired by Kamprad. If a member of the executive committee quits or dies, the other four members appoint his or her replacement.

The company is organized into four different main areas. The first area *Range* is primarily carried out by IKEA of Sweden. Second, *Purchasing* is undertaken by agents responsible for placing orders according to IKEA's specifications. Thirdly, the *Distribution and Wholesale* undertakes the transport and distribution of the finished products to IKEA's regional distribution centres and then globally. The *Sales* functions were carried out by ensuring uniformity of selling methods and customer service standards in all IKEA stores.

IKEA is a global organization which employs *co-workers* worldwide in the stores and where subcontracting is utilized for manufacturing, but some functions such as research and development remain in Sweden. Other functions such as human resources, finance and store construction are universal. Support functions including Information Technology, Communication, and IKEA Indirect Materials and Service also provide service to IKEA stores worldwide. As such, the current organizational structure can be regarded as 'highly functional with a global market strategy'. IKEA is therefore able to maintain centralized control over functional activities and at the same time take advantage of low cost and enhanced quality from international suppliers. Furthermore, control over strategic direction is improved.

Due to this organizational structure the traditional perception of the 'chain of command' is not obvious in IKEA. IKEA's management philosophy is that a practical approach to problem-solving and decision-making are important activities. Essentially coworkers at all levels of the organization structure are encouraged to take initiatives. This in turn makes the coworkers feel valued and an important part of the company. Equally, managers in turn are expected to share information with the coworkers. Essentially, as Oddou and Mendenhall say, 'A distaste for

bureaucratic procedures are basic managerial attitudes that have long been promoted within IKEA.' Status is not important in IKEA and therefore managers are expected to be close to their coworkers. As such, this egalitarian approach to management has allowed coworkers to gain promotion in IKEA without formal training. Oddou and Mendenhall further state that, 'To ensure that the IKEA way is understood, the organization relies heavily on managers to act as "missionaries"... This as much as anything else, provides the reason for the extensive presence of Swedish managers in IKEA's international units, as their knowledge stems from their direct exposure to Ingvar Kampard and IKEA's subtle way of doing business and managing people.'

Despite this consensus-driven approach, although being successful in day-to-day operational matters IKEA has not always been successful when dealing with change. Although managing change has been the norm at IKEA for a long time, due to both growth and restructuring, it has not always been viewed as a priority. As such there is a clear need for management to understand and cope with the change management process. As Albert A. Angehrn, Director of CALT states: 'One very distinct feature about IKEA is that it is an action orientated organization ... Emphasis is placed on how things are done, and less on how they can be understood differently ... Another issue that is special about conducting change in IKEA is that it is a consensus-driven organization. It was also found that IKEA needed to prioritize the sustainability of change processes. Many change processes at IKEA seems to be successful for a while, but after a while the organization seems to slip back into its old habits.'

A critical function in the management of change within IKEA is its commitment to its human resources. IKEA adopts a positive approach toward human resource management. For example, in the late 1990s and early 2000s, the company introduced several initiatives such as flexible work design, comprehensive benefits, quality of work life, and employee training and development. IKEA's unique work culture is seen to support its coworkers while encouraging creativity and diversity. As Pernille Spiers-Lopez, IKEA's President, says, 'We're delighted to be among Fortune's '100 Best Companies to Work For. At IKEA, we live by the philosophy that when coworkers have the support and flexibility to make their personal lives a success; they thrive in the workplace, too.'

Essentially, IKEA adopts a paternalistic stance toward employees and promoting empowerment globally in all the stores. As Spiers-Lopez highlights, 'At IKEA, we think of ourselves as a family. Just as one would look after their parents, siblings or children, our coworker family is encouraged to and excels at supporting and taking care of each other'. IKEA's human resource philosophy maintains that employees are more productive and committed when the company takes a more caring approach to their needs. However, this was not always the case as different employees had different needs. In the late 1990s IKEA realized that employees were not able to derive the maximum benefit from its beneficial HR policies, because the policies did not always match individual needs and requirements. This was felt more acutely in countries unfamiliar with the 'Swedish' way of doing things. IKEA felt that employees would benefit more if there were a greater amount of flexibility in its approach.

Nowadays IKEA pays close attention to the cultures of the countries that they have expanded into, especially when considering their employees in that foreign market. It is their intention to bring their values with them wherever they open up stores and this calls for a fundamental understanding of the different cultures in those countries. Also as part of IKEA's HR policy is its commitment to diversity. It is integral to IKEA's recruitment policy. This perspective can also be seen in corporate statements made by IKEA identified by Kling & Goteman, 'We see the diversity issue as a matter of creating a more challenging business atmosphere and of course expanding the recruitment base – including everyone and not just Swedish men. It also gives us a diverse workforce with a lot of positive business possibilities.' IKEA understands diversity management in the following way as Fajtová says, 'Diversity at IKEA is when people from different backgrounds feel comfortable and confident, when they can apply their perspectives and approaches at work and when they are included at all levels and functions in the organization.' IKEA argues that its HR diversity policy must be handled globally and be relevant to whatever country a store is opened in due to the difference in potential recruits and markets. As Fajtová says, 'As a global player it is very important for IKEA to be aware of what the world looks like today, and how it will change in the future. The only common thing for all of us is that we are different. If we accept and understand this fact we can start to use this diversity or the best of ourselves and for IKEA.'

Questions

1 Analyze the organizational structure of IKEA with reference to its functions, product and geography.

2 Discuss how IKEA's Human Resource Management policy may be attractive to prospective employees.

3 Explain how IKEA might value diversity in its global operations? How does IKEA deal with 'ethnocentrism'?

SOURCES 'How IKEA is Organized', online at: http://www.ikea.com/ms/en_US/about_ikea/facts_figures/ikea_is_organized.html; Angehern, A.A. (2007), 'A Common Language', Alpha Experiences, online at: http://www.alphaexperiences.org/DocFile/11917_Alpha%20Case%20Study%20Ikea%20M.PDF; Fajtová, E. (2007) Why Diversity? A global experience, Conference: Diversity Management & Inclusion: European Solutions to Common Problems. Prague, The Czech Republic: Human Resources Development Interface; Oddou, G.R. and Mendenhall, M.A. (1998) 'Cases in International Organizational Behaviour', Blackwell Publishing; 'IKEA Named to Working Mother Magazine's "100 Best Companies for Working Mothers" for Second Consecutive Year', Business Wire, September 2004, online at: http://findarticles.com/p/articles/mi_m0EIN/is_/ai_n6202287

PART 5

LEADING

Architects lead the construction process: They determine the size and shape of a building, how it will be built, where it will be built, and other salient choices. These choices often have a subtle impact in how that structure will embody and even influence the culture. Architecture has always been used as a means of cultural leadership, leading by the embodiment of foundational ideas.

The first permanent structures ever built were temples, shrines to ancient gods. Religion was the central rule of ancient life and the ancient temples embodied how those people saw themselves and the world around them. The people lived in temporary structures that were not expected to outlast the occupants, but the temples were built of stone, intended to survive for ages, which in fact, many of them did.

Many times architects are keenly aware of the culture into which a structure is being built, and that structure is designed specifically to either reinforce the current culture or to lead the culture in a new direction, to express new ideas. Roman and Greek architecture is similar, particularly since Rome borrowed heavily from Greek thought and architecture, but the ideas embodied differ vastly. Greek architecture displayed the Greek ideas of democracy, piety and independence; Roman architecture, however, valued authority and practicality. So where Greek architecture was largely concerned with temples, Roman architecture expanded to secular structures—law courts, theaters, and houses—exemplifying and reinforcing centralised Roman thinking and authority. Ironically, when the Byzantine Empire emerged from the ashes of the Roman Empire, around 500 a.d., the Christian churches were constructed in the same style as the surrounding buildings; instead of standing out, the early Byzantium churches blended in, a startling departure from Greek and Roman concepts of worship and deity.

Although a manager's job includes issuing directives, leadership is not simply ordering people: go here, do that. A leader must also guide the culture and spirit of a company or business. A manager must lead with ideas and be an embodiment of those ideas—a cultural leader.

CHAPTER OUTLINE

© MEDIAPHOTOS/ISTOCK

LEARNING OBJECTIVES

After reading this chapter, you should be able to:

1 Define attitudes, including their major components, and explain their relationship to personality, perception and behaviour.

2 Discuss the importance of work-related attitudes.

3 Identify major personality traits and describe how personality can influence workplace attitudes and behaviours.

4 Define the four components of emotional intelligence and explain why they are important for today's managers.

5 Explain how people learn in general and in terms of individual learning styles.

6 Discuss the effects of stress and identify ways individuals and organizations can manage stress to improve employee health, satisfaction and productivity.

CHAPTER 14

DYNAMICS OF BEHAVIOUR IN ORGANIZATIONS

Manager's Challenge

Since the day Chris Hall left a full-time marketing management career at Mars corporation to run his own company, Hallmark Consumer Services in Melton Mowbray, UK – a company making marketing materials for a range of local and national businesses – he's successfully solved many management problems. But suddenly Chris feels out of his league. Chris has been accustomed to thinking of himself as on top of his game, chief architect of the company's growing sales and profits. But lately he's noticed a disturbing situation. Managers at the company seem to have lost the drive to push through new ideas and proposals that can keep Hallmark thriving, and Chris catches himself complaining about his subordinates without taking steps to improve things. Realizing that everyone is under stress from several years of rapid growth, Chris hires a pack of new, young managers to reinforce his exhausted troops. Surprisingly, though, things just seem to get worse, with the new managers feeling adrift and the old-timers seeming even less focused than before. Then Chris has a revelation that both unnerves and excites him. Rather than complain about his managers' shortcomings, Chris realizes that he has to remake himself, change his own attitude. He wants to become a mentor who shapes positive attitudes in others and to knit the newcomers and long-time employees into a cohesive and productive team.[1]

If you were Chris Hall, how would you gain a better understanding of yourself and the personal changes you need to make to help people feel more satisfied and committed to Hallmark Consumer Services? Do you believe the personality and attitudes of a small company's CEO will affect economic performance?

TAKE A MOMENT

Are You Self-confident?

Self-confidence is the foundation for many important behaviours of a new manager. To learn something about your level of self-confidence, answer the following questions. Answer whether each item is Mostly True or Mostly False for you.

		Mostly True	Mostly False
1	I have lots of confidence in my decisions.	☐	☐
2	I would like to change some things about myself.	☐	☐
3	I am satisfied with my appearance and personality.	☐	☐
4	I would be nervous about meeting important people.	☐	☐
5	I come across as a positive person.	☐	☐
6	I sometimes think of myself as a failure.	☐	☐
7	I am able to do things as well as most people.	☐	☐
8	I find it difficult to believe nice things someone says about me.	☐	☐

SCORING AND INTERPRETATION: Many good things come from self-confidence. How self-confident are you? Give yourself one point for each *odd-numbered* item above marked as Mostly True and one point for each *even-numbered* item marked Mostly False. If you scored 3 or less, your self-confidence may not be very high. You might want to practise new behaviour in problematic areas to develop greater confidence. A score of 6 or above suggests a high level of self-confidence and a solid foundation on which to begin your career as a new manager.

If a new manager lacks self-confidence, he or she is more likely to avoid difficult decisions and confrontations and may tend to over-control subordinates, which is called micromanaging. A lack of self-confidence also leads to less sharing of information and less time hiring and developing capable people. Self-confident managers, by contrast, can more easily delegate responsibility, take risks, give credit to others, confront problems and assert themselves for the good of their team.

The situation at Hallmark Consumer Services illustrates the importance of understanding organizational behaviour. Managers' attitudes, and their ability to understand and shape the attitudes of employees, can profoundly affect the workplace and influence employee motivation, morale and job performance. People differ in many ways. Some are quiet and shy while others are gregarious; some are thoughtful and serious while others are impulsive and fun-loving. Employees – and managers – bring their individual differences to work each day. Differences in attitudes, values, personality and behaviour influence how people interpret an assignment, whether they like to be told what to do, how they handle challenges and how they interact with others. People are an organization's most valuable resource – and the source of some of managers' most difficult problems. Three basic leadership skills are at the core of identifying and solving people problems: (1) diagnosing, or gaining insight into the situation a manager is trying to influence; (2) adapting individual behaviour and resources to meet the needs of the situation; and (3) communicating in a way that others can understand and accept. Thus, managers need insight about individual differences to understand what a behavioural situation is now and what it may be in the future.

To handle this responsibility, managers need to understand the principles of organizational behaviour – that is, the ways individuals and groups tend to act in organizations. By increasing their knowledge of individual differences in the areas of attitudes, personality, perception, learning and stress management, managers can understand and lead employees and colleagues through many workplace challenges. This chapter introduces basic principles of organizational behaviour in each of these areas.

Organizational Behaviour

Organizational behaviour, commonly called OB, is an interdisciplinary field dedicated to the study of human attitudes, behaviour and performance in organizations. OB draws concepts from many disciplines, including psychology, sociology, cultural anthropology, industrial engineering, economics, ethics and vocational counselling, as well as the discipline of management. The concepts and principles of organizational behaviour are important to managers because in every organization human beings ultimately make the decisions that control how the organization acquires and uses resources. Those people may cooperate with, compete with, support or undermine one another. Their beliefs and feelings about themselves, their coworkers, and the organization shape what they do and how well they do it. People can distract the organization from its strategy by engaging in conflict and misunderstandings, or they can pool their diverse talents and perspectives to accomplish much more as a group than they could ever do as individuals.

By understanding what causes people to behave as they do, managers can exercise leadership to achieve positive outcomes. By creating a positive environment, for example, managers can foster **organizational citizenship**, which refers to the tendency of people to help one another and put in extra effort that goes beyond job requirements to contribute to the organization's success. An employee demonstrates organizational citizenship by being helpful to coworkers and customers, doing extra work when necessary, and looking for ways to improve products and procedures. These behaviours enhance the organization's performance and help to build *social capital*, as described in Chapter 12.[2] Organizational citizenship contributes to positive relationships both within the organization and with customers, leading to a high level of social capital and smooth organizational functioning. Managers can encourage organizational citizenship by applying their knowledge of human behaviour, such as selecting people with positive attitudes and personalities, helping them see how they can contribute, and enabling them to learn from and cope with workplace challenges.

Organizational behaviour
An interdisciplinary field dedicated to the study of how individuals and groups tend to act in organizations.

Organizational citizenship
Work behaviour that goes beyond job requirements and contributes as needed to the organization's success.

Attitudes

Most students have probably heard the expression that someone 'has an attitude problem', which means some consistent quality about the person affects his or her behaviour in a negative way. An employee with an attitude problem might be hard to get along with, might constantly gripe and cause problems, and might persistently

Attitude
A cognitive and affective evaluation that predisposes a person to act in a certain way.

resist new ideas. We all seem to know intuitively what an attitude is, but we do not consciously think about how strongly attitudes affect our behaviour. Defined formally, an **attitude** is an evaluation – either positive or negative – that predisposes a person to act in a certain way. Understanding employee attitudes is important to managers because attitudes determine how people perceive the work environment, interact with others, and behave on the job. Emerging research is revealing the importance of positive attitudes to both individual and organizational success. For example, studies have found that the characteristic most common to top executives is an optimistic attitude. People rise to the top because they have the ability to see opportunities where others see problems and can instil in others a sense of hope and possibility for the future.[3]

Good managers strive to develop and reinforce positive attitudes among all employees, because happy, positive people are healthier, more effective and more productive.[4] A person who has the attitude 'I love my work; it's challenging and fun' will typically tackle work-related problems cheerfully, while one who comes to work with the attitude 'I hate my job' is not likely to show much enthusiasm or commitment to solving problems.[5] Some companies, such as Alchimie Originelle, the French's wedding industry pioneer, are applying scientific research to improve employee attitudes – and sales performance.

Components of Attitudes

One important step for managers is recognizing and understanding the *components* of attitudes, which is particularly important when attempting to change attitudes.

Behavioural scientists consider attitudes to have three components: cognitions (thoughts), affect (feelings) and behaviour.[6] The cognitive component of an attitude

 INNOVATIVE WAY

Alchimie Originelle

Planning a wedding can be one of the most joyful experiences in a woman's life – and one of the most nerve-wracking. Launched in 2003 by both wedding and event professionals, Alchimie Originelle has been serving the needs of many of the world's couples. Thanks to their wedding planners' exceptional professional and ethical standards, Alchimie Originelle has become a famous trendsetter in the French Wedding Industry.

The Bridal Consultants, Designers and Coordinators at Alchimie Originelle based in many offices in the French Riviera and Loire Valley, bear the brunt of the intense emotions of their customers. For many, dealing with those emotions can be overwhelming and exhausting, translating into negative attitudes and impatience with already-stressed customers.

Managers turned to new research on happiness to help employees cope and develop more positive attitudes. Employees were taught how to feel more

cheerful with techniques such as 'emotion regulation', 'impulse control' and 'learned optimism', originally developed in the US by psychologist Martin Seligman. They learned coping techniques to use when dealing with a harried, indecisive bride-to-be, such as making a mental list of the top five things that bring her joy. These techniques enable the consultants to be more calm and centred, which helps customers stay calm and centred as well. That attitude/behaviour translates into better organized events, meaning employees make better commissions, which in turn contributes to more positive attitudes toward the job.

As the example at Alchimie Originelle shows, sometimes negative attitudes can result from characteristics of the job, such as a high stress level, but managers can find ways to help people have more positive attitudes. Managers should pay attention to negative attitudes because they can be both the result of underlying problems in the workplace as well as a contributor to forthcoming problems.[7]

Exhibit 14.1 Components of an Attitude

Cognitive...thoughts...

'My job is interesting.'

Affective...feelings...
'I love my job.'

Behavioural...intention to act...
'I'm going to get to work early with a smile on my face.'

Attitude: Job Satisfaction

includes the beliefs, opinions and information the person has about the object of the attitude, such as knowledge of what a job entails and opinions about personal abilities. The affective component is the person's emotions or feelings about the object of the attitude, such as enjoying or hating a job. The behavioural component of an attitude is the person's intention to behave toward the object of the attitude in a certain way. Exhibit 14.1 illustrates the three components of a positive attitude toward one's job. The cognitive element is the conscious thought that 'my job is interesting and challenging'. The affective element is the feeling that 'I love this job'. These elements, in turn, are related to the behavioural component – an employee might arrive at work early because he or she is happy with the job.

Often, when we think about attitudes, we focus on the cognitive component. However, it is important for managers to remember the other components as well. The emotional (affective) component is often the stronger factor in affecting behaviour. When people feel strongly about something, the affective component may influence them to act in a certain way no matter what someone does to change their thoughts or opinions. Recall the discussion of idea champions in Chapter 11. When someone is passionate about a new idea, he or she may go to great lengths to implement it, even when colleagues and superiors say the idea is stupid. Another example is an employee who is furious about being asked to work overtime on his birthday. The supervisor might present clear, rational reasons for the need to put in extra hours, but the employee might still act based on his anger – by failing to cooperate, lashing out at co-workers or even quitting. In cases such as these, effective leadership includes addressing

the emotions associated with the attitude. Are employees so excited that their judgement may be clouded, or so discouraged that they have given up trying? If nothing else, the manager probably needs to be aware of situations that involve strong emotions and give employees a chance to vent their feelings appropriately.

As a general rule, changing just one component – cognitions, affect or behaviour – can contribute to an overall change in attitude. Suppose a manager concludes that some employees have the attitude that the manager should make all the decisions affecting the department, but the manager prefers that employees assume more decision-making responsibility. To change the underlying attitude, the manager would consider whether to educate employees about the areas in which they can make good decisions (changing the cognitive component), build enthusiasm with pep talks about the satisfaction of employee empowerment (changing the affective component), or simply insist that employees make their own decisions (behavioural component) with the expectation that, once they experience the advantages of decision-making authority, they will begin to like it.

TAKE A MOMENT   As a new manager, be mindful of your own attitude and how it affects people who work for you. A positive attitude can go a long way toward helping others feel good about themselves and their work responsibilities. If you want to change employees' attitudes, don't underestimate the strength of the emotions.

High-Performance Work Attitudes

The attitudes of most interest to managers are those related to work, especially attitudes that influence how well employees perform. To lead employees effectively, managers logically seek to cultivate the kinds of attitudes that are associated with high performance. Two attitudes that might relate to high performance are satisfaction with one's job and commitment to the organization.

Job Satisfaction

Job satisfaction
A positive attitude toward one's job.

A positive attitude toward one's job is called job satisfaction. In general, people experience this attitude when their work matches their needs and interests, when working conditions and rewards (such as pay) are satisfactory, when they like their coworkers, and when they have positive relationships with supervisors. You can take the quiz in Exhibit 14.2 to better understand some of the factors that contribute to job satisfaction.

Many managers believe job satisfaction is important because they think satisfied employees will do better work. In fact, research shows that the link between satisfaction and performance is generally small and is influenced by other factors.[8] For example, the importance of satisfaction varies according to the amount of control the employee has; an employee doing routine tasks may produce about the same output no matter how he or she feels about the job. However, one internal study at Sears found a clear link between employee satisfaction, customer satisfaction and revenue. In particular, employees' attitudes about whether their workloads were manageable and well-organized ranked among the top ten indicators of company performance.[9]

Managers of today's knowledge workers often rely on job satisfaction to keep motivation and enthusiasm for the organization high. Organizations don't want to lose talented, highly skilled workers. In addition, most managers care about their employees and simply want them to feel good about their work – and almost

Exhibit 14.2 Rate Your Job Satisfaction

Think of a job – either a current or previous job – that was important to you, and then answer the following questions with respect to how satisfied you were with that job. Answer the six questions with a number 1–5 that reflects the extent of your satisfaction.

| 1 = Very dissatisfied | 3 = Neutral | 5 = Very satisfied |
| 2 – Dissatisfied | 4 – Satisfied | |

1. Overall, how satisfied are you with your job?	1	2	3	4	5
2. How satisfied are you with the opportunities to learn new things?	1	2	3	4	5
3. How satisfied are you with your boss?	1	2	3	4	5
4. How satisfied are you with the people in your work group?	1	2	3	4	5
5. How satisfied are you with the amount of pay you receive?	1	2	3	4	5
6. How satisfied are you with the advancement you are making in the organization?	1	2	3	4	5

Scoring and Interpretation: Add up your responses to the six questions to obtain your total score: _____. The questions represent various aspects of satisfaction that an employee may experience on a job. If your score is 24 or above, you probably feel satisfied with the job. If your score is 12 or below, you probably do not feel satisfied. What is your level of performance in your job, and is your performance related to your level of satisfaction?

SOURCE: These questions were adapted from Daniel R. Denison, *Corporate Culture and Organizational Effectiveness* (New York: John Wiley, 1990); and John D. Cook, Susan J. Hepworth, Toby D. Wall, and Peter B. Warr, *The Experience of Work: A Compendium and Review of 249 Measures and their Use* (San Diego, CA: Academic Press, 1981).

everyone prefers being around people who have positive attitudes. Regrettably, a survey by International Survey Research found that Gen X employees, those who are carrying the weight of much of today's knowledge work, are the least satisfied of all demographic groups.[10] Managers play an important role in whether employees have positive or negative attitudes toward their jobs.[11] The CEO of Vision Metrics, based in the Netherlands, recognizes that managers have to pay attention to their own attitudes and behaviours to influence the attitudes and performance of others.

By creating a positive environment, leaders such as Ference Liszkay contribute to higher job satisfaction for employees. A related attitude is organizational commitment.

Organizational Commitment

Organizational commitment refers to an employee's loyalty to and engagement with the organization. An employee with a high degree of organizational commitment is likely to say *we* when talking about the company. Such a person likes being a part of the organization and tries to contribute to its success. This attitude is illustrated by an incident at the A. W. Chesterton Company, a Massachusetts manufacturer of mechanical seals and pumps. When two Chesterton pumps that supply water on Navy ship *USS John F. Kennedy* failed on a Saturday night just before the ship's scheduled departure, Todd Robinson, the leader of the team that produces the seals, swung

Organizational commitment
Loyalty to and heavy involvement in one's organization.

INNOVATIVE WAY

Vision Metrics Consulting Group

As CEO of Vision Metrics, Ference Liszkay was reviewing his 360-degree feedback, and discovered that many managers thought he needed to do a better job of coaching his direct reports. Rather than becoming defensive, Ference adopted the attitude that he needed to improve himself in order to help others grow and improve.

When the top leader of a company displays arrogance and simply tells everyone else how they need to improve, that attitude and behaviour filters down to every level of management. An 'us-versus-them' mindset often develops between employees and managers and job satisfaction, motivation and performance decline.

Ference Liszkay, though, had an insight. By being open with people and admitting his own weaknesses and efforts to improve, he set an example for others to do the same. Ference is noted for his enlightened attitudes about how to help employees be successful both at work and in their personal lives. The first step, he knows, is for a leader to be aware of how his attitudes and behaviours influence others and create either a positive or a negative organizational environment.

into action. He and his fiancée, who also works for Chesterton, worked through the night to make new seals and deliver them to be installed before the ship left port.[12]

Most managers want to enjoy the benefits of loyal, committed employees, including low turnover and employee willingness to do more than the job's basic requirements. Results of a Towers Perrin-ISR survey of more than 360 000 employees from 41 companies around the world indicate that companies with highly committed employees perform better.[13] Alarmingly, another recent survey suggests that commitment levels around the world are relatively low. Only one-fifth of the respondents were categorized as fully engaged, that is, reflecting a high level of commitment. In the US, the percentage classified as fully engaged was 29 per cent, compared to 54 per cent in Mexico, 37 in per cent in Brazil, and 36 per cent in India. Countries where employees reflect similar or lower levels of commitment than the US include Canada at 23 per cent, Spain at 19 per cent, Germany at 17 per cent, China at 16 per cent, the UK at 14 per cent, France at 12 per cent and Japan at only 3 per cent.[14]

The high motivation and engagement that comes with organizational commitment is essential to the success of organizations that depend on employees' ideas and creativity. Trust in management's decisions and integrity is an important component of organizational commitment.[15] Unfortunately, in recent years, many employees have lost that trust, resulting in a decline in commitment. Just 28 per cent of employees surveyed by *Fast Company* magazine said they think the CEO of their company has integrity. Another recent survey by Ajilon Professional Staffing found that only 29 per cent of employees believe their boss truly cares about them and looks out for their interests.[16]

Managers can promote organizational commitment by keeping employees informed, giving them a say in decisions, providing the necessary training and other resources that enable them to succeed, treating them fairly and offering rewards they value. For example, recent studies suggest that employee commitment in today's workplace is strongly correlated with initiatives and benefits that help people balance their work and personal lives.[17]

Conflicts Among Attitudes

Sometimes a person may discover that his or her attitudes conflict with one another or are not reflected in behaviour. For example, a person's high level of organizational commitment might conflict with a commitment to family members. If employees routinely work evenings and weekends, their long hours and dedication to the job might conflict with their belief that family ties are important. This conflict can create a state of **cognitive dissonance**, a psychological discomfort that occurs when individuals recognize inconsistencies in their own attitudes and behaviours.[18] The theory of cognitive dissonance, developed by social psychologist Leon Festinger in the 1950s, says that people want to behave in accordance with their attitudes and usually will take corrective action to alleviate the dissonance and achieve balance.

In the case of working overtime, people who can control their hours might restructure responsibilities so that they have time for both work and family. In contrast, those who are unable to restructure workloads might develop an unfavourable attitude toward the employer, reducing their organizational commitment. They might resolve their dissonance by saying they would like to spend more time with their kids but their unreasonable employer demands that they work too many hours.

Perception

Another critical aspect of understanding behaviour is perception. Perception is the cognitive process people use to make sense out of the environment by selecting, organizing and interpreting information from the environment. Attitudes affect perceptions, and vice versa. For example, a person might have developed the attitude that managers are insensitive and arrogant, based on a pattern of perceiving arrogant and insensitive behaviour from managers over a period of time. If the person moves to a new job, this attitude will continue to affect the way he or she perceives superiors in the new environment, even though managers in the new workplace might take great pains to understand and respond to employees' needs.

Because of individual differences in attitudes, personality, values, interests and so forth, people often 'see' the same thing in different ways. A class that is boring to one student might be fascinating to another. One student might perceive an assignment to be challenging and stimulating, whereas another might find it a silly waste of time. Referring back to the topic of diversity discussed in Chapter 13, many African-Americans perceive that blacks are regularly discriminated against, whereas many white employees perceive that blacks are given special opportunities in the workplace.[19] Similarly, in a survey of financial profession executives, 40 per cent of women perceive that women face a 'glass ceiling' that keeps them from reaching top management levels, while only 10 per cent of men share that perception.[20]

We can think of perception as a step-by-step process, as shown in Exhibit 14.3. First, we observe information (sensory data) from the environment through our senses: taste, smell, hearing, sight and touch. Next, our mind screens the data and will select only the items we will process further. Third, we organize the selected data

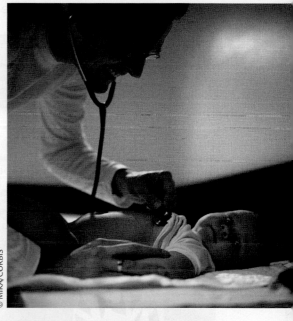

© MIKA/CORBIS

CONCEPT CONNECTION A team from the Health Economics Research Unit at Aberdeen University and NHS Education for Scotland North Deanery undertook a national survey of the working conditions and job satisfaction of doctors in NHS Scotland. Health Minister Andy Kerr said: 'Better patient care is delivered by doctors who are happier in the work they do. That's why I'm delighted to see the growing positive attitudes among our senior doctors. In recent years we have introduced high-profile new contracts for consultants and GPs. Rightly, that has meant improved pay and conditions, but in return it's also given us far more control over how our doctors work.' In addition to good pay and flexible working conditions, doctors relish the autonomy of the job, a chance to help others, the challenge of diagnosing and treating a variety of illnesses, and working as part of a team.

Cognitive dissonance
A condition in which two attitudes or a behaviour and an attitude conflict.

Perception
The cognitive process people use to make sense out of the environment by selecting, organizing and interpreting information.

Exhibit 14.3 The Perception Process

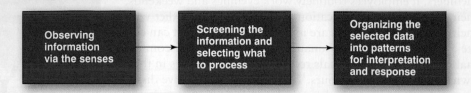

Exhibit 14.4 Perception – What Do You See?

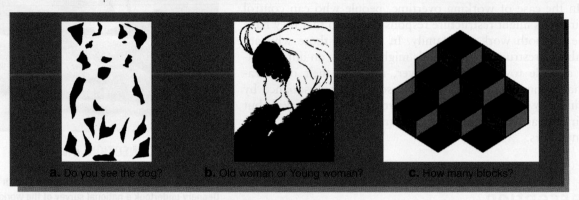

a. Do you see the dog?   b. Old woman or Young woman?   c. How many blocks?

into meaningful patterns for interpretation and response. Most differences in perception among people at work are related to how they select and organize sensory data. You can experience differences in perceptual organization by looking at the visuals in Exhibit 14.4. What do you see in part *a* of Exhibit 14.4? Most people see this as a dog, but others see only a series of unrelated ink blots. Some people will see the figure in part *b* as a beautiful young woman while others will see an old one. Now look at part *c*. How many blocks do you see – six or seven? Some people have to turn the figure upside down before they can see seven blocks. These visuals illustrate how complex perception is.

Perceptual Selectivity

We all are aware of our environment, but not everything in it is equally important to our perception of it. We tune in to some data (e.g. a familiar voice off in the distance) and tune out other data (e.g. paper shuffling next to us). People are bombarded by so much sensory data that it is impossible to process it all. The brain's solution is to run the data through a perceptual filter that retains some parts and eliminates others. **Perceptual selectivity** is the process by which individuals screen and select the various objects and stimuli that vie for their attention. Certain stimuli catch their attention, and others do not.

People typically focus on stimuli that satisfy their needs and that are consistent with their attitudes, values, and personality. For example, employees who need positive feedback to feel good about themselves might pick up on positive statements made by a supervisor but tune out most negative comments. A supervisor could use this understanding to tailor feedback in a positive way to help the employee improve work performance. The influence of needs on perception has been studied in laboratory experiments and found to have a strong impact on what people perceive.[21]

Perceptual selectivity
The process by which individuals screen and select the various stimuli that vie for their attention.

Characteristics of the stimuli themselves also affect perceptual selectivity. People tend to notice stimuli that stand out against other stimuli or that are more intense than surrounding stimuli. Examples would be a loud noise in a quiet room or a bright red dress at a party where most women are wearing basic black. People also tend to notice things that are familiar to them, such as a familiar voice in a crowd, as well as things that are new or different from their previous experiences. In addition, *primacy* and *recency* are important to perceptual selectivity. People pay relatively greater attention to sensory data that occur toward the beginning of an event or toward the end. Primacy supports the old truism that first impressions really do count, whether it be on a job interview, meeting a date's parents or participating in a new social group. Recency reflects the reality that the last impression might be a lasting impression. For example, Malaysian Airlines discovered its value in building customer loyalty. A woman travelling with a nine-month-old might find the flight itself an exhausting blur, but one such traveller enthusiastically told people for years how Malaysian Airlines flight attendants helped her with baggage collection and ground transportation.[22]

As these examples show, perceptual selectivity is a complex filtering process. Managers can use an understanding of perceptual selectivity to obtain clues about why one person sees things differently from others, and they can apply the principles to their own communications and actions, especially when they want to attract or focus attention.

Perceptual Distortions

Once people select the sensory data to be perceived, they begin grouping the data into recognizable patterns. Perceptual organization is the process by which people organize or categorize stimuli according to their own frame of reference. Of particular concern in the work environment are **perceptual distortions**, errors in perceptual judgement that arise from inaccuracies in any part of the perceptual process.

Some types of errors are so common that managers should become familiar with them. These include stereotyping, the halo effect, projection and perceptual defence. Managers who recognize these perceptual distortions can better adjust their perceptions to more closely match objective reality.

Stereotyping is the tendency to assign an individual to a group or broad category (e.g. female, black, elderly; or male, white, disabled) and then to attribute widely held generalizations about the group to the individual. Thus, someone meets a new colleague, sees he is in a wheelchair, assigns him to the category 'physically disabled', and attributes to this colleague generalizations she believes about people with disabilities, which may include a belief that he is less able than other coworkers. However, the person's inability to walk should not be seen as indicative of lesser abilities in other areas. Indeed, the assumption of limitations may not only offend him, it also prevents the person making the stereotypical judgement from benefiting from the many ways in which this person can contribute. Stereotyping prevents people from truly knowing those they classify in this way. In addition, negative stereotypes prevent talented people from advancing in an organization and fully contributing their talents to the organization's success.

The **halo effect** occurs when the perceiver develops an overall impression of a person or situation based on one characteristic, either favourable or unfavourable. In other words, a halo blinds the perceiver to other characteristics that should be used in generating a more complete assessment. The halo effect can play a significant role in performance appraisal, as we discussed in Chapter 12. For example, a person with an outstanding attendance record may be assessed as responsible, industrious and highly productive; another person with less-than-average attendance may be assessed

Perceptual distortions
Errors in perceptual judgement that arise from inaccuracies in any part of the perceptual process.

Stereotyping
The tendency to assign an individual to a group or broad category and then attribute generalizations about the group to the individual.

Halo effect
An overall impression of a person or situation based on one characteristic, either favourable or unfavourable.

as a poor performer. Either assessment may be true, but it is the manager's job to be sure the assessment is based on complete information about all job-related characteristics and not just his or her preferences for good attendance.

Projection
The tendency to see one's own personal traits in other people.

Projection is the tendency of perceivers to see their own personal traits in other people; that is, they project their own needs, feelings, values and attitudes into their judgement of others. A manager who is achievement oriented might assume that subordinates are as well. This assumption might cause the manager to restructure jobs to be less routine and more challenging, without regard for employees' actual satisfaction. The best guards against errors based on projection are self-awareness and empathy.

Perceptual defence
The tendency of perceivers to protect themselves by disregarding ideas, objects or people that are threatening to them.

Perceptual defence is the tendency of perceivers to protect themselves against ideas, objects or people that are threatening. People perceive things that are satisfying and pleasant but tend to disregard things that are disturbing and unpleasant. In essence, people develop blind spots in the perceptual process so that negative sensory data do not hurt them. For example, the director of a non-profit educational organization in Tennessee hated dealing with conflict because he had grown up with parents who constantly argued and often put him in the middle of their arguments. The director consistently overlooked discord among staff members until things would reach a boiling point. When the blow-up occurred, the director would be shocked and dismayed, because he had truly perceived that everything was going smoothly among the staff. Recognizing perceptual blind spots can help people develop a clearer picture of reality.

Attributions

Attributions
Judgements about what caused a person's behaviour – either characteristics of the person or of the situation.

As people organize what they perceive, they often draw conclusions, such as about an object or a person. Among the judgements people make as part of the perceptual process are attributions. Attributions are judgements about what caused a person's behaviour – something about the person or something about the situation. An *internal attribution* says characteristics of the person led to the behaviour ('My boss yelled at me because he's impatient and doesn't listen'). An *external attribution* says something about the situation caused the person's behaviour ('My boss yelled at me because I missed the deadline and the customer is upset'). Attributions are important because they help people decide how to handle a situation. In the case of the boss yelling, a person who blames the yelling on the boss's personality will view the boss as the problem and might cope by avoiding the boss. In contrast, someone who blames the yelling on the situation might try to help prevent such situations in the future.

Social scientists have studied the attributions people make and identified three factors that influence whether an attribution will be external or internal.[23] These three factors are illustrated in Exhibit 14.5.

1 *Distinctiveness*. Whether the behaviour is unusual for that person (in contrast to a person displaying the same kind of behaviour in many situations). If the behaviour is distinctive, the perceiver probably will make an *external* attribution.

2 *Consistency*. Whether the person being observed has a history of behaving in the same way. People generally make *internal* attributions about consistent behaviour.

3 *Consensus*. Whether other people tend to respond to similar situations in the same way. A person who has observed others handle similar situations in the same way will likely make an *external* attribution; that is, it will seem that the situation produces the type of behaviour observed.

Exhibit 14.5 Factors Influencing Whether Attributions Are Internal or External

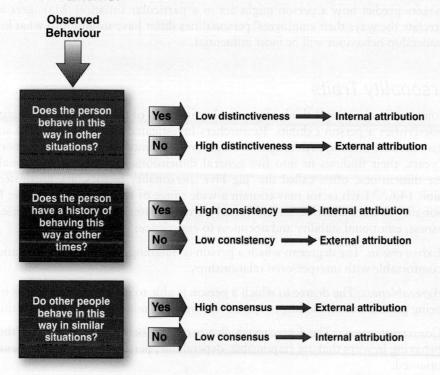

In addition to these general rules, people tend to have biases that they apply when making attributions. When evaluating others, we tend to underestimate the influence of external factors and overestimate the influence of internal factors. This tendency is called the **fundamental attribution error**. Consider the case of someone being promoted to CEO. Employees, outsiders and the media generally focus on the characteristics of the person that allowed him or her to achieve the promotion. In reality, however, the selection of that person might have been heavily influenced by external factors, such as business conditions creating a need for someone with a strong financial or marketing background at that particular time.

Another bias that distorts attributions involves attributions we make about our own behaviour. People tend to overestimate the contribution of internal factors to their successes and overestimate the contribution of external factors to their failures. This tendency, called the **self-serving bias**, means people give themselves too much credit for what they do well and give external forces too much blame when they fail. Thus, if your manager says you don't communicate well enough, and you think your manager doesn't listen well enough, the truth may actually lie somewhere in between.

Fundamental attribution error
The tendency to underestimate the influence of external factors on another's behaviour and to overestimate the influence of internal factors.

Self-serving bias
The tendency to overestimate the contribution of internal factors to one's successes and the contribution of external factors to one's failures.

Personality and Behaviour

Another area of particular interest to organizational behaviour is personality. In recent years, many employers showed heightened interest in matching people's personalities to the needs of the job and the organization.

In the workplace, we find people whose behaviour is consistently pleasant or aggressive or stubborn in a variety of situations. An individual's **personality** is the set

Personality
The set of characteristics that underlie a relatively stable pattern of behaviour in response to ideas, objects or people in the environment.

of characteristics that underlie a relatively stable pattern of behaviour in response to ideas, objects or people in the environment. Understanding personality can help managers predict how a person might act in a particular situation. Managers who appreciate the ways their employees' personalities differ have insight into what kinds of leadership behaviour will be most influential.

Personality Traits

In common usage, people think of personality in terms of traits, the fairly consistent characteristics a person exhibits. Researchers investigated whether any traits stand up to scientific scrutiny. Although investigators examined thousands of traits over the years, their findings fit into five general dimensions that describe personality. These dimensions, often called the 'Big Five' personality factors, are illustrated in Exhibit 14.6.[24] Each factor may contain a wide range of specific traits. The **Big Five personality factors** describe an individual's extroversion, agreeableness, conscientiousness, emotional stability and openness to experience:

Big Five personality factors
Dimensions that describe an individual's extroversion, agreeableness, conscientiousness, emotional stability and openness to experience.

1 *Extroversion.* The degree to which a person is outgoing, sociable, assertive and comfortable with interpersonal relationships.

2 *Agreeableness.* The degree to which a person is able to get along with others by being good-natured, likable, cooperative, forgiving, understanding and trusting.

3 *Conscientiousness.* The degree to which a person is focused on a few goals, thus behaving in ways that are responsible, dependable, persistent and achievement oriented.

4 *Emotional stability.* The degree to which a person is calm, enthusiastic and self-confident, rather than tense, depressed, moody or insecure.

5 *Openness to experience.* The degree to which a person has a broad range of interests and is imaginative, creative, artistically sensitive and willing to consider new ideas.

As illustrated in the exhibit, these factors represent a continuum. That is, a person may have a low, moderate, or high degree of each quality. Answer the questions in Exhibit 14.6 to see where you fall on the Big Five scale for each of the factors. Having a moderate-to-high degree of each of the Big Five personality factors is considered desirable for a wide range of employees, but this isn't always a key to success. For example, having an outgoing, sociable personality (extroversion) is considered desirable for managers, but many successful top leaders, including Richard Branson, Herbert Heiner, Phillip Rose, Bill Gates, Charles Schwab and Steven Spielberg, are introverts, people who become drained by social encounters and need time alone to reflect and recharge their batteries. One study found that four in ten top executives test out to be introverts.[25] Thus, the quality of extroversion is not as significant as is often presumed. Traits of agreeableness, on the other hand, seem to be particularly important in today's collaborative organizations. The days are over when a hard-driving manager can run roughshod over others to earn a promotion. Companies want managers who work smoothly with others and get help from lots of people inside and outside the organization. Today's successful CEOs are not the tough guys of the past but those men and women who know how to get people to like and trust them. Philip Purcell was forced out as CEO of Morgan Stanley largely because he was a remote, autocratic leader who treated many employees with contempt and failed to build positive relationships with clients. Purcell had little goodwill to back him up when things started going against him. Many people just didn't like him. In

Exhibit 14.6 The Big Five Personality Traits

Each individual's collection of personality traits is different; it is what makes us unique. But, although each *collection* of traits varies, we all share many common traits. The following phrases describe various traits and behaviours. Rate how accurately each statement describes you, based on a scale of 1 to 5, with 1 being very inaccurate and 5 very accurate. Describe yourself as you are now, not as you wish to be. There are no right or wrong answers.

	1	2	3	4	5
Very Inaccurate					Very Accurate

Extroversion

I am usually the life of the party.	1	2	3	4	5
I feel comfortable around people.	1	2	3	4	5
I am talkative.	1	2	3	4	5

Agreeableness

I am kind and sympathetic.	1	2	3	4	5
I have a good word for everyone.	1	2	3	4	5
I never insult people.	1	2	3	4	5

Conscientiousness

I am systematic and efficient.	1	2	3	4	5
I pay attention to details.	1	2	3	4	5
I am always prepared for class.	1	2	3	4	5

Neuroticism (Low Emotional Stability)

I often feel critical of myself.	1	2	3	4	5
I often envy others.	1	2	3	4	5
I am temperamental.	1	2	3	4	5

Openness to New Experiences

I am imaginative.	1	2	3	4	5
I prefer to vote for liberal political candidates.	1	2	3	4	5
I really like art.	1	2	3	4	5

Which are your most prominent traits? For fun and discussion, compare your responses with those of peers.

contrast, Sainsbury's CEO Justin King stresses good relationships with employees, suppliers, partners and customers as a key to effective management.[26]

One recent book argues that the secret to success in work and in life is *likeability*. We all know we're more willing to do something for someone we like than for someone we don't, whether it be a team-mate, a neighbour, a professor or a supervisor. Managers can increase their likeability by developing traits of agreeableness, including being friendly and cooperative, understanding other people in a genuine way, and striving to make people feel positive about themselves.[27]

Many companies, including HSBC, the UK's National Health Service, ToysRUs, Next, Lancôme and others, use personality testing to hire, evaluate or promote employees. Surveys show that at least 30 per cent of organizations use some kind of personality testing for hiring.[28] In the US, MultiCinema (AMC), one of the largest theatre chains in the US, looks for front-line workers with high conscientiousness and high emotional stability.[29] Marriott Hotels looks for people who score high on conscientiousness and agreeableness because they believe these individuals will provide better service to guests.[30] Companies also use personality testing for managers. Hewlett-Packard, Apple, Google, Dell Computer and General Electric all put candidates for top positions through testing, interviews with psychologists or both, to see whether they have the 'right stuff' for the job.[31] Executives at franchises such as Little Gym International and Yum Brands, which owns Pizza Hut and KFC are using personality testing to make sure potential franchisees can fit into their system and be successful.[32] A growing number of entrepreneurs are using sophisticated personality testing to match singles through online dating services. Match.com, for example, claims to have facilitated 30,000 marriages by matching people based on their compatible personalities.

Despite growing use of personality tests, little hard evidence shows them to be valid predictors of job or relationship success. The long-term tracking of data of romantic matchmaking sites has been referred to as 'the early days of a social experiment of unprecedented proportions, involving millions of couples and possibly extending over the course of generations'.[33] Similarly, scientific evidence for the valid use of personality testing for job success is still years away.

Emotional Intelligence

In recent years, new insights into personality are emerging through research in the area of *emotional intelligence*. Emotional intelligence (EQ) includes four basic components:[34]

1 *Self-awareness.* The basis for all the other components; being aware of what you are feeling. People who are in touch with their feelings are better able to guide their own lives and actions. A high degree of self-awareness means you can accurately assess your own strengths and limitations and have a healthy sense of self-confidence.

2 *Self-management.* The ability to control disruptive or harmful emotions and balance one's moods so that worry, anxiety, fear, or anger do not cloud thinking and get in the way of what needs to be done. People who are skilled at self-management remain optimistic and hopeful despite setbacks and obstacles. This ability is crucial for pursuing long-term goals. For example, MetLife found that applicants who failed the regular sales aptitude test but scored high on optimism made 21 per cent more sales in their first year and 57 per cent more in their second year than those who passed the sales test but scored high on pessimism.[35]

3 *Social awareness.* The ability to understand others and practice *empathy*, which means being able to put yourself in someone else's shoes, to recognize what others are feeling without them needing to tell you. People with social awareness are capable of understanding divergent points of view and interacting effectively with many different types of people.

CONCEPT CONNECTION Managers at French bank Credit Agricole SA routinely refer to their personality test results to gauge their progress toward improving the skills or personal characteristics that need work. CEO Georges Pauget firmly believes in the value of personality testing to help him gauge whether job applicants have the optimal traits for the position and to aid employees in their personal development. He's not alone. A 2005 Society for Human Resource Management survey revealed that more than a third of the respondents were already using behavioural or personality assessments, with more organizations planning to incorporate such tests in the near future.

© IMAGESEUROPE/ALAMY

4 *Relationship awareness.* The ability to connect to others, build positive relationships, respond to the emotions of others, and influence others. People with relationship awareness know how to listen and communicate clearly and they treat others with compassion and respect.

Studies find a positive relationship between job performance and high degrees of emotional intelligence in a variety of jobs. Numerous organizations, including the US Air Force and Canada Life, use EQ tests to measure such things as self-awareness, ability to empathize, and capacity to build positive relationships.[36] EQ seems to be particularly important for jobs that require a high degree of social interaction, which includes managers, who are responsible for influencing others and building positive attitudes and relationships in the organization. Managers with low emotional intelligence can undermine employee morale and harm the organization.

As a new manager, one thing that influences your EQ is agreeableness, and another is self-confidence – an important foundation for a good manager. At times of great change or crisis managers rely on a high EQ level to help employees cope with the anxiety and stress they may be experiencing. In China and Taiwan fears of typhoons and earthquakes, in the US fears of terrorism, in the Middle East anxiety and sorrow over the war in Palestine and Iraq, political rivalry in Zimbabwe, and continuing economic hardship through the credit crunch for many people, all make meeting the psychological and emotional needs of employees a new role for managers. It is important to remember that emotional intelligence is not an in-born personality characteristic, but something that can be learned and developed.[37]

✓ NEW MANAGER SELF-TEST

What's Your EQ?

Understanding yourself and others is a major part of new manager's job. To learn about your insights into self and others, answer each item below as Mostly True or Mostly False for you.

		Mostly True	Mostly False
1	I am aware of sensations and emotions within my body.	☐	☐
2	I am slow to react to others' slights or negative actions toward me.	☐	☐
3	I can tell my friends' moods from their behaviour.	☐	☐
4	I am good at building consensus among others.	☐	☐
5	I have a good sense of why I have certain feelings.	☐	☐
6	I calm down right away if upset and am quick to forgive.	☐	☐
7	I often sense the impact of my words or behaviour on others.	☐	☐
8	Other people are happier when I am around.	☐	☐

SCORING AND INTERPRETATION The categories of emotional intelligence are below. Give yourself one point for each item marked Mostly True.

Self-Awareness: Items 1, 5

Self-Management: Items 2, 6

Social Awareness: Items 3, 7

Relationship Management: Items 4, 8

These are the four dimensions of EQ described in the text. If you scored 2 on a dimension, you probably do well on it. If you scored 0 on a dimension, you may want to work on that aspect of your EQ before becoming a manager. The important thing as a manager is to know and guide yourself, to understand the emotional state of others and to guide your relationships in a positive direction.

Attitudes and Behaviours Influenced by Personality

An individual's personality influences a wide variety of work-related attitudes and behaviours. Four that are of particular interest to managers are locus of control, authoritarianism, Machiavellianism and problem-solving styles.

Locus of Control

Locus of control
The tendency to place the primary responsibility for one's success or failure either within oneself (internally) or on outside forces (externally).

People differ in terms of what they tend to accredit as the cause of their success or failure. Their **locus of control** defines whether they place the primary responsibility within themselves or on outside forces.[43] Some people believe that their own actions strongly influence what happens to them. They feel in control of their own fate. These individuals have a high *internal* locus of control. Other people believe that events in their lives occur because of chance, luck or outside people and events. They feel more like pawns of their fate. These individuals have a high *external* locus of control. Many top leaders of e-commerce and high-tech organizations possess a high internal locus of control. These managers have to cope with rapid change and uncertainty associated with internet business. They must believe that they and their employees can counter the negative impact of outside forces and events. John Chambers, CEO of Cisco Systems, is a good example. Despite a tough economy and a drastically diminished stock price in the early 2000s, Chambers maintained his belief that Cisco can defeat any challenge thrown its way.[44] A person with a high external locus of control would likely feel overwhelmed trying to make the rapid decisions and changes needed to keep pace with the industry, particularly when environmental conditions are unstable.

Research on locus of control shows real differences in behaviour across a wide range of settings. People with an internal locus of control are easier to motivate because they believe the rewards are the result of their behaviour. They are better able to handle complex information and problem solving, are more achievement oriented, but are also more independent and therefore more difficult to manage. By contrast, people with an external locus of control are harder to motivate, less involved in their jobs, more likely to blame others when faced with a poor performance evaluation, but more compliant and conforming and, therefore, easier to manage.[45]

Do you believe luck plays an important role in your life, or do you feel that you control your own fate? To find out more about your locus of control, read the instructions and complete the questionnaire in Exhibit 14.7.

Authoritarianism

Authoritarianism is the belief that power and status differences should exist within the organization.[46] Individuals high in authoritarianism tend to be concerned with power and toughness, obey recognized authority above them, stick to conventional values, critically judge others, and oppose the use of subjective feelings. The degree to which managers possess authoritarianism will influence how they wield and share power. The degree to which employees possess authoritarianism will influence how they react to their managers. If a manager and employees differ in their degree of authoritarianism, the manager may have difficulty leading effectively. The trend toward empowerment and shifts in expectations among younger employees for more equitable relationships contribute to a decline in strict authoritarianism in many organizations.

Authoritarianism
The belief that power and status differences should exist within the organization.

Machiavellianism

Another personality dimension that is helpful in understanding work behaviour is **Machiavellianism**, which is characterized by the acquisition of power and the manipulation of other people for purely personal gain. Machiavellianism is named after Niccolo Machiavelli, a sixteenth-century author who wrote *The Prince*, a book for noblemen of the day on how to acquire and use power. Psychologists developed instruments to measure a person's Machiavellianism (Mach) orientation.[47] Research shows that high Machs are predisposed to being pragmatic, capable of lying to achieve personal goals, more likely to win in win-lose situations, and more likely to persuade than be persuaded.[48]

Machiavellianism
The tendency to direct much of one's behaviour toward the acquisition of power and the manipulation of other people for personal gain.

Exhibit 14.7 Measuring Locus of Control

Your Locus of Control

This questionnaire is designed to measure locus-of-control beliefs. Researchers using this questionnaire in a study of college students found a mean of 51.8 for men and 52.2 for women, with a standard deviation of 6 for each. The higher your score on this questionnaire, the more you tend to believe that you are generally responsible for what happens to you; in other words, higher scores are associated with internal locus of control. Low scores are associated with external locus of control. Scoring low indicates that you tend to believe that forces beyond your control, such as powerful other people, fate, or chance, are responsible for what happens to you.

For each of these ten questions, indicate the extent to which you agree or disagree using the following scale:

1 = strongly disagree   4 = neither disagree nor agree   7 = strongly agree

2 = disagree   5 = slightly agree

3 = slightly disagree   6 = agree

	1	2	3	4	5	6	7
1. When I get what I want, it is usually because I worked hard for it.	1	2	3	4	5	6	7
2. When I make plans, I am almost certain to make them work.	1	2	3	4	5	6	7
3. I prefer games involving some luck over games requiring pure skill.	1	2	3	4	5	6	7
4. I can learn almost anything if I set my mind to it.	1	2	3	4	5	6	7
5. My major accomplishments are entirely due to my hard work and ability.	1	2	3	4	5	6	7
6. I usually don't set goals, because I have a hard time following through on them.	1	2	3	4	5	6	7
7. Competition discourages excellence.	1	2	3	4	5	6	7
8. Often people get ahead just by being lucky.	1	2	3	4	5	6	7
9. On any sort of exam or competition, I like to know how well I do relative to everyone else.	1	2	3	4	5	6	7
10. It's pointless to keep working on something that's too difficult for me.	1	2	3	4	5	6	7

Scoring and Interpretation

To determine your score, reverse the values you selected for questions 3, 6, 7, 8 and 10 (1 = 7, 2 = 6, 3 = 5, 4 = 4, 5 = 3, 6 = 2, 7 = 1). For example, if you strongly disagree with the statement in question 3, you would have given it a value of 1. Change this value to a 7. Reverse the scores in a similar manner for questions 6, 7, 8 and 10. Now add the point values for all ten questions together.

Your score _____

SOURCE: Adapted from J. M. Burger, *Personality: Theory and Research* (Belmont, CA: Wadsworth, 1986): 400–401, cited in D. Hellriegel, J. W. Slocum, Jr., and R. W. Woodman, *Organizational Behaviour*, 6th ed. (St. Paul, MN: West, 1992): 97–100. Original source: D. L. Paulhus, 'Sphere-Specific Measures of Perceived Control', *Journal of Personality and Social Psychology*, 44, 1253–1265.

Different situations may require people who demonstrate one or the other type of behaviour. In loosely structured situations, high Machs actively take control, while low Machs accept the direction given by others. Low Machs thrive in highly structured situations, while high Machs perform in a detached, disinterested way. High Machs are particularly good in jobs that require bargaining skills or that involve substantial rewards for winning.[49]

What's Your Crisis EQ?

Threats of terrorist attacks. Downsizing. Swine flu. Company failures. Stock market crashes. Rapid technological changes. Information overload. The turbulence of today's world has left lingering psychological and emotional damage in workplaces all across Europe, as well as in the rest of the world. When even a minor crisis hits an organization, uncertainty and fear are high. Today's managers need the skills to help people deal with their emotions and return to a more normal work routine. Although managers cannot take the place of professional counsellors, they can use patience, flexibility and understanding to assist people through a crisis. Here are some important elements of crisis EQ for managers:

■ Be visible and provide as much up-to-date, accurate information as possible about what's going on in the company and the industry. Rumour control is critical.

■ Find simple ways to get employees together. Order pizza for the entire staff. Invite telecommuters to come in to the office so they can connect with others and have a chance to share their emotions.

■ Give employees room to be human. It is natural for people to feel anger and other strong emotions, so allow those feelings to be expressed as long as they aren't directed at other employees.

■ Publicize the company's charitable endeavours and make employees aware of the various opportunities both within and outside the organization to volunteer and donate to charity.

■ Thank employees in person and with handwritten notes when they go above and beyond the call of duty during a difficult time.

■ Recognize that routine, structured work can help people heal. Postpone major, long-term projects and decisions to the extent possible, and break work into shorter, more manageable tasks. Listen to employees and determine what they need to help them return to a normal work life.

■ Provide professional counselling services for people who need it. Those with a history of alcohol abuse, trouble at home or previous mental or emotional problems are especially at risk, but anyone who has trouble gradually returning to his or her previous level of work may need outside counselling.

SOURCES Based on Matthew Boyle, 'Nothing Really Matters,' *Fortune* (October 15, 2001): 261–264; and Sue Shellenbarger, 'Readers Face Dilemma Over How Far to Alter Post-Attack Workplace', *The Wall Street Journal* (October 31, 2001): B1.

Problem-Solving Styles and the Myers–Briggs Type Indicator

Managers also need to understand that individuals differ in the way they solve problems and make decisions. One approach to understanding problem-solving styles grew out of the work of psychologist Carl Jung. Jung believed differences resulted from our preferences in how we go about gathering and evaluating information.[50] According to Jung, gathering information and evaluating information are separate activities. People gather information either by *sensation* or *intuition*, but not by both simultaneously. Sensation-type people would rather work with known facts and hard data and prefer routine and order in gathering information. Intuitive-type people would rather look for possibilities than work with facts and prefer solving new problems and using abstract concepts.

Evaluating information involves making judgements about the information a person has gathered. People evaluate information by *thinking* or *feeling*. These represent the extremes in orientation. Thinking-type individuals base their judgements on impersonal analysis, using reason and logic rather than personal values or emotional

Exhibit 14.8 Four Problem-Solving Styles

Personal Style	Action Tendencies	Likely Occupations
Sensation-Thinking	■ Emphasizes details, facts, certainty ■ Is a decisive, applied thinker ■ Focuses on short-term, realistic goals ■ Develops rules and regulations for judging performance	■ Accounting ■ Production ■ Computer programming ■ Market research ■ Engineering
Intuitive-Thinking	■ Prefers dealing with theoretical or technical problems ■ Is a creative, progressive, perceptive thinker ■ Focuses on possibilities using impersonal analysis ■ Is able to consider a number of options and problems simultaneously	■ Systems design ■ Systems analysis ■ Law ■ Middle/top management ■ Teaching business, economics
Sensation-Feeling	■ Shows concern for current, real-life human problems ■ Is pragmatic, analytical, methodical and conscientious ■ Emphasizes detailed facts about people rather than tasks ■ Focuses on structuring organizations for the benefit of people	■ Directing supervisor ■ Counselling ■ Negotiating ■ Selling ■ Interviewing
Intuitive-Feeling	■ Avoids specifics ■ Is charismatic, participative, people oriented and helpful ■ Focuses on general views, broad themes and feelings ■ Decentralises decision making, develops few rules and regulations	■ Public relations ■ Advertising ■ Human Resources ■ Politics ■ Customer service

aspects of the situation. Feeling-type individuals base their judgements more on personal feelings such as harmony and tend to make decisions that result in approval from others.

According to Jung, only one of the four functions – sensation, intuition, thinking or feeling – is dominant in an individual. However, the dominant function usually is backed up by one of the functions from the other set of paired opposites. Exhibit 14.8 shows the four problem-solving styles that result from these matchups, as well as occupations that people with each style tend to prefer.

Two additional sets of paired opposites not directly related to problem solving are *introversion–extroversion* and *judging–perceiving*. Introverts gain energy by focusing on personal thoughts and feelings, whereas extroverts gain energy from being around others and interacting with others. On the judging versus perceiving dimension, people with a judging preference like certainty and closure and tend to make decisions quickly based on available data. Perceiving people, on the other hand, enjoy ambiguity, dislike deadlines and may change their minds several times as they gather large amounts of data and information to make decisions.

A widely used personality test that measures how people differ on all four of Jung's sets of paired opposites is the **Myers–Briggs Type Indicator (MBTI)**. The

Myers–Briggs Type Indicator (MBTI)
Personality test that measures a person's preference for introversion vs. extroversion, sensation vs. intuition, thinking vs. feeling, and judging vs. perceiving.

MBTI measures a person's preferences for introversion versus extroversion, sensation versus intuition, thinking versus feeling, and judging versus perceiving. The various combinations of these four preferences result in 16 unique personality types.

Go to the Experiential Exercise on page 553 that pertains to evaluating your Myers–Briggs personality type.

TAKE A MOMENT

Each of the 16 different personality types can have positive and negative consequences for behaviour. Based on the limited research that has been done, the two preferences that seem to be most strongly associated with effective management in a variety of organizations and industries are thinking and judging.[51] However, people with other preferences can also be good managers. One advantage of understanding your natural preferences is to maximize your innate strengths and abilities. Dow Chemical manager Kurt Swogger believes the MBTI can help put people in the right jobs – where they will be happiest and make the strongest contribution to the organization.

Other organizations also use the MBTI, with 89 of the *Fortune* 100 companies recently reporting that they use the test when making hiring and promotion decisions.[52] Matching the right people to the right jobs is an important responsibility for managers, whether they do it based on intuition and experience or by using personality tests such as the MBTI. Managers strive to create a good fit between the person and the job he or she is asked to do.

 INNOVATIVE WAY

Dow Chemical

When Kurt Swogger arrived at Dow Chemical's plastics business in 1991, it took anywhere from 6 to 15 years to launch a new product – and the unit hadn't launched a single one for three years. Today, a new product launch takes just two to four years, and Swogger's R&D team has launched 13 product hits over the past decade.

How did Swogger lead such an amazing transformation? By making sure people were doing the jobs they were best suited for. The simple fact, Swogger says, 'is that some [people] do development better than others. The biggest obstacle to launching great new products was not having the right people in the right jobs'. Swogger began reassigning people based on his intuition and insight, distinguishing pure inventors from those who could add value later in the game and still others who were best at marketing the new products. Swogger says he was right-on about 60 per

cent of the time. If someone didn't work out after six months, he'd put them in another assignment.

Seeking a better way to determine people's strengths, Swogger turned to a former Dow employee, Greg Stevens, who now owns a consulting firm. Stevens and Swogger used the Myers–Briggs Type Indicator (MBTI), predicting which types would be best suited to each stage of the product development and launch cycles. After administering the test to current and former Dow plastics employees, they found some startling results. In 1991, when Swogger came on board, the match between the right personality type and the right role was only 29 per cent. By 2001, thanks to Swogger's great instincts, the rate had jumped to 93 per cent.

Swogger's next step is to administer the MBTI to new hires, so the job match is right to begin with. He believes the MBTI can help him assign people to jobs that match their natural thinking and problem-solving styles, leading to happier employees and higher organizational performance.[53]

COURTESY OF LORI REESE/REDUX PICTURES

CONCEPT CONNECTION Dogs are such a huge part of our lives that many of us dream of having them come to work with us. Well, more and more companies are allowing dogs in the office and yours may be next. At Google Headquarters (Googleplex) Googlers are permitted to bring their dogs to the workplace. Research has shown that having pets in the workplace reduces stress and increases the feeling of well-being. And that's precisely why Relay Recruitment, a company in West Yorkshire, UK brought in Rupert, a Cocker Spaniel. What management experienced was beyond their expectations. Rupert indeed helped with the post-holiday blues, but also encouraged four people to quit smoking and others to lose weight by going on walks during breaks. For a lot of companies with rules such as owner accountability, a dog review board and a dog-approval process, employees find that the dogs are a great release for stress. This dog policy helps managers make good recruitment decisions; candidates who respond favourably to the canine rule are likely to fit in with the existing office culture. It worked out so well that 'Bosses now plan to provide dogs for their staff in Leeds, Halifax and York.'[57]

Person–Job Fit

Given the wide variation among personalities and among jobs, an important responsibility of managers is to try to match employee and job characteristics so that work is done by people who are well suited to do it. This goal requires that managers be clear about what they expect employees to do and have a sense of the kinds of people who would succeed at various types of assignments. The extent to which a person's ability and personality match the requirements of a job is called **person–job fit**. When managers achieve person–job fit, employees are more likely to contribute and have higher levels of job satisfaction and commitment.[54] The importance of person–job fit became especially apparent during the dot-com heyday of the late 1990s. People who rushed to internet companies in hopes of finding a new challenge – or making a quick buck – found themselves floundering in jobs for which they were unsuited. One manager recruited by a leading executive search firm lasted less than two hours at his new job. The search firm, a division of Russell Reynolds Associates, later developed a 'Web Factor' diagnostic to help determine whether people have the right personality for the internet, including such things as a tolerance for risk and uncertainty, an obsession with learning, and a willingness to do whatever needs doing, regardless of job title.[55]

A related concern is *person–environment fit*, which looks not only at whether the person and job are suited to one another but also at how well the individual will fit in the overall organizational environment. An employee who is by nature strongly authoritarian, for example, would have a hard time in an organization such as W. L. Gore and Associates, which has few rules, no hierarchy, no fixed or assigned authority, and no bosses. Many of today's organizations pay attention to person–environment fit from the beginning of the recruitment process. Texas Instruments' webpage includes an area called Fit Check that evaluates personality types anonymously and gives prospective job candidates a chance to evaluate for themselves whether they would be a good match with the company.[56]

Person–job fit
The extent to which a person's ability and personality match the requirements of a job.

Learning

Years of schooling condition many of us to think that learning is something students do in response to teachers in a classroom. With this view, in the managerial world of time deadlines and concrete action, learning seems remote – even irrelevant. However, successful managers need specific knowledge and skills as well as the ability to adapt to changes in the world around them. Managers have to learn.

Learning is a change in behaviour or performance that occurs as the result of experience. Experience may take the form of observing others, reading or listening to sources of information, or experiencing the consequences of one's own behaviour. This important way of adapting to events is linked to individual differences in attitudes, perception and personality.

Learning
A change in behaviour or performance that occurs as the result of experience.

Two individuals who undergo similar experiences – for example, a business transfer to a foreign country – probably will differ in how they adapt their behaviours to (that is, learn from) the experience. In other words, each person learns in a different way.

The Learning Process

One model of the learning process, shown in Exhibit 14.9, depicts learning as a four-stage cycle.[58] First, a person encounters a concrete experience. This event is followed by thinking and reflective observation, which lead to abstract conceptualization and, in turn, to active experimentation. The results of the experimentation generate new experiences, and the cycle repeats.

The Best Buy chain of consumer electronics superstores owes its birth to the learning process of its founder, Richard M. Schulze. In the 1960s, Schulze built a stereo store called Sound of Music into a chain of nine stores in and near St. Paul, Minnesota. However, a tornado destroyed his largest and most profitable store, so he held a massive clearance sale in the parking lot. So many shoppers descended on the lot that they caused traffic to back up for two miles. Reflecting on this experience, Schulze saw great demand for a store featuring large selection and low prices, backed by heavy advertising. He tried out his idea by launching his first Best Buy superstore. Today Best Buy has nearly 800 retail stores in the US and Canada, as well as a thriving online division.[59]

The arrows in the model of the learning process in Exhibit 14.9 indicate that this process is a recurring cycle. People continually test their conceptualizations and adapt them as a result of their personal reflections and observations about their experiences.

Learning Styles

Individuals develop personal learning styles that vary in terms of how much they emphasize each stage of the learning cycle. These differences occur because the learning process is directed by individual needs and goals. For example, an engineer might place greater emphasis on abstract concepts, while a salesperson might emphasize concrete experiences. Because of these preferences, personal learning styles typically have strong and weak points.

Questionnaires can assess a person's strong and weak points as a learner by measuring the relative emphasis the person places on each of the four learning stages shown in Exhibit 14.10: concrete experience, reflective observation, abstract conceptualization and active experimentation. Some people have a tendency to overemphasize one stage of the learning process, or to avoid some aspects of learning. Not many people have totally balanced profiles, but the key to effective learning is competence in each of the four stages when it is needed.

Researchers identified four fundamental learning styles that combine elements of the four stages of the learning cycle.[61] Exhibit 14.10 summarizes the characteristics and dominant learning abilities of these four styles, labelled Diverger, Assimilator, Converger and Accommodator. The exhibit also lists occupations that frequently attract individuals with each of the learning styles. For example, people whose dominant style is Accommodator are often drawn to sales and marketing. A good example is Gertrude Boyle, who took over Columbia

© GETTY IMAGES

CONCEPT CONNECTION The South African company PDA (People Development Africa), has learnt and encourages their clients that it is not only useful to equip people with skills and knowledge but it is also critical to create an enabling environment where a trained workforce or managers are free to practise and demonstrate their newly learnt abilities in the organization. Thus they believe in continuous learning for both employees and clients. PDA further believes that it is of utmost importance for organizations to develop their workforce in such a manner that the process gives birth to employees that are achievers and who, together with their team, can produce the outstanding results required by the organization. Thelma Bowore, the Managing Member helps to turn this training philosophy into reality. PDA has carefully devised selected skills training programmes that will lead towards improved productivity within organizations.[60]

Exhibit 14.9 The Experiential Learning Cycle

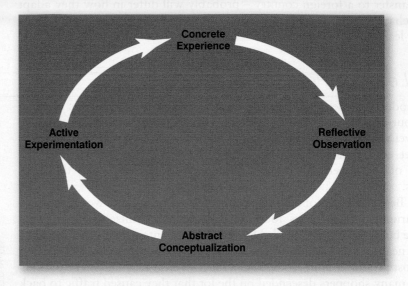

Exhibit 14.10 Learning Style Types

Learning Style Type	Dominant Learning Abilities	Learning Characteristics	Likely Occupations
Diverger	■ Concrete experience ■ Reflective observation	■ Is good at generating ideas, seeing a situation from multiple perspectives, and being aware of meaning and value ■ Tends to be interested in people, culture and the arts	■ Human resource management ■ Counselling ■ Organization development specialist
Assimilator	■ Abstract conceptualization ■ Reflective observation	■ Is good at inductive reasoning, creating theoretical models, and combining disparate observations into an integrated explanation ■ Tends to be less concerned with people than ideas and abstract concepts.	■ Research ■ Strategic planning
Converger	■ Abstract conceptualization ■ Active experimentation	■ Is good at decisiveness, practical application of ideas and hypothetical deductive reasoning ■ Prefers dealing with technical tasks rather than interpersonal issues	■ Engineering
Accommodator	■ Concrete experience ■ Active experimentation	■ Is good at implementing decisions, carrying out plans and getting involved in new experiences ■ Tends to be at ease with people but may be seen as impatient or pushy	■ Marketing ■ Sales

Sportswear after the death of her husband. She and her son, Tim, propelled the company from sales of $13 million to $358 million over a 13-year period by observing what competitors were doing and actively experimenting to find a novel sales approach. The 74-year-old Gert Boyle decided to star in her own 'Tough Mother' ads as a way to distinguish the company from competitors who advertised their products worn by fit, young models. Boyle believes in constantly pushing herself and her company, questioning everything, and trying new ideas.[62] Exhibit 14.10 lists other likely occupations for Divergers, Assimilators, Convergers and Accommodators.

As a new manager, determine your natural learning style to understand how you approach problems, recognize your learning strengths and better relate to people who have different learning styles. As you grow in your management responsibilities, strive for a balance among the four learning stages shown in Exhibit 14.10.

TAKE A MOMENT

Continuous Learning

To thrive in today's turbulent business climate, individuals and organizations must be continuous learners. For individuals, continuous learning entails looking for opportunities to learn from classes, reading and talking to others, as well as looking for the lessons in life's experiences. One manager who embodies the spirit of continuous learning is Larry Ricciardi, senior vice president and corporate counsel at IBM. Ricciardi is an avid traveller and voracious reader who likes to study art, literature and history. In addition, Ricciardi likes to add supermarket tabloids to his daily fare of *The Wall Street Journal*. On business trips, he scouts out side trips to exotic or interesting sites so he can learn something new.[63] Ricciardi never knows when he might be able to apply a new idea or understanding to improve his life, his job or his organization.

For organizations, continuous learning involves the processes and systems through which the organization enables its people to learn, share their growing knowledge and apply it to their work. In an organization in which continuous learning is taking place, employees actively apply comments from customers, news about competitors, training programmes, and more to increase their knowledge and improve the organization's practices. For example, at the BUPA Clinic, UK, doctors are expected to consult with doctors in other departments, with the patient, and with anyone else inside or outside the clinic who might help with any aspect of the patient's problem.[64] The emphasis on teamwork, openness and collaboration keeps learning strong at BUPA.

Managers can foster continuous learning by consciously stopping from time to time and asking, 'What can we learn from this experience'? They can allow employees time to attend training and reflect on their experiences. Recognizing that experience can be the best teacher, managers should focus on how they and their employees can learn from mistakes, rather than fostering a climate in which employees hide mistakes because they fear being punished for them. Managers also encourage organizational learning by establishing information systems that enable people to share knowledge and learn in new ways. Information technology will be discussed in detail in Chapter 20. As individuals, managers can help themselves and set an example for their employees by being continuous learners, listening to others, reading widely and reflecting on what they observe.

Stress and Stress Management

Stress
A physiological and emotional response to stimuli that place physical or psychological demands on an individual.

Just as organizations can support or discourage learning, organizational characteristics also interact with individual differences to influence other behaviours. In every organization, these characteristics include sources of stress. Formally defined, **stress** is an individual's physiological and emotional response to external stimuli that place physical or psychological demands on the individual and create uncertainty and lack of personal control when important outcomes are at stake.[65] These stimuli, called *stressors,* produce some combination of frustration (the inability to achieve a goal, such as the inability to meet a deadline because of inadequate resources) and anxiety (such as the fear of being disciplined for not meeting deadlines).

People's responses to stressors vary according to their personalities, the resources available to help them cope and the context in which the stress occurs. Thus, a looming deadline will feel different depending on the degree to which the individual enjoys a challenge, the willingness of co-workers to team up and help each other succeed, and family members' understanding of an employee's need to work extra hours, among other factors.

TAKE A MOMENT   Go to the Ethical Dilemma on page 556 that pertains to organizational sources of stress.

When the level of stress is low relative to a person's coping resources, stress can be a positive force, stimulating desirable change and achievement. However, too much stress is associated with many negative consequences, including sleep disturbances, drug and alcohol abuse, headaches, ulcers, high blood pressure and heart disease. People who are experiencing the ill effects of too much stress may become irritable or withdraw from interactions with their coworkers, take excess time off, and have more health problems. For example, a recent study of manufacturing workers in Bangladesh found a significant connection between job stress and absenteeism. Another study of 46,000 workers in the US found that health care costs are 147 per cent higher for individuals who are stressed or depressed.[66] People suffering from stress are less productive and may leave the organization. Clearly, too much stress is harmful to employees as well as to companies.

Type A and Type B Behaviour

Type A behaviour
Behaviour pattern characterized by extreme competitiveness, impatience, aggressiveness and devotion to work.

Type B behaviour
Behaviour pattern that lacks Type A characteristics and includes a more balanced, relaxed lifestyle.

Researchers observed that some people seem to be more vulnerable than others to the ill effects of stress. From studies of stress-related heart disease, they categorized people as having behaviour patterns called Type A and Type B.[67] The **Type A behaviour** pattern includes extreme competitiveness, impatience, aggressiveness and devotion to work. In contrast, people with a **Type B behaviour** pattern exhibit less of these behaviours. They consequently experience less conflict with other people and a more balanced, relaxed lifestyle. Type A people tend to experience more stress-related illness than Type B people.

Most Type A individuals are high-energy people and may seek positions of power and responsibility. One example is Simone Schwinger, Director for health care improvement at Clinic Birshof, a private hospital in Basel, Switzerland part of Hirslanden International Group. When Schwinger was in charge of establishing an information network of community-wide medical records to support patient care, she typically began her day at 6a.m. and worked until 11p.m. Her days were a blur of conference calls, meetings and email exchanges. 'I could move mountains if I put my mind to it,' she says. 'That's what good executives do.'[68]

By pacing themselves and learning control and intelligent use of their natural high-energy tendencies, Type A individuals can be powerful forces for innovation and leadership within their organizations, as Simone Schwinger has been at Hirslanden International. However, many Type A personalities cause stress-related problems for themselves, and sometimes for those around them. Schwinger eventually reached burnout. She couldn't sleep, she began snapping at colleagues, and she finally took a sabbatical and learned to lead a more balanced life.[69] Type B individuals typically live with less stress unless they are in high-stress situations. A number of factors can cause stress in the workplace, even for people who are not naturally prone to high stress.

Causes of Work Stress

Workplace stress is skyrocketing worldwide. A recent World Congress on Health and Safety at Work presented studies suggesting that job-related stress may be as big a danger to the world's people as chemical and biological hazards.[70] In the US, the number of people who say they are overworked has risen from 28 per cent in 2001 to 44 per cent in 2005, and one third of Americans between the ages of 25 and 39 say they feel burned out by their jobs. The UK's Health and Safety Executive says that half a million people in the UK are ill because of workplace stress, and stress-related illnesses are second only to back pain as a cause of work absences. In India, growing numbers of young software professionals and call-centre workers are falling prey to depression, anxiety and other mental illnesses because of increasing workplace stress.[71]

Most people have a general idea of what a stressful job is like: difficult, uncomfortable, exhausting, even frightening. Managers can better cope with their own stress and establish ways for the organization to help employees cope if they define the conditions that tend to produce work stress. One way to identify work stressors is to think about stress caused by the demands of job tasks and stress caused by interpersonal pressures and conflicts.

- *Task demands* are stressors arising from the tasks required of a person holding a particular job. Some kinds of decisions are inherently stressful: those made under time pressure, those that have serious consequences, and those that must be made with incomplete information. For example, emergency room doctors are under tremendous stress as a result of the task demands of their jobs. They regularly have to make quick decisions, based on limited information, that may determine whether a patient lives or dies. Almost all jobs, especially those of managers, have some level of stress associated with task demands. Task demands also sometimes cause stress because of role ambiguity, which means that people are unclear about what task behaviours are expected of them.

- *Interpersonal demands* are stressors associated with relationships in the organization. Although in some cases interpersonal relationships can alleviate stress, they also can be a source of stress when the group puts pressure on an individual or when conflicts arise between individuals. Managers can resolve many conflicts using techniques that will be discussed in Chapter 18. Role conflict occurs when an individual perceives incompatible demands from others. Managers

© TIME & LIFE PICTURES/GETTY IMAGES

CONCEPT CONNECTION
Sylvia Weinstock is founder of Sylvia Weinstock Cakes in New York City, known for celebrity wedding cakes, including those for Catherine Zeta-Jones, Liam Neeson and Donald Trump. Weinstock, named 'New York's reigning cake diva' by *InStyle* magazine, loves her job but feels the stress of task demands. 'This is an obsessive business because of the intensity and personal value that everyone places on their occasion,' she says. 'And I honour that. I fret. I worry. And unless I heard that the cake arrived happy, I'm checking that phone all the time.'

Role ambiguity
Uncertainty about what behaviours are expected of a person in a particular role.

Role conflict
Incompatible demands of different roles.

often feel role conflict because the demands of their superiors conflict with those of the employees in their department. They may be expected to support employees and provide them with opportunities to experiment and be creative, while at the same time top executives are demanding a consistent level of output that leaves little time for creativity and experimentation.

Almost everyone experiences some degree of job stress associated with these factors. For example, consider the stress caused by task demands on Aviva's call-centre representatives.

💡 INNOVATIVE WAY

Aviva Call Centre[72]

Nishant Patel loves his job as a call-centre representative for Aviva (previously Norwich Union) at the EXL call centre, in the new IT outpost of Noida, north of Delhi. He sees himself as a professional, and has a managerial position as a 'team fraud coordinator'. He enjoys connecting with customers; he makes good money and has good benefits. But he admits that it's not the job for everyone. About a third of the 100 or so calls a representative handles each day are stressful. Besides dealing with irate customers and handling calls regarding billing or other problems, representatives have to be able to rattle off Aviva's string of products and services, including terms and rates, and try to sell them to each and every call. It doesn't matter how angry or rude the customer on the other end of the line – pushing new services is a key requirement of the job.

What makes matters worse is that representatives often have to do these tasks under observation. Managers routinely sit next to a representative or listen in on a call to check whether the rep has hit on nearly 80 different points required in every customer contact. Call centre reps must meet precise performance specifications, and managers defend the observation practice as a way to ensure consistency and better customer service. However, employees almost always find the experience adds to their stress level. For some employees, particularly inexperienced ones, an observation can create a panic situation, causing heart pounding and profuse sweating, which, in turn, creates even greater stress.[73]

The true monotony of the work is disguised by 'camouflaging work as fun' – introducing cafés, popcorn booths and ping-pong tables into the offices. Meanwhile, quotas for calls or emails successfully attended to are often fixed at such a high level 'that the agent has to burn out to fulfil it'. With employees working through the night to cater for clients in different time zones, the work requires staff 'to live as Indian by day and Westerner after sundown' and takes a 'heavy toll' on agents' physical and mental health. But more importantly, call-centre work 'leads to a wastage of human resources and de-skilling of workers'.

In a windowless room in the basement of the building, half a dozen new employees are being tested on insurance claim scenarios. They give rote answers swiftly in clear English which has been 'neutralized' from any strong accent during a three-week voice-training programme. It is 10.45p.m., and in the dark streets outside preparations are being made for Diwali, the Hindu festival of light, but EXL works to English rhythms and even training sessions are conducted according to London time.

Nishant says : 'The pressure is tough. There's such a volume of calls that we don't have a second to pause, and the customers are often irate because they've been waiting so long,' she said. 'The hours are regimented. If you need to go to the loo, you have to wait until your allotted break period. My parents want me to leave because they can see how my health has suffered.'

The situation for call-centre representatives in other countries, who are handling calls for the US-based companies such as American Express, Citibank, Sprint and IBM, can be even more stressful. There, the high stress caused by task demands is compounded by interpersonal issues, primarily 'hate calls' from American customers angry over the loss of US jobs. A survey by the Indian magazine *Dataquest* found that most call centre employees find these calls 'psychologically disturbing' and identify them as a major cause of job stress.[74]

TAKE A MOMENT

As a new manager, learn to recognize the conditions that cause stress in the workplace and then change what you can to alleviate unnecessary or excessive stress for employees. Remember that not all stress is negative, but try to help people manage stress in a healthy way.

Innovative Responses to Stress Management

Organizations that want to challenge their employees and stay competitive in a fast-changing environment will never be stress-free. But because many consequences of stress are negative, managers need to make stress management a priority. In the UK, lawmakers implemented a new requirement that employers meet certain conditions that help to manage workplace stress, such as ensuring that employees are not exposed to a poor physical work environment, have the necessary skills and training to meet their job requirements, and are given a chance to offer input into the way their work is done.[75]

A variety of techniques can help individuals manage stress. Among the most basic strategies are those that help people stay healthy: exercising regularly, getting plenty of rest and eating a healthful diet.

Although individuals can pursue stress management strategies on their own, today's enlightened companies support healthy habits to help people manage stress and be more productive. Stress costs businesses billions of dollars a year in absenteeism, lower productivity, staff turnover, accidents, and higher health insurance and workers' compensation costs.[76] In today's workplace, taking care of employees has become a business as well as an ethical priority.

Supporting employees can be as simple as encouraging people to take regular breaks and vacations. Consider that more than a third of US employees surveyed by the Families and Work Institute currently don't take their full allotment of vacation time.[77] Some companies, including BellSouth, First Union and Tribble Creative Group, also have designated *quiet rooms* or meditation centres where employees can take short, calming breaks at any time they feel the need.[78] The time off is a valuable investment when it allows employees to approach their work with renewed energy and a fresh perspective.

Companies develop other programmes aimed at helping employees reduce stress and lead healthier, more balanced lives. Some have wellness programmes that provide access to nutrition counselling and exercise facilities. A worldwide study of wellness programmes conducted by the Canadian Government found that for each dollar spent, the company gets from $1.95 to $3.75 return payback from benefits.[79] Other organizations create broad work–life balance initiatives that may include flexible work options such as telecommuting and flexible hours, as well as benefits such as onsite day-care, fitness centres, and personal services such as pickup and delivery of dry cleaning. *Daily flexitime* is considered by many employees to be the most effective work–life practice, which means giving employees the freedom to vary their hours as needed, such as leaving early to take an elderly parent shopping or taking time off to attend a child's school play.[80]

The study of organizational behaviour reminds managers that employees are *human* resources with human needs. By acknowledging the personal aspects of employees' lives, work–life practices communicate that managers and the organization care about employees. In addition, managers' attitudes make a tremendous difference in whether employees are stressed out and unhappy or relaxed, energetic and productive.

A MANAGER'S ESSENTIALS: WHAT HAVE WE LEARNED?

- The principles of organizational behaviour describe how people as individuals and groups behave and affect the performance of the organization as a whole. Desirable work-related attitudes include job satisfaction and organizational commitment. Employees' and managers' attitudes can strongly influence employee motivation, performance and productivity. Three components of attitudes are cognitions, emotions and behaviour.

- Attitudes affect people's perceptions, and vice versa. Individuals often 'see' things in different ways. The perceptual process includes perceptual selectivity and perceptual organization. Perceptual distortions, such as stereotyping, the halo effect, projection and perceptual defence, are errors in judgement that can arise from inaccuracies in the perception process. Attributions are judgements that individuals make about whether a person's behaviour was caused by internal or external factors.

- Another area of interest is personality, the set of characteristics that underlie a relatively stable pattern of behaviour. One way to think about personality is the Big Five personality traits of extroversion, agreeableness, conscientiousness, emotional stability and openness to experience. Some important work-related attitudes and behaviours influenced by personality are locus of control, authoritarianism, Machiavellianism and problem-solving styles. A widely used personality test is the Myers–Briggs Type Indicator. Managers want to find a good person–job fit by ensuring that a person's personality, attitudes, skills, abilities and problem-solving styles match the requirements of the job and the organizational environment. New insight into personality has been gained through research in the area of emotional intelligence (EQ). Emotional intelligence includes the components of self-awareness, self-management, social awareness and relationship management.

- Even though people's personalities may be relatively stable, individuals can learn new behaviours. Learning refers to a change in behaviour or performance that occurs as a result of experience. The learning process goes through a four-stage cycle, and individual learning styles differ. Four learning styles are Diverger, Assimilator, Converger and Accommodator. Rapid changes in today's marketplace create a need for ongoing learning. They may also create greater stress for many of today's workers. The causes of work stress include task demands and interpersonal demands. Individuals and organizations can alleviate the negative effects of stress by engaging in a variety of techniques for stress management.

Returning to our opening example, Chris Hall at Hallmark Consumer Services realized that he had developed some negative attitudes that were affecting his managers' attitudes and performance. Rather than continuing to complain about the shortcomings of others, Hall adopted a new attitude that it was his responsibility as a leader to meld everyone into a cohesive, high-performing team. He eagerly began looking for classes he could take to learn new people skills and boost his emotional intelligence. Hall realized that the infusion of new, young managers into the organization had left some of the long-time executives feeling insecure about whether they were about to be replaced by the 'new kids'. Hall addressed the emotional component of managers' negative attitudes toward the new employees by reassuring them that they were valued and that their jobs were safe. He also met regularly with the new employees, rather than expecting other managers to do all the work of integrating them into the team. The long-time managers seemed reinvigorated and became more receptive to new ideas and more responsive to the new executives. The newcomers, in turn, developed more positive attitudes about the veteran managers, seeing them as team-mates who were eager to implement new ideas and improve the organization. By shifting his own attitude and acting as a mentor and coach, Chris Hall successfully united the two groups into a cohesive team in which each person appreciated the values and strengths of the others.[81]

DISCUSSION QUESTIONS

1 If you were trying to change a subordinate's attitude, which approach do you think would be more effective: changing cognition, affect or behaviour? Why? Why is it important for managers to have an understanding of organizational behaviour? Do you think a knowledge of OB might be more important at some managerial levels than at others? Discuss.

2 In what ways might the cognitive and affective components of attitude influence the behaviour of employees who are faced with learning an entirely new set of computer-related skills in order to retain their jobs at a manufacturing facility?

3 Suggest a way that a manager might be able to use his or her understanding of perceptual selectivity and organization to communicate more effectively with subordinates. What steps might managers at a company that is about to merge with another company take to promote organizational commitment among employees?

4 In the Big Five personality factors, extroversion is considered a 'good' quality to have. Why might introversion be an equally positive quality?

5 Why do you think surveys show that Generation X employees (those born between 1961 and 1981) experience the least job satisfaction of all demographic groups? Do you expect this finding to be true throughout their careers?

6 What is meant by perceptual selectivity? Explain some characteristics of the perceiver and of the stimuli that might affect perception?

7 Which of the four components of emotional intelligence do you consider most important to an effective manager in today's world? Why?

8 How might understanding whether an employee has an internal or an external locus of control help a manager better communicate with, motivate and lead the employee?

9 You are a manager, and you realize that one of your employees repeatedly teases coworkers born in India that they come from a backward country with pagan beliefs. How would you decide whether it's necessary to respond to the situation? If you decide to intervene, what would your response be? Why is it important for managers to achieve a person–job fit when they are hiring employees?

10 Review Exhibit 14.10. Which learning style best characterizes you? How can you use this understanding to improve your learning ability? To improve your management skills?

11 Describe a time when you experienced role ambiguity or role conflict. What stress management techniques did you use to cope with the stress this situation created?

12 Why do you think workplace stress seems to be skyrocketing? Do you think it is a trend that will continue? Explain the reasons for your answer. Do you think it is the responsibility of managers and organizations to help employees manage stress? Why or why not?

MANAGEMENT IN PRACTICE: EXPERIENTIAL EXERCISE

Personality Assessment: Jung's Typology and the Myers-Briggs Type Indicator

For each of the following items, circle either a or b. In some cases, both a and b may apply to you. You should decide which is more like you, even if it is only slightly more true.

1 I would rather:

  a. Solve a new and complicated problem
  b. Work on something that I have done before.

2 I like to:

  a. Work alone in a quiet place
  b. Be where 'the action' is.

3 I want a boss who:

a. Establishes and applies criteria in decisions
b. Considers individual needs and makes exceptions.

4 When I work on a project, I:

a. Like to finish it and get some closure
b. Often leave it open for possible change.

5 When making a decision, the most important considerations are:

a. Rational thoughts, ideas and data
b. People's feelings and values.

6 On a project, I tend to:

a. Think it over and over before deciding how to proceed
b. Start working on it right away, thinking about it as I go along.

7 When working on a project, I prefer to:

a. Maintain as much control as possible
b. Explore various options.

8 In my work, I prefer to:

a. Work on several projects at a time, and learn as much as possible about each one
b. Have one project that is challenging and keeps me busy.

9 I often:

a. Make lists and plans whenever I start something and may hate to seriously alter my plans
b. Avoid plans and just let things progress as I work on them.

10 When discussing a problem with colleagues, it is easy for me:

a. To see 'the big picture'
b. To grasp the specifics of the situation.

11 When the phone rings in my office or at home, I usually:

a. Consider it an interruption
b. Don't mind answering it.

12 The word that describes me better is:

a. Analytical
b. Empathetic.

13 When I am working on an assignment, I tend to:

a. Work steadily and consistently
b. Work in bursts of energy with 'downtime' in between.

14 When I listen to someone talk on a subject, I usually try to:

a. Relate it to my own experience and see whether it fits
b. Assess and analyse the message.

15 When I come up with new ideas, I generally:

a. 'Go for it'
b. Like to contemplate the ideas some more.

16 When working on a project, I prefer to:

a. Narrow the scope so it is clearly defined
b. Broaden the scope to include related aspects.

17 When I read something, I usually:

a. Confine my thoughts to what is written there
b. Read between the lines and relate the words to other ideas.

18 When I have to make a decision in a hurry, I often:

a. Feel uncomfortable and wish I had more information
b. Am able to do so with available data.

19 In a meeting, I tend to:

a. Continue formulating my ideas as I talk about them
b. Speak out only after I have carefully thought the issue through.

20 In work, I prefer spending a great deal of time on issues of:

a. Ideas
b. People.

21 In meetings, I am most often annoyed with people who:

a. Come up with many sketchy ideas
b. Lengthen the meeting with many practical details.

22 I tend to be:

  a. A morning person
  b. A night owl.

23 My style in preparing for a meeting is:

  a. To be willing to go in and be responsive
  b. To be fully prepared and sketch an outline of the meeting.

24 In meetings, I would prefer for people to:

  a. Display a fuller range of emotions
  b. Be more task-oriented.

25 I would rather work for an organization where:

  a. My job was intellectually stimulating
  b. I was committed to its goals and mission.

26 On weekends, I tend to:

  a. Plan what I will do
  b. Just see what happens and decide as I go along.

27 I am more:

  a. Outgoing
  b. Contemplative.

28 I would rather work for a boss who is:

  a. Full of new ideas
  b. Practical.

In the following, choose the word in each pair that appeals to you more:

29 a. Social   b. Theoretical

30 a. Ingenuity   b. Practicality

31 a. Organized   b. Adaptable

32 a. Active   b. Concentration

Scoring and Interpretation

Count one point for each of the following items that you circled in the inventory.

Score for I (Introversion)	Score for E (Extroversion)	Score for S (Sensing)	Score for N (Intuition)
2a	2b	1b	1a
6a	6b	10b	10a
11a	11b	13a	13b
15b	15a	16a	16b
19b	19a	17a	17b
22a	22b	21a	21b
27b	27a	28b	28a
32b	32a	30b	30a
Totals _____	_____	_____	_____

Circle the one with more points: Circle the one with more points:

S or N   I or E

(If tied on I/E, don't count #11)   *(If tied on S/N, don't count #16)*

Score for T (Thinking)	Score for F (Feeling)	Score for J (Judging)	Score for P (Perceiving)
3a	3b	4a	4b
5a	5b	7a	7b
12a	12b	8b	8a
14b	14a	9a	9b
20a	20b	18b	18a
24b	24a	23b	23a
25a	25b	26a	26b
29b	29a	31a	31b
Totals _____	_____	_____	_____

Circle the one with more points:
T or F
(If tied on T/F, don't count #24)
Your Score Is: I or E _____ S or N _____ T or F _____ J or P _____
Your MBTI type is _____ (example: INTJ; ESFP; etc.)

Circle the one with more points:
J or P
(If tied on J/P, don't count #23)

Characteristics Frequently Associated with Each Myers-Briggs Type

The Myers-Briggs Type Indicator (MBTI), based on the work of psychologist Carl Jung, is the most widely used personality assessment instrument in the world. The MBTI, which was described in the chapter text, identifies 16 different 'types', shown with their dominant characteristics in the chart above. Remember that no one is a pure type; how-ever, each individual has preferences for introversion versus extroversion, sensing versus intuition, thinking versus feeling, and judging versus perceiving. Read the description of your type as determined by your scores in the survey. Do you believe the description fits your personality?

SOURCE From *Organizational Behaviour: Experience and Cases*, 4th ed. by Dorothy Marcic. © 1995. Reprinted with permission of South-Western, a division of Thomson Learning: http://www.thomsonrights.com.

MANAGEMENT IN PRACTICE: ETHICAL DILEMMA

Should I Fudge the Numbers?

Sara MacIntosh recently joined MicroPhone, a large telecommunications company, to take over the implementation of a massive customer service training project. The programme was created by Kristin Cole, head of human resources and Sara's new boss. According to the grapevine, Kristin was hoping this project alone would give her the 'star quality' she needed to earn a coveted promotion. Industry competition was heating up, and Micro-Phone's strategy called for being the best at cus-tomer service, which meant having the most highly trained people in the industry, especially those who worked directly with customers. Kristin's new training programmr called for an average of one full week of intense customer service training for each of 3000 people and had a price tag of about $40 million.

Kristin put together a team of overworked staffers to develop the training programme, but now she needed someone well qualified and dedi-cated to manage and implement the project. Sara, with eight years of experience, a long list of accom-plishments, and advanced degrees in finance and organizational behaviour, seemed perfect for the job. However, during a thorough review of the pro-posal, Sara discovered some assumptions built into the formulas that raised red flags. She approached Dan Sotal, the team's coordinator, about her con-cerns, but the more Dan tried to explain how the financial projections were derived, the more Sara realized that Kristin's proposal was seriously flawed. No matter how she tried to work them out, the most that could be squeezed out of the $40 mil-lion budget was 20 hours of training per person, not the 40 hours everyone expected for such a high price tag.

Sara knew that, although the proposal had been largely developed before she came on board, it would bear her signature. As she carefully described the problems with the proposal to Kris-tin and outlined the potentially devastating conse-quences, Kristin impatiently tapped her pencil. Finally, she stood up, leaned forward, and inter-rupted Sara, quietly saying, 'Sara, make the num-bers work so that it adds up to 40 hours and stays within the $40 million budget.' Sara glanced up and replied, 'I don't think it can be done unless we either change the number of employees who are to be trained or the cost figure...' Kristin's smile froze on her face and her eyes began to snap as she again interrupted. 'I don't think you understand what I'm saying. We have too much at stake here. *Make the previous numbers work.*' Stunned, Sara belatedly began to realize that Kristin was ordering her to fudge the numbers. She felt an anxiety attack coming on as she wondered what she should do.

What Would You Do?

1 Make the previous numbers work. Kristin and the entire team have put massive amounts of time into the project, and they all expect you to be a team player. You don't want to let them down. Besides, this project is a great opportunity for you in a highly visible position.

2 Stick to your principles and refuse to fudge the numbers. Tell Kristin you will work overtime to help develop an alternative proposal that stays within the budget by providing more training to employees who work directly with customers and fewer training hours for those who don't have direct customer contact.

3 Go to the team and tell them what you've been asked to do. If they refuse to support you, threaten to reveal the true numbers to the CEO and board members.

SOURCE Adapted from Doug Wallace, 'Fudge the Numbers or Leave', *Business Ethics* (May–June 1996): 58–59. Copyright 1996 by New Mountain Media LLC. Reproduced with permission of New Mountain Media LLC in the format Textbook via Copyright Clearance Center.

CASE FOR CRITICAL ANALYSIS 14.1

Heinz Kettler GMBH

As the plane took off from Frankfurt Airport for home, Bert Schultz tried to unwind, something that didn't come naturally to the Kettler mechanical engineer. He needed time to think, and the flight from Frankfurt was a welcome relief. He went to Frankfurt to help two members of his project team solve technical glitches in the new treadmill design. Schultz had been pushing himself and his team hard for three months now, and he didn't know when they would get a break. He was responsible for the technical implementation of the new small size treadmill fitness equipment developed for urban customers in Europe. The new product was badly needed to improve sales for the company in big cities for home use. Kettler sold exercise equipment to gyms and sports stores through a international force of 310 salespeople.

Schultz knew that CEO Dr Katrin Kettler saw the new lightweight compact products as the answer to one of the exercise equipment manufacturer's most persistent problems. Even though Kettler's prices generated healthy sales, follow-up service was spotty. Consequently, getting repeat business from customers – gyms, hotels and corporate recreation centres – was an uphill battle, they were never able to convince urban clients in the need to have their equipment in their home. Excited by the prospect of finally removing this major roadblock, Kartin ordered the new product designed in just ten weeks, a goal Schultz privately thought was unrealistic. He also felt the project budget wasn't adequate. Schultz thought about meeting the next day with his three Dortmund team members, and about the status update he would give his boss, Nicolette Weiss, the senior vice president for sales and marketing. Schultz remembered that Weiss had scheduled ten weeks for this project. He had always been a top performer by driving himself hard, and had been in his management position three years now. He was good with technology, but was frustrated when members of his five-person team didn't seem as committed. Weiss told him last week that she didn't feel a sense of urgency from his team. How could she think that? Bert Schultz requested that team members work evenings and weekends because the budget was too tight to fill a vacant position. They agreed to put in the hours, although they didn't seem enthusiastic.

Still, Kettler was the boss, so if she wanted the job done in ten weeks, Schultz would do everything in his power to deliver, even if it meant the entire team worked nights and weekends. He wasn't

33. Lori Gottlieb, 'How Do I Love Thee?', *The Atlantic Monthly* (March 2006): 58–70.

34. Daniel Goleman, 'Leadership That Gets Results', *Harvard Business Review* (March–April 2000): 79–90; Richard E. Boyatzis and Daniel Goleman, *The Emotional Competence Inventory–University Edition*, The Hay Group, 2001; and Daniel Goleman, *Emotional Intelligence: Why It Can Matter More than IQ* (New York: Bantam Books, 1995).

35. Farnham, 'Are You Smart Enough to Keep Your Job?'

36. Hendrie Weisinger, *Emotional Intelligence at Work* (San Francisco: Jossey–Bass, 2000); D. C. McClelland, 'Identifying Competencies with Behavioural-Event Interviews', *Psychological Science* (Spring 1999): 331–339; Daniel Goleman, 'Leadership That Gets Results', *Harvard Business Review* (March–April 2000): 78–90; D. Goleman, *Working with Emotional Intelligence* (New York: Bantam Books, 1999); and Lorie Parch, 'Testing … 1, 2, 3', *Working Woman* (October 1997): 74–78.

37. D. Goleman, 'Leadership That Gets Results'.

38. F. Romanelli, J. Cain and K. M. Smith (2006) 'Emotional Intelligence as a Predictor of Academic and/or Professional Success', *American Journal of Pharmaceutical Education*, June 15; 70(3): 69.

39. C. S. Daus and N. M. Ashkanasy (2003) 'Will the Real Emotional Intelligence Please Stand Up? On Deconstructing the Emotional Intelligence "Debate"', *The Industrial-Organizational Psychologist* (October) 41(2): 69–72.

40. D. Goleman, (1995) *Emotional intelligence*, New York: Bantam Books.

41. Mayer, J. D., Salovey, P., Caruso, D. R. and Sitaraneos, G. (2003) 'Measuring emotional intelligence with the MSCEIT', V2.0. *Emotion, 3*, 97–105.

42. C.S. Daus and N.M. Ashkanasy, 'Will the real emotional intelligence please stand up? On deconstructing the emotional intelligence 'debate'', *The Industrial and Organizational Psychologist* 41 no 2 (2003): 69–72.

43. J. B. Rotter, 'Generalized Expectancies for Internal versus External Control of Reinforcement', *Psychological Monographs* 80, no. 609 (1966).

44. Andy Serwer, 'There's Something about Cisco', *Fortune* (May 15, 2000); Stephanie N. Mehta, 'Cisco Fractures Its Own Fairy Tale', *Fortune* (May 14, 2001): 104–112.

45. See P. E. Spector, 'Behaviour in Organizations as a Function of Employee's Locus of Control', *Psychological Bulletin* (May 1982): 482–497.

46. T. W. Adorno, E. Frenkel-Brunswick, D. J. Levinson and R. N. Sanford, *The Authoritarian Personality* (New York: Harper & Row, 1950).

47. Richard Christie and Florence Geis, *Studies in Machiavellianism* (New York: Academic Press, 1970).

48. R. G. Vleeming, 'Machiavellianism: A Preliminary Review', *Psychological Reports* (February 1979): 295–310.

49. Christie and Geis, *Studies in Machiavellianism*.

50. Carl Jung, *Psychological Types* (London: Routledge and Kegan Paul, 1923).

51. Mary H. McCaulley, 'Research on the MBTI and Leadership: Taking the Critical First Step', keynote address, The Myers–Briggs Type Indicator and Leadership: An International Research Conference, January 12–14, 1994.

52. Reported in Cullen, 'SATs for J-O-B-S'.

53. Alison Overhold, 'Are You a Polyolefin Optimizer? Take This Quiz!', *Fast Company* (April 2004): 37.

54. Charles A. O'Reilly III, Jennifer Chatman and David F. Caldwell, 'People and Organizational Culture: A Profile Comparison Approach to Assessing Person-Organization Fit', *Academy of Management Journal* 34, no. 3 (1991): 487–516.

55. Anna Muoio, 'Should I Go .Com?' *Fast Company* (July 2000): 164–172.

56. Leder, 'Is That Your Final Answer'?

57. Dogs at the Office – Good for Dogs, People and Business (online) available from http://www.bigpawsonly.com/dog-blog/dogs-at-the-office-good-for-dogs-people-and-business, (accessed November 15, 2008).

58. David A. Kolb, 'Management and the Learning Process', *California Management Review* 18, no. 3 (Spring 1976): 21–31.

59. De'Ann Weimer, 'The Houdini of Consumer Electronics', *BusinessWeek* (June 22, 1998): 88, 92; and http://www.bestbuy.com (accessed June 19, 2006).

60. South African Development Agency PDA, (online) available from http://www.peopledevelopmentafrica.co.za, accessed on November 15, 2008.

61. See David. A. Kolb, I. M. Rubin and J. M. McIntyre, *Organizational Psychology: An Experimental Approach*, 3rd ed. (Englewood Cliffs, NJ: Prentice Hall, 1984): 27–54.

62. Stephanie Gruner, 'Our Company, Ourselves', *Inc.* (April 1998): 127–128.

63. Ira Sager, 'Big Blue's Blunt Bohemian', *BusinessWeek* (June 14, 1999): 107–112.

64. Paul Roberts, 'The Best Interest of the Patient Is the Only Interest to be Considered', *Fast Company* (April 1999): 149–162.

65. T. A. Beehr and R. S. Bhagat, *Human Stress and Cognition in Organizations: An Integrated Perspective* (New York: Wiley, 1985); and Bruce Cryer, Rollin McCraty and Doc Childre, 'Pull the Plug on Stress', *Harvard Business Review* (July 2003): 102–107.

66. Ekramul Hoque and Mayenul Islam, 'Contribution of Some Behavioural Factors to Absenteeism of Manufacturing Workers in Bangladesh', *Pakistan Journal of Psychological Research* 18, no. 3–4 (Winter 2003): 81–96; US research study conducted by HERO, a not-for-profit coalition of organizations with common interests in health promotion, disease management, and health-related productivity research, and reported in Bruce Cryer, Rollin McCraty, and Doc Childre, 'Pull the Plug on Stress', *Harvard Business Review* (July 2003): 102–107.

67. M. Friedman and R. Rosenman, *Type A Behaviour and Your Heart* (New York: Knopf, 1974).

68. John L. Haughom, 'How to Pass the Stress Test', *CIO* (May 1, 2003): 50–52; Quote from Cora Daniels, 'The Last Taboo', *Fortune* (October 28, 2002): 137–144.

69. Haughom, 'How to Pass the Stress Test'.

70. Reported in 'Work Stress Is Costly', *Morning Call* (October 18, 2005): E1.

71. Families and Work Institute survey, reported in 'Reworking Work', *Time* (July 25, 2005): 50–55; Spherion survey, reported in Donna Callea, 'Workers Feeling the Burn: Employee Burnout a New Challenge to Productivity, Morale, Experts Say', *News Journal* (March 27, 2006): A11; 'Workplace Stress Now Causing Huge Loss of Working Days', *Birmingham Post* (April 19, 2006): 23; Vani Doraisamy, 'Young Techies Swell the Ranks of the Depressed', *The Hindu* (October 11, 2005): 1.

72. Gentelman, A. (2005) 'Painful truth of the call-centre cyber coolies', *Guardian online*, available from http://www.guardian.co.uk/business/2005/oct/30/india.internationalnews, accessed on (November 15, 2008).

73. Kris Maher, 'At Verizon Call Center, Stress Is Seldom on Hold', *The Wall Street Journal* (January 16, 2001): B1, B12.

74. Rama Lakshmi, 'India Call Centers Suffer Storm of 4-Letter Words; Executives Blame American Anger Over Outsourcing', *The Washington Post* (February 27, 2005): A22.

75. Donalee Moulton, 'Buckling Under the Pressure', *OH & S Canada* 19, no. 8 (December 2003): 36.

76. Claire Sykes, 'Say Yes to Less Stress', *Office Solutions* (July–August 2003): 26; and Andrea Higbie, 'Quick Lessons in the Fine Old Art of Unwinding', *The New York Times* (February 25, 2001): BU10.

77. Rosabeth Moss Kanter, 'Balancing Work and Life', *Knight-Ridder Tribune News Service* (April 8, 2005): 1.

78. Leslie Gross Klass, 'Quiet Time at Work Helps Employee Stress', *Johnson City Press* (January 28, 2001): 30.

79. Moulton, 'Buckling Under the Pressure'.

80. David T. Gordon, 'Balancing Act', *CIO* (October 15, 2001): 58–62.

81. N. Moguilnaia and C. Hall (2006) 'Hallmark Consumer Services' Case Study.

CHAPTER OUTLINE

© MBBIRDY/ISTOCK

LEARNING OBJECTIVES

After reading this chapter, you should be able to:

1 Define leadership and explain its importance for organizations.

2 Describe how leadership is changing in today's organizations.

3 Identify personal characteristics associated with effective leaders.

4 Define task-oriented behaviour and people-oriented behaviour and explain how these categories are used to evaluate and adapt leadership style.

5 Describe Hersey and Blanchard's situational theory and its application to subordinate participation.

6 Explain the path–goal model of leadership.

7 Discuss how leadership fits the organizational situation and how organizational characteristics can substitute for leadership behaviours.

8 Describe transformational leadership and when it should be used.

9 Identify the five sources of leader power and the tactics leaders use to influence others.

10 Explain servant leadership and moral leadership and their importance in contemporary organizations.

CHAPTER 15

LEADERSHIP

Manager's Challenge

Building a motivated, satisfied and committed workforce for low-skill, low-wage jobs such as food service, hospital cleaning and lawn mowing can be a nightmare. Vacman Cleaning from Scotland is involved in all those businesses and more as a leader in managed services carrying out daily office cleaning, industrial cleaning, hygiene services or house clearances for its customers. Alastair Irvine loves working for Vacman Cleaning, and he takes great pride in his new job as head of a service operation that cleans factories and offices in the Edinburgh area. Yet, he had no idea how hard it would be to keep 100 mostly non-English-speaking immigrants motivated and inspired to give their best to a minimum wage job. Morale is dismal, and turnover exceeds 50 per cent a year. People don't seem to take any pride in their work. Moreover, some of the valuables have a funny way of disappearing from the offices. Irvine is determined to turn the operation around by creating an environment where employees feel committed to the company, their fellow workers and customers. But how is he to do it? He's always believed that managers shouldn't get involved in the personal problems of their subordinates, but Irvine thinks he might need a different approach to tap into the energy and enthusiasm of his employees.[1]

TAKE A MOMENT

If you were in Alastair Irvine's position, what leadership approach would you take? Do you think it is possible for a leader to improve job satisfaction and organizational commitment for low-skilled, low-paid employees such as those Irvine is supervising?

What's Your Personal Style?

Ideas about effective leadership change over time. To understand your approach to leadership, think about your personal style toward others or toward a student group to which you belong, and then answer each item below as Mostly True or Mostly False for you.

		Mostly True	Mostly False
1	I am a modest, unassuming person.	☐	☐
2	When a part of a group, I am more concerned about how the group does than how I do.	☐	☐
3	I prefer to lead with quiet modesty rather than personal assertiveness.	☐	☐
4	I feel personally responsible if the team does poorly.	☐	☐
5	I act with quiet determination.	☐	☐
6	I resolve to do whatever needs doing to produce the best result for the group.	☐	☐
7	I am proactive to help the group succeed.	☐	☐
8	I facilitate high standards for my group's performance.	☐	☐

SCORING AND INTERPRETATION A recent view of leadership called Level Five Leadership says that the most successful leaders have two prominent qualities: humility and will. Give yourself one point for each item marked Mostly True.

Humility: Items 1, 2, 3, 4

Will: Items 5, 6, 7, 8

Humility means a quiet, modest, self-effacing manner. A humble person puts group or organizational success ahead of one's personal success. 'Will' means a quiet but fierce resolve to stay the course to achieve the group's desired outcome and to help the group succeed. The traits of humility and will are opposite the traditional idea of leadership as loud and self-centred. If you scored 3 or 4 on either humility or will, you are on track to level 5 leadership, which says that ordinary people often make excellent leaders.

In the previous chapter, we explored differences in attitudes and personality that affect behaviour. The attitudes and behaviours of leaders play an important role in shaping employee attitudes, such as their job satisfaction and organizational commitment. Yet there are as many variations among leaders as there are among other individuals, and many different styles of leadership can be effective.

Different leaders behave in different ways depending on their individual differences as well as their followers' needs and the organizational situation. For example, contrast the styles of Pat McGovern, founder and chair of International Data Group, a technology publishing and research firm that owns magazines such as *CIO*, *PC World* and *Computerworld*, with that of Tom Siebel, CEO of software company

Siebel Systems. McGovern treats each employee to lunch at the Ritz on his or her tenth anniversary with IDG to tell them how important they are to the success of the company. He personally thanks almost every person in every business unit once a year, which takes about a month of his time. Managers provide him with a list of accomplishments for all their direct reports, which McGovern memorizes the night before his visit so he can congratulate people on specific accomplishments. In addition to appreciating and caring about employees, McGovern also shows that he believes in them by decentralizing decision-making so that people have the autonomy to make their own decisions about how best to accomplish organizational goals. Tom Siebel, in contrast, is known as a disciplined and dispassionate manager who remains somewhat aloof from his employees and likes to maintain strict control over every aspect of the business. He enforces a dress code, sets tough goals and standards, and holds people strictly accountable. 'We go to work to realize our professional ambitions, not to have a good time,' Siebel says.[2] Both Siebel and McGovern have been successful as leaders, although their styles are quite different.

This chapter explores one of the most widely discussed and researched topics in management–leadership. Here we define leadership and explore the differences between leadership and management. We look at some important leadership approaches for contemporary organizations, as well as examine trait, behavioural and contingency theories of leadership effectiveness, discuss charismatic and transformational leadership, and consider how leaders use power and influence to get things done. The final section of the chapter discusses servant leadership and moral leadership, two enduring approaches that have received renewed emphasis in recent years. Chapters 16 through to 18 will look in detail at many of the functions of leadership, including employee motivation, communication and encouraging teamwork.

The Nature of Leadership

No topic is probably more important to organizational success today than leadership. Leadership matters. In most situations, a team, military unit or volunteer organization is only as good as its leader. Consider the war situation in Iraq, as military United Nations' advisors strive to build the Iraqi forces that can take over security duties without support from coalition troops. Many trainers say they encounter excellent individual soldiers and junior leaders but that many of the senior commanders are stuck in old authoritarian patterns that undermine their units. Whether an Iraqi unit succeeds or fails often comes down to one person – its commander – so advisors are putting emphasis on finding and strengthening good leaders.[3] Top leaders make a difference in business organizations as well. Baron Partners Fund, which picks stocks based largely on an evaluation of companies' senior executives, was the best-performing diversified stock fund of 2004, with a return of 42 per cent. Manager Ron Baron says top leaders who are smart, honourable, and treat their employees right typically lead their companies to greater financial success and greater shareholder returns.[4]

The concept of leadership continues to evolve as the needs of organizations change. Among all the ideas and writings about leadership, three aspects stand out – people, influence and goals. Leadership occurs among people, involves the use of influence, and is used to attain goals.[5] *Influence* means that the relationship among people is not passive. Moreover, influence is designed to achieve some end or goal. Thus, leadership as defined here is the ability to influence people toward the attainment of goals. This definition captures the idea that leaders are involved with other people in the achievement of goals.

Leadership
The ability to influence people toward the attainment of organizational goals.

© JACK SULLIVAN/ALAMY

Leadership is reciprocal, occurring *among* people.[6] Leadership is a 'people' activity, distinct from administrative paper shuffling or problem-solving activities. Leadership is dynamic and involves the use of power to influence people and get things done.

Contemporary Leadership

The concept of leadership evolves as the needs of organizations change. That is, the environmental context in which leadership is practiced influences which approach might be most effective, as well as what kinds of leaders are most admired by society. The technology, economic conditions, labour conditions, and social and cultural mores of the times all play a role. A significant influence on leadership styles in recent years is the turbulence and uncertainty of the environment in which most organizations are operating. Ethical and economic difficulties, corporate governance concerns, globalization, changes in technology, new ways of working, shifting employee expectations, and significant social transitions have contributed to a shift in how we think about and practice leadership.

Of particular interest for leadership in contemporary times is a *post-heroic approach* that focuses on the subtle, unseen, and often unrewarded acts that good leaders perform every day, rather than on the grand accomplishments of celebrated business heroes.[7] During the 1980s and 1990s, leadership became equated with larger-than-life personalities, strong egos and personal ambitions. In contrast, the post-heroic leader's major characteristic is humility.[8] **Humility** means being unpretentious and modest rather than arrogant and prideful. Humble leaders don't have to be in the centre of things. They quietly build strong, enduring companies by developing and supporting others rather than touting their own abilities and accomplishments. Two approaches that are in tune with post-heroic leadership for today's times are Level 5 leadership and interactive leadership, a style that is commonly used by women leaders.

Level 5 Leadership

A recent five-year study conducted by Jim Collins and his research associates identified the critical importance of what Collins calls *Level 5 leadership* in transforming companies from merely good to truly great organizations.[9] As described in his book *Good to Great: Why Some Companies Make the Leap … and Others Don't*, Level 5 leadership refers to the highest level in a hierarchy of manager capabilities, as illustrated in Exhibit 15.1. A key characteristic of Level 5 leaders is an almost complete lack of ego, coupled with a fierce resolve to do what is best for the organization. In contrast to the view of great leaders as larger-than-life personalities with strong egos and big ambitions, Level 5 leaders often seem shy and unpretentious. Although they accept full responsibility for mistakes, poor results or failures, Level 5 leaders give credit for successes to other people. For example, Joseph F. Cullman III, former CEO of Philip Morris,

CONCEPT CONNECTION
At a time when all business leaders are preoccupied with socially responsible leadership, John Bird has been leading the way since founding the Big Issue magazine in 1991 – now the UK's most successful social enterprise. Renowned for his original and often trenchant views on business and society, Bird has led a unique network of homeless vendors to circulation of 147,000 copies a week amidst a magazine industry in decline. It provides vendors with £8 million a year – providing an alternative to begging or crime – and is also published in Australia, Japan, South Africa, Kenya, Ethiopia, Malawi and Namibia with plans to launch in India and Pakistan well underway.

Humility
Being unpretentious and modest rather than arrogant and prideful.

TAKE A MOMENT Go to the Ethical Dilemma on page 596 that pertains to post-heroic leadership for turbulent times.

Exhibit 15.1 The Level 5 Leadership Hierarchy

Level 5: The Level 5 Leader

Builds an enduring great organization through a combination of personal humility and professional resolve.

Level 4: The Effective Executive

Builds widespread commitment to a clear and compelling vision; stimulates people to high performance.

Level 3: Competent Manager

Sets plans and organizes people for the efficient and effective pursuit of objectives.

Level 2: Contributing Team Member

Contributes to the achievement of team goals; works effectively with others in a group.

Level 1: Highly Capable Individual

Productive contributor; offers talent, knowledge, skills and good work habits as an individual employee.

SOURCE: 'The Level 5 Leadership Hierarchy' from, *Good to Great: Why Some Companies Make the Leap . . . and Others Don't*, by Jim Collins. Reprinted by permission of HarperCollins Publishers, Inc.

staunchly refused to accept credit for the company's long-term success, citing his great colleagues, successors and predecessors as the reason for the accomplishments. Another example is Enrico Bondi. When he was promoted to CEO of Parmalat spa, Bondi questioned whether the board really wanted to appoint him because he didn't believe he had the qualifications a CEO needed.

Women's Ways of Leading

The focus on minimizing personal ambition and developing others is also a hallmark of *interactive leadership*, which has been found to be common among female leaders. Research indicates that women's style of leadership is typically different from most men's and is particularly suited to today's organizations.[10] Using data from actual performance evaluations, one study found that when rated by peers, subordinates and bosses, female managers score significantly higher than men on abilities such as motivating others, fostering communication and listening.[11]

Interactive leadership means that the leader favours a consensual and collaborative process, and influence derives from relationships rather than position power and formal authority.[12] For example, Nancy Hawthorne, former chief financial officer at Continental Cablevision Inc., felt that her role as a leader was to delegate tasks and authority to others and to help them be more effective. 'I was being traffic cop and coach and facilitator,' Hawthorne says. 'I was always into building a department that hummed.'[13] Similarly, Terri Kelly, who took over as CEO of W. L. Gore in 2005, says her goal is to provide overall direction and guidance, not to micromanage and tell people how to do their jobs.[14] It is important to note that men can be interactive leaders as well, as demonstrated by the example of Pat McGovern of International Data Group earlier in the chapter. For McGovern, having personal contact with employees and letting them know they're appreciated is a primary responsibility of leaders. The characteristics associated with interactive leadership are emerging as valuable qualities for both male and female leaders in today's workplace. Values associated with interactive leadership include personal humility, inclusion, relationship building and caring.

Interactive leadership
A leadership style characterized by values such as inclusion, collaboration, relationship building and caring.

INNOVATIVE WAY

Parmalat[15]

Enrico Bondi, who led Parmalat since 2003, is a classic example of a Level 5 leader. Few people have ever heard of him – and that's probably just the way he wanted it. In Italy, Parmalat's main businesses are selling long-life milk, yogurts and fruit juices. The company's major plant in Collechio is one of the largest of its type in Europe.

Now the government-appointed administrator, Enrico Bondi, has almost completed his salvage operation. Bondi has won the confidence of the workers at the company's headquarters near Parma by often eating with them in the canteen after queuing for food. It strengthened team spirit when the workers feared they would all lose their jobs. For the New Year, Bondi sent them a message saying courage, cohesion and strength were still needed to assure their future.

Very quickly he put a new management team in place. Dubbed 'the Bondi boys', they had the job of salvaging something from the corporate wreckage of a scandal described as Europe's Enron. Most of the Bondi boys, like Mr Bondi himself, were outsiders to the company with proven track records in other corporate rescues.

However, one of the biggest problems that Enrico Bondi identified from the start when the company hit financial crisis was getting suppliers to maintain milk deliveries. This problem was solved by giving Parmalat's lorry drivers large wads of cash so they could pay farmers and wholesalers on the spot for their products.

Bondi was never featured in splashy articles in *Fortune* magazine or *The Wall Street Journal,* apart from the one which depicted the nature of financial scandal Parmalat was dealing with when Bondi took over the reins of power. Yet, far from being meek, Bondi demonstrated an aggressive determination to revive Parmalat, rebuilding confidence in a company that at the time was a stodgy entity that had seen years of falling stock prices. Anyone who interpreted his appearance and demeanour as a sign of ineptness soon learned differently, as Bondi made difficult decisions that set Parmalat on the path to recovery.

As the example of Enrico Bondi illustrates, despite their personal humility, Level 5 leaders have a strong will to do whatever it takes to produce great and lasting results for their organizations. They are extremely ambitious for their companies rather than for themselves. This goal becomes highly evident in the area of succession planning. Level 5 leaders develop a solid corps of leaders throughout the organization, so that when they leave the company it can continue to thrive and grow even stronger. Egocentric leaders, by contrast often set their successors up for failure because it will be a testament to their own greatness if the company doesn't perform well without them. Rather than an organization built around 'a genius with a thousand helpers', Level 5 leaders build an organization with many strong leaders who can step forward and continue the company's success. These leaders want everyone in the organization to develop to their fullest potential.

TAKE A MOMENT   As a new manager, will your interpersonal style fit the contemporary leadership approaches described above? To find out, complete the New Manager Self Test opposite.

Leadership versus Management

Much has been written in recent years about the leadership role of managers. Management and leadership are both important to organizations. Effective managers have to be leaders, too, because distinctive qualities are associated with management and leadership that provide different strengths for the organization, as illustrated in Exhibit 15.2. As shown in the exhibit, management and leadership reflect two

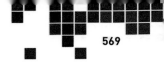

 NEW MANAGER SELF-TEST

Interpersonal Patterns

The majority of a new manager's work is accomplished through interpersonal relationships. To understand your relationship pattern, consider the following verbs. These 20 verbs describe some of the ways people feel and act from time to time. Think about your behaviour in groups. How do you feel and act in groups? Tick the five verbs that best describe your behaviour in groups as you see it.

☐ acquiesce	☐ coordinate	☐ lead
☐ advise	☐ criticize	☐ oblige
☐ agree	☐ direct	☐ relinquish
☐ analyze	☐ disapprove	☐ resist
☐ assist	☐ evade	☐ retreat
☐ concede	☐ initiate	☐ withdraw
☐ concur	☐ judge	

Two underlying patterns of interpersonal behaviour are represented in the preceding list: *dominance* (authority or control) and *sociability* (intimacy or friendliness). Most individuals tend either to like to control things (high dominance) or to let others control things (low dominance). Similarly, most persons tend either to be warm and personal (high sociability) or to be somewhat distant and impersonal (low sociability). In the following diagram, circle the five verbs in the list that you used to describe yourself. The set of ten verbs in either horizontal row (sociability dimension) or vertical column (dominance dimension) in which three or more are circled represents your tendency in interpersonal behaviour.

	High Dominance	Low Dominance
High Sociability	advises	acquiesces
	coordinates	agrees
	directs	assists
	initiates	concurs
	leads	obliges
Low Sociability	analyzes	concedes
	criticizes	evades
	disapproves	relinquishes
	judges	retreats
	resists	withdraws

Your behaviour pattern suggested in the diagram is a clue to your interpersonal style as a new manager. Which of the four quadrants provides the best description of you? Is that the type of leader you aspire to become? Generally speaking the high sociability and high dominance pattern reflects the type of leader to which many new managers aspire. How does your pattern correspond to the Level 5 and interactive leadership patterns described in the text?

SOURCE: David W. Johnson and Frank P. Johnson, *Joining Together: Group Theory and Group Skills,* 8th ed. (New York: Allyn and Bacon, 2003): 189–190. Used with permission.

Exhibit 15.3 Personal Characteristics of Leaders

Physical Characteristics	Personality	Work-Related Characteristics
Energy	Self-confidence	Achievement drive, desire to excel
Physical stamina	Honesty and integrity	Conscientiousness in pursuit of goals
	Enthusiasm	Persistence against obstacles, tenacity
	Desire to lead	
	Independence	

Intelligence and Ability	Social Characteristics	Social Background
Intelligence, cognitive ability	Sociability, interpersonal skills	Education
Knowledge	Cooperativeness	Mobility
Judgement, decisiveness	Ability to enlist cooperation	
	Tact, diplomacy	

SOURCE: Based on Bernard M. Bass, *Bass & Stogdill's Handbook of Leadership: Theory, Research, and Managerial Applications,* 3rd ed. (New York: The Free Press, 1990): 80–81; and S. A. Kirkpatrick and E. A. Locke, 'Leadership: Do Traits Matter?', *Academy of Management Executive* 5, no. 2 (1991): 48–60.

© GETTY IMAGES

CONCEPT CONNECTION Angela and David Hart, founders of Nappy Express, offer a comprehensive range of baby related products to their customers in and around London, and demonstrate many of the personal traits associated with effective leadership. For example, they displayed intelligence, ability, knowledge and judgment by knowing that to make their company successful, it had to be unique. Everything about Nappy Express is tailored to children and families. Nappy Express characters perch on lilac and teal colours and cater for the variety of family needs from baby care to groceries and even pet products.[25]

in organizing and directing people toward achieving the organization's goals. Yet Mulqueen knows that leaders don't get people to rally around them simply by issuing orders. He's never intimidating, and he's always willing to listen to other people's ideas, allow people autonomy in how they accomplish goals, and show appreciation and respect. Mulqueen's high consideration–high initiating structure leadership approach has turned the Greater Chicago Food Depository into one of the nation's most effective hunger-relief agencies.[22] Successful pro football coaches also often use a high–high style.[23] For example, coaches have to keep players focused on winning football games by scheduling structured practices, emphasizing careful planning, and so forth. However, the best coaches are those who genuinely care about and show concern for their players.

Some research, however, indicates that the high–high style is not necessarily the best. These studies suggest that effective leaders may be high on consideration and low on initiating structure or low on consideration and high on initiating structure, depending on the situation.[24]

Michigan Studies

Studies at the University of Michigan at about the same time took a different approach by comparing the behaviour of effective and ineffective supervisors.[26] The most effective supervisors were those who focused on the subordinates' human needs in order to 'build effective work groups with high performance goals'. The Michigan researchers used the term *employee-centred leaders* for leaders who established high performance goals and displayed supportive behaviour toward subordinates. The less-effective leaders were called *job-centred leaders*; these leaders tended to be less concerned with goal achievement and human needs in favour of meeting schedules, keeping costs low, and achieving production efficiency.

The Leadership Grid

Building on the work of the Ohio State and Michigan studies, Blake and Mouton of the University of Texas proposed a two-dimensional leadership theory called the leadership grid.[27] The two-dimensional model and five of its seven major management styles are depicted in Exhibit 15.4. Each axis on the grid is a nine-point scale, with 1 meaning low concern and 9 high concern.

Team management (9, 9) often is considered the most effective style and is recommended for managers because organization members work together to accomplish tasks. *Country club management* (1, 9) occurs when primary emphasis is given to people rather than to work outputs. *Authority-compliance management* (9, 1) occurs when efficiency in operations is the dominant orientation. *Middle-of-the-road management* (5, 5) reflects a moderate amount of concern for both people and production. *Impoverished management* (1, 1) means the absence of a management philosophy; managers exert little effort toward interpersonal relationships or work accomplishment.

Leadership grid
A two-dimensional leadership theory that measures the leader's concern for people and for production.

Exhibit 15.4 The Leadership Grid® Figure

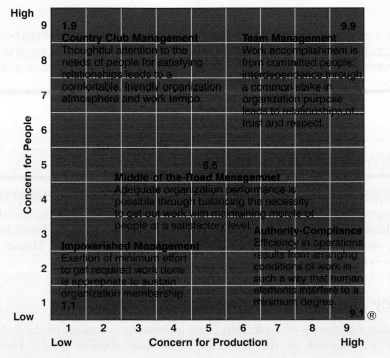

SOURCE: The Leadership Grid® figure, Paternalism figure and Opportunism from *Leadership Dilemmas-Grid Solutions*, by Robert R. Blake and Anne Adams McCanse (formerly the Managerial Grid by Robert R. Blace and Jase S. Mouton). Houston: Gulf Publishing Company. (Grid figure: p. 29, Paternalism figure: p. 30, Opportunism figure: p. 31.) Copyright © 1991, by Blake and Mouton, and Scientific Methods, Inc. Reproduced by permission of the owners.

INNOVATIVE WAY

Michelin Tyre and Tires Plus

Edouard Michelin – president and CEO of the famous tyre company that his great grandfather and a great great uncle founded 120 years ago – is in no doubt about the importance of the supply chain to his operation. 'The supply chain is everywhere,' he insists. 'Everything is about the supply chain.'

He complains that not enough people in companies understand how the supply chain works, and says it has to be considered in the strategic choices businesses make. That means he's fully aware that manufacturing companies the length and breadth of Europe are burning lots of rubber to move their production set-ups to the lowest-cost part of the globe that will have them. As a result he makes no apologies for his hard-driving leadership style. His emphasis on ambitious goals, tough standards and bottom-line results has brought renewed health and vitality to Michelin globally.

Compare Michelin's hard-nosed approach to that of Tom Gegax, who calls himself the head coach of Tires Plus, a fast-growing chain of retail tyre stores. Gegax believes that you cannot manage people the same way as you manage fixed assets. His emphasis is on treating employees just as well as they are expected to treat their customers. Gegax personally leads classes at Tires Plus University, where employees learn not just about changing tyres but about how to make their whole lives better. Gegax also makes sure stores are clean, bright and airy, so that employees have a pleasant work environment. He believes all these details translate into better service. Employees, as well as customers, like the approach. 'The last thing the world needs is another chain of stores,' Gegax says. 'What it does need is a company with a new business model – one that embraces customers and employees as whole people.'[28]

The leadership style of Edouard Michelin is characterized by high concern for tasks and production (task-oriented behaviour) and low-to-moderate concern for people (people-oriented behaviour). Tom Gegax, in contrast, is high on concern for people and moderate on concern for production. Both leaders are successful, although they display different leadership styles because of their different situations. The next group of theories builds on the leader-follower relationship of behavioural approaches to explore how organizational situations affect the leader's approach.

TAKE A MOMENT As a new manager, realize that both task-oriented behaviour and people-oriented behaviour are important, although some situations call for a greater degree of one over the other. Go to the Experiential Exercise on page 594 to measure your degree of task-orientation and people-orientation.

Contingency approach
A model of leadership that describes the relationship between leadership styles and specific organizational situations.

Situational theory
A contingency approach to leadership that links the leader's behavioural style with the task readiness of subordinates.

Contingency Approaches

Several models of leadership explain the relationship between leadership styles and specific situations. They are termed **contingency approaches** and include the situational theory of Hersey and Blanchard, the leadership model developed by Fiedler and his associates, the path–goal theory presented by Evans and House, and the substitutes-for-leadership concept.

Hersey and Blanchard's Situational Theory

The **situational theory** of leadership is an interesting extension of the behavioural theories summarized in the leadership grid (see Exhibit 15.4). Hersey and

Blanchard's approach focuses a great deal of attention on the characteristics of followers in determining appropriate leadership behaviour. The point of Hersey and Blanchard is that subordinates vary in readiness level. People low in task readiness, because of little ability or training, or insecurity, need a different leadership style than those who are high in readiness and have good ability, skills, confidence and willingness to work.[29] According to the situational theory, a leader can adopt one of four leadership styles, based on a combination of relationship (concern for people) and task (concern for production) behaviour. The appropriate style depends on the readiness level of followers.

Exhibit 15.5 summarizes the relationship between leader style and follower readiness. The *telling style* reflects a high concern for tasks and a low concern for people and relationships. This highly directive style involves giving explicit directions about how tasks should be accomplished. The *selling style* is based on a high concern for both people and tasks. With this approach, the leader explains decisions and gives subordinates a chance to ask questions and gain clarity and understanding about work tasks. The next leader behaviour style, the *participating style*, is based on a combination of high concern for people and relationships and low concern for production tasks. The leader shares ideas with subordinates, gives them a chance to participate and facilitates decision-making. The fourth style, the *delegating style*, reflects a low concern for both relationships and tasks. This leader style provides little direction and little support because the leader turns over responsibility for decisions and their implementation to subordinates.

Exhibit 15.5 Hersey and Blanchard's Situational Theory of Leadership

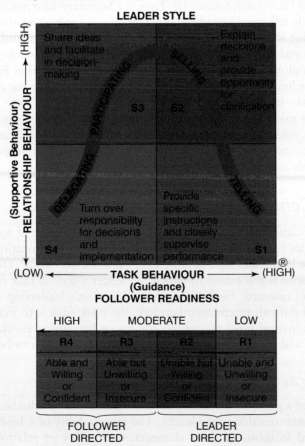

The bell-shaped curve in Exhibit 15.5 is called a prescriptive curve because it indicates when each leader style should be used. The readiness level of followers is indicated in the lower part of the exhibit. R1 is low readiness and R4 represents high readiness. The telling style is for low readiness followers because people are unable or unwilling, because of poor ability and skills, little experience or insecurity, to take responsibility for their own task behaviour. The leader is specific, telling people exactly what to do, how to do it, and when. The selling and participating styles work for followers at moderate readiness levels. For example, followers might lack some education and experience for the job but have high confidence, interest and willingness to learn. As shown in the exhibit, the selling style is effective in this situation because it involves giving direction but also includes seeking input from others and clarifying tasks rather than simply instructing that they be performed. When followers have the necessary skills and experience but are somewhat insecure in their abilities or lack high willingness, the participating style enables the leader to guide followers' development and act as a resource for advice and assistance. When followers demonstrate high readiness, that is they have high levels of education, experience and readiness to accept responsibility for their own task behaviour, the delegating style can effectively be used. Because of the high readiness level of followers, the leader can delegate responsibility for decisions and their implementation to subordinates who have the skills, abilities and positive attitudes to follow through. The leader provides a general goal and sufficient authority to do the task as followers see fit.

To apply the Hersey and Blanchard model, the leader diagnoses the readiness level of followers and adopts the appropriate style – telling, selling, participating or delegating. Using the incorrect style can hurt morale and performance. When president of Harvard University, former US Treasury Secretary Lawrence Summers, tried to use a primarily telling style with followers who were at high readiness levels, it led to serious conflict with some faculty members and eventual demands for his ouster. Summers employed an assertive top-down style with followers who think of themselves not as employees but as partners in an academic enterprise. Faculty members at Harvard have long been accustomed to decentralized, democratic decision-making and having a say in matters such as department mergers or new programmes of study. Summers made many decisions on his own that followers thought should be put to a faculty vote. Although students in general supported Summers, the conflicts and a vote of no-confidence from some faculty convinced Summers to resign with many of his goals and plans for the university unrealized.[30]

Fiedler's Contingency Theory

Whereas Hersey and Blanchard focused on the characteristics of followers, Fiedler and his associates looked at some other elements of the organizational situation to assess when one leadership style is more effective than another.[31] The starting point for Fiedler's theory is the extent to which the leader's style is task oriented or relationship (people) oriented. Fiedler considered a person's leadership style to be relatively fixed and difficult to change; therefore, the basic idea is to match the leader's style with the situation most favourable for his or her effectiveness. By diagnosing leadership style and the organizational situation, the correct fit can be arranged.

Situation: Favourable or Unfavourable?

The suitability of a person's leadership style is determined by whether the situation is favourable or unfavourable to the leader. The favourability of a leadership situation can be analyzed in terms of three elements: the quality of relationships between leader and followers, the degree of task structure, and the extent to which the leader has formal authority over followers.[32]

For example, a situation would be considered *highly favourable* to the leader when leader-member relationships are positive, tasks are highly structured, and the leader has formal authority over followers. In this situation, followers trust, respect and have confidence in the leader. The group's tasks are clearly defined, involve specific procedures, and have clear, explicit goals. In addition, the leader has formal authority to direct and evaluate followers, along with the power to reward or punish. A situation would be considered *highly unfavourable* to the leader when leader-member relationships are poor, tasks are highly unstructured, and the leader has little formal authority. In a highly unfavourable situation, followers have little respect for or confidence and trust in the leader. Tasks are vague and ill-defined, lacking in clear-cut procedures and guidelines. The leader has little formal authority to direct subordinates and does not have the power to issue rewards or punishments.

Matching Leader Style to the Situation

Combining the three situational characteristics yields a variety of leadership situations, ranging from highly favourable to highly unfavourable. When Fiedler examined the relationships among leadership style and situational favourability, he found the pattern shown in Exhibit 15.6. Task-oriented leaders are more effective when the situation is either highly favourable or highly unfavourable. Relationship-oriented leaders are more effective in situations of moderate favourability.

The task-oriented leader excels in the favourable situation because everyone gets along, the task is clear, and the leader has power; all that is needed is for someone to lead the charge and provide direction. Similarly, if the situation is highly unfavourable to the leader, a great deal of structure and task direction is needed. A strong leader will define task structure and establish authority over subordinates. Because leader-member relations are poor anyway, a strong task orientation will make no difference in the leader's popularity.

The relationship-oriented leader performs better in situations of intermediate favourability because human relations skills are important in achieving high group performance. In these situations, the leader may be moderately well liked, have some power, and supervize jobs that contain some ambiguity. A leader with good interpersonal skills can create a positive group atmosphere that will improve relationships, clarify task structure and establish position power.

A leader, then, needs to know two things in order to use Fiedler's contingency theory. First, the leader should know whether he or she has a relationship- or task-oriented style. Second, the leader should diagnose the situation and determine whether leader-member relations, task structure and position power are favourable or unfavourable.

Fiedler believed fitting leader style to the situation can yield big dividends in profits and efficiency.[33] On the other hand, the model has also been criticized.[34] For one thing, some researchers have challenged the idea that leaders cannot adjust their styles as situational characteristics change. Despite criticisms, Fiedler's model has continued to influence leadership studies. Fiedler's research called attention to the importance of finding the correct fit between leadership style and the situation.

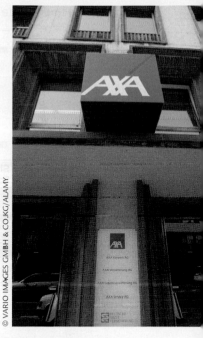

© VARIO IMAGES GMBH & CO.KG/ALAMY

CONCEPT CONNECTION
At AXA Investment Managers, an asset management firm in London, UK, the quality of leader-member relationships is high. CEO Dominique Carrel-Billiard has gained the respect and trust of colleagues and followers because he has proven that he has the integrity, skills and commitment to keep the company thriving. Carrel-Billiard can be characterized as a task-oriented leader because he is focused, prepared and competitive, and he expects others to be as well. According to Fiedler's contingency theory, Carrel-Billiard's style succeeds at AXA because of positive leader-member relations, strong leader position power and jobs that contain some degree of task structure.

Exhibit 15.6 How Leader Style Fits the Situation

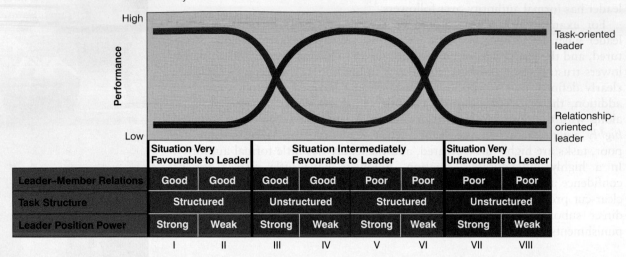

	Situation Very Favourable to Leader		Situation Intermediately Favourable to Leader				Situation Very Unfavourable to Leader	
Leader–Member Relations	Good	Good	Good	Good	Poor	Poor	Poor	Poor
Task Structure	Structured		Unstructured		Structured		Unstructured	
Leader Position Power	Strong	Weak	Strong	Weak	Strong	Weak	Strong	Weak
	I	II	III	IV	V	VI	VII	VIII

SOURCE: Based on Fred E. Fiedler, 'The Effects of Leadership Training and Experience: A Contingency Model Interpretation', *Administrative Science Quarterly* 17 (1972): 455.

TAKE A MOMENT

As a new manager, remember that different situations and different followers may require different approaches to leadership. Pay attention to the situation and the followers to determine how much structure and direction followers need.

Path–Goal Theory

Path–goal theory
A contingency approach to leadership specifying that the leader's responsibility is to increase subordinates' motivation by clarifying the behaviours necessary for task accomplishment and rewards.

Another contingency approach to leadership is called the path–goal theory.[35] According to the **path–goal theory**, the leader's responsibility is to increase followers' motivation and clarify the path to attain personal and organizational goals.[36] This model includes two sets of contingencies: leader behaviour and the use of rewards to meet subordinates' needs.[37] In the Fiedler theory the assumption would be to switch leaders as situations change, but the path–goal theory suggests that leaders can switch their behaviours to match the situation.

Leader Behaviour

The path–goal theory suggests a fourfold classification of leader behaviours.[38] These classifications are the types of leader behaviour the leader can adopt and include supportive, directive, achievement-oriented and participative styles.

Supportive leadership involves leader behaviour that shows concern for subordinates' well-being and personal needs. Leadership behaviour is open, friendly, and approachable, and the leader creates a team climate and treats subordinates as equals. Supportive leadership is similar to the consideration, people-centred or relationship-oriented leadership described earlier.

Directive leadership occurs when the leader tells subordinates exactly what they are supposed to do. Leader behaviour includes planning, making schedules, setting performance goals and behaviour standards, and stressing adherence to rules and regulations. Directive leadership behaviour is similar to the initiating-structure, job-centred or task-oriented leadership style described earlier.

Participative leadership means that the leader consults with his or her subordinates about decisions. Leader behaviour includes asking for opinions and suggestions, encouraging participation in decision-making, and meeting with subordinates in their workplaces. The participative leader encourages group discussion and written suggestions.

Achievement-oriented leadership occurs when the leader sets clear and challenging goals for subordinates. Leader behaviour stresses high-quality performance and improvement over current performance.

Achievement-oriented leaders also show confidence in subordinates and assist them in learning how to achieve high goals.

The four types of leader behaviour are not considered ingrained personality traits as in the Fiedler theory; rather, they reflect types of behaviour that every leader is able to adopt, depending on the situation.

Use of Rewards

Recall that the leader's responsibility is to clarify the path to rewards for subordinates or to increase the value of rewards to enhance satisfaction and job performance. In some situations, the leader works with subordinates to help them acquire the skills and confidence needed to perform tasks and achieve rewards already available. In others, the leader may develop new rewards to meet the specific needs of subordinates.

Exhibit 15.7 illustrates four examples of how leadership behaviour is tailored to the situation. In the first example situation, the subordinate lacks confidence; thus, the supportive leadership style provides the social support with which to encourage the subordinate to undertake the behaviour needed to do the work and receive the rewards. In the second situation, the job is ambiguous, and the employee is not performing effectively. Directive leadership behaviour is used to give

CONCEPT CONNECTION Southwest Airlines co-founder and chairman Herb Kelleher (shown here celebrating Southwest's new Philadelphia service with Ben Franklin) firmly believes that it's free-flowing communication that makes participative leadership possible. Southwest encourages employees to talk to anyone at anytime about anything on their minds. In addition to sending notes or emails, workers get the chance to share their opinions and ask questions when executives drop in on them periodically. When Gary Kelly, Kelleher's successor as CEO, visited an employee lounge at Chicago's Midway Airport, a mechanic who owns Southwest stock took him aside. 'What's happening here?', he asked, pointing to stock quotes on a computer screen. 'That's my retirement, and it's not moving.'

Exhibit 15.7 Path–Goal Situations and Preferred Leader Behaviours

SOURCE: Adapted from Gary A. Yukl, *Leadership in Organizations* (Englewood Cliffs, NJ: Prentice Hall, 1981): 146–152.

instructions and clarify the task so that the follower will know how to accomplish it and receive rewards. In the third situation, the subordinate is unchallenged by the task; thus, an achievement-oriented behaviour is used to set higher goals. In the fourth situation, an incorrect reward is given to a subordinate, and the participative leadership style is used to change this situation. By discussing the subordinates' needs, the leader is able to identify the correct reward for task accomplishment and help people know how to achieve the reward. In all four cases, the outcome of fitting the leadership behaviour to the situation produces greater employee effort by either clarifying how subordinates can receive rewards or changing the rewards to fit their needs.

At The Home Depot, CEO Bob Nardelli reinvigorated employee morale – and retail sales – with his achievement-oriented leadership, which cascades down from headquarters to the store level.

 INNOVATIVE WAY

The Home Depot

Things seemed a little shaky in 2007 when new CEO Frank Blake first started imposing high goals, order and discipline at The Home Depot, one of the world's largest retailers next to Wal-Mart. Many store managers, who were used to a more relaxed approach, left the company, and investors sent the stock price plummeting.

But Blake knew what he was after. Instead of a retail chain where employees were becoming complacent and bored, he wanted a company full of enterprizing people who thrive on challenge, responsibility and recognition. Blake slowly began building a cadre of talented people, from top to bottom, and instituting a 'no-bull performance culture' that gives people challenging goals and generous rewards for achieving them. Rigorous talent assessments, new approaches to hiring, new performance measurement systems, and programmes such as the Store Leadership Programme and Accelerated Leadership Programme have enhanced employee skills and reduced turnover in the USA, Canada, Mexico and even China. Blake can monitor stores in real time via computer, and he spends one week a quarter as a 'mystery shopper', popping in unannounced to as

many as ten stores a day. He makes clear to employees that he's not trying to 'catch anybody', he just wants to see the store from the eyes of customers and help people do a better job of serving them.

Blake's achievement-oriented leadership has helped to increase sales from $45.7 billion to about $80 billion within five years, increase earnings per share by 20 per cent annually and giving the retailer an edge in new segments such as the $410 billion professional construction market. 'His real ability,' says Jack Welch, who was Blake's boss at General Electric, 'is to motivate lots of people around a mission, excite them about it, and make it happen.'

Blake's achievement-oriented leadership is successful because it encourages every manager in the organization to focus on keeping people challenged and motivated to reach goals.[40] Path–goal theorizing can be complex, but much of the research on it has been encouraging.[41] Using the model to specify precise relationships and make exact predictions about employee outcomes may be difficult, but the four types of leader behaviour and the ideas for fitting them to situational contingencies provide a useful way for leaders to think about motivating subordinates.

Substitutes for Leadership

The contingency leadership approaches considered so far focus on the leaders' style, the subordinates' nature, and the situation's characteristics. The final contingency approach suggests that situational variables can be so powerful that they actually substitute for or neutralize the need for leadership.[39] This approach outlines those organizational settings in which a leadership style is unimportant or unnecessary.

Exhibit 15.8 Substitutes and Neutralizers for Leadership

Variable		Task-Oriented Leadership	People-Oriented Leadership
Organizational variables	Group cohesiveness	Substitutes for	Substitutes for
	Formalisation	Substitutes for	No effect on
	Inflexibility	Neutralises	No effect on
	Low position power	Neutralises	Neutralises
	Physical separation	Neutralises	Neutralises
Task characteristics	Highly structured task	Substitutes for	No effect on
	Automatic feedback	Substitutes for	No effect on
	Intrinsic satisfaction	No effect on	Substitutes for
Group characteristics	Professionalism	Substitutes for	Substitutes for
	Training/experience	Substitutes for	No effect on

Exhibit 15.8 shows the situational variables that tend to substitute for or neutralize leadership characteristics. A **substitute** for leadership makes the leadership style unnecessary or redundant. For example, highly professional subordinates who know how to do their tasks do not need a leader who initiates structure for them and tells them what to do. A **neutralizer** counteracts the leadership style and prevents the leader from displaying certain behaviours. For example, if a leader has absolutely no position power or is physically removed from subordinates, the leader's ability to give directions to subordinates is greatly reduced.

Situational variables in Exhibit 15.8 include characteristics of the group, the task and the organization itself. When followers are highly professional and experienced, both leadership styles are less important. People do not need much direction or consideration. With respect to task characteristics, highly structured tasks substitute for a task-oriented style, and a satisfying task substitutes for a people-oriented style. With respect to the organization itself, group cohesiveness substitutes for both leader styles. Formalized rules and procedures substitute for leader task orientation. Physical separation of leader and subordinate neutralizes both leadership styles.

The value of the situations described in Exhibit 15.8 is that they help leaders avoid leadership overkill. Leaders should adopt a style with which to complement the organizational situation. Consider the work situation for bank tellers. A bank teller performs highly structured tasks, follows clear written rules and procedures, and has little flexibility in terms of how to do the work. The head teller should not adopt a task-oriented style, because the organization already provides structure and direction. The head teller should concentrate on a people-oriented style to provide a more pleasant work environment. In other organizations, if group cohesiveness or intrinsic satisfaction meets employees' social needs, the leader is free to concentrate on task-oriented behaviours. The leader can adopt a style complementary to the organizational situation to ensure that both task needs and people needs of the work group will be met.

Substitute
A situational variable that makes a leadership style unnecessary or redundant.

Neutralizer
A situational variable that counteracts a leadership style and prevents the leader from displaying certain behaviours.

TAKE A MOMENT   As a new manager, avoid leadership overkill. Don't use a task-oriented style if the job already provides clear structure and direction. Concentrate instead on people and relationships. Remember that professional employees typically need less leadership.

Leading Change

In Chapter 1, we defined management to include the functions of leading, planning, organizing and controlling. But recent work on leadership has begun to distinguish leadership as something more: a quality that inspires and motivates people beyond their normal levels of performance. We are living in an era when leadership is needed more than ever. The environment today is turbulent, and organizations need to shift direction quickly to keep pace.[42] Leaders in many organizations have had to reconceptualize almost every aspect of how they do business to meet the needs of increasingly demanding customers, keep employees motivated and satisfied, and remain competitive in a rapidly changing global environment.

Research finds that some leadership approaches are more effective than others for bringing about change in organizations. Two types of leadership with a substantial impact are charismatic and transformational. These types of leadership are best understood in comparison to *transactional leadership*.[43] **Transactional leaders** clarify the role and task requirements of subordinates, initiate structure, provide appropriate rewards, and try to be considerate to and meet the social needs of subordinates. The transactional leader's ability to satisfy subordinates may improve productivity. Transactional leaders excel at management functions. They are hardworking, tolerant and fair minded. They take pride in keeping things running smoothly and efficiently. Transactional leaders often stress the impersonal aspects of performance, such as plans, schedules and budgets. They have a sense of commitment to the organization and conform to organizational norms and values. Transactional leadership is important to all organizations, but leading change requires a different approach.

Charismatic and Visionary Leadership

Charismatic leadership goes beyond transactional leadership techniques. Charisma has been referred to as 'a fire that ignites followers' energy and commitment, producing results above and beyond the call of duty'.[44] The **charismatic leader** has the ability to inspire and motivate people to do more than they would normally do, despite obstacles and personal sacrifice. Followers transcend their own self-interests for the sake of the team, department or organization. The impact of charismatic leaders is normally from (1) stating a lofty vision of an imagined future that employees identify with, (2) shaping a corporate value system for which everyone stands, and (3) trusting subordinates and earning their complete trust in return.[45] Charismatic leaders tend to be less predictable than transactional leaders. They create an atmosphere of change, and they may be obsessed by visionary ideas that excite, stimulate and drive other people to work hard.

Charismatic leaders are often skilled in the art of *visionary leadership*. A **vision** is an attractive, ideal future that is credible yet not readily attainable. Vision is an important component of both charismatic and transformational leadership. Visionary leaders speak to the hearts of employees, letting them be part of something

Transactional leader
A leader who clarifies subordinates' role and task requirements, initiates structure, provides rewards and displays consideration for subordinates.

Charismatic leader
A leader who has the ability to motivate subordinates to transcend their expected performance.

Vision
An attractive, ideal future that is credible yet not readily attainable.

bigger than themselves. Where others see obstacles or failures, they see possibility and hope. Bill Strickland, who built a centre of hope in a crumbling Pittsburgh area neighbourhood, is the epitome of a visionary and charismatic leader.

INNOVATIVE WAY

Manchester Bidwell

Bill Strickland was a rootless teenager about to flunk out of high school when he met a special teacher, Frank Ross, who changed his life by turning him on to the power of art and music. When Ross took the 16-year-old to see Fallingwater, the famous Frank Lloyd Wright-designed house that has a creek running through the middle of it, Strickland's life changed forever. 'It was a very interesting way of looking at water,' Strickland tells people now, 'and a very interesting way of looking at light. I said to myself, if I could ever bring that light to my neighbourhood … I thought, before I die, I am going to build that kind of place in Manchester.'

Thus were planted the seeds of a vision that eventually turned into Manchester Bidwell, a non-profit corporation that is a centre of light in the crumbling Pittsburgh area community of Manchester, Pennsylvania. One division, the Manchester Craftsman's Guild, is a bright, clean, attractive centre that provides after-school and summer programmes in ceramics, photography, digital imaging, drawing and painting to mostly at-risk middle and high school kids. Under the same gracefully-designed roof is the Bidwell Training Centre, which gives low-income adults training in fields such as culinary arts, horticultural technology, and medical coding, placing about 90 per cent of students in full time jobs with area employers such as Bayer, Heinz and the Pittsburgh Medical Center.

The way Strickland built Machester-Bidwell's state-of-the-art greenhouse is a lesson in the power of vision. Rep. Melissa Hart, a US congresswoman from Pennsylvania recalls: 'Ten years ago, he and I stood together in this bombed-out industrial area, and Bill was saying, "This is where we're going to have the irrigation system, and this is going to be the computerized control room, and we're going to sell our orchids to [supermarket chain] Giant Eagle." I said, "Sure, uh-huh, Bill." But he actually saw that greenhouse standing in that bombed-out field. He was absolutely convinced it was a done deal.' Giant Eagle helped finance the construction of the greenhouse and now buys top-grade orchids cultivated by Bidwell students, with all the revenue ploughed back into training programmes.

By spreading his vision of hope, Strickland established smaller Manchester Bidwell Centers in San Francisco, Cincinnati, and Grand Rapids, Michigan, His long-term goal is to open 25 more such centres in inner-city neighbourhoods around the country. Strickland isn't shy about admitting that he's out to save the world. Practically every member of every audience he speaks to hears the passion in his voice and wants to help make that vision a reality.[46]

An associate of Bill Strickland's said his power is that he doesn't just overcome obstacles, he refuses to even recognize them. Leaders like Bill Strickland see beyond current realities and problems and help followers believe in a brighter future as well.

Charismatic leaders typically have a strong vision for the future, almost an obsession, and they can motivate others to help realise it.[47] These leaders have an emotional impact on subordinates because they strongly believe in the vision and can communicate it to others in a way that makes the vision real, personal and meaningful. Charismatic and transformational leaders are passionate about a vision. This chapter's Manager's Shoptalk provides a short quiz to help you determine whether you have the potential to be a charismatic leader.

Charismatic leaders include Mother Theresa, Adolf Hitler, Sam Walton, Alexander the Great, Ronald Reagan, David Koresh, Martin Luther King Jr. and Osama bin

Laden. Charisma can be used for positive outcomes that benefit the group, but it can also be used for self-serving purposes that lead to deception, manipulation and exploitation of others. When charismatic leaders respond to organizational problems in terms of the needs of the entire group rather than their own emotional needs, they can have a powerful, positive influence on organizational performance.[48]

Transformational Leaders

Transformational leaders are similar to charismatic leaders, but are distinguished by their special ability to bring about innovation and change by recognizing followers' needs and concerns, helping them look at old problems in new ways, and encouraging them to question the status quo. Transformational leaders inspire followers not just to believe in the leader personally, but to believe in their own potential to imagine and create a better future for the organization. Transformational leaders create significant change in both followers and the organization.[49] They have the ability to lead changes in the organization's mission, strategy, structure and culture, as well as to promote innovation in products and technologies. Transformational leaders do not rely solely on tangible rules and incentives to control specific transactions with followers. They focus on intangible qualities such as vision, shared values and ideas to build relationships, give larger meaning to diverse activities, and find common ground to enlist followers in the change process.[50]

A recent study confirmed that transformational leadership has a positive impact on follower development and follower performance. Moreover, transformational leadership skills can be learned and are not ingrained personality characteristics.[51] However, some personality traits may make it easier for a leader to display transformational leadership behaviours. For example, studies of transformational leadership have found that the trait of agreeableness, as discussed in the previous chapter, is positively associated with transformational leaders.[52] In addition, transformational leaders are typically emotionally stable and positively engaged with the world around them, and they have a strong ability to recognize and understand others' emotions.[53] These characteristics are not surprising considering that these leaders accomplish change by building networks of positive relationships.

Richard Kovacevich, who steered mid-sized Norwest Corporation (now Wells Fargo & Co.) through numerous acquisitions to make it one of the largest and most powerful banking companies in the US, is an excellent example of a transformational leader.

Kovacevich's leadership style puts accountability for success in the hands of each and every employee. He leads with slogans such as, 'Mind share plus heart share equals market share.' Although some people might think it sounds hokey, Kovacevich and his employees don't care. It is the substance behind the slogans that matters. Kovacevich believes it's not what employees know that is important, but whether they care. Employees are rewarded for putting both their hearts and minds into their work. Kovacevich spends a lot of time out in the field, meeting employees, patting backs, and giving pep talks. He likes to personally remind people on the front lines that they are the heart and soul of Wells Fargo, and that only through their efforts can the company succeed.[54]

CONCEPT CONNECTION The real magic behind e-tailing company Amazon.com is the visionary leadership of founder and CEO Jeff Bezos. His passion and enthusiasm was the key to getting investors to give him millions of dollars in financing. Bezos continued to inspire employees with his vision of a new kind of retailer as the company struggled for years before finally achieving profitability. He keeps Amazon innovative with bold moves, such as his new vision to use Amazon's technological, operations, and logistics expertise to provide services to other companies and entrepreneurs. The company plans to rent out just about everything it uses to run its own business, from warehouse space to spare computing capacity and data storage.

Transformational leader
A leader distinguished by a special ability to bring about innovation and change.

© TOM BIBLE/ALAMY

 MANAGER'S SHOPTALK

Are You a Charismatic Leader?

If you were the head of a major department in a corporation, how important would each of the following activities be to you? Answer yes or no to indicate whether you would strive to perform each activity.

1 Help subordinates clarify goals and how to reach them.

2 Give people a sense of mission and overall purpose.

3 Help get jobs out on time.

4 Look for the new product or service opportunities.

5 Use policies and procedures as guides for problem solving.

6 Promote unconventional beliefs and values.

7 Give monetary rewards in exchange for high performance from subordinates.

8 Command respect from everyone in the department.

9 Work alone to accomplish important tasks.

10 Suggest new and unique ways of doing things.

11 Give credit to people who do their jobs well.

12 Inspire loyalty to yourself and to the organization.

13 Establish procedures to help the department operate smoothly.

14 Use ideas to motivate others.

15 Set reasonable limits on new approaches.

16 Demonstrate social nonconformity.

The even-numbered items represent behaviours and activities of charismatic leaders. Charismatic leaders are personally involved in shaping ideas, goals and direction of change. They use an intuitive approach to develop fresh ideas for old problems and seek new directions for the department or organization. The odd-numbered items are considered more traditional management activities, or what would be called *transactional leadership*. Managers respond to organizational problems in an impersonal way, make rational decisions, and coordinate and facilitate the work of others. If you answered yes to more even-numbered than odd-numbered items, you may be a potential charismatic leader.

SOURCES Based on 'Have You Got It?', a quiz that appeared in Patricia Sellers, 'What Exactly Is Charisma?', *Fortune* (January 15, 1996): 68–75; Bernard M. Bass, *Leadership and Performance Beyond Expectations* (New York: Free Press, 1985); and Lawton R. Burns and Selwyn W. Becker, 'Leadership and Managership', in S. Shortell and A. Kaluzny (eds), *Health Care Management* (New York: Wiley, 1986).

Followership

No discussion of leadership is complete without a consideration of followership. Leadership matters, but without effective followers no organization can survive. Leaders can develop an understanding of their followers and how to help them be most effective.[55] Many of the qualities that define a good leader are the same qualities as those possessed by a good follower. Understanding differences in followers can improve one's effectiveness as both a follower and a leader. One model of followership is illustrated in Exhibit 15.9. Robert E. Kelley conducted extensive interviews with managers and their subordinates and came up with five *follower styles*, which are categorized according to two dimensions, as shown in the exhibit.[56]

The first dimension is the quality of independent, **critical thinking** versus dependent, **uncritical thinking**. Independent critical thinkers are mindful of the effects of their own and others' behaviour on achieving organizational goals. They can weigh the impact of their boss's and their own decisions and offer constructive criticism, creativity, and innovation. Conversely, a dependent, uncritical thinker does not consider possibilities beyond what he or she is told, does not contribute to the cultivation of the organization, and accepts the supervisor's ideas without thinking.

The second dimension of follower style is active versus passive behaviour. An active follower participates fully in the organization, engages in behaviour that is beyond the limits of the job, demonstrates a sense of ownership and initiates problem solving and decision-making. A passive follower, by contrast, is characterized by a need for constant supervision and prodding by superiors. Passivity is often regarded as laziness; a passive person does nothing that is not required and avoids added responsibility.

The extent to which an individual is active or passive and is a critical, independent thinker or a dependent, uncritical thinker determines whether the person will be an alienated follower, a passive follower, a conformist, a pragmatic survivor or an effective follower, as illustrated in Exhibit 15.9:

1 The **alienated follower** is a passive, yet independent, critical thinker. Alienated employees are often effective followers who have experienced setbacks and obstacles, perhaps promises broken by their superiors. Thus, they are capable, but they focus exclusively on the shortcomings of their boss. Often cynical, alienated followers are able to think independently, but they do not participate in developing solutions to the problems or deficiencies they see. These people waste valuable time complaining about their boss without offering constructive feedback.

2 The **conformist** participates actively in a relationship with the boss but doesn't use critical thinking skills. In other words, a conformist typically carries out any and all orders regardless of the nature of the request. The conformist participates willingly, but without considering the consequences of what he or she is being asked to do – even at the risk of contributing to a harmful endeavour. A conformist is concerned only with avoiding conflict. This follower style might reflect an individual's over-dependent attitude toward authority, yet it can also result from rigid rules and authoritarian environments that create a culture of conformity.

3 The **pragmatic survivor** has qualities of all four extremes – depending on which style fits with the prevalent situation. This type of person uses whatever style best benefits his or her own position and minimizes risk. Pragmatic survivors often emerge when an organization is going through desperate times, and managers find themselves doing whatever is needed to get themselves through the difficulty. Within any given company, some 25 to 35 per cent of people tend to be pragmatic survivors, avoiding risks and fostering the status quo.[57]

4 The **passive follower** exhibits neither critical, independent thinking nor active participation. Being passive and uncritical, these people show neither initiative nor a sense of responsibility. Their activity is limited to what they are told to do, and they accomplish things only with a great deal of supervision. Passive followers leave the thinking to the boss. Often, this style is the result of a micromanaging boss who encourages passive behaviour. People learn that to show initiative, accept responsibility, or think creatively is not rewarded, and may even be punished by the boss, so they grow increasingly passive.

5 The **effective follower** is both a critical, independent thinker and active in the organization. Effective followers behave the same toward everyone,

© GETTY IMAGES

CONCEPT CONNECTION

UPS employees joke that when Mike Eskew became CEO, he'd only worked for the company for 30 years. This bit of office humour reflects UPS's long-standing promote-from-within approach to management development. Most UPS managers gain expert power by working their way up from the bottom. For example, when Eskew arrived as a young industrial engineer, his first assignment was to re-draw a parking lot so it could accommodate more trucks. Today, he's using his thorough understanding of the business to help move the $43 billion company from package delivery into global supply chain management. Eskew retired in 2008, having completed the five-year tenure that's become customary for UPS CEOs.

Exhibit 15.9 Styles of Followership

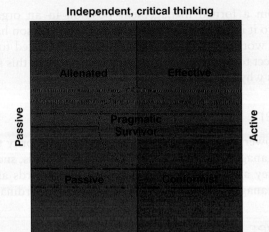

SOURCE: From 'The Power of Followership' by Robert E Kelley, p 97, copyright © by Consultants to Executives and Organizations, LTD. Used by permission of Doubleday, a division of Random House, Inc.

regardless of their position in the organization. They develop an equitable relationship with their leaders and do not try to avoid risk or conflict. These people are capable of self-management, they discern strengths and weaknesses in themselves and their bosses, they are committed to something bigger than themselves, and they work toward competency, solutions, and positive impact. Effective followers recognize that they have power in their relationships with superiors; thus, they have the courage to manage upward, to initiate change, and to put themselves at risk or in conflict with the boss if they believe it serves the best interest of the team or organization.

Power and Influence

Recall our definition of leadership, which is the ability to influence people to achieve goals. Particularly for leaders involved in major change initiatives, the effective and appropriate use of power is crucial. One way to understand how leaders get things done is to look at the sources of leader power and the interpersonal influence tactics leaders use.

Power is the potential ability to influence the behaviour of others.[58] Sometimes the terms *power* and *influence* are used synonymously, but the two are distinct in important ways. Basically, **influence** is the effect a person's actions have on the attitudes, values, beliefs, or behaviour of others. Whereas power is the capacity to cause a change in a person, influence may be thought of as the degree of actual change.

Power results from an interaction of leader and followers. Some power comes from an individual's position in the organization. Power may also come from personal sources that are not as invested in the organization, such as a leader's personal interests, goals, and values. Within organizations, five sources of power are typical: legitimate, reward, coercive, expert and referent.

Power
The potential ability to influence others' behaviour.

Influence
The effect a person's actions have on the attitudes, values, beliefs, or behaviour of others.

Position Power

The traditional manager's power comes from the organization. The manager's position gives him or her the power to reward or punish subordinates in order to influence their behaviour. Legitimate power, reward power, and coercive power are all forms of position power used by managers to change employee behaviour.

Legitimate Power

Legitimate power
Power that stems from a formal management position in an organization and the authority granted to it.

Power coming from a formal management position in an organization and the authority granted to it is called **legitimate power**. Once a person has been selected as a supervisor, most workers understand that they are obligated to follow his or her direction with respect to work activities. Subordinates accept this source of power as legitimate, which is why they comply.

Reward Power

Reward power
Power that results from the authority to bestow rewards on other people.

Another kind of power, **reward power**, stems from the authority to bestow rewards on other people. Managers may have access to formal rewards, such as pay increases or promotions. They also have at their disposal such rewards as praise, attention and recognition. Managers can use rewards to influence subordinates' behaviour.

Coercive Power

Coercive power
Power that stems from the authority to punish or recommend punishment.

The opposite of reward power is **coercive power**: it refers to the authority to punish or recommend punishment. Managers have coercive power when they have the right to fire or demote employees, criticize or withdraw pay increases. For example, if Sanjay, a salesperson, does not perform as expected, his supervisor has the coercive power to criticize him, reprimand him, put a negative letter in his file and hurt his chance for a pay increase.

Personal Power

In contrast to the external sources of position power, personal power most often comes from internal sources, such as a person's special knowledge or personal characteristics.

A good example of personal power is Charles Firneno, math teacher and football coach at Benjamin Franklin High School in New Orleans. After the school was devastated by Hurricane Katrina in 2005 and no one could get through to inspect the damage, Firneno took it upon himself to get things rolling. A former US Marine helicopter pilot, Firneno put on his uniform and convinced National Guardsmen to let him through. Firneno laid out a plan for fixing the building and began mobilizing people to help. Although before the flood, Firneno had been held in rather low esteem by his faculty colleagues with more advanced degrees, his commitment, knowledge, skills and ability to mobilize people in a crisis quickly won the support and respect of teachers, parents and community volunteers. Soon, Firneno was handed an extra set of keys to the building and the principal's authorization to spend school funds as he saw fit, helping to get the school open in record time.[59] Firneno's power came from his special knowledge and skills and from his personal commitment to the school, rather than from a formal position of authority.

Personal power is the primary tool of the leader, and it is becoming increasingly important as more businesses are run by teams of workers who are less tolerant of authoritarian management.[60] Two types of personal power are expert power and referent power.

Expert Power

Expert power
Power that stems from special knowledge of or skill in the tasks performed by subordinates.

Power resulting from a leader's special knowledge or skill regarding the tasks performed by followers is referred to as **expert power**. When the leader is a true expert, subordinates go along with recommendations because of his or her superior knowledge. Leaders at supervisory levels often have experience in the production process that gains them promotion. At top management levels, however, leaders may lack expert power because subordinates know more about technical details than they do.

Referent Power

The last kind of power, **referent power**, comes from a leader's personal characteristics that command followers' identification, respect and admiration so they wish to emulate the leader. Referent power does not depend on a formal title or position. When workers admire a supervisor because of the way she deals with them, the influence is based on referent power. Referent power is most visible in the area of charismatic leadership. In social and religious movements, for example, we often see charismatic leaders who emerge and gain a tremendous following based solely on their personal power.

Referent power
Power that results from characteristics that command subordinates' identification with, respect and admiration for, and desire to emulate the leader.

TAKE A MOMENT

As a new manager, you may not have a lot of position power. Build your personal power by strengthening your knowledge and skills and by developing positive relationships. Interpersonal influence tactics will serve you well throughout your career, even as your position power increases.

Interpersonal Influence Tactics

The next question is how leaders use their power to implement decisions and facilitate change. Leaders often use a combination of influence strategies, and people who are perceived as having greater power and influence typically are those who use a wider variety of tactics. One survey of a few hundred leaders identified more than 4000 different techniques these people used to influence others.[61]

However, these tactics fall into basic categories that rely on understanding the principles that cause people to change their behaviour and attitudes. Exhibit 15.10 lists seven principles for asserting influence. Notice that most of these involve the use of personal power rather than relying solely on position power or the use of rewards and punishments.[62]

1 *Use rational persuasion.* The most frequently used influence strategy is to use facts, data, and logical argument to persuade others that a proposed idea, request, or decision is appropriate. Using rational persuasion can often be highly effective, because most people have faith in facts and analysis.[63] Rational persuasion is

Exhibit 15.10 Seven Interpersonal Influence Tactics for Leaders

1. Use rational persuasion.

2. Make people like you.

3. Rely on the rule of reciprocity.

4. Develop allies.

5. Be assertive — ask for what you want.

6. Make use of higher authority.

7. Reward the behaviours you want.

most successful when a leader has technical knowledge and expertise related to the issue at hand (expert power), although referent power is also used. That is, in addition to facts and figures, people also have to believe in the leader's credibility.

2 *Make people like you.* Recall our discussion of *likeability* from the previous chapter. People would rather say yes to someone they like than to someone they don't. Effective leaders strive to create goodwill and favourable impressions. When a leader shows consideration and respect, treats people fairly, and demonstrates trust in others, people are more likely to want to help and support the leader by doing what he or she asks. In addition, most people like a leader who makes them feel good about themselves, so leaders should never underestimate the power of praise.

3 *Rely on the rule of reciprocity.* Leaders can influence others through the exchange of benefits and favours. Leaders share what they have – whether it be time, resources, services, or emotional support. The feeling among people is nearly universal that others should be paid back for what they do, in one form or another. This unwritten 'rule of reciprocity' means that leaders who do favours for others can expect that others will do favours for them in return.[64]

4 *Develop allies.* Effective leaders develop networks of allies, people who can help the leader accomplish his or her goals. Leaders talk with followers and others outside of formal meetings to understand their needs and concerns as well as to explain problems and describe the leader's point of view. They strive to reach a meeting of minds with others about the best approach to a problem or decision.[65]

5 *Ask for what you want.* Another way to influence others is to make a direct and personal request. Leaders have to be explicit about what they want, or they aren't likely to get it. An explicit proposal is sometimes accepted simply because others have no better alternative. Also, a clear proposal or alternative will often receive support if other options are less well-defined.

6 *Make use of higher authority.* Sometimes to get things done leaders have to use their formal authority, as well as gain the support of people at higher levels to back them up. However, research has found that the key to successful use of formal authority is to be knowledgeable, credible, and trustworthy – that is, to demonstrate expert and referent power as well as legitimate power. Managers who become known for their expertise, who are honest and straightforward with others, and who inspire trust can exert greater influence than those who simply issue orders.[66]

7 *Reward the behaviours you want.* Leaders can also use organizational rewards and punishments to influence others' behaviour. The use of punishment in organizations is controversial, but negative consequences almost always occur for inappropriate or undesirable behaviour. Leaders should not rely solely on reward and punishment as a means for influencing others, but combined with other tactics that involve the use of personal power, rewards can be highly effective. At General Electric, for example, CEO Jeff Immelt is having success in shifting managers' behaviour by using rewards for managers who demonstrate an ability to come up with innovative ideas and improve customer service and satisfaction.[67]

Research indicates that people rate leaders as 'more effective' when they are perceived to use a variety of influence tactics. But not all managers use influence in the same way. Studies have found that leaders in human resources, for example, tend to use softer, more subtle approaches such as building goodwill, using favours and developing allies, whereas those in finance are inclined to use harder, more direct tactics such as formal authority and assertiveness.[68]

Leadership as Service

To close our chapter, let's look at two timeless leadership approaches that are gaining renewed attention in today's environment of ethical scandals and weakened employee trust. Characteristics of servant leadership and moral leadership can be successfully used by leaders in all situations to make a positive difference.

Servant Leadership

Some leaders operate from the assumption that work exists for the development of the worker as much as the worker exists to do the work.[69] For example, a young David Packard, who co founded Hewlett-Packard, made a spectacle of himself in 1949 by standing up in a roomful of business leaders and arguing that companies had a responsibility to recognize the dignity and worth of their employees and share the wealth with those who helped to create it.[70]

The concept of servant leadership, first described by Robert Greenleaf, is leadership upside down, because leaders transcend self-interest to serve others and the organization.[71] **Servant leaders** operate on two levels: for the fulfilment of their subordinates' goals and needs and for the realization of the larger purpose or mission of their organization. Servant leaders give things away – power, ideas, information, recognition, credit for accomplishments, even money. Harry Stine, founder of Stine Seed Company in Adel, Iowa, casually announced to his employees at the company's annual post-harvest luncheon that they would each receive $1000 for each year they had worked at the company. For some loyal workers, that amounted to a $20000 bonus.[72] Servant leaders truly value other people. They are trustworthy and they trust others. They encourage participation, share power, enhance others' self-worth, and unleash people's creativity, full commitment, and natural impulse to learn and contribute. Servant leaders can bring their followers' higher motives to the work and connect their hearts to the organizational mission and goals.

Servant leaders often work in the non-profit world because it offers a natural way to apply their leadership drive and skills to serve others. But servant leaders also succeed in business. George Merck believed the purpose of a corporation was to do something useful. At Merck & Co., he insisted that people always come before profits. By insisting on serving people rather than profits, Merck shaped a company that averaged 15 per cent earnings growth for an amazing 75 years.[73]

Servant leader
A leader who works to fulfil subordinates' needs and goals as well as to achieve the organization's larger mission.

Moral Leadership

Another enduring issue in leadership is its moral component. Because leadership can be used for good or evil, to help or to harm others, all leadership has a moral component. Leaders carry a tremendous responsibility to use their power wisely and ethically. Sadly, in recent years, too many have chosen to act from self-interest and greed rather than behaving in ways that serve and uplift others. The disheartening ethical climate in American business has led to a renewed interest in moral leadership. **Moral leadership** is about distinguishing right from wrong and choosing to do right. It means seeking the just, the honest, the good, and the decent behaviour in the practice of leadership.[74] Moral leaders remember that business is about values, not just economic performance.

Distinguishing the right thing to do is not always easy, and doing it is sometimes even harder. Leaders are often faced with right-versus-right decisions, in which several responsibilities conflict with one another.[75] Commitments to superiors, for example, may mean a leader feels the need to hide unpleasant news about pending layoffs from followers. Moral leaders strive to find the moral answer or compromise, rather than

Moral leadership
Distinguishing right from wrong and choosing to do right in the practice of leadership.

31 I would persuade others that my ideas are to their advantage.

A F O S N

32 I would permit the group to set its own pace.

A F O S N

33 I would urge the group to beat its previous record.

A F O S N

34 I would act without consulting the group.

A F O S N

35 I would ask that group members follow standard rules and regulations.

A F O S N

T_____ P_____

Scoring and Interpretation

The T–P Leadership Questionnaire is scored as follows:
a. Circle the statements numbered 8, 12, 17, 18, 19, 30, 34 and 35.

b. Write the number 1 in front of the circled number if you responded S (seldom) or N (never) to that statement.
c. Also write a number 1 in front of the statement numbers not circled if you responded A (always) or F (frequently).
d. Circle the number 1s that you have written in front of the following statements: 3, 5, 8, 10, 15, 18, 19, 22, 24, 26, 28, 30, 32, 34 and 35.
e. Count the circled number 1s. This total is your score for concern for people. Record the score in the blank following the letter P at the end of the questionnaire.
f. Count uncircled number 1s. This total is your score for concern for task. Record this number in the blank following the letter T.

SOURCE The T–P Leadership Questionnaire was adapted by J. B. Ritchie and P. Thompson in *Organization and People* (New York: West, 1984). Copyright 1969 by the American Educational Research Association. Adapted by permission of the Publisher.

MANAGEMENT IN PRACTICE: ETHICAL DILEMMA

Newcomer Thirsts for Market Share[78]

Not long ago, André Hadji-Thomas, managing director for EIBCO, Egyptian International Beverages Company, hoping to carve a niche out of the company's beer and wine monopoly, made a point of stopping by Director for HR, Mahal El Dahan's office, and lavishly praising him for his volunteer work with school programme for disadvantaged children in a nearby urban neighbourhoods. Now he was about to summon him to his office so he could take him to task for dedication to the same volunteer work.

It was Hadji-Thomas's secretary who'd alerted him to the problem. 'Mahal told the local community representatives he'd take responsibility for a fundraising mass mailing. And then he asked me to edit the letter he'd drafted, make all the copies, stuff the envelopes and get it into the mail – most of this on my own time,'

she reported, still obviously indignant. 'When I told him, "I'm sorry, but that's not my job," he looked me straight in the eye and asked when I'd like to schedule my upcoming performance appraisal.'

Several of El Dahan's subordinates also volunteered with the programme. After chatting with them, Hadji-Thomas concluded most were volunteering out of a desire to stay on the boss's good side. It was time to talk to El Dahan.

'Oh, come on,' he responded impatiently when Hadji-Thomas confronted him. 'Yes, I asked for her help as a personal favour to me. But I only brought up the appraisal because I was going out of town, and we needed to set some time aside to do the evaluation.' El Dahan went on to talk about how important working for the school programme was to him personally. 'I grew up in that neighbourhood, and if it hadn't been for the people at the local community centre, I wouldn't be here today,' he said. Besides, even if he had pressured employees to help out – and he wasn't saying he had – didn't all the emphasis the company was putting on employee volunteerism make it okay to use employees' time and company resources?

After El Dahan left, Hadji-Thomas thought about the conversation. There was no question EIBCO needed to build reputation in the region and should actively encourage employee volunteerism – and not just because it was the right thing to do. It was a newly created company with a number of new product lines in winery and brewery sections that needed promoting.

Volunteering had the potential to help employees acquire new skills, create a sense of camaraderie and play a role in recruiting and retaining talented people. But most of all, it gave a badly needed boost to the company's public image. Recently, EIBCO took every opportunity to publicize its employees' extracurricular community work on its website and in company publications. And the company created the annual EIBCO Prize, which granted cash awards to outstanding volunteers.

So now that André Hadji-Thomas had talked with everyone concerned, just what was he going to do about the dispute between his secretary and Director for HR?

What Would You Do?

1 Tell the secretary that employee volunteerism is important to the company and that while her performance evaluation will not be affected by her decision, she should consider helping El Dahan because it is an opportunity to help a worthy community project.

2 Tell El Dahan that the employee volunteer programme is just that: a volunteer programme. Even though the company sees volunteerism as an important piece of its campaign to repair its tarnished image, employees must be free to choose whether to volunteer. He should not ask for the help of his direct reports with the after-school programme.

3 Discipline El Dahan for coercing his subordinates to spend their own time on his volunteer work at the community after-school programme. This action will send a signal that coercing employees is a clear violation of leadership authority.

CASE FOR CRITICAL ANALYSIS 15.1

Co-operative Insurance Company of Kenya Limited (CIC)

'Be careful what you wish for,' thought Johna Tomno, Assistant General Manager for the Nairobi-based health insurance company, Co-operative Insurance Company of Kenya, Ltd (CIC). When there was an opening for a new director of customer service last year due to Obisola Oboleme's retirement, he'd seen it as the perfect opportunity to bring someone in to control the ever-increasing costs of the labour-intensive department. He'd been certain he had found just the person in Gakere Kamau, a young man in his late twenties with a shiny new bachelor's degree in business administration.

A tall, unflappable woman, Obisola Oboleme consistently showed warmth and concern toward her mostly female, non-unionized employees as they sat in their noisy cubicles, fielding call after call about CIC's products, benefits, eligibility and claims. Because she had worked her way up from a customer service representative position herself, she could look her subordinates right in the eye after they'd fielded a string of stressful calls and tell them she knew exactly how they felt. She did her best to offset the low pay by accommodating the women's needs with flexible scheduling, giving them frequent breaks and offering plenty of training opportunities that kept them up-to-date in the health company's changing products and in the latest problem-solving and customer service techniques.

Her motto was: 'Always put yourself in the subscriber's shoes.' She urged representatives to take the time necessary to thoroughly understand the subscriber's problem and do their best to see that it was completely resolved by the call's completion. Their job was important, she told them. Subscribers counted on them to help them negotiate the complexities of their coverage. Obisola's subordinates adored her, as demonstrated by the 10 per cent

36. Robert J. House, 'A Path–Goal Theory of Leader Effectiveness', *Administrative Science Quarterly* 16 (1971): 321–338.

37. M. G. Evans, 'Leadership', in *Organizational Behavior*, ed. S. Kerr (Columbus, OH: Grid, 1974): 230–233.

38. Robert J. House and Terrence R. Mitchell, 'Path–Goal Theory of Leadership', *Journal of Contemporary Business* (Autumn 1974): 81–97.

39. S. Kerr and J. M. Jermier, 'Substitutes for Leadership: Their Meaning and Measurement', *Organizational Behavior and Human Performance* 22 (1978): 375–403; and Jon P. Howell and Peter W. Dorfman, 'Leadership and Substitutes for Leadership among Professional and Nonprofessional Workers', *Journal of Applied Behavioral Science* 22 (1986): 29–46.

40. Jennifer Reingold, 'Bob Nardelli Is Watching', *Fast Company* (December 2005): 76–83.

41. Charles Greene, 'Questions of Causation in the Path–Goal Theory of Leadership', *Academy of Management Journal* 22 (March 1979): 22–41; and C. A. Schriesheim and Mary Ann von Glinow, 'The Path–Goal Theory of Leadership: A Theoretical and Empirical Analysis', *Academy of Management Journal* 20 (1977): 398–405.

42. Anthony J. Mayo and Nitin Nohria, 'Double Edged Sword', *People Management* (October 27, 2005).

43. The terms *transactional* and *transformational* come from James M. Burns, *Leadership* (New York: Harper & Row, 1978); and Bernard M. Bass, 'Leadership: Good, Better, Best', *Organizational Dynamics* 13 (Winter 1985): 26–40.

44. Katherine J. Klein and Robert J. House, 'On Fire: Charismatic Leadership and Levels of Analysis', *Leadership Quarterly* 6, no. 2 (1995): 183–198.

45. Jay A. Conger and Rabindra N. Kanungo, 'Toward a Behavioral Theory of Charismatic Leadership in Organizational Settings', *Academy of Management Review* 12 (1987): 637–647; Walter Kiechel III, 'A Hard Look at Executive Vision', *Fortune* (October 23, 1989): 207–211; and William L. Gardner and Bruce J. Avolio, 'The Charismatic Relationship: A Dramaturgical Perspective', *Academy of Management Review* 23, no. 1 (1998): 32–58.

46. John Brant, 'What One Man Can Do', *Inc.* (September 2005): 145–153.

47. Robert J. House, 'Research Contrasting the Behavior and Effects of Reputed Charismatic vs. Reputed Non-Charismatic Leaders' (paper presented as part of a symposium), 'Charismatic Leadership: Theory and Evidence', Academy of Management, San Diego, 1985.

48. Robert J. House and Jane M. Howell, 'Personality and Charismatic Leadership', *Leadership Quarterly* 3, no. 2 (1992): 81–108; and Jennifer O'Connor, Michael D. Mumford, Timothy C. Clifton, Theodore L. Gessner and Mary Shane Connelly, 'Charismatic Leaders and Destructiveness: A Historiometric Study', *Leadership Quarterly* 6, no. 4 (1995): 529–555.

49. Bernard M. Bass, 'Theory of Transformational Leadership Redux', *Leadership Quarterly* 6, no. 4 (1995): 463–478; Noel M. Tichy and Mary Anne Devanna, *The Transformational Leader* (New York: John Wiley & Sons, 1986); and Badrinarayan Shankar Pawar and Kenneth K. Eastman, 'The Nature and Implications of Contextual Influences on Transformational Leadership: A Conceptual Examination', *Academy of Management Review* 22, no. 1 (1997): 80–109.

50. Richard L. Daft and Robert H. Lengel, *Fusion Leadership: Unlocking the Subtle Forces that Change People and Organizations* (San Francisco: Berrett-Koehler, 1998).

51. Taly Dvir, Dov Eden, Bruce J. Avolio and Boas Shamir, 'Impact of Transformational Leadership on Follower Development and Performance: A Field Experiment', *Academy of Management Journal* 45, no. 4 (2002): 735–744.

52. Robert S. Rubin, David C. Munz and William H. Bommer, 'Leading From Within: The Effects of Emotion Recognition and Personality on Transformational Leadership Behavior', *Academy of Management Journal* 48, no. 5 (2005): 845–858; and Timothy A. Judge and Joyce E. Bono, 'Five-Factor Model of Personality and Transformational Leadership', *Journal of Applied Psychology* 85, no. 5 (October 2000): 751ff.

53. Rubin *et al.*, 'Leading from Within'.

54. Paul Nadler, 'The Litttle Things That Help Make Wells a Giant', *American Banker* (December 10, 2003): 4; John R. Enger, 'Cross-Sell Campaign', *Banking Strategies* 77, no. 6 (November–December 2001): 34; Bethany McLean, 'Is This Guy the Best Banker in America?', *Fortune* (July 6, 1998): 126–128; and Jacqueline S. Gold, 'Bank to the Future', *Institutional Investor* (September 2001): 54–63.

55. Barbara Kellerman, 'What Every Leader Needs to Know About Followers', *Harvard Business Review* (December 2007): 84–91.

56. Robert E. Kelley, *The Power of Followership* (New York: Doubleday, 1992).

57. *Ibid.*, 117–118.

58. Henry Mintzberg, *Power In and Around Organizations* (Englewood Cliffs, NJ: Prentice Hall, 1983); and Jeffrey Pfeffer, *Power in Organizations* (Marshfield, MA: Pitman, 1981).

59. George Anders, 'Back to Class; How a Principal in New Orleans Saved Her School', *The Wall Street Journal* (January 13, 2006): A1, A6.

60. Jay A. Conger, 'The Necessary Art of Persuasion', *Harvard Business Review* (May–June 1998): 84–95.

61. D. Kipnis, S. M. Schmidt, C. Swaffin-Smith and I. Wilkinson, 'Patterns of Managerial Influence: Shotgun Managers, Tacticians, and Politicians', *Organizational Dynamics* (Winter 1984): 58–67.

62. These tactics are based on Kipnis *et al.*, 'Patterns of Managerial Influence' and Robert B. Cialdini, 'Harnessing the Science of Persuasion', *Harvard Business Review* (October 2001): 72–79.

63. *Ibid.*; and Pfeffer, *Managing with Power: Politics and Influence in Organizations* (Boston: Harvard Business School Press, 1992): Chapter 13.

64. *Ibid.*

65. V. Dallas Merrell, *Huddling: The Informal Way to Management Success* (New York: AMACOM, 1979).

66. Robert B. Cialdini, *Influence: Science and Practice,* 4th ed. (Boston: Pearson Allyn & Bacon, 2000).

67. Diane Brady, 'The Immelt Revolution', *BusinessWeek* (March 28, 2005): 64–71.

68. Harvey G. Enns and Dean B. McFarlin, 'When Executives Influence Peers, Does Function Matter?', *Human Resource Management* 4, no. 2 (Summer 2003): 125–142.

69. Daft and Lengel, *Fusion Leadership*.

70. Jim Collins, 'The 10 Greatest CEOs of All Time', *Fortune* (July 21, 2003): 54–68.

71. Robert K. Greenleaf, *Servant Leadership: A Journey into the Nature of Legitimate Power and Greatness* (Mahwah, NJ: Paulist Press, 1977).

72. Anne Fitzgerald, 'Christmas Bonus Stuns Employees', *The Des Moines Register* (December 20, 2003), http://www.desmoinesregister.com.

73. Collins, 'The 10 Greatest CEOs of All Time'.

74. Richard L. Daft, *The Leadership Experience*, 3rd ed. (Cincinnati, OH: South-Western, 2005), Chapter 6.

75. Badaracco, 'A Lesson for the Times: Learning From Quiet Leaders'.

76. Jim Collins, 'The 10 Greatest CEOs of All Time'.

77. Byrne, 'How to Lead Now'.

78. Maha El Dahan (2006) 'Spirited Newcomer Thirsts For Market Share', *ZAWYA: Business Monthly* (February 2006) online, available from https://www.zawya.com/printstory.cfm?storyid=ZAWYA20060208084639&l−000000060226 (accessed November 18, 2008).

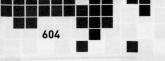

Are You Engaged or Disengaged?[1]

The term *employee engagement* is becoming popular in the corporate world. To learn what engagement means, answer the following questions twice – (1) once for a course you both enjoyed and performed well and (2) a second time for a course you did not enjoy and performed poorly. Mark a '1' to indicate whether each item is Mostly True or Mostly False for the course you enjoyed and performed well. Mark a '2' to indicate whether each item is Mostly True or Mostly False for the course you did not enjoy and performed poorly.

		Mostly True	Mostly False
1	I made sure to study on a regular basis.	☐	☐
2	I put forth effort.	☐	☐
3	I found ways to make the course material relevant to my life.	☐	☐
4	I found ways to make the course interesting to me.	☐	☐
5	I raised my hand in class.	☐	☐
6	I had fun in class.	☐	☐
7	I participated actively in small group discussions.	☐	☐
8	I helped fellow students.	☐	☐

SCORING AND INTERPRETATION   Engagement means that people involve and express themselves in their work, going beyond the minimum effort required. Engagement typically has a positive relationship with both personal satisfaction and performance. If this relationship was true for your classes, the number of '1s' in the Mostly True column will be higher than the number of '2s.' You might expect a score of 6 or higher for a course in which you were engaged, and possibly 3 or lower if you were disengaged.

The challenge for a new manager is to learn to engage subordinates in the same way your instructors in your favourite classes were able to engage you. Teaching is similar to managing. What techniques did your instructors use to engage students? Which techniques can you use to engage people when you become a new manager?

TAKE A MOMENT   Would this issue concern you if you were a manager at Currys? Long hours and hard work are often a part of corporate life. If people are paid good wages and rewarded with bonuses when they put in extra effort, shouldn't managers expect them to remain satisfied, motivated and productive?

The problem at Currys headquarters is that many experienced employees are losing their drive. Currys executives are continually looking for ways to do things better, faster and cheaper than the competition, but they realize that simply pushing for greater productivity is not the key to reviving employee morale and motivation. This situation can be a problem even for the most successful and admired of organizations, when experienced, valuable employees lose the motivation and commitment they once felt, causing a decline in their performance. One secret for success in organizations is motivated and enthusiastic employees. The challenge for Currys and other companies is to keep employee motivation consistent with organizational goals.

Motivation is a challenge for managers because motivation arises from within employees and typically differs for each person. For example, Janice Rennie makes $350 000 a year selling residential real estate in Toronto, Canada; she attributes her success to the fact that she likes to listen carefully to clients and then find houses to meet their needs. Greg Storey is a skilled machinist who is challenged by writing programmes for numerically controlled machines. After dropping out of college, he swept floors in a machine shop and was motivated to learn to run the machines. Frances Blais sells educational books and software. She is a top salesperson, but she doesn't care about the £50 000-plus commissions: 'I'm not even thinking money when I'm selling. I'm really on a crusade to help children read well.' In stark contrast, Rob Michaels gets sick to his stomach before he goes to work. Rob is a telephone salesperson who spends all day trying to get people to buy products they do not need, and the rejections are painful. His motivation is money; he earned $120 000 in the past year and cannot make nearly that much doing anything else.[2]

Rob is motivated by money, Janice by her love of listening and problem solving, Frances by the desire to help children read, and Greg by the challenge of mastering numerically controlled machinery. Each person is motivated to perform, yet each has different reasons for performing. With such diverse motivations, it is a challenge for managers to motivate employees toward common organizational goals.

This chapter reviews theories and models of employee motivation. First we examine various perspectives on motivation and consider several models that describe the employee needs and processes associated with motivation. We discuss goal-setting theory and the reinforcement perspective on motivation, as well as examine how *job design* – changing the structure of the work itself – can affect employee satisfaction and productivity. Finally, we discuss the trend of *empowerment*, where authority and decision-making are delegated to subordinates to increase employee motivation, and look at how managers can imbue work with a sense of meaning to inspire and motivate employees to higher performance.

The Concept of Motivation

Most of us get up in the morning, go to school or work, and behave in ways that are predictably our own. We respond to our environment and the people in it with little thought as to why we work hard, enjoy certain classes, or find some recreational activities so much fun. Yet all these behaviours are motivated by something. Motivation refers to the forces either within or external to a person that arouse enthusiasm and persistence to pursue a certain course of action. Employee motivation affects productivity, and part of a manager's job is to channel motivation toward the accomplishment of organizational goals.[3] The study of motivation helps managers understand what prompts people to initiate action, what influences their choice of action, and why they persist in that action over time.

A simple model of human motivation is illustrated in Exhibit 16.1. People have basic *needs* – for food, achievement or monetary gain – that translate into an internal tension that motivates specific behaviours with which to fulfil the need. To the extent that the behaviour is successful, the person is rewarded in the sense that the need is satisfied. The reward also informs the person that the behaviour was appropriate and can be used again in the future.

Motivation
The arousal, direction, and persistence of behaviour.

Exhibit 16.1 A Simple Model of Motivation

NEED Creates desire to fulfil needs (food, friendship, recognition, achievement) → BEHAVIOUR Results in actions to fulfil needs → REWARDS Satisfy needs; intrinsic or extrinsic rewards

FEEDBACK Reward informs person whether behaviour was appropriate and should be used again.

Intrinsic reward
The satisfaction received in the process of performing an action.

Extrinsic reward
A reward given by another person.

Rewards are of two types: intrinsic and extrinsic. Intrinsic rewards are the satisfactions a person receives in the process of performing a particular action. The completion of a complex task may bestow a pleasant feeling of accomplishment, or solving a problem that benefits others may fulfil a personal mission. For example, Frances Blais sells educational materials for the intrinsic reward of helping children read well. Extrinsic rewards are given by another person, typically a manager, and include promotions, pay increases and bonuses. They originate externally, as a result of pleasing others. Rob Michaels, who hates his sales job, nevertheless is motivated by the extrinsic reward of high pay. Although extrinsic rewards are important, good managers strive to help people achieve intrinsic rewards as well. The most talented and innovative employees are rarely motivated exclusively by rewards such as money and benefits, or even praise and recognition. Instead, they seek satisfaction from the work itself.[4] For example, at Google, people are motivated by an idealistic goal of providing 'automated universal transference', which basically means unifying data and information around the world and totally obliterating language barriers via the internet. People are energized by the psychic rewards they get from working on intellectually stimulating and challenging technical problems, as well as by the potentially beneficial global impact of their work.[5]

TAKE A MOMENT   As a new manager, remember that people will be more engaged when they do things they really like. Take the New Manager Self-Test opposite to understand what engages you in a class. You will read more about engagement later in the chapter.

The importance of motivation as illustrated in Exhibit 16.1 is that it can lead to behaviours that reflect high performance within organizations. Studies have found that high employee motivation goes hand-in-hand with high organizational performance and profits.[6] Managers can use motivation theory to help satisfy employees' needs and simultaneously encourage high work performance. With massive layoffs in many organizations all over the world in recent years and a decline in trust of corporate leadership, managers are struggling to keep employees focused and motivated. Finding and keeping talented workers is a growing challenge. Managers have to find the right combination of motivational techniques and rewards to keep people satisfied and productive in a variety of organizational situations.

Foundations of Motivation

A manager's assumptions about employee motivation and the use of rewards depend on his or her perspective on motivation. Four distinct perspectives on employee motivation have evolved: the traditional approach, the human relations approach, the human resource approach and the contemporary approach.[7]

NEW MANAGER SELF-TEST

Your Approach to Motivating Others

Think about situations in which you were in a student group or organization. Think about your informal approach as a leader and answer the questions below. Indicate whether each item below is Mostly False or Mostly True for you.

		Mostly True	Mostly False
1	I ask the other person what rewards they value for high performance.	☐	☐
2	I only reward people if their performance is up to standard.	☐	☐
3	I find out if the person has the ability to do what needs to be done.	☐	☐
4	I use a variety of rewards (treats, recognition) to reinforce exceptional performance.	☐	☐
5	I explain exactly what needs to be done for the person I'm trying to motivate.	☐	☐
6	I generously and publicly praise people who perform well.	☐	☐
7	Before giving somebody a reward, I find out what would appeal to that person.	☐	☐
8	I promptly commend others when they do a better-than-average job.	☐	☐

SCORING AND INTERPRETATION The questions above represent two related aspects of motivation theory. For the aspect of *expectancy theory*, sum the points for Mostly True to the odd-numbered questions. For the aspect of *reinforcement theory*, sum the points for Mostly True for the even-numbered questions. The scores for my approach to motivation are:

My use of expectancy theory _____

My use of reinforcement theory _____

These two scores represent how you apply the motivational concepts of expectancy and reinforcement in your role as an informal leader. Three or more points on *expectancy theory* means you motivate people by managing expectations. You understand how a person's effort leads to performance and make sure that high performance leads to valued rewards. Three or more points for *reinforcement theory* means that you attempt to modify people's behaviour in a positive direction with frequent and prompt positive reinforcement. New managers often learn to use reinforcements first, and as they gain more experience are able to apply expectancy theory.

SOURCES These questions are based on D. Whetten and K. Cameron, *Developing Management Skills*, 5th ed. (Upper Saddle River, NJ: Prentice-Hall, 2002), pp. 302–303; and P. M. Podsakoff, S. B. Mackenzie, R. H. Moorman, and R. Fetter, 'Transformational Leader Behaviors and Their Effects on Followers'; Trust in Leader, Satisfaction, and Organizational Citizenship Behaviors', *Leadership Quarterly* 1, no. 2 (1990): 107–142.

Traditional Approach

The study of employee motivation really began with the work of Frederick W. Taylor on scientific management. Recall from Chapter 2 that scientific management pertains to the systematic analysis of an employee's job for the purpose of increasing efficiency. Economic rewards are provided to employees for high performance. The emphasis on pay evolved into the notion of the *economic man* – people would work harder for higher pay. This approach led to the development of incentive pay systems, in which people were paid strictly on the quantity and quality of their work outputs.

Human Relations Approach

The economic man was gradually replaced by a more sociable employee in managers' minds. Beginning with the landmark Hawthorne studies at a Western Electric plant, as described in Chapter 2, noneconomic rewards, such as congenial work groups that met social needs, seemed more important than money as a motivator of work behaviour.[8] For the first time, workers were studied as people, and the concept of *social man* was born.

Human Resource Approach

Content theories
A group of theories that emphasize the needs that motivate people.

The human resource approach carries the concepts of economic man and social man further to introduce the concept of the *whole person*. Human resource theory suggests that employees are complex and motivated by many factors. For example, the work by McGregor on Theory X and Theory Y described in Chapter 2 argued that people want to do a good job and that work is as natural and healthy as play. Proponents of the human resource approach believed that earlier approaches had tried to manipulate employees through economic or social rewards. By assuming that employees are competent and able to make major contributions, managers can enhance organizational performance. The human resource approach laid the groundwork for contemporary perspectives on employee motivation.

CONCEPT CONNECTION Managers at Swedish retailer ICA in Sweden believe that creating a work environment that is rich in opportunity, challenge and reward motivates employees and is key to the company's success. By providing clear goals and objectives, performance reviews, formal and informal education programmes, functional training, lateral promotions, and individual mentoring, managers help employees such as Lars Bengtsson, find both intrinsic and extrinsic rewards in their work. Bengtsson has been assisting shoppers and winning hearts at ICA supermarket in Almhult since the store opened in 1976. 'He's the Mayor of ICA,' says Store Director Madelene Gummesson.

Contemporary Approach

The contemporary approach to employee motivation is dominated by three types of theories, each of which will be discussed in the following sections. The first are *content theories*, which stress the analysis of underlying human needs. Content theories provide insight into the needs of people in organizations and help managers understand how needs can be satisfied in the workplace. *Process theories* concern the thought processes that influence behaviour. They focus on how people seek rewards in work circumstances. *Reinforcement theories* focus on employee learning of desired work behaviours. In Exhibit 16.1, content theories focus on the concepts in the first box, process theories on those in the second and reinforcement theories on those in the third.

Content Perspectives on Motivation

Content theories emphasize the needs that motivate people. At any point in time, people have basic needs such as those for monetary reward, achievement or recognition. These needs translate into an internal drive that motivates specific

Exhibit 16.2 Maslow's Hierarchy of Needs

Fulfilment off the Job	Need Hierarchy	Fulfilment on the Job
Education, religion, hobbies, personal growth	Self-Actualization Needs	Opportunities for training, advancement, growth and creativity
Approval of family, friends, community	Esteem Needs	Recognition, high status, increased responsibilities
Family, friends, community groups	Belongingness Needs	Work groups, clients, coworkers, supervisors
Freedom from war, pollution, violence	Safety Needs	Safe work, fringe benefits, job security
Food, water, oxygen	Physiological Needs	Heat, air, basic salary

behaviours in an attempt to fulfil the needs. In other words, our needs are like a hidden catalogue of the things we want and will work to get. To the extent that managers understand employees' needs, they can design reward systems to meet them and direct employees' energies and priorities toward attaining organizational goals.

Hierarchy of Needs Theory

Probably the most famous content theory was developed by Abraham Maslow.[9] Maslow's hierarchy of needs theory proposes that people are motivated by multiple needs and that these needs exist in a hierarchical order, as illustrated in Exhibit 16.2. Maslow identified five general types of motivating needs in order of ascendance:

1 *Physiological needs.* These most basic human physical needs include food, water and oxygen. In the organizational setting, they are reflected in the needs for adequate heat, air and basic salary to ensure survival.

2 *Safety needs.* These needs include a safe and secure physical and emotional environment and freedom from threats – that is, for freedom from violence and for an orderly society. In an organizational workplace, safety needs reflect the needs for safe jobs, fringe benefits and job security.

3 *Belongingness needs.* These needs reflect the desire to be accepted by one's peers, have friendships, be part of a group and be loved. In the organization, these needs influence the desire for good relationships with coworkers, participation in a work group and a positive relationship with supervisors.

4 *Esteem needs.* These needs relate to the desire for a positive self-image and to receive attention, recognition and appreciation from others. Within organizations, esteem needs reflect a motivation for recognition, an increase in responsibility, high status and credit for contributions to the organization.

5 *Self-actualization needs.* These needs include the need for self-fulfilment, which is the highest need category. They concern developing one's full potential, increasing one's competence, and becoming a better person. Self-actualization needs can be met in the organization by providing people with opportunities to grow, be creative and acquire training for challenging assignments and advancement.

Hierarchy of needs theory
A content theory that proposes that people are motivated by five categories of needs – physiological, safety, belongingness, esteem and self-actualization – that exist in a hierarchical order.

According to Maslow's theory, low-order needs take priority – they must be satisfied before higher-order needs are activated. The needs are satisfied in sequence: physiological needs come before safety needs, safety needs before social needs, and so on. A person desiring physical safety will devote his or her efforts to securing a safer environment and will not be concerned with esteem needs or self-actualization needs. Once a need is satisfied, it declines in importance and the next higher need is activated.

A study of employees in the manufacturing department of a major health care company in the UK provides some support for Maslow's theory. Most line workers emphasized that they worked at the company primarily because of the good pay, benefits and job security. Thus, employees' lower level physiological and safety needs were being met. When questioned about their motivation, employees indicated the importance of positive social relationships with both peers and supervisors (belongingness needs) and a desire for greater respect and recognition from management (esteem needs).[10]

TAKE A MOMENT   As a new manager, recognize that some people are motivated primarily to satisfy lower-level physiological and safety needs, while others want to satisfy higher-level needs. Learn which lower- and higher-level needs motivate you by completing the Experiential Exercise on page 635.

ERG Theory

ERG theory
A modification of the needs hierarchy theory that proposes three categories of needs: existence, relatedness and growth.

Clayton Alderfer proposed a modification of Maslow's theory in an effort to simplify it and respond to criticisms of its lack of empirical verification.[11] His **ERG theory** identified three categories of needs:

1 *Existence needs.* The needs for physical well-being.

2 *Relatedness needs.* The needs for satisfactory relationships with others.

3 *Growth needs.* The needs that focus on the development of human potential and the desire for personal growth and increased competence.

Frustration–regression principle
The idea that failure to meet a high-order need may cause a regression to an already satisfied lower-order need.

The ERG model and Maslow's need hierarchy are similar because both are in hierarchical form and presume that individuals move up the hierarchy one step at a time. However, Alderfer reduced the number of need categories to three and proposed that movement up the hierarchy is more complex, reflecting a **frustration–regression principle**, namely, that failure to meet a high-order need may trigger a regression to an already fulfilled lower-order need. Thus, a worker who cannot fulfil a need for personal growth may revert to a lower-order need and redirect his or her efforts toward making a lot of money. The ERG model therefore is less rigid than Maslow's need hierarchy, suggesting that individuals may move down as well as up the hierarchy, depending on their ability to satisfy needs.

Need hierarchy theory helps explain why organizations find ways to recognize employees, encourage their participation in decision-making, and give them opportunities to make significant contributions to the organization and society. For example, Cahoot Bank, a subsidiary of Santander UK plc, is not using bank tellers or cashiers. These positions are now front-line managers who are expected to make decisions and contribute ideas for improving the business.[12] USAA, which offers insurance, mutual funds and banking services to five million members of the military and their families, provides another example.

INNOVATIVE WAY

USAA

USAA's customer service agents are on the front lines in helping families challenged by war and overseas deployment manage their financial responsibilities. Managers recognize that the most important factor in the company's success is the relationship between USAA members and these front-line employees.

To make sure that relationship is a good one, USAA treats customer service reps, who are often considered the lowest rung on the corporate ladder, like professionals. People have a real sense that they're making life just a little easier for military members and their families, which instils them with a feeling of pride and accomplishment. Employees are organized into small, tightly knit 'expert teams' and are encouraged to suggest changes that will benefit customers. One service rep suggested that the company offer insurance premium billing timed to coincide with the military's bi-weekly pay checks. Service reps don't have scripts to follow, and calls aren't timed. Employees know they can take whatever time they need to give the customer the best possible service.

Giving people the opportunity to make real contributions has paid off. In a study by Forrester Research, 81 per cent of USAA customers said they believe the company does what's best for them, rather than what's best for the bottom line. Compare that to about 20 per cent of customers for financial services firms such as JP Morgan Chase and Citibank.[13]

A recent survey found that employees who contribute ideas at work, such as those at USAA, are more likely to feel valued, committed, and motivated. In addition, when employees' ideas are implemented and recognized, a motivational effect often ripples throughout the workforce.[14]

Many companies are finding that creating a humane work environment that allows people to achieve a balance between work and personal life is also a great high-level motivator. Flexibility in the workplace, including options such as telecommuting, flexible hours and job sharing, is highly valued by today's employees because it enables them to manage their work and personal responsibilities. Flexibility is good for organizations too. Employees who have control over their work schedules are significantly less likely to suffer job burnout and are more highly committed to their employers, as shown in Exhibit 16.3. This idea was supported by a survey conducted at Deloitte, which found that client service professionals cited workplace flexibility as a strong reason for wanting to stay with the firm. Another study at Prudential Insurance found that work-life satisfaction and work flexibility directly correlated to job satisfaction, organizational commitment, and employee retention.[15]

Making work fun can play a role in creating this balance. One psychologist recently updated Maslow's hierarchy of needs for a new generation and included the need to have fun as a substantial motivator for today's employees.[16] Having fun at work relieves stress and enables people to feel more 'whole', rather than feeling that their personal lives are totally separate from their work lives. Something as simple as a manager's choice of language can create a lighter, more fun environment. Research suggests the use of phrases such as 'Play around with this ... Explore the possibility of ... Have fun with ... Don't worry about little mistakes ... View this as a game ...' and so forth can effectively build elements of fun and playfulness into a workplace.[17]

Two-Factor Theory

Frederick Herzberg developed another popular theory of motivation called the *two-factor theory*.[18] Herzberg interviewed hundreds of workers about times when they were highly motivated to work and other times when they were dissatisfied and

Exhibit 16.3 The Motivational Benefits of Job Flexibility

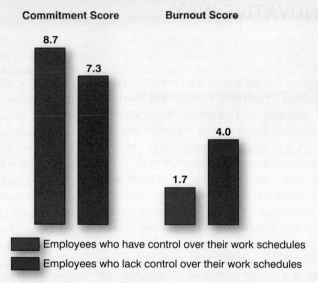

Commitment Score   Burnout Score

8.7

7.3

4.0

1.7

SOURCE: WFD Consulting data, as reported in Karol Rose, 'Work-Life Effectiveness', *Fortune* (September 29, 2003): S1–S17.

Employees who have control over their work schedules

Employees who lack control over their work schedules

un-motivated at work. His findings suggested that the work characteristics associated with dissatisfaction were quite different from those pertaining to satisfaction, which prompted the notion that two factors influence work motivation.

The two-factor theory is illustrated in Exhibit 16.4. The centre of the scale is neutral, meaning that workers are neither satisfied nor dissatisfied. Herzberg believed that two entirely separate dimensions contribute to an employee's behaviour at

Exhibit 16.4 Herzberg's Two-Factor Theory

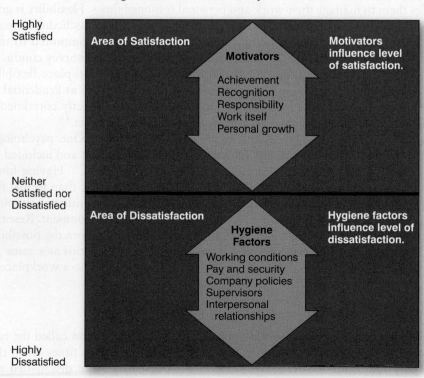

Highly Satisfied

Area of Satisfaction

Motivators

Achievement
Recognition
Responsibility
Work itself
Personal growth

Motivators influence level of satisfaction.

Neither Satisfied nor Dissatisfied

Area of Dissatisfaction

Hygiene Factors

Working conditions
Pay and security
Company policies
Supervisors
Interpersonal relationships

Hygiene factors influence level of dissatisfaction.

Highly Dissatisfied

work. The first, called hygiene factors, involves the presence or absence of job dissatisfiers, such as working conditions, pay, company policies and interpersonal relationships. When hygiene factors are poor, work is dissatisfying. However, good hygiene factors simply remove the dissatisfaction; they do not in themselves cause people to become highly satisfied and motivated in their work.

The second set of factors does influence job satisfaction. Motivators focus on high-level needs and include achievement, recognition, responsibility and opportunity for growth. Herzberg believed that when motivators are absent, workers are neutral toward work, but when motivators are present, workers are highly motivated and satisfied. Thus, hygiene factors and motivators represent two distinct factors that influence motivation. Hygiene factors work only in the area of dissatisfaction. Unsafe working conditions or a noisy work environment will cause people to be dissatisfied, but their correction will not lead to a high level of motivation and satisfaction. Motivators such as challenge, responsibility and recognition must be in place before employees will be highly motivated to excel at their work.

The implication of the two-factor theory for managers is clear. On one hand, providing hygiene factors will eliminate employee dissatisfaction but will not motivate workers to high achievement levels. On the other hand, recognition, challenge and opportunities for personal growth are powerful motivators and will promote high satisfaction and performance. The manager's role is to remove dissatisfiers – that is, to provide hygiene factors sufficient to meet basic needs – and then to use motivators to meet higher-level needs and propel employees toward greater achievement and satisfaction. Consider how Vision Express, one of the UK and Europe's largest providers of eye care benefits, uses both hygiene factors and motivators.

Hygiene factors
Factors that involve the presence or absence of job dissatisfiers, including working conditions, pay, company policies and interpersonal relationships.

Motivators
Factors that influence job satisfaction based on fulfilment of high-level needs such as achievement, recognition, responsibility and opportunity for growth.

 # INNOVATIVE WAY

Vision Express[19]

Based in Nottingham, UK, Vision Express has seen its workforce nearly triple over the past few decades. Despite the challenges of rapid growth, employee satisfaction levels have climbed to an astonishing high of 98 per cent. Vision Express is a subsidiary of GrandVision, which employs 3600 people and operates 873 store throughout Europe, including the GrandOptical, Generale D'Optique and Solaris multiple chains.

Vision Express doesn't offer outrageous salaries and stock options; it does make sure people are paid fairly and provided with solid benefits. The real key to high motivation and satisfaction at Vision Express, though, is that people feel valued and respected. The process starts the minute someone is hired. Managers use a checklist of items that should be waiting for the new employee upon arrival. Having such basics as a computer, voice mail and email accounts, a nameplate and business cards helps the newcomer feel like a member of the team. Supervisors give each new employee a picture frame with a note from the CEO encouraging them to use it to display the important people in their lives. A career development programme gives employees opportunities to examine their personal priorities, develop their skills and discuss their career objectives. If someone wants a new job in the company that he or she is not qualified for, Vision Express sets up an individualized training programme to help bridge the gap.

Open communication is another high-level motivator. Issues are raised, debated and dealt with openly, and people have all the information they need to do their best work. CEO Bryan Magraph personally answers emails from any employee, randomly sits with employees in the company cafeteria, and holds biannual employee meetings where he shares all company information and answers any employee question on the spot. This openness is motivating to employees, who appreciate the higher responsibility and the respect and trust that it implies.

By incorporating both hygiene factors and motivators, managers at Vision Express have created an environment where people are highly motivated and want to stay.

© CHRIS HONDROS/NEWSMAKERS/GETTY IMAGES

CONCEPT CONNECTION According to General Electric CEO Jeffrey Immelt, people who succeed at GE are usually those who have a strong need for achievement or need for affiliation. 'We lose people who just want to make a lot of money, or just want to be powerful. But if you like building stuff, and you like who you work with, this is a pretty energizing place to work.' Immelt is counting on those highly motivated employees as he tries to steer the multinational conglomerate toward unprecedented growth by transforming it into a customer-driven company that thrives on innovation as well as superior productivity.

Acquired Needs Theory

The final content theory was developed by David McClelland. The *acquired needs theory* proposes that certain types of needs are acquired during the individual's lifetime. In other words, people are not born with these needs but may learn them through their life experiences.[20] The three needs most frequently studied are these:

1 *Need for achievement*. The desire to accomplish something difficult, attain a high standard of success, master complex tasks and surpass others.

2 *Need for affiliation*. The desire to form close personal relationships, avoid conflict and establish warm friendships.

3 *Need for power*. The desire to influence or control others, be responsible for others and have authority over others.

Early life experiences determine whether people acquire these needs. If children are encouraged to do things for themselves and receive reinforcement, they will acquire a need to achieve. If they are reinforced for forming warm human relationships, they will develop a need for affiliation. If they get satisfaction from controlling others, they will acquire a need for power.

For more than 20 years, McClelland studied human needs and their implications for management. People with a high need for achievement are frequently entrepreneurs. The parents of social entrepreneur Bill Strickland, the charismatic leader who established Manchester Bidwell, described in the previous chapter, always encouraged him to follow his dreams. When he wanted to go south to work with the Freedom Riders in the 1960s, they supported him. His plans for tearing up the family basement and making a photography studio were met with equal enthusiasm. Strickland thus developed a need for *achievement* that enabled him to accomplish amazing results later in life.[21] People who have a high need for *affiliation* are successful integrators, whose job is to coordinate the work of several departments in an organization.[22] Integrators include brand managers and project managers who must have excellent people skills. People high in need for affiliation are able to establish positive working relationships with others.

A high need for *power* often is associated with successful attainment of top levels in the organizational hierarchy. For example, McClelland studied managers at AT&T for 16 years and found that those with a high need for power were more likely to follow a path of continued promotion over time. More than half of the employees at the top levels had a high need for power. In contrast, managers with a high need for achievement but a low need for power tended to peak earlier in their careers and at a lower level. The reason is that achievement needs can be met through the task itself, but power needs can be met only by ascending to a level at which a person has power over others.

In summary, content theories focus on people's underlying needs and label those particular needs that motivate behaviour. The hierarchy of needs theory, the ERG theory, the two-factor theory, and the acquired needs theory all help managers understand what motivates people. In this way, managers can design work to meet needs and hence elicit appropriate and successful work behaviours.

Process Perspectives on Motivation

Process theories explain how people select behavioural actions to meet their needs and determine whether their choices were successful. The two basic process theories are equity theory and expectancy theory.

Equity Theory

Equity theory focuses on individuals' perceptions of how fairly they are treated compared with others. Developed by J. Stacy Adams, equity theory proposes that people are motivated to seek social equity in the rewards they expect for performance.[23]

According to equity theory, if people perceive their compensation as equal to what others receive for similar contributions, they will believe that their treatment is fair and equitable. People evaluate equity by a ratio of inputs to outcomes. Inputs to a job include education, experience, effort and ability. Outcomes from a job include pay, recognition, benefits and promotions. The input-to-outcome ratio may be compared to another person in the work group or to a perceived group average. A state of **equity** exists whenever the ratio of one person's outcomes to inputs equals the ratio of another's outcomes to inputs.

Inequity occurs when the input-to-outcome ratios are out of balance, such as when a person with a high level of education or experience receives the same salary as a new, less-educated employee. Interestingly, perceived inequity also occurs in the other direction. Thus, if an employee discovers she is making more money than other people who contribute the same inputs to the company, she may feel the need to correct the inequity by working harder, getting more education or considering lower pay. Studies of the brain have shown that people get less satisfaction from money they receive without having to earn it than they do from money they work to receive.[24] Perceived inequity creates tensions within individuals that motivate them to bring equity into balance.[25]

The most common methods for reducing a perceived inequity are these:

- *Change inputs.* A person may choose to increase or decrease his or her inputs to the organization. For example, underpaid individuals may reduce their level of effort or increase their absenteeism. Overpaid people may increase effort on the job.
- *Change outcomes.* A person may change his or her outcomes. An underpaid person may request a salary increase or a bigger office. A union may try to improve wages and working conditions in order to be consistent with a comparable union whose members make more money.
- *Distort perceptions.* Research suggests that people may distort perceptions of equity if they are unable to change inputs or outcomes. They may artificially increase the status attached to their jobs or distort others' perceived rewards to bring equity into balance.
- *Leave the job.* People who feel inequitably treated may decide to leave their jobs rather than suffer the inequity of being under- or over-paid. In their new jobs, they expect to find a more favourable balance of rewards.

The implication of equity theory for managers is that employees indeed evaluate the perceived equity of their rewards compared to others'. An increase in salary or a promotion will have no motivational effect if it is perceived as inequitable relative to that of other employees.

Inequitable pay puts pressure on employees that is sometimes almost too great to bear. They attempt to change their work habits, try to change the system, or leave the job.[26] Consider Deb Allen, who went into the office on a weekend to catch up on work and found a document accidentally left on the copy machine. When she saw that some new employees were earning €200 000 more than her counterparts with more experience, and that 'a noted screw-up' was making more than highly competent people, Allen began questioning why she was working on weekends for less pay than many others were receiving. Allen became so demoralized by the inequity that she left her job three months later.[27]

TAKE A MOMENT

As a new manager, be aware of equity feeling on your team. Don't play favourites, such as regularly praising some while overlooking others making similar contributions. Keep equity in mind when you make decisions about compensation and other rewards.

© PHOTOLIBRARY

CONCEPT CONNECTION

BMW sales managers are using expectancy theory principles to help meet employee's needs while attaining organizational goals. By creating an incentive programme that is a commission-based plan designed to provide the highest compensation to sales counsellors who are committed to serving every customer, BMW achieves its volume and profitability objectives. The incentive programme is also used in other areas such as distribution, where employees are recognized for accomplishments in safety, productivity and attendance.

Expectancy Theory

Expectancy theory suggests that motivation depends on individuals' expectations about their ability to perform tasks and receive desired rewards. Expectancy theory is associated with the work of Victor Vroom, although a number of scholars have made contributions in this area.[28] Expectancy theory is concerned not with identifying types of needs but with the thinking process that individuals use to achieve rewards. Consider Amy Huang, a university student with a strong desire for a B in her accounting course. Amy has a C+ average and one more exam to take. Amy's motivation to study for that last exam will be influenced by (1) the expectation that hard study will lead to an A on the exam and (2) the expectation that an A on the exam will result in a B for the course. If Amy believes she cannot get an A on the exam or that receiving an A will not lead to a B for the course, she will not be motivated to study exceptionally hard.

Elements of Expectancy Theory

Expectancy theory is based on the relationship among the individual's *effort*, the individual's *performance* and the desirability of *outcomes* associated with high performance. These elements and the relationships among them are illustrated in Exhibit 16.5. The keys to expectancy theory are the expectancies for the relationships among effort, performance, and the value of the outcomes to the individual.

E → P expectancy involves determining whether putting effort into a task will lead to high performance. For this expectancy to be high, the individual must have the ability, previous experience, and necessary machinery, tools and opportunity to perform. For Amy Huang to get a B in the accounting course, the E → P expectancy is high if Amy truly believes that with hard work, she can get an A on the final exam. If Amy believes she has neither the ability nor the opportunity to achieve high performance, the expectancy will be low, and so will be her motivation.

P → O expectancy involves determining whether successful performance will lead to the desired outcome. In the case of a person who is motivated to win a job related award, this expectancy concerns the belief that high performance will truly lead to the award. If the P → O expectancy is high, the individual will be more highly motivated. If the expectancy is that high performance will not produce the desired outcome, motivation will be lower. If an A on the final exam is likely to produce a B in the accounting course, Amy Huang's P → O expectancy will be high. Amy might talk to the professor to see whether an A will

Exhibit 16.5 Major Elements of Expectancy Theory

be sufficient to earn her a B in the course. If not, she will be less motivated to study hard for the final exam.

Valence is the value of outcomes, or attraction to outcomes, for the individual. If the outcomes that are available from high effort and good performance are not valued by employees, motivation will be low. Likewise, if outcomes have a high value, motivation will be higher.

Expectancy theory attempts not to define specific types of needs or rewards but only to establish that they exist and may be different for every individual. One employee might want to be promoted to a position of increased responsibility, and another might have high valence for good relationships with peers. Consequently, the first person will be motivated to work hard for a promotion and the second for the opportunity of a team position that will keep him or her associated with a group. Recent studies by the Gallup Organization substantiate the idea that rewards need to be individualized to be motivating. A recent finding from the US Department of Labor shows that the number one reason people leave their jobs is because they 'don't feel appreciated'. Yet Gallup's analysis of 10 000 workgroups in 30 industries found that making people feel appreciated depends on finding the right kind of reward for each individual. Some people prefer tangible rewards or gifts, while others place high value on words of recognition. In addition, some want public recognition while others prefer to be quietly praised by someone they admire and respect. Many of today's managers are also finding that praise and recognition from one's peers often means more than a pat on the back from a supervisor, so they are implementing peer-recognition programmes that encourage employees to applaud one another for accomplishments.[29]

A simple sales department example illustrates how the expectancy model in Exhibit 16.5 works. If Carl, a salesperson at the Harrods, believes that increased selling effort will lead to higher personal sales, we can say that he has a high E $\rightarrow$ P expectancy. Moreover, if Carl also believes that higher personal sales will lead to a promotion or pay raise, we can say that he has a high P $\rightarrow$ O expectancy. Finally, if Carl places a high value on the promotion or pay raise, valence is high and he will have a high motivational force. On the other hand, if either the E $\rightarrow$ P or P $\rightarrow$ O expectancy is low, or if the money or promotion has low valence for Carl, the overall motivational force will be low. For an employee to be highly motivated, all three factors in the expectancy model must be high.[30]

Expectancy theory
A process theory that proposes that motivation depends on individuals' expectations about their ability to perform tasks and receive desired rewards.

E → P expectancy
Expectancy that putting effort into a given task will lead to high performance.

P → O expectancy
Expectancy that successful performance of a task will lead to the desired outcome.

Valence
The value or attraction an individual has for an outcome.

Implications for Managers

The expectancy theory of motivation is similar to the path–goal theory of leadership described in Chapter 15. Both theories are personalized to subordinates' needs and goals. Managers' responsibility is to help subordinates meet their needs and at the same time attain organizational goals. Managers try to find a match between a subordinate's skills and abilities, job demands, and available rewards. To increase motivation, managers can clarify individuals' needs, define the outcomes available from the organization, and ensure that each individual has the ability and support (namely, time and equipment) needed to attain outcomes.

Some companies use expectancy theory principles by designing incentive systems that identify desired organizational outcomes and give everyone the same shot at getting the rewards. The trick is to design a system that fits with employees' abilities and needs.

Goal-Setting Theory

Recall from Chapter 7 our discussion of the importance and purposes of goals. Numerous studies have shown that people are more motivated when they have specific targets or objectives to work toward.[31] You have probably noticed in your own life that you are more motivated when you have a specific goal, such as making an A on a final exam, losing 5 kilograms over the next three months or earning enough money during the summer to buy a used car.

Goal-setting theory, described by Edwin Locke and Gary Latham, proposes that managers can increase motivation by setting specific, challenging goals that are accepted as valid by subordinates, then helping people track their progress toward goal achievement by providing timely feedback. The four key components of goal-setting theory include the following:[32]

Goal-setting theory
A motivation theory in which specific, challenging goals increase motivation and performance when the goals are accepted by subordinates and these subordinates receive feedback to indicate their progress toward goal achievement.

- *Goal specificity* refers to the degree to which goals are concrete and unambiguous. Specific goals such as 'Visit one new customer each day', or 'Sell $1000 worth of merchandise a week' are more motivating than vague goals such as 'Keep in touch with new customers' or 'Increase merchandise sales'. The first, critical step in any pay-for-performance system is to clearly define exactly what managers want people to accomplish. Lack of clear, specific goals is a major cause of the failure of incentive plans in many organizations.[33]

- In terms of *goal difficulty*, hard goals are more motivating than easy ones. Easy goals provide little challenge for employees and don't require them to increase their output. Highly ambitious but achievable goals ask people to stretch their abilities.

- *Goal acceptance* means that employees have to 'buy into' the goals and be committed to them. Managers often find that having people participate in setting goals is a good way to increase acceptance and commitment. At Aluminio del Caroni, a state-owned aluminium company in south-eastern Venezuela, plant workers felt a renewed sense of commitment when top leaders implemented a *co-management* initiative that has managers and lower-level employees working together to set budgets, determine goals and make decisions. 'The managers and the workers are running this business together,' said one employee who spends his days shovelling molten aluminium down a channel from an industrial oven to a cast. 'It gives us the motivation to work hard.'[34]

- Finally, the component of *feedback* means that people get information about how well they are doing in progressing toward goal achievement. It is important for managers to provide performance feedback on a regular, ongoing basis.

However, self-feedback, where people are able to monitor their own progress toward a goal, has been found to be an even stronger motivator than external feedback.[35] Managers at Sanmina France S.A.S., which makes custom-printed circuit boards, steer employee performance toward goals by giving everyone ongoing numerical feedback about every aspect of the business. Employees are so fired up that they check the data on the intranet throughout the day as if they were checking the latest sports scores. The system enables people to track their progress toward achieving goals, such as reaching sales targets or solving customer problems within specified time limits.

Why does goal setting increase motivation? For one thing, it enables people to focus their energies in the right direction. People know what to work toward, so they can direct their efforts toward the most important activities to accomplish the goals. Goals also energize behaviour because people feel compelled to develop plans and strategies that keep them focused on achieving the target. Specific, difficult goals provide a challenge and encourage people to put forth high levels of effort. In addition, when goals are achieved, pride and satisfaction increase, contributing to higher motivation and morale.[36]

As a new manager, use specific, challenging goals to keep people focused and motivated. Have team members participate in setting goals and determining how to achieve them. Give regular feedback on how people are doing.

TAKE A MOMENT

Reinforcement Perspective on Motivation

The reinforcement approach to employee motivation sidesteps the issues of employee needs and thinking processes described in the content and process theories. Reinforcement theory simply looks at the relationship between behaviour and its consequences. It focuses on changing or modifying employees' on-the-job behaviour through the appropriate use of immediate rewards and punishments.

Reinforcement theory
A motivation theory based on the relationship between a given behaviour and its consequences.

Reinforcement Tools

Behaviour modification is the name given to the set of techniques by which reinforcement theory is used to modify human behavior.[37] The basic assumption underlying behaviour modification is the law of effect, which states that behaviour that is positively reinforced tends to be repeated, and behaviour that is not reinforced tends not to be repeated. Reinforcement is defined as anything that causes a certain behaviour to be repeated or inhibited. The four reinforcement tools are positive reinforcement, avoidance learning, punishment, and extinction. Each type of reinforcement is a consequence of either a pleasant or unpleasant event being applied or withdrawn following a person's behaviour. The four types of reinforcement are summarized in Exhibit 16.6.

Behaviour modification
The set of techniques by which reinforcement theory is used to modify human behaviour.

Law of effect
The assumption that positively reinforced behaviour tends to be repeated, and unreinforced or negatively reinforced behaviour tends to be inhibited.

Positive Reinforcement

Positive reinforcement is the administration of a pleasant and rewarding consequence following a desired behaviour. A good example of positive reinforcement is immediate praise for an employee who arrives on time or does a little extra work.

Reinforcement
Anything that causes a given behaviour to be repeated or inhibited.

Exhibit 16.6 Changing Behaviour with Reinforcement

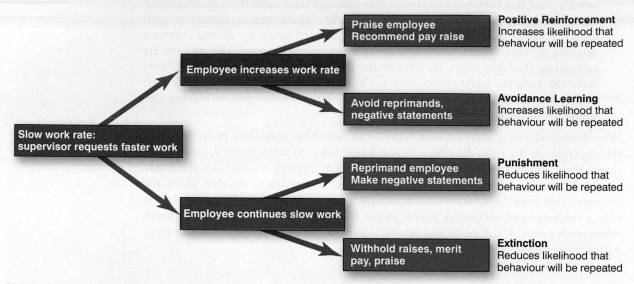

	Praise employee **Recommend pay raise**	**Positive Reinforcement** Increases likelihood that behaviour will be repeated
Employee increases work rate	**Avoid reprimands,** **negative statements**	**Avoidance Learning** Increases likelihood that behaviour will be repeated
Slow work rate: **supervisor requests faster work**	**Reprimand employee** **Make negative statements**	**Punishment** Reduces likelihood that behaviour will be repeated
Employee continues slow work	**Withhold raises, merit** **pay, praise**	**Extinction** Reduces likelihood that behaviour will be repeated

SOURCE: Based on Richard L. Daft and Richard M. Steers, *Organizations: A Micro/Macro Approach* (Scott, Foresman Glenview, IL;, 1986): 109.

© OWEN FRANKEN/CORBIS

CONCEPT CONNECTION Farm managers often use a fixed-rate reinforcement schedule by basing a fruit or vegetable picker's pay on the amount he or she harvests. A variation on this individual piece-rate system is a relative incentive plan that bases each worker's pay on the ratio of the individual's productivity to average productivity among all coworkers. A study of Eastern and Central European pickers in the UK found that workers' productivity declined under the relative plan. Researchers theorized that fast workers didn't want to hurt their slower colleagues, so they reduced their efforts. The study authors suggested a team-based scheme – where everyone's pay increased if the team did well – would be more effective.

The pleasant consequence will increase the likelihood of the excellent work behaviour occurring again. Studies have shown that positive reinforcement does help to improve performance. In addition, non-financial reinforcements such as positive feedback, social recognition and attention are just as effective as financial incentives.[38] Indeed, many people consider factors other than money to be more important. Nelson Motivation Inc. conducted a survey of 750 employees across various industries to assess the value they placed on various rewards. Cash and other monetary awards came in dead last. The most valued rewards involved praise and manager support and involvement.[39]

Avoidance Learning

Avoidance learning is the removal of an unpleasant consequence following a desired behaviour. Avoidance learning is sometimes called *negative reinforcement*. Employees learn to do the right thing by avoiding unpleasant situations. Avoidance learning occurs when a supervisor stops criticizing or reprimanding an employee once the incorrect behaviour has stopped.

Punishment

Punishment is the imposition of unpleasant outcomes on an employee. Punishment typically occurs following undesirable behaviour. For example, a supervisor may berate an employee for performing a task incorrectly. The supervisor expects that the negative outcome will serve as a punishment and reduce the likelihood of the behaviour recurring. The use of punishment in organizations is controversial and often criticized because it fails to indicate the correct behaviour. However, almost all managers report that they find it necessary to occasionally impose forms of punishment ranging from verbal reprimands to employee suspensions or firings.[40]

Extinction

Extinction is the withdrawal of a positive reward. Whereas with punishment, the supervisor imposes an unpleasant outcome such as a reprimand, extinction involves withholding pay raises, bonuses, praise or other positive outcomes. The idea is that behaviour that is not positively reinforced will be less likely to occur in the future. For example, if a perpetually tardy employee fails to receive praise and pay raises, he or she will begin to realize that the behaviour is not producing desired outcomes. The behaviour will gradually disappear if it is continually not reinforced.

Executives can use aspects of reinforcement theory to shape employees' behaviour. Garry Ridge, CEO of WD-40 Company, which makes the popular lubricant used for everything from loosening bolts to removing scuff marks from floors, wanted to encourage people to talk about their failures so the company could learn from them. He offered prizes to anyone who would email and share their 'learning moments', and each respondent would have the chance to win an all-expenses paid vacation. The positive reinforcement, combined with the company's 'blame-free' policy, motivated people to share ideas that have helped WD-40 keep learning and growing.[41]

Schedules of Reinforcement

A great deal of research into reinforcement theory suggests that the timing of reinforcement has an impact on how quickly employees learn and respond with the desired behaviour. Schedules of reinforcement pertain to the frequency with which and intervals over which reinforcement occurs. A reinforcement schedule can be selected to have maximum impact on employees' job behaviour. Five basic types of reinforcement schedules include continuous and four types of partial reinforcement.

Schedule of reinforcement
The frequency with which and intervals over which reinforcement occurs.

Continuous Reinforcement

With a continuous reinforcement schedule, every occurrence of the desired behaviour is reinforced. This schedule can be especially effective in the early stages of learning new types of behaviour, because every attempt has a pleasant consequence. Some companies use a continuous reinforcement schedule by offering people cash, game tokens, or points that can be redeemed for prizes each time they perform the desired behaviour. Barrie Stephen Hair Salon in Leicester, UK, tried a programme developed to cut inventory losses and to increase sales of additional hair product lines. Hair stylists and designers received tokens each time they sold an item from Kérastase, TGI Hair products and other ranges to the customer.[42] Many companies are developing continuous reinforcement programmes so that employees make a clear connection between their behaviour and the desired reward.

Continuous reinforcement schedule
A schedule in which every occurrence of the desired behaviour is reinforced.

Partial Reinforcement

However, in the real world of organizations, it is often impossible to reinforce every correct behaviour. With a partial reinforcement schedule, the reinforcement is administered only after some occurrences of the correct behaviour. The four types of partial reinforcement schedules are fixed interval, fixed ratio, variable interval and variable ratio.

Partial reinforcement schedule
A schedule in which only some occurrences of the desired behaviour are reinforced.

1 *Fixed-interval schedule.* The fixed-interval schedule rewards employees at specified time intervals. If an employee displays the correct behaviour each day, reinforcement may occur every week, for example. Regular pay cheques or quarterly bonuses are examples of fixed-interval reinforcement. At Mikael Grahn's Mini Maid franchise in Terjärv, Finland, workers are rewarded with an attendance bonus each pay period if they have gone to work every day on time and in uniform.[43]

2 *Fixed-ratio schedule.* With a fixed-ratio schedule, reinforcement occurs after a specified number of desired responses, say, after every fifth. For example, paying a field hand €2 for picking 10 pounds of peppers is a fixed-ratio schedule. Most piece-rate pay systems are considered fixed-ratio schedules.

3 *Variable-interval schedule.* With a variable-interval schedule, reinforcement is administered at random times that cannot be predicted by the employee. An example would be a random inspection by the manufacturing superintendent of the production floor, at which time he or she commends employees on their good behaviour.

4 *Variable-ratio schedule.* The variable-ratio schedule is based on a random number of desired behaviours rather than on variable time periods. Reinforcement may occur sometimes after 5, 10, 15 or 20 displays of behaviour. One example is random monitoring of telemarketers, who may be rewarded after a certain number of calls in which they perform the appropriate behaviours and meet call performance specifications. Employees know they may be monitored but are never sure when checks will occur and when rewards may be given.

The schedules of reinforcement are illustrated in Exhibit 16.7. Continuous reinforcement is most effective for establishing new learning, but behaviour is vulnerable to

Exhibit 16.7 Schedules of Reinforcement

Schedule of Reinforcement	Nature of Reinforcement	Effect on Behaviour When Applied	Effect on Behaviour When Withdrawn	Example
Continuous	Reward given after each desired behaviour	Leads to fast learning of new behaviour	Rapid extinction	Praise
Fixed-interval	Reward given at fixed time intervals	Leads to average and irregular performance	Rapid extinction	Weekly pay cheque
Fixed-ratio	Reward given at fixed amounts of output	Quickly leads to very high and stable performance	Rapid extinction	Piece-rate pay system
Variable-interval	Reward given at variable times	Leads to moderately high and stable performance	Slow extinction	Performance appraisal and awards given at random times each month
Variable-ratio	Reward given at variable amounts of output	Leads to very high performance	Slow extinction	Sales bonus tied to number of sales calls, with random cheques

INNOVATIVE WAY

PinnacleHealth System

Federal health regulations in the US are carefully designed to prevent hospitals from paying doctors to skimp on care. But one hospital system in Pennsylvania obtained special approval for an innovative programme.

Administrators at PinnacleHealth System wanted to make doctors cost-sensitive and reward them for saving money. So, they developed an incentive plan that allows doctors to share in any money they save the hospital, which is positive reinforcement to doctors for using cost-efficient procedures or less-expensive medical devices. For example, in the past, many cardiologists at PinnacleHealth hospitals would inflate a new artery-opening balloon each time they inserted a stent into a patient's clogged arteries. Now, when possible,

they use a single balloon throughout the procedure. The doctors say this poses no risk to the patient, and the simple step cuts a couple of hundred dollars per procedure, amounting to big savings over time. When they can, PinnacleHealth doctors also use stents, pacemakers and other medical devices that the hospital buys at a negotiated volume discount, rather than using more costly products. Doctors can use any device they feel is in the best interest of the patient, but incentives focus doctors on manufacturers with whom the company has low-cost supplier contracts.

It's working. Annual savings in 2004 amounted to about $1 million, with participating physicians each earning an estimated $10 000 to $15 000 from the payouts that year.[45]

extinction. Partial reinforcement schedules are more effective for maintaining behaviour over extended time periods. The most powerful is the variable-ratio schedule, because employee behaviour will persist for a long time due to the random administration of reinforcement only after a long interval.[44]

PinnacleHealth System provides an excellent, though somewhat controversial, example of the successful use of reinforcement theory.

Reinforcement also works at such organizations as Campbell Soup Co., Emery Air Freight, Hallmark Consumer Services, Michigan Bell, Barrie Stephen Hair and PC World, because managers reward the desired behaviours. They tell employees what they can do to receive rewards, tell them what they are doing wrong, distribute rewards equitably, tailor rewards to behaviours, and keep in mind that failure to reward deserving behaviour has an equally powerful impact on employees.

Reward and punishment motivational practices dominate organizations. According to the Society for Human Resource Management, 84 per cent of all companies in the US offer some type of monetary or non-monetary reward system, and 69 per cent offer incentive pay, such as bonuses, based on an employee's performance.[46] However, in other studies, more than 80 per cent of employers with incentive programmes have reported that their programmes are only somewhat successful or not working at all.[47] Despite the testimonies of organizations that enjoy successful incentive programmes, criticism of these 'carrot-and-stick' methods is growing, as discussed in the Manager's Shoptalk.

As a new manager, remember that reward and punishment practices are partial motivational tools because they focus only on extrinsic rewards and lower-level needs. Using intrinsic rewards to meet higher level needs is important too.

TAKE A MOMENT

see the outcomes of their efforts. A football coach knows whether the team won or lost, but a basic research scientist may have to wait years to learn whether a research project was successful.

The job characteristics model says that the more these five core characteristics can be designed into the job, the more the employees will be motivated and the higher will be performance, quality, and satisfaction.

Critical Psychological States

The model posits that core job dimensions are more rewarding when individuals experience three psychological states in response to job design. In Exhibit 16.9, skill variety, task identity and task significance tend to influence the employee's psychological state of *experienced meaningfulness of work*. The work itself is satisfying and provides intrinsic rewards for the worker. The job characteristic of autonomy influences the worker's *experienced responsibility*. The job characteristic of feedback provides the worker with *knowledge of actual results*. The employee thus knows how he or she is doing and can change work performance to increase desired outcomes.

Personal and Work Outcomes

The impact of the five job characteristics on the psychological states of experienced meaningfulness, responsibility and knowledge of actual results leads to the personal and work outcomes of high work motivation, high work performance, high satisfaction and low absenteeism and turnover.

Employee Growth-Need Strength

The final component of the job characteristics model is called *employee growth-need strength*, which means that people have different needs for growth and development. If a person wants to satisfy low-level needs, such as safety and belongingness, the job characteristics model has less effect. When a person has a high need for growth and development, including the desire for personal challenge, achievement and challenging work, the model is especially effective. People with a high need to grow and expand their abilities respond favourably to the application of the model and to improvements in core job dimensions.

One interesting finding concerns the cross-cultural differences in the impact of job characteristics. Intrinsic factors such as autonomy, challenge, achievement and recognition can be highly motivating in countries such as the US, the UK and other European countries. However, they may contribute little to motivation and satisfaction in a country such as Nigeria, China or India, and might even lead to *demotivation*. A recent study indicates that the link between intrinsic characteristics and job motivation and satisfaction is weaker in economically disadvantaged countries with poor governmental social welfare systems, and in high power distance countries, as defined in Chapter 4.[53] Thus, the job characteristics model would be expected to be less effective in these countries.

Innovative Ideas for Motivating

Despite the controversy over carrot-and-stick motivational practices discussed in the Manager's Shoptalk box earlier in this chapter, organizations are increasingly using

Exhibit 16.10 New Motivational Compensation Programmes

Program	Purpose
Pay for performance	Rewards individual employees in proportion to their performance contributions. Also called *merit pay.*
Gain sharing	Rewards all employees and managers within a business unit when predetermined performance targets are met. Encourages teamwork.
Employee stock ownership plan (ESOP)	Gives employees part ownership of the organisation, enabling them to share in improved profit performance.
Lump-sum bonuses	Rewards employees with a one-time cash payment based on performance.
Pay for knowledge	Links employee salary with the number of task skills acquired. Workers are motivated to learn the skills for many jobs, thus increasing company flexibility and efficiency.
Flexible work schedule	*Flextime* allows workers to set their own hours. *Job sharing* allows two or more part-time workers to jointly cover one job. *Telecommuting,* sometimes called *flex-place,* allows employees to work from home or an alternative workplace.
Team-based compensation	Rewards employees for behavior and activities that benefit the team, such as cooperation, listening, and empowering others.
Lifestyle awards	Rewards employees for meeting ambitious goals with luxury items, such as high-definition televisions, tickets to big-name sporting events and exotic travel.

various types of incentive compensation as a way to motivate employees to higher levels of performance. Exhibit 16.10 summarizes several popular methods of incentive pay.

Go to the Ethical Dilemma on page 636 that pertains to the use of incentive compensation as a motivational tool.

TAKE A MOMENT

Variable compensation and forms of 'at risk' pay are key motivational tools and are becoming more common than fixed salaries at many companies. These programmes can be effective if they are used appropriately and combined with motivational ideas that also provide employees with intrinsic rewards and meet higher-level needs. Effective managers don't use incentive plans as the sole basis of motivation. At steelmaker Nucor, for example, the amount of money employees and managers take home depends on company profits and how effective the plants are at producing defect-free steel.

Some organizations give employees a voice in how pay and incentive systems are designed, which boosts motivation by increasing people's sense of involvement and control.[54] Managers at Premium Standard Farms' pork-processing plant hired a consultant to help slaughterhouse workers design and implement an incentive programme. Annual payouts to employees in one recent year were around $1000 per employee. More important, though, is that workers feel a greater sense of dignity and purpose in their jobs, which has helped to reduce turnover significantly. As one employee put it, 'Now I have the feeling that this is my company, too.'[55] The most effective motivational programmes typically involve much more than money or other external rewards. Two recent motivational trends are empowering employees and framing work to have greater meaning.

Empowering People to Meet Higher Needs

One significant way managers can meet higher motivational needs is to shift power down from the top of the organization and share it with employees to enable them to achieve goals. **Empowerment** is power sharing, the delegation of power or authority to subordinates in an organization.[56] Increasing employee power heightens motivation for task accomplishment because people improve their own effectiveness, choosing how to do a task and using their creativity.[57] Most people come into an organization with the desire to do a good job, and empowerment releases the motivation that is already there. Research indicates that most people have a need for *self-efficacy*, which is the capacity to produce results or outcomes, to feel that they are effective.[58] By meeting this higher-level need, empowerment can provide powerful motivation.

Empowering employees involves giving them four elements that enable them to act more freely to accomplish their jobs: information, knowledge, power and rewards.[59]

Empowerment
The delegation of power and authority to subordinates.

1 *Employees receive information about company performance.* In companies where employees are fully empowered, all employees have access to all financial and operational information. At Reflexite Corporation, for example, which is largely owned by employees, managers sit down each month to analyze data related to operational and financial performance and then share the results with employees throughout the company. In addition to these monthly updates, employees have access to any information about the company at any time they want or need it.[60]

2 *Employees have knowledge and skills to contribute to company goals.* Companies use training programmes to help employees acquire the knowledge and skills they need to contribute to organizational performance. For example, when DMC, which makes pet supplies, gave employee teams the authority and responsibility for assembly-line shutdowns, it provided extensive training on how to diagnose and interpret line malfunctions, as well as data related to the costs of shutdown and start-up. People worked through several case studies to practice decision-making related to line shutdowns.[61]

3 *Employees have the power to make substantive decisions.* Empowered employees have the authority to directly influence work procedures and organizational performance, such as through quality circles or self-directed work teams. At Venezuela's Aluminio del Caroní, employees participate in roundtable discussions and make recommendations to management regarding new equipment purchases or other operational matters. In addition, workers vote to elect managers and board members.[62] The Brazilian manufacturer Semco, described in Chapter 3, pushes empowerment to the limits by allowing its employees to choose what they do, how they do it, and even how they get compensated for it. Many employees set their own pay by choosing from a list of 11 different pay options, such as set salary or a combination of salary and incentives.[63]

4 *Employees are rewarded based on company performance.* Organizations that empower workers often reward them based on the results shown in the company's bottom line. For example, at Semco, in addition to employee-determined compensation, a company profit-sharing plan gives each employee an even share of 23 per cent of his or her department's profits each quarter.[64] Organizations may also use other motivational compensation programmes described in Exhibit 16.10 to tie employee efforts to company performance.

Exhibit 16.11 A Continuum of Empowerment

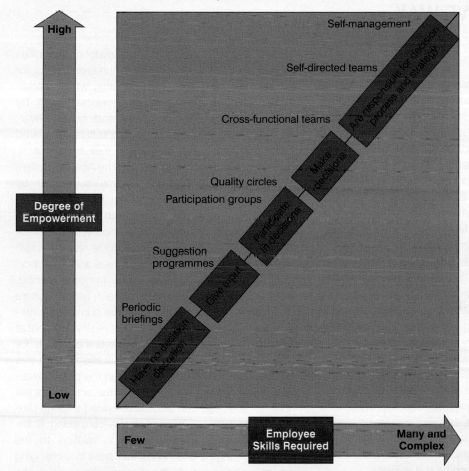

SOURCE: Based on Robert C. Ford and Myron D. Fottler, 'Empowerment: A Matter of Degree', *Academy of Management Executive* 9, no. 3 (1995), 21–31; Lawrence Holpp, 'Applied Empowerment', *Training* (February 1994), 39–44; and David P. McCaffrey, Sue R. Faerman, and David W. Hart, 'The Appeal and Difficulties of Participative Systems', *Organization Science* 6, no. 6 (November–December 1995), 603–627.

Many of today's organizations are implementing empowerment programmes, but they are empowering workers to varying degrees. At some companies, empowerment means encouraging workers' ideas while managers retain final authority for decisions; at others it means giving employees almost complete freedom and power to make decisions and exercise initiative and imagination.[65] Current methods of empowerment fall along a continuum, as illustrated in Exhibit 16.11. The continuum runs from a situation in which front-line workers have almost no discretion, such as on a traditional assembly line, to full empowerment, where workers even participate in formulating organizational strategy. Studies indicate that higher-level empowerment programmes, where employees have input and decision making power related to both everyday operational issues and higher-level strategic decisions, are still relatively rare.[66]

Giving Meaning to Work

Another way to meet higher-level motivational needs and help people get intrinsic rewards from their work is to instil a sense of importance and meaningfulness. *Fortune* magazine finds that one of the primary characteristics shared by companies on its annual list of 'The 100 Best Companies to Work For' is that they are *purpose-driven*, that is, people have a sense that what they are doing matters and makes a positive difference in the world.[68] Consider the motivation of employees at Swarovski.

It is easy to understand why employees at Swarovski feel they are serving an important cause. But managers in any organization can tap into people's desire to

INNOVATIVE WAY

Swarovski[67]

Since 1895, Swarovski has held true to its vision of maintaining a balance between economic success, social responsibility and stewardship of the environment. Throughout the Swarovski group, there is a strong emphasis on respect for all cultures, ethical business practice and generosity towards others. From the upper management to production, Swarovski employees take pride in living up to the axiom of the founder – 'continually improve on what is good.' This axiom, in fact, is regarded as a driving force behind the company's innovativeness, entrepreneurship and success.

In daily working lives, Swarovski stays faithful to the founder's vision by cultivating ways to improve on successes and by looking towards the future at all times. As a family-run company, Swarovski feels that sustainable growth is as important as generating profits. The latter is reinvested in the company in order to keep the future secure. All employees benefit from this sustainability.

There is another way personal growth and economic success is kept in balance at Swarovski: development. By offering employees ongoing opportunities to fine-tune and enhance existing skills and also acquire new ones, the company ensures that at the end of the day everyone has the opportunity to contribute to the company's success according to their strengths and abilities.

These opportunities are available through line managers. In addition, it is up to every employee to seek out and take advantage of the growth opportunities appropriate to them. This can take numerous forms, for instance through Swarovski Academy, where leadership and management skills are developed for all. By acting as a company-wide competence centre, Swarovski Academy builds a 'leadership culture' of shared values that employees embody in their behaviour — improving on-the job performance. The Academy offers customized, multi-cultural programs supported by preparation and a follow-up process, helps leaders develop 'their' style in accordance with company principles and core competencies, improves speakers' effectiveness and fosters a dialogue across businesses, regions and functions. There is also an opportunity for employees to sign up for in-house training, which is tailored to the needs of each region, culture and location. On top of this there are numerous external training opportunities and Executive development at well-known business schools. There is a possibility for employees to be sent on international assignments that expose them to other cultures within the global Swarovski environment. The learning of the way things are done at Swarovski can also be cultivated through project assignments and general on-the-job training. Naturally, all training courses stand in relation to the personal strengths and needs that arise in a changing market environment. All these programmes have one aim at their heart – to appropriately prepare staff for this constant change.

contribute and make a difference. Former Coca-Cola CEO Roberto Goizueta spent a lot of time talking to employees about the company's charitable work and emphasized that millions of small merchants could make a living because they sold Coca-Cola. Employees at FedEx take pride in getting people the items they need on time, whether it be a work report that is due, a passport for a holiday trip to Jamaica or an emergency order of medical supplies.[69]

Another example is Les Schwab Tire Centers, where employees feel like partners united toward a goal of making people's lives easier. Stores fix flats for free, and some have been known to install tyres hours before opening time for an emergency trip. Employees frequently stop to help stranded motorists. Schwab rewards people with a generous profit-sharing plan for everyone and promotes store managers solely from within. However, these external rewards only supplement, not create, the high motivation employees feel.[70]

In recent years, managers have focused on employee *engagement*, which has less to do with extrinsic rewards such as pay and much more to do with fostering an environment in which people can flourish. Engaged employees are more satisfied and motivated because they feel appreciated by their supervisors and the organization, and they thrive on work challenges rather than feeling frustrated by them.[71] Engaged employees are motivated, enthusiastic and committed employees. In addition, there is a growing recognition that it is the behaviour of managers that makes the biggest difference in whether people feel engaged at work. When David A. Brandon took over as CEO of Domino's Pizza, he commissioned research to identify the factors that contributed to a store's success. What he learned was that the quality of the manager and how he or she treats employees has a much greater impact than neighbourhood demographics, packaging, marketing or other factors.[72] Indeed, a Gallup Organization study conducted over 25 years found that the single most important variable in whether employees feel good about their work is the relationship between employees and their direct supervisors.[73]

The role of today's manager is not to control others but to organize the work-place in such a way that each person can learn, contribute, and grow. Good managers channel employee motivation toward the accomplishment of organizational goals by tapping into each individual's unique set of talents, skills, interests, attitudes and needs. By treating each employee as an individual, managers can put people in the right jobs and provide intrinsic rewards to every employee every day. Then, managers make sure people have what they need to perform, clearly define the desired outcomes and get out of the way.

One way to evaluate how a manager or a company is doing in engaging employees by meeting higher-level needs is a metric developed by the Gallup researchers called the Q12. When a majority of employees can answer these 12 questions positively, the organization enjoys a highly motivated and productive workforce:

1 Do I know what is expected of me at work?

2 Do I have the materials and equipment that I need in order to do my work right?

3 At work, do I have the opportunity to do what I do best every day?

4 In the past seven days, have I received recognition or praise for doing good work?

5 Does my supervisor, or someone at work, seem to care about me as a person?

6 Is there someone at work who encourages my development?

7 At work, do my opinions seem to count?

8 Does the mission or purpose of my company make me feel that my job is important?

9 Are my coworkers committed to doing quality work?

10 Do I have a best friend at work?

11 In the past six months, has someone at work talked to me about my progress?

12 This past year, have I had opportunities to learn and grow?[74]

Results of the Gallup study show that organizations where employees give high marks on the Q12 have less turnover, are more productive and profitable, and enjoy greater employee and customer loyalty.[75] Many companies have used the Q12 to pinpoint problems with motivation in the organization. Best Buy, for example, uses the survey and includes employee engagement as a key item on each manager's score-card. Eric Taverna, the general manager of a Best Buy store in Manchester, Connecticut, took to heart the finding that his employees didn't think their opinions mattered. Taverna responded by implementing significant changes based on employee ideas and suggestions. The Manchester store's engagement levels improved significantly, as did the store's financial performance, while turnover has been

7 The prestige of the job outside the company (i.e., the regard received from others not in the company)

   1   2   3   4   5   6   7

8 The feeling of worthwhile accomplishment in that job

   1   2   3   4   5   6   7

9 The opportunity in that job to give help to other people

   1   2   3   4   5   6   7

10 The opportunity in that job for participation in the setting of goals

   1   2   3   4   5   6   7

11 The opportunity in that job for participation in the determination of methods and procedures

   1   2   3   4   5   6   7

12 The authority connected with the job

   1   2   3   4   5   6   7

13 The opportunity to develop close friendships in the job

   1   2   3   4   5   6   7

Scoring and Interpretation

Score the exercise as follows to determine what motivates you:

Rating for question 5 =	_____.	
Divide by 1 =	_____	security.
Rating for questions =	_____.	
9 and 13		
Divide by 2 =	_____	social.
Rating for questions =	_____.	
1, 3, and 7		
Divide by 3 =	_____	esteem.
Rating for questions =	_____.	
4, 10, 11, and 12		
Divide by 4 =	_____	autonomy.
Rating for questions =	_____.	
2, 6, and 8		
Divide by 3 =	_____	self-actualization.

Your instructor has national norm scores for presidents, vice presidents and upper middle-level, lower middle-level and lower-level managers with which you can compare your mean importance scores. How do your scores compare with the scores of managers working in organizations?

SOURCE Lyman W. Porter, *Organizational Patterns of Managerial Job Attitudes* (New York: American Foundation for Management Research, 1964): 17, 19. Used with permission.

MANAGEMENT IN PRACTICE: ETHICAL DILEMMA

To Renege or Not To Renege?

Joseon Kim, Vice President of Sales for Samshin Trade Co., a South Korean merchant in building materials, wasn't all that surprised by what company president Samguk Gok and CFO Yeon Chong had to say during their meeting that morning.

Last year, launching a major expansion made sense to everyone at Samshin, a well-established company that provided building materials as well as manufacturing and installation services to residential builders in the Seoul area. Samshin Trade looked at the record new housing starts and decided it was time to move into the Suweon markets, especially concentrating on Suweon and Incheon – two of the hottest housing markets in the country. Jeseon Kim carefully hired promising new sales representatives and offered them hefty bonuses if they reached the goals set for the new territory over the next 12 months. All of the representatives had performed well, and three of them had exceeded Samshin's goal – and then by more. The incentive system he'd put in place had worked well. The sales reps were expecting handsome bonuses for their hard work.

Early on, however, it became all too clear that Samshin Trade had seriously underestimated the time it took to build new business relationships and the costs associated with the expansion, a mistake that was already eating into profit margins. Even more distressing were the most recent figures for new housing starts, which were heading in the wrong direction. The credit crunch in the US had a knock-on effect in South Korea. As Samguk said, 'Granted, it's too early to tell if this is just a pause or the start of a real long-term downturn. But I'm worried. If things get worse, Samshin Trade could be in real trouble.'

Yeon looked at Joseon and said, 'Our lawyers built enough contingency clauses into the sales reps' contracts that we're not really obligated to pay those bonuses you promised. What would you think about not paying them?' Joseon turned to the president, who said, 'Why don't you think about it, and get back to us with a recommendation?'

Joseon felt torn. On the one hand, he knew the CFO was correct. Samshin Trade wasn't, strictly speaking, under any legal obligation to pay out the bonuses, and the eroding profit margins were a genuine cause for concern. The president clearly did not want to pay the bonuses. But Joseon had created a first-rate sales force that had done exactly what he'd asked them to do. He prided himself on being a man of his word, someone others could trust. Could he go back on his promises?

What Would You Do?

1 Recommend to the president that a meeting be arranged with the sales representatives entitled to a bonus and tell them that their cheques were going to be delayed until Samshin Trade's financial picture clarified. The sales reps would be told that the company had a legal right to delay payment and that it may not be able to pay the bonuses if its financial situation continues to deteriorate.

2 Recommend a meeting with the sales representatives entitled to a bonus and tell them the company's deteriorating financial situation triggers one of the contingency clauses in their contract so that the company won't be issuing their bonus cheques. Samshin Trade will just have to deal with the negative impact on sales rep motivation.

3 Recommend strongly to the president that Samshin Trade pay the bonuses as promised. The legal contracts and financial situation don't matter. Be prepared to resign if the bonuses are not paid as you promised. Your word and a motivated sales team mean everything to you.

SOURCE Based on Doug Wallace, 'The Company Simply Refused to Pay', *Business Ethics* (March–April 2000): 18; and Adam Shell, 'Over-heated Housing Market Is Cooling', *USA Today* (November 2, 2005): www.usatoday.com/money/economy/housing/2005-11-01-real-estate-usat_x.htm; http://yjflex.en.ec21.com/company_info.jsp.

CASE FOR CRITICAL ANALYSIS 16.1

C&A Department Store

C&A is one of the leading fashion retailers in Europe and Latin America. Indeed, it has been for decades. Having started trading in 1841 as a textile warehouse, it has a history spanning over 160 years and five generations of the same family making it one of the pioneers of the retail industry. C&A's motto is 'Fashion for young and old, fashion that fits every occasion and suits every style'. That is how C&A makes life more pleasant for millions of customers. C&A has been providing Europe with quality clothing at reasonable prices for more than 100 years.

Frank Maher, the new C&A's CEO, looked at the latest 'Sales by Manager' figures on his daily Web-based sales report. What did these up-to-the-minute numbers tell her about the results of C&A's trial of straight commission pay for its salespeople?

As a European chain of department stores based in Brussels, C&A faces the challenge shared by most department stores these days: how to stop losing share of overall retail sales to discount store chains. A key component of the strategy the company formulated to counter this long-term trend is the revival of great customer service on the floor, once a hallmark of upscale stores. Frank knows C&A has its work cut out for it. When he dropped in on several stores incognito a few years ago, he was dismayed to discover that finding a salesperson actively engaged with a customer was rare. In fact, finding a salesperson when a customer wanted to pay for an item was often difficult.

About a year and a half ago, the CEO read about a quiet revolution sweeping department store retailing. At stores in the US such as Bloomingdale's and Bergdorf Goodman, managers put all salespeople on straight commission. Frank decided to give the system a year long try in two area stores.

Such a plan, he reasoned, would be good for C&A if it lived up to its promise of attracting better salespeople, improving their motivation and making them more customer-oriented. It could also potentially be good for employees. Salespeople in departments such as boutique clothing lines and jewellery, where expertise and highly personalized services paid off, had long worked solely on commission. But the majority of employees earn an hourly wage plus a 0.5 per cent commission on total sales. Under the new scheme, all employees earn a 7 per cent commission on sales. When he compared the two systems, he saw that a new salesclerk in women's wear would earn €35 000 on €500 000 in sales, as opposed to only €18 000 under the old scheme.

Now, with the trial period about to end, Frank notes that while overall sales in the two stores have increased modestly, so also has employee turnover. When the CEO examined the sales-by-manager figures, it was obvious that some associates had thrived and others had not. Most fell somewhere in the middle.

For example, Birgitta Bern is enthusiastic about the change – and for good reason. She works in women's designer shoes and handbags, where a single item can cost upwards of €500. Motivated largely by the desire to make lots of money, she's a personable, outgoing individual with an entrepreneurial streak. Ever since the straight commission plan took effect, she has put even more time and effort into cultivating relationships with wealthy customers, and it shows. Her pay has increased an average of €150 per week.

It's a different story in the lingerie department, where even luxury items have more modest price tags. The lingerie department head, Maria Weinholtz, said salespeople in her department are demoralized. Several valued employees had quit, and most miss the security of a salary. No matter how hard they work, they cannot match their previous earnings. 'Yes, they're paying more attention to customers,' conceded Maria, 'but they're so anxious about making ends meet, they tend to pounce on the poor women who wander into the department.' Furthermore, lingerie sales associates are giving short shrift to duties such as handling complaints or returns that don't immediately translate into sales. 'And boy, do they ever resent the sales superstars in the other departments,' said Maria.

The year is nearly up. It's time to decide. Should Frank declare the straight commission experiment a success on the whole and roll it out across the chain over the next six months?

Questions

1 What theories about motivation underlie the switch from salary to commission pay?

2 What needs are met under the commission system? Are they the same needs in the shoes and handbag department as they are in lingerie? Explain.

3 If you were Frank Maher, would you go back to the previous compensation system, implement the straight commission plan in all C&A stores, or devise and test some other compensation method? If you decided to test another system, what would it look like?

SOURCES Based on Cynthia Kyle, 'Commissions question – to pay … or not to pay'? *Michigan Retailer* (March 2003): www.retailers.com/news/retailers/03mar/mr0303commissions.html; 'Opinion: Effective Retail Sales Compensation', *Furniture World Magazine* (March 7, 2006): www.furninfo.com/absolutenm/templates/NewsFeed.asp?articleid=6017; Terry Pristin, 'Retailing's Elite Keep the Armani Moving Off the Racks', *The New York Times* (December 22, 2001): D1; Francine Schwadel, 'Chain Finds Incentives a Hard Sell', *The Wall Street Journal* (July 5, 1990): B4; and Amy Dunkin, 'Now Salespeople Really Must Sell for Their Supper', *BusinessWeek* (July 31, 1989): 50–52.

ENDNOTES

1. Questions based on Mitchell M. Handelsman, William L. Briggs, Nora Sullivan and Annette Towler, 'A Measure of College Student Course Engagement', *Journal of Educational Research* 98 (January/ February 2005): 184–191.

2. David Silburt, 'Secrets of the Super Sellers', *Canadian Business* (January 1987): 54–59; 'Meet the Savvy Supersalesmen', *Fortune* (February 4, 1985): 56–62; Michael Brody, 'Meet Today's Young American Worker', *Fortune* (November 11, 1985): 90–98; and Tom Richman, 'Meet the Masters. They Could Sell You Anything', *Inc.* (March 1985): 79–86.

3. Richard M. Steers and Lyman W. Porter, eds, *Motivation and Work Behavior*, 3rd ed. (New York: McGraw-Hill, 1983); Don Hellriegel, John W. Slocum, Jr. and Richard

W. Woodman, *Organizational Behavior*, 7th ed. (St. Paul, MN: West, 1995): 170; and Jerry L. Gray and Frederick A. Starke, *Organizational Behavior: Concepts and Applications*, 4th ed. (New York: Macmillan, 1988): 104–105.

4. Carol Hymowitz, 'Readers Tell Tales of Success and Failure Using Rating Systems', *The Wall Street Journal* (May 29, 2001): B1.

5. Alan Deutschman, 'Can Google Stay Google?', *Fast Company* (August 2005): 62–68.

6. See Linda Grant, 'Happy Workers, High Returns', *Fortune* (January 12, 1998): 81; Elizabeth J. Hawk and Garrett J. Sheridan, 'The Right Stuff', *Management Review* (June 1999): 43–48; Michael West and Malcolm Patterson, 'Profitable Personnel', *People Management* (January 8, 1998): 28–31; Anne Fisher, 'Why Passion Pays', *FSB* (September 2002): 58; and Curt Coffman and Gabriel Gonzalez-Molina, *Follow This Path: How the World's Great Organizations Drive Growth By Unleashing Human Potential* (New York: Warner Books, 2002).

7. Steers and Porter, *Motivation*.

8. J. F. Rothlisberger and W. J. Dickson, *Management and the Worker* (Cambridge, MA: Harvard University Press, 1939).

9. Abraham F. Maslow, 'A Theory of Human Motivation', *Psychological Review* 50 (1943): 370–396.

10. Sarah Pass, 'On the Line', *People Management* (September 15, 2005).

11. Clayton Alderfer, *Existence, Relatedness, and Growth* (New York: Free Press, 1972).

12. Robert Levering and Milton Moskowitz, '2004 Special Report: The 100 Best Companies To Work For', *Fortune* (January 12, 2004): 56–78.

13. Jena McGregor, 'Employee Innovator; Winner: USAA', *Fast Company* (October 2005): 57.

14. Jeff Barbian, 'C'mon, Get Happy', *Training* (January 2001): 92–96.

15. Karol Rose, 'Work-Life Effectiveness', *Fortune* (September 29, 2003): S1–S17.

16. W. Glaser, *The Control Theory Manager* (New York: Harper-Business, 1994); and John W. Newstrom, 'Making Work Fun: An Important Role for Managers', *SAM Advanced Management Journal* (Winter 2002): 4–8, 21.

17. Newstrom, 'Making Work Fun'.

18. Frederick Herzberg, 'One More Time: How Do You Motivate Employees?', *Harvard Business Review* (January 2003): 87–96.

19. 'Vision Express appoints CEO', online available from http://www.opticianonline.net/Articles/2007/11/16/19855/Vision+Express+appoints+CEO.html, (accessed November 2008); 'Vision Express sets sights on franchising', *Small Business*, online available from http://www.smallbusiness.co.uk/channels/start-a-business/news/22294/vision-express-sets-sights-on-franchising.thtml, (accessed November 2008).

20. David C. McClelland, *Human Motivation* (Glenview, IL: Scott, Foresman, 1985).

21. John Brant, 'What One Man Can Do', *Inc.* (September 2005): 145–153.

22. David C. McClelland, 'The Two Faces of Power', in *Organizational Psychology*, ed. D. A. Colb, I. M. Rubin, and J. M. McIntyre (Englewood Cliffs, NJ: Prentice Hall, 1971): 73–86.

23. J. Stacy Adams, 'Injustice in Social Exchange', in *Advances in Experimental Social Psychology*, 2d ed., ed. L. Berkowitz (New York: Academic Press, 1965); and J. Stacy Adams, 'Toward an Understanding of Inequity', *Journal of Abnormal and Social Psychology* (November 1963): 422–436.

24. 'Study: The Brain Prefers Working Over Getting Money for Nothing', *TheJournalNews.com* (May 14, 2004), www.thejournalnews.com/apps/pbcs.dll/frontpage.

25. Ray V. Montagno, 'The Effects of Comparison to Others and Primary Experience on Responses to Task Design', *Academy of Management Journal* 28 (1985): 491–498; and Robert P. Vecchio, 'Predicting Worker Performance in Inequitable Settings', *Academy of Management Review* 7 (1982): 103–110.

26. James E. Martin and Melanie M. Peterson, 'Two-Tier Wage Structures: Implications for Equity Theory', *Academy of Management Journal* 30 (1987): 297–315.

27. Jared Sandberg, 'Why You May Regret Looking at Papers Left on the Office Copier', *The Wall Street Journal* (June 20, 2006): B1.

28. Victor H. Vroom, *Work and Motivation* (New York: Wiley, 1964); B. S. Gorgopoulos, G. M. Mahoney and N. Jones, 'A Path-Goal Approach to Productivity', *Journal of Applied Psychology* 41 (1957): 345–353; and E. E. Lawler III, *Pay and Organizational Effectiveness: A Psychological View* (New York: McGraw-Hill, 1981).

29. Erin White, 'Theory & Practice: Praise from Peers Goes a Long Way – Recognition Programs Help Companies Retain Workers as Pay Raises Get Smaller', *The Wall Street Journal* (December 19, 2005): B3.

30. Richard L. Daft and Richard M. Steers, *Organizations: A Micro/Macro Approach* (Glenview, IL: Scott, Foresman, 1986).

31. See Edwin A. Locke and Gary P. Latham, 'Building a Practically Useful Theory of Goal Setting and Task Motivation: A 35-Year Odyssey', *The American Psychologist* 57, no. 9 (September 2002): 705+; Gary P. Latham and Edwin A. Locke, 'Self-Regulation through Goal Setting', *Organizational Behavior and Human Decision Processes* 50, no. 2 (1991): 212+; G. P. Latham and G. H. Seijts, 'The Effects of Proximal and Distal Goals on Performance of a Moderately Complex Task', *Journal of Organizational Behavior* 20, no. 4 (1999): 421+; P. C. Early, T. Connolly, and G. Ekegren, 'Goals, Strategy Development, and Task Performance: Some Limits on the Efficacy of Goal Setting', *Journal of Applied Psychology* 74 (1989): 24–33; E. A. Locke, 'Toward a Theory of Task Motivation and Incentives', *Organizational Behavior and Human Performance* 3 (1968): 157–189; Gerard H. Seijts, Ree M. Meertens and Gerjo Kok, 'The Effects of Task Importance and Publicness on the Relation Between Goal Difficulty and Performance', *Canadian Journal of Behavioural Science* 29, no. 1 (1997): 54+.

32. Locke and Latham, 'Building a Practically Useful Theory of Goal Setting and Task Motivation'.

33. Edwin A. Locke, 'Linking Goals to Monetary Incentives', *Academy of Management Executive* 18, no. 4 (2005): 130–133.

34. Brian Ellsworth, 'Making a Place for Blue Collars in the Boardroom', *The New York Times* (August 3, 2005), www.nytimes.com.

35. J. M. Ivanecevich and J. T. McMahon, 'The Effects of Goal Setting, External Feedback, and Self-Generated Feedback on Outcome Variables: A Field Experiment', *Academy of Management Journal* (June 1982): 359+; G. P. Latham and E. A. Locke, 'Self-Regulation Through Goal Setting', *Organizational Behavior and Human Decision Processes* 50, no. 2 (1991): 212+.

36. Gary P. Latham, 'The Motivational Benefits of Goal-Setting', *Academy of Management Executive* 18, no. 4 (2004): 126–129.

37. Alexander D. Stajkovic and Fred Luthans, 'A Meta-Analysis of the Effects of Organizational Behavior Modification on Task Performance, 1975–95', *Academy of Management Journal* (October 1997): 1122–1149; H. Richlin, *Modern Behaviorism* (San Francisco: Freeman, 1970); and B. F. Skinner, *Science and Human Behavior* (New York: Macmillan, 1953).

38. Stajkovic and Luthans, 'A Meta-Analysis of the Effects of Organizational Behavior Modification on Task Performance, 1975–95', and Fred Luthans and Alexander D. Stajkovic, 'Reinforce for Performance: The Need to Go Beyond Pay and Even Rewards', *Academy of Management Executive* 13, no. 2 (1999): 49–57.

39. Reported in Charlotte Garvey, 'Meaningful Tokens of Appreciation', *HR Magazine* (August 2004): 101–105.

40. Kenneth D. Butterfield and Linda Klebe Treviño, 'Punishment from the Manager's Perspective: A Grounded Investigation and Inductive Model', *Academy of Management Journal* 39, no. 6 (December 1996): 1479–1512; and Andrea Casey, 'Voices from the Firing Line: Managers Discuss Punishment in the Workplace', *Academy of Management Executive* 11, no. 3 (1997): 93–94.

41. Gwendolyn Bounds, 'Boss Talk: No More Squeaking By – WD-40 CEO Garry Ridge Repackages a Core Product', *The Wall Street Journal* (May 23, 2006): B1.

42. Barrie Stephen Hair online available from http://www.barriestephenhair.co.uk/about/ accessed on November 2008.

43. Roberta Maynard, 'How to Motivate Low-Wage Workers', *Nation's Business* (May 1997): 35–39.

44. L. M. Sarri and G. P. Latham, 'Employee Reaction to Continuous and Variable Ratio Reinforcement Schedules Involving a Monetary Incentive', *Journal of Applied Psychology* 67 (1982): 506–508; and R. D. Pritchard, J. Hollenback and P. J. DeLeo, 'The Effects of Continuous and Partial Schedules of Reinforcement on Effort, Performance, and Satisfaction', *Organizational Behavior and Human Performance* 25 (1980): 336–353.

45. Reed Abelson, 'To Fight Rising Costs, Hospitals Seek Allies in the Operating Room', *The New York Times* (November 18, 2005), www.nytimes.com.

46. Amy Joyce, 'The Bonus Question; Some Managers Still Strive to Reward Merit', *The Washington Post* (November 13, 2005): F6.

47. Survey results from World at Work and Hewitt Associates, reported in Karen Kroll, 'Benefits: Paying for Performance', *Inc.* (November 2004): 46; and Kathy Chu, 'Firms Report Lackluster Results from Pay-for-Performance Plans', *The Wall Street Journal* (June 15, 2004): D2.

48. Barbian, 'C'mon, Get Happy'.

49. Norm Alster, 'What Flexible Workers Can Do', *Fortune* (February 13, 1989): 62–66.

50. Christine M. Riordan, Robert J. Vandenberg and Hettie A. Richardson, 'Employee Involvement Climate and Organizational Effectiveness', *Human Resource Management* 44, no. 4 (Winter 2005): 471–488.

51. Glenn L. Dalton, 'The Collective Stretch', *Management Review* (December 1998): 54–59.

52. J. Richard Hackman and Greg R. Oldham, *Work Redesign* (Reading, MA: Addison-Wesley, 1980); and J. Richard Hackman and Greg Oldham, 'Motivation through the Design of Work: Test of a Theory', *Organizational Behavior and Human Performance* 16 (1976): 250–279.

53. Xu Huang and Evert Van de Vliert, 'Where Intrinsic Job Satisfaction Fails to Work: National Moderators of Intrinsic Motivation', *Journal of Organizational Behavior* 24 (2003): 157–179.

54. Ann Podolske, 'Giving Employees a Voice in Pay Structures', *Business Ethics* (March–April 1998): 12.

55. Rekha Balu, 'Bonuses Aren't Just for the Bosses', *Fast Company* (December 2000): 74–76.

56. Edwin P. Hollander and Lynn R. Offermann, 'Power and Leadership in Organizations', *American Psychologist* 45 (February 1990): 179–189.

57. Jay A. Conger and Rabindra N. Kanungo, 'The Empowerment Process: Integrating Theory and Practice', *Academy of Management Review* 13 (1988): 471–482.

58. *Ibid.*

59. David E. Bowen and Edward E. Lawler III, 'The Empowerment of Service Workers: What, Why, How, and When', *Sloan Management Review* (Spring 1992): 31–39; and Ray W. Coye and James A. Belohav, 'An Exploratory Analysis of Employee Participation', *Group and Organization Management* 20, no. 1, (March 1995): 4–17.

60. William C. Taylor, 'Under New Management; These Workers Act Like Owners (Because They Are)', *The New York Times* (May 21, 2006), www.nytimes.com.

61. Russ Forrester, 'Empowerment: Rejuvenating a Potent Idea', *Academy of Management Executive* 14, no. 3 (2000): 67–80.

62. Ellsworth, 'Making a Place for Blue Collars in the Boardroom'.

63. Ricardo Semler, 'How We Went Digital Without a Strategy', *Harvard Business Review* (September–October 2000): 51–58.

64. Podolske, 'Giving Employees a Voice in Pay Structures'.

65. This discussion is based on Robert C. Ford and Myron D. Fottler, 'Empowerment: A Matter of Degree', *Academy of Management Executive* 9, no. 3 (1995): 21–31.

66. Bruce E. Kaufman, 'High-Level Employee Involvement at Delta Air Lines', *Human Resource Management* 42, no. 2 (Summer 2003): 175–190.

67. Adapted from Swarovski Sparkles online available from http://www.swarovskisparkles.com/fashion/armani/n-189.html#docs acceded on November 2008; Svarovski Cristall – The Story online available from http://www.swarovski.com/is-bin/INTERSHOP. enfinity/WFS/SCO-Web_GB-Site/en_US/-/GBP/SPAG_TheStory-ViewPage?origin=landing accessed on November 2008.

68. Geoff Colvin, 'The 100 Best Companies to Work For'.

69. Colvin, 'The 100 Best Companies to Work For'; Levering and Moskowitz, 'And the Winners Are . . .'; and Daniel Roth, 'Trading Places', *Fortune* (January 23, 2006): 120–128.

70. Cheryl Dahle, 'Four Tires, Free Beef', *Fast Company* (September 2003): 36.

71. Jerry Krueger and Emily Killham, 'At Work, Feeling Good Matters', *Gallup Management Journal* (December 8, 2005).

72. Erin White, 'New Recipe; To Keep Employees, Domino's Decides It's Not All About Pay', *The Wall Street Journal* (February 17, 2005): A1, A9.

73. This discussion is based on Tony Schwartz, 'The Greatest Sources of Satisfaction in the Workplace are Internal and Emotional', *Fast Company* (November 2000): 398–402; Marcus Buckingham and Curt Coffman, *First, Break All the Rules: What the World's Greatest Managers Do Differently* (New York: Simon and Schuster, 1999); and Krueger and Killham, 'At Work, Feeling Good Matters'.

74. This discussion is based on Tony Schwartz, 'The Greatest Sources of Satisfaction in the Workplace are Internal and Emotional', *Fast Company* (November 2000): 398–402; Marcus Buckingham and Curt Coffman, *First, Break All the Rules: What the World's Greatest Managers Do Differently* (New York: Simon and Schuster, 1999); and Krueger and Killham, 'At Work, Feeling Good Matters'.

75. Curt Coffman and Gabriel Gonzalez-Molina, *Follow This Path: How the World's Greatest Organizations Drive Growth by Unleashing Human Potential* (New York: Warner Books, 2002), as reported in Anne Fisher, 'Why Passion Pays', *FSB* (September 2002): 58.

76. Rodd Wagner, ''One Store, One Team' at Best Buy', *Gallup Management Journal* (August 12, 2004).

77. Thottam, 'Reworking Work'.

CHAPTER OUTLINE

© WEBPHOTOGRAPHEER/ISTOCK

LEARNING OBJECTIVES

After reading this chapter, you should be able to:

1   Explain why communication is essential for effective
    management and describe how non-verbal behaviour and
    listening affect communication among people.

2   Explain how managers use communication to persuade and
    influence others.

3   Describe the concept of channel richness, and explain how
    communication channels influence the quality of
    communication.

4   Explain the difference between formal and informal
    organizational communications and the importance of each for
    organization management.

5   Identify how structure influences team communication
    outcomes.

6   Explain why open communication, dialogue and feedback are
    essential approaches to communication in a turbulent
    environment.

7   Identify the skills managers need for communicating during a
    crisis situation.

8   Describe barriers to organizational communication and
    suggest ways to avoid or overcome them.

CHAPTER 17

COMMUNICATION

Personal networking is an important skill for managers because it enables them to get things done more smoothly and rapidly than they could do in isolation. Networking builds social, work and career relationships that facilitate mutual benefit. How do managers build a personal network that includes a broad range of professional and social relationships? One key is knowing how to communicate effectively. In fact, communication is a vital factor in every aspect of the manager's job.

Manager's Challenge

As a doctor, Robert Bells knows first hand what it's like to lose patients that he thought could be saved. As chief executive of Royal Brompton & Harefield National Health Service (NHS) Trust in the UK, he knows what it's like to see hospitals losing millions of pounds due to inefficiencies and waste. Because the two issues come together most dramatically in the operating room, that's where NHS trust administrators are looking to see what issues contribute to inefficiencies and errors in patient care. They decide to conduct a survey at 20 hospitals, based on recent studies suggesting that the intense atmosphere of operating rooms, where surgeons typically call all the shots, is a big part of the problem. Administrators – and most surgeons – are stunned by the results. As many as 60 per cent of nurses and support staff members say they find it difficult to speak up if they perceive a problem with patient care in the operating room. Something has to be done to improve communications between surgeons and support staff or hospitals will continue to unnecessarily lose patients' lives, as well as waste money due to mistakes that could have been prevented.[1]

If you were a manager at Royal Brompton & Harefield NHS Trust, what steps would you take to improve communications between surgeons and hospital support staff? How would you overcome the communication barriers that exist and get people to communicate across functional and hierarchical boundaries?

TAKE A MOMENT

Are You Building a Personal Network?

How much effort do you put into developing connections with other people? Personal networks may help a new manager in the workplace. To learn something about your networking skills, answer the questions below. Indicate whether each item is Mostly True or Mostly False for you in college or at work.

		Mostly True	Mostly False
1	I learn early on about changes going on in the organization and how they might affect me or my position.	☐	☐
2	I network as much to help other people solve problems as to help myself.	☐	☐
3	I am fascinated by other people and what they do.	☐	☐
4	I frequently use lunches to meet and network with new people.	☐	☐
5	I regularly participate in charitable causes.	☐	☐
6	I maintain a list of friends and colleagues to whom I send holiday greeting cards.	☐	☐
7	I maintain contact with people from previous organizations and school groups.	☐	☐
8	I actively give information to subordinates, peers and my boss.	☐	☐

SCORING AND INTERPRETATION Give yourself one point for each item marked as Mostly True. A score of 6 or higher suggests active networking and a solid foundation on which to begin your career as a new manager. When you create a personal network, you become well connected to get things done through a variety of relationships. Having sources of information and support helps a new manager gain career traction. If you scored 3 or less, you may want to focus more on building relationships if you are serious about a career as a manager. People with active networks tend to be more effective managers and have broader impact on the organization.

Effective communication, both within the organization and with people outside the company, is a major challenge and responsibility for managers. Although in most companies, poor communication doesn't risk people's lives, as it does in hospital operating rooms, ineffective communication can cause significant problems, including poor employee morale, lack of innovation, decreased performance and a failure to respond to new threats or opportunities in the environment. Many managers are trying to improve their communications knowledge and skills.

To stay connected with employees and customers and shape company direction, managers must excel at personal communications. At Paris-based Buffulo Grill – 'US steak house style' French restaurant chain – CEO Christian Picart set up numerous processes to make sure he stays in touch with employees, including surveys, leadership discussion groups and small quality circles that involve people from all levels of the company. Guidant Corporation, with locations in the US, Ireland and Puerto Rico, now owned by Eli Lilly, has a 'reverse mentoring' programme in which each top manager is assigned a mentor from lower organizational levels to help them stay in touch with what's going on in the organization. Jürgen Grossmann, CEO of RWE AG, one of the power producers in Europe, and number one in Germany, encourages employees to send him emails, and he reads every one. They often alert him to such issues as festering problems in the organization, what the competition is doing, or pending legislation that could affect energy prices. Grossmann is by no means alone. A survey for *The Wall Street Journal* found that 39 out of 44 companies responding said their CEOs personally read and answer employees' emails.[2]

Non-managers often are amazed at how much energy successful executives put into communication. Consider the comment about Robert Strauss, former chairman of the Democratic National Committee and former ambassador to Russia:

> One of his friends says, 'His network is everywhere. It ranges from bookies to bank presidents.'
>
> He seems to find time to make innumerable phone calls to 'keep in touch'; he cultivates secretaries as well as senators; he will befriend a middle-level White House aide whom other important officials won't bother with. Every few months, he sends candy to the White House switchboard operators.[3]

This chapter explains why executives such as Robert Strauss, Christian Picart and Jürgen Grossmann are effective communicators. First, we examine communication as a crucial part of the manager's job and describe a model of the communication process. Next, we consider the interpersonal aspects of communication, including communication channels, persuasion, listening skills and non-verbal communication that affect managers' ability to communicate. Then, we look at the organization as a whole and consider formal upward, downward and horizontal communications as well as personal networks and informal communications. We discuss the importance of keeping multiple channels of communication open and examine how managers can effectively communicate during times of turbulence, uncertainty and crisis. Finally, we examine barriers to communication and how managers can overcome them.

Communication and the Manager's Job

How important is communication? Consider this: managers spend at least 80 per cent of every working day in direct communication with others. In other words, 48 minutes of every hour is spent in meetings, on the telephone, communicating online or talking informally while walking around. The other 20 per cent of a typical manager's time is spent doing desk work, most of which is also communication in the form of reading and writing.[4]

Exhibit 17.1 illustrates the crucial role of managers as communication champions. Managers gather important information from both inside and outside the organization and then distribute appropriate information to others who need it. Managers' communication is *purpose-directed*, in that it directs everyone's attention toward the vision, values and desired goals of the team or organization, and influences people to act in a way to achieve the goals. Managers facilitate *strategic conversations* by using open communication, actively listening to others, applying the practice of dialogue and using feedback for learning and change. Strategic conversation refers to people talking across boundaries and hierarchical levels about the team or organization's vision, critical strategic themes and the values that help achieve important goals.[5] For example, at Royal Philips Electronics, president Gerald Kleisterlee defined four strategic technology themes that he believes

Strategic conversation
Dialogue across boundaries and hierarchical levels about the team or organization's vision, critical strategic themes and the values that help achieve important goals.

Exhibit 17.1 The Manager as Communication Champion

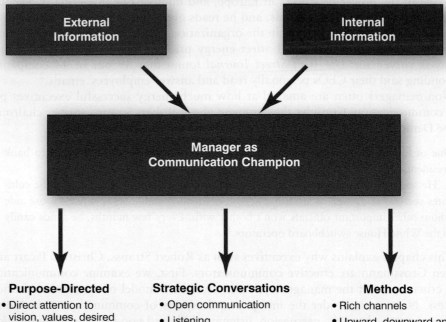

SOURCES: Adapted from
Henry Mintzberg, *The Nature
of Managerial Work* (New
York; Harper and Row, 1973);
and Richard L. Daft, *The
Leadership Experience*, 3rd
ed. (Cincinnati, OH: South-
Western, 2005): 346.

Purpose-Directed
- Direct attention to vision, values, desired outcomes
- Influence employee behaviour

Strategic Conversations
- Open communication
- Listening
- Dialogue
- Feedback

Methods
- Rich channels
- Upward, downward and horizontal channels
- Nonverbal communication
- Personal networks

should define Philips's future in the industry: display, storage, connectivity and digital video processing. These themes intentionally cross technology boundaries, which requires that people communicate and collaborate across departments and divisions to accomplish goals.[6] Effective managers use many communication methods, including selecting rich channels of communication; facilitating upward, downward and horizontal communication; understanding and using non-verbal communication; and building informal communication networks that cross organization boundaries.

Communication permeates every management function described in Chapter 1.[7] For example, when managers perform the planning function, they gather information; write letters, memos and reports; and meet with other managers to formulate the plan. When managers lead, they communicate to share a vision of what the organization can be and motivate employees to help achieve it. When managers organize, they gather information about the state of the organization and communicate a new structure to others. Communication skills are a fundamental part of every managerial activity.

What is Communication?

A professor at Harvard once asked a class to define communication by drawing pictures. Most students drew a manager speaking or typing on a computer keyboard. Some placed 'speech balloons' next to their characters; others showed pages flying from a printer. 'No', the professor told the class, 'none of you has captured the essence of communication.' He went on to explain that communication means 'to share' – not 'to speak' or 'to write'.

Communication thus can be defined as the process by which information is exchanged and understood by two or more people, usually with the intent to motivate or influence behaviour. Communication is not just sending information. Honouring this distinction between *sharing* and *proclaiming* is crucial for successful management. A manager who does not listen is like a used-car salesperson who claims, 'I sold a car – they just did not buy it.' Management communication is a two-way street that includes listening and other forms of feedback. Effective communication, in the words of one expert, is as follows:

> When two people interact, they put themselves into each other's shoes, try to perceive the world as the other person perceives it, try to predict how the other will respond. Interaction involves reciprocal role-taking, the mutual employment of empathetic skills. The goal of interaction is the merger of self and other, a complete ability to anticipate, predict, and behave in accordance with the joint needs of self and other.[8]

It is the desire to share understanding that motivates executives to visit employees on the shop floor, hold small informal meetings, or eat with employees in the company cafeteria. The things managers learn from direct communication with employees shape their understanding of the organization.

The Communication Process

Many people think communication is simple. After all, we communicate every day without even thinking about it. However, communication usually is complex, and the opportunities for sending or receiving the wrong messages are innumerable. No doubt, you have heard someone say, 'But that's not what I meant!' Have you ever received directions you thought were clear and yet still got lost? How often have you wasted time on misunderstood instructions?

To more fully understand the complexity of the communication process, note the key elements outlined in Exhibit 17.2. Two essential elements in every communication situation are the sender and the receiver. The *sender* is anyone who wishes to convey an idea or concept to others, to seek information, or to express a thought or emotion. The *receiver* is the person to whom the message is sent. The sender **encodes** the idea by selecting symbols with which to compose a message. The **message** is the tangible formulation of the idea that is sent to the receiver. The message is sent through a **channel**, which is the communication carrier. The channel can be a formal report, a telephone call or email message, or a face-to-face meeting. The receiver

Communication
The process by which information is exchanged and understood by two or more people, usually with the intent to motivate or influence behaviour.

Encode
To select symbols with which to compose a message.

Message
The tangible formulation of an idea to be sent to a receiver.

Channel
The carrier of a communication.

Exhibit 17.2 A Model of the Communication Process

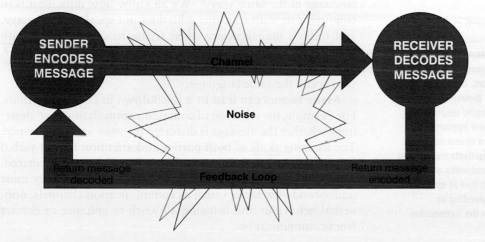

Decode
To translate the symbols used in a message for the purpose of interpreting its meaning.

Feedback
A response by the receiver to the sender's communication.

decodes the symbols to interpret the meaning of the message. Encoding and decoding are potential sources for communication errors, because knowledge, attitudes and background act as filters and create *noise* when translating from symbols to meaning. Finally, feedback occurs when the receiver responds to the sender's communication with a return message. Without feedback, the communication is *one-way*; with feedback, it is *two-way*. Feedback is a powerful aid to communication effectiveness, because it enables the sender to determine whether the receiver correctly interpreted the message.

TAKE A MOMENT

As a new manager, be a communication champion by communicating across boundaries, actively listening to others and using feedback to make improvements. Remember that effective communication requires sharing and achieving mutual understanding.

Managers who are effective communicators understand and use the circular nature of communication. Consider Nortel Networks' *Virtual Leadership Academy*, a monthly televised programme hosted by Dan Hunt, president of Nortel's Caribbean and Latin American operations, and Emma Carrasco, vice president of marketing and communications. Hunt and Carrasco use a talk-show format to get people talking. Employees from about 40 different countries watch the show from their regional offices and call in their questions and comments. 'We're always looking for ways to break down barriers', says Carrasco. 'People watch talk shows in every country, and they've learned that it's okay to say what's on their minds.'[9] The television programme is the channel through which Hunt and Carrasco send their encoded message. Employees decode and interpret the message and encode their feedback, which is sent through the channel of the telephone hook-up. The communications circuit is complete.

CONCEPT CONNECTION

Videoconferencing systems, such as the one shown here, use increasingly sophisticated hardware and software to transmit both visual and verbal cues and provide feedback. On large screens in the front of the room, managers not only see and hear colleagues thousands of miles away, but they can also scrutinize displays of relevant information. These new systems provide channel richness once characteristic of only face-to-face meetings. Analysts expect that terrorism threats, possible pandemics and expensive business travel will fuel at least a 20 per cent annual increase in spending on videoconferencing systems in the foreseeable future.

© DAN KRAUSS/GETTY IMAGES

Communicating Among People

The communication model in Exhibit 17.2 illustrates the components of effective communication. Communications can break down if sender and receiver do not encode or decode language in the same way.[10] We all know how difficult it is to communicate with someone who does not speak our language, and today's managers are often trying to communicate with people who speak many different native languages. However, communication breakdowns can also occur between people who speak the same language.

Many factors can lead to a breakdown in communications. For example, the selection of communication channel can determine whether the message is distorted by noise and interference. The listening skills of both parties and attention to non-verbal behaviour can determine whether a message is truly shared. Thus, for managers to be effective communicators, they must understand how factors such as communication channels, non-verbal behaviour and listening all work to enhance or detract from communication.

Communication Channels

Managers have a choice of many channels through which to communicate to other managers or employees. A manager may discuss a problem face-to-face, make a telephone call, use instant messaging, send an email, write a memo or letter, or put an item in a newsletter, depending on the nature of the message. Research has attempted to explain how managers select communication channels to enhance communication effectiveness.[11] The research has found that channels differ in their capacity to convey information. Just as a pipeline's physical characteristics limit the kind and amount of liquid that can be pumped through it, a communication channel's physical characteristics limit the kind and amount of information that can be conveyed through it. The channels available to managers can be classified into a hierarchy based on information richness.

The Hierarchy of Channel Richness

Channel richness is the amount of information that can be transmitted during a communication episode. The hierarchy of channel richness is illustrated in Exhibit 17.3. The capacity of an information channel is influenced by three characteristics: (1) the ability to handle multiple cues simultaneously; (2) the ability to facilitate rapid, two-way feedback; and (3) the ability to establish a personal focus for the communication. Face-to-face discussion is the richest medium, because it permits direct experience, multiple information cues, immediate feedback and personal focus. Face-to-face discussions facilitate the assimilation of broad cues and deep, emotional understanding of the situation. Telephone conversations are next in the richness hierarchy. Although eye contact, posture and other body language cues are missing, the human voice can still carry a tremendous amount of emotional information.

Electronic messaging, such as email and instant messaging, is increasingly being used for messages that were once handled via the telephone. However, in a survey by researchers at the Ohio State University, most respondents said they preferred the telephone or face-to-face conversation for communicating difficult news, giving advice or expressing affection.[12] Because email messages lack both visual and verbal cues and don't allow for interaction and feedback, messages can sometimes be misunderstood. Using email to discuss disputes, for example, can lead to an escalation rather than a resolution of conflict.[13] Studies have found that email messages tend to be much more blunt than other forms of communication, even other written

Channel richness
The amount of information that can be transmitted during a communication episode.

Exhibit 17.3 The Pyramid of Channel Richness

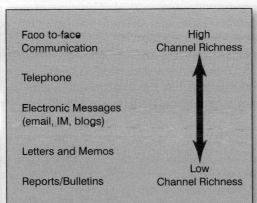
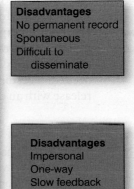

Advantages
Personal
Two-way
Fast feedback

Face-to-face Communication — High Channel Richness

Telephone

Electronic Messages (email, IM, blogs)

Letters and Memos

Reports/Bulletins — Low Channel Richness

Disadvantages
No permanent record
Spontaneous
Difficult to disseminate

Advantages
Permanent record
Premeditated
Easy to disseminate

Disadvantages
Impersonal
One-way
Slow feedback

communications. This bluntness can cause real problems when communicating cross-culturally, because some cultures consider directness rude or insulting.[14] Instant messaging alleviates the problem of miscommunication to some extent by allowing for immediate feedback. **Instant messaging (IM)** allows users to see who is connected to a network and share short-hand messages or documents with them instantly. A growing number of managers are using IM, indicating that it helps people get responses faster and collaborate more smoothly.[15] Over reliance on email and IM can damage company communications because people stop talking to one another in a rich way that builds solid interpersonal relationships. However, some research indicates that electronic messaging can enable reasonably rich communication if the technology is used appropriately.[16] Organizations are also using interactive meetings over the internet, sometimes adding video capabilities to provide visual cues and greater channel richness.

Still lower on the hierarchy of channel richness are written letters and memos. Written communication can be personally focused, but it conveys only the cues written on paper and is slower to provide feedback. Impersonal written media, including fliers, bulletins and standard computer reports, are the lowest in richness. These channels are not focused on a single receiver, use limited information cues and do not permit feedback.

Instant messaging (IM) Electronic communication that allows users to see who is connected to a network and share information instantly.

Selecting the Appropriate Channel

It is important for managers to understand that each communication channel has advantages and disadvantages, and that each can be an effective means of communication in the appropriate circumstances.[17] Channel selection depends on whether the message is routine or non-routine. *Non-routine messages* typically are ambiguous, concern novel events and involve great potential for misunderstanding. They often are characterized by time pressure and surprise. Managers can communicate non-routine messages effectively by selecting rich channels. *Routine* messages are simple and straightforward. They convey data or statistics or simply put into words what managers already agree on and understand. Routine messages can be efficiently communicated through a channel lower in richness, such as email or memorandum. Written communications should also be used when the communication is official and a permanent record is required.[18]

Consider the alert to consumers issued by the Department for Environment, Food and Rural Affairs regarding mad cow disease when more than 179 000 cattle had been infected and 4.4 million slaughtered during the eradication programme. Grocers immediately pulled the product from shelves, and widespread news coverage warned the public not to consume any beef until the cause of the contamination could be identified. An immediate response was critical. This type of non-routine communication forces a rich information exchange. The group will meet face-to-face, brainstorm ideas and provide rapid feedback to resolve the situation and convey the correct information. If, in contrast, an agency director is preparing a press release about a routine matter such as a policy change or new department members, less information capacity is needed. The director and public relations people might begin developing the press release with an exchange of memos, telephone calls and email messages.

TAKE A MOMENT   As a new manager, take care in choosing how to send a message. Don't use email for difficult or emotional conversations that should be dealt with face-to-face or via the telephone. Email is preferable for more routine communications.

The key is to select a channel to fit the message. During a major acquisition, one firm decided to send top executives to all major work sites of the acquired company, where most of the workers met the managers in person, heard about their plans for the company, and had a chance to ask questions. The results were well worth the time and expense of the personal face-to-face meetings because the acquired workforce saw their new managers as understanding, open and willing to listen.[19] Communicating their non-routine message about the acquisition in person prevented damaging rumours and misunderstandings. The choice of a communication channel can also convey a symbolic meaning to the receiver; in a sense, the medium becomes the message. The firm's decision to communicate face-to-face with the acquired workforce signalled to employees that managers cared about them as individuals.

Communicating to Persuade and Influence Others

Communication is not just for conveying information, but to persuade and influence people. Although communication skills have always been important to managers, the ability to persuade and influence others is even more critical today. Businesses are run largely by cross-functional teams who are actively involved in making decisions. Issuing directives is no longer an appropriate or effective way to get things done.[20]

To persuade and influence, managers have to communicate frequently and easily with others. Yet some people find interpersonal communication experiences unrewarding or difficult and thus tend to avoid situations where communication is required. The term **communication apprehension** describes this avoidance behaviour, and is defined as 'an individual's level of fear or anxiety associated with either real or anticipated communication'. With training and practice, managers can overcome their communication apprehension and become more effective communicators.

Communication apprehension
An individual's level of fear or anxiety associated with interpersonal communications.

Go to the Experiential Exercise on page 674 that pertains to your level of communication apprehension.

TAKE A MOMENT

Effective persuasion doesn't mean telling people what you want them to do; instead, it involves listening, learning about others' interests and needs, and leading people to a shared solution.[21] Managers who forget that communication means *sharing*, as described earlier, aren't likely to be as effective at influencing or persuading others, as the founder and president of the executive coaching firm Valuedance learned the hard way (see the Innovative Way box).

As this example shows, people stop listening to someone when that individual isn't listening to them. By failing to show interest in and respect for the boss's point of view, Cramm and her client lost the boss's interest from the beginning, no matter how suitable the ideas they were presenting. To effectively influence and persuade others, managers have to show they care about how the other person feels. Persuasion requires tapping into people's emotions, which can only be done on a personal, rather than a rational, impersonal level.

Managers who use symbols, metaphors and stories to deliver their messages have an easier time influencing and persuading others. Stories draw on people's imaginations and emotions, which helps managers make sense of a fast-changing environment in ways that people can understand and share. If we think back to our early school years, we may remember that the most effective lessons often were couched in

INNOVATIVE WAY

Valuedance

When Susan Cramm, who has worked with executives from a number of Fortune Global 200 clients, including Toyota, Sony and Time Warner, was asked by a client to help persuade the client's boss to support an initiative she wanted to launch, Cramm readily agreed. They scheduled a meeting with the boss, then held a series of planning sessions where the two discussed the current situation at the client's firm, weighed the options, and decided on the best approach for launching the initiative. Filled with enthusiasm and armed with a Power-Point presentation, Cramm was sure the client's boss would see things their way.

An agonizing 15 minutes later, she was out the door, PowerPoint deck and all, having just had a lesson about the art of persuasion. What went wrong? Cramm had focused on the hard, rational matters and ignored the soft skills of relationship building, listening and negotiating that are so critical to persuading others. 'Never did we consider the boss's views,' Cramm said later about the planning sessions she and her client held to prepare for the meeting. 'Like founding members of the "it's all about me" club, we fell upon our swords, believing that our impeccable logic, persistence and enthusiasm would carry the day.'

With that approach, the meeting was over before it even began. The formal presentation shut down communications because it implied that Cramm had all the answers and the boss was just there to listen and agree.[22]

stories. Presenting hard facts and figures rarely has the same power. Evidence of the compatibility of stories with human thinking was demonstrated by a study at Stanford Business School.[23] The point was to convince MBA students that a company practiced a policy of avoiding layoffs. For some students, only a story was used. For others, statistical data were provided that showed little turnover compared to competitors. For other students, statistics and stories were combined, and yet other students were shown the company's official policy statements. Of all these approaches, the students presented with a vivid story alone were most convinced that the company truly practised a policy of avoiding layoffs. Managers can learn to use elements of storytelling to enhance their communication.[24] Stories need not be long, complex or carefully constructed. A story can be a joke, an analogy or a verbal snapshot of something from the manager's own past experiences.[25]

Non-verbal Communication

Managers also use symbols to communicate what is important. Managers are watched, and their behaviour, appearance, actions and attitudes are symbolic of what they value and expect of others.

Most of us have heard the saying that 'actions speak louder than words'. Indeed, we communicate without words all the time, whether we realize it or not. Non-verbal communication refers to messages sent through human actions and behaviours rather than through words.[26] Most managers are astonished to learn that words themselves carry little meaning. A significant portion of the shared understanding from communication comes from the non-verbal messages of facial expression, voice, mannerisms, posture and dress.

Non-verbal communication occurs mostly face to face. One researcher found three sources of communication cues during face-to-face communication: the *verbal*, which are the actual spoken words; the *vocal*, which include the pitch, tone and timbre of a person's voice; and *facial expressions*. According to this study, the relative

Non-verbal communication
A communication transmitted through actions and behaviours rather than through words.

weights of these three factors in message interpretation are as follows: verbal impact, 7 per cent; vocal impact, 38 per cent; and facial impact, 55 per cent.[27] To some extent, we are all natural *face readers*, but facial expressions can be misinterpreted, suggesting that managers need to ask questions to make sure they're getting the right message. Managers can hone their skills at reading facial expressions and improve their ability to connect with and influence followers. Studies indicate that managers who seem responsive to the unspoken emotions of employees are more effective and successful in the workplace.[28]

This research also strongly implies for managers that 'it's not what you say but how you say it'. Non-verbal messages and body language often convey our real thoughts and feelings with greater force than do our most carefully selected words. Thus, while the conscious mind may be formulating a vocal message such as 'Congratulations on your promotion', body language may be signalling true feelings through blushing, perspiring or avoiding eye contact. When the verbal and non-verbal messages are contradictory, the receiver will usually give more weight to behavioural actions than to verbal messages.[29]

A manager's office sends non-verbal cues as well. For example, what do the following seating arrangements mean? (1) The supervisor stays behind her desk, and you sit in a straight chair on the opposite side. (2) The two of you sit in straight chairs away from her desk, perhaps at a table. (3) The two of you sit in a seating arrangement consisting of a sofa and easy chair. To most people, the first arrangement indicates, 'I'm the boss here', or 'I'm in authority'. The second arrangement indicates, 'This is serious business'. The third indicates a more casual and friendly, 'Let's get to know each other'.[30] Non-verbal messages can be a powerful asset to communication if they complement and support verbal messages. Managers should pay close attention to non-verbal behaviour when communicating. They can learn to coordinate their verbal and non-verbal messages and at the same time be sensitive to what their peers, subordinates and supervisors are saying non-verbally.

Listening

One of the most important tools of manager communication is listening, both to employees and customers. Most managers now recognize that important information flows from the bottom up, not the top down, and managers had better be tuned in.[31] The next Innovative Way box describes how a new managing director and human resources director transformed Kwik-Fit Financial Services by listening to employees who were tired of feeling as though no one in the organization cared about them. Some organizations use innovative techniques for finding out what's on employees' and customers' minds. Cabela's, a retailer for outdoor enthusiasts, lets employees borrow and use any of the company's products for a month, as long as they provide feedback that helps other employees better serve customers. The employee fills out a form detailing the product's pros and cons, gives a talk to other employees or customers about the product, and provides feedback in the form of 'Item Notes' that are fed into a knowledge sharing system.[32]

In the communication model in Exhibit 17.2, the listener is responsible for message reception, which is a vital link in the communication process. Listening involves the skill of grasping both facts and feelings to interpret a message's genuine meaning. Only then can the manager provide the appropriate response. Listening requires attention, energy and skill. Although about 75 per cent of effective communication is

© PICTURE CONTACT/ALAMY

CONCEPT CONNECTION About a year ago, Dominic Odipo became the editor of *The Standard*, a famous newspaper based in Nairobi, Kenya. Describing his new responsibilities, Odipo emphasizes the importance of listening. 'Whenever someone walks into my office with a knitted brow and an open mouth, I say, pre-emptively, "Would you like a cup of tea?" Whatever the answer, this creates a pause and sets the tone for the discussion to follow.' Odipo is convinced that listening to employees, although time consuming, is essential to her success as a manager.

Listening
The skill of receiving messages to accurately grasp facts and feelings to interpret the genuine meaning.

INNOVATIVE WAY

Managers at Kwik-Fit Learn that it Pays to Listen[33]

When Keren Edwards took over as human resources director at Kwik-Fit Financial Services, the work environment was dour indeed. Staff turnover at the insurance company call centre, located near Glasgow, was 52 per cent. So Edwards rolled up her sleeves and got to work.

Her efforts have clearly paid off. The Chartered Institute of Personnel and Development (CIPD) awarded Kwik-Fit its prestigious 2005 People Management Award, and *The Sunday Times* named it one of Britain's 100 best places to work. Kwik-Fit's 2005 turnover rate dropped to about 34 per cent, profits nearly doubled, and more than seven out of ten employees said they enjoyed working there. What accounts for this turnaround? According to Edwards, it all comes down to listening: 'Listening to your people and making changes based on their views, opinions and feedback is very powerful.'

With the support of new managing director Martin Oliver, who vowed to make Kwik-Fit a 'fantastic place to work', Edwards supervised a series of one-day workshops that called on the entire workforce to tackle the company's human resource problems. She and her staff primed the idea pump by making it a competition, posting the number of suggestions generated by each

session outside the company cafeteria. In all, 32 workshops generated 6500 proposals, some admittedly more fanciful than practical – for example, a pet day care and a rooftop helicopter pad. But there were plenty of potentially workable suggestions. The company then charged teams consisting of both senior managers and rank-and-file volunteers with the task of implementing selected employee-generated ideas.

As a result, Kwik-Fit employees now work in a completely renovated building and enjoy bonuses, performance-based pay, flexitime, flexible benefits, and an onsite day care. In addition, they counter job stress by taking advantage of the free corporate gym; a cheerful chill-out room complete with TV, pool tables and computer games; yoga and tai chi classes; and a massage service. And then there's Rob Hunter, the company's first 'minister of fun', who organizes special theme days, social evenings and the holiday party, not to mention the annual sales awards he hosts in a sparkly jacket. 'Staff need to work hard and play hard to be motivated and productive,' he observes.

Kwik-Fit has gone from being perceived as a company that doesn't care about its workers to one where employees feel they matter. Its 'Mail Martin' programme, which encourages people to send ideas straight to the managing director by awarding £250 monthly for the best idea, guarantees that Kwik-Fit call centre employees will continue to feel they're being heard.

listening, most people spend only 30 to 40 per cent of their time listening, which leads to many communication errors.[34] One of the secrets of highly successful salespeople is that they spend 60 to 70 per cent of a sales call letting the customer talk. However, listening involves much more than just not talking. Many people do not know how to listen effectively. They concentrate on formulating what they are going to say next rather than on what is being said to them. Our listening efficiency, as measured by the amount of material understood and remembered by subjects 48 hours after listening to a 10-minute message, is, on average, no better than 25 per cent.[35]

TAKE A MOMENT   As a new manager, use stories and metaphors to tap into people's imagination and emotions. When influencing or persuading, first listen and strive to understand the other person's point of view. And pay attention to non-verbal communication.

Exhibit 17.4 Ten Keys to Effective Listening

Keys	Poor Listener	Good Listener
1. Listen actively.	Is passive, laid back	Asks questions, paraphrases what is said
2. Find areas of interest.	Tunes out dry subjects	Looks for opportunities, new learning
3. Resist distractions.	Is easily distracted	Fights or avoids distraction, tolerates bad habits, knows how to concentrate
4. Capitalize on the fact that thought is faster.	Tends to daydream with slow speakers	Challenges, anticipates, mentally summarises; weighs the evidence; listens between the lines to tone of voice
5. Be responsive.	Is minimally involved	Nods, shows interest, give and take, positive feedback
6. Judge content, not delivery.	Tunes out if delivery is poor	Judges content; skips over delivery errors
7. Hold one's fire.	Has preconceptions, starts to argue	Does not judge until comprehension is complete
8. Listen for ideas.	Listens for facts	Listens to central themes
9. Work at listening.	Shows no energy output; fakes attention	Works hard, exhibits active body state, eye contact
10. Exercise one's mind.	Resists difficult material in favour of light, recreational material	Uses heavier material as exercise for the mind

SOURCES: Adapted from Sherman K. Okum, 'How to Be a Better Listener', *Nation's Business* (August 1975): 62; and Philip Morgan and Kent Baker, 'Building a Professional Image: Improving Listening Behavior', *Supervisory Management* (November 1985): 34–38.

What constitutes good listening? Exhibit 17.4 gives ten keys to effective listening and illustrates a number of ways to distinguish a bad from a good listener. A good listener finds areas of interest, is flexible, works hard at listening, and uses thought speed to mentally summarize, weigh and anticipate what the speaker says. Good listening means shifting from thinking about self to empathizing with the other person and thus requires a high degree of emotional intelligence.

Few things are as maddening to people as not being listened to. Executives at health-insurer Humana Inc. realized they could grab a bigger share of the Medicare drug benefits business simply by listening to America's senior citizens.

Humana, Inc.

Sixty-eight-year-old Helen Arnold tells how she spent hours trying to research a Medicare drug benefit plan over the phone without ever being able to get through to a person. 'This recorded voice just kept giving me all these numbers to punch,' she said, her voice rising as she recalled the frustration. It's a frustration that was shared by seniors all over the US as they struggled to comprehend the new Medicare plans.

Arnold is part of a consumer gripe session, sponsored by Humana, Inc., the nation's number five health insurer. Humana decided to take an approach unique in the health insurance industry – listening to what customers want and designing products and services around their needs. The company holds consumer focus groups, solicits the input of employees, and observes people in their homes as they make health-care decisions. Humana learned for example, that many people got frustrated researching the new Medicare plans online or over the phone, so it set up kiosks at Wal-Marts, hired sales representatives to sell the plans in people's homes, and made a deal with 17 000 State Farm insurance agents to offer Humana's Medicare plans through their offices.

Humana is the first major health insurer to create a culture that emphasizes actively listening to customers. Consumer products company Procter & Gamble effectively used these techniques for finding out what people want. P&G also learned that listening to employees translates into business success. Managers emphasize the importance of listening to both internal as well as external customers. 'Gaining the hearts and minds of every employee . . . is no small challenge, and it's one that managers have to wrestle with every day to succeed,' says P&G's global marketing officer James Stengel. 'That's what we do with our customers – and now we're making sure we do it with our own employees.'[36]

Listening has paid off. In early 2006, Humana had signed up 2.4 million people to its Medicare plans, second only to much-larger United Health Group. The company is using listening to better serve other customers as well, such as by setting up kiosks at employers' offices so people can talk to someone face-to-face.

Organizational Communication

Another aspect of management communication concerns the organization as a whole. Organization-wide communications typically flow in three directions – downward, upward and horizontally. Managers are responsible for establishing and maintaining formal channels of communication in these three directions. Managers also use informal channels, which means they get out of their offices and mingle with employees.

Formal Communication Channels

Formal communication channel
A communication channel that flows within the chain of command or task responsibility defined by the organization.

Formal communication channels are those that flow within the chain of command or task responsibility defined by the organization. The three formal channels and the types of information conveyed in each are illustrated in Exhibit 17.5.[37] Downward and upward communications are the primary forms of communication used in most traditional, vertically organized companies. However, many of today's organizations emphasize horizontal communication, with people continuously sharing information across departments and levels.

Electronic communication such as email and instant messaging have made it easier than ever for information to flow in all directions. For example, the British Army is using technology to rapidly transmit communications about weather conditions, the latest intelligence on the insurgency, and so forth to lieutenants in the field in Afghanistan and Iraq. Similarly, the Navy uses instant messaging to communicate within ships, across Navy divisions. 'Instant messaging has allowed us to keep our crew members on the same page at the same time,' says Commander Houston, who oversees the Navy's communications programme. 'Lives are at stake in real time, and we're seeing a new level of communication and readiness.'[38]

Downward Communication

Downward communication
Messages sent from top management down to subordinates.

The most familiar and obvious flow of formal communication, downward communication, refers to the messages and information sent from top management to subordinates in a downward direction.

Exhibit 17.5 Downward, Upward and Horizontal Communication in Organizations

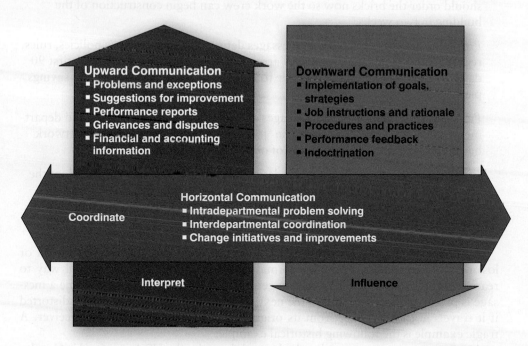

Upward Communication
- Problems and exceptions
- Suggestions for improvement
- Performance reports
- Grievances and disputes
- Financial and accounting information

Downward Communication
- Implementation of goals, strategies
- Job instructions and rationale
- Procedures and practices
- Performance feedback
- Indoctrination

Horizontal Communication
- Intradepartmental problem solving
- Interdepartmental coordination
- Change initiatives and improvements

Coordinate

Interpret

Influence

Managers can communicate downward to employees in many ways. Some of the most common are through speeches, messages in company newsletters, email, information leaflets tucked into pay envelopes, material on bulletin boards and policy and procedures manuals. Managers sometimes use creative approaches to downward communication to make sure employees get the message. John Adamson, project manager at Process Line, Leeds based engineering company, noticed that workers were dropping expensive power tools, so he hung price tags on the tools to show the replacement cost. Employees solved the problem by finding a way to hook up the tools so they wouldn't be dropped. Adamson's symbolic communication created a climate of working together for solutions.

Managers also have to decide what to communicate about. It is impossible for managers to communicate with employees about everything that goes on in the organization, so they have to make choices about the important information to communicate.[39] Unfortunately, many US managers could do a better job of effective downward communication. The results of one survey found that employees want open and honest communication about both the good and the bad aspects of the organization's performance. But when asked to rate their company's communication effectiveness on a scale of 0 to 100, the survey respondents' score averaged 69. In addition, a study of 1500 managers, mostly at first and second management levels, found that 84 per cent of these leaders perceive communication as one of their most important tasks, yet only 38 per cent believe they have adequate communications skills.[40]

Managers can do a better job of downward communication by focusing on specific areas that require regular communication. Recall our discussion of purpose-directed communication from early in this chapter. Downward communication usually encompasses these five topics:

1 *Implementation of goals and strategies.* Communicating new strategies and goals provides information about specific targets and expected behaviours. It gives direction for lower levels of the organization. *Example:* 'The new quality campaign is for real. We must improve product quality if we are to survive.'

2 *Job instructions and rationale.* These directives indicate how to do a specific task and how the job relates to other organizational activities. *Example:* 'Purchasing should order the bricks now so the work crew can begin construction of the building in two weeks.'

3 *Procedures and practices.* These messages define the organization's policies, rules, regulations, benefits, and structural arrangements. *Example:* 'After your first 90 days of employment, you are eligible to enrol in our company-sponsored savings plan.'

4 *Performance feedback.* These messages appraise how well individuals and departments are doing their jobs. *Example:* 'Joe, your work on the computer network has greatly improved the efficiency of our ordering process.'

5 *Indoctrination.* These messages are designed to motivate employees to adopt the company's mission and cultural values and to participate in special ceremonies, such as picnics. *Example:* 'The company thinks of its employees as family and would like to invite everyone to attend the annual picnic and fair on March 3.'

A major problem with downward communication is *drop off*, the distortion or loss of message content. Although formal communications are a powerful way to reach all employees, much information gets lost – 25 per cent or so each time a message is passed from one person to the next. In addition, the message can be distorted if it travels a great distance from its originating source to the ultimate receiver. A tragic example is the following historical example:

A reporter was present at a hamlet burned down by the US Army 1st Air Cavalry Division in 1967. Investigations showed that the order from the Division headquarters to the brigade was: 'On no occasion must hamlets be burned down.'

The brigade radioed the battalion: 'Do not burn down any hamlets unless you are absolutely convinced that the Viet Cong are in them.'

The battalion radioed the infantry company at the scene: 'If you think there are any Viet Cong in the hamlet, burn it down.'

The company commander ordered his troops: 'Burn down that hamlet.'[41]

Information drop off cannot be completely avoided, but the techniques described in the previous sections can reduce it substantially. Using the right communication channel, consistency between verbal and non-verbal messages, and active listening can maintain communication accuracy as it moves down the organization.

Upward Communication

Upward communication
Messages transmitted from the lower to the higher levels in the organization's hierarchy.

Formal upward communication includes messages that flow from the lower to the higher levels in the organization's hierarchy. Most organizations take pains to build in healthy channels for upward communication. Employees need to air grievances, report progress and provide feedback on management initiatives. Coupling a healthy flow of upward and downward communication ensures that the communication circuit between managers and employees is complete.[42] Five types of information communicated upward are the following:

1 *Problems and exceptions.* These messages describe serious problems with and exceptions to routine performance in order to make senior managers aware of difficulties. *Example:* 'The printer has been out of operation for two days, and it will be at least a week before a new one arrives.'

2 *Suggestions for improvement.* These messages are ideas for improving task-related procedures to increase quality or efficiency. *Example:* 'I think we should

eliminate step 2 in the audit procedure because it takes a lot of time and produces no results.'

3 *Performance reports*. These messages include periodic reports that inform management how individuals and departments are performing. *Example:* 'We completed the audit report for Smith & Smith on schedule but are one week behind on the Jackson report.'

4 *Grievances and disputes*. These messages are employee complaints and conflicts that travel up the hierarchy for a hearing and possible resolution. *Example:* 'The manager of operations research cannot get the cooperation of the Lincoln plant for the study of machine utilization.'

5 *Financial and accounting information*. These messages pertain to costs, accounts receivable, sales volume, anticipated profits, return on investment, and other matters of interest to senior managers. *Example:* 'Costs are 2 per cent over budget, but sales are 10 per cent ahead of target, so the profit picture for the third quarter is excellent.'

Many organizations make a great effort to facilitate upward communication. Mechanisms include suggestion boxes, employee surveys, open-door policies, management information system reports and face-to-face conversations between workers and executives. Consider how one entrepreneur, Pat Croce, keeps the upward communication flowing.

In today's fast-paced world, many managers find it hard to maintain constant communication. Ideas such as the Five-Fifteen help keep information flowing upward so managers get feedback from lower levels.

Despite these efforts, however, barriers to accurate upward communication exist. Managers might resist employee feedback because they don't want to hear negative information, or employees might not trust managers sufficiently to push information upward.[43] At *The New York Times*, for example, poor upward communication was partly to blame for the Jayson Blair scandal. Some people in the newsroom knew or suspected that the rising reporter was fabricating elements of his news stories, but the environment of separation between reporters and editors prevented the information

 INNOVATIVE WAY

Pat Croce, Entrepreneur

Pat Croce is involved in several business ventures, including the development of Pirate Soul, 'the ultimate pirate museum', in Key West, Florida. Like many entrepreneurs, Croce spends a lot of time on the road, travelling all across the country from his home office in Philadelphia.

To make sure he stays in touch with what's going on in his various businesses, Croce implemented a key communication tool he calls the Five-Fifteen. Each Friday, all employees and managers take 15 minutes to write brief progress reports and forward them to their immediate supervisors. Within a few

days, all the information trickles up to Croce in a sort of 'corporate Cliff Notes' version. The idea is that the reports take Croce only five minutes to read (hence the name Five-Fifteen). Croce says the Five-Fifteens have enabled him to keep in touch with the little details that make a big difference in the success of his businesses.

Employees typically look at the Five-Fifteens as a chance to be heard, while Croce looks at them as a way to keep his finger on the pulse of each business. In addition, the reports give him a chance to compliment and thank people for their accomplishments and offer questions or suggestions in areas that need improvement.[44]

from being transmitted upward.[45] Innovative companies search for ways to ensure that information gets to top managers without distortion. A report reviewing the Blair scandal at the *Times*, for instance, recommended techniques such as cross-hierarchical meetings, office hours for managers, and informal brainstorming sessions among reporters and editors to improve upward communication.[46] At Nando's, a South African restaurant chain with a Portuguese theme, top managers spend at least one weekend a year in the trenches – cutting steaks, washing glasses, setting tables and taking out the rubbish. By understanding the daily routines and challenges of waiters, chefs and other employees at their restaurants, Nando's executives increase their awareness of how management actions affect others.

Horizontal Communication

Horizontal communication
The lateral or diagonal exchange of messages among peers or co-workers.

Horizontal communication is the lateral or diagonal exchange of messages among peers or co-workers. It may occur within or across departments. The purpose of horizontal communication is not only to inform but also to request support and coordinate activities. Horizontal communication falls into one of three categories:

1   *Intradepartmental problem solving.* These messages take place among members of the same department and concern task accomplishment. *Example:* 'Kelly, can you help us figure out how to complete this medical expense report form?'

2   *Interdepartmental coordination.* Interdepartmental messages facilitate the accomplishment of joint projects or tasks. *Example:* 'Bob, please contact marketing and production and arrange a meeting to discuss the specifications for the new sub-assembly. It looks like we might not be able to meet their requirements.'

3   *Change initiatives and improvements.* These messages are designed to share information among teams and departments that can help the organization change, grow and improve. *Example:* 'We are streamlining the company travel procedures and would like to discuss them with your department.'

Horizontal communication is particularly important in learning organizations, where teams of workers are continuously solving problems and searching for better ways of doing things. Recall from Chapter 10 that many organizations build in horizontal communications in the form of task forces, committees, or even a matrix or horizontal structure to encourage coordination. At Woodend Hospital, two doctors created a horizontal task force to solve a serious patient health problem.

© JHB PHOTOGRAPHY/ALAMY

CONCEPT CONNECTION Despite having a strong external brand, several rapid changes of ownership left many Orange employees with a confused sense of their corporate identity. "We'd defined what we stood for as a business looking out," says David Roberts, employer brand manager at Orange, "but a brand is also about the promise and it was felt this needed explaining internally – to form part of our HR identity." Roberts and his colleagues played on this duality by creating two cartoon characters: one displaying a light bulb (representing the rational outward looking dimension) and the other a heart (representing the company's internal emotions). Embedded across internal and external communications (you can see them here: www.orange.co.uk/whyworkhere), the characters have subtly helped Orange to develop a more coherent organization.

Team Communication Channels

A special type of horizontal communication is communicating in teams. Teams are the basic building block of many organizations. Team members work together to accomplish tasks, and the team's communication structure influences both team performance and employee satisfaction.

Research into team communication has focused on two characteristics: the extent to which team communications are

⊙ INNOVATIVE WAY

Woodend Hospital[47]

We've all heard of it happening – a patient checks into the hospital for a routine procedure and ends up getting sicker instead of better. Hospital-borne infections afflict about two million patients – and kill nearly 100 000 – each year. Greater antibiotic use causes the germs to develop greater resistance. The infection epidemic is growing worse worldwide, but a task force at Woodend Hospital, Aberdeen, Scotland has reversed the trend by breaking down communication barriers.

When a cancer patient became Woodend's first victim of a new strain of deadly bacteria – superbug, infectious-disease specialists Lawrence McDermit and Gordon Bray realized it would take everyone's help to defeat the insidious enemy. As infection spread throughout the hospital, they launched a regular Monday morning meeting to plot countermoves. Although some doctors and staff members were offended at having their procedures questioned, the goal of

preventing needless deaths overrode their concerns. Absolute candour was the rule at the Monday morning meetings, which involved not only doctors and nurses, but also lab technicians, pharmacists, computer technicians and admissions representatives. One pharmacist, for example, recognized that antibiotics act as fertilizer for many bacteria, which encouraged physicians to decrease their use of antibiotics in favour of alternative treatments. Computer representatives and admissions people got together to develop software to identify which returning patients might pose a threat for bringing infection back into the hospital. Eventually, the task force even included maintenance staff when studies showed that a shortage of sinks was inhibiting hand-washing.

Increasing horizontal communication paid off at Woodend Hospital, saving millions in annual medical costs and at least a few lives. Over three years, Woodend's rate of hospital-borne infections plunged 22 per cent.

centralized and the nature of the team's task.[48] The relationship between these characteristics is illustrated in Exhibit 17.6. In a **centralized network**, team members must communicate through one individual to solve problems or make decisions. In a **decentralized network**, individuals can communicate freely with other team members. Members process information equally among themselves until all agree on a decision.[49]

In laboratory experiments, centralized communication networks achieved faster solutions for simple problems. Members could simply pass relevant information to a central person for a decision. Decentralized communications were slower for simple

Centralized network
A team communication structure in which team members communicate through a single individual to solve problems or make decisions.

Decentralized network
A team communication structure in which team members freely communicate with one another and arrive at decisions together.

Exhibit 17.6 Effectiveness of Team Communication Networks

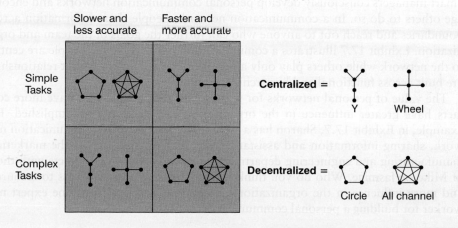

SOURCES: Adapted from A. Bavelas and D. Barrett, 'An Experimental Approach to Organization Communication', *Personnel* 27 (1951): 366–371; M. E. Shaw, *Group Dynamics: The Psychology of Small Group Behavior* (New York: McGraw-Hill, 1976); and E. M. Rogers and R. A. Rogers, *Communication in Organizations* (New York: Free Press, 1976).

problems because information was passed among individuals until someone finally put the pieces together and solved the problem. However, for more complex problems, the decentralized communication network was faster. Because all necessary information was not restricted to one person, a pooling of information through widespread communications provided greater input into the decision. Similarly, the accuracy of problem solving was related to problem complexity. The centralized networks made fewer errors on simple problems but more errors on complex ones. Decentralized networks were less accurate for simple problems but more accurate for complex ones.[50]

The implication for organizations is as follows: In a highly competitive global environment, organizations typically use teams to deal with complex problems. When team activities are complex and difficult, all members should share information in a decentralized structure to solve problems. Teams need a free flow of communication in all directions.[51] Teams that perform routine tasks spend less time processing information, and thus communications can be centralized. Data can be channelled to a supervisor for decisions, freeing workers to spend a greater percentage of time on task activities.

Personal Communication Channels

Personal communication channels
Communication channels that exist outside the formally authorized channels and do not adhere to the organization's hierarchy of authority.

Personal communication channels exist outside the formally authorized channels. These informal communications coexist with formal channels but may skip hierarchical levels, cutting across vertical chains of command to connect virtually anyone in the organization. In most organizations, these informal channels are the primary way information spreads and work gets accomplished. Three important types of personal communication channels are *personal networks*, *management by wandering around* and the *grapevine*.

TAKE A MOMENT

As a new manager, it is essential to build and nurture a personal communication network. Take the New Manager Self-Test on page 663 to learn how you are as a networker. Networking plugs you into the grapevine, and supplements your formal communication channels.

Developing Personal Communication Networks

Personal networking
The acquisition and cultivation of personal relationships that cross departmental, hierarchical and even organizational boundaries.

Personal networking refers to the acquisition and cultivation of personal relationships that cross departmental, hierarchical and even organizational boundaries.[52] Smart managers consciously develop personal communication networks and encourage others to do so. In a communication network, people share information across boundaries and reach out to anyone who can further the goals of the team and organization. Exhibit 17.7 illustrates a communication network. Some people are central to the network while others play only a peripheral role. The key is that relationships are built across functional and hierarchical boundaries.

The value of personal networks for managers is that people who have more contacts have greater influence in the organization and get more accomplished. For example, in Exhibit 17.7, Sharon has a well-developed personal communication network, sharing information and assistance with many people across the marketing, manufacturing and engineering departments. Contrast Sharon's contacts with those of Mike or Jasmine. Who do you think is likely to have greater access to resources and more influence in the organization? Here are a few tips from one expert networker for building a personal communication network:[53]

1 *Build it before you need it.* Smart managers don't wait until they need something to start building a network of personal relationships – by then, it's too late. Instead, they show genuine interest in others and develop honest connections.

2 *Never eat lunch alone.* People who excel at networking make an effort to be visible and connect with as many people as possible. Master networkers keep their social as well as business conference and event calendars full.

3 *Make it win-win.* Successful networking isn't just about getting what *you* want; it's also about making sure other people in the network get what *they* want.

4 *Focus on diversity.* The broader your base of contacts, the broader your range of influence. Build connections with people from as many different areas of interest as possible (both within and outside of the organization).

✅ NEW MANAGER SELF-TEST

What is Your Social Disposition?

How do you come across to others? What is your social disposition? To find out, mark whether each item below is Mostly True or Mostly False for you.

		Mostly True	Mostly False
1	I want to climb the corporate ladder as high as I can.	☐	☐
2	I confront people when I sense a conflict.	☐	☐
3	People consider me cooperative and easy to work with.	☐	☐
4	I like to get right to the point.	☐	☐
5	I make quick decisions usually without consulting others.	☐	☐
6	I make a real effort to understand other peoples' point of view.	☐	☐
7	I enjoy competing and winning.	☐	☐
8	I like to get to the bottom line.	☐	☐
9	I take a personal interest in people.	☐	☐

SCORING AND INTERPRETATION Give yourself one point for items 1, 2, 4, 5, 7 and 8 that you marked Mostly True and one point for items 3, 6 and 9 that you marked Mostly False. The questions pertain to whether your social disposition is one of being focused and driven toward personal success or whether you tend to come across as affable and friendly. If you scored 7 or higher, you are probably ambitious and goal oriented. A score of 3 or less would mean that you probably are empathic, ask questions and enjoy collaborating with others.

A person with a driven disposition may be promoted to manager, but may not be a good listener, fail to pick up on body language or take time to engage in dialogue. A manager has to get things done through other people, and it helps to slow down, listen, build relationships, and take the time to communicate. Too much focus on your personal achievement may come across as uncaring. A new manager with a friendly disposition is often a good listener, makes inquiries and experiences fewer communication mistakes.

SOURCE Based on 'Social Styles', in Paula J. Caproni, *Management Skills for Everyday Life: The Practical Coach,* 2nd ed. (Upper Saddle River, NJ: Prentice-Hall, 2005), pp. 200–203.

Exhibit 17.7 An Organizational Communication Network

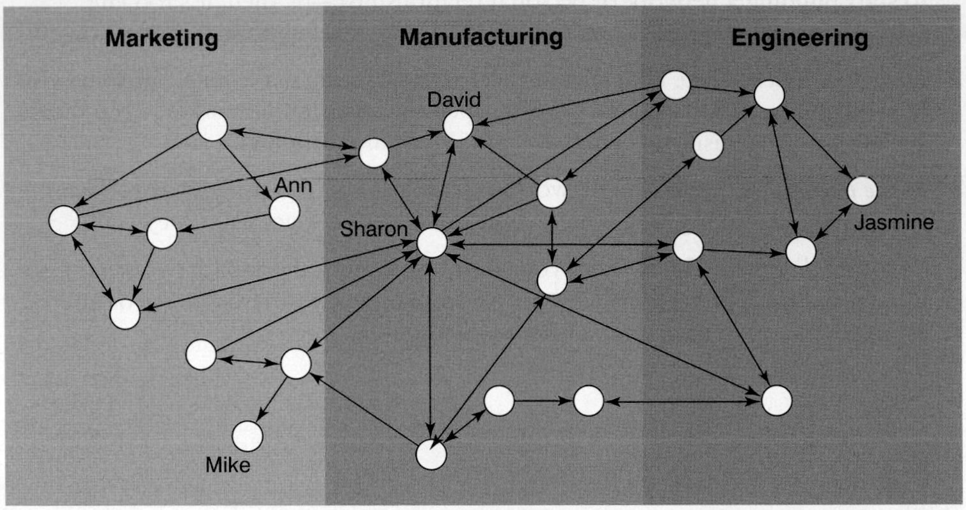

Most of us know from personal experience that 'who you know' sometimes counts for more than what you know. By cultivating a broad network of contacts, managers can significantly extend their influence and accomplish greater results.

The Grapevine

Grapevine
An informal, person-to-person communication network of employees that is not officially sanctioned by the organization.

One type of informal, person-to-person communication network that is not officially sanctioned by the organization is referred to as the **grapevine**.[54] The grapevine links employees in all directions, ranging from the CEO through middle management, support staff and line employees. The grapevine will always exist in an organization, but it can become a dominant force when formal channels are closed. In such cases, the grapevine is actually a service because the information it provides helps makes sense of an unclear or uncertain situation. Employees use grapevine rumours to fill in information gaps and clarify management decisions. One estimate is that as much as 70 per cent of all communication in a firm is carried out through its grapevine.[55] The grapevine tends to be more active during periods of change, excitement, anxiety and sagging economic conditions. For example, a survey by professional employment services firm Randstad found that about half of all employees reported first hearing of major company changes through the grapevine.[56] Consider what happened at Jel, Inc., an auto supply firm that was under great pressure from Ford and GM to increase quality. Management changes to improve quality – learning statistical process control, introducing a new compensation system, buying a fancy new screw machine from Germany – all started out as rumours, circulating days ahead of the actual announcements, and were generally accurate.[57]

Surprising aspects of the grapevine are its accuracy and its relevance to the organization. About 80 per cent of grapevine communications pertain to business-related topics rather than personal gossip. Moreover, from 70 to 90 per cent of the details passed through a grapevine are accurate.[58] Many managers would like the grapevine to be destroyed because they consider its rumours to be untrue, malicious, and harmful, which typically is not the case. Managers should be aware that almost five of every six important messages are carried to some extent by the grapevine rather than through official channels. In a survey of 22 000 shift workers in varied industries, 55 per cent said they get most of their information via the grapevine.[59] Smart managers understand the company's grapevine. They recognize who's connected to whom and which employees are key players in the informal spread of information. In all cases, but particularly in times of crisis, executives need to manage communications effectively so that the grapevine is not the only source of information.[60]

Management by Wandering Around

The communication technique known as **management by wandering around** (MBWA) was made famous by the books *In Search of Excellence* and *A Passion for Excellence*.[61] These books describe executives who talk directly with employees to learn what is going on. MBWA works for managers at all levels. Managers mingle and develop positive relationships with employees and learn directly from them about their department, division or organization. The president of Hewlett-Packard had a habit of visiting a district field office. Rather than schedule a big strategic meeting with the district supervisor, he would come in unannounced and chat with the lowest-level employees. In any organization, both upward and downward communications are enhanced with MBWA. Managers have a chance to describe key ideas and values to employees and, in turn, learn about the problems and issues confronting employees.

When managers fail to take advantage of MBWA, they become aloof and isolated from employees. For example, Peter Anderson, president of Ztel, Inc., a maker of television switching systems, preferred not to personally communicate with employees. He managed at arm's-length. As one manager said, 'I don't know how many times I asked Peter to come to the lab, but he stayed in his office. He wasn't that visible to the troops.' This formal, impersonal management style contributed to Ztel's troubles and eventual bankruptcy.[62]

Management by wandering around (MBWA)
A communication technique in which managers interact directly with workers to exchange information.

Using the Written Word

Not all manager communication is face-to-face, or even verbal. Managers frequently have to communicate in writing, via memorandums, reports or everyday emails. The memo, whether it is sent on paper or electronically, remains a primary way of communicating within companies, and email has become the main way most organizations communicate with customers and clients. Yet evidence shows that the writing skills of US employees and managers in general are terrible. One study found that at least a third of workers in the US don't have the writing skills they need to perform their jobs. A report from The National Commission on Writing says that states spend nearly $250 million a year on remedial writing training for government workers.[63]

Good writing matters. Consider this story told by the president of Opus Associates, a written communications consulting company. After attorney Brian Puricelli won a major case for a client, he petitioned the court to recover his fees. Magistrate Judge Jacob Hart agreed, but he deemed the petition so full or errors and misspellings that he declared it disrespectful to the court and slashed the amount due to Puricelli by nearly $30 000.[64]

Managers can learn to be good writers. Here are a few tips from experts on how to effectively communicate in written form:[65]

- *Respect the reader*. The reader's time is valuable; don't waste it with a rambling, confusing memo or email that has to be read several times to try to make sense of it. Pay attention to your grammar and spelling. Sloppy writing indicates that you think your time is more important than that of your readers. You'll lose their interest – and their respect.

- *Know your point and get to it.* What is the key piece of information that you want the reader to remember? Many people just sit and write, without clarifying in their own mind what it is they're trying to say. To write effectively, know what your central point is and write to support it.
- *Write clearly rather than impressively.* Don't use pretentious or inflated language, and avoid jargon. The goal of good writing for business is to be understood the first time through. State your message as simply and as clearly as possible.
- *Get a second opinion.* When the communication is highly important, such as a formal memo to the department or organization, ask someone you consider to be a good writer to read it before you send it. Don't be too proud to take their advice. In all cases, read and revise the memo or email a second and third time before you hit the send button.

A former manager of communication services at consulting firm Arthur D. Little Inc. has estimated that around 30 per cent of all business memos and emails are written simply to get clarification about an earlier written communication that didn't make sense to the reader.[66] By following these guidelines, you can get your message across the first time.

Communicating During Turbulent Times

During turbulent times, communication becomes even more important. To build trust and promote learning and problem solving, managers incorporate ideas such as open communication, dialogue, and feedback and learning. In addition, they develop crisis communication skills for communicating with both employees and the public in exceptionally challenging or frightening circumstances.

Open Communication

Open communication
Sharing all types of information throughout the company, across functional and hierarchical levels.

A recent trend that reflects managers' increased emphasis on empowering employees, building trust and commitment, and enhancing collaboration is open communication. **Open communication** means sharing all types of information throughout the company, across functional and hierarchical levels. Many companies, such as British Petroleum, Tata Group and BirdsEye Frozen Foods, are opening the financial books to workers at all levels and training employees to understand how and why the company operates as it does. At Volvo, one of the world's leading truck-trailer manufacturers, employees complete several hours of business training and attend regular meetings on the shop floor to review the company's financial performance.[67]

Open communication runs counter to the traditional flow of selective information downward from supervisors to subordinates. By breaking down conventional hierarchical barriers to communication, the organization can gain the benefit of all employees' ideas. The same ideas batted back and forth among a few managers do not lead to effective learning or to a network of relationships that keep companies thriving. New voices and conversations involving a broad spectrum of people revitalize and enhance organizational communication.[68] Open communication also builds trust and a commitment to common goals, which is essential in organizations that depend on collaboration and knowledge-sharing to accomplish their purpose. Of the executives surveyed, 50 per cent reported that open communication is a key to building trust in the organization.[69]

Dialogue

Another popular means of fostering trust and collaboration is through dialogue. The 'roots of dialogue' are *dia* and *logos*, which can be thought of as *stream of meaning*.

Exhibit 17.8 Dialogue and Discussion: The Differences

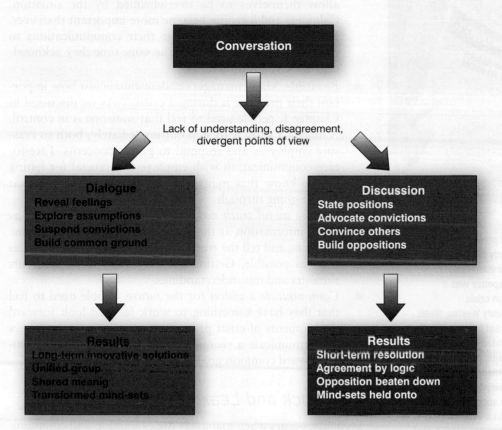

```
                    ┌─────────────────────┐
                    │   Conversation      │
                    └─────────────────────┘
                              │
                              ▼
                Lack of understanding, disagreement,
                      divergent points of view
           ┌──────────────────────────────────────┐
           ▼                                        ▼
┌─────────────────────┐              ┌─────────────────────┐
│   Dialogue          │              │   Discussion        │
│   Reveal feelings   │              │   State positions   │
│   Explore assumptions│             │   Advocate convictions│
│   Suspend convictions│             │   Convince others   │
│   Build common ground│             │   Build oppositions │
└─────────────────────┘              └─────────────────────┘
           │                                        │
           ▼                                        ▼
┌─────────────────────┐              ┌─────────────────────┐
│   Results           │              │   Results           │
│   Long-term innovative solutions│  │   Short-term resolution│
│   Unified group     │              │   Agreement by logic│
│   Shared meanig     │              │   Opposition beaten down│
│   Transformed mind-sets│           │   Mind-sets held onto│
└─────────────────────┘              └─────────────────────┘
```

SOURCE: Adapted from Edgar Schein, 'On Dialogue, Culture, and Organizational Learning', *Organizational Dynamics* (Autumn 1993): 46.

Dialogue is a group communication process in which people together create a stream of shared meaning that enables them to understand each other and share a view of the world.[70] People may start out at polar opposites, but by talking openly, they discover common ground, common issues, and shared goals on which they can build a better future.

A useful way to describe dialogue is to contrast it with discussion (see Exhibit 17.8). The intent of discussion, generally, is to deliver one's point of view and persuade others to adopt it. A discussion is often resolved by logic or 'beating down' opponents. Dialogue, by contrast, asks that participants suspend their attachments to a particular viewpoint so that a deeper level of listening, synthesis and meaning can evolve from the group. A dialogue's focus is to reveal feelings and build common ground. Both forms of communication – dialogue and discussion – can result in change. However, the result of discussion is limited to the topic being deliberated, whereas the result of dialogue is characterized by group unity, shared meaning and transformed mind-sets. As new and deeper solutions are developed, a trusting relationship is built among team members.[71]

Dialogue
A group communication process aimed at creating a culture based on collaboration, fluidity, trust and commitment to shared goals.

Crisis Communication

Over the past few years, the sheer number and scope of crises have made communication a more demanding job for managers. Organizations face small crises every day, such as charges of racial discrimination, a factory fire or a flu epidemic. Moreover, acts of intentional evil, such as bombings or kidnappings, continue to increase, causing serious repercussions for people and organizations. Managers can develop four primary skills for communicating in a crisis.[72]

© GREG WOOD/AFP/GETTY IMAGES

CONCEPT CONNECTION When an extortionist claimed to have placed seven pesticide-contaminated candy bars in Sydney area stores, manufacturer MasterFoods Australia-New Zealand's response was a textbook example of effective crisis communication. President Andy Weston-Webb announced, 'It's not safe to eat Mars or Snickers bars' and immediately activated recall plans. MasterFoods launched a public relations campaign, which included interviews with Weston-Webb, full-page newspaper ads, a company hotline and media access to the burial of three million candy bars in a deep pit. The two-month absence of the popular snacks cost the company more than $10 million. But MasterFoods emerged with its reputation intact. During the first week of the products' return, sales surged 300 per cent.

■ *Maintain your focus.* Good crisis communicators don't allow themselves to be overwhelmed by the situation. Calmness and listening become more important than ever. Managers also learn to tailor their communications to reflect hope and optimism at the same time they acknowledge the current difficulties.

■ *Be visible.* Many managers underestimate just how important their presence is during a crisis.[73] As we discussed in Chapter 1, people need to feel that someone is in control. A manager's job is to step out immediately, both to reassure employees and respond to public concerns. Face-to-face communication with employees is crucial for letting people know that managers care about them and what they're going through.

■ *Get the awful truth out.*[74] Effective managers gather as much information as they can, do their best to determine the facts, and tell the truth to employees and the public as soon as possible. Getting the truth out quickly prevents rumours and misunderstandings.

■ *Communicate a vision for the future.* People need to feel that they have something to work for and look forward to. Moments of crisis present opportunities for managers to communicate a vision of a better future and unite people toward common goals.

Feedback and Learning

Feedback occurs when managers use evaluation and communication to help individuals and the organization learn and improve. It enables managers to determine whether they have been successful in communicating with others. Recall from Exhibit 17.2 that feedback is an important part of the communication process. However, despite its importance, feedback is often neglected. Giving and receiving feedback is typically difficult for both managers and employees. Yet, by avoiding feedback, people miss a valuable opportunity to help one another learn, develop, and improve.[75]

Successful managers focus their feedback to help develop the capacities of subordinates, and they encourage critical feedback from employees. When managers enlist the whole organization in reviewing the outcomes of activities, they can quickly learn what works and what doesn't and use that information to improve the organization. Consider how the Russian Army's feedback system promotes whole-system learning.

Managing Organizational Communication

Many of the ideas described in this chapter pertain to barriers to communication and how to overcome them. Exhibit 17.9 lists some of the major barriers to communication, along with some techniques for overcoming them.

Barriers to Communication

Barriers can be categorized as those that exist at the individual level and those that exist at the organizational level.

INNOVATIVE WAY

Russian Ground Forces[76]

At the National Training Centre just south of Moscow, Russia, ground troops engage in a simulated battle. The 'enemy' has sent unmanned aerial vehicles (UAVs) to gather targetting data. When the troops fire on the UAVs, they reveal their location to attack helicopters hovering just behind a nearby ridge. After the exercise, unit members and their superiors hold an *after-action review* to review battle plans, discuss what worked and what didn't, and talk about how to do things better. Gen. Pavel Grachev suggests that inexpensive decoy UAVs might be just the thing to make a distracted enemy reveal its location. The observation became a 'lesson learned' for the entire army, and UAVs became an important part of battle operations in Afghanistan.

Many researchers attribute the transformation of the army from a demoralized, dysfunctional organization following the Afghanistan War into an solid force capable of feedback and learning system. In the Russian Army, after-action reviews take just 15 minutes, and they occur after every identifiable event – large or small, simulated or real. The review involves asking four simple questions: what was supposed to happen? What actually happened? What accounts for any difference? What can we learn? It is a process of identifying mistakes, of innovating, and of continually learning from experience. The lessons are based not only on simulated battles, but also on real-life experiences of soldiers in the field.

In this example, the organization is learning by communicating feedback about the consequences of field operations and simulated battles. Compiling what is learned and using communication feedback create an improved organization. After-action reviews are also used in corporate world. Steelcase Inc., an office furniture manufacturer, and oil giant BP are among the companies adopting similar system to create a process of continuous learning and improvement. BP credits the feedback system for $700 million in cost savings and other gains.

Exhibit 17.9 Communication Barriers and Ways to Overcome Them

Barriers	How to Overcome
Individual	
Interpersonal dynamics	Active listening
Channels and media	Selection of appropriate channel
Semantics	Knowledge of other's perspective
Inconsistent cues	MBWA
Organisational	
Status and power differences	Climate of trust, Dialogue
Departmental needs and goals	Development and use of formal channels
Lack of formal channels	Encouragement of multiple channels, formal and informal
Communication network unsuited to task	Changing organisation or group structure to fit communication needs
Poor coordination	Feedback and learning

Individual Barriers

First, *interpersonal barriers* include problems with emotions and perceptions held by employees. For example, rigid perceptual labelling or stereotyping prevents people from modifying or altering their opinions. If a person's mind is made up before the communication starts, communication will fail. Moreover, people with different backgrounds or knowledge may interpret a communication in different ways.

Second, *selecting the wrong channel* or *medium* for sending a communication can be a problem. When a message is emotional, it is better to transmit it face to face rather than in writing. Email can be particularly risky for discussing difficult issues because it lacks the capacity for rapid feedback and multiple cues. On the other hand, email is highly efficient for routine messages.

Semantics
The meaning of words and the way they are used.

Third, *semantics* often causes communication problems. Semantics pertains to the meaning of words and the way they are used. A word such as *effectiveness* may mean achieving high production to a factory superintendent, but to a human resources staff specialist it might mean employee satisfaction. Many common words have an average of 28 definitions; thus, communicators must take care to select the words that will accurately encode ideas.[77] Language differences can also be a barrier in today's organizations. This chapter's Manager's Shoptalk offers some guidelines for how managers can better communicate with people who speak a different language.

TAKE A MOMENT   Go to the Ethical Dilemma on page 676 that pertains to individual barriers to communication.

Fourth, sending *inconsistent cues* between verbal and non-verbal communications will confuse the receiver. If one's facial expression does not reflect one's words, the communication will contain noise and uncertainty. The tone of voice and body language should be consistent with the words, and actions should not contradict words.

Organizational Barriers

Organizational barriers pertain to factors for the organization as a whole. One of the most significant barriers relates to *status and power differences*. Low-power people may be reluctant to pass bad news up the hierarchy, thus giving the wrong impression to upper levels.[78] High-power people may not pay attention or may think that low-status people have little to contribute.

Second, *differences across departments in terms of needs and goals* interfere with communications. Each department perceives problems in its own terms. The production department is concerned with production efficiency whereas the marketing department's goal is to get the product to the customer in a hurry.

Third, the *absence of formal channels* reduces communication effectiveness. Organizations must provide adequate upward, downward and horizontal communication in the form of employee surveys, open-door policies, newsletters, memos, task forces and liaison personnel. Without these formal channels, the organization cannot communicate as a whole.

Fourth, the *communication flow* may not fit the team's or organization's task. If a centralized communication structure is used for non-routine tasks, not enough information will be circulated to solve problems. The organization, department or team is most efficient when the amount of communication flowing among employees fits the task.

MANAGER'S SHOPTALK

Leaping over Language Barriers

In today's global business environment, odds are good you'll find yourself conversing with an employee, colleague or customer who has limited skills in your native language. Here are some guidelines that will help you speak – and listen – more effectively.

1 **Keep your message simple.** Be clear about what you want to communicate, and keep to the point.

2 **Select your words with care.** Don't try to dazzle with your vocabulary. Choose simple words, and look for opportunities to use cognates – that is, words that resemble words in your listener's language. For example, *banco* in Spanish means 'bank' in English. Assemble those simple words into equally simple phrases and short sentences. And be sure to avoid idioms, slang, jargon and vague terminology such as *soon, often* or *several.*

3 **Pay close attention to non-verbals.**

 ■ Don't cover your mouth with your hand. Being able to see your lips helps your listener decipher what you're saying.
 ■ Speak slowly and carefully. In particular, avoid running words together. 'Howya-doin?' won't make any sense to someone still struggling with the English language, for example.
 ■ Allow for pauses. If you're an American, your culture has taught you to avoid silence whenever possible, but pauses give your listener time to take in what you've said, ask a question or formulate a response.
 ■ Fight the urge to shout. Speaking louder doesn't make it any easier for someone to

understand you. It also tends to be intimidating and could give the impression that you're angry.

 ■ Pay attention to facial expressions and body language, but keep in mind that the meaning of such cues can vary significantly from culture to culture. For example, Americans may view eye contact as a sign you're giving someone your full attention, but the Japanese consider prolonged eye contact rude.

4 **Check for comprehension frequently, and invite feedback.** Stop from time to time and make sure you're being understood, especially if the other person laughs inappropriately, never asks a question or continually nods and smiles politely. Ask the listener to repeat what you've said in his or her own words. If you find the other person hasn't understood you, restate the information in a different way instead of simply repeating yourself. Similarly, listen carefully when the non-native speaks, and offer feedback so the person can check your understanding of his or her message.

Above all, when communicating with someone who doesn't speak your language well, be patient with yourself and the listener, be encouraging and be persistent.

SOURCES 'How to Communicate with a Non Native English Speaker', wikiHow, www.wikihow.com/Communicate-With-a-Non-Native-English-Speaker; Sondra Thiederman, 'Language Barriers: Bridging the Gap', www.thiederman.com/articles_detail.php?id=39; 'Communicating with Non-native Speakers', Magellan Health Services, www.magellanassist.com/mem/library/default.asp?TopicId=95&CategoryId=0&ArticleId=5.

A final problem is *poor coordination*, so that different parts of the organization are working in isolation without knowing and understanding what other parts are doing. Top executives are out of touch with lower levels, or departments and divisions are poorly coordinated so that people do not understand how the system works together as a whole.

Overcoming Communication Barriers

Managers can design the organization so as to encourage positive, effective communications. Designing involves both individual skills and organizational actions.

© REUTERS/CORBIS

CONCEPT CONNECTION 'I've taken an oath to serve and protect all in my county', says Clark County, Ohio, Sheriff Gene Kelly. He uses the Phraselator P2, shown here, to overcome barriers to communication with the county's growing Spanish-speaking population. The Phraselator is a PDA-sized translation device originally developed by Maryland-based VoxTec for the military. The hand-held computer translates English phrases such as 'Halt' or 'Show me where it hurts' and then broadcasts them in one of approximately 60 languages. Troops and medical personnel in Afghanistan, Iraq, Haiti and Southeast Asia use Phraselators, and they're beginning to make their way into US emergency rooms and county health departments in addition to law enforcement agencies.

Individual Skills

Perhaps the most important individual skill is *active listening*. Active listening means asking questions, showing interest and occasionally paraphrasing what the speaker has said to ensure accurate interpretation. Active listening also means providing feedback to the sender to complete the communication loop.

Second, individuals should select the *appropriate channel* for the message. A complicated message should be sent through a rich channel, such as face-to-face discussion or telephone. Routine messages and data can be sent through memos, letters or email, because the risk of misunderstanding is lower.

Third, senders and receivers should make a special effort to *understand* each other's perspective. Managers can sensitize themselves to the information receiver so they can better target the message, detect bias and clarify misinterpretations. When communicators understand others' perspectives, semantics can be clarified, perceptions understood and objectivity maintained.

The fourth individual skill is *management by wandering around*. Managers must be willing to get out of the office and check communications with others. Sheikh Ahmed bin Saeed Al-Maktoum, the CEO of Emirates Airline, takes every opportunity to introduce himself to employees and customers and find out what's on their minds. He logs more airplane time than many of his company's pilots, visits passenger lounges, and chats with employees on concourses, galleys and airport terminals. Through direct observation and face-to-face meetings, managers like him gain an understanding of the organization and are able to communicate important ideas and values directly to others.

Organizational Actions

Perhaps the most important thing managers can do for the organization is to create a *climate of trust and openness*. Open communication and dialogue can encourage people to communicate honestly with one another. Subordinates will feel free to transmit negative as well as positive messages without fear of retribution. Efforts to develop interpersonal skills among employees can also foster openness, honesty and trust.

Second, managers should develop and use *formal information channels* in all directions. Scandinavian Design uses two newsletters to reach employees. Dana Corporation has developed innovative programmes such as the 'Here's a Thought' board – called a HAT rack – to get ideas and feedback from workers. Other techniques include direct mail, bulletin boards and employee surveys.

Third, managers should encourage the use of *multiple channels*, including both formal and informal communications. Multiple communication channels include written directives, face-to-face discussions, MBWA and the grapevine. For example, managers at Renault and GM plants use multimedia, including a monthly newspaper, frequent meetings of employee teams, and an electronic news display in the cafeteria. Sending messages through multiple channels increases the likelihood that they will be properly received.

Fourth, the structure should *fit communication needs*. An organization can be designed to use teams, task forces, project managers or a matrix structure as needed to facilitate the horizontal flow of information for coordination and problem solving. Structure should also reflect information needs. When team or department tasks are difficult, a decentralized structure should be implemented to encourage discussion and participation.

A system of organizational *feedback and learning* can help overcome problems of poor coordination. Harrah's created a *communication team* as part of its structure at the Casino/Holiday Inn in Las Vegas. The team includes one member from each department. This cross-functional team deals with urgent company problems and helps people think beyond the scope of their own departments to communicate with anyone and everyone to solve those problems.

A MANAGER'S ESSENTIALS: WHAT HAVE WE LEARNED?

- A manager's communication is purpose-directed in that it unites people around a shared vision and goals and directs attention to the values and behaviours that achieve goals. Managers facilitate strategic conversations by using open communication, actively listening to others, applying the practice of dialogue and using feedback for learning and change.

- Communication is the process in which information is exchanged and understood by two or more people. Two essential elements in every communication situation are the sender and the receiver. The sender encodes the idea by selecting symbols with which to compose a message and selecting a communication channel. The receiver decodes the symbols to interpret the meaning of the message. Feedback occurs when the receiver responds to the sender's communication with a return message.

- Communication among people can be affected by communication channels, gender differences, non-verbal communication and listening skills. An important aspect of management communication is persuasion. The ability to persuade others to behave in ways that help accomplish the vision and goals is crucial to good management.

- Organization-wide communication typically flows in three directions: downward, upward and horizontally. Managers are responsible for maintaining formal channels of communication in all three directions. Teams with complex tasks need to communicate successfully in all directions through a decentralized communication network.

- Personal communication channels exist outside formally authorized channels and include personal networks, the grapevine and written communication. Managers with more contacts in their personal network have greater influence in the organization. The grapevine carries workplace gossip, a dominant force in organization communication when formal channels are closed. The ability to write clearly and quickly is increasingly important in today's collaborative work environment.

To enhance organizational communication, managers should understand how to engage in dialogue, manage crisis communication, use feedback and learning to improve employee performance, and create a climate of trust and openness. The final part of this chapter described several individual and organizational barriers to communication. These barriers can be overcome by active listening, selecting appropriate channels, engaging in MBWA, using dialogue, developing a climate of trust, using formal channels, designing the correct structure to fit communication needs, and using feedback for learning. Status and power differences can be a significant barrier to communications, as they have been at the Woodend hospital described earlier in the chapter, where people are afraid to speak up to surgeons because of their status and unique skills. Administrators took the first step toward breaking down barriers with a survey that gave people a chance to be heard. Woodend then launched a programme called Transforming the Operating Room, which includes team-building activities, pre- and post-surgical briefing sessions where everyone is expected to participate, and required 'safety pauses' to encourage anyone in the operating room to delay or even suspend surgery if there is a concern. By establishing these formal mechanisms, administrators significantly improved horizontal and upward communications at Woodend hospital. However, the idea of

Exhibit 18.1 Differences Between Groups and Teams

Group	Team
• Has a designated strong leader	• Shares or rotates leadership roles
• Holds individuals accountable	• Holds team accountable to each other
• Sets identical purpose for group and organisation	• Sets specific team vision or purpose
• Has individual work products	• Has collective work products
• Runs efficient meetings	• Runs meetings that encourage open-ended discussion and problem solving
• Measures effectiveness indirectly by influence on business (such as financial performance)	• Measures effectiveness directly by assessing collective work
• Discusses, decides, delegates work to individuals	• Discusses, decides, shares work

SOURCE: Adapted from Jon R. Katzenbach and Douglas K. Smith, 'The Discipline of Teams', *Harvard Business Review* (March–April 1995): 111–120.

importance of teamwork. But the coaches of teams tend to look not for the best players but a mix of the right players.[12] The 2008 Beijing Olympic Chinese athletes have taken the highest number of medals not only in individual competitions, but also in team events. Similarly the Russian football team Zenit St. Petersburg won the UEFA cup in 2008 with a cohesive team of unknown players led by Andrey Arshavin, who in February 2009 joined Arsenal, a London team in the Premier League, and in the first few months of playing for this team has learnt to play with other strong players and was voted the player of the month.

Model of Work Team Effectiveness

Some of the factors associated with team effectiveness are illustrated in Exhibit 18.2. Work team effectiveness is based on three outcomes – productive output, personal

Exhibit 18.2 Work Team Effectiveness Model

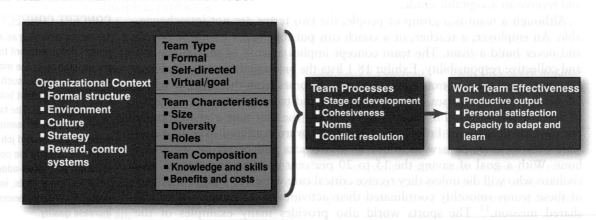

satisfaction and the capacity to adapt and learn.[13] *Satisfaction* pertains to the team's ability to meet the personal needs of its members and hence maintain their membership and commitment. *Productive output* pertains to the quality and quantity of task outputs as defined by team goals. *Capacity to adapt and learn* refers to the ability of teams to bring greater knowledge and skills to job tasks and enhance the potential of the organization to respond to new threats or opportunities in the environment.

The factors that influence team effectiveness begin with the organizational context.[14] The organizational context in which the team operates is described in other chapters and includes such factors as structure, strategy, environment, culture and reward systems. Within that context, managers define teams. Important team characteristics are the type of team, the team structure and team composition. Managers must decide when to create permanent teams within the formal structure and when to use a temporary task team. Factors such as the diversity of the team in terms of gender and race, as well as knowledge, skills and attitudes, can have a tremendous impact on team processes and effectiveness.[15] Team size and roles also are important. Managers strive for the right mix of knowledge and skills for the task to be performed and consider whether a team is the best way to accomplish the task. If costs outweigh benefits, managers may wish to assign an individual employee to the task.

These team characteristics influence processes internal to the team, which, in turn, affect output, satisfaction, and the team's contribution to organizational adaptability. Good team leaders understand and manage stages of team development, cohesiveness, norms and conflict in order to build an effective team. These processes are influenced by team and organizational characteristics and by the ability of members and leaders to direct these processes in a positive manner.

The model of team effectiveness in Exhibit 18.3 is the basis for this chapter. In the following sections, we will examine types of organizational teams, team structure, internal processes and the benefits of effective work teams.

Exhibit 18.3 Five Common Dysfunctions of Teams

Dysfunction	Effective Team Characteristics
Lack of Trust — People don't feel safe to reveal mistakes, share concerns or express ideas.	**Trust** — Members trust one another on a deep emotional level; feel comfortable being vulnerable with one another.
Fear of Conflict — People go along with others for the sake of harmony; don't express conflicting opinions.	**Healthy Conflict** — Members feel comfortable disagreeing and challenging one another in the interest of finding the best solution.
Lack of Commitment — If people are afraid to express their true opinions, it's difficult to gain their true commitment to decisions.	**Commitment** — Because all ideas are put on the table, people can eventually achieve genuine buy-in around important goals and decisions.
Avoidance of Accountability — People don't accept responsibility for outcomes; engage in finger-pointing when things go wrong.	**Accountability** — Members hold one another accountable rather than relying on managers as the source of accountability.
Inattention to Results — Members put personal ambition or the needs of their individual departments ahead of collective results.	**Results Orientation** — Individual members set aside personal agendas; focus on what's best for the team. Collective results define success.

SOURCE: Based on Patrick Lencioni, *The Five Dysfunctions of a Team* (New York: John Wiley & Sons, 2002).

Problem-solving team
Typically five to 12 hourly employees from the same department who meet to discuss ways of improving quality, efficiency, and the work environment.

Self-directed team
A team consisting of five to 20 multi-skilled workers who rotate jobs to produce an entire product or service, often supervized by an elected member.

Problem-solving teams typically consist of five to 12 hourly employees from the same department who voluntarily meet to discuss ways of improving quality, efficiency and the work environment. Recommendations are proposed to management for approval. Problem-solving teams usually are the first step in a company's move toward greater employee participation. The most widely known application is *quality circles*, first used by Japanese companies, in which employees focus on ways to improve quality in the production process. USX adopted this approach in several of its steel mills, recognizing that quality takes a team effort. Under the title All Product Excellence program (APEX), USX set up APEX teams of up to 12 employees who met several times a month to solve quality problems.[23]

As a company matures, problem-solving teams can gradually evolve into self-directed teams, which represent a fundamental change in how work is organized. Self-directed teams enable employees to feel challenged, find their work meaningful, and develop a strong sense of identity with the company.[24] Self-directed teams typically consist of five to 20 multi-skilled workers who rotate jobs to produce an entire product or service or at least one complete aspect or portion of a product or service (e.g. engine assembly, insurance claim processing). The central idea is that the teams themselves, rather than managers or supervisors, take responsibility for their work, make decisions, monitor their own performance, and alter their work behaviour as needed to solve problems, meet goals and adapt to changing conditions.[25] For example, at Dublin's Kellogg's plant in Ireland which produces cereals, production workers are divided into teams of about ten. Some of the teams function entirely without designated leaders and handle all issues and problems that arise in their areas, including hiring and firing, scheduling, budgeting, quality and disciplinary problems. Other teams have leaders assigned by management as they continue to learn how to work in a team environment, but the teams that have progressed to total self-direction actually outperform teams with assigned leaders.[26]

Self-directed teams are permanent teams that typically include the following elements:

- The team includes employees with several skills and functions, and the combined skills are sufficient to perform a major organizational task. A team may include members from the foundry, machining, grinding, fabrication and sales departments, with members cross-trained to perform one another's jobs. The team eliminates barriers among departments, enabling excellent coordination to produce a product or service.
- The team is given access to resources such as information, equipment, machinery and supplies needed to perform the complete task.
- The team is empowered with decision-making authority, which means that members have the freedom to select new members, solve problems, spend money, monitor results and plan for the future.[27]

CONCEPT CONNECTION John Hallam, Gillian Hayes and Jose Carmena from Edinburgh University, Scotland are part of the Mobile Robotics research group, a special purpose team, that is researching how robots can benefit mankind. The projects already developed by the group include gait and face recognition technology. The group also includes research students, who work temporarily on individual projects until these are completed.[28]

© WILLIAM WHITEHURST/CORBIS

In a self-directed team, team members take over managerial duties such as scheduling or ordering materials. They work with minimum supervision, perhaps electing one of their own as supervisor, who may change each year. The most effective self-directed teams are those that are fully empowered, as described in the discussion of empowerment in Chapter 16. In addition to having increased responsibility

Orpheus Orchestra

Most orchestras are strongly hierarchical and structured around a conductor who wields almost complete power and control. Not Orpheus, a world-renowned chamber orchestra started in the 1970s by a small group of musicians committed to democratic power sharing.

Orpheus operates completely without a conductor! Teams of musicians determine the repertoire, schedule concerts, select new musicians, interpret musical works and handle all the other artistic and performance duties a conductor usually controls. The instrument sections constitute natural, specialized self-directed teams. Leadership rotates among different members, who are elected by their team-mates.

The actual structure of teams at Orpheus is quite complex and is designed to facilitate participative leadership, avoid hierarchical control and allow everyone to participate in decision-making.[31]

and discretion, empowered teams are those that have a strong belief in their team's capabilities, find value and meaning in their work, and recognize the impact the team's work has on customers, other stakeholders and organizational success.[29] Managers create the conditions that determine whether self-directed teams are empowered by giving teams true power and decision-making authority, complete information, knowledge and skills, and appropriate rewards. The manager to whom the team and team leaders report, sometimes referred to as the *external leader*, has a tremendous impact on the team's success. In addition to creating conditions for empowerment, effective external leaders serve as an active link between the team and the organization, building constructive relationships and getting the team what it needs to do its best work.[30] An interesting example of the use of self-directed teams is the Orpheus Orchestra of New York City.

The Orpheus Orchestra has found that using self-directed teams provides a number of advantages. The greater information flow and diverse artistic input contributes to a superb performance. In addition, members typically feel a high degree of commitment, and turnover is quite low.

One business organization that succeeds with teamwork is Consolidated Diesel's engine factory in Whitakers, North Carolina. In its 20 or so years of operation as a team-based organization, the plant has had higher revenues, lower turnover and significantly lower injury rates than the industry average. In addition, while most plants average one supervisor for every 25 workers, Consolidated Diesel has one for every 100 employees because the plant workers themselves handle many supervisory duties. The difference yields a savings of about $1 million a year.[32]

Teams in the New Workplace

Some exciting new approaches to teamwork have resulted from advances in information technology, shifting employee expectations and the globalization of business. Two types of teams that are increasingly being used are virtual teams and global teams.

Virtual Teams

A **virtual team** is made up of geographically or organizationally dispersed members who are linked primarily through advanced information and telecommunications technologies.[33] Although some virtual teams may be made up of only organizational

Virtual team
A team made up of members who are geographically or organizationally dispersed, rarely meet face to face and do their work using advanced information technologies.

© MARMADUKE ST. JOHN/ALAMY

CONCEPT CONNECTION When commercial air traffic was grounded immediately after September 11, 2001, DreamWorks CEO Jeffrey Katzenbach had to assemble a virtual team of creative designers. He discovered that existing videoconferencing technology didn't allow team members to hold multiple conversations or get a good look at an object's details. The experience inspired the animation studio to join forces with Hewlett-Packard to produce the Halo Collaboration Studio. In addition to HP, companies such as Cisco Systems and Polycom are now offering these high-end 'telepresence' systems that use studio-quality cameras and sound equipment, high-speed data transmission and rooms carefully designed to be identical, giving geographically dispersed teams a lifelike virtual meeting room.

members, virtual teams often include contingent workers, members of partner organizations, customers, suppliers, consultants or other outsiders. Team members use email, instant messaging, voice mail, videoconferencing, internet and intranet technologies, and various types of collaboration software to perform their work, although they might also sometimes meet face-to-face. Many virtual teams are cross-functional teams that emphasize solving customer problems or completing specific projects. Others are permanent self-directed teams.

With virtual teams, team leadership is typically shared or rotated, depending on the area of expertise needed at each stage of the project.[34] In addition, team membership in virtual teams may change fairly quickly, depending on the tasks to be performed. One of the primary advantages of virtual teams is the ability to rapidly assemble the most appropriate group of people to complete a complex project, solve a particular problem or exploit a specific strategic opportunity. Virtual teams present unique challenges. Managers as team leaders should consider these critical issues when building virtual teams:[35]

- *Select the right team members.* The first step is creating a team of people who have the right mix of technical and interpersonal skills, task knowledge and personalities to work in a virtual environment. Interviews with virtual team members and leaders indicate that the ability to communicate and a desire to work as a team are the most important personal qualities for virtual team members.[36]
- *Manage socialization.* People need to get to know one another and understand the appropriate behaviours and attitudes. Smart team leaders establish team norms and ground rules for interaction early in the team's formation.
- *Foster trust.* Trust might be the most important ingredient in a successful virtual team. Teams that exhibit high levels of trust tend to have clear roles and expectations of one another, get to know one another as individuals, and maintain positive action-oriented attitudes.
- *Effectively manage communications.* Frequent communication is essential. Team leaders need to understand when and how to use various forms of communication to best advantage. Some experts suggest regular face-to-face meetings, while others believe virtual teams can be successful even if they interact only electronically. One time when face-to-face communication might be essential is when misunderstandings, frustrations or conflicts threaten the team's work.[37]

Global Teams

Global team
A work team made up of members of different nationalities whose activities span multiple countries; may operate as a virtual team or meet face-to-face.

Virtual teams are also sometimes global teams. **Global teams** are cross-border work teams made up of members of different nationalities whose activities span multiple countries.[38] Generally, global teams fall into two categories: intercultural teams, whose members come from different countries or cultures and meet face-to-face, and virtual global teams, whose members remain in separate locations around the world and conduct their work electronically.[39] For example, global teams of software developers at Tandem Services Corporation coordinate their work electronically so that the team is productive around the clock. Team members in London code a project and transmit the code each evening to members in the US for testing. US team members then forward the code they've tested to Tokyo for debugging. The next

INNOVATIVE WAY

Nokia

In a study of 52 virtual teams in 15 leading multinational companies, London Business School researchers found that Nokia's teams were among the most effective, even though they were made up of people working in several different countries, across time zones and cultures. What makes Nokia's teams so successful?

Nokia managers are careful to select people who have a collaborative mind-set, and they form many teams with volunteers who are highly committed to the task or project. The company also tries to make sure some members of a team have worked together before, providing a base for trusting relationships. Making the best use of technology is critical. In addition to a virtual work space that team members can access 24 hours a day, Nokia provides an online resource where virtual workers are encouraged to post photos and share personal information. With the inability of members to get to know each another one of the biggest barriers to effective virtual teamwork, encouraging and supporting social networking has paid off for Nokia.[40]

morning, the London team members pick up with the code debugged by their Tokyo colleagues, and another cycle begins.[41] The trend toward creating virtual teams that cross geographical boundaries has grown tremendously in recent years. In some organizations, such as open-source software maker MySQL, most employees are scattered around the world and never see one another face-to-face.

Global teams present enormous challenges for team leaders, who have to bridge gaps of time, distance and culture. In some cases, members speak different languages, use different technologies and have different beliefs about authority, decision-making and time orientation. For example, some cultures, such as the US, are highly focused on 'clock time', and tend to follow rigid schedules, whereas many other cultures have a more relaxed, cyclical concept of time. These different cultural attitudes toward time can affect work pacing, team communications, and the perception of deadlines.[42] Members from different countries may also have varied attitudes about teamwork itself. Multinational organizations have found that many team phenomena are culture-specific. Some countries, such as Mexico, value high power distance, as described in Chapter 4, meaning that differences in power and status are seen as appropriate and desirable. This viewpoint conflicts with the American idea of teamwork, which emphasizes shared power and authority. Thus, the acceptance and effectiveness of team-based systems can vary widely across different cultures, which makes implementing and evaluating teams quite complex.[43]

Organizations using global teams invest the time and resources to adequately educate employees. Managers make sure all team members appreciate and understand cultural differences, are focused on goals and understand their responsibilities to the team. For a global team to be effective, all team members must be willing to deviate somewhat from their own values and norms and establish new norms for the team.[44] As with virtual teams, carefully selecting team members, building trust, and sharing information are critical to success.

© MARK LEONG/REDUX

CONCEPT CONNECTION To update Lotus Symphony, a package of PC software applications, IBM assigned the project to teams in Beijing, China; Austin, Texas; Raleigh, North Carolina; and Boeblingen, Germany. Leading the project, the Beijing group – shown here with Michael Karasick (centre), who runs the Beijing lab, and lead developer Yue Ma (right) – navigated the global team through the programming challenges. To help bridge the distance gap, IBM uses Beehive, a corporate social network similar to Facebook, where employees create profiles, list their interests, and post photos.

Team Characteristics

The next issue of concern to managers is designing the team for greatest effectiveness. One factor is *team characteristics*, which can affect team dynamics and performance. Characteristics of particular concern are team size, diversity and member roles.

Size

More than 30 years ago, psychologist Ivan Steiner examined what happened each time the size of a team increased, and he proposed that team performance and productivity peaked at about five – a quite small number. He found that adding additional members beyond five caused a decrease in motivation, an increase in coordination problems and a general decline in performance.[45] Since then, numerous studies have found that smaller teams perform better, though most researchers say it's impossible to specify an optimal team size. One recent investigation of team size based on data from 58 software development teams found that the five best-performing teams ranged in size from three to six members.[46] Results of a recent Gallup poll in the US show that 82 per cent of employees agree that small teams are more productive.[47]

Teams need to be large enough to incorporate the diverse skills needed to complete a task, enable members to express good and bad feelings and aggressively solve problems. However, they should also be small enough to permit members to feel an intimate part of the team and to communicate effectively and efficiently. In general, as a team increases in size, it becomes harder for each member to interact with and influence the others.

A summary of research on group size suggests the following:[48]

1 Small teams (2–5 members) show more agreement, ask more questions, and exchange more opinions. Members want to get along with one another. Small teams report more satisfaction and enter into more personal discussions. They tend to be informal and make few demands on team leaders.

2 Large teams (ten or more) tend to have more disagreements and differences of opinion. Subgroups often form, and conflicts among them occur. Communication becomes more difficult, and demands on leaders are greater because of the need for stronger coordination, more centralized decision-making and less member participation. Large teams also tend to be less friendly. Turnover and absenteeism are higher in a large team, especially for blue-collar workers. Because less satisfaction is associated with specialized tasks and poor communication, team members have fewer opportunities to participate and feel like an important part of the team.

Free rider
A person who benefits from team membership but does not make a proportionate contribution to the team's work.

3 As teams increase in size, so does the number of *free riders*. The term **free rider** refers to a team member who attains benefits from team membership but does not actively participate in and contribute to the team's work. The problem of free riding has likely been experienced by people in student project groups, where some students put more effort into the group project but everyone benefits from the result. Free riding is sometimes called *social loafing* because members do not exert equal effort.[49] A classic experiment by German psychologist Ringelmann found that the pull exerted on a rope was greater by individuals working alone than by individuals in a group.[50] Similarly, experiments have found that when people are asked to clap and make noise, they make more noise on a per person basis when working alone or in small groups than they do in a large group.[51]

As a general rule, large teams make need satisfaction for individuals more difficult; thus, people feel less motivation to remain committed to their goals. Large projects can be split into components and assigned to several smaller teams to keep the benefits of small team size. At Amazon.com, CEO Jeff Bezos established a 'two-pizza rule'. If a team gets so large that members can't be fed with two pizzas, it needs to be split into smaller teams.[52]

Diversity

Because teams require a variety of skills, knowledge, and experience, it seems likely that heterogeneous teams would be more effective than homogeneous ones. In general, research supports this idea, showing that diverse teams produce more innovative solutions to problems.[53] Diversity in terms of functional area and skills, thinking styles and personal characteristics is often a source of creativity. In addition, diversity may contribute to a healthy level of disagreement that leads to better decision-making. At Southern Company, a new CIO made a conscious effort to build a diverse senior leadership team, recruiting people to build in gender, racial, educational, religious, cultural and geographical diversity. 'The differences we bring to the table sometimes mean we have long, heated discussions,' says Becky Blalock. 'But once we make a decision, we know we've viewed the problem from every possible angle.'[54]

Research studies have confirmed that both functional diversity and gender diversity can have a positive impact on work team performance.[55] Racial, national and ethnic diversity can also be good for teams, but in the short term these differences might hinder team interaction and performance. Teams made up of racially and culturally diverse members tend to have more difficulty learning to work well together, but, with effective leadership, the problems fade over time.[56]

As a new manager, remember that team effectiveness depends on selecting the right type of team for the task, getting people with the right mix of knowledge and skills, and balancing the team's size and diversity.

TAKE A MOMENT

Member Roles

For a team to be successful over the long run, it must be structured so as to both maintain its members' social well-being and accomplish its task. In successful teams, the requirements for task performance and social satisfaction are met by the emergence of two types of roles: task specialist and socioemotional.[57]

People who play the **task specialist role** spend time and energy helping the team reach its goal. They often display the following behaviours:

- *Initiate ideas*. Propose new solutions to team problems.
- *Give opinions*. Offer opinions on task solutions; give candid feedback on others' suggestions.
- *Seek information*. Ask for task-relevant facts.
- *Summarize*. Relate various ideas to the problem at hand; pull ideas together into a summary perspective.
- *Energize*. Stimulate the team into action when interest drops.[58]

Task specialist role
A role in which the individual devotes personal time and energy to helping the team accomplish its task.

Socioemotional role
A role in which the individual provides support for team members' emotional needs and social unity.

People who adopt a **socioemotional role** support team members' emotional needs and help strengthen the social entity. They display the following behaviours:

- *Encourage.* Are warm and receptive to others' ideas; praise and encourage others to draw forth their contributions.
- *Harmonize.* Reconcile group conflicts; help disagreeing parties reach agreement.
- *Reduce tension.* Tell jokes or in other ways draw off emotions when group atmosphere is tense.
- *Follow.* Go along with the team; agree to other team members' ideas.
- *Compromise.* Will shift own opinions to maintain team harmony.[59]

Exhibit 18.5 illustrates task specialist and socioemotional roles in teams. When most individuals in a team play a social role, the team is socially oriented. Members do not criticize or disagree with one another and do not forcefully offer opinions or try to accomplish team tasks, because their primary interest is to keep the team happy. Teams with mostly socioemotional roles can be satisfying, but they also can be unproductive. At the other extreme, a team made up primarily of task specialists will tend to have a singular concern for task accomplishment. This team will be effective for a short period of time but will not be satisfying for members over the long run. Task specialists convey little emotional concern for one another, are unsupportive and ignore team members' social and emotional needs. The task-oriented team can be humourless and unsatisfying.

Dual role
A role in which the individual both contributes to the team's task and supports members' emotional needs.

As Exhibit 18.5 illustrates, some team members may play a dual role. People with **dual roles** both contribute to the task and meet members' emotional needs. Such people often become team leaders. A study of new-product development teams in high-technology firms found that the most effective teams were headed by leaders who balanced the technical needs of the project with human interaction issues, thus meeting both task and socioemotional needs.[60] Exhibit 18.5 also shows the final type of role, called the **non-participator role**, in which people contribute little to either the task or the social needs of team members. These people are free riders, as defined earlier, and typically are held in low esteem by the team.

Non-participator role
A role in which the individual contributes little to either the task or members' socioemotional needs.

The important thing for managers to remember is that effective teams must have people in both task specialist and socioemotional roles. Humour and social concern are as important to team effectiveness as are facts and problem solving. Managers also should remember that some people perform better in one type of role; some are inclined toward social concerns and others toward task concerns. A well-balanced team will do best over the long term because it will be personally satisfying for team members as well as permit the accomplishment of team tasks.

Exhibit 18.5 Team Member Roles

Task Specialist Role Focuses on task accomplishment over human needs Important role, but if adopted by everyone, team's social needs will not be met	**Dual Role** Focuses on task and people May be a team leader Important role, but not essential if members adopt task specialist and socioemotional roles
Non-participator Role Contributes little to either task or people needs of team; also called free riding Not an important role; if adopted by too many members, team will disband	**Socioemotional Role** Focuses on people needs of team over task Important role, but if adopted by everyone, team's tasks will not be accomplished

Member Task Behaviour (High / Low) — Member Social Behaviour (Low / High)

Team Processes

Now we turn our attention to internal team processes. Team processes pertain to those dynamics that change over time and can be influenced by team leaders. In this section, we discuss the team processes of stages of development, cohesiveness and norms. The fourth type of team process, conflict, will be covered in the next section.

Stages of Team Development

After a team has been created, it develops through distinct stages.[61] New teams are different from mature teams. Recall a time when you were a member of a new team, such as a fraternity or sorority pledge class, a committee or a small team formed to do a class assignment. Over time the team changed. In the beginning, team members had to get to know one another, establish roles and norms, divide the labour and clarify the team's task. In this way, each member became part of a smoothly operating team. The challenge for leaders is to understand the stages of team development and take action that will help the group improve its functioning.

Research findings suggest that team development is not random but evolves over definitive stages. One useful model for describing these stages is shown in Exhibit 18.6. Each stage confronts team leaders and members with unique problems and challenges.[62]

Forming

The **forming** stage of development is a period of orientation and getting acquainted. Members break the ice and test one another for friendship possibilities and task orientation. Team members find which behaviours are acceptable to others. Uncertainty is high during this stage, and members usually accept whatever power or authority is offered by either formal or informal leaders. Members are dependent on the team until they find out what the ground rules are and what is expected of them. During this initial stage, members are concerned about such things as 'What is expected of me?' 'What is acceptable?' 'Will I fit in?' During the forming stage, the team leader should provide time for members to get acquainted with one another and encourage them to engage in informal social discussions.

Forming
The stage of team development characterized by orientation and acquaintance.

Storming

During the **storming** stage, individual personalities emerge. People become more assertive in clarifying their roles and what is expected of them. This stage is marked by conflict and disagreement. People may disagree over their perceptions of the team's mission. Members may jockey for position, and coalitions or subgroups based on common interests may form. One subgroup may disagree with another over the total team's goals or how to achieve them. Unless teams can successfully move beyond this stage, they may get bogged down and never achieve high performance. During the storming stage, the team leader should encourage participation by each team member. Members should propose ideas, disagree with one another, and work through the uncertainties and conflicting perceptions about team tasks and goals.

Storming
The stage of team development in which individual personalities and roles, and resulting conflicts, emerge.

Norming

During the **norming** stage, conflict is resolved, and team harmony and unity emerge. Consensus develops on who has the power, who are the leaders, and members' roles.

Norming
The stage of team development in which conflicts developed during the storming stage are resolved and team harmony and unity emerge.

Exhibit 18.6 Five Stages of Team Development

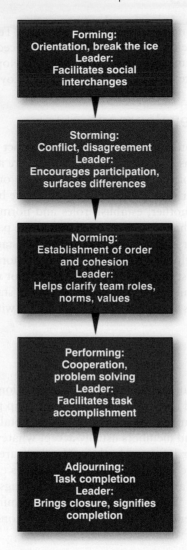

> **Forming:**
> Orientation, break the ice
> **Leader:**
> Facilitates social interchanges

> **Storming:**
> Conflict, disagreement
> **Leader:**
> Encourages participation,
> surfaces differences

> **Norming:**
> Establishment of order
> and cohesion
> **Leader:**
> Helps clarify team roles,
> norms, values

> **Performing:**
> Cooperation,
> problem solving
> **Leader:**
> Facilitates task
> accomplishment

> **Adjourning:**
> Task completion
> **Leader:**
> Brings closure, signifies
> completion

Members come to accept and understand one another. Differences are resolved, and members develop a sense of team cohesion. This stage typically is of short duration. During the norming stage, the team leader should emphasize unity within the team and help to clarify team norms and values.

Performing

Performing

The stage of team development in which members focus on problem solving and accomplishing the team's assigned task.

During the **performing** stage, the major emphasis is on problem solving and accomplishing the assigned task. Members are committed to the team's mission. They are coordinated with one another and handle disagreements in a mature way. They confront and resolve problems in the interest of task accomplishment. They interact frequently and direct their discussions and influence toward achieving team goals. During this stage, the leader should concentrate on managing high task performance. Both socioemotional and task specialists contribute to the team's functioning.

As a new manager, help people on a new team get to know one another, clarify expectations, work out differences and learn to work together. Encourage team members both to accomplish the task and meet the social needs of team members.

Adjourning

The **adjourning** stage occurs in committees and teams that have a limited task to perform and are disbanded afterward. During this stage, the emphasis is on wrapping up and gearing down. Task performance is no longer a top priority. Members may feel heightened emotionality, strong cohesiveness and depression or regret over the team's disbandment. They may feel happy about mission accomplishment and sad about the loss of friendship and associations. At this point, the leader may wish to signify the team's disbanding with a ritual or ceremony, perhaps giving out plaques and awards to signify closure and completeness.

The five stages of team development typically occur in sequence. In teams that are under time pressure or that will exist for only a short period of time, the stages may occur quite rapidly. The stages may also be accelerated for virtual teams. For example, bringing people together for a couple of days of team building can help virtual teams move rapidly through the forming and storming stages. McDevitt Street Bovis, one of the country's largest construction management firms, uses an understanding of the stages of team development to put teams on a solid foundation.

Team Cohesiveness

Another important aspect of the team process is cohesiveness. **Team cohesiveness** is defined as the extent to which members are attracted to the team and motivated to remain in it.[63] Members of highly cohesive teams are committed to team activities, attend meetings, and are happy when the team succeeds. Members of less cohesive teams are less concerned about the team's welfare. High cohesiveness is normally considered an attractive feature of teams.

Determinants of Team Cohesiveness

Characteristics of team structure and context influence cohesiveness. First is *team interaction*. The greater the contact among team members and the more time spent together, the more cohesive the team. Through frequent interactions, members get to know one another and become more committed to the team.[64] Second is the concept of *shared goals*. If team members agree on goals, they will be more cohesive. Agreeing on purpose and direction binds the team together. Third is *personal attraction to the team*, meaning that members have similar attitudes and values and enjoy being together.

Two factors in the team's context also influence group cohesiveness. The first is the presence of competition. When a team is in moderate competition with other

© BEN RADFORD/CORBIS

CONCEPT CONNECTION To accomplish their goals – whether in the business world or on the football field – teams have to successfully advance to the performing stage of team development. The Manchester United football team-mates shown here blend their talents and energies so effortlessly that they play the game not like separate people but like a coordinated piece of a whole. Manchester United recently began using psychological testing as part of the appraisal of new coaches and potential draft picks. Managers think testing gives them another tool for building a high-performance team. As current coach Sir Alex Fergusson puts it, 'If a person isn't dotting the I's and crossing the T's, we know why, and we can surround that person with people who complement that.'

Adjourning
The stage of team development in which members prepare for the team's disbandment.

Team cohesiveness
The extent to which team members are attracted to the team and motivated to remain in it.

INNOVATIVE WAY

McDevitt Street Bovis

The team-building process at McDevitt Street Bovis is designed to take teams to the performing stage as quickly as possible by giving everyone an opportunity to get to know one another; explore the ground rules; and clarify roles, responsibilities and expectations. The company credits this process for quickly and effectively unifying teams, circumventing damaging and time-consuming conflicts, and preventing lawsuits related to major construction projects.

Rather than the typical construction project characterized by conflicts, frantic scheduling and poor communications, Bovis wants its collection of contractors, designers, suppliers and other partners to function like a true team – putting the success of the project ahead of their own individual interests. The team is first divided into separate groups that may have competing objectives – such as the clients in one group, suppliers in another, engineers and architects in a third, and so forth – and asked to come up with a list of their goals for the project. Although interests sometimes vary widely in purely accounting terms, common themes almost always emerge. By talking about conflicting goals and interests, as well as what all the groups share, facilitators help the team gradually come together around a common purpose and begin to develop shared values that will guide the project. After jointly writing a mission statement for the team, each party says what it expects from the others, so that roles and responsibilities can be clarified. The intensive team-building session helps take members quickly through the forming and storming stages of development. 'We prevent conflicts from happening,' says facilitator Monica Bennett. Leaders at McDevitt Street Bovis believe building better teams builds better buildings.[65]

teams, its cohesiveness increases as it strives to win. Finally, team success and the favourable evaluation of the team by outsiders add to cohesiveness. When a team succeeds in its task and others in the organization recognize the success, members feel good, and their commitment to the team will be high.

Consequences of Team Cohesiveness

The outcome of team cohesiveness can fall into two categories – morale and productivity. As a general rule, morale is higher in cohesive teams because of increased communication among members, a friendly team climate, maintenance of membership because of commitment to the team, loyalty and member participation in team decisions and activities. High cohesiveness has almost uniformly good effects on the satisfaction and morale of team members.[66]

With respect to team performance, research findings are mixed, but cohesiveness may have several effects.[67] First, in a cohesive team, members' productivity tends to be more uniform. Productivity differences among members are small because the team exerts pressure toward conformity. Noncohesive teams do not have this control over member behaviour and therefore tend to have wider variation in member productivity.

With respect to the productivity of the team as a whole, research findings suggest that cohesive teams have the potential to be productive, but the degree of productivity depends on the relationship between management and the working team. Thus, team cohesiveness does not necessarily lead to higher team productivity. One study surveyed more than 200 work teams and correlated job performance with their cohesiveness.[68] Highly cohesive teams were more productive when team members felt management support and less productive when they sensed management hostility and negativism. Management hostility led to team norms and goals of low performance, and the highly cohesive teams performed poorly, in accordance with their norms and goals.

Exhibit 18.7 Relationship Among Team Cohesiveness, Performance Norms and Productivity

Moderate Productivity Weak norms in alignment with organization goals	**High Productivity** Strong norms in alignment with organization goals
Low/Moderate Productivity Weak norms in opposition to organization goals	**Low Productivity** Strong norms in opposition to organization goals

Team Performance Norms — High / Low
Team Cohesiveness — Low / High

The relationship between performance outcomes and cohesiveness is illustrated in Exhibit 18.7. The highest productivity occurs when the team is cohesive and also has a high performance norm, which is a result of its positive relationship with management. Moderate productivity occurs when cohesiveness is low, because team members are less committed to performance norms. The lowest productivity occurs when cohesiveness is high and the team's performance norm is low. Thus, cohesive teams are able to attain their goals and enforce their norms, which can lead to either very high or very low productivity. A good example of team cohesiveness combined with high performance norms occurred at Motorola, where a highly cohesive team created a new cell phone that revived the company.

 INNOVATIVE WAY

Motorola

The mood inside Motorola was bleak. Managers and engineers alike knew the company needed a hot new product to regain its reputation – and maybe even some of its lost market share. In the concept phone unit, engineers started talking about building an impossibly thin clamshell phone that would be as beautiful as a piece of fine jewellery and just as desirable – and they wanted it done in a year.

Engineer Roger Jellicoe aggressively promoted himself to lead the team and quickly put together a group of engineers, designers and other specialists who were fired up by the ambitious project. The 'thin clam' team, as they came to be known, rapidly became viewed almost as a rebellious cult within Motorola. The team worked at a facility 50 miles from Motorola's central research unit and kept the details of the project top-secret, even from their colleagues within the company. The need for secrecy and speed, as well as the relative isolation, contributed to the quick, tight bond that developed among team members. Time and again, the thin clam team flouted Motorola's rules for developing new products and followed their own instincts. Top management looked the other way. They wanted the team to have the freedom to be creative and take chances. Because Motorola badly needed a hit, money was not an object; top management gave the team whatever they needed in terms of support and resources to accomplish their goal.

The result was the RAZR, a name based on the team's humorous reference to it as *siliqua patula*, Latin for razor clam. Unlike any other cell phone the world had seen, the RAZR wowed the industry and consumers alike – and rejuvenated the company in the process.[69]

At Motorola, a combination of team cohesiveness and management support that created high performance norms led to amazing results. The phone wasn't originally conceived to be a blockbuster, but it proved to be just that. Between the time the RAZR was launched in late 2004 and mid-2006, the stylish phone sold almost as many units as the red-hot Apple iPod.[70]

Team Norms

Team norm
A standard of conduct that is shared by team members and guides their behaviour.

A **team norm** is a standard of conduct that is shared by team members and guides their behavior.[71] Norms are informal. They are not written down, as are rules and procedures. Norms are valuable because they define boundaries of acceptable behaviour. They make life easier for team members by providing a frame of reference for what is right and wrong. Consider norms associated with the gruelling three-week-long Tour de France. Each team is out to win the 2700-mile bike race, but cooperation among competing teams is necessary for survival. When a team leader crashes, informal norms dictate that everyone slows down and waits. And when someone calls for a bathroom break, no formal rule says other riders have to pull to the side or slow down, but norms suggest they do so. When Dante Coccolo decided instead to go on the attack, putting a large time gap between him and the group, he learned the power of norms. When it came his own turn for a break, several other riders slowed down – but their purpose was to grab Coccolo's bike and toss it into a ditch. The chastened rider finished second to last, and never again rode in the Tour de France.[72]

Norms identify key values, clarify role expectations, and facilitate team survival. Norms begin to develop in the first interactions among members of a new team.[73] Thus, it is important for leaders, especially those of virtual teams, to try to shape early interactions that will lead to norms that help the team succeed. Norms that apply to both day-to-day behaviour and employee output and performance gradually evolve, letting members know what is acceptable and directing their actions toward acceptable performance. Four common ways in which norms develop for controlling and directing behaviour are illustrated in Exhibit 18.8.[74]

Exhibit 18.8 Four Ways Team Norms Develop

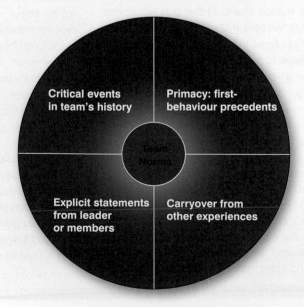

Critical events in team's history

Primacy: first-behaviour precedents

Team Norms

Explicit statements from leader or members

Carryover from other experiences

Critical Events

Often, *critical events* in a team's history establish an important precedent. One example occurred when an employee at a forest products plant was seriously injured while standing too close to a machine being operated by a team-mate. This incident led to a norm that team members regularly monitor one another to make sure all safety rules are observed. Any critical event can lead to the creation of a norm.

Primacy

Primacy means that the first behaviours that occur in a team often set a precedent for later team expectations. For example, at one company a team leader began his first meeting by raising an issue and then 'leading' team members until he got the solution he wanted. The pattern became ingrained so quickly into an unproductive team norm that members dubbed meetings the 'Guess What I Think' game.[75]

Carryover Behaviours

Carryover behaviours bring norms into the team from outside. One current example is the strong norm against smoking in many management teams. Some team members sneak around, gargling with mouthwash and fear expulsion because the team culture believes everyone should kick the habit. Carryover behaviour also influences small teams of college students assigned by instructors to do class work. Norms brought into the team from outside suggest that students should participate equally and help members get a reasonable grade.

Explicit Statements

With *explicit statements*, leaders or team members can initiate norms by articulating them to the team. Explicit statements symbolize what counts and thus have considerable impact. Making explicit statements can be a highly effective way for leaders to influence or change team norms. One division of ABB was about to go bankrupt partly because team members had developed norms of politeness that made people hesitant to express disagreement or bring up negative information. The unit's leader turned things around by making an explicit statement that everyone was expected to speak their minds about problems. Similarly, Ryanair's CEO Michael O'Leary established a norm of cooperation and mutual support among his top leadership team by telling them bluntly every week that if he caught anyone trying to undermine the others, the guilty party would be fired.

Managing Team Conflict

The final characteristic of team process is conflict. Of all the skills required for effective team management, none is more important than handling the conflicts that inevitably arise among members. Conflict can arise among members within a team or between one team and another. **Conflict** refers to antagonistic interaction in which one party attempts to block the intentions or goals of another.[76] Competition, which is rivalry among individuals or teams, can have a healthy impact because it energizes people toward higher performance.[77]

Whenever people work together in teams, some conflict is inevitable. Bringing conflicts out into the open and effectively resolving them is one of the team leader's

Conflict
Antagonistic interaction in which one party attempts to thwart the intentions or goals of another.

most challenging jobs. For example, studies of virtual teams indicate that how they handle internal conflicts is critical to their success, yet conflict within virtual teams tends to occur more frequently and take longer to resolve because people are separated by space, time and cultural differences. Moreover, people in virtual teams tend to engage in more inconsiderate behaviours such as name-calling or insults than do people who work face-to-face.[78]

Balancing Conflict and Cooperation

Groupthink
The tendency for people to be so committed to a cohesive team that they are reluctant to express contrary opinions.

Some conflict can actually be beneficial to teams.[79] A healthy level of conflict helps to prevent groupthink, in which people are so committed to a cohesive team that they are reluctant to express contrary opinions. Author and scholar Jerry Harvey tells a story of how members of his extended family in Texas decided to drive 40 miles to Abilene on a hot day when the car's air conditioning didn't work. Everyone was miserable. Later, each person admitted they hadn't wanted to go but went along to please the others. Harvey used the term *Abilene paradox* to describe this tendency to go along with others for the sake of avoiding conflict.[80] Similarly, when people in work teams go along simply for the sake of harmony, problems typically result. Thus, a degree of conflict leads to better decision-making because multiple viewpoints are expressed. Among top management teams, for example, low levels of conflict have been found to be associated with poor decision-making.[81]

However, conflict that is too strong, that is focused on personal rather than work issues, or that is not managed appropriately can be damaging to the team's morale and productivity. Too much conflict can be destructive, tear relationships apart, and interfere with the healthy exchange of ideas and information.[82] Team leaders have to find the right balance between conflict and cooperation, as illustrated in Exhibit 18.9. Too little conflict can decrease team performance because the team doesn't benefit from a mix of opinions and ideas – even disagreements – that might lead to better solutions or prevent the team from making mistakes. At the other end of the spectrum, too much conflict outweighs the team's cooperative efforts and leads to a decrease in employee satisfaction and commitment, hurting team performance. A moderate amount of conflict that is managed appropriately typically results in the highest levels of team performance.

Exhibit 18.9 Balancing Conflict and Cooperation

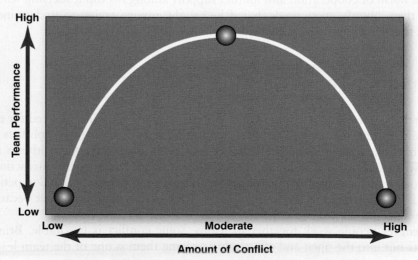

Go to the Ethical Dilemma on page 717 that pertains to team cohesiveness and conflict.   **TAKE A MOMENT**

Causes of Conflict

Several factors can cause people to engage in conflict:[83]

Scarce Resources

Resources include money, information, and supplies. Whenever individuals or teams must compete for scarce or declining resources, conflict is almost inevitable. The introduction of fast-cycle teams, as described earlier, for example, frequently leads to conflict because it creates a new competition for resources.[84] Some projects may be delayed because managers reallocate resources to fast-cycle projects, potentially creating conflicts.

Communication Breakdown

Poor communication results in misperceptions and misunderstandings of other people and teams. In some cases, information is intentionally withheld, which can jeopardize trust among teams and cause long-lasting conflict. Faulty communication can occur in any team, but virtual and global teams are particularly prone to communication breakdowns. For one thing, the lack of nonverbal cues, as described in the previous chapter, leads to more misunderstandings among virtual team members. In addition, trust issues are a major source of conflict in virtual teams because members may fear that they are being left out of important communication interactions.[85]

Personality Clashes

A personality clash occurs when people simply do not get along or do not see eye-to-eye on any issue. Personality clashes are caused by basic differences in personality, values, and attitudes. In one study, personality conflicts were the number-one reported cause preventing front-line management teams from working together effectively.[86] Some personality differences can be overcome. However, severe personality clashes are difficult to resolve. Often, it is a good idea to simply separate the parties so that they need not interact with one another.

Goal Differences

Conflict often occurs simply because people are pursuing conflicting goals. Goal differences are natural in organizations. Individual salespeople's targets may put them in conflict with one another or with the sales manager. Moreover, the sales department's goals might conflict with those of manufacturing. When team members don't have a clear understanding of and commitment to the team goal and how their individual tasks contribute, they may be pursuing their own agendas, which can lead to conflicts.

As a new manager, appreciate that some conflict can be healthy, but don't let conflict reduce the team's effectiveness and well-being. Take the New Manager Self-Test to learn about your personal style for handling conflict.   **TAKE A MOMENT**

✓ NEW MANAGER SELF-TEST

Managing Conflict

Conflicting opinions and perspectives occur in every team. The ability to handle conflict and disagreement is one mark of a successful new manager. To understand your approach to managing conflict, think about disagreements you have had with people on student teams or in other situations, then answer each of the following items as Mostly True or Mostly False for you.

	Mostly True	Mostly False
1 I typically assert my opinion to win a disagreement.	☐	☐
2 I often suggest solutions that combine others' points of view.	☐	☐
3 I prefer to not argue with team members.	☐	☐
4 I raise my voice to get other people to accept my position.	☐	☐
5 I am quick to agree when someone makes a good point.	☐	☐
6 I tend to keep quiet rather than argue with other people.	☐	☐
7 I stand firm in expressing my viewpoints during a disagreement.	☐	☐
8 I try to include other people's ideas to create a solution they will accept.	☐	☐
9 I like to smooth over disagreements so people get along.	☐	☐

SCORING AND INTERPRETATION Three categories of conflict-handling strategies are measured in this instrument: competing, accommodating and collaborating. By comparing your scores you can see your preferred conflict-handling strategy.

Give yourself 1 point for each item marked Mostly True.

Competing: Items 1, 4, 7

Accommodating: Items 2, 5, 8

Collaborating: Items 3, 6, 9

   For which conflict-handling strategy do you score highest? New managers may initially be accommodating to get along with people until they size up the situation. A too-strong competing style may prevent subordinates from having a say in important matters. The collaborating style tries for a win-win solution and has the long-run potential to build a constructive team. How would your strategy differ if the other people involved in a disagreement were family members, friends, subordinates or bosses?

Styles to Handle Conflict

Teams as well as individuals develop specific styles for dealing with conflict, based on the desire to satisfy their own concern versus the other party's concern. A model that describes five styles of handling conflict is in Exhibit 18.10. The two major dimensions are the extent to which an individual is assertive versus cooperative in his or her approach to conflict.

Exhibit 18.10 A Model of Styles to Handle Conflict

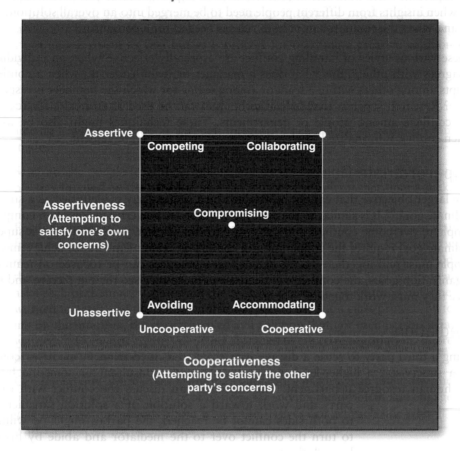

SOURCE: Adapted from Kenneth Thomas, 'Conflict and Conflict Management', in *Handbook of Industrial and Organizational Behavior*, ed. M. D. Dunnette (New York: John Wiley, 1976): 900.

Effective team members vary their style of handling conflict to fit a specific situation. Each of these five styles is appropriate in certain cases.[87]

1 The *competing style* reflects assertiveness to get one's own way, and should be used when quick, decisive action is vital on important issues or unpopular actions, such as during emergencies or urgent cost cutting.

2 The *avoiding style* reflects neither assertiveness nor cooperativeness. It is appropriate when an issue is trivial, when there is no chance of winning, when a delay to gather more information is needed, or when a disruption would be costly.

3 The *compromising style* reflects a moderate amount of both assertiveness and cooperativeness. It is appropriate when the goals on both sides are equally important, when opponents have equal power and both sides want to split the difference, or when people need to arrive at temporary or expedient solutions under time pressure.

4 The *accommodating style* reflects a high degree of cooperativeness, which works best when people realize that they are wrong, when an issue is more important to others than to oneself, when building social credits for use in later discussions, and when maintaining harmony is especially important.

5 The *collaborating style* reflects both a high degree of assertiveness and cooperativeness. The collaborating style enables both parties to win, although it may require substantial bargaining and negotiation. The collaborating style is

PART 6

CONTROLLING

Castles, fortresses, and fortifications were designed both to project power and for defense. The need to project power and control areas of interest leads to innovative designs in such structures. Sometimes changing technology can overcome what was once innovative. Or a line of defense that seems impenetrable is found to have an unexpected weakness. Two examples include Edinburgh Castle in Scotland and the Maginot Line in France.

Since the 7th century, some form of stronghold has been on the site of present-day Edinburgh Castle. The modern castle is the result of centuries of both expansion and destruction. In 1386, a tower was build to serve as the main entrance to what was then the castle. Called David's Tower after David II of Scotland who commissioned it, the tower was roughly 3 stories tall and enormous by the current standards. But in 1573, rebels loyal to the ousted Queen Mary of Scotland seized the castle. The legitimate Scot rulers called on Elizabeth I of England to assist them, and she sent heavy guns. The nearly 200 year old tower was no match for the modern armament and collapsed, forcing the rebels to surrender.

The Maginot Line was built during the peace following World War I along the border between France and Germany as an attempt to prevent another frontal German invasion. It is a hallmark of architecture and engineering. Connected by underground tunnels, most of the fortresses that comprise the Maginot Line are not even visible from the surface but blend with the surrounding countryside. The fortresses themselves run three or four stories below ground. The line was designed to turn back a frontal German assault and there is little doubt it would have succeeded if that is what the Germans had tried. But when the time came, Germany simply went around the line, through occupied Holland and Belgium.

Managers must project power and maintain standards, but even the best control mechanism will prove useless if can be easily circumvented. Quality controls make certain that goals are still being met, products are being made to specification, customers are getting the desired service, and employees are upholding company ethics and standards. But changing technology requires innovation and imagination both in applying to technology to solve problems as well as addressing new problems that come along with the new technology. So along with the efficiencies gained by the computer age, managers must also address concerns such as inappropriate emails or employees misusing access to the internet.

CHAPTER OUTLINE

© NIKADA/ISTOCK

LEARNING OBJECTIVES

After reading this chapter, you should be able to:

1   Define organizational control and explain why it is a key
    management function.

2   Explain the benefits of using the balanced scorecard to track
    performance and control of the organization.

3   Explain the four steps in the control process.

4   Discuss the use of financial statements, financial analysis and
    budgeting as management controls.

5   Contrast the hierarchical and decentralized methods of
    control.

6   Identify the benefits of open-book management.

7   Describe the concept of total quality management and major
    TQM techniques, such as quality circles, benchmarking, Six
    Sigma principles, reduced cycle time and continuous
    improvement.

8   Identify current trends in quality and financial control, including
    ISO 9000, economic value-added and market value-added
    systems, activity-based costing and corporate governance,
    and discuss their impact on organizations.

CHAPTER 19

MANAGING QUALITY AND PERFORMANCE

Control is an important issue facing every manager in every organization, but new managers sometimes have a hard time finding the correct degree of control that will keep people productive without squelching their motivation and creativity. Managers face many control issues, including controlling work processes, regulating employee behaviour, setting up basic systems for allocating financial resources, developing human resources, analyzing financial performance and evaluating overall profitability. Another important aspect is quality control.

Manager's Challenge

Rude, insensitive or condescending doctors have been around for as long as the medical profession, and the US-based Rochester Independent Practice Association, like other medical groups, has its fair share. But medical director Dr Howard Beckman fears that uncaring doctors are becoming more common as cost pressures put greater demands on them to see more patients. With less time to spend on each client, some doctors rely more on technology than on human interaction. Patients are rarely comfortable confronting a doctor when they feel they've been treated with indifference or disrespect. Those who are sufficiently offended or embarrassed simply never return, which hurts the doctor, the association and the patient. With growing demands from patients, health insurers and employers who purchase health plans for better customer service as well as increased efficiency, Dr Beckman knows something must be done to boost doctors' communication skills and improve the overall quality of patient care.[1]

What advice would you give Dr Beckman and other administrators about using control systems and strategies to improve the quality of the doctor-patient interaction? What is the first step you would recommend they take?

TAKE A MOMENT

What is Your Attitude Toward Organizational Regulation and Control?[2]

Managers have to control people for organizations to survive, yet control should be the right amount and type. Companies are often less democratic than the society of which they are a part. Think honestly about your beliefs toward the regulation of other people and answer each item that follows as Mostly True or Mostly False.

		Mostly True	Mostly False
1	I believe people should be guided more by feelings and less by rules.	☐	☐
2	I think employees should be on time to work and to meetings.	☐	☐
3	I believe efficiency and speed are not as important as letting everyone have their say when making a decision.	☐	☐
4	I think employees should conform to company policies.	☐	☐
5	I let my significant other make the decision and have his or her way most of the time.	☐	☐
6	I like to tell other people what to do.	☐	☐
7	I am more patient with the least capable people.	☐	☐
8	I like to have things running 'just so'.	☐	☐

SCORING AND INTERPRETATION Give yourself one point for each Mostly True answer to the odd-numbered questions and one point for each Mostly False answer to the even-numbered questions. A score of 6 or above suggests you prefer decentralized control for other people in organizations. A score of 3 or less suggests a preference for more control and bureaucracy in a company. Enthusiastic new managers may exercise too much of their new control and get a negative backlash. However, too little control may mean less accountability and productivity. The challenge for new managers is to strike the right balance for the job and people involved.

Control is an important issue facing every manager in every organization. At Rochester Independent Practice Association, administrators have implemented new systems for cutting costs and increasing efficiency, but they also need to find new ways to maintain the quality of care, including the quality of the doctor-patient relationship. Other organizations face similar challenges, such as improving product quality, minimizing the time needed to resupply goods in retail stores, decreasing the number of steps needed to process an online order, or improving the tracking procedures for overnight package delivery. Control, including quality control, also involves office productivity, such as elimination of bottlenecks and reduction in paperwork mistakes. In addition, every organization needs basic systems for allocating financial resources, developing human resources, analyzing financial performance and evaluating overall profitability.

This chapter introduces basic mechanisms for controlling the organization. We begin by summarizing the objectives of the control process and the use of the balanced scorecard to measure performance. Then we discuss the four steps in the control process and methods for controlling financial performance, including the use of budgets and financial statements. The next sections examine the changing philosophy of control, today's approach to total quality management and recent trends such as ISO certification, economic value-added and market value-added systems, activity-based costing and corporate governance.

The Meaning of Control

It seemed like a perfect fit. In the chaotic aftermath of 2005's Hurricane Katrina, the Red Cross needed private-sector help to respond to the hundreds of thousands of people seeking emergency aid. Spherion Corporation, a staffing company that operates throughout North America, Europe, Australia and Asia, had the expertise to hire and train temporary workers fast, and the company had a good track record working with the Red Cross. Yet Red Cross officials soon noticed something odd: an unusually large number of Katrina victim money orders, authorized by employees at the Spherion-staffed call centre, were being cashed near the call centre itself – far from the hurricane-ravaged area. A federal investigation found that some call-centre employees were issuing money orders to fake hurricane victims and cashing the orders for themselves. Fortunately, the fraud was discovered quickly, but the weak control systems that allowed the scam to occur got both the Red Cross and Spherion into a public relations and political mess.[3]

A lack of effective control can have repercussions that damage an organization's health, hurt its reputation and threaten its future. Consider Enron, which was held up as a model of modern management in the late 1990s but came crashing down a couple of years later. Numerous factors contributed to Enron's shocking collapse, including unethical managers and an arrogant, free-wheeling culture. But it ultimately comes down to a lack of control. No one was keeping track to make sure managers stayed within acceptable ethical and financial boundaries. Although former chairman and CEO Kenneth Lay claimed he didn't know the financial shenanigans were going on at the company, a jury disagreed and found him guilty, along with former CEO Jeffrey Skilling, of conspiracy and fraud. Some still believe that Lay – who died of a heart attack less than six weeks after the verdict – was telling the truth. However, at a minimum, he and other top leaders neglected their responsibilities by failing to set up and maintain adequate controls on the giant corporation. Since Enron, numerous organizations have established more clear-cut standards for ethical conduct and more stringent control systems regarding financial activities.

One area in which many managers are implementing stronger controls is employee use of the internet and email, as described in the Manager's Shoptalk.

Organizational control refers to the systematic process of regulating organizational activities to make them consistent with the expectations established in plans, targets and standards of performance. In a classic article on the control function, Douglas S. Sherwin summarizes the concept as follows: 'The essence of control is action which adjusts operations to predetermined standards, and its basis is information in the hands of managers.'[4] Thus, effectively controlling an organization requires information about performance standards and actual

Organizational control
The systematic process through which managers regulate organizational activities to make them consistent with expectations established in plans, targets and standards of performance.

© PAUL MCERLANE/ALAMY

CONCEPT CONNECTION Guinness, the world famous Dublin brewery, helped found the field of quality control when at the start of the twentieth century it launched a progressive recruitment policy of hiring statisticians, chemists and other scientists to improve the quality of their beer. One of these statisticians was William Gosset who developed the t-test, a statistical formula that allows organizations to check the wider quality of a population using only a small sample.

performance, as well as actions taken to correct any deviations from the standards. To effectively control an organization, managers need to decide what information is essential, how they will obtain that information, and how they can and should respond to it. Having the correct data is essential. Managers decide which standards, measurements and metrics are needed to effectively monitor and control the organization and set up

 ## MANAGER'S SHOPTALK

Cyberslackers Beware: The Boss is Watching

When employees have access to the internet's vast resources, and the ability to communicate quickly via email and instant messaging with anyone in the world, that's got to be good for productivity, right?

Not necessarily, as many organizations are discovering. Many companies are experiencing a growing problem with 'cyberslackers', people who spend part of their workday sending personal emails, visiting social networking sites, shopping or downloading music and videos that hog available bandwidth and sometimes introduce viruses. In addition, it takes just a few bad apples engaging in harmful and possibly illegal activities, such as harassing other employees over the Web, to cause serious problems for their employers. So it's not surprising that the use of sophisticated software to both block employees' access to certain sites and monitor their internet and email use has grown exponentially.

A certain degree of vigilance is clearly warranted. However, enlightened managers strive for a balanced approach that protects the organization's interests while at the same time maintaining a positive, respectful work environment. Surveillance overkill can sometimes cost more than it saves, and it can also have a distinctly negative impact on employee morale. At the very least, employees may feel as though they're not being treated as trustworthy, responsible adults.

Here are some guidelines for creating an effective but fair 'acceptable use policy' for workplace internet use.

- **Make sure employees understand that they have no legal right to privacy in the workplace.** The courts so far have upheld an organization's right to monitor any and all employee activities on computers purchased by an employer for work purposes.
- **Create a written internet policy.** Make sure you clearly state what qualifies as a policy violation

by giving clear, concrete guidelines for acceptable use of email, the internet and any other employer-provided hardware or software. For example, spell out the types of websites that are never to be visited while at work and what constitutes acceptable email content. Are employees ever permitted to use the Web for personal use? If so, specify what they can do, for how long, and whether they need to confine their personal use to lunchtime or breaks. List the devices you'll be checking and tell them the filtering and monitoring procedures you have in place. Get employees to sign a statement saying they've read and understand the policy.

- **Describe the disciplinary process.** Give people a clear understanding of the consequences of violating the organization's internet and electronic use policy. Make sure they know the organization will cooperate if a criminal investigation arises.
- **Review the policy at regular intervals.** You'll need to modify your guidelines as new technologies and devices appear.

Managers should remember that monitoring email and internet use doesn't have to be an all-or-nothing process. Some organizations use continuous surveillance; others only screen when they believe a problem exists, or they disseminate a policy and leave enforcement to the honour system. Look carefully at your workforce and the work they're doing, and assess your potential liability and security needs. Then come up with a policy and monitoring plan that makes sense for your organization.

SOURCES Lorraine Cosgrove Ware, 'People Watching', *CIO* (August 15, 2005): 24; Art Lambert, 'Technology in the Workplace: A Recipe for Legal Trouble', *Workforce.com* (February 14, 2005): www.workforce.com Technical Resource Group, 'Employee E-mail and Internet Usage Monitoring: Issues and Concerns', www.picktrg.com; Pui-Wing Tam, Erin White, Nick Wingfield and Kris Maher, 'Snooping E-Mail by Software Is Now a Workplace Norm', *The Wall Street Journal*, March 9, 2005; and Ann Sherman, 'Firms Address Worries over Workplace Web Surfing', *Broward Daily Business Review* (May 17, 2006): 11.

systems for obtaining that information. For example, an important metric for a pro football or basketball team might be the number of season tickets, which reduces the organization's dependence on more labour-intensive box-office sales.[5]

Choosing Standards and Measures

Most organizations focus on measuring and controlling financial performance, such as sales, revenue, and profit. Yet managers increasingly recognize the need to measure other intangible aspects of performance to manage the value-creating activities of the contemporary organization.[6] British Airways, for example, measures its performance in key areas of customer service because its strategy is to compete on superior service in an industry dominated by companies that compete on price. Underpinning this strategy is a belief that delivery of excellent service will result in higher levels of customer retention and profitability. Thus, British Airways measures and controls areas of customer service that have the greatest impact on a customer's service experience, including in-flight service, meal rating, baggage claim and executive club membership.[7] Instead of relying only on financial measures to judge the company's performance, British Airways uses a number of different operational measures to track performance and control the organization.

The Balanced Scorecard

Like British Airways, many firms are now taking a more balanced perspective of company performance, integrating various dimensions of control that focus on markets and customers as well as employees and financials.[8] Organizations recognize that relying exclusively on financial measures can result in short-term, dysfunctional behaviour. Non-financial measures provide a healthy supplement to the traditional financial measures, and companies are investing significant sums in developing more balanced measurement systems as a result.[9] The balanced scorecard is a comprehensive management control system that balances traditional financial measures with operational measures relating to a company's critical success factors.[10]

A balanced scorecard contains four major perspectives, as illustrated in Exhibit 19.1: financial performance, customer service, internal business processes and the organization's capacity for learning and growth.[11] Within these four areas, managers identify key performance metrics the organization will track. The *financial performance* perspective reflects a concern that the organization's activities contribute to improving short- and long-term financial performance. It includes traditional measures such as net income and return on investment. *Customer service* indicators measure such things as how customers view the organization, as well as customer retention and satisfaction. *Business process* indicators focus on production and operating statistics, such as order fulfilment or cost per order. A good example of business process indicators comes from Facebook, one of the fastest-rising dot-coms in history. One of the internal activities it measures is the number of minutes visitors spend at its site. In March 2008, Facebook visitors spent a whopping 20 billion minutes at the site, compared to 6.4 billion minutes a year earlier. By measuring 'minutes per visitor', Facebook is able to track its performance and adjust its strategy in response.[12]

The final component of the balanced scorecard looks at the organization's *potential for learning and growth*, focusing on how well resources and human capital are being managed for the company's future. Metrics may include such things as employee retention and the introduction of new products. The components of the scorecard are designed in an integrative manner, as illustrated in Exhibit 19.1.

Managers record, analyze and discuss these various metrics to determine how well the organization is achieving its strategic goals. The balanced scorecard is an effective

Balanced scorecard
A comprehensive management control system that balances traditional financial measures with measures of customer service, internal business processes and the organization's capacity for learning and growth.

Exhibit 19.1 The Balanced Scorecard

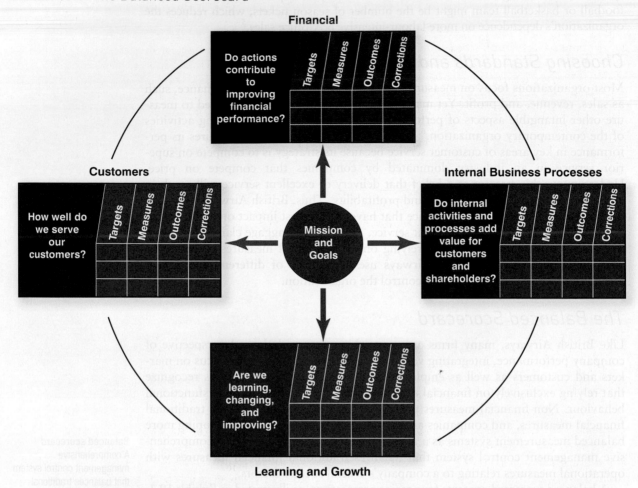

SOURCES: Based on Robert S. Kaplan and David P. Norton, 'Using the Balanced Scorecard as a Strategic Management System', *Harvard Business Review* (January–February 1996): 75–85; and Chee W. Chow, Kamal M. Haddad and James E. Williamson, 'Applying the Balanced Scorecard to Small Companies', *Management Accounting* 79, no. 2 (August 1997): 21–27.

tool for managing and improving performance only if it is clearly linked to a well-defined organizational strategy and goals.[13] At its best, use of the scorecard cascades down from the top levels of the organization so that everyone becomes involved in thinking about and discussing strategy.[14] The scorecard has become the core management control system for many organizations, including well-known organizations such as ExxonMobil, and Hilton Hotels, as well as being adapted for use by local government.[15] The widest use of Balanced Scorecard is found in the US, UK, Northern Europe and Japan. A study by Bain and Co. suggests that 44 per cent of organizations in North America use a Balanced Scorecard as part of their control system, while a similar study in Germany, Switzerland and Austria suggests around 26 per cent of companies use there use it. As with all management systems, the balanced scorecard is not right for every organization in every situation. The simplicity of the system causes some managers to underestimate the time and commitment that is needed for the approach to become a truly useful management control system. If managers implement the balanced scorecard using a *performance measurement* orientation rather than a *performance management* approach that links targets and measurements to corporate strategy, use of the scorecard can actually hinder or even decrease organizational performance.[16]

Feedback Control Model

All well-designed control systems involve the use of feedback to determine whether performance meets established standards. Managers need feedback, for example, in each of the four categories of the balanced scorecard. British Airways ties its use of the balanced scorecard to a feedback control model. Scorecards are used as the agenda for monthly management meetings. Managers focus on the various elements of the scorecard to set targets, evaluate performance, and guide discussion about what further actions need to be taken.[17] In this section, we examine the key steps in the feedback control model and then look at how the model applies to organizational budgeting.

Steps of Feedback Control

Managers set up control systems that consist of the four key steps illustrated in Exhibit 19.2: Establish standards, measure performance, compare performance to standards, and make corrections as necessary.

Establish Standards of Performance

Within the organization's overall strategic plan, managers define goals for organizational departments in specific, operational terms that include a *standard of performance* against which to compare organizational activities. A standard of performance could include 'reducing the reject rate from 15 to 3 per cent', 'increasing the corporation's return on investment to 7 per cent' or 'reducing the number of accidents to one per each 100 000 hours of labour'. Managers should carefully assess what they will measure and how they will define it. In the car industry, crash test ratings provide a standard of performance established by government. When crash test ratings are below standard, managers rethink design and manufacturing processes to improve crash test results. Although Daimler's ultra-tiny Smart ForTwo car won a Five Star rating for driver protection, it won just a Three Star rating for passenger protection, indicating the need for improved passenger safety features.[18]

Tracking such measures as customer service, employee involvement, or, for car manufacturers, crash test results, is an important supplement to traditional financial and operational performance measurement, but many companies have a hard time identifying and defining non-financial measurements.[19] To effectively evaluate and

Exhibit 19.2 Feedback Control Model

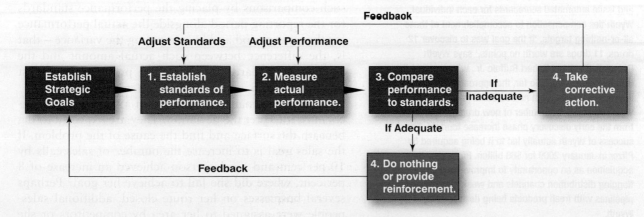

reward employees for the achievement of standards, managers need clear standards that reflect activities that contribute to the organization's overall strategy in a significant way. Standards should be defined clearly and precisely so employees know what they need to do and can determine whether their activities are on target.[20]

Measure Actual Performance

Most organizations prepare formal reports of quantitative performance measurements that managers review daily, weekly, or monthly. These measurements should be related to the standards set in the first step of the control process. For example, if sales growth is a target, the organization should have a means of gathering and reporting sales data. If the organization has identified appropriate measurements, regular review of these reports helps managers stay aware of whether the organization is doing what it should. Technology is aiding many organizations in measuring performance. For example, GPS tracking devices installed on company vehicles are helping some organizations, especially in the public sector, reduce waste and abuse, in part by catching employees shopping, working out at the gym or otherwise loafing about while on the clock. Although some claim this technology is intrusive, others claim that tracking the whereabouts of employees has deterred abuses and saved money.[21]

In most companies, managers do not rely exclusively on quantitative measures. They get out into the organization to see how things are going, especially for such goals as increasing employee participation or improving customer satisfaction. Managers have to observe for themselves whether employees are participating in decision-making and have opportunities to add to and share their knowledge. Interaction with customers is necessary for managers to really understand whether activities are meeting customer needs.

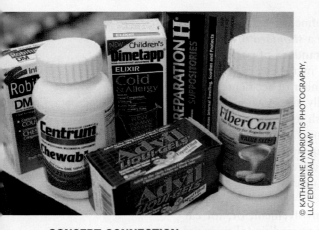

© KATHARINE ANDRIOTIS PHOTOGRAPHY, LLC/EDITORIAL/ALAMY

CONCEPT CONNECTION Is it possible to make scientific discovery efficient? Managers at pharmaceuticals company Wyeth think so. They devised a streamlined research and development system driven by ambitious, quantifiable standards of performance. Managers routinely compare performance to standards and issue automated scorecards for each individual. Wyeth ties compensation to accomplishment of these all-or-nothing targets. 'If the goal was to discover 12 drugs, 11 drugs are worth no points,' says Wyeth Research President Robert Ruffolo Jr., who oversaw the re-engineering effort. So far, the approach has yielded impressive results. With no additional investment, Wyeth has seen the number of new drugs that emerge from the early discovery phase increase fourfold. The success of Wyeth actually led to it being acquired by Pfizer in January 2009 for $68 billion. Pfizer saw the acquisition as an opportunity to improve its own flagging distribution channels and weak research pipelines with fresh products being developed by Wyeth.

Compare Performance to Standards

The third step in the control process is comparing actual activities to performance standards. When managers read computer reports or walk through the plant, they identify whether actual performance meets, exceeds or falls short of standards. Typically, performance reports simplify such comparisons by placing the performance standards for the reporting period alongside the actual performance for the same period and by computing the variance – that is, the difference between each actual amount and the associated standard. To correct the problems that most require attention, managers focus on variances.

When performance deviates from a standard, managers must interpret the deviation. They are expected to dig beneath the surface and find the cause of the problem. If the sales goal is to increase the number of sales calls by 10 per cent and a salesperson achieved an increase of 8 per cent, where did she fail to achieve her goal? Perhaps several businesses on her route closed, additional salespeople were assigned to her area by competitors or she needs training in making cold sales calls more effectively. Managers should take an inquiring approach to deviations to gain a broad understanding of factors that influence performance. Effective management control involves subjective judgement and employee discussions, as well as objective analysis of performance data.

TAKE A MOMENT

As a new manager, apply the feedback control model to determine whether your team is functioning well or if changes are needed. Define clear standards of performance, measure outcomes regularly and work with team members to take corrective actions when necessary.

Take Corrective Action

Managers also determine what changes, if any, are needed. In a traditional top-down approach to control, managers exercise their formal authority to make necessary changes. They may encourage employees to work harder, redesign the production process or fire employees. In contrast, managers using a participative control approach collaborate with employees to determine the corrective action necessary. As an example, Toyota's commitment to continuous improvement is reflected in its philosophy of 'Problems First'. In staff meetings, factory managers are asked to present their 'problems first', triggering problem-solving sessions with managers that generate solutions. This approach reflects the company's commitment to seeking out better ways to manufacture cars. 'Even with projects that had been a general success, we would ask, "What didn't go well so we can make it better?"' says James Wiseman, vice president of corporate affairs for Toyota manufacturing in North America.[22]

Managers may wish to provide positive reinforcement when performance meets or exceeds standards. For example, they may reward a department that has exceeded its planned goals or congratulate employees for a job well done. Managers should

---

 INNOVATIVE WAY

eBay

As CEO of eBay, one of Meg Whitman's guiding rules was 'If you can't measure it, you can't control it.' Whitman has moved on to other pursuits, but eBay is still a company obsessed with performance measurement. Top managers personally monitor a slew of performance metrics, including standard measurements such as site visitors, new users, and time spent on the site, as well as the ratio of eBay's revenues to the value of goods traded.

Managers and employees throughout the company also monitor performance almost obsessively. Category managers, for example, have clear standards of performance for their auction categories (such as sports memorabilia, jewellery and watches, health and beauty and fashion). They are constantly measuring,

tweaking and promoting their categories to meet or outperform the targets.

Top managers believe getting a firm grip on performance measurement is essential for a company to know where to spend money, where to assign more personnel, and which projects to promote or abandon. But performance measurement isn't just about numbers. At eBay, 'it's all about the customer', and gauging customer (user) satisfaction requires a mix of methods, such as surveys, monitoring eBay's discussion boards and personal contact. Managers get their chance to really connect with users at the annual eBay Live conference. There, they wander the convention hall floor talking with anyone and everyone about their eBay experiences.[23]

not ignore high-performing departments at the expense of taking corrective actions elsewhere. The online auction company eBay provides a good illustration of the feedback control model.

By defining standards, using a combination of measurement approaches, and comparing performance to standards, eBay managers are able to identify trouble spots and move quickly to take corrective action when and where it's needed.

Application to Budgeting

Budgetary control, one of the most commonly used methods of managerial control, is the process of setting targets for an organization's expenditures, monitoring results and comparing them to the budget, and making changes as needed. As a control device, budgets are reports that list planned and actual expenditures for cash, assets, raw materials, salaries and other resources. In addition, budget reports usually list the variance between the budgeted and actual amounts for each item.

TAKE A MOMENT   Go to the Experiential Exercise on page 760 that pertains to budgetary control.

A budget is created for every division or department within an organization, no matter how small, as long as it performs a distinct project, programme or function. The fundamental unit of analysis for a budget control system is called a responsibility centre. A responsibility centre is defined as any organizational department or unit under the supervision of a single person who is responsible for its activity.[24] A three-person appliance sales office in Cape Town or Lagos, is a responsibility centre, as is a quality control department in London or Tokyo, a marketing department in Paris or New York, and an entire refrigerator manufacturing plant in Shanghai or Mumbai. The manager of each unit has budget responsibility. Top managers use budgets for the company as a whole, and middle managers traditionally focus on the budget performance of their department or division. Budgets that managers typically use include expense budgets, revenue budgets, cash budgets, and capital budgets.

Responsibility centre
An organizational unit under the supervision of a single person who is responsible for its activity.

Expense Budget

An expense budget includes anticipated and actual expenses for each responsibility centre and for the total organization. An expense budget may show all types of expenses or may focus on a particular category, such as materials or research and development expenses. When actual expenses exceed budgeted amounts, the difference signals the need for managers to identify whether a problem exists and take corrective action if needed. The difference may arise from inefficiency, or expenses may be higher because the organization's sales are growing faster than anticipated. Conversely, expenses below budget may signal exceptional efficiency or possibly the failure to meet some other standards, such as a desired level of sales or quality of service. Either way, expense budgets help identify the need for further investigation but do not substitute for it.

Expense budget
A budget that outlines the anticipated and actual expenses for a responsibility centre.

Revenue Budget

A revenue budget lists forecasted and actual revenues of the organization. In general, revenues below the budgeted amount signal a need to investigate the problem to see whether the organization can improve revenues. In contrast, revenues above budget

Revenue budget
A budget that identifies the forecasted and actual revenues of the organization.

would require determining whether the organization can obtain the necessary resources to meet the higher-than-expected demand for its products or services. Managers then formulate action plans to correct the budget variance.

Cash Budget

The cash budget estimates receipts and expenditures of money on a daily or weekly basis to ensure that an organization has sufficient cash to meet its obligations. The cash budget shows the level of funds flowing through the organization and the nature of cash disbursements. If the cash budget shows that the firm has more cash than necessary to meet short-term needs, the company can arrange to invest the excess to earn interest income. In contrast, if the cash budget shows a payroll expenditure of £20 000 coming at the end of the week but only £10 000 in the bank, the organization must borrow cash to meet the payroll.

Cash budget
A budget that estimates and reports cash flows on a daily or weekly basis to ensure that the company has sufficient cash to meet its obligations.

Capital Budget

The capital budget lists planned investments in major assets such as buildings, heavy machinery or complex information technology systems, often involving expenditures over more than a year. Capital expenditures not only have a large impact on future expenses, they also are investments designed to enhance profits. Therefore, a capital budget is necessary to plan the impact of these expenditures on cash flow and profitability. Controlling involves not only monitoring the amount of capital expenditures but also evaluating whether the assumptions made about the return on the investments are holding true. Managers can evaluate whether continuing investment in particular projects is advisable, as well as whether their procedures for making capital expenditure decisions are adequate. Some companies, including Boeing, BP, RWE, Royal Dutch Shell and United Technologies evaluate capital projects at several stages to determine whether they are still in line with the company's strategy.[25]

Capital budget
A budget that plans and reports investments in major assets to be depreciated over several years.

Budgeting is an important part of organizational planning and control. Many traditional companies use top-down budgeting, which means that the budgeted amounts for the coming year are literally imposed on middle- and lower-level managers.[26] These managers set departmental budget targets in accordance with overall company revenues and expenditures specified by top executives. Although the top-down process provides some advantages, the movement toward employee empowerment, participation and learning means that many organizations are adopting bottom-up budgeting, a process in which lower-level managers anticipate their departments' resource needs and pass them up to top management for approval.[27] Companies of all kinds are increasingly involving line managers in the budgeting process. At the San Diego Zoo, scientists, animal keepers and other line managers use software and templates to plan their department's budget needs because, as CFO Paula Brock says, 'Nobody knows that side of the business better than they do.'[28] Each of the 145 zoo departments also does a monthly budget close and reforecast so that resources can be redirected as needed to achieve goals within budget constraints. Thanks to the bottom-up process, for example, the zoo was able to quickly redirect resources to protect its valuable exotic bird collection from an outbreak of a highly infectious bird disease without significantly damaging the rest of the organization's budget.[29]

Top-down budgeting
A budgeting process in which middle- and lower-level managers set departmental budget targets in accordance with overall company revenues and expenditures specified by top management.

Bottom-up budgeting
A budgeting process in which lower-level managers budget their departments' resource needs and pass them up to top management for approval.

Financial Control

In every organization, managers need to watch how well the organization is performing financially. Not only do financial controls tell whether the organization is on sound financial footing, but they can be useful indicators of other kinds of performance problems. For example, a sales decline may signal problems with products, customer service or sales force effectiveness.

Financial Statements

Financial statements provide the basic information used for financial control of an organization. Two major financial statements – the balance sheet and the income statement – are the starting points for financial control.

Balance sheet
A financial statement that shows the firm's financial position with respect to assets and liabilities at a specific point in time.

The balance sheet shows the firm's financial position with respect to assets and liabilities at a specific point in time. An example of a balance sheet is presented in Exhibit 19.3. The balance sheet provides three types of information: assets, liabilities and owners' equity. *Assets* are what the company owns, and they include *current assets* (those that can be converted into cash in a short time period) and *fixed assets* (such as buildings and equipment that are long term in nature). *Liabilities* are the firm's debts, including both *current debt* (obligations that will be paid by the company in the near future) and *long-term debt* (obligations payable over a long period). *Owners' equity* is the difference between assets and liabilities and is the company's net worth in stock and retained earnings.

Income statement
A financial statement that summarizes the firm's financial performance for a given time interval; sometimes called a profit-and-loss statement.

The income statement, sometimes called a profit-and-loss statement or P&L for short, summarizes the firm's financial performance for a given time interval, usually

Exhibit 19.3 Balance Sheet

New Creations Landscaping Consolidated Balance Sheet December 31, 2009					
Assets			**Liabilities and Owners' Equity**		
Current assets:			Current liabilities:		
Cash	$ 25,000		Accounts payable	$200,000	
Accounts receivable	75,000		Accrued expenses	20,000	
Inventory	500,000		Income taxes payable	30,000	
Total current assets		$ 600,000	Total current liabilities		$ 250,000
Fixed assets:			Long-term liabilities:		
Land	250,000		Mortgages payable	350,000	
Buildings and fixtures	1,000,000		Bonds outstanding	250,000	
Less depreciation	200,000		Total long-term liabilities		$ 600,000
Total fixed assets		1,050,000	Owners' equity:		
			Common stock	540,000	
			Retained earnings	260,000	
			Total owners' equity		800,000
Total assets		$1,650,000	Total liabilities and net worth		$1,650,000

Exhibit 19.4 Income Statement

New Creations Landscaping Income Statement For the Year Ended December 31, 2009		
Gross sales	$3,100,000	
Less sales returns	200,000	
Net sales		$2,900,000
Less expenses and cost of goods sold:		
Cost of goods sold	2,110,000	
Depreciation	60,000	
Sales expenses	200,000	
Administrative expenses	90,000	2,460,000
Operating profit		440,000
Other income		20,000
Gross income		460,000
Less interest expense	80,000	
Income before taxes		380,000
Less taxes	165,000	
Net income		$ 215,000

one year. A sample income statement is shown in Exhibit 19.4. Some organizations calculate the income statement at three-month intervals during the year to see whether they are on target for sales and profits. The income statement shows revenues coming into the organization from all sources and subtracts all expenses, including cost of goods sold, interest, taxes and depreciation. The *bottom line* indicates the net income – profit or loss – for the given time period.

The owner of Aahs!, a specialty retailing chain used the income statement to detect that sales and profits were dropping significantly during the summer months.[30] He immediately evaluated company activities and closed two money-losing stores. He also began a training programme to teach employees how to increase sales and cut costs to improve net income. This use of the income statement follows the control model described in the previous section, beginning with setting targets, measuring actual performance and then taking corrective action to improve performance to meet targets.

Financial Analysis: Interpreting the Numbers

A manager needs to be able to evaluate financial reports that compare the organization's performance with earlier data or industry norms. These comparisons enable the manager to see whether the organization is improving and whether it is competitive with others in the industry. The most common financial analysis focuses on

Exhibit 19.5 Common Financial Ratios

Liquidity Ratios	
Current ratio	Current assets/Current liabilities
Activity Ratios	
Inventory turnover	Total sales/Average inventory
Conversion ratio	Purchase orders/Customer inquiries
Profitability Ratios	
Profit margin on sales	Net income/Sales
Gross margin	Gross income/Sales
Return on assets (ROA)	Net income/Total assets
Leverage Ratios	
Debt ratio	Total debt/Total assets

ratios, statistics that express the relationships between performance indicators such as profits and assets, sales and inventory. Ratios are stated as a fraction or proportion. Exhibit 19.5 summarizes some financial ratios, which are measures of an organization's liquidity, activity, profitability and leverage. These ratios are among the most common, but many measures are used. Managers decide which ratios reveal the most important relationships for their business.

Liquidity Ratios

Liquidity ratio
A financial ratio that indicates the organization's ability to meet its current debt obligations.

A liquidity ratio indicates an organization's ability to meet its current debt obligations. For example, the *current ratio* (current assets divided by current liabilities) tells whether the company has sufficient assets to convert into cash to pay off its debts, if needed. If a hypothetical company, Oceanographics plc, has current assets of £600 000 and current liabilities of £250 000, the current ratio is 2.4, meaning it has sufficient funds to pay off immediate debts 2.4 times. This level for the current ratio is normally considered a satisfactory margin of safety.

Activity Ratios

Activity ratio
A financial ratio that measures the organization's internal performance with respect to key activities defined by management.

An activity ratio measures internal performance with respect to key activities defined by management. For example, *inventory turnover* is calculated by dividing total sales by average inventory. This ratio tells how many times the inventory is used up to meet the total sales figure. If inventory sits too long, money is wasted. Dell Inc. achieved a strategic advantage by minimizing its inventory costs. Dividing Dell's annual sales by its small inventory generates an inventory turnover rate of 35.7, a significant improvement from its ratio of 14 in 1997.[31]

Another type of activity ratio, the *conversion ratio*, is purchase orders divided by customer inquiries. This ratio is an indicator of a company's effectiveness in converting inquiries into sales. For example, if IKEA moves from 26.3 to 28.5 per cent conversion ratio, more of its inquiries are turned into sales, indicating better sales activity.

Profitability Ratios

Managers analyze a company's profits by studying profitability ratios, which state profits relative to a source of profits, such as sales or assets. One important profitability ratio is the *profit margin on sales*, which is calculated as net income divided by sales. Similarly, *gross margin* is the gross (before-tax) profit divided by total sales. Managers at Tesco.com, the online grocery service of Britain's top supermarket chain, pay close attention to the profit margin. Tesco.com managers implemented strict financial controls from the beginning. The online division was immediately profitable, earning about £3 on the average online sale, whereas US-based Webvan, which eventually failed, lost about $100 per sale because of its huge start-up costs and high operating expenses.[32]

Another profitability measure is *return on total assets (ROA)*, which is a percentage representing what a company earned from its assets, computed as net income divided by total assets. ROA is a valuable yardstick for comparing a company's ability to generate earnings with other investment opportunities. In basic terms, the company should be able to earn more by using its assets to operate the business than it could by putting the same investment in the bank. Caterpillar Inc., which produces construction and mining equipment, uses return on assets as its main measure of performance. It sets ROA standards for each area of the business and uses variances from the standards to identify whether the company is fully using its assets and improving operational efficiency. Since it began using ROA standards, Caterpillar has enjoyed double-digit returns.[33]

Profitability ratio
A financial ratio that describes the firm's profits in terms of a source of profits (e.g. sales or total assets).

Leverage Ratios

Leverage refers to funding activities with borrowed money. A company can use leverage to make its assets produce more than they could on their own. However, too much borrowing can put the organization at risk such that it will be unable to keep up with repayment of its debt. Managers therefore track their *debt ratio*, or total debt divided by total assets, to make sure it does not exceed a level they consider acceptable. Lenders may consider a company with a debt ratio above 1.0 to be a poor credit risk.

The Changing Philosophy of Control

Managers' approach to control is changing in many of today's organizations. In connection with the shift to employee participation and empowerment, many companies are adopting a *decentralized* rather than a *hierarchical* control process. Hierarchical control and decentralized control represent different philosophies of corporate culture, which was discussed in Chapter 3. Most organizations display some aspects of both hierarchical and decentralized control, but managers generally emphasize one or the other, depending on the organizational culture and their own beliefs about control.

Hierarchical versus Decentralized Approaches

Hierarchical control involves monitoring and influencing employee behaviour through extensive use of rules, policies, hierarchy of authority, written documentation, reward systems and other formal mechanisms.[34] In contrast, decentralized control relies on cultural values, traditions, shared beliefs and trust to foster compliance

Hierarchical control
The use of rules, policies, hierarchy of authority, reward systems and other formal devices to influence employee behaviour and assess performance.

Exhibit 19.6 Hierarchical and Decentralized Methods of Control

	Hierarchical Control	Decentralized Control
Basic Assumptions	People are incapable of self-discipline and cannot be trusted. They need to be monitored and controlled closely.	People work best when they are fully committed to the organization.
Actions	Uses detailed rules and procedures; formal control systems.	Features limited use of rules; relies on values, group and self-control, selection and socialization.
	Uses top-down authority, formal hierarchy, position power, quality control inspectors.	Relies on flexible authority, flat structure, expert power; everyone monitors quality.
	Relies on task-related job descriptions.	Relies on results-based job descriptions; emphasizes goals to be achieved.
	Emphasizes extrinsic rewards (pay, benefits, status).	Emphasizes extrinsic and intrinsic rewards (meaningful work, opportunities for growth).
	Features rigid organizational culture; distrust of cultural norms as means of control.	Features adaptive culture; culture recognized as means for uniting individual, team and organizational goals for overall control.
Consequences	Employees follow instructions and do *just* what they are told.	Employees take initiative and seek responsibility.
	Employees feel a sense of indifference toward work.	Employees are actively engaged and committed to their work.
	Employee absenteeism and turnover is high.	Employee turnover is low.

SOURCES: Based on Naresh Khatri, Alok Bavega, Suzanne A. Boren, and Abate Mammo, 'Medical Errors and Quality of Care: From Control to Commitment', *California Management Review* 48, no. 3 (Spring, 2006): 118; Richard E. Walton, 'From Control to Commitment in the Workplace', *Harvard Business Review* (March–April 1985): 76–84; and Don Hellriegel, Susan E. Jackson, and John W. Slocum, Jr., *Management,* 8th ed. (Cincinnati, Ohio: South-Western, 1999), p. 663.

with organizational goals. Managers operate on the assumption that employees are trustworthy and willing to perform effectively without extensive rules and close supervision.

Exhibit 19.6 contrasts the use of hierarchical and decentralized methods of control. Hierarchical methods define explicit rules, policies and procedures for employee behaviour. Control relies on centralized authority, the formal hierarchy and close personal supervision. Responsibility for quality control rests with quality control inspectors and supervisors rather than with employees. Job descriptions generally are specific and task related, and managers define minimal standards for acceptable employee performance. In exchange for meeting the standards, individual employees are given extrinsic rewards such as wages, benefits and possibly promotions up the hierarchy. Employees rarely participate in the control process, with any participation being formalized through mechanisms such as grievance procedures. With hierarchical control, the organizational culture is somewhat rigid, and managers do not consider culture a useful means of controlling employees and the organization. Technology often is used to control the flow and pace of work or to monitor employees, such as by measuring the number of minutes employees spend on phone calls or how many keystrokes they make at the computer.

Hierarchical control techniques can enhance organizational efficiency and effectiveness. Many employees appreciate a system that clarifies what is expected of them, and they may be motivated by challenging, but achievable goals.[35] However, although many managers effectively use hierarchical control, too much control can backfire. Employees resent being watched too closely, and they may try to sabotage the control system. One veteran truck driver expressed his unhappiness with electronic monitoring to a *Wall Street Journal* reporter investigating the use of devices that monitor truck locations. According to the driver, 'It's getting worse and worse all the time. Pretty soon they'll want to put a chip in the drivers' ears and make them robots.' He added that he occasionally escapes the relentless monitoring by parking under an overpass to take a needed nap out of the range of the surveillance satellites.[36]

Decentralized control is based on values and assumptions that are almost opposite to those of hierarchical control. Rules and procedures are used only when necessary. Managers rely instead on shared goals and values to control employee behaviour. The organization places great emphasis on the selection and socialization of employees to ensure that workers have the appropriate values needed to influence behaviour toward meeting company goals. No organization can control employees 100 per cent of the time, and self-discipline and self-control are what keep workers performing their jobs up to standard. Empowerment of employees, effective socialization and training all can contribute to internal standards that provide self-control.

Decentralized control
The use of organizational culture, group norms and a focus on goals, rather than rules and procedures, to foster compliance with organizational goals.

With decentralized control, power is more dispersed and is based on knowledge and experience as much as position. The organizational structure is flat and horizontal, as discussed in Chapter 10, with flexible authority and teams of workers solving problems and making improvements. Everyone is involved in quality control on an ongoing basis. Job descriptions generally are results-based, with an emphasis more on the outcomes to be achieved than on the specific tasks to be performed. Managers use not only extrinsic rewards such as pay, but the intrinsic rewards of meaningful work and the opportunity to learn and grow. Technology is used to empower employees by giving them the information they need to make effective decisions, work together and solve problems. People are rewarded for team and organizational success as well as their individual performance, and the emphasis is on equity among employees. Employees participate in a wide range of areas, including setting goals, determining standards of performance, governing quality and designing control systems.

With decentralized control, the culture is adaptive, and managers recognize the importance of organizational culture for uniting individual, team and organizational goals for greater overall control. Ideally, with decentralized control, employees will pool their areas of expertise to arrive at procedures that are better than managers could come up with working alone.

What is your philosophy of control? As a new manager, will you tend to watch things closely or give others freedom to perform? Complete the New Manager Self-Test on page 749 to get some feedback on your own approach to control.

TAKE A MOMENT

Open-Book Management

One important aspect of decentralized control in many organizations is open-book management. An organization that promotes information sharing and teamwork admits employees throughout the organization into the loop of financial control and responsibility to encourage active participation and commitment to goals.

© VITO PALMISANO

CONCEPT CONNECTION Honest Tea co-founder and CEO Seth Goldman (left) practises open book management – sharing with employees information on sales, profit and loss, growth rate, expenses, salaries as a lump sum, stock price and capitalization. Here, Goldman tours Castle's Co-Packer, which produces and bottles organic brewed teas for his company, with *Beverage World* magazine editor Sarah Theodore (centre) and Brian Dworkin of Castle's. When Coca-Cola bought 40 per cent of Honest Tea, Goldman says, 'We insisted on an arrangement that allowed all of our employees to invest alongside Coke in the transaction – there's no question that this structure has contributed to the passion and entrepreneurial spirit of our team.'

Open-book management Sharing financial information and results with all employees in the organization.

Open-book management allows employees to see for themselves – through charts, computer printouts, meetings, and so forth – the financial condition of the company. Second, open-book management shows the individual employee how his or her job fits into the big picture and affects the financial future of the organization. Finally, open-book management ties employee rewards to the company's overall success. With training in interpreting the financial data, employees can see the interdependence and importance of each function. If they are rewarded according to performance, they become motivated to take responsibility for their entire team or function, rather than merely their individual jobs.[37] Cross-functional communication and cooperation are also enhanced.

The goal of open-book management is to get every employee thinking and acting like a business owner. To get employees to think like owners, management provides them with the same information owners have: what money is coming in and where it is going. Open-book management helps employees appreciate why efficiency is important to the organization's success as well as their own. Open-book management turns traditional control on its head. Development Counsellors International, a New York City public relations firm, found an innovative way to involve employees in the financial aspects of the organization.

DCI has been profitable ever since Levine began the CFO-of-the-day programme. In addition, employees are happier with their jobs, so turnover has decreased. Clients tend to stick around longer too, because employees put more effort into building relationships. 'Nobody wants to see a zero next to their client in the income column,' Levine says.[38]

Managers in some countries have more trouble running an open-book company because prevailing attitudes and standards encourage confidentiality and even secrecy concerning financial results. Many businesspeople in countries such as China, Russia and India, for example, are not accustomed to publicly disclosing financial details, which can present problems for multinational companies operating there.[39] Exhibit 19.7 lists a portion of a recent *Opacity Index*, which offers some indication of the degree to which various countries are open regarding economic matters. The higher the rating, the more opaque, or hidden, the economy of that country. In the partial index in Exhibit 19.7 (see overleaf), Nigeria has the highest opacity rating at 57, and Finland the lowest at 9. The US has an opacity rating of 23, a slight increase since the previous ratings. In countries with higher ratings, financial figures are typically closely guarded and managers may be discouraged from sharing information with employees and the public. Globalization is beginning to have an impact on economic opacity in various countries by encouraging a convergence toward global accounting standards that support more accurate collection, recording and reporting of financial information. Thus, most countries have improved their ratings over the past few years. Indonesia, Singapore and Ireland all show significant decreases in opacity since the 2005–2006 ratings, for example.

Total quality management (TQM) An organization-wide commitment to infusing quality into every activity through continuous improvement.

Total Quality Management

Another popular approach based on a decentralized control philosophy is total quality management (TQM), an organization-wide effort to infuse quality into every activity in a company through continuous improvement. Managing quality is a

NEW MANAGER SELF-TEST

What is Your Control Approach?

As a new manager, how will you control your work unit? What is your natural control approach? Answer whether each item below is Mostly True or Mostly False for you.

		Mostly True	Mostly False
1	I find myself losing sight of long-term goals when there is a short-term crisis.	☐	☐
2	I prefer complex to simple problems and projects.	☐	☐
3	I am good at mapping out steps needed to complete a project.	☐	☐
4	I make most decisions without needing to know an overall plan.	☐	☐
5	I keep my personal books and papers in good order.	☐	☐
6	I prefer tasks that challenge my thinking ability.	☐	☐
7	I think about how my behaviour relates to outcomes I desire.	☐	☐
8	I like to be part of a situation where results are measured and count for something.	☐	☐

SCORING AND INTERPRETATION Control systems are designed and managed via a manager's 'systems' thinking. Systems thinking considers how component parts of system interact to achieve desired goals. Systems thinking means seeing the world in an organized way and thinking about underlying cause-effect relationships. Give yourself one point for each Mostly True answer to items 2, 3, 5 to 8 and one point for each Mostly False answer to items 1 and 4. A score of 6 or above means that you appear to have a natural orientation toward systems thinking and control. You see the world in an organized way and focus on cause-effect relationships that produce outcomes. If you scored 3 or less, you probably are not very focused on control issues and relationships. You may not be interested or have the time to understand complex relationships. As a new manager, you may have to put extra effort into understanding control relationships to produce the outcomes you and the organization desire.

 INNOVATIVE WAY

Development Counsellors International

When Andrew Levine took over as president of Development Counsellors International (DCI), the public relations firm founded by his father in 1960, he was eager to try open-book management. His first step was to add a financial segment to the monthly staff meeting, but employees just seemed bored. Most of them had no interest or skills in finance, statistics and ratios.

Rather than providing standard training, Levine had an idea: why not appoint a different staffer each month to be CFO for the day. That person would be required to figure out the financials and then present the financial reports at the monthly staff meeting. His first appointment was the receptionist, Sergio Barrios, who met with Levine and the company's chief financial officer to go over the figures, look at any unusual increases or decreases in revenue or expenses, and talk about ideas to spark discussion. Levine was astounded by the reaction of staffers at the monthly meeting. Unlike Levine or another manager, Barrios was new to accounting and consequently explained things in a way that any layperson could understand. In addition, employees wanted to support Barrios as 'one of their own', so they paid more attention and asked more questions.

At each monthly meeting, the CFO of the day goes through a breakdown of the company's sales and expenses, points out irregularities and trends in the numbers, takes questions from other staff members, and sparks discussion of current financial issues. At the end of the report, the person reveals the bottom line, indicating whether the company met its profit goal for the month. Each time DCI's accumulated profit hits another $100 000 increment during the course of the year, 30 per cent is distributed to employees.[40]

Exhibit 19.7 International Opacity Index: Which Countries Have the Most Secretive Economies?

Country	2007–2008 Opacity Score	2005–2006 Score
Nigeria	57	60
Venezuela	48	50
Saudi Arabia	47	52
China	45	48
India	44	44
Indonesia	41	56
Russia	41	45
Mexico	37	43
Taiwan	34	33
South Korea	31	35
South Africa	26	32
Japan	25	26
United States	23	21
Canada	22	24
Germany	17	27
Ireland	16	25
Singapore	14	28
Hong Kong	12	19
Finland	9	17

SOURCE: Joel Kurtzman and Glenn Yago, 'Opacity Index, 2007–2008: Measuring Global Business Risks', published by (April 2008), http://www.milkeninstitute. org/pdf/2008OpacityIndex. pdf (accessed June 16, 2008).

The higher the opacity score, the more secretive the national economy, meaning that prevailing attitudes and standards discourage openness regarding financial results and other data.

concern for every organization. The Yugo was the lowest-priced car on the market when it was introduced in the US in 1985 from Yugoslavia, yet four years later, the division went bankrupt, largely as a result of quality problems in both products and services.[41] In contrast, Toyota has steadily gained market share over the past several decades and has taken over General Motors as the world's top-selling car maker. The difference comes down to quality. Toyota is a model of what happens when a company makes a strong commitment to total quality management.

TQM became attractive to European and American managers in the 1980s because it had been successfully implemented by Japanese companies, such as Toyota, Canon and Honda, which were gaining market share and an international reputation for high quality. The Japanese system was based on the work of researchers and consultants as Deming, Juran and Feigenbaum, whose ideas attracted Western executives after the methods were tested overseas.[42] The TQM philosophy focuses on team-work, increasing customer satisfaction, and lowering costs.

Organizations implement TQM by encouraging managers and employees to collaborate across functions and departments, as well as with customers and suppliers, to identify areas for improvement, no matter how small. Each quality improvement is a step toward perfection and meeting a goal of zero defects. Quality control becomes part of the day-to-day business of every employee, rather than being assigned to specialized departments.

TQM Techniques

The implementation of total quality management involves the use of many techniques, including quality circles, benchmarking, Six Sigma principles, reduced cycle time and continuous improvement.

Quality Circles

One technique for implementing the decentralized approach of TQM is to use quality circles. A **quality circle** is a group of six to 12 volunteer employees who meet regularly to discuss and solve problems affecting the quality of their work.[43] At a set time during the workweek, the members of the quality circle meet, identify problems, and try to find solutions. Circle members are free to collect data and take surveys. Many companies train people in team building, problem solving and statistical quality control. The reason for using quality circles is to push decision-making to an organization level at which recommendations can be made by the people who do the job and know it better than anyone else.

> **Quality circle**
> A group of six to 12 volunteer employees who meet regularly to discuss and solve problems affecting the quality of their work.

Benchmarking

Introduced by Xerox in 1979, benchmarking is now a major TQM component. **Benchmarking** is defined as 'the continuous process of measuring products, services, and practices against the toughest competitors or those companies recognized as industry leaders to identify areas for improvement'.[44] The key to successful benchmarking lies in analysis. Starting with its own mission statement, a company should honestly analyze its current procedures and determine areas for improvement. As a second step, a company carefully selects competitors worthy of copying. For example, Xerox studied the order fulfilment techniques of L. L. Bean, the US, mail-order firm, and learned ways to reduce warehouse costs by 10 per cent. Companies can emulate internal processes and procedures of competitors, but must take care to select companies whose methods are compatible. Once a strong, compatible programme is found and analyzed, the benchmarking company can then devise a strategy for implementing a new programme.

> **Benchmarking**
> The continuous process of measuring products, services and practices against major competitors or industry leaders.

Six Sigma

Six Sigma quality principles were first introduced by Motorola in the 1980s and were later popularized by General Electric, where former CEO Jack Welch praised Six Sigma for quality and efficiency gains that saved the company billions of dollars. Based on the Greek letter *sigma*, which statisticians use to measure how far something deviates from perfection, **Six Sigma** is a highly ambitious quality standard that specifies a goal of no more than 3.4 defects per million parts. That essentially means being defect-free 99.9997 per cent of the time.[45] However, Six Sigma has deviated from its precise definition to become a generic term for a quality-control approach that takes nothing for granted and emphasizes a disciplined and relentless pursuit of higher quality and lower costs. The discipline is based on a five-step methodology referred to as DMAIC

> **Six Sigma**
> A quality control approach that emphasizes a relentless pursuit of higher quality and lower costs.

COURTESY OF STARWOOD HOTELS PHOTO PROVIDED BY BUSINESS WEEK

CONCEPT CONNECTION The idea for 'Unwind' events, such as this performance of traditional dance in the lobby of the Westin Kuala Lumpur in Malaysia, came from the staff of the Westin Chicago River North as a way to improve profitability and guest service. Unwind events are aimed at business travellers and designed to encourage guest interaction. Six Sigma specialists at each unit of Starwood Hotels & Resorts Worldwide facilitate the development of projects from the ideas of local staff. After rolling out a prototype, performance metrics are used to gauge the success or failure of the new projects. The Unwind programme alone produced 120 new events, one for each Westin hotel.

(Define, Measure, Analyze, Improve and Control, pronounced 'deMay-ick' for short), which provides a structured way for organizations to approach and solve problems.[46]

Effectively implementing Six Sigma requires a major commitment from top management, because Six Sigma involves widespread change throughout the organization. Hundreds of organizations have adopted some form of Six Sigma programme in recent years. Highly committed companies, including Amazon, Dell, DHL, HSBC, Motorola, General Electric, Network Rail, Samsung, Siemens AG and Vodafone, send managers to weeks of training to become qualified as Six Sigma 'black belts'. These black belts lead projects aimed at improving targeted areas of the business.[47] Although originally applied to manufacturing, Six Sigma has evolved to a process used in all industries and affecting every aspect of company operations, from human resources to customer service. The Neo Derm Group, based in Hong Kong, has used Six Sigma since 2005 to identify a defined sequence to ensure error-free staff performance and consistent quality customer service. The CEO, Lim Meng-teng explains that 'within three days after a client finishes her treatment, we will call her over a telephone, asking her to rate her therapists between one to five, depending on their overall satisfaction level'. The results appear on Neo Derm's central computer and can be accessed by all employees. Underperforming staff are counselled on how to improve their service levels. These management systems helped Neo Derm achieve a 390 per cent revenue growth in 2005, and it now employs over 700 employees at 15 treatment centres and six retail outlets in Hong Kong, and has just opened its first centre in Shanghai. However, high-profile Six Sigma failures like Home Depot and 3M also demonstrate that companies cannot focus on implementing Six Sigma in isolation, but also need human involvement in corporate change. Clearly, Six Sigma is a set of process tools that should only be part of a more holistic process improvement strategy. Exhibit 19.8 lists some statistics that illustrate why Six Sigma is important for both manufacturing and service organizations.

Exhibit 19.8 The Importance of Quality Improvement Programmes

99 Percent Amounts to:	Six Sigma Amounts to:
117,000 pieces of lost first-class mail per hour	1 piece of lost first-class mail every two hours
800,000 mishandled personal cheques each day	3 mishandled cheques each day
23,087 defective computers shipped each month	8 defective computers shipped each month
7.2 hours per month without electricity	9 seconds per month without electricity

SOURCE: Based on data from *Statistical Abstract of the United States*, US Postal Service, as reported in Tracy Mayor, 'Six Sigma Comes to IT: Targeting Perfection', *CIO* (December 1, 2003): 62–70.

Reduced Cycle Time

Cycle time has become a critical quality issue in today's fast-paced world. Cycle time refers to the steps taken to complete a company process, such as making an airline reservation, processing an online order or opening a retirement fund. The simplification of work cycles, including dropping barriers between work steps and among departments and removing worthless steps in the process, enables a TQM programme to succeed. Even if an organization decides not to use quality circles or other techniques, substantial improvement is possible by focusing on improved responsiveness and acceleration of activities into a shorter time. Reduction in cycle time improves overall company performance as well as quality.[48]

L. L. Bean is a recognized leader in cycle time control. Workers used flowcharts to track their movements, pinpoint wasted motions and completely redesign the order-fulfilment process. Today, a computerized system breaks down an order based on the geographic area of the warehouse in which items are stored. Items are placed on conveyor belts, where electronic sensors re-sort the items for individual orders. After orders are packed, they are sent to a FedEx facility on site. Improvements such as these have enabled L. L. Bean to process most orders within two hours after the order is received.[49]

© TRAVELSTOCKCOLLECTION – HOMER SYKES/ALAMY

CONCEPT CONNECTION Leyland Trucks uses *kaizen* at the heart of its corporate strategy, enabling major improvements to its business processes by continually taking and reviewing smaller steps. For example, before installing a robotic paint spray booth – the first of its kind in the world and a major leap forward – managers at Leyland's Preston plant ensured the views of everyone involved in previous changes were heard and fed into the process of installing the booth. As Jim Sumner, Managing Director of Leyland Trucks explains: "the key to continual renewal and development of our production system is organisational learning. The process of reflecting on what has and hasn't worked shapes the way we move forward."[50]

Continuous Improvement

In North America, crash programmes and designs have traditionally been the preferred method of innovation. Managers measure the expected benefits of a change and favour the ideas with the biggest payoffs. In contrast, Japanese companies have realized extraordinary success from making a series of mostly small improvements. This approach, called **continuous improvement**, or *kaizen*, is the implementation of a large number of small, incremental improvements in all areas of the organization on an ongoing basis. In a successful TQM programme, all employees learn that they are expected to contribute by initiating changes in their own job activities. The basic philosophy is that improving things a little bit at a time, all the time, has the highest probability of success. Innovations can start simple, and employees can build on their success in this unending process. The Innovative Way box shows how one car parts plant has tried to benefit from a TQM and continuous improvement philosophy.

Cycle time
The steps taken to complete a company process.

Continuous improvement
The implementation of a large number of small, incremental improvements in all areas of the organization on an ongoing basis.

Unfortunately, despite the effectiveness of the Franklin plant and the quality of its parts and service, the global downturn has resulted in massive production cutbacks by the major car manufacturers, along with pressure from the them for ever-lower prices even as the cost of raw materials was skyrocketing, pushed parent company Dana into bankruptcy. The company is now struggling to restructure and survive in an increasingly tough industry.[51] Yet Dana remains committed to a strong continuous improvement programme. 'As we pursue improved financial performance, we are taking aggressive actions to enhance our operational excellence. Chief among these are the establishment of shared, targeted metrics across all of our businesses; the implementation of the Dana Operating System, a coordinated approach to drive continuous improvement throughout our operations; and the review of our global manufacturing footprint to ensure that we are producing the right products in the

💡 INNOVATIVE WAY

Dana Corporation's Perfect Circle Products Franklin Steel Products Plant

The Dana Corporation' is a world leader in the supply of axles, driveshafts and other vehicle service parts. The company's customer base includes virtually every major vehicle manufacturer around the world. Based in Toledo, Ohio, the company employs over 32 000 people across 26 countries worldwide, with sales in 2007 of $8.7 billion. Dana's Perfect Circle Products Franklin Steel Products Plant in Franklin, Kentucky, manufactures as many as 3500 different part numbers, primarily for automakers Ford, General Motors, and Daimler-Chrysler, as well as thousands of after-market products. In one recent year, the company churned out about 60 million oil-ring expanders, for example.

Despite the high-volume, high-mix environment, Dana Franklin has maintained a 99 per cent on-time delivery rate to customers since 2001. For the first six months of 2004, customer complaints were zero per million products sold, and the customer reject rate was zero parts per million. The plant has been named one

of *Industry Week* magazine's Ten Best North American Manufacturing Facilities a record-setting six times. These results are amazing accomplishments for the plant's small workforce (just 44 production and management personnel), especially considering that some of the equipment they use is more than 50 years old. Yet the philosophy here is that with each unit produced, with each hour, with each day and each week, the plant gets just a little bit better. As plant manager Tim Parys says, 'We've sort of adopted the Japanese philosophy in that the worst that the equipment ever runs is the day that you put it on the floor.'

In addition to continuous improvement on the plant floor, typically two or three active Six Sigma initiatives are underway at any time in the plant. Almost everyone in the plant is a Six Sigma green belt or black belt. Dana Franklin holds regular four-day *kaizen* events, in which team members selected from the entire workforce focus on eliminating wasteful materials, activities and processes. Production technician Ronnie Steenbergen is convinced that *kaizen* works and can enable the factory to squeeze out even more improvements from its 'old machines'.[52]

right places to best serve the needs of our customers,' said CEO Gary Convis, a retired Toyota Motor Corp executive, recently appointed to introduce some of Toyota's lean manufacturing systems at Dana.[53]

TQM Success Factors

Despite its promise, total quality management does not always work. A few firms have had disappointing results. In particular, Six Sigma principles might not be appropriate for all organizational problems, and some companies have expended tremendous energy and resources for little payoff.[54] Many contingency factors (listed in Exhibit 19.9) can influence the success of a TQM programme. For example, quality circles are most beneficial when employees have challenging jobs; participation in a quality circle can contribute to productivity because it enables employees to pool their knowledge and solve interesting problems. TQM also tends to be most successful when it enriches jobs and improves employee motivation. In addition, when participating in the quality programme improves workers' problem-solving skills, productivity is likely to increase. Finally, a quality programme has the greatest chance of success in a corporate culture that values quality and stresses continuous improvement as a way of life, as at the Dana Franklin plant just described.

There are now many excellent examples of continuous improvement in action throughout Corus worldwide. The Kalzip team at Haydock, UK, began its continuous improvement programme by improving material flow. To enable this to happen the team moved big machines, such as a nine metre guillotine with a six-metre

Exhibit 19.9 Quality Programme Success Factors

Positive Factors	Negative Factors
■ Tasks make high skill demands on employees.	■ Management expectations are unrealistically high.
■ TQM serves to enrich jobs and motivate employees.	■ Middle managers are dissatisfied about loss of authority.
■ Problem-solving skills are improved for all employees.	■ Workers are dissatisfied with other aspects of organizational life.
■ Participation and teamwork are used to tackle significant problems.	■ Union leaders are left out of QC discussions.
■ Continuous improvement is a way of life.	■ Managers wait for big, dramatic innovations.

production foundation, relocated welding bays and re-routed workshops. It was estimated the job would take eight months. It actually took two months, as the changes were implemented after detailed value stream mapping discovered a lot of 'work in progress' (unproductive activity) as well as potentially unsafe ways of working. It was taking the forklift truck 45 minutes to reach one steel coil as it had to move many others out of the way. Reorganization of the coils into a new racking system has doubled storage capacity.

The Port Talbot strip products site has also taken on continuous improvement with many ensuing benefits. It was estimated that one man was spending 39 weeks a year looking for spare parts. This related to a pilot project at the central engineering workshop's bond stores. Engineering spare parts, gearboxes and rolls are received here ready to be assembled or used in repairs on the Port Talbot site. Complicated ways of working had developed over the years and no-one had ever changed these.

Within a short period 194 items were sorted out, relocated, tagged or scrapped, to the value of £30 000. Continuous improvement work at Port Talbot has now yielded benefits to the value of £350 000. The new system of palletizing spare parts, scheduled by a planner and then removed by forklift for storage in colour-coded bays has also provided big benefits. Orders can be cross-referenced to the pallet and fitters can find what they are looking for easily.[55]

CONCEPT CONNECTION Corus, an international metals company, and part of the giant Indian conglomerate Tata Steel, established a 'virtual' Corus Academy in April 2005. The Academy was designed to provide an open learning environment based on sharing best practice and maximizing the use of common approaches. As Corus is a global company, it needs to communicate internationally and this is where virtual learning is helpful. Examples of best practice can be conveyed in electronic format and shared in databases across the entire organization. For example, a Corus plant in the Netherlands or UK can learn from the practice of improvements in similar processes in Canada or the US.

Trends in Quality and Financial Control

Many companies are responding to changing economic realities and global competition by reassessing organizational management and processes – including control mechanisms. Some of the major trends in quality and financial control include international quality standards, economic value-added and market value-added systems, activity-based costing and increased corporate governance.

International Quality Standards

ISO 9000 standards
A set of standards that represent an international consensus of what constitutes effective quality management, as outlined by the International Organization for Standardization.

One impetus for total quality management in the US and Western Europe is the increasing significance of the global economy. Many countries have adopted a universal benchmark for quality management practices, ISO 9000 standards, which represent an international consensus of what constitutes effective quality management as outlined by the International Organization for Standardization.[56] Hundreds of thousands of organizations in 157 countries have been certified against ISO 9000 standards to demonstrate their commitment to quality. Europe continues to lead in the total number of certifications, but the greatest number of new certifications in recent years has been in the US. ISO certification has become the recognized standard for evaluating and comparing companies on a global basis, and more companies are feeling the pressure to participate to remain competitive in international markets. In addition, many countries and companies require ISO certification before they will do business with an organization.

TAKE A MOMENT

As a new manager, be aware of current trends in financial and quality control. Learn quality principles, new financial control systems and open-book management, and apply what works for your situation.

New Financial Control Systems

In addition to traditional financial tools, managers are using systems such as economic value-added, market value-added, activity-based costing and corporate governance to provide effective financial control.

Economic Value-Added (EVA)

Economic value-added (EVA)
A control system that measures performance in terms of after-tax profits minus the cost of capital invested in tangible assets.

Hundreds of companies, including Tesco, Quaker Oats, the Coca-Cola Company and Philips Petroleum Company, have set up economic value-added (EVA) measurement systems as a new way to gauge financial performance. EVA can be defined as a company's net (after-tax) operating profit minus the cost of capital invested in the company's tangible assets.[57] Measuring performance in terms of EVA is intended to capture all the things a company can do to add value from its activities, such as run the business more efficiently, satisfy customers and reward shareholders. Each job, department, process, or project in the organization is measured by the value added. EVA can also help managers make more cost-effective decisions. At Boise Cascade, they used EVA to measure the cost of replacing the company's existing storage devices against keeping the existing storage assets that had higher maintenance costs. Using EVA demonstrated that buying new storage devices would lower annual maintenance costs significantly and easily make up for the capital expenditure.[58]

Market Value-Added (MVA)

Market value-added (MVA)
A control system that measures the stock market's estimate of the value of a company's past and expected capital investment projects.

Market value-added (MVA) adds another dimension because it measures the stock market's estimate of the value of a company's past and projected capital investment projects. For example, when a company's market value (the value of all outstanding stock plus the company's debt) is greater than all the capital invested in it from shareholders, bondholders and retained earnings, the company has a positive MVA, an indication that it has increased the value of capital entrusted to it and thus created shareholder wealth. A positive MVA usually, although not always, goes hand-in-hand with a high overall EVA measurement.[59] For example, in one study, General Electric had both the highest MVA and the highest EVA in its category (companies were categorized by size). Microsoft was ranked second in MVA but had a lower EVA rating than GE and many other companies. This comparison indicates that the stock market believes Microsoft has greater opportunities for further growth, which will, in turn, increase its EVA.[60]

Activity-Based Costing (ABC)

Managers measure the cost of producing goods and services so they can be sure they are selling those products for more than the cost to produce them. Traditional methods of costing assign costs to various departments or functions, such as purchasing, manufacturing, human resources, and so on. With a shift to more horizontal, flexible organizations has come a new approach called activity-based costing (ABC), which allocates costs across business processes. ABC attempts to identify all the various activities needed to provide a product or service and allocate costs accordingly. For example, an activity-based costing system might list the costs associated with processing orders for a particular product, scheduling production for that product, producing it, shipping it and resolving problems with it. Because ABC allocates costs across business processes, it provides a more accurate picture of the cost of various products and services.[61] In addition, it enables managers to evaluate whether more costs go to activities that add value (meeting customer deadlines, achieving high quality) or to activities that do not add value (such as processing internal paperwork). They can then focus on reducing costs associated with non-value-added activities.

Activity-based costing (ABC)
A control system that identifies the various activities needed to provide a product and allocates costs accordingly.

Corporate Governance

Today, many organizations are moving toward increased control from the top in terms of corporate governance, which refers to the system of governing an organization so that the interests of corporate shareholders are protected. The matter of corporate governance has come to the forefront in light of the failure of top executives and corporate directors to provide adequate oversight and control at failed companies such as Northern Rock, Enron, Parmalat and WorldCom. In some cases, financial reporting systems were manipulated to produce false results and hide internal failures. The financial reporting systems and the roles of boards of directors are being scrutinized in organizations around the world to ensure that top leaders are keeping a close eye on the activities of lower-level managers and employees.

Corporate governance
The system of governing an organization so the interests of corporate owners are protected.

Some of the corporate failures could be attributed to *under control* because top managers did not keep personal tabs on everything in a large, global organization. Many of the CEOs who have been indicted in connection with financial misdeeds have claimed that they were unaware that misconduct was going on. In some cases, these claims might be true, but they reflect a significant breakdown in control.

The government response in the UK has been to introduce the Combined Code on Corporate Governance 2008 which sets out standards of good practice in relation to issues such as board composition and development, remuneration, accountability and audit and relations with shareholders. All companies incorporated in the UK and listed on the Main Market of the London Stock Exchange are required under the Listing Rules to report on how they have applied the Combined Code in their annual report and accounts. Overseas companies listed on the

Main Market are required to disclose the significant ways in which their corporate governance practices differ from those set out in the Code.[62] This is a very similar approach to that adopted in South Africa through the King Report on Corporate Governance.[63]

By contrast, the US government enacted the Sarbanes-Oxley Act of 2002, often referred to as SOX, which requires several types of reforms, including better internal monitoring to reduce the risk of fraud, certification of financial reports by top leaders, improved measures for external auditing and enhanced public financial disclosure. SOX has been unpopular with many business leaders, largely because of the expense of complying with the act. In addition, some critics argue that SOX is creating a culture of *over control* that is stifling innovation and growth. Even among those who agree that government regulation is needed, calls for a more balanced regulatory scheme in the US that requires transparency and objectivity without restraining innovation are growing.[64] Overall, it is interesting to contrast the UK approach with the emphasis has been more on voluntary codes of conduct rather than the statutory approach in the US.

TAKE A MOMENT   As a new manager, keep in mind that over control can be just as detrimental to your team's performance as under control. Find a balance between oversight and control on the one hand and mutual trust and respect on the other. Go to the Ethical Dilemma on page 761 that pertains to new workplace control issues.

Over control of employees can be damaging to an organization as well. Managers might feel justified in monitoring email and internet use, as described in the Manager's Shoptalk earlier in this chapter, for example, yet employees often resent and feel demeaned by close monitoring that limits their personal freedom and makes them feel as if they are constantly being watched. Excessive control of employees can lead to demotivation, low morale, lack of trust and even hostility among workers. Managers have to find an appropriate balance, as well as develop and communicate clear policies regarding workplace monitoring. Although oversight and control are important, good organizations also depend on mutual trust and respect among managers and employees.

A MANAGER'S ESSENTIALS: WHAT HAVE WE LEARNED?

- Organizational control is the systematic process through which managers regulate organizational activities to meet planned goals and standards of performance. Most organizations measure and control performance using financial measures. Increasingly, more organizations are measuring less tangible aspects of performance.
- The balanced scorecard is a comprehensive management control system that balances traditional measures with operational measures relating to a company's critical success factors. The four major perspectives of the balanced scorecard are financial performance, customer service,

internal business processes and the organization's capacity for learning and growth.

- The feedback control model involves using feedback to determine whether performance meets established standards. Well-designed control systems include four key steps: establish standards, measure performance, compare performance to standards and make corrections as necessary.
- Budgetary control is one of the most commonly used forms of managerial control. Managers might use expense budgets, revenue budgets, cash budgets and capital budgets. Other financial controls include use of the balance sheet,

income statement and financial analysis of these documents.

■ The philosophy of controlling has shifted to reflect changes in leadership methods. Traditional hierarchical controls emphasize establishing rules and procedures, then monitoring employee behaviour to make sure the rules and procedures are followed. With decentralized control, employees assume responsibility for monitoring their own performance.

■ Open-book management is used in decentralized organizations to share with all employees the financial condition of a company. Open-book management encourages active participation in achieving organizational goals, helps the employee understand how his or her job affects the financial success of the organization, and allows employees to see the interdependence and importance of each business function.

■ Total quality management is an organization-wide effort to infuse quality into every activity in a company through continuous improvement. Although based on work of US researchers and consultants, TQM was initially adopted and made popular by Japanese firms. TQM techniques include quality circles, benchmarking, Six Sigma, reduced cycle time and continuous improvement.

■ Recent trends in control include the use of international quality standards, economic value-added (EVA) and market value-added (MVA) systems, activity-based costing (ABC), and corporate governance.

At the Rochester Independent Practice Association, described in the chapter opening, Dr Howard Beckman realized that, for doctors to improve the quality of their interaction with patients, they needed objective feedback about how they were doing. Beckman tapped into a growing trend among medical groups to use scientific methods to survey patient satisfaction and rate doctors on how well they're communicating. Many doctors were surprised by their low scores. To take corrective action, Beckman taught doctors communication skills, such as how to be a better listener and get patients to tell their complete story rather than immediately jumping in to suggest tests or medication. One doctor was sceptical but called Beckman later and enthusiastically reported, 'I can't believe how different it is. I hear things I don't usually hear.' By giving doctors feedback, the Rochester Association is enabling them to provide better service, and most of them are happier with their patient interactions.[65]

DISCUSSION QUESTIONS

1 You're a manager who employs a participative control approach. You've concluded that corrective action is necessary to improve customer satisfaction, but first you need to convince your employees that the problem exists. What kind of evidence do you think employees will find more compelling: quantitative measurements or anecdotes from your interactions with customers? Explain your answer.

2 Describe the advantages of using a balanced scorecard to measure and control organizational performance. Suppose you created a balanced scorecard for McDonald's. What specific customer service measures would you include?

3 In bottom-up budgeting, lower-level managers anticipate their departments' resource needs and pass them up to top management for approval. Identify the advantages of bottom-up budgeting.

4 In the chapter example of eBay, CEO Meg Whitman is quoted as saying, 'If you can't measure it, you can't control it.' Do you agree with this statement? Provide examples from your school or business experience that support your argument.

5 Think of a class or module you've taken in the past. What standards of performance did your professor establish? How was your actual performance measured? How was your performance compared to the standards? Do you think the standards and methods of measurement were fair? Were they appropriate to your assigned work? Why or why not?

6 Some critics argue that Six Sigma is a collection of superficial changes that often result in doing a superb job of building the wrong product or

offering the wrong service. Do you agree or disagree? Explain.

7 What types of analysis can managers perform to help them diagnose a company's financial condition? How might a review of financial statements help managers diagnose other kinds of performance problems as well?

8 Why is benchmarking an important component of total quality management (TQM) programmes? Do you believe a company could have a successful TQM programme without using benchmarking?

9 How might activity-based costing provide better financial control tools for managers of a

company such as Kellogg that produces numerous food products?

10 What is ISO certification? Why would a global company like General Electric want ISO certification?

11 What are some examples of feedback control that might be used in a family-style restaurant? In the police service?

12 In what ways could a university benefit from hierarchical control? In what ways might it benefit from decentralized control? Overall, which approach do you think would be best at your college or university? Why?

MANAGEMENT IN PRACTICE: EXPERIENTIAL EXERCISE

Is Your Budget in Control?

By the time you are in college, you are in charge of at least some of your own finances. How well you manage your personal budget may indicate how well you will manage your company's budget on the job. Respond to the following statements to evaluate your own budgeting habits. If the statement doesn't apply directly to you, respond the way you think you would behave in a similar situation.

1 I spend all my money as soon as I get it.   Yes No

2 At the beginning of each week (or month, or term), I write down all my fixed expenses.   Yes No

3 I never seem to have any money left over at the end of the week (or month).   Yes No

4 I pay all my expenses, but I never seem to have any money left over for fun.   Yes No

5 I am not putting any money away in savings right now; I'll wait until after I graduate from university.   Yes No

6 I can't pay all my bills.   Yes No

7 I have a credit card, but I pay the balance in full each month.   Yes No

8 I take cash advances on my credit card.   Yes No

9 I know how much I can spend on eating out, movies and other entertainment each week.   Yes No

10 I pay cash for everything.   Yes No

11 When I buy something, I look for value and determine the best buy.   Yes No

12 I lend money to friends whenever they ask, even if it leaves me short of cash.   Yes No

13 I never borrow money from friends.   Yes No

14 I am putting aside money each month to save for something that I really need.   Yes No

Scoring and Interpretation

Yes responses to statements 2, 9, 10, 13 and 14 point to the most disciplined budgeting habits; *yes* responses to 4, 5, 7 and 11 reveal adequate budgeting habits; yes responses to 1, 3, 6, 8 and 12 indicate the poorest budgeting habits. If you have answered honestly, chances are you'll have a combination of all three. Look to see where you can improve your budgeting.

MANAGEMENT IN PRACTICE: ETHICAL DILEMMA

The Wages of Sin?

Chris Dykstra, responsible for loss prevention at West-End Electronics, took a deep breath before he launched into making his case for the changes he was proposing in the company's shoplifting policy. He knew convincing Ross Chenoweth was going to be a hard sell. Ross, the CEO, was the son of the founder of the local, still family-owned consumer electronics chain. He'd inherited not only the company but also his father's strict moral code.

'I think it's time to follow the lead of other stores,' Chris began. He pointed out that most other retailers didn't bother calling the police and pressing charges unless the thief had shoplifted merchandize worth more than £20–£50. In contrast, West-End currently had the zero-tolerance policy toward theft that Ross's father had put in place when he started the business. Chris wanted to replace that policy with one that only prosecuted individuals between 18 and 65, had stolen more than £15 worth of goods, and had no previous history of theft at West-End. In the case of first-time culprits under 18 or over 65, he argued for letting them off with a strict warning regardless of the value of their ill-gotten goods. Repeat offenders would be arrested.

'Frankly, the local police are getting pretty tired of having to come to our stores every time a teenager sticks a CD in his jacket pocket,' Chris pointed out. 'And besides, we just can't afford the costs associated with prosecuting everyone.' Every time he pressed charges against a shoplifter who'd made off with a £5 item, West-End lost money. The company had to engage solicitors and pay employees overtime for their court appearances. In addition, Chris was looking at hiring more security guards to keep up with the workload. West-End was already in a battle it was losing at the moment with the mass retailers who were competing all too successfully on price, so passing on the costs of its zero-tolerance policy to customers wasn't really an option. 'Let's concentrate on catching dishonest employees and those organized theft rings. They're the ones who are really hurting us,' Chris concluded.

There was a long pause after Chris finished his carefully prepared speech. Ross thought about his recently deceased father, both an astute businessman and a person for whom honesty was a key guiding principle. If he were sitting here today, he'd no doubt say that theft was theft, and that setting a minimum was tantamount to saying that stealing was acceptable just as long as you don't steal too much. He looked at Chris. 'You know, we've both got teenagers. Is this really a message you want to send out, especially to kids? You know as well as I do that there's nothing they like better than testing limits. It's almost an invitation to see if you can beat the system.' But then Ross faltered as he found himself glancing at the latest financial figures on his desk – another in a string of quarterly losses. If West-End went under, a lot of employees would be looking for another way to make a living. In his heart, he believed in his father's high moral standards, but he had to ask himself: just how moral could West-End afford to be?

What Would You Do?

1 Continue West-End's zero-tolerance policy toward shoplifting. It's the right thing to do – and it will pay off in the end in higher profitability because the chain's reputation for being tough on crime will reduce overall losses from theft.

2 Adopt Chris Dykstra's proposed changes and show more leniency to first-time offenders. It is a more cost-effective approach to the problem than the current policy, plus it stays close to your father's original intent.

3 Adopt Chris Dykstra's proposed changes with an even higher limit of £25 or £50, which is still less than the cost of prosecution. In addition, make sure the policy isn't publicized. That way you'll reduce costs even more and still benefit from your reputation for prosecuting all shoplifters.

SOURCE Based on Michael Barbaro, 'Some Leeway for the Small Shoplifter', *The New York Times*, July 13, 2006.

CASE FOR CRITICAL ANALYSIS 19.1

Lincoln Electric

Imagine having a management system that is so successful people refer to it with capital letters – the Lincoln Management System – and other businesses benchmark their own systems by it. That is the situation of Ohio-based Lincoln Electric. For a number of years, other companies have tried to figure out Lincoln Electric's secret – how management coaxes maximum productivity and quality from its workers, even during difficult financial times. Lately, however, Lincoln Electric has been trying to solve a mystery of its own: why is the company having such difficulty exporting a management system abroad that has worked so well at home?

Lincoln Electric was founded in 1895, and is today the world leader in the design, development and manufacture of arc welding products, robotic welding systems, plasma and oxyfuel cutting equipment, with more than $1 billion in sales and 6000 workers worldwide. The company's products are used for cutting, manufacturing and repairing other metal products. Although it is now a publicly traded company, members of the Lincoln family still own more than 60 per cent of the stock.

Lincoln uses a diverse control approach. Tasks are precisely defined, and individual employees must exceed strict performance goals to achieve top pay. The incentive and control system is powerful. Production workers are paid on a piece-rate basis, plus merit pay based on performance. Employees also are eligible for annual bonuses, which fluctuate according to the company's profits, and they participate in stock purchase plans. A worker's bonus is based on four factors: work productivity, work quality, dependability and cooperation with others. Some factory workers at Lincoln have earned more than $100 000 a year.

However, the Lincoln system succeeds largely because of an organizational culture based on openness and trust, shared control and an egalitarian spirit. To begin with, the company has earned employee trust with its no layoff policy. In fact, the last time it laid off anyone was in 1951. Although the line between managers and workers at Lincoln is firmly drawn, managers respect the expertise of production workers and value their contributions to many aspects of the business. The company has an open-door policy for all top executives, middle managers and production workers, and regular face-to-face communication is encouraged. Workers are expected to challenge management if they believe practices or compensation rates are unfair. Most workers are hired right out of high school, then trained and cross-trained to perform different jobs. Some eventually are promoted to executive positions, because Lincoln believes in promoting from within. Many Lincoln workers stay with the company for life.

One of Lincoln's founders felt that organizations should be based on certain values, including honesty, trustworthiness, openness, self-management, loyalty, accountability and cooperativeness. These values continue to form the core of Lincoln's culture, and management regularly rewards employees who manifest them. Because Lincoln so effectively socializes employees, they exercise a great degree of self-control on the job. Each supervisor oversees 100 workers, and less tangible rewards complement the piece-rate incentive system. Pride of workmanship and feelings of involvement, contribution and esprit de corps are intrinsic rewards that flourish at Lincoln Electric. Cross-functional teams, empowered to make decisions, take responsibility for product planning, development and marketing. Information about the company's operations and financial performance is openly shared with workers throughout the company.

Lincoln emphasizes anticipating and solving customer problems. Sales representatives are given the technical training they need to understand customer needs, help customers understand and use Lincoln's products, and solve problems. This customer focus is backed by attention to the production process through the use of strict accountability standards and formal measurements for productivity, quality and innovation for all employees. In addition, a software programme called Rhythm helps streamline the flow of goods and materials in the production process.

Lincoln's system worked so well in the US that senior executives decided to extend it overseas. Lincoln built or purchased eleven plants in Japan, South America and Europe, with plans to run the plants from the US using Lincoln's expertise with management control systems. Managers saw the opportunity to beat local competition by applying manufacturing control incentive systems to reduce costs and raise production in plants around the world. The results were abysmal and nearly sunk the company. Managers at international plants failed to meet their production and financial goals every year they exaggerated the goals sent to Lincoln's managers to receive more resources, especially during the recession in Europe and South America. Many overseas managers had no innate desire to increase sales, and workers were found sleeping on benches because not enough work was available. The European labour culture was hostile to the piece-work and bonus control system. The huge losses in the international plants, which couldn't seem to adopt Lincoln's vaunted control systems, meant the company would have to borrow money to pay US workers' bonuses, or forgo bonuses for the first time in Lincoln's history. Top managers began to wonder: had they simply done a poor job of applying the Lincoln Management System to other cultures, or was it possible that it simply wasn't going to work abroad?

Questions

1 Does Lincoln follow a hierarchical or decentralized approach to management? Explain your answer and give examples.

2 Based on what you've just read, what do you think makes the Lincoln System so successful in the US?

3 What is the problem with transporting Lincoln's control systems to other national cultures? What suggestions would you make to Lincoln's managers to make future international manufacturing plants more successful?

4 Should Lincoln borrow money and pay bonuses to avoid breaking trust with its US workers? Why or why not?

SOURCES Based on Herb Greenberg, 'Why Investors May Do Well with Firms That Avoid Layoffs', *The Wall Street Journal*, September 9, 2006; Mark Gottlieb, 'Feeding the Dragon', *Industry Week* 251, no. 1 (February 2002): 54–55; Donald Hastings, 'Lincoln Electric's Harsh Lessons from International Expansion', *Harvard Business Review* (May–June, 1999): 3–11; and Joseph Maciariello, 'A Pattern of Success: Can This Company Be Duplicated'? *Drucker Management* 1, no. 1 (Spring 1997): 7–11.

ENDNOTES

1. Gina Kolata 'When the Docter Is In, But You Wish He Wasn't', *The New York Times*, (November 30 2005) www.nytimes.com. http://query.nytimes.com/gst/fullpage. html?res=9F06E3DE1531F933A05752C1A9639C8B63&sec=&spon=&pagewanted=3 (accessed February 18, 2010).
2. Adapted from J. J. Ray, 'Do Authoritarians Hold Authoritarian Attitudes?' *Human Relations* 29 (1976): 307–325.
3. Yochi J. Dreazen, 'More Katrina Woes: Incidents of Fraud at Red Cross Centres', *The Wall Street Journal* (October 19, 2005).
4. Douglas S. Sherwin, 'The Meaning of Control,' *Dunn's Business Review* (January 1956).
5. Russ Banham, 'Nothin' But Net Gain', *eCFO* (Fall 2001): 32–33.
6. 'On Balance', a *CFO* Interview with Robert Kaplan and David Norton, *CFO* (February 2001):73–78; and Bill Birchard, 'Intangible Assets + Hard Numbers — Soft Finance', *Fast Company* (October 1999): 316–336.
7. Andy Neely and Mohammed Al Najjar, 'Management Learning Not Management Control: The True Role of Performance Measurement', *California Management Review* 48, no. 3 (Spring 2006): 105.
8. This discussion is based on a review of the balanced scorecard in Richard L. Daft, *Organization Theory and Design*, 7th ed. (Cincinnati, OH: South-Western, 2001), pp. 300–301.
9. Neely and Al Najjar, pp. 105 and 112.
10. Robert Kaplan and David Norton, 'The Balanced Scorecard: Measures That Drive Performance', *Harvard Business Review* (January–February 1992): 71–79; and Chee W. Chow, Kamal M. Haddad and James E. Williamson, 'Applying the Balanced Scorecard to Small Companies', *Management Accounting* 79, no. 2 (August 1997): 21–27.
11. Based on Kaplan and Norton, 'The Balanced Scorecard'; Chow, Haddad and Williamson, 'Applying the Balanced Scorecard'; and Cathy Lazere, 'All Together Now', *CFO* (February 1998): 28–36.
12. Jessi Hempil, 'Finding Cracks in Facebook', *Fortune* (May 13, 2008), http://money.cnn.com/2008/05/12/technology/cracks_facebook_hempel.fortune/index.htm?postversion=2008051308 (accessed May 14, 2008).
13. Geert J. M. Braam and Edwin J. Nijssen, 'Performance Effects of Using the Balanced Scorecard: A Note on the Dutch Experience', *Long Range Planning* 37 (2004): 335–349; Kaplan and Norton, 'The Balanced Scorecard'; and Cam Scholey, 'Strategy Maps: A Step-by-Step Guide to Measuring, Managing, and Communicating the Plan', *Journal of Business Strategy* 26, no. 3 (2005): 12–19.
14. Nils-Göran Olve, Carl-Johan Petri, Jan Roy and Sofie Roy, 'Twelve Years Later: Understanding and Realizing the Value of Balanced Scorecards', *Ivey Business Journal* (May–June 2004); Eric M. Olson and Stanley F. Slater, 'The Balanced Scorecard, Competitive Strategy, and Performance', *Business Horizons* (May–June 2002): 11–16; and Eric Berkman, 'How to Use the Balanced Scorecard', *CIO* (May 15, 2002): 93–100.
15. *Ibid.*; and Brigitte W. Schay, Mary Ellen Beach, Jacqueline A. Caldwell and Christelle LaPolice, 'Using Standardized Outcome Measures in the Federal Government', *Human Resource Management* 41, no. 3 (Fall 2002): 355–368.
16. Braam and Nijssen, 'Performance Effects of Using the Balanced Scorecard'.
17. Olve *et al.*, 'Twelve Years Later: Understanding and Realizing the Value of Balanced Scorecards'.

CHAPTER OUTLINE

© SHIRONOSOV/ISTOCK

LEARNING OBJECTIVES

After reading this chapter, you should be able to:

1 Explain the importance of information technology for organizations and discuss specific ways in which IT has changed the manager's job.

2 Describe new developments in information technology and identify the different types of IT systems used in organizations.

3 Tell how information systems support daily operations and decision-making.

4 Summarize the key components of e-business and explain e-business strategies.

5 Describe enterprise resource planning and customer relationship management systems.

6 Explain the importance of knowledge management and business intelligence in today's organizations.

CHAPTER 20

INFORMATION TECHNOLOGY AND E-BUSINESS

Manager's Challenge

As the public relations firm for Wal-Mart, Edelman is facing a tough challenge. The giant corporation has been under steady assault, with critics accusing the retailer of all manner of evil, from driving local retailers out of business, to paying workers piti-ful wages, to squeezing suppliers to death. Protestors carrying signs outside stores started the criticism decades ago, but the internet has intensified the damage. A single Wal-Mart detractor can go from zero to global in just a few minutes, using websites and blogs to spread negative opinions, rumours, or company mistakes. Bloggers had a field day after the group Wal-Mart Watch leaked an internal draft memo about health benefits to *The New York Times*, then posted excerpts on its website. In the memo, Wal-Mart's executive vice president for benefits indicated that the company's health plan requires such high out-of-pocket payments that employees hit by a costly illness 'almost certainly end up declaring personal bankruptcy'. The memo also pro-posed that the company rewrite job descriptions to involve more physical activity to 'dissuade unhealthy people from coming to work at Wal-Mart'. These revelations added fuel to the already raging storm in the blogosphere over the company's alleged poor treatment of its workers. Considering how fast bad publicity spreads on the internet, some of Edelman's PR staff began wondering how the company might use the internet to more quickly tell its side of the story.[1]

If you were a PR consultant to Wal-Mart, what would you suggest the company do to rapidly respond to new charges of wrongdoing and get its side of the story out to the public? Do you think Wal-Mart can use the power of the internet to improve its battered image? **TAKE A MOMENT**

Which Side of Your Brain Do You Use?[2]

The following questions ask you to describe your behaviour. For each question, tick the answer that best describes you.

1 I am usually running late for class or other appointments:
_____ **a.** Yes

_____ **b.** No

2 When taking a test I prefer:
_____ **a.** Subjective questions (discussion or essay)

_____ **b.** Objective questions (multiple choice)

3 When making decisions, I typically:
_____ **a.** Go with my gut – what feels right

_____ **b.** Carefully weigh each option

4 When solving a problem, I would more likely:
_____ **a.** Take a walk, mull things over, then discuss

_____ **b.** Write down alternatives, prioritize them, then pick the best

5 I consider time spent daydreaming as:
_____ **a.** A viable tool for planning my future

_____ **b.** A waste of time

6 To remember directions, I typically:
_____ **a.** Visualize the information

_____ **b.** Make notes

7 My work style is mostly:
_____ **a.** To juggle several things at once

_____ **b.** To concentrate on one task at a time until complete

8 My desk, work area, or laundry area are typically:
_____ **a.** Cluttered

_____ **b.** Neat and organized

SCORING & INTERPRETATION People have two thinking processes – one visual and intuitive, which is often referred to as *right-brained thinking*, and the other verbal and analytical, referred to as *left-brained thinking*. The thinking process you prefer predisposes you to certain types of knowledge and information – visual charts and operations dashboards vs. written reports, intuitive suggestions vs. quantitative data – as effective input to your thinking and decision-making.

Count the number of ticked 'a' items and 'b' items. Each 'a' represents right-brain processing, and each 'b' represents left-brain processing. If you scored 6 or higher on either, you have a distinct processing style. If you ticked less than 6 for either, you probably have a balanced style. New managers typically need left-brain processing to handle data and to justify decisions. At middle and upper management levels, right-brain processing enables visionary thinking and strategic insights.

The internet, little more than a curiosity to many managers just a decade ago, now influences their lives and jobs in myriad ways. Managers at e-courier Europe's fastest growing same day courier service fuses innovative technologically-advanced transport control systems with a customer-orientated business philosophy. Using the latest GPS technology, their patented technology tracks exactly where each courier is located at any given time, with 10 metre accuracy. Trinchero Family Estates, producer of Sutter Hill wines, uses an online system to track the processing of grapes from harvesting to bottling to selling. And in the public sector strategic programmes for e-governance have been established recently in African countries such as Egypt, Kenya, Senegal and South Africa.[3]

Many companies, such as Wal-Mart, are profiting by using websites to sell more products, but, as discussed at the opening of this chapter, are also discovering that the internet has drawbacks aswell.

Almost every company uses the internet to some extent as part of its information technology system. The strategic use of information technology is one of the defining aspects of organizational success in today's world. Indeed, Wal-Mart is a classic example of the effective use of information technology to improve operational efficiency and manage every aspect of the business. Managers use information systems that rely on a massive data warehouse to make decisions about what to stock, how to price and promote it, and when to reorder or discontinue items. Handheld scanners enable managers to keep close tabs on inventory and monitor sales; at the end of each workday, orders for new merchandize are sent by computer to headquarters, where they are automatically organized and sent to regional distribution centres, which have electronic linkages with key suppliers for reordering. A recent innovation is using tiny chips with identification numbers on shipments of products (called radio-frequency identification, or RFID), which enables close tracking of inventory all through the supply chain. Back at headquarters, top Wal-Mart executives analyze buying patterns and other information, enabling them to spot problems or opportunities and convey the information to stores.[4] Numerous other companies, in industries from manufacturing to entertainment, as well as not-for-profit and government organizations, are using information technology to get closer to customers, enter new markets, and streamline business processes.

Information technology and e-business have changed the way people and organizations work and thus present new challenges for managers. The internet continues to disrupt and transform the traditional ways of business as well as convulse entire industries by giving advantages to nimble upstarts. Yet existing businesses are using e-business to cut costs, increase efficiency, improve customer service, speed up innovation and improve productivity.[5] This chapter explores the management of information technology and e-business. We begin by looking at the management implications of using advanced information technology. Next, we examine some recent technology trends and the types of information systems frequently used in organizations. Then, the chapter looks at the growing use of the internet and e-business, including a discussion of fundamental e-business strategies, business-to-business marketplaces, use of information technology in business operations and the importance of knowledge management.

Information Technology has Transformed Management

Advanced information technology makes just-in-time inventory management work seamlessly, but it has also transformed management in many other ways. An organization's **information technology (IT)** consists of the hardware, software,

Internet
A global collection of computer networks linked together for the exchange of data and information.

Information technology (IT)
The hardware, software, telecommunications, database management, and other technologies used to store, process and distribute information.

telecommunications, database management and other technologies it uses to store data and make them available in the form of information for organizational decision-making. In general, information technology has positive implications for the practice of management.

Boundaries Dissolve; Collaboration Reigns

Walk into the video conference room at Infosys Technologies, a leader in India's outsourcing and software industry, and the first thing you'll see is a wall-size flat-screen television. On that screen, Infosys can hold virtual meetings between the key players from its entire global supply chain for any project at any time of the day or night.[6]

Time, distance and other boundaries between individuals, departments and organizations are irrelevant in today's business world. Collaboration is what it's all about. Information technology can connect people around the world for the sharing and exchange of information and ideas. As historian Thomas L. Friedman puts it, 'Wherever you look today ... hierarchies are being flattened and value is being created less and less within vertical silos and more and more through horizontal collaboration within companies, between companies, and among individuals.'[7]

Knowledge Management

Knowledge management
The process of systematically gathering knowledge, making it widely available throughout the organization and fostering a culture of learning.

Information technology plays a key role in managers' efforts to support and leverage organizational knowledge. **Knowledge management** refers to the efforts to systematically gather knowledge, organize it, make it widely available throughout the organization, and foster a culture of continuous learning and knowledge sharing.[8]

Knowledge is not the same thing as data or information, although it uses both. **Data** are simple, absolute facts and figures that, in and of themselves, may be of little use. A company might have data that show 30 per cent of a particular product is sold to customers in Florida. To be useful to the organization, the data are processed into finished *information* by connecting them with other data – for example, nine out of ten of the products sold in Florida are bought by people over the age of 60. **Information** is data that have been linked with other data and converted into a useful context for specific use. **Knowledge** goes a step further; it is a conclusion drawn from the information after it is linked to other information and compared to what is already known. Knowledge, as opposed to information and data, always has a human factor. Books can contain information, but the information becomes knowledge only when a person absorbs it and puts it to use.[9]

Knowledge management portal
A single point of access for employees to multiple sources of information that provides personalized access on the corporate intranet.

IT systems facilitate knowledge management by enabling organizations to collect and store tremendous amounts of data, analyze that data so it can be transformed into information and knowledge, and share knowledge all across the enterprise. The most common organizational approach to knowledge management is sharing knowledge via information technology.[10] A variety of new software tools support collaboration and knowledge sharing through services such as Web conferencing, knowledge portals, content management and the use of *wikis*. A **knowledge management portal** is a single, personalized point of access for employees to multiple sources of information on the corporate intranet. A **wiki** uses software to create a website that allows anyone with access to create, share and edit content through a simple browser-based user interface. Organizations typically use a variety of IT systems to facilitate the collection, analysis and sharing of information and knowledge.

Wiki
Website that allows anyone with access, inside or outside the organization, to create, share and edit content through a simple, browser-based user interface.

Another IT application for knowledge management is the use of **business intelligence software** that analyzes data and extracts useful insights, patterns and relationships that might be significant.

Business Intelligence

Today's organizations can collect and store tremendous amounts of data. Some companies use data warehousing, which refers to the use of a huge database that combines all of a company's data and allows business users to access the data directly, create reports, and obtain answers to what-if questions. Others have data stored in multiple sources. In addition, companies have access to numerous sources of outside data. How do managers make sense of it all? They do so through the use of business intelligence.

Business intelligence (BI) is an umbrella term that refers to a variety of software applications that analyze a company's data and extract useful insights to help managers make better strategic decisions.[11] Business intelligence includes activities such as *data mining*, which searches out and analyzes data from multiple sources across the enterprise, and sometimes from outside sources, to identify patterns and relationships that might be significant, as well as online statistical analysis, querying and reporting. Many managers like getting BI information via a business performance dashboard, as described earlier in the chapter, because it provides a user-friendly way to view and navigate through information.[12]

Business intelligence tools are the hottest area of software right now, with companies spending billions on powerful new tools that can manipulate trillions of pieces of data and provide managers with targeted information to help them improve efficiency, increase customer satisfaction and loyalty, and pump up sales and profits.[13] Managers can, for example, identify sets of products that particular market segments purchase, patterns of transactions that signal possible fraud, or patterns of product performance that may indicate defects. The application of business intelligence helped managers at Staples, the office-supply chain, create a more profitable product mix in its stores. Managers had thought that devoting a large part of their floor space to desks, file cabinets and other big-ticket items made sense. However, the BI system indicated that the overall profitability of the furniture category was actually less than that for smaller goods such as paper and pens. Staples now devotes more of its floor space to such items as paper clips, highlighters, mailing labels, Post-it notes, and yellow pads, helping to keep the chain's net income growing at a 12 per cent compounded rate for five straight years.[14]

In addition, BI is being applied to improve day-to-day operations. Unlike early BI applications that often produced reports too late for managers to make needed changes, newer versions connect with other IT systems to let managers or others throughout the organization keep track of business intelligence in real-time. See Innovative Way for an example of how Anheuser-Busch InBev makes profitable use of business intelligence.

> **Data warehousing**
> The use of a huge database that combines all of a company's data and allows users to access the data directly, create reports and obtain answers to what-if questions.

> **Business intelligence (BI)**
> The high-tech analysis of data from multiple sources to identify patterns and relationships that might be significant.

People Do Better Work

Information technology can provide employees with all kinds of information about their customers, competitors, markets and service, as well as enable them to instantly share information and insights with colleagues. In addition, with time and geographic boundaries dissolving, a team can work throughout the day on a project in Switzerland or South Africa and, while they sleep, a team in the US can continue where the Swiss or South African team left off.

In general, information technology enables managers to design jobs to provide people with more intellectual engagement and more challenging work. The availability of information technology does not guarantee increased job performance, but when implemented and used appropriately, it can have a dramatic influence on employee effectiveness. For example, in November 2003, KLM became the first carrier

💡 INNOVATIVE WAY

Anheuser Busch

The Belgian owned Anheuser-Busch InBev is the leading global brewer and one of the world's top five consumer products companies. A true consumer-centric, sales driven company, Anheuser-Busch InBev manages a portfolio of over 200 brands that includes global flagship brands Budweiser, Stella Artois and Beck's, and has 120 000 employees based in operations in over 30 countries across the world.

Only a few years ago, the company's beer distributors and sales reps were turning their information in on stacks of paper invoices and sales orders. Keeping track of what products were selling and what marketing campaigns were effective was an arduous and time-consuming process. If a certain product wasn't going over well in a particular market, managers wouldn't even know it for months.

But all that changed at Anheuser-Busch with the introduction of BudNet, a corporate data network through which distributors and sales reps report in excruciating detail on everything from new orders and level of sales to competitors' shelf stock and current promotional efforts. Sales reps use handheld PDAs and laptops to enter data that are compiled and transmitted nightly to Anheuser corporate headquarters. Then, business intelligence software goes to work, helping brand managers find out what beer drinkers are buying, as well as when, where and why. Managers use the intelligence to constantly alter marketing strategies, design promotions to target the ethnic makeup of various markets, and get an early warning when rivals may be gaining an edge. For example, by cross-analyzing company data with US Census figures on the ethnic and economic makeup of neighbourhoods, Anheuser can tailor marketing campaigns with local precision. For instance, it knows that Tequiza sells well in San Antonio, and that the Fourth of July is a big beer sales holiday in Atlanta but St. Patrick's Day isn't; and that beer drinkers in blue-collar neighbourhoods prefer cans over bottles.[15]

Anheuser-Busch InBev now hopes to apply the same techniques in other international markets such as China, the largest beer market in the world. With strong local brands such as Harbin and Sedrin and global brands such as Budweiser, it is well positioned to benefit from the significant potential in this important market.

in Europe to introduce bar-coded boarding passes, resulting in quicker service for passengers and greater efficiency for KLM and from Schiphol Airport, Amsterdam, as well as from 46 other countries. The KLM internet Check-In tool enables passengers using an e-ticket departing from any of these enabled airports to print their boarding passes from their personal computers. The barcode offers a mechanism instead of using common boarding passes, so passengers do not need to use those anymore. Besides the barcode makes it possible to print from the internet, decreasing time spent in lines at the airport and thus increasing customer satisfaction.[16]

Things are More Efficient

Information technology can significantly speed work processes, cut costs and increase efficiency. Outsourcing continues to expand, often into unexpected areas McDonald's has been experimenting with a system where when you pull up to the drive-through at a few innovative McDonald's locations in the US and place your order, the person you talk to through the speakerphone is no longer in the restaurant where your order is being prepared. Instead, she is in a call centre thousands of miles away, in Colorado Springs, Colorado.

At the call centre, the operator takes your order and takes a digital picture of you in your car. She then sends the information back to the people preparing your order at the restaurant. The system saves just a few seconds per order, but over the course of time at a busy drive-through, that adds up to significant cost savings and increased sales.[17] As global communications systems become as cheap and reliable as those in the US, perhaps the next call centre for McDonald's drive-throughs will be offshore. In a couple of years, when you order at the drive-through window of a McDonald's restaurant, the voice coming out of the loudspeaker might originate in Mumbai or Delhi.

Sweeping away administrative paperwork, automating mundane tasks, and standardizing services are other advantages of information technology. For example, at IBM, automating customer service helped reduce the number of call centre employees and saved $750 million in one year alone. Hennes & Mauritz (H&M) is well known throughout Europe as a highly successful company selling low-priced fashion clothing and accessories. H&M was a pioneer in pursuing a strategy of vertical integration with the distribution network. This strategy has allowed the company to directly collect and fully exploit information about sales and consumers in order to improve and accelerate response to the market.

 INNOVATIVE WAY

Hennes & Mauritz – Virtualization of the Workplace

A central part of the Hennes & Mauritz success is the IT system that connects the individual stores with the logistics and procurement department. This system keeps track of sales and stock management centrally. Whenever an item is sold in a given store it is registered in the central system, which keeps track of the need for restocking and procurement.

There is also IT-integration between the central office in Stockholm and the 21 production offices. All communication between the departments takes place by IT, including the distribution of design sketches. It is foreseen that this integration will eventually include those suppliers with whom the most long-term relationships exist.

IT plays an important role in Hennes & Mauritz's efforts to reduce lead times. It is of the utmost competitive importance that there are always new goods on the shelves, that stores do not run out of items and that stores do not keep unsellable stock (i.e. having capital tied up in stock). This requires good market intelligence as well as tools for market prediction and inventory status, and for this IT is essential.

The common IT system facilitates this integration throughout the enterprise through both front-end and back-end data sharing and integration. Hennes & Mauritz can keep track of sales and integrate this

directly with procurement. Very little human interaction is needed as data are sent to a central database as soon as one given item is sold in a shop. This facilitates the tracking of local and central stock and integration with the production facilities, and it provides Hennes & Mauritz with market intelligence – e.g. which products seems to be a 'hit' and those which are more difficult to sell.

Market intelligence can also come from other sources. In order to gain insight into new trends in the fashion market. Hennes & Mauritz representatives spend much time at trade shows and exhibitions, and in Europe designers attend the main design exhibitions. Another source of information on market development is found in the countries (mainly Asia) where production takes place.

Hennes & Mauritz has local production offices whose main responsibility is negotiation with subcontractors and supervision of the code of conduct. However, an additional aspect of their work is to monitor local market development and send information back to the central administration in Stockholm.

A final aspect of virtualization is the new eCommerce initiative, which is currently only being offered to customers in Scandinavian countries. This is considered as an additional distribution channel, but is not expected to replace or abolish the need for the more traditional channels – the stores will continue to be regarded as the main distribution channel.[18]

H&M sells clothes and cosmetics in about 950 stores in 19 countries. The group has more than 40 000 employees and the turnover was SEK 56 550 million (€6.1 million) in 2003. Central functions are based in Sweden, but there is a national office in most of the sales countries. IT is a crucial tool along the entire value chain. Individual stores are connected with the logistics and procurement departments and the central warehouse. From central departments, it is possible to follow sales of individual items, thus feeding an intelligent procuring system. The company relies on IT integration between the central office and the production offices. Communication between departments takes place electronically, including design and product development.

Every stage in the logistic chain is controlled by H&M, acting as importer and wholesaler, as well as a retailer. Continuous IT development provides support to H&M logistics.

Employees are Engaged

Information technology is profoundly affecting the way organizations are structured. With IT, managers can change the locus of knowledge by providing information to people who would not otherwise receive it. Lower-level employees are increasingly challenged with more information and more interesting jobs. Nurses, truck drivers, utility repair workers, and warehouse staff all need easy access to information to do their jobs well in today's fast-paced environment.[19]

IT enables empowers employees to make decisions and provide better customer service. To empower employees, Staples, the world's largest office supply retails store chain, with over 2000 stores worldwide in 27 countries, wants to put the Web at their fingertips.

When a customer in a Staples store wants more details on a product or warranty, the retailer doesn't want store assistants scurrying off to a desktop PC to check a corporate database. Instead, the assistants will now be able to research what they need from a hand-held web-based device, the iPAD from Fujitsu Transaction Solutions Inc. 'The iPAD will improve the operational productivity of our store associates, enabling them to spend more time interacting with our customers,' says Staples CIO Scott Floeck.

Staples is rolling out iPAD devices to all its stores. Fujitsu says the iPADs can be used anywhere in a store for virtually any back-office retail operation, including checking inventory, verifying prices, processing mobile POS transactions and accessing gift registries. The iPADs can also be used to log onto Staples.com to show a store shopper how to use the site or to check online merchandizing.[20]

People can Suffer from Information Overload

Getting data and information to people who need it and can use it to improve their performance and decision-making is important, but it's possible to have too much of a good thing. One major problem associated with advances in technology is that the company can become a quagmire of information, with employees so overwhelmed by the sheer volume that they are unable to sort out the valuable from the useless.[21]

In many cases, the ability to produce data and information is outstripping employees' ability to process it. One British psychologist claims to have identified a new mental disorder caused by too much information; he has termed it *information fatigue syndrome*.[22] Information technology is a primary culprit in contributing to this new 'disease'. However, managers have the ability to alleviate the problem and improve information quality. The first step is to ensure that suppliers of information technology and CIOs work closely with employees to identify the kinds of questions they must answer and the kinds of data and information they really need. Specialists often are enamoured with the volume of data a system can produce and overlook the need to provide small amounts of quality information in a timely and useful manner for decision-making. Top executives should be actively involved in setting limits by focusing the organization on key strategies and on the critical questions that must be answered to pursue those strategies.[23]

Management Information Systems

A **management information system (MIS)** is a computer-based system that provides information and support for effective managerial decision-making. The central elements of a management information system are illustrated in Exhibit 20.1.

MISs typically support strategic decision-making needs of mid-level and top management. However, as technology becomes more widely accessible, more employees are wired into networks, and organizations push decision-making downward in the hierarchy, these kinds of systems are seeing use at all levels of the organization. For example, when a production supervisor needs to make a decision about production scheduling, he or she may need data on the anticipated number of orders in the coming month, inventory levels, and availability of computers and personnel. The MIS can provide these data.

Management information systems typically include decision support systems executive information systems and groupware.

Decision support systems (DSSs) are interactive, computer-based **information reporting systems** that rely on decision models and specialized databases to support decision-makers. With electronic spreadsheets and other decision support software, users can pose a series of what-if questions to test alternatives they are considering. Based on the assumptions used in the software or specified by the user, managers

> **Management information system (MIS)**
> A computer-based system that provides information and support for effective managerial decision-making.

> **Decision support system (DSS)**
> An interactive, computer-based system that uses decision models and specialized databases to support organization decision-makers.

> **Information reporting system**
> A system that organizes information in the form of prespecified reports that managers use in day-to-day decision-making.

Exhibit 20.1 Basic Elements of Management Information Systems

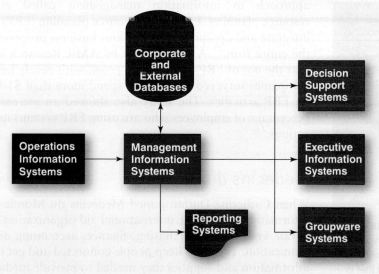

SOURCE: Adapted from Ralph M. Stair and George W. Reynolds, *Principles of Information Systems: A Managerial Approach*, 4th ed. (Cambridge, MA: Course Technology, 1999), p. 391.

Executive information system (EIS)
A management information system designed to facilitate strategic decision-making at the highest levels of management by providing executives with easy access to timely and relevant information.

Business performance dashboard
A system that pulls data from a variety of organizational systems and databases; gauges the data against key performance metrics; pulls out the right nuggets of information; and delivers information to managers in a graphical, easy-to-interpret format.

Groupware
Software that works on a computer network or the internet to facilitate information sharing, collaborative work, and group decision-making.

Enterprise resource planning (ERP) system
A networked information system that collects, processes, and provides information about an organization's entire enterprise, from identification of customer needs and receipt of orders to distribution of products and receipt of payments.

can explore various alternatives and receive tentative information to help them choose the alternative with the best outcome. Big retailers such as Tesco, Carrefour and Gap use decision support systems to help them gauge when to mark down prices and what items to discount, for example.

Executive information systems (EISs) are management information systems to facilitate strategic decision-making at the highest level of management. These systems are typically based on software that provides easy access to large amounts of complex data and can analyze and present information in a timely fashion. EISs provide top management with quick access to relevant internal and external information and, if designed properly, can help them diagnose problems as well as develop solutions. Many companies use executive information systems that enable top managers to view a *dashboard* of key performance indicators on their PCs or laptops. A **business performance dashboard** uses software to present key business information (e.g. sales data, fill rates for orders or profits per product line) in graphical, easy-to-interpret form and can alert managers to any deviations or unusual patterns in the data. Dashboards pull data from a variety of organizational systems and databases, gauge the data against key performance metrics, and pull out the right nuggets of information to deliver to top managers for analysis and action.[24] The effective use of business performance dashboards is further discussed in this chapter's Manager's Shoptalk.

Modern information technology systems also recognize that many organizational and managerial activities involve groups of people working together to solve problems and meet customer needs. **Groupware** is software that works on a computer network or via the internet to link people or workgroups across a room or around the globe. The software enables managers or team members to communicate, share information, and work simultaneously on the same document, chart or diagram and see changes and comments as they are made by others. Sometimes called *collaborative work systems*, groupware systems allow people to interact with one another in an electronic meeting space and at the same time take advantage of computer-based support data.

Enterprise Resource Planning Systems

Another key IT component for many companies is an approach to information management called enterprise resource planning. **Enterprise resource planning (ERP) systems** integrate and optimize all the various business processes across the entire firm.[25] A recent study by AMR Research indicates that the use of ERP continues to grow, with nearly half of the companies surveyed planning to spend more than $10 million on ERP activities. The study also showed an increase in the percentage of employees who are using ERP systems in organizations.[26]

Medecins du Monde

When Catherine Duffau joined Medecins du Monde as chief information officer, the international aid organization had disparate systems for purchasing, finance, accounting and communication. Trying to keep people connected and get them the information and supplies they needed to provide medical services to victims of war, famine and drought in 59 countries was overwhelming the staff and its limited resources.

CONCEPT CONNECTION When carefully implemented, ERP can cut costs, shorten cycle time, enhance productivity and improve relationships with customers and suppliers. One organization that is reaping benefits from an ERP system is Medecins du Monde (Doctors of the World).

MANAGER'S SHOPTALK

Putting Performance Dashboards to Work

It's first thing in the morning. You sit down at your computer, coffee cup in hand, and click on an icon. Attractively arrayed on the screen is current information organized under various headings – for example, 'Calendar', 'Tasks', 'Key Performance Indicators', 'Sales by Manager', and those always eye-catching 'Alerts'. Critical information about your business is presented in colourful tables, pie charts, graphs and other visual displays. With just a glance, you're up-to-date on everything you need to know before you start your day. If you're puzzled by a particular figure or alarmed by an alert, you just click on the item and start 'drilling down' into the data until you get a detailed picture of exactly what is going on. Welcome to the world of business performance dashboards.

Estimates suggest that nearly half of the world's 2000 largest companies already use Web-based business performance dashboards, and observers expect dashboards to become even more ubiquitous. In addition, organizations are increasingly sharing this new tool – originally designed to help top executives steer their organizations toward strategic goals – with lower-level managers and employees to help them be more effective and in control. However, as impressive as the technology is, it's the way organizations design and use these tools that determines whether they turn out to be a boon or a distracting bane. Here are some tips.

- **Don't contribute to information overload.** Because dashboards collate information from many databases and programmes, it's all too easy to construct a webpage that delivers too much information. To make dashboards useful, carefully choose what data will be tracked and what information will be displayed. Make sure it's what employees need to know to do their jobs better.

- **Let line managers and employees drive the development.** Always remember that designing a

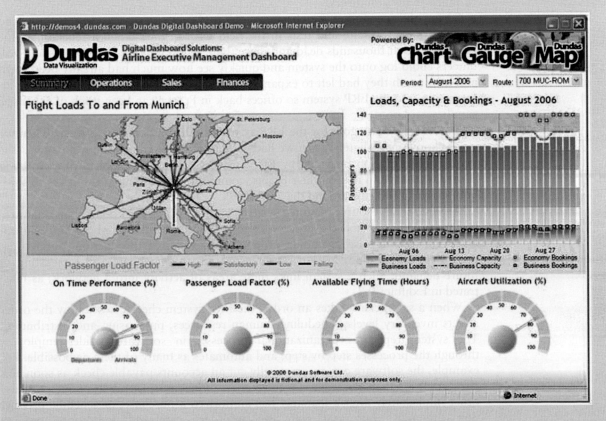

SOURCE: Dundas Data Visualization, www.dundas.com.

dashboard is primarily a strategic project, not a technical one. The IT department can help implement the dashboard, but it is the responsibility of managers to determine its content. One way to make sure people get the right information is to solicit input from end users during the design process.

■ *Carefully assess who needs a dashboard.* At General Electric, business unit chiefs use dashboards, but CEO Jeffrey Immelt rarely does. Immelt doesn't want to get so mired in the details that he loses sight of the big picture. On the other hand, using dashboards to push information farther down into the organization can help employees at all levels see from day to day in concrete terms exactly how their actions contribute to an organization's success or failure in achieving its goals.

■ *Don't forget the human touch.* Having all the latest facts and figures at your fingertips is certainly valuable, but it's only part of what managers need to know to run an effective organization. Getting out and talking to employees and customers is still just as important.

SOURCES: Spencer E. Ante, 'Giving the Boss the Big Picture', *BusinessWeek* (February 13, 2006): 48–51; Tad Leahy, 'Warming Up to Performance Dashboards', *Business-FinanceMag.com* (June 1, 2006), http://businessfinancemag.com/article/warming-performance-dashboards-0601; and Doug Bartholomew, 'Gauging Success', *CFO-IT* (Summer 2005): 17–19.

Duffau believed an ERP system would solve the problem by helping integrate functions as well as collect precise data on doctors' needs and expenses in the field. She selected a small ERP system provided by French software maker Qualiac, which was known for its ease of use, thus making it more manageable for Medecins du Monde's many volunteers.

So far, the accounting, purchasing, stock and investment records are set up and running on the system, and tests in the field have begun. When a rebellion in the Ivory Coast left thousands dead and more than a million homeless, doctors and volunteers could log onto the system and quickly see how much had already been spent and how much they had left to expand treatment when needed. Volunteers enter information into the ERP system so offices back in France can keep track of expenses, supplies, and needs.

Duffau's ultimate goal for the ERP system is information in real time. 'Then we would know immediately when we had enough money to expand our missions,' she says. The integration provided by ERP answers the urgent problem of connecting people who have to rely on their brains, commitment and limited resources to solve huge human problems around the world.[27]

An enterprise resource planning system can become the backbone of an organization's operations. It collects, processes and provides information about an organization's entire enterprise, including orders, product design, production, purchasing, inventory, distribution, human resources, receipt of payments and forecasting of future demand. Such a system links these areas of activity into a network, as illustrated in Exhibit 20.2.

When a salesperson takes an order, the ERP system checks to see how the order affects inventory levels, scheduling, human resources, purchasing and distribution. The system replicates organizational processes in software, guides employees through the processes step by step, and automates as many of them as possible. For example, the software can automatically cut an accounts payable check as soon as a clerk confirms that goods have been received in inventory, send an online purchase order immediately after a manager has authorized a purchase, or schedule production at the most appropriate plant after an order is received.[28] In addition, because the system integrates data about all aspects of operations, managers and employees

Exhibit 20.2 Example of ERP Applications

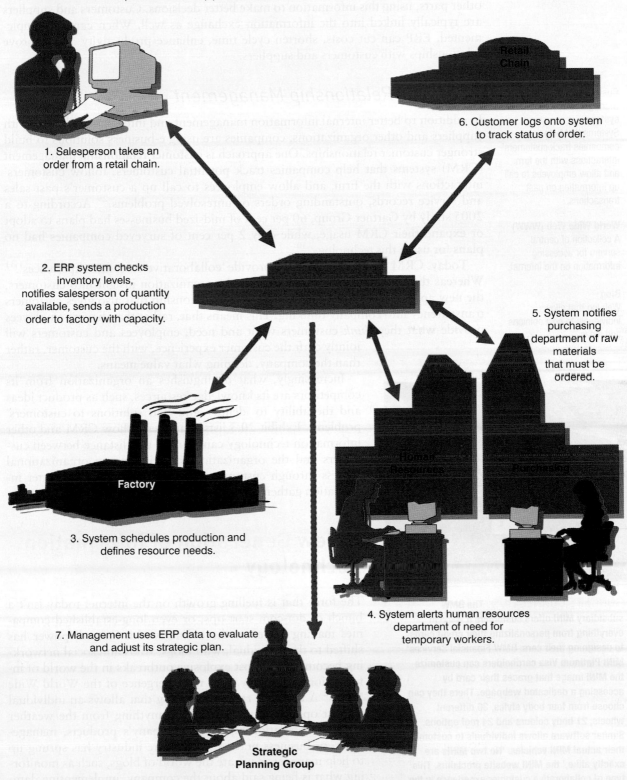

1. Salesperson takes an order from a retail chain.

2. ERP system checks inventory levels, notifies salesperson of quantity available, sends a production order to factory with capacity.

6. Customer logs onto system to track status of order.

5. System notifies purchasing department of raw materials that must be ordered.

3. System schedules production and defines resource needs.

4. System alerts human resources department of need for temporary workers.

7. Management uses ERP data to evaluate and adjust its strategic plan.

Retail Chain

Factory

Human Resources

Purchasing

Strategic Planning Group

SOURCE: Adapted from Gail Edmondson, 'Silicon Valley on the Rhine', *BusinessWeek* (November 2, 1997): 162–166.

at all levels can see how decisions and actions in one part of the organization affect other parts, using this information to make better decisions. Customers and suppliers are typically linked into the information exchange as well. When carefully implemented, ERP can cut costs, shorten cycle time, enhance productivity and improve relationships with customers and suppliers.

Customer relationship management (CRM) systems
Systems that help companies track customers' interactions with the firm and allow employees to call up information on past transactions.

World Wide Web (WWW)
A collection of central servers for accessing information on the internet.

Blog
Web log that allows individuals to post opinions and ideas.

Customer Relationship Management

In addition to better internal information management and information sharing with suppliers and other organizations, companies are using e-business solutions to build stronger customer relationships. One approach is **customer relationship management (CRM) systems** that help companies track potential customers, follow customers' interactions with the firm, and allow employees to call up a customer's past sales and service records, outstanding orders or unresolved problems.[29] According to a 2005 study by Gartner Group, 60 per cent of midsized businesses had plans to adopt or expand their CRM usage, while only 2 per cent of surveyed companies had no plans for using this technology.[30]

Today, CRM tools are evolving to provide 'collaborative customer experiences'.[31] Whereas the traditional CRM model gives the organization insight into customers, the new approach will provide for a two-way relationship that also gives customers transparency into company thinking. This means that, rather than having employees provide what they *think* customers want and need, employees and customers will jointly craft the customer experience, with the customer, rather than the company, defining what value means.

Increasingly, what distinguishes an organization from its competitors are its knowledge resources, such as product ideas and the ability to identify and find solutions to customers' problems. Exhibit 20.3 lists examples of how CRM and other information technology can shorten the distance between customers and the organization, contributing to organizational success through customer loyalty, superior service, better information gathering and organizational learning.

© SERGIO DIONISIO/GETTY IMAGES

CONCEPT CONNECTION The BMW subsidiary MINI offers customers a voice in everything from personalizing their credit cards to designing their cars. BMW Financial Services' MINI Platinum Visa cardholders can customize the MINI image that graces their card by accessing a dedicated webpage. There they can choose from four body styles, 36 different wheels, 21 body colours and 24 roof options. Similar software allows individuals to customize their actual MINI vehicles. 'No two MINIs are exactly alike,' the MINI website proclaims. This type of collaborative customer experience is the next step in customer relationship management (CRM), as companies court internet-savvy Gen X and Gen Y consumers.

A New Generation of Information Technology

The force that is fuelling growth on the internet today isn't a bunch of dot-com start-ups, or even long-established companies making waves in the online world. Instead, power has shifted to the individual, with blogs, wikis and social networking becoming the most explosive outbreaks in the world of information technology since the emergence of the **World Wide Web**.[32] A **blog** is a running web log that allows an individual to post opinions and ideas about anything from the weather and dating relationships to a company's products, management, or business practices. An entire industry has sprung up to help managers navigate the world of blogs, such as monitoring what is being said about the company, implementing damage control strategies and tracking what the majority of the world is thinking, minute by minute, to help the organization respond to emerging trends and opportunities.[33] In addition,

Exhibit 20.3 Competitive Advantages Gained from Customer Relationship Management (CRM) Systems

Competitive advantage	Example
• **Increase in customer loyalty**	Full information about customer profile and previous requests or preferences is instantly available to sales and service representatives when a customer calls.
• **Superior service**	Customer representatives can provide personalized service, offer new products and services based on customer's purchasing history.
• **Superior information gathering and knowledge sharing**	The system is updated each time a customer contacts the organization, whether the contact is in person, by phone or via the Web. Sales, marketing, service and technical support have access to shared database.
• **Organizational learning**	Managers can analyze patterns to solve problems and anticipate new ones.

Social networking
Online interaction in a community format where people share personal information and photos, produce and share all sorts of information and opinions, or unify activists and raise funds.

managers at companies such as McDonald's, Marriott International, and even the once-secretive Boeing are posting blogs of their own to communicate with employees and customers and present the company's side of the story to the public.[34]

Companies are also tapping into the power of new IT applications as powerful collaboration tools within organizations, using group blogs, wikis, social networking and peer-to-peer file sharing. The simplicity and informality of blogs make them an easy and comfortable medium for people to communicate and share ideas, both with colleagues and outsiders. As described earlier, a *wiki* is similar to a blog and uses software to create a website that allows people to create, share, and edit content through a browser-based interface. Rather than simply sharing opinions and ideas as with a blog, wikis are free-form, allowing people to edit what they find on the site and add content.[35] The best-known example of a wiki is the online encyclopedia Wikipedia, where thousands of volunteer contributors have written, edited and policed more than nine million entries in more than a hundred languages.[36] Boeing and BMW both use wiki software to open much of their design work to partner organizations.

Social networking, also referred to as *social media* or *user-generated content*, is an extension of blogs and wikis.[37] Sites such as MySpace, Facebook and Friendster provide an unprecedented peer-to-peer communication channel, where people interact in an online community, sharing personal data and photos, producing and sharing all sorts of information and opinions, or unifying activists and raising funds. MySpace, now owned by News Corp., had 72 million members within only two years, with an estimated quarter of a

© ALEX SEGRE/ALAMY

CONCEPT CONNECTION Jeffrey Kalmikoff and Jake Nichell, owners of Threadless, built a $30 million business through a social network where users are both customers and part of the supply chain. Their online T-shirt business uses Facebook, Twitter, Flickr, MySpace and the company website to interact with the Threadless community. Designers submit designs for T-shirts, and online participants vote for the best designs. Winners receive a cash prize of $2500 and reprint fees for designs that are printed on T-shirts. Threadless has been connecting online with designers since 2000 and opened its first retail location in Chicago in 2007.

Exhibit 20.4 Types of Information Systems

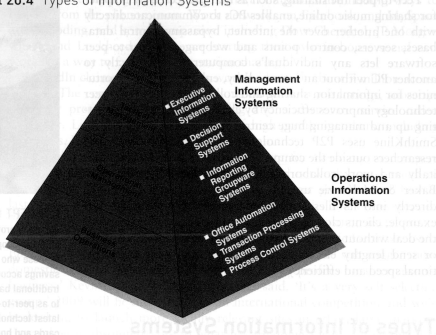

Management
Information
Systems

- Executive Information Systems
- Decision Support Systems
- Information Reporting Groupware Systems

Operations
Information
Systems

- Office Automation Systems
- Transaction Processing Systems
- Process Control Systems

© JIM WILEMAN/ALAMY

CONCEPT CONNECTION Just how completely will the internet and information technology revolutionize banking? Egg Banking plc is a British internet bank, established in 1996, and is now the world's largest internet bank in that it is only possible to operate an Egg account over the internet, or via their call centre. Egg specializes in savings, credit cards and loans but also offers mortgage and insurance products. To be sure, Egg does have to overcome security concerns, compensate for the lack of ATM machines, and compete against improved online services at traditional banks. Still they believe that the new internet bank model can prosper through lower overheads and by targeting affluent, computer-savvy professionals who value its time-saving convenience.

parts of the country such as holiday towns like Blackpool might need a larger percentage of slightly irreverent, youth-oriented products.

Mobile Banking in Africa with M-Pesa

Kenya pioneered mobile banking with M-Pesa, for 'mobile money', the world's first cellular money-transfer service. Offered by Safaricom – a subsidiary of the British giant Vodafone and Kenya's dominant cell-phone company – M-Pesa allows customers to send anywhere from $1.25 to $440 to any cell phone number in Kenya, with fees that start at less than 40 cents. In less than two years, the service has registered 5.5 million customers, one-sixth of the country. The average transaction is only about $30, yet each day M-Pesa moves more than $4 million among Kenyans through a network of licensed agents.

Before, when Malit Kuronoi needed to pay the cowherd who watched over his cattle in faraway northern Kenya, he made the 500-mile round trip himself. For four days, Mr Kuronoi rode ramshackle buses across roads patrolled by bandits and bribe-seeking cops, sometimes sleeping by the roadside when a bus broke down, just to deliver the money. Now he sends it by mobile phone. The Kenyan farmer is among millions who are at the forefront of a pocket-sized financial revolution that's sweeping Africa. Mobile banking, powered by cell phones, is allowing people who could never afford traditional bank accounts to send, receive and save money, often just by writing text messages.

Cheap and efficient m-banking services are cropping up from South Africa to Senegal. They're the latest example of how the cell phone has transformed life in sub-Saharan Africa, where over the past decade mass-market mobile networks have stitched together countries and families long separated by distance, poverty and shoddy infrastructure. Less than one-fifth of Africans have bank accounts, and far fewer access the internet. The continent, however, recently surpassed the US and Canada with 340 million cell phone users and is adding another 70 million each year, according to Wireless Intelligence, a market research group.

Cell phone companies are racing to capitalize by offering banking tools that make it easier for city dwellers to send money to rural relatives, small businesses to pay their employees, and parents to deposit their children's school fees. The amounts are relatively small, and the commissions are a fraction of those that major banks and wire services such as Western Union charge. 'It's absolutely changed lives,' said Aly Khan Satchu, a Kenyan financial analyst. 'This is bringing banking services to the "un-banked" and the poor. It's very empowering.'

Safaricom doesn't expect M-Pesa to become a major profit earner – it only recently ended its first month in the black – but it's spawned a host of imitators. Vodafone has introduced the concept in Afghanistan and Tanzania, and the rival Orange network plans to launch mobile banking in Cote d'Ivoire, Senegal, and Mali. Safaricom is exploring a low-cost service to transfer money to and from Britain, which is home to tens of thousands of expatriate Kenyans. Experts say that the services have improved financial security dramatically for rural families because urban relatives, freed from having to travel to deliver the money themselves, can send more cash more often.[44]

Operations Information Systems

A variety of tools referred to as operations information systems support the information-processing needs related to a business's day-to-day operations. Types of operations information systems include transaction-processing systems, process control systems, and office automation systems. Each of these supports daily operations and decisions that typically are made by non-management employees or lower-level managers.

Transaction-processing systems (TPSs) record and process data resulting from business operations, including such data as sales to customers, purchases from suppliers, inventory changes and wages to employees. A TPS collects data from these transactions and stores them in a database. Employees use the database to produce reports and other information, such as customer statements and employee pay cheques. Most of an organization's reports are generated from these databases. Transaction-processing systems identify, collect and organize the fundamental information from which an organization operates.

While a transaction-processing system keeps track of the size, type and financial consequences of the organization's transactions, companies also need information about the quantity and quality of their production activities. Therefore, they may use process control systems to monitor and control ongoing physical processes. For example, petroleum refineries, pulp and paper mills, food manufacturing plants, and electric power plants use **process control systems** with special sensing devices that monitor and record physical phenomena such as temperature or pressure changes. The system relays the measurements or sensor-detected data to a computer for processing; employees and operations managers can check the data to look for problems requiring action.

Office automation systems combine modern hardware and software such as word processors, desktop publishers, email and teleconferencing to handle the tasks of publishing and distributing information. Office automation systems can also use data from other operations systems to transform manual accounting procedures to

Transaction-processing system (TPS)
A type of operations information system that records and processes data resulting from routine business transactions such as sales, purchases and payroll.

Information
Data that have been converted into a meaningful and useful context for the receiver.

Process control system
A computer system that monitors and controls ongoing physical processes, such as temperature or pressure changes.

Office automation systems
Systems that combine modern hardware and software to handle the tasks of publishing and distributing information.

strategic approaches for traditional organizations setting up an internet operation are illustrated in Exhibit 20.6. Some companies embrace e-business primarily to expand into new markets and reach new customers. Others use e-business as a route to increased productivity and cost efficiency.

E-business Strategy: Market Expansion

Print media organizations use websites as an expansion strategy to reach new customers, as well. An internet division allows a company to establish direct links to customers and expand into new markets. The organization can provide access around the clock to a worldwide market. *The Economist* is an English-language weekly news and international affairs publication owned by The Economist Newspaper Ltd and edited in London. Continuous publication began in September 1843. *The Economist* once bragged about its limited circulation. In 1920 it only had 6000 readers. After the second world war, it rose rapidly, but from a base of barely 18 000, and not reaching 100 000 until 1970. However, today circulation is over a million, more than four-fifths of it outside Britain. Sales inside North America were around 54 per cent of the total, with sales in the UK making up 14 per cent of the total and continental Europe 19 per cent. *The Economist* claims sales, both by subscription and on newsstands, in over 200 countries. Global sales have doubled since 1997 and much of this growth has been linked to the launch of an online edition, Economist.com.

CONCEPT CONNECTION The BBC recently launched the iPlayer, its long-promised video on demand service, which will allow viewers to catch up with any TV or radio show from the past seven days. The download service, essentially a TV version of the BBC's 'listen again' radio service, which allows licence fee payers to tune in to live radio or any show from the previous seven days over the Web, will transfer selected shows to computers to be viewed at will.

Economist.com

Economist.com publishes all articles from *The Economist* print edition (including those printed only in British copies) plus a searchable archive of all *The Economist*'s articles back to June 1997. Links to other articles and to relevant sources on the Web are included with many of the stories.

However, the online edition is not simply an internet copy of the printed magazine. Other Economist.com services include:

- **News analysis** – analysis of important news stories and issues, updated throughout the working week (http://www.economist.com).
- **Today's views** – comprising online-only columns, Correspondent's Diary and Fair Exchange, a forum for debating economics (http://www.economist.com).
- **Country Briefings** – articles, background profiles, forecasts and statistics, market and currency updates, newswires and links on 60 countries (http://www.economist.com/countries).
- **Global Executive** – articles on management reading and business education (http://www.economist.com/business/globalexecutive).
- **Backgrounders** – concise briefings on key issues in the news, with links to relevant articles in Economist.com's archive (http://www.economist.com/research/backgrounders).
- **Currency data** – currency comparison and conversion tools.
- **Web feeds** – news headlines from around the web.

- **Diversions** – Infrequently Asked Questions: a daily news and current affairs multiple-choice quiz, articles on sports and games, crosswords and more (http://www.economist.com/diversions).
- **Mobile Edition** – Daily articles published on Economist.com can be viewed on a PDA or mobile device (http://www.economist.com/mobile/).
- **Email newsletters and alerts** – (http://www.economist.com/email).
- **RSS feeds** – Notifies users when new articles or audio content are published on Economist.com (http://www.economist.com/rss).

Since July 2007, there has also been a complete audio edition of the magazine available 5p.m. London time on Fridays, the next day after the print magazine is published. It is free for subscribers and available for a fee for non-subscribers.

 ## INNOVATIVE WAY

JC Penney

Not so long ago, the century-old JC Penney department store chain had so many troubles that some analysts predicted it wouldn't survive. Today, however, the retailer is thriving, thanks in part to managers' mastery of e-business.

Penney was one of the first traditional retailers to launch a website in 1994. Though that initial site sold only one product – Power Rangers – it gave the company invaluable experience for expansion once the internet really took off. Today, Penney has one of the most productive online stores among mainstream retailers. The website has enabled the company to attract a younger customer base than those who typically shop at Penney and find ways to lure them into bricks-and-mortar stores. Penney embraced the internet wholeheartedly, encouraging cooperation between its website and stores from the beginning. It was the one of the first to allow customers to pick up and return items bought online at their local store, and it was the first to give online shoppers a way to check which clothes are in stock at local stores. It's no wonder Penney's ranks among the top five websites in terms of the number of paying customers it attracts.[49]

Many retailers have also been big winners with a market expansion strategy. For example, as illustrated above, US department store chain JC Penney was one of the first traditional retailers to launch a website.

Like JC Penney, most retailers selling products online also now use their websites to drive more traffic into stores. Bloomingdale's tapped into the social networking phenomenon by sponsoring a three-day event that allowed people to try on outfits in front of an interactive mirror that connected them to their friends via the internet. Many other big retailers, such as Argos, also now let online shoppers pick up purchases at the local store. Getting people to the store gives staff a chance to push accessory items and increase sales.[50]

Go to the Ethical Dilemma on page 795 that pertains to using the internet for market expansion.

TAKE A MOMENT

E-business Strategy: Increasing Efficiency

With this approach, the e-business initiative is seen primarily as a way to improve the bottom line by increasing productivity and cutting costs. Automakers such as Toyota,

General Motors and Ford, for example, use e-business to reduce the cost of ordering and tracking parts and supplies and to implement just-in-time manufacturing.

Several studies attest to real and significant gains in productivity from e-business.[51] Even the smallest companies can realize gains. Rather than purchasing parts from a local supplier at premium rates, a small firm can access a worldwide market and find the best price, or negotiate better terms with the local supplier.[52] Service firms and government agencies can benefit too. Research by Maliranta and Rouvinen found is strong evidence for the productivity-enhancing impacts of e-technology in Finland. After controlling for industry and time effects, the additional productivity of e-technology equipped labour ranges from 8 per cent to 18 per cent.[53]

Implementing E-Business Strategies

When traditional organizations such as Ikea, BBC or Toyota want to establish an internet division, managers have to decide how best to integrate bricks and clicks – that is, how to blend their traditional operations with an internet initiative.[54] One approach is to set up an *in-house division*. This approach offers tight integration between the online business and the organization's traditional operation. Managers create a separate department or unit within the company that functions within the structure and guidance of the traditional organization. This approach gives the new division several advantages by piggybacking on the established company, including brand recognition, purchasing leverage with suppliers, shared customer information and marketing opportunities. Office Depot, for example, launched an online unit for market expansion as a tightly integrated in-house part of its overall operation. Managers and employees within the company are assigned to the unit to handle website maintenance, product offerings, order fulfilment, customer service and other aspects of the online business.[55]

A second approach is through *partnerships*, such as joint ventures or alliances. Safeway partnered with the British supermarket chain Tesco, described in the previous chapter, to establish its online grocery business in the US. Safeway first tried to go it alone, but found that it needed the expertise of an established online player with a proven business model.[56] In many cases, a traditional company will partner with an established internet firm to reach a broader customer base or to handle activities such as customer service, order fulfilment, and website maintenance. Companies such as Timberland and Reebok partner with GSI Commerce, which stores goods, takes orders and then picks, packs and ships orders directly to customers. The bricks-and-mortar companies get the expertise and services of a world-class internet business without having to hire more people with IT expertise and build the capabilities themselves.[57]

Going International

When businesses were first rushing to set up websites, managers envisioned that doing business all over the world would be easy. Soon, though, they awakened to the reality that national boundaries matter just as much as they ever did. The global e-market can't be approached as if it were one homogeneous area.[58]

© SIMELA PANTZARTZI/EPA/CORBIS

CONCEPT CONNECTION Many of the world's largest corporations depend on Siemens Business Services to manage their advanced information technology infrastructures. Turning to outside experts such as Siemens helps companies keep up with constantly-evolving technology as they keep their IT costs down. This advertisement promotes Siemens' SieQuence solution, which provides an integrated suite of services, from managing networks and knowledge management systems, to integrated enterprise resource planning and real-time management of the entire IT infrastructure. Within a year of its introduction in the US, SieQuence was making up 30 per cent of the company's total US revenue, prompting a global launch in 2004.

Organizations that want to succeed with international e-business are tailoring their websites to address differences in language, regulations, payment systems and consumer preferences in different parts of the world. For example, Amazon, Dell, Google, Tesco and Walt Disney have all set up country-specific sites in the local language. Washingtonpost.com gives its news a broader global flavour during the overnight hours when international readers frequent the site. EBay is struggling with currency issues, as it has alienated many potential users in other countries by quoting prices only in US dollars. And companies with online stores are finding that they may need to offer a different product mix and discounts tailored to local preferences. The internet is a powerful way to reach customers and partners around the world, and managers are learning to address the cross-national challenges that come with serving a worldwide market.

E-marketplaces

The biggest boom in e-commerce has been in business-to-business (B2B) transactions, or buying and selling between companies. Business-to-business transactions are at $2.4 trillion and growing, according to Forrester Research Inc.[59] One significant trend is the development of **B2B marketplaces**, in which an intermediary sets up an electronic marketplace where buyers and sellers meet, acting as a hub for B2B commerce. Exhibit 20.7 illustrates a B2B marketplace, where many different sellers offer products and services to many different buyers through a *hub*, or online portal. Conducting business through a Web marketplace can mean lower transaction costs, more favourable negotiations, and productivity gains for both buyers and sellers. For example, the high technology manufacturer and defence contractor United Technologies, which does business in over 180 countries and generates 64 per cent of its $58.7 annual sales from outside the US, buys around $450 million worth of metals, motors and other products annually via an e-marketplace and gets prices about 15 per cent less than what it once paid.[60]

Alibaba, the Chinese company, which is the world's largest online platform for trade between businesses, intends to take advantage of the global financial crisis as an opportunity to transform itself from a China-focused e-commerce provider into a global Web marketplace. As part of its drive for geographical diversification, Alibaba is moving its European headquarters from Geneva to London this month, as it sees the UK as one of the most promising markets for picking up suppliers.

B2B marketplace
An electronic marketplace set up by an intermediary where buyers and sellers meet.

Exhibit 20.7 B2B Marketplace Model

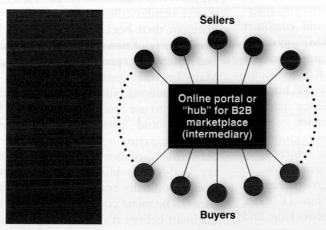

Alibaba Group, which also includes Taobao, China's leading consumer e-commerce website, and Yahoo China, plans to increase its current workforce of 12 000 by more than 4000 this year. Alibaba.com, the Hong Kong-listed flagship which operates the business-to-business trading platform, reported revenues of Rmb2.2 billion ($321 million) for the first nine months of 2008.

Although Alibaba serves buyers and sellers all over the world, Chinese companies seeking buyers overseas account for the bulk of its revenues so far. But as demand from the US and Europe has dropped off, the company has launched programmes to support domestic trade and exports from other countries to China.[61]

In addition to open, public B2B marketplaces such as eBay, some companies set up private marketplaces to link with a specially invited group of suppliers and partners.[62] For example, General Motors spends billions a year on public marketplaces, but it also operates its own private marketplace, GMSupplyPower, to share proprietary information with thousands of its parts suppliers. E-marketplaces can bring efficiencies to many operations, but some companies find that they don't offer the personal touch their type of business needs.

A MANAGER'S ESSENTIALS: WHAT HAVE WE LEARNED?

- This chapter described several points about information technology and e-business. Managers rely on information technology for the efficient management and control of operations. Information technology and e-business has transformed management and contributes to enhanced collaboration and knowledge sharing. Sophisticated information technology systems can gather huge amounts of data and transform them into useful information for decision-makers. Management information systems that support operations and decision-making include decision support systems, executive information systems and collaborative work systems.

- Important IT solutions for improving business operations and customer relations are enterprise resource planning (ERP) and customer relationship management (CRM) systems. Knowledge management is also an important application for new technology. Key technologies for knowledge management are business intelligence software and knowledge management portals on the corporate intranet.

- Collaborative work systems allow groups of managers or employees to share information, collaborate electronically, and have access to computer-based support data for group decision-making and problem solving. New IT tools, including blogs, wikis, social networking and peer-to-peer file sharing, extend the power of the organization's collaborative systems.

- Most organizations have incorporated the internet and e-business as part of their information technology strategy. Traditional organizations use an online division primarily for market expansion or to increase productivity and reduce costs.

In the opening example, Wal-Mart learned how quickly bad news can spread on the internet. Marshall Manson, a senior account supervisor at Edelman, the company's PR firm, decided to turn the power of blogs to Wal-Mart's advantage. Manson emailed a number of bloggers who were known to support Wal-Mart and asked if they would like to receive regular communications from the company. Edelman then began feeding these bloggers exclusive nuggets of news, suggesting topics for postings and promoting positive aspects of the company. Many organizations have used blogs to help shape public opinion, but Wal-Mart was the first major company to use blogging as a general PR tool. Some bloggers and observers are incensed by the approach, saying a blog should be about the blogger's own voice, not someone else's. Others, though, say Wal-Mart's blogging initiative is no different from a company sending a press release to a newspaper. The tactic could backfire, but Wal-Mart and Edelman believe it's a valid approach to telling the retailer's side of the story. 'As more and more Americans go to the internet to get information from varied, credible, trusted sources,' a Wal-Mart spokeswoman said, 'Wal-Mart is committed to participating in that online conversation.'[63]

DISCUSSION QUESTIONS

1 Business writer Nicholas Carr argued that because computers and software have become so available and affordable, it's getting harder to achieve a competitive edge by being a technology leader. Do you agree or disagree? Explain your answer.

2 What types of information technology do you as a student use on a regular basis? How might your life be different if this technology were not available to you?

3 How do you think the growth of sophisticated management information systems (MIS) has changed the importance of personal experience and intuition in decision-making? In other words, does MIS make decision-making more of a science than an art? Discuss.

4 How might the organizers of an upcoming Olympics use an extranet to get all the elements of the event up and running on schedule?

5 If you were a manager in charge of new product marketing, what are some ways you might harness the power of blogs and social networking sites to help market your latest products?

6 The openness of wikis is both their strength and their weakness. As a business owner, why might you want to take advantage of this new technology? How might you guard against potential problems, such as vulnerability to mistakes, pranks, self-serving posts or cyber-vandalism?

7 You are a manager assigned the task of deciding how to blend your organization's traditional operations with a new internet initiative for both purchasing and sales. What are the main factors you would consider? What information would you collect?

8 Define the difference between explicit knowledge and tacit knowledge and give an example of each from your own experience. How can knowledge management systems be designed to promote the sharing of both explicit and tacit knowledge?

9 Do you believe information overload is a problem for today's students? For managers or employees in an organization where you have worked? How might people deal with information overload?

10 How is e-business affecting the way organizations are structured and the way jobs are designed?

11 Have you ever used peer-to-peer (P2P) file-sharing technology? Discuss your experiences – positive and negative – with P2P.

12 How might large organizations such as Wal-Mart use technology to effectively monitor and respond to what is being discussed about them in the media and on internet blogs?

MANAGEMENT IN PRACTICE: EXPERIENTIAL EXERCISE

What is Your MIS Style?

For each of the following 14 statements, circle the number that indicates how much you agree that each statement is characteristic of you. The questions refer to how you use information and make decisions.

Disagree Strongly 1 2 3 4 5 Agree Strongly

1 I like to wait until all relevant information is examined before deciding something.

1 2 3 4 5

2 I prefer information that can be interpreted in several ways and leads to different but acceptable solutions.

1 2 3 4 5

3 I like to keep gathering data until an excellent solution emerges.

1 2 3 4 5

4 To make decisions, I often use information that means different things to different people.

1 2 3 4 5

5 I want just enough data to make a decision quickly.

1 2 3 4 5

6 I act on logical analysis of the situation rather than on my 'gut feelings' about the best alternative.

1 2 3 4 5

7 I seek information sources or people that will provide me with many ideas and details.

1 2 3 4 5

8 I try to generate more than one satisfactory solution for the problem faced.

1 2 3 4 5

9 When reading something, I confine my thoughts to what is written rather than search for additional understanding.

1 2 3 4 5

10 When working on a project, I try to narrow, not broaden, the scope so it is clearly defined.

1 2 3 4 5

11 I typically acquire all possible information before making a final decision.

1 2 3 4 5

12 I like to work on something I've done before rather than take on a complicated problem.

1 2 3 4 5

13 I prefer clear, precise data.

1 2 3 4 5

14 When working on a project, I like to explore various options rather than maintain a narrow focus.

1 2 3 4 5

Scoring and Interpretation

Your information-processing style determines the extent to which you will benefit from computer-based information systems. First, subtract each of your scores for questions 5, 6, 9, 10, 12 and 13 from the number 6 and indicate the adjusted score next to each question. Use the adjusted scores to calculate your totals as follows:

The odd-numbered questions pertain to the 'amount of information' you like to use. Your total score for odd-numbered questions: _____. A score of 28 or more suggests you prefer a large amount of information. A score of 14 or less indicates you like a small amount.

The even-numbered questions pertain to the 'focus of information' you prefer. Your total score for even-numbered questions: _____. A score of 28 or more suggests you are comfortable with ambiguous, multi-focused information, while a score of 14 or less suggests you like clear, uni-focused data.

If you are a person who likes a large amount of information and clear, focused data, you will tend to make effective use of management information systems. You could be expected to benefit greatly from an EIS or MIS in your company. If you are a person who prefers a small amount of information and data that are multi-focused, you would probably not get the information you need to make decisions through formal information systems. You probably won't utilize EIS or MIS to a great extent, preferring instead to get decision data from other convenient sources, including face-to-face discussions.

SOURCES: This questionnaire is adapted from Richard L. Daft and Norman B. Macintosh, 'A Tentative Exploration into the Amount and Equivocality of Information Processing in Organizational Work Units', *Administrative Science Quarterly* 26 (1981): 207–224; and Dorothy Marcic, *Organizational Behavior: Experiences and Cases*, 4th ed. (St. Paul, MN: West, 1995).

MANAGEMENT IN PRACTICE: ETHICAL DILEMMA

Manipulative or not?

As head of the marketing department for Butter Crisp Snack Foods, 55-year-old Frank Bellows has been forced to learn a lot about the internet in recent years. Although he initially resisted the new technology, Frank has gradually come to appreciate the potential of the internet for serving existing customers and reaching potential new ones. In fact, he has been one of the biggest supporters of the company's increasing use of the internet to stay in touch with customers.

However, something about this new plan just doesn't feel right. At this morning's meeting, Keith Deakins, Butter Crisp's CEO, announced that the company would soon be launching a website geared specifically to children. Although Deakins has the authority to approve the site on his own, he has asked all department heads to review the site and give their approval for its launch. He then turned the meeting over to the information technology team that developed the new site, which will offer games and interactive educational activities. The team pointed out that although it will be clear that Butter Crisp is the sponsor of the site, the site will not include advertising of Butter Crisp products. So far, so good, Frank thinks. However, he knows that two of the young hotshot employees in his department have been helping to develop the site and that they provided a list of questions that children will be asked to answer online. Just to enter the website, for example, a user must provide name, address, gender, email address and favourite TV show. In return, users receive 'Crisp Cash', a form of virtual money that they can turn in for toys, games, Butter Crisp samples and other prizes. After they enter the site, children can earn more Crisp Cash by providing other information about themselves and their families.

Frank watched the demonstration and agreed that the website does indeed have solid educational content. However, he is concerned about the tactics for gathering information from children when that information will almost certainly be used for marketing purposes. So far, it seems that the other department heads are solidly in favour of launching the website. Frank is wondering whether he can sign his approval with a clear conscience. He also knows that several groups, including the Children's Charities Coalition for Internet Safety are calling for stricter governmental controls regarding collecting information from children via the internet.

What would you do?

1 Stop worrying about it. There's nothing illegal about what Butter Crisp is proposing to do, and any personal information gathered will be closely guarded by the company. Children can't be harmed in any way by using the new website.

2 Begin talking with other managers and try to build a coalition in support of some stricter controls, such as requiring parental permission to enter areas of the site that offer Crisp Cash in exchange for personal information.

3 Contact the Children's Charities Coalition for Internet Safety and tell them you suspect Butter Crisp intends to use the website to conduct marketing research. The lobby group might be able to apply pressure that would make it uncomfortable enough for Deakins to pull the plug on the new kid's website.

SOURCE: Based on Denise Gellene, 'Internet Marketing to Kids Is Seen as a Web of Deceit', *Los Angeles Times*, March 29, 1996.

CASE FOR CRITICAL ANALYSIS 20.1

Acme Equipment and Leasing

Ravi Ahmed, managing director of Acme Equipment and Leasing, which owns several agricultural equipment dealerships across the European Union, tried computers 15 years ago. He didn't like them, and he didn't think he needed information technology to run his business.

But as the company grew, Ravi realized he had taken on more debt than he was comfortable with, so he hired a chief financial officer named Sarah Kennedy. Ravi also got back into the information technology, investing £150 000 in a proprietary inventory and accounting system. When Ravi and Sarah approached AgriBank's Global Equipment Finance Division seeking better financing for the company, Ravi was surprised that Agribank seemed to be more interested in Acme's information technology capacity than it was in how many million-euro machines the company had sold. As an Agribank representative explained, 'The theory goes that if you can trust the computer systems, you can trust the company's numbers.'

Acme wanted to borrow a significant amount of money, so Agribank sent information technology consultants to evaluate the company's systems and make sure they were capable of generating the sort of accurate monthly financial reports required by the firm for such a sizable loan. Acme was already on the right track with the new inventory and accounting system, so the necessary data were in the database. However, the consultants soon learned that it was difficult to translate the data into quality information. For instance, if someone wanted a list of accounts receivable that were past due, the database would spit out 500 pages of indecipherable codes and numbers. 'None of the answers just popped out of the computer,' recalls Kennedy.

Kennedy began using a software program called Kingdom (ironically, already installed on the computer) to turn the data into useful information printed on neat, readable spreadsheets. In the process, Acme not only qualified for a £5 million loan, but also discovered some of its own poor business practices. For example, Ravi and Sarah found more than £100 000 worth of outdated, unused parts that could be returned to manufacturers. As Acme's ability to turn data into quality information has increased, the leaders are able to see at a moment's notice how the company is performing. They can see immediately which pieces of equipment are being sold or leased and which are not – and on which sales lots. In addition, salespeople, who now carry laptops, can enter sales figures directly into a customer's file using contract management software. When a salesperson gives a customer a quote, it is automatically emailed to Ravi. As soon as Ravi opens the email, the quote is deposited in the central database for later reference.

With the success of Kingdom and other management information systems, Ravi is now thinking about moving into the world of e-business. He has read about extranets, webpages, customer relationship management software, and the like, and he wonders how these new technologies might help his business.

Questions

1 With its newfound reliance on information technology, do you think Acme might fall into a trap of poor information quality or information overload? Why or why not?

2 How does information technology contribute to Acme's knowledge management? What other strategic advantages does MIS provide?

3 What would you recommend to Acme as a first step into e-business? Why?

SOURCES: Adapted from Joshua Macht, 'The Accidental Automator', *Inc. Tech*, no. 2 (1997): 66–71.

ENDNOTES

1. Michael Barbaro, 'Wal-Mart Enlists Bloggers in P.R. Campaign', *The New York Times* (March 7, 2006): www.nytimes.com; Daniel McGinn, 'Wal-Mart Hits the Wall', *Newsweek* (November 14, 2005): 42; Reed Abelson, 'One Giant's Struggle Is Corporate America's Too; Rewriting the Social Contract – The Wal-Mart Challenge', *The New York Times* (October 29, 2005): C1; www.walmartwatch.com; and Jerry Useem, 'Should We Admire Wal-Mart?' *Fortune* (March 8, 2004): 118ff.

2. Adapted from Carolyn Hopper, *Practicing Management Skills*, (New York, Houghton Mifflin, 2003) and Jacquelyn Wonder and prescilla Donovan, 'Mind Openers', *Self* (March 1984).

3. http://www.commissionforafrica.org/english/report/background/coleman_background.pdf (accessed February 18, 2010).

4. Christopher Palmeri, 'Believe in Yourself, Believe in the Merchandise', *Continental* (December 1997): 49–51; Timothy J. Mullaney with Heather Green, Michael Arndt, Robert D. Hof and Linda Himelstein, 'The E-Biz Surprise', *Business Week*, (May 12, 2003): 60–68.

5. 'The Web Smart 50'; Timothy J. Mullaney, 'E-Biz Strikes Again', *Business Week* (May 10, 2004): 80–82; and Mullaney *et al.*, 'The E-Biz Surprise'.

6. Thomas L. Friedman, 'It's a Flat World, After All', *The New York Times Magazine* (April 3, 2005): www.nytimes.com/2005/04/03/magazine.

7. *Ibid.*

8. Based on Andrew Mayo, 'Memory Bankers', *People Management* (January 22, 1998): 34–38; William Miller, 'Building the Ultimate Resource', *Management Review* (January 1999), 42–45; and Todd Datz, 'How to Speak Geek', *CIO Enterprise*, Section 2 (April 15, 1999), 46–52.

9. Richard McDermott, 'Why Information Technology Inspired But Cannot Deliver Knowledge Management', *California Management Review* 41, no. 4 (Summer 1999), 103–117.

10. Thomas H. Davenport, Laurence Prusak and Bruce Strong, 'Business Insight (A Special Report): Organization; Putting Ideas to Work: Knowledge Management Can Make a Difference – But It Needs to Be More Pragmatic', *The Wall Street Journal* (March 10, 2008).

11. Meridith Levinson, 'Business Intelligence: Not Just for Bosses Anymore', *CIO* (January 15, 2006): 82–86.

12. John Edwards, 'Picture This', *CFO* (November 2005): 80–83.

13. Julie Schlosser, 'Looking for Intelligence in Ice Cream', *Fortune* (March 17, 2003): 114–120.

14. Reported in Schlosser, 'Looking for Intelligence in Ice Cream' *Fortune* (March 17, 2003): 114–120.

15. Kevin Kelleher, '66,207,896 Bottles of Beer on the Wall', *Business 2.0* (January–February 2004): 47–49.

16. http://www.accenture.com/NR/rdonlyres/53CE5486-4A48-4F3A-85F7-B0B8475103EB/0/KLMathighaltitudes.pdf (accessed February 18, 2010).

17. Matt Richtel, 'The Long-Distance Journey of a Fast-Food Order', *The New York Times* (April 11, 2006): www.nytimes.com.

18. http://www.eurofound.europa.eu/emcc/content/source/eu04013a.htm (accessed February 18, 2010).

19. Liz Thach and Richard W. Woodman, 'Organizational Change and Information Technology: Managing on the Edge of Cyberspace', *Organizational Dynamics* (Summer 1994): 30–46; and Elizabeth Horwitt, 'Going Deep: Empowering Employees', *Microsoft Executive Circle* (Summer 2003): 24–26.

20. http://www.internetretailer.com/internet/marketing-conference/23306-empower-employees-staples-puts-web-at-their-fingertips.html (accessed February 18, 2010).

21. Tonya Vinas, 'Surviving Information Overload', *Industry Week* (April 2003): 24–29.

22. Joseph McCafferty, 'Coping with Infoglut', *CFO* (September 1998): 101–102.

23. Leonard M. Fuld, 'The Danger of Data Slam', *CIO Enterprise* (September 15, 1998): 28–33.

24. Spencer E. Ante, 'Giving the Boss the Big Picture', *BusinessWeek* (February 13, 2006): 48–51; Doug Bartholomew, 'Gauging Success', *CFO-IT* (Summer 2005): 17–19; Russ Banham, 'Seeing the Big Picture: New Data Tools Are Enabling CEOs to Get a Better Handle on Performance Across Their Organizations', *Chief Executive* (November 2003): 46.

25. This discussion is based on Judy Sweeney and Simon Jacobson, 'ERP Breaks', *Industry Week* (January 2007): 11a–13a; and Vincent A. Mabert, Ashok Soni and M. A. Venkataramanan, 'Enterprise Resource Planning: Common Myths Versus Evolving Reality', *Business Horizons* (May–June 2001): 69–76.

26. Sweeney and Jacobson, 'ERP Breaks'.

27. Susannah Patton, 'Doctors' Group Profits From ERP', *CIO* (September 1, 2003): 32.

28. Derek Slater, 'What Is ERP?', *CIO Enterprise* (May 15, 1999): 86.

29. Brian Caulfield, 'Facing Up to CRM', *Business 2.0* (August–September 2001): 149–150; and 'Customer Relationship Management: The Good. The Bad. The Future'. *BusinessWeek* (April 28, 2003): 53–64.

30. Ellen Neuborne, 'A Second Act for CRM', *Inc.* (March 2005): 40.

31. The discussion of collaborative customer experiences is based on Paul Greenberg, 'Applied Insight: Move Over, Baby Boomers', *CIO* (March 1, 2006), http://www.cio.com.

32. Anya Kamenetz, 'The Network Unbound', *Fast Company* (June 2006): 68ff; and Stephen Baker and Heather Green, 'Blogs Will Change Your Business', *BusinessWeek* (May 2, 2005): 56–67.

33. Baker and Green, 'Blogs Will Change Your Business'.

34. Stanley Holmes, 'Into the Wild Blog Yonder', *BusinessWeek* (May 22, 2006): 8486; and Erin White, Joann S. Lublin and David Kesmodel, 'Executives Get the Blogging Bug', *The Wall Street Journal*, July 13, 2007.

35. Cindy Waxer, 'Workers of the World – Collaborate', *FSB* (April 2005): 57–58.

36. Evelyn Nussenbaum, 'Technology to Boost Teamwork', *Forbes Small Business* (February 2008): 51–54; and Russ Juskalian, 'Wikinomics Could Change Everything As Concept of Sharing Spreads', *USA Today*, January 2, 2007, http://www.usatoday.com (accessed January 2, 2007).

37. This discussion of social networks is based on Kamenetz, 'The Network Unbound'.

38. Brad Stone, 'Facebook Expands Into MySpace's Territory', *The New York Times* (May 25, 2007); and Heather Green, 'The Water Cooler is Now on the Web', *BusinessWeek* (October 1, 2007).

39. Kevin J. Delaney, 'Garage Brand; With NBC Pact, YouTube Site Tries to Build a Lasting Business', *The Wall Street Journal* (June 27, 2006): A1, A13.

40. *Ibid.*

41. Spencer E. Ante *et al.*, 'In Search of the Net's Next Big Thing' *BusinessWeek* (March 26, 2001): 140–141; Amy Cortese, 'Peer to Peer: P2P Taps the Power of Distant Computers in a Way That Could Transform Whole Industries', *The BusinessWeek 50, Supplement to BusinessWeek* (Spring 2001): 194–196.

42. Mark Roberti, 'Peer-to-Peer Isn't Dead', *The Industry Standard* (April 23, 2001): 58–59.

43. Thomas H. Davenport and Jeanne G. Harris, 'Automated Decision Making Comes of Age', *MIT Sloan Management Review* (Summer 2005): 83–89.

44. http://www.csmonitor.com/2009/0213/p25s19-woaf.html (accessed February 18, 2010).

45. John P. Mello Jr., 'Fly Me to the Web', *CFO* (March 2000): 79–84.

46. Heather Harreld, 'Pick-Up Artists', *CIO* (November 1, 2000): 148–154; and Carol J. Loomis, 'The Big Surprise Is Enterprise', *Fortune* (July 24, 2006): 140–150.

47. Jim Turcotte, Bob Silveri, and Tom Jobson, 'Are You Ready for the E-Supply Chain?', *APICS–The Performance Advantage* (August 1998): 56–59.

48. This discussion is based on Long W. Lam and L. Jean Harrison-Walker, 'Toward an Objective-Based Typology of E-Business Models', *Business Horizons* (November–December 2003): 17–26; and Detmar Straub and Richard Klein,

'E-Competitive Transformations', *Business Horizons* (May–June 2001): 3–12.

49. Robert Berner, 'J. C. Penney Gets the Net', *Business Week* (May 7, 2007): 70; and 'jppeney.Com Celebrates 10th Anniversary Of Online Shopping', *Business Wire* (November 8, 2004).

50. Nanette Byrnes, 'More Clicks at the Bricks', *Business Week* (December 17, 2007): 50–52.

51. Jonathan L. Willis, 'What Impact Will E-Commerce Have on the US Economy?', *Economic Review – Federal Reserve Bank of Kansas City* 89, no. 2 (Second Quarter 2004): 53ff; 2005 productivity gains reported in Mullaney *et al.*, 'The E-Biz Surprise'.

52. Straub and Klein, 'E-Competitive Transformations'.

53. http://ideas.repec.org/a/taf/ecinnt/v15y2006i6p605-616.html (accessed February 18, 2010).

54. This discussion of implementation approaches is based on Ranjay Gulati and Jason Garino, 'Get the Right Mix of Bricks and Clicks', *Harvard Business Review* (May–June 2000): 107–114.

55. *Ibid.*

56. 'Business: Surfing USA', *The Economist* (June 30, 2001): 58; and James R. Hagerty and James Hall, 'British Supermarket Giant Cooks Up Plans to Go Global – Tesco's Move to Duplicate High Growth at Home Comes with Big Risks', *The Wall Street Journal* (July 5, 2001): A9.

57. Banham, 'Old Dogs, New Clicks'.

58. This discussion is based on Mauro F. Guillén, 'What Is the Best Global Strategy for the Internet?', *Business Horizons* (May–June 2002): 39–46; and Bob Tedeschi, 'American Web Sites Speak the Language of Overseas Users', *The New York Times* (January 12, 2004): www.nytimes.com.

59. Statistic reported in Mullaney *et al.*, 'The E-Biz Surprise'. This discussion is based on Pamela Barnes-Vieyra and Cindy Claycomb, 'Business-to-Business E-Commerce: Models and Managerial Decisions', *Business Horizons* (May–June 2001): 13–20.

60. http://www.ft.com/cms/s/0/3d1ec800-e5b2-11dd-afe4-0000779fd2ac.html (accessed February 18, 2010).

61. Reported in Hamm *et al.*, 'E-Biz: Down But Hardly Out'.

62. Eric Young, 'Web Marketplaces That Really Work', *Fortune/CNET Tech Review* (Winter 2001): 78–86.

63. Barbaro, 'Wal-Mart Enlists Bloggers in P.R. Campaign'; and David Watkins, 'Media: How Big Business Barged In on the Bloggers: Companies Once Saw Them as a Nuisance', *The Guardian* (March 20, 2006): 6.

CHAPTER OUTLINE

© STEVECOLECCS/ISTOCK

LEARNING OBJECTIVES

After reading this chapter, you should be able to:

1 Define *operations management* and describe its application within manufacturing and service organizations.

2 Discuss the role of operations management strategy in the company's overall competitive strategy.

3 Explain the role of e-business in today's partnership approach to supply chain management.

4 Summarize considerations in designing an operations system, including product and service design, facilities layout and capacity planning.

5 Explain why small inventories are preferred by most organizations.

6 Discuss major techniques for the management of materials and inventory.

7 Describe what is meant by lean manufacturing.

8 Define *productivity* and explain why and how managers seek to improve it.

CHAPTER 21

OPERATIONS AND VALUE CHAIN MANAGEMENT

Manager's Challenge

After nearly 30 years in business, West Marine is thriving. Randy Repass started the company from his garage, selling nylon rope by mail order, and gradually expanded into a robust wholesale business and then opening of retail stores, offering everything from foul weather gear and boat safety equipment to electronics. Now, West has acquired one of its oldest and most respected competitors, E&B Marine. Whereas West's target customer has always been a sailor with a large, coastal boat, E&B has served primarily power boaters with small craft. The merger gives West 150 stores across the country, making it nearly 300 per cent larger than its closest competitor and a one-stop shopping destination for everything to do with boating except the boat itself. But managers wonder whether business has been a little too good. Distribution has become chaotic, and stores are having trouble keeping items in stock, with out-of-stock levels during peak season climbing to more than 12 per cent. As the business has expanded, getting the right orders from suppliers at the right time has also become a nightmare. The on-time fill rate for vendor orders at West's distribution centres has dropped to about 35 per cent. Sales have started to decline because the stores don't have the right equipment and supplies when customers want them.[1]

If you were a manager at West Marine, how would you help the retail stores get the equipment and supplies they need when they need them? How can West's managers get suppliers to do a better job of delivering the right products to distribution centres on time, and then make sure products get from the centres into the stores where they're needed?

TAKE A MOMENT

Networking and Political Skills

Managing a supply chain, for example, means asserting influence and gaining cooperation without having formal authority over suppliers, which requires interpersonal and political skills. How good are you at influencing people horizontally across an organization? To learn something about your skills, answer the questions that follow. Answer whether each item that follows is Mostly True or Mostly False for you.

		Mostly True	Mostly False
1	I am able to communicate easily and effectively with others.	☐	☐
2	I spend a lot of time at work developing connections with people outside my area.	☐	☐
3	I instinctively know the right thing to say or do to influence others.	☐	☐
4	I am good at using my connections outside my area to get things done at work.	☐	☐
5	When communicating with others, I am absolutely genuine in what I say and do.	☐	☐
6	It is easy for me to reach out to new people.	☐	☐
7	I make strangers feel comfortable and at ease around me.	☐	☐
8	I am good at sensing the motivations and hidden agendas of others.	☐	☐

SCORING AND INTERPRETATION Give yourself one point for each item marked as Mostly True. A score of 6 or higher suggests active political skills and a good start for your career as a new manager. If you scored 3 or less, you may want to focus more on building horizontal relationships as you progress in your career.

Political skills help a new manager build personal and organizational networks and relationships that enhance the team's outcomes. New managers often learn task and people skills first. Political and networking skills tend to be subtle and are typically mastered after gaining management experience.

SOURCE Adapted from Gerald R. Ferris, Darren C. Treadway, Robert W. Kolodinsky, Wayne A. Hochwarter, Charles J. Kacmer, Ceasar Douglas and Dwight D. Frink, 'Development and Validation of the Political Skill Inventory', *Journal of Management* 31 (February 2005): 126–152.

Like West Marine, many companies with successful products and services find themselves with out-of-date, inefficient operations systems that contribute to performance problems. Strategic success depends on efficient operations. The importance of operational efficiency is illustrated by the chaos that surrounds many relief efforts following major disasters. Aid groups are typically deluged with donated supplies but have a hard time getting them to where they're needed. The global cargo industry, including companies such as express shipper DHL and the giant logistics company TNT, has embarked on an innovative volunteer effort to help governments and private aid groups improve their operations to respond faster and more effectively to major disasters. As a repository of knowledge on how to move huge loads to remote places fast, these companies can help in areas such as improving air-traffic logistics after a disaster, keeping track of supplies and effectively and rationally distributing aid.[2]

For all organizations, operational concerns such as obtaining parts and supplies, updating production technology and implementing efficient delivery systems take on extreme importance in today's competitive, global environment. Production costs are a major expense for organizations, especially for manufacturers, but service organizations such as West Marine have to be concerned with productivity and efficiency too. Organizations therefore try to limit costs and increase quality by improving how they obtain materials, set up production facilities, and produce goods and services. Likewise, companies are seeking a strategic advantage in the ways they deliver products and services to consumers. In the manufacturing sector, the efficiency of Toyota's car production is legendary. Wal-Mart is a leader in operations excellence in the service sector, with executives using sophisticated technology to manage a supremely efficient supply and distribution network that enables the company to keep costs and prices at rock bottom. Manufacturing and service operations such Wal-Mart, Toyota and West Marine are important because they signify the company's basic purpose – indeed, its reason for existence. Without the ability to produce products and services that are competitive in the global marketplace, companies cannot expect to succeed.

Whereas the two preceding chapters described overall control concepts, including management information systems, this chapter will focus on the management and control of production operations. First we define operations management. Then we look at how some companies bring operations into strategic decision-making and provide an overview of the integrated enterprise, in which managers use electronic linkages to manage interrelated operations activities. Next, we consider specific operational design issues, such as product and service design, procurement, location planning and facilities layout, production technology and capacity planning. We give special attention to inventory management, including a discussion of just-in-time inventory systems and logistics. Finally, we look at how managers measure and improve productivity.

The Organization as a Value Chain

In Chapter 1, the organization was described as a system used for transforming inputs into outputs. At the centre of this transformation process is the **technical core**, which is the heart of the organization's production of its product or service.[3] In an automobile company, the technical core includes the plants that manufacture automobiles. In a university, the technical core includes the academic activities of teaching and research.

As illustrated in Exhibit 21.1, the organization can be thought of as a *value chain* that receives inputs from the environment, such as raw materials and other resources, and adds value by transforming them into products and services for customers. Inputs into the technical core typically include materials and equipment, human resources, land and buildings and information. Outputs from the technical core are the goods and services produced by the organization and sold or provided to customers and clients. Operations strategy and control feedback shape the quality of outputs and the efficiency of operations within the technical core.

The topic of operations management pertains to the day-to-day management of the technical core, as illustrated in Exhibit 21.1, including acquiring inputs, transforming them, and distributing outputs. **Operations management** is formally defined as the field of management that specializes in the production of goods and services and uses special tools and techniques for solving production problems. In essence, operations managers are concerned with all the activities involved in converting inputs into outputs, including decisions about matters such as how and where to obtain raw materials, where to locate facilities and what equipment to install in

Technical core
The heart of the organization's production of its product or service.

Operations management
The field of management that focuses on the physical production of goods or services and uses specialized techniques for solving manufacturing problems.

Exhibit 21.1 The Organization as a Value Chain

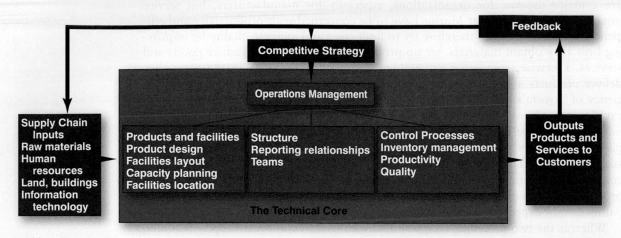

them, and how to get products or services to customers. For example, PepsiCo has got into the farming business in order to get the raw materials it needs to build its snack foods business in emerging markets. Sales of Western-style snack foods are growing fast in China and other developing countries, and Pepsi wants to be the global leader. However, getting the tens of millions of potatoes needed to serve the Chinese market alone turned out to be a major problem. Today, Pepsi is the largest private potato grower in China and also has potato programmes in Russia, South Africa and Poland.[4] Pepsi's operations managers also have to consider the best location to manufacture snack foods for global markets, how to get raw materials to manufacturing facilities, and how to efficiently produce products and get them onto store shelves.

As with all areas of management, operations management also requires the ability to lead people. For example, Toyota's operations are admired worldwide as a model of quality and efficiency, but this success is not merely a result of using the right machines or setting the right standards. US car makers have had difficulty duplicating Toyota's success with *lean manufacturing* because they have focused primarily on the technical elements of the system and failed to implement the necessary cultural and leadership changes.[5] Toyota's system combines techniques, systems and philosophy, such as commitment to employee empowerment and a creative culture. Besides installing the methodology for running an efficient assembly line, such as *just-in-time* shipments of supplies, managers must instil the necessary attitudes, such as concern for quality and a desire to innovate.

Manufacturing and Service Operations

Although terms such as *production* and *operations* seem to imply manufacturing organizations, operations management applies to all organizations. The service sector has increased three times as fast as the manufacturing sector in some economies such as the US and the UK. Today, more than half of all businesses are service organizations and with two-thirds of the US workforce is employed in services, such as hospitals, hotels and resorts, retail, financial services or telecommunications firms. Operations management tools and techniques apply to services as well as manufacturing. Exhibit 21.2 shows differences between manufacturing and service organizations.

Exhibit 21.2 Differences Between Manufacturing and Service Organizations

Manufacturing Organizations	Service Organizations
Produce physical goods	Produce nonphysical outputs
Goods inventoried for later consumption	Simultaneous production and consumption
Quality measured directly	Quality perceived and difficult to measure
Standardized output	Customized output
Production process removed from consumer	Consumer participates in production process
Facilities site moderately important to business success	Facilities site crucial to success of firm
Capital intensive	Labour intensive
Examples:	*Examples:*
Automobile manufacturers	Airlines
Steel companies	Hotels
Soft-drink companies	Law firms

SOURCES: Based on Richard L. Daft, *Organization Theory and Design* (Cincinnati, OH: South-Western, 2005): 256; and Byron J. Finch and Richard L. Luebbe, *Operations Management* (Fort Worth, TX: The Dryden Press, 1995): 50.

Manufacturing organizations are those that produce physical goods, such as cars, books, computers or tennis balls. In contrast, **service organizations** produce nonphysical outputs, such as medical, educational, communication or transportation services provided for customers. Doctors, consultants, online auction companies and the local barber all provide services. Services also include the sale of merchandize. Although merchandize is a physical good, the service company does not manufacture it but merely sells it as a service to the customer.

Services differ from manufactured products in two ways. First, the service customer is involved in the actual production process.[6] The patient actually visits the doctor to receive the service, and it's difficult to imagine a hairstylist providing services without direct customer contact. The same is true for airlines, restaurants and banks. Second, manufactured goods can be placed in inventory, whereas service outputs, being intangible, cannot be stored. Manufactured products such as clothes, food, cars or iPods all can be put in warehouses and sold at a later date. However, a hairstylist cannot wash, cut and style hair in advance and leave it on the shelf for the customer's arrival, nor can a doctor place examinations in inventory. The service must be created and provided for the customer exactly when he or she wants it.

Despite the differences between manufacturing and service firms, they face similar operational problems. First, each kind of organization needs to be concerned with scheduling. A medical clinic must schedule appointments so that doctors' and patients' time will be used efficiently. Second, both manufacturing and service organizations must obtain materials and supplies. Third, both types of organizations should be concerned with quality and productivity. Because many operational problems are similar, operations management tools and techniques can and should be applied to service organizations as readily as they are to manufacturing operations.

Manufacturing organization
An organization that produces physical goods.

Service organization
An organization that produces non-physical outputs that require customer involvement and cannot be stored in inventory.

As a new manager, think about your team as part of a value chain that receives inputs, adds value, and provides outputs to customers or clients. Help your team implement operating techniques to achieve superior customer responsiveness, innovation, quality, and efficiency.

Operations Management and Competitive Strategy

Many operations managers are involved in day-to-day problem solving and lose sight of the fact that the best way to control operations is through strategic planning. When operations managers become enmeshed in operational details, they are less likely to see the big picture with respect to inventory build-ups, parts shortages and seasonal fluctuations. To manage operations effectively, managers understand the importance of competitive strategy.

Operations strategy
The recognition of the importance of operations to the firm's success and the involvement of operations managers in the organization's strategic planning.

Operations strategy means that operations managers are directly involved in the organization's strategic planning by developing plans and tactics that increase operational effectiveness and help the company attain its strategic goals. Superior operations effectiveness can support existing strategy, as well as contribute to new strategic directions that can be difficult for competitors to copy.[7] When an organization's operations effectiveness is based on capabilities that are ingrained in its employees, its culture, and its operating processes, the company can be tough to beat.[8]

Managers focus on four major outcomes to build a highly effective operations system:[9]

- *Achieving superior customer responsiveness.* The operations system should be designed so that the organization can satisfy customer needs, giving customers what they want, when they want it, at an acceptable price. Companies that are more responsive to customers and provide good value are more competitive. Enterprise has become the largest and most profitable rental car company in the US based largely on an intense focus on customers, especially those who have lost the use of their vehicles due to a traffic accident. The idea of picking customers up at their homes was a stroke of genius, and Enterprise has successfully transferred this business model into other countries.[10]

- *Achieving superior innovation with speed and flexibility.* Innovation leads to new and better products and services as well as better ways of producing them and delivering them to customers. Innovation is a top priority for many organizations today, including big, established companies like John Deere, the leading manufacture of agricultural machinery in the world. Deere is building tractors with computer systems that enable farmers to analyze fertilizer, soil composition and yields in each section of their fields, and producing forestry equipment that allows operators to select and cut trees in a way that fosters regrowth.[11] As discussed in Chapter 11, successful innovation, including the ability to introduce new or improved products fast, means a company can differentiate itself from rivals and attract more customers.

- *Achieving superior quality.* Quality means producing products or services that are highly reliable and have features or characteristics that customers desire. Offering high-quality products builds brand-name reputation, which means the company can typically charge higher prices for its products or services. For example, Hyundai Motor Company's high-volume, low-cost Hyundai brand jumped from eleventh place to third place, behind Porsche and Toyota, in the 2006 J. D. Power & Associates Initial Quality Study. Hyundai's reputation for quality is growing rapidly, nearly approaching that of Toyota, enabling the company to increase prices and profits.[12] Today's organizations are using a variety of techniques, such as quality circles, Six Sigma principles and benchmarking, as described in Chapter 19, to improve quality in products, service, and processes.

■ *Achieving superior efficiency*. As discussed in Chapter 1, efficiency refers to the amount of resources used to achieve organizational goals. As applied to the operations system, efficiency measures the amount of inputs used to produce a given amount of outputs, as illustrated in Exhibit 21.1. An organization that uses fewer inputs for a given level of outputs is more efficient, meaning its costs will be lower and it can provide outputs to customers at a more competitive price and still make money. Enterprise improved efficiency with an innovative computer system called ARMS (automated rental management system), as described in Chapter 20. ARMS, which links all of the car rental's locations and connects Enterprise to major car insurers, saves employees an average of eight to nine phone calls per rental, which adds up to time and money for Enterprise.[13]

The Integrated Enterprise

To adopt a strategic approach, operations managers appreciate that their operations are not independent of other activities. To operate efficiently, innovate and produce high-quality items that meet customers' needs, the organization must have reliable deliveries of high-quality, reasonably priced supplies and materials. It also requires an efficient and reliable system for distributing finished products, making them readily accessible to customers.

Supply Chain Management

Operations managers with a strategic focus therefore recognize that they need to manage the entire supply chain. **Supply chain management** is the term for managing the sequence of suppliers and purchasers covering all stages of processing from obtaining raw materials to distributing finished goods to final consumers.[14]

The most recent advances in supply chain management involve using internet technologies to achieve the right balance of low inventory levels and customer responsiveness. An e-supply chain creates a seamless, integrated link that stretches from customers to suppliers, by establishing electronic linkages between the organization and these external partners for the sharing and exchange of data.[15] Dell's integrated supply chain, illustrated in Exhibit 21.3 provides an excellent example. Dell has struggled in recent years due to poor strategic decisions, but it thrived for decades because managers found the most efficient way to make, sell, and deliver personal computers.

Despite Dell's recent problems, AMR Research still ranks it as the third best-performing supply chain in the world, with Apple ranked at number 1, Nokia at number 2, Wal-Mart at number 6, and the British supermarket chain Tesco at number 12.[16]

Enterprise integration through the use of electronic linkages is creating a level of cooperation not previously imaginable for many organizations. Supplier relationships used to be based on an *arm's-length* approach, in which an organization spreads purchases among many suppliers and encourages them to compete with one another. With integration, more companies are opting for a *partnership* approach, which involves cultivating intimate relationships with a few carefully selected suppliers and collaborating closely to coordinate tasks that benefit both parties.

Supply chain management
Managing the sequence of suppliers and purchasers, covering all stages of processing from obtaining raw materials to distributing finished goods to final consumers.

Exhibit 21.3 Dell Computer's Integrated Supply Chain

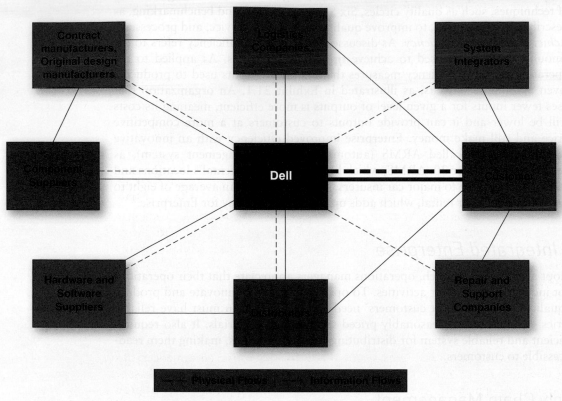

SOURCE: Jason Dedrick and Kenneth L. Kraemer, 'The Impacts of IT on Firm and Industry Structure: The Personal Computer Industry', *California Management Review* 47, no. 3 (Spring 2005); 132. Used with permission.

 INNOVATIVE WAY

Dell Inc.

Dell is electronically connected to suppliers, contract manufacturers, and distributors, as shown in Exhibit 21.3, so that everyone along the supply chain has almost completely transparent information about sales, orders, shipments and other data. That means, for instance, that suppliers have data about orders and production levels and know what parts Dell's factories are going to need and when they'll need them. Distributors know when computers will be ready for shipment and where they'll be going. At the end of the supply chain, Dell develops close connections to customers through a range of channels, including online sales and services, call centres, and a direct sales force and technical personnel serving larger customers. Dell's role in the supply chain is to manage the electronic information flows and physical connections among suppliers, partners, and customers.[17]

Integrating every company along the supply chain also means a quicker response to end consumers by reducing the time it takes to move critical data through the information pipeline. Manufacturers have immediate access to sales data and can deliver new products, even custom orders, as needed. An integrated supply chain enables managers at fashion chain Zara stores to order hot selling items and have them in stock two days later.[18] Ford Motor Company has been undergoing a

supply-chain makeover intended to enable the company to manufacture cars on a reasonable build-to-order basis, so that customers no longer have to wait months for delivery of the car of their dreams.[19]

Managing a supply chain requires interpersonal influence and good networking and political skills because of the lack of direct control over outside suppliers.

TAKE A MOMENT

Designing Operations Management Systems

Every organization must design its production system. This process starts with the design of the product or service to be produced. A restaurant designs the food items on the menu. An automobile manufacturer designs the cars it produces. A management consulting firm designs the various types of services it will offer to clients. Other considerations in designing the production system include purchasing raw materials, layout of facilities, designing production technology, facilities location and capacity planning.

Product and Service Design

The way a product or service is designed affects its appeal for customers; it also affects how easy or expensive operations will be. Design has become a critical aspect of product development for many companies, even old-line manufacturers of products such as appliances and tools. Whirlpool's Duet line of washers and dryers, with soft curves and splashes of colour, captured 19 per cent of the front-loading washer market in only two years.[20] Solo Cup's sales of disposable plates began growing at a double-digit pace after a design company observed people picnicking and suggested adding deep wells and indented hand grips to make the plates easier to manage with one hand.[21]

However, some product designs are difficult to execute properly. When Volant began making an unconventional type of skis from steel, skiers began snapping them up, delighted with their flexibility and tight grip of the snow. However, producing the skis turned out to be a nightmare, and many pairs had to be scrapped or reworked. Expenses mounted, and the company failed to meet promised delivery dates. Eventually, Volant hired Mark Soderberg, an engineer with experience at Boeing. Soderberg made a small design change that allowed more generous manufacturing tolerances (variances from the design specifications). After the tooling was adjusted to accommodate the design change, Volant began producing the modified skis – and forecast its first year of operating in the black – subsequently leading to its acquisition by the Finnish company Amer Sports Oyj, the largest manufacturer of sporting equipment in the world.

To prevent such problems in the first place, a growing number of businesses are using *design for manufacturability and assembly* (DFMA). In the past, many engineering designers fashioned products with disdain for how they would be produced. Elegant designs nearly always had too many parts. The watchword today is simplicity, making the product easy and inexpensive to manufacture. At Seagate Technology, the largest and most efficient maker of hard drives in the world, with its drives used in computers and cameras, MP3 players and cell phones, and Xboxes and Tivos, all products have at least 75 per cent of their parts and machinery in common

Exhibit 21.4 Basic Production Layouts

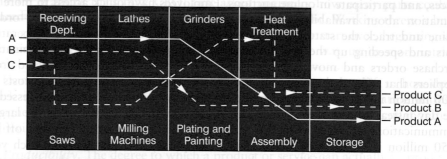

(a) Process Layout

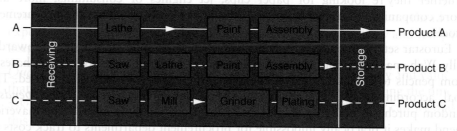

(b) Product Layout

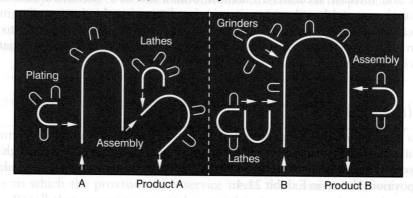

(c) Cellular Layout

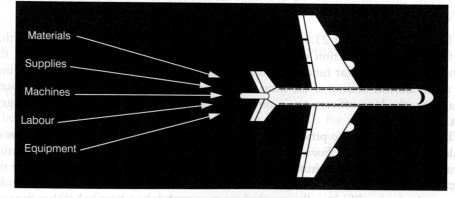

(d) Fixed-Position Layout

SOURCES: Based on J. T. Black, 'Cellular Manufacturing Systems Reduce Setup Time, Make Small Lot Production Economical', *Industrial Engineering* (November 1983): 36–48; and Richard J. Schonberger, 'Plant Layout Becomes Product-Oriented with Cellular, Just-in-Time Production Concepts', *Industrial Engineering* (November 1983): 66–77.

Product Layout

Exhibit 21.4(b) illustrates a **product layout** – one in which machines and tasks are arranged according to the progressive steps in producing a single product. The automobile assembly line is a classic example, because it produces a single product starting from the raw materials to the finished output. Many fast-food restaurants use the product layout, with activities arranged in sequence to produce hamburgers or fried chicken, depending on the products available.

The product layout is efficient when the organization produces huge volumes of identical products. Note in Exhibit 21.4(b) that two lines have paint areas. This duplication of functions can be economical only if the volume is high enough to keep each paint area busy working on specialized products.

Cellular Layout

Illustrated in Exhibit 21.4(c) is an innovative layout, called cellular layout, based on group-technology principles. In a manufacturing plant, all machines dedicated to sequences of operations are grouped into cells, as shown in the exhibit. In a service organization, all the people who work on a process, such as insurance claims processing, are organized into cells where they can see and easily communicate with one another. Work flows from one station to another, similar to materials movement in the manufacturing plant.[27] Grouping technology into cells provides some of the efficiencies of both process and product layouts. Even more important, the U-shaped cells in Exhibit 21.4(c) provide efficiencies in material and tool handling and inventory movement. Employees work in clusters that facilitate teamwork and joint problem solving. Staffing flexibility is enhanced because people are cross-trained so that each worker can perform all the tasks, assisting co-workers as needed.

As the need for speed and responsiveness increased, many organizations designed facilities layout to allow for a high level of flexibility. This chapter's Manager's Shoptalk offers some tips from a German factory that is on the cutting edge of a new way of working.

Fixed-Position Layout

As shown in Exhibit 21.4(d), the fixed-position layout is one in which the product remains in one location, and employees and equipment are brought to it. The fixed-position layout is used to create a product or service that is either large or one of a kind. Product examples include aircraft, ships, and buildings. The product cannot be moved from function to function or along an assembly line; rather, the people, materials, and machines all come to the fixed-position site for assembly and processing. London-based Imagination Ltd, Europe's largest independent design and communications agency, provides an interesting service example.

The fixed-position layout is not good for high volume, but it is often necessary for large, bulky products, special events, and custom orders like the one-of-a-kind launch of the *Harry Potter and the Prisoner of Azkaban* DVD. Many manufacturers are adapting the fixed-position layout to speed up production. Boeing now builds many of its planes on a type of moving assembly line, which cut in half the time it takes to assemble a single-aisle 737. Airbus uses assembly stations, moving the plane only from one major workstation to the next, with the idea that a glitch in one plane won't slow a whole production line.[28]

Technology Automation

A goal for many of today's operations managers is to find the right combination of technology and management to most efficiently produce goods and services. Let's look at three advances in manufacturing and service operations.

Product layout
A facilities layout in which machines and tasks are arranged according to the sequence of steps in the production of a single product.

Cellular layout
A facilities layout in which machines dedicated to sequences of production are grouped into cells in accordance with group-technology principles.

Fixed-position layout
A facilities layout in which the product remains in one location and the required tasks and equipment are brought to it.

MANAGER'S SHOPTALK

A German Factory Shows How to Be Fast and Flexible

Many students might think a factory that makes polymer bearings and power-supply chains is not the best place to get a view of the factory of the future, but they'd be wrong. Cologne, Germany's igus Inc. manufacturing plant represents a highly innovative approach to facilities design. The plant's flexible design enables the factory to shrink or expand at a moment's notice, keeping pace with an unpredictable market. Almost nothing is bolted down on the plant floor, so that machines, modules, and entire departments can be rearranged. Other design features, such as exposed overhead wiring and few support columns, mean the company can redesign itself as needed with little disruption to the 24-7 production flow. Over the past five years, igus has made at least 50 significant changes to the factory's configuration to accommodate strategic shifts, facilitate fast growth or meet new customer needs.

Fast, agile organizations do not occur on their own. Managers have to make decisions that include considering the physical as well as the human environment. Frank Blase, president of igus, offers the following tips for building a nimble organization:

1 *Create a flexible environment.* A plant's space, facilities design, and layout should accommodate the business, not the other way around.

2 *Recruit carefully.* Not everyone is comfortable working in a highly flexible, fast-changing environment. Human resource managers should screen job candidates carefully and make sure they understand the nature of the workplace. At igus, candidates are given a *schnuppertag*, or sniffing-around day, to explore, observe and ask questions.

3 *Practise being fast.* Every aspect of the company should be designed to encourage speed and agility. All igus employees are equipped with mobile phones and get around on shiny, motorized scooters. An open physical environment encourages collaboration and information transparency. Department teams conduct quick daily huddles to review what went well and what didn't the day before.

4 *Inspire your staff.* This last tip may be the most important of all. Flexibility hinges on innovation and creativity, Blase says, which depends on employees who are inspired to think differently and express their ideas and opinions. 'We're trying to be a different kind of company,' he adds, 'and our building helps us tremendously in doing that. It creates a holistic system for how to behave.'

SOURCE Chuck Salter, 'This Is One Fast Factory', *Fast Company* (August 2001): 32–33.

 INNOVATIVE WAY

Imagination Ltd.

Imagination Ltd. has made a name for itself by producing highly theatrical and award-winning events and programmes. Consider the event staged for the launch of the *Harry Potter and the Prisoner of Azkaban* DVD and video. There were 800 guests invited to Middle Temple, an historic London building where Imagination employees had recreated four movie sets, among them the Great Hall at the Hogwarts School of Witchcraft and Wizardry.

Getting the décor right was a top priority, but Imagination's employees faced a challenge because Middle Temple is a working dining room during the week. They had to work outside regular dining hours and keep everything top-secret, not so easy to do when you're suspending 200 battery-powered candles from the ceiling and making arrangements to transport Harry Potter himself to the party. The event, designed to attract international media for client Warner Home Video, was a resounding success and generated more than $9.5 million worth of free advertising.[29]

Radio-Frequency Identification (RFID)

Radio-frequency identification (RFID) uses electronic tags that can identify and track individual items such as books, jugs of laundry detergent, automobiles or even people. One of the best-known uses of RFID is OnStar, which is a satellite-based RFID system used in motor vehicles. RFID tags emit radio signals that can be read remotely by electronic readers and provide precise, real-time information about the location of specific items, whether it be a Ford with a dead battery, a misplaced book in a bookstore or a pallet of merchandise in a warehouse.[30] Although RFID is also used by manufacturing firms, the technology has revolutionized services. The biggest names in retail, including Wal-Mart, Home Depot, Carrefour and Tesco, are taking advantage of the new technology. Dutch bookseller Selexyz tags every book on its shelves with RFID, which increases profits and cuts costs since there's no more taking inventory by hand, fewer lost books and fewer returns to publishers.[31] The potential of RFID for streamlining inventory management and cutting costs for retailers is enormous, which has prompted many companies to require that suppliers use the new technology.

Other service firms use RFID as well. Amusement parks put RFID wrist bands on children so they can be quickly located if they get separated from their parents.[32] The technology might even ameliorate the age-old problem of lost luggage, which is maddening for passengers and costly for airlines. An RFID baggage-tagging system in use at the Las Vegas McCarran International Airport reduced lost luggage by about 20 per cent, and bags that do go astray are located more quickly.[33]

In addition to providing employees with more satisfying jobs and giving customers better service, the technology has other operational benefits for Lloyds Pharmacy. For example, it means stores need only 400 square feet, whereas most pharmacies occupy at least 1000. That saves money, and it means Lloyds Pharmacy can squeeze into small spaces in supermarkets and other retail outlets. Lloyds Pharmacy stocks about 2000 drugs, more than in an average pharmacy, but most inventory is stored in a vertical 14-foot-high carousel that reaches up into the ceiling. Push a button and, with the aid of bar coding, the desired item descends to eye level. The storage system works in conjunction with other technologies, such as a dispensing device that quickly and accurately counts and sorts tablets for up to 400 prescriptions a day, and workflow management software that increases overall efficiency. Each prescription goes through numerous checks for accuracy.

Judging by the fledgling pharmacy's rapid growth – with representation in 14 countries and prescription sales growing at four to five times the national average – Lloyds Pharmacy's sophisticated use of technology is doing the job.

CONCEPT CONNECTION Because its manufactured goods are too large and cumbersome to move along a traditional assembly line, Boeing Corporation typically uses a fixed-position layout. Products, such as this 787 Dreamliner, remain in one location, and employees, components and equipment are brought to them for assembly. To increase speed and flexibility, Boeing has begun implementing a hybrid system for some of its products. After the wings and landing gear have been attached, a plane such as the 737 is dragged toward the door at two inches a minute, with workers moving along it on a float-like apparatus. Boeing's goal is to push a 737 out the door in only five days.

Flexible Manufacturing Systems

Advanced technology has also revolutionized manufacturing. The use of automated production lines that can be quickly adapted to produce more than one kind of

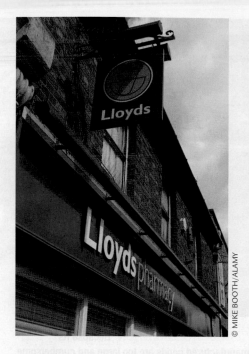

© MIKE BOOTH/ALAMY

CONCEPT CONNECTION At Lloyds pharmacy, Smaller Is Better. Lloyds pharmacy has over 1600 pharmacies across the UK. These are based predominantly in community and health centre locations. The company employs over 16 000 staff, of which 80 per cent are women, and dispenses 120 million prescription items annually. Does the world need another drugstore? The owners of Lloyds pharmacy – Celesio AG based in Stuttgart – think it does – but not the kind where you have to wait half an hour for a prepack-aged antibiotic, or fight for a few minutes of a stressed-out pharmacist's time to answer your questions. The aim was to build a different kind of drugstore, one that uses sophisticated integrated technology to achieve maximum efficiency, improve customer service, reduce prescription errors, and free pharmacists from mundane chores such as counting pills or checking technicians' work. At Lloyds pharmacy you won't see many people counting pills. That task is handled by automated devices that dispense the most-frequently prescribed drugs, combined with a rigid bar-code scanning system that assures pharmacists of accuracy. That means the pharmacist can actually come out from behind the counter and talk to customers about their health care issues and drug concerns. It's the dream of what every pharmacist wants to practise.[34]

© MOTORING PICTURE LIBRARY/ALAMY

CONCEPT CONNECTION At its East Liberty, Ohio, facility, Honda can shift within minutes from making a Ridgeline truck to making the subcompact Civic. A flexible manufacturing system enables this quick-changeover and lets Honda build the Civic Sedan, Civic GX (natural gas powered), Element, Honda CR-V and Ridgeline truck on the same assembly line with little disruption. As part of the system, the factory has 200-plus robots for welding, which can be quickly reprogrammed by an operator as they shift from one model to another. This flexibility helps Honda respond faster than competitors to changing consumer interests as fuel prices fluctuate.

product is called a flexible manufacturing system.[35] The machinery uses sophisticated computer technology to coordinate and integrate the machines. Automated functions include loading, unloading, storing parts, changing tools and machining. The computer can instruct the machines to change parts, machining and tools when a new product must be produced. Human operators make adjustments to the computer, not the production machinery itself, dramatically cutting the time and expense of making changes. This approach is a breakthrough compared with the traditional assembly line in which a single line is restricted to a single product. With a flexible manufacturing system, a single production line can be readily adapted to small batches of different products based on computer instructions.

At a Nissan factory, for example, minivans, pickup trucks, and sport utility vehicles can all be sent down the same assembly line. Robotic arms on machines are programmed to weld in the spots needed for different vehicles. Highly automated painting machines are programmed to paint all kinds of vehicles one after another, with no down time for reconfiguration.[36] Many of Matsushita Electric's Factories did away with assembly lines altogether in favour of clusters of robots controlled by software that can quickly shift gears to make the hottest electronic gadgets and ease up on slow sellers.[37]

CAD/CAM

Operations management in most businesses today employs computers for the design of products, and often for their manufacture as well. CAD (computer-aided design) enables engineers to develop new-product designs in about half the time required with traditional methods. Computers provide a visual display for the engineer and illustrate the implications of any design change.

CAM (computer-aided manufacturing) uses computers to direct manufacturing processes, as in flexible manufacturing systems. Typically, the CAM system is linked to CAD, so that the product specifications drive the manufacturing specifications. The computer system thus guides and controls the manufacturing process. For example, a sportswear manufacturer can use computers to mechanize the entire sequence of manufacturing operations – pattern scaling, layout and printing. Computer-controlled cutting tables are installed. Once the computer has mathematically defined the geometry, it guides the cutting blade, eliminating the need for paper patterns. Computer programs also can direct fabric requisitions, production orders for cutting and sewing operations, and sewing line work.

The most advanced factories are using product life-cycle management (PLM) software, which manages a product from creation through development, manufacturing, testing, and even maintenance in the field. PLM can coordinate people and facilities around the world for the design, development, and manufacture of products as small as a pair of roller skates, or as large as Boeing's new 787 Dreamliner passenger jet. PLM connects design and development of new products to the design of tools, assembly lines, and even entire factories. In addition, it links employees to a digital repository of project data so that ideas and parts can be accessed and used efficiently.[38] The software can link well-known older programs, such as CAD/CAM, with newer tools that perform tasks such as simulating an assembly line or an entire factory. The most efficient manufacturing layout can be created even as the product is being designed.

Facility Location

At some point, almost every organization must decide on the location of facilities. Commerce Bank like HSBC needs to open a new branch office, a fast food franchise like KFC or McDonalds needs to find locations for new restaurants, or Intel needs to find locations somewhere in the world for a new research facility and a new chip assembly and testing plant. When these decisions are made unwisely, they are expensive and troublesome for the organization.

The most common approach to selecting a site for a new location is to do a cost-benefit analysis. For example, managers at bank headquarters may identify four possible locations. The costs associated with each location are the land (purchase or lease); moving from the current facility; and construction, including zoning laws, building codes, land features and size of the parking lot. Taxes, utilities, rents and maintenance are other cost factors to be considered in advance. Each possible bank location also will have certain benefits. Benefits to be evaluated are accessibility of customers, location of major competitors, general quality of working conditions and nearness to restaurants and shops, which would be desirable for both employees and customers. Once the bank managers have evaluated the worth of each benefit, they can divide total benefits by total costs for each location, then select the location with the highest ratio.

New location scouting software is helping managers turn facilities location from guesswork into a science. These programmes use sophisticated number crunching tools, for example, to help fast-food chains determine the best areas for expansion. However, most companies don't rely on technology alone, but also use human location scouts, who combine heaps of research with an eye for details and a honed

Flexible manufacturing system
A small or medium-sized automated production line that can be adapted to produce more than one product line.

CAD
A production technology in which computers perform new-product design.

CAM
A production technology in which computers help guide and control the manufacturing system.

Product life-cycle management (PLM)
Manufacturing software that manages a product from creation through development, manufacturing, testing, and even maintenance in the field.

instinct about where the business will succeed. John Batty is the top scout for Domino's Pizza UK and IRL.

 INNOVATIVE WAY

Domino's Pizza

Whenever a new franchisee for Domino's needs to locate a site, John Batty is likely to get a call. He's the top location scout for Domino's and travels about 15 days a month looking for locations.

Batty uses mapping software, demographic analysis, and personal observation to pick good new locations. When scouting for a new store, John drives thousands of miles criss-crossing the same streets, watching traffic patterns, chatting up people in McDonald's and other competitors, and seeing where people spend their time during weekdays and weekends. He likes to locate near booming retail areas, high streets in towns, because this generates traffic. However, for Domino's, which is trying to position itself as more upmarket than competing fast-food chains, finding the right *type* of location is important, too. Once, John thought the mapping technology had pinpointed a good site near a new developing shopping area in Nottingham – until personal investigation revealed a Pizza Express nearby. Further investigation confirmed John's hunch that the neighbourhood had also had a

variety of top fast-food restaurants within a two mile radius. Similarly, if one glance at the parking lot of a shopping centre reveals a lot of Jaguars, John moves on. 'Too high end,' he says. 'I'm not going in.'

Although John Batty appreciates the support of new analytical tools, he believes personal investigation and 'gut instinct' play a big part in location selection as well. So far his instincts are right on in picking good locations for restaurants. He picked hot spots for drive-in burger chain Burger King for years before being lured away by Domino's Pizza.

Particularly for global corporations, selecting facility location is an important and complex consideration. When locating facilities in other countries, managers must take into account cost-based variables such as transportation, exchange rates and cost of labour. In addition, the skill levels of potential workers, the development of regional infrastructure, a good quality of life and a favourable business climate are important considerations in selecting a location overseas. For high-tech firms, proximity to world-class research institutions and access to venture capital are also essential criteria.

Capacity Planning

Capacity planning
The determination and adjustment of the organization's ability to produce products and services to match customer demand.

Capacity planning is the determination and adjustment of an organization's ability to produce products or services to match demand. For example, if an automaker anticipates a 15 per cent increase in sales over the next year, capacity planning is the procedure whereby it will ensure that it has sufficient capacity to service that demand.

Organizations can do several things to increase capacity. One is to create additional shifts and hire people to work on them. A second is to ask existing people to work overtime to add to capacity. A third is to outsource or subcontract extra work to other firms. A fourth is to expand a plant and add more equipment. Each of these techniques will increase the organization's ability to meet demand without risk of major excess capacity.

The biggest problem for most organizations, however, is excess capacity. When misjudgements occur, transportation companies have oil tankers sitting empty in the harbour, oil companies have refineries sitting idle, semiconductor companies have plants shuttered, developers have office buildings half full, and the service industry may have hotels or amusement parks operating at partial capacity. Consider movie theatre chains, which have grossly overbuilt in recent years, more than doubling the number of screens in Finland, Sweden, Russia, the UK, the USA and many other countries in a 20-year period adopting an American movie theatre model. Some theatres show films to only one or two people at a time because of excess capacity. The challenge is for managers to add capacity as needed without excess. For many companies, the solution is contracting work out to other organizations. Outsourcing and new organizational forms such as the virtual network organization described in Chapter 10 enable companies to quickly ramp up production to increase capacity and dissolve partnerships when extra help is no longer needed.

CONCEPT CONNECTION In an industry where changing fashions can quickly leave finished goods untouched on the racks, Zara has made inventory management the creative heart of its "fast fashion" business. Sophisticated information technology in every store, including handheld computers, provide a non-stop flow of data back to the company's headquarters in La Coruña, Spain, enabling not just precise inventory management but also guiding Zara's 200-person strong creative team. Responding to the latest information on what is – and isn't – selling allows Zara to bring cutting-edge finished goods back to their stores in as little as four to five weeks, where the cycle continues.

Inventory Management

A large portion of the operations manager's job consists of inventory management. Inventory is the goods the organization keeps on hand for use in the production process. Most organizations have three types of inventory: finished goods prior to shipment, work in process and raw materials.

Finished-goods inventory includes items that have passed through the entire production process but have not been sold. This inventory is highly visible. The new cars parked in the storage lot of an automobile factory are finished-goods inventory, as are the hamburgers and French fries stacked under the heat lamps at a McDonald's restaurant. Finished-goods inventory is expensive, because the organization has invested labour and other costs to make the finished product.

Work-in-process inventory includes the materials moving through the stages of the production process that are not completed products. Work-in-process inventory in an automobile plant includes engines, wheel and tyre assemblies, and dashboards waiting to be installed. In a fast-food restaurant, the French fries in the fryer and hamburgers on the grill are work-in-process inventory.

Raw materials inventory includes the basic inputs to the organization's production process. This inventory is cheapest, because the organization has not yet invested labour in it. Steel, wire, glass, and paint are raw materials inventory for an auto plant. Meat patties, buns and raw potatoes are the raw materials inventory in a fast-food restaurant.

The Importance of Inventory

Inventory management is vitally important to organizations, because inventory sitting idly on the shop floor or in the warehouse costs money. Many years ago, a firm's wealth was measured by its inventory. Today inventory is recognized as an unproductive asset in cost-conscious firms. Money not tied up in inventory can be used in other productive ventures. Keeping inventory low is especially important for high-tech firms, because so many of their products lose value quickly as they are

Inventory
The goods that the organization keeps on hand for use in the production process up to the point of selling the final products to customers.

Finished-goods inventory
Inventory consisting of items that have passed through the complete production process but have yet to be sold.

Work-in-process inventory
Inventory composed of the materials that still are moving through the stages of the production process.

Raw materials inventory
Inventory consisting of the basic inputs to the organization's production process.

Exhibit 21.5 Large Inventories Hide Operations Management Problems

SOURCE: R. J. Schonberger, Japanese Manufacturing Techniques: Nine Hidden Lessons in Simplicity (New York: The Free Press, 1982).

replaced by more innovative and lower-cost models. For example, the value of a completed personal computer falls rapidly; even if shelf space for PCs were free, a company would lose money on its PC inventory. Service firms are concerned with inventory too, which is a big part of the reason for the growth of RFID, as described earlier.

Services are concerned with inventory too. Managers at retail giants such as Wal-Mart, Toys R Us, Carrefour, and Tesco understand that efficient inventory management is essential to their ability to keep prices low and attract more customers. State-of-the-art, integrated e-business systems, including the use of new wireless RFID technology as described earlier, allow tight inventory control and enable the retailers to eliminate excess inventory. Their suppliers have refined their delivery systems so that the stores receive only the products needed to meet customer purchases.

The Japanese analogy of rocks and water describes the current thinking about the importance of inventory. As illustrated in Exhibit 21.5, the water is the inventory in the organization. The higher the water, the less managers have to worry about the rocks, which represent problems. In operations management, these problems apply to scheduling, facilities layout, product or service design and quality. When the water level goes down, managers see the rocks and must deal with them. When inventories are reduced, the problems of a poorly designed and managed operations process also are revealed. The problems then must be solved. When inventory can be kept at an absolute minimum, operations management is considered excellent.

We now consider specific techniques for inventory management. Four important concepts are economic order quantity, material requirements planning, just-in-time inventory systems and distribution management.

Economic Order Quantity

Two basic decisions that can help minimize inventory are how many raw materials to order and when to order from outside suppliers. Ordering the minimum amounts at the right time keeps the raw materials, work-in-process, and finished-goods inventories at low levels. One popular technique is **economic order quantity** (EOQ), which is designed to minimize the total of ordering costs and holding costs for inventory items. *Ordering costs* are the costs associated with actually placing the order, such as postage, receiving and inspection. *Holding costs* are costs associated with keeping the item on hand, such as storage space charges, finance charges and materials-handling expenses.

The EOQ calculation indicates the order quantity size that will minimize holding and ordering costs based on the organization's use of inventory. The EOQ formula

Economic order quantity (EOQ)
An inventory management technique designed to minimize the total of ordering and holding costs for inventory items.

includes ordering costs *(C)*, holding costs *(H)*, and annual demand *(D)*. For example, consider a hospital's need to order surgical dressings. Based on hospital records, the ordering costs for surgical dressings are $15, the annual holding cost is $6 and the annual demand for dressings is 605. The following is the formula for the economic order quantity:

$$EOQ = \sqrt{\frac{2DC}{H}} = \sqrt{\frac{2(605)(15)}{6}} = 55$$

The EOQ formula tells us that the best quantity to order is 55.

The next question is when to make the order. For this decision, a different formula, called **reorder point (ROP)**, is used. ROP is calculated by the following formula, where *D* is the annual demand for dressings, *T* is the time period (365 days in the year), and *L* is the lead time, or number of days between ordering and receiving the product. In this example, we assume that it takes three days to receive the order after the hospital has placed it:

Reorder point (ROP)
The most economical level at which an inventory item should be reordered.

$$ROP = \frac{D}{T}(L) = \frac{605}{365}(3) = 4.97, \text{ or } 5$$

The reorder point tells us that because it takes three days to receive the order, at least five dressings should be on hand when the order is placed. As nurses use surgical dressings, operations managers will know that when the level reaches the point of five, the new order should be placed for a quantity of 55.

This relationship is illustrated in Exhibit 21.6. Whenever the reorder point of five dressings is reached, the new order is initiated, and the 55 arrive just as the inventory is depleted. In a typical hospital, however, some variability in lead time and use of surgical dressings will occur. Thus, a few extra items of inventory, called safety stock, are used to ensure that the hospital does not run out of surgical dressings. In general, companies keep more safety stock when demand for items is highly variable. When demand is easy to predict, the safety stock may be lower. However, a careful inventory manager may take into account other criteria as well. A sizable price cut or volume discount might make a large purchase economically more attractive, especially in the case of a product the company is almost certain to need in the future.

Exhibit 21.6 Inventory Control of Surgical Dressings by EOQ

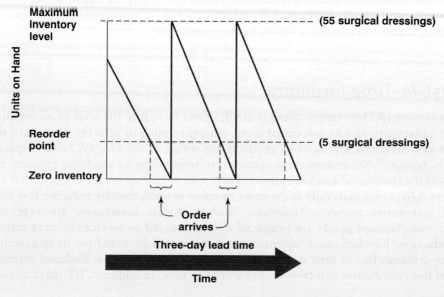

Material Requirements Planning

Dependent demand inventory
Inventory in which item demand is related to the demand for other inventory items.

Material requirements planning (MRP)
A dependent demand inventory planning and control system that schedules the precise amount of all materials required to support the production of desired end products.

The EOQ formula works well when inventory items are not dependent on one another. For example, in a restaurant the demand for hamburgers is independent of the demand for milkshakes; thus, an economic order quantity is calculated for each item. A more complicated inventory problem occurs with **dependent demand inventory**, meaning that item demand is related to the demand for other inventory items. For example, if Ford Motor Company decides to make 100 000 cars, it will also need 400 000 tyres, 400 000 rims, and 400 000 hubcaps. The demand for tyres is dependent on the demand for cars.

The most common inventory control system used for handling dependent demand inventory is **material requirements planning (MRP)**. MRP is a dependent demand inventory planning and control system that schedules the exact amount of all materials required to support the desired end product. MRP is computer based and requires sophisticated calculations to coordinate information on production scheduling, inventory location, forecasting and ordering. Unlike with EOQ, inventory levels are not based on past consumption; rather, they are based on precise estimates of future needs for production. MRP can dramatically reduce inventory costs. With MRP, managers can better control the quantity and timing of deliveries of raw materials, ensuring that the right materials arrive at approximately the right time they are needed in the production process. The computerized MRP system can slow or accelerate the inflow of materials in response to changes in the production schedule. These controls result in lower labour, materials, and overhead costs.

As competitive pressures increased, MRP gradually evolved into the broader enterprise resource planning (ERP) systems described in Chapter 20. MRP is focused only on manufacturing and inventory, while ERP incorporates computerized links to other business functions, such as human resources, finance and sales, enabling managers to evaluate trade-offs such as the balance between workload and the human resources and manufacturing capacity. ERP systems can integrate, track and optimize functions across the entire organization. MRP systems are a valuable subset of ERP, enabling managers to have greater insight into operations so they can optimize the use of human and material resources.

TAKE A MOMENT   As a new manager, recognize the financial importance of inventory management. Use economic order quantity and material requirements planning to minimize inventory levels. Consider a just-in-time inventory system for your organization.

Just-In-Time Inventory

Just-in-time (JIT) inventory system
An inventory control system that schedules materials to arrive precisely when they are needed on a production line.

Just-in-time (JIT) inventory systems are designed to reduce the level of an organization's inventory and its associated costs, aiming to push to zero the amount of time that raw materials and finished products are sitting in the factory, being inspected, or in transit.[39] Sometimes these systems are referred to as *stockless systems*, *zero inventory systems* or *kanban systems*. Each system centres on the concept that suppliers deliver materials only at the exact moment needed, thereby reducing raw material inventories to zero. Moreover, work-in-process inventories are kept to a minimum because goods are produced only as needed to service the next stage of production. Finished-goods inventories are minimized by matching them exactly to sales demand. Just-in-time systems have tremendous advantages. Reduced inventory level frees productive capital for other company uses. In addition, JIT plays a crucial role in enhancing flexibility. A study of manufacturing firms in seven countries found that those that were performing better in terms of flexibility ranked just-in-time as one of their top two improvement initiatives, along with total quality management, as defined in Chapter 19.[40]

Recall the analogy of the rocks and the water. To reduce inventory levels to zero means that all management and coordination problems will surface and must be resolved. Scheduling must be scrupulously precise and logistics tightly coordinated. For example, follow the movement of a shipment of odometers and speedometers from a supplier to a Nissan plant:

Thursday, 9a.m.:	A truck arrives at the supplier. As workers load the parts, drivers check on-board computers for destination, route and estimated time of arrival (ETA) data.
Friday, 3a.m.:	The truck arrives at Canton, Mississippi, and approaches a switching yard two miles from the Nissan plant, parking in a computer-assigned spot. The driver downloads a key-shaped floppy disk from the on-board computer into the trucking company's mainframe, which relays the performance report directly to Nissan.
Friday, 12:50p.m.:	The trailer leaves the switching yard at a designated time and arrives at a predetermined receiving dock at the Nissan plant, where workers unload the parts and send them to the production line just in time.[41]

Logistics
The activities required to physically move materials into the company's operations facility and to move finished products to customers.

The coordination required by JIT demands that information be shared among everyone in the supply chain. Communication between only adjoining links in the supply chain is too slow. Rather, coordination requires a kind of information web in which members of the supply chain share information simultaneously with all other participants, often using internet technologies and perhaps RFID.[42] For example, Dell's factory uses online information exchange so effectively that it can order only the materials needed to keep production running for the next two hours. In addition, web hook-ups to shipping companies mean that finished inventory can often be loaded onto trucks less than 15 hours after a customer submits an order.[43]

Just-in-time inventory systems also require excellent employee motivation and cooperation. Workers are expected to perform at their best because they are entrusted with the responsibility and authority to make the zero inventory system work. Employees must help one another when they fall behind and must be capable of doing different jobs. Workers experience the satisfaction of being in charge of the system and making useful improvements in the company's operations.[44]

Logistics and Distribution Management

A critical aspect of managing inventory is efficiently moving raw materials into the facility and moving finished products out to customers. Some companies develop the necessary logistics expertise in house. **Logistics** refers to managing the movement of materials within the facility, the shipment of incoming

© MIKE CLARKE/AFP/GETTY IMAGES

CONCEPT CONNECTION The 2005 publication of J.K. Rowling's eagerly-awaited *Harry Potter and the Half-Blood Prince* placed massive demands on the distribution and order fulfilment systems of everyone involved. First of all, they handled a huge volume of product: Scholastic, the novel's American publisher, had an initial print run of 10.8 million copies. On top of that, Scholastic – together with retailers, wholesale distributors and delivery companies – had to put stringent security measures in place so that, in accordance with Rowling's wishes, no customers got their hands on the book a moment before 12:01a.m. on July 16. Here Barnes & Noble employees inspect the shipment brought to a company warehouse by a caravan of 124 tractor-trailers.

materials from suppliers, and the shipment of outgoing products to customers. For example, Wal-Mart uses regional distribution centres, which has more than 1 million square feet of floor space, 96 dock doors for loading and unloading trailers, and 5.62 miles of conveyors for moving merchandize.[45] These regional centres receive incoming shipments from suppliers, receive orders from the retail stores, make up the orders, and load and ship merchandize orders to stores throughout the region. Distribution centre employees coordinate the entire system and schedule inbound trucks from suppliers and company-owned trucks outbound to the retail stores. Using computers, the system can be so precisely coordinated that the stores don't need warehouses; orders of merchandize go directly from the trucks to the shelves, usually within 48 hours.

Distribution
Moving finished products to customers; also called *order fulfilment*.

Moving finished products out to customers is usually referred to as **distribution** or *order fulfilment*. The faster and more accurately a company can fill customer orders, the lower the costs for the organization and the greater the likelihood that the customer will return. Many firms are shifting some of their warehouses and distribution facilities to China so that imported goods can go straight to retailers and manufacturers, bypassing a stop at a US warehouse and saving time and money. UPS had about 50 warehouses in China in 2005 with plans to add ten more by the end of 2006.[46]

Organizations are finding ways to deliver products faster and less expensively by using the internet. In the latest advance, some companies share transportation information and resources with unrelated companies, even competitors, so they can share truck space and avoid hauling an empty trailer on a return trip. Subaru of America is talking with a rival automaker about the possibility of sharing rail and truck space so cars will get to dealers faster. Dell has moved all its external suppliers into their own premises, which allows them to save time dramatically and ensure quality control.

Lean Manufacturing and Productivity

Productivity is significant because it influences the well-being of the entire society as well as of individual companies. The only way to increase the output of goods and services to society is to increase organizational productivity.

Lean Manufacturing

Many of the concepts we have discussed, including just-in-time inventory and an emphasis on quality, are central to the philosophy of lean manufacturing. Today's organizations are trying to become more efficient, and implementing the lean manufacturing philosophy is one popular approach to doing so. **Lean manufacturing**, sometimes called *lean production*, combines advanced technology with innovative management methods, using highly trained employees who take a painstaking approach to problem solving at every stage of the production process to cut waste and improve quality and productivity. Lean manufacturing was pioneered by Toyota, and the concept has spread around the world to both manufacturing and service organizations.

Lean manufacturing
Manufacturing process using highly trained employees at every stage of the production process to cut waste and improve quality.

Technology plays a key role in lean manufacturing. Companies make full use of flexible manufacturing systems, and equipment is often designed to stop automatically so that a defect can be fixed. However, the heart of the process is not machines or technology, but people.[47] For example, Toyota's operations are admired worldwide as a model of quality and efficiency, but this success is not merely a result of using the right machines or setting the right standards. Toyota's system combines techniques, systems and management philosophy, such as commitment to employee

empowerment and a creative culture. Besides installing the methodology for running an efficient assembly line, such as *just-in-time* shipments of supplies, managers must instil the necessary attitudes, such as concern for quality and a desire to innovate.[48]

Measuring Productivity

One important question when considering productivity improvements is: What is productivity, and how do managers measure it? In simple terms, **productivity** is the organization's output of goods and services divided by its inputs. This means that productivity can be improved by either increasing the amount of output using the same level of inputs or reducing the number of inputs required to produce the output. Sometimes a company can even do both. Ruggieri & Sons, for example, invested in mapping software to help it plan deliveries of heating fuel. The software plans the most efficient routes based on the locations of customers and fuel reloading terminals, as well as the amount of fuel each customer needs. When Ruggieri switched from planning routes by hand to using the software, its drivers began driving fewer miles but making 7 per cent more stops each day – in others words, burning less fuel in order to sell more fuel.[49]

The accurate measure of productivity can be complex. Two approaches for measuring productivity are total factor productivity and partial productivity. **Total factor productivity** is the ratio of total outputs to the inputs from labour, capital, materials and energy:

$$Total\ factor\ productivity = \frac{Output}{Labour + Capital + Materials + Energy}$$

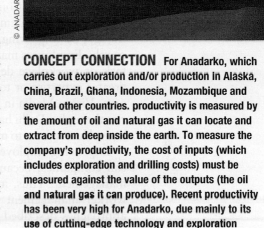

CONCEPT CONNECTION For Anadarko, which carries out exploration and/or production in Alaska, China, Brazil, Ghana, Indonesia, Mozambique and several other countries. productivity is measured by the amount of oil and natural gas it can locate and extract from deep inside the earth. To measure the company's productivity, the cost of inputs (which includes exploration and drilling costs) must be measured against the value of the outputs (the oil and natural gas it can produce). Recent productivity has been very high for Anadarko, due mainly to its use of cutting-edge technology and exploration techniques. For instance, while exploring in a part of Algeria that bigger competitors had given up on, Anadarko workers used an unorthodox imaging technique to discover a three-billion barrel field of oil.[50]

Total factor productivity represents the best measure of how the organization is doing. Often, however, managers need to know about productivity with respect to certain inputs. **Partial productivity** is the ratio of total outputs to a major category of inputs. For example, many organizations are interested in labour productivity, which would be measured as follows:

$$Labour\ productivity = \frac{Output}{Cost\ of\ labour}$$

Productivity
The organization's output of products and services divided by its inputs.

Total factor productivity
The ratio of total outputs to the inputs from labour, capital, materials, and energy.

Partial productivity
The ratio of total outputs to the inputs from a single major input category.

Calculating this formula for labour, capital or materials provides information on whether improvements in each element are occurring. However, managers often are criticized for relying too heavily on partial productivity measures, especially direct labour.[51] Measuring direct labour misses the valuable improvements in materials, work processes, and quality. Labour productivity is easily measured, but may show an increase as a result of capital improvements. Thus, managers will misinterpret the reason for productivity increases.

Improving Productivity

When an organization decides that improving productivity is important, managers can look at two critical areas, employee productivity and managerial productivity.

TAKE A MOMENT　　As a new manager, take personal responsibility for improving productivity. Go to the Experiential Exercise on page 829 that pertains to your personal orientation toward productivity improvements.

Employee Productivity

Increased *employee productivity* means having workers produce more output in the same time period. Companies can improve employee productivity by establishing the means for existing employees to do more, such as by acquiring more efficient technology, by improving work processes or by training employees to work more efficiently. Employees may simply need more knowledge, better technology or improved task or workplace design. The company may also decide to hire employees with greater expertise or to outsource certain operations to a firm with expertise in that area. Virgin Media in the UK, for example, outsourced customer services and enquiries through a Delhi based call centres as it has the computer applications and technological know-how to more efficiently handle the task.

Improving employee productivity has sometimes been a real challenge for American companies, because too often workers have an antagonistic relationship with management. Thus, increasing employee productivity often requires improving the worker–management relationship. Many of the leadership and management approaches described in this book can enhance worker productivity by motivating and inspiring employees.

Managerial Productivity

Increased managerial productivity simply means that managers do a better job of running the business. Leading experts in productivity and quality often have stated that the real reason for productivity problems in the US is poor management.[52] One of these authorities, W. Edwards Deming, proposed specific points for telling management how to improve productivity. These points are listed in Exhibit 21.7.

Managerial productivity improves when managers emphasize quality over quantity, break down barriers and empower their employees, and do not over manage using numbers. Managers can learn to use reward systems, employee involvement, teamwork and other management techniques that have been described throughout this book. However, it is important for managers to consider the linkage between these techniques and the company's strategy – not just to blindly insert a technique into the organization's activities. For example, although many managers have encouraged their employees to share knowledge, their efforts often fail because employees see no benefits and they lose interest. In contrast, knowledge management efforts succeed when managers establish a strategy-related focus for what information is to be shared, then measure the results. At General Electric, for example, employees focused on learning about how to improve response time. Management determined that improvements in this area would significantly improve the company's performance. When GE instituted its knowledge management system, managers looked for – and found – improvements in such performance measures as sales per employee.[53] In this example, as in many others throughout this chapter, the difference can be attributed to better management, not to specific techniques.

Exhibit 21.7 Condensation of the 14 Points for Management

1. Create constancy of purpose toward improvement of product and service, with the aim to become competitive and to stay in business, and to provide jobs.

2. Adopt the new philosophy. We are in a new economic age. Western management must awaken to the challenge, must learn its responsibilities and take on leadership for change.

3. Cease dependence on inspection to achieve quality. Eliminate the need for inspection on a mass basis by building quality into the product in the first place.

4. End the practice of awarding business on the basis of price tag. Instead, minimize total cost. Move toward a single supplier for any one item, on a long-term relationship of loyalty and trust.

5. Improve constantly and forever the system of production and service, to improve quality and productivity, and thus constantly decrease costs.

6. Institute training on the job.

7. Institute leadership (see Point 11). The aim of supervision should be to help people and machines and gadgets do a better job. Supervision of management is in need of overhaul as well as supervision of production workers.

8. Drive out fear, so that everyone may work effectively for the company.

9. Break down barriers between departments. People in research, design, sales, and production must work as a team, to foresee problems of production and in use that may be encountered with the product or service.

10. Eliminate slogans, exhortations and targets for the workforce asking for zero defects and new levels of productivity. Such exhortations only create adversarial relationships, as the bulk of the causes of low quality and low productivity belong to the system and thus lie beyond the power of the workforce.

11. a. Eliminate work standards (quotas) on the factory floor. Substitute leadership.
    b. Eliminate management by objective. Eliminate management by numbers, numerical goals. Substitute leadership.

12. a. Remove barriers that rob hourly workers of their right to pride of workmanship. The responsibility of supervisors must be changed from sheer numbers to quality.
    b. Remove barriers that rob people in management and in engineering of their right to pride of workmanship. This means, *inter alia,* abolishment of the annual merit rating and of management by objective.

13. Institute a vigorous programme of education and self-improvement.

14. Put everybody in the company to work to accomplish the transformation. The transformation is everybody's job.

A MANAGER'S ESSENTIALS: WHAT HAVE WE LEARNED?

- This chapter described several points about operations management and the use of information for management and control. Operations management pertains to the tools and techniques used to manage the organization's core production process. These techniques apply to both manufacturing and service organizations.

- Supply chain management is a crucial area for operations, and today's managers use internet and computer-based technology to manage the sequence of suppliers and purchasers covering all stages of processing from obtaining raw materials to distributing finished goods to consumers. Other important considerations for operations management include facilities layout and technology automation, including RFID, flexible manufacturing systems, and lean manufacturing.

■ The chapter also discussed inventory management. Three types of inventory are raw materials, work in process, and finished goods. Just-in-time inventory is an effective technique for minimizing inventory levels.

Operations management has a great impact when it influences competitive strategy, applying strategic tools such as supply chain management.

At West Marine, described in the chapter opening, managers applied new technology to integrate the supply chain, dramatically improving effectiveness and efficiency. West undertook a three-year project that linked its distribution centres with store-level replenishment systems, so that the centres had real-time data about what products were sold and when store levels were getting low. The stores and centres were also linked electronically to suppliers. By quickly sharing sales data with a limited number of key suppliers, on-time fill rates for vendor orders improved from 35 per cent to 80 per cent. Stores have been able to maintain peak season in-stock levels at 96 per cent or better because of the enhanced coordination.[54]

DISCUSSION QUESTIONS

1 What are the major differences between manufacturing and service organizations? Give examples of each type.

2 To what extent is each of the four major outcomes of a highly effective operations system – superior customer responsiveness, innovation, quality and efficiency – equally important? Does it make a difference if you are considering a manufacturing versus a service organization?

3 In today's fast-changing environment, manufacturers need their supply chains to be flexible, speedy, and lower the cost of producing a product. Yet sometimes, in an effort to cut costs, organizations outsource to distant locations such as China or India, perhaps sacrificing some degree of flexibility and speed in the process. Do you think outsourcing to distant countries is a worthwhile trade-off? Why or why not?

4 Why is procurement considered such an important part of operations management? What are some of the major changes in the procurement process in recent years?

5 What type of production layout do you think would work best in a car dealership? What type would work best for a company that produces handmade pottery? Discuss reasons for your answers.

6 If you were asked to identify a location for a new resort catering to retirees, what steps would you take? How would you plan for the new resort's capacity?

7 What are the three types of inventory? Which type is most likely to be affected by the just-in-time inventory system? Explain.

8 Some companies are using both lean manufacturing and Six Sigma (Chapter 19) methods simultaneously to improve their operations. How do you think the two approaches might complement or conflict with each other? Explain.

9 Discuss the importance of logistics and distribution in managing inventory. Why do you think many of today's companies outsource this function?

10 If you were a consultant to a local manufacturing plant that wants to improve productivity, what advice would you give managers?

11 Critics argue that *radio-frequency identifications* (RFIDs) can potentially jeopardize consumer privacy by making it possible to link purchases to individuals. Should this concern prevent companies from adopting RFIDs? Explain.

12 Boeing's 787 Dreamliner was seriously delayed because of slow deliveries from suppliers who were responsible for large chunks of the jet. Outsourcing has become an important aspect of supply chain management as companies strive to cut costs, yet the practice gives managers less control, as at Boeing, and may decrease speed and flexibility. As an operations manager, how would you decide if a multinational supply chain is a better approach than trying to manufacturing as much as possible in-house?

MANAGEMENT IN PRACTICE: EXPERIENTIAL EXERCISE

What is Your Attitude Toward Productivity?

Complete the following questions based on how you think and act in a typical work situation. For each item, circle the number that best describes you.

Disagree Strongly 1 2 3 4 5 Agree Strongly

1 I spend time developing new ways of approaching old problems.

1   2   3   4   5

2 As long as things are done correctly and efficiently, I prefer not to take on the hassle of changing them.

1   2   3   4   5

3 I always believe the effort to improve something should be rewarded, even if the final improvement is disappointing.

1   2   3   4   5

4 A single change that improves things 30 per cent is much better than 30 improvements of 1 per cent each.

1   2   3   4   5

5 I frequently compliment others on changes they have made.

1   2   3   4   5

6 I let people know in a variety of ways that I like to be left alone to do my job efficiently.

1   2   3   4   5

7 I am personally involved in several improvement projects at one time.

1   2   3   4   5

8 I try to be a good listener and be patient with what people say, except when it is a stupid idea.

1   2   3   4   5

9 I am always proposing unconventional techniques and ideas.

1   2   3   4   5

10 I usually do not take risks that would create a problem for me if the idea failed.

1   2   3   4   5

Scoring and Interpretation

Subtract each of your scores for questions 2, 4, 6, 8 and 10 from the number 6. Then, using the adjusted scores, add the scores from all ten items for your total score.

This scale indicates the extent to which your orientation toward productivity is based on *efficiency* or *continuous improvement*. Efficiency sometimes can be maximized by eliminating change. This approach may be appropriate in a stable organizational environment. Continuous improvement is an attitude that productivity can always get better and you take personal responsibility to improve it. This attitude is appropriate for a quality-conscious company experiencing frequent change.

A score of 40 or higher indicates that you take personal responsibility for improving productivity and frequently initiate change. A score of 20 or less indicates you make contributions through efficient work in a stable environment. Discuss the pros and cons of the efficiency versus continuous improvement orientations for organizations and employees.

MANAGEMENT IN PRACTICE: ETHICAL DILEMMA

A Friend For Life?

Priscilla Dennis has always loved her job as managing director of Smallworld's, a small company that produces and markets toys for young children. As a mother, Priscilla appreciates the care that goes into producing safe, high-quality toys. Late last year, Holly's designer invented a small, cuddly talking bear. Called the Binky-Bear, the toy was made of soft brown simulated fur and had a digital chip inside that played 50 messages. To see what kind of appeal the Binky-Bear might have, Holly produced 50 of the toys and placed them in kindergartens and nurseries. Results were better than managers had hoped, with many of the kindergartens reporting that the toy quickly became the most popular in the school.

Based on these results, Smallworld's decided to produce 1000 of the bears, and they developed a catchy marketing slogan: 'A Friend for Life'. The bear was marketed as a toy that children could play with for years and years, and perhaps still have around as a keepsake when they had long outgrown toys. The first batch sold out within a week, so the company scheduled another production run of 25 000. However, during the run, the production manager discovered a problem. In the excitement over the new product, the designer and managers had failed to look carefully at manufacturing considerations. It turned out that the process needed to make Binky-Bear's soft fur was much more expensive than anticipated. Using the original fur will cost the company £4.98 per bear, but the manufacturing department can produce a substitute that will cut the cost to only £1.25 per bear. However, as compared with the original fur, which should last approximately eight years, the alternative, less-expensive fur will last for only eight months.

Market research indicates that a price increase to cover the greater expense of the original fur would significantly hurt sales; the Binky-Bear is already considered rather costly for a stuffed animal toy. In an emergency meeting to discuss the problem, Smallworld's managers are considering two options: absorb the extra cost, or use the cheaper substitute fur that will not last nearly as long. Many of the managers emphasize that children aren't interested in playing with toys for more than a few months – or even weeks – anyway, so substituting the less-expensive fur shouldn't be a problem. Others, including the production manager, believe the company's reputation for quality will be severely damaged. 'We're going to have complaints within eight months, and we will rue the day we agreed to a cheaper substitute,' the production manager said. The manufacturing director agreed, asking, 'What are we going to do about our slogan – change it to 'A Friend for Eight Months'? The marketing and sales managers forcefully argued the opposite viewpoint, pointing out that Smallworld already had a fortune tied up in the bear. 'If you stop production now or continue with the expensive fur, we'll lose our shirts,' the sales manager said. 'The bear looks the same. I say we substitute the cheaper fur and no one will ever know the difference.'

The final decision about how to handle the problem rests with Priscilla Dennis. She knows Smallworld can't afford to absorb the extra production costs, but can it afford to lose its reputation for quality? Also, she wonders whether she can look her young daughter in the eye if she goes along with what the sales manager is suggesting.

What Would You Do?

1 Substitute the less expensive fur but insist on a revised marketing campaign and advise buyers about the change in the production process.

2 Substitute the less expensive fur and wait to see what happens. The company would not be doing anything illegal, and most customers probably will never notice that the fur wears out so quickly.

3 Absorb the extra production costs. It's the right thing to do, and besides, the company's reputation for quality is too important to risk.

SOURCE Based on 'A Friend for Life', in Donald F. Kuratko and Richard M. Hodgetts, *Entrepreneurship: A Contemporary Approach*, 4th ed. (Fort Worth, TX: The Dryden Press, 1998): 172–173.

CASE FOR CRITICAL ANALYSIS 21.1

SunBright Outdoor Furniture

James Cowart started making and selling outdoor furniture in 1984. He built up the business to 300 employees and £28 million in sales in 2003. SunBright operates a single factory, where it fabricates and assembles a wide range of outdoor furniture, including tables, chairs, umbrellas and matching accessories. SunBright's major production tasks include extruding the aluminium furniture parts, bending and shaping the extruded parts, finishing and painting the parts, and then assembling the parts into completed furniture. Cloth and leather upholstery, glass for tabletops, wood finishing and hardware such as screws and bolts are purchased from outside vendors.

Running this business was an almost 24-hour-a-day job for Cowart, because manufacturing or sales problems arose constantly. Cowart seemed to be the only person who could solve them. In 2003, Cowart decided to hire a general manager to run the manufacturing and sales department so he could have more time for other interests, including his grandchildren. To his good fortune, he was approached by Eva Rucker, who offered to invest in the business and grow it from a regional manufacturer to one that sold to major national retailers. Rucker had excellent experience in sales and understood manufacturing. After a few months of getting to know each other, Cowart sold Rucker 25 per cent of the business and installed her as general manager. Cowart retained for himself the position of managing director. Although he would not be at work full time, he would retain final authority on major decisions.

After just two months, Rucker started adding salespeople, with the goal of doubling the sales force in one year in order to reach new regional and national retail accounts. As sales began to increase, she also hired additional support staff, including a purchasing agent, two furniture designers, and an accountant. By the end of Rucker's first year, SunBright was carried by three national retail chains on a trial basis. However, new problems started to surface. SunBright was missing the delivery dates promised by sales reps and a few orders had been returned for not meeting quality standards. With the consolidation of retail stores into fewer chains, the national retailers had the power to demand high quality, low prices, and rapid delivery from SunBright or they would order outdoor furniture from other suppliers.

At the end of her first year, Rucker was struggling to improve operations to meet the demands of national retailers, but with little success. She invited a consultant to evaluate SunBright's operations. The consultant's report contained the following elements.

1 Cooperation among departments is minimal or nonexistent. For example, the purchasing manager changed to a new supplier for paint because it saved a few pence per gallon. But the paint had to be applied in a thicker coat to wear as long in outdoor use. The additional labour and paint actually cost more than the few pence saved in purchasing, and no one in the manufacturing department had been consulted.

2 Salespeople frequently run promotions and promise sales delivery dates that are impossible for manufacturing to meet. The department head of manufacturing emphasizes that it takes time to work out the bugs when introducing new products or increasing production levels.

3 The furniture designers have added features that are difficult and expensive to produce. On the new 'Monarch' line, for example, the table legs required a new die that cost £26 000. The designers could have designed a table leg that would be produced on one of the existing dies.

4 The accounting department reports that productivity for the plant is low. Equipment utilization is too low. The operation is not lean enough to make acceptable profits.

5 The comptroller reports that inventory is too high. Too much capital is tied up in raw materials. Too much capital is also tied up in excessive in-process inventory waiting at machines to be finished and processed for delivery to customers.

6 Salespeople want to use the internet to publicize SunBright product information and to make routine sales, freeing them to call on new customers. This approach would entail hiring people who could design and manage a sophisticated SunBright webpage.

Eva Rucker discussed these six issues with the consultant and agreed with the report's findings. She met with James Cowart to report the findings and ask for his support and financial resources to make corrections. Cowart listened to the presentation and then said he had some other things to attend to. 'I don't think it's as serious as you say,' he told Rucker, 'but you can have a meeting with the department heads if you want to discuss it with them. Remember that our production problems are no worse than our competitors' issues. You don't have to fix everything overnight. Things worked pretty well before we started to grow so fast, and I'm sure they'll work well again.'

Questions

1 At what stage of operations strategy is Sun-Bright? Explain.

2 Which of the problems outlined by the consultant do you consider the highest priority? Second priority? Why? What steps would you take to solve them?

3 If you were James Cowart, how would you have responded to the report from Eva Rucker? If you were Rucker, what would you do now?

SOURCE Adapted from 'Taracare, Inc.', in Jack R. Meredith and Scott M. Shafer, *Operations Management for MBAs* (New York: John Wiley, 2002): 17–18.

ENDNOTES

1. Susannah Patton, 'The Perfect Order', *CIO* (August 1, 2005): 38–44; and West Marine Company History: A Lesson in Navigation, www.westmarine.com.
2. Glenn R. Simpson, 'Just in Time: In Year of Disasters, Experts Bring Order to Chaos of Relief', *The Wall Street Journal* (November 22, 2005): A1, A12; and Ellen Florian Kratz, 'For FedEx, It Was Time to Deliver', *Fortune* (October 3, 2005): 83–84.
3. James D. Thompson, *Organizations in Action* (New York: McGraw-Hill, 1967).
4. Chad Terhune, 'Growing Pains; To Bag China's Snack Market, Pepsi Takes Up Potato Farming', *The Wall Street Journal* (December 19, 2005): A1, A6.
5. Brian Heymans, 'Leading the Lean Enterprise', *Industrial Management* (September–October 2002): 28–33; and Norihiko Shirouzu, 'Gadget Inspector: Why Toyota Wins Such High Marks on Quality Surveys', *The Wall Street Journal* (March 15, 2001): A1, A11.
6. Gregory B. Northcraft and Richard B. Chase, 'Managing Service Demand at the Point of Delivery', *Academy of Management Review* 10 (1985): 66–75; and Richard B. Chase and David A. Tanski, 'The Customer Contact Model for Organization Design', *Management Science* 29 (1983): 1037–1050.
7. Robert H. Lowson, 'Strategic Operations Management – The New Competitive Advantage?' *Journal of General Management* 28, no. 1 (Autumn 2002): 36–56; and Everett E. Adam Jr. and Paul M. Swamidass, 'Assessing Operations Management from a Strategic Perspective', *Journal of Management* 15 (1989): 181–203.
8. Robert H. Hayes and David M. Upton, 'Operations-Based Strategy', *California Management Review* 40, no. 4 (Summer 1998): 8–25.
9. This section is based on Charles W. L. Hill and Gareth R. Jones, *Strategic Management: An Integrated Approach*, 6th edn. (Boston: Houghton Mifflin, 2004): Chapter 4.
10. Carol J. Loomis, 'The Big Surprise Is Enterprise', *Fortune* (July 24, 2006): 140–150.
11. Carol Hymowitz, 'For Now, the Focus Is More on Innovation Than on Budget Cuts', *The Wall Street Journal* (July 17, 2006): B1.
12. Terry Kosdrosky, 'Porsche Jumps to No.1 in Auto-Quality Survey', *The Wall Street Journal (Europe)*, (June 8, 2006): 6.
13. Heather Harreld, 'Pick-Up Artists', *CIO* (November 1, 2000): 148–154; Cheryl Rosen, 'Online Repair Updates with a Click', *InformationWeek* (July 30, 2001): 67; and Loomis, 'The Big Surprise Is Enterprise'.
14. Definition based on Steven A. Melnyk and David R. Denzler, *Operations Management: A Value-Driven Approach* (Burr Ridge, IL: Richard D. Irwin, 1996): 613.
15. Based on Jim Turcotte, Bob Silveri and Tom Jobson, 'Are You Ready for the E-Supply Chain?', *APICS–The Performance Advantage* (August 1998): 56–59.
16. AMR Research rankings reported in Patton, 'The Perfect Order'.
17. Jason Dedrick and Kenneth L. Kraemer, 'The Impacts of IT on Firm and Industry Structure: The Personal Computer Industry', *California Management Review* 47, no. 3 (Spring 2005): 122–142; Kathryn Jones, 'The Dell Way', *Business 2.0* (February 2003): 61–66; and Stewart Deck, 'Fine Line', *CIO* (February 1, 2000): 88–92.
18. Jeffrey McCracken, 'Ford Seeks Big Savings by Overhauling Supply System' *The Wall Street Journal* (September 29, 2005): A1, A11.
19. Russ Banham, 'Caught in the Middle', *CFO* (May 2001): 69–74.
20. Jason Tanz, 'From Drab to Fab', *Fortune* (December 8, 2003): 178–184.
21. David Goldenberg, 'Fresh Breath, Fresher Packaging', *Business 2.0* (December 2005): 74–76
22. Erika Brown, 'Drive Fast, Drive Hard', *Forbes* (January 9, 2006): 92.

23. Christopher Koch, 'The Big Payoff', *CIO* (October 1, 2000): 101–112; Norman Gaither and Greg Frazier, *Operations Management*, 9th edn. (Cincinnati, OH: South-Western Publishing, 2002): 428–429.

24. Gaither and Frazier, *Operations Management*, 429.

25. David Rocks, 'The Net as a Lifeline', *BusinessWeek e.biz* (October 29, 2001): EB16–EB28.

26. Scott Leibs, 'First Pencils, Now People', *CFO* (November 2001): 91–94.

27. Nancy Lea Hyer and Karen A. Brown, 'Work Cells with Staying Power: Lessons for Process–Complete Operations', *California Management Review* 46, no. 1 (Fall 2003): 27–52.

28. Daniel Michaels and J. Lynn Lunsford, 'Streamlined Plane Making', *The Wall Street Journal* (April 1, 2005): B1, B2.

29. Kelly Wardle, 'One Enchanted Evening', *Special Events*, http://www.specialevents.com/corporate/events_one_enchanted_evening_20060203/index.html (accessed May 27, 2008).

30. Dean Elmuti and Michael Abebe, 'RFID Reshapes the Global Supply Chain', *Industrial Management* (March–April 2005): 27–31; John Teresko, 'Plant Strategies: Winning with Wireless', *Industry Week* (June 2003): 60–66; and Meridith Levinson, 'The RFID Imperative', *CIO* (December 1, 2003): 78–91.

31. Erick Schonfeld, 'Tagged for Growth', *Business 2.0* (December 2006): 58–61.

32. 'ZDNet Definition for: RFID'.

33. Scott McCartney, 'The Middle Seat: A New Way to Prevent Lost Luggage', *The Wall Street Journal*, (February 27, 2007).

34. http://www.lloydspharmacy.com/wps/portal/aboutus/about lloydspharmacy; Jena McGregor, 'The Starbucks of Pharmacies'? *Fast Company* (April 2005): 62–63; Sandra Levy, 'PrairieStone Pharmacy: Drug Topics' Chain of the Year', *Drug Topics* (April 18, 2005): www.drugtopics.com/drug topics/article/articleDetail.jsp?id=1564 90; www.prairiestonerx.com; and 'PrairieStone Pharmacy Makes Its Debut', *Chain Drug Review* (May 2, 2005): 69.

35. Sumer C. Aggarwal, 'MRP, JIT, OPT, FMS?' *Harvard Business Review* 63 (September–October 1985): 8–16; and Paul Ranky, *The Design and Operation of Flexible Manufacturing Systems* (New York: Elsevier, 1983).

36. David Welch, 'How Nissan Laps Detroit', *BusinessWeek* (December 22, 2003): 58–60.

37. Kenji Hall, 'No One Does Lean Like the Japanese', *BusinessWeek* (July 10, 2006): 40–41.

38. This discussion of product life-cycle management software is based on Gene Bylinsky, 'Not Your Grandfather's Assembly Line', *Fortune* special section, 'Industrial Management and Technology', (June 28, 2004): www.fortune.com.

39. Luciana Beard and Stephen A. Butler, 'Introducing JIT Manufacturing: It's Easier Than You Think', *Business Horizons* (September–October 2000): 61–64.

40. Robert J. Vokurka, Rhonda R. Lummus and Dennis Krumwiede, 'Improving Manufacturing Flexibility: The Enduring Value of JIT and TQM', *SAM Advanced Management Journal* (Winter 2007): 14–21.

41. Based on Ronald Henkoff, 'Delivering the Goods', *Fortune* (November 28, 1994): 64–78.

42. Noel P. Greis and John D. Kasarda, 'Enterprise Logistics in the Information Era', *California Management Review* 39, no. 4 (Summer 1997): 55–78; 'Kanban: The Just-in-Time Japanese Inventory System', *Small Business Report* (February 1984): 69–71; and Richard C. Walleigh, 'What's Your Excuse for Not Using JIT?', *Harvard Business Review* 64 (March–April 1986): 38–54.

43. David Rocks, 'Dell's Second Web Revolution', *BusinessWeek e.biz* (September 18, 2000): EB62–EB63.

44. 'Kanban: The Just-in-Time Japanese Inventory System', *Small Business Report* (February 1984): 69–71; and Richard C. Walleigh, 'What's Your Excuse for Not Using JIT?', *Harvard Business Review* 64 (March–April 1986): 38–54.

45. Gaither and Frazier, *Operations Management*, 150–151.

46. Andrew Ward, Dan Roberts, and Alexandra Harney, 'US Groups Shift Their Warehouses to China', *Financial Times* (November 17, 2005): www.ft.com.

47. Peter Strozniak, 'Toyota Alters Face of Production', *Industry Week* (August 13, 2001): 46–48; and Jeffrey K. Liker and James M. Morgan, 'The Toyota Way in Services: The Case of Lean Product Development', *Academy of Management Perspectives* (May 2006): 5–20.

48. Art Kleiner, 'Leaning Toward Utopia', *Strategy + Business*, no. 39 (Second Quarter 2005): 76–87; Fara Warner, 'Think Lean', *Fast Company* (February 2002): 40, 42; Norihiko Shirouzu, 'Gadget Inspector: Why Toyota Wins Such High Marks on Quality Surveys', *The Wall Street Journal*, March 15, 2001; and James P. Womack and Daniel T. Jones, *The Machine That Changed the World: The Story of Lean Production* (New York: HarperCollins, 1991).

49. Emily Esterson, 'First-Class Delivery', *Inc. Technology* (September 15, 1998): 89.

50. W. Bouce Chew, 'No-Nonsense Guide to Measuring Productivity', *Harvard Business Review* (January–February 1988): 110–118.

51. The Outsourcing Institute, 'Outsourcing: The New Midas Touch', *BusinessWeek* (December 15, 1997): special advertising section.

52. W. E. Deming, *Quality, Productivity, and Competitive Position* (Cambridge, MA: Center for Advanced Engineering Study, MIT, 1982); and P. B. Crosby, *Quality Is Free* (New York: McGraw-Hill, 1979).

53. Charles E. Lucier and Janet D. Torsilieri, 'Why Knowledge Programs Fail: A C.E.O.'s Guide to Managing Learning', *Strategy + Business* (Fourth Quarter 1997): 14–16, 21–27.

54. Patton, 'The Perfect Order'.

IKEA
PART SIX: IN CONTROL WITH IT SYSTEMS

IKEA has always been at the forefront when it comes to using the latest information technology for all areas of its business processes. One of the main reasons is that IKEA has always been able to adapt quickly to change. Also, as has been previously noted, their competitive advantage relies on keeping prices low; therefore, the objective of every step of production and sale is to keep low costs without affecting quality. To do this IKEA has developed methods which are both cost-efficient and innovative, enhanced by using Information Technology (IT). IKEA's IT division is called *IKEA IT*. This central division provides IKEA with all its systems requirements such as common business solutions, architecture, infrastructure, service and support. IKEA invests approximately 1.5 per cent of its yearly sales in its IT functions. These functions include over 60 IT systems, each one created for a specific business process including product development, administration finance, order management, inventory control, logistics and transport, sales follow-up, warehousing, invoicing, electronic commerce, etc. IT also helps in managing the product range that includes 12 000 products, innovating in technologies and products, and cutting costs in production and distribution. One of the central IT tools is the PIA (Product Information Assistance) system. This IT system is used in developing IKEA's products, and in this phase IKEA works with suppliers in developing products to obtain the lowest production costs possible. PIA has a large database which includes supplier identities and contracts, production technology and quality certifications, technical descriptions of the product and the related Computer Aided Design (CAD) files. PIA's key contribution is in the launch of the modified or new version of a product. Any product modification can't be launched before sending retailers two documents that only PIA can create: with those documents, retailers are able to order and sell the products. Also consumers are reached by PIA information in assembly instructions, price tags and packaging information. Coupled with PIA there are also many other area specific IT initiatives. For example Dairy Farm International's IKEA franchise in Hong Kong and Taiwan recently deployed an Enterprise Resource Planning system, *The Lawson M3,* for optimizing business processes in its seven IKEA stores and two warehouses. These processes include replenishment, inventory, finance, distribution and logistics and procurement. In Hong Kong, IKEA employs a centralized warehouse and store replenishment model and Taiwan utilizes a hybrid distribution model where a centralized warehouse is coupled with real-time replenishment of inventory. Another important feature is the point-of-sales system which integrates with the backend inventory and distribution functions. Essentially, *The Lawson M3* ERP links the point-of-sale with the supply chain including functions such as inventory statistics, warehouse management, distribution order processing, transportation management and sales budget planning. To date, 550 users and 100 point-of-sale tills in IKEA's Hong Kong and Taiwan operations are linked by the ERP. John Shelton, Group IT Director of Dairy Farm, representing the IKEA franchise business states that: 'The Lawson M3 solutions also offer a low Total Cost of Ownership (TCO), which presents a good case for achieving return-on-investment (ROI). As a retailer of furnishing for everyday people, we want to be able to derive the best value out of our IT solutions so that the savings can be passed on to our customers. With Lawson M3, we are able to do this and enhance the store and customer experience at the same time.' Delivery time is also shortened because of the increased supply chain visibility. David Hope, Regional Managing Director, Lawson Software Asia and Japan says, 'We're proud to enable Dairy Farm's IKEA business in enhancing supply chain efficiency to deliver their world famous home furnishing products to even more satisfied customers in Hong Kong and Taiwan.'

IKEA have not only adopted technology for those business processes mentioned above but also subscribe to other technologies for activities such as project management and design. For example IKEA has hired Aconex to provide its online information management service to aid in the building of five stores in China. Aconex provides a Web-based platform for managing project information such as drawings, documents and correspondence. This allows IKEA and its partners access to their files from at any in any location. As Leigh Jasper, Aconex Chief Executive Officer, says, 'The design and construction of these stores will involve thousands of documents being exchanged between team members in China and IKEA's headquarters in Europe. Aconex will improve productivity by enabling project participants to access and share their information in real-time. IKEA will also be able to control its risk exposure by having the ability to track the status of tasks and "who did what and when" on the project.'

Another recent innovation is that all of IKEA's global warehouses and their largest suppliers will start to use GS1 DataBar's system of barcodes and Serial Shipping Container Codes (SSCCs). This consists of 18 digits and is bar-coded using GS1-128. Using this key a package can be uniquely identified by everybody involved in the supply chain, e.g. suppliers, transporters and IKEA's warehouses and stores. IKEA is also considering initiating the use of Radio Frequency Identification (RFID). Jan Ståhl, business developer at IKEA's Supply Chain Development says, 'The introduction of the system reduces costs considerably. This means both lower prices and higher product quality for IKEA's customers. This trend will continue when we introduce RFID.' The system was piloted at IKEA's warehouses in Älmhult and Torsvik in cooperation with their three largest suppliers and the initial results were positive. Fundamentally, a barcode is read as the pallet is unloaded allowing it to be fetched immediately by a truck driver and put into the store. The results showed that the time to unload a truck was reduced by 44 per cent and the turnover in the warehouse's dock area increased by 55 per cent. Stahl says, 'Inventory control is improved, stock information is more accurate, and the pallets' traceability is much better. This also applies to the three suppliers who have started to use the system for internal traceability in their own warehouses.' Referring to product quality Stahl also notes that, 'The idea is that, due to the different legal demands on product quality and product content in different countries, we can easily trace the raw materials from which our products are made thus further improving quality.'

IKEA, recognizing the importance of managing its workforce, also recently facilitated a fully automated employee scheduling system. This system analyses historical trading data, projected sales figures, labour standards and employee availability before creating the optimum staffing schedule for each department. This optimized scheduling will be available at all 17 IKEA stores in the UK. Keith Statham, Managing Director, Kronos UK, who supplied the system said, 'Retailers work hard to optimize everything from the supply chain to store merchandizing, yet optimizing every aspect of managing the workforce is often overlooked. I'm delighted that IKEA has taken this step to automate and optimize employee scheduling. It's the step that all retailers need to take to truly create an efficient store environment and keep their customers happy'.

In regard to ecommerce and ebusiness systems IKEA is also willing to adapt its business processes. For example in 2007 it launched its online shopping service in the UK. Prior to this IKEA's shoppers could only browse the internet before going to the stores. Now the new the website carries a wide range of IKEA products, including sofas, bedding and lighting that can be purchased online. At the time Mr Högsted of IKEA stated that, 'We will test it very softly in the summer and autumn and then full-scale later this year or early next year. It is a way to be more accessible for our customers.' However, he did recognize that, 'If you want to make this a future business strategy then it can work in a very big way. It is all about the logistics and supply from our suppliers'. As such it should be noted that the e-commerce system should have a direct link with those systems already identified.

As an adjunct its e-commerce activities, and in line with its policy on its continuing IT initiatives, IKEA is also involved in *social networking*. For example IKEA's (business) Facebook page includes a store profile, photos, stories, discussion board, customer reviews and 'wall posts'. IKEA has over 32 000 'Fans' who can upload photos of their rooms. IKEA added the 'notes' application that can be used to add information about just about anything including policies, profiles and community involvement.

The above systems indicate how IKEA is willing to embrace a variety of IT initiatives in all areas of its business. These included enterprise resource planning, customer relationship management, supply chain management and staff management, and even social networking.

Questions

1 Identify where the following types of control would be best employed within the IKEA systems discussed in the Case: *feedforward control, concurrent control and feedback control.* Give examples.

2 What important issues would IKEA's management have had to consider prior to their decision to invest in an e-business strategy?

3 Explain how IKEA's Enterprise Resource Planning (ERP) system can benefit the company's supply chain.

SOURCES 'Lawson Software Delivers ERP Solutions to IKEA' (2007), Phillipines Hardware Zone, online at: http://ph.hardware zone.com/news/view.php?id=8040&cid=11; 'IKEA selects Aconex online information management service for five store developments in China' (2008), *Bulding Talk,* online at: http://www.buildingtalk. com/news/acx/acx132.html; 'IKEA chooses Kronos scheduling solution' (2007), *Personnel Today,* online at: http://www.person neltoday.com/articles/2007/12/07/43623/ikea-chooses-kronos-scheduling-solution.html; Lopez-Gines, A. (2007),'Computers in Management', online at: https://www.socialtext.net/lite/page/cim/ ikea; Raattamaa, B. (2007), 'IKEA adopts GS1 standards', online at: http://209.85.229.132/search?q=cache:uSYBbOy60DEJ:bar codes.gs1us.org/dnn_bcec/Documents/tabid/136/DMXModule/ 731/Command/Core_Download/Default.aspx%3FEntryId%3D165+ IKEA+adopts+GS1+standards&hl=en&ct=clnk&cd=1&gl=uk.

GLOSSARY

360-degree feedback A process that uses multiple raters, including self-rating, to appraise employee performance and guide development.

accountability The fact that the people with authority and responsibility are subject to reporting and justifying task outcomes to those above them in the chain of command.

achievement culture A results-oriented culture that values competitiveness, personal initiative, and achievement.

activity ratio A financial ratio that measures the organization's internal performance with respect to key activities defined by management.

activity-based costing (ABC) A control system that identifies the various activities needed to provide a product and allocates costs accordingly.

adaptability culture A culture characterized by values that support the company's ability to interpret and translate signals from the environment into new behaviour responses.

adjourning The stage of team development in which members prepare for the team's disbandment.

administrative model A decision-making model that describes how managers actually make decisions in situations characterized by non-programmed decisions, uncertainty, and ambiguity.

administrative principles A subfield of the classical management perspective that focuses on the total organization rather than the individual worker, delineating the management functions of planning, organizing, commanding, coordinating, and controlling.

affirmative action A policy requiring employers to take positive steps to guarantee equal employment opportunities for people within protected groups.

ambidextrous approach Incorporating structures and processes that are appropriate for both the creative impulse and for the systematic implementation of innovations.

ambiguity A condition in which the goals to be achieved or the problem to be solved is unclear, alternatives are difficult to define, and information about outcomes is unavailable.

angel financing Financing provided by a wealthy individual who believes in the idea for a start-up and provides personal funds and advice to help the business get started.

application form A device for collecting information about an applicant's education, previous job experience, and other background characteristics.

assessment centre A technique for selecting individuals with high managerial potential based on their performance on a series of simulated managerial tasks.

attitude A cognitive and affective evaluation that predisposes a person to act in a certain way.

attributions Judgements about what caused a person's behaviour – either characteristics of the person or of the situation.

authoritarianism The belief that power and status differences should exist within the organization.

authority The formal and legitimate right of a manager to make decisions, issue orders, and allocate resources to achieve organizationally desired outcomes.

B2B marketplace An electronic marketplace set up by an intermediary where buyers and sellers meet.

balance sheet A financial statement that shows the firm's financial position with respect to assets and liabilities at a specific point in time.

balanced scorecard A comprehensive management control system that balances traditional financial measures with measures of customer service, internal business processes, and the organization's capacity for learning and growth.

bargaining zone The range between one party's minimum reservation point (the point beyond which the party is willing to accept a deal) and the other party's maximum reservation point.

BATNA The 'best alternative to a negotiated agreement'; a previously determined choice of what a party will do if an acceptable agreement cannot be reached through negotiation.

BCG matrix A concept developed by the Boston Consulting Group that evaluates strategic business units with respect to the dimensions of business growth rate and market share.

behaviour modification The set of techniques by which reinforcement theory is used to modify human behaviour.

behavioural sciences approach A subfield of the humanistic management perspective that applies social science in an organizational context, drawing from economics, psychology, sociology, and other disciplines.

behaviourally anchored rating scale (BARS) A rating technique that relates an employee's performance to specific job-related incidents.

benchmarking The continuous process of measuring products, services, and practices against major competitors or industry leaders.

biculturalism The socio-cultural skills and attitudes used by racial minorities as they move back and forth between the dominant culture and their own ethnic or racial culture.

Big Five personality factors Dimensions that describe an individual's extroversion, agreeableness, conscientiousness, emotional stability, and openness to experience.

blog Web log that allows individuals to post opinions and ideas.

Blue Ocean Strategy is a creative battle where the players of a particular segment don't compete with each other remaining in the same market space; instead explore, create and acquire new market spaces by dealing with new demand.

bottom of the pyramid concept The idea that large corporations can both alleviate social problems and make a profit by selling goods and services to the world's poorest people.

bottom-up budgeting A budgeting process in which lower-level managers budget their departments' resource needs and pass them up to top management for approval.

boundary-spanning roles Roles assumed by people and/or departments that link and coordinate the organization with key elements in the external environment.

bounded rationality The concept that people have the time and cognitive ability to process only a limited amount of information on which to base decisions.

brainstorming A technique that uses a face-to-face group to spontaneously suggest a broad range of alternatives for decision-making.

bureaucratic organizations A subfield of the classical management perspective that emphasized management on an impersonal, rational basis through such elements as clearly defined authority and responsibility, formal record-keeping, and separation of management and ownership.

business incubator An innovation that provides shared office space, management support services, and management advice to entrepreneurs.

business intelligence (BI) The high-tech analysis of data from multiple sources to identify patterns and relationships that might be significant.

business performance dashboard A system that pulls data from a variety of organizational systems and databases; gauges the data against key performance metrics; pulls out the right nuggets of information; and delivers information to managers in a graphical, easy-to-interpret format.

business plan A document specifying the business details prepared by an entrepreneur prior to opening a new business.

business-level strategy The level of strategy concerned with the question 'How do we compete'? Pertains to each business unit or product line within the organization.

CAD A production technology in which computers perform new-product design.

CAM A production technology in which computers help guide and control the manufacturing system.

capacity planning The determination and adjustment of the organization's ability to produce products and services to match customer demand.

capital budget A budget that plans and reports investments in major assets to be depreciated over several years.

cellular layout A facilities layout in which machines dedicated to sequences of production are grouped into cells in accordance with group-technology principles.

central planning department A group of planning specialists who develop plans for the organization as a whole and its major divisions and departments and typically report directly to the president or CEO.

centralization The location of decision authority near top organizational levels.

centralized network A team communication structure in which team members communicate through a single individual to solve problems or make decisions.

ceremony A planned activity at a special event that is conducted for the benefit of an audience.

certainty The situation in which all the information the decision-maker needs is fully available.

chain of command An unbroken line of authority that links all individuals in the organization and specifies who reports to whom.

change agent An OD specialist who contracts with an organization to facilitate change.

changing The intervention stage of organization development in which individuals experiment with new workplace behaviour.

channel The carrier of a communication.

channel richness The amount of information that can be transmitted during a communication episode.

charismatic leader A leader who has the ability to motivate subordinates to transcend their expected performance.

chief ethics officer A company executive who oversees ethics and legal compliance.

classical model A decision-making model based on the assumption that managers should make logical decisions that will be in the organization's best economic interests.

classical perspective A management perspective that emerged during the nineteenth and early twentieth centuries that emphasized a rational, scientific approach to the study of management and sought to make organizations efficient operating machines.

closed system A system that does not interact with the external environment.

coalition An informal alliance among managers who support a specific goal.

code of ethics A formal statement of the organization's values regarding ethics and social issues.

coercive power Power that stems from the authority to punish or recommend punishment.

cognitive dissonance A condition in which two attitudes or a behaviour and an attitude conflict.

collectivism A preference for a tightly knit social framework in which individuals look after one another and organizations protect their members' interests.

committee A long-lasting, sometimes permanent team in the organization structure created to deal with tasks that recur regularly.

communication The process by which information is exchanged and understood by two or more people, usually with the intent to motivate or influence behaviour.

communication apprehension An individual's level of fear or anxiety associated with interpersonal communications.

compensation Monetary payments (wages, salaries) and nonmonetary goods/commodities (benefits, vacations) used to reward employees.

compensatory justice The concept that individuals should be compensated for the cost of their injuries by the party responsible and also that individuals should not be held responsible for matters over which they have no control.

competitive advantage What sets the organization apart from others and provides it with a distinctive edge in the marketplace.

competitors Other organizations in the same industry or type of business that provide goods or services to the same set of customers.

conceptual skill The cognitive ability to see the organization as a whole and the relationships among its parts.

conflict Antagonistic interaction in which one party attempts to thwart the intentions or goals of another.

consideration A type of behaviour that describes the extent to which the leader is sensitive to subordinates, respects their ideas and feelings, and establishes mutual trust.

consistency culture A culture that values and rewards a methodical, rational, orderly way of doing things.

content theories A group of theories that emphasize the needs that motivate people.

contingency approach A model of leadership that describes the relationship between leadership styles and specific organizational situations.

contingency plans Plans that define company responses to specific situations, such as emergencies, setbacks, or unexpected conditions.

contingency view An extension of the humanistic perspective in which the successful resolution of organizational problems is thought to depend on managers' identification of key variations in the situation at hand.

contingent workers People who work for an organization, but not on a permanent or full-time basis, including temporary placements, contracted professionals, or leased employees.

continuous improvement The implementation of a large number of small, incremental improvements in all areas of the organization on an ongoing basis.

continuous process production A type of technology involving mechanization of the entire work flow and non-stop production.

continuous reinforcement schedule A schedule in which every occurrence of the desired behaviour is reinforced.

controlling The management function concerned with monitoring employees' activities, keeping the organization on track toward its goals, and making corrections as needed.

coordination The quality of collaboration across departments.

core competence A business activity that an organization does particularly well in comparison to competitors.

corporate governance The system of governing an organization so the interests of corporate owners are protected.

corporate social responsibility The obligation of organization management to make decisions and take actions that will enhance the welfare and interests of society as well as the organization.

corporate university An in-house training and education facility that offers broad-based learning opportunities for employees.

corporate-level strategy The level of strategy concerned with the question 'What business are we in'? Pertains to the organization as a whole and the combination of business units and product lines that make it up.

corporation An artificial entity created by the state and existing apart from its owners.

cost leadership A type of competitive strategy with which the organization aggressively seeks efficient facilities, cuts costs, and employs tight cost controls to be more efficient than competitors.

countertrade The barter of products for other products rather than their sale for currency.

courage The ability to step forward through fear and act on one's values and conscience.

creativity The generation of novel ideas that might meet perceived needs or offer opportunities for the organization.

cross-functional teams A group of employees from various functional departments that meet as a team to resolve mutual problems.

cultural competence The ability to interact effectively with people of different cultures.

cultural intelligence (CQ) A person's ability to use reasoning and observation skills to interpret unfamiliar gestures and situations and devise appropriate behavioural responses.

cultural leader A manager who uses signals and symbols to influence corporate culture.

culture change A major shift in the norms, values, attitudes, and mindset of the entire organization.

culture shock Feelings of confusion, disorientation, and anxiety that result from being immersed in a foreign culture.

culture The set of key values, beliefs, understandings, and norms that members of an organization share.

customer relationship management (CRM) systems Systems that help companies track customers' interactions with the firm and allow employees to call up information on past transactions.

customers People and organizations in the environment who acquire goods or services from the organization.

cycle time The steps taken to complete a company process.

data Raw, unsummarized, and unanalyzed facts and figures.

data warehousing The use of a huge database that combines all of a company's data and allows users to access the data directly, create reports, and obtain answers to what-if questions.

debt financing Borrowing money that has to be repaid at a later date in order to start a business.

decentralization The location of decision authority near lower organizational levels.

decentralized control The use of organizational culture, group norms, and a focus on goals, rather than rules and procedures, to foster compliance with organizational goals.

decentralized network A team communication structure in which team members freely communicate with one another and arrive at decisions together.

decentralized planning Managers work with planning experts to develop their own goals and plans.

decision A choice made from available alternatives.

decision styles Differences among people with respect to how they perceive problems and make decisions.

decision support system (DSS) An interactive, computer-based system that uses decision models and specialized databases to support organization decision-makers.

decision-making The process of identifying problems and opportunities and then resolving them.

decode To translate the symbols used in a message for the purpose of interpreting its meaning.

delegation The process managers use to transfer authority and responsibility to positions below them in the hierarchy.

departmentalization The basis on which individuals are grouped into departments and departments into the total organization.

dependent demand inventory Inventory in which item demand is related to the demand for other inventory items.

descriptive An approach that describes how managers actually make decisions rather than how they should make decisions according to a theoretical ideal.

devil's advocate A decision-making technique in which an individual is assigned the role of challenging the assumptions and assertions made by the group to prevent premature consensus.

diagnosis The step in the decision-making process in which managers analyze underlying causal factors associated with the decision situation.

dialogue A group communication process aimed at creating a culture based on collaboration, fluidity, trust, and commitment to shared goals.

differentiation A type of competitive strategy with which the organization seeks to distinguish its products or services from that of competitors.

digital technology Technology characterised by use of the internet and other digital processes to conduct or support business operations.

direct investing An entry strategy in which the organization is involved in managing its production facilities in a foreign country.

discretionary responsibility Organizational responsibility that is voluntary and guided by the organization's desire to make social contributions not mandated by economics, law, or ethics.

discrimination When someone acts out their prejudicial attitudes toward people who are the targets of their prejudice.

distribution Moving finished products to customers; also called *order fulfilment.*

distributive justice The concept that different treatment of people should not be based on arbitrary characteristics. In the case of substantive differences, people should be treated differently in proportion to the differences among them.

distributive negotiation A competitive and adversarial negotiation approach in which each party strives to get as much as it can, usually at the expense of the other party.

diversification A strategy of moving into new lines of business.

diversity All the ways in which employees differ.

diversity training Special training designed to educate employees about the importance of diversity, make people aware of their own biases, and teach them skills for communicating and working in a diverse workplace.

divisional structure An organization structure in which departments are grouped based on similar organizational outputs.

downsizing Intentional, planned reduction in the size of a company's workforce.

downward communication Messages sent from top management down to subordinates.

dual role A role in which the individual both contributes to the team's task and supports members' emotional needs.

dynamic capabilities Leveraging and developing more from the firm's existing assets, capabilities, and core competencies in a way that will provide a sustained competitive advantage.

E → P expectancy Expectancy that putting effort into a given task will lead to high performance.

e-business Any business that takes place by digital processes over a computer network rather than in physical space.

e-commerce Business exchanges or transactions that occur electronically.

economic dimension The dimension of the general environment representing the overall economic health of the country or region in which the organization operates.

economic forces Forces that affect the availability, production, and distribution of a society's resources among competing users.

economic order quantity (EOQ) An inventory management technique designed to minimize the total of ordering and holding costs for inventory items.

economic value-added (EVA) A control system that measures performance in terms of after-tax profits minus the cost of capital invested in tangible assets.

effectiveness The degree to which the organization achieves a stated goal.

efficiency The use of minimal resources – raw materials, money, and people – to produce a desired volume of output.

electronic brainstorming Bringing people together in an interactive group over a computer network to suggest alternatives; sometimes called *brainwriting*.

electronic data interchange (EDI) A network that links the computer systems of buyers and sellers to allow the transmission of structured data primarily for ordering, distribution, and payables and receivables.

employee network groups Groups based on social identity, such as gender or race, and organized by employees to focus on concerns of employees from that group.

employment test A written or computer-based test designed to measure a particular attribute such as intelligence or aptitude.

empowerment The delegation of power and authority to subordinates.

encode To select symbols with which to compose a message.

enterprise resource planning (ERP) system A networked information system that collects, processes, and provides information about an organization's entire enterprise, from identification of customer needs and receipt of orders to distribution of products and receipt of payments.

entrepreneur Someone who recognizes a viable idea for a business product or service and carries it out.

entrepreneurship The process of initiating a business venture, organizing the necessary resources, and assuming the associated risks and rewards.

entropy The tendency for a system to run down and die.

equity A situation that exists when the ratio of one person's outcomes to inputs equals that of another's.

equity financing Financing that consists of funds that are invested in exchange for ownership in the company.

equity theory A process theory that focuses on individuals' perceptions of how fairly they are treated relative to others.

ERG theory A modification of the needs hierarchy theory that proposes three categories of needs: existence, relatedness, and growth.

escalating commitment Continuing to invest time and resources in a failing decision.

ethical dilemma A situation that arises when all alternative choices or behaviours are deemed undesirable because of potentially negative consequences, making it difficult to distinguish right from wrong.

ethics The code of moral principles and values that governs the behaviours of a person or group with respect to what is right or wrong.

ethics or corporate responsibility committee A group of executives assigned to oversee the organization's ethics by ruling on questionable issues and disciplining violators.

ethics training Training programmes to help employees deal with ethical questions and values.

ethnocentrism A cultural attitude marked by the tendency to regard one's own culture as superior to others.

ethno-relativism The belief that groups and subcultures are inherently equal.

euro A single European currency that replaced the currencies of 15 European nations.

executive information system (EIS) A management information system designed to facilitate strategic decision-making at the highest levels of management by providing executives with easy access to timely and relevant information.

exit interview An interview conducted with departing employees to determine the reasons for their termination.

expatriates Employees who live and work in a country other than their own.

expectancy theory A process theory that proposes that motivation depends on individuals' expectations about their ability to perform tasks and receive desired rewards.

expense budget A budget that outlines the anticipated and actual expenses for a responsibility centre.

expert power Power that stems from special knowledge of or skill in the tasks performed by subordinates.

exporting An entry strategy in which the organization maintains its production facilities within its home country and transfers its products for sale in foreign countries.

external locus of control The belief by individuals that their future is not within their control but rather is influenced by external forces.

extranet An external communications system that uses the internet and is shared by two or more organizations.

extrinsic reward A reward given by another person.

fast-cycle team A multi-functional team that is provided with high levels of resources and empowerment to accomplish an accelerated product development project.

feedback A response by the receiver to the sender's communication.

femininity A cultural preference for relationships, cooperation, group decision-making, and quality of life.

finished-goods inventory Inventory consisting of items that have passed through the complete production process but have yet to be sold.

first-line manager   A manager who is at the first or second management level and is directly responsible for the production of goods and services.

fixed-position layout   A facilities layout in which the product remains in one location and the required tasks and equipment are brought to it.

flat structure   A management structure characterized by an overall broad span of control and relatively few hierarchical levels.

flexible manufacturing system   A small or medium-sized automated production line that can be adapted to produce more than one product line.

focus   A type of competitive strategy that emphasizes concentration on a specific regional market or buyer group.

force-field analysis   The process of determining which forces drive and which resist a proposed change.

formal communication channel   A communication channel that flows within the chain of command or task responsibility defined by the organization.

formal team   A team created by the organization as part of the formal organization structure.

forming   The stage of team development characterized by orientation and acquaintance.

franchising   A form of licensing in which an organization provides its foreign franchisees with a complete package of materials and services.

free rider   A person who benefits from team membership but does not make a proportionate contribution to the team's work.

frustration-regression principle   The idea that failure to meet a high-order need may cause a regression to an already satisfied lower-order need.

functional manager   A manager who is responsible for a department that performs a single functional task and has employees with similar training and skills.

functional structure   The grouping of positions into departments based on similar skills, expertise, and resource use.

functional-level strategy   The level of strategy concerned with the question 'How do we support the business-level strategy'? Pertains to all of the organization's major departments.

fundamental attribution error   The tendency to underestimate the influence of external factors on another's behaviour and to overestimate the influence of internal factors.

general environment   The layer of the external environment that affects the organization indirectly.

general manager   A manager who is responsible for several departments that perform different functions.

glass ceiling   Invisible barrier that separates women and minorities from top management positions.

global outsourcing   Engaging in the international division of labour so as to obtain the cheapest sources of labour and supplies regardless of country; also called *offshoring*.

global team   A work team made up of members of different nationalities whose activities span multiple countries; may operate as a virtual team or meet face-to-face.

globalization   The standardization of product design and advertising strategies throughout the world.

goal   A desired future state that the organization attempts to realize.

goal-setting theory   A motivation theory in which specific, challenging goals increase motivation and performance when the goals are accepted by subordinates and these subordinates receive feedback to indicate their progress toward goal achievement.

grapevine   An informal, person-to-person communication network of employees that is not officially sanctioned by the organization.

greenfield venture   The most risky type of direct investment, whereby a company builds a subsidiary from scratch in a foreign country.

groupthink   The tendency for people to be so committed to a cohesive team that they are reluctant to express contrary opinions.

groupware   Software that works on a computer network or the internet to facilitate information sharing, collaborative work, and group decision-making.

halo effect   A type of rating error that occurs when an employee receives the same rating on all dimensions regardless of his or her performance on individual ones.

Hawthorne studies   A series of experiments on worker productivity begun in 1924 at the Hawthorne plant of Western Electric Company in Illinois; attributed employees' increased output to managers' better treatment of them during the study.

hero   A figure who exemplifies the deeds, character, and attributes of a strong corporate culture.

hierarchical control   The use of rules, policies, hierarchy of authority, reward systems, and other formal devices to influence employee behaviour and assess performance.

hierarchy of needs theory   A content theory that proposes that people are motivated by five categories of needs – physiological, safety, belongingness, esteem, and self-actualization – that exist in a hierarchical order.

high-context culture   A culture in which communication is used to enhance personal relationships.

high-performance culture   A culture based on a solid organizational mission or purpose that uses shared adaptive values to guide decisions and business practices and to encourage individual employee ownership of both bottom-line results and the organization's cultural backbone.

horizontal communication   The lateral or diagonal exchange of messages among peers or co-workers.

horizontal linkage model   An approach to product change that emphasizes shared development of innovations among several departments.

horizontal team   A formal team composed of employees from about the same hierarchical level but from different areas of expertise.

human capital   The economic value of the knowledge, experience, skills, and capabilities of employees.

human relations movement   A movement in management thinking and practice that emphasizes satisfaction of employees' basic needs as the key to increased worker productivity.

human resource information system   An integrated computer system designed to provide data and information used in HR planning and decision-making.

human resource management (HRM)   Activities undertaken to attract, develop, and maintain an effective workforce within an organization.

human resource planning   The forecasting of human resource needs and the projected matching of individuals with expected job vacancies.

human resources perspective   A management perspective that suggests jobs should be designed to meet higher-level needs by allowing workers to use their full potential.

human skill   The ability to work with and through other people and to work effectively as a group member.

humanistic perspective   A management perspective that emerged near the late nineteenth century and emphasized understanding human behaviour, needs, and attitudes in the workplace.

humility   Being unpretentious and modest rather than arrogant and prideful.

hygiene factors   Factors that involve the presence or absence of job dissatisfiers, including working conditions, pay, company policies, and interpersonal relationships.

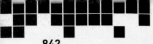

idea champion   A person who sees the need for and champions productive change within the organization.

idea incubator   An in-house programme that provides a safe harbour where ideas from employees throughout the organization can be developed without interference from company bureaucracy or politics.

implementation   The step in the decision-making process that involves using managerial, administrative, and persuasive abilities to translate the chosen alternative into action.

income statement   A financial statement that summarizes the firm's financial performance for a given time interval; sometimes called a profit-and-loss statement.

individualism   A preference for a loosely knit social framework in which individuals are expected to take care of themselves.

individualism approach   The ethical concept that acts are moral when they promote the individual's best long-term interests.

influence   The effect a person's actions have on the attitudes, values, beliefs, or behaviour of others.

information   Data that have been converted into a meaningful and useful context for the receiver.

information reporting system   A system that organizes information in the form of prespecified reports that managers use in day-to-day decision-making.

information technology (IT)   The hardware, software, telecommunications, database management, and other technologies used to store, process, and distribute information.

infrastructure   A country's physical facilities that support economic activities.

initiating structure   A type of leader behaviour that describes the extent to which the leader is task oriented and directs subordinate work activities toward goal attainment.

instant messaging (IM)   Electronic communication that allows users to see who is connected to a network and share information instantly.

integrative negotiation   A collaborative approach to negotiation that is based on a win-win assumption, whereby the parties want to come up with a creative solution that benefits both sides of the conflict.

intelligence team   A cross-functional group of managers and employees who work together to gain a deep understanding of a specific competitive issue and offer insight and recommendations for planning.

interactive leadership   A leadership style characterized by values such as inclusion, collaboration, relationship building, and caring.

interim manager   A manager who is not affiliated with a specific organization but works on a project-by-project basis or provides expertise to organizations in a specific area.

internal environment   The environment that includes the elements within the organization's boundaries.

internal locus of control   The belief by individuals that their future is within their control and that external forces have little influence.

international dimension   Portion of the external environment that represents events originating in foreign countries as well as opportunities for U.S. companies in other countries.

international human resource management (IHRM)   A subfield of human resource management that addresses the complexity that results from recruiting, selecting, developing, and maintaining a diverse work-force on a global scale.

international management   The management of business operations conducted in more than one country.

internet   A global collection of computer networks linked together for the exchange of data and information.

intranet   An internal communications system that uses the technology and standards of the internet but is accessible only to people within the organization.

intrinsic reward   The satisfaction received in the process of performing an action.

intuition   The immediate comprehension of a decision situation based on past experience but without conscious thought.

inventory   The goods that the organization keeps on hand for use in the production process up to the point of selling the final products to customers.

involvement culture   A culture that places high value on meeting the needs of employees and values cooperation and equality.

ISO 9000 standards   A set of standards that represent an international consensus of what constitutes effective quality management, as outlined by the International Organization for Standardization.

job analysis   The systematic process of gathering and interpreting information about the essential duties, tasks, and responsibilities of a job.

job characteristics model   A model of job design that comprises core job dimensions, critical psychological states, and employee growth-need strength.

job description   A concise summary of the specific tasks and responsibilities of a particular job.

job design   The application of motivational theories to the structure of work for improving productivity and satisfaction.

job enlargement   A job design that combines a series of tasks into one new, broader job to give employees variety and challenge.

job enrichment   A job design that incorporates achievement, recognition, and other high-level motivators into the work.

job evaluation   The process of determining the value of jobs within an organization through an examination of job content.

job rotation   A job design that systematically moves employees from one job to another to provide them with variety and stimulation.

job satisfaction   A positive attitude toward one's job.

job simplification   A job design whose purpose is to improve task efficiency by reducing the number of tasks a single person must do.

job specification   An outline of the knowledge, skills, education, and physical abilities needed to adequately perform a job.

joint venture   A variation of direct investment in which an organization shares costs and risks with another firm to build a manufacturing facility, develop new products, or set up a sales and distribution network.

justice approach   The ethical concept that moral decisions must be based on standards of equity, fairness, and impartiality.

just-in-time (JIT) inventory system   An inventory control system that schedules materials to arrive precisely when they are needed on a production line.

knowledge management portal   A single point of access for employees to multiple sources of information that provides personalized access on the corporate intranet.

knowledge management   The efforts to systematically find, organize, and make available a company's intellectual capital and to foster a culture of continuous learning and knowledge sharing.

labour market   The people available for hire by the organization.

large-group intervention   An approach that brings together participants from all parts of the organization (and may include key outside

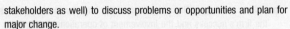

stakeholders as well) to discuss problems or opportunities and plan for major change.

law of effect The assumption that positively reinforced behaviour tends to be repeated, and unreinforced or negatively reinforced behaviour tends to be inhibited.

leadership The ability to influence people toward the attainment of organizational goals.

leadership grid A two-dimensional leadership theory that measures the leader's concern for people and for production.

leading The management function that involves the use of influence to motivate employees to achieve the organization's goals.

lean manufacturing Manufacturing process using highly trained employees at every stage of the production process to cut waste and improve quality.

learning A change in behaviour or performance that occurs as the result of experience.

learning organization An organization in which everyone is engaged in identifying and solving problems, enabling the organization to continuously experiment, improve, and increase its capability.

legal-political dimension The dimension of the general environment that includes federal, state, and local government regulations and political activities designed to influence company behaviour.

legitimate power Power that stems from a formal management position in an organization and the authority granted to it.

licensing An entry strategy in which an organization in one country makes certain resources available to companies in another to participate in the production and sale of its products abroad.

line authority A form of authority in which individuals in management positions have the formal power to direct and control immediate subordinates.

liquidity ratio A financial ratio that indicates the organization's ability to meet its current debt obligations.

listening The skill of receiving messages to accurately grasp facts and feelings to interpret the genuine meaning.

locus of control The tendency to place the primary responsibility for one's success or failure either within oneself (internally) or on outside forces (externally).

logistics The activities required to physically move materials into the company's operations facility and to move finished products to customers.

long-term orientation A greater concern for the future and high value on thrift and perseverance.

low-context culture A culture in which communication is used to exchange facts and information.

Machiavellianism The tendency to direct much of one's behaviour toward the acquisition of power and the manipulation of other people for personal gain.

management The attainment of organizational goals in an effective and efficient manner through planning, organizing, leading, and controlling organizational resources.

management by objectives (MBO) A method of management whereby managers and employees define goals for every department, project, and person and use them to monitor subsequent performance.

management by wandering around (MBWA) A communication technique in which managers interact directly with workers to exchange information.

management information system (MIS) A computer-based system that provides information and support for effective managerial decision-making.

management science perspective A management perspective that emerged after World War II and applied mathematics, statistics, and other quantitative techniques to managerial problems.

managing diversity Creating a climate in which the potential advantages of diversity for organizational or group performance are maximized while the potential disadvantages are minimized.

manufacturing organization An organization that produces physical goods.

market entry strategy An organizational strategy for entering a foreign market.

market value-added (MVA) A control system that measures the stock market's estimate of the value of a company's past and expected capital investment projects.

masculinity A cultural preference for achievement, heroism, assertiveness, work centrality, and material success.

mass production A type of technology characterized by the production of a large volume of products with the same specifications.

matching model An employee selection approach in which the organization and the applicant attempt to match each other's needs, interests, and values.

material requirements planning (MRP) A dependent demand inventory planning and control system that schedules the precise amount of all materials required to support the production of desired end products.

matrix approach An organization structure that utilizes functional and divisional chains of command simultaneously in the same part of the organization.

matrix boss The product or functional boss, responsible for one side of the matrix.

mediation The process of using a third party to settle a dispute.

mentor A higher-ranking, senior organizational member who is committed to providing upward mobility and support to a protégé's professional career.

merger The combining of two or more organizations into one.

message The tangible formulation of an idea to be sent to a receiver.

middle manager A manager who works at the middle levels of the organization and is responsible for major departments.

mission The organization's reason for existence.

mission statement A broadly stated definition of the organization's basic business scope and operations that distinguishes it from similar types of organizations.

modular approach The process by which a manufacturing company uses outside suppliers to provide large components of the product, which are then assembled into a final product by a few workers.

monoculture A culture that accepts only one way of doing things and one set of values and beliefs.

moral leadership Distinguishing right from wrong and choosing to do right in the practice of leadership.

moral-rights approach The ethical concept that moral decisions are those that best maintain the rights of those people affected by them.

motivation The arousal, direction, and persistence of behaviour.

motivators Factors that influence job satisfaction based on fulfilment of high-level needs such as achievement, recognition, responsibility, and opportunity for growth.

multicultural teams Teams made up of members from diverse national, racial, ethnic, and cultural backgrounds.

multidomestic strategy The modification of product design and advertising strategies to suit the specific needs of individual countries.

multinational corporation (MNC) An organization that receives more than 25 per cent of its total sales revenues from operations outside the parent company's home country; also called global corporation or *transnational corporation*.

Myers–Briggs Type Indicator (MBTI) Personality test that measures a person's preference for intro-version vs. extroversion, sensation vs. intuition, thinking vs. feeling, and judging vs. perceiving.

natural dimension The dimension of the general environment that includes all elements that occur naturally on earth, including plants, animals, rocks, and natural resources such as air, water, and climate.

need to achieve A human quality linked to entrepreneurship in which people are motivated to excel and pick situations in which success is likely.

negotiation A conflict management strategy whereby people engage in give-and-take discussions and consider various alternatives to reach a joint decision that is acceptable to both parties.

neutralizer A situational variable that counteracts a leadership style and prevents the leader from displaying certain behaviours.

new-venture fund A fund providing resources from which individuals and groups can draw to develop new ideas, products, or businesses.

new-venture team A unit separate from the mainstream of the organization that is responsible for developing and initiating innovations.

nonparticipator role A role in which the individual contributes little to either the task or members' socioemotional needs.

non-programmed decision A decision made in response to a situation that is unique, is poorly defined and largely unstructured, and has important consequences for the organization.

nonverbal communication A communication transmitted through actions and behaviours rather than through words.

normative An approach that defines how a decision-maker should make decisions and provides guidelines for reaching an ideal outcome for the organization.

norming The stage of team development in which conflicts developed during the storming stage are resolved and team harmony and unity emerge.

office automation systems Systems that combine modern hardware and software to handle the tasks of publishing and distributing Information.

on-the-job training (OJT) A type of training in which an experienced employee 'adopts' a new employee to teach him or her how to perform job duties.

open communication Sharing all types of information throughout the company, across functional and hierarchical levels.

open innovation Extending the search for and commercialization of new ideas beyond the boundaries of the organization.

open system A system that interacts with the external environment.

open-book management Sharing financial information and results with all employees in the organization.

operational goals Specific, measurable results expected from departments, work groups, and individuals within the organization.

operational plans Plans developed at the organization's lower levels that specify action steps toward achieving operational goals and that support tactical planning activities.

operations information system A computer-based information system that supports a company's day-to-day operations.

operations management The field of management that focuses on the physical production of goods or services and uses specialized techniques for solving manufacturing problems.

operations strategy The recognition of the importance of operations to the firm's success and the involvement of operations managers in the organization's strategic planning.

opportunity A situation in which managers see potential organizational accomplishments that exceed current goals.

organization A social entity that is goal directed and deliberately structured.

organization chart The visual representation of an organization's structure.

organization development (OD) The application of behavioural science techniques to improve an organization's health and effectiveness through its ability to cope with environmental changes, improve internal relationships, and increase learning and problem-solving capabilities.

organization structure The framework in which the organization defines how tasks are divided, resources are deployed, and departments are coordinated.

organizational behaviour An interdisciplinary field dedicated to the study of how individuals and groups tend to act in organizations.

organizational change The adoption of a new idea or behaviour by an organization.

organizational citizenship Work behaviour that goes beyond job requirements and contributes as needed to the organization's success.

organizational commitment Loyalty to and heavy involvement in one's organization.

organizational control The systematic process through which managers regulate organizational activities to make them consistent with expectations established in plans, targets, and standards of performance.

organizational environment All elements existing outside the organization's boundaries that have the potential to affect the organization.

organizing The management function concerned with assigning tasks, grouping tasks into departments, and allocating resources to departments.

outsourcing Contracting out selected functions or activities of an organization to other organizations that can do the work more cost-efficiently.

P → O expectancy Expectancy that successful performance of a task will lead to the desired outcome.

partial productivity The ratio of total outputs to the inputs from a single major input category.

partial reinforcement schedule A schedule in which only some occurrences of the desired behaviour are reinforced.

partnership An unincorporated business owned by two or more people.

path–goal theory A contingency approach to leadership specifying that the leader's responsibility is to increase subordinates' motivation by clarifying the behaviours necessary for task accomplishment and rewards.

pay-for-performance Incentive pay that ties at least part of compensation to employee effort and performance.

peer-to-peer file sharing File sharing that allows PCs to communicate directly with one another over the internet, bypassing central databases, servers, control points, and web pages.

people change A change in the attitudes and behaviours of a few employees in the organization.

perception The cognitive process people use to make sense out of the environment by selecting, organizing, and interpreting information.

perceptual defence The tendency of perceivers to protect themselves by disregarding ideas, objects, or people that are threatening to them.

perceptual distortions Errors in perceptual judgement that arise from inaccuracies in any part of the perceptual process.

perceptual selectivity The process by which individuals screen and select the various stimuli that vie for their attention.

performance The organization's ability to attain its goals by using resources in an efficient and effective manner.

performance appraisal The process of observing and evaluating an employee's performance, recording the assessment, and providing feedback to the employee.

performance gap A disparity between existing and desired performance levels.

performing The stage of team development in which members focus on problem solving and accomplishing the team's assigned task.

permanent teams A group of participants from several functions who are permanently assigned to solve ongoing problems of common interest.

personal communication channels Communication channels that exist outside the formally authorized channels and do not adhere to the organization's hierarchy of authority.

personal networking The acquisition and cultivation of personal relationships that cross departmental, hierarchical, and even organizational boundaries.

personality The set of characteristics that underlie a relatively stable pattern of behaviour in response to ideas, objects, or people in the environment.

person–job fit The extent to which a person's ability and personality match the requirements of a job.

plan A blueprint specifying the resource allocations, schedules, and other actions necessary for attaining goals.

planning The management function concerned with defining goals for future organizational performance and deciding on the tasks and resources needed to attain them.

pluralism An environment in which the organization accommodates several subcultures, including employees who would otherwise feel isolated and ignored.

point-counterpoint A decision-making technique in which people are assigned to express competing points of view.

political forces The influence of political and legal institutions on people and organizations.

political instability Events such as riots, revolutions, or government upheavals that affect the operations of an international company.

political risk A company's risk of loss of assets, earning power, or managerial control due to politically based events or actions by host governments.

portfolio strategy The organization's mix of strategic business units and product lines that fit together in such a way as to provide the corporation with synergy and competitive advantage.

power The potential ability to influence others' behaviour.

power distance The degree to which people accept inequality in power among institutions, organizations, and people.

prejudice The tendency to view people who are different as being deficient.

pressure group An interest group that works within the legal-political framework to influence companies to behave in socially responsible ways.

problem A situation in which organizational accomplishments have failed to meet established goals.

problem-solving team Typically 5 to 12 hourly employees from the same department who meet to discuss ways of improving quality, efficiency, and the work environment.

procedural justice The concept that rules should be clearly stated and consistently and impartially enforced.

process An organized group of related tasks and activities that work together to transform inputs into outputs and create value.

process control system A computer system that monitors and controls ongoing physical processes, such as temperature or pressure changes.

process layout A facilities layout in which machines that perform the same function are grouped together in one location.

process theories A group of theories that explain how employees select behaviours with which to meet their needs and determine whether their choices were successful.

procurement Purchasing supplies, services, and raw materials for use in the production process.

product change A change in the organization's product or service outputs.

product layout A facilities layout in which machines and tasks are arranged according to the sequence of steps in the production of a single product.

product life-cycle management (PLM) Manufacturing software that manages a product from creation through development, manufacturing, testing, and even maintenance in the field.

productivity The organization's output of products and services divided by its inputs.

profitability ratio A financial ratio that describes the firm's profits in terms of a source of profits (for example, sales or total assets).

programmed decision A decision made in response to a situation that has occurred often enough to enable decision rules to be developed and applied in the future.

project manager A manager responsible for a temporary work project that involves the participation of other people from various functions and levels of the organization.

projection The tendency to see one's own personal traits in other people.

quality circle A group of 6 to 12 volunteer employees who meet regularly to discuss and solve problems affecting the quality of their work.

raw materials inventory Inventory consisting of the basic inputs to the organization's production process.

realistic job preview A recruiting approach that gives applicants all pertinent and realistic information about the job and the organization.

recruiting The activities or practices that define the desired characteristics of applicants for specific jobs.

reengineering The radical redesign of business processes to achieve dramatic improvements in cost, quality, service, and speed.

referent power Power that results from characteristics that command subordinates' identification with, respect and admiration for, and desire to emulate the leader.

refreezing The reinforcement stage of organization development in which individuals acquire a desired new skill or attitude and are rewarded for it by the organization.

reinforcement Anything that causes a given behaviour to be repeated or inhibited.

reinforcement theory A motivation theory based on the relationship between a given behaviour and its consequences.

related diversification Moving into a new business that is related to the company's existing business activities.

reorder point (ROP) The most economical level at which an inventory item should be reordered.

responsibility The duty to perform the task or activity an employee has been assigned.

responsibility centre An organizational unit under the supervision of a single person who is responsible for its activity.

revenue budget A budget that identifies the forecasted and actual revenues of the organization.

reward power Power that results from the authority to bestow rewards on other people.

risk A situation in which a decision has clear-cut goals and good information is available, but the future outcomes associated with each alternative are subject to chance.

risk propensity The willingness to undertake risk with the opportunity of gaining an increased payoff.

role A set of expectations for one's behaviour.

role ambiguity Uncertainty about what behaviours are expected of a person in a particular role.

role conflict Incompatible demands of different roles.

satisficing To choose the first solution alternative that satisfies minimal decision criteria, regardless of whether better solutions are presumed to exist.

scenario building Looking at trends and discontinuities and imagining possible alternative futures to build a framework within which unexpected future events can be managed.

schedule of reinforcement The frequency with which and intervals over which reinforcement occurs.

scientific management A subfield of the classical management perspective that emphasized scientifically determined changes in management practices as the solution to improving labour productivity.

selection The process of determining the skills, abilities, and other attributes a person needs to perform a particular job.

self-directed team A team consisting of 5 to 20 multi-skilled workers who rotate jobs to produce an entire product or service, often supervised by an elected member.

self-serving bias The tendency to overestimate the contribution of internal factors to one's successes and the contribution of external factors to one's failures.

semantics The meaning of words and the way they are used.

servant leader A leader who works to fulfil subordinates' needs and goals as well as to achieve the organization's larger mission.

service organization An organization that produces non-physical outputs that require customer involvement and cannot be stored in inventory.

service technology Technology characterized by intangible outputs and direct contact between employees and customers.

short-term orientation A concern with the past and present and a high value on meeting social obligations.

single-use plans Plans that are developed to achieve a set of goals that are unlikely to be repeated in the future.

situational theory A contingency approach to leadership that links the leader's behavioural style with the task readiness of subordinates.

Six Sigma A quality control approach that emphasizes a relentless pursuit of higher quality and lower costs.

skunkworks A separate small, informal, highly autonomous, and often secretive group that focuses on breakthrough ideas for the business.

slogan A phrase or sentence that succinctly expresses a key corporate value.

small-batch production A type of technology that involves the production of goods in batches of one or a few products designed to customer specification.

social entrepreneur Entrepreneurial leaders who are committed to both good business and changing the world for the better.

social facilitation The tendency for the presence of others to influence an individual's motivation and performance.

social forces The aspects of a culture that guide and influence relationships among people – their values, needs, and standards of behaviour.

social networking Online interaction in a community format where people share personal information and photos, produce and share all sorts of information and opinions, or unify activists and raise funds.

sociocultural dimension The dimension of the general environment representing the demographic characteristics, norms, customs, and values of the population within which the organization operates.

socioemotional role A role in which the individual provides support for team members' emotional needs and social unity.

sole trader or proprietorship An unincorporated business owned by an individual for profit.

span of management The number of employees reporting to a supervisor; also called *span of control*.

special-purpose team A team created outside the formal organization to undertake a project of special importance or creativity.

staff authority A form of authority granted to staff specialists in their area of expertise.

stakeholder Any group within or outside the organization that has a stake in the organization's performance.

standing plans Ongoing plans that are used to provide guidance for tasks performed repeatedly within the organization.

stereotype A rigid, exaggerated, irrational belief associated with a particular group of people.

stereotype threat A psychological experience of a person who, usually engaged in a task, is aware of a stereotype about his or her identify group suggesting that he or she will not perform well on that task.

stereotyping The tendency to assign an individual to a group or broad category and then attribute generalizations about the group to the individual.

storming The stage of team development in which individual personalities and roles, and resulting conflicts, emerge.

story A narrative based on true events and repeated frequently and shared among organizational employees.

strategic business unit (SBU) A division of the organization that has a unique business mission, product line, competitors, and markets relative to other SBUs in the same corporation.

strategic conversation Dialogue across boundaries and hierarchical levels about the team or organization's vision, critical strategic themes, and the values that help achieve important goals.

strategic goals Broad statements of where the organization wants to be in the future; pertain to the organization as a whole rather than to specific divisions or departments.

strategic management The set of decisions and actions used to formulate and implement strategies that will provide a competitively superior fit between the organization and its environment so as to achieve organizational goals.

strategic plans The action steps by which an organization intends to attain strategic goals.

strategy The plan of action that prescribes resource allocation and other activities for dealing with the environment, achieving a competitive advantage, and attaining organizational goals.

strategy execution The stage of strategic management that involves the use of managerial and organizational tools to direct resources toward achieving strategic outcomes.

strategy formulation The stage of strategic management that involves the planning and decision-making that lead to the establishment of the organization's goals and of a specific strategic plan.

strategy map A visual representation of the key drivers of an organization's success, showing the cause-and-effect relationships among goals and plans.

stress A physiological and emotional response to stimuli that place physical or psychological demands on an individual.

stretch goal A reasonable yet highly ambitious, compelling goal that energizes people and inspires excellence.

substitute A situational variable that makes a leadership style unnecessary or redundant.

subsystems Parts of a system that depend on one another for their functioning.

superordinate goal A goal that cannot be reached by a single party.

suppliers People and organizations who provide the raw materials the organization uses to produce its output.

supply chain management Managing the sequence of suppliers and purchasers, covering all stages of processing from obtaining raw materials to distributing finished goods to final customers.

survey feedback A type of OD intervention in which questionnaires on organizational climate and other factors are distributed among employees and their results reported back to them by a change agent.

sustainability Economic development that generates wealth and meets the needs of the current population while preserving the environment for the needs of future generations.

SWOT analysis Analysis of the strengths, weaknesses, opportunities, and threats (SWOT) that affect organizational performance.

symbol An object, act, or event that conveys meaning to others.

synergy The condition that exists when the organization's parts interact to produce a joint effect that is greater than the sum of the parts acting alone.

system A set of interrelated parts that function as a whole to achieve a common purpose.

systems theory An extension of the humanistic perspective that describes organizations as open systems characterized by entropy, synergy, and subsystem interdependence.

tactical goals Goals that define the outcomes that major divisions and departments must achieve for the organization to reach its overall goals.

tactical plans Plans designed to help execute major strategic plans and to accomplish a specific part of the company's strategy.

tall structure A management structure characterized by an overall narrow span of management and a relatively large number of hierarchical levels.

task environment The layer of the external environment that directly influences the organization's operations and performance.

task force A temporary team or committee formed to solve a specific short-term problem involving several departments.

task specialist role A role in which the individual devotes personal time and energy to helping the team accomplish its task.

team A unit of two or more people who interact and coordinate their work to accomplish a specific goal.

team building A type of OD intervention that enhances the cohesiveness of departments by helping members learn to function as a team.

team cohesiveness The extent to which team members are attracted to the team and motivated to remain in it.

team norm A standard of conduct that is shared by team members and guides their behaviour.

team-based structure Structure in which the entire organization is made up of horizontal teams that coordinate their activities and work directly with customers to accomplish the organization's goals.

technical complexity The degree to which complex machinery is involved in the production process to the exclusion of people.

technical core The heart of the organization's production of its product or service.

technical skill The understanding of and proficiency in the performance of specific tasks.

technological dimension The dimension of the general environment that includes scientific and technological advancements in the industry and society at large.

technology change A change that pertains to the organization's production process.

telecommuting Using computers and telecommunications equipment to perform work from home or another remote location.

tolerance for ambiguity The psychological characteristic that allows a person to be untroubled by disorder and uncertainty.

top leader The overseer of both the product and functional chains of command, responsible for the entire matrix.

top manager A manager who is at the top of the organizational hierarchy and is responsible for the entire organization.

top-down budgeting A budgeting process in which middle- and lower-level managers set departmental budget targets in accordance with overall company revenues and expenditures specified by top management.

total factor productivity The ratio of total outputs to the inputs from labour, capital, materials, and energy.

total quality management (TQM) A concept that focuses on managing the total organization to deliver quality to customers. Four significant elements of TQM are employee involvement, focus on the customer, benchmarking, and continuous improvement.

traits Distinguishing personal characteristics, such as intelligence, values, and appearance.

transactional leader A leader who clarifies subordinates' role and task requirements, initiates structure, provides rewards, and displays consideration for subordinates.

transaction-processing system (TPS) A type of operations information system that records and processes data resulting from routine business transactions such as sales, purchases, and payroll.

transformational leader A leader distinguished by a special ability to bring about innovation and change.

transnational strategy A strategy that combines global coordination to attain efficiency with flexibility to meet specific needs in various countries.

two-boss employees Employees who report to two supervisors simultaneously.

Type A behaviour Behaviour pattern characterized by extreme competitiveness, impatience, aggressiveness, and devotion to work.

Type B behaviour Behaviour pattern that lacks Type A characteristics and includes a more balanced, relaxed lifestyle.

uncertainty The situation that occurs when managers know which goals they wish to achieve, but information about alternatives and future events is incomplete.

uncertainty avoidance A value characterized by people's intolerance for uncertainty and ambiguity and resulting support for beliefs that promise certainty and conformity.

unfreezing The stage of organization development in which participants are made aware of problems to increase their willingness to change their behaviour.

unrelated diversification Expanding into a totally new line of business.

upward communication Messages transmitted from the lower to the higher levels in the organization's hierarchy.

utilitarian approach The ethical concept that moral behaviours produce the greatest good for the greatest number.

valence The value or attraction an individual has for an outcome.

validity The relationship between an applicant's score on a selection device and his or her future job performance.

venture capital firm A group of companies or individuals that invests money in new or expanding businesses for ownership and potential profits.

vertical integration Expanding into businesses that either produce the supplies needed to make products or that distribute and sell those products.

vertical team A formal team composed of a manager and his or her subordinates in the organization's formal chain of command.

virtual network structure An organization structure that disaggregates major functions to separate companies that are brokered by a small headquarters organization.

virtual team A team made up of members who are geographically or organizationally dispersed, rarely meet face-to-face, and do their work using advanced information technologies.

vision An attractive, ideal future that is credible yet not readily attainable.

wage and salary surveys Surveys that show what other organizations pay incumbents in jobs that match a sample of 'key' jobs selected by the organization.

whistle-blowing The disclosure by an employee of illegal, immoral, or illegitimate practices by the organization.

wholly owned foreign affiliate A foreign subsidiary over which an organization has complete control.

wiki Website that allows anyone with access, inside or outside the organization, to create, share, and edit content through a simple, browser-based user interface.

work redesign The altering of jobs to increase both the quality of employees' work experience and their productivity.

work specialization The degree to which organizational tasks are subdivided into individual jobs; also called division of labour.

workforce optimization Implementing strategies to put the right people in the right jobs, make the best use of employee talent and skills, and develop human capital for the future.

work-in-process inventory Inventory composed of the materials that still are moving through the stages of the production process.

World Wide Web (WWW) A collection of central servers for accessing information on the internet.

INDEX